Crystal Reports® XI:
The Complete Reference

George Peck

McGraw-Hill/Osborne
New York   Chicago   San Francisco
Lisbon   London   Madrid   Mexico City
Milan   New Delhi   San Juan
Seoul   Singapore   Sydney   Toronto

The **McGraw·Hill** Companies

McGraw-Hill/Osborne
2100 Powell Street, 10th Floor
Emeryville, California 94608
U.S.A.

To arrange bulk purchase discounts for sales promotions, premiums, or fund-raisers, please contact **McGraw-Hill**/Osborne at the above address.

Crystal Reports® XI: The Complete Reference

7890 CUS CUS 019

ISBN 0-07-226246-X

Acquisitions Editor
Lisa McClain

Project Editor
Carolyn Welch

Acquisitions Coordinator
Alex McDonald

Contributing Writer
Brian Norris

Technical Editors
Blair Harvey
Herb Hess

Copy Editor
Bob Campbell

Proofreader
Susie Elkind

Indexer
Claire Splan

Composition
Apollo Publishing Services

Illustrators
Apollo Publishing Services

Series Design
Peter F. Hancik, Lyssa Wald

This book was composed with Adobe® InDesign®.

For Denise

Thanks for XVIII wonderful years.

About the Author

After more than ten years as an internal consultant and trainer in a large corporation, George founded his own consulting and training firm, The Ablaze Group, in 1994 (www.AblazeGroup.com). He has trained, consulted, and developed custom software for large and small organizations throughout the United States, Canada, the United Kingdom, and Puerto Rico.

George works as both a trainer and consultant exclusively with Crystal Reports, Crystal Enterprise, and Crystal Reports Server/BusinessObjects Enterprise. This is his sixth title in the *Crystal Reports: The Complete Reference* series, best-sellers published by McGraw-Hill/Osborne. He is also the author of *Crystal Reports Professional Results*, also published by McGraw-Hill/Osborne.

Prior to his computer career, George was a broadcaster. His voice may still be heard on various national radio and TV commercial and promotional campaigns.

Contents

Acknowledgments

This sixth edition of *Crystal Reports: The Complete Reference* brought an even more difficult task of trying to creatively acknowledge those who helped make it possible. This is especially true because those who work so hard to help make this effort a success are helpful over and over again from edition to edition.

Despite having to deal with significant "adversity" within the Business Objects organization this time around, the first acknowledgment still goes to Jaylene Crick at Business Objects. You came to the rescue on more than one occasion and probably went out on a limb for me on more than one occasion, too. Thanks!

Contributing writer Brian Norris came through once again, helping with some Crystal Reports Server chapters and some other material. In particular, I'm deeply grateful for your taking the VS .NET chapter off my hands. One of these days, I'll get my "assemblies" together.

And, the team at McGraw-Hill/Osborne put up with some extra difficulties this time around, for which I'm eternally grateful. Once again, my acquisitions editor Lisa McClain endured the excuses and the tardiness, while being professional and understanding. Thanks, also, to acquisitions coordinator Alex McDonald. Appreciation goes out again to wordsmith Bob Campbell for having a dictionary and thesaurus handy. And, once again, my heartfelt thanks go to Carolyn Welch who keeps the whole project on track and keeps me in great conversation, even if only via e-mail.

Technical editors Blair Harvey and Herb Hess were of great help. Thanks for double checking the nit-picky technical stuff, and for confirming that product documentation isn't always correct!

And, for the sixth time, the last, and most special, acknowledgment goes to Dad. I think of you with every word I write.

George Peck, September 2005
author@CrystalBook.com
www.CrystalBook.com

Introduction

Crystal Reports XI introduces some very fundamental broad changes—some which are immediately obvious, while others are not. The version number is one of the first departures from past versions. The Roman XI has been substituted for the prior Arabic version numbering scheme (however, you'll still find the number 11 appearing on the Start menu, in some documentation, and in most programming interfaces). The Roman numbering scheme not only signifies a new approach to the number 11 but it also ties in to "Extreme Insight" marketing hyperbole also released with the software. And, XI is the first version released completely under the umbrella of the new Business Objects organization, after the acquisition of Crystal Decisions by Business Objects about two-thirds of the way through the Crystal Reports 10 development cycle. The file directory structure (within the Program Files directory), registry entries, documentation, and logos now all reflect the Business Objects name.

An initial look at Crystal Reports XI also reveals major changes to the user look and feel, and minor to moderate changes to functionality and software capabilities. The "Office XP User Interface" catches the eye right away, requiring long-time users of earlier versions to get used to subtle shading, push pins, and reorganized toolbars. And, XI now includes more "tabs" than you'll find in the Library of Congress card catalog!

While some organization changes exist in this XI book, the title largely maintains the layout of previous editions. Part I covers general report design techniques that will apply to virtually everybody who uses the tool. The everyday report designer will find this section the most valuable. However, even web or Windows coders charged with integrating reports into their custom applications will find this section useful, as report design knowledge is critical when incorporating reports into custom applications.

Part II covers various techniques and methods to place your Crystal Reports on the Web. From simple HTML export to complex techniques for administering Crystal Reports Server XI, this section provides detailed help for web-based report audiences. A large portion of this section deals with the new Crystal Reports Server XI enterprise reporting tool. Replacing the previous Crystal Enterprise product, a small-user edition of Crystal Reports Server XI is included with Crystal Reports XI Professional and Developer editions. Use chapters in Part II to help you explore this powerful web-based reporting tool.

Part III is for the Active Server Page, Visual Basic, or Visual Studio .NET developer who is charged with integrating Crystal Reports into a web and Windows applications. In this section, the Report Designer Component is covered for use with both Active Server Page Web and Visual Basic Windows applications. And, a dedicated chapter covers using Crystal Reports with custom Visual Studio .NET web and Windows applications.

As with previous book editions, sample reports and sample developer applications can be found online. Many of the sample reports illustrated in Part I, as well as sample RDC and VS .NET applications from Part III, can be found on this book's companion web site at www.CrystalBook.com.

And, while the previous edition of this book offered a Formula Language Reference as an online extra, it has now been added to the book as an appendix. This covers all functions in the formula language (including new functions added to version XI), along with my own personal descriptions and examples that I hope best illustrate each function and operator.

What's New in Crystal Reports XI

In addition to the vendor-related and version numbering changes, Crystal Reports XI presents a fairly substantial set of functional changes. A short description of most of these additions and updates follows, with chapter number references (although, some minor new features may be mentioned only here and not covered extensively in the rest of the book). Crystal Reports Server XI new features are discussed in Chapters 22, 23, and 24.

- **New Look and Feel**   The first obvious change is the look and feel of Crystal Reports XI. Overall screen organization and appearance, the addition of a Start Page, toolbar changes, and the new Dependency Checker and Workbench dialog boxes all fall within this category. These changes are discussed in Chapter 1.

- **Dynamic and Cascading Pick Lists**   Probably one of the most anticipated updates to Crystal Reports XI are Dynamic and Cascading Pick Lists. This feature (used when report viewers are prompted for Parameter Field values) allows drop-down pick lists to be populated on-the-fly from the database. Chapter 13 covers this new feature as it relates to standalone reports, and Chapter 16 discusses special pick list requirements when integrating reports with Dynamic Pick Lists into Crystal Reports Server XI.

- **New Formula Language Functions**   Several new formula language rounding functions, additional functions relating to time zones, and additional functions pertaining to hierarchical grouping are available in the new formula language. These are covered in the appendix, the Formula Language Reference.

- **Dynamic Graphic Location**   This new feature allows a report to dynamically assign the location of an external bitmap image as the report runs, based on a formula, database data, and so forth. This new image feature is covered in Chapter 7.

- **Drag-and-Drop Charts and Cross-Tabs**   Crystal Reports XI introduces the ability to simply drag and chart or cross-tab onto the report from toolbar or menu, automatically supplying an initial set of chart or cross-tab options. This new charting capability is discussed in Chapter 10, with the new cross-tab discussion appearing in Chapter 9.

- **Tighter Integration with Enterprise Reporting Products**   Not only has Business Objects' web-based enterprise reporting suite changed in version XI (both Crystal Reports Server XI and BusinessObjects Enterprise XI replace the previous Crystal Enterprise product), but Crystal Reports XI itself provides tighter integration with these products. For example, if you have a properly configured enterprise reporting system available, you can now preview your Crystal Reports in a web browser right from within Crystal Reports. You may now also log off and on to multiple systems without closing Crystal Reports. And, the new Workbench integrates with enterprise Report Packages. The Repository Explorer in covered in Chapter 17 and the Workbench is discussed in Chapter 1.

- **Exporting Enhancements, Formula-Driven TopN Value and Group Sorting Direction, and Formula-By-Formula Null Handling**   Various and sundry other changes are sprinkled throughout the book. Changes to report exporting, such as additional RTF export options, and the ability to save export options with the report, are discussed in Chapter 14. The ability to supply group sorting direction with a formula is discussed in Chapter 3, as is the ability to provide a TopN value with a formula. And, the ability to choose how to handle null database values on a formula-by-formula basis is covered in Chapter 5.

PART

Designing Reports

Getting a Feel for Crystal Reports XI

Information technology has come a long way from the mainframe era, through minicomputer "green screens," to personal computer-based systems, into Internet- and intranet-based web applications, and on to today's portable wireless devices and personal digital assistants. One old tried-and-true acronym still remains very applicable, however: *GIGO,* or *garbage in, garbage out,* is still an important concept to keep in mind whenever you are designing an information-oriented system.

No matter what type of device or interface is used to initially connect a human being with an information system, the *output* from the device is often the most critical element of the whole system. Hence, the *O* in GIGO is arguably the most important letter of the acronym. No matter how much data goes into an information system, or how elegantly or accurately it is added, the system is rarely of much use unless usable output results down the line.

While avoiding the "garbage" portion of this scenario is typically the job of input business rules and logic, as well as plain old common sense and training, the transformation of the input to the output, as well as its storage along the way, is the focus of this book. In particular, the vast bulk of business data today is stored in a centralized *database system* for use in generating output. Getting that data to the end user, garbage free, is one of the most critical portions, if not *the* most critical portion, of the information processing cycle.

This is where the *database report writer* comes in. While there are many ways to present database output to a human being, a comprehensive reporting tool is one of the most popular approaches available. Version XI continues the tradition of many previous versions of Crystal Reports in attaining this goal.

Introducing Crystal Reports XI

Crystal Reports remains the market leader and de facto standard for business and corporate report writing. In 1984, a Canadian shipping company wanted to produce custom reports from its accounting system. When the vendor said "We can't help you," the company created Quick Reports, the precursor to Crystal Reports. Crystal Reports' first "bundle" was with that vendor's next version of its accounting software. The acquisition of the Crystal series of tools by former competitor Business Objects is testament to the ubiquity of this long-popular tool. Version XI is the first version to be fully developed and released under the Business Objects umbrella.

NOTE *The "XI" moniker of this release exhibits more significance than just the "Extreme Insight" designation given the software in marketing hyperbole. XI is the 11th major release of Crystal Reports. In fact, you'll still find it referred to as Crystal Reports 11 on many screens, including the Windows Start menu.*

Crystal Reports is now bundled with close to 200 leading software packages, including many enterprise resource planning and accounting packages from vendors such as ACCPAC International (the outgrowth of the first software package to use Crystal), PeopleSoft/Oracle, and SAP. Versions of Crystal Reports are also included with various Microsoft packages, including their latest development environment, Visual Studio .NET.

Crystal Reports is aimed at several general types of users:

- Casual business users, such as data analysts, executive assistants, and marketing directors, who will design reports around their corporate data to make intelligent business decisions.
- Information technology professionals, who will use Crystal Reports to integrate sophisticated reporting right inside their own Microsoft Windows programs.
- Webmasters, who will use Crystal Reports to provide print-quality reports and graphics over their intranets or the Internet.

Figure 1-1 shows the Crystal Reports XI screen when the program is first started. While Crystal Reports XI maintains the standard Windows user interface from previous versions, users of older Crystal Reports versions will immediately notice the new "Office 2003" smooth gradient screen layout and color/shading scheme. Also, a new Start page appears when you first launch Crystal Reports, replacing the older Welcome dialog box. This new initial presentation includes online content from the Business Objects web site if your computer is connected to the Internet. And, you'll probably notice a new Workbench window on the right side of the screen (the Workbench is covered later in this chapter).

TIP *If you prefer a more "classic" Windows appearance, you may choose other shading and layout schemes from the View | Toolbars menu option. New options in version XI allow you to choose a Standard XP or Classic Flat Style look, in addition to Smooth Gradients.*

When you first start the program, you may want to navigate to some of the online hyperlinks presented on the new Start page. However, the only two main functions that you'll usually want to perform are creating a new report and opening an existing report. Like most functions in Crystal Reports, these functions can be accomplished in several ways. By choosing options in the Start screen, you can choose from several new report options, choose from a list of recently opened reports, or click the Open File link to navigate through a standard Open File dialog box for an existing report. You can even choose Help | Report Samples from the pull-down menus to choose from two folders of sample reports installed with Crystal Reports.

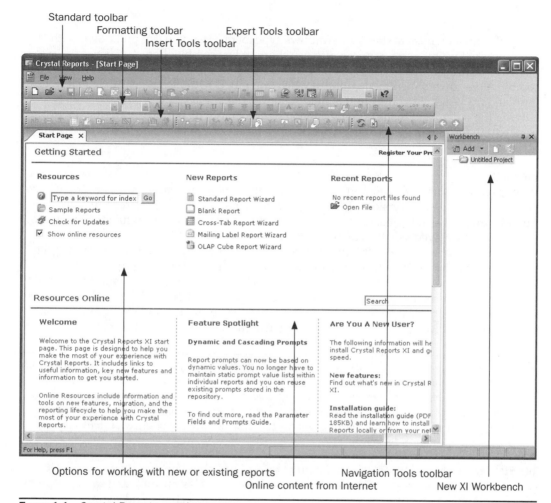

FIGURE 1-1   Crystal Reports opening screen

If you've closed the Start page, you may redisplay it from the Help menu and choose from the variety of options on it. And, whether the Start page is displayed or not, you may also open an existing report or create a new report with pull-down menu options, keyboard shortcuts, or toolbar buttons, as described later in the chapter.

Crystal Reports Screen Elements

While the general look, feel, and layout of Crystal Reports XI had changed from previous versions, the overall location of key screen elements remains the same. Aside from the Start page (which you may close by clicking the small *X* on the Start Page tab below the toolbars), the Crystal Reports screen consists of several main parts you'll want to familiarize yourself with: the pull-down menus, the toolbars, the report design/preview area, and the status bar. The Workbench window (covered later in this chapter) initially appears on the right side of the screen.

Pull-Down Menus

The pull-down menus are standard Windows-type menus that you can pull down with your mouse. In some cases, you can also use shortcut key combinations (such as CTRL-O to open an existing report) to choose pull-down menu options. You'll notice these shortcut key combinations next to their menu options when you pull down the menus. You can also use the standard Windows convention of holding down the ALT key and typing the underlined letter in the menu, and then choosing a menu option by typing another underlined letter from within the menu. For example, you can open an existing report (File menu, Open option) by typing ALT-F-O.

Toolbars

When you first start Crystal Reports, all five available toolbars (including the new Navigation Tools toolbar added to version XI) are displayed across the top of the screen by default. Initially, the first two toolbars are displayed by themselves vertically, while the last three toolbars are displayed side by side below the first two.

To selectively turn on or off individual toolbars, choose View | Toolbars from the pull-down menus. The toolbars contain buttons for almost all of Crystal Reports' available functions (some options still require the use of pull-down menu options, but not many). Many of the icons on the toolbars are self-explanatory. In addition, tooltips are available for each toolbar button—just point to a toolbar button with your mouse and wait a few seconds. A small yellow box containing a short description of the toolbar button's function will appear.

TIP *You may "undock" the toolbars from their default positions and place them anywhere you want. Just click the dotted or gray line at the left of the toolbar and drag it to the desired location. If you move it left or right within its current location, it will simply move to a different position. If you move it away from the top of the screen, it will become its own "window." If you place it near the top or bottom of the Crystal Reports screen (or back near its original position), it will snap into place along the edge of the screen.*

The Standard Toolbar   This toolbar is the first toolbar just below the pull-down menus. It contains the most often-used Crystal Reports functions, such as opening and saving report files, printing and exporting the report, undoing and redoing actions, and so on.

The Formatting Toolbar   This toolbar is the toolbar just below the Standard toolbar. You should be familiar with this toolbar if you've used most any office suite type of tool, such as word processors or spreadsheets. This toolbar enables you to change the format (color, font, size, alignment, and so forth) of one or more objects that you have selected on your report.

The Insert Tools Toolbar   The third toolbar (initially, the first toolbar in the third row) contains options to insert new objects onto your reports, such as text objects, charts, maps, and cross-tab objects.

The Expert Tools Toolbar   The fourth toolbar (initially, the middle toolbar in the third row) presents buttons that display various Crystal Reports "experts" that guide you through different report functions usually presented with a tabbed dialog box. Such experts include the Database Expert, Group Expert, and Select Expert.

The Navigation Tools Toolbar   The fifth toolbar (initially, the last toolbar in the third row) is new in Crystal Reports XI. It includes buttons that refresh the report's data, stop report formatting that's in progress, and navigate among various report pages.

Report Design/Preview Area

The large gray area in the middle of the Crystal Reports screen (you won't see this area until you close the Start page) is the report design/preview area. Here, you actually manipulate fields and objects that make up your report. When you want to have a look at the way the report will eventually appear when printed on paper or exported to another file format, you can preview the actual report in this area, as well.

You'll soon see that you can choose between multiple reports that you may have open simultaneously, as well as different views of the selected report, by clicking a number of tabs that appear at the top of the report design/preview area. When you initially create a new report or open an existing report, you'll see a tab for that report. Below the tab for the currently selected report, you will see one or more other tabs. In particular, you'll always see a Design tab, which shows a design view, or "layout," of your report, simply indicating the location of objects in different report sections. When you preview the report, a Preview tab appears that shows actual data from the database as it will appear in the final report. In addition, as you progress with your report work, you'll see additional tabs for subreports and drill-down views. Simply click the tab you wish to see.

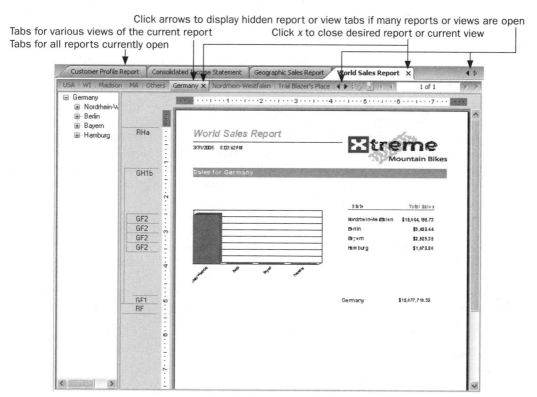

Figure 1-2   New XI tab layout

Status Bar

The status bar appears at the very bottom of the Crystal Reports screen. Although you can hide the status bar by unchecking the Status Bar option on the View menu, you'll probably want to leave it displayed, because it displays very helpful information for you as you design and preview reports. In particular, the status bar will show more detailed descriptions of menu options and toolbar buttons. While the short tooltip that appears when you point to a button is handy, it may not offer a good enough description of what the toolbar button does. Just look in the status bar for more information.

Also, the status bar contains more helpful information on its right side, such as the date and time the report was last "refreshed" from the database, how many database records are being used in your report, what percentage of the report processing is finished, and at what location (X-Y coordinates) on the report page a currently selected object is located.

Starting Out: Opening or Creating a Report

To open an existing report, you may use options from the Start page, choosing a recently used report from the list, or choosing the Open File option. Whether or not you've closed the Start page, you can also use the File menu or Open button in the Standard toolbar. If you want to choose from a list of recently used reports, choose from the recent file list (a list of numbered report filenames) from the File menu, or click the small down arrow on the Open toolbar button in the Standard toolbar.

To choose a report from an Open File dialog box, select File | Open, use the shortcut key combination CTRL-O, or click the Open button in the Standard toolbar. A standard File Open dialog box will appear, showing any files with an .RPT extension in the drive and folder. Navigate to any alternate drives or folders to find the existing Crystal Report .RPT file that you wish to open.

To create a new report, choose options from the Start page, the File menu, or the Standard toolbar. The Start page includes several options for creating new reports, including four report "wizards" and the Blank Report option. Click the desired choice.

Whether or not the Start page is displayed, you can also start a new report by using pull-down menu options or a toolbar button. If you choose File | New, a submenu will appear presenting the four possible wizards, as well as the blank report option. Pressing the CTRL-N keyboard shortcut or clicking the New Report button in the Standard toolbar will display the Standard Report Creation Wizard.

Using the Report Wizards

The four standard *report wizards* allow you to create "quick and dirty" reports with minimal effort. They're helpful when you want to create a simple report or put together the beginning elements of a more complex report. Using the Start page or File | Menu submenu, choose the wizard that most closely matches the type of report that you want to create.

To create a simple, general-purpose report (for example, an employee phone list or your last year's sales totals), use the Standard Report Wizard (see Figure 1-3). The Standard Report Wizard presents a type of dialog box that's probably familiar to you if you've used other office suites or productivity products. You build your report by choosing options from the different screens in a dialog box. You advance to the next screen by clicking the Next button at the bottom of the dialog box.

PART I

FIGURE 1-3
The Standard Report
Wizard

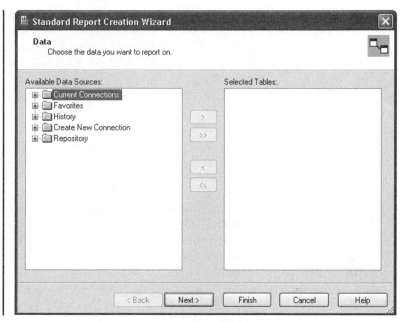

To create a report with the Standard Report Wizard, follow these steps:

1. First, choose the database tables (or other data source) you want to use for the report using one of the categories from the Available Data Sources list. This list allows you to choose any data source Crystal Reports supports, including data connections that you are already connected to from previous reports (from the Current Connections category), that you've specifically added to your Favorites folder, that you've used recently (from the History category), that are available in the Create New Connection category, or that are stored in the Crystal Reports Server or BusinessObjects Enterprise repository. Click the plus sign next to the folder you wish to open to see the available options. For example, if you click the Create New Connection folder, you'll see a list of database types that Crystal Reports can connect to, including PC-style "local" databases, client/server databases (such as Oracle or Informix), BusinessObjects Enterprise Universes, and many other categories (see Chapter 20 for more information on special database types).

2. As you add tables, you'll see them appear in the Selected Tables list. Once you're finished adding tables, click the Next button. You'll be taken to the Link portion of the wizard (provided that you chose more than one table). This area shows you the tables you've chosen in a visual format, allowing you to *link* the tables together, using common fields. Crystal Reports will *autolink* the tables automatically, showing you lines indicating the fields and tables that are linked. If these links are correct (in the real world they rarely are), you may leave them as is.

3. If you need to delete a link that Crystal Reports added, click the line that connects the tables, and press the DEL key to remove the existing link or click the Delete Link

button. If you want to delete all existing links, you may click the Clear Links button. You may then create your own link by dragging from the "from" field and table and dropping on the "to" field and table. A line will appear, indicating your new link. Once you've linked the tables correctly, click the Next button at the bottom of the Wizard.

TIP *Linking tables has quite a few fine points. Look for more information in Chapter 15.*

---

4. Choose the database fields you actually want to appear on your report. You may choose single fields simply by clicking the field name under the Available Fields list. If you want to choose multiple fields, hold down the CTRL key and click. You'll notice that fields are "multiselected" when you click them. To deselect an already selected field, hold down CTRL and click the field name again. To select a range of fields, click the first field in the range. Then, hold down the SHIFT key and select the last field in the range. Both fields, plus all fields in between, will be selected. Then, click the right-arrow button to move your selected fields to the Fields To Display box. If you, per chance, would like to add all fields from the tables to the report, click the double-right arrow.

5. To search for a particular field (in case the tables you chose contain many fields), click the Find Field button under the Available Fields list. You can enter a full or partial field name to search for. If that field is in any tables in the Available Fields list, the field will be highlighted. If you select a field in the field list and then click the Browse Data button, you'll see a sample of actual data from that database field. This may be helpful in determining whether or not this is the correct field to add to your report.

6. If you'd like to change the order in which the fields appear on the report, you can make those changes in the Fields To Display box by choosing the field you want to move and clicking the up or down arrows above the list. When you're finished, click Next to move on.

TIP *This is all the information the Standard Report Wizard needs to display the report. From this point forward, if you don't want to specify any other report features, such as grouping, totaling, charting, or record selection, you may click the Finish button to display the report.*

---

7. If you wish to have your report contain report groups, choose one or more fields from the Available Fields list on the Grouping portion of the wizard and click the right-arrow button. *Grouping* puts all report records together on the report whose chosen grouping fields are the same. Grouping is similar to just sorting records, but groups can have subtotals, counts, averages, or other summaries at the end. Grouping is covered in more detail in Chapter 3.

8. If you choose to group the report, the Next button will then display the Summaries section, where you'll add an entry in the Summarized Fields list for every group you created previously. This is where you choose subtotals, averages, counts, or other summaries that you want to appear at the end of the group. Crystal Reports assumes that you wish to create "sum" summaries for any numeric fields you've

placed on your report. You'll notice that these have already been added. You may leave these as-is, change the type of summary by selecting the summary field and choosing from the drop-down list at the bottom of the wizard, or delete the summaries by selecting them and clicking the left arrow. To add new summaries, begin by clicking the group that you wish to create a summary for in the Summarized Fields list. Then, click the field in the Available Fields list that you wish to summarize for that group and click the right-arrow button. The wizard will choose a default summary type (such as Sum or Maximum) and display it below the Summarized Fields list. If you wish to change the type of summary for the field you just added, choose the different summary function from this drop-down list. Note that you'll see more limited summary types for nonnumeric or noncurrency fields.

9. Clicking Next will display the Group Sorting area of the wizard (assuming that you have summary fields on your report). Usually, any groups on your report are presented in alphabetical order (for example, Arizona precedes California, followed by Oregon, Texas, and Wyoming). However, if you want to see the "top or bottom five states in order of sales," select the appropriate radio button to show groups in order of the subtotal or summary amount that you choose in the drop-down list, rather than by the name of the group. Click the Next button.

10. The Chart area lets you show your report data graphically in a bar, line, or pie chart. If you choose one of these options, specify the title for the chart, as well as the fields that the chart should be based on and should use for the size of the bar, wedge, or line. Do this with the Chart Title, On Change Of, and Show Summary options. Chapter 10 explains charting options in more detail.

11. When you click Next, the Record Selection area of the wizard will appear. Use this to limit your report to a desired set of meaningful database records. You likely won't ever want to include every record in the database tables in your report. Many tables contain large numbers of records, and your reports will be much more meaningful if they contain only the relevant set of records. Choose one or more fields to select, and move them to the Filter Fields list by clicking the right-arrow button. When you click a field in the Filter Fields list, an additional drop-down list appears below. You can choose the comparison operator you need in the pull-down list (such as equal to, less than, one of, between, and so on). Then, choose the value you want to compare against in the additional drop-down lists that appear. You may type a comparison value directly in the drop-down list box, or you can click the down arrow in the box to choose from a sample of data that will be read from the database field.

TIP   *More detailed information on selecting records is contained in Chapter 4.*

---

12. Click Next to show the final area of the wizard, the Template area. This area lets you determine the general appearance of your report. When you choose one of the available templates, a thumbnail view of the template appears to the right. If you wish to use an existing Crystal Report .RPT file as a template, click the Browse button to locate that .RPT file. Once chosen, the thumbnail view of that report will also appear to the right.

You may now click the Back button if you wish to move backward through the wizard to make any changes. Once you're satisfied with all your choices, click Finish to show the entire report in the Preview tab.

Once you have created the report using the Standard Report Wizard, you can print it on a printer, export it to another file format, save it to the Crystal Reports .RPT file format, or use any other function that Crystal Reports provides. You can click the Design tab to make any manual adjustments to the report that you wish.

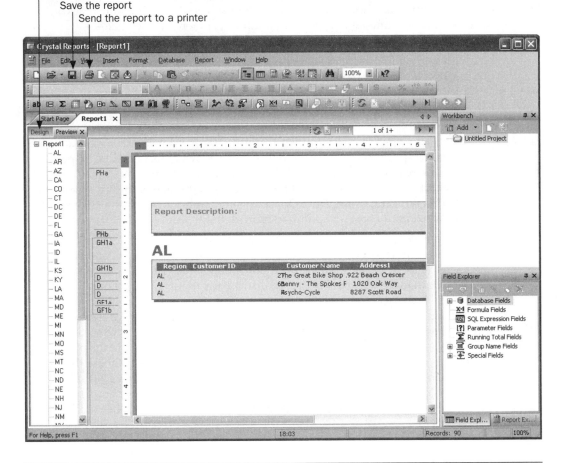

Click the Design tab to make manual adjustments to the report
Save the report
Send the report to a printer

CAUTION *Crystal Reports will not allow you to rerun the Report Wizard to make changes to the report you've already created—you must use the Design tab and make manual adjustments. While the Report Wizard does make "quick and dirty" reporting easier than manually creating reports, you'll probably want to familiarize yourself with general report formatting options in the Design tab so that you can modify reports you create with the wizard.*

Using the Blank Report Option

While the report wizards simplify the report design process by presenting a step-by-step approach, they limit your flexibility to create a report exactly as you'd like it to look. Among other limitations, you are required to accept the fonts, colors, and layout that the wizard chooses. Group total and summary fields are labeled haphazardly, and group fields are repeated over and over again in every report line within the group.

Although it's initially more labor intensive, using the Blank Report option to create a report gives you absolute control over what you put on your report, where you put it, and how it looks. Even if you use the report wizards, it's important to understand the concepts involved in the Blank Report option, because you'll need to use those concepts to refine many reports that the report wizards create.

To use the Blank Report option, choose Blank Report from the New Reports section of the Start page. You may also choose File | New from the pull-down menus and choose the Blank Report option from the submenu. In each case, a new empty report will be created and the Database Expert will appear.

The Database Expert

The *Database Expert,* shown in Figure 1-4, is where you choose the database tables you wish to include in your report. Here, you can select from any database type that Crystal Reports supports, including PC-type "local" databases, such as Microsoft Access, dBASE, Paradox, Btrieve, and others. You can also choose from virtually all popular client/server or SQL databases, such as Microsoft SQL Server, Oracle, Informix, and Sybase. Crystal Reports even supports proprietary data types, such as web server activity logs, the Windows NT/2000 event log, Microsoft Exchange systems, and XML-formatted data. These data types are all chosen here.

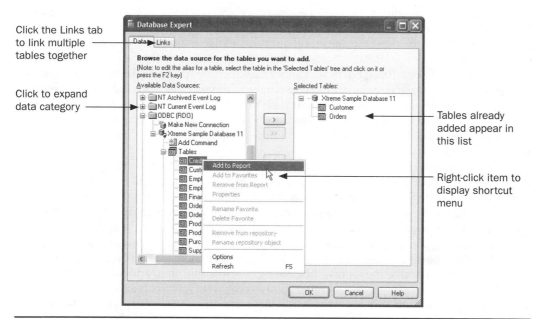

Figure 1-4   The Database Expert

The Database Expert categorizes types of databases, shown as small folder icons with plus signs next to them. Depending on the type of database you want to report on, click the plus sign next to one of the following database categories:

- **Current Connections** Displays a list of any databases you may already have connected to when working with previous reports. These connections will be closed when you close Crystal Reports.

- **Favorites** Contains data sources that you've previously added to your Favorites folder—if you use a data source on a regular basis, you may want to add it to the Favorites category to make it easy to find.

- **History** Shows data sources that you've recently connected to.

- **Create New Connection** Displays another set of subcategories that show types of databases that Crystal Reports will connect to. The folders that appear here are based on what database connection options you chose when you installed Crystal Reports, as well as on database connection software you may have installed on your computer, such as an existing program that contains an Oracle or DB2 client database driver.

- **Repository** Requests Crystal Reports Server or BusinessObjects Enterprise logon info, and then displays a list of any database connections that you have added to the Crystal/Business Objects Repository (the Repository is covered in more detail in Chapter 17).

NOTE *A more thorough discussion of the different data types that Crystal Reports supports can be found in Chapter 20.*

After you click the plus sign next to the category you wish to use, you may see a list of available databases under that category. If you're already logged on to a database in that category, you'll see the database name and all the available tables underneath the database name. Choose the desired database or subcategory. Depending on the category or database you choose, additional dialog boxes will appear, asking you to choose a particular database filename, log in to the database, or choose a database server. Eventually, you'll be able to choose one or more *database tables* that you wish to include in your report. You may also see a selection of database object types, such as tables, views, and stored procedures, that you can choose from. Click the plus sign next to the desired object type and choose an object from within the category.

To add a table to the report, select the table and click the right-arrow button. You can also just double-click the table name. When the table has been added to the report, the table name will appear in the rightmost Selected Tables list. If you add a table by mistake, just select it and click the left-arrow button to remove it—it will disappear from the Selected Tables list. If you want to select and add multiple tables, you may multiselect additional tables by holding down the CTRL key while clicking table names. Or, you may SHIFT-click tables to select those two tables, as well as all tables in between. When you've chosen the tables you want to add to the report, click the right-arrow button to add them all at once. And finally, you may simply add all tables in the Available Data Source list to the Selected Tables list by clicking the double-right-arrow key. Once you've selected all the tables you want to include in your report, close the Database Expert with the Close button.

PART I

> **TIP**   *There may be several different ways to connect to the same database. If, for example, you wish to report on a corporate Oracle database, you may connect via ODBC, via OLE DB, or by using a Crystal Reports "native" driver in the More Data Sources category within Create New Connection. If you're unsure of how to connect to your database, check with your database administrator.*

If you choose more than one table for your report, a Links tab will appear in the Database Explorer. You must click this tab to link the tables you've added to your report together. If you don't link tables, you'll be presented with the Links tab when you click OK on the Database Explorer dialog box. Use the Links tab to join or link your tables together. Table linking is discussed in detail in Chapter 15.

The Design Tab and Field Explorer

Once you've chosen and linked tables, Crystal Reports will display the Design tab. This is the "template" view that you use to begin designing the look and feel for your report. The first step to beginning report design is choosing fields for the report from the *Field Explorer,* shown in Figure 1-5. If you don't already see the Field Explorer, you can display it by clicking the Field Explorer button in the Standard Toolbar, or by choosing View | Field Explorer from the pull-down menus. Begin designing your report simply by dragging fields from the Field Explorer and dropping them on the report where you want them to appear.

The Field Explorer contains categories of fields that are available to place on your report. You'll see a plus sign next to the Database Fields category, indicating that more choices are

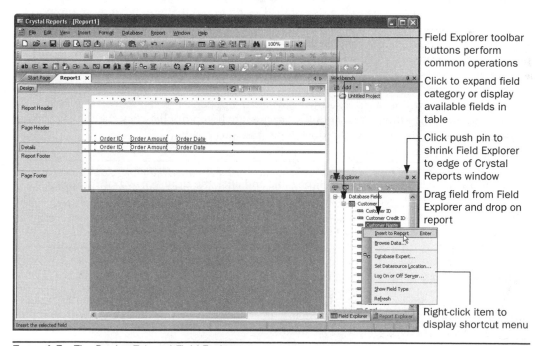

FIGURE 1-5   The Design Tab and Field Explorer

available in that category. Clicking the plus sign next to it will expand the category, showing all the tables you added from the Database Expert. Plus signs next to the table names, as well as next to the Special Fields category, indicate that fields are available below those levels—click the plus sign to see available fields. The other categories of the Field Explorer will not have any plus signs next to them, unless you've opened an existing report that already contains fields of these types. Once you begin creating new formulas, parameter fields, and so on, you'll see plus signs next to these categories as well. Click the plus signs to see available fields in these other categories.

The simplest way to add a field to the report is to drag and drop the field from the Field Explorer to the report's Design tab. When you drag, you'll see an outline of the field object appear on the report as you drag. When you have positioned the field where you want it to appear, simply release the mouse button to drop the field on the report. As an alternative, you may right-click a field and choose Insert To Report from the pop-up menu, select the desired field, and click the Insert To Report button (the first toolbar button) from the Field Explorer toolbar, or just press ENTER. The field will be attached to the mouse cursor, which you can then position to drop the field.

You're not limited to dragging and dropping one field at a time to the report. If you see several fields you'd like to drag and drop at once, use CTRL-click to select or deselect multiple fields. If you wish to select a range of fields, click the first field in the range and then hold down the SHIFT key and click the last field in the range. Both fields, as well as all of those in between, will be selected. After you CTRL- or SHIFT-click the desired fields, drag and drop them as a group. After you add a field to the report, you see a small green check mark next to the field in the Field Explorer. This indicates that the field is in use somewhere on the report.

You do not have to leave the Field Explorer docked to the side of the Crystal Reports window. If you'd like to expand the size of the Design tab so that you have more room to work without scrolling, "undock" the Field Explorer by pointing to its title bar area at the top. Then, either double-click the title bar or drag the Field Explorer away until you see the outline of a separate, free-floating window. The Design tab will expand to the full width of the Crystal Reports window, and the Field Explorer will now display in its own free-floating window. To redock the Field Explorer, drag it back toward the edge of the Crystal Reports window until the outline of a docked window again appears. You can redock the Field Explorer to the left, bottom, or right of the Design tab. If you double-click the title bar of the free-floating Field Explorer, it will redock to its previous position.

TIP *One of the new user interface elements in many Crystal Reports XI dialog boxes (including the Field Explorer) is the push pin. Clicking this icon in the upper right-hand corner of a dialog box will "shrink" the dialog box to the edge of the Crystal Reports screen, freeing up more screen space for report design. Then, if you simply point to the name of the dialog box on the edge of the screen, the dialog box will expand from the edge of the screen. If you wish to return the dialog box to its always-displayed state, just click the push pin again when the dialog box is expanded.*

Report Sections

When you first create a new report, Crystal Reports shows five default sections in the Design tab. Table 1-1 outlines where and how many times each section appears in a report, and the types of objects you may want to place in them.

Section	Where It Appears	What to Place in the Section
Report header	Once only, at the beginning of the report	Title page, company logo, introductory information that you want to appear once only, at the beginning of the report, charts or cross-tabs that apply to the whole report
Page header	At the top of every page	Field titles, print date/time, report title
Details	Every time a new record is read from the database	Database fields and formulas that you want to appear for every record
Report footer	Once only, at the end of the report	Grand totals, closing disclaimers, charts, or cross-tabs that apply to the whole report
Page footer	At the bottom of every page	Page numbers, report name, explanations for figures in the report

TABLE 1-1   Default Report Sections

If you drag a database field into the details section, Crystal Reports places a field heading in the page header automatically and aligns it with the database field. If you drag a database field into any other section, no field heading will be inserted, even if you drag the field into the details section later—automatic field headings are only created if you drag a field directly into the details section (and, if you haven't turned off the Insert Detail Field Headings option in File | Options).

Previewing the Report

When you see objects depicted in the Design tab, Crystal Reports is displaying only "placeholders." You'll see the names of fields and objects surrounded by outline symbols, indicating how wide and tall they are. You won't ever see actual data in the Design tab. To see the report containing real data as it might appear when printed on a printer or exported to a web page, you need to preview the report.

There are several ways of previewing a report. Choose View | Print Preview or click the Print Preview button on the Standard toolbar to preview the entire report. To preview a limited number of records, choose View | Preview Sample and specify the number of records you wish to see.

When you preview a report, the Preview tab appears next to the Design tab, as shown in Figure 1-6. You can scroll up and down through the report, use the Zoom control to change the Zoom level of the report, and use the page navigation buttons to move through various pages of the report (Crystal Reports XI now displays page navigation buttons both at the top of the report preview screen and in the new Navigation Tools toolbar). You can easily move back and forth between the Design and Preview tabs by clicking them.

Return to the Design tab without removing the Preview tab
Preview the report when the Design tab is active
Remove the Preview tab and return to the Design tab
Cancel data retrieval and show what's been formatted so far
Change preview zoom levels
Page navigation buttons

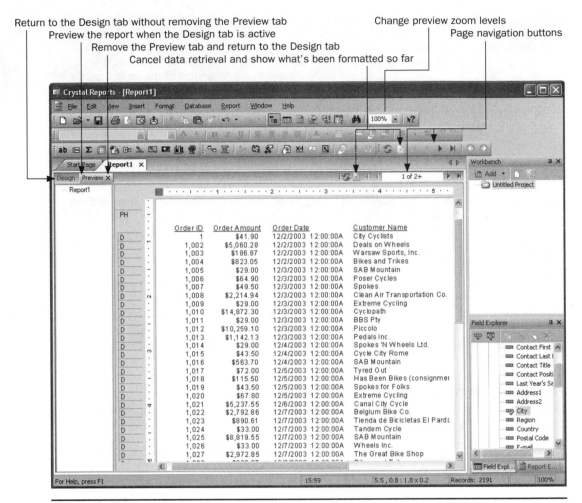

FIGURE 1-6 Previewing a report

Moving and Sizing Objects

Once you've placed objects on your report, you will probably want to move them around the report as your design progresses. Crystal Reports estimates how much horizontal space is required to display string database fields. This may result in string fields on the report that may appear too narrow or too wide. Also, if you change the font size of an object, you'll usually have to adjust the object size accordingly.

The first step in moving or sizing an object is to select the object. Simply click it. A shaded outline and four blocks appear around the object, indicating that it is selected. Now you can move or size it.

Pointing inside the selected object causes your mouse pointer to turn into a four-way pointer. You can then click and drag the object to a new location with the mouse. If you point at one of the little blue blocks—the *sizing handles* at the top, bottom, left, and right of the object—your mouse pointer turns into a two-way size pointer. Clicking and dragging these handles stretches or shrinks the object. Sizing objects requires very precise accuracy with your mouse! Laptop users with trackpads will probably opt for an external mouse after trying this a few times.

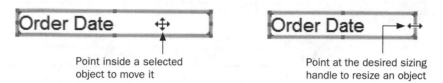

Point inside a selected   Point at the desired sizing
object to move it   handle to resize an object

You're not limited to moving or sizing one object at a time. You can select multiple objects before moving or sizing them. CTRL-click or SHIFT-click to select more than one field or field title. You can also surround multiple objects with an elastic box. Before you start to draw the elastic box, make sure you deselect any already-selected objects by clicking an area of the report where there are no objects.

TIP *When the Design tab is displayed, you don't have to use the mouse to move or resize objects. For very fine control of object placement and sizing, use your keyboard's cursor keys. Using the cursor keys by themselves will move selected objects in the direction of the key. If you hold down SHIFT and use the cursor keys, objects will be widened, narrowed, made taller, or made shorter in the direction of the keys.*

Using Guidelines to Move Objects

When you insert a database field into the details section, Crystal Reports inserts two other things automatically. The first, the field heading, appears directly above the field in the page header. What might not be so obvious is the *vertical guideline*. You'll notice a little "upside-down tent" (officially known as a *guideline handle*) in the ruler above the report. The guideline is actually a vertical line extending from the guideline handle all the way down the report. Crystal Reports automatically placed this in the ruler, and it attached the field in the details section and the field heading in the page header to the guideline.

NOTE *By default, only the guideline handles are visible when you first install Crystal Reports. If you'd like to see the dashed guidelines themselves in the Design tab, choose View | Guidelines | Design from the pull-down menus. To see guidelines in the Preview tab, choose View | Guidelines | Preview from the pull-down menus. Note that even if you make the latter choice, you'll see the dashed guidelines in the Preview tab only if you click any object to select it in the preview window.*

You may move objects as a group by dragging the guideline handle left or right inside the ruler. All objects attached to that guideline will move at the same time. If you've placed a database field in the details section and an associated field heading in the page header, and you have inserted several group subtotals in groups and grand totals in the report footer, they will typically all be attached to the same guideline. Just move the guideline left or right to move all the objects together.

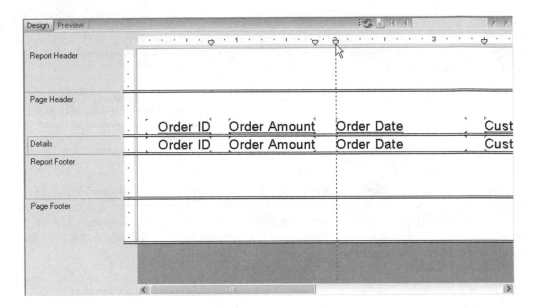

With a little experience, you'll probably quickly develop a love-hate relationship with guidelines. If you have lots of smaller objects positioned closely together on a report, you'll probably give up on the guidelines and just move them by CTRL-clicking or using an elastic box. If you have fewer objects spaced a little farther apart on your report, or lots of aligned objects in several report sections, you'll probably like using the guidelines to rearrange objects. Table 1-2 shows some of the guideline issues that may crop up in your report-design process, along with ways of solving the problems.

NOTE *If you created the report with a report wizard, you'll see that Crystal Reports inserted horizontal guidelines on the left side of the Design tab. You can add these yourself if you use the Blank Report option. Just click in the side ruler to add a horizontal guideline. Then attach objects to them on the top, bottom, or middle. Move the guideline to move whole lines of objects up or down at the same time.*

Formatting Objects

When you place objects on your report, Crystal Reports applies default font faces, sizes, colors, and formatting to the objects. You'll usually want to change some of this formatting to suit your particular report style or standards. There are several ways of formatting objects. As you use Crystal Reports, you may find that one way suits you better than another. Also, all formatting options aren't available with every method, so you may need to use a certain one to perform a specific kind of formatting.

Using the Formatting toolbar is the quickest way to apply standard formatting. The Formatting toolbar is similar to other toolbars you may have used in word processors or spreadsheet programs. To format using the Formatting toolbar, first select the object or objects you want to format, and then change their formatting by clicking Formatting toolbar buttons or choosing items in drop-down lists.

What Happened	How Is It Fixed?
You mistakenly dragged a guideline off the ruler when you just wanted to move it left or right. The objects attached to it haven't moved, and the guideline is now gone.	Click the Undo button on the Standard toolbar, or choose Edit | Undo Remove Guideline. This will bring the guideline back. If you notice the missing guideline after you've completed other tasks, and you don't want to Undo, just add a guideline back into the ruler by clicking in the ruler; reattach the objects by dragging them to the new guideline.
You selected and moved an individual object or objects with your mouse, but the guideline didn't move with them. Now, when you move the guideline in the ruler, the objects don't move.	You detach an object from a guideline when you move the object in the Design tab. You cannot reattach guidelines to objects by moving the guideline in the ruler. You have to reattach *objects to guidelines* by moving the objects until they snap to the guidelines. You can tell when an object has been reattached to a guideline by looking at the very small red marks on the edge of the object where it's attached to the guideline.
You've resized or moved objects and they now appear to be attached to two guidelines: one on the left and one on the right. When you move either guideline, the objects stretch rather than move.	Resize the objects away from the guideline you don't want them attached to. By resizing, you detach them from one guideline while leaving them attached to the other.
You notice that when you delete objects from the report, the guidelines stay and clutter up the ruler. When you move other objects around on the report, they're always snapping to the stray guidelines.	Remove any unwanted guidelines simply by dragging them off the ruler.

TABLE 1-2   Guideline Issues

   Some formatting options, such as formatting a date field to print in a long date format or designating that only one dollar sign should print at the top of each page, aren't available on the Formatting toolbar. These formatting options, along with all the options available on the Formatting toolbar, can be chosen in the Format Editor, shown in Figure 1-7. To use the Format Editor, first choose the object or objects that you wish to format, and then do one of the following:

- Click the Format button on the Expert Tools toolbar.
- Choose Format Field from the Format menu.
- Right-click the object and choose Format Field from the pop-up menu.

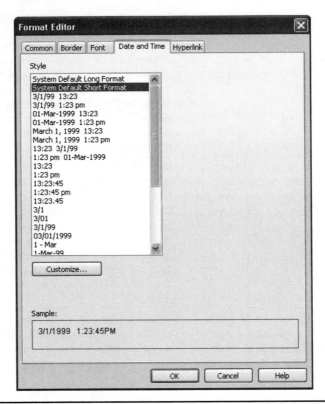

FIGURE 1-7 The Format Editor

All of these options display the Format Editor. Choose the desired tab on the Format Editor, and make formatting selections by choosing one of the built-in styles, by using a custom style, or by choosing other specific formatting options on the desired tab. Click OK on the Format Editor to apply all the formatting you chose and close the Format Editor.

There are two general ways you can choose formats in the Format Editor—with a default style, or by customizing the style. In particular, you'll notice a selection of predefined formats for most non-string data types in the Style list. You can just choose one of these default formats from the list. If, however, the exact format you want isn't in the Style list, click the Customize button at the bottom of the Style list. A Custom Style dialog box will appear where you can make more detailed choices about how to format the field. You'll need to use the Customize button to conditionally format some aspects of the field as well (conditional formatting is discussed in Chapter 7).

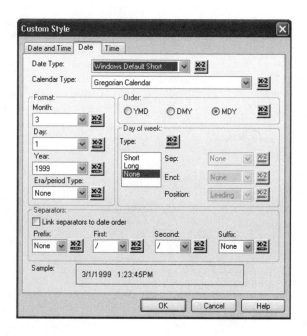

TIP   *You can add new objects, or move, size, and format existing objects, just as easily in the Preview tab as in the Design tab. Be careful, though, that you move or size objects accurately in the Preview tab. You may inadvertently move an object from the details section to the page header, or make some similar undesirable move, without realizing it. Formatting objects in the Preview tab is great, but it may be better to size or move them in the Design tab.*

Customizing Crystal Reports Behavior

When you first install Crystal Reports, it behaves in a certain way that should serve most report designers well. However, you will probably want to customize the behavior of some Crystal Report options. Other software typically has a Preferences or Options menu item to accomplish this. Crystal Reports has two options that work together to control how the program behaves: Options and Report Options, both chosen from the File menu.

Most often, you will use the Options dialog box, shown in Figure 1-8, to change the default behavior of Crystal Reports. For example, to change the default font face and size from Arial 10 point to something else, you would click the Fonts tab in the Options dialog box, click the button for the type of object you want to change, and choose a different font or size. To change the default format of date fields from the default specified in the Windows Control Panel to mm/dd/yy, you would click the Fields tab in the Options dialog box and then click the Date button.

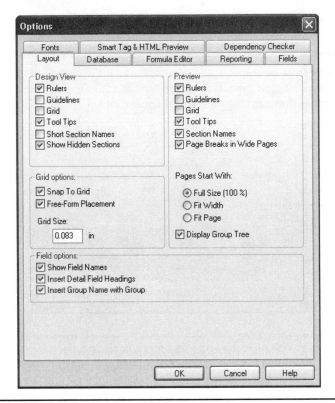

FIGURE 1-8   Options dialog box

CAUTION *Many options you choose here don't change items already placed on the current report, or any existing reports—they will affect only new items added to the report. For example, if you change the default font to 8-point Times New Roman, only new objects that you add to the report from that point forward will take on that new formatting.*

There are a number of options that benefit the new user and make report creation a bit easier. You may want to choose File | Options and set each of the following options to your own personal preference.

The Options dialog box is divided into a series of tabs, each categorizing the various options that are available. What follows is a summary of the more often-used options.

Layout Tab

- **Design View – Guidelines**   You may wish to turn this option on to display dashed guidelines in the Design tab. The majority of report designing should occur in the Design tab, and guidelines can be useful.

- **Design View – Short Section Names**   Once you're more familiar with the Design tab, you may turn this option on to give you more design area. This will change the fully spelled section names at the left of the Design tab to smaller abbreviations.

- **Preview – Section Names**   You'll probably want to leave this option on to help you troubleshoot sectional problems when you're in preview mode. This will show abbreviated section names to the left of the Preview tab.

- **Grid Options – Snap To Grid**   Great to turn off when you want to be able to truly use freeform placement of objects. This will allow precise placement without objects snapping to the predetermined grid.

- **Design View – Grid**   If you leave Snap To Grid turned on, this will actually show the grid in the Design tab as a series of dots, so you can see exactly where objects you are moving will snap.

- **Preview – Grid**   You'll probably want to leave this option turned off to improve clarity. You may turn it on if you are moving and resizing objects in the Preview tab and want to see where they will snap.

Reporting Tab

- **Save Data With Report**   Checks the File | Save Data With Report option automatically when you create a new report. This saves data in the Preview tab along with the report design in the report .RPT file. If you don't want this option turned on when you create a new report, uncheck it here in File | Options.

- **Suppress Printing If No Records Selected**   If the particular combination of data and record selection chosen returns no records, this option will suppress printing of every object on the report. If you leave this option turned off and no records are returned, text objects in page/report headers, and other "fixed" objects, will still print.

- **Show All Headers On Drill Down**   Shows all headers above the group being drilled into inside the drill-down tab. See Chapter 8 for information on drill-down reporting.

- **Autosave Reports After *x* Minutes**   This will automatically save your report files every few minutes, preventing a loss of data if you suffer a power failure or your computer hangs. You may choose how often to automatically save reports. Reports are saved in the drive/folder specified as your Windows "Temp" folder with the file extension .AUTOSAVE.RPT.

- **Save Preview Picture**   This will automatically save a small "thumbnail view" of your report along with the .RPT file when you save the report (you must preview the report before you save it for the Preview Picture to be saved). This is helpful if you plan on posting the report in BusinessObjects Enterprise (discussed in Part II of this book).

Formula Editor Tab

- **Default Formula Language**   This feature allows you to choose the default formula language for Crystal Reports formulas. You may change the language used for formulas within each formula, but this allows you to choose the default. Chapter 5 discusses the different formula language options in more detail.

- **Text Options/Color**   These choices will change the default font and color scheme used in the Formula Editor. You may, for example, wish to increase or decrease the size and style of the font that appears when you create formulas.

Database Tab

- **Sort Tables Alphabetically/Sort Fields Alphabetically**   This will sort tables in the Database Expert and fields in the Field Explorer alphabetically, rather than in the order the database returns them. This may be helpful with large databases when you need to find a particular table or field.

- **Database Server Is Case-Insensitive**   If you check this option, SQL databases that you use (such as Microsoft SQL Server, Oracle, and Informix) will ignore the case of any record selection you may provide. For example, if you supply a record selection or Select Expert comparison value of "USA", the report will still include records if they include "Usa", "usa", or "uSa".

- **Select Distinct Data For Browsing**   You may notice that browsing for sample data in the Select Expert, in the Field Explorer, and in other parts of Crystal Reports takes a significant amount of time. This is probably because the report is set to Select Distinct Data For Browsing. If you turn off this option, only the first 500 records of the report will be read when browsing, instead of reading records until 500 unique values are retrieved. Although this may not supply as many sample values when browsing, it can be significantly faster.

- **Perform Query Asynchronously**   Checking this option will allow you to stop a query sent to a SQL database before it begins returning records to the report. You can do this with the Stop button in the Preview tab (the square button to the right of the page navigation buttons). If you leave this option unchecked, you will have to wait until the server completes the query and begins to return records to the report before you may stop report processing.

Fonts/Fields Tabs

These tabs will allow you to choose formatting options for different Crystal Reports data types (such as string, numeric, dates, and so forth) and different types of Crystal Reports objects (such as database fields, summary fields, field titles, and so forth). Click the desired button and choose desired formatting options for the default Format Editor. New objects placed on reports from that point forward will take on the new formatting.

A subset of items from the Options dialog box appears on the File | Report Options dialog box.

Report Options

General Settings

- ☐ Convert Database NULL Values to Default
- ☐ Convert Other NULL Values to Default
- ☐ Show All Headers On Drill Down
- ☐ Always Sort Locally
- ☑ Database Server is Case-Insensitive
- ☐ Perform Grouping On Server
- ☑ Use Indexes Or Server For Speed
- ☑ Verify on First Refresh
- ☐ Verify Stored Procedures on First Refresh
- ☐ Respect Keep Group Together On First Page

- ☑ Save Data With Report
- ☐ Suppress Printing If No Records
- ☐ Perform Query Asynchronously
- ☑ Create Group Tree
- ☑ Display Alerts on Refresh
- ☐ Read-only
- ☐ Select Distinct Records
- ☑ Select Distinct Data for Browsing
- ☐ Retain Original Image Color Depth
- ☑ Prompt For Hyperlinks

Initial Report Part Settings

Paste the Report Part link: 📋   Paste Link ▼

Object Name:

Data Context:

Preview Pages Start With :   Full Size

[OK]   [Cancel]   [Help]

When you create a new report, these options are based on what's set in the File | Options dialog box. Later, though, these options can be set to be different from the corresponding File | Options dialog box items. When the report is saved, these options are saved along with the report. The next time the report is retrieved, they will *supersede* the corresponding File | Option items.

The Report Explorer

The *Report Explorer* is a tree-like view of all the sections in your report (Report Header, Details section, Page footer, and so forth) and the report objects within them (database fields, text objects, and so forth). Navigating through the Report Explorer is another way to format or delete individual report objects or entire report sections.

To display the Report Explorer, choose View | Report Explorer from the pull-down menus or click the Report Explorer button in the Standard Toolbar. If the Field and Report Explorers are combined in the single dialog box, you may also click the Report Explorer tab to display the Report Explorer.

The Report Explorer will appear, as shown in Figure 1-9. As with other similar dialog boxes (such as the Field Explorer), Crystal Reports XI now displays the push pin in the upper right-hand corner. You may click this to shrink the Report Explorer to the side of the Crystal Reports window.

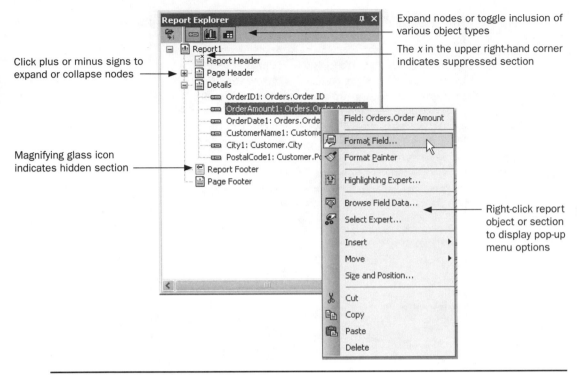

Click plus or minus signs to expand or collapse nodes

Magnifying glass icon indicates hidden section

Expand nodes or toggle inclusion of various object types

The *x* in the upper right-hand corner indicates suppressed section

Right-click report object or section to display pop-up menu options

FIGURE 1-9   The Report Explorer

NOTE *By default, the Field Explorer and Report Explorer are combined into a single tabbed dialog box. You may separate them by dragging the desired tab away from the combined dialog box. If you then wish to redock the explorer, you may discover that the two are no longer combined with their respective tabs. While this may be the way you prefer to display the dialog boxes (especially if you make use of the new push pin feature), you may wish to recombine the two explorer dialogs into a single tabbed dialog. To do this, drag either the Field Explorer or the Report Explorer on top of the other dialog box until a box-with-tab outline appears. When you release the mouse button, the two dialog boxes will recombine. You may actually use this technique to combine other explorers (such as the Workbench or the Dependency Checker) with existing explorers.*

The very top "node" in the Report Explorer represents the report itself—everything else appears within this node. Click the plus sign to expand the report, which will then display a list of report sections (Page Header, Details section, and so forth). If you click the plus sign next to a report section, you'll be presented with either additional sections (if you've created them) or report objects within that section. A different icon will appear for suppressed or hidden sections. And, the type of each report object within a section will also be indicated by a unique icon—a small picture image will appear next to bitmap graphics, the "ab" characters will appear next to a text object, and so on. Report objects will display either their default names, such as "Graph1", or specific names you've given them in the Common tab of the Format Editor (discussed in more detail in Chapter 7).

If you select a report section, the corresponding gray section name will be highlighted at the left of the Design or Preview tab. If you click a report object, the object will be selected on the Design or Preview tab of Crystal Reports. Once you've selected the section or object you wish to modify, right-click. A pop-up menu will appear giving you several choices, depending on whether you've selected a report section or an object (this is the same pop-up menu that you'll see if you right-click the report object itself or the gray section area in the Design or Preview tab). You may choose, among other things, to format a section (which will display the Section Expert), format a report object (which will display the Format Editor), or delete the object or section. If you wish to format multiple report objects at the same time, you may CTRL-click more than one object to select them. Then, options you choose from the pop-up menu will apply to all selected objects (note that you can't multiselect report sections or a combination of sections and objects).

TIP *More information on formatting sections with the Section Expert is presented in Chapter 8. More detailed information on formatting individual objects with the Format Editor can be found in Chapter 7.*

The New Workbench

New in Crystal Reports XI is the Workbench. The *Workbench* is an additional "explorer" (similar to the Field Explorer and Report Explorer discussed earlier in the chapter) that allows you to organize sets of reports into "projects."

When you first start Crystal Reports, the Workbench window appears on the right side of the Crystal Reports screen. If this is the first time you've started Crystal Reports, or if you have done no previous work with the Workbench, the screen will simply display a Create New Project entry. Ultimately, you may simply choose not to use the Workbench, or you may wish that the Workbench "shrink" to provide more screen space for other report design elements. As with the other explorers mentioned earlier in the chapter, you may click the small *x* or push pin in the upper right-hand corner of the Workbench to close or shrink the dialog box.

If you shrunk the Workbench, click the icon on the side of the Crystal Reports screen to expand it. If you closed the Workbench, you may choose View | Workbench from the pull-down menus, or click the Workbench toolbar button in the Standard toolbar. The Workbench will reappear.

The Workbench, shown in Figure 1-10, allows you to organize any number of report files into a series of projects. A *project* simply displays as a folder inside the Workbench. You may then add any number of existing reports to a project folder. If you are using Crystal Reports Server or BusinessObjects Enterprise, you may also add Report Packages to the Workbench. By making use of the Workbench, you can organize a series of reports that you wish to treat in some organized fashion, such as a batch of reports that you may be developing for a new Data Warehouse project or a custom software package.

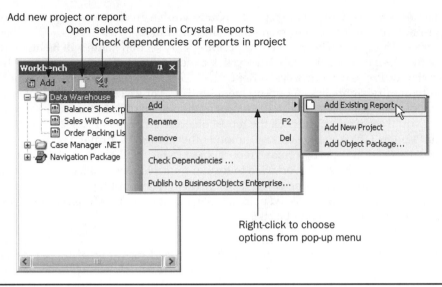

Figure 1-10   The Workbench

Creating Projects and Adding Existing Reports

You must create at least one project folder before you add reports to the Workbench. If you add reports before you create a project folder, an "Untitled Project" folder will be created for the report automatically. To create a new project, either click the down arrow next to the Add button in the Workbench toolbar and choose Add New Project, or right-click in the Workbench and choose Add | Add New Project from the pop-up menu. An "Untitled Project" folder will be added to the Workbench. The project name will automatically be placed in edit mode so that you can type the desired name for the project folder as soon as you create it. If you wish to rename an existing project folder, select the desired folder and press the F2 key, hold your mouse button down for a short period of time, or right-click and choose Rename from the pop-up menu. The project folder name will be placed in edit mode so that you can type a new name.

NOTE *Unlike the Crystal Reports Server/BusinessObjects Enterprise folder/subfolder model, the Crystal Reports Workbench allows projects to be created only one level deep. In other words, a project folder will contain only reports—it cannot contain lower-level folders or "subprojects."*

Once you've created a new project folder, you may add one or more reports to the folder. First, select the project folder you wish to add reports to. Then, click the Add toolbar button in the Workbench toolbar or right-click the desired project folder and choose Add | Add Existing Report from the pop-up menu. An Open dialog box will appear displaying existing .RPT files. Navigate to the desired folder on your local hard disk or network drive and choose the report you wish to add. Once you click Open, the report will be added to the Workbench in the chosen project folder. You may also open a separate Windows Explorer window and select one or more .RPT files. Then, simply drag the files to the desired project folder in the Workbench. The report or reports will be added to the Workbench.

Deleting projects and reports from the Workbench is similarly straightforward. Select either the project folder or report you wish to delete. Then, just press the DEL key or right-click and choose Remove from the pop-up menu. The selected report or project will be deleted from the Workbench. If you delete a project folder, all reports in that folder will be deleted.

NOTE *When you delete reports from the Workbench, you are only deleting their reference in the Workbench dialog box. The actual .RPT file will not be deleted from your hard disk or network drive.*

Once you have organized reports and projects in the Workbench, it's simple to reorganize them by dragging and dropping. You may, for example, wish to move a report from one project folder to another. Just select the desired report and drag with your mouse. You'll see a small underline indicating where the report will be dropped. Drop it underneath the desired folder and the report will be placed in that folder. You may also reorder the lists of project folders by dragging and dropping the folders to different locations.

Opening a report you've added to the Workbench is accomplished by merely double-clicking its name. You may also select the desired report and click the Open toolbar button from the Workbench toolbar, or right-click the desired report and choose Open from the pop-up menu. The report will be opened in Crystal Reports for viewing or editing. If you have renamed, moved, or deleted a report since adding it to the Workbench, the Workbench will be unable to find the report and an error message will appear when you attempt to open the report.

NOTE *You can also publish reports from a project folder in the Workbench to Crystal Reports Server or BusinessObjects Enterprise—either as individual reports, or as a report package. More information on publishing reports can be found in Chapter 24.*

Adding Report Packages

Crystal Reports Server and BusinessObjects Enterprise feature the ability to store a group of related reports as a *report package.* A report package allows multiple reports to be scheduled and viewed as a single unit (more information on report packages can be found in Chapter 24).

The Workbench allows you to connect to your Crystal Reports Server or BusinessObjects Enterprise system and add a report package as a separate entry. Right-click in the Workbench and choose Add | Add Object Package from the pop-up menu (no toolbar button option is available to add report packages). Once you've supplied proper logon credentials to your Crystal Reports Server or BusinessObjects Enterprise system, a list of folders will appear. Navigate to the desired location and choose the report package you wish to add to the Workbench.

A report package will appear in the Workbench as a separate entry with a unique icon (it won't be placed in a project folder). Click the plus sign next to the report package name to see the group of reports that make it up. As with individual reports you added to the Workbench, you may open a report contained in a report package by double-clicking it, selecting it and clicking the Open toolbar button in the Workbench toolbar, or right-clicking it and choosing Open from the pop-up menu. And, as with reports added to the Workbench from disk drives, any report package reports that are removed or renamed in their source Crystal Reports Server or BusinessObjects Enterprise systems won't open if they're chosen in the Workbench.

TIP *All Crystal Reports Workbench information is stored in the ProjectExplorer.XML data file created in your private "Documents and Settings" folder maintained by Windows. Even if you uninstall and reinstall Crystal Reports, the Workbench will still retain its layout and contents if this file is left intact.*

The New Dependency Checker

Crystal Reports XI adds the Dependency Checker as a new feature. The *Dependency Checker* will analyze one or more reports and return a list of potential problems the report may have, including:

- Errors in formulas, SQL Expressions, or Custom Functions
- Hyperlinks set in the Format Editor that are broken
- Invalid database connections that are identified by the Verify Database command
- Repository objects that can't be found in the source repository
- Report part hyperlinks that are broken
- External subreports that can't be found in their original locations

The Dependency Checker can check a single report that is currently open for viewing or editing. It can also be used to check one or more reports as a group from the Workbench (discussed earlier in the chapter). When the Dependency Checker is run, a list of potential problems is presented in a separate dialog box. When you double-click an individual error, the specific part of the report (formula, repository object, and so forth) referenced by the error will be displayed. You may then take steps to resolve the error.

NOTE *The new Crystal Reports XI Dependency Checker is not related to the Business View Manager function of the same name. Information on checking dependencies in Business Views is discussed in Chapter 16.*

Checking Dependencies in the Current Report

You may check dependencies in the report you currently have open for editing or viewing. You may, for example, have created a large number of formulas and wish to ensure that they all reference proper fields. Or, you may have just opened a report developed by a colleague and wish to look for any obvious problems that the Dependency Checker looks for.

Choose Report | Check Dependencies from the pull-down menus (there is no equivalent toolbar button). A dialog box will appear that indicates the progress of the checking process—the more complex a report, the longer it will take to check dependencies.

The Dependency Checker Dialog Box

Once the dependency checking process is complete, results will be displayed in the Dependency Checker dialog box, shown in Figure 1-11. This dialog box, like other "explorers" discussed in this chapter (Field Explorer, Report Explorer, Workbench, and so forth), can be docked or undocked to the side or bottom of the Crystal Reports screen, as well as being shrunk and expanded by clicking the push pin icon.

An icon will appear next to each error message, indicating the type of error encountered. These error icons include a green check mark that indicates no errors in the report, a yellow explanation point that indicates a potential problem that generally won't prevent the report from running, and a red *x* that indicates a problem that may prevent the report from running at all.

To display the specific object that resulted in the error message, do one of these things: double-click the error message, select the error message and press ENTER, or else right-click the error and choose Go To from the pop-up menu. The report will display the object referenced by the error (for example, the formula that has an error or the bitmap image that can't be found in the repository). You may then take steps to resolve the problem identified by the Dependency Checker.

Once you've finished viewing Dependency Checker entries, you may close the Dependency Checker dialog box by clicking the small *x* in the upper right-hand corner. However, even closing the Dependency Checker will not clear the entries in it from a previous checking process. You may redisplay the Dependency Checker by choosing View | Dependency Checker from the pull-down menus, or clicking the Dependency Checker toolbar button in the Standard toolbar.

To actually clear errors from the Dependency Checker, select the desired error you no longer wish to display and press the DEL key. You may also right-click the desired error and choose Clear from the pop-up menu. Or, if you'd like to clear all errors in the Dependency Checker, right-click and choose Clear All from the pop-up menu. Once you've cleared errors, running the Dependency Checker process again with the Report | Check Dependencies option will redisplay any leftover errors in the report.

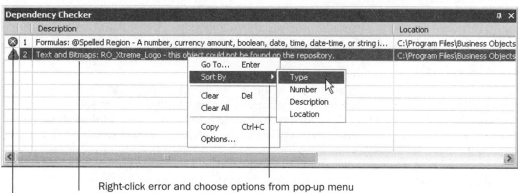

Right-click error and choose options from pop-up menu

Double-click error to highlight suspect object

Icon indicates type of error

FIGURE 1-11 The Dependency Checker

Dependency Checker Options

By default, the Dependency Checker will check all possible types of errors, including those based on the Crystal Reports Server/BusinessObjects Enterprise repository, hyperlinks, and so forth. You may, however, prefer that the Dependency Checker only check for certain types of errors in your report. To make these choices, check or uncheck options in the Dependency Checker Options dialog box. You may display this dialog box by choosing File | Options from the pull-down menus and then clicking the Dependency Checker tab. Or, you may right-click in the Dependency Checker dialog box and choose Options from the pop-up menu.

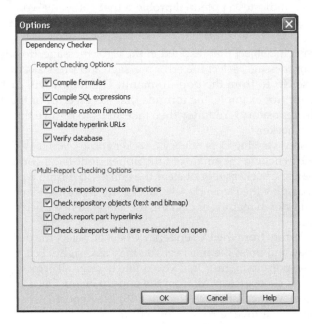

Checking Dependencies for Workbench Projects

Not only can you check dependencies in the currently open report, but you can check a single report or group of reports that you've organized in the Workbench (the Workbench is covered in more detail earlier in the chapter). You can even check dependencies in one or all reports contained in a report package that you've added to the Workbench from Crystal Reports Server or BusinessObjects Enterprise.

To check a report or reports contained within a Workbench project, select the desired item you want to check in the Workbench. For example, to check a single report, select it in the Workbench. If you want to check all reports in a project, select the project folder. If you want to check a single report in a report package, select the individual report within the package. Or, select the report package name if you wish to check all reports within the package. Once you've made your selection, click the Check Dependencies button in the Workbench toolbar, or right-click and choose Check Dependencies from the pop-up menu.

Crystal Reports will open all selected reports and check dependencies in each one. The Dependency Checker dialog box will appear with all errors found in all reports. You can determine which report an error belongs to by looking at the Location column in the Dependency Checker. To evaluate or correct a particular error, double-click the error, select the error and press ENTER, or right-click on the error and choose Go To from the pop-up menu.

Adding Text to Reports

There are many times during the report design process that you need to just drop some *literal text* into your report. This could be a report title that you place in the report header, a label next to a subtotal in the group footer, or a whole paragraph that you place in the report footer (perhaps explaining the methodology of the report). You can accomplish this with *text objects*.

To insert a text object, choose Insert | Text Object or click the Text Object button on the Insert Tools toolbar. Crystal Reports XI now behaves differently than previous versions by displaying a cross-hair cursor. Move this cursor to where you want the text object to appear. Then hold down your mouse button to drag the text object to its desired width and height. The text object will be dropped at that location, and you'll be immediately placed in *edit mode*. You'll always know when you're in edit mode because you'll see a flashing cursor inside the text object and a small ruler at the top of the Design or Preview tab, as shown here:

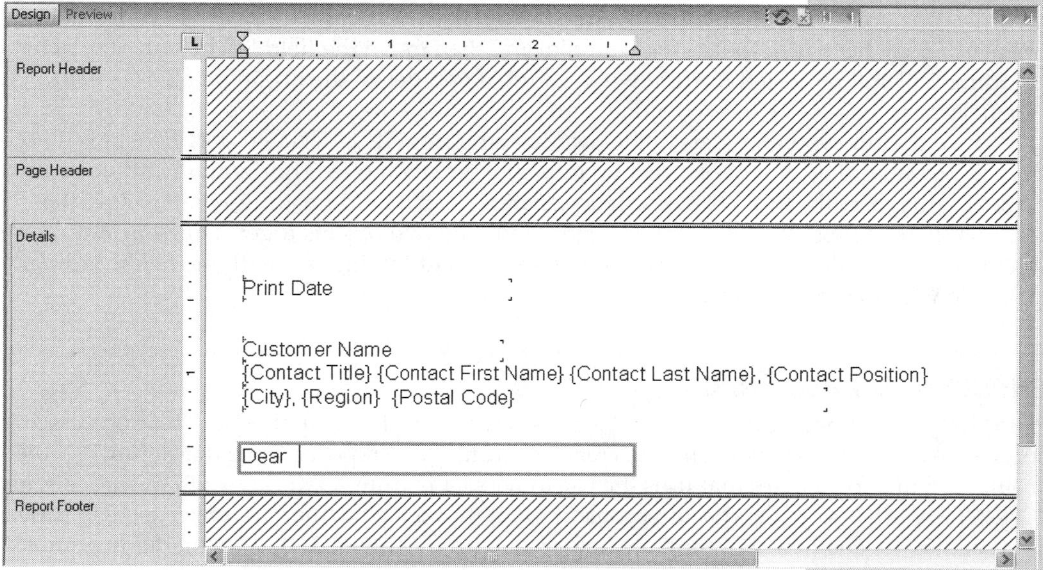

Now, just start typing. The material you type will appear inside the text object. When you're finished, just click outside the text object to save your changes.

There are several ways to edit the contents of an existing text object. To use the "long way," select the text object and then choose Edit | Edit Text from the pull-down menus, or right-click the text object and choose Edit Text from the pop-up menu. The "short way" is simply to double-click a text object, which places you in edit mode. Once in edit mode, use the cursor keys, BACKSPACE key, and DEL key to move around and edit the text. You may also use the CTRL key, in combination with cursor keys, to move forward and backward an entire word. And, to highlight portions of the text object (perhaps to delete a group of text), use the SHIFT key in combination with cursor keys.

CAUTION *It's commonplace to attempt to exit edit mode by pressing the ENTER key. Not only will this not end editing, it will start a new line in the text object. This can often cause the contents of the text object to partially or completely disappear. If you want to put line breaks in your text object, go ahead and press ENTER, but make sure you resize the text object when you're finished so that you can see all of your text. You may also format a multiline text object with the Can Grow formatting option.*

The Field Heading Text Object

A special kind of text object is the *field heading text object*. This is created in the page header automatically by Crystal Reports when you place a field from the Field Explorer into the details section. If you then select the text object in the page header, you'll notice that the Crystal Reports status bar indicates that you've selected a field heading. While this object can be edited and formatted just like a regular text object, it will now move along with its matching details field—if you move the field in the details section left or right, the field heading will follow. Even if you move the details field vertically to a new section (to the page or report header or footer, for example) and then move the field left or right, the field heading will still move left or right with it. And, if you delete the original database field, the field heading will be deleted along with it.

The only time you may detach the field heading from its associated details field is if you move the detail field out of one section into another *and* move it horizontally at the same time. In this case, the two objects will be separated—the field heading won't follow the original details field anymore. However, to hook the two objects together again, simply move the details field left or right in its new section until it lines up with the field heading. The two will become "reattached."

Combining Database Fields

Simply typing literal text into text objects is a waste of their capabilities! Text objects are powerful elements that can help you create very attractive reports. Consider Figure 2-1, the beginning of a form letter that uses the Customers table from XTREME.MDB (included with Crystal Reports). Note the spacing problems with the contact name, city, state, and ZIP code. These lines are composed of separate fields from the Customers table. No matter how much you try or how creative you get sizing and moving these fields, they will not line up properly for every customer. They appear in the same horizontal location in every details section, no matter how wide or narrow the fields are sized.

FIGURE 2-1 Spacing problems using database fields

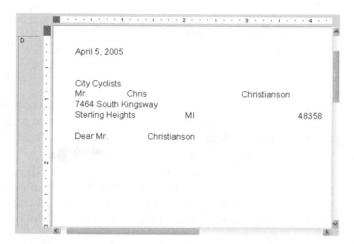

This type of problem is a dead giveaway that this is a computer-generated letter. Although most consumers are savvy enough to assume that a computer had something to do with the form letters they receive, you don't want to make it obvious. Crystal Reports gives you a better way with text objects.

In addition to containing literal text, text objects allow you to *embed* database fields inside text objects with literal text. When the text object appears, it automatically sizes the contents of these embedded fields so that there is no extra space. Figure 2-2 shows the same form letter as Figure 2-1, but text objects are used to combine the database fields with literal text and spaces.

To combine fields inside a text object, follow these steps:

1. Insert a text object, as described previously. If you need to include any literal text, you may type it either now or after you've inserted the database fields. It doesn't matter whether you leave the text object in edit mode or end editing.

2. From the Field Explorer, choose the field or fields you want to combine in the text object. Drag them from the Field Explorer into the text object. Note that your mouse

FIGURE 2-2 Spacing problems solved with text objects

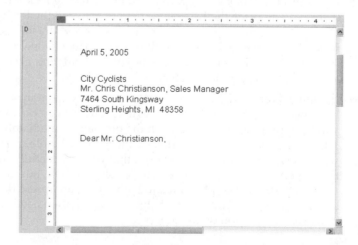

cursor will change when you move over the text object, and a blinking cursor will appear in the text object at the same time:

3. Before dropping the database field or fields in the text object, look very carefully at the location of the blinking text object cursor. Wherever the cursor is located is where the field or fields will go when you release the mouse button. Release the button when the cursor is in the proper position.

4. If you were already editing the text object when you dragged the field into it, it will stay in edit mode. You may now type more literal text or add another field, if you need to. If the text object wasn't in edit mode, the field will be dropped inside without going into edit mode. If you wish to add more text, double-click the text object to place it in edit mode.

5. When you're finished combining fields and literal text, end editing by clicking outside the text object.

Combining Special Fields

You're not limited to combining database fields inside text objects. You can use *special fields* as well. Special fields are system-generated fields, such as the print date, print time, page number, and total page count. You may place them directly on the report, just like database fields. And, like database fields, they'll give you spacing problems if you try to place them near literal text.

To combine special fields with literal text inside text objects, perform the same steps as for database fields. Just drag the fields from the Special Fields category of the Field Explorer, instead of from the Database Field category. In fact, you can embed any type of field from the Field Explorer in a text object just by dragging and dropping from the desired category. Figure 2-3 shows the benefits of combining special fields with literal text in text objects.

The following pointers will help you as you combine fields and literal text inside text objects:

- If you place a database or special field in the wrong location inside the text object (suppose you place the Last Name field in between the letters *a* and *r* in the word "Dear"), you can simply use your cursor keys and the BACKSPACE or DEL key to make the correction. In this case, it is easier to just delete the text following the special field, and reenter it before the special field. You may also use CTRL-C to cut text and CTRL-V to paste text inside the text object.

- If you inadvertently drop a subtotal, a summary, a database field, or some other item inside a text object by mistake (it's pretty easy to do, even if you're careful), you have two choices. If you catch the problem immediately, you can choose Edit | Undo, or click the Undo button on the Standard toolbar. The field will move back where it was. However, if you notice that you accidentally dropped a field inside the text object after it's too late to reasonably undo it, edit the text object, click the field that was mistakenly added to highlight it, and press the DEL key. The field will be removed from inside the text object. You will then need to re-create it and place it in its correct position on the report.

FIGURE 2-3
Combining special
fields inside text
objects

Special fields and text
as separate objects

Special fields
combined with literal
text inside text objects

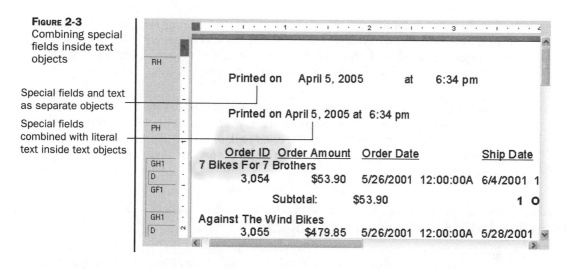

The Can Grow Formatting Option

When you combine database fields or special fields inside text objects, you may often find that the text object is no longer wide enough to show its entire contents. Crystal Reports features the Can Grow formatting option that allows a text object to grow vertically, if necessary, to show its entire contents. You may choose this option, as well as change the Maximum Number Of Lines option that the text object can grow from the Format Editor.

To display the Format Editor, use one of these options:

- Select the text object, and then select Format | Format Text from the pull-down menus.
- Right-click the text object and choose Format Text from the pop-up menu.
- Click the Format button on the Expert Tools toolbar.

The Can Grow option is found on the Common tab of the Format Editor.

With Can Grow turned on, the text object will automatically grow taller to show all the text inside it. You can specify the maximum number of lines that the text object will grow, or leave the number set to zero for unlimited size. When Can Grow is turned on, the text object will display only as wide as it appears on the report. However, it will word-wrap at spaces in the text, creating additional vertical space up to the maximum number of lines.

This automatic behavior lets you size a text object so that it's only one line high. If the contents of the text object can be displayed in one line, the text object will remain one line tall. If it needs more lines, it will expand only by the amount of vertical space necessary to show the material inside the text object (limited by the maximum number of lines).

TIP *Can Grow is helpful for other types of objects as well, not just text objects. You can set the Can Grow formatting option for string fields and memo fields. This is particularly helpful for "description" or "narrative" types of fields that could contain as little as a few characters and as much as several paragraphs of text. Can Grow isn't available for any type of object other than a text object, string field, or memo field.*

Formatting Individual Parts of Text Objects

You can format a text object as you would any other object, using the Formatting toolbar or Format Editor. When you select a text object and change the formatting, as by setting a color or font size, the entire text object takes on that format. This may be the behavior you want.

However, at other times you may want certain characters or words in a text object to take on different formatting than the rest of the text object. Even more prevalent is a situation in which you need to format individual database fields or special fields that are embedded *inside* a text object.

For example, when you insert the Print Date special field inside a text object, it takes on the default formatting from File | Options (perhaps an mm/dd/yyyy format). If you select the text object and display the Format Editor, there is no Date tab in which to choose an alternate date format—this is a text object you're formatting! Similarly, if you've placed a number field inside a text object, you may want to change the formatting to show no decimal places or to add a currency symbol.

To accomplish these types of formatting tasks, you must format individual parts of the text object. This is actually quite simple. Start editing the text object by double-clicking it. You are then free to select individual characters or words by dragging over them with your mouse or by holding down the SHIFT key while using the cursor keys. You can then use the Format toolbar or Format Editor to change the formatting for just those selected characters.

To change the formatting of a database or special field inside a text object, edit the text object and then click the field you wish to format. You'll know you've selected the field when it becomes highlighted inside the text object. You can then use the Format Editor (either from the Format menu or by right-clicking—the number-formatting buttons on the Formatting toolbar won't work here) to change the formatting of the object.

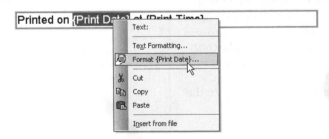

Importing Text from a File

If you have large amounts of text that you want to use in Crystal Reports text objects, you may either type it into a text object directly or copy and paste from the Windows Clipboard. However, data for text objects can also be imported directly from plain text, Rich Text Format (RTF), or Hypertext Markup Language (HTML) files.

To import text into a text object, add a text object as described previously in the chapter (using the Insert menu or toolbar button). If the text object isn't already in edit mode, double-click it to place it in edit mode. Then, right-click and choose Insert From File from the pop-up menu.

A File Open dialog box will appear. Navigate to the drive and folder where the text, RTF, or HTML file is that you wish to import into the text object. Choose the desired file and click OK. The file will be imported into the text object, alongside any existing text that may already be in the text object. If the text file contains plain text, it will simply be displayed in the text object in the default font style for text objects (set on the Fonts tab of File | Options). If the imported text is in HTML or RTF format, Crystal Reports automatically interprets most (but not all) of the embedded font and formatting specifications and includes them in the text object. If you wish to reformat portions of the text object, simply use techniques described previously in the chapter for formatting individual parts of text objects.

Sorting and Grouping

When you first create and preview a report, the report shows details sections in *natural order*; that is, the records appear in whatever order the database sends them to Crystal Reports. This order can vary widely, depending on what database you are using, how you link tables, and the actual order in which records were entered into the database.

You'll probably want to control the order in which information appears on your report. An employee listing, for example, isn't very useful if it isn't in alphabetical order. A sales breakdown is probably more helpful if you see your sales figures in a particular order. You're probably interested in a highest-to-lowest sequence of order quantities if you're about to send gifts to your best customers at the holidays. On the other hand, lowest-to-highest sequence is probably more appropriate if you're about to send your marketing department out to talk to lower-performing customers.

Sorting Your Report

If you simply want to reorder your report's details sections into a particular order, you need to *sort* the report. Sorting is useful for simple reports that need to present information in a certain order. To sort a report, choose Report | Record Sort Expert from the pull-down menus, or click the Record Sort Expert button on the Expert Tools toolbar. This displays the Record Sort Order dialog box.

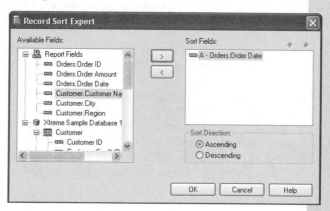

The left Available Fields box shows all the report fields that you've placed on the report, followed by a list of all tables and fields you initially added to the report. If you wish to sort on a field you haven't placed on the report, scroll down through the Report Fields list until you find the list of tables and fields you added to your report. Choose one or more fields to control how you want your report sorted. Simply double-click the field you wish to sort on, or select the field and then click the right arrow button. Either method moves the field to the Sort Fields box on the right. You may then choose between the Ascending and Descending radio buttons to choose the sort order.

An *ascending* sort organizes the records alphabetically in A to Z order; if the records start with numbers, they will appear before any letters, sorted 0 through 9. In a *descending* sort, the order is reversed. Records appear in Z to A order, followed by any numbers in 9 to 0 order.

You may sort by as many fields as you like—you're not limited to one. This is handy, for example, if you want to sort your customers by state, and within state by customer name. Simply add the additional sort fields to the Sort Fields box and choose the Ascending or Descending radio button for each field. The first field in the list will be the *primary*, or first, sorting field, the second field will be *secondary* (will be used to sort multiple records that have the same primary field), and so forth. If you wish to change the order of sorting priority, select a field in the Sort Fields list and click the up or down arrow above the list to reorder the sort fields. When you click OK, Crystal Reports will sort by the higher (primary) field first, and then the lower fields.

TIP *You can sort just as easily on formula fields (covered in Chapter 5) as you can on database fields. This is often required if you want to customize some aspect of the way records are sorted. Just remember that if you're using a SQL database, such as SQL Server or Oracle, sorting on a formula field makes Crystal Reports sort the records instead of having the database server do the work, which may affect the performance of your report (albeit slightly). This is covered in more detail in Chapter 15.*

Grouping Records

Sorting records is handy for lists or other simple reports that just need records to appear in a certain order. It's more common, however, to want not only to have your report sorted by certain fields, but also to have subtotals, counts, averages, or other summary information appear when the sort field changes. To accomplish this, you must use Crystal Reports *groups*. In other reporting tools and mainframe development languages, this was often referred to as report *level breaks*.

When you create a report group, you both sort the records on the report and create two additional report sections every time the group field changes. You may place subtotals, averages, counts, and many other types of summary information in these sections. In addition, grouping your report enables the *group tree*, an Explorer-like window on the left side of the Preview tab. The group tree gives you a quick overview of the organization of your report and enables you to navigate directly to a particular group that you want to see.

To create a report group, you may either choose Insert | Group from the pull-down menus or click the Insert Group button from the Insert Tools toolbar. The Insert Group dialog box appears. It contains two tabs: Common (shown here) and Options (discussed later).

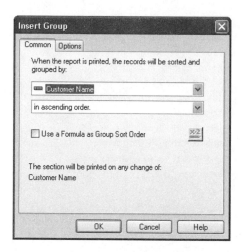

There are two drop-down lists and a checkbox/conditional formula button in the Common tab that you use to insert a group. Follow these steps to complete the dialog box:

1. Click the top drop-down list to select the field you want to group on. The list will display fields on your report, as well as other fields in the tables that the report is using. You can group by a field already on the report or by a database field that you didn't put on the report. You can also group by a formula field.

2. Click the second drop-down list to select the order in which your groups will appear on the report. There are four options: *ascending order* shows the groups in A to Z order alphabetically; *descending order* shows the groups in Z to A order; *specified order* lets you create your own groups (described later in this chapter); and *original order* groups records in the order in which they appear in the database. (This last option is an interesting feature, but rarely useful in most reports.)

3. Crystal Reports XI adds the ability to choose to sort groups in ascending or descending order by use of a formula, rather than the choice made in the second drop-down list. This is helpful if, for example, you wish to prompt your report viewer to choose an ascending or descending group order via a parameter field and create a formula using the parameter field to control group sorting. Should you desire to provide this level of control, check Use a Formula as Group Sort Order and click the conditional formula button. Create a formula that returns the values crAscendingOrder (for ascending order grouping), crDescendingOrder (for descending order grouping), or crOriginalOrder (for original order grouping).

NOTE *Parameter Fields are discussed in more detail in Chapter 13, while conditional formatting formulas are discussed in Chapter 7.*

If you wish to allow Crystal Reports to make "typical" choices for the way groups appear, you may simply click OK now to create the new group. However, if you want to set additional options for the group, click the Options tab.

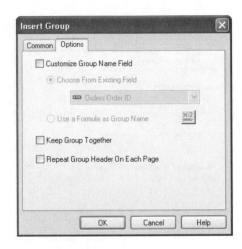

Make Options tab choices as follows:

1. If you simply want to have the database field itself appear in the groups on the report and the group tree, leave the Customize Group Name Field check box empty. However, if you'd like to customize the way the groups appear (perhaps you'd like a month fully spelled out along with a four-digit year for a date field), click the Customize Group Name Field check box. You can then make additional choices to determine what appears for the group. "Customizing Group Name Fields" appears later in the chapter.

2. Click the Keep Group Together option if you want Crystal Reports to try to keep your groups from breaking at the end of a page. If you leave this option unchecked, the beginning of a group and just a few detail records in the group may print at the bottom of a page, while the rest of the group's detail records and its subtotals may appear at the top of the next page.

3. Click the Repeat Group Header on Each Page option if you think you will have large groups that will span more than a single page. This option will print the group header section (described later) at the top of each page where a group continues. This allows you to look at details sections on subsequent pages and know which group they belong to.

CAUTION *Clicking Keep Group Together can cause odd behavior if the first group in your report won't fit on a page by itself. In this case, Crystal Reports will detect that it can't fit the group on the first page of the report and will start a new page before it starts printing the group. The result will be a blank first page. If this happens, you may resolve the problem by un-checking Respect Keep Group Together on First Page in File | Report Options.*

Figure 3-1 shows the two new sections that are added to the Design tab, the group header and group footer. These sections appear at the beginning and end of every group. Note that Crystal Reports places an object in the group header section automatically. This *group name* object will automatically print the contents of the field on which the group is based in each group header. The group footer section is empty.

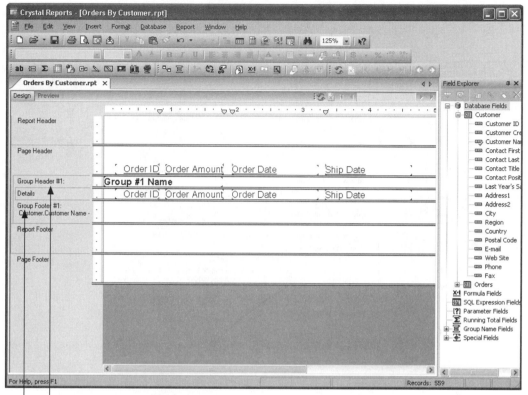

Group Header will print at the start of each group
Group Footer will print at the end of each group

FIGURE 3-1   Group added to a report

TIP   *You may turn off the Insert Group Name with Group option in File | Options if you don't want Crystal Reports to automatically insert a group name object in the group header when a group is created. If this is turned off, or if you inadvertently delete a group name object, you can insert a group name from the Field Explorer by dragging and dropping a group name object after opening the Group Name Fields category.*

Figure 3-2 shows the Preview tab with the now-active group tree. You can see your groups in an outline form and navigate directly to the beginning of one of the groups by clicking the group in the group tree. You can also turn the display of the group tree on and off by clicking the Toggle Group Tree button on the Standard toolbar.

TIP   *In addition to the steps previously outlined, you may use the Group Expert (discussed later in the chapter) to create a new group.*

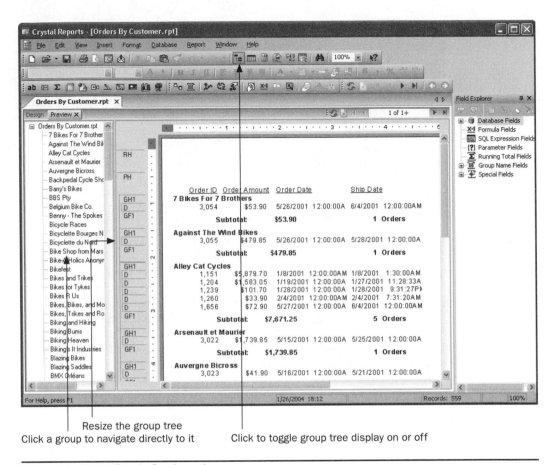

Resize the group tree
Click a group to navigate directly to it   Click to toggle group tree display on or off

FIGURE 3-2   Group Tree in Preview tab

Manipulating Existing Groups

After you create a group, you may wish to delete it so that only detail records print again without grouping. Or, you may wish to change the field that the group is based on, change the order of the groups from ascending to descending, customize the group name field, or choose one of the formatting options to control the way Crystal Reports deals with page breaks inside groups.

One way to do this is to point your mouse to a group header or footer section in the "gray section area" of the left side of the Design or Preview tab (the section will be abbreviated "GH" and "GF" in the Preview tab). You must point to the group header or group footer for the group you wish to delete, right-click, and choose Delete Group from the pop-up menu. The group header and group footer sections will be removed from the report, along with any objects in them. You may also use the Group Expert, discussed in the following section, to delete a group.

Group Header #1: Customer.Customer Name - A

Hide (Drill-Down OK)

Suppress (No Drill-Down)

Se*c*tion Expert...

Change *G*roup...

Show Short Section Names

I*n*sert Line

*D*elete Last Line

Ar*r*ange Lines

*F*it Section

*I*nsert Section Below

De*l*ete Group

Select *A*ll Section Objects

There are also several ways to change existing groups by redisplaying the dialog box that appeared when you created the group. You may change the field that the group is based on, change the order of groups (ascending, descending, specified, original), add a formula to conditionally set the order, customize the group name field, or select the Keep Group Together or Repeat Group Header on Each New Page option.

As when deleting groups, you may point to the group header or group footer section of the group you want to change in the Design or Preview tab. Then right-click and choose Change Group from the pop-up menu. The Change Group Options dialog box will reappear, where you can change group settings on either the Common or Options tab and then click OK when you're finished. You may also use the new Group Expert, discussed in the following section, to change a group.

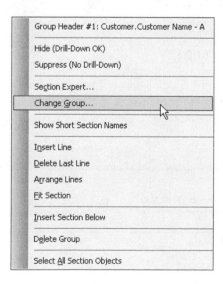

Group Header #1: Customer.Customer Name - A

Hide (Drill-Down OK)

Suppress (No Drill-Down)

Se*c*tion Expert...

Change *G*roup...

Show Short Section Names

I*n*sert Line

*D*elete Last Line

Ar*r*ange Lines

*F*it Section

*I*nsert Section Below

De*l*ete Group

Select *A*ll Section Objects

The Group Expert

Another Crystal Reports approach to group manipulation is the *Group Expert,* which is designed to let you perform most of the grouping options described previously in the chapter, such as creating new groups, modifying existing groups, reordering groups, and deleting groups. To display the Group Expert, choose Report | Group Expert from the pull-down menus, or click the Group Expert button in the Expert Tools toolbar. The Group Expert will appear, as shown in Figure 3-3.

Here, you can add a new group to the report by selecting the field from the Available Fields list that you want to use, and clicking the right arrow to add the group. If you have an existing group on the report that you wish to remove, select that group in the Group By list and click the left arrow to remove it. And, if you want to choose options for a group on the report (either a new group you just added or an existing group that was added previously), select the group in the Group By list that you want to modify and click the Options button. The Group Options dialog box will appear. Choose the Common or Options tab and choose or change appropriate options.

If your report contains more than one group (discussed in more detail later in the chapter under "Multiple Groups"), you may wish to change the order in which the groups appear. For example, you may have initially grouped your report first by Customer, and within Customer by Region. If you want to change the order of the groups to be by Region and then Customer, you would select a group in the Group By list and use the up and down arrows above the Group By list to change the order of the groups.

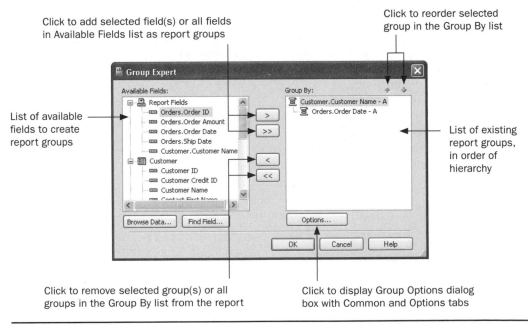

FIGURE 3-3   The Group Expert

Adding Summaries

So, what's the difference between just sorting the report and creating a group? Not only is the group tree useful with grouped reports, but you now have a section available for subtotals, averages, counts, and other summary functions at the end of each group. Although the group footer is empty when first created, you can insert summary functions into it with ease.

Inserting summaries in your report requires several steps:

1. Choose Insert | Summary from the pull-down menus, or right-click the field you want to summarize in the Details section and choose Insert Summary from the pop-up menu. To insert a summary, you can also click the Summary button on the Insert Tools toolbar. The Insert Summary dialog box will appear.

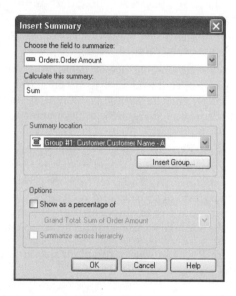

2. If you selected a field on the report before you chose an Insert Summary option, that field will be preselected in the Choose Field To Summarize drop-down list. Otherwise, choose the field you wish to total, average, or otherwise summarize in this list.

3. Choose the summary function (sum, average, and so on) that you wish to use. Then, either choose to insert a grand total for the entire report (the default), or choose the existing group in which you want to place the summary. If you wish to create a new group on the report for your summary, click the Insert Group button to create a new group.

4. If you want to create a percentage summary field, click the Show As A Percentage Of check box and choose from the drop-down list the field that you want to show the percentage of (percentage summary fields are discussed in detail later in the chapter). You must choose a report group before you can check this box—Percentage Summaries can't be created in the report footer.

5. If the group you've chosen is a hierarchical group (discussed later in the chapter under "Hierarchical Groups"), you may check the Summarize Across Hierarchy check box to include the summary in all hierarchical groups.

6. Click OK to place the subtotal or summary in the group footer or report footer directly below the detail field that you're summarizing.

7. Since Crystal Reports doesn't label group summaries for you, you should add text objects next to the summaries to indicate what they display. For example, a subtotal won't be confused with an average if you place a text object containing "Subtotal:" next to the subtotal object.

Here are a few pointers to keep in mind when inserting summaries:

- Although Crystal Reports places subtotals and summaries in the group footer or report footer by default, you don't have to leave them there. If you move them to the group header or report header, they'll print the same information, but at the beginning of groups or the report.

- Once a summary or subtotal has been created, you don't have to delete it and insert a new summary if you want to change its function (for example, to change a subtotal to an average). Simply click the subtotal or summary and choose Edit | Edit Summary from the pull-down menus, or right-click the summary and choose Edit Summary from the pop-up menu.

- If you want to insert a summary in one or more group footers and the report footer (to summarize for multiple groups and the entire report), you don't have to use the Insert Summary options over and over for each group and the entire report. Just insert the summary into one group and then copy the summary from that group footer to the other groups or the report footer by using Edit menu options, or just CTRL-dragging the summary from a group footer to copy it to another section.

Table 3-1 shows the different summary functions that are available in Crystal Reports and what each does.

CAUTION *If the details field that you summarize contains null values (a special database value where the field actually contains nothing, as opposed to a zero or empty string), the summary function won't "count" that record. For example, a Count or Average won't figure the null record into its calculation. If you wish to avoid this problem with the current report, you can convert database null values to zero or empty string values by choosing File | Report Options and clicking Convert Database NULL Values To Default. If you want this to be the default option for all new reports, you can choose the same option on the Reporting tab from File | Options.*

Percentage Summary Fields

Although the default summary functions satisfy most needs for analytical reporting, sometimes you may prefer to calculate percentages rather than whole numbers. For example, if your report groups sales by sales rep within each month, you may want to know both the actual dollars and the *percentage* of revenues each sales rep is responsible for in that month. And, you may also want to calculate the percentage of total sales for the entire year that each month is responsible for. Such an example is shown in Figure 3-4. Crystal Reports features the *percentage summary field*, which creates this type of calculation without the need for a formula.

Function	Results
	Returns the subtotal of the chosen field; available only for number or currency fields.
Average	Returns the average of the chosen field; available only for number or currency fields.
Sample Variance Sample Standard Deviation Population Variance Population Standard Deviation	For number of currency fields only, these functions return the statistical result for the group or report values. For detailed descriptions on the specific steps performed to arrive at the results, consult a statistics text or Crystal Reports online help.
Maximum	For number or currency fields, returns the highest number in the group. For string fields, returns the last member of the group alphabetically. For date fields, returns the latest date in the group.
Minimum	For number or currency fields, returns the lowest number in the group. For string fields, returns the first member of the group alphabetically. For date fields, returns the earliest date in the group.
Count	Simply counts the records in the details section and returns the number of records in the group. Although you are required to choose a database field before selecting this option, the Count function will return the same number no matter which field you choose (with the exception of fields that contain null values).
Distinct Count	Similar to the Count function, but returns only the distinct number of occurrences of the field. As opposed to Count, the field you choose in the details section before choosing Distinct Count is very significant. For example, if five records contain the strings Los Angeles, Chicago, Vancouver, Chicago, and Miami, the Count function would return 5, whereas Distinct Count would return 4.
Correlation Covariance	For number of currency fields only, these functions return the statistical result for the group or report values. When you choose these functions, an additional drop-down list appears where you may choose an additional report field to complete the function. For detailed descriptions on the specific steps performed to arrive at the results, consult a statistics text or Crystal Reports online help.
Median	For number and currency fields only. Returns the median, or middle, number in the group. If there is one number in the group, it is returned. If there are two numbers, their average is returned.

TABLE 3-1   Summary Functions

Function	Results
Mode	Returns the most frequently occurring value from all the detail records in the group. For numeric fields, Mode returns the most frequently occurring number. For string fields, Mode returns the most frequently occurring string (for example, with detail records containing five occurrences of FedEx, three occurrences of UPS, and eight occurrences of Parcel Post, Mode would return Parcel Post).
Nth Largest	Returns the third, fifth, or tenth (and so forth) largest value in the group, depending on the value you enter for N. For example, Nth largest, with N equaling 1, returns the largest value in the group. When you choose this function, an additional box appears in which you can enter the value for N. For numeric fields, this function returns the Nth-highest numeric value. With string fields, it returns the Nth value alphabetically (for example, if there are three records containing FedEx and two records containing UPS, Nth largest when N equals 2 will be UPS, and Nth largest when N equals 3 will be FedEx).
Nth Smallest	Returns the third, fifth, tenth (and so forth) smallest value in the group. For example, Nth smallest with N equaling 1 returns the smallest value in the group. When you choose this function, an additional box appears in which you can enter the value for N. This function behaves similarly to Nth highest with both numeric and string fields.
Nth Most Frequent	Returns the third, fifth, tenth (and so forth) most frequent occurrence in the group. This is similar to Mode, except that you're not limited to just the most frequent occurrence.
Pth Percentile	For number and currency fields only. When you choose this function, an additional box appears in which you can enter a number between 0 and 100 for P. This function returns the number that indicates what the percentile is for P, based on all the numbers in the group.
Weighted average	For number and currency fields only. This will calculate an average of group or report values, but apply the "weight" of another field to adjust the average. When you choose this function, an additional drop-down list appears where you may choose an additional report field to complete the function.

TABLE 3-1   Summary Functions *(continued)*

To create a percentage summary field, follow the steps previously outlined to insert a summary field. Choose the field you want to use to calculate the percentage (the "numerator") and the group in which you want the percentage placed, as though you were creating a regular summary. Then, click the Show As A Percentage Of check box and use the drop-down

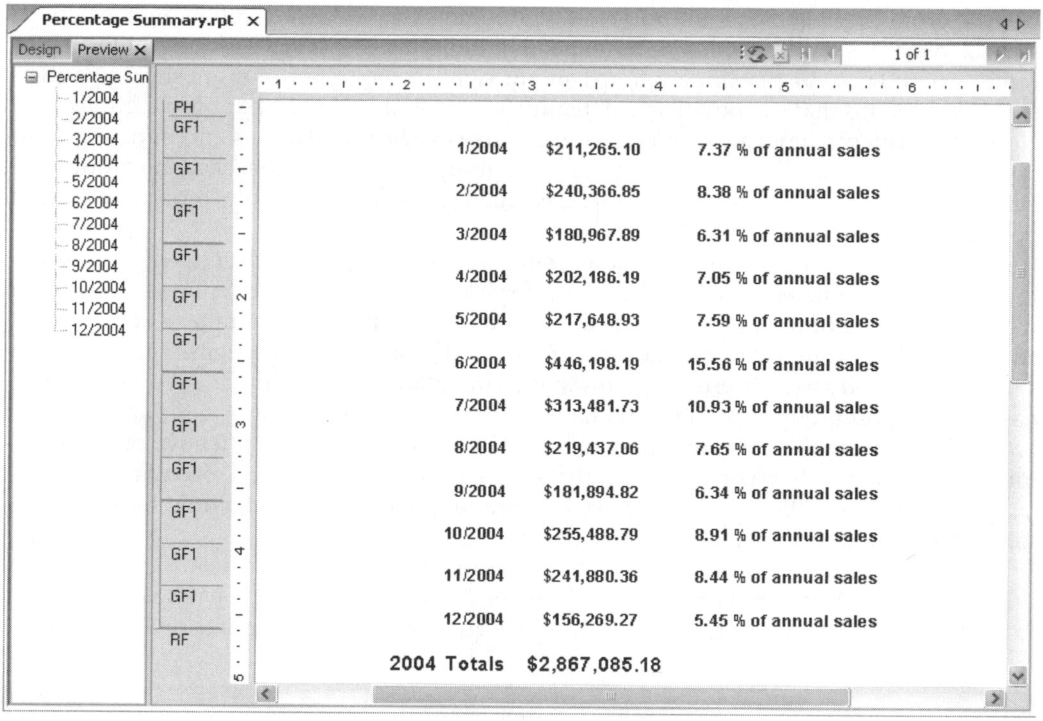

Figure 3-4 Percentages created with Percentage Summary field

list to choose the higher-level group or grand total you want used as the "denominator." If you are placing the percentage in the highest-level (or only) group on the report, you'll only be able to choose a grand total for the denominator. Click OK.

Crystal Reports will place a summary field in the group footer of the group you specified. When you preview the report, however, you'll see a percentage number rather than a count, subtotal, or other number. The percentage summary field will already be formatted to display a percent sign.

Multiple Groups

Crystal Reports does not limit your report to just one level of grouping. In fact, many powerful reporting features can be provided to your report viewer by creative use of multiple groups. The key to many sophisticated reporting requirements lies in creative use of formulas (covered in Chapter 5) in conjunction with multiple levels of grouping.

Multiple groups form a report hierarchy, with increasing levels of detailed information being presented by inner groups. For example, a report might be grouped by country first. Within the country group would be a geographic region group (Northwest, Southwest, and so forth), and then a group by state, a group by county or township, a group by city, and finally detail records showing individual customers or orders within that city. Each group has its own group header and group footer sections, and subtotals and summaries can exist for each group.

The group tree handles multiple levels of grouping very elegantly, following the general style of Windows Explorer. Plus signs (expand buttons) are displayed next to groups that can be expanded to display inner groups; minus signs (collapse buttons) are shown beside expanded groups that can be collapsed. Figure 3-5 shows a report with multiple groups. Notice that you can navigate through the group tree by clicking the plus and minus signs to open and close group levels. When you find the group you want to see, click the group name in the group tree to go directly to the beginning of that group in the report, no matter how deep the group is in the hierarchy.

To create additional levels of grouping, simply repeat the process described previously for inserting a group, either using the Group Expert or the Insert Group options. The groups will appear in the order that you create them. You can use the Insert Summary options to add subtotals and summaries to the group footer and group header sections.

You may inadvertently create groups in the wrong order. For example, if you wish to have your report grouped by state and then by city, make sure to create the groups in that order. If you create the city group first, followed by the state group, you'll have one group for each city, with whatever state that city is in as a lower-level group. You'd have, for example, a group for Boulder containing a Colorado group. Below that, you'd have a group for Denver containing another Colorado group.

This isn't as much of a problem as it might seem. You don't have to delete groups and reinsert them in the desired order—moving them around is surprisingly easy. Simply return to the Design tab and point to the gray Group Header or Group Footer area on the left side

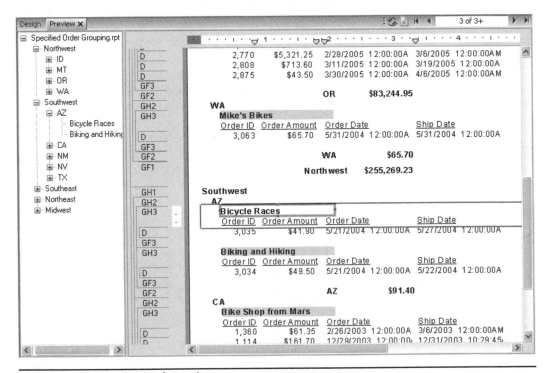

FIGURE 3-5 Multiple levels of grouping

of the screen. Point to the group that needs to be moved, and hold down the left mouse button—the mouse cursor turns into a hand symbol.

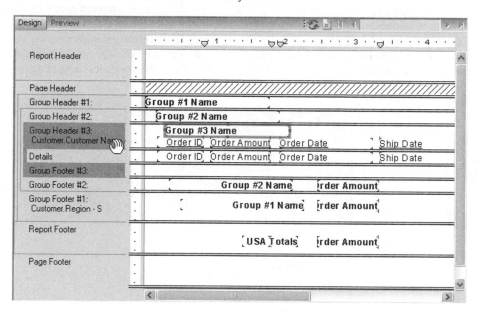

You can now simply drag and drop the group header or group footer on top of the group that you wish to swap it with. When you release the mouse button, the groups swap locations. Don't be confused by the fact that the groups stay numbered in sequential order— the groups have been moved. In the preceding example, simply dropping the state group header (Group Header #2) on the city group header (Group Header #1) will swap the groups. The state group header becomes Group Header #1, and the city group header becomes Group Header #2.

TIP   *The Group Expert also allows you to easily change the order of groups.*

Specified Order Grouping

Sometimes, you may need data grouped on your report in a special order that the database doesn't offer. For example, the database may contain a state field, but not a field indicating what geographic location the record belongs to (Northwest, Southwest, and so on). One option that may be appropriate for more sophisticated customized grouping is basing a group on a sophisticated formula. However, if your customized grouping is not particularly complicated, *specified order grouping* may be more straightforward. This allows you to create customized groups without having to know the Crystal Reports formula language.

Specified order grouping lets you use a dialog box similar to the Select Expert (discussed in Chapter 4) to create your own groups, based on an existing database field. In the geographic location example used previously, you could create a Northwest group consisting of Washington, Oregon, Idaho, and Montana. The Southwest group could include Nevada, California, Texas, and Arizona. The Northeast group could consist of New York, Maine,

Vermont, and New Hampshire. Southeast could include Florida, Alabama, Louisiana, and Mississippi. All the other states not in these four groups could either be ignored, placed in their own individual groups, or lumped together in one final group given a name of your choice, such as Midwest.

To specify your own groups, choose Specified Order in the Group dialog box instead of Ascending or Descending order when you create a new group or change an existing group. When you choose Specified Order, a Specified Order tab is added to the Change Group Options dialog box.

NOTE *Crystal Reports XI's new Use A Formula As Group Sort option does not allow you to choose Specified Order based on a formula. You may only choose Specified Order grouping with the formula option unchecked.*

Click the New button to create a new named group. This will display the Define Named Group dialog box. Type the name the group should have on the report, such as Northwest. Then, using options in the tabs, indicate which records will be included in the group. For example, you may want the Northwest group to include records in which Customer.Region is one of WA, MT, and ID.

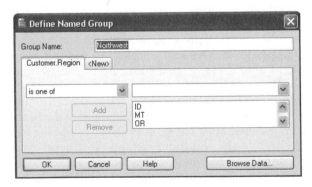

If you need to use several different criteria for the named group, you can click the <New> tab and add additional criteria for the group. When you're finished, click OK on the Define Named Group dialog box. The named group will be created and will appear in the list of named groups in the Group Options dialog box. You can now click the New button again to add additional named groups (for example, Southwest, including AZ, CA, and TX).

TIP Remember that clicking the <New> tab to create more than one selection tab still only allows you to select by one field—the field your group is created on. The criteria on the tabs will be joined using a logical Or operation—this is different from the Select Expert.

As you add new named groups, they appear in the Specified Order tab of the Change Group Options dialog box in the order that you created them, *not* in alphabetical order. If you wish to change the order in which the named groups appear on the report, select a named group and use the up or down arrow next to the list of named groups to change its position. The Others group, however, will always be last, no matter what you name it or how you position named groups with the arrow buttons.

After you create at least one named group, the Others tab appears in the Group dialog box. You use this tab to deal with any records that haven't been caught by your specific named groups. You can discard the remaining records, place them in one "catchall" group with the name of your choice, or leave them in their own groups based on the database field. In the geographic example, Northwest, Southwest, Northeast, and Southeast have all been created as named groups. The Others tab is used to lump any regions that weren't otherwise specified into a Midwest group.

TIP You might have noticed the Named Group drop-down list on the Specified Order tab. This list will browse the database, showing you samples of the actual field you're grouping on. If you choose one of these samples, Crystal Reports will create a named group with the same name as the actual database field. This is handy if you want to create the same groups as you would by using Ascending or Descending order, but place the groups in the specific order you desire.

After you create your named groups and click OK on the Change Group Options dialog box, the report will reflect your new grouping. Figure 3-6 shows a report grouped by the five geographic areas described previously. If you wish to change any of your specified grouping options, or remove them altogether so that records appear in their own groups, just use the steps mentioned previously to change an existing group. The Change Group Options dialog box will open, and you can edit your specified groups or change grouping to ascending or descending order, which will remove specified grouping.

Drilling Down on Data

One of the most powerful features of Crystal Reports is its online reporting capability. Although you can print reports on a printer and export them to other file formats, such as Word or Excel, the real power of many reports becomes available only when users can view and interact with them *online*. This means that the user directly views the .RPT file that Crystal Reports creates. This affords two benefits:

- A user can rerun the report whenever they want, seeing an updated view of the database at that moment.

- A user can interact with the report by using the group tree and drill-down capabilities.

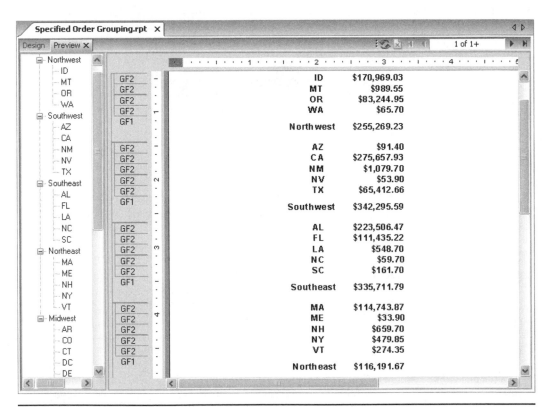

FIGURE 3-6   Report with Specified Order grouping

Various Crystal Reports editions offer online interactive reporting to users in several ways:

- Giving users their own copy of Crystal Reports, letting them open, view, and modify reports at will
- Reporting with a web browser and Crystal Reports Server or BusinessObjects Enterprise (covered in Part II)
- Including a Crystal Report in a custom Windows application (covered in Part III)
- Providing any one of a number of available third-party tools to users to allow them to run reports online (many of these tools are highlighted on this book's companion web site. Visit CrystalBook.com for information).

All of these interactive methods allow a user to *drill down* on data in the report. This technique, a feature that has been carried over from early PC-based decision-support system software, allows a report viewer to initially look at higher-level data. For example, a report might start at the country level. If the viewer sees a subtotal or summary number (or an element in a pie chart or other chart) for a particular country that interests them, they can double-click that number. This will drill down to the next level in the report, possibly the region or state level, where they can see summary numbers for each of those states or regions. If the report is designed with several levels of drill-down ability, the user could then double-click a region that piqued their interest to display all the cities in that region. The drilling down could progress further, allowing users to drill down on cities and finally ZIP codes, where individual detail items at the ZIP-code level would appear.

Crystal Reports automatically sets up a drill-down hierarchy when you create groups. Every group you create can be drilled into, exposing the lower-level group and finally the details section. So, for the just-described drill-down example to work, you would create multiple groups on the report in the following order: country, region (state), city, and finally, ZIP code.

After you create groups, you can drill down on the group name (automatically placed in the group header) or any summary or subtotal that you place in a group header or group footer. When you point at these objects, you'll notice that the mouse pointer changes from an arrow to a magnifying glass (or a finger cursor in a web page), called a *drill-down cursor*. This indicates that you can drill down on the group by double-clicking this object (or single-clicking in a web page). When you double-click, a *drill-down tab* appears next to the main Preview tab, containing the lower-level group or detail data. Every time you drill down, a separate drill-down tab appears.

If you drill down enough times, there won't be enough room to see all the drill-down tabs, along with the main Preview and Design tabs. In this situation, two small arrows appear next to the last drill-down tab. You can click these arrows to move back and forth among the tabs to see tabs that have disappeared off the screen. You can also close any drill-down tab by clicking the small *X* on the selected tab. This closes the current tab and displays the tab to the left. You can close every tab this way (including the Preview tab), except for the Design tab.

TIP If you wish to print the report to a printer or export it to another file format, only the material appearing in the current tab will print or export. If you're displaying the Preview tab at the time, the summarized report will print or export. If, however, you have a drill-down tab selected when you print or export, only the material in that drill-down tab will be included.

Figure 3-7 shows a report with several drill-down tabs visible. Notice that there isn't enough room to show all the tabs, so small arrows appear to the right of the last drill-down tab. Also notice that the mouse cursor has changed to a magnifying glass because it is over a group name object.

You can drill down on any report that has at least one group on it, even if all the details sections are showing already. Drill-down ability is really helpful with summary reports that start out showing only high-level data. A viewer will only want to see the lower-level groups and the detail when they drill down. Therefore, you'll want to hide the details section, as well as the lower-level group headers and group footers, to create a truly useful drill-down report. You'll see how to hide or suppress sections in Chapter 8.

TIP *Controlling detailed drill-down behavior, such as deciding if you want to show all higher-level group headers when you drill down, or whether to show a particular group header in some drill-down tabs, but not others, may require use of Crystal Reports formulas or conditional formatting. A DrillDownGroupLevel function is available in Crystal Reports to help with this custom drill-down behavior. Look in the Print State category of the Formula Editor Function Tree to find this function. Formulas are covered in more detail in Chapter 5, and conditional formatting is covered in more detail in Chapters 7 and 8.*

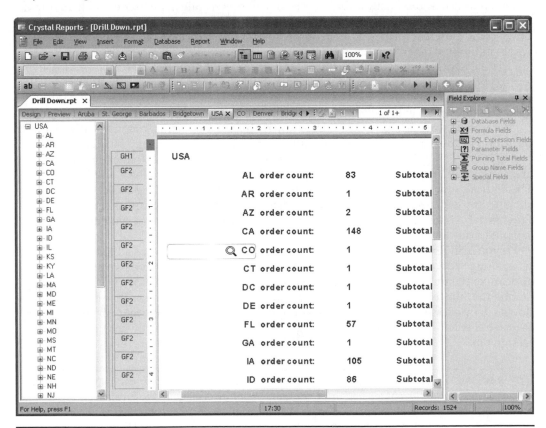

FIGURE 3-7 Drill-down report

Grouping on Date Fields

When you create report groups based on date fields, you probably don't want a new group to appear every time the date changes from one day to another. You may only want a new group for every week, month, or calendar quarter. You could create a complicated formula that breaks down groups in this manner and groups on the formula, but Crystal Reports provides a much easier way.

When you select a date field to group on, Crystal Reports automatically adds an additional drop-down list to the Insert Group dialog box.

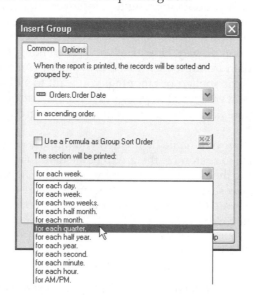

You can choose how often a new group will be created by selecting the appropriate item from the list. Then click OK. The groups will now appear in the group tree for every month, quarter, year, or whatever period was chosen. The group name in the group header will indicate the beginning date for each group (the first month of the quarter, the first day of the week, and so forth).

Customizing Group Name Fields

The group name field takes on the Crystal Reports default format for the data type of the group field. For example, the default format for date fields is the same as your Windows default date format. Thus, a group name for a calendar quarter group may show up as 1/2005, 4/2005, and so on. What if you prefer the group names to appear as "January, 2005" and "April, 2005"?

You can format a group name field just like any other field or object. Click the group name field and then format it just like any other object (by using the Format menu, by using the Format toolbar button in the Expert Tools toolbar, or by right-clicking and using the pop-up menu). For a group name based on a date field, for example, you can choose how the month and year appear, as well as what character should be used as the separator between them.

However, you'll notice that even when you format the group name field as mentioned here, the group tree will not reflect the change. It continues to use the default formatting regardless of how you format the group name field. Also, you may find situations in which you want to show information for the group that is different from what is actually supplied by the field you group on. For example, you may be grouping by a fiscal month number in a database. You'll want to show the spelled-out month name despite the fact that the group tree and group headers will show the number (1 for January, 8 for August, and so on). Or, you may be grouping by employee number rather than employee name, to avoid the possibility of lumping employee data together for employees that share the same name. But, you still want the report to show the employee name instead of the number.

You may create a formula and group on it instead of the database field to accomplish this type of specialized group display. However, you'll often not get exactly the results you want (in the numeric month example mentioned previously, you will need to add the month number in front of the spelled-out month if you want to still show the months in chronological order). However, Crystal Reports provides the *customized group name field*, which gives you much more flexibility in controlling what the group tree and group header display.

You may customize the group name field when you initially create a group. Or, if you decide later that you'd like to customize the group name field in an existing group, you can change the group by using the Group Expert, or by right-clicking the appropriate group header or group footer gray section name and choosing Change Group from the pop-up menu. Once the Change Group Options dialog box appears, perform the following steps to customize the group name field:

1. Click the Options tab.
2. Click the Customize Group Name Field check box.
3. To choose an alternate database field to display (for example, if you'd like to show an employee name field instead of the employee number field the group is based on), click the Choose From Existing Field radio button and then pick the desired database field in the associated drop-down list.
4. To create a specialized formula to display instead of the field the group is based on, click the Use A Formula As Group Name radio button. Then, click the Conditional Formula button next to the radio button. The group name Formula Editor appears, in which you can create a string formula to display instead of the field the group is based on. For example, to show an employee's last name, a comma, and then the employee's first name, you could create the following formula:

```
{Employee.Last Name} & ", " & {Employee.First Name}
```

Look at Chapter 5 for details on creating formulas.

Grouping on Formula Fields

As your reports become more sophisticated, you'll find more and more often that you won't be able to create the groups you need just from database fields. You may be able to use specified order grouping, but even it is limited by its simple Select Expert-like approach. When your "creative grouping with database fields" runs out of steam, you need to create formula fields and group on them. Creating formula fields is covered in Chapter 5.

Grouping on a formula field is very simple (at least the grouping is, after you create the formula). The formula appears at the end of the list of report fields in the Insert Group or Change Group Options dialog box. Simply choose it as the formula field you wish to group on.

One of the immediate benefits of grouping on a formula is being able to change your report grouping on the fly by use of Crystal Reports parameter fields (covered in Chapter 13). By using a parameter field to change the value that a formula returns, and then grouping on the formula, you can dynamically change report grouping depending on user input.

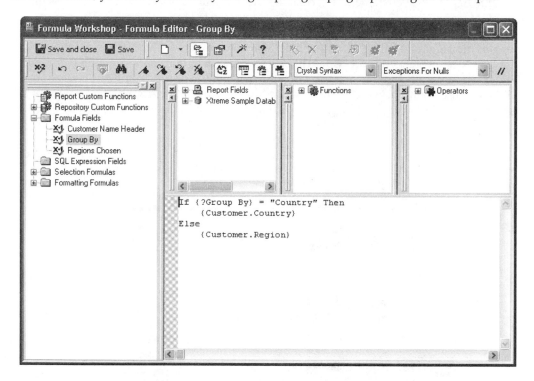

The @Group By formula field can now be used instead of the database field to dynamically group the report on Country or Region, as chosen by the report viewer.

CAUTION *Although you gain great flexibility when you group on a formula field, you may lose a little performance along the way. When you group on a database field, Crystal Reports can have the database server (SQL Server, Oracle, and so on) sort records in the proper group order before sending them to Crystal Reports. When you group on a formula field, the server won't be able to sort the records in advance, leaving that for Crystal Reports to do once the records begin to arrive from the server. You may or may not notice any performance degradation, depending on the size of the report and the speed of your computer. If you really want to maximize performance and still have a customized group, you may be able to substitute a SQL expression for a formula as the source for your group. SQL expressions are covered in Chapter 15.*

Top N Reporting

Figure 3-8 shows a typical order summary report by customer name. This is a great drill-down report example—the details section is hidden, and only the summary information for each customer is showing (hiding sections is covered in Chapter 8). This is a good report for the sales manager who is asked, "How did Barry's Bikes do last year?" All the viewer has to do is click Barry's Bikes in the group tree to go directly to its summaries.

However, what if the sales manager has ten boxes of Godiva chocolates that she wants to send to her ten best customers? Or, consider the new sales associate who's been assigned the task of visiting the 15 worst-performing customers to try to bolster sales. The report shown in Figure 3-8 is not very useful if you want to find the top 10 or bottom 15 customers. The sales manager and sales associate would be much happier with a Top *N* report.

A Top *N* report lets you sort your groups by a subtotal or summary function (subtotal of order amount, for example), instead of by the name of the group. That way, your groups will appear, for example, in order of highest to lowest sales or lowest to highest sales. In addition, Top *N* reporting enables you to see only the top or bottom *N* groups, where you specify the *N*.

Crystal Reports uses the Group Sort Expert to reorder your groups by a subtotal or summary. Choose this option from the pull-down menus by selecting Report | Group Sort Expert. You can also click the Group Sort Expert button in the Expert Tools toolbar.

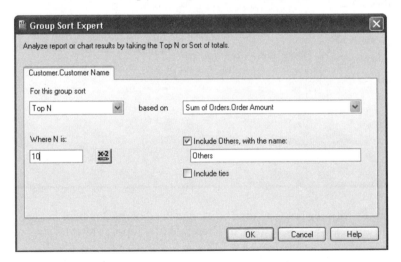

The Group Sort Expert presents a tab for every group you've created on your report (provided that group has at least one summary created for it). Click the tab for the group that you want to reorder. When you first open the Group Sort Expert, the default setting for the first drop-down list is No Sort. This simply indicates that this group initially will not be a Top *N* group and that groups will appear in the order you chose when you created the groups. If none of the groups on your report have subtotal or summary fields in them, the Group Sort Expert won't be available, as it uses summary fields to sort the groups.

There are several choices available in the For This Group Sort drop-down list. Choose the desired option from the following choices:

All	Displays all groups on report, but uses one or more summary fields to determine the order of the groups. You have a choice of whether to show groups in ascending order (lowest to highest) or descending order (highest to lowest).
Top N	Displays only the top N (top 5, top 10) groups based on a summary field in order of highest to lowest.
Bottom N	Displays only the bottom N (bottom 5, bottom 10) based on a summary field in order of lowest to highest.
Top Percentage	Displays the top N percent (top 10 percent, top 25 percent) of groups based on a summary field.
Bottom Percentage	Displays the bottom N percent (bottom 10 percent, bottom 25 percent) of groups based on a summary field.

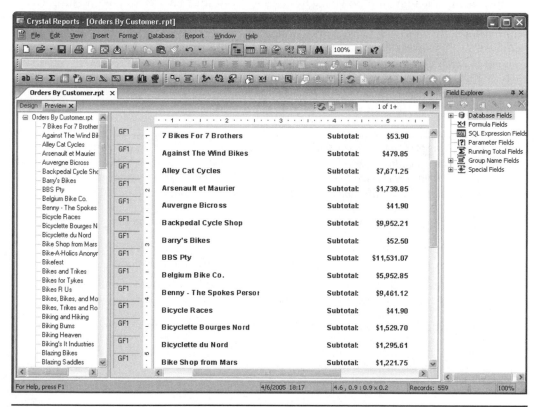

FIGURE 3-8 Order summary by customer

When you click the down arrow of the second drop-down list, you see all the summaries you've created for that group (only summaries you created with Insert Summary will be there—you won't see any formulas or other fields). Choose the one that you want the Top *N* report to be based on. For example, if you want to see the top ten customers according to last year's sales, choose Sum of Customer.Last Year's Sales. If you leave the first drop-down list set to All, all groups will remain on the report, but they will be sorted in ascending or descending order, based on the radio buttons at the bottom of the dialog box. If you want the groups sorted by more than one summary (for example, first by sum of order amount and then by count of order ID), select additional summaries from the drop-down list and choose an ascending or descending sort for each.

TIP *Using the All option to sort groups in a different order can be a very innovative way to solve unique reporting problems. If you need to create a group based on one field but then have the groups appear in a different order, insert a summary field in the group footer based on the field you want to sort the groups by. Then, using the All option, choose the summary field you created.*

If you are only interested in the Top *N*, Bottom *N*, Top Percentage, or Bottom Percentage groups, change the first drop-down list from All to the desired choice. The second drop-down list enables you to select one summary or subtotal to use to sort the groups. Choose the summary you want to use. Once you've done that, type the value of *N* or the percentage in the appropriate text box. You also have a check box and text box that let you choose whether to include other groups not in the Top or Bottom *N* or percentage in the report. If you do include them, they will be lumped together in one other group with the name you type. If you want to not increment the *N* or percentage when group summaries are tied (this may change a top 10 to a top 12 if two of the groups are tied), check the Include Ties check box.

TIP *Crystal Reports XI adds the capability to provide the value for N or the percentage by way of a formula. This is helpful if you, for example, want to supply the value for N from a parameter field (Parameter Fields are covered in Chapter 13). Click the Conditional Formula button next to the N text box and supply a formula or numeric parameter field name.*

Using the Godiva and worst-performing-customer example earlier:

- The sales manager's Godiva chocolate report would be Top *N* of Sum of Orders. Order Amount, where *N* is 10 and other groups are not included.

- The sales associate's follow-up visit report would be a Bottom *N* of Sum of Orders. Order Amount, where *N* is 15 and other groups are not included.

The following Top *N* report shows who will be getting chocolates this year:

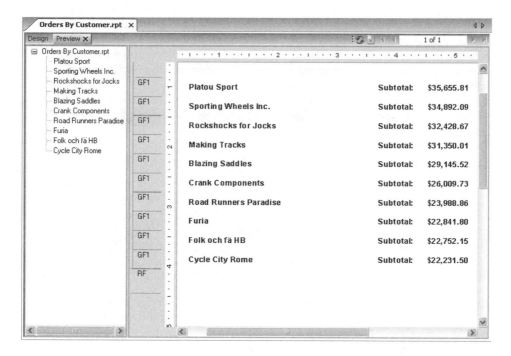

If you wish to change the report from Top *N* to Bottom *N*, change the value of *N*, or remove the Top/Bottom *N* sorting altogether and show all of your groups sorted in the order you originally chose, simply redisplay the Group Sort Expert and change the values. Remember that a group will be sorted in its original ascending or descending order if you set the first drop-down list to No Sort.

CAUTION   If you create a Top N report and don't include others, any grand totals you place in the report footer will still include all records on the report. If you want to include accurate grand totals in a Top N report, either include others or use a running total instead of grand totals (as explained in Chapter 5).

Hierarchical Groups

Crystal Reports also features *hierarchical groups,* which can be helpful in certain reporting situations where two fields relate to each other hierarchically. A specific example would be an organizational relationship between employees and supervisors, where the database would contain a single record containing both an employee ID and a supervisor ID. Without hierarchical grouping, creating an organizational chart utilizing this data would be difficult. While you could group by supervisor ID to see all the employees that reported to that supervisor, you still wouldn't see any hierarchical levels, where that supervisor would appear underneath *their* supervisor, and so forth.

With Crystal Reports, you may simply choose hierarchical grouping options to indicate the relationship between the two fields in the same set of data, and to specify how much indentation you wish to show between the hierarchies. As an example, you may create a simple report using the Employee table from the XTREME sample database included with Crystal Reports. If you create a group based on Employee ID, you'll simply see one group for each employee in the table. To show the reporting relationship among the employees, choose Report | Hierarchical Grouping Options. This displays the Hierarchical Options dialog box.

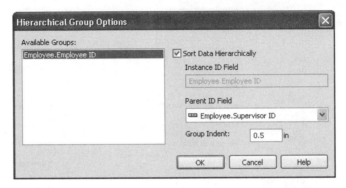

Choose the group (if there is more than one) for which you want to show the hierarchy. Then, click the Sort Data Hierarchically check box and choose the field that relates to the group field in the Parent ID Field drop-down list. Finally, type the distance by which you wish to indent the lower-level hierarchies. Click OK.

The report will now create additional occurrences of groups to show the hierarchies created by the relationship of the two chosen fields. Here's an example of hierarchical reporting using the XTREME sample database:

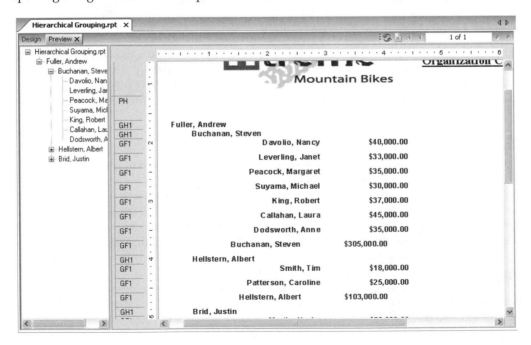

Crystal Reports includes the ability to add subtotals or summaries in hierarchical groups. Once you've created your group hierarchy with the features discussed previously, just use the same Insert Subtotal, Insert Summary, and Insert Grand Total features covered earlier in the chapter to summarize data in hierarchical groups. The Summarize Across Hierarchy check box will appear.

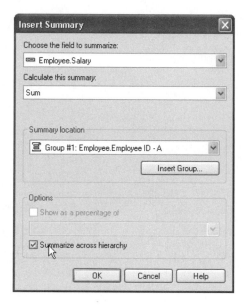

New Crystal Reports XI Hierarchical Formula Functions

Crystal Reports XI introduces new functions to the formula language that are helpful with hierarchical grouping. These functions help you determine where in the hierarchy a group appears (both the level of grouping in a multigroup report, as well as how many levels deep a value is within a single hierarchy). The *GroupingLevel* and *HierarchyLevel* functions can be used to determine where, within the hierarchy, a particular group resides (one level deep, two levels deep, and so forth).

In addition, Crystal Reports XI now allows the horizontal position of a field to be supplied via a conditional formula. By choosing the Size and Position option from the Format menu or pop-up menu after selecting the desired field, you can specify the horizontal (or X) position via a conditional formula, rather than just a typed-in number. By using the aforementioned hierarchy formula functions in a conditional formula, you may change the horizontal position of certain fields according to their hierarchy. This gives you more granular formatting control than that provided by the Group Indent setting in the Hierarchical Grouping Options dialog box (which controls indentation of the entire group, not just a single object).

TIP *A detailed explanation of the GroupingLevel and HierarchyLevel functions can be found in the appendix, the Formula Language Reference.*

Analyzing with Advanced Selection Criteria

reating a simple report is as quick as choosing tables, dragging and dropping fields on the report, and clicking the Preview button. However, if you perform only those few steps, you may have a much larger report show up than you bargained for! One important step missing is *record selection*. If you don't enter some record selection criteria, every record that exists in the tables you choose will appear on the report.

In the case of a small PC-type database with, say, 1,000 records, this won't be terribly time- or resource-intensive. However, if you're connected to a large SQL database with potentially millions of records, the consequences of not including record selection will probably be felt on your network and will certainly be felt on your desktop PC. Since Crystal Reports needs to store the data that makes up a report somewhere, you may run out of memory or temporary disk space in such a situation. Regardless of these concerns, your report will be terribly slow, and probably not very useful, if you have that many records on the report.

Virtually all reports will need record selection criteria. You may want to limit the report to only U.S.A. customers, only orders placed in 2004, or only invoices that are more than 30 days past due. Record selection criteria can be used to limit your report to any of these sets of records. In any event, it's very wise to apply your record selection criteria early on in your report design process—probably *before* you preview or print the report.

The Select Expert

Crystal Reports provides the *Select Expert* to help you create useful record selection criteria. You can use the Select Expert for simple, straightforward record selection, and as a starting point for more sophisticated record selection. The Select Expert can be run from the Record Selection section of any of the report wizards, or after you have chosen and linked tables using the Blank Report option. In either case, you'll want to make sure to use it before you preview the report.

To use the Select Expert while using one of the report wizards, choose at least one table in the Data section and, if necessary, link the tables in the Link section (table linking is covered in more detail in Chapter 15). Then progress through the other sections until you reach the Record Selection section, which looks like this:

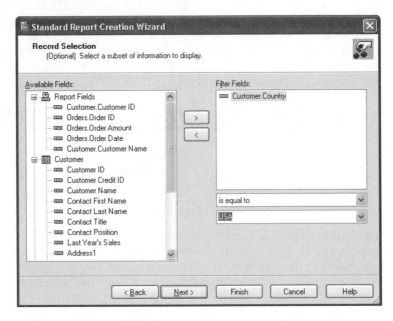

If you are using the Blank Report option to create a report, you must initially select and link tables. Once the Design tab appears, you can either immediately run the Select Expert or add fields to the report before running the Select Expert. Again, you'll want to run the Select Expert before you preview the report.

Run the Select Expert by clicking the Select Expert button in the Expert Tools toolbar. You can also choose Report | Select Expert from the drop-down menus. If you have already added fields to the report and want to use one of them from the Design tab or Preview tab for record selection, select the field on the report before you start the Select Expert. You can also right-click your selected field and choose Select Expert from the pop-up menu. In each case, the Select Expert will start with a tab already created for the chosen field.

CAUTION *You may use this feature unintentionally. If you start the Select Expert and see a tab for a field that you don't want to select on, just click the Delete button on the right side of the expert to delete the current tab. Then, click the <New> tab or the New button to choose the correct field to select.*

If this is the first time you've run the Select Expert, and you haven't chosen an existing report field, you'll see a Choose Field dialog box listing all report and database fields. You'll also see this dialog box if you are already displaying the Select Expert and click the <New> tab or the New button to add additional criteria.

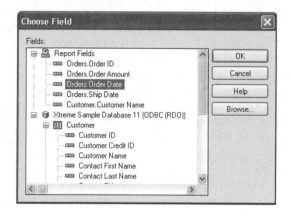

Click the report or database field that you want your record selection to be based on. If you want to see sample data from the database for that field, click Browse. Once you're satisfied with the field you want to use for record selection, select it and click OK. The Select Expert will appear with a tab for that field.

Once you've chosen a field to base record selection on, a drop-down list will appear displaying the default Is Any Value criteria. You will use this list to choose the comparison operation you want to use for your record selection. The drop-down list will reveal all the comparisons you can use to select records; it may vary somewhat based on the type of field you've chosen for record selection. Table 4-1 explains the different operators that may appear in the drop-down list. In addition to those listed in the table, the Select Expert will also provide "Is Not" versions of most of the comparisons. As you might imagine, choosing the "Not" version of the comparison will include records where the condition is *not* true, instead of where the condition is true.

Once you've chosen a comparison operator in the drop-down list, the Select Expert will change based on the selection you've made. If you've chosen an operator that only compares to one item (such as Equal To, Less Than, or Greater Than), one additional drop-down list will appear. If you've chosen an operator that can compare to multiple items (such as One Of, Like, or Starts With), a drop-down list will appear, along with a multiple-item box. You can add and remove items from the multiple-item box by clicking the Add and Delete buttons that appear next to the box.

Operator	Description
Is Any Value	This is the same as having no selection criteria at all. Is Any Value means it doesn't matter what's in the field—all records will be included in the report.
Is Equal To	The field must be exactly equal to what you specify.
Is One Of	You can specify more than one item to compare to by adding multiple comparison items to a list. If the field is exactly equal to any of them, the record will be included.
Is Less Than	The field must be less than the item you're comparing to. If you are comparing numbers, the field must be smaller numerically. If you are comparing dates, the field must be an earlier date. If you're comparing strings, the field must be lower in the alphabet. If you choose the Less Than Or Equal To option, the field can be equal to or less than what you're comparing to.
Is Greater Than	The field must be greater than the item you're comparing to. If you are comparing numbers, the field must be larger numerically. If you're comparing dates, the field must be a later date. If you're comparing strings, the field must be higher in the alphabet. If you choose the Greater Than Or Equal To option, the field can be equal to or greater than what you're comparing to.
Is Between	Allows you to select two items to create a comparison range. The field must be between the two items, or equal to one of them. Is Between uses the same type of comparison that is used with less and greater comparisons: numbers compare numerically, dates compare chronologically, and strings compare alphabetically.
Starts With	Allows you to specify "leading" characters to compare to. If the first characters in the field equal the specified characters, the record will be returned. If you want to perform several Starts With comparisons, you can add multiple criteria to a list. This operator will only appear when you are using a string field.
Is Like	You can look for partial text matches using wildcard characters to search for records that contain particular characters or groups of characters. When you specify your comparisons, you can use a question mark to indicate that one character in the field at that position can contain anything. You can use an asterisk to indicate that the rest of the field from that point on can contain anything. If you want to perform several Like comparisons, you can add multiple criteria to a list. This operator will appear only when you are using a string field.
Is In the Period	Allows you to compare a date field to a group of built-in date ranges, such as the last week, last month, last quarter, current year, etc. These built-in ranges are all based on the system clock of your computer when you run the report. This operator will appear only when you are using a date or date-time field.
Is True	Includes records where the field equates to true. This operator will appear only when you are using a Boolean field.
Is False	Includes records where the field equates to false. This operator will appear only when you are using a Boolean field.
Formula	Allows you to enter any Boolean formula using the Crystal Reports formula language. Similar to the Show Formula button in the lower-right corner of the Select Expert.

TABLE 4-1   Select Expert Comparison Operators

The new drop-down list allows you to choose the item you want to compare the field to in either of two ways: you can type it directly or choose it from the drop-down list. You can simply type the literal item you want to compare to directly in the drop-down list.

If you click the arrow on the drop-down list, the Select Expert will browse the database and list sample items from that database field. You may choose one of the items in the drop-down list for comparison.

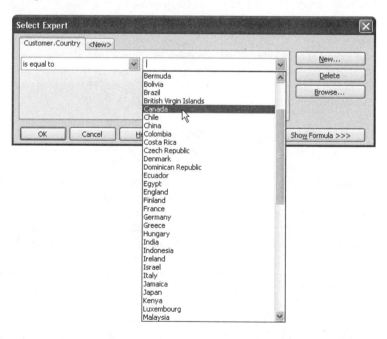

If the comparison operator you've chosen allows multiple entries, you can add an item you've typed to the multiple-item box by clicking Add. If you choose a browsed database item from the drop-down list, it will be added to the multiple-item box automatically. In either case, you can remove an item from the multiple-item box by selecting it and then clicking Remove.

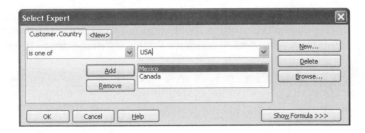

Note that you can choose *Is Not* versions of the comparison operators as well. This will, in essence, *reverse* the selection criteria you've chosen. If, for example, you chose a country field, selected the Is Not Equal To operator, and specified "USA" as the item to compare to, your report will now include records for every country *except* the U.S.A.

The Select Expert does not limit you to comparing just one field. Once you have added one database field, you can click the <New> tab or the New button. This will redisplay the Choose Field dialog box, from which you can pick another field to compare to. Once you pick this field, a new tab will display in the Select Expert, enabling you to create another comparison. You may create as many tabs and comparisons as you need.

TIP *Crystal Reports applies a logical AND to all the tabs in the Select Expert—all the criteria have to be true for a record to be selected. If you would rather have a logical OR applied to some or all of the tabs (so that if any one of them is true, but not all of them, a record is returned), you must manually edit the selection formula created by the Select Expert. This is discussed later in this chapter in "Manipulating the Record Selection Formula Directly."*

Refreshing the Report Versus Using Saved Data

When you preview a report on the screen for the first time, Crystal Reports has to actually read the database and perform record selection, and only thereafter can it format and display the report. To enhance future performance while you work with the report, Crystal Reports creates a set of *saved data.* This saved data consists of the records that were retrieved from the database, which are then kept either in memory or in temporary files on your hard drive. If you perform simple formatting changes, move fields around, or make other minor modifications that won't require the database to be re-queried, Crystal Reports will use the saved data every time you preview the modified report, thus improving performance. If you add new fields to the report, Crystal Reports knows it has to re-query the database, and it does so without prompting. You may notice a bit of a wait (or maybe a long wait, depending on your database) while it runs the new query.

But when you change record selection criteria, Crystal Reports doesn't know whether or not it needs to re-query the database. You will be given the option to Refresh or Use Saved Data. The choice you make is dependent upon whether you widened or narrowed the selection criteria. If you *narrowed* your selection criteria so that the new selection criteria can be completely satisfied with the existing saved data, you can choose to use the saved data. Since the database doesn't have to be re-queried, the changes will appear very quickly in the Preview tab.

If, however, you *widened* the selection criteria so that the saved data won't contain all the records you're specifying, you need to refresh the report so that the database can be re-queried. Choosing to use saved data in this situation will result in your report showing too few (if any) records, even though they actually exist in the database. However, the new query will take time to perform. If you make the wrong choice and end up with too few, or no, records, you can refresh the report manually by clicking the Refresh button in the Navigation Tools toolbar or in the upper-right of the Preview tab next to the page navigation buttons, pressing the F5 key, or choosing Report | Refresh Report Data from the drop-down menus.

When you save a report, you have the option to store the saved data in the .RPT file. If you include the saved data, the report will immediately display the Preview tab showing the saved data the next time you open the .RPT file—no database re-query will be required. However, this will also make the .RPT file larger (sometimes significantly so), since it has to keep the saved data along with the report design specifications.

Tip *Even if you open a report with saved data, the saved data will be discarded and only the Design tab will appear if the Discard Saved Data On Open option is checked on the Reporting tab of File | Options.*

To choose whether or not to save data, check or uncheck File | Save Data with Report from the drop-down menus, and then resave the report after making your choice. You can also make the choice with the appropriate check box on File | Report Options. If you wish to set default behavior for this option for all new reports in the future, turn on or off the Save Data with Report option on the Reporting tab of File | Options.

Record Selection with Date Fields

Many reporting requirements can be satisfied by creatively using date fields in record selection. Crystal Reports provides a good selection of built-in date ranges you can use to compare to, or you can use other operators to compare date fields. When you choose a date or date/time field in the Choose Field dialog box, the Select Expert makes the In the Period comparison operator available. If you choose this operator, another drop-down list containing Crystal Reports' built-in date ranges appears.

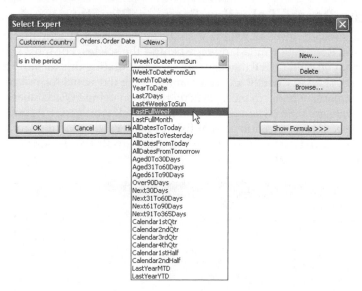

By using these built-in ranges, you can create a report that will return, say, only orders in the previous month by comparing to the LastFullMonth. What's particularly appealing about using built-in date range functions is the "self-maintenance" of the report. When you use the LastFullMonth range, for example, the report will always use the system clock in your computer to include orders from the previous month, no matter when the report is run. You don't have to manually change the date range every month.

There may be times, however, when you have to manually enter a date range for record selection. If, for example, you want to see all orders for 2003, you need to specify those dates manually. There is no built-in X Years Ago date range. In this case, you choose the date field you want to select on (for example, Order Date) and use a Between comparison operator to indicate orders between January 1, 2003, and December 31, 2003. You can enter a beginning date of 1/1/2003 and an ending date of 12/31/2003.

TIP *Crystal Reports allows a fair amount of flexibility in date formatting with the Select Expert, generally allowing you to type in free-form dates as you wish. However, you'll still receive error messages if you type in dates that Crystal Reports isn't sure about, such as dates that include only a two-digit year.*

Even if you choose a date/time field for record selection, you may supply just a date (without a time) as the comparison value. While Crystal Reports will allow this, understand that a time of midnight will be assumed with the date you specified. With a Between comparison in particular, this can cause confusing results. Since both dates will be compared to as of midnight, all records on or after midnight for the *first* specified date will be included. However, only records that include times of exactly midnight for the *second* date will be included—any times of even one second after midnight for the second date won't be included. Therefore, make sure you include a time value alongside a date value if you want to select records based on some time other than midnight.

Manipulating the Record Selection Formula Directly

When you create record selection criteria with the Select Expert, it actually creates a formula using the Crystal Reports formula language behind the scenes. For most simple record selection criteria, you won't have to worry about manipulating this formula directly. Also, by using the Select Expert directly and not manipulating the actual formula that it creates, you will often maximize performance, particularly when using SQL databases.

However, there are times when the Select Expert itself won't provide enough flexibility for the record selection you need to accomplish. Consider the following scenario—you have two fields on their own tabs included in the Select Expert: Region Is Equal to CO and Order Amount Is Greater than 2500.

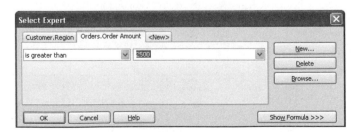

Since the Select Expert performs a logical AND between the tabs, what do you do if you want to see all orders from Colorado, regardless of the order amount, as well as orders from any other state over $2,500?

In this case, the Select Expert doesn't provide sufficient flexibility to create this type of special record selection. Thus, you must use a *record selection formula*. The Select Expert creates a record selection formula automatically as you add tabs and selection criteria. You can modify the formula it creates in one of three ways:

- By clicking the Show Formula button on the Select Expert itself
- By choosing Report | Selection Formulas | Record from the drop-down menus
- By displaying the Formula Workshop (discussed in more detail in Chapter 5) and choosing Record Selection in the Selection Formulas category

---

TIP *If you know you'll need extra features that the Select Expert doesn't provide, you can skip it entirely and create your record selection formula right in the Formula Editor or Formula Workshop. Choose Report | Selection Formulas | Record from the drop-down menus or choose Record Selection in the Formula Workshop's Selection Formulas category to create the formula this way.*

In the scenario previously mentioned, you need to change the relationship that exists between the two criteria from an And to an Or. This is a simple process that you can apply either right from the Select Expert or by using the Formula Editor. To use the Select Expert, simply click Show Formula.

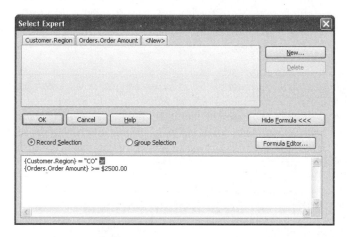

You can now modify the formula created by the Select Expert to show you all Colorado orders, regardless of amount, and other orders over $2,500. Notice that the Select Expert has placed the And operator between the two parts of the selection formula. Simply position the cursor in the formula and change the And to Or, and then click OK.

TIP *If you click Show Formula in the Select Expert and then decide you want to use the full-featured Formula Editor, just click the Formula Editor button in the expanded Select Expert dialog box. The formula will be transferred to the Formula Editor, where you can modify or enhance it.*

Since you will ultimately be using the Crystal Reports formula language for your record selection, most of the features of the language are available for record selection. In this situation, it may be preferable to edit the selection formula in the Formula Editor so that you can see and use all the built-in functionality. The formula that the Select Expert created will appear when you choose Report | Selection Formulas | Record from the drop-down menus.

You can modify this formula to your heart's content, provided that the ultimate finished formula is a Boolean formula—it will ultimately just return true or false (refer to Chapter 5 for more information on Boolean formulas). The formula will be evaluated for each record in the database. If the formula evaluates to true, the record will be included in the report; otherwise, the record will be ignored.

Case Sensitivity with Record Selection

A question that you will probably ask yourself fairly quickly when using record selection is, "Is it case sensitive?" In other words, if you ask to see records where the country is "USA," will a record be returned if the database field contains mixed-case characters, such as "Usa"?

Case sensitivity is generally ignored when using SQL databases and PC databases via ODBC, as well as certain databases using a direct database driver. Although this case insensitivity is the default behavior "out of the box," be sure to check the Database Server Is Case-Insensitive option in the File | Report Options dialog box to affect the current report, or check the same option on the Database tab of File | Options to set the default for all new reports you create in the future.

Even if this option is checked, some databases and ODBC drivers may not support case insensitivity with Crystal Reports. It's best to run a test with your own database to make sure you're retrieving all desired records with your record selection.

NOTE *If you modify the formula the Select Expert created, or you create your own formula, running the Select Expert again is fine. However, if the Select Expert is unable to fully interpret the formula you created, you'll see slightly different behavior for one or more tabs. You may see a tab with a field set to Is Formula and part of the selection formula showing in the third list box. You may also see a message indicating that the formula uses a "composite expression" and prompting you to edit the formula directly.*

Limiting Data with a Group Selection Formula

When you use the Select Expert or create a record selection formula with the Formula Editor, you affect the way Crystal Reports initially selects data from the database. Record selection occurs during the *first pass* of the report, before data has been sorted or grouped. Because of this, you can't use record selection to limit your report, say, to groups where the total sales exceeds $100,000—the record selection occurs before these totals are calculated.

You may also want to use an existing report formula in record selection. However, if you use the WhilePrintingRecords function or a summary function in the formula, it will evaluate in the report's *second pass* and won't show up in the Field

Tree box when you create a record selection formula. Again, the record selection occurs during the first pass, and second-pass formulas can't be used (see Chapter 5 for a discussion of report passes and Chapter 3 for information on Grouping).

If you want to limit the report according to group subtotals or summaries, or somehow limit the report using second-pass formulas, you must use a *group selection formula* instead of a record selection formula. You may actually create a group selection formula inadvertently and not even know it. If you use a subtotal or summary field you create on your report in the Select Expert (perhaps you choose the Sum of Customer.Last Years Sales instead of the Customer.Last Years Sales database field itself), you will be using group selection instead of record selection.

You may also create a group selection formula from the Select Expert by clicking Show Formula and then clicking the Group Selection radio button. If you want to make use of a typed-in formula, you have two choices: Select Report | Selection Formulas | Group from the drop-down menus or Group Selection in the Selection Formulas category of the Formula Workshop. You can now create a Boolean formula to limit records using group summaries or second-pass formulas.

One word of caution: Group selection occurs *after* the group tree, subtotals, and grand totals have been calculated. This can lead to apparent inaccuracies on your report. For example, look at the report shown in Figure 4-1.

You'll notice that the group tree shows many more regions than actually appear on the report. And, it doesn't take a math degree to see that the grand totals don't quite add up. Don't forget that selection of a summary or subtotal field in the Select Expert will create a group

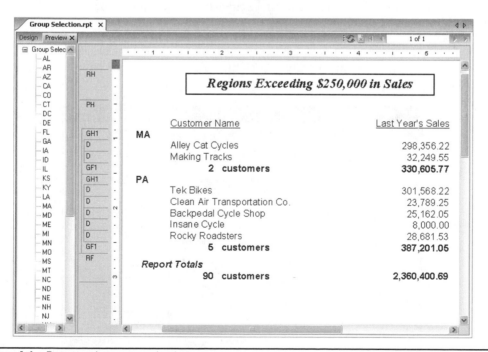

FIGURE 4-1 Report using group selection

selection formula instead of a record selection formula. You may see this kind of odd behavior and not fully understand why. Look back at the Select Expert to see if your selection is based on a subtotal or summary field.

This report applies a group selection formula to limit the report to groups where the sum of Last Year's Sales exceeds $250,000. This group selection is applied after the group tree and grand totals have been created. Although there is no way to change the group tree in this situation, you can correct the totaling problem by using running totals instead of grand totals. Look at Chapter 5 for information on running total fields.

Performance Considerations with Record Selection

In many cases, record selection is the most time-consuming portion of the report process, particularly with larger databases. If you're using a PC-style database located on a local or network hard drive, Crystal Reports performs the record selection itself, reading every record in the database and keeping only those that match. If you are using a server-based database (such as SQL Server or Oracle), Crystal Reports will attempt to create a WHERE clause in the query that's sent to the database server, which will cause the database server to perform the query and send only the desired records to Crystal Reports.

In either situation, you'll probably see overall improved performance if you use *indexed fields* for your record selection (with PC-style databases, this is often very critical). Indexed fields are fields that are specially designated when the database is designed. The field's index stores all the values in the field in a presorted state that makes it much faster to select records based on the field. To determine if a field is indexed, you may wish to consult the database designer.

You can also see which fields are indexed by using the Links tab of the Database Expert. Click the Database Expert button on the Expert Tools toolbar, or choose Database | Database Expert from the pull-down menus. Then, click the Links tab (you must have added at least two tables to your report to see it).

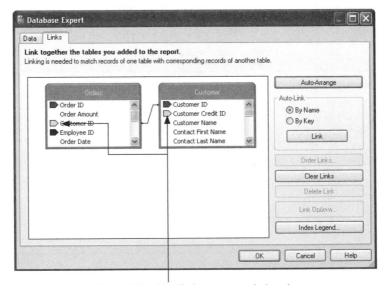

Fields with a "tent" character are indexed

You'll notice a small "tent" character appearing next to every indexed field (the different colors you may see are generally insignificant to record selection, as long as you select on a field with the symbol). Make note of the indexed fields and attempt to use them in record selection. If the field you need to select on is not indexed, and record selection appears very sluggish, you may wish to consult the database designer about adding an index for that field.

TIP *Crystal Reports versions prior to 9 did not show the tent characters when using SQL databases. New Crystal Reports versions now display index designations for popular SQL databases, as well as PC-style databases. However, depending on the database driver you are using, you still may not see the "tent" index designators in some instances.*

Finally, double-check the setting of the Use Indexes Or Server For Speed option. To check the option for the current report, look in the File | Report Options dialog box. If you wish to check the option for all new reports in the future, look for the option on the Database tab of File | Options. If this is turned off, Crystal Reports won't use field indexes at all.

SQL databases (or PC-style databases accessed via ODBC) present a different set of performance considerations when compared to performance with PC-style databases. As a general reporting rule, you want to always have the database server perform the record selection (via the aforementioned WHERE clause), if at all possible. This can typically be accomplished by using only the Select Expert to create selection criteria—using the Formula Editor makes it entirely too easy to introduce functions that Crystal Reports can't move to the database server. Also, making changes to what the Select Expert creates with an Is Formula operator or the Show Formula button may seriously degrade database server record selection performance. As with PC-style databases, make sure the Use Indexes or Server for Speed option is turned on in File | Report Options.

TIP *More in-depth discussion and examples of performance issues, including record selection, are found in Chapter 15.*

Using Formulas

When you first start using Crystal Reports, you'll be able to write some simple reports using data that comes entirely from the database. You simply drag fields from the Field Explorer onto the report, and away you go. However, it won't be long until you find that you want some information to appear on your report that isn't contained in the database. Or, you may find that you want to display a field differently on the report than it appears in the database. For these, and many similar situations, use Crystal Reports *formulas*.

A formula can be thought of as a math calculation or a small piece of computer programming code. If you're not used to them at first, creating formulas can appear to be very complicated. Depending on your background, you may like the fact that some formulas are very much like programming, or this may be one characteristic of formulas that you would prefer not to deal with. Formulas can be as simple or as complex as you want to make them—you can start with simple math computations and, as you get more comfortable, graduate to full Basic-like formulas using Case statements, variables, and other advanced programming techniques. You can even share your formula expertise with your coworkers using Crystal Reports custom functions (covered in Chapter 6) and the Repository (covered in Chapter 17). Formulas bring the ultimate power and flexibility to Crystal Reports.

You can create formulas with either the Design or the Preview tab displayed, although creating them in the Design tab is probably better because you will have a more accurate idea of where the formulas will really end up when you place them on your report. You may create a new formula or modify an existing formula in two places in Crystal Reports—either the Field Explorer's Formula Fields category, or from the Formula Workshop.

The Formula Workshop

The *Formula Workshop* is a dialog box that presents a unified approach to examining, creating, and modifying different types of formulas in your reports. The Formula Workshop not only allows you to display and modify standard report formulas, but also allows creation of report custom functions (covered in Chapter 6) and provides the capability to store custom functions in the central repository (covered in Chapter 17). The Formula Workshop provides access to record and group selection and custom formatting formulas.

To display the Formula Workshop, either choose Report | Formula Workshop from the mail pull-down menus, or click the Formula Workshop toolbar button from the Expert Tools toolbar. The Formula Workshop will appear, as shown in Figure 5-1.

The Formula Workshop consists of a folder "tree" view on the left, two toolbars on the top, and a large area below the toolbars and to the right of the tree view where the Formula Expert or Formula Editor (both discussed later in the chapter) will appear when actually working with a formula.

The tree view contains a list of formula categories available in the Formula Workshop.

- **Report Custom Functions**   "Sharable" functions that can be used by any formula in your report (covered in Chapter 6).

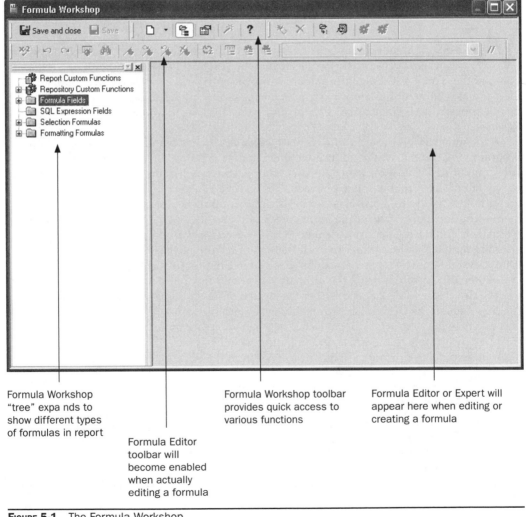

FIGURE 5-1   The Formula Workshop

- **Repository Custom Functions**   "Sharable" functions that have been saved in the repository to be used by every copy of Crystal Reports connected to the repository (the repository is covered in Chapter 17).

- **Formula Fields**   Formulas that you create for use in just this report (covered in the rest of this chapter).

- **SQL Expression Fields**   Server-based formulas, using the Structured Query Language (covered in Chapter 15).

- **Selection Formulas**   Formulas used to control record and group selection. These are the same formulas created using the Select Expert, or the Report | Selection Formulas pull-down menu options (covered in Chapter 4).

- **Formatting Formulas**   Formulas that set appearance of report objects and sections conditionally. These are the same formulas created using the conditional buttons in the Format Editor and Section Expert (covered in Chapters 7 and 8).

If there are available formulas or functions in the desired category, a plus sign will appear next to that category—just click the plus sign to open up that category and show the available formulas or functions in it. The lack of a plus sign next to a category indicates that no formulas or functions in that category have yet been created.

As Table 5-1 shows, the Formula Workshop toolbar at the top of the dialog box provides quick ways to perform more common Formula Workshop options.

Not all of the toolbar buttons will be enabled all of the time. Certain buttons and their functions are enabled only when an appropriate formula is selected in the tree view. For example, you can't rename custom functions in the repository or click the Delete button when the record selection formula is highlighted.

TIP *The Formula Workshop toolbar actually consists of several separate toolbars, each of which can be "undocked" from the top of the Formula Workshop window. Just click on the small gray vertical bar to the left of the different parts of the toolbar and drag to a new location.*

You're not limited to using the Formula Workshop to create, rename, and delete formulas. You can also use the Field Explorer. By choosing the Formula Fields category of the Field Explorer, you can access Field Explorer toolbar buttons, right-click pop-up menus, and keyboard shortcuts as well. Accordingly, there are numerous ways to create a new report formula by using the Field Explorer's Formula Fields category or the Formula Workshop. Once you've chosen to create a new formula, you'll be asked to supply a formula name. Remember that you're *not* creating a file on disk when you add a formula, so you don't need to worry about file-naming conventions—the formula is simply stored inside the .RPT file of your report. Your formula names can contain upper- and lowercase letters, spaces, and anything else that makes them descriptive. Use an easy-to-understand formula name—not only does it help you to recognize what the formula is when you look at the list of formulas you've created, but it also is used for the field title when you place a formula in the details section.

Icon	Description
or **CTRL-S**	Saves the current formula or function and closes the Formula Workshop. If Crystal Reports detects any errors in the formula or function, you'll be prompted whether or not you wish to save with the error. You may also close the Formula Workshop by clicking the X in the window's upper right-hand corner.
or **ALT-S**	Saves the current formula or function but leaves the Formula Workshop open. If Crystal Reports detects any errors in the formula or function, you'll be prompted whether or not you wish to save with the error.
or **CTRL-N**	Creates a new formula. If you click the button directly, you'll create a new formula or function based on the category selected in the tree view. If you click the small down arrow next to the button, you'll be given a choice of type of formula to create. You may also create a new formula by right-clicking the desired tree view category and choosing New from the pop-up menu.
	Toggles display of the Formula Workshop tree view on and off.
	Toggles between viewing the actual code of a selected custom function or the custom function's properties, such as arguments, author, and so forth (this button has no effect when editing a formula). See Chapter 6 for more information on this button.
or **ALT-X**	Toggles between displaying the formula in the Formula Expert (discussed later in the chapter and in Chapter 6) or in the Formula Editor. If you are displaying a formula that consists of something other than use of a single custom function, you'll be warned that clicking this button will erase the current formula. Also, this button won't work while you're creating a custom function.
? or **F1**	Displays context-sensitive Formula Workshop, Formula Expert, or Formula Editor online help (depending on which portion of the Formula Workshop is currently displayed, which function or operator is highlighted, or where the cursor appears).
or **F2**	Renames the formula currently selected in the tree view. Clicking this button will place the formula name in the tree view in Edit mode. You may also rename a formula by right-clicking the formula in the tree view and choosing Rename from the pop-up menu, or by just holding your mouse button down for a few seconds after selecting the formula name in the tree.
X or **DEL**	Deletes the formula from the Formula Workshop and the report. You may be notified that the formula is being used in the report or that repository function deletions can't be undone and asked to confirm the deletion. You may also delete by right-clicking the formula in the tree view and choosing Delete from the pop-up menu.
	Expands the folder you currently have selected in the tree view. For example, if you have the Formula Fields folder selected, clicking this button will open that category and show all the report formulas within the category. If the folder is already expanded, clicking the button again will do nothing.

TABLE 5-1   Formula Workshop Toolbar Buttons

Icon	Description
	Toggles between showing all Formatting Formula category report objects in the report or only those objects that already contain formatting formulas. For example, if you click this button while viewing the expanded Formatting Formulas category, a limited set of report objects will appear (or none, if there are no existing formatting formulas in the report). This button affects only the Formatting Formulas category in the tree view.
	Adds the selected report custom function to the repository (see Chapter 17 for more information on adding your own custom functions to the repository).
	Copies the selected repository custom function to the current report. The custom function will then appear in the Custom Functions portion of the Formula Editor functions tree. See Chapter 17 for more information on adding repository custom functions to your report.

TABLE 5-1   Formula Workshop Toolbar Buttons *(continued)*

The Formula Expert

When you initially create a new formula, the Formula Editor will appear (the Formula Editor is discussed in detail later in the chapter). However, if you click the "magic wand" toolbar button in the Formula Workshop toolbar before you type any formula text, the Formula Expert will appear instead. Also, if you edit an existing formula that's based on a single custom function, the Formula Expert will also appear.

The Formula Expert is shown in Figure 5-2. This expert is designed to help you create a formula without having to use the Crystal Reports formula language. While this sounds tempting to those who may, at least initially, be slightly put off by the Crystal formula language, the Formula Expert immediately introduces one substantial caveat: only formulas using a single custom function can be created in the expert. If you want to create a formula using regular Crystal Reports formula language functions or math operators, the Formula Expert won't provide appropriate capabilities. And even if you are using a custom function, the Formula Expert won't allow you to enclose it inside another custom function or use the custom function with any other Crystal Reports formula language syntax. In any situation where you can't use the Formula Expert, you'll need to use the Formula Editor to create your desired formula.

The first step in using the Formula Expert is to determine the custom function you want to base your formula on. Choose this function in the Custom Function list. You may choose a function from either the Report Custom Functions category (these are custom functions that are already part of your report) or the Repository Custom Functions category (these are custom functions that reside in your BusinessObjects Enterprise or Crystal Reports Server repository). In either case, click the plus sign next to the desired category and navigate through the tree until you find the desired custom function you wish to use. Once you select that custom function, a description of the function will appear in the Summary area (if the description was added when the custom function was created). The data type that the function will return (string, number, and so forth) will appear in the Return Type area.

Custom function chosen to
base formula on

Description of custom function (if added
when custom function was created)

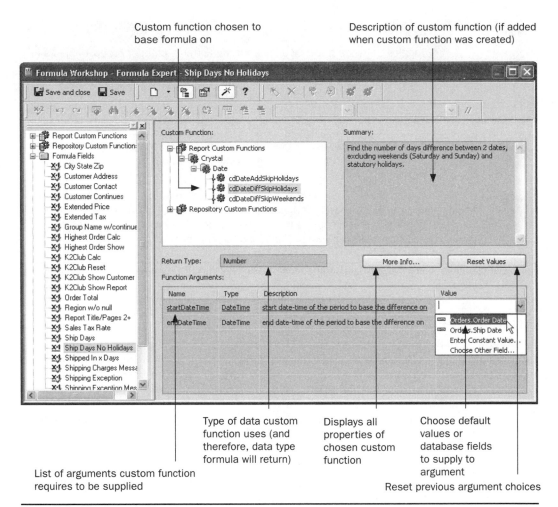

Type of data custom
function uses (and
therefore, data type
formula will return)

Displays all
properties of
chosen custom
function

Choose default
values or
database fields
to supply to
argument

List of arguments custom function
requires to be supplied

Reset previous argument choices

FIGURE 5-2   The Formula Expert

And, any necessary parameters or *arguments* that the function requires to be supplied will
be added to the Function Arguments area at the bottom of the Formula Expert.

Then, simply choose the database fields, other formula fields, or typed-in values that
you want to supply as arguments to the custom function. You may do this by typing in a
number, string, date, or other value directly in the Value area for the desired argument. Or if
you click the down arrow to display a drop-down list, you'll see a list of fields you've
previously added to the report that match the data type of the argument (for example, if the
argument requires a date-time value, only date-time fields that you've previously added to
the report will appear in the drop-down list). You may also choose drop-down list options
to Enter Constant Value, which will display a separate dialog box where you may choose

or type a value (which is just the same as typing the value in directly without clicking the down arrow). You may also select Choose Other Field from the drop-down list, which will display a separate dialog box listing all fields in all database tables that match the data type of the argument.

If you've supplied several values to arguments in the Function Arguments list and wish to discard them all, click the Reset Values button above the Function Arguments list. All previously supplied arguments will be discarded, and you'll need to choose arguments again. If you want more general information on the custom function you've chosen to base your formula on, click More Info to see a dialog box showing all the function's properties.

Once you've supplied all the necessary arguments, click the Save And Close button in the Formula Workshop toolbar. If the formula you're creating in the Expert is based on a function from the repository, you'll be reminded that creating this formula will add the chosen repository custom function (and any other repository functions that it may be based on) to the report. This will be required to use this formula, so click Yes to acknowledge this message.

The formula will be created and added to the Field Explorer, where it may be dragged to your report just like any other field. If you later wish to edit this formula, either right-click the formula in the report's Design or Preview tab and choose Edit Formula from the pop-up menu, choose Field Explorer options to edit the existing formula, or display the Formula Workshop and choose and edit the formula from within the Formula Fields tree. The Formula Workshop containing the Formula Expert will reappear with the formula already in it. If you wish to see the formula displayed in the Formula Editor instead of the Formula Expert, click the "magic wand" button in the Formula Workshop toolbar—the formula will be displayed in the Formula Editor instead.

NOTE   *Creating custom functions that you may base Formula Expert formulas on is covered in more detail in Chapter 6.*

The Formula Editor

When you first create a new formula or edit an existing formula that is based on something other than a single custom function, the Formula Editor will appear inside the Formula Workshop, as shown in Figure 5-3. It may look a little foreboding at first, but don't worry—it will soon become second nature to you as you create and edit more formulas.

TIP   *If you wish to customize the font face, size, colors, and other appearance options that the Formula Editor uses, select File | Options on the pull-down menus and make your choices on the Formula Editor tab.*

Before you actually create a formula, familiarize yourself with the layout of the Formula Editor. Notice that the Field Tree, Function Tree, and Operator Tree boxes can be closed, resized, moved, and undocked (detached from the main window and put in their own windows). You have a great deal of flexibility in customizing the way the Formula Editor looks. You may also undock the Formula Editor toolbar (the second toolbar at the top of the Formula Workshop) and move it to another location on the screen.

Formula Editor toolbar provides access to the most common Formula Editor functions

Choose the formula language syntax to use for this formula

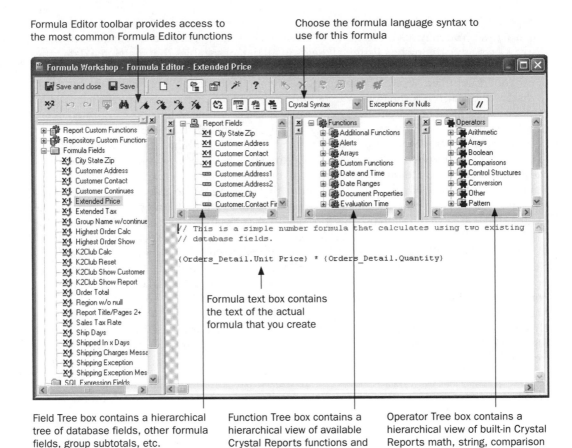

Formula text box contains the text of the actual formula that you create

Field Tree box contains a hierarchical tree of database fields, other formula fields, group subtotals, etc.

Function Tree box contains a hierarchical view of available Crystal Reports functions and custom functions

Operator Tree box contains a hierarchical view of built-in Crystal Reports math, string, comparison operators, etc.

FIGURE 5-3   The Formula Editor inside the Formula Workshop

TIP *If you mistakenly undock and then close the toolbar, you can get it back by closing and re-opening the Formula Workshop. The toolbar will then reappear.*

When you're working with the Formula Editor, you'll want to familiarize yourself with the Formula Editor toolbar (titled the *Expression Editor toolbar* if you undock it), because you'll need to use it on a regular basis. There are buttons to check for proper formula syntax; undo and redo editing changes; hide and show the field, function, and operator trees; and so forth. If you're unfamiliar with a toolbar button's function, point to it with your mouse and wait a second or two—a tooltip for that button will appear. Table 5-2 shows the functions of the Formula Editor's toolbar buttons.

TIP *There are many other shortcut keys you can use while in the Formula Editor. Search Crystal Reports online Help for "Key controls for Formula Editor."*

Button/Key Combo	Name	Function
x·2 or ALT-C	Check	Checks the syntax of the formula and reports any errors.
or CTRL-Z	Undo	Undoes the latest editing or typing.
or CTRL-Y	Redo	Redoes the latest editing or typing.
or ALT-B	Browse Data	Displays sample data from the database for the selected database field. This button will work only when you've highlighted a database field, not a custom function.
or CTRL-F	Find/Replace	Allows searching and replacing for specific characters in the current formula.
or CTRL-F2	Toggle Bookmark	Places a bookmark at the current line of formula text. If a bookmark is already there, removes it.
or CTRL-ALT-F2	Next Bookmark	Moves the cursor to the next bookmark in the current formula.
or SHIFT-F2	Previous Bookmark	Moves the cursor to the previous bookmark in the current formula.
or CTRL-SHIFT-F2	Clear All Bookmarks	Removes all bookmarks from the current formula.
or ALT-O	Sort Trees	Sorts the contents of the three Tree boxes alphabetically, instead of in the default logical order.
or ALT-F	Field Tree	Displays/hides the Field Tree box.
or ALT-U	Function Tree	Displays/hides the Function Tree box.
or ALT-P	Operator Tree	Displays/hides the Operator Tree box.
Crystal Syntax or CTRL-T	Syntax	Chooses syntax (Crystal or Basic) to use for this formula only.
Exceptions For Nulls (new in version XI)	Null Treatment	Chooses to treat null values encountered in a formula as nulls, or to convert nulls to the default value for the data type of the null field.
// or ALT-M	Comment/ Uncomment	Adds comment characters (two slashes for Crystal Syntax, an apostrophe for Basic Syntax) to all formula lines that are highlighted. If the lines already are commented, this button removes the comment characters. Lines that are preceded with comment characters are ignored by the formula.

TABLE 5-2 Formula Editor Toolbar Buttons

PART I

There are two general approaches to building a formula: type in the parts of the formula directly or double-click in the tree boxes. Once you become more familiar with the Crystal Reports formula language, you will probably create at least some parts of your formula by typing the formula text right into the Formula text box at the bottom of the Formula Editor. For example, simply typing an asterisk when you want to multiply numbers often is easier than clicking around in the Operator Tree box to find the multiplication operator.

Other parts of your formula, however, are best created automatically by double-clicking elements in one of the three tree boxes. For example, to include a database field as part of your formula, just find the field you want to include in the Field Tree box and double-click it. The field will be placed at the cursor position in the Formula text box, using proper formula language syntax.

Using the trees is easy. Simply find the general area of the tree that you are interested in and click the plus sign next to the category that you want to use. All the functions or operators within that category will appear. Double-click the one you want to use and it will be placed at the cursor position in the Formula text box. If you click a function that requires *arguments* (or parameters), such as an UpperCase function that needs to know what you want to convert to uppercase, the function name and parentheses will be placed in the formula with the cursor positioned at the location of the first argument. You can either type it in or move to another tree (the field tree, for example) and double-click the field you want to add as the argument. After a while, you'll be able to find the functions or operators you're looking for quickly and create fairly large formulas simply by pointing and double-clicking.

Notice the syntax that Crystal Reports uses when it places objects in the Formula text box (the small formula illustrated in Figure 5-3 is a good example). If you decide to type material into the formula yourself, you'll need to adhere to proper formula language syntax. Table 5-3 identifies special characters and other syntactical requirements of the formula language.

Crystal Syntax	Basic Syntax	Uses
. (period)	. (period)	Used to separate the table name from the field name when using a database field. You must always include the table name, a period, and the field name—the field name by itself is not sufficient.
{} ("curly" or French braces)	{} ("curly" or French braces)	Used to surround database fields, other formula names, and parameter fields. The formula won't understand fields if they're not surrounded by curly braces.
// (two slashes)	' (apostrophe) or Rem	Denotes a comment. These can be used at the beginning of a line in a formula, in which case the Formula Editor ignores the whole line. You can also place two slashes or an apostrophe anywhere in a formula line, in which case the rest of the line will be ignored. You may use the Formula Editor Comment/Uncomment toolbar button to add these characters to multiple selected lines at one time.

TABLE 5-3 Formula Editor Special Characters

Crystal Syntax	Basic Syntax	Uses

" " or ' ' (quotation marks or apostrophes)	" " (quotation marks)	Used to surround string or text literals (fixed-string characters) in formulas. With Crystal syntax, you can use either option, as long as they're used in matched pairs. For example:
		`If {Customer.Country} = "USA" Then`
		`"United States" Else 'International'`
		If you are using Basic syntax, you must use quotation marks only—an apostrophe will be interpreted as a comment.

() (parentheses)	() (parentheses)	Used to force certain parts of formulas to be evaluated first, as in the following:
		`({Orders.Amount} +`
		`{Orders.Amount}) * {@Tax Rate}`
		Also used to denote arguments of built-in functions, as in this example:
		`UpperCase({Customer.Customer`
		`Name})`

@ ? # %	@ ? # %	Crystal Reports automatically precedes certain fields with these characters. The @ sign precedes formulas, ? precedes parameter fields, # precedes running total fields, and % precedes SQL expression fields. When including these types of fields in a formula, make sure you surround the field with curly braces.
# (pound sign)	# (pound sign)	If you don't include curly braces around a pound sign, Crystal Reports will expect a value appearing between two pound signs that can be converted to a date/time value, as in this example: #2/10/2000 1:15 pm#

, (comma)	, (comma)	Used to separate multiple arguments in functions. For example:
		`ToText({Orders.Amount},0," ")`
		Don't add a comma as a thousands separator when using a numeric constant in a formula. For example:
		`{Orders.Amount} + 2,500`
		`will cause a syntax error.`

; (semicolon)	: (colon)	If your formula contains multiple statements, you must separate them with a semicolon in Crystal syntax (putting statements on separate lines without a semicolon will still cause a syntax error). With Basic syntax, you must either put each statement on a separate line or separate multiple statements on the same line with a colon. Note that in Basic syntax, some statements (such as those making up For loops) must be placed on separate lines—separating these statements with a colon will still cause a syntax error.

TABLE 5-3   Formula Editor Special Characters *(continued)*

Crystal Syntax	Basic Syntax	Uses

ENTER key	_ (space followed by underscore)	In Crystal syntax, you may press ENTER to start a new line in your formula anywhere between a field or function and an operator (don't put new lines or spaces in the middle of field or function names). Long formulas are more readable on multiple lines. For example:
		
		`If {Order.Amount} > 5000 Then`
		`    "Qualifies for bonus"`
		`Else`
		`    "Not eligible for bonus"`
		
		In Basic syntax, you may press ENTER only at the end of a complete statement. If you want a line break in the middle of a statement, you must use a line continuation sequence (a space, followed by the underscore). For example:
		
		`If {Order.Amount} > 5000 Then`
		`    Formula = _`
		`       "Qualifies for bonus"`
		`Else Formula = _`
		`       "Not eligible for bonus"`
		`End If`

:= (colon followed by equal sign)	= (equal sign)	Used for variable assignment, such as:
		`NumberVar Quota := 1`
		In Crystal syntax, don't confuse this with the equal sign alone, which is used for comparison:
		`If {Customer.Region} = "BC"`
		`Then`
		`"Canadian Customer"`
		In Basic syntax, the equal sign is used for both comparison and assignment, as in
		`If {Customer.Region} _`
		`    = "BC" Then`
		`Formula = "Canadian Customer"`
		`End If`

TABLE 5-3 Formula Editor Special Characters *(continued)*

Formula Syntax Choices in Crystal Reports

The syntax you use for individual formulas can be chosen with the syntax drop-down list, located at the right end of the Formula Editor toolbar. When you choose the desired syntax, you'll notice that the function and operator trees will change, showing all the built-in functions and operators for the chosen syntax. When you check the formula with the Check button, the formula must conform to the syntax chosen in the drop-down list. If, for example, you create a formula that is correct for Crystal syntax and then choose Basic syntax in the drop-down list, you'll probably get an error message if you check the formula. Crystal Reports will not automatically convert from one syntax to the other when you change the syntax drop-down value in an already existing formula.

The choice of syntax is largely one of personal preference. If you are a Basic programmer who often encounters syntax errors with Crystal syntax because you instinctively use Basic, you'll probably be pleased with Basic syntax. If you've used previous versions of Crystal Reports and aren't a Basic programmer, you'll most likely want to continue to use Crystal syntax because you're familiar with it. You don't have to do this at the expense of flexibility, either—virtually all of the Basic-like constructs in Basic syntax are also available in Crystal syntax. You can always choose which syntax to use in each formula that you create (the notable exceptions being record- and group-selection formulas—these can use only Crystal syntax, and you aren't given a choice). You may choose the default syntax for all new formulas by choosing File | Options and clicking the Formula Editor tab.

The remainder of this chapter focuses largely on Crystal syntax, showing most examples in the Crystal Reports "original" formula language. This choice has been made for two reasons:

- If you are using previous versions of Crystal Reports, most of this chapter will still apply to you.

- The Basic language is well documented in many other texts. Since this book is specific to Crystal Reports, language syntax that is specific to Crystal Reports is best documented here.

Any examples or issues that are specific to Basic syntax will be so noted.

Crystal Reports Formula Autocomplete

If you develop computer programs in certain programming languages, or develop web pages with certain tools, you may be familiar with autocompletion, which will often anticipate what you are typing and complete portions of your code for you. Crystal Reports features a limited form of this technology as part of the Formula Editor.

In addition to double-clicking functions in the group tree, you may begin typing portions of your formula directly in the formula text area of the Formula Editor. If you'd like to choose from a list of possible formula functions you can use, press CTRL-SPACE. A list will appear with possible functions you can use.

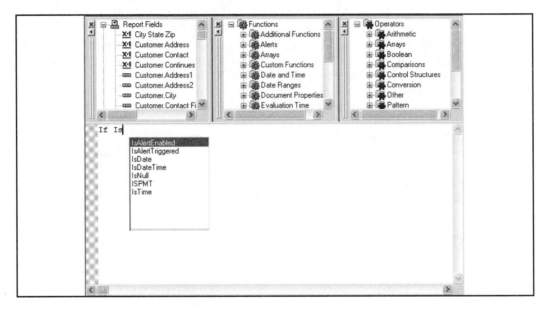

The list of functions you see in the drop-down list will be based on what you've typed so far before pressing CTRL-SPACE—if you've typed enough letters to narrow down the list of available functions to a small group, only the few that fit will appear. If you type CTRL-SPACE with no characters typed beforehand, the whole list of Crystal Reports functions will appear in the drop-down list. And, if you have typed enough characters to narrow the available functions to just one, the drop-down list won't be displayed at all—the complete function name will just be typed in for you.

To choose a function from the drop-down list, use the DOWN ARROW key to choose the desired function and press SPACE or ENTER, or click on the desired function with your mouse. You may also just continue to type, narrowing down the list of available functions as you go. When you get to a single unique choice, the completed function name will be typed for you.

Data Types

As you begin to work with formulas, it's very important to understand the concept of *data types*. Every database field has a certain data type, and every formula you create will result in a single data type. These concepts are important, because if the formula you create doesn't deal with data types properly, you'll get errors when you try to save the formula, or the formula won't give you the result you're looking for. You can't, for example, add the contents of a number field to the contents of a string field with a plus sign—both fields have to be numbers. You can't convert a date field to uppercase characters, because only a string field can be converted to uppercase.

By default, Crystal Reports doesn't display objects in the Design tab by their data types. It shows their names instead. You may prefer to see the data-type representation instead of the field name. To do this, choose File | Options from the pull-down menus and turn off the Show Field Names check box in the Field Options section of the Layout tab. Notice the difference between showing field names and showing data types:

Order ID	Order Amount	Order Date		Courier Website	
-5,555,555	($55,555.56)	3/1/1999 1:23:45PM		XXXXXXXXXXXXXXXXXXXXXXXXX	

You may want to turn off Show Field Names when you first start working with formulas. Seeing the data types can help you determine the types of operators and functions that will work with the database fields you're including in your formulas. Also, whenever you *browse* database fields in the Formula Editor, the data type shows up in the Browse dialog box. In the preceding illustration, the fields have the following data types:

- **Order ID** A *number* data type, which can contain only numbers (along with a period to indicate a decimal point, and a hyphen or minus sign if it's a negative number). You can add, subtract, multiply, divide, and perform other math operations on number data types.

- **Order Amount** A *currency* data type (available only from certain databases). This is similar to a number data type, but it avoids rounding errors that sometimes occur when performing math operations on number data types.

- **Order Date** A combined *date/time* data type (again, supported only by certain databases). This can contain a date, a time, or a combination of both. Other databases have date-only data types, and some have time-only data types.

- **Courier Website** A *memo* data type. The memo data type, like another type called *string*, allows any combination of characters to be placed in the field. However, because letters and punctuation marks can reside in the field, you normally can't perform mathematical calculations with the field.

You may encounter other data types in your databases that aren't shown in this example:

- **Boolean** Represents data that can have only a true or false value.
- **BLOB** Designed to contain photos, graphics, or large amounts of plain ASCII text. Sometimes these appear as "Picture" data types.

CAUTION BLOB (Binary Large Object) fields can be placed on the report only for display. They cannot be used or manipulated inside formulas. While they may show up in the Formula Editor Field Tree box, you'll receive an error message if you attempt to use them inside a formula.

You may also show data types alongside field names in the Field Explorer. Just select the Database Fields category, a table name, or an individual database field and then right-click. Choose the Show Field Type option from the resulting pop-up menu (the option will then show a check mark next to it). The data type will then appear next to each field name in any database table.

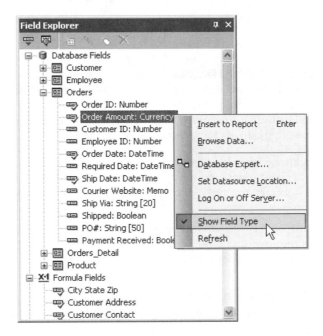

Creating a New Formula

Creating a simple math calculation is easy. Using the Orders Detail table of the sample XTREME sample database included with Crystal Reports, you can calculate the extended price of each order-line item with the following formula.

To create this formula, follow these steps:

1. Create a new report using the XTREME sample database included with Crystal Reports (you can use the XTREME Sample Database ODBC data source if you choose). Choose the Orders Detail table from this database.

2. Select the Formula Fields category, and then click the New button in the Field Explorer toolbar. Or, you may launch the Formula Workshop and create the new formula from there.

3. When asked to name the formula, call it **Extended Price** and click OK.

4. When the Formula Editor appears, double-click the Orders Detail.Unit Price report field in the Field Tree box (you may need to click the plus sign next to the database name to be able to see the Orders Detail table) to add it to the Formula text box. If the field you want to add has already been placed on the report, you will actually find it in the field tree under both the Report Fields section and the database name—there is absolutely no difference if you choose the field from either area.

5. Click the plus sign next to Arithmetic in the Operator Tree box to see all the arithmetic operators that are available. Double-click the multiply operator. (You can save yourself some mouse clicks by typing an asterisk directly in the Formula text box, if you'd like. Although you don't have to put a space before or after the asterisk, the formula is easier to read if you do.)

6. Double-click the Orders Detail.Quantity field in the Field Tree box to place it after the asterisk.

7. If you wish to add a comment explaining the use of the formula (for your own information, or perhaps for others who may be working with your report later), you may precede the comment lines with two slashes, or just type the comment lines, highlight them with your mouse, and click the Comment button in the Formula Editor toolbar.

After you finish the formula, you have several ways to save it and close the Formula Editor and the Formula Workshop. When you first start to use formulas, you'll probably want to check for correct syntax of the formula before you save it. This will ensure that Crystal Reports can at least understand the different parts of the formula and how they are supposed to be calculated or manipulated. Check the formula's syntax by clicking the Check button in the Formula Editor toolbar, or press ALT-C. If Crystal Reports can understand all parts of the formula, a dialog box will appear indicating that no errors were found. (If you've ever written computer programs or used spreadsheet formulas before, though, you know that correct syntax doesn't guarantee that the formula will return the right answer!)

If there is a syntax error in the formula, Crystal Reports will display an error message and highlight the portion of the formula where it stopped understanding it. As you can see here, sometimes these messages may be very descriptive:

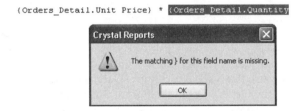

or they can be very cryptic:

even though both of these examples result from simply forgetting curly braces. You'll learn over time what most error messages indicate and how to resolve them.

CAUTION *Even though you may not get any syntax errors when you first check the formula after you create it, you may still get an error when the report runs, depending on the actual data in the database. This may happen, for example, if you create a formula that divides two fields, but the "divided by" field returns a zero during a certain record. You'll then get a Can't Divide by Zero syntax error in the middle of the report process. If there's a chance that this type of error may occur given particular data, you'll probably want to add some type of "If {field} > 0 Then..." logic to ensure that these types of run-time syntax errors won't occur.*

After you determine that there are no syntax errors, it's time to save the formula. You may either save the formula and remain in the Formula Workshop or save the formula and close the Formula Workshop by using the appropriate buttons in the Formula Workshop toolbar. If you try to create a new formula or edit another formula without first saving the current formula, you'll be asked if you want to save the current formula before you proceed to the next formula.

If you choose to skip the syntax check and immediately save the formula, Crystal Reports will check the syntax anyway. If there is an error, you'll be given the opportunity to save the formula with the error. This makes little sense, because Crystal Reports will stop as soon as you try to run the report and display the error message in the Formula Editor. If you try to save and get a syntax error, correct the error and try to save the formula again. If there are no errors, you'll no longer get a syntax error message and the formula will be saved.

Once the formula has been saved and the Formula Workshop has closed, you will see the formula name under the Formula Fields category of the Field Explorer. You can simply drag and drop the formula on the report, just like a database field. In the case of the Extended Price formula, notice that the formula has taken on the currency data type. This occurred because a currency field was multiplied by a number field, resulting in a currency formula.

Run-Time Debugging Features

As mentioned previously in the chapter, it's possible that an error may occur when the report actually runs, but not be detected when you initially create a formula. It's frustrating to create a formula, click Check, and receive a "No Errors Found" message, only to have the formula return with an error when the report runs. This situation is known as a *run-time error*. Run-time errors are often caused by formulas not anticipating the type of data that may be encountered as the report progresses. For example, the formula may perform division on a database field that could possibly return zero for certain records. Or, the formula might extract certain specific characters from a string, only to encounter an error at run time when a record contains a null value for a string, or not enough characters to satisfy the formula's requirements.

In Crystal Reports 8.5 and earlier, you would just receive the error message and the Formula Editor would appear showing the offending formula. However, there would be no indication of what part of the formula was actually causing the error. Now, however, run-time errors can be more easily debugged using the *call stack*. If you encounter a run-time error, you'll first see the error message indicating what the error is (such as "Divide By Zero"), followed by the Formula Workshop showing the offending formula. However, the left-hand tree of the workshop will now show the formulas and functions that led up to the error.

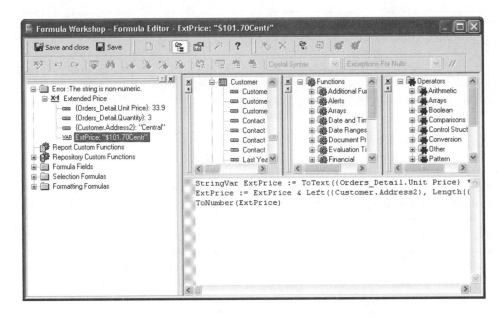

By viewing different entries in the call stack, you can see what the values of variables, fields, and other parts of the formula currently contain. This can be helpful in determining the cause of the error more quickly so that you can supply additional logic to avoid the error in the future.

Editing, Renaming, or Deleting an Existing Formula

After you create a formula, you may wish to change its calculation or add to its function. There are many ways for you to *edit* the existing formula in either the Field Explorer or Formula Workshop. To edit by using the Field Explorer, perform any of these steps:

- Select the formula you wish to change and click the Edit button in the Field Explorer toolbar.
- Right-click the formula and choose Edit from the pop-up menu.

Or, you may display the Formula Workshop by clicking the Formula Workshop toolbar button or choosing Report | Formula Workshop from the pull-down menus. You may then expand the Formula Fields category and click the formula you want to edit.

Any of these options will redisplay the Formula Workshop and Formula Editor with the formula in it.

An even quicker method of editing is available after you've placed the formula on your report. In either the Design or Preview tab, click the formula. Notice in the status bar that the formula name is preceded by the @ sign. Crystal Reports automatically adds this symbol to the beginning of all formulas you create. Now that you've selected the formula, simply right-click and choose Edit Formula from the pop-up menu. The formula will reappear in the Formula Editor, ready for you to modify.

If you wish to *rename* a formula, you may do so either from the Formula Fields category of the Field Explorer or the Formula Workshop. If you are using the Field Explorer, begin by selecting the formula you want to rename. Then, you may either click the Rename button in the Field Explorer toolbar or press the F2 key. You may also right-click the formula and choose Rename from the pop-up menu or even just click on the formula and then hold the mouse button down for a second or two. The name will become "editable"—type the new name and either click outside the formula name or press ENTER. If you've used this formula inside other formulas or elsewhere on your report, Crystal Reports will change the name there, too. To rename a formula in the Formula Workshop, use identical steps to select and rename the formula in the workshop tree.

If you select a formula on the report and press the DEL key, you remove that particular occurrence of the formula from the report. However, the formula remains in the Field Explorer and takes up memory and storage space when you save the report. If you're sure you no longer need the formula, delete it entirely. This must be done from the Formula Fields category of the Field Explorer or the Formula Workshop. Select the formula you want to delete and press the DEL key. You can also choose the Delete button from the appropriate toolbar, or right-click the formula name and choose Delete from the pop-up menu. The formula will be removed from the dialog box.

CAUTION *If you remove a formula that is in use somewhere else on the report, such as in another formula or in a hidden section, you'll be given a warning, as deleting a formula that other formulas depend upon may stop the report from working properly. In some cases, Crystal Reports won't even allow you to delete a formula if it is being referenced in some other formula in the report. While a message will indicate that you cannot undo a formula deletion, you may perform a single undo that returns the formula to the Field Explorer. However, anything prior to this in the "undo stack" will no be longer available.*

Number Formulas

Probably the most common type of formula is a number formula, such as the Extended Price formula discussed earlier. Number formulas can be as simple as multiplying a database field by 1.1 to increase its amount by 10 percent, or as complex as calculations that include sophisticated statistical math. There is no special procedure required to declare a formula as a "number formula"—the formula simply takes on that data type because of the fields and operators that you use in the formula. The Extended Price sample formula (shown here), multiplying a currency field by a number field, will return a resulting currency data type:

```
{Orders Detail.Unit Price} * {Orders Detail.Quantity}
```

Many number formulas will use a mathematical *operator*, such as a plus sign, a hyphen or minus sign, an asterisk for multiplication, or a slash for division. You may also need to use built-in *functions* that Crystal Reports supplies or custom functions that you create yourself or that others create for you. You'll find all these functions listed in the Function Tree box (you may need to add a custom function to your report from the repository first—see Chapter 17 for more information). When you double-click a function, the function name is placed in the Formula text box with the cursor located in between the opening and closing parentheses. You can then either type in the function's arguments, or double-click other fields or formulas in the Field Tree box to add them as arguments to the function.

For example, if you have a group on the report and want to include a group subtotal in a formula, you would use the Sum function. You'll find that three Sum functions actually are available, with one, two, or three arguments. Here are some examples:

```
Sum({Orders.Order Amount})
```

returns a total of all order amounts for the entire report.

```
Sum({Orders.Order Amount},{Customer.Region})
```

returns a total of just the order amounts in the region group where the formula is evaluated. If the formula was evaluated in the Colorado group, the formula returns the order amount subtotal for Colorado only.

```
Sum({Orders.Order Amount},{Orders.Order Date}, "weekly")
```

returns the order amount subtotal for the current order date group, calculating the subtotal based on a week of orders. Note that this third argument corresponds to the time periods that are available when creating a group based on a date field. (Refresh your memory about date-field grouping by looking at Chapter 3.)

So, you could calculate each order amount's percentage of the region subtotal by using the percentage operator and the Sum function as follows:

```
{Orders.Order Amount} % Sum({Orders.Order Amount},{Customer.Region})
```

There are built-in functions to calculate all the summary-type information discussed in Chapter 3, such as average, subtotal, *P*th percentile, and on and on. By opening the Arithmetic category of functions in the Function Tree box, you'll also find functions to calculate remainders, determine absolute value, and round numbers.

TIP   *If you need to calculate a group subtotal as a percentage of a grand total or higher-level group total, there's no need to create a formula. Instead, use percentage summary fields as described in Chapter 3. However, you'll still need to create a formula, as described previously, if you want to determine what percentage of a group subtotal a particular detail field is responsible for.*

The Basic Syntax Formula Variable

When you use Crystal syntax, the formula simply returns the results of the last statement in the formula. If the formula consists of only one statement, such as the multiplication in one of the previous examples, the formula returns the results of the multiplication. If the formula contains several statements separated by semicolons, the last statement determines what's returned to the report.

But if you are using Basic syntax, you must keep in mind one slight difference from any Basic-like programming languages you've used. In a Basic computer language, you typically assign and manipulate variables throughout your code. When you wish to display the value of a variable, you may use a Debug.Print (or similar) statement or set the value of a text box or other form element to the value of the variable. Because Crystal Reports has no Print statement, you need an alternative method of displaying a value on the report. This is accomplished with the *Formula variable*.

The word "Formula" is a reserved word in Basic syntax—you can't use it for any other purpose, such as using it as your own variable name with a Dim statement. By assigning a value to the Formula variable, you determine what the formula returns to the report. You can use the Formula variable over and over within a formula, just like any other variable (as an accumulator, for example). The last occurrence in the formula where a value is assigned to the Formula variable determines what the formula returns to the report. Consider the following Basic syntax formula:

```
' Calculates extended price
Formula = {Orders Detail.Unit Price} * {Orders Detail.Quantity}
If {Customer.Region} = "CO" Then
    ' add 4.25% sales tax to Colorado orders
    Formula = Formula * 1.0425
End If
```

Here, the Formula variable is used like a regular variable (it doesn't even have to be declared with a Dim statement first). It's first used just to calculate the extended price. Then, it's included in an If statement to add sales tax for Colorado orders. If the If statement is true, the existing value of the Formula variable is multiplied by 1.0425 to add 4.25 percent. If the If test fails, the last statement that assigns a value to the Formula variable (the extended price calculation) will be what's returned to the report.

Order of Precedence

You'll sometimes find situations where you're unsure of the order in which Crystal Reports evaluates a formula's operators. For example, if you wish to add sales tax to an extended price, you might use the following formula, which is supposed to add 8 percent sales tax to the extended price of an order (already calculated in the @Extended Price formula):

```
{@Extended Price} + {@Extended Price} * .08
```

The question of how Crystal Reports calculates this is crucial. Does it perform the addition operation first and then the multiplication operation, or does it perform the multiplication operation first and then the addition operation? The results will vary dramatically, depending on the calculation order. Consider an Extended Price of $100 with addition performed first:

```
100 + 100 = 200
200 * .08 = 16.00
```

or with multiplication performed first:

```
100 * .08 = 8.00
100 + 8.00 = 108.00
```

While your customer might be very pleasantly surprised by the first calculation showing up on their invoice, the second calculation is certainly the correct one. But looking at the formula, you'll notice that the multiplication operator is the second operator. Will it be evaluated second?

The answer is no, because of the *order of precedence.* Although it may sound like a computer concept, order of precedence is actually a concept that you should recall from your ninth-grade math class. In this formula, multiplication and division are evaluated first from left to right across the formula; then, addition and subtraction are evaluated from left to right across the formula.

The order of precedence for both Crystal syntax and Basic syntax is as follows:

- Exponentiation (^)
- Negation (–)
- Multiplication, division, left to right (*, /)
- For Crystal syntax only, percent (%) is evaluated at the same time as multiplication and division
- Integer division (\)
- Modulus (Mod)
- Addition and subtraction, left to right (+, –)

Given this syntax, the formula to add tax to the Extended Price shown earlier will work just fine. But what if, for some reason, you want the addition performed first, not the multiplication? Again, thinking back to ninth-grade math, you surround the part of the formula you want evaluated first with *parentheses*. The following formula will perform the addition before the multiplication:

```
({@Extended Price} + {@Extended Price}) * .08
```

NOTE *If you use one formula inside another formula, as in this example, Crystal Reports calculates the embedded formula first (using the order of precedence) and then calculates the outer formula.*

String Formulas

Many times, the database will contain string or text data that is insufficient for your reporting needs. For example, you may want to sort a report by ZIP code, but the database contains ZIP codes only as part of a combined City_State_Zip field. Or, you may want to write a report to print checks, spelling out the dollar amount in words, using a number or currency field in the database. All of these are applications for a formula that either manipulates or creates string data.

Strings can be *concatenated,* or "tacked together," using the plus sign or the & sign (ampersand). Although the plus operator is the same one used to add numbers, the results will be very different depending on the data type. For example, the formula

```
25 + 7 + 100
```

returns a numeric result of 132. Because all the elements of the formula are numbers, the plus sign will add the numbers together and return a numeric answer.

Contrast that with this formula:

```
"25" + "7" + "100"
```

or

```
"25" & "7" & "100"
```

which returns a string result of 257100. When you enclose the numbers in quotation marks, Crystal Reports interprets the values in the formula as strings, not numbers. When you use a plus sign or ampersand with strings, the result is the concatenation of the individual string elements.

This is very useful for many situations you'll encounter when reporting against databases. The following illustration shows the beginning of a form letter that simply uses database fields on the report.

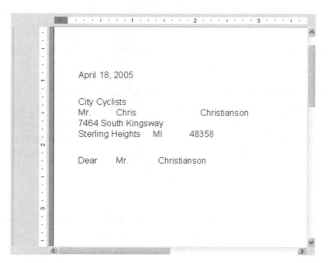

Notice the spacing problems for the contact name, city-state-ZIP line, and salutation. While you may be able to improve the appearance of this report slightly by resizing and moving the individual database fields, you'll never achieve a perfect result. By placing the database fields on the report in fixed locations, the report will never be able to accommodate varying widths of first names, last names, cities, and so on.

The next illustration shows the same report using formulas to concatenate the database fields together.

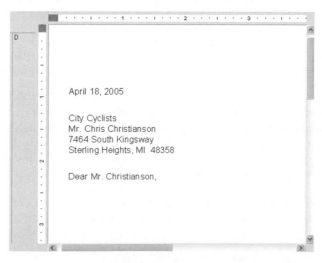

The results are obvious: No matter how wide or narrow names or cities are, they are placed right next to the other items (with a space in between).

While you can conceivably combine these database fields in text objects to accomplish the same result (refer to Chapter 2 for information about combining data in text objects), formulas give you a lot more flexibility as to how your report looks. For example, you can display only the first initial of a contact name on the report using a formula. You can't do that with a text object.

Concatenating string fields is as simple as using the ampersand (&) operator, as in the following:

```
{Customer.Contact Title} & " " & {Customer.Contact First Name} &
" " & {Customer.Contact Last Name}
```

Notice that a space is hard-coded into the formula using a *string literal,* which is simply a fixed string surrounded by quotation marks. You'll use string literals often in concatenation formulas and If-Then-Else formulas (discussed later in this chapter). So, the literal space in this formula will separate the title from the first name, and the first name from the last name.

You could create a salutation line using several string literals, as follows:

```
"Dear " & {Customer.Contact Title} & " " &
{Customer.Contact Last Name} & ","
```

Notice that the word "Dear" and a space precede the title, a space separates the title from the last name, and a comma follows the last name.

NOTE *The ampersand concatenation operator is available in both Crystal and Basic syntaxes. An concatenation operator held over from earlier Crystal Reports versions, the plus sign (+), is also available in Crystal syntax.*

There are many situations in which you may want to use only certain parts of strings in a formula, not the whole string. For example, you may want to use only a first initial as part of the contact name on a form letter. By following a string field with a number or range of numbers enclosed in square brackets (Crystal syntax) or parentheses (Basic syntax), you can extract certain characters from the string field. This function is known as the *subscript* function. For example, look at this formula in Crystal syntax:

```
{Customer.Contact Title} & " " & {Customer.Contact First Name}[1] &
". " & {Customer.Contact Last Name}
```

Notice that only the first character from the first name will be included in the formula, and a period has been added to the space literal between the first and last names.

Many older database systems contain date information in string fields because earlier versions of mainframe systems or older database systems did not include a date data type. To allow dates to sort correctly, the year needs to precede the month and day in these fields as well. Thus, it is very common to find January 10, 1999, coded into a string database field as 19990110.

If you want to display the date in an mm/dd/yyyy format to make the date more readable, you could use string subscript operators to pick out the individual parts of the date, add some string literals, and rearrange the date's appearance. Assuming that the hire date in a "legacy" database is an eight-character string field in the form yyyymmdd, this formula will redisplay it as mm/dd/yyyy:

```
{EMP.HIRE_DATE}[5 to 6] & "/" & {EMP.HIRE_DATE}[7 to 8] &
"/" & {EMP.HIRE_DATE}[1 to 4]
```

Notice that the subscript operator can also return a *range* of characters, not just one.

In addition to the subscript operator, there are many built-in string functions that you can use in your formulas. There are functions to return characters from the left of a string, the middle of a string, and the right of a string. Using these, the preceding date formula could be rewritten in Crystal syntax as follows:

```
Mid({EMP.HIRE_DATE},5,2) & "/" & Right({EMP.HIRE_DATE},2) &
"/" & Left({EMP.HIRE_DATE,4})
```

In this case, the Mid function takes three arguments: the field or string to use, the position in the string from which to start reading, and the number of characters to return (there's also a two-argument version of Mid). The Right and Left functions take two arguments: the field or string to use and the number of characters to return.

TIP *You can find complete explanations of all built-in Crystal Reports formula functions, including samples of usage, in the appendix.*

Dealing with Null Database Values

Crystal Reports may return odd results with formulas that encounter a database field containing a *null value* (a special database value equating to empty, as opposed to zero for a number field, or an empty string for a string/text field). Several factors determine whether or not the database will contain null values. In many cases, this is determined by the way the database is initially designed. If you prefer to avoid null values appearing on the report, Crystal Reports allows you to convert them en masse to a "default" format (typically a zero for number fields, and an empty string for string fields). To do this for all new reports in the future, check Convert Database NULL Values To Default on the Reporting tab of the File | Options pull-down menu. You'll also find the Convert Other NULL Values To Default option to deal with other non-database values (such as other formulas) that may return null values. To set these options for just the current report, check the same options after choosing File | Report Options from the pull-down menus.

String formulas are particularly susceptible to problems resulting from null values. If any field in the string formula that you're using returns a null, the entire formula will return null (this type of formula is sometimes referred to as a formula that returns an *exception*).

There are several ways of dealing with nulls and the resulting oddities in formulas. One way is to use an If-Then-Else formula, along with the IsNull built-in function (described later in the chapter), to deal with potential null situations. Or, you may check the Convert Database NULL Values To Default options described earlier in this box.

Crystal Reports XI adds yet one additional way of dealing with nulls in formulas (string or otherwise). A new drop-down option choice appears in the Formula Editor toolbar presenting two choices for dealing with nulls: Exceptions For Nulls and Default Value For Nulls. The first point to keep in mind is that *neither* of these options will be relevant if your formula doesn't encounter any nulls. Thus, if you've chosen to Convert Database NULL Values To Default as described previously, no formulas in your report will ever encounter a Null and neither of these options will have any effect.

If, however, you may encounter null values in a formula, this new option allows you to make a choice, on a formula-by-formula basis, on how to deal with them. If you choose Exceptions For Nulls, nulls will be treated as an *exception* if they are encountered in a formula. For example, a string concatenation formula that encounters a null anywhere within it will return a null (or *exception*) to the report—no data will actually appear. By choosing Default Value For Nulls, you in essence choose the Convert Database NULL Values To Default for *this one formula only.* In this case, a string concatenation formula that would otherwise return a null "exception" value will, instead, return the results of the string concatenation with an empty string appearing for the field that would have otherwise evaluated to a null.

If you wish to set a default choice for this setting for all new formulas you create in the future, you may make this choice by choosing File | Options from the pull-down menus. Then, make your desired default choice on the Formula Editor tab.

The ToText Function

A crucial built-in function that you will probably use very often in string formulas is ToText, which is used to convert other data types to a string data type so that you can use them in concatenation or comparison formulas. You can use ToText to convert numbers, dates, times—virtually any other data type—to strings. You need this functionality to avoid the type of problem shown here:

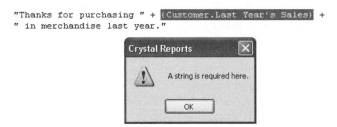

This problem occurs because you can't concatenate a number field onto a string literal (or any other combination of mismatched data types). To convert a number or currency field to a string, such that you can concatenate it to another string, use ToText. The following will solve this problem:

```
"Thanks for purchasing " + ToText({Customer.Last Year's Sales}) +
" in merchandise last year."
```

That formula will return

```
Thanks for purchasing $32,421.27 in merchandise last year.
```

If you look in the Function Tree box under Strings, you'll see several permutations of ToText, with anywhere from one to five arguments. You may also notice the CStr function containing the same set of arguments. CStr and ToText are equivalent—you may use either function.

TIP *If you use the ampersand operator (&) to concatenate strings, you reduce your need to use ToText, as this operator performs an automatic conversion if you are mixing data types in your formula. However, if you want to control formatting of the converted values in your formula, you'll still need to use ToText to provide customized formatting.*

While the best place to look for all the ToText details is Crystal Reports online Help or the appendix, here are a few additional ToText examples:

- Determine the number of decimal places.

```
"Thanks for purchasing " & ToText({Customer.Last Year's Sales},0) &
" in merchandise last year."
```

  will return

```
Thanks for purchasing $32,421 in merchandise last year.
```

  A second number argument to ToText determines how many decimal places Crystal Reports uses when it converts the number or currency field to a text string.

- Determine the thousands separator.

```
"Thanks for purchasing " & ToText({Customer.Last Year's Sales},0,"")
&
" in merchandise last year."
```

  will return

```
Thanks for purchasing $32421 in merchandise last year.
```

  A third string argument to ToText determines what thousands separator Crystal Reports uses when it converts a number or currency field to a text string. In this example, the two quotation marks side-by-side indicate an empty string, so ToText doesn't use a thousands separator.

- Format date fields.

```
"Your order was placed on " +
ToText({Orders.Order Date},"dddd, MMMM d, yyyy.")
```

  will return

```
Your order was placed on Monday, January 12, 2004.
```

  This version of ToText uses a *format string* as the second argument. The format string (sometimes referred to as a *mask*) uses special characters—pound signs; zeros; decimal points; the letters *d, m, y*; and so forth—as placeholders to indicate how data should be formatted when converted to a string. In this example, the *dddd* characters specify the day of the week to be spelled out fully. *MMMM* specifies a fully spelled month, *d* specifies the day of the month without a leading zero, and *yyyy* specifies a four-digit year. Any characters included in the format string that can't be translated into placeholders (such as the commas and periods) are simply added to the string as literals.

TIP *It's important to remember that the case of the placeholder characters is significant. When formatting time fields, for example, lowercase* h *characters indicate hours with a 12-hour clock, whereas uppercase* H *characters indicate hours with a 24-hour military clock. Apart from that, if you use placeholder characters of the wrong case, Crystal Reports will just include the characters in the resulting string as literals.*

Another built-in function, ToWords, comes in handy when writing checks with Crystal Reports. Consider the following formula:

```
ToWords({PAYROLL.NET_CHECK_AMT})
```

When placed on the report, this formula returns the following for an employee record with net pay of $1,231.15:

```
one thousand two hundred thirty-one and 15/100
```

Picking Apart Strings

In more complex reports, you may wish to pick out only certain parts of strings (the first initial of a name was mentioned previously as an example). Crystal Reports contains many interesting formula functions to handle even more complex "substring" requirements.

For example, you may wish to make use of the ToWords function discussed previously, but not to print checks. If you are printing legal contracts, real estate documents, or bank notes, for example, you may need to print both the numeric and text forms of the same number, as in

```
This contact expires in thirty (30) days.
```

For the sake of this example, assume that the data indicating the number of "expire days" is contained in a numeric database field. Accordingly, you may try creating a formula to print the previous example. The formula might initially look like this:

```
"This contract expires in " & ToWords({Contracts.Expires}) & " (" &
ToText({Contracts.Expires},0) & ") days."
```

In this example, the ToWords function is used to convert the numeric field to "spelled out" text, and ToText is used to convert the number to a numeric string, with no decimal places.

However, the result of this formula will be

```
This contract expires in thirty and xx / 100 (30) days.
```

Because ToWords is designed for printing checks, it returns not only the "whole number" part of the numeric field, but the hundredths part as well. For the contract example shown previously, this won't work. How, then, can you create a formula to return just the whole number portion?

If you look closely at ToWords, you'll notice that the whole number portion is always separated from the hundredths portion with the word "and." If you can search through the result of ToWords for the "and" characters, and return just the portion *before* these characters, you will have a successful formula.

Look at this example:

```
"This contract expires in " &
Left(ToWords({Contracts.Expires}),
    InStr(ToWords({Contracts.Expires}), " and "))
& "(" & ToText({Contracts.Expires},0) & ") days."
```

There are several functions and techniques used in this formula that require further explanation:

- **The Left function**   The Left function returns a certain number of characters from the left side of another string (and as you might imagine, there is also an available Right function to return characters from the right side of a string). In this formula, the desire is to return the left portion of the words returned by ToWords up until the characters "and" are encountered. So, if ToWords returns "thirty and xx / 100", you wish to extract the first six characters from the left (up until the "and" is encountered). But, how do you determine where the characters "and" are?

- **The InStr function**   There are several different versions of InStr in the formula language. The version shown in the previous example takes two arguments: the string you want to search, and the "substring" you want to search for within the first string. By supplying the ToWords function as the first argument, and the characters "and" as the second argument, you are asking InStr to find the *numeric position* in "thirty and xx / 100" where the word "and" is. Here the word "and" begins at position 8, which is the numeric result from the InStr function.

So, by using the InStr function within the Left function, you can extract the proper number of characters to get just the whole number portion of the spelled-out number. The only adjustment you must consider is that InStr returns a value of 8, but you want only the first 6 characters (or 7, if you don't mind having a trailing space). This is why you see the "– 1" subtraction of the value returned by InStr. This will return the leftmost 7 characters, including the trailing space, resulting in the characters "thirty" appearing as the spelled-out text.

There are many other built-in string functions that can perform similar functions. Look in the functions tree under Strings, or in the appendix, for information on other versions of ToText, InStr, Mid, and many others.

Date/Time Formulas

There are many reporting situations in which you need to manipulate date, time, or date/time data types. Most modern PC and SQL databases support some or all of these data types. Although date and time fields don't appear on the report as pure numbers (they often include other characters and words, depending on how they're formatted), they are actually stored by the database and Crystal Reports as numbers. Therefore, it's possible to do mathematical calculations on date fields. There are also built-in date and time functions that return just parts of date and time fields and that convert other data types to date or time fields.

Number of Days Between Dates

When Crystal Reports performs math on date-only fields, the result of the calculation is in whole days. Crystal Reports returns fractional days if fields in the formula are date/time fields. For example, if you subtract a date-only field containing the value May 1, 2005, from a date-only field containing the value May 5, 2005, the result will be the whole number 4. If the fields are date/time fields and the May 1 field contains a time of 12 noon and the May 5 field contains a time of midnight, the result will be the fractional number 3.5.

So, determining how long it took to ship an order is as simple as creating the following formula:

```
{Orders.Ship Date} - {Orders.Order Date}
```

Even though both the database fields in this formula are dates (or date/time if these fields are coming from the sample XTREME database included with Crystal Reports), the result of the formula will be a number—the number of days between the two dates. This formula will return the number of calendar days between the two dates—it uses all days in the calendar. When you perform this type of date arithmetic, you may find fractional days returned, if the date/time fields contain actual time values. This can cause differences between two dates to be "3.5" or "5.75." This can sometimes be difficult if you really want to know just the number of days between two dates, not including time. In these cases, you can use the *Date* built-in function to convert the Date/Time data types to just dates. It may be preferable, for instance, to use the following formula to determine the number of days between two dates:

```
Date({Orders.Ship Date}) - Date({Orders.Order Date})
```

Or, you may also consider using the Round or Truncate function to adjust the numeric result. *Round* (not a Date-related formula function, but helpful in this example) will round a number to a specified number of decimal places—rounding up or down, depending on the fractional value. *Truncate* will simply "throw away" the fractional portion of the result, not rounding in the process. Accordingly, this would also work to avoid fractional dates resulting from time values in the date/time fields:

```
Truncate({Orders.Ship Date} - {Orders.Order Date}, 0)
```

If you wish to exclude weekends from this calculation, it gets a little trickier. Crystal Reports provides the Visual Basic–like function DateDiff in both syntaxes to do more flexible date math. An example of using DateDiff to exclude weekends from this type of calculation can be found in Crystal Reports online Help. Search for "DateDiff function."

You can calculate a date in the future. If, for example, you want to create an accounts receivable report that shows the actual due date of an invoice, the date itself could be calculated by using the invoice date (a date field) and terms (a number field), as follows:

```
{AR.INV_DATE} + {AR.TERMS}
```

Although you don't explicitly define this formula as a date formula, it returns a date data type showing the date on which the invoice is due, provided the terms field contains the number of days required for payment (30, 45, and so forth).

Another function in both Crystal Reports formula syntaxes can be a lifesaver with future and past date calculations. The DateAdd function operates much like its Visual Basic counterpart. For example, to determine a date exactly one month prior to today's date, you would use this formula:

```
DateAdd("m", -1, CurrentDate)
```

The "m" argument indicates an interval of a month. The second argument indicates the number of "time intervals" to add (in this case, a negative one, thereby subtracting a month). The third argument is the date or date/time value to add to (Crystal Reports' *CurrentDate* function returns the date from your PC's system clock). What's particularly powerful about DateAdd is the automatic adjustment for various numbers of days in months and years. For example, if you evaluated this formula on March 31, 2000, it would return February 29, 2000 (there is no February 31, but 2000 was a leap year, therefore resulting in February 29).

TIP *Crystal Reports includes a set of date-related custom functions in the default repository that comes with BusinessObjects Enterprise and Crystal Reports Server. Some of these custom functions will automatically exclude weekends from date calculations. There's even a custom function you can modify with your own company holidays to exclude these from date calculations, as well as weekends. See Chapter 17 for more information on adding these custom functions to your reports.*

Number of Hours and Minutes Between Times

You can also perform mathematical functions directly on time fields. When you calculate two time fields together, the result is in seconds. For example, the following formula will return the elapsed time, in seconds, between a starting time field and ending time field in a college database's course table:

```
{COURSE.EndTime} - {COURSE.StartTime}
```

If the fields containing the time are actually date/time data types, you won't want to return days between the dates, but seconds between the times. In this situation, you'll need to use the built-in *Time* function to return just the time portion of a field. For example,

```
Time({COURSE.EndTime}) - Time({COURSE.StartTime})
```

You may not want the time returned as seconds, but perhaps as hours and minutes, minutes and seconds, or any combination separated with colons. To accomplish this, you have a bit more work to do, but not as much as you might think. Examine the following:

```
Time(0,0,0) + ({COURSE.EndTime} - {COURSE.StartTime})
```

You'll notice that parentheses force the time calculation to be performed first, resulting in the number of seconds between the two times. The Time built-in function (used in a different format in this example) is also being used to return a time data type using three arguments: hour, minute, and second. The particular time being returned by the Time function is midnight. By adding the seconds between the two times to midnight, you essentially have the number of hours, minutes, and seconds that have elapsed since midnight.

When you place this on your report, you'll see hours, minutes, and seconds, followed by AM or PM (AM if the time difference is less than 12 hours, PM if more, assuming that you're using Crystal Reports' default *hh:mm:ss AM/PM* date format). Now it's simply a matter of using the Format Editor to suppress the AM/PM indicator by choosing 24-hour time display. You can also suppress any combination of hours, minutes, and seconds to show the elapsed time the way you wish.

TIP *The DateDiff function is not limited to just calculating differences between dates. You can also do time calculations similar to the previous example with DateDiff.*

Month, Day, Year, Hour, Minute, and Seconds Functions

There are many built-in functions to help you use date and time fields. You can use the Month, Day, and Year functions with a date or date/time field as an argument to return just the month, day, or year of the date as a number. Conversely, with the Hour, Minute, and Seconds functions, you can supply a time or date/time field as a single argument and have just the hour, minute, or second of the field returned as a number.

DateValue Function

Two very important functions are DateValue and CDate, both of which are functionally equivalent. While there are several variations on DateValue, probably the most intriguing is the variation that accepts one string argument. This string can contain several variations of date-like strings, such as 10/1/99, March 17, 2000, 21 Feb 2003, and so on. Crystal Reports will evaluate the string to determine where the month, day, and year portions reside, returning a "real" date value as the result.

NOTE *If you supply a two-digit year to DateValue, Crystal Reports applies a "sliding scale" approach to determining the century. If the two-digit year is between 0 and 29, Crystal Reports assumes the century is 2000. Otherwise, the two-digit year will be converted to the 1900s.*

This greatly simplifies date conversion in Crystal Reports. For example, if your legacy database contains dates in string fields formatted as "mm/dd/yyyy," simply use the following:

```
DateValue({EMP.HIRE_DATE})
```

There may be times when DateValue can't properly evaluate a date string, due to misspellings or other nonconforming string contents in a database field. This is a prime

candidate for a run-time formula error. When you check the formula in the Formula Editor with the Check button, you'll get the popular No Errors Found message. However, when the report runs and the formula encounters the nonconforming string value, you'll get an error.

To avoid these run-time errors, use an If-Then-Else statement (described later in the chapter) in conjunction with another function,

IsDate, to perform the conversion to a Date value only if the string can be interpreted by Crystal Reports as a date.

TIP *A number of related Time and DateTime conversion and detection functions are also available in Crystal Reports. Look in the functions tree, online help, or the appendix for DateTimeValue, TimeValue, IsDateTime, and IsTime.*

If-Then-Else Formulas

One of the complaints that's sometimes heard in the competitive community of database report writers is, "Crystal Reports is too complex—it's made for programmers." While this complaint may or may not ring true, there is no doubt that elements of common programming languages can be found in the Crystal Reports formula languages. The first of these programming-oriented features is If-Then-Else logic. The If-Then-Else combination is the cornerstone of much computer programming code, so once you learn If-Then-Else concepts, you'll be on your way to performing really sophisticated report customization.

If-Then-Else formulas perform a test on a database field, another formula, or some combination of them. Your test can be as simple or as complex as you need it to be—perhaps just checking to see if a sales figure exceeds the $1,000 bonus threshold. Or, you may want to check the number of days a product took to ship, in conjunction with the carrier who shipped the product and the sales level of the customer, to determine if a shipment met your company's shipping goals. If the test passes (returns *true*), the formula will return a certain result. If the test fails (returns *false*), a different result will be returned.

If-Then-Else formulas are created with the following syntax:

```
If <test> Then <result if true> Else <result if false>
```

The test portion of an If-Then-Else formula must use comparison operators found in the Operator Tree box (or a Boolean formula, discussed later in the chapter). You'll find a Comparisons section of the box that, when opened, shows operators that test for equal, less than, greater than, and other combinations of conditions. These can be used in conjunction with And, Or, and Not Boolean operators to combine multiple conditional tests together. Here's a simple If-Then-Else formula that will return a string based on an order amount:

```
If {Orders.Order Amount} > 5000 Then "Bonus Order"
Else "Regular Order"
```

The Order Amount database field is tested to see if its value is greater than 5,000. If the test is true, the formula returns the "Bonus Order" string. Otherwise, the formula returns the "Regular Order" string.

Boolean operators can also be used to combine multiple comparisons together. You can use And, Or, and Not Boolean operators. The preceding formula has been slightly enhanced in the following formula, using a Boolean operator to combine two comparisons:

```
If {Orders.Order Amount} > 5000 And Month({Orders.Order Date}) = 12 Then
    "Holiday Bonus Order"
Else
    "Regular Order"
```

Here, the order amount has to exceed 5,000 *and* the order must have been placed in December for the formula to return Holiday Bonus Order. Orders over 5,000 in other months will still be regular orders. If you change the And to an Or in the preceding formula, then *all* orders in December will be bonus orders, regardless of amount. Orders over 5,000 will also be considered bonus orders the rest of the year.

Data Types in If-Then-Else Formulas

While creating If-Then-Else formulas, you must pay special attention to the data types that you're using in the formula. In the If test of the formula, make sure you use similar data types in each individual comparison operation. For example, if you want to test whether Customer.Country is USA, the test will be

```
If {Customer.Country} = "USA"
```

Since Customer.Country is a string field, you need to compare it with a string literal, enclosed in quotation marks or apostrophes (just quotation marks in Basic syntax). If the field you are testing is numeric, you need to use a number constant, as in the Orders.Order Amount sample shown previously. If you mismatch data types, such as these:

```
If {Orders.Order Amount} > "5000"
```

you'll receive an error.

If you use multiple comparisons separated by Boolean operators, each comparison can have a different data type. For example, if you want to combine the two tests mentioned previously, your formula would start out as follows:

```
If {Customer.Country} = "USA" And {Orders.Order Amount} > 5000
```

In this case, the different data types in the If part of the formula are fine, as long as each "side" of each comparison is of the same data type.

For example, you may have an existing formula on your report, @Ship Days, that calculates the number of days it took to ship an order. But since @Ship Days is a numeric formula, it will display a zero on your report if the order was placed and shipped on the same day. Therefore, you would write the following If-Then-Else formula to show the words "Same Day" on the report if @Ship Days is zero, or to show just the contents of the @Ship Days formula if it is not zero:

```
If {@Ship Days} = 0 Then
    "Same Day"
Else
    {@Ship Days}
```

But if you use the Check button in the Formula Editor to check the syntax of this formula, you'll receive an error:

The problem is that Crystal Reports doesn't know what data type to assign to the formula. If the test returns true, the formula will return a string for the words "Same Day". However, if the test returns false, the formula will return @Ship Days, which is a number. Crystal Reports must assign a data type to a formula when it's first created—it can't wait until the report is running. Therefore, even though the If part of a formula can contain various data type tests, the Then and Else parts must contain the same data types.

Remember the function that converts other data types to strings? The following will solve this problem:

```
If {@Ship Days} = 0 Then
    "Same Day"
Else
    ToText({@Ship Days},0)
```

This result is better, because it doesn't show zero as the number of ship days. But we want to take it a step further to make the report more readable. Look at the enhanced version of this formula:

```
If {@Ship Days} = 0 Then
    "Shipped Same Day"
Else
    "Shipped in " + ToText({@Ship Days},0) + " days"
```

This looks better on the report, particularly if the report isn't a straight columnar report. You might want to put this in a group header for an order, before the individual line items for the order show up in the details section. But there's just one more problem. What will this formula return if it took only one day to ship the order?

```
Shipped in 1 days
```

While this probably won't mean your dismissal from the report development team, why not go one easy step further to make the report look even better? Try the following:

```
If {@Ship Days} = 0 Then
    "Shipped Same Day"
Else
    If {@Ship Days} = 1 Then
        "Shipped in 1 day"
    Else
        "Shipped in " + ToText({@Ship Days},0) + " days"
```

This is an example of a *compound* or *nested* If-Then-Else statement. Notice that you're not limited to one If, Then, or Else clause in a formula. You can make another If statement the result of the first Then, or the result of the first Else, and on and on. There is no specific limit to how many levels you can nest these, but obviously the formula becomes hard to follow after only one or two levels. Also, don't forget that the Else clause isn't required, so when you nest these, you won't have to always have a matching Else clause for every If.

Multiple Actions with One If-Then-Else Statement

You'll notice in all the preceding examples that only one action occurred as the result of the Then and Else parts of the statement. While this is okay for many types of formulas, sometimes you may want several things to happen, particularly when you need to set the contents of several variables as the results of a single Then or Else clause (variables are discussed later in this chapter). In this situation, you can simply repeat the If-Then-Else test several times, with a different result for each Then and Else clause. Just be sure to separate each If-Then-Else statement from the next with a semicolon. For example, to set the contents of several variables in one formula, you might use the following:

```
NumberVar GroupBonus;
NumberVar GroupFollowUpCount;
NumberVar ReportBonus;
NumberVar ReportFollowUpcount;
StringVar GoodCustomer;

If {Orders.Order Amount} > 5000 Then
    GroupBonus := GroupBonus + 1
Else
    GroupFollowUpCount := GroupFollowUpCount + 1 ;

If {Orders.Order Amount} > 5000 Then
    ReportBonus := ReportBonus + 1
Else
    ReportFollowUpCount := ReportFollowUpCount + 1 ;

If {Orders.Order Amount} > 5000 Then
    GoodCustomer := {Customer.Customer Name}
```

All of these If statements will be evaluated and the resulting variables will be set. The formula will display the result of the last action in the If statement on the report. In this example, if the Order Amount is over $5,000, all the bonus variables will be incremented by one and the GoodCustomer variable will be assigned the customer name. But because the GoodCustomer variable assignment is the last action that executes, the customer name is what the formula actually displays on the report. If the Order Amount is less than $5,000, then the two FollowUpCount variables will be incremented by one. But because the last statement still tries to set the GoodCustomer variable and fails (and there's no Else clause), the GoodCustomer variable won't be assigned a value and the formula will return an empty string.

If you look at the previous example, you see quite a bit of duplicate typing (the If test is repeated three times). This duplication can be eliminated by creating just one If-Then-Else statement, but supplying several actions to the Then and Else clauses, separating the action statements with a semicolon and surrounding them all with parentheses. Here's the same formula created using this shortened approach:

```
NumberVar GroupBonus;
NumberVar GroupFollowUpCount;
NumberVar ReportBonus;
NumberVar ReportFollowUpcount;
StringVar GoodCustomer;
```

```
If {Orders.Order Amount} > 5000 Then
    (GroupBonus := GroupBonus + 1 ;
    ReportBonus := ReportBonus +1 ;
    GoodCustomer := {Customer.Customer Name})
Else
    (GroupFollowUpCount := GroupFollowUpCount + 1 ;
    ReportFollowUpCount := ReportFollowUpCount + 1;
    GoodCustomer := "")
```

CAUTION *In the preceding example, you'll need to make sure to include the statement to assign the GoodCustomer variable an empty string in the Else clause. Otherwise, you'll receive the "A String Is Required Here" error. This is because the Then and Else clauses must still return the same data type. Without the GoodCustomer assignment in the Else clause, the Then clause will return a string value (a string variable is being assigned) and the Else clause will return a numeric value (a numeric variable is being assigned).*

Enhanced Crystal Reports If-Then-Else Options

If the If-Then-Else logic described so far isn't enough to propel you toward (or perhaps away from) a programming career, Crystal Reports includes a bevy of other If-Then-Else possibilities to help you reconsider!

First, the If-Then-Else statements in Basic syntax differ from those Crystal syntax versions described previously. Basic syntax follows the more typical If-Then-Else-EndIf approach familiar to Basic language programmers. In particular, this makes performing multiple actions as the result of a single If-Then-Else statement more straightforward by introducing the End If clause:

```
If <test> Then
    <statement>
    <statement>
    <more statements...>
Else
    <statement>
    <statement>
    <more statements...>
End If
```

Also, you can use the Basic syntax ElseIf clause (don't forget it's one word—no space) to allow nesting of multiple If conditions in one statement:

```
If <first test> Then
    <statements...>
ElseIf <second test> Then
    <second test statements...>
Else
    <statements if first test fails...>
End If
```

Yet another permutation of If-Then-Else logic exists in both Crystal and Basic syntaxes. If you've used Microsoft Office products, such as Microsoft Access, you may be familiar with the IIF *Immediate If* function. This shortened version of protracted If-Then-Else logic is actually a single function, similar to ToText or UpperCase (it appears in the function tree under Programming Shortcuts) that accepts three arguments. The function syntax is as follows:

```
IIF(<boolean expression>, <result if true>, <result if false>)
```

This function can simplify If-Then-Else logic for small, simple formulas, or when you want to perform a "mini" If-Then-Else statement as part of a larger formula. For example, consider the following string formula using traditional If-Then-Else logic:

```
If {Customer.Country} = "USA" Then
    {Customer.Customer Name} & " requires domestic shipping charges"
Else
    {Customer.Customer Name} & " requires international shipping charges"
```

By using the Immediate If function, this can be simplified to the following:

```
{Customer.Customer Name} & " requires " &
IIF({Customer.Country} = "USA", "domestic", "international") &
" shipping charges"
```

Helpful Built-in Functions for If-Then-Else Formulas

If you look in the Function Tree box of the Formula Editor, you'll notice a Print State category. Opening this category shows a variety of built-in functions that you can use in If-Then-Else (and other) formulas to enhance your reporting flexibility. For example, the special fields found in the Field Explorer, such as Page Number, Total Page Count, Print Date and Time, Record Number, and Group Number, are available. There are other special functions that you can use to test for a null database value in the current, next, or last record; to check whether the current database record is the first or last; or to check whether the formula appears in a repeated group header. By using these special built-in functions, you can create formulas that make your reports more intuitive and easier to read.

Here are some examples:

- IsNull function

```
If IsNull({Customer.Region}) Then
    ""
Else
    ", " + {Customer.Region}
```

The IsNull function is critical if you want to actually test for null values in database fields that you include in your formulas. By using the If-Then-Else test with the IsNull function, you can check whether the region field contains a null value. If so, the formula will return an empty string (denoted by the two sets of quotation marks). Otherwise, the formula will return a comma, a space, and then the region name. This formula can then be concatenated with city and ZIP database fields in another formula to form a city-state-ZIP line. If the region in the database is null, the other formula won't become null.

TIP *A more complete discussion of null values and how to deal with them can be found earlier in this chapter under "Dealing with Null Database Values."*

- Next function

```
If {Customer.Customer Name} = Next({Customer.Customer Name}) Then
    {Customer.Customer Name} + " continues on next page..."
```

The Next function reads a field in the next record of the database. This formula compares the field in the next record to the same field in the current record. If the values are the same, you know that the same customer will appear in the first record on the next page, and you can note this with a text message. This formula would typically be placed in the page footer.

TIP *Notice that there is no Else clause in this formula. Crystal Reports doesn't require an Else clause in an If-Then-Else formula in Crystal syntax. If you leave the Else off and the test returns false, the formula will produce an empty string.*

- InRepeatedGroupHeader function

```
If InRepeatedGroupHeader Then
    GroupName ({Customer.Customer Name}) + "   - continued -"
Else
    GroupName ({Customer.Customer Name})
```

If you place this formula in the group header of a group with the Repeat Group Header On Each New Page option turned on (this can be set when you create or change a group— see Chapter 3), "- continued -" appears only when the group header is repeated. This also uses the GroupName function to return the group name field for a particular group. An InRepeatedGroupHeader test also comes in handy if you are resetting variables in formulas you are placing in the group header (assuming that you'll always be encountering a new group when the group header prints). Because you don't want to reset your variables in a *repeated* group header, you can condition your variable assignment statement on the value of InRepeatedGroupHeader. You might use something similar to the following:

```
If Not InRepeatedGroupHeader Then GroupBonus := 0
```

Other Crystal Reports Logic Constructs

Many advanced users (particularly those with programming backgrounds) will often find some of the procedural capabilities of high-level computer languages useful when designing reports. If you fall into this category (perhaps you are a Basic programmer), not only will the typical procedural constructs in Basic syntax open up enhanced flexibility for you, but similar logic constructs in Crystal syntax will also make your reporting life easier. Even if you're not a programmer, you'll probably soon find that these features come in handy in the more advanced reporting situations you'll encounter.

The term *logic construct* refers to the features of the Crystal Reports formula language that enable you to go beyond basic If-Then-Else logic. For example, it can be tedious to write long repetitive If-Then-Else formulas to perform tasks such as testing for more than a small number of conditions, picking apart strings, or cycling through multiple-value parameter fields or other arrays. Crystal Reports logic functions such as Select Case, For loops, and Do loops make these tasks much easier. These functions enable Crystal Reports formulas to move closer and closer to a full procedural language, such as Visual Basic.

Select Case Statement

Select Case is very similar to its Visual Basic counterpart. It provides a much simpler and cleaner approach to testing for multiple conditions and returning appropriate results—those complex If-Then-Else statements can now be replaced with more readable and easy-to-maintain logic.

Look at the following compound If-Then-Else statement:

```
If {@Ship Days} = 0 Then
    "Shipped Same Day"
Else
    If {@Ship Days} = 1 Then
        "Shipped in 1 day"
    Else
        "Shipped in " & ToText({@Ship Days},0) & " days"
```

This is a relatively simple formula that checks whether the @Ship Days formula returns a 0 or a 1, returning a different string value in each case. If neither of these conditions is true, a catchall Else clause displays another string value. While this particular example isn't particularly complicated, it could quickly become much more difficult to interpret and maintain if more than two conditions have to be tested for.

Select Case is much better suited to this type of logic. Consider the following:

```
Select {@Ship Days}
    Case 0:
        "Shipped Same Day"
    Case 1:
        "Shipped in 1 day"
    Default:
        "Shipped in " & ToText({@Ship Days},0) & " days"
```

You may choose Select Case from the Control Structures category of the Formula Editor Operator Tree or simply by typing the correct syntax. Begin with the word "Select" followed by a database field, formula, or other expression. Then, supply multiple Case clauses, each testing the value of the Select expression (make sure the value you supply to each Case clause is the same data type as the Select expression). If you want to have the formula return the same result for several different values of the Select expression, you may separate the values after the Case clause with commas. You may also supply one value, the To operator, and a second value to supply a range of values. After the Case clause, supply a colon (don't use a semicolon—this isn't the end of the statement) and then supply the expression you want the formula to return if the Select value equals the Case clause. Remember that all expressions that result from a Case clause must be the same data type—you can't have one Case clause return a string and another Case clause return a number. After the Case clauses have been defined, you may supply an optional Default clause, followed by a colon, and the expression you want the formula to return if none of the Case clauses match the Select value.

For Loop

Basic programmers have always enjoyed the capability to loop through fragments of program code over and over to perform repetitive logic. This also becomes helpful in certain reporting situations (if, for example, you need to cycle through a multiple-value parameter field or iterate through a number array).

Crystal Reports includes the ubiquitous For loop in both syntaxes (except there's no Next clause in the Crystal syntax version). The For loop uses a counter variable to keep track of how many times a specified piece of logic has been cycled through. The For clause sets both the beginning and ending values of the counter variable. The optional Step clause tells the For statement how to increment the counter variable (the default is 1 if the Step clause is left out). The For statement is closed off by the word Do, followed by one or more statements enclosed in parentheses (use a semicolon to separate more than one statement within the parentheses). The statements inside the parentheses will be executed once for every increment of the counter variable.

The following formula displays all the entries a user has chosen in the multiple-value Region parameter field:

```
NumberVar Counter;
StringVar Message := "Regions Chosen: ";

// cycle through all members of the multivalue
// ?Region parameter field
For Counter := 1 to Count({?Region}) Step 1 Do
(
    // build the Message variable, along with comma/space
    Message := Message & {?Region}[Counter] + ", "
);

// strip off last comma/space added by the loop
Left(Message, Length(Message) - 2)
```

First, this formula declares two variables: Counter to increment the For loop, and Message to accumulate the parameter field values (look at the next section of the chapter for information on using variables). The For loop then cycles Counter from 1 to the number of elements in the parameter field (returned by the Count function). For each loop, Counter is used to retrieve the next element of the parameter field and accumulate it, along with a comma and a space, in Message. The final statement of the formula, which is not associated with the loop, strips off the last comma and space that were added inside the last occurrence of the loop.

NOTE *Although Crystal Reports now allows string formulas and variables to return up to 64K of characters (only 254 characters could be returned by strings prior to version 9), good formula logic dictates adding a test in this formula that uses the Exit For statement to exit the For loop if the Message variable may ever approach approximately 64,000 characters in length. If the loop tries to accumulate more than 64K characters in the variable, a run-time error will occur.*

Using the Join and Split Functions to Avoid Loops

While the previous code is a great For loop example, there's actually another built-in formula function that negates the need for the variable declarations, the looping logic, and the removal of the trailing comma/space when creating a single string containing multivalue parameter field entries. Look at the following code:

```
"Regions chosen: " + Join({?Region}, ", ")
```

This formula uses the *Join* function, similar to its Visual Basic counterpart, which takes all the *elements* of the array supplied in the first argument (a multivalue parameter field actually is an array), concatenates them together, and optionally separates each with the string supplied in the second argument. Join performs the same thing as all the looping logic and variable manipulation demonstrated earlier, with one simple function.

Conversely, you may wish to take a string value or variable that contains multiple strings separated by a common delimiter (such as a slash) and create an array of string values. You could create a loop that cycles through the string one character at a time, looking for the delimiter (the slash), and performing complex logic to extract the substring and add it to an array. But the *Split* function, like its equivalent in Visual Basic, will perform all this logic for you automatically. Look at the following code fragment (this is not a complete formula):

```
StringVar array Regions;
Regions :=
Split("Northwest/Southwest/Northeast/Southeast/Midwest", "/")
```

The second line of code will populate the Regions array variable with five elements by looking through the string and separating the five substrings that are separated by slashes.

But, don't forget your looping capabilities just yet—the Join and Split function work only with string values. If you have a multivalue parameter field that is designated as a number, date, or other non-string type, you'll still need to use loops to extract the individual elements. And if you want to build a non-string array, you may need to use loops as well, as Split works only with strings.

While Do Loop

A looping construct similar to the For loop described previously can be used to repeat statements while a certain condition is met. Whereas the For loop uses a counter variable to determine how many times the loop executes, the While Do loop evaluates a condition before each occurrence of the loop and stops if the condition is no longer true. This construct is similar to Do and While loops used in Visual Basic and other procedural languages.

The following listing is a formula that sets a variable to a phone number database field and then uses a While Do loop to look for hyphens in the variable. As long as a hyphen exists in the variable, the Do loop will execute a statement to "pick out" the hyphen, leaving behind only the pure numbers from the phone number. When there are no more hyphens in the variable, the While condition will fail and the statement after the closing parenthesis of the While Do loop (the variable name, which will display the number without the hyphens) will execute.

```
StringVar NewPhone := {Customer.Phone};

While Instr(NewPhone,"-") > 0 Do
(
    NewPhone := Left(NewPhone, Instr(NewPhone,"-") - 1) &
    Right(NewPhone, Length(NewPhone) - Instr(NewPhone, "-"));
);

NewPhone
```

Although this is a good example of how a While Do loop can cycle while a condition is true, it's a fairly complex process for the relatively simple "search and replace" function that it performs. For a more streamlined formula, you can use the Crystal Reports Replace function, as in the following example:

```
Replace({Customer.Phone}, "-", "")
```

In this case, the Replace function makes use of three arguments: the first being the string field or value that you want to modify, the second being the character or characters you want to search for, and the third being the character or characters you want to replace the search characters with.

NOTE *The previous logic construct examples are presented in Crystal syntax. Basic syntax logic constructs are very similar, if not identical, to their Visual Basic counterparts. Just remember that you must use at least one instance of the Formula intrinsic variable in Basic syntax to return a result to the report.*

Boolean Formulas

The one remaining type of formula that you may need to create is the *Boolean formula,* which can return just two values, true and false. You can think of a Boolean formula as just the "test" part of an If-Then-Else formula. When the formula is evaluated, it ultimately returns only one of the two states.

Here's a simple Boolean formula:

```
{@Ship Days} > 3
```

In this formula, the existing @Ship Days formula (a number formula) is tested to be greater than 3 (indicating a shipping exception). It simply *is* or *is not* greater than 3. If it is greater than 3, the formula returns a true value—if it's not, the formula returns a false value.

When you then place this formula on your report, it will appear with a Boolean data type. If you have Show Field Names turned off in File | Options (discussed earlier in the chapter), then you'll see the formula show up with the word "True" in the Design tab.

If you format the field, you'll notice a Boolean tab in the Format Editor that lets you choose how you want the true/false values to appear on the report.

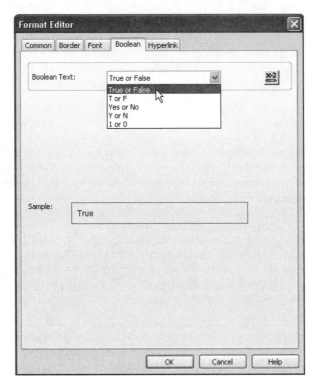

Although you may occasionally find Boolean formulas helpful when they're actually placed on the report, you'll probably use them much more often as a cornerstone for other formulas. For example, the Boolean formula shown previously indicates that Xtreme Mountain Bikes considers orders that took longer than three days to ship as exceptions. But, Xtreme really wants to break down the shipping exception rule according to Last Year's Sales. If the customer purchased more than $50,000 in merchandise last year, the three-day shipping exception will apply. However, if a customer purchased less, a six-day shipping exception applies.

This requires a *compound* Boolean formula, such as

```
({@Ship Days} > 3 And {Customer.Last Year's Sales} > 50000)
Or {@Ship Days} > 6
```

which uses a combination of And and Or operators, along with the comparison operators, to create a more complex Boolean formula. What's important to remember, though, is that the ultimate result will still be either true or false. You can make a Boolean formula as complex as you want, using combinations of comparison operators along with And, Or, and Not operators, but in the end, only true or false will result.

TIP *Notice the parentheses around the first part of this compound Boolean formula. They ensure that both @Ship Days is less than 3 and Last Year's Sales is greater than $50,000 before "Or'ing" the @Ship Days greater than 6 test. Although this may make the formula more understandable, it is optional. Crystal Reports considers all Boolean operators (And, Or, and Not) equally in the order of precedence (discussed previously in this chapter). That is, it evaluates them equally as it travels through the formula from left to right.*

There are several benefits to creating Boolean formulas in this fashion:

- After you create a complex Boolean formula, you can include it in other formulas as the test part of an If-Then-Else formula, as in the following:

```
If {@Shipping Exception} Then
    "*** Shipping Exception ***"
Else
    "Shipped Within Goal"
```

This makes the second formula much easier to read and understand.

- By using the Boolean formula throughout the report, you eliminate the need to retype the complex Boolean test repeatedly, thus reducing the chance of errors. Even more important, you have only one formula to change if the report requirements change down the road. For example, if you use the @Shipping Exception formula as the cornerstone for 50 other formulas in your report, and you later decide to reduce the Last Year's Sales qualification from $50,000 to $35,000, you have only *one* formula to change on your report, not 50. All the rest will follow the change.

- You can use the Boolean formula in advanced record selection (covered in Chapter 4) and conditional formatting (covered in Chapter 7) to limit the report to certain records or to have certain objects on the report appear with different formatting.

TIP *Every Crystal Reports built-in formula function and operator is illustrated in the appendix. Also, you can find extended online help for these when displaying the Formula Editor. Just select the function or operator you want more information on in the appropriate Function or Operator Tree and press F1.*

Variables in Formulas and Evaluation Times

As a general rule, formulas maintain the results of their calculation only for the duration of one database record. If you put a formula in the details section, it will evaluate every time a new record is processed and put its result in the details section. If you put a formula in a group footer, it will be evaluated when each group footer prints. In every case, the formula will not "remember" anything from the previous record or previous group footer. Once the next record or footer comes along, the formula evaluates completely "from scratch."

Sometimes, though, you may need a formula to remember material from record to record or from group to group. You may want to accumulate some value as the report progresses so that you can print a total in a group footer or report footer. For example, you may want to check the value of a subtotal in a group footer. If it exceeds a certain threshold, you may want to increment a counter so that you can show how many groups exceeded the threshold at the end of the report.

To accomplish this, you need to somehow store information from record to record or from group to group. This can be accomplished by using *variables*. A variable is simply a "placeholder" that Crystal Reports sets aside in the computer's memory. As the report progresses from record to record or from group to group, your formula can refer back to the variable or change its contents. You can then use the variable in other formulas or display its accumulated contents in a group or report footer.

Declaring a Variable

The first step in any formula that uses a variable is to *declare* the variable. This sets aside a specific amount of memory for the variable, based on its data type. You'll find variable declarations listed in the Operator Tree box of the Formula Editor under Variable Declarations.

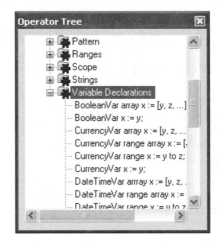

Notice that a different variable declaration statement exists for each Crystal Reports data type. You must consider in advance what kind of data your variable is going to hold, and declare the correct type of variable accordingly. If, for example, you want to keep track of a customer name from record to record, and the customer name field in the database is a string data type, you need to declare a string variable to hold the information.

NOTE *Crystal syntax and Basic syntax use different statements to maintain variables. Just like in Microsoft Visual Basic, Crystal's Basic syntax requires use of the Dim statement to declare a variable before use. And as when working in Visual Basic, you can either assign a data type to a variable when you Dim it, or simply assign a value to it after you have used Dim without a data type (and the variable will automatically take on the data type of the value you assign it). Because of this similarity to Visual Basic, Basic syntax variables won't be discussed here, because they are well documented in Visual Basic texts. The rest of the discussion on variables applies to Crystal syntax.*

You must also give each variable a name. You can give it any descriptive name you wish, provided it doesn't start with a number, contain spaces, or conflict with another Crystal Reports formula language *reserved word*. You can't, for example, use variable names such as Date, ToText, or UpperCase—these are reserved by the formula language for its own built-in functions (you'll know if your variable names are reserved words by looking at their color in the Formula Editor—Crystal Reports turns all reserved words blue).

To declare a variable, type the appropriate variable declaration keyword followed by the variable name, such as this example:

```
NumberVar BonusAmount;
```

This declares a number variable called BonusAmount that can later be assigned a numeric value. The semicolon at the end of the statement separates this statement from the next one in the formula (presumably a statement to assign or test the contents of the variable).

If you wish to use more than one variable in the formula, you may declare them together, again separated by semicolons. For example,

```
NumberVar BonusAmount;
StringVar BonusCustName;
DateVar DateBonusReached;
```

TIP You may be used to assigning variables in other programming languages. Remember that Crystal Reports probably treats variables differently. You must declare a variable in each formula where you want to refer to the variable. However, even if you declare a variable and assign it a value in one formula, and then declare it again in a formula that appears later in the report, it will retain the value from the first formula. Unlike in many other languages, declaring a variable more than once in Crystal Reports does not reset its value to zero or empty (with the exception of local variables, as described in the following section). These considerations apply to both syntaxes, Crystal and Basic. Even if you're used to using the Dim statement only once in Visual Basic, you must use it with Basic syntax in every formula where you want to refer to a variable. If the variable has been declared with a Dim statement in another formula, declaring it again will not reset its value.

Variable Scope

The whole idea and benefit of variables is that they retain their values as the report progresses from record to record or from group to group. So, for variables to be of real benefit, they need to keep their values throughout the report process. And because you may have several formulas that you want to refer to the same variable, you need to be able to refer to a variable in one formula that was already declared and assigned a value in another.

Exactly how long and where a variable keeps its value is determined by the variable's *scope*. If a variable has a narrow scope, it will retain its value only in the formula where it is initially declared—any other formula that refers to a variable with the same name will be referring to a brand-new variable. If a variable has a wide scope, its value will be retained for use not only in other formulas, but also in subreports within the main report. (Subreports are covered in Chapter 12.) The following are three additional words you can place in front of your variable declarations (or use in place of the Dim statement in Basic syntax) to determine the variable's scope.

Local	The variable remains in scope only for the formula in which it is defined. If you declare a variable with the same name in another formula, it won't use the value from the first formula.
Global	The variable remains in scope for the duration of the entire main report. You can declare a global variable in one formula, and another formula will be able to use the contents placed in the variable by the first formula. Global variable values, however, are not retained in subreports.
Shared	The variable not only remains in scope for the duration of the entire main report but can also be referred to in formulas in subreports. You can use shared variables to pass data around the main report, back and forth between the main report and subreports, and from subreport to subreport.

Add these keywords in front of variable declarations to determine their scope, as follows:

```
Local NumberVar BonusAmount; //will only be visible in this formula
Global StringVar BonusCustName; //available to the whole main report
Shared DateVar DateBonusReached; //available to main and subreports
```

TIP *If you leave off the variable scope keyword in Crystal syntax, the default scope for a variable will be global—it will be available to other formulas in the main report, but not to subreports. If you use the Dim statement in Basic syntax, the default scope for the variable will be local—it will be available for use only in the rest of the formula where it's declared. If you don't want to use the default scope, make sure you always add the proper scope keyword. And, make sure you add the keyword to the declaration in every formula that will be using the variable.*

Assigning a Value to a Variable

After you declare a variable, it won't do you much good if you don't assign a value to it. You may want to use it as an accumulator (to "add one" to it each time some condition is met for the database record). You may want to assign a string value to it, concatenating additional string values onto the variable as records progress. You then might display the value of the accumulated variable in the group footer, and assign the variable an empty string in the group header to start the whole process over again for the next group.

TIP *If you declare a variable but don't assign a value to it, it takes on a default value based on its data type. Numeric and Currency variables default to 0, string variables default to an empty string, Boolean variables default to false, and Date variables default to a "0/0/00" date. Date/ Time and Time variables have no default value.*

Crystal syntax provides two instances in which you can assign a variable a value: at the same time the variable is declared, or on a separate line later in the formula. In either event, you must use the assignment operator, consisting of a colon followed by an equal sign, to assign a value to a variable. This is important—it's easy to get confused and just use the equal sign by itself. The equal sign works only for comparison—you must place a colon in front of the equal sign to make assignment work properly unless you are using Basic syntax, in which case the equal sign by itself is used for both assignment and comparison. Here's a Crystal syntax example of assigning a variable a value on a separate line:

```
NumberVar CustomerCount;
CustomerCount := CustomerCount + 1
```

Here, the CustomerCount variable is declared on the first line (terminated with a semicolon) and assigned a value on the second line. In this particular formula, the CustomerCount variable will keep its value from record to record (remember that Crystal syntax variables take on Global scope by default), so it will be incremented by one every time the formula executes.

   If you want to reset the value of the CustomerCount variable in a group header, you need to reset it to 0. Here's a Crystal syntax example of how to declare and assign a variable at the same time:

```
NumberVar CustomerCount := 0
```

Here, the variable is declared, followed by the assignment operator and the value to assign the variable. In this example, placing this formula in the group header will reset the CustomerCount variable at the beginning of each group.

TIP *Keep in mind that a semicolon doesn't have to appear at the end of the last line of a formula, because it is used to separate one statement from another. If your formula only declares and assigns a variable, you don't need the semicolon at the end of the declaration/assignment statement.*

You don't have to assign a value to a variable every time the formula executes, nor do you need to assign the same value every time. Creative use of logic constructs, such as If-Then-Else or Select Case, along with variable assignment, provides report flexibility that rivals that of many programming languages. Look at the following formula, which declares and conditionally assigns several variables:

```
CurrencyVar BonusAmount;
StringVar HighestCustName;
DateTimeVar DateBonusReached;

If {Orders.Order Amount} > BonusAmount Then
    (HighestCustName := {Customer.Customer Name};
    DateBonusReached := {Orders.Order Date};
    BonusAmount := {Orders.Order Amount})
```

Look at this formula closely. Assuming it's placed in the details section, it keeps track of the highest order amount as the records progress. When an order exceeds the previous high amount, the customer who placed the order and the date the order was placed are added to variables. Then, the new high order amount is assigned to the bonus amount. The following are some important points to note about the formula:

- There are multiple variable assignments separated by semicolons inside the parentheses. They will all execute, but only the last statement will determine how the formula appears on the report. In this example, the last statement uses a currency data type, so the formula will appear on the report as currency.

- If you are keeping track of the bonus amounts, dates, and customer names for a certain group, such as a region or country, make sure to reset the variables in the group header. If you fail to reset the variables, and the next group doesn't have an order as high as the top value in the previous group, the previous group's values will appear for the following group as well.

- If you want to keep track of quotas or similar values for both group and report levels (for example, you want to see the bonus customer for each region and for the entire report), you'll need to assign and maintain two sets of variables: one for the group level that is reset in the group header, and one for the report level that's not reset.

Displaying a Variable's Contents

In the preceding example, you saw how to accumulate values in variables in the details section, and how to reset them by assigning them a value of 0 in the group header (or in another area of the report). You also need to have a way to show exactly what's contained in a variable on the report, or to use the variable's value in a formula some other way.

To show the contents of a variable, you simply need to declare it. If the formula contains no other statements, declaring the variable will also return it as the formula value. For example, you might place the following formula in the group footer to show the customer who reached the bonus in the region group:

```
StringVar HighestCustName
```

You neither need to place any other statements in the formula to show the value of the variable nor even need the semicolon at the end of the declaration line—it's the last line in the formula.

You may have situations in which you want to show the contents of a variable but are using other statements to assign the variable in the formula. In that case, just declaring the variable won't display it, because the declaration statement won't be the last line in the formula. In this situation, just add the name of the variable as the last line of the formula. This will then display the contents of the variable when the formula executes. Here's an example:

```
CurrencyVar BonusAmount;
StringVar HighestCustName;
DateTimeVar DateBonusReached;

If {Orders.Order Amount} > BonusAmount Then
    (HighestCustName := {Customer.Customer Name};
     DateBonusReached := {Orders.Order Date};
     BonusAmount := {Orders.Order Amount});

HighestCustName
```

This formula performs the test and variable assignments as before, but the last line of the formula simply shows the HighestCustName variable, a string variable. So, this formula shows up with small *x*'s in the Design tab (if Show Field Names is turned off in File | Options), and the contents of the HighestCustName variable will be shown whenever the formula executes.

You can go even one step further by testing and assigning variables and then using them later in other calculations or concatenations. Here's another permutation of this formula:

```
CurrencyVar BonusAmount;
StringVar HighestCustName;
DateTimeVar DateBonusReached;

If {Orders.Order Amount} > BonusAmount Then
    (HighestCustName := {Customer.Customer Name};
     DateBonusReached := {Orders.Order Date};
     BonusAmount := {Orders.Order Amount});

"As of this order, the amount to beat is " & ToText(BonusAmount) &
" set by " & HighestCustName & " on " &
ToText(DateBonusReached, "M/d/yy")
```

This formula not only declares variables, it also conditionally assigns them and then concatenates and displays them, converting them to text as necessary.

Evaluation Times and Report Passes

As you may have gathered by this time, formulas that contain variables are often affected by where they are placed physically on the report. If you want to check values and assign variables during record-by-record processing, you must put the formula in the details section. If you want to show the accumulated totals for each group, you place a formula in the group footer to show the total variables. To reset the variables for the next group, you need to place the formula that resets them in the group header.

However, just placing the formulas in these sections doesn't necessarily guarantee that they will actually evaluate in that section or during the logical "formatting" process of the report (during which a group header prints, then the detail sections for that group print, then the group footer prints, and so on). Consider the following example. Figure 5-4 contains a report that calculates a "running total" using a variable. The variable accumulates the order amounts in each details section as the report progresses.

As you can see, the report is a simple detail report—there are no groups. The running total is accumulating the orders as the report progresses. The formula contains the following variable assignment:

```
CurrencyVar MonthlyTotal := MonthlyTotal + {Orders.Order Amount}
```

In Figure 5-5, the report is grouped by Order Date, using "for each month" grouping. In this situation, the desire is to reset the running total for each month, as the viewer evaluates each month on its own. Accordingly, the running total variable "MonthlyTotal" must be reset in each group header with the following formula:

```
CurrencyVar MonthlyTotal := 0
```

However, even when this formula is placed in the group header of the report, the desired result is not achieved.

Notice that not only did the running total not get reset to zero from the group header, but that it's showing a *lower* value than it was in the previous group. Why does adding a

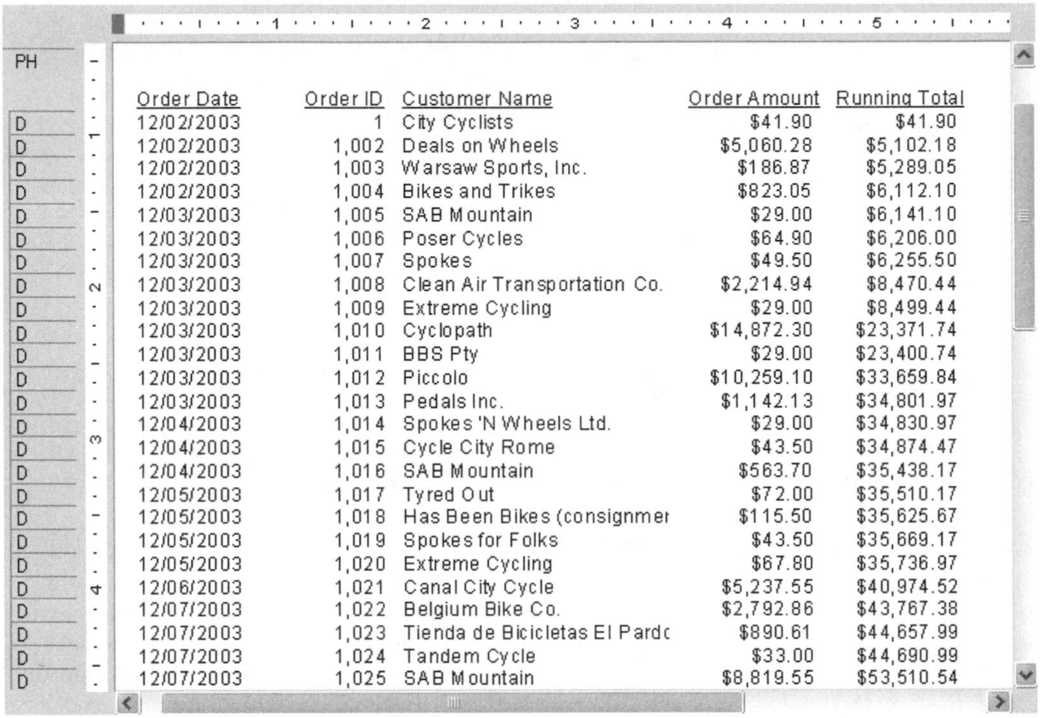

Order Date	Order ID	Customer Name	Order Amount	Running Total
12/02/2003	1	City Cyclists	$41.90	$41.90
12/02/2003	1,002	Deals on Wheels	$5,060.28	$5,102.18
12/02/2003	1,003	Warsaw Sports, Inc.	$186.87	$5,289.05
12/02/2003	1,004	Bikes and Trikes	$823.05	$6,112.10
12/03/2003	1,005	SAB Mountain	$29.00	$6,141.10
12/03/2003	1,006	Poser Cycles	$64.90	$6,206.00
12/03/2003	1,007	Spokes	$49.50	$6,255.50
12/03/2003	1,008	Clean Air Transportation Co.	$2,214.94	$8,470.44
12/03/2003	1,009	Extreme Cycling	$29.00	$8,499.44
12/03/2003	1,010	Cyclopath	$14,872.30	$23,371.74
12/03/2003	1,011	BBS Pty	$29.00	$23,400.74
12/03/2003	1,012	Piccolo	$10,259.10	$33,659.84
12/03/2003	1,013	Pedals Inc.	$1,142.13	$34,801.97
12/04/2003	1,014	Spokes 'N Wheels Ltd.	$29.00	$34,830.97
12/04/2003	1,015	Cycle City Rome	$43.50	$34,874.47
12/04/2003	1,016	SAB Mountain	$563.70	$35,438.17
12/05/2003	1,017	Tyred Out	$72.00	$35,510.17
12/05/2003	1,018	Has Been Bikes (consignmer	$115.50	$35,625.67
12/05/2003	1,019	Spokes for Folks	$43.50	$35,669.17
12/05/2003	1,020	Extreme Cycling	$67.80	$35,736.97
12/06/2003	1,021	Canal City Cycle	$5,237.55	$40,974.52
12/07/2003	1,022	Belgium Bike Co.	$2,792.86	$43,767.38
12/07/2003	1,023	Tienda de Bicicletas El Pardc	$890.61	$44,657.99
12/07/2003	1,024	Tandem Cycle	$33.00	$44,690.99
12/07/2003	1,025	SAB Mountain	$8,819.55	$53,510.54

Figure 5-4   Running total using a variable

group result in the oddities with the running total? This happens because the formula is accumulating the running total at a different time from when it's actually displaying it on the report, and because the formula to reset the running total is evaluating at yet another time during report processing.

The formula to accumulate the running total is calculating while records are being read from the database, not when records have been grouped and are actually being printed or formatted. Also, the formula that resets the running total is actually being processed only once, at the very beginning of report processing, not when each group header prints. These formulas are said to be calculating in different *report passes* than the pass that actually formats the report. So, the running total has already been calculated for every record before Crystal Reports sorts the records to be placed in groups. Besides, the running total is actually being reset to zero only once before anything else happens on the report.

Crystal Reports generally breaks down its report processing into the following three passes, during which certain types of formulas automatically evaluate.

Before Reading Records	Occurs before any records are read from the database. If formulas don't include any references to database fields or summary functions, they calculate in this pass. These formulas are sometimes referred to as flat or constant formulas.

While Reading Records	Occurs as records are being read from the database, but before any record selection, sorting, or grouping is performed. Formulas that include references to database fields, but don't contain any subtotal or summary functions, are calculated in this pass. These formulas are often called first-pass or recurring formulas.
While Printing Records	Occurs after records have been read and are being formatted for display or printing. Sorting and grouping occurs during this pass. Formulas that include sum, average, or other summary functions are included in this pass. These formulas are often called second-pass or print-time formulas.

In most cases, you can trust Crystal Reports to accurately determine in which pass it needs to evaluate a formula. The glaring exception, however, is when a formula uses variables. If a formula simply declares a variable, or declares the variable and assigns it a literal or constant value, Crystal Reports evaluates that formula in the Before Reading Records pass, because it makes no reference to database fields or summary functions. If you assign a variable a database value, Crystal Reports evaluates that formula in the While Reading Records pass (the formula will become a first-pass formula). Only if you have some type of summary or subtotal function in the formula will Crystal Reports automatically evaluate

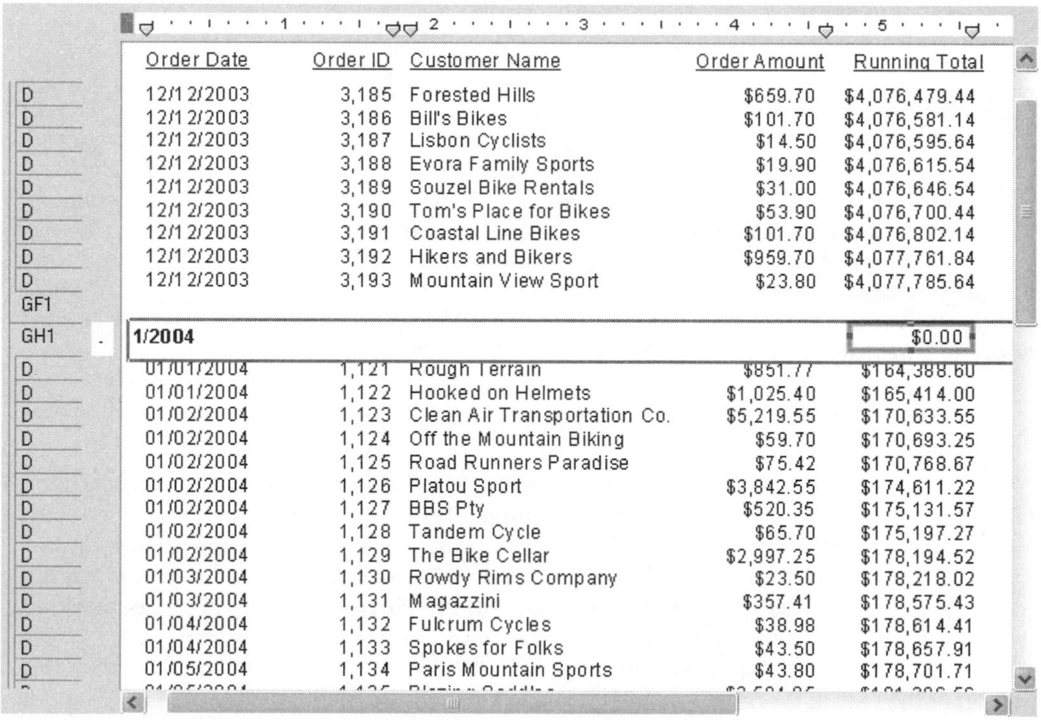

FIGURE 5-5 Formula in group header to reset running total doesn't work

the formula in the While Printing Records pass (the formula then becomes a second-pass formula).

This default behavior can cause very strange results, as the previous running total example illustrates. The formula to accumulate the running total makes reference to the Order Amount database field and therefore evaluates in the first pass (WhileReadingRecords). This accumulated the running total just fine before the report was grouped. However, when the report was grouped by the Order Date, records appeared on the report in a different order than they were read from the database, resulting in the running totals no longer appearing in a logical order. And to complicate matters even further, the formula that reset the running total variable made no references to database fields at all, so it became a flat formula (BeforeReadingRecords) and processed only once at the very beginning of report processing, instead of at the beginning of every group.

When you use variables in a formula, you may need to force the formula to evaluate in a different pass than it would by default. You do this by changing the formula's *evaluation time*. To do this, add an evaluation-time statement as the first statement in the formula. Look in the Formula Editor Function Tree box and you'll notice an Evaluation Time section. Open that section to see several evaluation-time statements that should now be mostly self-explanatory.

To force the formula that accumulates the running total to the second pass, where it will calculate the running total correctly after the records have been grouped, add the WhilePrintingRecords evaluation-time statement to the formula, as follows:

```
WhilePrintingRecords;
CurrencyVar MonthlyTotal := MonthlyTotal + {Orders.Order Amount}
```

CAUTION *Don't get confused if you can't insert a subtotal, summary, or grand total on a second-pass formula. When you click this type of formula in the details section, no subtotal, summary, or grand total options will be available on the pull-down or pop-up menus, because subtotals, summaries, and grand totals are calculated in the WhilePrintingRecords pass. If the formula is already evaluating in that pass, you can't create a summary or grand total on it.*

Now, to ensure that the formula that resets the running total actually happens when the groups are being formatted, instead of one time only at the beginning of the report, force it to the WhilePrintingRecords pass as well.

```
WhilePrintingRecords;
CurrencyVar MonthlyTotal := 0
```

The one evaluation-time function that may not be self-explanatory is EvaluateAfter, which takes one argument: the name of another formula. This forces one formula to evaluate after another formula when they evaluate in the same pass and are in the same section of the report. Because Crystal Reports automatically evaluates formulas that contain other formulas in the proper order, you'll use this function very rarely. However, it may be necessary to use it with formulas that contain variables.

When Crystal Reports evaluates two formulas that contain the same variable in the same section of the report, the order in which it will evaluate them is not predictable. One example is if you place two formulas in a group footer. The first formula shows the values of the variables (assuming that those values have been set in other formulas in the details section):

```
WhilePrintingRecords;

CurrencyVar BonusAmount;
StringVar HighestCustName;
DateTimeVar DateBonusReached;
"The highest order of " + ToText(BonusAmount) +
" was placed by " + HighestCustName + " on " +
ToText(DateBonusReached,"M/d/yy")
```

The second resets the variables to zero or an empty string to prepare for the next group:

```
WhilePrintingRecords;

CurrencyVar BonusAmount := 0;
StringVar HighestCustName := "";
DateTimeVar DateBonusReached := DateTime(0,0,0);
```

Because there's a chance that the formula that resets the variables will evaluate before the formula that shows them, you have two choices. The first (and probably most logical) is simply to move the formula that resets the variables to the group header. That way, the variables will be reset when a new group begins, after they have been displayed in the previous group footer. Or if there is some logical reason why both formulas must exist in the group footer, you can use EvaluateAfter in the formula that resets the variables, as follows:

```
EvaluateAfter ({@Bonus Show});

CurrencyVar BonusAmount := 0;
StringVar HighestCustName := "";
DateTimeVar DateBonusReached := DateTime(0,0,0);
```

By placing EvaluateAfter as the first statement in the formula, you force the reset formula to evaluate after the display formula. Because you are forcing this formula to evaluate after a formula that's in the second pass, there's no need to include WhilePrintingRecords in this formula (although the formula will work fine if you do).

TIP As you begin to add formulas that calculate and reset variables, you may find quite a few instances of things appearing in details and group header sections that show zeros or other unnecessary information. You can't delete the formulas from these sections, because then they won't evaluate properly. To hide them, just suppress their display by using the Suppress button on the Formatting Toolbar or the Suppress check box on the Common tab of the Format Editor. You'll then see them on the Design tab, but not on the Preview tab or any other report output.

When Not to Use Variables

It's fairly common to learn how to use certain "spiffy" features of a tool, and then to use them to excess! Variables have that potential. Although they are fast and, if used judiciously, don't consume significant extra memory or resources, they can sometimes be "overkill." If you find a use for variables, first look closely at your report to see whether an easier, quicker way exists to accomplish the same task.

Figure 5-6 is an example of a report that counts orders that exceed a $1,000 bonus level. The number of orders needs to be shown both at the group level and at the end of the report.

Using variables to accomplish this requires the creation of several formulas. Two variables are also required: one to accumulate the bonus order count for each group, and one to count for the whole report. Following are the formulas.

@Bonus Calc is placed in the details section and suppressed:

```
WhilePrintingRecords;
NumberVar CountCustomer;
NumberVar CountReport;
If {Orders.Order Amount} > 1000 Then
    (CountCustomer := CountCustomer + 1;
     CountReport := CountReport + 1)
```

@Show Group Bonus is placed in the group footer:

```
WhilePrintingRecords;
NumberVar CountCustomer;
"This customer had " + ToText(CountCustomer,0) + " bonus orders."
```

@Reset Group Bonus is placed in the group header and suppressed:

```
WhilePrintingRecords;
NumberVar CountCustomer := 0;
```

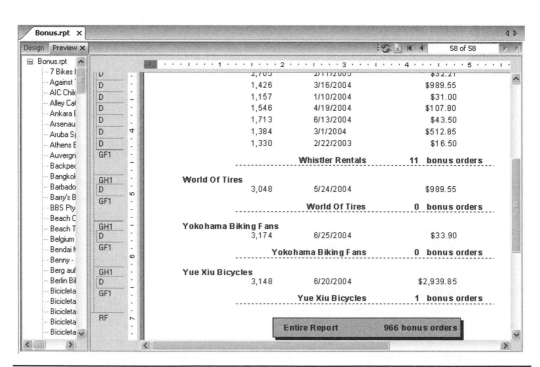

FIGURE 5-6   Over $1,000 Bonus report

@Show Report Bonus is placed in the report footer:

```
WhilePrintingRecords;
NumberVar CountReport;
"This report had " + ToText(CountReport,0) + " bonus orders."
```

While this will work, there is a much simpler way to accomplish the same task with just one formula using no variables. Create a single formula, place it in the details section, and suppress it. It will simply consist of the following:

```
If {Orders.Order Amount} > 1000 Then 1
```

When you place this in the details section, it will return a number constant of 1 when an order exceeds $1,000. If an order is under $1,000, the number formula will return 0 (because the formula is numeric and there is no Else clause, it will return 0 if the If test fails). You then simply need to insert a group subtotal and a report grand total on the formula to calculate group and report totals.

The result: the same totals with much less effort. This simple technique of assigning a formula a value of 1 if a test is passed can become the cornerstone for a lot of statistics-type reports you may have to write.

You may also be able to save time by using running total fields instead of formulas with variables. The running total report earlier in the chapter that illustrates evaluation times is a perfect example. In this type of report, there's no need to create formulas to calculate the running total. Running total fields are covered later in this chapter.

TIP *Many of the types of formulas illustrated in this chapter are included in samples report on this book's accompanying web site. Look at www.CrystalBook.com for FORMULAS.RPT and BONUS.RPT to see how these, and similar formulas, are implemented.*

User Function Libraries

Crystal Reports has been designed as an *extensible* reporting tool. With respect to formulas, that means that you can develop your own functions to add to the Function Tree box if Crystal Reports doesn't provide one that you need. In Crystal Reports 9 and later, this capability has been enhanced with custom functions that you can create directly in your report, or add to the repository to be shared with other Crystal Reports users (custom functions are covered in Chapter 6).

However, versions of Crystal Reports prior to 9 didn't feature custom functions. Also, in some cases, Custom Functions still may not provide sufficient capabilities for your particular business needs. For these situations, you'll still need to create your own functions that appear in the Formula Editor. Look at an example of the built-in functions that appear under the Additional Functions category.

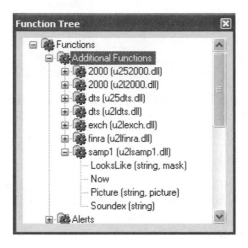

The functions in this category aren't really "built-in." These functions are being supplied to Crystal Reports by *user function libraries (UFLs).* The UFL is supplied to Crystal Reports by an external dynamic link library developed in another programming language. You can write your own custom functions using a Windows programming language, such as C++, Visual Basic, Delphi, or Java, and have them appear in this section of the Function Tree box. For example, you could write a function that calculates the number of business days between two dates you supply, excluding any weekends and company holidays that are contained in an external database. Or, you might write a UFL that reads a value from an external piece of proprietary measurement equipment and supplies a value to your report.

The filename that supplies the UFL appears as a category in the Additional Functions list—you may click the plus sign next to the filename to see the available functions supplied by that file. As with other functions, double-click the function name and supply the necessary arguments inside your formula.

Crystal Reports XI adds support for Java-developed UFLs. With this support comes a new choice in the Formula Editor tab of File | Options. As Windows-oriented UFLs (Windows-based UFL development typically occurs with Visual Basic, Visual Studio .NET, Delphi, and so forth) can't reside in Crystal Reports at the same time as Java-developed UFLs, you must choose which UFLs you wish to be visible to Crystal Reports. You may choose to include COM/C (Windows-oriented) UFLs, Java UFLs, or no UFLs. Once you make the choice and restart Crystal Reports, only UFLs of the chosen type installed on your computer will appear in the Additional Functions category of the Function Tree box.

Tip *Although the need for external UFLs is probably greatly reduced by Crystal Reports custom function and repository capabilities, you may still need to use them to connect to external databases, external equipment, or any other capability that is not provided by the Crystal Reports formula language (which is what Crystal Reports custom functions use). Information on creating User Functions Libraries with Visual Basic can be found on this book's web site. Look at www. CrystalBook.com.*

Running Total Fields

In certain situations, the use of formulas with variables (discussed earlier in the chapter) is inevitable. However, many of the examples shown previously can actually be accomplished without even creating a formula. If you need to accumulate, display, and reset running totals, you will probably prefer the *running total field*. A running total field can be inserted just like a database field. It gives you great flexibility to accumulate or increment values as the report progresses, without the need for formulas or variables.

Figure 5-7 shows a Top *N* report (discussed in Chapter 3) that shows regional subtotals for the top five regions in the U.S. This particular Top *N* report does not include Others. As mentioned in Chapter 3, this causes the report grand totals not to agree with the sum of all the group totals. The grand totals are based on all report records, not just those that fall into the top five groups. Using running total fields is the perfect answer to this problem.

All new running total fields are created from the Field Explorer. First, select the Running Total Fields category in the Field Explorer. Click the New button in the Field Explorer toolbar or right-click the Running Total Fields category and choose New from the pop-up menu. You may also select an existing field in the Details section, right-click, and choose Insert | Running Total from the pop-up menu. The Create Running Total Field dialog box appears, as shown in Figure 5-8.

Start by giving the running total field a name (if you don't like the default name given by Crystal Reports). It can contain mixed-case characters and spaces and won't conflict with formula or database field names. Crystal Reports will precede the running total field name with a pound sign (#).

If you select a detail field and use the right-click method to insert the running total field, the field you choose will already appear in the Field To Summarize drop-down list, and

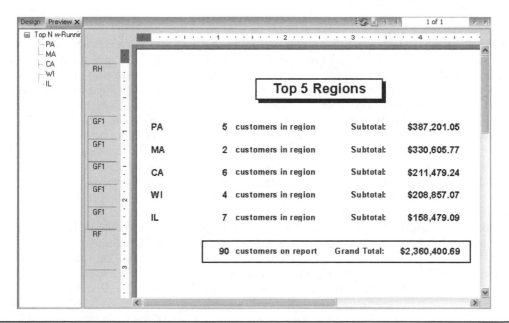

FIGURE 5-7   Grand total problem with Top *N* report and no Others group

When the running total will be incremented

Fields available to use
in running total

Field and type of summary used to calculate running total

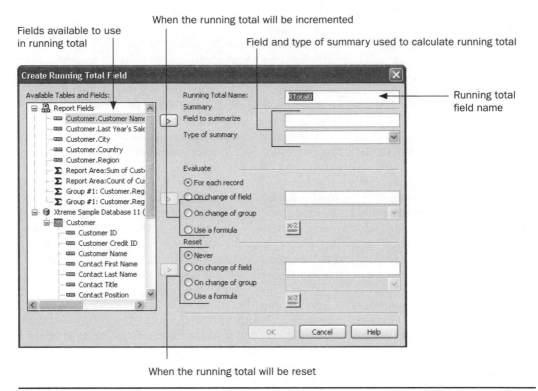

Running total
field name

When the running total will be reset

FIGURE 5-8   Create Running Total Field dialog box

a default summary function will appear in the Type Of Summary drop-down list. If you're creating a new running total field from the Field Explorer, choose the report, database, or formula field that you want to use to calculate the running total by selecting the field in the Available Tables and Fields list and clicking the right arrow next to the Field to Summarize box. Choose the type of calculation you want to use from the Type Of Summary pull-down list. If you just want to increment the running total by one for certain records, use the Count or DistinctCount summaries, depending on how "unique" the field you are summarizing is, along with any field from the report that won't contain null values (nulls don't increment counts). Other functions available in running totals are the same as those available for summaries. Look back at Chapter 3 for a detailed description of available summaries.

Choose when you want the running total to increment, by making choices in the Evaluate section. Then, choose when you want the running total to reset, by making choices in the Reset section. If you select a field in the Available Tables And Fields list and then click the arrow next to the On Change Of Field radio button, the running total will increment or reset every time a new value appears in that field. If you click the On Change Of Group radio button, you can then choose an existing report group in the pull-down list. The running total will increment or reset every time the chosen group changes. If you click the Use A Formula radio button, you can then click the Formula button next to it. The Formula Editor will appear, in which you can enter a Boolean formula that will trigger when the running total field is incremented or reset.

Click OK when you've completed the Create Running Total Field dialog box. The running total will now appear in the Field Explorer and can be dragged and dropped on the report just like a database field. If you'd like to edit, rename, or delete the running total field, you have these choices in the Field Explorer. You can also right-click a running total field in either the Design or Preview tab and choose Edit Running Total from the pop-up menu.

To solve the problem with the Top *N* report without "Others," simply create two running total fields: one to calculate the number of customers:

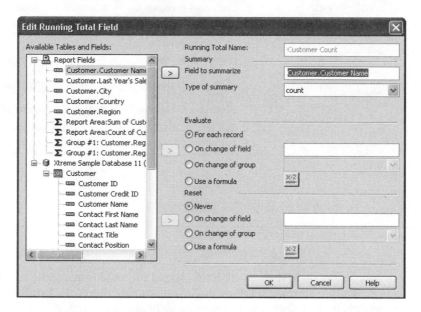

and one to calculate the sale grand total:

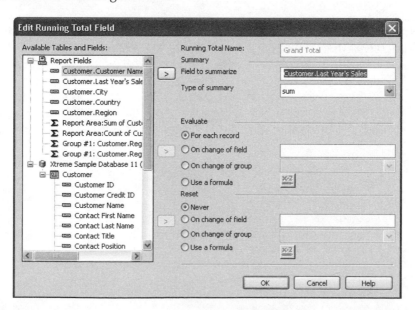

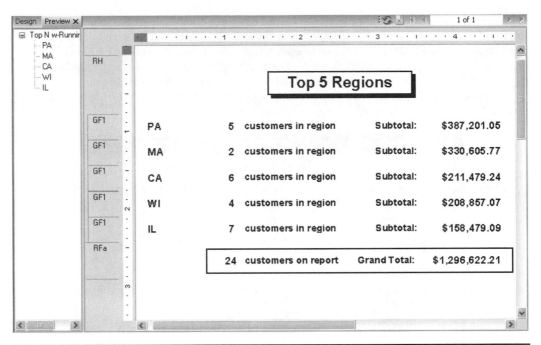

FIGURE 5-9 Correct Top *N* report using running totals

Place these running totals in the report footer instead of grand totaling the fields from the details section. Because running totals evaluate only during the While Printing Records pass, the extra records in the Others group won't be included in the report footer. Figure 5-9 shows the correct totals now displayed on the Top *N* report.

CAUTION *Because running total fields are calculated in the While Printing Records pass of the report, you cannot create running total fields based on second-pass formulas.*

Creating Custom Functions

One of the most often-heard questions from Crystal Reports users is "How can I share a formula I write with other reports or with other Crystal Reports users?" Often, too, a report designer will find a set of formula logic that is particular to their type of business or type of reports that must be used over and over again in many other formulas. The question then becomes, "Is there any way of reducing the need to type these same parts of the formula over and over again?"

In earlier versions of Crystal Reports, the solutions to these requirements typically weren't very elegant. Some users would open two reports side by side, reduce the size of the windows inside the Crystal Report designer, and drag a formula from one report to another. Others would open a report, edit a formula, copy the contents to the clipboard, and paste the contents to a new formula. Or a user might copy the contents of a formula in a report, close the first report, open a second report, create a new formula, and paste the formula text from the first report into the Formula Editor. Still others would keep their own "library" of formulas in a text file or word processing document, cutting and pasting between various formulas in various reports and this document on a regular basis.

Now, Crystal Reports makes this much easier by providing the ability to create your own "reusable functions," called *custom functions*. Not only can custom functions be used over and over again in different formulas in the same report, but they can be added to the BusinessObjects Enterprise or Crystal Reports Server repository for use in other reports and for use by other Crystal Reports users.

Custom Functions Defined

A custom function is very similar to a regular function you will already find in the function tree of the Crystal Reports Formula Editor (learn more about formulas and the function tree in Chapter 5). For example, the built-in ToText function in the Crystal Reports formula language will convert from any non-text data type (such as numbers) to a text data type. The built-in Left function will return a certain number of characters from the left side of a string value. And the built-in Round function will round a numeric value to a specified number of decimal places.

But what if you have a special need in your company to use a function that's not included as part of the built-in Crystal Reports functions? You may, for example, need to calculate the number of business days between two dates, excluding weekends and company holidays.

Or you may want to calculate a discount for customers in a large number of formulas. However, you want to base this discount on several factors, including the size of the order amount, the number of orders the customer placed last year, and the length of time they have been a customer. While you can most probably make use of Crystal Reports' extensive formula language to create these special formulas, making use of the logic over and over again in more than one formula, or sharing the logic with other report designers, is where a custom function becomes really useful.

Available custom functions (either that you built after creating the report, or added from the repository) will appear in the Formula Editor just like built-in functions. However, custom functions appear in their own Custom Functions area of the function tree, as shown in Figure 6-1.

A custom function can accept arguments (or parameters), just like a regular function (arguments are discussed in more detail later in the chapter). And as with regular functions, you can use the custom function over and over in as many formulas as you desire. If the core logic of your custom function changes (perhaps business holidays or a discount percentage tier change with the new year), changing the custom function in its one location will be

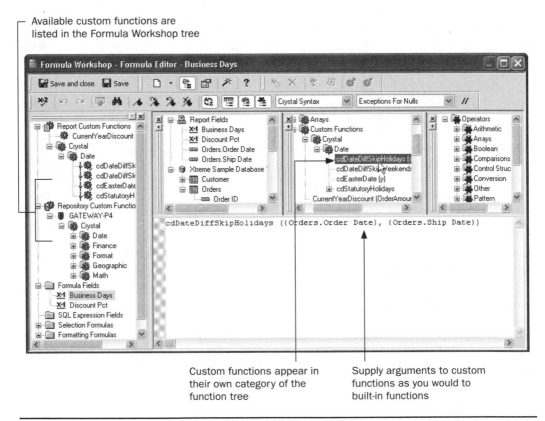

Available custom functions are listed in the Formula Workshop tree

Custom functions appear in their own category of the function tree

Supply arguments to custom functions as you would to built-in functions

FIGURE 6-1   A custom function used in a formula

reflected in all formulas that make use of that function—you won't have to edit each and every formula to change the formula logic.

Creating Your Own Custom Functions

If you install BusinessObjects Enterprise XI or Crystal Reports Server XI, its repository ships with a "starter set" of custom functions. However, you'll probably soon discover a use for your own. Creating a custom function is very similar to creating a Crystal Reports formula— most of the typical built-in functions and operators otherwise available in regular formulas are available for your use in a custom function (Chapter 5 covers formula creation in more detail).

There are two ways to create a new custom function: base it on an existing formula or create it from scratch.

Extracting Custom Functions from Existing Formulas

If you have an existing formula in a report that contains the "core" set of logic that you wish to use for your custom function, you may base your custom function on it by *extracting* the custom function from the formula. Do this by performing these steps:

1. Launch the Formula Workshop by clicking the Formula Workshop button in the Expert Tools toolbar, or choosing Report | Formula Workshop from the pull-down menus.

2. In the Formula Workshop tree, right-click the Report Custom Functions category and choose New from the pop-up menu. You may also just click the Report Custom Functions category to select it and click the New button in the Formula Workshop toolbar, or click the down arrow next to the New toolbar button and choose Custom Function from the drop-down list.

3. Type in a name for your custom function. Choose a name within the naming limitations discussed later in this chapter.

4. Click the Use Extractor button to base your custom function on an existing report formula. The Extract Custom Function From Formula dialog box will appear, as shown in Figure 6-2.

5. Make any desired changes to arguments that are substituted for database fields in the original formula. You may also add descriptive text to the function definition that will appear when you use the function in the Formula Expert (discussed in Chapter 5).

6. If you wish to change the original formula to use the function, check the Modify Formula To Use New Custom Function check box.

7. Click the Enter More Info button to supply optional items, such as default argument values and other descriptive text.

8. Click OK to save the new custom function.

Choose an existing report formula for your function

Change the previously given function name here

Type in a description of the function (optional)

Give arguments substituted for formula database fields names and descriptions (optional)

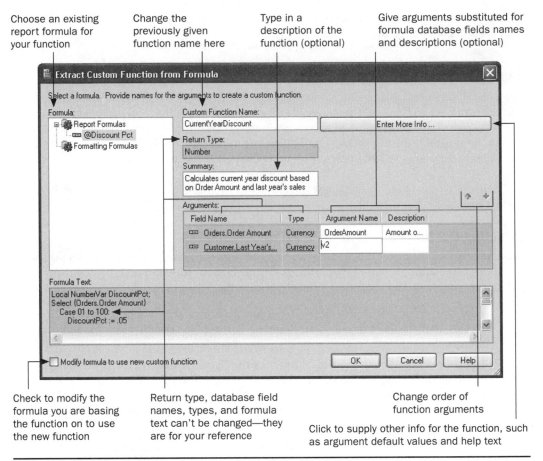

Figure 6-2 Creating a custom function based on a formula

Check to modify the formula you are basing the function on to use the new function

Return type, database field names, types, and formula text can't be changed—they are for your reference

Change order of function arguments

Click to supply other info for the function, such as argument default values and help text

Custom Function Arguments

One of the first adjustments you'll need to make when creating custom functions, as opposed to formulas, is handling function arguments. An *argument* is a parameter that you create within your function to accept a value from the formula that calls it. It then uses this value (possibly along with other arguments that are also supplied) to perform some calculation or logic and return a result to the calling formula.

If you think of Crystal Reports built-in functions, most require that you supply arguments when you use them in formulas. For example, if you use the ToText function to convert a number, date, or other non-string data type to a string, you must supply at least one argument: the non-string value to be converted. And the Left function, which returns a certain number of characters from the left side of a larger string, requires you to supply two arguments: the string to retrieve a subset of characters from and the number of characters to retrieve. In cases of built-in functions, arguments you supply must conform to specific data types. The single-argument ToText example requires a string argument to be supplied. The Left function requires a string argument and a number argument.

Custom Function Naming Limitations

You are more restricted in choosing names for your custom functions than you are for formulas. Because custom functions appear in the Formula Editor's function tree alongside all the built-in functions, there are several limitations:

- Custom function names must begin with a letter—you can't start a function name with a number. Also, you can include only letters, numbers, and the underscore character in your custom function name—other special characters (such as the % or # signs) cannot be included.

- Custom function names cannot contain spaces—you can use only underscores to separate a multiword custom function name. However, you can use mixed upper- and lowercase letters to help delineate multiword custom function names.

- You cannot use a name that is already used by a Crystal Reports built-in function. For example, you'll receive an error message if you try to create a custom function named ToText or Left.

- You may notice that Business Objects–supplied custom function names include a two-character "cd" prefix (left over from previous Crystal Decisions references). Although adding your own prefix is certainly not required, it may be a handy way of identifying a certain group of custom functions. Prefixing custom function names may also help avoid naming conflicts with other custom functions contained in the repository, as well as conflicts with built-in function names.

When you create your own custom functions (by either extracting logic from an existing formula or creating the function from scratch), you must consider if your function will need to accept arguments from the calling formula, how many arguments your function requires, what data types the arguments will be, and if you want to supply one or more default values for each argument.

When extracting a custom function from a formula, such as the function illustrated in Figure 6-2, the number and data types of arguments in your function are automatically determined by the number of unique database fields included in the original formula. In the example shown in the figure, the original formula the custom function is based upon contains two database fields: {Orders.Order Amount} and {Customer.Last Year's Sales}. When the custom function is extracted from this formula, the database fields are removed from the function and replaced with two arguments, both of which require currency data types (the data types of the original database fields) to be supplied.

The arguments that the extract process identifies are listed in the Arguments list of the Extract Custom Function From Formula dialog box. You'll see the original database fields that are being replaced with arguments, the data type of the argument (both of these columns are for your information and can't be changed), the name of the argument in the custom function, and the description of the argument. By default, the extract process will number arguments successively from the number 1, preceding the argument number with the letter *v*.

If you simply wish to allow the default v-numbered arguments to remain, you may ignore this section of the Extract Custom Function From Formula dialog box. However, in that case, the function illustrated in Figure 6-2 would appear like this in the function tree of the Formula Editor:

```
CurrentYearDiscount(v1, v2)
```

It's more likely that you will want arguments in your custom function to have more meaningful names, perhaps replacing v1 with OrderAmount and v2 with PreviousSaleAmount. To accomplish this, rename the v1 and v2 argument names in the dialog box. You may optionally add descriptions to each argument that will appear in the Formula Expert (described in Chapter 5).

The More Info Button

When you extract a custom function from a formula, you'll notice the Enter More Info button on the Extract Custom Function From Formula dialog box. If you click this button, the Custom Function Properties dialog box appears.

The shaded areas of this dialog box are just for reference—they can't be changed here. The Summary and Argument descriptions are interchangeable with those in the Extract Custom Function From Formula dialog box—changing the descriptions of the function and arguments in either place will change it in the other. However, the Category, Author, Display In Experts check box, argument default values, and help text can be changed only on this dialog box.

Category   If you look at the custom functions supplied with the BusinessObjects Enterprise XI/Crystal Reports Server XI default repository, you'll notice that they are categorized in a hierarchy several levels deep (for example, the cdDateDiffSkipHolidays custom function is within the Date category, which is within the Crystal category). You may set up categories and hierarchies for your own custom functions. Do this by specifying the category in the Category text box. If you wish to build a hierarchy for the categories, separate the category names with slashes. For example, placing a function in the Sales/Orders category will show a Sales entry in the Formula Workshop tree with a plus sign. When you click the plus sign, the Orders subcategory will appear with the CurrentYearDiscount custom function in it.

Author   This is, in essence, a comment field that you can either leave blank or fill with text of your choice (probably the name of the person who developed the custom function). This value will appear only when you edit the custom function or use it in the Formula Expert. This text won't be available in the Formula Editor.

Display In Experts   This check box determines whether or not the custom function will appear in the list of available functions when using the Formula Expert (covered in Chapter 5). If you uncheck this box, then you'll see the custom function in the function tree of the Formula Editor, but not in the list of available custom functions when using the Formula Expert.

Argument Default Values   For certain arguments, such as those that may accept department codes, months of the year, or other common values (the order amount/previous period sales examples here probably don't fall into this category), you may wish to supply a list of one or more default values that a user can choose from when they use the custom function in the Formula Expert. To supply these, click the Default Values box for the argument that you want to set the defaults for. This will display the Default Values dialog box.

Here, you may type in a default value that you want a user to be able to choose; then click the Add button. This will add the value to a list in the lower part of the dialog box. If you want to add additional values, type them in and click the Add button. If you wish to remove a value that's already been added, choose it in the lower list and click the Remove button. And if you wish to change the order of the default values you've already added, choose the value in the list that you wish to move and click the up or down arrow to the right of the list.

When you click OK, the default value list will be added to the custom function and will appear in the argument list on the original Custom Function Properties dialog box.

Help Text   Clicking the Help Text button will simply display yet another dialog box where you can type in free-form text describing the custom function, providing more detail on its arguments or return value, or other helpful information. This help text will be visible only when editing this function later, or using it in the Formula Expert. This text won't be available in the Formula Editor.

CAUTION   *There are certain requirements an existing report formula must meet to be used as the basis for a custom function. For example (and this list is not all-inclusive), the formula cannot contain any evaluation time functions (such as WhilePrintingRecords), any summary functions used with database fields (such as Sum({Orders.Order Amount})), or any variables scoped other than Local. If you attempt to extract a custom function from such a formula, you'll either receive an error message indicating that the formula can't be used, and explaining why, or a function that may not perform the way you expected it to. You may either copy the formula to the clipboard and paste it into the Custom Function Editor when creating the function from scratch (making modifications to the copied formula to allow it to work as a function), or edit the report formula (perhaps explicitly setting variable scope to Local), and then extract the function from the updated formula.*

Creating Custom Functions from Scratch

There may be times when an existing report formula isn't available as the basis for your custom function. Also, you may have a need for a custom function that is more sophisticated than an existing formula, or the existing formula might contain elements that prohibit it from being used as the basis for a custom function (it may use global variables, evaluation time functions, or other limiting features). In these cases, you will want to create a custom function "from scratch" using the Custom Function editor.

In this case, the steps for initially creating the custom function are the same. Create and name the new custom function in the Formula Workshop as described previously in the chapter. However, in the Custom Function Name dialog box, click the Use Editor button to display the Custom Function Editor inside the Formula Workshop, as shown in Figure 6-3.

The Custom Function Editor is almost identical to the Formula Editor discussed in detail in Chapter 5. The difference is that the field tree, containing a list of database fields, is not visible. And the function tree, which contains a list of built-in Crystal Reports functions, contains a slightly reduced set of built-in functions. This variance is because custom functions are designed to be independent of any particular report they are placed in; you can't include database fields in a custom function—there would be no way of ensuring these fields would be available when the function is called from another report. You are also prevented from including the limited set of built-in functions (such as Evaluation Time, Print State, and others) because of the "stateless" nature of a custom function.

TIP   *Even though the function tree contains a reduced set of options, it will still display a Custom Function category where you can choose another existing custom function to use in the current custom function.*

You may now just create the custom function logic by double-clicking built-in functions in the function tree and operators in the operator tree. You may, of course, type in these

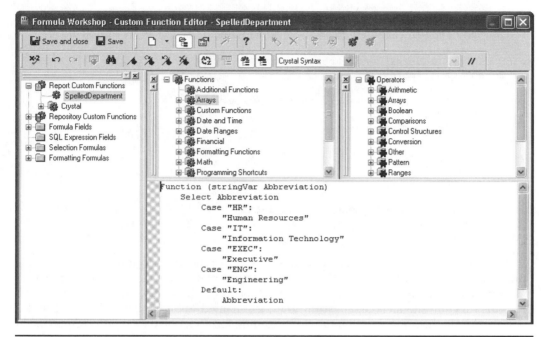

FIGURE 6-3   The Custom Function Editor

items yourself, as well as associated formula code. And as with the Formula Editor, you can check the syntax of your custom function before saving by clicking the Check button in the toolbar or typing ALT-C.

Syntax Choices and Requirements

When you create a custom function, you have the choice of both Crystal Reports formula languages (or syntaxes) just like you do when creating a report formula. Choose the desired syntax from the drop-down list toward the right of the Custom Function Editor toolbar. The function tree and the operator tree will adjust to the chosen syntax. You'll also see a commensurate difference in the formula text that is automatically added by Crystal Reports.

The basic premise of creating a custom function directly in the Custom Function Editor is to design a formula to accept any necessary values passed into the function arguments from the calling formula; perform evaluations, calculations, If-Then-Else tests, and so forth within the custom function; and return a value back to the calling formula. If you have created functions in a programming language, such as Visual Basic, then this should be a fairly straightforward process. If you haven't programmed in a programming language in the past, then getting the "hang" of custom function creation may take some time. But, if you're familiar with Crystal Reports formulas in general, you should be able to apply your existing knowledge to custom function creation pretty quickly.

Here is an example of a Basic Syntax custom function that returns the spelled-out name of a company department based on an abbreviated name passed in as an argument:

```
Function SpelledDepartment (Abbreviation As String) As String
    Select Case Abbreviation
        Case "HR"
            SpelledDepartment = "Human Resources"
        Case "IT"
            SpelledDepartment = "Information Technology"
        Case "EXEC"
            SpelledDepartment = "Executive"
        Case "ENG"
            SpelledDepartment = "Engineering"
        Case Else
            SpelledDepartment = Abbreviation
    End Select
End Function
```

The basic (no pun intended) layout of a Basic syntax function is formula code within a Function and End Function block. The Function statement declares the name of the function (the same name you used when you created the function), a list of any arguments and data types the function should accept (a string argument named Abbreviation in this case), and the type of data the function will return to the calling formula (the data type "As" portion is optional—if you don't include it, the data type the function returns will be determined by the data type you assign to the function name later inside the function).

The last statement within the Function–End Function block that assigns a value to the function name will determine what the function returns to the calling formula. In this case, the function uses a Select Case construct (from the Control Structures category of the operator tree) to test for various values of the passed Abbreviation argument, setting the function name to a string literal based on the value of the argument.

Here is the same function in Crystal syntax (this is illustrated in Figure 6-3):

```
Function (StringVar Abbreviation)
Select Abbreviation
    Case "HR" :
        "Human Resources"
    Case "IT" :
        "Information Technology"
    Case "EXEC" :
        "Executive"
    Case "ENG" :
        "Engineering"
    Default:
        Abbreviation
```

In this case, there is no Function–End Function block—all the formula text included in the function is implicitly considered to be within this "block." The argument being passed to the function is included in parentheses immediately after the Function keyword, preceded by the data type that the argument is assigned (data type keywords are the same as those for declaring variables—see the Variable Declarations section of the operator tree for proper spelling). Similar to the Basic syntax example, the last statement inside the function to evaluate will determine what the function returns to the calling formula. In this example, the Case statement that matches the passed argument will return a string value to the calling formula.

Complex Data Types and Optional Arguments

In the preceding examples, the custom function accepted a single "simple" string value as an argument and returned a single simple string value as a result. However, you may have more complex custom functions that need to deal with more than one argument, or *complex data types*, such as array and range values. While the Formula Extractor (discussed earlier in the chapter) can create custom functions with multiple arguments, it can't create functions that accept or return complex data types. To accept range values or arrays as arguments, or pass similar data types back to the calling formula, you must use the Custom Function editor.

You also may create a special kind of argument in the Custom Function editor called an *optional argument*. By placing the Optional keyword in front of an argument name, you specify that the formula calling the function does not have to supply this argument. If the formula does supply the argument, it will override the default value for the argument that you must supply if you declare an argument as optional.

For example, if you create the following as the *first* line of a Basic syntax function:

```
Function DaysBetweenDates _
(BDate As Date, Optional EDate As Date = CurrentDate)
```

You will be able to call the function in a formula using one *or two* arguments, as the second argument is optional. If you call the function using two arguments, both will be supplied to the function. If you call the function using only one argument, that argument will be supplied as the BDate argument and the current date from the computer's system clock (CurrentDate is a built-in function) will be supplied as the second argument. Adding optional arguments will create multiple occurrences of the function in the function tree to indicate the ability to call the function with multiple arguments. For example, the single custom function created with the Function statement illustrated previously will appear in the function tree twice.

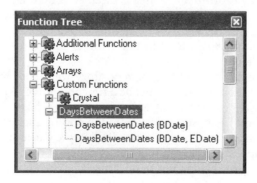

Optional arguments are declared in Crystal syntax with the Optional keyword as well, but with the standard Crystal syntax data type spellings and colon-equal operator used to assign the default value.

```
Function (DateVar BDate, Optional DateVar EDate := CurrentDate)
```

TIP Finer points on Crystal and Basic syntax when used in custom functions, such as how to declare complex data types in arguments and syntax differences between custom functions and report formulas, can be found in Crystal Reports online help. Search for Custom Functions | Basic Syntax, or Custom Functions | Crystal Syntax.

Modifying Existing Custom Functions

Once you've created a custom function, you may wish to change it later. One of the benefits of custom functions over copying and pasting the same formula logic over and over again in multiple formulas is that all formulas based on a custom function will automatically reflect the change made in the one custom function. As such, a great deal of effort can be eliminated by sharing custom functions in the repository and making a single change to the repository. The change will automatically be reflected in all formulas in all reports that make use of that function. Storing custom functions in the repository is covered later in this chapter and in Chapter 17.

If you've added the custom function just to one report, you may change a custom function in the same way you would change a formula: select it in the Formula Workshop and make changes directly to the formula text in the Custom Function Editor. When you save changes, any formulas using the function will immediately reflect the change.

NOTE Even though you were able to initially extract a custom function from a formula using a dialog box, you will need to make changes to the custom function in the Custom Function Editor. Once you've saved any custom function, even by extracting it from a formula, editing must be done in the Custom Function Editor.

If you've added custom functions to your report from the repository, you'll notice that the Custom Function Editor formula text area is disabled for editing when you select the custom function in the Formula Workshop tree. This is because you have not disconnected the custom function from the repository. In order to change the contents of a repository-based function, you must *disconnect* the function—this is similar to "checking out" the function from the repository.

To disconnect a custom function from the repository, right-click the function you wish to edit in the Formula Workshop tree (this must be a function in the Report Custom Functions category—you can't disconnect or edit a custom function that hasn't first been added to the report). Choose Disconnect From Repository from the pop-up menu. You'll notice two changes: first, the custom function can now be edited in the Custom Function Editor, and second, the small icon appearing next to the custom function name in the Formula Workshop tree will no longer display the small "linked" icon.

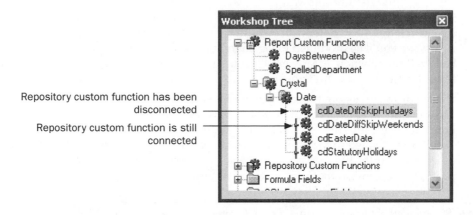

Repository custom function has been disconnected

Repository custom function is still connected

You may not only edit the formula text of an existing custom function, but the summary, author, category, and other nonformula items that you specified when first creating the function. With the function you wish to edit displayed in the Custom Function Editor, click the Toggle Properties Display button in the Formula Workshop toolbar, or right-click the function name in the Formula Workshop tree and choose Toggle Property Display from the pop-up menu. The Custom Function Editor will be replaced with a dialog box summarizing all the other properties that can be set for the function. Make any necessary changes on this screen and click the same toolbar button or use the same pop-up menu choice to toggle back to the Custom Function Editor.

Once you've made changes to the custom function and saved the changes, you may wish to add your new custom function to the repository for sharing with other reports or users. If the custom function is a modified version of an existing repository function, you will probably want to "reconnect" the custom function back to the repository with changes. The following section describes how to add a custom function to the repository.

Sharing Custom Functions with Other Users

One of the main benefits of Crystal Reports custom functions is the ability to share them not only among reports you may design, but among reports that other Crystal Reports users design as well. This is accomplished by saving the custom function or functions you wish to share in the repository. And if you've disconnected a custom function from the repository to change it, you'll most probably want to save the updated function back to the repository again. The steps to add a new custom function to the repository for the first time, or to update a custom function that you disconnected, are largely the same. There are actually three different ways to accomplish the same thing:

- Right-click the custom function you wish to add to the repository in the Formula Workshop tree. Select Add To Repository from the pop-up menu. If you have not already logged on to your BusinessObjects Enterprise XI/Crystal Reports Server XI system to access the repository, you'll be prompted to do so. If the function already exists (you disconnected it earlier), you'll be prompted to confirm that you want to overwrite the existing repository function.

- Select the custom function you wish to add to the repository in the Formula Workshop tree. Click the Add To Repository button in the Formula Workshop toolbar. If necessary, you'll be prompted to log on to BusinessObjects Enterprise/Crystal Reports Server. If the function already exists (you disconnected it earlier), you'll be prompted to confirm that you want to overwrite the existing repository function.

- Simply drag the custom function you wish to add to the repository from the Report Custom Functions category of the Formula Workshop tree to the Repository Custom Functions category. This will automatically add the function to the selected repository. You'll be prompted to log on to BusinessObjects Enterprise/Crystal Reports Server, if necessary. If the function already exists (you disconnected it earlier), you'll be prompted to confirm that you want to overwrite the existing repository function.

CAUTION *You may not be able to add a custom function to the repository—either a new custom function you created yourself, or a custom function you disconnected from the repository to edit. Depending on the BusinessObjects Enterprise or Crystal Reports Server system you are connected to, and the rights you have been granted, you may not be able to add or update custom functions. If you get an error message when attempting to add a custom function to the repository, contact your system administrator to verify that you have the right to modify the repository.*

Using Custom Functions in Your Formulas

Once you've created a custom function, either for use in just the current report, or to be shared from the repository, using the function in a formula is easy. You may create a formula that makes use of the function with the Formula Expert (covered in detail in Chapter 5). Or if you create a formula with the Formula Editor, custom functions you've created in the current report will appear in the Custom Functions category of the function tree.

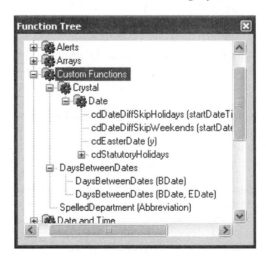

Custom functions in the repository, however, won't automatically appear in the function tree unless you add them to the report first. To add a repository custom function to the report, expand the Repository Custom Functions category of the Formula Workshop until you find the custom function that you wish to use (you may be prompted to log on to BusinessObjects Enterprise or Crystal Reports Server first). Select the function you wish to add and click the Add To Report toolbar button in the Formula Workshop toolbar. You can also right-click the function name in the Formula Workshop tree and choose Add To Report from the pop-up menu. And finally, you may simply drag the custom function you wish to add to the report from the Repository Custom Functions category to the Report Custom Functions category of the Formula Workshop tree.

If the custom function you choose to add to the report calls other custom functions as well (remember, one custom function can call another), you'll be notified that additional custom functions will be added as well. The custom functions will now appear in the Custom Functions category of the function tree for you to add to formulas.

CHAPTER 7

Making Your Reports Visually Appealing

Crystal Reports, as a Windows-based report writer, has many features that can help you create eye-catching, visually effective reports. You can often use Crystal Reports to create reports right from the database, whereas you formerly had to use a word processor or page publishing program to create such reports. The next time you're tempted to export database records to a text file and merge them in a word processing or page publishing document, use some of the techniques covered in this chapter and save yourself the extra work.

You may consider using geographic maps (discussed in Chapter 11) and charts and graphs (discussed in Chapter 10) as visual elements to make your reports more appealing. But even using just the textual elements of Crystal Reports can be very creative. Not only can you use a variety of fonts and typefaces in your reports, you also can set object foreground and background colors, choose unique borders on all four sides of objects, add drop shadows, and use other graphical features. You can then copy that formatting en masse from one object to others. You can include bitmap pictures on your report, either reading them directly from the database (if the database you're using supports and includes them) or adding graphics files right into a report section. You can draw lines and boxes around the report to highlight important portions. You can use Report Alerts to trigger a message when a certain condition is met, as well as highlight portions of the report that met that condition. You can choose a predefined set of object and report formatting and apply it to other reports in one step by use of templates.

General Formatting

Crystal Reports gives you considerable flexibility in customizing the appearance of objects that you place on your report, such as database fields, text objects, and formulas. By using various formatting options for these objects, you can change many aspects of their appearance, such as font face, size, color, alignment, and more. The most basic type of formatting is known as *absolute formatting,* in which you simply select the object and make formatting changes with the Formatting toolbar or the Format Editor. In either case, the change applies to all occurrences of the object on the report—if you format a field in the details section absolutely, that field will appear the same every time it prints.

The Formatting Toolbar

The quickest way to format one or more objects on the report is to select the object or objects you want to format and then choose options from the Formatting toolbar. To choose a single object, just click it with the mouse. To choose multiple objects to format at once, CTRL-click or SHIFT-click on more than one object (you'll notice that all objects you've selected will have a shaded outline around them). Then, click buttons in the Formatting toolbar to format the selected objects. Table 7-1 outlines each Formatting toolbar button.

Button	Function
Arial ▾ Font Face	Choose a different font face (such as Arial, Times Roman, etc.) from the drop-down list
10 ▾ Font Size	Choose the font size, in points, from the drop-down list, or enter a value directly in the box
A⁺ Increase Font Size	Increase the font size (each click of this button increases the font size by one point)
A⁻ Decrease Font Size	Decrease the font size (each click of this button decreases the font size by one point)
B Bold (or CTRL-B)	Format object using bold emphasis
I Italic (or CTRL-I)	Format the object using italic letters
U Underline (or CTRL-U)	Add an underline to the object
≡ Align Left	Align text to the left of the object's defined width
≡ Align Center	Align text to the center of the object's defined width
≡ Align Right	Align text to the right of the object's defined width
≡ Justify	Align on both the left and right side of the object's defined width. This provides "fully justified" text, similar to that often found in newspaper columns.

TABLE 7-1 Formatting Toolbar Options

Button	Function
A Font Color	Change font color. If you click the button itself, it will set the font color to that displayed on the small line in the button. If you click the down arrow, a dialog box will appear giving you a choice of colors. Once you choose a color that becomes the default color for the button, you will see the small line in the button change to that color.
Outside Borders	Add border lines on sides of the object. If you click the face of the button, all four sides of the object will initially be given a border. If you click the face of the button again, the borders will be turned off. If you click the down arrow, a subset of buttons will appear, which allow you to choose combinations of left, right, top, or bottom borders, all, or none.
Suppress	Toggle display of the object on and off. This is equivalent to clicking the Suppress check box on the Common tab of the Format Editor.
Lock Format	Toggle ability to change other formatting properties on the object. If formatting is locked, all other formatting options, including width and height, will be disabled. This is equivalent to clicking the Read Only check box on the Common tab of the Format Editor.
Lock Size/Position	Toggle ability to change the width or height, or to move the object. This is equivalent to clicking the Lock Position and Size check box on the Common tab of the Format Editor.
$ Currency	Toggle display of a currency symbol (the symbol chosen as the default currency symbols in the Windows Control Panel) with the object. This button will be enabled only if all objects you've selected are currency or numeric fields.
, Thousands Separator	Toggle display of a thousands separator (the symbol chosen as the default thousands separator in Windows Control Panel) within the object. This button will be enabled only if all objects you've selected are currency or numeric fields.
% Percent Sign	Toggle display of a percent sign on the right side of the object. This option actually adds a currency symbol, but it changes the symbol to the percent sign and the position to the right side of the object. This button will be enabled only if all objects you've selected are currency or numeric fields.
Increase Decimals	Increase the number of decimal places displayed. For example, if the object is displayed as $121.22 and this button is clicked, the number might display as $121.223. This button will be enabled only if all objects you've selected are currency or numeric fields.
Decrease Decimals	Decrease the number of decimal places displayed. For example, if the object is displayed as $121.22 and this button is clicked, the number will display as $121.2. This button will be enabled only if all objects you've selected are currency or numeric fields, and if at least one decimal place is already showing.

TABLE 7-1 Formatting Toolbar Options *(continued)*

The Format Editor

Although Crystal Reports offers a large number of formatting choices on the Formatting toolbar, there are still quite a few formatting options that you can't perform with toolbar buttons. For these formatting requirements, you must use the Format Editor. The *Format Editor* is not an "editor" per se, but a tabbed dialog box that displays a varying set of tabs, depending upon the data type of the object you're formatting.

To display the Format Editor, select objects as described earlier in this chapter and then choose one of the following options:

- Choose Format | Format Text, Format | Format Field, or Format | Format Objects from the pull-down menus (the choice of Text, Field, or Objects is determined by the number and data type of objects selected before you choose the option).

- Right-click the selected object and choose Format Text, Format Field, or Format Objects from the pop-up menu.

 • Click the Format toolbar button in the Expert Tools toolbar.

The tab that displays in the Format Editor will vary, depending on the data type of the object you're formatting. For example, if you selected one or more date/time fields before displaying the Format Editor, the Date/Time tab will initially display. Number fields will result in the Number tab displaying, and string fields or text objects will cause the Paragraph Formatting tab to initially display. If you select multiple objects of varying data types, the Common tab will display by default, and you'll be able to change only formatting options that apply to all objects you've selected: data type–specific options will be unavailable until you cancel the Format Editor, select one or more objects with the same data type, and reformat them.

In some of the Format Editor tabs (such as the Number tab or Date/Time tab), you'll be able to choose from predefined formatting "styles" that appear in a list. These styles provide more commonly used formatting styles that you may select with one mouse click. If, however, you'd like to use some combination of formatting that these styles don't provide, a Custom Style button at the bottom of the Format Editor will display additional dialog boxes where you can format individual pieces of the field, such as the leading day-of-week for a date field, or the currency symbol for a number or currency field.

Most Format Editor options are fairly self-explanatory in terms of the data type being formatted. For those options that aren't self-explanatory, Crystal Reports online help will provide additional information. Also, additional discussion of various Format Editor options can be found throughout this book in sections and chapters relating to the different types of fields being formatted.

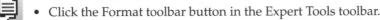

The Highlighting Expert

While the absolute formatting options on the Format Editor will solve many reporting needs, you'll soon find that you may wish object formatting to change according to the data being displayed. This is called *conditional formatting*, which lets you change the appearance of objects depending on their contents or the contents of other fields, objects, or formulas. Although the possibilities of conditional formatting are limited only by your imagination and creativity, some immediate uses of conditional formatting that may come to mind are

- Showing sales figures in red if they fall below a predefined level
- Using a different font to highlight long-time customers
- Adding a border around an invoice number if it's past due
- Showing a report title that's different on the first page than on the rest of the pages
- Graphically indicating with file-folder icons whether a case file has been opened or closed

Probably the simplest conditional formatting tool with Crystal Reports is the *Highlighting Expert,* which lets you vary the appearance of a field when a certain condition is met. If a sales figure falls below a preset goal for the department, you can have it stand out with a white font color on a red background. Or, you can change the border on a Days Overdue formula that exceeds, say, 60 days.

To use the Highlighting Expert with a field, select the field you want to change. Start the Highlighting Expert by clicking the Highlighting button on the Expert Tools toolbar, choosing Format | Highlighting Expert from the pull-down menus, or right-clicking the object and choosing Highlighting Expert from the pop-up menu. Figure 7-1 shows the Highlighting Expert.

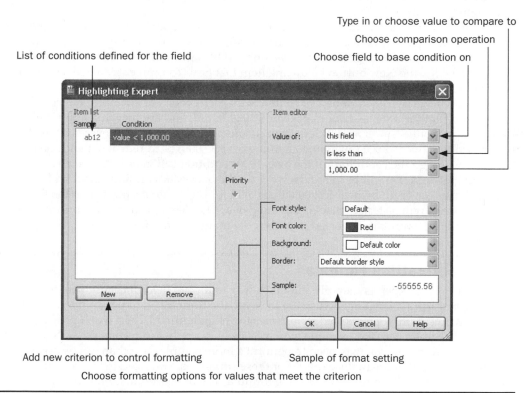

FIGURE 7-1 The Highlighting Expert

The idea of the Highlighting Expert is to allow conditional formatting of a field without intricate knowledge of the Crystal Reports formula language. By using the drop-down lists in the dialog box, you choose a series of conditions (by clicking the New button multiple times) and specific formatting for each condition. Begin by clicking the New button to add a new condition. Then, choose the field you want to use in a comparison test from the first drop-down list in the Value Of section of the dialog box (you may choose any field on the report for this test, not just the field you are highlighting). Then, choose a comparison operator in the second drop-down list. You'll find most of the standard comparison operators you've used in formulas or in the Select Expert, such as Less Than, Greater Than, Equal To, Not Equal To, and so forth. After making this choice, enter a constant value to compare to in the third drop-down list (you can also click the drop-down arrow and choose a value from the sample data in the list). Finally, choose any combination of font and background styles, colors, and border styles you want the field to display if the comparison is true.

For example, to format the sales figure to show up as white text on a red background if it falls below the preset sales figure of $1,000, choose "this field" in the first drop-down list, choose a comparison of Less Than, type **1000**, and then choose a Font Color of White and a Background of Red. You will see a sample in the Sample box in the lower right of the Highlighting Expert, as well as to the left of the now-created condition in the Item List box on the left. When you click OK, the field will show white text on a red background for any sales figures less than $1,000.

You may want to set up multiple conditions if you want more than one formatting option displayed. To expand on the previous example, suppose you want to show bonus sales (over $5,000) in blue, in addition to the existing red background for those that fall below $1,000. Just click the New button below the Item List box. You can enter a new condition and another set of formatting options. Both will apply to the field.

You may have two conditions that conflict with each other. For example, you could have a condition that formats field contents over $1,000 in red, and another that applies blue formatting for contents over $5,000. Since both conditions would satisfy the over-1000 condition, will everything over $1,000 (including anything over $5,000) be in red? It depends on the *priority* you assign the conditions. If the over-1000 condition is higher in the Item List box, everything over $1,000 will be in red. However, if the over-5000 condition is set higher, then it has priority—everything over $5,000 will be in blue. Then, the second item in the list (the over-1000 item) will be tested, placing anything over $1,000 in red. To change priority, click the condition you want to move and then click the up or down Priority arrow.

Conditional Formatting Formulas

The Highlighting Expert is a simple and quick way to format fields, because you don't have to know the formula language to use it. However, the trade-off is in flexibility. As your reports become more sophisticated, sometimes the Highlighting Expert won't provide all the flexibility you need. For example, you may need to apply formatting other than just color and borders. Or, you may need to perform a more complex test than can be done with the comparisons that are in the expert. For these situations, you need to use *conditional formatting formulas.* Conditional formatting formulas use the Formula Editor to create one or more conditions to determine how the object appears.

Absolute Versus Conditional Formatting

Before you learn how to set formatting conditionally, it's important to have a fundamental grasp of absolute formatting, which simply refers to applying normal formatting to objects with the Format Editor. This type of formatting, described earlier in the chapter, makes use of the Formatting toolbar or the Format Editor to apply the same formatting to all occurrences of the field. If you right-click an object and choose Format Field from the pop-up menu, the Format Editor will appear. You can then click the Font tab to change the font face, style, size, or color. If you change the color of the font to Red, *all* occurrences of the object on the report will be red. If you click the Border tab and select the Drop Shadow check box, *all* occurrences of the object will have a drop shadow. This is the process of absolute formatting.

The first rule to follow when it comes to conditional formatting is remembering that you must use the Format Editor. While you can perform absolute formatting with either the Formatting toolbar or the Format Editor, you can set up conditional formatting only with the Format Editor—the Formatting toolbar won't work.

As you approach conditional formatting, it's important to distinguish between two types of Format Editor formatting properties: *multiple-choice* properties and *on-off* properties. On the Font tab, Font and Color are good examples of multiple-choice properties. You can click a drop-down list and choose from any one of several fonts or colors. An example of an on-off property is Drop Shadow on the Border tab, which just has a check box: it can only be turned on or off. Whether a formatting property is multiple choice or on-off determines the type of formula you'll use to set it conditionally. Multiple-choice properties are conditionally formatted with If-Then-Else or Select Case formulas, while on-off properties are conditionally formatted with Boolean formulas.

TIP *You need to be familiar with the Crystal Reports formula language to use conditional formatting effectively. To refresh your memory, look for information on If-Then-Else and Boolean formulas, as well as Select Case in Chapter 5.*

To set formatting conditionally, click the Conditional Formula button that appears on the Format Editor next to the property that you want to format.

This will display the *Format Formula Editor* inside the Formula Workshop (essentially the same Formula Editor discussed in Chapter 5, but with a new title), shown in Figure 7-2. Notice that you can set conditional formatting with either Crystal or Basic syntax by making your choice from the Syntax drop-down list. If you are formatting a multiple-choice property, all the available options for the property appear at the top of the Function Tree box. If, for example, you are conditionally formatting the Color property, you'll see all the available colors listed. If you're formatting a border, you'll see the different available line styles. And, Crystal Reports XI will display available options as comments (lines preceded by two slashes in Crystal syntax or an apostrophe in Basic syntax) in many formatting formulas to help you choose proper values.

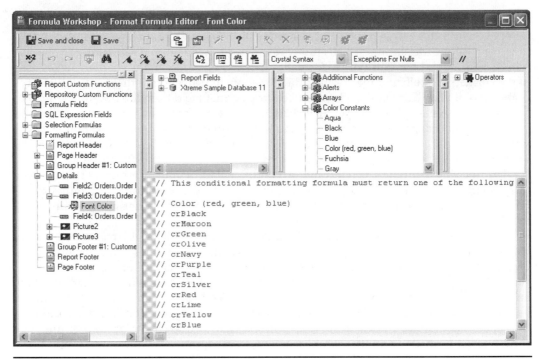

FIGURE 7-2 The Format Formula Editor

Use an If-Then-Else or Select Case formula to determine the formatting of the object. Your formula can be as simple or as complex as you need. For example, you may have a formula to set font color that is as simple as the following:

```
If {Customer.Last Year's Sales} > 5000 Then crBlue Else crBlack
```

or a formula to set a bottom border as complex as this:

```
If {Orders.Order Amount} > 5000 And {Orders.Ship Via} = "Fedex" Then
    crDoubleLine
Else
    If {Orders.Order Amount} > 1000 And {@Ship Days} < 3 Then
        crSingleLine
    Else
        crNoLine
```

TIP *In most cases, you may type formatting values, such as color or line type, into the formula directly. You may also double-click values shown in the Function Tree box of the Formula Editor. If you double-click, the prefix "cr" will appear in front of the formatting value in the formula. With few exceptions, either the value name by itself or the value name preceded by "cr" is acceptable.*

You can use any type of simple or compound If-Then-Else formula, or a Select Case formula, as long as the results of every Then, Else, or Case are one of the available formatting properties in the Function Tree box.

When you have finished with the formula, you can use the Check button to check for correct syntax of the formula, or save the formula and close the Format Formula Editor with the Save And Close button. The Format Editor will remain on the screen. Notice that the Conditional Formula button changes from blue to red, and the pencil character inside the button points at a different angle. This indicates that a conditional formula is set for this property.

To change the existing formula, click the Conditional Formula button again and change the formula that appears in the Format Formula Editor. To delete conditional formatting and return to absolute formatting (or no formatting at all), just highlight and delete the whole conditional formula. Then, click the Save And Close button. You'll notice that the Conditional Formula button has returned to a blue color with the pencil pointed in its original direction.

NOTE *While most conditional formulas must use a built-in formatting function for the Then, Else, or Case clauses of your formula, the Size property is a little different from other properties. In this case, the result of your conditional formula must be a number, which will indicate the font size to be used.*

If you're formatting an on-off property, the general procedure for conditional formatting is the same. But when you click the Conditional Formula button next to the property, you won't see any additional functions in the Function Tree box of the Format Formula Editor, because you generally won't use an If-Then-Else or Select Case formula to format this property. Because the property can have only one of two states, on or off, you must format it with a Boolean formula that can return only one of two results: true or false.

To add a drop shadow to Customer Name fields of customers who have last year's sales greater than $100,000, start by right-clicking the Customer Name field. Choose Format Field from the pop-up menu, choose the Border tab, and click the Conditional Formula button next to the Drop Shadow property. When the Format Formula Editor appears, type in the following Boolean formula:

```
{Customer.Last Year's Sales} > 100000
```

The Boolean formula will evaluate to only one of two states: true or false. If the formula returns true, the formatting property will be turned on and the field will have a drop shadow around it. If the formula returns false, the property will be turned off and the field won't have a drop shadow.

TIP *If you find If-Then-Else or Select-Case logic simpler to remember, you can use it with a Boolean conditional formula. Just make sure the result of every Then or Else, or every Case clause, is the word True or False. Conditions that return True will turn on the formatting property, while False conditions won't.*

You may be curious about how conditional formatting and absolute formatting interrelate. Consider the following scenario. You choose an absolute color of Red on the Font tab of the

Format Editor and click OK. Of course, every occurrence of the field will be red. You then return to the Format Editor and, without changing the absolute formatting, click the Conditional Formula button next to the Color property and add the following formula:

```
If {Customer.Last Year's Sales} > 50000 Then Blue
```

Note the missing Else clause. Remember that Crystal Reports does *not* require an Else clause in an If-Then-Else formula. In a regular formula, if the If test fails and there's no Else clause, the formula returns an empty string, zero, or other default value based on the data type of the formula. But what color will the font take on here if there's no Else clause and absolute formatting is set to red?

Contrary to what might seem logical, when the If test fails in this case, the font will show up in black type, despite the absolute formatting of red. This is by design—if conditional formatting is applied, absolute formatting is ignored. If the conditional formula fails (and there's no condition to "catch" the failure, like an Else clause), the Windows Control Panel default color or format for that type of object will be used. Be careful with this if you don't use Else clauses, especially if you're formatting background colors. A font color of black isn't necessarily problematic, but a background color of black will often cause your report to look like someone plastered electrical tape all over it!

The exception to this rule, and a way to combine absolute and conditional formatting, is to use the DefaultAttribute function, located in the Formatting Functions category of the Function Tree box in the Format Formula Editor. If you use this function with the Then, Else, or Case clause, the formula will use the setting from the absolute formatting property. Hence,

```
If {Customer.Last Year's Sales} > 50000 Then
    Blue
Else
    DefaultAttribute
```

will show sales figures over $50,000 in blue and others in red (provided that the absolute color chosen in the Format Editor is red). If you change the absolute color, then figures over $50,000 will still show up in blue, but the rest will take on whatever color you specified as absolute.

TIP *If you've applied conditional formatting to a field that's also being formatted with the Highlighting Expert, the Highlighting Expert will take precedence. Only if it doesn't change the formatting of a field will conditional formatting be visible.*

Creative Use of the Suppress Property

If you search through the Format Editor, you'll notice that virtually all formatting properties can be set conditionally. One of the most flexible is the Suppress property on the Common tab. You may consider that absolutely setting the Suppress property is of limited usefulness. (Why even bother putting the object on the report if you're just going to suppress it?) There are some good reasons for suppressing the object; for example, a formula that sets a variable to zero in a group header has to be physically placed in the header to work properly, but you don't want zeros showing up at the top of every group.

There are many more situations in which *conditionally suppressing* an object can be useful. Here are some examples, and the corresponding Boolean formulas you will apply to the Suppress property:

- **Placing the word "continued" in a repeated group header**   In Chapter 3, the repeated group header was introduced. If you select this option in the Group Options dialog box, a group header section will repeat at the top of a page if a group continues from the previous page. Indicating that this group continues from the previous page adds readability to your report. Place a text object that contains the word "continued," or something similar, in the group header close to the Group Name field. You must now suppress it if it is *not* in a repeated group header. Conditionally suppress the text object with the following Boolean formula:

```
Not InRepeatedGroupHeader
```

TIP   *When you conditionally suppress an object, you use a Boolean formula; when your formula returns true, the object will be suppressed. So, you may have to think "backward" when conditionally suppressing.*

- **Showing a bonus message only for certain records**   You may want a report to indicate that a certain record (for example, a certain order or a certain salesperson) has exceeded a predefined goal amount. Simply create a text object that displays something like "Congratulations! You've exceeded the sales goal." Again, you have to think about when you *don't* want the text object to appear, not when you do. Assuming a $10,000 sales goal, conditionally suppress the text object with the following Boolean formula:

```
{AccountRep.Sales} <= 10000
```

- **Showing a different heading on page 2 and later**   You may want to have a larger report title, perhaps including the company logo and a large font, on page 1 of the report. However, every other page needs to contain a smaller title without the logo, and perhaps include the word "continued." If you put the large title in the report header, you'll only see it at the beginning of the report. Putting the smaller title in the page header, on the other hand, will result in it showing up on every page, including page 1. Create the text object that contains the smaller title and place it in the page header along with any column headings or other objects you want to appear on every page, but conditionally suppress the text object containing the title with the following Boolean formula (PageNumber is a built-in function from the Print State category of the Formula Editor Function Tree box that returns the current page number):

```
PageNumber = 1
```

TIP   *You can also create string formulas that provide roughly the same functionality as these examples and place them in appropriate report sections. However, to minimize potential "formula clutter," it sometimes may be preferable to just create text objects and conditionally suppress them.*

Special Fonts, Graphics, and Line Drawing

As mentioned at the beginning of the chapter, Crystal Reports is a true Windows report writer. This means that it can use most of the fonts and graphical capabilities of Windows.

Using Special Fonts

Don't hesitate to use symbol fonts that are installed on your computer. In particular, the Symbol and Wingdings symbol fonts are included as part of Windows and should be available to most "target" systems that will be running your report.

CAUTION *Don't forget that any fonts you use when designing your reports must also be present on the machine that runs your reports if you expect the report to look identical on both machines. Using Times Roman, Arial, Symbol, and Wingdings fonts, at a minimum, is pretty safe, because they are installed by default on all Windows systems.*

Both Symbol and Wingdings fonts contain typographical symbols instead of letters and numbers. Although you type letters and numbers into a text object or formula formatted with a text font initially, you'll see them replaced with the symbol characters once you change the font from a text font to one of the symbol fonts. You'll need either a font table (typically available from Windows Control Panel) or a little extra time to experiment and figure out what symbols display when you type certain letters, numbers, or special characters.

Figure 7-3 shows a report using the Wingdings font. In this example, the following formula is being displayed on the report next to the order amount, formatted using the Wingdings font:

```
If {Orders.Order Amount} < 1000 Then
    "L"
Else
    If {Orders.Order Amount} In 1000 To 2500 Then
        "K"
    Else
        "J"
```

Using Bitmap Graphics

If you are planning to create reports that approach the quality of output from page publishing programs, you'll soon have a need to use *bitmap graphics* in your reports. Bitmap graphics are common graphics files most often associated with the Web (such as .JPG files) or Windows paint program files (such as .BMP and .PCX, and .WMF files). You may have a company logo that you want included on the title page of the report. Or, you may want to add a smaller graphical element, such as an icon, to another section of the report.

To insert a bitmap graphic, first make sure you are displaying the Design tab. Although it's possible to add a graphic while viewing the Preview tab, this is risky, because you won't always be sure which report section the graphic will end up in. Click the Insert Picture button on the Insert Tools toolbar or choose Insert | Picture from the pull-down menus. A familiar File Open dialog box will appear, asking you to choose a bitmap format file. Navigate to the necessary drive and folder, and the dialog box will show any files at that location that can be added to the report. Choose the correct file and click OK.

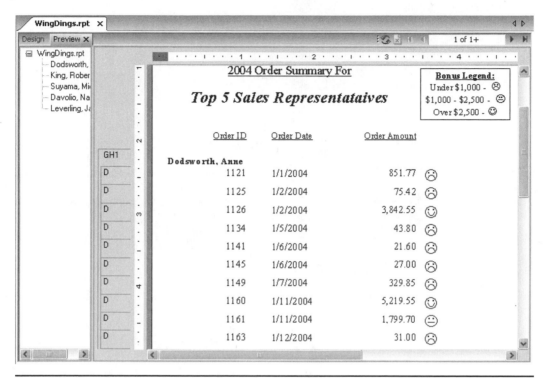

FIGURE 7-3 Report using symbols as well as text

An outline will appear alongside your mouse cursor. Drag the outline to the section of the report where you want the graphic to be placed, and click the left mouse button to drop it there. If the graphic happens to cover more than one report section, it will be dropped in the section where the upper-left corner of the outline is when the mouse is clicked. Once you drop the graphic, you'll see it appear in the Design tab.

You have complete control over how the graphic is sized and cropped. You can simply drag the graphic to a new location on the report, or resize it using the sizing handles on the sides and corners. You can also position the graphic (or any other object on the report, for that matter) with the Object Size and Position dialog box. Select the object that you want to position, right-click, and choose Size and Position from the pop-up menu. You can also choose Format | Size and Position from the pull-down menus.

To format the graphic more precisely, you can use the Format Editor. Make sure the graphic is still selected. Then, click the Format button in the Expert Tools toolbar, right-click the graphic, and choose Format Graphic from the pop-up menu; or choose Format | Format Graphic from the pull-down menus. The Picture tab allows you to specify exact cropping and scaling specifications.

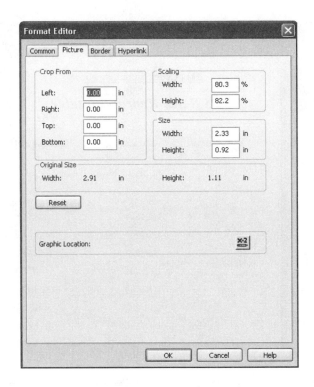

TIP *Only common bitmap graphic formats are supported in Crystal Reports. It will not recognize specialized formats, such as Adobe Photoshop, or vector formats (other than Windows Metafile), such as those from CorelDRAW or Adobe Illustrator. If you wish to use these graphics in a report, you need to convert them to common bitmap formats before adding them to your report. And if you wish to include graphics from web pages, you must use .JPG format—Crystal Reports won't recognize .GIF files.*

Although using symbol fonts, such as Wingdings, is very powerful, you are limited to what is included in the font itself. Also, the symbols are generally simple two-dimensional images and can be displayed only in a single color. Wouldn't it be nice if you could use smaller bitmap files, such as icon-like graphics that look more three-dimensional and include several colors, on your report?

Because you can suppress bitmap files conditionally, just like other objects, you have real power and flexibility in creating visually appealing and interesting reports using bitmap graphics. Figure 7-4 shows a report with unique icons indicating the status of an order. Orders that have been shipped (or are "closed") have a closed file folder next to them. Open orders (not shipped) have an open file folder next to them.

This report uses a technique that could be called *mutually exclusive suppression*. There are two different bitmap files on the report: an open-file bitmap and a closed-file bitmap. They are placed right on top of each other in the details section. They are conditionally suppressed in such a way that only one will ever be displayed at a time. In this case, they are suppressed using the Shipped field (a Boolean field that returns true or false) from the XTRME Sample Database Orders table.

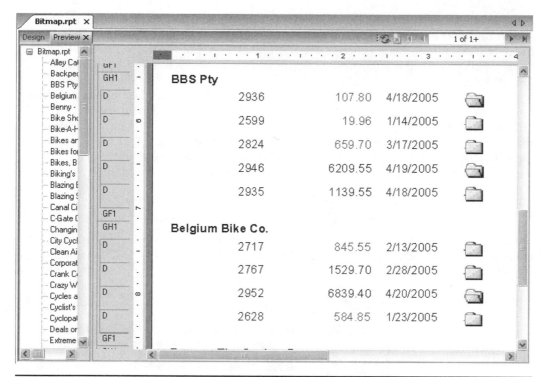

FIGURE 7-4   Using bitmap files formatted conditionally

The open-file bitmap is conditionally suppressed using this formula:

{Orders.Shipped}

while the closed-file bitmap is conditionally suppressed using this formula:

Not {Orders.Shipped}

Because of this, only one bitmap will ever be visible at a time.

The success of this technique depends on Crystal Reports allowing multiple objects to be placed right on top of each other. You have the ability to do this with any text or graphic object whenever and wherever you choose. Just make sure you implement some technique similar to this to prevent them from splattering all over each other. You can also use the Move to Back, Move Backward, Move Forward, and Move to Front options from the Format pull-down menu or from the pop-up menu that appears when you right-click an object. These options determine which objects have "priority" when they are placed on top of each other.

Crystal Reports XI Dynamic Graphic Locations

While Crystal Reports version 10 and earlier allows you to place bitmap images on the report using techniques described earlier in this chapter, Crystal Reports XI adds additional flexibility to change the actual source file of the bitmap image dynamically as the report runs. This *dynamic graphic location* capability allows you to use a conditional formula to specify an external graphic image filename and location "on the fly." Previous to version XI, the only way to have images change dynamically as the report processed to was to use image fields contained in a database table (sometimes known as Binary Large Object, or "BLOB," fields).

To set the location of a graphic file dynamically, click the Graphic Location conditional formula button on the Picture tab of the Format Editor. The Formula Workshop/Formula Editor will appear. Create a formula using any available formula field, function, or operator that returns a string value equating to the location and filename of an image file. For example, the following formula uses a database field to derive the filename of an external .JPG file containing a unique image for each DVD in a DVD collection database record:

```
"C:\Program Files\InterVocative Software\DVD Profiler\Images\"
& {Collection.ID} & "f.jpg"
```

This formula concatenates a drive and pathname to a number taken from the database to the letter "f", followed by the ".jpg" extension. The result is a unique JPEG filename for each record in the database.

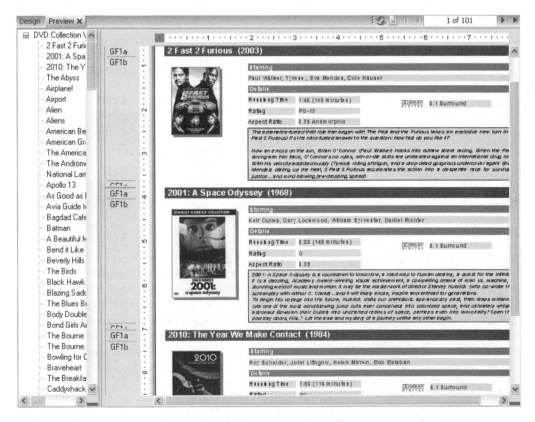

Remember to consider how a "target" computer that runs your report will find images you specify in dynamic graphic location formulas. For example, if the images are stored on a network drive mapped to drive H on your computer, they may not be found when another computer on the network runs the report if the same drive H mapping isn't defined. To reduce this probability, you may choose to use Universal Naming Convention (UNC) path- and filenames, such as:

```
"\\x23\c\Program Files\InterVocative Software\DVD Profiler\Images\"
& {Collection.ID} & "f.jpg"
```

Or, if an image is stored on a web server or Internet web site, you may use a web URL to specify the graphic name:

```
"http://www.ablazegroup.com/DVDData/Images/"
& {Collection.ID} & "f.jpg"
```

Line and Box Drawing

You can use the Border tab on the Format Editor to control line appearance on all four sides of individual objects. While this lets the individual objects stand out by having lines or boxes appear around them, you may want more flexibility to have groups of objects highlighted with boxes or to have lines stretch partially or completely across sections.

Crystal Reports lets you use line and box drawing tools to create these boxes and lines. To create a line or box, ensure that you have the Design tab chosen. Inserting lines or boxes in the Preview tab may give you undesirable results if you don't put them in the right section.

To add a line or box to your report, perform these steps:

1. Click the Insert Line or Insert Box button in the Insert Tools toolbar. You can also choose Insert | Line or Insert | Box from the pull-down menus.

2. When you make either of these choices, your mouse cursor changes to a pencil. Point the pencil to where you want to begin the line or box and hold down the left mouse button.

3. Drag the line or box to its ending position and release the button. Notice that you can draw only perfectly vertical or horizontal lines—diagonal lines can't be drawn.

The line or box will appear on the report, complete with sizing handles. You can now drag or resize the line or box just like any other object. You may also format the line or box with the Format Editor (using options from the Format pull-down menu, or by right-clicking the line or box and choosing Format from the pop-up menu). You can choose the color, size, and style of the line or box, along with other options (Crystal Reports allows you to create rounded boxes, for example). Figure 7-5 shows a report that uses a horizontal line to delineate group footers, and places a filled, rounded box around report totals.

TIP *You can draw lines and boxes that traverse multiple report sections. This is handy if you want to have a single box enclose a column starting in the page header and ending in the page footer, including all the sections in between. However, this can sometimes result in odd behavior if, for example, you start a line in the page header but end it in the details section or a group footer. If your lines or boxes traverse sections, make sure you preview the report to check that you get the desired results.*

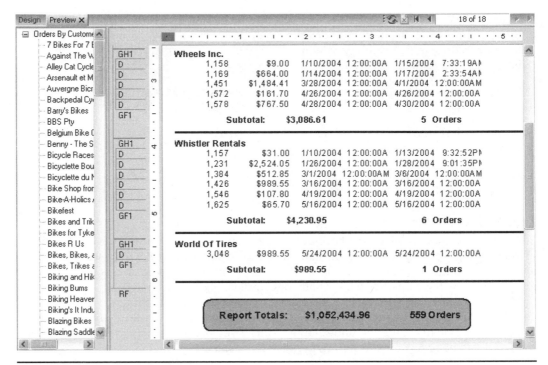

Figure 7-5 Line and box drawing

Text and Paragraph Formatting

Crystal Reports includes various text formatting features that enhance reporting capabilities. Some are designed for use with foreign-language versions of the report writer (such as Japanese), while others simply provide enhanced functionality for more reporting situations.

A subtle feature that may not be immediately noticeable is *fractional point sizes* for fonts. If you use the Point Size drop-down list either in the Format toolbar or from the Font tab of the Format Editor, you'll see that only whole-number point-size values are available. However, if you click inside the drop-down list, you can then type values directly into the drop-down list, rather than choosing predefined numbers. If you want to use a 10.5 point size instead of a whole number, simply type **10.5** and press ENTER. You may type in sizes in ½-point increments (10.5 will work, but 10.25 will round to 10.5).

You'll also notice a *Text Rotation* option on the Format Editor Common tab. This allows you to rotate objects based on TrueType or built-in printer fonts to 90 degrees (sideways from bottom to top) or 270 degrees (sideways from top to bottom). Just choose the desired rotation from the drop-down list. You'll probably need to adjust the height and width of the now-rotated text to properly show all the material in the object.

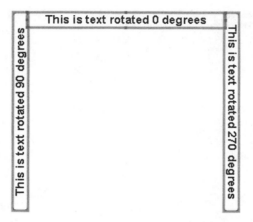

TIP *You can make innovative use of text rotation by using multiple report sections and the Underlay section formatting option, described in Chapter 8. For example, by placing a rotated text object in Page Header b (which is formatted with the Underlay option), you can have vertical text flow down alongside the rest of your report on every page. This technique can be helpful for replicating special forms, for example.*

Format Editor Paragraph Formatting Tab

If you format a string or memo database field or a text object, Crystal Reports presents an additional *Paragraph* tab on the Formula Editor, as shown in Figure 7-6. Use these options to determine how multiple lines of text or data will be formatted:

- **Indentation—First Line**   Indicates the amount of space the first line in each paragraph will be indented. The first line of the text or any line after a carriage return is considered the first line of a paragraph.

- **Indentation—Left**   Indicates the amount of space that the entire field will be indented from the left side of the object.

- **Indentation—Right**   Indicates the amount of space that the entire field will be indented from the right side of the object.

- **Spacing—Line Spacing**   Adds vertical blank space between each line in the paragraph. Choose the Multiple option to choose a multiple of the normal spacing (for example, two times normal spacing). Choose the Exact option to choose a specific point size for line spacing (for example, 5 points).

- **Spacing—Of *x* Times Normal**   Specifies the associated number for the Multiple or Exact Line Spacing option.

- **Reading Order**   Specifies whether the text in the object that's being formatted will be read from left to right, or right to left. This option generally applies to non-English versions of Crystal Reports, and while it doesn't reverse the display of characters that make up a field, it does rearrange placement of punctuation marks that appear at the end of fields.

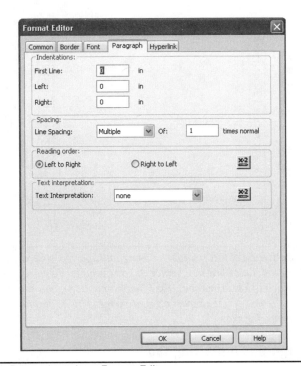

Paragraph Formatting tab on Format Editor

Using HTML and RTF Text Interpretation

Figure 7-6 also shows the *Text Interpretation* drop-down list on the Paragraph Formatting tab
(you'll see this option only with string or memo database fields—not with text objects).

Available options in this drop-down list are None (the default), HTML Text (Hypertext
Markup Language), and RTF Text (Rich Text Format). HTML text is often associated with
the Web—web pages are encoded in HTML. RTF is a standard text format that is
interchangeable between most popular word processors and page publishing programs.

If you leave the default Text Interpretation option of None chosen, Crystal Reports
simply displays the value from the database as it actually appears in the database. If the
field contains special formatting codes, they'll just appear on the report directly. If your
database string or memo fields contain text with special HTML or RTF formatting codes to
describe fonts, colors, and special formatting, choose the appropriate HTML or RTF Text
Interpretation option. Crystal Reports will convert these formatting codes into actual
typeface, point size, color, and formatting options. Notice how a Text Interpretation setting
of None (as opposed to a setting of HTML) displays a database field that's encoded using
the Hypertext Markup Language.

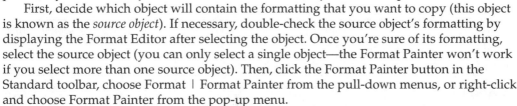

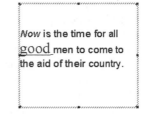

Tip *Not all HTML tags and attributes are supported. For a list of specific HTML tags that Crystal Reports interprets, search online help for "Paragraph Formatting tab."*

The Crystal Reports Format Painter

The *Format Painter,* which provides capabilities like those of similarly named features in standard office suites, allows you to copy a large number of formatting properties from one previously formatted object to one or more additional objects with simple mouse clicks.

First, decide which object will contain the formatting that you want to copy (this object is known as the *source object*). If necessary, double-check the source object's formatting by displaying the Format Editor after selecting the object. Once you're sure of its formatting, select the source object (you can only select a single object—the Format Painter won't work if you select more than one source object). Then, click the Format Painter button in the Standard toolbar, choose Format | Format Painter from the pull-down menus, or right-click and choose Format Painter from the pop-up menu.

The mouse cursor will change to the Format Painter paintbrush. Now, move the mouse cursor to the report object (known as the *target object*) you want to copy the source formatting to. If you move the mouse cursor over an object that the Format Painter won't work with, a "no-drop" cursor (a circle with a line through it) will appear. For example, you won't be able to copy formatting from a database field to a bitmap image. Objects that can accept Format Painter formatting will show the paintbrush cursor. Click on the target object to apply the copied formatting. If you want to copy Format Painter formatting to *more* than one object, make sure to hold down the ALT key while clicking on object. The paintbrush icon will continue to appear as you click on subsequent objects.

Data types play a significant role in Format Painter behavior. If you've set a combination of formatting properties for the source object that both are and are not dependent upon data type (for example, font color is not dependent upon data type, but number of decimal places is), some of the properties will not "stick" to the target object. Continuing with the previous example, using a numeric field that contains a red font color and three decimal places will only result in the red font color sticking on a non-numeric field—the three decimal place formatting will stick only when the target object is a numeric or currency field.

Conditional formatting is also a consideration when using the Format Painter. First and foremost, any conditional formatting applied with the Highlighting Expert (discussed earlier in the chapter) *will not* be copied to target objects by the Format Painter. However, conditional formatting applied with formulas set with Format Editor conditional formatting buttons will be copied. Again, only those conditional formulas that are applicable to the target data type will be copied—a conditional formula setting the number of decimal places won't be copied to a non-numeric field, while a conditional formula setting font size will.

While data types play a role in determining what will be copied to target objects, the *type* of report object (database field, text object, bitmap image, cross-tab, and so forth) determines whether or not the Format Painter will even work. If you attempt to copy formatting with the Format Painter, you may find the no-drop cursor (circle with line) appearing more often than you might expect. This is often because you are attempting to copy formatting to a dissimilar type of report object.

For example, if you click a database field prior to clicking the Format Painter toolbar button, you'll encounter a no-drop cursor if you hover the mouse over a text object, bitmap field, or other dissimilar report object. Sometimes, this behavior will be completely understandable (you can't change the font color of a bitmap). In other cases, you may wish to paste some common formatting properties (font color, size, or face) onto the text object target from the source database field. Because the objects are dissimilar, the Format Painter won't work. This is a limitation of Crystal Reports.

TIP *For a complete object type–by–object type description of Format Painter behavior, search online help for "Format Painter, using."*

Report Alerts

In addition to some of the conditional reporting features discussed elsewhere in this chapter, Crystal Reports allows you to highlight records that meet a requirement using Report Alerts. *Report Alerts* enable you to set up a condition that Crystal Reports checks for every time you refresh the report (by clicking the Refresh button in the Navigation Tools toolbar or next to page navigation buttons), by selecting Report | Refresh Report Data from the pull-down menus, or by pressing the F5 key). Report Alerts can also be used to highlight desired conditions or send an e-mail when reports are scheduled with the BusinessObjects Enterprise or Crystal Reports Server web-based reporting systems (covered in Part II of this book).

While you've always been able to conditionally format report sections and objects in terms of a condition, you might not have always known which customers, sales reps, months, and so forth had "triggered" this condition without going through the report page by page looking for the conditionally formatted sections. Now when a report with Report Alerts defined runs, a separate dialog box will pop up if any of the conditions on the report have been met. You can then click a button on the dialog box to display a separate tab (similar to a drill-down tab) that shows only report records that meet the alert condition.

To work with Report Alerts, choose Report | Alerts | Create or Modify Alerts from the pull-down menus. The Create Alerts dialog box will appear, as shown in Figure 7-7. If any existing alerts have already been created in the report, they'll appear inside this dialog box. If you wish to modify any existing alert, select it in the dialog box and click the Edit button. To delete an existing alert, select it and click the Delete button. If there are no alerts in the report yet, the dialog box will be empty.

FIGURE 7-7   The Create Alerts dialog box

To create a new alert, click the New button. The Create Alert dialog box will appear, as shown in Figure 7-8. At minimum, you must specify the name of the Report Alert in the Name text box, and the condition that will trigger the alert by clicking the Condition button. You may optionally type a message that will appear when the alert is triggered in the Message text box, or customize the message with a string formula you create by clicking the conditional formula button. Clicking the Condition button will display the Formula Editor, where you enter a Boolean formula that determines when the alert will be triggered (see Chapter 5 for information on Boolean formulas). If you wish to temporarily disable the alert without deleting it entirely, deselect the Enabled check box.

For example, you may wish to create a simple report showing orders that were placed. If the order amount exceeds a certain level ($5,000, for example), you wish to trigger a report alert. Create the report as you usually would and then create a new Report Alert. Give the alert a name of your choosing (perhaps "Order Exceeds 5,000"), type any message you want

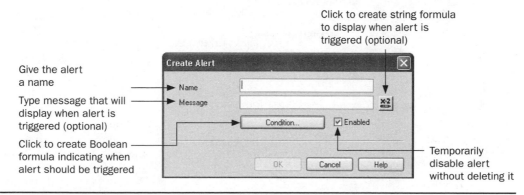

FIGURE 7-8   The Create Alert dialog box

to appear when the alert is triggered, and then click the Condition button. Enter a Boolean formula to indicate what records should trigger the alert, such as

```
{Orders.Order Amount} > 5000
```

Once you've saved the alert, simply refresh the report. If any order amounts in the report exceed $5,000, you'll receive an alert dialog box indicating that the alert has been triggered.

To see a separate tab showing all report records with orders that exceed $5,000, just click the View Records button. A separate tab (similar to a drill-down tab, discussed in Chapters 3 and 8) will appear showing just the relevant records.

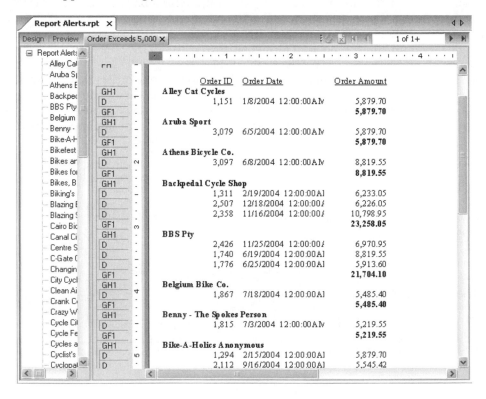

You don't have to just base Report Alerts on database fields, as in the previous example. You can also base report alerts on summaries or subtotals in group footers (although you can't base Report Alerts on WhilePrintingRecords or "second pass" formulas). For example, you may prefer to create a parameter field (discussed in Chapter 13) to prompt the user for a customer total threshold. You can then create a Report Alert that will be triggered if an order subtotal in a customer name group footer exceeds the value supplied by the parameter field. In this situation, the Boolean formula used to trigger the alert will look something like this:

```
Sum ({Orders.Order Amount}, {Customer.Customer Name}) >
{?Report Alert Threshold}
```

Basing Report Formulas or Conditional Formatting on Report Alerts

While it's helpful to see a dialog box showing that a Report Alert has been triggered, and see a separate tab of report items that triggered the alert, you may appreciate the additional power afforded to your formulas by Report Alerts as well. Three functions exist in the formula language in Crystal Reports to support alerts: *IsAlertEnabled, IsAlertTriggered,* and *AlertMessage.* Each of these new functions takes one argument, the name of a previously created report alert:

- **IsAlertEnabled**   Returns a true or false value, depending on the state of the Enabled check box in the Create Alert dialog box (shown in Figure 7-8, earlier in the chapter). If the alert is enabled, then this function will return true. Otherwise, it will return false.

- **IsAlertTriggered**   Returns a true or false value, depending on whether the record the formula is evaluating for triggers the alert or not. For example, if you create a formula containing the IsAlertTriggered("Order Exceeds 5,000") function, the function will return true for records with order amounts greater than $5,000, and false for records with order amounts equal to or less than $5,000.

- **AlertMessage**   Returns the message specified for the Report Alert. This is either the "hard-coded" message that was typed into the Message text box when the alert was created, or the results of the message string formula that was created with the alert.

For the previously discussed customer subtotal example, you may wish to create a formula that displays a message in group footers that trigger the alert. The formula might look similar to this:

```
If IsAlertTriggered ("Beat 2004 Goal") Then
    GroupName ({Customer.Customer Name}) & " beat the 2004 goal"
```

You may also wish to highlight the entire group footer with a different background color if the group triggered a Report Alert. You can use these new formula functions in conditional formatting formulas, as well as report formulas. For example, you could conditionally set the background color of the Customer Name Group Footer to aqua by using the Section Expert. The conditional formula would be similar to this:

```
If IsAlertTriggered ("Beat 2004 Goal") Then
    crAqua
Else
    crNoColor
```

NOTE *For complete information on formatting sections and the Section Expert, refer to Chapter 8.*

Crystal Reports Templates

You may have created a report that contains a large amount of custom formatting that you'd like to apply to other reports all at once. You may user Report Templates for this purpose. *Report Templates* are just existing .RPT files that are used to format other reports. One of the first places you may notice use of report templates is on the last screen of report wizards that you can use when first creating a new report.

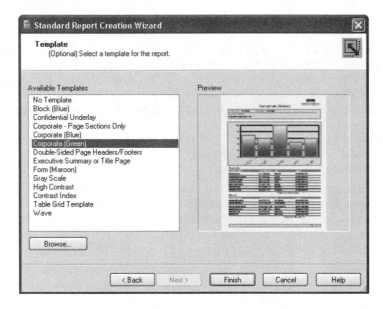

To apply a template in a report wizard, simply select one of the predefined templates in the Available Templates list. When you choose one of the templates in the list, a thumbnail view of the template is shown in the Preview section of the report wizard. You may also choose another .RPT file to use as a template by clicking the Browse button. This will launch a standard open file dialog box, where you can navigate to the existing .RPT file you wish to use as a template.

Once you've chosen the report, it will be added to the template list, where you may select it to control the formatting of the new report. If the report you added has a value in the File | Summary Info Title field, it will appear as the name of the template. And if the Save Preview Picture check box is checked in the File | Summary Info dialog box of the report you just added, the preview of the report will appear in the Preview area of the report wizard.

NOTE *Any .RPT files you add to the template list won't remain in the list the next time you use the report wizards. You'll need to navigate to the report with the Browse button again if you want to use it as a template.*

The Template Expert

If you want to apply a template to a report you've already created (either with a report wizard or without), you can use the Template Expert to apply a template or undo the previous application of a template. To display the Template Expert, either click the Template Expert toolbar button in the Expert Tools toolbar or choose Report | Template Expert from the pull-down menus. The Template Expert will appear, as shown in Figure 7-9.

The Template Expert looks very similar to the Template section of the report wizards, with a few additional features. As with the report wizards, you can pick a template from the list to add to your current report. When you select a template in the list, a preview of the template will appear in the Preview area of the Template Expert. And you may also click the Browse button to add an existing .RPT file to the template list to use to reformat the current report.

However, the Template Expert includes a few more features that don't apply to the report wizards. In particular, if you've already applied a template and aren't satisfied with its results (and this is a real possibility—templates can dramatically change the formatting of your report), you can undo the template application by clicking the Undo the Current Template radio button in the Template Expert. This is the only way to undo a template application—the Undo feature on the Edit menu or the Undo toolbar button won't undo a template application. If you've already undone a template and wish to redo it, you may either choose it in the template list again or click the Re-Apply the Last Template radio button.

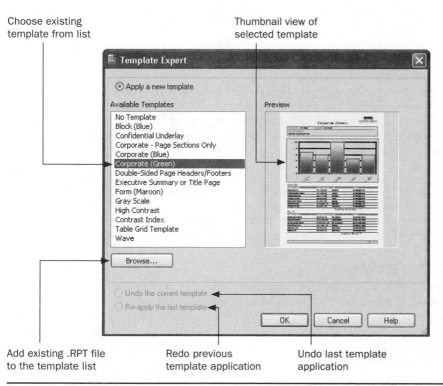

FIGURE 7-9   The Template Expert

It's important to remember that the Undo and Redo features will be available only during the current Crystal Reports session. If you apply a template, save the report, and then exit Crystal Reports, you'll be stuck with the template's formatting when you next reopen the report.

TIP The predefined templates in the Template Expert are supplied by existing .RPT files. By default, Crystal Reports looks in \Program Files\Business Objects\Crystal Reports 11\Templates\ <language> for template reports. If you wish to change the location that Crystal Reports uses to populate the Template Expert, you must change the Registry key HKEY_LOCAL_MACHINE/ Software/Business Objects/Suite 11.0/Crystal Reports/Templates/TemplatePath. Ensure you are familiar with manipulating Registry settings before attempting this change.

Once you've chosen a template to apply to your current report, the report's formatting will change, often drastically. How Crystal Reports applies all the individual object and section reporting of the source template to your current report is not necessarily predictable—you'll want to experiment with several templates to see how they affect formatting. However, as a general rule, Crystal Reports will compare report objects and report sections between the template and the current report, applying many of the formatting properties of both report sections and individual objects in the template to the current report. If, for example, the template report contains two details sections (Details a and Details b) and the current report contains only a single detail section, the current report will have an additional details section added when the template is applied. If you have a chart in the template but not in your current report, a chart will be added when the template is applied. And if your template contains ten details section fields formatted with different colors, you can generally expect the template's formatting to be applied to the first ten objects in the details section of your current report.

If you plan on using a template, you probably won't want to do a great deal of formatting to your original report before you apply the template—your pre-template formatting will be discarded. If you are generally pleased with a report's formatting, you would be well advised to save the report before applying templates. While the Undo capability exists in the Template Expert, you'll want to play it safe in case you may not want to permanently accept a template's formatting changes.

TIP You are not limited to applying one template to a report, but may apply as many as you'd like by following the previous steps more than once. Depending on which templates you apply, these multiple template applications will "blend" together to form a report that combines the formatting options from all templates applied. In other cases, one template will completely replace another.

Creating Your Own Templates

As was mentioned previously, templates are merely other Crystal Report .RPT files whose formatting is copied to the current report. While the few sample templates that are already provided by Business Objects are acceptable for exploring the capabilities of adding templates, you'll probably want to develop a set of templates that conform to your company's "look and feel," perhaps including a company logo, preferred font face and size, and various object and section formatting standards that you wish to commonly apply to reports.

You may want to begin by just picking some already-created "standard" reports that approximate the look and feel you desire. You can then experiment with using them as templates. You may wish to save them in a temporary folder and modify the original reports to make better use of them as templates. Once you've modified the existing "template" reports to meet your needs, you may add an appropriate name to the Title field in the File | Summary Info dialog box, as well as checking the Save Preview Picture check box in the same dialog box. Then, preview the report (this is required to generate the preview picture) and save the report into the template directory. That report will now appear as a template in the Template Expert and Report Wizard Template section.

You may also wish to create a new report from scratch to act as a template. Crystal Reports includes a special type of field known as the template field to help in this endeavor. A *template field* is a special kind of field you can add to a report to act as a placeholder for a report object when applying the template to the main report. A template field doesn't initially display any data—it just contains formatting information that is carried over when the template is applied to the main report. To insert a template field, choose Insert | Template Field Object from the pull-down menus. An object outline will be placed on your mouse cursor. Drag the object to its desired location on the report and click to drop it. The template field will be added to the report.

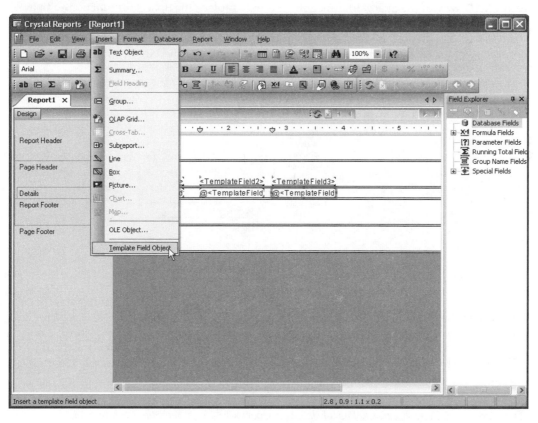

You now select the template field and format it with any of the methods discussed earlier in this chapter. However, you'll notice one unique difference between template fields and regular database fields when you format them with the Format Editor: tabs for every possible data type will appear in the Format Editor when formatting a template field. This additional template field flexibility lets you set up formatting for various target report fields that you may use with this template report. For example, if you're not sure whether the first field in the details section of the target report will be a string, number, or date, you can use the Paragraph tab, the Number tab, and the Date and Time tab to set formatting for the template field. When the template field is used to apply formatting in the target report, the formatting you've chosen in the appropriate tab will filter to the target fields.

When using template fields in a template report, it may be difficult to see what the actual target report formatting may look like. This is because template fields, by default, aren't connected to any database fields. As such, they won't show any data if you try to view your template report in the Preview tab. However, you can set template fields to display a value in the Preview tab by using the Formula Workshop. Notice that when you add a template field to the report, a corresponding formula is added to the Field Explorer. If you edit the template field formulas (editing formulas is discussed in detail in Chapter 5), you can change the formula to return something other than ten spaces, which are initially returned by the formula by way of the Space(10) function. You may replace the Space(10) function with a database field from the Field tree, or another function from the Function tree that will return data. When you display the template report in the Preview tab, you'll now be able to more accurately determine how the resultant formatting will be applied in the target report.

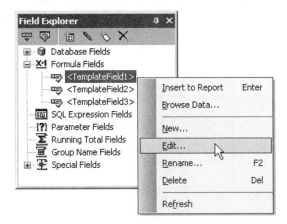

Once you've used template fields to create the template report, supply a name for the template in the Title field of File | Summary Info. You may also wish to check Save Preview Picture, preview the template report (which is required to save the preview picture), and then save the template report to the folder where other template reports are located. You will then see the new template appear the next time you need to apply a template with the Template Expert or in the report wizards.

TIP *A detailed chart discussing how objects and report sections in templates interact with the main report can be found in Crystal Reports online help. Search help for "templates, considerations."*

Using Sections and Areas

In previous chapters, you learned how to change the appearance of individual objects on the report, such as by changing the color of a field or adding a drop shadow to a text object. However, you also have the ability to format *entire sections* of your report. Just a few of the section formatting options available to you are to

- Add a gray background to every other details section
- Format a group header so that every group starts anew on its own page
- Create multiple columns in your details section for labels
- Add a light-colored watermark graphic in its own page header section that appears behind the rest of your report

Formatting Sections with the Section Expert

There are several ways to change the appearance of an entire report section. You'll often just want to change the *size* of a section. Consider this "single-spaced" report:

Order ID	Order Amount	Order Date	Ship Date
1	$41.90	12/2/2003 12:00:00AM	12/10/2003 5:32:23PM
1,002	$5,060.28	12/2/2003 12:00:00AM	12/2/2003 6:45:32AM
1,003	$186.87	12/2/2003 12:00:00AM	12/5/2003 12:10:12AM
1,004	$823.05	12/2/2003 12:00:00AM	12/2/2003 3:24:54PM
1,005	$29.00	12/3/2003 12:00:00AM	12/3/2003 1:54:34AM
1,006	$64.90	12/3/2003 12:00:00AM	12/5/2003 7:58:01PM
1,007	$49.50	12/3/2003 12:00:00AM	12/3/2003 9:05:46AM
1,008	$2,214.94	12/3/2003 12:00:00AM	12/7/2003 10:10:12PM
1,009	$29.00	12/3/2003 12:00:00AM	12/10/2003 6:47:47AM
1,010	$14,872.30	12/3/2003 12:00:00AM	12/3/2003 11:11:11PM
1,011	$29.00	12/3/2003 12:00:00AM	12/3/2003 5:00:00AM
1,012	$10,259.10	12/3/2003 12:00:00AM	12/5/2003 4:59:00PM
1,013	$1,142.13	12/3/2003 12:00:00AM	12/8/2003 3:56:56PM
1,014	$29.00	12/4/2003 12:00:00AM	12/4/2003 4:52:12AM
1,015	$43.50	12/4/2003 12:00:00AM	12/7/2003 1:00:00AM
1,016	$563.70	12/4/2003 12:00:00AM	12/6/2003 3:00:00PM
1,017	$72.00	12/5/2003 12:00:00AM	12/5/2003 2:30:00AM
1,018	$115.50	12/5/2003 12:00:00AM	12/6/2003 2:22:39PM
1,019	$43.50	12/5/2003 12:00:00AM	12/7/2003 12:01:00PM
1,020	$67.80	12/5/2003 12:00:00AM	12/10/2003 4:00:00PM
1,021	$5,237.55	12/6/2003 12:00:00AM	12/12/2003 7:30:23AM
1,022	$2,792.86	12/7/2003 12:00:00AM	12/7/2003 5:40:35AM
1,023	$890.61	12/7/2003 12:00:00AM	12/8/2003 7:00:00PM
1,024	$33.00	12/7/2003 12:00:00AM	12/7/2003 8:32:37AM
1,025	$8,819.55	12/7/2003 12:00:00AM	12/8/2003 11:23:43AM
1,026	$33.00	12/7/2003 12:00:00AM	12/11/2003 4:57:02PM

Design Preview ✕

Report1

1 of 1+

Notice the details sections appearing very close to each other. Maybe you'll just want to "double-space" the report. However, there is no double-space, space-and-a-half, or similar function available in Crystal Reports. Instead, you choose how tall you want a section to be by using one of several techniques.

The simplest technique is simply to drag the bottom border of a section down to make the section taller. Point to the line at the bottom of the section you want to resize—the mouse cursor will turn into two lines with up and down arrows. This section-sizing cursor indicates that you can drag the section border down to make a section taller, or drag the border up to make the section shorter.

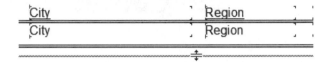

When you simply make the details section taller, the white space that's exposed becomes the "double-space" when you re-preview the report, as shown here:

Although this is the most straightforward way to resize a section, you have other options available. By right-clicking in the gray section name on the left side of the Design tab, you display the section pop-up menu. For example, right-clicking the Details section brings up this menu.

This pop-up menu contains four additional features for resizing sections, as listed here:

Insert Line	Adds an additional horizontal guideline to the section ruler on the left side of the section. If the section isn't tall enough to show the additional guideline, the section grows taller.
Delete Last Line	Removes the bottom guideline in the section and shrinks the size of the section proportionally. If you choose this option and a report object is attached to the guideline that you would remove, you'll receive an error message.
Arrange Lines	Rearranges any horizontal guidelines in an even fashion. If there aren't enough horizontal guidelines to fill the section, additional guidelines will be added.
Fit Section	Automatically shrinks the size of the section to the bottommost object in the section. If there are any horizontal guidelines below the bottom object, they are removed before the section is resized.

Although you may sometimes use the Insert Line, Delete Last Line, or Arrange Lines option from the section pop-up menu, you'll most likely find Fit Section the only useful option. It's particularly useful if the section is very tall (perhaps you've deleted a large map, chart, or picture from the section and all the white space it took up is still there), and you want to shrink it without having to scroll down to find the bottom section border.

The Section Expert

Whereas the Format Editor is used to format individual objects, you use the *Section Expert*, shown in Figure 8-1, to format entire sections of your report. The Section Expert has a large number of options for formatting individual report sections. Using these options provides a high level of flexibility for your reports.

The Section Expert can be displayed in several ways. You can click the Section Expert button on the Standard toolbar, choose Report | Section Expert from the pull-down menus, or right-click in the gray area of the section you wish to format and choose Section Expert from the pop-up menu. If you choose the toolbar button or menu option, the first section will be highlighted in the Section Expert. If you right-click in the gray area of a section and use the pop-up menu, that particular section will be highlighted.

By selecting different sections of the report in the Section Expert, you can view and set formatting properties for the section. Note that the properties will vary slightly, some new properties may appear, and some won't be available, depending on which section you select. For example, the New Page Before property doesn't make much sense for a page header section, so it will be grayed out when a page header is selected. And if you select the Page Footer section, an additional "Reserve Minimum Page Footer" option will appear. Table 8-1 explains the different section formatting properties available in the Section Expert's Common tab.

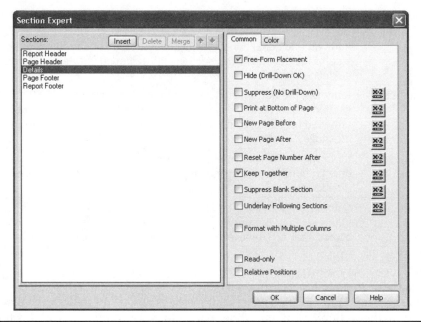

FIGURE 8-1   The Section Expert

CAUTION *Don't confuse the Keep Together section property and the Keep Group Together group property on the Options tab of the Change Group dialog box. Keep Together in the Section Expert just prevents the particular section from splitting over two pages; whereas Keep Group Together will attempt to keep the group header, all details sections, and the group footer for the same group from printing across multiple pages.*

You'll also notice Conditional Formula buttons for many properties on the Common tab. These properties can be set conditionally with a Boolean formula, if necessary. There are many uses for both absolute and conditional properties on the Common tab. Here are some common examples.

Starting a Group on Its Own Page

Checking New Page Before in a group header or New Page After in a group footer (but not both) will cause each group to start on a new page. There is one problem with setting this property absolutely—you can end up with "stranded" pages. If you set New Page Before on a group header, you'll often encounter a stranded first page, because the report header will print and Crystal Reports will skip to the next page before printing the first group header. Conversely, if you set New Page After on a group footer, you'll often encounter a stranded last page, because the last group footer will be followed by a page break before the report footer prints.

To avoid these pitfalls, you have two choices:

- Suppress the report header and/or report footer if you have no data in them to show.

- Set the New Page Before or New Page After properties conditionally.

PART I

Property	Function
Free-Form Placement	Allows objects to be moved freely throughout the section without snapping to horizontal guidelines. If this is turned off, horizontal guidelines are added to the left of the section and objects snap to them when moved.
Hide (Drill-Down OK)	Hides a section and all objects in it. However, if the section is within a higher-level group and that group is drilled into, this section *will* appear in the drill-down tab.
Suppress (No Drill-Down)	Suppresses a section and all objects in it. If the section is within a higher-level group and that group is drilled into, this section *will not* appear in the drill-down tab, even though a drill-down tab will appear.
Print at Bottom of Page	Prints the section at the bottom of the page. This is typically used for invoices, statements, or other, similar reports that require a group footer with a total to print at the bottom of the page, regardless of how many details sections print above it.
New Page Before	Starts a new page before printing this section. This is useful in a group header if you want each group to start on its own page.
New Page After	Starts a new page after printing this section. This is useful in a group footer if you want the next group to start on its own page.
Reset Page Number After	Resets the page number back to 1 after printing this section. This is useful in a group footer if you want each group to have its own set of page numbers, regardless of the total number of pages on the report. This also resets the Total Page Count field.
Keep Together	Prevents Crystal Reports from putting a page break in the middle of this section. For example, this would avoid having the first few lines of a multiple-line details section appear on the bottom of one page and the last few lines appear on the next page.
Suppress Blank Section	Suppresses the entire section if all the objects inside it are blank. This is useful in situations where you want to avoid white gaps appearing in your report if all the objects in a section have been conditionally suppressed or suppressed "if duplicated."
Underlay Following Sections	Prints the section, and then all following sections print right on top of the section. This is useful for printing maps, charts, or pictures alongside data or underneath the following sections.
Format with Multiple Columns	Creates multiple newspaper- or phonebook-style columns. The Layout tab will appear when this property is checked. This is only available when the details section is chosen.
Reserve Minimum Page Footer	Reserves only enough vertical space to show the largest page footer section (if you have added multiple page footers, such as Page Footer a, Pager Footer b, and so on, and have conditionally suppressed them). If you have multiple conditionally suppressed page footers and don't check this option, Crystal Reports will leave enough vertical space for all the combined page footers, even if they are not all displayed.

TABLE 8-1   Section Expert Common Tab Formatting Properties

Property	Function
Read Only	Prevents formatting, moving, or sizing of all objects in the report section. This is, in essence, the same as selecting all objects in the section and using the Lock Format and Lock Size And Position options from the Formatting Toolbar or Format Editor.
Relative Positions	When selected, this will automatically move any objects that are placed to the right of a cross-tab or OLAP grid in the section, according to the size of the cross-tab or OLAP grid. For example, if you place report fields or text objects to the right of a cross-tab, the cross-tab may very well print right over the top of the other object, as it grows horizontally to match the data it shows. By checking this option, you assure that any objects to the right of the cross-tab or OLAP grid will automatically move right to avoid being overprinted.

TABLE 8-1   Section Expert Common Tab Formatting Properties *(continued)*

If you have material in the report header or report footer that you want to print on the same page as the first group header or last group footer, you must do some conditional formatting. To avoid a stranded first page, you can use a conditional formula to set the New Page Before property only on the second and subsequent groups—the first group will stay on the first page with the report header. Since the first group header will print at the same time the first record is printing, you can use the following Boolean conditional formula for New Page Before:

```
Not OnFirstRecord
```

To avoid a stranded last page, you want a new page after every group footer *except the last one.* Since the last group footer will only occur on the last record of the report, you can use this conditional formula for New Page After:

```
Not OnLastRecord
```

Printing an Invoice Total at the Bottom of the Page

You may be creating invoices grouped by invoice number, or statements grouped by customer number. You want the invoice or statement total, located in the group footer, to print at the bottom of the page, regardless of how many detail records print. Crystal Reports' normal behavior is to print the group footer immediately following the last detail record. If there are only a few invoice items or statement lines, the total will print high up the page, right after the last detail line. If you want the total to print at the bottom of the page in this situation, check the Print at Bottom of Page property for the group footer.

Starting Page Numbers Over for Each New Group

You might have a large report grouped by department that you want to "burst" apart and distribute to each individual department. Initially, you'll want to make sure to use the New Page Before property with the group header or the New Page After property with the group footer so that you won't ever have the end of one department appearing on the same page as the beginning of the next.

However, you also don't want to confuse those who may look at page numbers on later groups in the report. Even though a page may be the first one for the IT department, it will probably have a much larger page number than 1. Simply check the Reset Page Number After property for the department group footer. Page numbers will then start over at 1 for each department.

Changing Color for Entire Sections

The Color tab in the Section Expert, shown in Figure 8-2, lets you change the background color for an entire section, separate from any color formatting that individual objects in the section may have.

If you check the Background Color property, you can then choose from various colors from the color palette below it. This will set the background color for the entire section. This lets you highlight entire sections with different colors, if you choose—for example, a report with the group footer section showing a different background color:

Creating a "Banded" Report

Notice the Conditional Formula button on the Color tab. This lets you set the background color conditionally, which can be helpful if you want to base a background color on some particular condition.

Mainframe reports often were printed on "green bar" or "blue bar" paper with alternating shades of color and white. This was designed to make columns of numbers easy to follow across the page. Now that many PC-based reports are printed by laser printers on plain paper, you must create your own "banded" reports if your reports would benefit from this kind of look.

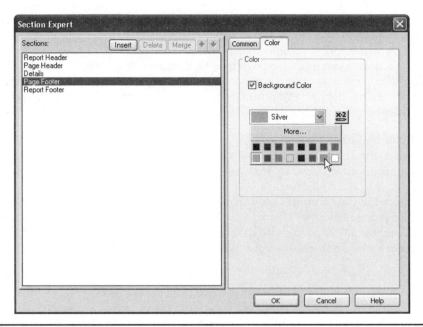

FIGURE 8-2 Setting the background color for a section

Simply giving the details section a silver background color isn't visually appealing, as shown here:

However, setting every other details section to silver provides a good way to help report readers follow columns of material across the page. You can set the background color conditionally to accomplish this. Use the following conditional formula:

```
If RecordNumber Mod 2 = 0 Then
    crSilver
Else
    crNoColor
```

This uses several built-in Crystal Reports functions. The Mod function (which performs Modulus arithmetic) divides one number by another but returns the *remainder* of the division operation, not the result of the division. The RecordNumber built-in function simply counts records consecutively, starting at 1. Therefore, *every other* record number, when divided by 2, will return 0 as the remainder. This will alternate the details section background color for every record.

You can make modifications to this formula to shade more than just every other line. If you want *every two* lines shaded, you could change the formula slightly:

```
If RecordNumber Mod 4 In [1,2] Then
    crSilver
Else
    crNoColor
```

This divides the record number by 4 and checks for remainders of 1 or 2. This will be true for every two records. The result is shown here:

You probably get the general idea of how this works. You can now modify the formula in any number of ways to change the way background shading works.

TIP *When setting the background color of a section, as well as background colors for individual objects, you may want to use NoColor instead of White to indicate a normal color. By using White, you will have solid white colors that can sometimes look unpleasant in combination with other solid colors. If you use NoColor, you often achieve a certain amount of transparency that will look better when mixing colors on the report or when using watermarks (discussed later in the chapter).*

Creating Summary and Drill-Down Reports

A *details report* shows every individual detail record in the database. This may often be preferable for certain listings or smaller transaction-type reports. Often, however, a viewer will only want to see subtotals, counts, averages, or other summary information for certain groups on the report. The details information used to arrive at those summaries isn't as important. This calls for a *summary report.*

In its simplest form, a summary report is a report with one or more groups with the details section hidden or suppressed. Consider Figure 8-3, a details report of orders, grouped by customer.

This shows every order for the customer, with order count and order amount subtotals appearing in the group footer. While this may be useful for a report viewer concerned about individual orders, the sales manager or account representative may often just be interested

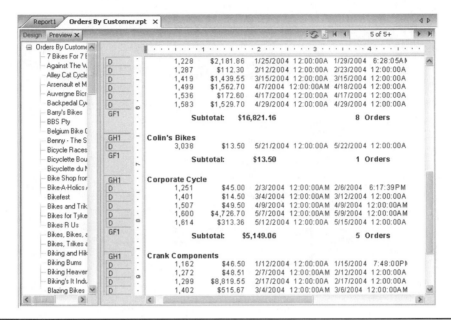

FIGURE 8-3   Orders detail report

in the summary information for each customer—just the *bottom line*. All the order details just get in the way of their analysis.

In this case, simply hiding or suppressing the details section will create a much more meaningful report for these viewers. You can hide or suppress the details section from the Section Expert. As a shortcut, there are Hide and Suppress options available right in the section pop-up menu, as well. Just right-click the gray details section name at the left of the Design or Preview tab and choose Hide (Drill-Down OK) or Suppress (No Drill-Down) from the pop-up menu.

The details section will simply disappear from the Preview tab, while the group header and footer still show up. Figure 8-4 shows the resulting summary report, which is much more succinct and meaningful to a viewer looking at the big picture.

If you later want to change your report back to a details report, you need to have the details section reappear. Just display the Section Expert by using the toolbar button or pull-down menu option. Select the details section and turn off the Hide or Suppress property. You can also display the Design tab and right-click the gray area to the left of the screen where the details section is hidden or suppressed. To redisplay the details section, choose the opposite of the Suppress or Hide option you initially set.

TIP   *You can choose how a hidden or suppressed section appears in the Design tab. Choose File |*
Options from the pull-down menus and look for the Show Hidden Sections option in the Design
View section of the Layout tab. If this is checked (the default), hidden or suppressed sections will
still appear in the Design tab, but they will have gray shading. If you turn this option off, they
will only show the bottom border of the hidden or suppressed section in the Design tab.

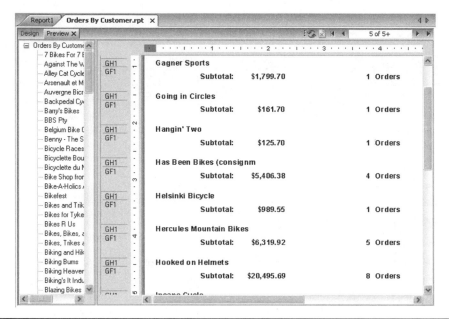

FIGURE 8-4   Orders summary report

Choosing whether to hide or suppress a section determines whether or not you want a report viewer to drill down into the section. Also, note that the Suppress property can be conditionally set in the Section Expert, while the Hide property cannot.

Drill-Down Reports

One of the most powerful features of an online reporting tool like Crystal Reports is interactive reporting. You may be creating a report to distribute to a large audience via a web page in a BusinessObjects Enterprise or Crystal Reports Server (covered in Part II of this book), or as part of a custom Web or Windows application (covered in Part III). A truly useful report will initially present viewers with higher-level summary or total information. If the viewer sees a number or other characteristic of the report that interests them, you want them to be able to drill down into just that particular area.

NOTE *Drill-down is an interactive feature only applicable to viewers looking at a Crystal Report in its "native" format. Drill-down isn't available in any reports exported to another format, such as Word or Excel. And obviously, drill-down isn't a feature that applies to reports printed on paper!*

In its simplest form, a drill-down report can be created by hiding the details section (hence, the Drill-Down OK notation alongside the Hide property) in a report that has one or more groups. When you point at the group name field, or a subtotal or summary object in a group header or footer, you'll notice your mouse cursor change to a magnifying glass, or *drill-down cursor*. When you double-click, a separate drill-down tab will appear, showing the group header, footer, and details sections for that group. You can then navigate to the main

Preview tab to see the summary report, or back to individual drill-down tabs to see the details information. You can double-click in the Preview tab as many times as you want in order to create additional drill-down tabs.

More complicated drill-down reports can be created by using multiple levels of grouping, along with creative use of section hiding. Figure 8-5 shows a drill-down report containing a details section and three groups: country, region, and city. Initially, the report just shows countries and their totals. If you drill down on a country, you'll find region subtotals for that country. Drilling down on a region will show city totals. And finally, drilling down on a city total will show individual orders placed from that city.

Click the Design, Preview, or any
drill-down tab to display it

Click the x on a tab
to close that tab

Moves among the tabs, if there are
too many to display at once

Click to print or export the contents of the current tab

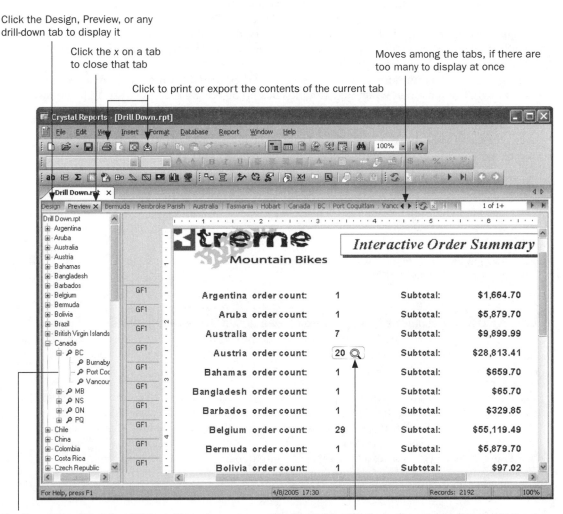

The Group Tree shows the drill-down hierarchy

Double-click to drill down when you see the magnifying glass

FIGURE 8-5   A more complex drill-down report

TIP *Make note of the Show All Headers On Drill Down option. When you turn this option on (it's off by default), your report will display all higher levels of group headers when you drill into a group, instead of showing just the previous level of group headers. Choose this option for the current report only by selecting File | Report Options. To choose the option for all new reports in the future, set the option on the Reporting tab after choosing File | Options.*

If you're interacting with a report, it's important to remember what will print or export if you click the Print or Export button on the Standard toolbar, or choose File | Print or File | Export from the pull-down menus. Only what's shown in the current drill-down tab (or Preview tab) will print or export. If you want to just print one drill-down tab, choose the drill-down tab and then click the Print button. If you want to print all the summary information in the main Preview tab, make sure it's selected before you print or export. If you want to print or export both summary and details information *in the same report,* you must either display the details section and print from the Preview tab, or create a separate report more appropriate for printing.

Using Tool Tip text (under the common section of the Format Editor) can help a viewer determine what will happen when they double-click an object. By creating a string formula with the Tool Tip text Conditional Formula button in the Format Editor, you can give a viewer more information about what the object contains. For example, this tooltip will appear when you enter the following Tool Tip text conditional formula. This formula is added to the Tool Tip Text property of the summary field in the Country group footer:

```
"Double-click to see regional totals within " &
    GroupName ({Customer.Country})
```

Creative Use of Column Headings and Group Headers in Drill-Down Reports

If you leave Crystal Reports' default column headings in the page header and simply hide or suppress lower-level group headers in your drill-down reports, you may get undesirable results when the viewer sees the initial Preview tab.

Column Heading Problems   The first problem will be the appearance of column headings in the Preview tab above the first group header, but with no matching detail records. But when you eventually drill down to the details level, the page header won't appear, so the viewer won't see the column headings.

There are two ways of resolving this problem, depending on how many levels of grouping exist on the report. If you only have one level of grouping, perform the following steps:

1. Move the column headings from the page header to the group header, either above or below the group name field (or remove the group name field altogether), depending on how you want the drill-down tab to appear.

2. Copy the group name field from the group header into the group footer.

3. Hide the group header along with the details section.

This way, the summary report will just show one line per group until you drill down. Then, the group header (containing the column headings) will appear inside the drill-down tab, along with the details sections.

However, if you have more than one level of grouping, the previous technique won't work properly—you'll see the column headings appear over and over again at the last group level. In this case, use this approach:

1. Create a second details section (Details b) and move the column headings into it.

2. Swap Details b and Details a so that the column headings are on top of the details section that contains database fields.

3. Select the text objects that comprise the column headings. You may multiselect them with CTRL-click or an elastic box. Using the Format Editor, choose the Suppress If Duplicated formatting option.

4. Using the Section Expert, choose the Suppress Blank Section formatting option for Details a.

This technique, while a little more time-consuming, provides perfect results. When the lowest level of grouping appears, there will be no column headings (because they've been moved to the details section). But when you drill down to the details level, the column headings only show up once at the top of the drill-down tab, because of the Suppress If Duplicated/Suppress Blank Section formatting combinations.

Repeating Group Headers   If you simply choose the Hide (Drill-Down OK) formatting option on group header sections, your report may suffer from extra sets of group headers that appear when you drill down. For example, if you drill down into a country group to see all the regions within the country, the region group header will print before every group footer. To solve this problem, you may try to suppress the region group header so that it will never show up. However, when you then drill into a region group to see cities within the region, the region group header won't print at the top of the list of cities.

In theory, you'd like the region group header to show up when you've drilled into the region group to see cities, but *not* show up when you're looking at the region group at its summary level. But, what conditional formula can you use to suppress the region group header so that it only shows up when there isn't a country group header there as well?

Crystal Reports features the *DrillDownGroupLevel* function in the Crystal Reports formula language. This function allows you to test for a certain drill-down level and conditionally suppress a group header (or perform any other functions or calculations, for that matter), depending on the level of the drill-down. Making use of this function to conditionally suppress group headers will allow you the ultimate control over your report behavior when the viewer drills down.

Using the previous Country/Region/City drill-down scenario as an example, you suppress the region group header (Group Header 2) conditionally so that it won't appear when you drill down to the country level, but will appear when you drill down to the region level. This is simply a matter of using this formula to conditionally suppress Group Header 2:

```
DrillDownGroupLevel = 1
```

This will suppress the group header when a Country drill-down occurs (level 1), but will not suppress it when a Region drill-down occurs (level 2). You may also use the DrillDownGroupLevel function to determine if the main Preview tab is being displayed. If the DrillDownGroupLevel function returns a zero, no drill-down is occurring at all.

Examples of the drill-down techniques discussed here can be found in a sample report on this book's companion web site. Look for the Drill Down.RPT sample report at www.CrystalBook.com.

Multiple-Column Reports for Labels and Listings

Crystal Reports is designed to replace much of the repetitive printing that you may have used a word processor for in the past. Immediate uses include form letters and mailing labels. You can also use the multicolumn feature of Crystal Reports to create newspaper-style columns in your reports. If you have just a few fields that you'd like to print in columnar form, the Section Expert provides the necessary section formatting.

To create mailing labels in Crystal Reports, choose Mailing Label Report from the Start Page or File | New menu when first creating a new report. This brings up the Mailing Labels Report Creation Wizard. This wizard takes you step-by-step through the process of choosing the table and fields that make up your mailing label, and choosing from a predefined list of continuous-feed and laser printer labels. Figure 8-6 shows the section of this wizard where you may select predefined labels or make fine adjustments to label specifications.

Since there is no similar expert for creating newspaper-style reports, you have to create such reports using the Blank Report option and the Section Expert. Recall from Table 8-1 one of the Section Expert's formatting properties, Format with Multiple Columns. This property is only available for the details section—it won't even appear in the Section Expert if you have any other section selected. Once you check this property, the Layout tab appears in the Section Expert, as shown in Figure 8-7.

On the Layout tab, you determine the specifics of the columns you want to create. Although you might expect to see a "number of columns" setting, this is actually determined by page margins (set with File | Page Setup), the width of the details section, and the horizontal gap between details. For example, if you have quarter-inch margins with standard letter-size paper in portrait orientation, you'll have 8 full inches of printable space. If you choose a details-size width of 2.5 inches and a horizontal gap of a quarter inch, you'll have three evenly spaced columns with a quarter inch on all sides.

When you choose to format the details section with multiple columns, the Design tab changes slightly. You'll notice that the width of the details section's bottom border shrinks to equal the width you set in the Layout tab. The other sections of the report retain the full width of the page.

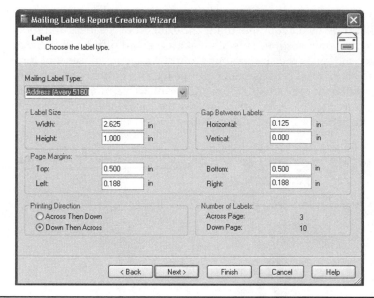

FIGURE 8-6   Mail Label Report Creation Wizard

Specify width of the column (height is unused here—details section height is determined in the Design tab)

Specify horizontal gap (gutter) between columns and vertical gap between details sections

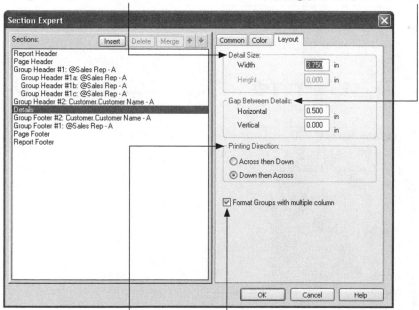

Choose the order in which to print details sections

Choose whether to print group headers and footers in the same columnar format as the details sections

FIGURE 8-7   Section Expert for multicolumn report

The exception to this rule occurs when you check the Format Groups With Multiple Column check box on the Layout tab. In this case, all group headers and footers take on the same width as the details section. This can make a marked difference in the appearance of your report, depending on the size of your groups. As a general rule, not formatting groups with multiple columns will cause smaller groups to print only in one column on the left side of the page. Usually, the only small groups that print across multiple columns are ones that start at the bottom of the page. Figure 8-8 shows the difference. You'll typically experience more predictable behavior by formatting groups with multiple columns.

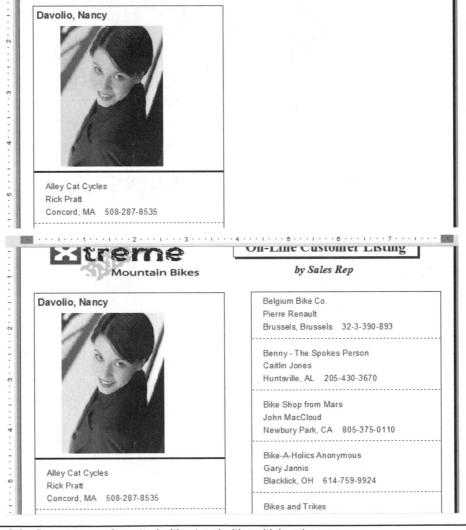

FIGURE 8-8 Report groups formatted without and with multiple columns

Using Multiple Sections

To be precise, the five default sections that first appear in a new report, and any additional group headers and footers that are added later, are referred to as *areas.* This is in contrast to

the term "section," which really refers to "subareas." Because Crystal Reports lets you create multiple occurrences of the same area, such as multiple details or multiple group headers, each of the individual occurrences is called a *section.* Creating multiple sections can be accomplished from the Section Expert or by using the pop-up menu that appears when you right-click in the gray area on the left side of the screen.

To insert an additional details section, for example, right-click in the details gray area on the left side of the Design tab and choose Insert Section Below from the pop-up menu. Or, from the Section Expert, select the area that you wish to duplicate and click the Insert button. You'll see the details area split into two sections: Details a and Details b. Once you've created multiple sections in an area, the pop-up menu (shown here) and Section Expert (shown in Figure 8-9) take on a great deal of additional capability.

Deletes the current section, and all objects in it

Merges the current section with the section below it. All objects in the section below will be placed in the current section

Creates a new section directly below the currently selected one

Rearranges the order in which sections appear

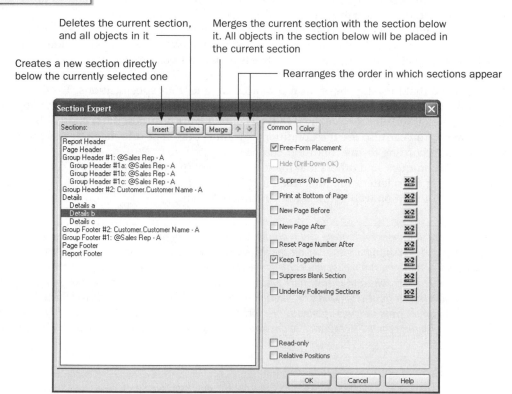

FIGURE 8-9   Manipulating multiple sections in the Section Expert

You can insert as many sections in an area as you wish—there can be Details a, b, c, d, and on and on (when Crystal Reports runs out of letters, it starts doubling them up, as in "Details ab"). Any area can consist of multiple sections. Nothing prevents you from having three report headers, five details sections, two group footer #1s, or any other combination.

Once you've created the multiple sections, you can add objects to any of the sections. You can even add the same object to some, or all, of them. When the report prints, the sections will simply print one right after the other, with the objects showing up one below the other. Probably the biggest question you have right now is, "What's the benefit of multiple sections anyway? Everything just prints as though it were in one bigger section!"

Figure 8-10 is a great example of the benefit of multiple sections. This shows portions of a form letter based on the Customer table from the sample XTREME Mountain Bike database included with Crystal Reports. Notice that the letter consists of four different details sections. Details a contains the logo, print date, customer name, and address 1; Details b contains address 2; Details c contains the city-state-ZIP and salutation; and Details d contains the body of the form letter. When you preview the report, it just shows the details sections one on top of the other, as though everything were in one big details section.

But what will happen to a customer with no address 2 data? You would see an empty line where the Address 2 database field would appear. This behavior, again, is identical to what you'd expect if you had put all the objects in one tall details section.

Here's the benefit: you may *conditionally suppress* individual sections—in this case, Details b—so that they appear or disappear according to your specifications. To eliminate the blank line that appears when there's nothing in address 2, format Details b with Suppress Blank Section. If the objects contained in it all contain empty values, the section will not appear at all. You can also use the Conditional Formula button next to the Suppress property to suppress according to any condition you need.

These techniques, and others that make good use of multiple sections and conditional formatting for form letters, are illustrated in the sample Form Letter.rpt report. Find it on this book's companion web site at www.CrystalBook.com.

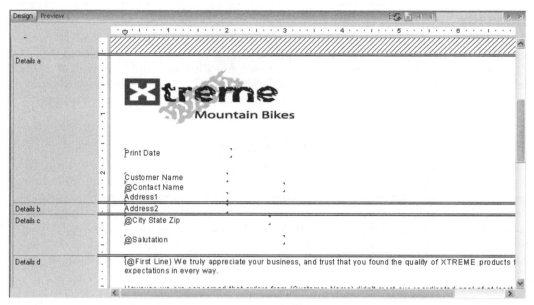

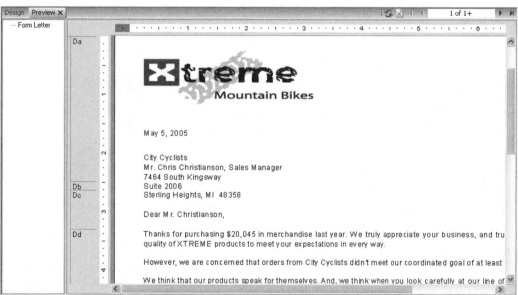

Figure 8-10 Multiple details sections

Conditionally Suppressing Sections

There may be times when conditionally suppressing a single section is beneficial (for example, you may wish to conditionally suppress a single group header, depending on DrillDownGroupLevel). But, conditional suppression really comes in handy with multiple section reports. Using the Conditional Formula button next to the Suppress property lets you supply a Boolean formula to determine when the section appears or doesn't appear. Consider the following examples.

Printing a Bonus Message for Certain Records

You are designing a list of orders by salesperson. You want a bonus message and a "lots o' money" graphic to appear below the order if it exceeds $2,500. However, if the order doesn't exceed the bonus level, you *don't* want the large blank space to appear where the graphic and message are located. If you just use the Format Editor to conditionally suppress the graphic and text object containing the message, they won't appear, but the empty space still will.

Simply create a Details b section and place the graphic and text object in it. Then, suppress Details b when the bonus isn't met, using the following conditional formula for the Suppress property:

```
{Orders.Order Amount} < 2500
```

Figure 8-11 shows the result.

FIGURE 8-11   Multiple details sections with conditional suppression

Printing a Different Page Header on Page 2 and Later

You may wish to print a title page or other large page header on page 1 of the report, perhaps containing a logo and large formatted title. However, on subsequent pages of the report, you want a less flashy header with smaller type and no graphic. You want column headings and the print date and time to show up on all pages of the report, including the first.

This presents a special reporting problem. The flashy page header can simply be put in the report header section. It will then appear only on the first page. However, if you put the smaller report title in the page header along with the column headings and other information, it will appear on page 1 along with the report header. You can use the Format Editor to suppress the object containing the smaller header, but then extra white space will appear on page 1.

The solution is to create a second page header section. Put the smaller report title in Page Header a and put the column headings and print date/time in Page Header b. Then, conditionally suppress Page Header b so that it won't show up on page 1. Here's the conditional formula, which uses the PageNumber built-in function:

```
PageNumber = 1
```

Printing Odd and Even Page Headers or Footers

You may be printing your report on a "duplex" laser printer that can print on both sides of the paper. Or, you may want to photocopy your report from one to two sides and place it in a three-ring binder or other bound format. Crystal Reports lets you create separate odd and even page headers and footers to add a real page-published look to your report.

Simply create separate Page Headers a and b (and, perhaps, Page Footers a and b). Place the appropriate material in each section and position it properly for odd/even appearance. Now, conditionally suppress the sections. The sections containing the material for odd page numbers will be suppressed for even page numbers with the following conditional formula:

```
PageNumber Mod 2 = 0
```

Also, the sections containing the material for even page numbers will be suppressed for odd page numbers with the following conditional formula:

```
PageNumber Mod 2 = 1
```

These formulas use the PageNumber built-in function illustrated previously. In addition, they use the Mod function, which will indicate whether a page number is even or odd (even page numbers divided by 2 return a remainder of 0, and odd page numbers return a remainder of 1, as explained earlier in the chapter).

Underlaying Sections

The Section Expert includes the Underlay Following Sections property. As described earlier in Table 8-1, this property prints the underlaid section in its usual position but prints the following sections right over the top. Initially, this may seem of limited usefulness. How readable will a report be if sections are printing right over the top of earlier sections?

Look at Figure 8-12 to get an idea. This report includes a large, light "Draft" graphic that has been placed in the page header. When Underlay Following Sections is checked for the page header in the Section Expert, all the other sections will print right over the top of the page header, creating the watermark effect.

If you want to include column headings in the page header, along with the watermark, you experience a problem. The watermark will be underlaid as you desire, but so will the column headings! The solution, as you might expect, is to add a Page Header b. Place the watermark graphic in one page header section and format it to Underlay Following Sections. Place the column headings in the other page header section and don't underlay it. Which page header you place the objects in will determine whether or not the column headings are underlaid. If you put the watermark in Page Header a (which is formatted to Underlay Following Sections) and the column headings in Page Header b (not underlaid), the watermark will underlay the column headings. If you choose the other way around, the column headings won't be underlaid.

NOTE *When you underlay a section, all sections will print over the top of it, until Crystal Reports comes to its "companion" section, which will not underlay it. For example, if you underlay a page header, all sections will print on top until Crystal Reports gets to the matching page footer. If you underlay Group Header b, all other sections will print on top until the report hits Group Footer b, which will not be underlaid.*

You can also use the Underlay Following Sections feature to place maps or charts beside the data they refer to, rather than on top or bottom of the related data. Figure 8-13 shows

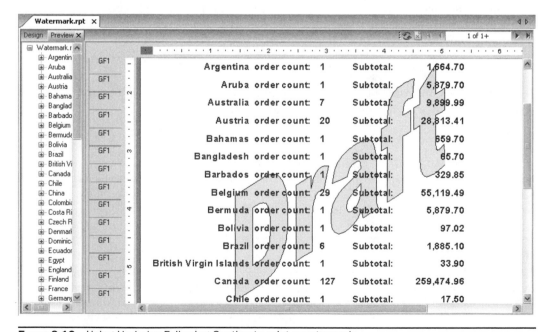

FIGURE 8-12   Using Underlay Following Section to print a watermark

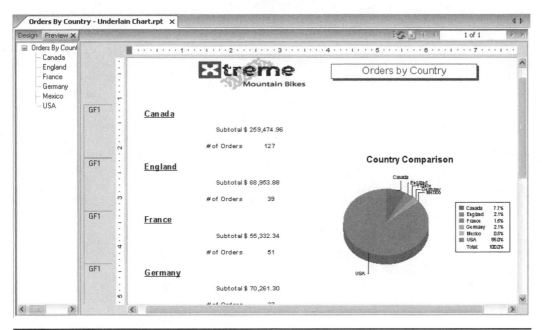

FIGURE 8-13   Chart in an underlaid section

a report containing a chart. Notice that the chart appears alongside the data that the chart refers to, rather than above. The chart is contained in a second report header (Report Header b), but the chart object has been moved to the right of the section, and the report header section is formatted to Underlay Following Sections.

Placing the chart in Report Header b permits the report title and logo to remain in Report Header a (which isn't underlaid) so that the report title and logo aren't also underlaid along with the chart.

Analyzing with Cross-Tabs

Database report writers and spreadsheet programs are typically considered to be two completely separate products. The database report writer sorts and selects data very well, while the spreadsheet is great for analyzing, totaling, and trending in a compact row-and-column format. Crystal Reports provides a tool that, to a limited extent, brings the two features together: the cross-tab object. A *cross-tab* is a row-and-column object that looks similar to a spreadsheet. It summarizes data by using at least three fields in the database: a row field, a column field, and a summarized field. For each intersection of the row and column fields, the summarized field is aggregated (summed, counted, or subjected to some other type of calculation).

Consider two common summary reports. The first summary report shows total sales in dollars for each state in the United States. The second report shows total units sold by product type. If a marketing analyst wanted to combine these two reports to more closely analyze both sales in dollars by state and units sold by product type, you would be limited in what you could offer with the standard grouped summary report.

You can create a report, similar to that shown in Figure 9-1 (initially grouped by state, and within state grouped by product type), which provides the information the analyst desires. But if the analyst wanted to compare total mountain bikes sold in the country with total kids' bikes sold in the country, this report would make the process very difficult. Product type is the inner group, so there are no overall totals by it. Also, comparing Alabama totals with Illinois totals would be difficult, because they would be several pages apart on the report.

This scenario is a perfect example of where a cross-tab object would be useful. A cross-tab is a compact, row-and-column report that can compare subtotals and summaries by two or more different database fields. Whenever someone requests data to be shown by one thing and by another, it's a cross-tab candidate. Just listen for the "by this and by that" request. Figure 9-2 will probably be much more useful to the analyst.

Creating a Cross-Tab Object

When you look at a cross-tab, it's tempting to think of it as an entire report unto itself, much as an Excel spreadsheet is entirely independent. In fact, a cross-tab is just an object that resides in an existing report section. Even when you choose the Cross-Tab choices from the Start Page or the File | New menu item, Crystal Reports just creates a cross-tab object and puts it in the report header. You can create more than one cross-tab per report, if you wish.

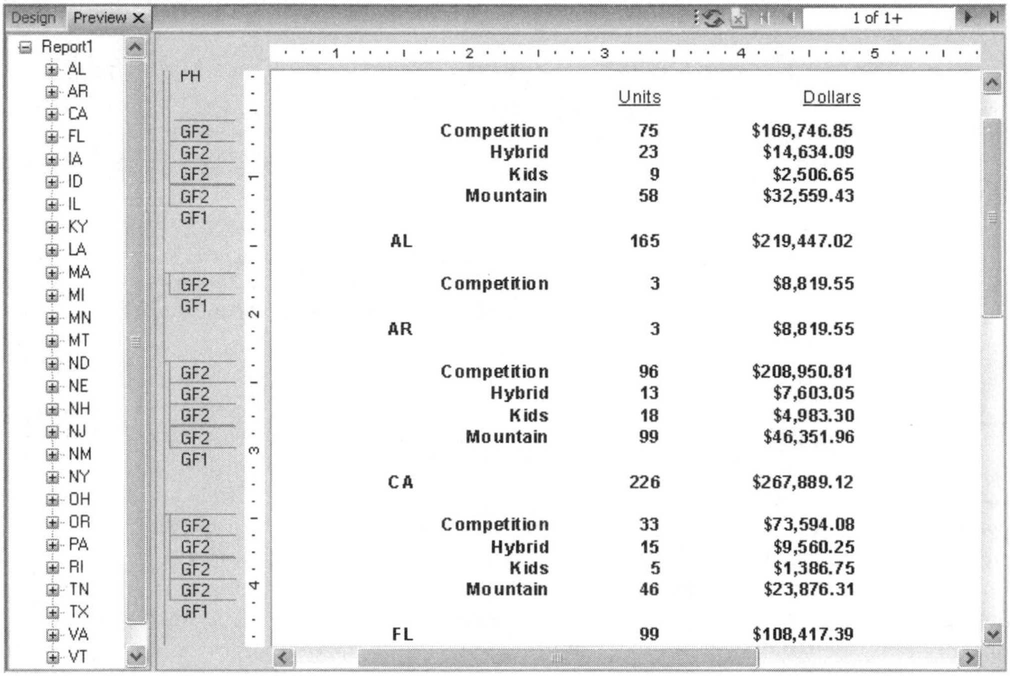

Design | Preview ✕   1 of 1+

Report1
- AL
- AR
- CA
- FL
- IA
- ID
- IL
- KY
- LA
- MA
- MI
- MN
- MT
- ND
- NE
- NH
- NJ
- NM
- NY
- OH
- OR
- PA
- RI
- TN
- TX
- VA
- VT

	Units	Dollars
Competition	75	$169,746.85
Hybrid	23	$14,634.09
Kids	9	$2,506.65
Mountain	58	$32,559.43
AL	**165**	**$219,447.02**
Competition	3	$8,819.55
AR	**3**	**$8,819.55**
Competition	96	$208,950.81
Hybrid	13	$7,603.05
Kids	18	$4,983.30
Mountain	99	$46,351.96
CA	**226**	**$267,889.12**
Competition	33	$73,594.08
Hybrid	15	$9,560.25
Kids	5	$1,386.75
Mountain	46	$23,876.31
FL	**99**	**$108,417.39**

FIGURE 9-1   Standard summary report with two groups

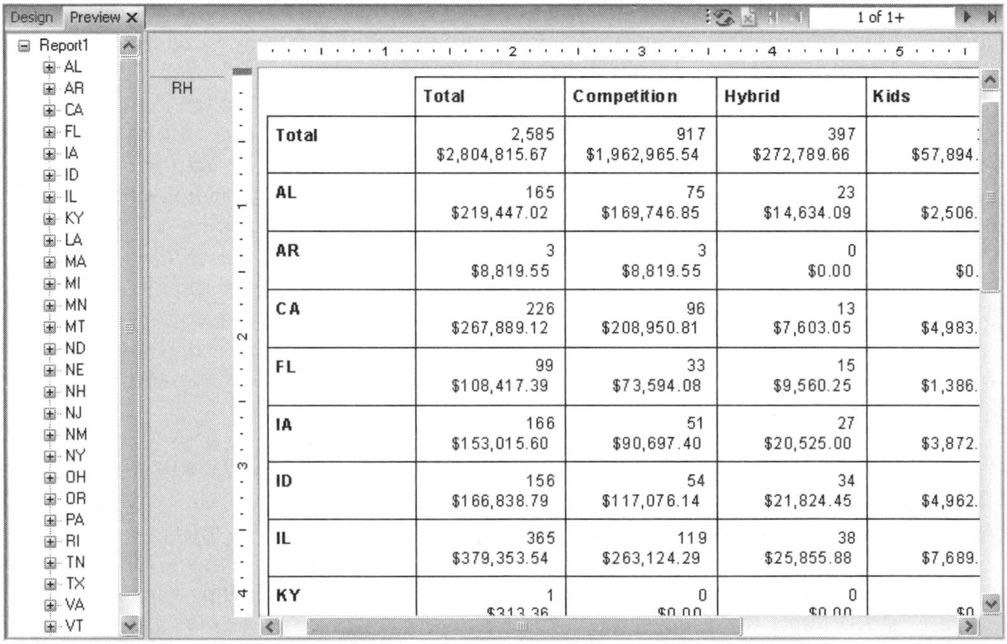

Design | Preview ✕   1 of 1+

Report1
- AL
- AR
- CA
- FL
- IA
- ID
- IL
- KY
- LA
- MA
- MI
- MN
- MT
- ND
- NE
- NH
- NJ
- NM
- NY
- OH
- OR
- PA
- RI
- TN
- TX
- VA
- VT

	Total	Competition	Hybrid	Kids
Total	2,585 $2,804,815.67	917 $1,962,965.54	397 $272,789.66	$57,894.
AL	165 $219,447.02	75 $169,746.85	23 $14,634.09	$2,506.
AR	3 $8,819.55	3 $8,819.55	0 $0.00	$0.
CA	226 $267,889.12	96 $208,950.81	13 $7,603.05	$4,983.
FL	99 $108,417.39	33 $73,594.08	15 $9,560.25	$1,386.
IA	166 $153,015.60	51 $90,697.40	27 $20,525.00	$3,872.
ID	156 $166,838.79	54 $117,076.14	34 $21,824.45	$4,962.
IL	365 $379,353.54	119 $263,124.29	38 $25,855.88	$7,689.
KY	1 $313.36	0 $0.00	0 $0.00	$0.

FIGURE 9-2   Cross-tab showing units/dollars by region and by product type

In fact, you can even copy an existing cross-tab and put it in several different sections of the same report. It's just an object, like a text object, chart, or database field.

A cross-tab can exist by itself on a report (as evidenced by the Cross-Tab Report Wizard, which creates a report containing nothing but a cross-tab), or it can be placed on a report that already contains fields in the details section, as well as one or more groups. The report can be completely functional in every respect before the cross-tab is added—the cross-tab is simply dropped in.

The first step in creating a cross-tab is to ensure that the tables you've chosen and linked for your report contain enough data to populate the cross-tab. If, for example, you want to look at order totals for the years 1995, 1996, 1997, and 1998 by state, make sure you choose tables that include the order amount, the year the order was placed, and the state of the customer who placed the order. While this may seem rather obvious, you may not have enough data to adequately populate your cross-tab if you don't think ahead carefully.

You may or may not want to use actual report fields as cross-tab fields. If the fields are already on the report, you can add them to the cross-tab object. Or if you've added completely different fields to the report, you can still base the cross-tab on other fields that exist in the tables you chose when creating the report.

You can use the Cross-Tab Report Creation Wizard from the Start page or File | New menu, or add a cross-tab to an existing report you've already created. To begin with the Cross-Tab Report Creation Wizard, simply choose it from the Start page or choose File | New | Cross-Tab Report. In addition to the familiar Data, Link, Chart, and Record Selection dialogs seen in other report wizards, the Cross-Tab Wizard displays a Cross-Tab row/column dialog and a Grid Style dialog similar to those discussed in more detail later in the chapter.

 If you've already created another report using another wizard or the Blank Report option, you may insert a cross-tab object whenever you want. To create a cross-tab object, it's best to select the Design tab first. Although you can place a cross-tab on the report in the Preview tab, you may not be able to accurately tell where it's being placed. In the Design tab, there's no question. Click the Insert Cross-Tab button on the Insert Tools toolbar, or choose Insert | Cross-Tab from the pull-down menus. An object outline will be attached to your cursor. Drop the outline where you'd like the cross-tab to appear. You can drop the cross-tab object in the report header or footer, or in a group header or footer. Cross-tabs can't be placed in the details section or in a page header or footer—you'll get a "no-drop" cursor (a circle with a line through it) if you try to position the cross-tab in these sections.

This "drop attached cross-tab object" behavior is new in Crystal Reports XI (previously, choosing the Insert options would immediately display the Cross-Tab Expert, described later in this chapter). Once you've dropped the empty cross-tab object in the desired reports section, you may drag fields directly from the Field Explorer onto the Cross-Tab object to determine your row, column, and summarized field selections.

Begin by choosing the field you wish to appear as the cross-tab row or column field. Drag it from the Field Explorer to the right of the Total column (to make it the column field) or below the Total row (to make it the row field). The mouse cursor will appear as a piece of paper with a plus sign, and a small arrow will appear beside the column total or below the row total. Release the mouse button to drop the field in the cross-tab. You may add additional row or column fields (when using multiple rows or columns, a cross-tab will create a hierarchy between the two fields) by dragging them from the Field Explorer. Drop a field above an existing column or to the left of an existing row to place that field at the top of the hierarchy.

Or, drop a field below an existing column or to the right of an existing row to place it at the bottom of the hierarchy (hierarchical relationships based on multiple row and column fields are discussed later in the chapter).

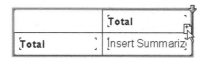

Once you've chosen row and columns fields, drag the field you wish to summarize (sum, average, and so forth) on top of the Insert Summarized Field cell. The cell will turn a different shade when you have the field properly positioned. Release the mouse button to drop the field in the summary cell. As with rows and columns, you may include more than one summary field in a cross-tab (for example, you may choose to summarize both quantity and extended price for the cross-tab). Just drag the additional field on top of the existing summary in a summary cell. The additional summary will be added to the cross-tab.

NOTE   *A default behavior of using the drag-and-drop cross-tab creation method is that a total row and column will appear before any data rows or columns, rather than after them. If this is not the desired appearance for your cross-tab, select the desired row or column name object in the cross-tab, right-click, and uncheck Totals On Top from the Row Grand Totals or Column Grand Totals pop-up menu choice. You can also display the Cross-Tab Expert (discussed later in the chapter) and turn off the Row Totals On Left and Column Totals On Top options on the Customize Style tab.*

To choose more detailed cross-tab options, use the Cross-Tab Expert. First, you must select the entire cross-tab object (you can't display the Cross-Tab Expert if you've selected an individual cross-tab field or summary). Do this by clicking either the small white space in the upper-left corner of the cross-tab (above the first row and to the left of the first column) or one of the grid lines between cells. You'll know you've selected the entire cross-tab if the status bar displays "Cross-Tab" (you can select the cross-tab in either the Design tab or the Preview tab). Then, choose Format | Cross-Tab Expert from the pull-down menus, or right-click the cross-tab and choose Cross-Tab Expert from the pop-up menu. The Cross-Tab Expert dialog box will appear, as shown in Figure 9-3.

The Cross-Tab Expert dialog box has three tabs: Cross-Tab, Style, and Customize Style. The Cross-Tab tab is used to define the database fields or formulas that make up the rows and columns of the cross-tab. The Style tab lets you choose a predefined formatting style for the grid on the cross-tab. And, the Customize Style tab displays a large number of custom formatting options to precisely control the appearance of the cross-tab.

You'll notice fields you've already dragged and dropped onto the cross-tab appearing in the Rows, Columns, and Summarized Fields boxes on the Cross-Tab tab. If you wish to change a row, column, or summarized field item, you may select existing items and remove them with the small left arrows, or choose additional fields in the Available Fields box to add. Just drag your chosen field from the Available Fields box and drop it on the Rows or Columns box. You can also select the field in the Available Fields box and click the right arrow button beside the Rows or Columns box. If you don't want to scroll the Available Fields box to find your field, you can click the Find Field button and type all or part of the

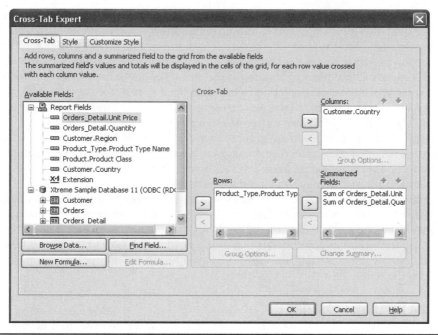

FIGURE 9-3   The Cross-Tab Expert dialog box

field name in the resulting dialog box. The first field name containing that string will be highlighted in the Available Fields box.

You may also remove fields from or add fields to the Summarized Fields box. These will typically be number or currency fields, such as Quantity Sold or Order Amount, but they don't have to be. If you choose a number field, the default summary type will be a sum (subtotal) of the field for each cell. If you choose a field with another data type, the default summary type is a count of the number of occurrences of the field for each row/column combination. Drag the field to be summarized from the Available Fields box to the Summarized Field box, or select the field and click the right arrow next to the Summarized Fields list. If you need a different summary type, use the Change Summary button, as discussed in more detail later in this chapter.

If you'd like to use an existing formula for a row, column, or summarized field, just select the formula in the Available Fields box. If you'd like to create a new formula or edit an existing formula before using it in the cross-tab, click the New Formula button or Edit Formula button, either of which launches the Formula Editor, where you can create or edit the formula. The formula will then appear in the Available Fields box; you can then drag it to the Rows, Columns, or Summarized Field box.

If you're not concerned initially about doing any customized formatting for your cross-tab object, you can click OK to close the Cross-Tab Expert (formatting options on the other two tabs of the Cross-Tab Expert dialog box are discussed later in the chapter). When you click OK on the Cross-Tab Expert dialog box, you are returned to the report.

When you preview the report, Crystal Reports will cycle through report data to properly summarize the totals for all row and column combinations—you may note some extra time required to do this. The cross-tab will then appear in the section where you placed it.

The section in which you place a cross-tab is critical in determining the data that the cross-tab will encompass. If you place a cross-tab in the report header or footer, only one occurrence of the cross-tab will appear on the report (remember, the report header and footer appear only once, at the beginning and end of the report, respectively). This cross-tab will encompass all the data on the report. If you place a cross-tab in a group header or footer, you get as many cross-tabs on your report as there are groups, each encompassing only data for that group.

Figure 9-4 shows a cross-tab created using the XTREME sample database included with Crystal Reports. This cross-tab includes product names as the rows, and cities as the columns. Notice that all cities in all states show up in the cross-tab.

Contrast this with Figure 9-5, which is the exact same cross-tab object that's just been moved to a state group footer. Now there will be a cross-tab on the report for every state group, but each cross-tab will contain data only for that particular group. If you choose to, you can copy the cross-tab object between a group header or footer to the report header or footer and actually see cross-tabs for individual groups, as well as an all-encompassing cross-tab for the whole report.

Editing an Existing Cross-Tab

After you create a cross-tab and drop it on your report, making changes to it is easy. If you wish to add an additional row, column, or summarized field, you may drag and drop desired fields or formulas from the Field Explorer just as you could when you initially created the cross-tab. Or, you may make more detailed changes using the Cross-Tab Expert.

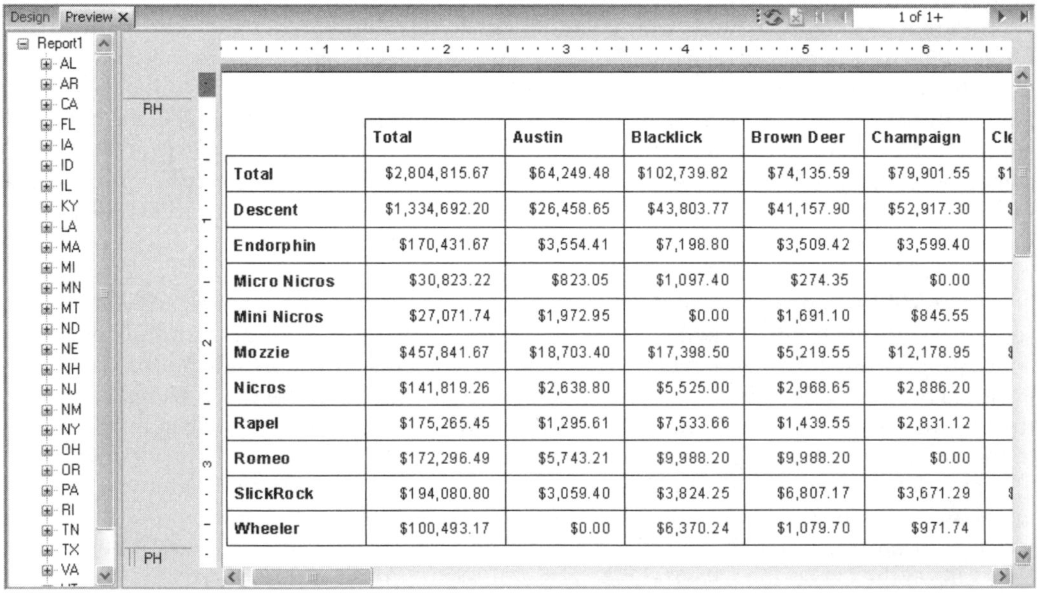

	Total	Austin	Blacklick	Brown Deer	Champaign	Cl
Total	$2,804,815.67	$64,249.48	$102,739.82	$74,135.59	$79,901.55	$1
Descent	$1,334,692.20	$26,458.65	$43,803.77	$41,157.90	$52,917.30	
Endorphin	$170,431.67	$3,554.41	$7,198.80	$3,509.42	$3,599.40	
Micro Nicros	$30,823.22	$823.05	$1,097.40	$274.35	$0.00	
Mini Nicros	$27,071.74	$1,972.95	$0.00	$1,691.10	$845.55	
Mozzie	$457,841.67	$18,703.40	$17,398.50	$5,219.55	$12,178.95	
Nicros	$141,819.26	$2,638.80	$5,525.00	$2,968.65	$2,886.20	
Rapel	$175,265.45	$1,295.61	$7,533.66	$1,439.55	$2,831.12	
Romeo	$172,296.49	$5,743.21	$9,988.20	$9,988.20	$0.00	
SlickRock	$194,080.80	$3,059.40	$3,824.25	$6,807.17	$3,671.29	
Wheeler	$100,493.17	$0.00	$6,370.24	$1,079.70	$971.74	

FIGURE 9-4   Cross-tab in report header

| | | Design Preview × | | | 2 of 2+ | |

Units		Dollars
Competition	96	$208,950.81
Hybrid	13	$7,603.05
Kids	18	$4,983.30
Mountain	99	$46,351.96
CA	226	$267,889.12

	Total	Irvine	Newbury Park	San Diego	Santa Ana
Total	$267,889.12	$97,415.83	$67,325.12	$68,555.99	$34,592.18
Descent	$147,727.50	$52,917.30	$17,198.13	$54,093.27	$23,518.80
Endorphin	$17,727.06	$6,298.95	$9,718.39	$0.00	$1,709.72
Micro Nicros	$3,292.20	$548.70	$2,743.50	$0.00	$0.00
Mini Nicros	$1,691.10	$281.85	$845.55	$563.70	$0.00
Mozzie	$43,496.25	$17,398.50	$20,878.20	$5,219.55	$0.00
Nicros	$15,189.64	$8,064.86	$4,189.11	$1,946.12	$989.55
Rapel	$13,723.73	$2,399.25	$7,149.77	$1,919.40	$2,255.31

FIGURE 9-5   Cross-tab in group footer

As mentioned earlier, you must first select the entire cross-tab object, not just one of its individual pieces, before you can start the Cross-Tab Expert. Once you've selected the desired cross-tab, choose Format | Cross-Tab Expert from the pull-down menus, or right-click and choose Cross-Tab Expert from the pop-up menu. This simply displays the Cross-Tab Expert dialog box, where you may also change row, column, or summarized fields on the Cross-Tab tab, or format cross-tab styles with the Style tab or the Customize Style tab.

You can also *pivot* the cross-tab, which simply means swapping the rows and columns around so that what used to be the row will now be the column, and vice versa. Choose Format | Pivot Cross-Tab from the pull-down menus, or right-click the selected cross-tab object and choose Pivot Cross-Tab from the pop-up menu.

Creative Use of Grouping and Formulas

As discussed previously, Crystal Reports chooses a default calculation for the summarized field when it creates the cross-tab. If you choose a number or currency field for a summarized field, Crystal Reports will use the Sum function to subtotal the numbers in each cell. This typically is what you want for this type of field (for example, the total sales figure for Green Bikes in the U.S.A.). If you use any other type of field (string, date, Boolean, and so forth), Crystal Reports will default to the Count function to count the occurrences of the particular summarized field for each row/column combination.

You are, however, completely free to change the function that Crystal Reports assigns to the summarized field. If you want to see the average sales figure in each cell instead of the total figure, it's easy to change. In either the Design or Preview tab, click the object in the cell (the intersection of the row and column). The status bar will indicate that you've selected

Sum or Count of <summarized field>. Change the summary operation to any other available summary by choosing Edit | Edit Summary from the pull-down menus or by right-clicking and choosing Edit Summary from the pop-up menu. This brings up the Edit Summary dialog box.

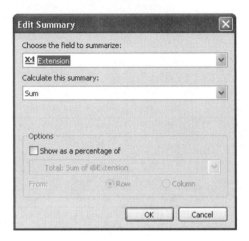

You can change the field that's summarized, if desired, or just the summary operation itself. If you've used a nonnumeric field for the cross-tab summarized field, you can change the summary operation from Count to Minimum, Maximum, Distinct Count, or any other summary function that is available for nonnumeric fields. You can also choose to express the summary as a percentage of another total or summary. These options are similar to how you can change the summary operation with existing group summaries and subtotals, as discussed in Chapter 3. In fact, the cross-tab, in essence, groups database records for every row/column combination, creating the summary or subtotal field for each cross-tab "group." Chapter 3 has more information on available summary functions and what they calculate.

TIP *Although cross-tabs are typically used for numeric analysis, you may sometimes find them of value when using string fields. For example, by using Minimum or Maximum summary functions with string fields, you can display textual information within a cross-tab cell. This may be helpful for certain types of string-oriented cross-tabs, such as schedules.*

Changing Cross-Tab Grouping
Because Crystal Reports uses a procedure to create cross-tabs that's similar to its procedure for creating groups, you have some of the same flexibility to change the way the cross-tab is organized. You can change a cross-tab "group" when first creating the cross-tab or when editing an existing cross-tab. This can be done with a pop-up menu from the cross-tab object, or through the Cross-Tab Expert.

If you want to change group options when displaying the cross-tab in the Design or Preview tabs, select the desired row or column name object (at the top of a column or left of a row) and right-click. Choose Row Options | Group Options or Column Options | Group Options from the pop-up menu. If you're using the Cross-Tab Expert, select the row or column field you want to change in the Cross-Tab tab, and then click the Group Options button. The Cross-Tab Group Options dialog box appears.

The Common tab allows you to change the field the cross-tab is grouped on, as well as the order in which the groups are displayed. For a non-date field, there are three order choices, along with the choice to determine order by using a formula:

- **Ascending Order**   Shows the cross-tab row or column in A to Z order.
- **Descending Order**   Shows the cross-tab row or column in Z to A order.
- **Specified Order**   Lets you create custom rows or columns, based on the contents of the database field you chose for the row or column. This works identically to Specified Order Grouping, discussed in Chapter 3.
- **Use A Formula As Group Sort Order**   Displays the Formula Editor, where you can create a formula that chooses between ascending and descending order.

NOTE   *Even though the crOriginalOrder option is available in the Formula Editor, you'll receive an error if your formula returns this option. Original Order is not a valid choice for cross-tab grouping.*

On the Options tab, the Customize Group Name Field check box, radio buttons, and formula button work the same as the identical options in the Change Group dialog box discussed in Chapter 3. You may customize the appearance of the text that displays in the row or column of the cross-tab with these options.

If the row or column field is a date field, time field, or date/time field, the Cross-Tab Group Options dialog box offers additional options that give you even greater flexibility, similar to creating report groups with similar fields.

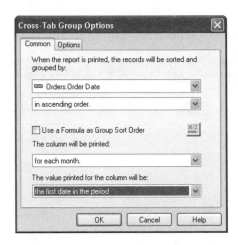

The pull-down list under "The row/column will be printed:" gives you a choice of how often you want a new row or column to appear in the cross-tab. Choices include every day, every week, every two weeks, every hour, every minute, and so on. Again, these are identical to the date/time grouping choices discussed in Chapter 3.

The pull-down list under "The value printed for the row/column will be:" gives you two choices: the first date in the period and the last date in the period. If you choose the first-date option with, say, a quarterly date period for 2001, the cross-tab will show 1/2001, 4/2001, 7/2001, and 10/2001. If you choose the last-date option, the cross-tab will show the exact same data in the cells, but the dates will be 3/2001, 6/2001, 9/2001, and 12/2001.

NOTE *Remember that cross-tab row and column settings have no relation to any existing report groups. Changes you make in the Cross-Tab Expert will have no bearing on existing report grouping, and vice versa.*

Using Formulas in Cross-Tabs

Even with the powerful grouping options and the ability to change the summary function used to calculate cell values, you may not always be able to display material in a cross-tab exactly the way you want using just fields available in the database. You are completely free to use formulas in your cross-tabs as a row, column, or summarized field. You can create the formulas in advance with the Formula Editor and drag them to the cross-tab. Or, if you are using the Cross-Tab Expert, you can use an existing formula in the Available Fields box, or click the New Formula button right in the Cross-Tab Expert dialog box to display the Formula Editor. After you create the formula, it will appear in the Available Fields box under the Report Fields category. Simply drag it to the Rows, Columns, or Summarized Field box.

TIP *You may also use running totals as summarized fields in a cross-tab. Just drag and drop the running total from the Field Explorer to the summary area of a cross-tab in the Design or Preview tab. You'll also find running totals in the Available Fields box in the Cross-Tab Expert— just drag the running total to the Summarized Fields box. Note, however, that you can't use a running total as a row or column field in a cross-tab.*

Multiple Rows, Columns, and Summarized Fields

If you drag and drop a field onto an existing row, column, or summary cell in a cross-tab, you'll notice that the arrow icon or plus-sign icon still appears, indicating that you can add more than one field to a row, column, or summarized field. And, if you are using the Cross-Tab Expert, the Rows, Columns, and Summarized Field boxes obviously are more than one field tall. Yes, that means that you can add more than one database field or formula to any of these cross-tab sections. It's important to understand, though, how this will affect cross-tab behavior and appearance.

Probably the simplest place to start is with multiple summarized fields. If you add more than one summarized field, the cross-tab will simply calculate the additional summary or subtotal in each cell. You could, for example, use Product Name as the row, Region as the column, and both Quantity and Price as summarized fields. The cross-tab would simply include two numbers in each cell—the total quantity and total price for that particular product and region.

You can even add the same field as a summarized field more than once and choose a different summary function for each occurrence, using the change summary option (by right-clicking the summarized field in the cross-tab and choosing Edit Summary from the pop-up menu, or using the Change Summary button in the Cross-Tab Expert). You could, for example, add both the Quantity and Price fields as summarized fields again, and then choose a different summary operation for these summaries, such as Average. Alternatively, you might add them as Sum functions again, but this time choose the Percentage Of summary function for the second occurrence of the summed fields.

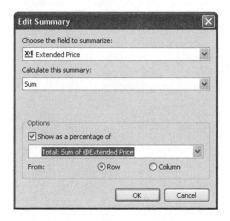

In the Edit Summary dialog box, when you select the Show As A Percentage Of option, you are given a choice between the Row total and the Column total as the target comparison number. In this example, the sums will be shown as a percentage of the column totals, so the resulting cross-tab shows four numbers in every cell: total quantity, total price, percentage of total quantity for the quarter, and percentage of total price for the quarter. It's interesting to note that the Row totals also display their percentage of the column totals, so the report is very effective as an analysis of each product by quarter:

	1/2004	4/2004	7/2004	10/2004	Total
Competition	207 37.23% $444,161.41 71.74 %	293 40.19% $625,777.60 74.36 %	238 35.52% $478,281.91 68.74 %	208 34.44% $427,784.15 67.66 %	946 36.97% $1,976,005.07 70.86 %
Hybrid	83 14.93% $54,999.16 8.88 %	76 10.43% $53,859.33 6.40 %	119 17.76% $80,494.11 11.57 %	108 17.88% $76,180.30 12.05 %	386 15.08% $265,532.90 9.52 %
Kids	42 7.55% $11,690.43 1.89 %	48 6.58% $13,257.70 1.58 %	54 8.06% $14,878.15 2.14 %	43 7.12% $11,869.84 1.88 %	187 7.31 % $51,696.12 1.85 %
Mountain	224 40.29% $108,284.64 17.49 %	312 42.80% $148,707.69 17.67 %	259 38.66% $122,151.72 17.56 %	245 40.56% $116,396.02 18.41 %	1,040 40.64% $495,540.07 17.77 %
Total	556 100.00% $619,135.64 100.00 %	729 100.00% $841,602.32 100.00 %	670 100.00% $695,805.89 100.00 %	604 100.00% $632,230.31 100.00 %	2,559 100.00% $2,788,774.16 100.00 %

Adding multiple row or column fields causes a little different behavior that is important to understand. Whereas multiple summarized fields simply calculate and print in the same cell, multiple row or column fields don't just print over and over, side-by-side. When you add multiple row or column fields, you create a grouping hierarchy between the fields. Consider a cross-tab in which you add the Product Type field as the first row field, and the Product Name field as the second row field. Crystal Reports will create a group hierarchy by Product Type, and within that, by Product Name. The resulting cross-tab would look like this:

		1/2004	4/2004	7/2004	10/2004	Total
Competition	**Descent**	$313,682.06	$448,915.16	$284,283.56	$271,789.16	$1,318,669.94
	Endorphin	$42,877.87	$66,903.88	$49,851.72	$44,992.55	$204,626.02
	Mozzie	$87,601.48	$109,958.56	$144,146.63	$111,002.44	$452,709.11
	Total	$444,161.41	$625,777.60	$478,281.91	$427,784.15	$1,976,005.07
Hybrid	**Romeo**	$30,921.83	$37,663.83	$47,860.15	$53,020.68	$169,466.49
	Wheeler	$24,077.33	$16,195.50	$32,633.96	$23,159.62	$96,066.41
	Total	$54,999.16	$53,859.33	$80,494.11	$76,180.30	$265,532.90
Kids	**Micro Nicros**	$3,840.90	$7,338.85	$6,831.31	$6,556.96	$24,568.02
	Mini Nicros	$7,849.53	$5,918.85	$8,046.84	$5,312.88	$27,128.10
	Total	$11,690.43	$13,257.70	$14,878.15	$11,869.84	$51,696.12
Mountain	**Nicros**	$29,505.11	$44,744.27	$36,959.74	$36,580.42	$147,789.54
	Rapel	$39,083.81	$45,681.81	$42,130.89	$34,957.13	$161,853.64
	SlickRock	$39,695.72	$58,281.61	$43,061.09	$44,858.47	$185,896.89
	Total	$108,284.64	$148,707.69	$122,151.72	$116,396.02	$495,540.07
Total		$619,135.64	$841,602.32	$695,805.89	$632,230.31	$2,788,774.16

Notice that rows are created for both the "inner" and "outer" groups—each product name has its own row within its product type, and each product type has its own subtotal row. And, at the end of the cross-tab is a grand total row for everything.

You can set up this multiple-field group hierarchy for either rows or columns with as many fields as you want (although it may not make much sense if you go beyond two or three levels).

So, a cross-tab that consists of two related row fields, two related column fields, and two summarized field might look like this in the Cross-Tab Expert:

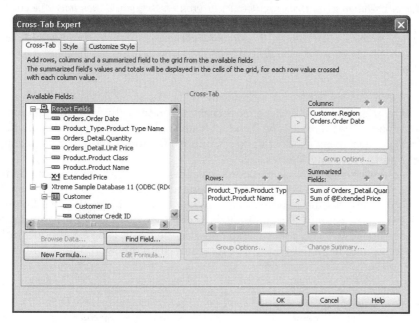

Here's a portion of the resulting cross-tab:

| | | AL | | | | | AR | |
		1/2004	4/2004	7/2004	10/2004	Total	4/2004	Total
Competition	Descent	0.00 $0.00	11.00 $32,338.35	7.00 $20,578.95	6.00 $17,639.10	24.00 $70,556.40	3.00 $8,819.55	3.00 $8,819.55
	Endorphin	3.00 $2,699.55	4.00 $3,419.44	2.00 $1,799.70	0.00 $0.00	9.00 $7,918.69	0.00 $0.00	0.00 $0.00
	Mozzie	0.00 $0.00	2.00 $3,479.70	6.00 $9,917.16	5.00 $8,699.25	13.00 $22,096.11	0.00 $0.00	0.00 $0.00
	Total	3.00 $2,699.55	17.00 $39,237.49	15.00 $32,295.81	11.00 $26,338.35	46.00 $100,571.20	3.00 $8,819.55	3.00 $8,819.55
Hybrid	Romeo	3.00 $2,247.36	1.00 $790.73	2.00 $1,498.24	1.00 $832.35	7.00 $5,368.68	0.00 $0.00	0.00 $0.00
	Wheeler	2.00 $1,079.70	2.00 $1,079.70	0.00 $0.00	0.00 $0.00	4.00 $2,159.40	0.00 $0.00	0.00 $0.00
	Total	5.00 $3,327.06	3.00 $1,870.43	2.00 $1,498.24	1.00 $832.35	11.00 $7,528.09	0.00 $0.00	0.00 $0.00
Kids	Micro Nicros	0.00 $0.00	1.00 $274.35	3.00 $823.05	0.00 $0.00	4.00 $1,097.40	0.00 $0.00	0.00 $0.00
	Mini Nicros	0.00 $0.00	0.00 $0.00	3.00 $845.55	2.00 $563.70	5.00 $1,409.25	0.00 $0.00	0.00 $0.00
	Total	0.00	1.00	6.00	2.00	9.00	0.00	0.00

NOTE *What section of the report you place the cross-tab in is particularly important when you are using multiple row or column fields. If you create a cross-tab that's based on Country, and then Region, you'll see different behavior depending on where you put the cross-tab. If you put it in the report header or footer, you'll have rows or columns for each country, and all the regions within those countries. However, if you have already grouped your report by country, and you place the cross-tab in a country group header or group footer, you'll then have one cross-tab for every country. However, that cross-tab will have only one country row or column in it, followed by any regions within that country. If you find cross-tabs at group levels with only one high-level row or column, there's not a great deal of benefit to using multiple row or column fields in that cross-tab.*

If you plan to use multiple row or column fields, choosing fields that have a logical, hierarchical relationship with each other is crucial. You may think of this relationship as being one-to-many. The Product Type/Product Name relationship is a good example—every one product type has many product names. Country/Region is another good example—every one country has many regions.

Using two row or column fields that don't have this relationship will cause an odd-looking cross-tab. For example, if you add Customer Name and Address fields to the same row or column, you'll simply see the customer name row or column, immediately followed by a single address row or column. The summaries in each will be exactly the same, because there's no logical one-to-many relationship between the fields. (The exception would be if a single customer had more than one office location—then this would be a valid multiple-field cross-tab example.)

NOTE *You may yearn for a cross-tab that allows multiple row or column fields that don't act as groups. You might, for example, want to see Actual $, Budget $, Variance $, and Variance % all as separate column fields that just calculate and print side by side. Sorry, but any time you add multiple row or column fields, Crystal Reports displays the fields in a grouping hierarchy from top to bottom.*

Reordering Fields in the Rows, Columns, or Summarized Field Boxes

The multiple fields you add as rows or columns not only have to have a logical relationship, they also need to appear in the right order. Using the previous Country/Region example, Country must be the first field row or column, followed by Region. If they're added the other way around, then each region will appear first, followed by a single row or column containing numbers from the country the region is in.

If you happen to add fields in the wrong order, you may reorder them either directly in the cross-tab object on the report or by using the Cross-Tab Expert. If you wish to reorder them directly on the report, simply drag and drop one row or column name on top of the other (you may do this either in the Design or Preview tabs). A small "double-swap-arrow" cursor will appear, indicating that the fields will swap locations. Or, if you use the Cross-Tab Expert, you can reorder them by one of two methods: either click one of the fields and then click the up or down arrow for that box to move it up or down, or click and drag a field in any of the boxes and drop it in a different location in the box.

Customizing Cross-Tab Appearance

So far, this chapter has concentrated on the basic steps required to create cross-tabs, on grouping options, and on some of the finer points of multiple row, column, and summarized fields. In all of these examples, the resulting cross-tab object looks fairly plain. In keeping with the ability of Crystal Reports to create publication-quality reports, you have numerous options available to help you improve the appearance of your cross-tab reports.

The most basic type of formatting options for cross-tabs lies in the individual cross-tab objects themselves. A cross-tab actually consists of a series of individual objects. The best way to see this is to look at a cross-tab in the Design tab.

	Column #1 Name	Total
Row #1 Name	of @Extended Price	Extended Price
Total	of @Extended Price	Extended Price

Notice the row and column name fields, which are similar to group name fields in a regular report—they display the database fields that make up the row and column headings. The Total text objects indicate the subtotal and total rows and columns. These are standard text objects—simply double-click them to change their contents, if you wish. And, in the actual cells, notice the subtotal or summary functions that calculate the cross-tab totals.

Each of these individual objects can be resized or formatted to change the appearance of the cross-tab. For example, if a column in the cross-tab isn't wide enough to show its contents, the contents will just be cut off or truncated. Examine the following cross-tab:

	1/2004	4/2004	7/2004	10/2004	Total
Compet	#########	#########	#########	#########	#########
Hybrid	$37,515.27	$23,902.97	$57,585.41	$56,495.59	#########
Kids	$9,717.48	$7,693.14	$10,821.47	$11,074.23	$39,306.32
Mountai	$78,354.83	$96,699.68	$85,004.71	$83,914.27	#########
Total	#########	#########	#########	#########	#########

Notice that the row labels are being truncated. Also, note that many of the cells contain pound signs, indicating that the cells aren't wide enough to show all the data in them. (Remember that if Allow Field Clipping is turned on, you won't see pound signs when numbers are truncated.)

Although you may be tempted to point to a line between columns in the cross-tab object to get a sizing cursor, or look on one of the tabs of the Cross-Tab Expert dialog box for some sort of column width setting, you simply need to select the individual object that makes up the column and resize it. This can be done in either the Design or Preview tab. Simply select the object, noting that all other similar cells are selected as well. Then, point to the desired sizing handle (one of the small blue blocks on all sides of a selected object) until the mouse cursor changes to the two-way sizing cursor. Then, simply resize the object to its desired width.

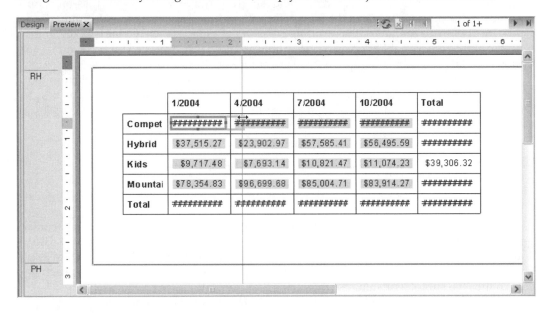

Tip *If the summarized values in your cross-tab are just too large to fit into a tidy grid, there is also a function you can use to abbreviate thousands or millions with the standard "K" or "M" notation. See "Conditionally Formatting Cross-Tabs" later in this chapter.*

You can format the individual pieces of the cross-tab just like any other text object or number field, using either the Formatting toolbar or the Format Editor. You can change the object's color, font face and size, horizontal alignment, or any other standard formatting option. If you choose one of the summary or subtotal objects in the middle, you can choose one of the default formatting styles, or choose a custom style to specify the number of decimal places, whether to include a thousands separator or currency symbol, or any other formatting option available to numeric or currency fields. If you base a row or column on a date or time field, you can choose how the field is displayed—month/year, month/day/year, hour: minute, hour:minute:second, or any other variation provided by the Format Editor.

Tip *You can select multiple objects in a cross-tab by using* CTRL-*click or* SHIFT-*click. You can then format them all at the same time with the Formatting toolbar or the Format Editor. Note, however, that the elastic box selection method doesn't select multiple objects within a cross-tab. You'll need to* CTRL-*click or* SHIFT-*click to do this.*

The Style Tab

When you select a cross-tab object and choose Format | Cross-Tab Expert or right-click and choose Cross-Tab Expert from the pop-up menu, the Cross-Tab Expert dialog box will appear.

Two tabs in this dialog box control formatting: Style and Customize Style. The Style tab lets you choose from several predefined formatting styles for the cross-tab object.

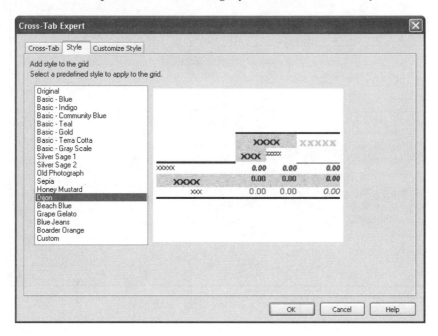

The Original option simply displays the cross-tab object with no special formatting—this is the original formatting option when a cross-tab is first created. You may choose from any of the predefined styles in the list. When you click a style, a sample of the style appears in the right side of the Style tab. Then, just click OK. The cross-tab will be formatted according to the built-in style that you chose.

CAUTION   *Crystal Reports behaves somewhat oddly when using the Style tab on the Cross-Tab Expert dialog box. Even if you haven't chosen any customized settings, you'll always receive a warning that you'll lose customized settings when you choose one of the built-in styles. And if you return to the Style tab later after choosing one of the built-in styles, the Custom setting will be highlighted, not the built-in style you chose before. Just remember that if you don't like a style setting, you may simply press CTRL-Z or use Edit | Undo to revert to your previous formatting.*

The Customize Style Tab

For very specific formatting of a cross-tab object, you need to use the Customize Style tab on the Cross-Tab Expert dialog box. This tab contains advanced cross-tab options that more precisely control cross-tab behavior. The Customize Style tab is shown in Figure 9-6.

If you've already chosen one of the built-in styles on the Style tab, you'll see the settings for that built-in style when you choose the Customize Style tab. For example, you'll see

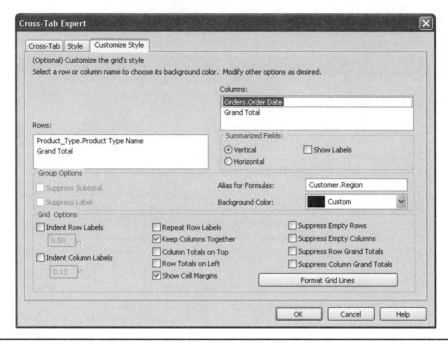

Figure 9-6   The Customize Style tab of the Cross-Tab Expert dialog box

background colors for each row or column item that the built-in style selected. If the built-in style shows totals before rows and columns instead of after, you'll see those options chosen. If you haven't chosen one of the built-in styles, or you want to change some of the settings that the built-in style selected, you may choose the various options in the Custom Style tab. The various options are explained in Table 9-1.

Several of the options on the Customize Style tab, particularly the Repeat Row Labels and Keep Columns Together options, dictate how a cross-tab appears when printed on paper. This is significant, because Crystal Reports displays cross-tabs differently in the Preview tab than it will print them on a printer. Even if the cross-tab width exceeds the width of the page, the Preview tab will show the entire cross-tab across the screen. You can continue to scroll farther right to see the rest of the cross-tab.

When Crystal Reports prints the cross-tab on paper, however, it must add page breaks if the cross-tab exceeds the width of the printed page. You can control how Crystal Reports formats the cross-tab across multiple pages with the options in the Customize Style tab. When you display the cross-tab in the Preview tab, you can see where Crystal Reports will insert page breaks when the cross-tab is printed on paper. In Figure 9-7, notice that the page break occurs between columns (it's not running right through the numbers of a column) and that the row labels are repeating after the page break. This is the result of turning on both Keep Columns Together and Repeat Row Labels.

Option	Description
Customize Grid's Style	
Rows list	Select the row that you want to format. If you've added multiple row fields, you'll see each row field listed. You can also choose separate formatting options for the row grand total.
Columns list	Select the column that you want to format. If you've added multiple column fields, you'll see each column field listed. You can also choose separate formatting options for the column grand total.
Summarized fields	When you have multiple fields summarized, you can choose whether to display them in a vertical stack (this is the default) or horizontally side-by-side. The Show Labels option prints the summarized field name(s) in the column header area (you can't customize the labels here, but can edit them in the Design or Preview tabs just like text objects). Figure 9-7 shows the horizontal summaries with labels.
Group Options	
Suppress Subtotal	If you select this option, the subtotal row or column (depending on what's selected in the Rows or Columns list) won't appear. In this case, the cross-tab still shows the hierarchical grouping relationship among the multiple row or column fields, but the subtotals for the selected field won't appear. This option is available only for higher-level fields when you've chosen multiple row or column fields—the option is disabled if you select the lowest-level (or if you added only one) row or column field.
Suppress Label	If you choose the Suppress Subtotal option, this option becomes enabled. Checking this option will completely eliminate the field you chose from the row or column. The grouping hierarchy will remain, but the higher-level group won't appear at all in the cross-tab. If you have also checked Indent Row Labels (described later in this table), this option will be checked and you can't change it.
Alias for Formulas	Used to refer to an entire row or column when performing conditional formatting on the cross-tab. See "Conditionally Formatting Cross-Tabs" later in the chapter.
Background Color	Sets the background color for the entire row or column that's chosen in the Rows or Columns list. This color is independent of any individual cell colors you may choose by selecting an object in the cross-tab and using the Format Editor.

TABLE 9-1   Customize Style Tab Options

Option	Description
Grid Options	
Indent Row Labels	Checking this option will indent the label for the chosen row from the left of the cross-tab. You may specify how much to indent the row in the text box after the Indent Row Labels check box. This is typically used to highlight a hierarchical grouping relationship when you've added multiple row fields to the cross-tab.
Indent Column Labels	Checking this option will indent the label for the chosen column from the top of the cross-tab. You may specify how much to indent the column in the text box after the Indent Column Labels check box.
Repeat Row Labels	If Keep Columns Together is checked, this option will repeat the row labels when a cross-tab exceeding the width of the page is printed on two or more pages.
Keep Columns Together	Prevents columns from being cut in half when a cross-tab exceeding the width of the page is printed.
Column Totals on Top	Displays column totals on top of the actual columns containing the data being totaled, rather than at the bottom of the columns (this is the default when dragging fields directly from the Field Explorer to a new cross-tab object).
Row Totals On Left	Displays row totals to the left of the actual rows containing the data being totaled, rather than on the right of the rows (this is the default when dragging fields directly from the Field Explorer to a new cross-tab object).
Show Cell Margins	Pads cells with white space on all sides. Turning this option off will place cells right next to each other.
Suppress Empty Rows	Rows with no data will not appear in the cross-tab.
Suppress Empty Columns	Columns with no data will not appear in the cross-tab.
Suppress Row Grand Totals	Prevents row grand totals from appearing in the cross-tab.
Suppress Column Grand Totals	Prevents column grand totals from appearing in the cross-tab.
Format Grid Lines button	Displays the Format Grid Lines dialog box (described later in the chapter) to customize where and how grid lines appear in the cross-tab.

TABLE 9-1 Customize Style Tab Options *(continued)*

TIP *In Crystal Reports XI, some of the options available on the Custom Style tab are also available by right-clicking directly on a column or row name field in the cross-tab and choosing options from the pop-up menu.*

Summarized field names appear when "Show Labels" activated

Summaries print side-by-side with horizontal option

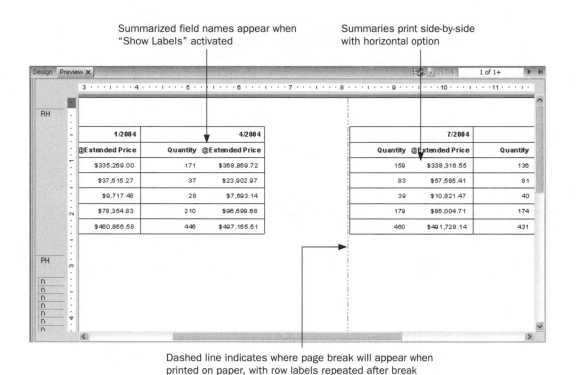

Dashed line indicates where page break will appear when printed on paper, with row labels repeated after break

FIGURE 9-7 Cross-tab with Repeat Row Labels, Show Labels, and Horizontal summaries activated on Customize Style tab

Formatting Grid Lines

Crystal Reports provides the ability to customize grid line appearance, including which grid lines appear and how they look. To customize the grid lines, select the entire cross-tab (you can't just select an individual cross-tab cell), right-click, and choose Grid Options | Format Grid Lines from the pop-up menu. If you are using the Cross-Tab Expert, click the Format Grid Lines button in the Grid Options area of the Customize Style tab. The Format Grid Lines dialog box will appear, as shown in Figure 9-8.

You may simply choose to not show any grid lines at all by unchecking the Show Grid Lines option. Or to control individual grid lines, you may either select the grid line you want to customize in the grid line list or actually click a particular line in the grid lines diagram at the top of the dialog box. Then, choose individual options for the grid line in the Line Options portion of the Format Grid Lines dialog box.

Labels or Legends with Cross-Tabs

If you add multiple summarized fields to a cross-tab, it may not be clear to your viewer what the numbers mean—they may be totals, averages, or counts. The Show Labels option, demonstrated earlier in Figure 9-7, is effective with one or two summaries. With more than one or two summaries, they may become unwieldy and hard to fit in the column or row headers.

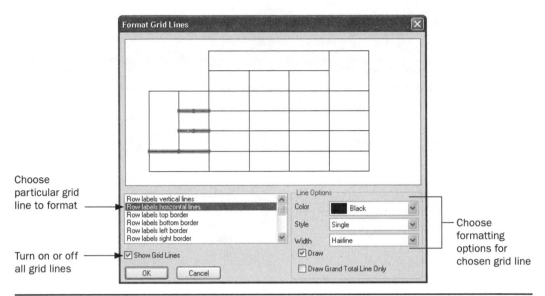

Choose particular grid line to format

Turn on or off all grid lines

Choose formatting options for chosen grid line

FIGURE 9-8 The Format Grid Lines dialog box

One way of reducing the size of labels is to change their content. Initially, they display the field name of the summarized field, including any special characters (such as the @ sign that precedes formula names). These labels are actually special text objects added to the cross-tab that you can manually change. As with other text objects, you may edit cross-tab row and column labels by simply double-clicking on them.

	1/2004		4/2004	
	Quantity	@Extended Price	Quantity	Extended Price
Competition	156	$335,269.00	171	$368,869.72
Hybrid	54	$37,515.27	37	$23,902.97
Kids	35	$9,717.48	28	$7,693.14
Mountain	166	$78,354.83	210	$96,699.68
Total	411	$460,856.58	446	$497,165.51

Conditionally Formatting Cross-Tabs

You may wish to conditionally format cross-tab cells, depending on their contents. Conditional formatting (discussed in more detail in Chapter 7) is the process of changing the appearance of a cross-tab cell according to its contents. You may wish to highlight certain cells that exceed a certain sales goal or shipping level; you can change the color, shading, or border of just those cells.

Select the summary or subtotal object that you want to conditionally format. Then, choose Format | Highlighting Expert from the pull-down menus, or right-click the cell and choose Highlighting Expert from the pop-up menu. You can choose Highlighting Expert conditions and formats to highlight certain cells.

You can also use conditional formulas. After selecting a summary or subtotal object in the cross-tab, display the Format Editor by choosing options from the Format pull-down menu or by right-clicking and choosing options from the pop-up menu. You can click a Conditional Formula button anywhere on the Format Editor to set that formatting property conditionally.

What Is CurrentFieldValue?

When you choose to use conditional formulas instead of the Highlighting Expert, you must be careful about the tests you use to conditionally format cross-tab summaries. Since the summaries are calculations based on database fields, but are not actually the database fields themselves, you can't just test a database field to conditionally format the cross-tab. And contrary to what you see if you've placed subtotals or summaries in a group footer, you won't see the summaries or subtotals that make up the cells in the field list of the Formula Editor.

You must test the built-in CurrentFieldValue function when conditionally formatting cross-tabs. CurrentFieldValue, as its name suggests, returns whatever the cell or "field"

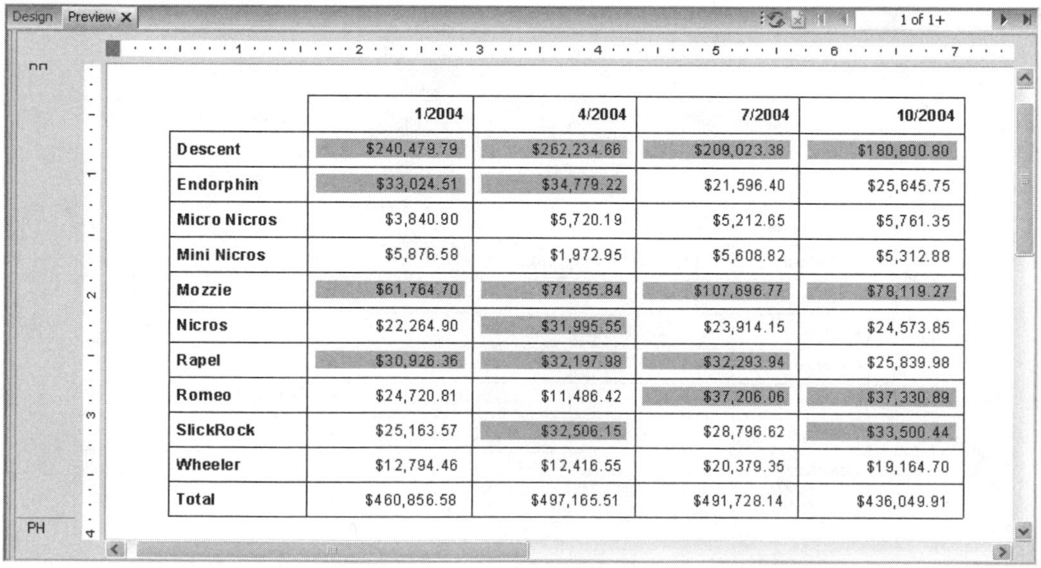

	1/2004	4/2004	7/2004	10/2004
Descent	$240,479.79	$262,234.66	$209,023.38	$180,800.80
Endorphin	$33,024.51	$34,779.22	$21,596.40	$25,645.75
Micro Nicros	$3,840.90	$5,720.19	$5,212.65	$5,761.35
Mini Nicros	$5,876.58	$1,972.95	$5,608.82	$5,312.88
Mozzie	$61,764.70	$71,855.84	$107,696.77	$78,119.27
Nicros	$22,264.90	$31,995.55	$23,914.15	$24,573.85
Rapel	$30,926.36	$32,197.98	$32,293.94	$25,839.98
Romeo	$24,720.81	$11,486.42	$37,206.06	$37,330.89
SlickRock	$25,163.57	$32,506.15	$28,796.62	$33,500.44
Wheeler	$12,794.46	$12,416.55	$20,379.35	$19,164.70
Total	$460,856.58	$497,165.51	$491,728.14	$436,049.91

FIGURE 9-9   Cross-tab conditional formatting with CurrentFieldValue

being tested contains. You can, therefore, use a conditional formula similar to the following to apply a silver background color to cross-tab subtotals that exceed $30,000:

```
If CurrentFieldValue > 30000 Then crSilver Else crNoColor
```

Figure 9-9 shows a cross-tab with this formatting.

What Are GridRowColumnValue and the Alias for Formulas?

Using the CurrentFieldValue function described in the preceding section, you can set conditional formatting in the cross-tab only based on the value of the current cell. However, you may also want to set conditional formatting based on the row or column that the cell is in, not just the value in the cell. Crystal Reports provides this capability using two functions: GridRowColumnValue and Alias for Formulas.

When you conditionally format a cell, notice the GridRowColumnValue function in the Formatting Functions category of the Functions box in the Format Formula Editor. By using this function with an If-Then-Else formula (when setting a multiple-choice formatting property) or a Boolean formula (when setting an on/off formatting property), you can determine which row or column the cell is in and format accordingly. Consider the following Boolean formula that conditionally sets the Drop Shadow property on the Format Editor Border tab:

```
GridRowColumnValue("Product.Product Name") = "Nicros"
```

The result is shown in Figure 9-10. Notice that only cells in the Nicros row have drop shadows applied to them. By supplying an alias name as the parameter for the GridRowColumnValue function, you can determine which row or column the formula will refer to. In this scenario, Product.Product Name is supplied as the alias name. So the

	1/2004	4/2004	7/2004	10/2004
Descent	$240,479.79	$262,234.66	$209,023.38	$180,800.80
Endorphin	$33,024.51	$34,779.22	$21,596.40	$25,645.75
Micro Nicros	$3,840.90	$5,720.19	$5,212.65	$5,761.35
Mini Nicros	$5,876.58	$1,972.95	$5,608.82	$5,312.88
Mozzie	$61,764.70	$71,855.84	$107,696.77	$78,119.27
Nicros	$22,264.90	$31,995.55	$23,914.15	$24,573.85
Rapel	$30,926.36	$32,197.98	$32,293.94	$25,839.98
Romeo	$24,720.81	$11,486.42	$37,206.06	$37,330.89
SlickRock	$25,163.57	$32,506.15	$28,796.62	$33,500.44
Wheeler	$12,794.46	$12,416.55	$20,379.35	$19,164.70
Total	$460,856.58	$497,165.51	$491,728.14	$436,049.91

FIGURE 9-10   Cross-tab conditional formatting with GridRowColumnValue

GridRowColumnValue for the Product Name row is tested. If the value of the row is Nicros, the drop shadow is applied.

By default, each row or column's alias is the field or formula name of the row or column (without the curly braces). If you want to change the alias name to something more meaningful (perhaps just the field name instead of the entire table/field name combination), you may change it on the Customize Style tab of the Cross-Tab Expert dialog box (refer back to Figure 9-6).

Select a row or column field in the Rows or Columns list. Then, type a new value in the Alias for Formulas text box. You may then use the new text you typed as the parameter for the GridRowColumnValue function to refer to the row or column. If you're unsure of the row or column name aliases that are available, you may expand the Row or Column names subcategory of the Formatting Functions function tree category to see them.

CAUTION *As much as you might like to, you cannot drill down on a cross-tab object. If you include a cross-tab in a summary report, you can drill down on the summary report groups, but not on the cross-tab.*

Cross-Tab Virtual Page Formatting Options

Crystal Reports deals with cross-tabs that span multiple pages in an inconsistent manner between the Preview tab and what actually is printed or exported from the finished report. If a cross-tab contains so many columns that it exceeds the chosen Crystal Reports page width, it simply expands the Preview tab horizontally and shows the cross-tab across a single page. However, when you print or export the report, the cross-tab will actually be broken into multiple pages that print one after the other.

Several options are available to make these "virtual pages" appear more palatable when printed or exported. A formatting option in the Format Editor, as well as a horizontal page number special field, are available to enhance cross-tab appearance.

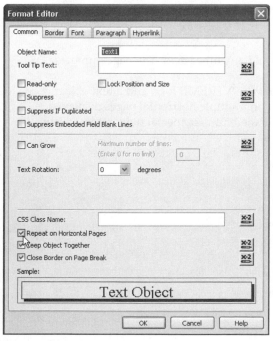

The Repeat on Horizontal Pages formatting option appears on the Format Editor Common tab. You may select this formatting property for virtually all Crystal Reports object types—database fields, bitmap graphics, text objects, and so forth. Any object that you apply this formatting option to will repeat on each subsequent page that a cross-tab object appears on, whether in the Preview tab or on a printed or exported report.

The other feature that's helpful with multipage cross-tabs is the Horizontal Page Number special field. Available along with other special fields in the Field Explorer, Horizontal Page Number will increment as cross-tabs span multiple pages, whereas the standard Page Number special field won't. Simply drag and drop the Horizontal

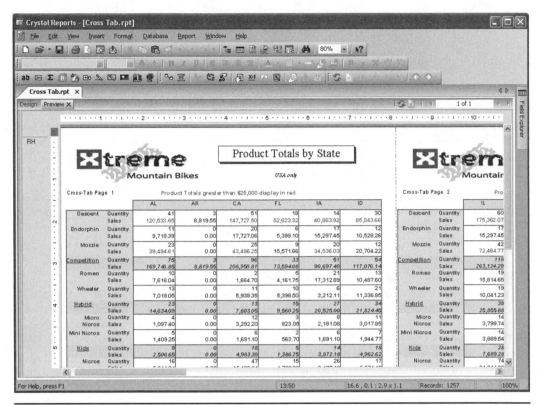

Figure 9-11   Multipage cross-tab

Page Number special field onto the report as you would any other field. The page numbers will increment as cross-tabs span pages.

Figure 9-11 illustrates these features. Notice that the XTREME logo and a text object indicating custom formatting in the cross-tab appear on multiple horizontal pages displayed in the Preview tab. Also, notice that the Horizontal Page Number special field automatically increments when the cross-tab spans multiple pages.

Creating Charts

Depending on your reporting audience requirements, you may find that graphical representation of data either supplements, or perhaps even replaces, traditional textual presentation—sometimes "a picture is worth a thousand words." Crystal Reports' rich charting capability complements its complete formatting capabilities for textual information. Not only can you create attractive, meaningful text-based reports, you can present the information graphically as well. Using Crystal Reports charting and graphing capabilities, you can see your database data presented in colorful bar charts, in pie charts, in three-dimensional area charts, and in many other ways (one additional chart type has been added to version XI). These charts can be seen in the Preview tab right inside Crystal Reports, on web reports, included in reports exported to other external file formats, or printed on a black-and-white or color printer.

There are some very fundamental questions you should initially ask before you add a chart to a report. Either you or your reporting audience should answer these questions satisfactorily before you proceed:

- Will my viewers really benefit from a graphical representation of the data?
- What kind of chart best matches the information to be shown?

While it's tempting to load up reports with lots of pretty, colorful charts, they aren't always an appropriate way to get across the "message" of the report. But for the many instances when a chart will add value to a report, you have a great number of charting options available to you.

Types and Layouts of Charts

Once you've decided to use a chart, you have two general choices to make about how you'll create your chart: what type of chart to use, and how the chart will be laid out. The *chart type* refers to what the chart will look like—whether it will show the data in bars, lines, a pie, or some other graphical representation. The *chart layout* refers to the data that will be used to make up the chart, whether it comes from the details section, group summaries, or a cross-tab or OLAP grid (OLAP reporting is discussed in Chapter 19).

Chart Type

The first consideration is which type of chart best represents the data to be charted. Although some types may be prettier than others, you again need to consider what type of chart will add real meaning to the data, allowing the viewer to get the most benefit from the report. Table 10-1 discusses the main types of charts available in the Crystal Reports Chart Expert and where they are best used. When you begin to use the Chart Expert, you'll notice that many of these main chart types actually have several variations.

Chart Type	Usage
Bar	Shows a series of bars side by side on the page, which is effective for showing how items compare to each other in terms of volume, size, dollars, etc., and may also be effective in plotting growth over time.
Line	Shows trends over time, particularly for multiple groups of data.
Area	Similar to a line chart, except that the area below the line is filled in with a color. Like the line chart, it is helpful for showing trends over time, but for just one or a few groups of data.
Pie	A circle with colored slices for each item, which is good for showing which item is the biggest "piece of the pie." The pie chart represents percentages for each item and is effective for small to moderate numbers of items.
Doughnut	Similar to a pie chart, showing who has the biggest bite of the donut. The only difference from a pie chart is that the doughnut has a hole in the middle, where the grand total for the chart is displayed.
3-D riser	A three-dimensional version of the bar chart. You can choose what shape you want for the bars—a cone, a pyramid, etc. Because this chart is three-dimensional, it can show multiple groups of data side by side.
3-D surface	A three-dimensional version of the area chart; it shows multiple groups of data in a three-dimensional view.
XY scatter	Plots data as points on two axes, allowing you to see if a correlation exists between the individual items.
Radar	Looks a little like a radar screen, with concentric circles expanding from the center. Each group of data is drawn as a line from the center to the outside of the chart, with the subtotal of that group displayed on the line in its relative location.
Bubble	Very similar to an XY scatter chart, plotting individual points within two axes, but provides more quantitative information by varying the size of the plotted points as well.
Stock	Similar to a bar chart in that it displays side-by-side bars. However, all the bars don't start at the bottom of the chart. Both the tops and bottoms of the bars are based on data supplied. This chart is helpful for viewing minimum and maximum financial data, such as stock prices.

TABLE 10-1 Crystal Reports Chart Types

Chart Type	Usage
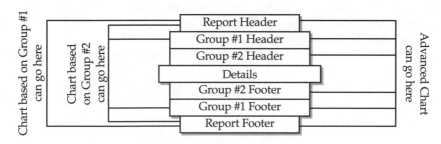 **Numeric Axis**	An alternative way of creating bar, line, or area charts (discussed previously in this table), a Numeric Axis chart allows you to use a numeric value or date/time field as the X-axis value for the charts.
Gauge	A gauge chart shows values much as a gauge on an auto dashboard shows the amount of fuel left or the speed of the automobile—a needle points to the value represented by the chart. One gauge appears for each group or single "on change of" value. If there are multiple "on change of" values, multiple needles appear in each gauge.
Gantt	This is the quintessential "project schedule" chart, showing one bar for each "task," plotting the start and end dates. This chart type can only be used with an Advanced Chart (no Group charting is available), and two date or date/time fields must be used with the chart.
Funnel	This chart type, which is very similar to a stacked bar chart where multiple elements make up a single bar, shows multiple elements in a funnel shape. A funnel chart is sometimes used to illustrate sales processes or potential, such as where each sales rep or time element sits "in the funnel."
Histogram	This standard statistical chart breaks down the data being charted into buckets or "bins," displaying a count of occurrences that fall into each bin as a bar in the chart. The number of bin bars typically is seven or eight, regardless of how many different occurrences or ranges are being charted. Values being charted are then dropped into the appropriate bin, based on where they fall in the ranges represented by the bins.

TABLE 10-1   Crystal Reports Chart Types *(continued)*

Chart Layout

In addition to the type of chart, you have a choice as to what data the chart will represent. *Cross-Tab charts* and *OLAP charts* are fairly easy to understand—they graph data in existing cross-tab objects or OLAP grids on your report. A *Group chart* graphs data contained in subtotal or summary fields in existing group headers or footers. An *Advanced chart* graphs data based on individual database records. The choice you make will be based on your individual report design and the way you want to graphically display the data.

It's particularly important to understand the difference between a Group chart and an Advanced chart, and to know where they can be placed on a report. Consider the following illustration:

In essence, a chart must always be placed *at least one level higher* than the data it's graphing. An Advanced chart must be placed in a group header or footer or the report header or footer. A Group chart must be placed in a group header or footer of a higher-level group (if there is one), or the report header or footer. Because of the one-level-higher requirement, you can *never* place an Advanced chart or Group chart in the details section—cross-tab and OLAP charts can't go there either.

Cross-Tab and OLAP charts don't fit the one-level-higher scenario. Because they depict data in a specific cross-tab or OLAP grid, they make sense only if they're in the same section as the cross-tab or OLAP grid they're based on. If you base a chart on a cross-tab or OLAP grid, it must be placed in the same section. If you later move the cross-tab or OLAP grid to another report section, the chart will automatically move along with it. If you try to move a cross-tab or OLAP grid chart to a mismatching section, you'll be unable to drop the chart.

Where you place a chart determines the data that it depicts. If you create an Advanced chart and place it in a group header, it will depict just the database records for that group— a different chart will appear for each group. If you place the same Advanced chart in the report header or footer, it will depict data for the entire report. You'll see the same behavior for a Group chart. If you place it in a higher-level group, it will graph data only for subgroups within the group where it is located. If you place the Group chart in a report header or footer, it will include data for all groups on the report.

Creating Charts

You can create a limited set of chart types within the Standard, Cross-Tab, or OLAP Report Wizard from the Start Page or wizards available on the File | New pull-down menu. If you're using one of the report wizards, you will eventually arrive at a Chart section that contains a reduced set of charting options. To take advantage of all charting capabilities, you'll need to edit the existing chart or insert a new chart after using the wizards. You may also insert a new chart when creating a report with the Blank Report option.

 If you've already created a report with a wizard and simply want to add a chart to it, or if your report is designed with the Blank Report option, you may add a new chart in one of two ways. While you can insert a chart when the Preview tab is displayed, you'll probably find better results if you first display the Design tab. Then, either click the Insert Chart button on the Insert Tools toolbar or choose Insert | Chart from the pull-down menus.

The way Crystal Reports XI responds to either of these methods has changed from previous versions. Now, as soon as you choose either Insert Chart option, an outline of the chart will be placed on your mouse pointer to be dropped into a particular report section. As discussed earlier in the chapter, charts cannot be placed in all report sections—if you drag a chart over a prohibited section, a "no-drop" cursor (a circle with a line through it) will appear. Once you click the mouse to drop the chart onto the report, two different behaviors can result: either a bar chart will be placed on the report with most options automatically chosen, or the Chart Expert will appear for you to choose specific charting choices. The different behavior is determined by where you drop the chart and how your existing report is designed.

For example, if you insert a chart into the report header or footer when there are no groups on the report (or groups with no associated summary fields), the Chart Expert will appear with the Advanced Chart button selected. However, if you perform the same insertion with a report containing a group with a summary field, a bar chart based on that group will immediately appear in the report header or footer. If your report contains a Cross-Tab or OLAP Grid object and you select it before inserting a chart, Crystal Reports will create an additional section above that containing the Cross-Tab or OLAP Grid and place a bar chart based on the Cross-Tab or OLAP Grid in the new section. You will find other instances of direct placement of bar charts versus display of the Chart Expert too. Ultimately, if you're not happy with the default behavior, just make other choices in the Chart Expert (if necessary, you'll need to select the default chart and select Format | Chart Expert from the pull-down menus or right-click the chart and choose Chart Expert from the pop-up menu).

The *Chart Expert* is a tabbed dialog box that gives you tremendous flexibility for designing your charts. You specify chart options by progressing through the Chart Expert's six tabs: Type, Data, Axes, Options, Color Highlight, and Text (some of which may not appear, depending on the chart type chosen).

The Type Tab

When the Chart Expert first appears, the Type tab will be displayed, as shown in Figure 10-1.

First, choose the general type of chart (such as pie, bar, or area) that you want to use from the list. When you make a general choice, you typically see a more specific set of choices shown as thumbnails on the right. To use the specific type of chart, click the thumbnail that best represents what you want to use. You'll see a description of the layout and uses of the chart in the scroll box below.

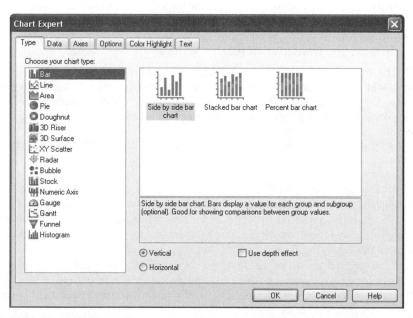

FIGURE 10-1 The Chart Expert Type tab

Certain chart types give you a choice of horizontal or vertical direction. If you choose vertical with a bar chart, for example, the bars will grow out of the bottom of the chart. If you choose horizontal, they will spread from the left of the chart toward the right. By default, all chart types display in a flat, non-dimensional form. However, most chart types will provide a Use Depth Effect check box to allow the chart to be displayed with a three-dimensional appearance. Checking this box will display the thumbnails with a 3-D appearance so that you can get a better idea of how your chart will ultimately appear.

The Data Tab

The Data tab is where you choose the layout for the chart—whether it will be an Advanced, Group, Cross-Tab, or OLAP chart. You also use the Data tab to select the actual summary, database, or formula fields you want Crystal Reports to use when creating your chart, and to specify when you want the chart to "change" graphically (when you want a new bar or pie slice to be created, when you want a new point plotted on the line, and so on).

Begin by choosing the chart layout you want to use. The following four buttons on the left side of the Data tab may or may not be enabled, depending on other elements in your report:

- **Group**   Available only if at least one group with at least one summary field has been created on your report.

- **Advanced**   Always available, although it is the default button only if nothing else is available.

- **Cross-Tab**   Available only if one or more cross-tab objects already are on the report in the same section as the chart (or "companion" section, such as a corresponding header or footer section). If you have more than one cross-tab but haven't selected the cross-tab you want to chart first, this button will be disabled.

- **OLAP**   Available only if one or more OLAP grids already are on the report in the same section as the chart (or in a "companion" section, such as a corresponding header or footer section). If you have more than one OLAP grid but haven't selected the grid you want to chart first, this button will be disabled.

Portions of the Data tab will change as you click different chart layout buttons.

Group

A Group chart will graph data from fields in an existing report group. You have to have at least one group defined, with at least one subtotal or summary field, before you can use this button. You also must have placed the chart in the report header or footer or in a higher-level group header or footer (above another group) for this button to be enabled. Figure 10-2 shows the Data tab when the Group button is clicked.

The On Change Of drop-down list lets you choose when you want the graph to start a new element. If, for example, you choose Customer.Country, a new bar will show up in a bar chart for every country. Or for another example, if you choose Employee.Last Name, a new slice in a pie chart will appear for every employee.

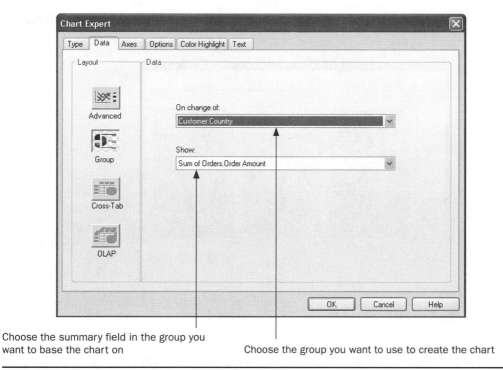

Choose the summary field in the group you
want to base the chart on

Choose the group you want to use to create the chart

FIGURE 10-2   Data tab for Group button

The On Change Of drop-down list's contents change in correlation with where you placed
the chart on the report, how many groups are on the report, and which groups contain
summary fields. In essence, the On Change Of drop-down list shows you one or two levels
lower than where you placed your chart. For example, if you placed the chart in a report
header or footer, the On Change Of drop-down list will show the highest-level group on the
report. If there is more than one group, it will also show an additional option of showing the
highest-level group and the next-highest-level group (assuming both groups contain at least
one summary field). If you placed the report in a group header or footer, On Change Of will
show the next two lower-level groups, and so on.

Here's an example of what shows up in the On Change Of drop-down list when the chart
is placed in the report header and there are country and customer name groups on the report,
both containing at least one summary field:

If you choose a single group, your chart will just summarize the values in that group, as shown here:

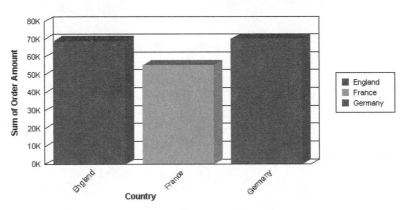

If you choose the two-group option, Crystal Reports actually creates multiple sections of the chart—the first section based on the first group, each containing individual chart elements based on the second group, like this:

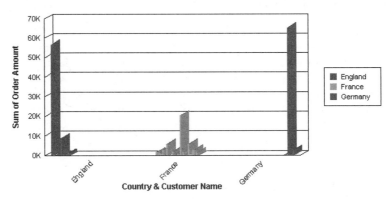

The Show drop-down list lets you choose what makes up the chart element. If, for example, you create a bar chart with On Change Of set to Customer.Country, and Show set to Sum of Orders.Order Amount, you'll see a new bar for every country. The bar's height or width (depending on whether you chose a horizontal or vertical bar chart) will be based on the subtotal of Order Amount for the group.

The Show drop-down list is populated according to what subtotal and summary fields you place in the group header or footer of the group chosen in On Change Of. For a group graph to work, you must have at least one summary or subtotal for the group—if you don't, the Group layout button won't even be available.

Advanced

An Advanced chart graphs data from individual database records in your report. Although you can create an Advanced chart even if you have groups defined, it won't be affected by the groups at all. Figure 10-3 shows the Data tab when the Advanced button is clicked.

This rather busy dialog box lets you choose data from the report or database to create a chart (fields don't have to be placed on the report to be used to create the chart). Because so many different choices are available, a little more forethought is required when using this dialog box.

The Available Fields list shows report, formula, subtotal/summary, running total, and database fields in the report. You can select any of these fields that you need for creating your chart (except summary/subtotal fields, which can be used only in the Show Value(s) list). If you're unsure what kind of data is in a field, select it and click the Browse button to see a sample of database data. Once you're ready to use a field as either an On Change Of or Show Value(s) field, select the field and click the right arrow next to the box where you want the field placed. It will be copied to the box on the right.

The drop-down list in the upper right gives you three choices: On Change Of, For Each Record, and For All Records. The choice you make here determines how often a new chart element (bar, pie slice, and so on) will appear in the chart.

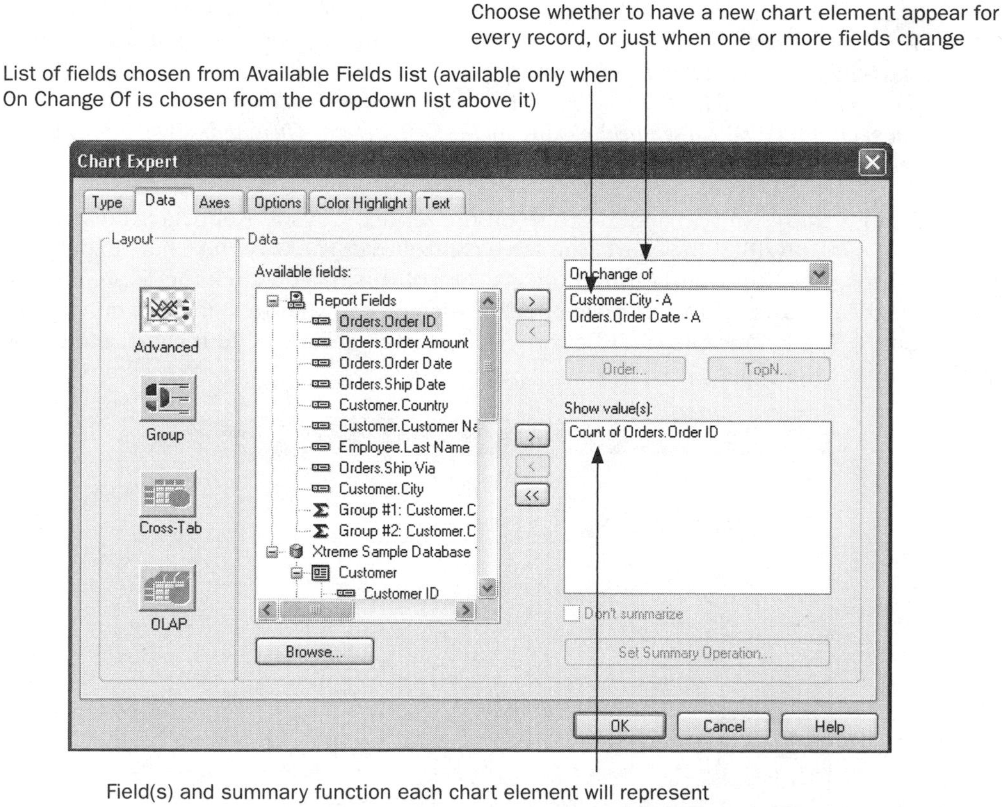

Choose whether to have a new chart element appear for every record, or just when one or more fields change

List of fields chosen from Available Fields list (available only when On Change Of is chosen from the drop-down list above it)

Field(s) and summary function each chart element will represent

FIGURE 10-3   Data tab for the Advanced button

If you choose For Each Record, a new element appears in the chart for every record in the report. This may be useful for very small tables that have only a few records in them. However, if your database has more than a few records, making this choice will probably render a chart that's too crowded to be of any real value. If you choose For All Records, you essentially create a *grand total* chart, showing just one element that displays a total of all records on the report. If you choose this option, the box below the drop-down list remains empty—you won't be able to add any fields to it from the Available Fields list. If you choose For Each record, you may add one field from the Available Fields list that will label each chart element.

By choosing On Change Of in the drop-down list and choosing one or more fields from the Available Fields list (except group summary or subtotal fields), you can create a chart that summarizes values for the chosen field or fields. This option basically creates an invisible group within the chart, creating a new chart element every time the chosen field changes. For example, if your report contains no groups but you choose On Change Of Customer. Country, your chart will have a new element appear for each unique country that appears in the database. Whatever field you add to the Show Value(s) list will be summarized or subtotaled by country, and the result will be used as the value for the chart.

TIP *You can choose one or two fields to add to the On Change Of list. This works like the Group chart option, described previously, in which you can choose to show the highest-level group and the next-highest-level group. If you choose one field, the chart will contain only one section with all the elements located in it. If you choose two fields, the chart will be broken into side-by-side sections, with the first-chosen field making up the first section. Then, individual elements for the second field will appear within each of the sections based on the first field.*

Although there isn't an actual group on the report, Crystal Reports is creating an "invisible" group within the chart. You have control over the way the Chart Expert uses these groups. The TopN and Order buttons control this. If you click the TopN button, you'll see the Group Sort Expert dialog box, where you can choose to include only the top *N*, bottom *N*, Top *N* Percentage, or Bottom *N* percentage groups in your chart, and choose which number to use for *N*.

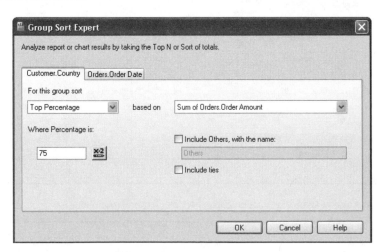

If you click the Order button, you'll see the Chart Sort Order dialog box with a drop-down list containing Ascending, Descending, Specified Order, and Original Order options. You may choose to show the chart elements in A to Z order, Z to A order, or using specified grouping (and, if you recall from Chapter 3, although Original Order is an option, it's probably of little use). If the chosen field is a date, time, or date/time field, you can choose how often you want a new chart element to appear (monthly, weekly, every minute, hourly, and so on). Refer to Chapter 3 for information on Top N, Specified Order grouping, and grouping on date/time fields.

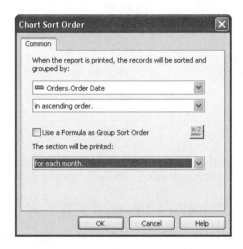

Once you've chosen a field in the On Change Of box to determine when a new chart element will appear, you can add a field or fields to the Show Value(s) list to indicate which values Crystal Reports will use to size the chart element. If you add multiple fields to this list, the chart will contain multiple bars, lines, and so forth—one for each field you add to the list.

If you add a number or currency field to this list (and you haven't chosen For Each Record in the top drop-down list), Crystal Reports automatically uses the Sum function to subtotal the field for each invisible group. If you choose another type of field, Crystal Reports automatically uses the Count function. If you wish to change the summary function (for example, to graph the average sales amount instead of the total), you can select the field you want to change in the Show Value(s) list and click the Set Summary Operation button. A dialog box will appear with a drop-down list containing the available summary functions for that type of field. Choose the summary function you want used to size the chart element. The Percentage Summary Field option for group summaries, discussed in Chapter 3, is also available here. By checking the Show As A Percentage Of check box, you can choose a higher-level group total or grand total, and chart elements will display the percentage of the higher totals that each of the invisible group totals represents.

NOTE *If you choose On Change Of for an Advanced Chart and add a formula field to the Show value(s) list, the Don't Summarize check box will be enabled when you select the formula. Clicking this check box for the formula (probably a formula that already does some sort of summarization) allows you to display the formula's value directly in the chart without its being summarized again.*

If you choose For Each Record in the top drop-down list, Crystal Reports will display a new chart element for every record on the report—no invisible group will be created. In this case, any fields you add to the Show Value(s) list won't be summarized—whatever value the fields return for each record will be charted.

Cross-Tab

The Cross-Tab button is available only if you have one or more cross-tab objects in the same section (or a "companion" header or footer) as the chart. If you have only one cross-tab object, this button will be enabled even if you haven't selected the cross-tab first. However, if you have more than one cross-tab, you must select the cross-tab that you want to chart *before* you display the Chart Expert (Chapter 9 discusses cross-tab objects). Figure 10-4 shows the Data tab when the Cross-Tab button is clicked.

The On Change Of drop-down list includes the two outer fields you chose for the cross-tab row and column; if you used multiple row and column fields, only the first row or field can be used. Crystal Reports will create one chart element (bar, pie slice, and so on) for each occurrence of this field in the cross-tab.

The Subdivided By drop-down list is initially set to None. If you leave it this way, the chart will create only one series of chart elements, based on the field in the On Change Of drop-down list. If, however, you want to create two series of elements for side-by-side comparison, or if you're using a 3-D riser or 3-D area chart and want to see multiple elements three-dimensionally, choose the other row/column field in the Subdivided By drop-down list.

The Show drop-down list shows the summary field or fields you placed in your cross-tab. Choose the field that you want to use in your chart. This field determines the size of the chart elements (height of a bar, size of a pie slice, and so forth).

Choose row or column field to
determine chart element

Optionally choose other row/
column for multipart chart

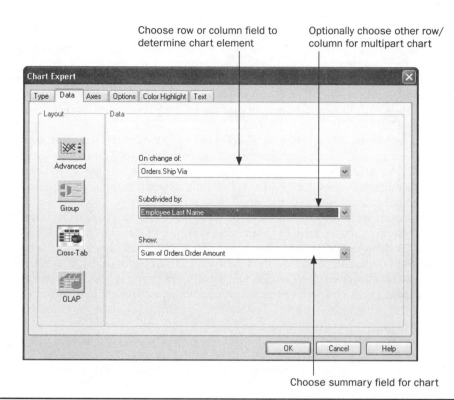

Choose summary field for chart

FIGURE 10-4 Data tab for the Cross-Tab button

The following illustration shows the resulting 3-D riser chart for the Data tab shown in
Figure 10-4:

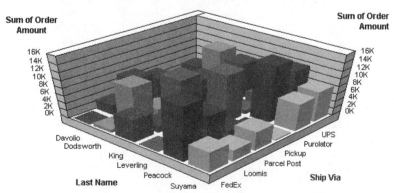

OLAP

The OLAP button is available only if you have one or more OLAP grid objects in the same section (or a "companion" header or footer) as the chart. If you have only one OLAP grid object, this button will be enabled even if you haven't selected the grid first. However, if you have more than one OLAP grid, you must select the grid that you want to chart *before* you display the Chart Expert (Chapter 19 discusses OLAP reporting). Figure 10-5 shows the Data tab when the OLAP button is clicked.

Creating a chart based on an OLAP grid is very similar to creating a chart based on a cross-tab. There are just a couple of differences between the two. There is no summary field to choose (OLAP grids display only one value, so there is no choice to make). Also, the dimension hierarchy of your OLAP grid may be a little different than the multiple row/column fields you added to a cross-tab object.

Choose a dimension on which to base the chart from the On Change Of drop-down list. A new chart element will be created for every occurrence of this dimension. If you leave the Subdivided By drop-down list set to None, the chart creates only one series of chart elements, based on the dimension in the On Change Of drop-down list. If, however, you want to create two series of elements for side-by-side comparison, or if you're using a 3-D riser or 3-D area chart and want to see multiple elements three-dimensionally, choose

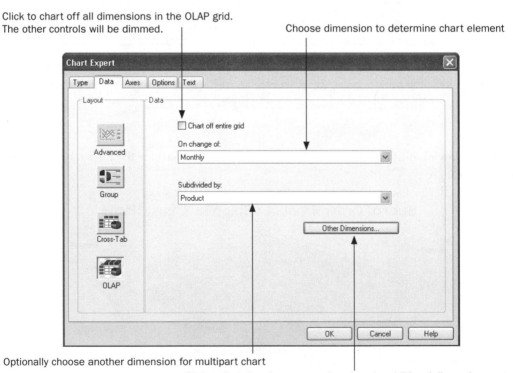

Click to chart off all dimensions in the OLAP grid. The other controls will be dimmed.

Choose dimension to determine chart element

Optionally choose another dimension for multipart chart

Click to limit the chart to certain values in additional dimensions not included in the On Change Of and Subdivided By drop-down lists

FIGURE 10-5 Data tab for the OLAP button

another dimension in the Subdivided By drop-down list. You can choose a next "deeper" level dimension here if you've created multiple levels of dimensions in your OLAP grid.

Depending on how many dimensions your OLAP grid contains, and how the fields that make up the dimension relate to each other (their *hierarchy*), you may need to filter the chart to just certain field values in a dimension. To do this, click the Other Dimensions button in the lower right of the Data tab. This displays the Format Other Dimensions dialog box, where you can choose the particular subdimension of the OLAP grid that you want the chart filtered by.

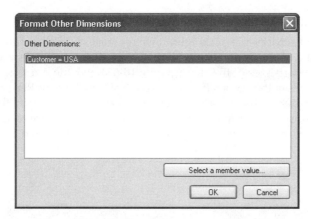

Click one of the available Other Dimensions and click the Select A Member Value button. The Member Selector dialog box appears, with the dimension hierarchy displayed in an Explorer-like fashion.

Navigate through the dimension hierarchy and choose a level that you want to limit the chart to. For example, if you navigate down from USA and choose CO, your OLAP chart will just contain totals for the Colorado region in the OLAP grid.

TIP *You can experiment with OLAP grids and charts by using a sample OLAP cube file installed with Crystal Reports. Create an OLAP grid (using the steps described in Chapter 19) based on the Holos HDC cube file Program Files\Business Objects\Crystal Reports 11\Samples\En\ Databases\Olap Data\Xtreme.hdc. Note that you must have included the OLAP Cube data access type when you installed Crystal Reports in order to create an OLAP grid. You can then create a chart based on this OLAP grid.*

The Axes Tab

The Axes tab will appear if you have chosen a chart type that makes use of X and Y axes (for example, a bar or line chart—pie or doughnut chart choices will eliminate the Axes tab). The Axes tab gives you complete control over how Crystal Reports displays the X, Y, and Z (if you're using a 3-D chart) axes of the chart. Figure 10-6 shows the Axes tab.

By making choices in the Axes tab, you can control how Crystal Reports displays axes on your charts. The *axes* are the areas of the chart that describe or depict the data values in the chart. If, for example, you have a bar chart in which each bar represents sales volume for a country, the bottom of the chart where each country is listed is called the *group axis* (also

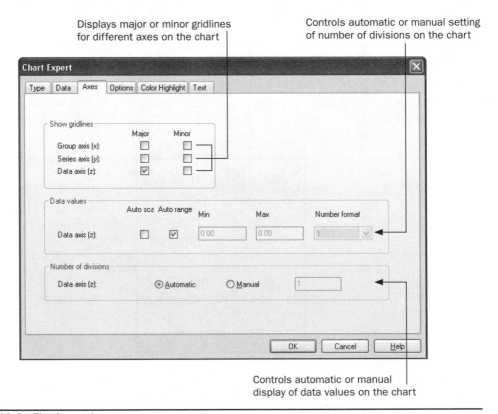

FIGURE 10-6 The Axes tab

sometimes called the *X axis*). The left side of the chart where the numbers representing the volume appear is called the *data axis* (sometimes called the *Y axis*), as shown here:

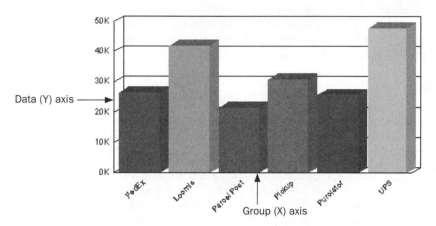

If you are using a 3-D chart, the data axis is the Z axis, and a new axis called the *series axis* is the Y axis, like this:

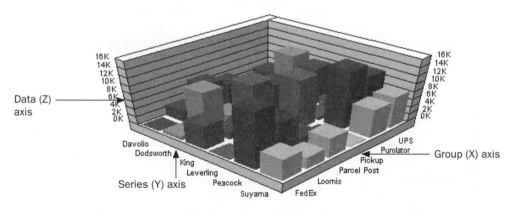

Click the Major or Minor check box to add gridlines to the chosen axes. *Major gridlines* fall directly in line with the axis labels that Crystal Reports assigns to the axis. *Minor gridlines* appear in between the axis labels and work only for numeric labels. Depending on the type of chart you're using, you may not notice any difference between major and minor gridlines. Also, some charts will always have a group axis gridline, regardless of what you choose on the Axes tab.

If you leave the Auto Range check box for the Data Values option on, Crystal Reports automatically formats the chart according to the number of elements it includes. If you wish to customize this, you can turn off the Auto Range option and add starting and ending values for the axes, as well as choose the number format (decimals, currency symbols, and so on) to use for the labels. If you choose a certain number format, such as a currency symbol, and then recheck Auto Range, the axes will be automatically renumbered, but the number format you chose will stay in place. The Auto Scale option affects the beginning numeric value that the data axis starts with. If you choose Auto Scale, Crystal Reports uses the values of the chart elements to choose an appropriate starting number for the data axis.

If you leave the Number of Divisions set to Automatic, Crystal Reports will create a predefined number of labels and gridlines for the data axes. Clicking the Manual radio button and specifying a number in the text box will create your specified number of divisions, along with labels and gridlines, for the data axes.

The Options Tab

The Options tab allows you to customize general options for your chart, such as whether to display it in color or black and white, whether to show a legend and where to place it, and other options. The Options tab will change based on the type of chart you've chosen. Figure 10-7 shows the Options tab for a bar chart.

TIP *If you are printing your reports on a black-and-white printer, it may be preferable to leave the chart in color and let the printer assign gray tones to the chart elements. These may actually look better than the ones Crystal Reports assigns. Experiment to determine what works best with your particular printer.*

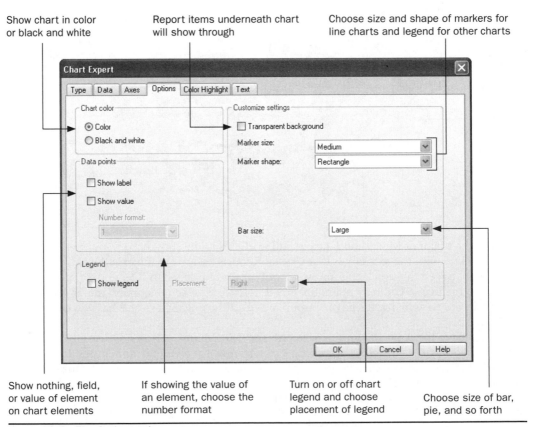

FIGURE 10-7   The Options tab

The Data Points section lets you choose whether you want labels, numbers, or both to appear on your chart elements. If, for example, you choose Show Label with a pie chart, each of the slices of the pie will be labeled with the item that the slice refers to. If you choose Show Value with a bar chart and choose a number format of $1, you'll see the actual dollar amounts (with no decimal places) appear above each bar.

The Marker Size and Marker Shape drop-down lists let you choose how markers look on a line chart. *Markers* are the points on the line chart that are connected by the lines.

The Show Legend check box determines whether or not a legend appears on your chart. The *legend* is the color-coded key that indicates what the elements of your chart refer to. You can also choose where to place the legend with options in the Placement drop-down list. You might want legends for a pie chart with no labels, for example. However, if you are using a bar chart with labels already appearing along the bottom of the chart, a legend is redundant and should be turned off.

The Color Highlight Tab

The Color Highlight tab, new in version XI, allows conditional formatting of chart element colors (previously, this choice was available via a button on the Options tab). While you can pick individual chart elements, such as an individual pie wedge, or an individual bar, and change the color (as discussed later in the chapter under "Changing Colors and Shades of Chart Elements"), your change will always affect the same wedge or bar in each chart, regardless of what the value of that element is. In other words, if you change the pie wedge for Colorado, which happens to be the second wedge in the chart, to a light blue color, the second wedge in the chart will be light blue no matter what data populates the chart. If the data changes so that Colorado becomes the fourth wedge, the second wedge will still be formatted as light blue.

The Color Highlight tab works with charts in much the same way that the Highlighting Expert works with text (the Highlighting Expert is discussed in detail in Chapter 7). You may choose one or more conditions that determine the color of a chart element. The Color Highlight tab is shown in Figure 10-8.

By choosing either the "On Change Of" field that the chart is based on or the summary field used to determine the weight of the chart element, you can conditionally set the color of the chart element.

For example, Figure 10-8 shows a condition set up to change the color of the chart element (in this case, the bar of a bar chart) to Red if the value shown by the bar exceeds $70,000. To set this condition, click the New button, which will add a new condition to the Item list. Then, choose the field you want to base the condition on and the comparison operator (such as equal to, greater than, and so forth) from the first two drop-down lists of the Value Of section. Type the value you want to compare to in the text box in the same section. Then, choose the color you wish the chart element to display if the condition is true from the color list on the lower right. Any chart elements that meet the condition will be given the chosen color.

You may add as many conditions as you wish by clicking the New button multiple times. If you have multiple conditions that may conflict, such as a condition that looks for a value between 100 and 1,000, and another condition that looks for a value greater than 500, you can set the priority of the conditions by using the up and down arrows at the top of the item list. Conditions toward the top of the item list take priority.

Reorder priority of conditions
if there are more than one

Choose field and condition
to determine element color

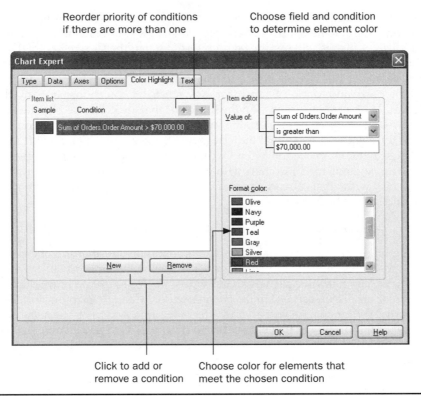

Click to add or
remove a condition

Choose color for elements that
meet the chosen condition

FIGURE 10-8 The Color Highlight tab

The Text Tab

The Text tab, shown in Figure 10-9, allows you to assign text to different parts of your chart, and change the appearance of these text items. You can add a chart title, subtitle, and footnote. Also, you can place titles on the group, data, and series (or data2) axes of your chart.

By default, the Auto-Text check boxes are all selected and the text boxes next to them are dimmed. You'll notice that Crystal Reports has added titles into certain items automatically, depending on the data that the chart is based on. If you don't wish to use Crystal Reports' default titles on the chart, uncheck the Auto-Text check box for the desired title and then type the material you want to appear on the chart in the associated text boxes on the Text tab. If you leave a text box blank, that title won't appear on the chart.

To change the appearance of the different items, select the item you want to change in the list on the lower right of the Text tab. Then, click the Font button to choose the font face, size, and appearance for that item. A sample of the font you choose appears in the shaded box above the Font button.

Figure 10-10 shows a chart with all the labels set. You can see where each of the labels appears on a typical chart.

Check to automatically generate
text based on data in the chart

If you turn off Auto-Text, type in titles
for various parts of the chart

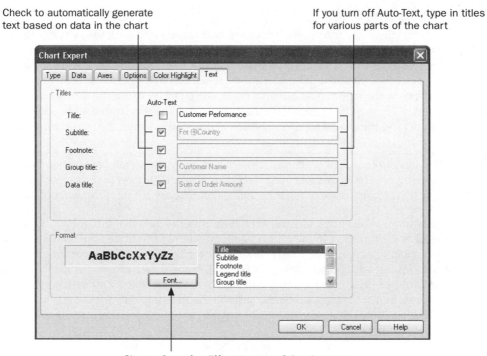

Choose fonts for different parts of the chart text

FIGURE 10-9 The Text tab

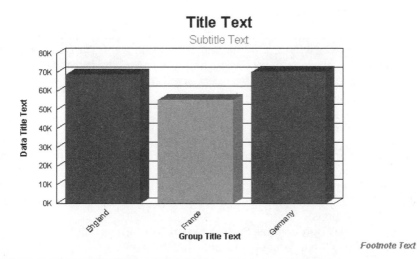

FIGURE 10-10 Labels from the Text tab

Placing and Sizing Charts

Once you complete all the information on the Chart Expert and click OK, Crystal Reports redisplays the chart with any changes you chose in the Chart Expert. The chart remains selected after you close the Chart Expert—you'll notice the shaded outline and sizing handles around the chart. You can now drag it to another location in the same section, or move it to another section on the report. You can also resize the chart by using the sizing handles, or move and resize the chart by choosing Format | Size And Position from the pull-down menus, or by right-clicking the chart and choosing Size And Position from the pop-up menu.

CAUTION *Make sure you have the entire chart selected before you attempt to move or resize it. If you see sizing handles around any individual chart elements, such as the title or an individual bar or pie wedge, you'll move or resize the individual element instead of the entire chart.*

Remember that where you place a chart determines the data that it displays. If you place an Advanced or Group chart in the report header or footer, it will display data for the whole report. If you place the chart in a group header or footer, the chart will appear for every group, showing data for only that particular group. Cross-Tab and OLAP charts display the data from the particular objects they're based on. If you place a cross-tab object and matching chart in a group header or footer, the cross-tab and chart will display data only for the group they're in. Since OLAP grids don't change with their location on the report, a matching OLAP chart won't change if you move it.

Cross-Tab and OLAP charts are always in the same section (or a "companion" section, such as a matching footer or header) as their corresponding cross-tab object or OLAP grid object. You may have an OLAP grid in the report footer and its matching chart in the report header, but if you try to move the chart into a group header or footer, it won't work. And if you then move the OLAP grid from the report footer to a group footer, the chart will automatically move to the matching group header.

TIP *If you create a chart based on, say, a Region field, but years appear in the Design tab, don't be surprised. The charts that appear in the Design tab are "dummy" charts that don't depict actual data in the database. When you preview the report, however, you will see live data depicted in the chart.*

Placing Charts Alongside Text

If you initially place a chart in a report or group header, the chart will print before the rest of the report or the group, because the section containing the chart prints first. Sometimes, you may want a chart to appear *alongside* the data it's referring to. Typically, this might be an Advanced chart that you've placed in a group header. Instead of having the chart print by itself, followed by the details that belong to the group, you may want the chart to print alongside the details sections.

By using the Underlay option in the Section Expert, you can format the group header section to underlay the following details sections, thereby printing the chart alongside the other items. For this to work effectively, you need to size and move the details section objects so that they won't be overprinted by the chart. Then, move and size the chart so that it will appear to the side of the details section objects. Using the Section Expert, choose the Underlay

Following Sections option for the section containing the chart. If there is a group name, column headings, or other information in the group header that you *don't* want to be underlaid, you need to create a second group header section for the chart that you underlay. Format it to use the Underlay feature and format the first group header containing the textual information with Underlay turned off. See Chapter 8 for more information on multiple sections and the Underlay feature.

Figure 10-11 shows a chart placed in the Report Header with Underlay Following Sections turned on.

Modifying Existing Charts

Once you've created a chart, you may wish to change it. You may not agree with the default choices Crystal Reports makes when it inserts certain charts for you. Perhaps you prefer to see a pie chart instead of a bar chart. Or, you may want to change the titles that appear on the chart. You may even want to change the chart from an Advanced chart to a Group chart, or vice versa.

First, select the chart you want to change in either the Design or Preview tab (make sure you select the entire chart, not just an embedded chart element). Then, choose Format | Chart Expert from the pull-down menus, or right-click the selected chart and choose Chart Expert from the pop-up menu. The Chart Expert will reappear, and you can make any desired changes before clicking OK.

If you place a single chart on the report that may appear multiple times (for example, you place a chart in a group header that prints for multiple report groups), you'll find that a submenu will appear when you attempt to redisplay the Chart Expert. The submenu's

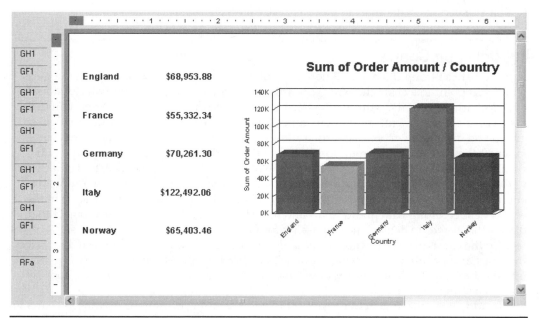

FIGURE 10-11   Chart placed alongside text with the Underlay feature

choices, Applied To Group Template and Applied To This Instance, determine whether the Chart Expert will apply to *all* charts in all groups (the Group Template choice) or to the individual chart in the group you selected (the This Instance choice).

TIP   *The Crystal Reports Format Painter works with charts, as well as textual elements. However, note that only the few formatting items that appear on the chart Format Editor, such as border, drop shadow, and so forth, will be copied from one chart to another. No chart-specific items, such as chart type, legend, or titles, will be copied by the Format Painter.*

Zooming In and Out on Charts

You may zoom in and out on a limited number of chart types. If you have created a Bar or Line chart, you'll notice additional options, such as Select Mode and Zoom In, available on the pop-up menu when you right-click. You may also select a chart and use the Zoom options from the Chart pull-down menu.

If you choose the Zoom In option, your mouse cursor will change to a magnifying glass with a plus sign. While you may be tempted to just click somewhere inside the chart expecting to zoom in, you must actually hold down your mouse button and draw an elastic box with the mouse. When you release the mouse button, the chart will zoom in to the area you surrounded. You may continue to highlight additional areas to zoom in further on the chart.

To zoom back out, right-click the chart and choose Zoom Out from the pop-up menu, or choose the associated option from the Chart pull-down menu. The mouse cursor will change to a magnifying glass with a minus sign. Just click anywhere on the chart to zoom back out.

When you're finished zooming in or out on a chart, choose Select Mode from the chart pop-up or pull-down menus. Your mouse cursor will return to its default "four-arrow" state so that you can select the chart to move or resize it on the report.

Drilling Down on Charts

If you create a Group chart, you'll notice the mouse cursor change to a magnifying glass when you point to a chart element. This drill-down cursor indicates that you can double-click a chart element that you're interested in to drill down on the chart. When you drill down on a chart element, another tab appears next to the Preview tab for the particular group you drilled down on. Drill-down allows your report viewer to interact with charts, much as they interact with group footer and group header subtotal and summary fields.

By creative use of Group charts and hiding of details and group header/footer sections, you can make a very visually appealing interactive report for use in online reporting environments. You could, for example, create a large Group pie chart and place it in the report header, along with grand totals and text objects. You might add a text object that directs the viewer to double-click a pie slice for more information. You may also set Tool Tip text for the chart, prompting the viewer to double-click the slice they're interested in. Select the chart and right-click, choosing Format Chart from the pop-up menu. Then, type text into the Tool Top Text box directly, or use the Conditional Formula button to add Tool Tip text via a string formula.

To add even more interactivity, you could add lower-level Group or Advanced charts in the report's group headers or footers, hiding them with the Section Expert. When the user drills down on the higher-level chart in the report header, a drill-down tab showing a more detailed chart will open. You can create drill-down levels until the user eventually reaches details sections to see low-level transaction data.

Get more information about creating multiple groups, drill-down, and hidden sections in Chapters 3 and 8.

TIP *Drill-down is available and useful only when viewing a report in its native format. Viewers can drill down on reports displayed right on the Preview tab of Crystal Reports, by using a report integrated with a custom Windows application, or by using Crystal Reports web-based viewers, including Crystal Reports Server (discussed in Part II of this book). Drill-down doesn't work with reports exported to other file formats, such as Word and Excel. Obviously, drill-down won't be effective with printed reports.*

Finer Points of Chart Formatting

So far, the discussion on chart formatting has been limited to what can be accomplished in the Chart Expert. However, Crystal Reports provides more granular formatting options by way of in-place chart formatting. *In-place* formatting allows you to select individual parts of the chart, such as chart or axis titles, individual chart elements, or the chart legend, and perform additional formatting functions.

CAUTION *While in-place chart formatting reduces the number of steps required to format individual chart elements, it also makes it easier to inadvertently move or resize an individual chart element when you mean to move or resize the entire chart. Pay close attention to what has been highlighted (the entire chart or an individual chart element) before you move or resize with your mouse.*

One of the first chart formatting options that you should become familiar with is the *Auto Arrange Chart* option. Once you've selected a chart, you may choose this option either from the Chart pull-down menu or by right-clicking on the chart and choosing it from the pop-up menu. This option will use default placement, sizing, and formatting for chart elements. If you haven't done any individual element formatting since you've created the chart, this option very well may not do anything at all. However, if you changed positions of certain items (such as the chart title, legend, or axes titles), you may see them snap back to other positions that you didn't intend. Don't worry too much about this behavior—if you don't like the changes that Auto Arrange makes to the chart, you may undo its effects with Edit | Undo from the pull-down menus, the Undo toolbar button in the Standard toolbar, or by pressing CTRL-Z.

Customizing Charts with Chart Options

While you can control a good deal of chart formatting from within the Chart Expert, there will probably be many times when you wish to have more detailed control over chart appearance. Crystal Reports allows you either to select individual elements of the chart (such as the title, individual bars or pie wedges, the legend, and so forth) and apply formatting to them, or to make more specific changes that affect the overall chart appearance.

To perform generalized formatting on the entire chart, choose Chart | Chart Options from the pull-down menus or right-click the chart and choose Chart Options from the pop-up menu. A tabbed dialog box will appear, showing various detailed options for changing overall chart appearance.

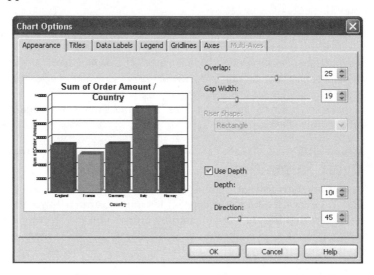

In most cases, you'll notice a thumbnail miniature picture of the chart in the dialog box. As you make changes to the dialog box, you'll see the changes immediately reflected in the thumbnail. When you click OK, the chart will reflect the changes.

TIP *Any changes you make to a chart using chart formatting options will apply to only that one instance of the chart back on the Preview tab. If, for example, you choose a chart in the Canada group header and customize it with Chart Options, the other charts in the USA and Mexico group headers won't be affected. If you want to have these changes propagate to all other chart instances, right-click the chart and choose Apply Changes To All Charts from the pop-up menu, or choose Chart | Apply Changes To All Charts from the pull-down menus.*

In addition to general chart formatting options available on the Chart Options dialog box, various individual customization options are available for individual portions of the chart, including individual elements (such as line/pie/bar elements), the chart "frame," and individual text portions of the chart (such as titles, axes labels, and footnote text).

Changing Colors and Shades of Chart Elements

When you create a chart in the Chart Expert, your only choices for affecting chart colors are the Color and Black And White radio buttons on the Options tab, and the Color Highlight tab for conditional color selection. By choosing the Color radio button in the Options tab, you have no control over what individual colors or shades the chart elements will have. And, while you can set conditions for coloring chart elements in the Color Highlight tab, this is an unduly complicated task if your desire is to simply change the default colors. The ability to completely customize element colors and shades is a feature available with Chart Options.

Begin by selecting the element you wish to color. This can be an individual bar, pie slice, or line. Note that it may look as though you've selected only part of an element—for example, just one side or just the top of the bar. Whenever you change the color, however, it will apply to the entire element.

Then, choose the appropriate format option from the Chart pull-down menu, or right-click the element and choose the Format option from the pop-up menu. For example, if you select an individual bar in a bar chart and choose Format Series Riser, the following dialog box appears:

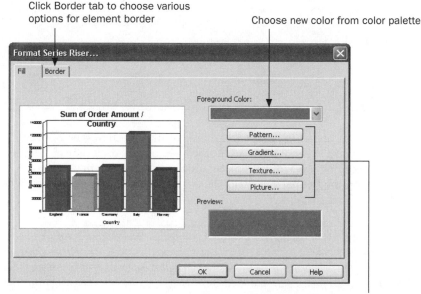

Click Border tab to choose various options for element border

Choose new color from color palette

Click one of these buttons to fill with a pattern, gradient, texture, or picture

You may change not only the color of the chosen chart element, but also the pattern displayed in the element. By default, all charts created with the Chart Expert contain solid colors. However, you may want to replace the solid color with a graduated color, a pattern, or maybe even a picture. You may change the solid color to use for the element by choosing a predefined color from the palette. If you want to use a color that's not in the standard palette, click the More button at the bottom of the palette. A Custom Color dialog box appears, in which you can choose a custom color.

To apply a pattern, gradient, or texture, or to fill the chart element with a picture, choose one of the corresponding buttons on the right side of the dialog box. For example, clicking the gradient button displays a dialog box showing preset color gradients. If you click the Advanced Options button, the gradient dialog box displays an extra section that lets you design your own gradients.

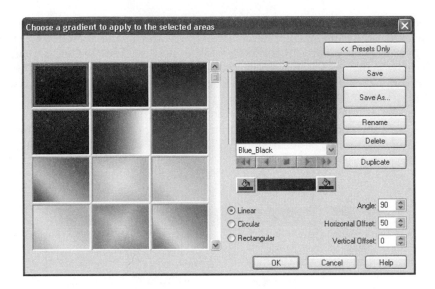

Either choose one of the preset gradients or use the dialog box options to customize your own gradient. When you click OK, the solid color previously appearing in the preview portion of the dialog box will be replaced by the selected gradient.

Click OK on the Formatting dialog box to apply your selected color, pattern, gradient, or picture to the chart element.

TIP *Often, gradients and patterns, or even certain solid background colors, can add visual appeal if applied to the whole background of the chart. To do this, select the entire chart, making sure no individual chart elements are selected. Then, right-click or use the Chart menu options to format the chart background. Color and gradient/pattern options you choose will then apply to the chart background.*

Customizing and Moving Chart Titles, Labels, and the Legend

When you add a title, labels, and legend to your chart with the Options and Text tabs of the Chart Expert, Crystal Reports places them in specific locations, using specific colors and alignment. If you choose to display a legend on your chart, you have only a few predefined locations on the Options tab where you can place it. Also, if you choose the Auto Arrange Chart option discussed earlier, chart elements will be repositioned to default locations.

However, chart titles and labels are all objects that you can select by pointing and clicking within the chart in either the Design or Preview tab. Once you've selected an object (as denoted by the "sizing handle" blocks on all sides), you can reposition the text simply by pointing inside the text frame and dragging it to a new location. To resize the object, position the cursor on one of the sizing handles and narrow or stretch the object. Then, use the appropriate Chart menu or pop-up menu format option to display the Formatting dialog box. You may choose alternate colors, fonts, alignment, and other text-related options on the Font and Text tabs of the Formatting dialog box.

If you want to move the legend to a specific place on the chart, just drag it (you can't resize it) to its new location. You can actually select and format three different parts of the legend: the frame, the textual items, and the symbols. Select each piece and use the Chart pull-down menu or pop-up menu formatting option to change them. Note that if you change certain properties of the symbol, the associated chart element (bar, pie slice, and so forth) changes along with it.

Changing 3-D Viewing Angles

Some of the more impressive chart types that Crystal Reports can create are 3-D charts. There are several types of 3-D charts, some of which actually chart only one data item, such as the 3-D bar, pie, and doughnut charts, and others that chart two data items, such as 3-D riser and 3-D surface charts.

Once you create these types of charts, you have a great deal of control over the three-dimensional appearance of the chart. For example, if you choose a single doughnut chart, Crystal Reports gives it a certain 3-D appearance by default. Using choices from Chart Options, you can completely change the viewing aspects of the chart. To make these selections, choose Chart Options from the pop-up or pull-down menus. The Chart Options dialog box will appear.

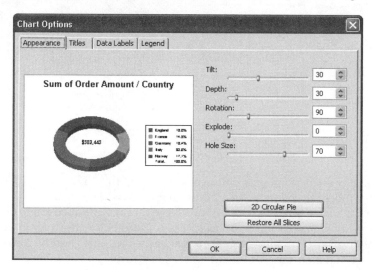

The Appearance tab contains various sliders and spin boxes that allow you to change all visual aspects of the 3-D doughnut chart.

Dual-data-item 3-D charts, such as the 3-D riser and 3-D surface charts, have even more "whiz-bang" 3-D capabilities. Not only can you choose from a variety of viewing angles right on the Chart Expert's Options tab when you create the chart, but you also can perform almost unlimited 3-D customizations using pull-down or pop-up menu formatting options.

Select the 3-D riser chart you want to adjust. Then, choose 3D Viewing Angle from either the pull-down or pop-up menus. The Choose A Viewing Angle dialog box appears. If you click the Advanced Options button, the dialog box displays an extra section that lets you completely customize the viewing angle, rather than just choosing presets, as shown in Figure 10-12.

Choose from one of the preset viewing angles

Choose from one of the saved viewing angles

Save, delete, and rename saved viewing angles from the drop-down list

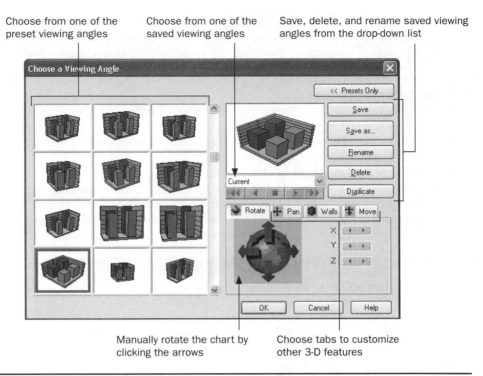

Manually rotate the chart by clicking the arrows

Choose tabs to customize other 3-D features

FIGURE 10-12   The Choose a Viewing Angle dialog box

This dialog box offers numerous options for changing the 3-D appearance of the chart. You can simply choose from any of the 12 built-in angles by clicking one of the 12 boxes on the left side of the dialog box, or choose from a large number of saved angle definitions by clicking the drop-down list or forward/backward buttons below the main thumbnail. You can also manually change all kinds of 3-D viewing aspects of the chart by making manual adjustments on the Rotate, Pan, Walls, and Move tabs. You'll see the main thumbnail in the middle of the dialog box change as you choose alternative viewing options.

You may be confused by the prompt to name and save a viewing angle that you've customized when you click OK. If you make manual changes to the viewing angle with options on the tab, rather than choosing one of the built-in presets or named angles, you'll be prompted to save the settings before you apply them. While you can replace an existing named angle, or create a new one, before you actually apply the viewing angle to the chart, you don't have to. Just click the Cancel button on the Enter 3D Viewing Angle Preset name dialog box. The changes will still be applied to the chart.

Choosing Additional Chart Types

Although the Chart Expert contains many different types and variations of charts (bubble, scatter, and so forth), the Format Chart option contains even more (provided you selected the Custom Charting option when you installed Crystal Reports). To look at the available additional chart types, select the chart that you want to potentially apply a new chart type to. Then, choose Load Template from either the pull-down or pop-up menu. The Choose A Chart Type dialog box will appear.

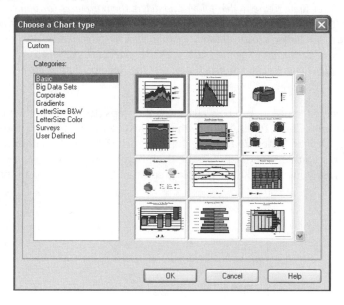

This dialog box presents a list of chart categories on the left. When you click each category, a large assortment of chart thumbnails from within that category appears on the right. Scroll down through the different thumbnails until you find a custom chart type that appeals to you. Select it and click OK. The new chart type will be applied to the selected chart. If you want to customize the look of the chart further, use any of the techniques discussed earlier in the chapter.

NOTE *You must have chosen the Custom Charting option when you installed Crystal Reports for these additional chart types to be available. If they're not available, rerun Crystal Reports setup and choose the Custom Charting option.*

Saving and Reusing Chart Templates

If you have a particular set of formatting settings you'd like to use on more than one chart, you can save the settings in a chart *template*. You can then apply the template to another chart that you create or edit.

To save a template, make any desired changes to your chart, such as changing label positions, element colors, perhaps the legend position, and any other settings you want to make. Then, either choose Save As Template from the pull-down or pop-up menu. A Save As dialog box will appear where you can give your chart a name (the template will be saved with a .3tf file extension).

Tip *By default, templates are saved in the \Program Files\Common Files\Business Objects\3.0\ ChartSupport\Templates\User Defined folder. If you need to delete a user-defined template, use Windows Explorer to navigate to that folder and delete the templates (or you can delete them directly from the Save Template As dialog box when saving a new template). If you wish to point your copy of Crystal Reports to an alternate location for Chart Templates, use the Registry Editor and look for the ChartSupport key in HKEY_LOCAL_MACHINE/Software/Business Objects/ Suite 11.0/Crystal Reports/ChartSupportPath. Use the Registry Editor only if you are sure how it works.*

To apply the saved template to a new chart, use the steps described in the preceding section, "Choosing Additional Chart Types." Notice that the last category on the Choose A Chart type dialog box is *User Defined*. When you choose that category, the collection of thumbnails consists of all the templates you've saved. Choose the thumbnail that you wish to apply to your current chart. When you click OK, the template settings will be applied to the existing chart.

Creating Geographic Maps

Business Objects retains the Geographic Map feature in Crystal Reports XI, although no major changes in this feature appear. Your reports can include not only textual information (for example, states, cities, and sales totals), but also a colorful map that, for example, plots sales totals by state. Using maps, you can display information in a way that helps to analyze geographical data more easily. In addition to regular groups and details section fields, Crystal Reports allows you to create maps based on online analytical processing (OLAP) grids and groups using specified order grouping.

NOTE *Crystal Reports XI's installation program does not install geographic map capabilities by default. You must choose a custom installation method and specifically choose the mapping component.*

Different Map Types

Crystal Reports provides five different types of maps. The type you should choose depends on the data that you'll be depicting in the map and the way you wish to show it. Table 11-1 discusses the different types of maps and their uses.

CAUTION *Crystal Reports XI contains a limited number of maps. If you use a field that contains geographic values that Crystal Reports can't resolve to an existing map, the map may not show any meaningful data, or it may show up as a blank area on your report. Crystal Reports mapping modules are provided by a third party, MapInfo. You may also get more information from MapInfo at http://www.mapinfo.com.*

- **Group map**   Requires you to use existing groups with their subtotals and summaries for the map. A report grouped by country, for example, can be used to show the concentration of customers by country if you include a summary function that counts customers for each group.

- **Advanced map**   Allows you to create a map based on data in the report's details section. You may have a detail report containing a sales figure for each customer. If you include the state each customer is in, you can create an advanced map based on the state and the amount of sales for that state. The map will show how sales compare by state. In effect, the map will group and subtotal your records by state, even if no state group exists on the report. You also would use an advanced map when you need to map multiple values per geographic region (as in the pie chart and bar chart explained in Table 11-1).

- **Cross-Tab map or OLAP map**   Plots data from a cross-tab object (covered in Chapter 9) or an OLAP grid (covered in Chapter 19). The cross-tab object must have at least one row or column field that's based on a geographic item, such as a country or state. OLAP grids must have a certain type and organization of dimensions (see "OLAP Maps" later in the chapter for details). Because cross-tabs and OLAP grids can contain multiple summary fields, you can use them to create pie chart or bar chart maps.

Map Type	Description	Uses and Comments
Ranged	Assigns different colors to ranges of numbers. For example, a state that contains over $500,000 in sales would be bright red, a state that contains between $250,000 and $500,000 in sales would be orange, and a state that contains less than $250,000 in sales would be a deep magenta.	Useful for comparing different regions or countries to each other by shade or color. There are four ways to choose how the ranges are colored: **Equal count** Evenly divides the number of map ranges so that an equal number (or as close as possible to an equal number) of mapped values appear in each range. This avoids map views containing almost all one color, which may occur if the data you are mapping is heavily concentrated on the low or high end of the overall range of values. **Equal ranges** Divides the map ranges by the summary numbers being shown on the map. This option assigns equal ranges of summary values, regardless of how many groups or regions make up each range. **Natural break** Also uses the summary numbers to determine map ranges, but bases range breakdowns on the average amounts of the ranges. **Standard deviation** Divides the map ranges such that the middle interval breaks at the average of the summary values. The ranges above and below the middle break at one "standard deviation" above or below the middle.
Dot density	Displays a dot on the map for every occurrence of the item being mapped. A higher concentration of dots appears in areas of the map that have the most occurrences.	Used to show a concentration of activity (for example, quantities or subtotals) in certain states or countries.

TABLE 11-1   Crystal Reports Map Types

Map Type	Description	Uses and Comments
Graduated	A symbol (a circle, by default) represents data, and the size of the symbol is based on the concentration or level of the amount: small amounts are represented by small circles, large amounts by large ones.	Shows just one symbol per country, state, etc., but shows a different size depending on the number the map is based on. The default symbol is a circle, but you can choose from other characters, as well as apply special effects (for example, a drop shadow, halo, etc.) to the symbol.
Pie chart	Displays a pie chart over the related geographic area.	Only useful when comparing multiple related data points for the same geographic area. A pie chart is better for comparing items against each other, where all items total 100 percent. For example, if you are graphing sales by account rep, grouped by state, you would see a pie chart on each state showing how much of the "state pie" each rep has.
Bar chart	Displays a bar chart over the related geographic area.	Only useful when comparing multiple related data points for the same geographic area. A bar chart is better for comparing items over time, or other comparisons that aren't "piece of the pie" oriented. For example, if you are graphing sales for the past five years, grouped by state, you would see a bar chart on each state comparing the sales for the past five years.

TABLE 11-1   Crystal Reports Map Types *(continued)*

Adding a Map

To insert a map on your report, choose Insert | Map from the pull-down menus, or click the Insert Map button on the Insert Tools toolbar. The Map Expert appears, containing three main tabs: Data, Type, and Text.

The Data Tab

The Data tab is where you choose the type of map you want to create, as well as the fields and summaries from the report that you want to base your map on.

Group Maps

To create a group map, click the Group button on the Data tab.

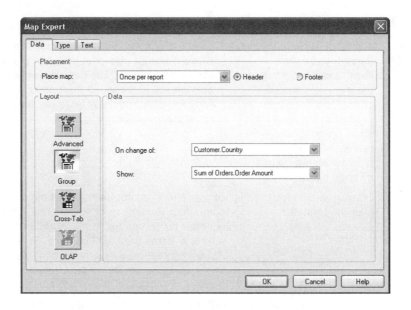

The Place Map drop-down list lets you choose how often you want the map to appear on the report. The options in this list will vary according to how many groups you have on your report. If you only have one group on your report, the only option available in the drop-down list is Once Per Report. If you have more than one group, you also have For Each *Group Field* options for every group, *except* for the bottom-level group, because you must always place a map at least one level higher in your report than the group your map is based on.

For example, if you only have a state group on your report, the only option for a group map is Once Per Report, because you must have the map at a level higher than the group. However, if you have a country group, and a region group within the country group, the drop-down list allows you to choose Once Per Report or For Each Customer.Country. If you choose this lower country level, you'll have a map appearing in every country group, showing the geographic breakdown *by region* for that country.

You can then choose whether to have Crystal Reports initially place the map in the group or report header or footer, by clicking the desired radio button. After the map has been created initially, you can drag the map object from the header to the footer, or vice versa.

Use the On Change Of drop-down list to choose the geographic group that you want the map to be based on. Continuing with the preceding example, if you choose once per report, then the options are on change of Customer.Country or on change of Customer.Country and Customer.Region. However, if you choose to place the map per country, then the only option in the On Change Of list is Customer.Region.

From the Show drop-down list, choose the summary or subtotal field you want the map to depict.

TIP *Because Group Maps must be based on a summary or subtotal field in a group, any groups that don't have at least one subtotal or summary field won't show up in the Map Expert. If you only have one group on your report and it doesn't contain a subtotal or summary field, the Group button in the Map Expert will be dimmed.*

Advanced Maps

To create an advanced map, click the Advanced button on the Data tab.

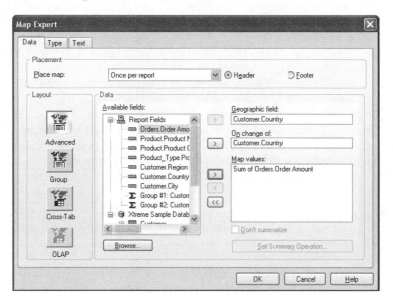

The Place Map drop-down list lets you choose how often you want the map to appear on the report. The options in this list will vary according to how many groups (if any) you have on your report. If there are no groups, the only option available in the drop-down list is Once Per Report. If you have one or more groups, you also have For Each *Group Field* options for every group.

You can then choose whether to have Crystal Reports initially place the map in the group or report header or footer, by clicking the desired radio button. You are also free to drag the map object from the header to the footer, or vice versa, after the map has been created.

The Available Fields list contains all the report, database, and formula fields available for the map. Choose the geographic field that you want your map to use, and then click the right arrow next to the Geographic Field box to choose the field. The same field will also automatically be placed in the On Change Of box. If you wish to just summarize values for the geographic field (for a range or dot density map, for example), simply leave the same field in the two boxes. If, however, you wish to show a pie or bar chart on the map for another field (for example, to show a pie chart in each country comparing states), then choose the field you want to "compare" in the Available Fields list and click the right arrow next to the On Change Of text box. Finally, click one or more fields (using CTRL-click or SHIFT-click) in the Available Fields list that you want summarized in the map. Use the right arrow next to the Map Values box to add them. If you wish to remove a Map Value field or fields, click it in the Map Values box and click the left arrow. If you wish to remove all the Map Value fields, click the double left arrow.

Even though this is an advanced map (based on individual report records), Crystal Reports still summarizes values by default, as though report groups exist for the fields you've placed in the Geographic Field and On Change Of boxes. You can choose the summary function

(Sum, Average, Count, and so on) you want the map to use when summarizing the detail fields you've added to the Map Values box. Select a field in the box, click the Set Summary Operation button, and choose the function (Sum, Average, Count, and so on) that you wish to use.

Crystal Reports mapping can be picky about the geographic field you base your map on. For example, if the field contains USA, the map will recognize it. If it just contains US, the map won't recognize it. The same holds true for state names. Two-letter abbreviations and completely spelled state names are recognized, whereas inconsistently abbreviated state names or standard two-letter state names followed by periods may not be recognized. Sometimes you'll need to experiment, and in some cases you may want to create a formula (discussed in Chapter 5) that changes the way the geographic data is presented, and then base the map on the formula field. Also, Crystal Reports provides the ability to resolve data mismatches that exist between the geographic names that maps recognize and the actual data in the database (see "Resolving Data Mismatches" later in the chapter).

TIP *If you add a nonnumeric field to the Map Values box, it is automatically summarized with a count function. The only other choice in the Change Summary Operation list is DistinctCount.*

Cross-Tab Maps

To create a cross-tab map, click the Cross-Tab button on the Data tab (this button will be grayed out unless you have a cross-tab object in your report).

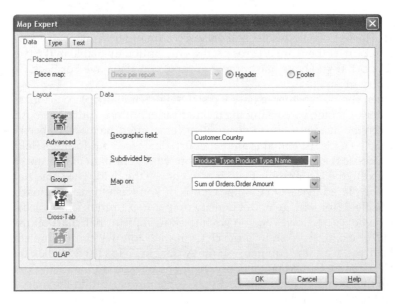

The Place Map drop-down list will be dimmed, because you must place the map on the same level as the cross-tab (in the same group, once per report, and so forth). You can choose whether to have Crystal Reports initially place the map in the group or report header or footer, by clicking the desired radio button. You can also drag the map object from the header to the footer, or vice versa, after the map has been created.

In the Geographic Field drop-down list, choose the row or column of the cross-tab that contains the geographic field the map will be based on. If you want the cross-tab to be mapped as a pie or bar chart map, choose the other row or column in the Subdivided By drop-down list. In the Map On drop-down list, choose the summary field from the cross-tab that you want depicted. If you have multiple summary fields, you'll have multiple options here.

OLAP Maps

To create an OLAP map, click the OLAP button on the Data tab.

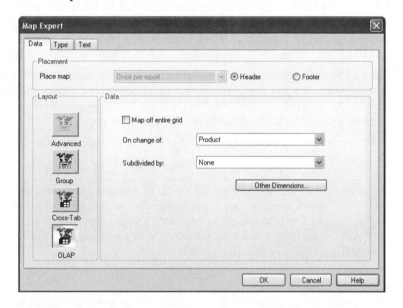

The Place Map drop-down list will be dimmed, because you must place the map on the same level as the OLAP grid (in the same group, once per report, and so forth). You can choose whether to have Crystal Reports initially place the map in the group or report header or footer, by clicking the desired radio button. You can also drag the map object from the header to the footer, or vice versa, after the map has been created.

In the On Change Of drop-down list, choose the dimension of the OLAP grid that contains the geographic field the map will be based on (this may be a "lower-level" dimension; go back and look at the results of your OLAP grid if you're unsure where the geographic data is). If you want the OLAP grid to be mapped as a pie or bar chart map, choose another dimension in the Subdivided By drop-down list. Checking the Map Off Entire Grid check box will disable the On Change Of and Subdivided By drop-down lists and will create a map based on all row and column dimensions in the OLAP grid.

NOTE *Cross-tab and OLAP maps aren't available if you don't already have a cross-tab or OLAP grid on the report before you launch the Map Expert. The Cross-Tab and OLAP buttons will be dimmed in the Map Expert in these cases.*

The Type Tab

After you've chosen the data elements for your map, click the Type tab to choose the type of map you want to display. Click one of the following buttons to select a map type:

- **Ranged**   Presents options for a ranged map, including how many intervals the map will contain, how the intervals are broken down, the beginning and ending color for the intervals, and whether the map should show empty intervals.

- **Dot Density**   Enables you to choose large or small dots for the map.

- **Graduated**   Presents the symbol used for the graduated map. A circle symbol is chosen by default, but you can click the Customize button to change the symbol and color and add special effects to the symbol, such as a halo or drop shadow.

- **Pie Chart**   Presents options for a pie chart map. You can choose small, medium, or large pies. If you click the Proportional Sizing check box, the pies will be sized according to the quantities contained in the data being mapped: larger quantities create larger pies, and smaller quantities create smaller pies.

- **Bar Chart**   Enables you to choose the size of the bars: large, medium, or small.

TIP   You are restricted to either the first three or the second two buttons, depending on how many data elements you've chosen for your map. If you chose only one data element to map, you can use only the Ranged, Dot Density, or Graduated option. If your map contains multiple elements from a detail report, or you chose a Subdivided By item with a cross-tab object or OLAP grid, you can use only the Pie Chart or Bar Chart option.

The Text Tab

The Text tab lets you customize textual elements, such as the title and legend, which appear with the map. Type in the Map Title box the title you wish the map to display. Crystal Reports automatically creates a legend for the map. You can choose whether to display a full legend, a compact legend, or no legend at all by clicking the appropriate radio button. If you choose to include a legend, you can display the map-generated legend or specify your own by using the radio buttons and text boxes in the Legend Title section.

After you choose all the necessary options, click OK. Crystal Reports creates the map and places it in the report or group header or footer that you specified. To modify an existing map, simply click the map to select it in either the Design or Preview tab. Then, choose Format | Map Expert from the pull-down menus or right-click the map and choose Map Expert from the pop-up menu.

Drilling Down on Maps

Crystal Reports lets you drill down on Group maps, just like on group names and summaries (discussed in Chapter 3) and on charts and graphs (covered in Chapter 10). When you view a map in the Preview tab, simply point your mouse to the geographic region you wish to look at in more detail. The mouse cursor turns into a magnifying glass (or a finger cursor in a web page). Double-click (single-click in a web page) the desired area of the map to open up a drill-down tab next to the Preview tab. This drill-down tab will contain just the information for the report group represented by that map segment. If you attempt to drill down on a geographic element that doesn't include any data (perhaps you drill down on a city that's plotted on a map, but there's no group for that city), you'll receive a message indicating the lack of detail data for that city.

To close a drill-down tab, click the small *x* that appears on the right of the drill-down tab. The current tab closes and the next tab to the left is displayed.

TIP *Because an Advanced map is already mapping the lowest level of information on your report, you cannot drill down on this type of map. Nor can you drill down into Cross-Tab or OLAP maps.*

Changing the Map View

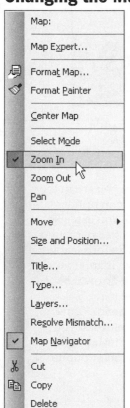

While viewing a particular map, you may wish to change your "view" of the map, such as zooming in or out on the map, or panning left, right, up, or down on the map. You may do this by selecting the map you want to change the view of and choosing options from the Map pull-down menu. Or, simply right-click on the map in the Preview tab and choose options from the pop-up menu.

- **To zoom in on a map**   Choose the Zoom In option. This will change the mouse cursor to a magnifying glass with a plus sign. Draw an elastic box around the portion of the map you want to zoom in on. The map will resize to show your chosen area.

- **To zoom out from the map**   Choose the Zoom Out option. This will change the mouse cursor to a magnifying glass with a minus sign. Every time you click on the map, it will zoom out a predetermined level.

- **To pan left, right, up, or down**   Choose the Pan option. This will change the mouse cursor to an arrow/pan cursor. Hold down the mouse button on the map and move your mouse left, right, up, or down. The map will reposition accordingly.

- **To recenter the map to its original position**   Choose the Center Map option.

The Map Navigator

Another way to change your view of a map in Crystal Reports is the Map Navigator. When you click on a map to select it in the Preview tab, a smaller "thumbnail" of the map appears in its own window in the lower right of the map. You may drag the Map Navigator by its title bar to move it around inside the map, as well as resize the window by dragging a border of the window.

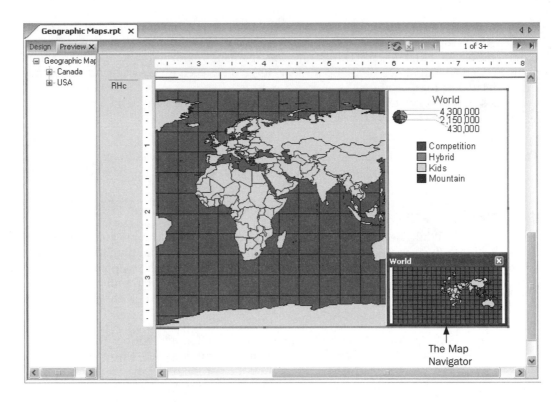

A shaded outline in the Map Navigator shows the portion of the map that you see in the rest of the map view. If you zoom in or out on the map (using the pop-up menu options), the outline shrinks or expands, outlining the zoomed-in portion of the map. You can also use the outline in the Map Navigator to zoom in, zoom out, and pan the view to a particular area of the map. If you point inside the outline, your mouse cursor changes to a four-arrow move cursor; simply drag the outline around to pan to a different area of the map. If you point to a corner of the outline, the mouse cursor changes into a diagonal two-arrow cursor. Drag the corner to expand or contract the outline. This zooms in or out on the map.

You may hide the Map Navigator by clicking the X on its upper right-hand corner. However, if you then deselect and reselect the map, the Map Navigator will return. If you want to turn the Map Navigator display off on a more permanent basis for all instances of maps, you may uncheck the Map Navigator option in the Map pull-down menu or pop-up menu that appears when you right-click on a map.

Resolving Data Mismatches

One of the peculiarities of geographic maps is potential mismatches of geographic data in the database to what the map understands. If your database contains, for example, spelled-out state names instead of two-letter abbreviations, the map will not be able to resolve the names to actual states. Crystal Reports allows you to resolve data mismatches that may cause database data to be improperly mapped, or not mapped at all.

If you suspect that the map may not be interpreting database data correctly, first select the map that you wish to work with in the Preview tab (you can't resolve data mismatches in the Design tab). Then, choose Map | Resolve Mismatch from the pull-down menus or right-click on the map and choose Resolve Mismatch from the pop-up menu. This will display the Resolve Map Mismatch dialog box, with the Change Map tab shown first.

The map definition used to display the particular map you are working with will appear as both the "current map" and selected in the Available maps list. If you wish to display a different map definition, scroll through the list of available maps and choose another map. If, however, the mismatch involves a misspelling or misinterpretation of a particular country, state, city, or other geographical field, you'll need to resolve the mismatch on the Resolve Mismatch tab, shown in Figure 11-1 (it may take some time for this tab to appear, as Crystal Reports must build several lists on the fly when you choose this tab).

You'll notice that any database values that have already been matched to map values by Crystal Reports will appear in the Match Results list. However, if there are database values that could not be matched, they will appear in the Assign This Field Name list in the upper left-hand corner. And, you'll find a list of all the available geographic values that the map understands in the To This Map Name list in the upper right-hand corner.

To match an unmatched database value to a map value, select the value you want to match in the Assign This Field name list. Then, scroll up and down in the To This Map Name list until you find the substitute data, which you can then select (typing letters on the

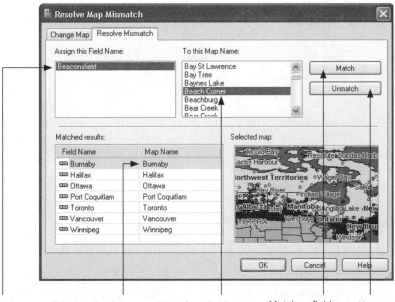

List of database fields that have no match in the current map

Existing database-to-map matches already made by Crystal Reports

List of available geographic areas already understood by the map

Matches fields selected in the Assign This Field Name and To This Map Name lists

Unmatches selected pair chosen in Matched Results list

FIGURE 11-1 The Resolve Mismatch tab

keyboard will often select items in the list more quickly than using the scroll bar). Click the Match button, which adds the match to the Matched Results list. Each match you create is added to the bottom list, along with all assignments that Crystal Reports made previously. If you decide that you don't want to use an assignment (that either you made or was made automatically), select it in the Matched Results list and click the Unmatch button.

When you're finished assigning values, click the OK button to show the map with the updated mapping assignments.

Map Layers

A map is displayed in the Preview tab using *layers*. If you are looking at a USA map, for example, the map may be composed of layers consisting of USA, US Highways, and US Major Cities. You can think of a map layer as a transparency containing just that layer's information that lies on top of the lower layers, which lie on top of the map. By using layers, the map can be displayed showing different levels of detail, usually determined by how far in the map is zoomed. If you are fully zoomed out on the map, you'll only see the states. As you zoom in, you eventually see highways appear across the states. And, as you zoom in even further, you see dots and the names of cities within the states.

Although maps include layers in a default order with default settings, you can choose which layers to display, hide, include, or not include. You can also change the order in which the layers "lie" on the map, and change the zoom level at which layers become visible. To work with map layers, select the map you wish to work with in the Preview tab (you can't work with layers in the Design tab). Then, choose Map | Layers from the pull-down menus, or right-click on the map and choose Layers from the pop-up menu. The Layer Control dialog box is displayed.

You see all the layers included in the map by default. You can change the order in which the layers appear by selecting an individual layer and then clicking the Up or Down button to change the order of the layers. If you want to hide a layer so that it doesn't show in the map, select the layer and clear the

Visible check box. If you decide that you no longer want the layer at all, select it and click the Remove button.

If you later decide you want to redisplay a layer you removed earlier, or you want to add a new layer not already on the map, click the Add button. A File Open dialog box appears.

Additional layers are located in \Program Files\Business Objects\MapInfo Mapx\Maps. Point to that folder and look for the appropriate .TAB file. After you choose it, it appears in the Layer Control dialog box.

To change the zoom level at which a layer appears, select the layer and click the Display button. The Display Properties dialog box for that layer opens.

If you uncheck Display Within Zoom Range, the layer appears in the map at all times, regardless of the Zoom level. If you leave it checked, you can set the minimum and maximum Zoom levels at which the layer will become visible. After you make your choices, you can zoom in or out on the map to see the layer changes.

Figure 11-2 shows the same map at the same Zoom level with different settings for the US Highways layer.

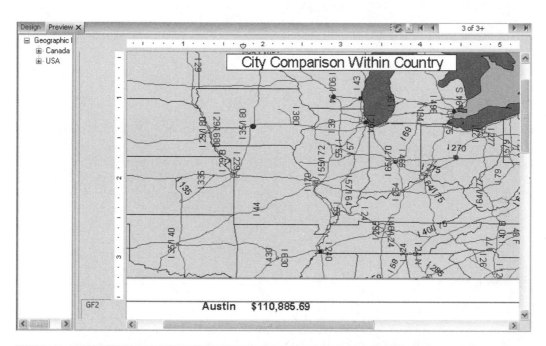

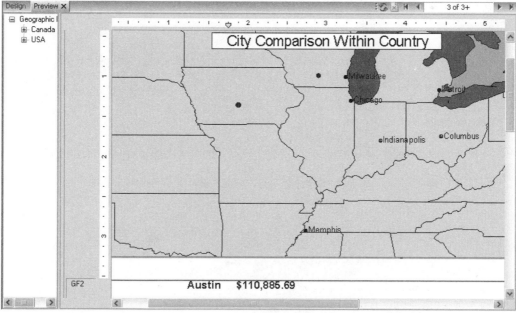

FIGURE 11-2   Maps with different US Highways layer zoom settings

Using Subreports

As you become more sophisticated in your report designing abilities, you will find at times that it's difficult, if not impossible, to create certain kinds of reports. For example, you might want to create one of the following:

- A single-page Company Condition report that contains an accounts receivable summary in the upper left, an accounts payable summary in the upper right, a payroll expense summary in the lower left, and a sales summary in the lower right. At the bottom of the report, you'd like some grand totals for each of the summary reports.

- A listing of orders by customer for the month that also has a summary of the top five products sold during the month, regardless of customer.

- A sales report grouped by state, with a list of all credit granted in the same state in the group footer.

- A report that combines tables in such a way that duplicate records from certain tables repeat when matching to other tables (often referred to as a "many-to-many" relationship). You wish to properly subtotal records from the affected tables.

- A report that contains a report title, logo, and company information from a separate Company Information table in the database that doesn't contain any field that can be linked to other fields in other tables.

In each of these cases, you can't create the report using traditional Crystal Reports methods. The first three instances are prohibitive because a report, by nature, can use only a single result set, or a single group of fields returned all at once, from the database. The fourth instance exhibits a common problem that occurs when multiple tables contain more than one matching record. And the fifth instance (a fairly common situation) exhibits the problem encountered when there are no common fields that can be linked between the two tables.

Crystal Reports provides an innovative way to deal with these types of reporting challenges. *Subreports* allow you to solve these problems by, in essence, placing one report inside another report. A subreport is simply another report that appears inside the original *main report* as an object. Even though both reports have separate layouts and separate Design tabs, they appear together in the same place. The main report is created initially, after which one or more subreports are added to the main report.

Each subreport is designed separately, based on its own database tables and fields. You can preview each subreport in its own Preview tab, format individual objects in each subreport, and create unique selection criteria for the subreport. However, when you return to the main report's Preview tab or print the main report, the subreports will be processed and printed at the same time, appearing inside the main report.

There are two main types of subreports:

- **Unlinked subreports**   Have no tie-in to the main report at all—they exist completely on their own and don't typically communicate with the main report. The Company Condition report mentioned previously falls into this category. Each of the unlinked subreports stands on its own and won't change based on any controlling field in the main report.

- **Linked subreports**   Controlled by the main report. The subreport will "follow" the main report, returning only a certain set of records based on the main report's controlling field or fields. The previously mentioned subreport, containing sales by state followed by matching credit, is an example of a linked subreport. When the state group changes in the main report, the subreport will return only records for that particular state.

You can also choose when subreports are processed by the main report. *In-place* subreports process at the same time as the main report and return their results at the same time. *On-demand* subreports appear in the Preview tab only with a placeholder and don't process until a viewer double-clicks them (or single-clicks in a web page). This improves the performance of the main report, because all the subreports don't have to be processed at the same time as the main report.

Unlinked Subreports

The most straightforward subreport is an unlinked subreport. An unlinked subreport can be thought of as a completely separate report that just shows up on the main report—there's no logical connection between them at all. The subreport has its own layout, its own database connection, and its own selection criteria. It is not affected at all by what appears on the main report.

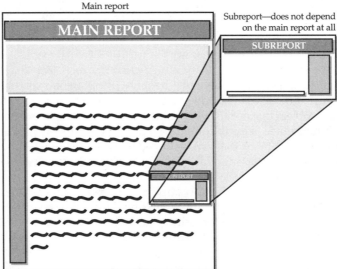

Main report

MAIN REPORT

Subreport—does not depend
on the main report at all

SUBREPORT

NOTE *Crystal Reports will not create another .RPT file when you create a subreport. Even though you will see another Design tab with separate tables and record selection, the subreport definitions are all contained in the main .RPT file.*

To create an unlinked subreport, you must first create or open at least the skeleton for the main report, and then use the Insert Subreport function to create or import a subreport. Although you can insert a subreport on the report in the Preview tab, you may not be able to accurately tell where it's being placed, so it's best to display the Design tab before you add a subreport.

Start to create the subreport by clicking the Insert Subreport button on the Insert Tools toolbar, or by choosing Insert | Subreport from the pull-down menus. The Insert Subreport dialog box will appear.

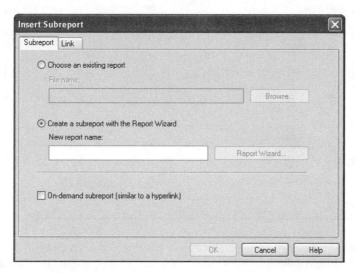

The Insert Subreport dialog box contains two tabs: Subreport and Link. The Link tab, discussed later in the chapter, is used to create a linked subreport. The Subreport tab contains two radio buttons, Choose A Report and Create A Subreport, and one check box, On-Demand Subreport (on-demand subreports are discussed later in this chapter). If you've already created another report that you would like to import as a subreport now, you can click the Choose A Report radio button and type in the path and filename of the existing report, or use the Browse button to navigate to the existing report. When you click OK, a subreport object outline will be attached to your mouse cursor. Place the subreport object in the desired location on the main report. If you double-click the subreport outline, choose Edit | Edit Subreport from the pull-down menus, or right-click on the subreport and choose Edit Subreport from the pop-up menu, another Design tab will appear. If you click it, you'll find the report layout for the report you just imported.

If you wish to create a new subreport from scratch, click the Create A Subreport radio button and give the subreport a descriptive name in the Report Name text box. Remember that you are not creating a new .RPT file when you create a subreport, so the subreport name doesn't have to conform to file-naming conventions. It should be descriptive of the subreport, because the name will appear on the main report Design tab wherever the subreport object is placed. Notice that once you enter a name, the only button that becomes enabled is the Report Wizard button. The OK button at the bottom of the dialog box is still dimmed. This indicates that you must use the Report Wizard to create at least a minimal portion of your subreport. (Once you close the Report Wizard and return to the Insert Subreport dialog box, the OK button will be enabled.) When you click the Report Wizard button, the Standard Report Creation Wizard appears.

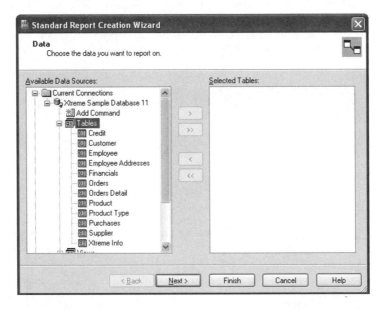

Don't forget that one of the powerful features of subreports is the ability to create reports based on entirely different databases and tables. You can select completely different databases, tables, and fields than are used on the main report. You don't have to complete any of the dialogs in the wizard in order to click Finish and place the subreport on the main report—you can have a completely empty subreport as a placeholder while you work on other things—but usually you would choose options in at least the Data and Fields dialogs. All of the same dialogs available in the Standard Report Creation Wizard when creating a main report are available when you're creating a subreport, including Grouping, Summarizing, Group Sorting (TopN), Chart, Record Selection, and Template. You can refine your subreport before you click Finish, or enter minimal information and work in the subreport Design tab directly.

When you've selected your desired options in the Wizard and clicked Finish, you'll be returned to the Insert Subreport dialog box. Notice that the OK button is now enabled, because you have created enough of a report in the Wizard. When you click OK, you will be returned to the main report Design tab, and a box-like subreport object will be attached to your mouse cursor. Drop the object by clicking in the report section of the main report where you want the subreport to appear. Choose this section carefully; it typically makes no sense for an unlinked subreport to appear more than once in the main report. For example, if you place the subreport in the details section, the same unlinked subreport will appear over and over again, once for each details record. You'll typically place an unlinked subreport in a report header or footer, unless you want it to repeat on more than one page.

TIP *Don't forget the Underlay formatting option on the Section Expert (discussed in detail in Chapter 8). You can, for example, easily create a second page header section for your subreport object and format the second page header to Underlay Following Sections. That way, your subreport will print alongside—not on top of—any data on the main report.*

When you place your subreport in the main report Design tab, it simply shows up as a box with the subreport name centered inside it. When you double-click the subreport outline, choose Edit | Edit Subreport from the pull-down menus, or right-click on the subreport and choose Edit Subreport from the pop-up menu another Design tab labeled with the subreport name will appear alongside the main report Design tab. If you click the new tab, the subreport Design tab will appear.

Main report
Design tab

Main report Preview tab visible if
main report has been previewed

Subreport Design tab labeled
with name of subreport

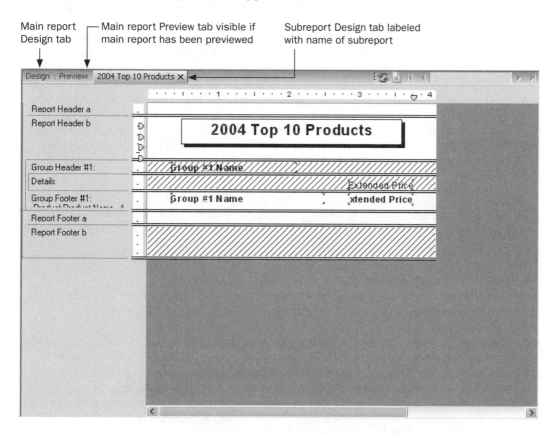

You can now move, resize, reformat, and otherwise modify objects in the subreport just as you would in the main report. The subreport will present its own Database Expert and Field Explorer, allow a separate set of formulas to be created, and allow you all the flexibility you have on the main report. However, the subreport Design tab has one limitation: You cannot add another subreport to it—subreports can be created only one level deep.

CAUTION *Since subreports can be only one level deep, an existing report that already contains subreports will not include those subreports when it is imported from the Insert Subreport dialog box. The report will be imported into the subreport Design tab, but the lower-level subreports won't show up. You may need to modify the imported report to make up for the empty space that appears where the subreport used to be.*

You can even preview a subreport in its own Preview tab. With the subreport Design tab displayed, preview the report using the Preview toolbar button, the Refresh button, the F5 key, or the pull-down menu options. A separate Preview tab for the subreport will appear next to the subreport Design tab. This tab will simply add the subreport to the word Preview.

When you now preview the main report, you'll see the subreport where you placed it. By default, subreports are surrounded by a border, so you'll see a box around the subreport. If you do not want to see a box around the subreport, right-click the subreport object and select Format Subreport. On the border tab, you can remove all or some of the four border lines. You can also modify border appearance with the appropriate Formatting Toolbar button after selecting the subreport.

If the subreport is not entirely visible (it may be pushed off the right side of the page, or it may be overwriting main report data if you use the Underlay Following Sections section formatting option), return to the main report Design tab and reposition or resize the subreport object. The width of the subreport design tab is based on how wide you make the subreport object in the main report. If you don't have sufficient room in the subreport Design tab to properly place objects, return to the main report Design tab and resize the subreport object.

TIP *You may save a subreport in its own .RPT file to use elsewhere or on its own. Select the subreport object in the main report Design or Preview tab and choose File | Save Subreport As, or right-click the subreport object and choose Save Subreport As from the pop-up menu.*

Drilling Down on Subreports

You have the same flexibility for drill-down reporting in subreports as you do in the main report. If you design a subreport with grouping, hidden sections, or charts, you can drill down in the subreport, too.

When you first preview the main report, the subreport will appear inside it. If you point to the subreport, you'll notice the mouse cursor change to a drill-down cursor, indicating drill-down capability. When you double-click the subreport, it will be displayed in its own Preview tab (but no actual subreport drill-down will occur). If you've designed the subreport to allow drill-down, you'll notice the mouse cursor displaying a drill-down cursor again in the subreport Preview tab. If you then double-click again, additional drill-down tabs will appear for groups you've created in the subreport.

If Crystal Reports runs out of room to display all the tabs, two small left-right arrows will appear to the right of the group of tabs. You can use the arrows to cycle through the tabs from the left or right. If you wish to close some of your drill-down tabs, click the small *X* in the desired tab. This will close the tab you are currently viewing and display the tab to the left. Figure 12-1 shows an unlinked subreport with more tabs than can be displayed at once.

TIP *When you add a subreport to the main report, a Design tab for the subreport is created automatically. You can close the subreport Design tab by clicking the small X in the tab. To redisplay a subreport Design tab, display the Design tab for the main report and then double-click the subreport object. You may also select the subreport and choose Edit | Edit Subreport from the pull-down menus, or right-click the subreport object and choose Edit Subreport from the pop-up menu.*

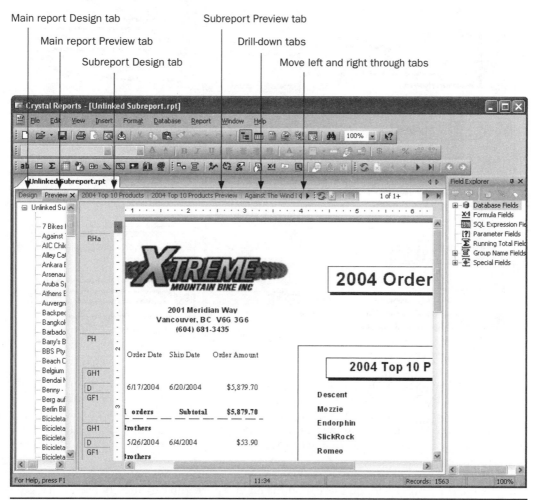

FIGURE 12-1 Unlinked subreport with Design tab, Preview tab, and drill-down tabs

Linked Subreports

A linked subreport is handy when you need to display related data elements from more than one database table on a report but can't tie the tables together properly for one reason or another (such reasons are discussed in detail at the beginning of the chapter). A report that encounters a many-to-many relationship when it attempts to show multiple sales records in a region, followed by multiple credits in the same region, fits this category. The subreports follow along with the main report.

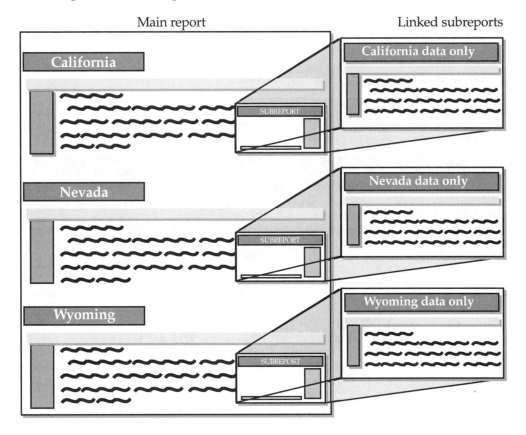

The initial steps for creating a linked subreport are the same as for creating an unlinked subreport. Use the Insert Subreport toolbar button or menu options to create a subreport. Then, import an existing report or create a new subreport with the Subreport Expert. However, before you click OK in the Insert Subreport dialog box, click the Link tab. This will display the Subreport Links dialog box where you can choose how to link the subreport to the main report.

If you inadvertently click OK in the Insert Subreport dialog box before linking, you can still link the subreport after you place it on the main report. You can also choose to change links for an existing linked subreport or link a previously unlinked subreport. Choose Edit | Subreport Links from the pull-down menus, or right-click the subreport object and choose

Change Subreport Links from the pop-up menu. The Subreport Links dialog box is shown in Figure 12-2.

If you are linking directly from the Link tab on the Insert Subreport dialog box, the For Subreport drop-down list will be dimmed—you will be setting links for the subreport you are currently creating. If you are linking a subreport already on the main report, you can choose the subreport you want to set links for (don't forget—there can be more than one subreport on a main report).

The Available Fields list shows fields and formulas available in the main report. Select the field from the list you want to link from, and add it to the Field(s) To Link To list by clicking the right arrow button. If you later decide you don't want to link on that field, select it in the Field(s) To Link To list and remove it with the left arrow button.

Once you've added a main report field to link on, three additional options appear at the bottom of the Subreport Links dialog box. The Subreport Parameter Field To Use drop-down list contains any parameter fields you have created in the subreport (see Chapter 13 for information on parameter fields). In addition to any that you have created, Crystal Reports will create a parameter field consisting of the main report field prefixed with Pm-. If you want to link the subreport so that it shows only matching records for the main report field, just leave this automatically created parameter field selected.

The general approach of linked subreports is to limit the subreport to records that match the linking field from the main report. If this is the behavior you want, make sure Select Data In Subreport Based On Field is checked. Then, use the drop-down list below the check box to choose the field in the subreport that you want to use to limit records (Crystal Reports

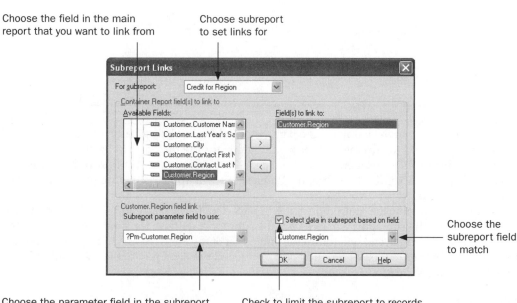

Choose the field in the main report that you want to link from

Choose subreport to set links for

Choose the subreport field to match

Choose the parameter field in the subreport that will hold information from the main report

Check to limit the subreport to records that match the main report link field

FIGURE 12-2   Subreport Links dialog box

will automatically show any subreport field that has the same field name as the main report linking field). If you want to use more than one field to link the main report to the subreport, just add additional fields to the Field(s) To Link To list and match them up to the corresponding subreport fields.

Clicking OK closes the Subreport Links or Insert Subreport dialog box and creates the links between the main report and the subreport. If you're just creating the subreport, its outline will be attached to the mouse cursor. Drop it in the appropriate main report section, typically the section that matches the field you linked the subreport on. A subreport link is based on two concepts: passing data from the main report into a subreport parameter field and creating a record-selection formula in the subreport based on the parameter field. This way, every time the main report runs the subreport, it places the value of the main report linking field in the parameter field, which is used to select records for the subreport.

Because of this method of subreport linking, whenever you try to preview a linked subreport on its own, you'll be prompted to supply a parameter field.

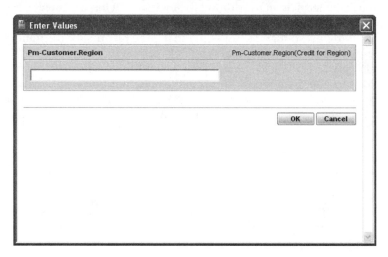

This indicates that the value for the parameter field is not being passed from the main report and you need to provide it. Type a valid value for the linked field (such as a state abbreviation, customer number, department code—whatever value is appropriate for the linked field) and click OK. The subreport Preview tab will appear showing just the records that you specified.

When you preview the main report, it will pass data to the subreport via the parameter field every time the subreport is processed; the subreport will use the parameter field in its record-selection formula and will return the limited set of resulting records to the main report. Figure 12-3 shows the customer/credit report mentioned previously, with the credit subreport appearing in the state group footer.

Linking Based on Formula Fields

If you use the Database Expert (discussed in Chapter 15) to link tables together in the main report, you can link only on actual database fields. This may be a problem if a field in one table doesn't exactly match the data type or organization in another table. For example, you

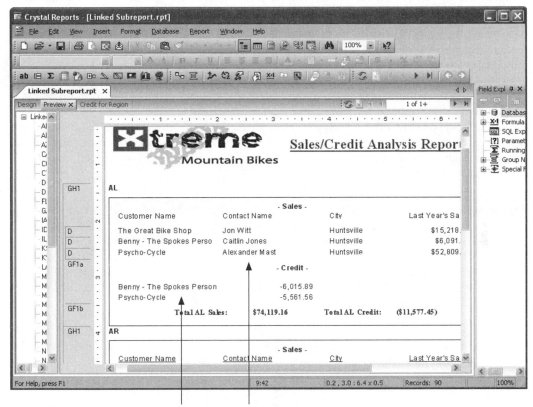

Credits (grouped & summed by customer)   Customers in main report details section
in subreport

FIGURE 12-3   Linked subreport placed in group footer

may want to link two tables together based on a First/Last Name field because there is no other common number field or other linkable field. The problem, however, might be that the fields are separated into individual First and Last Name fields in one table and contained in a single Name field in the other table. The link will never work in the Database Expert because of the differences in the data layout.

One of the benefits of using subreports is their ability to link based on a formula field, instead of just using database fields. By creating a subreport, you can link the two tables together. The key is to use a formula to concatenate the individual First and Last Name fields together into one combined formula field. Once you've created the formula in the report that contains the separate Name fields, the Name formula field will appear in the Subreport Links dialog box and you can choose it as a From or To linking field.

NOTE *Chapter 5 discusses concatenating string fields and other formula-creation techniques.*

Subreport Formatting with the Format Editor

There are a number of settings and features in the Format Editor you can use to further format and control subreport objects. On the main report Design or Preview tab, select the subreport object. Then, display the Format Editor by clicking the Format button in the Expert Tools toolbar, by choosing Format | Format Subreport from the pull-down menus, or by right-clicking the subreport object and choosing Format Subreport from the pop-up menu. The Format Editor appears with the Common tab appearing.

Some items on the Common tab may be of particular use with subreports. For example, changing the object name for the subreport will make the Report Explorer more meaningful, as well as assisting you in Report Part navigation with web reporting (discussed in more detail in Part II of the book).

TIP *If you are planning on passing values from a subreport to the main report (discussed later in the chapter), don't use the Suppress check box. Unlike a suppressed formula field (which will still calculate but won't display), a suppressed subreport does not process and will not generate values to pass to the main report. If you need to suppress a subreport from displaying, you will need to display the subreport Design tab and hide or suppress every section of the subreport. Then, returning to the main report, shrink the subreport object size as much as possible to reduce its height. The subreport will still run and pass values as if it were visible.*

By default, the Can Grow option is checked whenever you create a subreport. This allows the subreport to grow vertically based on the actual data returned in the subreport. You'll typically want to leave this check box on for most subreports.

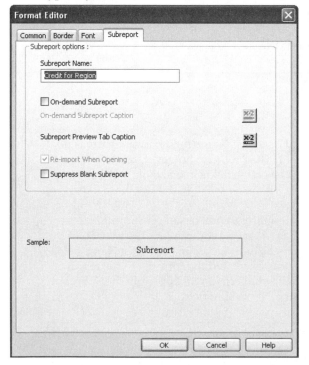

Formatting options particular to subreports appear on the Format Editor Subreports tab. While most of the options on the Subreport tab apply to on-demand subreports (discussed later in this chapter), three of the options bear further discussion here: Subreport Name, Re-import When Opening, and Suppress Blank Subreport.

If you'd like a more user-friendly name to display on the Preview and Design tabs for the subreport, you can change the Subreport Name here. The change applies as soon as you close and redisplay subreport related tabs, and it applies to both in-place and on-demand subreports.

The Re-import When Opening option is available only for subreports that were imported, rather than created, during the Insert Subreport dialog (this option will be dimmed if you format a subreport that you created from scratch). When you import an existing report as the subreport, Crystal Reports does not create a real-time link to

PART I

the original .RPT file. The report design characteristics of the existing report are just imported into the main report and then "forgotten." If you later make changes to the original report that you imported, the changes won't be reflected here. However, Crystal Reports provides the ability to automatically or manually update (re-import) the subreport to reflect any changes to the original .RPT file.

To manually re-import a subreport that has had changes made to the original .RPT file, right-click the subreport object on the main report Design tab. Choose Re-import Subreport on the pop-up menu. The .RPT file that was used to originally import the subreport will be read again, and any changes will now be reflected in this report.

To have Crystal Reports automatically update imported subreports every time the main report is opened, format the subreport by selecting the subreport object in the main report Design tab or Preview tab. Then either use the Format menu or right-click the subreport object and choose Format Subreport, which will display the Format Editor. On the Subreport tab, check the Re-import When Opening check box. You may also set this option globally by choosing File | Options and then checking the Re-import Subreports When Opening Reports option on the New Report tab.

CAUTION *The automatic re-import option will cause problems if the original .RPT file is missing, if changes have been made to it for other purposes, or if the main report/subreports have been maintained with database changes but the original subreport .RPT file hasn't. And if you re-import a subreport, any changes you made to the originally imported subreport structure will be overwritten by the updated subreport. You will be warned that your changes are going to be overwritten, and you cannot undo the import. If you realize that you've overwritten subreport changes that you wanted to keep, close the report without saving it. Then, reopen the report.*

The last option on the Subreport tab of the Format Editor is Suppress Blank Subreport. This option evaluates the subreport and suppresses its display entirely if it returns no records. However, note that the blank subreport object still takes up room in its main report section. Also, and any values passed from the subreport to the main report in shared variables will not be updated (passing data from a subreport to the main report is discussed later in the chapter). The "Handling Empty Subreports" section later in this chapter describes steps to correct these display issues.

On-Demand Versus In-Place Subreports

By default, a subreport will process *in-place* as soon as Crystal Reports encounters it during main-report processing. For example, if you place a subreport in a group footer and preview the report, the subreport will process every time Crystal Reports comes to a group footer. If the report contains 75 groups and you click the last page-navigation button, 75 subreports will have to be processed before you see the page.

Depending on subreport size, database speed, or any of a number of other factors, this subreport processing may present a prohibitive performance problem. That's why Crystal Reports provides the *on-demand* subreport. An on-demand subreport simply exists as a placeholder on the main report (similar to a web hyperlink), but it doesn't process as the main report progresses. Only when you click the subreport placeholder does the subreport actually process and appear in its own Preview tab.

There are two ways to denote a subreport as on-demand versus in-place. When you first create the subreport, check the On-Demand Subreport check box in the Insert Subreport dialog box. Or, you may change the settings for the subreport on the Subreport tab of the Format Editor. Check On-Demand Subreport to make the currently selected subreport on-demand. Now, when you preview the main report, only a placeholder outline will appear where the subreport would be. When the viewer clicks the placeholder, the on-demand subreport will process and appear in its own Preview tab.

CAUTION *Since data is not saved in on-demand subreports, you may wish to avoid them if you distribute a report to a viewer who doesn't have access to the database. Even if a viewer opens a report with File | Save Data With Report checked, on-demand subreports will have to connect to the database to be shown.*

There are two helpful text options that make on-demand subreports more intuitive and interactive. The On-Demand Subreport Caption and Subreport Preview Tab Caption properties also exist on the Format Editor's Subreport tab. Both of these properties are set via Conditional Formula buttons, which allow you to create a conditional string formula that determines what appears inside the subreport placeholder in the main report and in the subreport Preview tab, respectively.

Since both are conditional formulas, you can use the complete Crystal Reports formula language to create a string formula to display. This gives you the flexibility to include actual database data in the formulas. For example, to prompt the user to click a subreport placeholder to see credit information for a particular state, you could enter the following formula for the On-Demand Subreport Caption:

```
"Click to see Credit records for " & GroupName ({Customer.Region})
```

To show the state name in the Preview tab for the particular on-demand subreport that a viewer chooses, you could use the following conditional formula for the Subreport Preview Tab Caption:

```
GroupName ({Customer.Region}) & " credits"
```

TIP *The Subreport Preview Tab Caption option is available with either on-demand or in-place subreports. If you double-click on an in-place subreport, it will appear in its own Preview tab with the caption formula displayed. The On-Demand Subreport Caption option is only available if you check On-Demand Subreport.*

You can use other options on the Format Editor to choose the font face, size, and color; the border style; and the background color that appear on the placeholder. By using these formatting options creatively, you can make an on-demand subreport placeholder look clickable. Also, when you mouse over an on-demand subreport in the Preview tab, the mouse pointer changes to the standard Windows hand, which denotes a clickable object. You may also set Tool Tip Text in the Format Editor's Common tab to customize the tool tip that appears when you mouse over an on-demand subreport.

Figure 12-4 shows the resulting main report Preview tab. Notice that several subreports have been clicked and their Preview tabs have been customized.

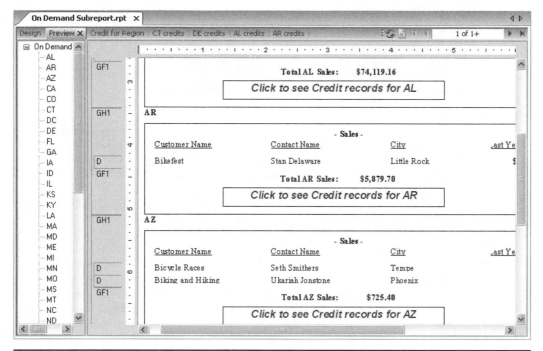

FIGURE 12-4   On-demand subreport

CAUTION *If you are passing data back to the main report from a subreport (discussed later in the chapter), making the subreport on-demand will prevent the data from being passed back when the main report runs. Since the subreports aren't processing as the main report runs, there's nothing for them to pass back.*

Passing Data Between Main Reports and Subreports

In addition to passing a linking field to a subreport from a main report to limit the subreport's record selection, you may want to pass data from a main report to a subreport for other purposes. Or, you may want to pass data from a subreport back to the main report to use in summary calculations or similar functions. You can pass data to a subreport from the main report by using a parameter field. Crystal Reports also provides the *shared variable*, which allows you to pass data back and forth between main reports and subreports.

Passing data to a subreport from the main report without the subreport using it in record selection is fairly straightforward. Display the Subreport Links dialog box, as explained earlier in this chapter. Choose a linking field from the main report and add it to the Field(s) To Link To list. This will automatically add a parameter field prefixed with Pm- (all parameter fields automatically begin with a question mark) to the Subreport Parameter Field To Use drop-down list. Now, simply uncheck Select Data in Subreport Based On Field.

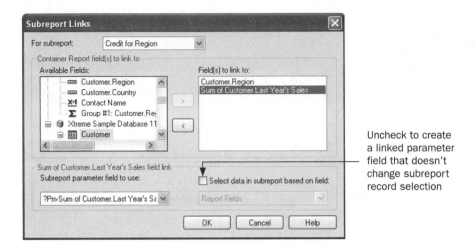

Uncheck to create
a linked parameter
field that doesn't
change subreport
record selection

These steps will create the Pm-parameter field in the subreport and pass data to it, but the parameter field won't be used for subreport record selection. Then, just use the parameter field in subreport formulas or place it on the subreport for display, as desired. For example, if you added a parameter for the summary field for the last year's sales by region figure in the sample report, your subreport would "know" the region's sales subtotal even though the subreport is not grouped by region. You could then add, in the footer of the subreport, a formula that compared the credit sum for the region and the sales sum for the region, and conditionally display appropriate text.

NOTE *Chapter 13 discusses how to use parameter fields in your reports.*

Using shared variables is a consistent way to pass data back and forth between the main report and one or more subreports, or even from subreport to subreport. You'll need to create formulas that declare the same shared variable in both the main report and the subreport. You can assign the variable a value in the subreport and then read the contents of the variable in the main report. Or, you can assign a value in the main report and read it in the subreport.

Here's an example of a formula in a subreport that places the sum of a currency field into a shared variable:

```
WhilePrintingRecords;
Shared CurrencyVar CreditTotal := Sum ({Credit.Amount})
```

Here's the corresponding formula in the main report that retrieves the value of the shared variable:

```
WhilePrintingRecords;
Shared CurrencyVar CreditTotal
```

An important step in using shared variables is determining if and when you need to reset the value contained in the shared variable. This may be necessary if, for example, you are passing the credit total from the subreport to the main report, and your data set includes regions that have no credit records. Should this be the case, the subreport won't encounter any data records and therefore won't evaluate the report section containing the formula that places a value in the shared variable. The variable will retain its value from the previous region that did process, resulting in incorrect calculations for the region with no credit records. To avoid this problem, create a formula to reset the shared variable to zero for each new region:

```
WhilePrintingRecords;
Shared CurrencyVar CreditTotal := 0
```

After you place this formula on the main report (in the region group header, for this example) and verify that it's producing the correct results, you can use the Format Editor to suppress it so that the zeros don't display.

For more information on assigning and using variables, and other formula topics, refer to Chapter 5.

NOTE *Because subreports process after formulas in the main report processing cycle, you must take special steps to retrieve the proper contents of a shared variable set by the subreport. For example, if you place both the subreport and a formula to retrieve the contents of a shared variable set in that subreport in a group footer, you'll notice odd behavior. Typically, you'll find that the formula returns the value of the shared variable from the previous group, instead of the current group. This is because the subreport is setting the value of the shared variable after the formula to retrieve the variable has already processed. To resolve this problem, insert an additional section (for example, a Group Footer #1 b) as described in Chapter 8. Then, place the formula that retrieves the value of the shared variable in the second section (Group Footer #1 b), while leaving the subreport in the first section (Group Footer #1 a). The formula that retrieves the contents of the shared variable will then retrieve the value from the correct subreport.*

Handling Empty Subreports

When you link subreports, there may be situations in which the subreport won't retrieve any records that match the linking field from the main report. Typically, this will just result in a subreport showing up without any details sections. If there are column headings or other information in other sections, they may appear with zeros for subtotals.

There are two graceful ways to handle empty subreports: suppress them and any related totals or display an informational message denoting the lack of data.

If you want to suppress the blank subreport altogether, check that option on the Subreport tab of the Format Editor. For this solution to work effectively, the subreport should reside alone in its own section. You may then format the section with the Section Expert and choose Suppress Blank Section. The entire section of the main report will then be suppressed if the subreport contains no data.

You may prefer to display an informational message instead of suppressing the blank subreport, similar to what's shown in Figure 12-5.

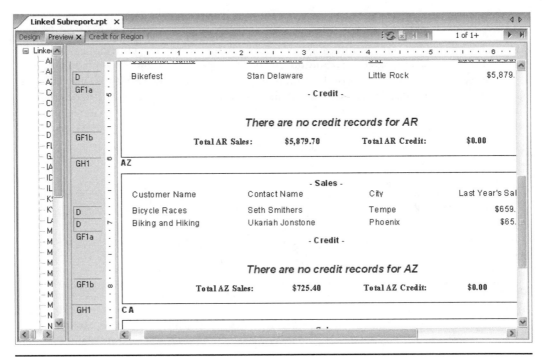

FIGURE 12-5 An empty subreport showing an informational message

This is accomplished by conditionally suppressing different sections of the subreport based on the presence or absence of database records. Look at the Design tab for the subreport.

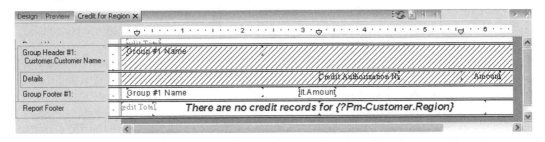

The group footer contains objects that you want to appear if the subreport actually returns records. The report footer contains the object (the text message) that you want to appear if the subreport doesn't return records. Conditional suppression of these two sections is done within the Section Expert.

Conditionally suppress the section containing the informational message by adding the following formula with the Conditional Formula button next to the Section Expert's Suppress property:

```
Not IsNull({Credit.Credit Authorization Number})
```

Then, conditionally suppress the sections that contain the actual subreport data with the following conditional formula applied to the Suppress property:

```
IsNull({Credit.Credit Authorization Number})
```

Don't forget—you are conditionally *suppressing* these sections (not displaying them), so you may need to think backward. If the subreport is empty because no records were returned based on the linked field from the main report, the Credit Authorization Number will be null. In this case, you'll want to suppress the actual subreport data but not the informational message. If data is returned, then the Credit Authorization Number will contain data and will not be null. In this case, you want to suppress the informational message but not the actual subreport data.

TIP *You can use this technique for all of your Crystal Reports, not just subreports. If you may encounter main reports that return no records, you can display an informational message in them. See Chapter 8 for more information on conditionally formatting sections.*

Performance Considerations

Subreports create potential performance problems for your reporting projects. Here are some tips to help maximize performance for your report viewer. Obviously, these considerations are more important if a viewer will be viewing a report online using Crystal Reports or as an on-demand report on the Web with BusinessObjects Enterprise/Crystal Reports Server. If a report is being printed or exported, subreports affect performance as well, but the user won't be staring at the screen waiting for them.

- Use on-demand subreports when appropriate. That way, a viewer won't have to wait for many subreports to process. Viewers can click the individual subreports they want to see when they want to see them.

- If you are creating a linked subreport, try to base the link on an indexed field in the subreport. This will cause record selection in the subreport to occur substantially faster. If the subreport is based on an ODBC or SQL database, make sure you are keeping as much of the SQL query on the server as possible (see Chapter 15 for SQL database performance considerations).

- If you are linking subreports with formula fields, try to keep the formula field in the main report and use a database field in the subreport. Using formula fields in the subreport, particularly with subreports based on SQL databases, will move part or all of the subreport query off the server, impeding performance.

Interactive Reporting with Parameter Fields

If you are designing reports to distribute to a viewer audience that may not be familiar with Crystal Reports or the Select Expert, you will soon have the need to prompt the viewer for values that affect record selection, conditional formatting, or some other ad hoc information. This becomes even more crucial when the viewer doesn't actually have a copy of Crystal Reports but wants to view a report presented in some "turnkey" fashion, such as an on-demand report run on the Web with Crystal Reports Server/BusinessObjects Enterprise. In these situations, the viewer won't have the ability to make changes with the Select Expert anyway.

The ideal solution for these types of ad hoc reporting requirements would be to present the viewer with a dialog box prompt, preferably including a choice of default values or a range of values, to help the user enter the correct values for the prompt. The response the viewer provides could then be passed to the Select Expert to customize record selection and formatting, and the values the viewer supplied could also be included on the report to indicate what data makes up the report.

This ideal solution is made possible by *parameter fields*: prompts that are presented to the viewer when he or she refreshes the report. The value the viewer provides is then passed on to the Select Expert, report formulas, or conditional-formatting formulas to customize the way the report appears, based on the viewer's response. The viewer doesn't have to know how to enter selection criteria or conditional formulas to customize the way the report behaves.

Parameter fields are one of the most changed, if not *the* most changed, features of Crystal Reports XI. In addition to a new look and feel to the parameter field creation process, Crystal Reports XI provides the long sought-after feature of dynamic and cascading parameter field prompts. These features allow parameter field prompts or "pick lists" to be dynamically generated every time the report viewer is presented with a parameter field—new values added to the source database will be presented in the pick list immediately after they've been added to the database. And, cascading prompts or "pick lists" allow one prompt to control another—if you choose Colorado for one prompt, only cities within Colorado will appear in a subsequent prompt. Details on new dynamic and cascading prompt features are covered later in this chapter.

Consider the following report:

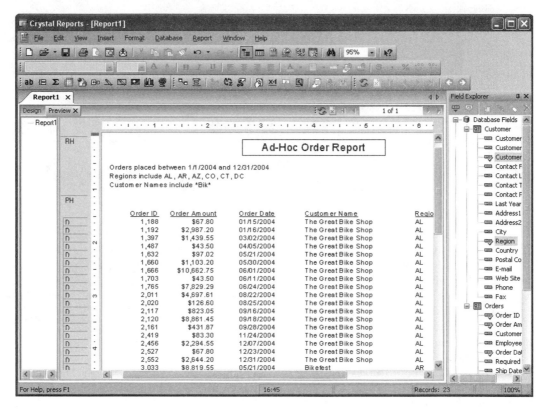

This report uses three fields in record selection:

- **Order Date**   Filtered with a Between selection criterion to include orders that were placed during 2004 (between January 1 and December 31).

- **Region**   Filtered with a One Of selection criterion to include orders placed from AL, AR, AZ, CO, CT, and DC.

- **Customer Name**   Filtered with a Like selection criterion to include customer names that contain the string *Bik*.

These criteria are hard-coded into the Select Expert, and text objects appear in the report header to indicate the restrictions.

The difficulty comes when you want the person reviewing the report to be able to easily change these criteria whenever the report is refreshed. The way this report is currently designed, the viewer must have the ability to alter record selection (and know enough about its intricacies to be able to change it). That person also must be able to edit the text object that displays what records are included. Even in this case, it's time-consuming to change this information every time the viewer wants to change these options. Parameter fields are the answer.

Using parameter fields to provide flexibility in this scenario is, at minimum, a two-step process. The third step is optional:

1. Create the parameter field.
2. Use the parameter field in record selection.
3. Place the parameter field on the report, perhaps embedded in a text object, to indicate what is included on the report.

Creating a Parameter Field

Parameter fields are created from the Field Explorer, which can be displayed when either the Design or Preview tab is selected. You can click the Field Explorer button in the Standard toolbar, or choose View | Field Explorer from the pull-down menus. Or, if you shrunk the Field Explorer with the push pin earlier, just click the push pin again to redisplay it. Then, click the plus sign next to the Parameter Fields category to show existing parameter fields, if any.

If there are parameter fields in the report already, you can edit them by selecting the desired parameter field and clicking the Edit button on the Field Explorer toolbar. You can also rename or delete existing parameter fields with the Rename and Delete buttons on the toolbar. If there are no existing parameter fields, or if you wish to create a new parameter field, ensure that the Parameter Fields category of the Field Explorer is selected (click it), then click the New button. You can also right-click the Parameter Fields category of the Field Explorer and choose New from the pop-up menu. The Create New Parameter Field dialog box appears, as shown in Figure 13-1.

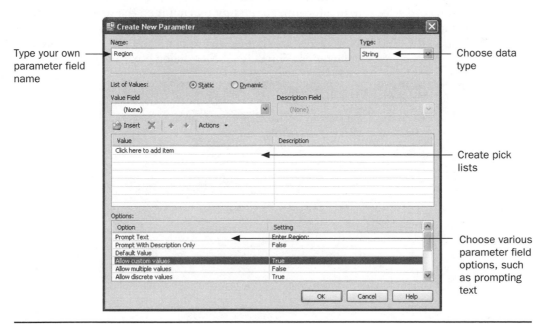

FIGURE 13-1   The Create New Parameter Field dialog box

Choose a name for your parameter field (presumably the "My Parameter" default name won't be appropriate in most cases). It can be the same name as other database or formula fields, because Crystal Reports distinguishes parameter fields by preceding their names with a question mark. Choose a descriptive yet reasonably short name for your parameter field.

You may want to consider changing the default descriptive message that will appear in the Enter Values dialog box when a viewer is prompted to provide the value. This is done by changing the default Prompt Text value in the Options list at the bottom of the Create New Parameter Field dialog box. Choose something that is easy to understand and helpful to the user, such as "Enter the state code (2 characters only) for this report." You can enter up to 254 characters of prompting text, although excessive prompting text will probably look unsightly when the parameter value is prompted for. Crystal Reports will word-wrap the prompting text when the viewer is prompted, if the prompting text won't all fit on one line.

Choose a data type for the parameter field from the Type drop-down list. This is a crucial step, as it determines how your parameter field can be used in record selection, formulas, and conditional formatting. For example, if you are planning on using the parameter field to compare to a string database field in the Select Expert, choose a String data type. If you are going to limit the report to a certain date range, based on a date/time field in the database, choose a DateTime data type.

These are the only items that are actually required for using a parameter field (and, changing the prompt text is optional). However, there are many features in Crystal Reports that enhance the flexibility of parameter fields.

Responding to Parameter Field Prompts

Once you've created a parameter field, you must make some use of the parameter field on the report—in record selection, in a formula, or just by placing it on the report—before you'll be prompted to supply a value (if a green check mark doesn't appear next to the parameter field in the Field Explorer, you have not made use of it). You will be prompted for it the first time you preview the report. The Enter Values dialog box will be displayed.

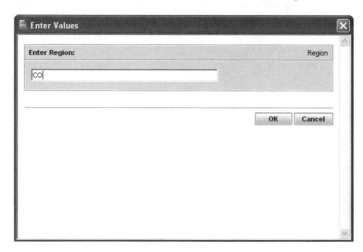

If you haven't entered any default values or created a pick list (discussed later in the chapter), the viewer will need to type their response to the prompt. If you've created a pick list, the prompt will appear as a drop-down list from which one of the predefined values can be selected. If you have created more than one parameter field for the report, only one Enter Values dialog box will appear, but each parameter field will appear in the list. Click the parameter field you want to select.

TIP *Parameter fields will appear in the Enter Values dialog box in the order you created them. If you'd like to change the order in which they appear, either select the Parameter category of the Field Explorer or select an individual parameter within the category. Right-click and choose Set Parameter Order from the pop-up list. The Parameter Order dialog box will appear. Select the desired parameter field and click the desired up or down arrow to reposition the parameter field.*

When you refresh the report, the Refresh Report Data dialog box will ask whether to use the currently set parameter field values or to prompt for new values. If you use the current values, the database will be reread with the current values in the parameter fields. If you choose to prompt for new values, the Enter Values dialog box will appear again, and you may specify new values for any necessary parameter fields. Values you entered previously will reappear in the Enter Values dialog box, so you only need to change values that you wish to differ from the last report refresh.

Data Type Considerations

The data type you choose for your parameter field determines how the parameter field can be used in the rest of the report. If, for example, you need to compare a parameter field to a date database field, you'll need to use a date parameter field. The data type will also determine how the report viewer must respond to the parameter field prompt.

String and number/currency parameter fields are fairly straightforward. In the case of strings, a viewer can respond with any combination of letters, numbers, or special characters. For numbers, only characters appropriate for numeric data, such as the numbers 0 through 9 and a minus sign, can be used—other characters will result in an error message when you click OK. Using date, time, date/time, or Boolean parameter fields will introduce some new features and limitations.

TIP *Ranges and edit masks can be used to limit or format what a viewer can enter into a parameter field. These special features are discussed later in this chapter.*

Dates and Times

You'll often want to use date or time parameter fields to limit your report to certain date or time ranges. You can choose data types of Date, Time, or DateTime. When you are prompted for a date or time parameter field, a few special features are available to you.

Make the selected range inclusive of exact date/time
entered; otherwise, entered values are not included

Click to see date picker (calendar)

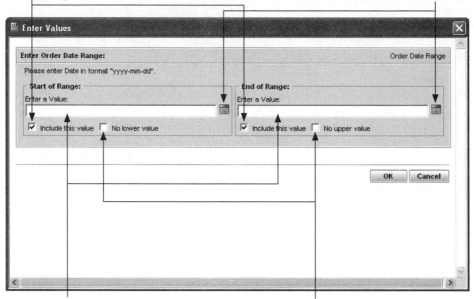

Type in date and/or time values directly,
using format specified at top of box

Use only one value to limit the range (useful for
"everything up to x" or "x and everything higher")

Preformatted dates and times may appear in the dialog box (perhaps from a pick list or a previous report refresh)—just type the correct date and time over any existing default value. If no pick list or default has been specified, or no previous value remains from an earlier report refresh, follow the example at the top of the box for entering date/time information. If you enter it incorrectly (for example, the standard U.S. date format of m/d/yyyy isn't allowed), an error message will appear when you click OK.

Boolean Parameter Fields

You may find a Boolean parameter field helpful when using record selection based on a Boolean database field or when conditionally formatting according to a parameter field value. A Boolean parameter field, like a Boolean formula (discussed in Chapter 5), can contain one of only two values: true or false.

When you choose a data type of Boolean in the Parameter dialog box, you may make certain choices to accommodate the special features of a Boolean parameter field, as shown in Figure 13-2. Specify the Name of the field and the Prompt Text for the parameter field just as you would for other parameter fields. You can also choose a True or False default value, as well as typing custom descriptions for the True and False options under the Description column.

The Options section differs slightly for a Boolean parameter field. If you type a number for the Boolean Group # option, you will add this parameter field to a grouping of one or more other Boolean parameter fields. Boolean parameter field groups allow you to simulate

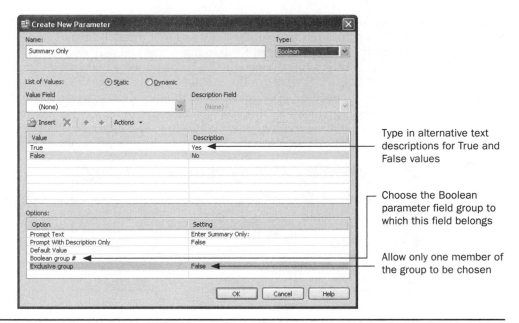

Type in alternative text descriptions for True and False values

Choose the Boolean parameter field group to which this field belongs

Allow only one member of the group to be chosen

FIGURE 13-2   Special features of a Boolean parameter field

the "radio button" behavior you see in Crystal Reports and other Windows applications. Since you can have more than one group of Boolean parameter fields, specify a unique number here for each group of Boolean parameter fields you wish to create—if, for example, you create four Boolean parameter fields with the number 1 specified here, all four will be prompted for together.

If you choose True for the Group Is Exclusive option, a single drop-down list consisting of all group parameters will appear when you're prompted to supply a value. The chosen field will return true, and all others will return false. If you choose False for the Group Is Exclusive option, two boxes will appear when you're prompted to supply a value—the box on the left will contain all parameters in the group, and the box on the right will contain parameters that you've specifically added. Each added parameter field will return true, while others will return false.

Using Parameter Fields in Record Selection

Probably the most common use for a parameter field is in report record selection. By creating a parameter field and using it with the Select Expert or a record-selection formula, you can prompt the viewer to provide variable information when the report runs, and have the report record selection reflect the viewer's choices.

After creating the desired parameter fields, use the toolbar button or pull-down menu option to display the Select Expert. Add a selection tab for the database field you want to compare to the value the viewer enters into the parameter field. In the operation drop-down list, choose the appropriate operation for the parameter action you need, such as "is equal to" for a region selection parameter, "greater than" for an order threshold parameter, or "is like" for a string-matching name parameter. Keep in mind that you may need to use a different Select Expert operation with parameter fields than you would otherwise. You'll typically use "is equal to" even if you want to allow multiple values or range values (discussed later in the chapter) to be supplied by a parameter. Even though you might be tempted to use "is between" for a range parameter or "is one of" for a multivalue parameter, you should just use "is equal". When you choose the drop-down list to see sample database values, you'll see parameter fields of the same data type in the list. Choose the correct parameter field.

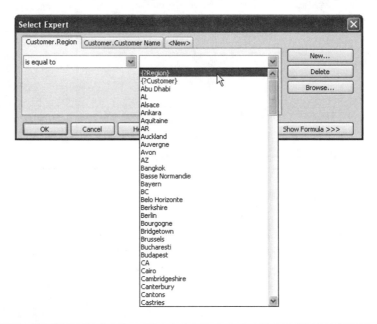

CAUTION *Only parameter fields of the same data type as the database field will show up in the Select Expert. If you don't see the parameter field you expect in the Select Expert, it wasn't created with the same data type as the database field you are using. Change the data type of the parameter field and rerun the Select Expert.*

If you use the Formula Editor to edit the record-selection formula, you'll see all parameter fields (regardless of data type) in the Field Tree box. Choose the parameter field you want to use in the record-selection formula. The formula may look something like this:

```
{Customer.Region} = {?Region}
```

Make sure you choose a parameter field of the same data type, or use functions to convert the parameter field to the correct data type. If you try, for example, to compare a numeric parameter field to a string database field, you'll receive an error in the Formula Editor.

Displaying Parameter Fields on the Report

One of the other major benefits of using parameter fields is that you can place them on your report just like database or formula fields. Whatever value the viewer placed in them before the report ran will appear on the report. By creatively using parameter fields, you can have a customized report that changes record selection and shows the values used in record selection on the report.

To place a parameter field on the report, drag and drop it from the Field Explorer just as you would a database or formula field. Depending on the data type of the parameter field, you can format it using the usual Format toolbar or Format Editor features discussed elsewhere in this book. You can also combine parameter fields with other fields and literal text inside text objects (as discussed in Chapter 2). A text object combining a parameter field looks like this in the Design tab:

Orders over {?Order Level} are highlighted

and will use the value supplied by the viewer when the report runs:

Orders over $2,500.00 are highlighted

TIP *Only single-value (discrete) parameters are effectively displayed this way. To display multiple values or ranged values, you must create a formula that extracts the whole set or range of values the user has entered. Solutions for these cases are discussed later in this chapter.*

Creating Pick Lists

If you don't add any default values when you first create a parameter field, the viewer will have to type in the value for the parameter field. While this sometimes may be desirable, it requires that the viewer know enough about the parameter field and the way the report and database are designed that they can type the value correctly. They may make a mistake by misspelling a name or entering an incorrect code for the field. By creating a pick list, you can let the viewer choose from a predefined list of default values.

NOTE *Crystal Reports documentation and dialog boxes refer to these lists variously as "Prompts" and "Lists of Values." However, the term "pick list" is used in this book, as it is a more common term to refer to a list of available options chosen from a drop-down list.*

Parameter field pick lists have changed dramatically in Crystal Reports XI. Not only is the Create Parameter dialog box entirely different than in previous versions, but the procedures for building pick lists have changed dramatically. And, after being an often-requested feature in previous Crystal Reports editions, dynamic and cascading pick lists (pick lists that are populated by live, on-the-fly database queries) have been added to Crystal Reports XI.

The first choice you'll encounter when you decide to create a parameter field pick list is whether the pick list should be static or dynamic. A *static* pick list contains a list of default values that doesn't change until you modify the parameter field. The list can contain default values that you type in manually, import from a text file, or import from a database field. These lists do not change as new data is added to a database—the only way to change a static pick list is to edit the parameter field and change the list.

A *dynamic* pick list is refreshed every time a viewer is prompted to supply the parameter field value. This real-time pick list allows additional values to be added to the pick list automatically as they are added to a source database. For example, if you create a dynamic pick list based on a sales rep name in a database, the pick list will show a current list of sales reps in the database every time a sales rep parameter field is prompted for. As sales reps are added or removed from the database, their names will appear or disappear from the pick list automatically.

A variation on a dynamic pick list, called a *cascading* pick list, has also been added to Crystal Reports XI. A cascading pick list is one of a series of related pick lists that depend on each other. While there is no practical limit to the number of related pick lists that can cascade, an example might be two dynamic pick lists that apply to two different parameter fields. These pick lists can relate to each other such that one pick list's values are based on another. To illustrate, the previously described sales rep pick list could be used to "cascade" a customer name pick list. When a specific sales rep is chosen from the sales rep pick list, the customer name dynamic pick list will only show customers that belong to the just-chosen sales rep. Both pick lists are dynamic—their contents are refreshed from the source database in real time.

Static Pick Lists

The simplest pick list is a static pick list. In this scenario, a fixed set of values appears to the report viewer in a drop-down list when they are prompted for the parameter field in the Add Values dialog box. This pick list will always be the same until you manually edit the parameter field and change the list. Static pick lists can merely be typed in manually, can be imported from a text file, can be gathered from a table and field contained in the report, or can be created with a combination of these methods.

The first step in creating a static pick list is to ensure that the Static radio button is chosen in the Create New Parameter dialog box. You may then perform various steps to create or import the list of values that will make up your pick list. The simplest way to add a value to the pick list is to click the Insert button at the top of the Value/Description table or click Click Here To Add Item in the Value/Description table. You may then manually type in a value to appear in the pick list. Repeat these steps to manually add additional list values.

Optionally, you may add descriptions for your pick list values by typing in the matching description column. This may be helpful if your parameter field requires codes or abbreviations to be provided to the report (for example, sales rep numbers instead of names), but you'd like descriptions of the codes or abbreviations to appear next to them, or in place of them, in the pick list. The Prompt With Description Only option further down in the dialog box controls whether the pick list will show only the descriptions you've typed in (if you set the option to true), or the values and descriptions together (if you set the option to false).

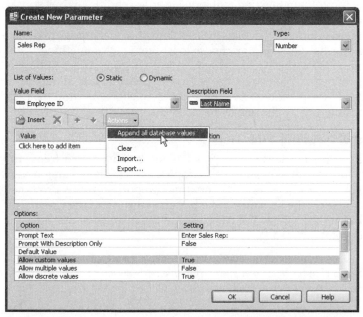

You may also populate your pick list from a field used in the report. To do this, choose the desired field in the Value Field drop-down list. Optionally, you may choose a description field from the report as well by choosing the desired field in the Description Field drop-down list. Once you've made these choices, click the Actions button above the Value/Description table. Choose Append All Database Values from the pop-up menu. This will fill the Value/Description table with sample data from the database (adding this data to any existing non-duplicative values already in the list).

If you have a large number of default values (and potentially descriptions) that you'd like to add to your pick list, you may want to import a pick list file. When you click the Actions button and choose Import from the pop-up menu, you are presented with a standard File Open dialog box that asks you to select the ASCII text file containing your pick list data. When you choose the appropriate pick list text file and click OK, the Default Values list will be populated with the data from the text file (adding this data to any existing non-duplicative values already in the list). If you wish to create a pick list file from the existing values that you've already added to the list (to use in another report, for example), click the Actions button and choose Export from the pop-up menu. A standard File Save dialog box will appear in which you can specify the filename for the pick list file to export to.

Once you've built a static pick list using these procedures, you may later decide that you don't want some existing values to be included in the pick list. You can remove one or more specific items by selecting them in the Value/Description table with click, CTRL-click, or SHIFT-click combinations. Once you've chosen the values you wish to remove, click the X button above the table. Or, you can remove all the values in the pick list by choosing Clear from the pop-up menu after clicking the Actions button.

CAUTION *Removing individual items from a pick list or using the Clear option can't be undone. Make sure you really want to remove these pick list values before making these choices.*

You may also wish to change the order that pick list items appear in the list. For example, if you've typed several values in manually, or you've combined manually typed entries with other values from the database or a text import, you may wish to reorder some individual values. Simply select the value in the table that you wish to move and click the small up or down arrow above the Value/Description table. The value you chose will move up or down in the list. Or, you may want to sort the entire list by the value or description. To sort the entire pick list, merely click the Value or Description column name in the Value/Description table. A small arrow will appear in that column, and the pick list will be sorted by that column. An up arrow in the column heading will indicate an ascending (a to z) sort, while a down arrow in the column heading will indicate a descending (z to a) sort.

Once you create your pick list, you may wish to ensure that report viewers only pick items from the pick list. Or, you may choose to let them pick something from the list, or type in their own value. Make this choice with the Allow Custom Values option in the Options section of the Parameter dialog box. Choose True for this option to allow the viewer to supply their own values to the parameter field, in addition to choosing from the pick list. Choose False for this option to force the viewer to pick values only from the pick list.

Dynamic and Cascading Pick Lists

If you create a parameter field whose pick list will be based on a frequently changing database field, you'll want to create a *dynamic* pick list. This new version XI feature allows pick lists to be dynamically generated every time a report viewer is prompted to supply a parameter value. Select the Dynamic radio button at the top of the Create New Parameter dialog box to begin the process. The remainder of the dialog box will adjust to settings you make from this point forward.

NOTE *Steps in this chapter refer to creating dynamic and cascading pick lists with reports that are not published to Crystal Reports Server/BusinessObjects Enterprise. If you plan on publishing a* *report to either of these tools, dynamic and cascading pick lists are managed within the enterprise server environment using Business Views. Chapter 16 covers server-based pick lists in more detail.*

If this is your first dynamic pick list in the report, the only available radio button in the Choose A Data Source section is New. If there are existing dynamic pick lists in this report, you may click the Existing radio button and choose an existing value from the associated drop-down list as the source for this pick list. With the New radio button selected, click the Insert button just below to choose the desired report field to act as the data source for the pick list. Pick a field in the Value drop-down list to act as the data source for the pick list.

Optionally, you may choose a report field to provide descriptions for your chosen value field. This may be helpful if your parameter field requires codes or abbreviations to be provided to the report (for example, sales rep numbers instead of names), but you'd like descriptions of the codes or abbreviations to appear next to them, or in place of them, in the pick list. The Prompt With Description Only option further down in the dialog box controls whether the pick list will show only the descriptions (if you set the option to true), or the values and descriptions together (if you set the option to false).

You may sort your dynamic pick list by the value or description field supplied. In the Options area of the dialog box, choose the desired ascending or descending sort choice for either the value or description field. The pick list will appear in the chosen order when the Enter Values dialog prompts for the parameter field.

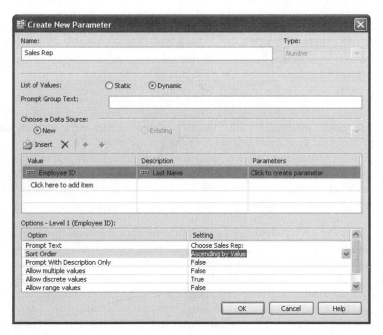

TIP *While you may enter text into the Prompt Group Text box, it's not particularly beneficial with a single dynamic pick list. You may, instead, simply supply regular parameter prompting text in the Options section once the pick list has been defined. Prompt Group Text is more appropriate for cascading pick lists, discussed later in the chapter.*

Creating a Cascading Pick List

A *cascading* pick list is similar to a single dynamic pick list, in that data is retrieved from the database in real time when the parameter field prompt is displayed. However, a cascading pick list consists of two or more pick lists that relate to each other. For example, you can create a higher-level customer name pick list and a lower-level order number pick list that are related. Only order numbers that belong to the customer (or customers) that are chosen in the first pick list will appear in the second pick list.

Steps for creating a cascading pick list are largely the same as for a dynamic pick list (described earlier in the chapter). However, you must add additional fields to create the cascading "hierarchy." Following the customer name/order number example, you wish to create a cascading pick list to determine an order number, but you want to limit order numbers in the pick list to match a previously chosen customer name. To do this, you must first add the customer name field to the Create New Parameter dialog box. Then, add the order number below it. By creating this hierarchy, what's known as a *prompt group* (a collection of one or more dynamic pick lists treated as a single unit) will be created, displaying a customer name dynamic pick list first, and then limiting the second order number dynamic pick list to the customer chosen. Once you've defined the last pick list in the hierarchy, click the "Click To Create Parameter" message under the Parameters column to assign the last pick list to the parameter field. This will assign the value chosen from the last pick list in the hierarchy to the parameter field you are creating.

You may create as many levels in the cascading hierarchy as necessary. For example, you might start with a Country field, followed by a State field, followed by a City field, followed by a ZIP Code field, and finally, a Store ID field—each lower-level dynamic pick list would be limited by the pick list above it. Just select the desired fields in the proper order and assign the parameter field to the last pick list in the hierarchy.

CAUTION *When you create a cascading pick list, you will find that Crystal Reports changes the name of the parameter field you are creating, using a combination of the original name you gave the field and the report field it's connected to in the prompt group. If you wish to rename the parameter field back to its original name, return to the Field Explorer and either hold the mouse button down on the parameter name for a few seconds until it goes into edit mode or select the parameter and click the rename button in the Field Explorer toolbar. You may then return the parameter field to its original name.*

Since your prompt group contains more than one pick list, you may customize two different sets of prompting text. First, you may change the default prompt text for each individual pick list in the Prompt Text area of the Options portion of the dialog box. Furthermore, you can set one additional Prompt Group Text value by typing in text just below the Static/Dynamic radio buttons. The text you add here will apply to the overall prompt group, whereas the individual prompt text options you set for each pick list will appear next to the drop-down for that particular list. Using the just-discussed Customer Name/Order Number example, you might set prompt text for the Customer pick list to "Choose Customer:", prompt text for the Order Number pick list to "Choose Order Number:", and Prompt Group Text to "Choose Customer/Order Number Combination:".

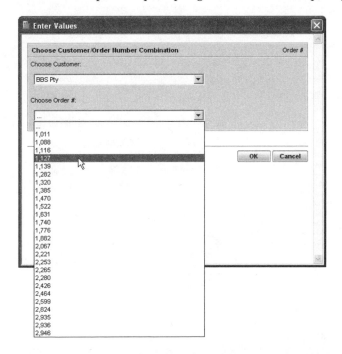

When the report is run and the parameter field using the cascading pick list is prompted for, you'll be presented with multiple pick lists, in the order of the cascading hierarchy. Pick lists lower in the hierarchy won't be enabled until you've chosen values from higher pick lists. And, lower pick lists will show limited sets of values based on choices in the higher pick lists. You'll also notice the individual pick list prompting text, as well as the prompt group text.

Using a SQL Command or Stored Procedure to Populate a Pick List

There are times when fields already included on the report may not be sufficient for dynamic pick list data sources. For example, inherent Crystal Reports limitations may not present a large enough pick list if large amounts of duplicate data are encountered in the report field you base your pick list on. A separate SQL query containing a SELECT DISTINCT clause may solve this problem. Or, you may want to base a pick list on data that comes from another database table, a stored procedure, or custom SQL that's not used in the current report.

In these cases, you can add a database stored procedure or create a SQL Command to be used as a data source for your dynamic pick lists (a detailed discussion on creating SQL Commands is contained in Chapter 15). Add either of these database connections by redisplaying the Database Expert and adding a stored procedure or creating a SQL Command. These will simply appear as additional tables in the Database Expert's Selected Tables list.

Once you've added the desired stored procedure or SQL Command, just click OK to close the Database Expert. If you aren't using the stored procedure or SQL Command as part of your regular report's data, you will not need to link the stored procedure or SQL Command to other tables in the report—you may ignore the error message that indicates that this non-linking is "generally not supported." You'll also be presented with a message confirming that your report contains mixed database connections.

When you create a parameter field that contains a dynamic or cascading pick list, you'll find the SQL Command or stored procedure appearing as another table in the list of available fields. Simply choose the desired field from the stored procedure or SQL Command you wish to use to populate your pick list.

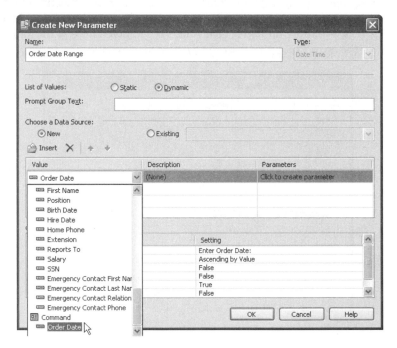

TIP *Stored procedures and SQL Commands can, themselves, be parameterized. These parameters are automatically added to the Parameter Fields category of the Field Explorer. You may edit these parameters and create static, dynamic, or cascading pick lists for them as well.*

Reusing a Pick List or Prompt Group

Once you've created a dynamic pick list or prompt group, you may wish to reuse it with additional parameter fields you create later. Or, you may initially create a cascading pick list that includes several pick lists in the hierarchy, and later wish to add an additional parameter field that uses one of the higher-level pick lists in the existing prompt group. In these types of cases, you can reuse either the "data source" created with an earlier dynamic or cascading pick list or add an additional parameter field to an existing prompt group.

Create a parameter field as discussed earlier in the chapter. Click the Dynamic radio button. However, instead of clicking New under Choose A Data Source, click Existing. The drop-down list next to the Existing radio button will show existing pick lists and prompt groups belonging to other parameter fields. If you want to use the existing set of data from the pick list, but create *an additional* prompt group, choose the first entry in the existing data source list without the words "prompt group." This will create a new prompt group, including the parameter field you are creating, along with additional copies of parameter fields that existed in the initial prompt group. If, however, you merely wish to add this new parameter field so that it's part of an existing prompt group (perhaps you want to retrieve the value selected in a higher-level pick list in a cascading pick list hierarchy), choose an entry in the existing data source list that includes the words "prompt group." Then, click the "Click To Create Parameter" entry next to the field in the prompt group that you want to assign the new parameter field to (as discussed earlier, Crystal Reports will rename your parameter field to indicate the field in the pick list you are assigning it to—you may rename it in the Field Explorer if you wish).

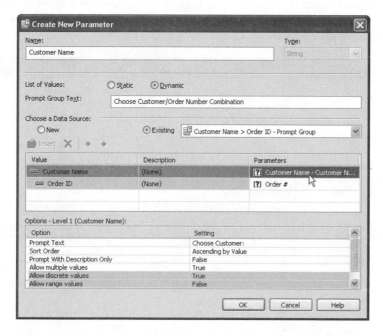

Special Parameter Field Features

Parameter fields provide a good deal of flexibility for various prompting scenarios. For example, a viewer can choose multiple values for a single parameter field to allow one-of types of record selection. Parameter fields can be specified to include entire ranges of values, so a viewer can, for example, include all orders placed between January 1, 2004, and December 31, 2004. Also, string parameter fields can be limited to certain lengths (for example, no less than three nor more than six characters) or limited to certain formats with edit masks.

Multiple Values

Often, you may want to be able to choose more than one value for a parameter field and have the report recognize the multiple values in record selection. You may, for example, want to initially specify only one region for a report and later run the same report including ten different regions. If you're not using parameter fields, you'll need to change the Select Expert operator from Equal To to One Of and select the multiple regions.

By setting the Allow Multiple Values option to True in the Options section of the Parameter dialog box, you allow multiple entries to be added to a parameter list—you, in essence, turn the parameter field into a single object called an *array* that contains more than one value. Even if you choose an Equal To operator in the Select Expert with a multiple-value parameter field, all the values in the array will be included in record selection.

When you are prompted for a multiple-value parameter field, you select one or more values in the Available Values list of the Enter Values dialog box (CTRL-clicking will select multiple values) and click the single arrow to add them to the Selected Values list. If the parameter field is using a static pick list with the Allow Custom Values option set to True, the values that are added to the list can be either chosen from the pick list or typed in the Enter A Value text box and then added with the right arrow (dynamic and cascading pick lists only allow you to pick a value from the list). You may remove a set of selected values with the Remove button (again, CTRL-click will multiselect in the Selected Values list) or remove all values with the Remove All button.

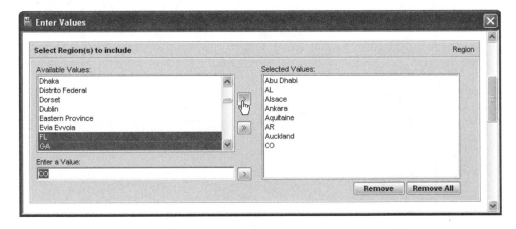

CAUTION *If you simply drag a multiple-value parameter field to your report to attempt to display chosen values, only the first value will actually appear on the report, even though all values will be used by the Select Expert. Use array functions in a formula, such as the Join function, to retrieve all the values in the parameter field. The Join function is described in detail in Chapter 5.*

Range Values

Crystal Reports provides *range-value* parameter fields, which allow you to create just one parameter field that can contain both low and high values. When this parameter field is supplied to the Select Expert with the Equals operator, it effectively supplies both the low and high values and changes the operator to Between.

To create a range-value parameter field, set the Allow Range Values option to True in the Options section of the Parameter dialog box (this and the Allow Discrete Values option are mutually exclusive—only one of these options can be set to True). This will change the way the parameter field prompt appears when the report is refreshed.

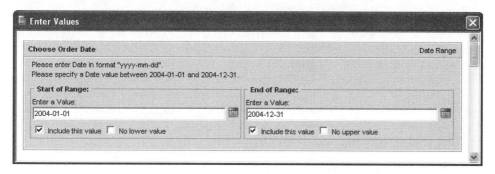

There are now two prompts for choosing or entering values: the Start of Range prompt and the End of Range prompt. These two prompts behave the same way a single prompt would behave, being based on pick list creation, allowing custom values, and so forth. However, when the viewer clicks OK, both prompts will be supplied to the Select Expert or record-selection formula, and all records between and including the selected values will be returned.

Normally, range-value parameter fields are "inclusive"; that is, the values returned to the report *include* the two values that are specified in the Enter Values dialog box. If you uncheck Include This Value, however, the chosen value *will not* be included in the range. For example, if you choose the number 300 as the Start of Range and leave Include Value checked, any records including the number 300 will be included in the report. If you uncheck Include Value, anything over 300 will be included, but not 300 itself.

There are also No Lower Value and No Upper Value check boxes to allow you to make the range an open-ended range. If you leave both boxes unchecked (the default), the range will be limited to the finite values you enter as Start of Range and End of Range. If you check No Lower Value or No Upper Value (you can't select both), the corresponding range value will be discarded and the range will include only the other value. For example, if you specify a range of 100 to 1000, checking No Lower Value will discard 100 and return records where the value is simply less than 1000 (or less than and including 1000 if you leave Include This Value checked). Checking No Upper Value will return records exceeding 100 (or equal to or greater than 100 if you leave Include This Value checked).

If you drag a range-value parameter field directly onto your report to display supplied values, the parameter field will not show anything, because the parameter field is actually a range value. A *range* value is a single object (in this case, the parameter field) that actually contains the entire range of values specified by the parameter field. If you just put the object on the report by itself, Crystal Reports won't display anything, because it's not sure which value in the range you want to display. You can use range functions in the Formula Editor to return the first or last entries in the range. For example, the following formula will display the starting and ending dates of a date-range parameter field:

```
"Orders between " & Minimum({?Date Range})
& " and " & Maximum({?Date Range})
```

The Minimum and Maximum functions return the first and last entries in the range, respectively. Even though the Minimum and Maximum functions return date data types in this example, the ampersand concatenation operator (&) automatically converts them to strings.

However, when either No Lower Value or No Upper Value is selected for a date range, the corresponding Minimum or Maximum value is displayed oddly—it may appear to return a nonsensical or blank value. To display a more helpful message, you can use a formula to evaluate the date using the HasLowerBound and HasUpperBound functions and display text in place of the beginning or ending date:

```
"Orders placed between " &
IIf(HasLowerBound({?Date Range}),
    ToText(Minimum({?Date Range})),
    "beginning of time")
& " and " &
IIf(HasUpperBound({?Date Range}),
    ToText(Maximum({?Date Range})),
    "into the future")
```

NOTE *The usage of techniques used in this formula is explained more fully in Chapter 5.*

If, in addition to setting the Allow Range Values option to True, you also set the Allow Multiple Values option to True in the Parameter dialog box, the parameter field will allow entry of multiple range values, or an *array of ranges*. For example, you could choose to see orders placed between January 1, 2003, and March 31, 2003, January 1, 2004, and March 31, 2004, and January 1, 2005, and March 31, 2005. When you are prompted for a range-value parameter field that allows multiple values, a list will appear in which you can add multiple ranges.

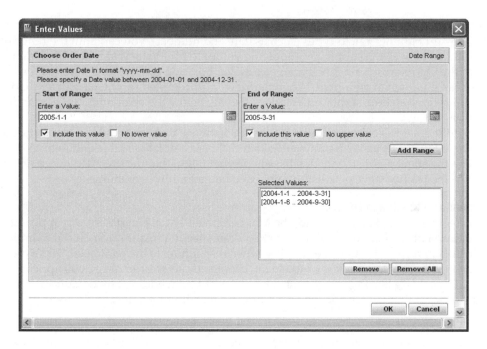

Different values can be specified in the Start of Range and End of Range areas and added to the list with the Add Range button. If you want to delete one or more existing ranges, select them in the Selected Values list and click the Remove button. You may delete all ranges with the Remove All button.

This single parameter field, when supplied to the Select Expert or record-selection formula, will effectively change the selection operator to Between *and* One Of at the same time.

CAUTION *The Minimum and Maximum array functions demonstrated earlier behave a little differently with combination range/multiple-value parameter fields and combination range and discrete-value/multiple-value parameter fields. In these cases, you may use the Minimum and Maximum function, as well as an array subscript (a number inside square brackets after the parameter field name), to extract the beginning and ending values of different elements of the array.*

Controlling Parameter Field Data Entry

One of the issues Crystal Reports users face is how to best customize the user interface for "turnkey" report users—those who aren't familiar with the intricacies of Crystal Reports. In an ideal world, the user interface will contain business rules, limits, and customized formatting to guide an end user through proper choices of parameters. While this ideal world is best provided with a customized "front end" program developed, perhaps, in Visual Studio .NET, Crystal Reports still gives the report developer a fair amount of control over how end users can enter data into parameter fields.

Limiting Entry to Certain Ranges of Values

With relevant parameter field types (such as date and number), you can limit the range of entries that a viewer can supply. By supplying values to Min Value/Start and Max Value/End, in the Options section of the Parameter dialog box, you can limit the values a report viewer can enter when prompted. When the viewer is prompted for the parameter field, they will receive an error if they enter values that are below the beginning range or above the ending range.

An added feature of range limiting is the set of values that can be added to a static pick list. When you range-limit a parameter field and choose a database table and field to help populate the static pick list, only database items that fall within the specified range will be added to the list (dynamic pick lists do not have range limiting capabilities).

Minimum and Maximum Lengths

If you create a string parameter field, the Min Length and Max Length options appear in the Options area of the Parameter dialog box. You can specify the minimum and maximum number of characters that must be supplied when responding to the parameter field's prompt. If a report viewer enters too few or too many characters, an error message will appear.

If you supply a length limit, you are also restricted from adding any default values to a static pick list that fall outside the minimum and maximum lengths.

Edit Masks

The most flexibility for controlling string parameter field entry comes from *edit masks*. An edit mask is a string of characters that controls many different aspects of data entry. One example might be an edit mask that allows only two uppercase characters to be entered (perhaps for a state abbreviation). Another example would be an edit mask that sets up the parameter field to accept data in a social security number format, accepting only number characters, and automatically adding hyphens between the third and fourth characters and between the fifth and sixth characters.

The key to using edit masks is learning the correct use of masking characters, listed in Table 13-1. Note that not only is the character you use significant, but so is the *case* of the character—uppercase and lowercase versions of the same character perform different masking functions.

So, an edit mask of (000) 000-0000 when used with a phone number parameter field will require entry of the area code and phone number portions, including the parentheses, the space, and the hyphen. The resulting content of the {?Phone} parameter value will include the literal characters, as well as the numbers.

An edit mask of Password will replace characters typed in the parameter prompting field with circles. This is commonly used for entry of passwords or other sensitive information to prevent the information from being learned by someone looking at the screen. When the viewer clicks OK, the actual characters typed will be passed to report formulas in the parameter value. However, if you simply drag and drop a password-formatted parameter to the report, it will not display anything.

Character	Usage
A	Requires entry of an alphanumeric character.
a	Allows an alphanumeric character to be entered, but doesn't require it.
0 (zero)	Requires a digit between 0 and 9 to be entered.
9	Allows a digit between 0 and 9 or a space to be entered, but doesn't require it.
#	Allows a digit, space, or plus or minus sign to be entered, but doesn't require it.
L	Requires entry of a letter between A and Z to be entered.
?	Allows a letter between A and Z to be entered, but doesn't require it.
&	Requires entry of any character or space.
C	Allows entry of any character or space, but doesn't require it.
>	Requires any subsequent characters to be typed in as uppercase characters (any resulting error message is unclear about this requirement).
<	Requires any subsequent characters to be typed in as lowercase characters (any resulting error message is unclear about this requirement).
\	Requires the next character to be typed into the parameter field in the exact position—you use this option if you want to actually include masking characters (such as A, a, <, and so forth) in the parameter field.
. , : ; - / ( ) or any character not listed in this table	These characters must be typed into the parameter field in the same position they are placed in the mask. They will be returned in the parameter field result exactly as typed.
Password	Causes characters typed in the parameter field to be displayed with circles instead of their actual characters; the actual characters are passed to report formulas but are not displayed on the report if the parameter field is simply dragged to the report.

TABLE 13-1   Parameter Field Masking Characters

Conditional Formatting with Parameter Fields

Parameter fields can be used to customize other parts of the report, not just record selection. If a viewer wishes to highlight orders over a certain amount, they can specify the amount in a parameter field and use the parameter field to set conditional formatting. If they wish to see summary data instead of detail data, they can respond to a Boolean parameter field that is used to suppress the details section. Basically, any place you can specify formatting conditionally, you can base formatting on parameter fields just as easily as you can on database or formula fields.

Highlighting Data Based on Parameter Fields

Once a parameter field has been created, it can be used for conditional formatting just as easily as any database or formula field. As with any parameter field, you need to consider the data type used to create the parameter field. For example, you might wish to prompt the viewer for an order amount threshold to highlight orders over that amount in red. If the Order Amount field in the database is contained in a currency data type, you'll need to either create the parameter field with the currency data type or do some data-type conversion in the conditional formula.

For example, you may wish to change various formatting properties of both report objects and sections based on a parameter. A currency parameter field will prompt the viewer to enter an order amount threshold. Then, two conditional formulas can be created: one to set the background color of the details section and one to set the font color of the order amount and customer name fields. The details section background color can be formatted to display in silver if the order exceeds the parameter value, as follows:

```
If {Orders.Order Amount} > {?Order Level} Then crSilver Else crNoColor
```

Then, another conditional formula, when applied to the font color of both the order amount and customer name, will display the fields in red if the order amount exceeds the threshold:

```
If {Orders.Order Amount} > {?Order Level} Then crRed Else crBlack
```

So, supplying a value of $2,500 to the Order Level parameter will highlight sections and change the font color for orders that exceed $2,500.

CAUTION Since the Highlighting Expert allows you only to compare to actual database values to set formatting conditionally, the Highlighting Expert will not work with parameter fields. You must use the Conditional Formula buttons that appear in the Format Editor if you wish to conditionally format with parameter fields.

Conditional Suppression Based on Parameter Fields

Use a parameter field just like a database or formula field to conditionally suppress individual objects or sections. Since the Suppress property requires a Boolean formula when being set conditionally, you can create a Boolean parameter field and supply it as the sole part of the Boolean formula, or you can create a Boolean formula by using a comparison operator with another type of parameter field.

You could, for example, create a Boolean parameter field called Summary Only that returns a true or false value based on the viewer's choice. By simply supplying the Boolean parameter field as the only item in a section or object's Suppress conditional formula, you could control whether the details section or a page header section containing column headings for the details section appears or doesn't appear.

When prompted for this parameter field, the viewer could select a True or False option for the Summary Only parameter field. You could then place this parameter field directly in the Suppress conditional formula for the details section. If the Summary Only parameter were true (indicating that the viewer wants a summary-only report), the details section would be suppressed. You could also suppress the page header section that contains column headings for the details fields.

A Password parameter can be used to conditionally format a sensitive data field, such as Salary, to suppress if {?Password} does not equal a certain value. Since the password is masked by circles when the viewer enters it, it's protected from inadvertent "over-the-shoulder" viewing, and only people who enter it correctly will see the sensitive data. Note, however, that anyone with access to the report and to the Crystal Reports Designer can simply view the conditional formatting formula to determine the password value required, so the password edit mask is not, in itself, a security measure for sensitive data.

Using Parameter Fields with Formulas

There will be many situations in which you need to prompt for a parameter field in a certain way or choose a particular data type for a parameter field so that it will work properly with record selection. However, you might want to display the parameter field on the report in a different way, perform some calculation based on the parameter field, or otherwise manipulate the parameter field in a formula. Or, you may want to provide some variable information to a formula, such as a sales tax rate. By setting up a parameter field to prompt for the tax rate, it's very easy to run the report for different states or cities that have varying sales tax rates.

When you create a parameter field, it will appear in the Formula Editor's Field Tree box under Report Fields. It can be added to a formula just like a database field or another formula. Just remember the data type you choose when creating the parameter field—you must use it correctly inside the formula to avoid type-mismatch errors. You may need to use ToText, ToNumber, or other conversion functions.

Using a Parameter Field for Partial Text Matches

A handy capability of the Select Expert is the Like operator that can be used when selecting records based on string database fields. Like allows you to supply *wildcard characters*, such as the question mark (?) and asterisk (*) to indicate single-character and partial-field matches, respectively. For example, supplying a Select Expert operator of Like with the literal *?eor?e* would return George, Jeorge, Jeorje, or Georje. Using the Like operator with an asterisk in the literal *Je** would return Jean, Jenny, Jennifer, and Jerry.

NOTE *A more complete discussion of record selection is contained in Chapter 4.*

By allowing question marks and asterisks to be included in parameter fields, and by using the Like operator in the Select Expert, you give your report viewer great flexibility in choosing only the records they want to see. However, if you want a meaningful message to appear on the report indicating what the user has chosen, you'll need to use a formula to display different information than the parameter field actually supplies to the Select Expert.

Consider a parameter field called Customer Name that will prompt the viewer to add question marks or asterisks for partial-match searches:

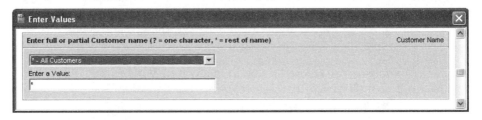

If you wish to place a descriptive message in the page header indicating which customers have been chosen, you can create the following formula:

```
If {?Customer Name} = "*" Then
    "All Customers"
Else
    If Instr({?Customer Name},"?") > 0 or
        Instr({?Customer Name},"*") > 0 Then
        "Customers matching the pattern " + {?Customer Name}
    Else
        "Customer: " + {?Customer Name}
```

This formula simply uses the Customer Name parameter field as you would another database or formula field in an If-Then-Else statement. If the parameter field contains only an asterisk, it will return all records, so the formula returns "All Customers." Otherwise, if the parameter field contains at least one asterisk or question mark (the Instr function will return the location of the first occurrence of the character, or zero if there isn't any occurrence), the formula indicates that the report is based on a partial pattern. Finally, if there are no asterisks or question marks at all, the report will be returning an exact text match to the parameter field, and this formula indicates that.

To make it easy for the report to default to all customers without the viewer knowing or remembering to enter an asterisk in the prompt, you may wish to add it as a default value for the parameter prompt, with the description All Customers.

NOTE *If you make use of this type of parameter field in the Select Expert, remember that you'll need to use the Like operator instead of Equal To. This will ensure that record selection interprets asterisk and question mark characters properly.*

Using a Parameter Field to Change Sorting or Grouping

You may often wish to have a report viewer choose the report sorting or grouping on the fly. Since a parameter field can't actually return a database or formula-field name itself, you need to create a formula based on the parameter field, and use that formula as the sort or group field in the report.

You could, for example, create a parameter field called Group By that prompts for grouping by Country, Region, or City. These would be the only three options, as the viewer will not be allowed to enter custom values. The prompt for this parameter field would look like this:

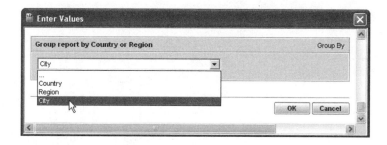

Because the parameter field will contain only the string Country, Region, or City, you can't use the parameter field directly as a sort or group field. You need to create a formula based on the parameter field and supply it as the sort or group field. Look at this formula:

```
If {?Group By} = "Region" Then {Customer.Region}
Else
If {?Group By} = "City" Then {Customer.City}
Else {Customer.Country}
```

This will actually return a different database field based on the parameter field's value. Then, this formula can be supplied as the grouping or sorting field, and the group or sort will change according to the viewer's response to the parameter field.

Using a Parameter Field to Control Top N Reporting

In Crystal Reports versions prior to XI, Top N reporting (covered in more detail in Chapter 3) only accepted a "hard-coded" value for N. That is, if you wanted to see the top 5 groups, or the bottom 10 groups, you had to choose Top N or Bottom N and type an actual "5" or "10" into the Group Sort Expert dialog box.

Crystal Reports XI introduces the ability to supply the value of N with a conditional formula. By supplying the value of a parameter field within the conditional formula, you may now allow a report viewer to specify the value of N every time the report is refreshed.

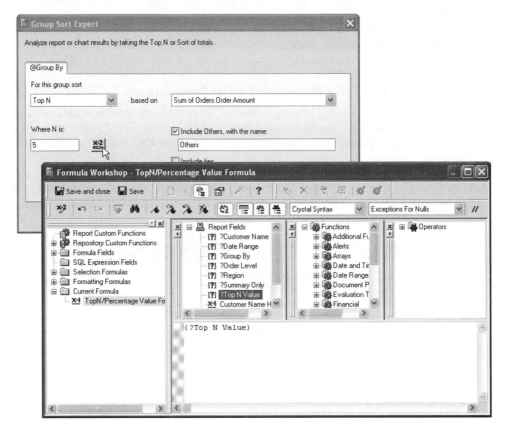

Exporting Reports to Different Formats

When you save a Crystal Report, your report file is saved on disk with an .RPT extension. This Crystal Reports native format can be used only with another copy of Crystal Reports, with Crystal Reports Server/BusinessObjects Enterprise, with a web-based application using a native Crystal Reports programming interface, or with a customized Windows application (both are discussed in Part III of the book). Since everyone who might ever need to view a report probably won't have their own copy of Crystal Reports, there are many ways to *export* a report to a different file format for use with such products as Microsoft Word, Microsoft Excel, Acrobat Reader, and others. You can also export your reports in HTML format for viewing in a web browser. Furthermore, you can attach these differently formatted files to e-mail messages or place them in a Lotus Domino database or a Microsoft Exchange public folder.

Although exporting is a handy way of distributing reports to non–Crystal Reports viewers, your exported reports are *static,* meaning they contain a picture of the database as it existed when the report was exported. As soon as the source database changes (perhaps the second after the report was exported), the report becomes outdated. If your viewers have their own copies of Crystal Reports, they can solve this problem by opening and refreshing the report, but this also means that they can *change* the report. This solution also assumes that your viewers know enough about Crystal Reports to be able to open and refresh a report.

If your viewers do not have their own copies of Crystal Reports and do need real-time data reporting, you may want to consider implementing Crystal Reports Server/BusinessObjects Enterprise to allow real-time running of reports in a web browser (see Part II of this book for more information). Or, you may develop a custom-programmed Windows or web application to integrate the report for viewing by your target audience (see Part III of this book for more information). Also, there are third-party utility programs available to help distribute reports to viewers (this book's companion web site, www.CrystalBook.com, features a large number of these utilities).

The examples in this chapter are based on a report, shown in Figure 14-1, containing both text and a chart placed beside the text with the Underlay feature. In addition, some of the text contains special formatting, such as drop shadows. The report also contains additional

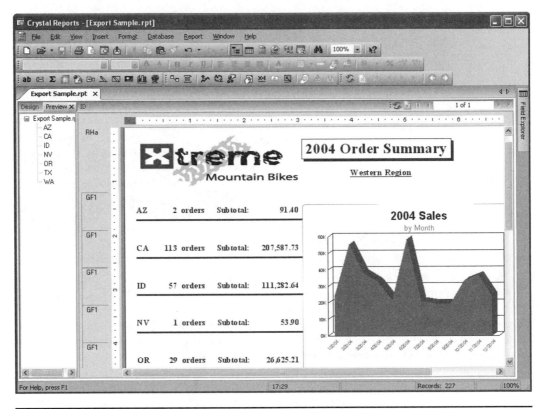

FIGURE 14-1   Sample report for exporting

graphical elements, such as line and box drawing. The report also contains hyperlinks to external web site and e-mail addresses.

Exporting Reports to Office Applications

You'll often wish to convert or export a report you've designed to a popular office file format, such as Excel, Word, WordPerfect, or Acrobat Reader. With Crystal Reports, this is as simple as choosing an option from the File menu. You can also export the file to a temporary location and immediately launch the application you want to use to view the file, provided it's installed on your PC.

Exporting to Different File Formats

To export a file, first open the report you wish to export. Refresh and preview the report, if necessary, to ensure that it contains the most up-to-date data from the database. Then, click the Export button on the Standard toolbar or choose File | Export | Export Report from the pull-down menus. The Export dialog box will appear.

You have two simple choices to make for your export: the file format of the export and the destination of the export. The Format drop-down list lets you choose from the large number of file formats to which Crystal Reports will export. You can choose from several different ASCII or "straight-text" formats, several Microsoft Excel formats, Microsoft Word, Acrobat Reader, and others.

The Destination drop-down list lets you choose how you want the report exported: to a disk file, attached to an e-mail message, placed in a Microsoft Exchange public folder, added to a Lotus Domino database, or launched in an application on your workstation. If you choose Disk File, the Choose Export File dialog box will prompt you for the folder and filename to export to. Choose a folder and type a filename, if the default folder and filename aren't sufficient.

CAUTION *If your report contains several drill-down tabs or subreport Preview tabs, ensure that the tab you want exported is selected before you begin exporting. Whatever appears in the current tab (and all pages you specify that are generated by that tab) is what will be exported by Crystal Reports.*

Figure 14-2 shows the sample report from Figure 14-1 after it has been exported to a Microsoft Word document. Notice that it, for the most part, accurately depicts the source report—the sole exception being the much subtler drop shadow on the report title. Both the web and e-mail hyperlinks are accurately exported.

TIP *While most Crystal Reports XI export formats exhibit accurate reproduction of original report formatting, you'll still find that some of the Crystal Reports formatting doesn't always translate to other file formats. You should export to your ultimate destination format throughout your report design process to make sure everything you want to include will be exported correctly. You'll also find variations on the same file format available, such as Excel and Excel – Data Only. These variations will retain different levels of formatting when exporting. For example, Crystal Reports XI has added an Editable RTF format that doesn't retain as much formatting as other RTF formats but makes Word documents created with the Editable RTF format easier to modify.*

If you drill down on a report, a different report "view" will appear inside the drill-down tab. Only the material inside the open drill-down tab will be exported. The main Preview tab won't be included. Exporting the Idaho (ID) drill-down tab will result in a Microsoft Excel file, shown in Figure 14-3.

Depending on the file format you choose, you may receive an additional dialog box prompting you for the page range to be exported, as well as other extended information

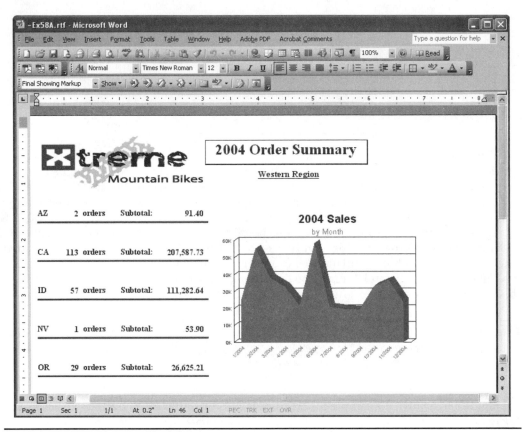

FIGURE 14-2   Exporting to a Word document

about the export. If, for example, you choose one of the Excel formats, a dialog box will allow you to choose more customized information when exporting to Excel.

Exporting to various text file formats, such as Character Separated Values, will present additional dialog boxes prompting you for, among other things, the characters to surround and separate fields.

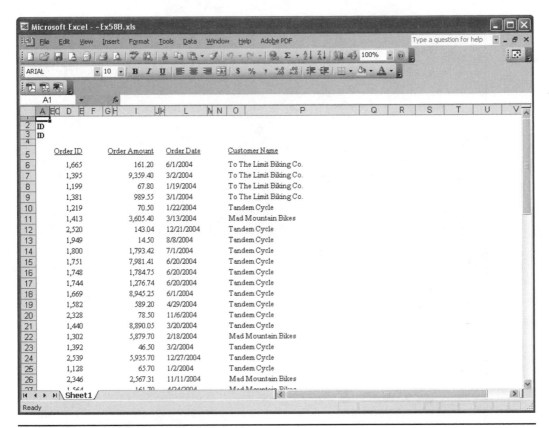

FIGURE 14-3   Drill-down tab exported to Excel

TIP *Crystal Reports XI allows you to set default values for many options on these dialog boxes so that they will be automatically set for subsequent exports. By choosing File | Export | Export Options, you may set defaults for many individual export format options.*

Exporting to an Adobe Portable Document Format, or *PDF*, file may be the most effective way to export a report that contains complex formatting and graphics, including underlaid sections, as shown in Figure 14-4. As PDF files are generally accepted formats for Windows, the Web, and other cross-platform applications, you'll find that its accurate formatting representation of the original report will often benefit a wide audience. In this example, both hyperlinks are accurately passed on to the PDF file as well.

NOTE *You may notice that some file formats and export destinations display a small number "1" beside them in the Export dialog box. This indicates that these formats and destinations were given an Install on first use attribute when Crystal Reports was initially installed. When you choose these formats or destinations for the first time, you'll be prompted to insert the original Crystal Reports program CD to install the necessary export drivers.*

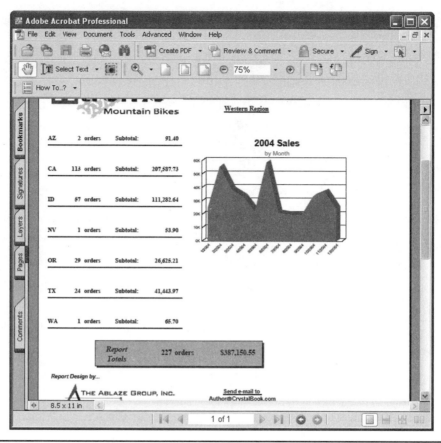

FIGURE 14-4   Exporting to an Acrobat PDF format

Exporting and Launching an Application

If you choose Application in the Destination drop-down list, Crystal Reports will export the file to a temporary folder and immediately open the file in the corresponding Windows application. If you choose a file format for an application that isn't installed on your computer, you may be presented with a dialog box asking you to choose an application to open the file with. If there is an alternative application that will open that file type, choose it from the list.

NOTE *The temporary files that Crystal Reports creates will be located in the Windows temporary folder (typically, your private folder underneath the Documents and Settings folder) and may not automatically be deleted when you close the application. If you wish to periodically "clean out" your Windows temporary folder, use Disk Cleanup or another appropriate utility or measure to remove temporary files.*

Exporting to an ODBC Data Source

You can export a Crystal Report to an ODBC data source, such as a Microsoft SQL Server or Oracle database. Typically, you'll want to do this with a simple columnar details report that you might be using to transport data from one database to another.

To export to an ODBC data source, choose the data source you want to export to in the Format drop-down list. You'll then be asked to supply a table name, which Crystal Reports will create in the database referred to by the data source. If the data source refers to a secure database, you will be asked to supply a database logon user ID and password before the export starts. And if the data source does not contain a specific database reference, you may be asked to choose a database in addition to the table name.

Crystal Reports will create a new table in the ODBC database and define fields to hold data from the exported report. If you want to change field names or the layout of the table, you need to use a utility specific to the ODBC database that you exported to. You may also notice that the fields and data that are exported to your ODBC database may not be what you initially expect. You may need to modify the original Crystal Report to accurately export data via ODBC.

Creating a Report Definition File

When you create reports, you may want to keep documentation that details the report design, such as the tables that are included, what formulas you've created, and what objects are contained in the report sections.

The Export dialog box in Crystal Reports provides a Report Definition format in the Format drop-down list. When you choose this format, Crystal Reports will save a text file containing a great deal of helpful information about the makeup of the report. You may wish to create and keep these text files in a central location to document the design of your reports. You may also open the text files in a word processor and reformat them to look more appealing.

```
~Ex592.txt - Notepad
File Edit Format View Help
           Crystal Report Professional v11.0 (32-bit) - Report Definition

1.0 File Information

        Report File:
        Version: 11.0

2.0 Record Sort Fields

3.0 Group Sort Fields

4.0 Formulas

4.1 Record Selection Formula
        {Customer.Region} in ["CA","WA","OR","ID","AZ","NV","TX"] and
{Orders.Order Date} in #1/1/2004# to #12/31/2004#

4.2 Group Selection Formula

4.3 Other Formulas

5.0 Sectional Information

5.1 Page Header Section
        Hidden, Keep Together

5.2 Page Footer Section
        Visible, New Page After, Keep Together, Print At Bottom of Page

5.3 Report Header Section
        Visible, New Page Before

    Subsection.1
            Visible, Keep Together

    Subsection.2
            Visible, Keep Together, Underlay

    2004 Order Summary
            String, Visible, Horizontal Centre Alignment, Top Alignment,
            Keep Together


    Western Region
            String, Visible, Horizontal Centre Alignment, Top Alignment,
            Keep Together
```

Exporting to XML

Crystal Reports provides the capability of exporting to Extensible Markup Language, or *XML*. XML, which is an extension of Hypertext Markup Language (HTML—the original "language" of the World Wide Web), is gaining more acceptance as a method of data exchange among disparate organizations and companies. XML describes the data that it encompasses with a set of descriptors, or *tags*, similar to HTML. These tags format the report content according to standardized language rules established (and still under development) by a consortium of technology and business organizations. XML files can vary in content from very simplified data output to formatted definitions of hierarchically organized data. Each element in an XML file is identified by tags, which define the name of the element, the type of element, and additional optional attributes.

Crystal Reports provides two basic XML output format options: the Crystal ML Schema, which provides a standard set of tags and structure that includes extensive formatting content, and the Custom Format, which allows you to suppress elements, change the names of elements, and add attributes to elements.

When using the Crystal ML Schema, the resulting XML file can be viewed by a web browser, but it will not be interpreted or formatted by the browser the way an HTML file will be, as XML does not, by its nature, include any font, color, or formatting attributes. Figure 14-5 shows the XML file output from a simple columnar Orders report (similar to the one in Figure 14-3), using Crystal ML Schema. This schema is published at http://www.businessobjects.com/xml/schema.xsd.

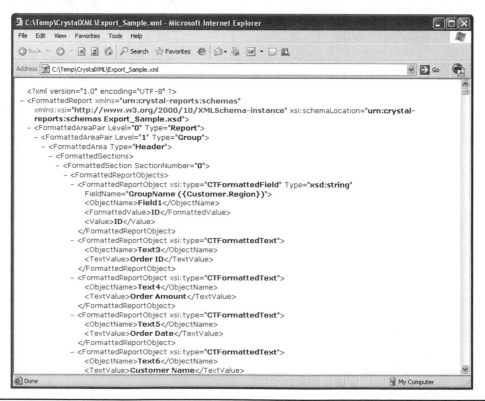

FIGURE 14-5   XML export, viewed in web browser

If you wish to add to the default Crystal ML schema, or customize the XML output format entirely, not using the standard format, use the XML Expert before exporting your report. The *XML Expert* is actually a flexible dialog box that allows you to customize the attributes and XML tags Crystal Reports will use when exporting to XML. Choose Report | XML Expert from the Crystal Reports pull-down menus. When the XML Format dialog box is displayed, click the Options tab.

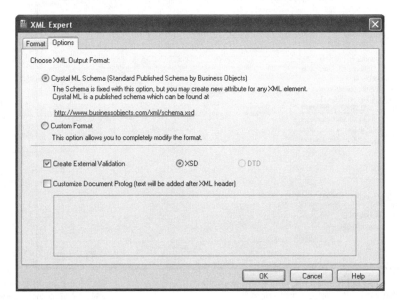

On the Options tab, initially choose whether to use the standard Crystal ML Schema or a custom format. You may also choose whether to create an external validation file, consisting of either an XSD (XML Schema Definition) or DTD (Document Type Definition). You may also enter any custom text you want to insert after the header in the XML file to further define the output. This custom text might, for example, reference an external DTD file or a standard HTML style sheet.

NOTE *Using the default Crystal ML Schema will only allow creation of an external XSD document—the DTD option will be dimmed.*

Once you've made schema, external validation, and custom text choices, click the Format tab to concisely control individual elements and tags used when exporting to XML. The Format tab is shown in Figure 14-6.

To limit the XML file to just data elements, rather than report/formatting elements, you'll want to suppress some or all of the report section parent elements, such as ReportArea: Report Area and Detail:Detail. To do this, select the desired parent element or section and click the Suppress XML Tag check box beneath the tree. You can use the Suppress All Children check box when you don't want to produce XML tags for *any* subsets of a section/element. However, don't use the Suppress All Children check box for any of the Details area elements, as it will also suppress tags for the data layer of the Details section. When an element is suppressed, the element can no longer be customized.

The Report Definition Tree displays each parent section of the report. Expand them to see the subsection elements.

Change the name of the element if the XML output needs different tag names than the default name.

Click here to create a new element for the selected report object that shares another object's element name.

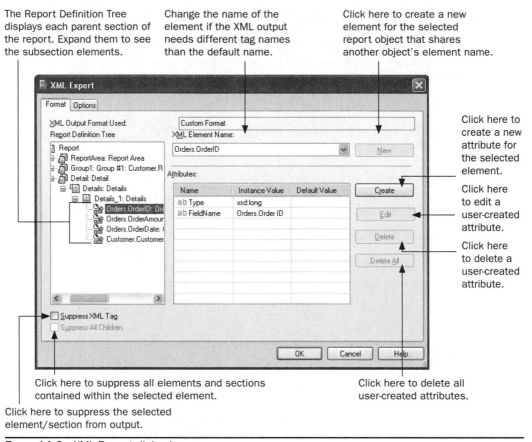

Click here to create a new attribute for the selected element.

Click here to edit a user-created attribute.

Click here to delete a user-created attribute.

Click here to suppress all elements and sections contained within the selected element.

Click here to delete all user-created attributes.

Click here to suppress the selected element/section from output.

FIGURE 14-6   XML Format dialog box

To customize attributes or element names, select the element you wish to customize. The element name and the attributes of the element are displayed on the right side of the dialog box. In the example illustrated in Figure 14-7, the selected element is the data field containing the order ID. If desired, the name of the element (Orders.OrderID) can be changed for output purposes by simply entering the modified name in the XML Element Name field. By default, Crystal has assigned two attributes to each data field element: Type and FieldName. The gray "ab" designation beside the attribute name indicates that these cannot be changed or deleted. However, additional attributes can be created, changed, and deleted as needed according to the XML output required. For example, if you need to add a "use" attribute to this field, you can click the Create button to produce the XML Attribute Dialog box seen in Figure 14-7.

For this example, supplying an attribute name of "use" and text of "required" will result in the standard XML field use attribute being inserted into the OrderID data element tag:

```
<Orders.OrderID FieldName="{Orders.Order ID}"
use="required">1128.00</Orders.OrderID>
```

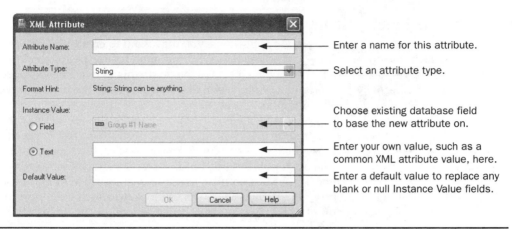

Enter a name for this attribute.

Select an attribute type.

Choose existing database field
to base the new attribute on.

Enter your own value, such as a
common XML attribute value, here.

Enter a default value to replace any
blank or null Instance Value fields.

FIGURE 14-7   XML Attribute dialog box

Once you've made any desired customizations, close the XML Expert. Then, export using
XML as the desired format with the File Export toolbar button or File menu option. When
you choose XML as the format, you'll be prompted to choose a file directory, rather than just
a filename. As XML exports can result in more than one file actually being created (for
example, if you choose to create an external XSD or DTD), you'll need to choose a specific
directory in which to place all exported files. You can also replace the default filename for
the main XML file—the name of the source report will be used by default.

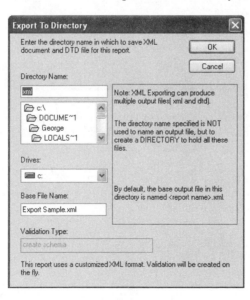

Sending Reports Electronically

In addition to exporting reports to office applications, you may want to create an exported report and attach it to an e-mail message, place it in a Lotus Domino database, or send to a Microsoft Exchange public folder. You might expect to have to do this in two steps: export to your chosen file format and then run a separate e-mail package to send the file. However, Crystal Reports lets you do it all in one step.

Use the Export toolbar button or choose the File | Export menu option to display the Export dialog box. Choose the desired format from the Format drop-down list. From the Destination drop-down list, choose the e-mail system you wish to send the report with. Choosing Lotus Domino will place a report in your Lotus Domino database; choosing Exchange Folder will add the report to a Microsoft Exchange; and choosing MAPI will use a Microsoft-compatible e-mail program, such as Microsoft Outlook, to attach the report to an e-mail message. Note that you need to have the appropriate "client" software installed on your PC for any of these options to work.

For example, if Microsoft Outlook is installed on your PC and you choose MAPI as the destination, the following dialog box will appear (you may be prompted to choose an Outlook profile first):

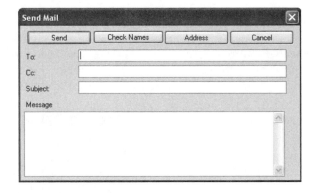

Specify the e-mail address or addresses you want the message to go to, along with the message you want to appear in the e-mail body. The message will be sent with the report file attached (in the format you specified).

Reporting from SQL Databases

A s newer leading-edge database applications are released, fewer and fewer make use of PC-style databases. The performance and capacity limitations of local PC databases often limit their usefulness for larger, performance-dependent applications. Instead, most newer applications rely on *client/server* database systems. A client/server system includes two parts: a *client*, typically a PC running software such as Crystal Reports or a data-entry application, and a *server*, typically a larger, high-end PC running Windows 2000 or 2003 Server, a midrange, or even a mainframe computer. The server maintains the database, and the client makes requests of the server for database access. Many different client/server databases exist, with Microsoft SQL Server, Oracle, IBM DB/2, and Informix being among the more popular ones.

CAUTION *Some SQL databases and database connectivity methods can be used only with the Professional or Developer edition of Crystal Reports. The Standard Edition reports only on a limited set of databases. If you want complete database flexibility, you should probably purchase the Professional or Developer edition.*

It's important to understand and contrast the differences between a client/server database system and a PC-style database system that is installed on a shared local area network (LAN). For reporting purposes, in particular, a LAN-based database system presents a much more serious performance hurdle than a client/server database. Figure 15-1 shows a PC reporting on two database environments. The first depicts a Microsoft Access database on a LAN server. The second depicts the same database on a SQL Server system.

The LAN-based scenario places heavy burdens on both the network and the PC making the reporting request. In this scenario, the PC must read the entire 100,000-record Access database across the network, picking and choosing the records that meet the report-selection criteria. This requires large amounts of data to be passed across the network, and the PC has to perform all the selection logic itself.

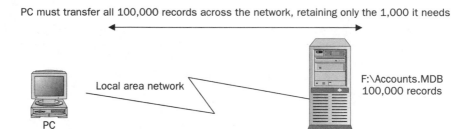

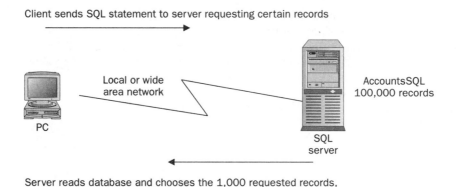

FIGURE 15-1   Retrieving 1,000 specific records from a LAN-based database vs. a client/server database

The client/server environment is much more efficient. The client PC simply makes a request to the database server via a Structured Query Language (SQL) request. The database server, presumably a larger, high-powered PC, Unix computer, or mainframe, runs database software designed to process such queries very efficiently. It directly queries the 100,000-record database and sends only the required 1,000 records back across the network. This places less demand on the client and the network, and the whole process typically takes less time.

Logging On to SQL Databases

The first step to creating a Crystal Report is to select the SQL database that you want to base your report on. There are three general communication methods you can use to connect to a client/server database with Crystal Reports: direct database drivers, ODBC, and OLE DB (pronounced oh-LAY-dee-bee).

Direct Database Drivers

Crystal Reports provides direct database drivers that work with many industry-standard client/server databases, including, among others, Oracle and IBM DB2 (the Microsoft SQL Server Direct Database driver has been eliminated from Crystal Reports, however). A direct database driver uses the native communication methods provided by the server vendor to communicate with the database server. This typically requires installing the specific client software provided by the database vendor on the PC, such as SQL*Plus for Oracle.

Crystal Reports will recognize the existence of these packages and provide a direct database driver to connect to the database. In addition, Crystal Reports provides other direct drivers to allow you to report from non-SQL data sources, such as Microsoft Outlook folders, Microsoft Exchange folders, Lotus Domino databases, Internet web server activity logs, and the Windows 2000/XP/2003 event log. You can even write reports based on the *local file system,* which consists of the file and directory structure of your C drive or a network drive. More details on these specialized types of reports can be found in Chapter 20.

Using direct database drivers to connect to the database server has two general advantages:

- Because fewer layers of communications protocols are being used, there may be a slight performance improvement when reporting.

- The direct database driver may allow more flexibility for creating more server-specific SQL statements or other query features for reporting.

ODBC

Although many companies standardize on database servers that Crystal Reports provides direct database drivers for, many other database systems and specialized data systems exist that you may want to report on. Some standard method of communication is needed to connect standard PC clients with the myriad specialized servers and systems that exist. Microsoft designed open database connectivity (ODBC) to accomplish this communication.

As a general rule, any server or proprietary data platform that is ODBC-compliant can be used with Crystal Reports. If the database or system vendor provides a Windows ODBC driver for its system, Crystal Reports should be able to report against that server or system. Because it has been accepted as an industry standard, ODBC is in widespread use.

TIP   Crystal Reports installs some generic ODBC data sources for common database files and formats, including an ODBC data source for using the sample XTREME.MDB database. Before you can use Crystal Reports to report against other ODBC data systems, you must set up an ODBC data source. Use the ODBC Administrator from Windows Control Panel to set up the data source.

OLE DB

Microsoft has added an additional standard, OLE DB, to extend its previous universal data connectivity method, ODBC. OLE DB provides data access in much the same manner as ODBC. A *data provider* acts as an interface between disparate client and server systems. Data providers are available not only for typical relational database systems, but also for more nontraditional data sources, such as spreadsheets, web servers, and multidimensional OLAP data sources.

Crystal Reports supports OLE DB data sources that are installed on your client PC. Various client applications, such as OLAP client software, will automatically install OLE DB data providers.

NOTE *You may also use Crystal Reports Server/BusinessObjects Enterprise Business Views or Universes as data sources. In these cases, the Business View or Universe will simply "point" to a Crystal Reports data source, such as a direct, ODBC, or OLE DB connection to the target SQL database.*

Choosing the Database

When you first start Crystal Reports, you can immediately choose and log on to a client/server database before you open an existing report or create a new report. If you don't log on but open a report based on a client/server database, you will be prompted to log on as soon as you try to refresh the report or choose any other function that requires the database to be read.

If you want to create a new report based on a client/server database, you can use a report wizard or the Blank Report option. If you use a report wizard, the first section of the wizard will display your database connection choices.

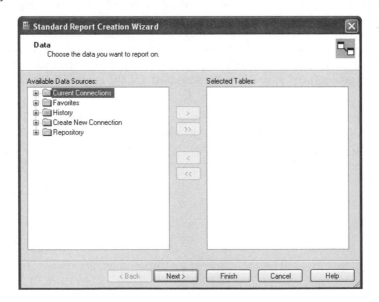

If you choose the Blank Report option to create a new report, the Database Expert will appear immediately.

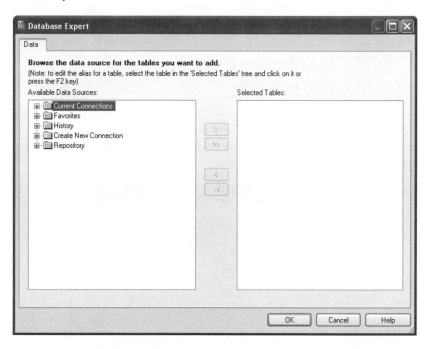

The Database Expert combines in one place all data sources, including direct database drivers, ODBC, and OLE DB. You may choose from one of these connection types from several places, depending on whether you've used data sources in the past (recently used data sources will appear in the History category), whether you're already logged into a data source from using another report (currently connected data sources will appear in the Current Connections category), or whether you've added a database connection to the Favorites folder. To maintain connections in your Favorites folder through the Database expert, simply right-click the desired database entry and select Add To Favorites from the pop-up menu.

You'll also find a Data Explorer folder entry for the repository, where you can choose a SQL Command or Crystal Reports Server/BusinessObjects Enterprise Business View as a data source (SQL Commands are covered later in this chapter, and Business Views are covered in Chapter 16). Click the plus sign next to the repository category to log on to the Crystal Reports Server/BusinessObjects Enterprise repository and choose the desired SQL Command or Business View.

If you don't see the data source you wish to connect to in any of these categories, you can create a new connection to a database by clicking the plus sign next to the Create New Connection category. This will display an additional set of database categories that you can choose from. Again, click the plus sign next to the desired category to create a connection using that connection type. Particular categories that you'll probably use to connect to standard client/server databases include ODBC, OLE DB, and More Data Sources.

Tip *As if ODBC and OLE DB aren't enough "alphabet soup" in the Database Expert, you are also presented with the abbreviations "RDO" and "ADO" after the ODBC and OLE DB categories. These are abbreviations for yet more Microsoft standards for database connectivity. RDO (which stands for Remote Data Objects) and ADO (which stands for ActiveX Data Objects) are technical terms to describe the internal method Crystal Reports uses to connect to ODBC and OLE DB data sources.*

Clicking the plus sign next to the ODBC will display a separate dialog box listing all the predefined ODBC data sources (use the ODBC Administrator from Windows Control Panel to add a data source if you don't see the desired data source here). Choose the desired data source and click the Next button in the dialog box. Depending on the data source you've chosen, as well as the database type it connects to, you'll probably see additional dialog boxes asking you to supply valid logon credentials.

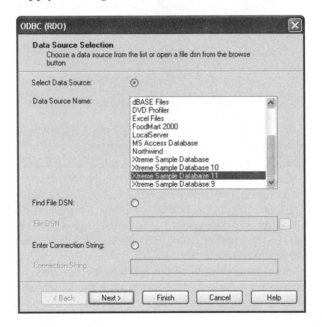

Clicking the plus sign next to the OLE DB category will also launch a separate OLE DB dialog box. You'll initially see a list of installed OLE DB *providers*, or database-specific connection drivers, that have been installed on your PC. Choose the provider you wish to use and click the Next button. As with ODBC, the remaining options in the OLE DB dialog box, such as those to choose a specific database and supply logon credentials, will vary according to the provider you choose.

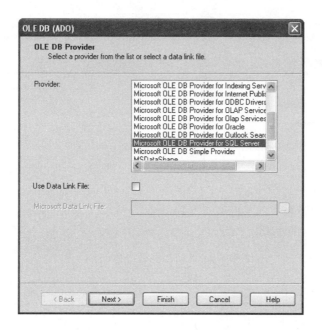

If you wish to use a direct database driver, click the plus sign next to the More Data Sources category. This will expand the Database Expert with yet another level of subfolders. Look for a description that matches the type of direct driver you wish to use, such as "Exchange Folders" or "Lotus Domino" (other non-SQL data sources will appear in this category as well—these other data sources are covered in more detail in Chapter 20). As with other connection methods, these drivers will provide database-specific dialog boxes asking you to provide logon credentials.

If the entry "no items found" appears below the chosen direct driver folder, it may be that you haven't properly installed necessary database client software on your PC. For example, you may see this message underneath the Oracle category if you haven't installed the Oracle SQL Plus client software on your PC.

TIP *Not all database drivers will be installed by default when you install Crystal Reports. The first time you choose one of these data sources in the Database Expert, you may be prompted to insert the original Crystal Reports CD to install the specific driver. Also, if you add an additional data source from Crystal Reports Setup, you'll often see an additional, related category appear within the Create New Connection category.*

Once you've successfully logged on to the database, the Database Expert will expand the folder you originally selected and display a list of databases, schemas, tables, views, or stored procedures available in the database (the display will vary depending on the type of database chosen). Figure 15-2 shows the Database Expert with a list of available SQL Server database tables with two tables already having been added to the report.

Remove highlighted
table from report

Add highlighted table in Available
Data Sources to report

Tables already
added to report

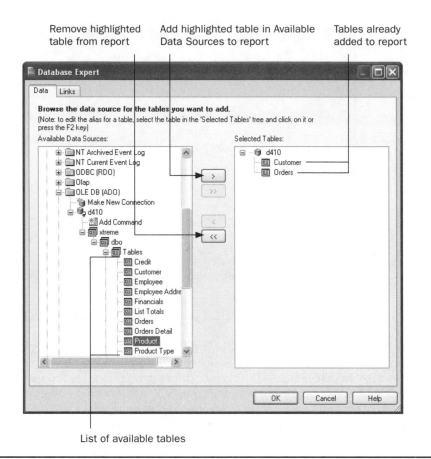

FIGURE 15-2   The Database Expert

Select the table, stored procedure, or view that you want to include in your report, either by double-clicking it or by selecting it and clicking the single right arrow. You can also CTRL-click more than one table and add them at once with the right arrow, or you can select one or more tables and simply drag them to the Selected Tables box. And if you want to add all the tables to the report (probably not a very common occurrence), you can click the double-right arrow. As you add tables, they will appear under the Selected Tables list on the right side of the Database Expert. If you accidentally add the wrong table or tables, you may highlight them in the Selected Tables list and remove them with the left arrow. You may remove all previously added tables with the double-left arrow.

TIP   *You may also right-click different entries in the Available Data Sources list to display a pop-up menu to perform many of the operations discussed in this section.*

If you don't see all the tables you expect, or you wish to limit the set of available tables to a certain database owner or certain table name pattern, right-click while pointing to the

Available Data Source list and choose Options from the pop-up menu. This will display the Database Options dialog box (discussed next in the chapter, under "Changing SQL Options"). After choosing options in this dialog box, you may then choose from any additional entries that appear in the Available Data Sources list. Once you've added the desired tables to the report, click the Links tab in the Database Expert to link the tables together on common fields (more detailed information on linking fields is found in the "Linking Tables" section later in this chapter). Once you've chosen and linked tables, close the Database Expert by clicking the OK button.

Keep in mind that once you log on to a SQL database from the Database Expert, you remain connected to that database even if you close any reports that are based on that database connection. If you then begin a new report and display the Database Expert, the database you are already connected to will appear in the Current Connections category of the Database Expert. If you don't want to use these tables in your report, you may merely ignore them and choose another database entry. If you'd prefer to release your connection to this existing database and not see it in the Current Connections category, you need to log off the original server, either by closing and restarting Crystal Reports or by using the Log On/ Off Server option. If you have a report open, choose Database | Log On/Off Server. If you don't have a report open, choose File | Log On/Off Server. In either case, choose the database you wish to log off from in the Current Connections category and click the Log Off button.

Changing SQL Options

Depending on the data source you choose, you may not see all the database elements you're looking for in the Database Expert. In particular, if your database supports *SQL stored procedures* (precompiled SQL statements that may contain parameters) or *views* (virtual tables that may combine several actual database tables together into one group), you will want to make sure you can see these in the Database Expert if your reports require using them. Or, you may want to limit the tables that you see in the Database Expert to only the table names that match a certain pattern or that are owned by a certain database user.

To make these choices, right-click anywhere in the Available Data Sources list on the left side of the Database Expert. Choose Options from the pop-up menu. The Database Options dialog box will appear, as shown in Figure 15-3.

TIP *You may also make changes to this dialog box when the Database Expert isn't being displayed. Choose File | Options from the pull-down menus and make changes to the Database tab of the Options dialog box.*

The Tables and Fields section lets you determine how tables and fields appear in the Database Expert and Field Explorer. You have several choices for how you want table and field names sorted, such as the ability to list tables in the Database Explorer and fields in the Field Explorer alphabetically.

The Data Explorer area of this dialog box lets you limit the tables that appear in the Database Expert when you log on to a database. Check the table types (Tables, Views, Synonyms, Stored Procedures, and System Tables) to determine the types of database elements you want to appear. You can also add a table name or table owner *pattern* to limit the list of tables to those that are named like the pattern or owned by a database user who matches a pattern.

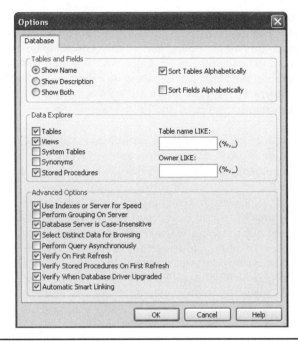

FIGURE 15-3 Database Options dialog box

Advanced options determine various database behaviors, depending on the type of database you're using and how you want it to behave. These advanced options are

- **Use Indexes or Server for Speed** Choose this option to use index files for PC-style databases (such as Microsoft Access and Paradox), and use a SQL WHERE clause with SQL databases. In most cases, choosing this option dramatically improves reporting performance.

- **Perform Grouping on Server** Choose this option to have Crystal Reports "push" as much of the subtotaling and aggregation as possible to the database server, to improve reporting performance. Certain conditions required to take full advantage of this feature are discussed later in the chapter, under "Enabling Server-Based Grouping."

- **Database Server Is Case-Insensitive** Choose this option to ignore case when doing record selection with a database (this option may not affect your particular database, as all databases cannot be made case-insensitive).

- **Select Distinct Data for Browsing** This option will continuously read the database until it has retrieved the first 500 *unique* values of a field when you browse the field in the Field Explorer or Formula Editors. If you leave this option turned off, Crystal Reports reads only the first 500 records in the table, even if there are a few (or no) unique values. Although you'll have bigger browse lists with this option turned on, you may also suffer from slower performance.

- **Perform Query Asynchronously**   This option allows you to stop a query from processing on the database server before database records are returned to Crystal Reports. In some cases, queries submitted to the SQL database can take minutes (sometimes hours) to run. By selecting this option, you can click the Stop button (the black square) at the right of the Preview tab to cancel the query on the database server. Note that this option applies only to certain databases and database drivers—not all databases and drivers support this option.

- **Verify Options**   These options determine when Crystal Reports reads the database layout to determine if additional fields have been added, field names or data types have changed, and so forth. If database fields have changed, a message will appear and the Field Explorer will reflect the changes once you respond to the message. If you leave these options turned off, you must manually verify from the Crystal Reports Database pull-down menu if you want database changes to be recognized.

Changing to a Different Database

You may initially create a report based on a PC-style database, such as Microsoft Access, and then decide later to convert the report to use a similarly organized SQL database. Perhaps the Access database has been upsized to SQL Server, or you may initially be developing reports against a test database in Btrieve, but the reports will eventually have to run against an identical Oracle database. Or else you may encounter other situations in which you initially develop a report against a specific database type, such an ODBC database, which now needs to be "pointed" to an alternate ODBC database.

In any case, Crystal Reports provides a single, streamlined choice for choosing a different database. Choose Database | Set Datasource Location from the pull-down menus, which will display the Set Datasource dialog box, as shown in Figure 15-4.

If you wish to replace a single table with a new table, select the particular table you wish to replace in the Current Data Source List. Or, you can replace an entire database, including all its tables, by selecting the actual database name above the Properties and individual table entries. Then, expand the database category in the Replace With list where the new database or table resides. Select a like object type (if you selected the entire database above, select a database name below—if you chose a single table above, select a single table below). If you choose a database in the Replace With list that requires logon credentials, supply proper credentials. Once you've chosen the desired tables or database, click the Update button.

If table or field names have changed in the new database, you'll be prompted to remap old fields to their new names. This is covered in more detail in Chapter 18.

Adding Additional Tables to the Report

Once you've initially chosen and linked tables and continued with report design, you will often find that you need to add and link additional tables to your report afterward. To do so, click the Database Expert toolbar button in the Expert Tools toolbar, or choose Database | Database Expert from the pull-down menus. The Database Expert will return, where you can add additional tables from the Available Data Sources list. Once you've added the additional tables, click the Database Expert Links tab to link the tables together (linking is discussed in detail later in the chapter, under "Linking Tables").

Choose original table or database
that you wish to replace

Click Update to update the report

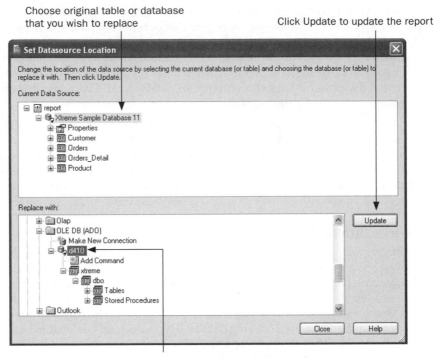

Choose replacement table or database

FIGURE 15-4 Set Datasource dialog box

Any tables that you've previously added to your report will already appear in the Selected Tables list. If you attempt to add one of these existing tables again, you'll be prompted to give the second occurrence of the table an *alias*, because each table used in the Database Expert Links tab must have a unique name.

TIP *You may want to intentionally add the same table to a report more than once. If, for instance, you have a common lookup table that is used with several master or transaction tables, you won't be able to retrieve lookup information by linking all the transaction or master tables to the same lookup table. You'll need to add the lookup table to the report multiple times, using a different alias each time. You can then link each transaction or master table to the different aliased versions of the lookup table.*

Removing Unused Tables from the Report

You may inadvertently add too many tables to your report, or you may no longer need tables that you used earlier in the report design process. If the Database Expert is displayed, just select the table you want to remove from the Selected Tables list and click the left arrow.

If you want to remove all tables from the Selected Tables list and start table additions over from scratch, click the double-left arrow. If any of the tables you attempt to remove are in use on the report, you will be so notified and prompted to confirm their removal.

If you have proceeded to report design and are currently working in the Design or Preview tabs, redisplay the Database Expert with the toolbar button or Database menu option and delete tables from the Selected Tables list.

CAUTION *Make sure you really want to remove the table before you click the left arrows and close the Database Expert. You can't undo a table removal. Also, if you remove a table that is referenced in any formulas, the formulas will no longer work after the table is gone. If you remove a table by mistake, redisplay the Database Expert to re-add and link the table. Or, if you had a known good copy of the report saved on disk, you may wish to close the existing report without saving changes and open the known good copy.*

Linking Tables

Although you may have rare instances in which you design a report based on just one database table, you usually need to use at least two, and often more, tables in your report, because most modern relational databases are *normalized.* Database normalization refers to breaking out repetitive database information into separate tables in the database for efficiency and maintenance reasons. Consider the following Employee table:

Employee Name	Department Name	Salary
Bill	Information Technology	50,000
Karen	Human Resources	32,500
Renee	Information Technology	37,500
John	Executive	85,000
Carl	Mail Room	24,000
Jim	Information Technology	48,000
Julie	Executive	87,000
Sally	Mail Room	23,500

Although this makes for a simple reporting environment, because you don't need to choose more than one table to print an employee roster or paycheck, it becomes more difficult to maintain. Notice that department names repeat several times throughout this small table. (Think about this same scenario for a 50,000-employee company!) This not only takes up a large amount of storage space, but if a department name changes, much work has to be done to make the change in this table. For example, if the Information Technology department changes its name to Information Systems, a search-and-replace function must be performed through the entire Employee table, replacing every occurrence of the old name with the new name.

Contrast this single-table layout with the following database environment:

Employee Table:

Employee Name	Department Number	Salary
Bill	25	50,000
Karen	17	32,500
Renee	25	37,500
John	8	85,000
Carl	13	24,000
Jim	25	48,000
Julie	8	87,000
Sally	13	23,500

Department Table:

Department Number	Department Name
8	Executive
13	Mail Room
17	Human Resources
25	Information Technology

Here, you can see that the database has been normalized by placing the department information in its own lookup table. In this environment, much less storage is used by the Employee table, because only a department number is stored for each employee, not the entire department name. And if the Information Technology department's name changes, only one record in the Department table has to be changed in the entire database.

Database Expert Links Tab

Using multiple tables complicates the reporting environment, because you need more than just the Employee table to print an employee roster or paycheck. In the preceding example, you not only have to include the two tables in your report, but you must also link them together with a common field. *Linking* tables (often also known as *joining* tables) consists of choosing a common field or fields that will allow the second table to follow the main table as the main table is read record by record. You link tables in Crystal Reports with the Database Expert Links tab, illustrated in Figure 15-5.

The Database Expert Links tab appears if you initially choose two or more tables when you first create a report, or whenever you choose additional tables within the Database Expert later in the report design process. If you want to work with database links at other times, simply display the Database Expert by clicking the Database Expert toolbar button or by choosing Database | Database Expert from the pull-down menus (as discussed earlier in the chapter). Then, click the Links tab.

Tables chosen from the Data tab

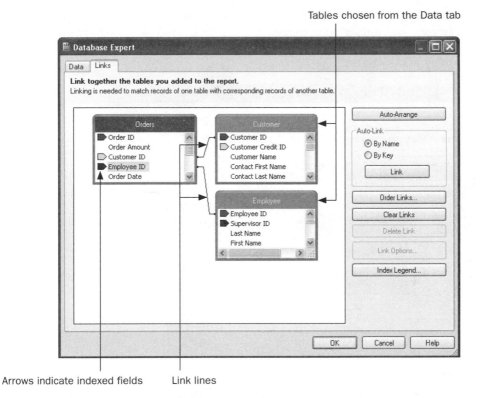

Arrows indicate indexed fields   Link lines

FIGURE 15-5   The Database Expert Links tab

You are free to move the individual tables around in the Links tab if you wish to see them in a different organization. You can also resize each table window to make it taller, shorter, narrower, or wider. If you wish to have Crystal Reports automatically rearrange the tables according to the way they're linked, click the Auto-Arrange button.

The Database Expert Links tab typically chooses links between the tables when you first display it. If you see lines connecting fields in the tables, the Database Expert Links tab has already automatically linked the tables for you (automatic linking is discussed later in the chapter). You may need to delete these existing links if they are incorrect, or add new links yourself.

To delete a link, click the line connecting the two tables. The link line, along with the fields it connects, will be highlighted. Click the Delete Link button or press the DEL key. If you want to change link options, such as the join type (discussed later in the chapter, under "Join Types, Link Types, and Join Enforcement") or multiple-table link behavior, click the Link Options button, double-click the selected link, or right-click the link and choose Link Options from the pop-up menu.

To draw a new link, click a field in the table you want to link from, drag your mouse to the other table you want to link, and then drop onto the field you want to link to. A link line will be drawn between the two tables and fields.

If Crystal Reports detects no potential problems with the link you've drawn, the link line simply appears and you see no messages. If, however, Crystal Reports detects a potential problem with the link, such as mismatched field types, you'll receive a warning message and the link may not be created.

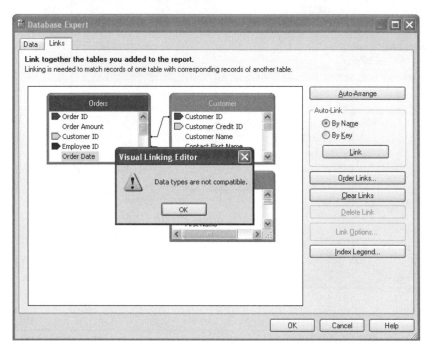

Significance of the Index Arrows

Most database systems allow database fields to be indexed by the database designer. These indexed fields are indicated by colored arrows. An *index* is a special setting that the database designer creates to speed up access to a table. Searching for specific records from that table will be much faster when the search is based on an indexed field. The different colors of the index arrows indicate that different indexes have been created by the database designer for the table. To display a key to the index arrow colors, click the Index Legend button. The window will appear showing the different colors and their indexes.

When linking database tables together, you may link on any field you choose—there is no requirement to link to or from an indexed field. For performance reasons, however, you may still want to try to link *to* indexed fields anyway. You may see improved record retrieval speeds.

So, Which Tables and Fields Should I Link?

You'll quickly figure out that you have to be very familiar with the database you are reporting against to accurately link tables and fields. You have to know the layout of the tables and the data that the common fields contain to successfully link them. This task is complicated even further by database designers who insist on protecting their jobs by creating confusing and cryptic table and field names.

Probably the most expeditious approach is to consult reliable database documentation, or perhaps chat with someone who either designed the database or is familiar with its layout and contents. Barring that, you may be able to discern the proper tables and fields to link if they are named logically. If nothing else, you can browse individual fields in the Database Expert Links tab by right-clicking a field name and choosing Browse Field from the pop-up menu. By looking for similar data types and sample data that seems to match up in both tables, you can find good candidates for links.

Always make sure you test your report and verify that correct data is being returned once you've linked tables. It's *very easy* to create an incorrect link that displays no error message but doesn't return the correctly matched data to the report.

Link Order

When you add tables to the report and then display the Links tab, Crystal Reports makes an assumption about the order in which you wish to link tables (this assumption is made only if Crystal Reports automatically links tables, which it will often do). If you are only linking two tables together, this will not be an issue, as there is only one link between two tables.

However, if you link three or more tables (tables A, B, and C in this example), Crystal Reports will link the tables in a certain order: perhaps first linking table A to table B on one field, and then linking table A to table C on another field. If the database you've used in the report is based on Structure Query Language, or SQL (discussed in more detail later in the chapter), you'll be able to view the SQL query that Crystal Reports sends to the database and see the order in which these links will occur.

In most cases, the link order won't be significant and you won't need to change it. However, in certain situations with certain types of table structures and database systems or connection drivers, you may notice a difference in the resulting data if you choose an "an A to C, then A to B order" instead of the "A to B, then A to C order." If this is significant, you can change the order by clicking the Order Links button. Clicking this button will display the Order Links dialog box.

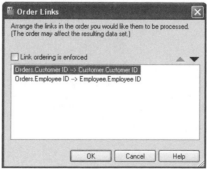

Select the link that you want to move up or down in the order and click the up or down arrow at the top of the dialog box. Click the Link Ordering Is Enforced check box to ensure that Crystal Reports reorders the link statements in the SQL query being sent to the database.

Using Multiple Database Types in the Same Report

Crystal Reports doesn't limit you to using just one type of database per report. You may, for example, wish to get the main transaction table for your report from a client/server database using a direct access database driver, one smaller lookup table from a Microsoft Access database on a shared LAN drive, and another lookup table from a Microsoft Excel spreadsheet on your C drive via the Access/Excel (DAO) connection.

To accomplish this, simply choose all the different tables from different categories of the Database Expert when you first create the report. Or, to add additional tables (even from different database types) after you've already started designing a report, simply redisplay the Database Expert using the toolbar button or pull-down menu options discussed earlier. After choosing the additional table or tables, click the Links tab and link them appropriately.

In general, this type of mixed reporting is perfectly acceptable. However, because connections to the different database types cannot be accomplished with a single SQL query (this is because a SQL query, by its nature, can't cross database boundaries), Crystal Reports will link the tables itself internally. In limited cases, this may require you to only link on string fields. Most often, however, mixed database usage will result in a warning message that your report contains more than one database type and that you can't use SQL Expressions or server-based grouping (both topics are discussed later in this chapter).

CAUTION *While the ability to include multiple database types in a single report greatly adds to Crystal Reports flexibility, it may impair report performance. Because several different database queries have to be performed, with Crystal Reports combining them together locally, reports may take longer to process.*

Does Crystal Reports Automatic Linking Work?

When you initially add tables to a report, Crystal Reports will attempt to link the tables automatically. The result will often be link lines appearing in the Links tab when you first display it, even before you draw any manual links in yourself. This is a feature with good intentions, but it is often more trouble than it's worth. This linking automatically links fields in two adjacent tables if the fields meet these criteria:

- The field names are exactly the same.
- The data types are identical.
- In the case of string fields, the field lengths are the same.

In an ideal setting (such as the XTREME sample database provided with Crystal Reports), automatic linking works perfectly. In the real world, however, things are usually quite different.

Consider, for example, a report that includes a Vendor table and a Customer table. Both tables contain fields named Address, City, State, and Zip_Code. It's perfectly conceivable that these fields have identical data types and field lengths. Automatic linking will dutifully link the two tables together on all four fields. But, these aren't the proper fields with which to link these two tables together.

Another type of automatic linking that Crystal Reports will attempt is linking by key. In this scenario, Crystal Reports attempts to determine a "primary key/foreign key" relationship between tables by reading the internal database structure provided by the database driver. You must typically choose this form of automatic linking yourself by clicking the By Key radio button, and then clicking the Auto-Link button in the Link tab. If the specific set of primary key/foreign key settings can't be found by Crystal Reports, you'll receive a message indicating that key linking can't be performed and asking if you wish to link via the field name scenario.

You'll probably find that automatic linking, either by key or by field name, often results in incorrect link lines being drawn. You then are forced to delete the incorrect links and draw in the correct ones. While version 10 only allowed automatic linking to be turned off by editing a registry entry, version XI returns this choice to File | Options. You may now uncheck Automatic Smart Linking on the Database tab.

Join Types, Link Types, and Join Enforcement

When you link two tables, you must consider carefully what records will be returned from both tables. Consider a slight modification to the normalized table structures illustrated earlier in this chapter.

Employee Table:

Employee Name	Department Number	Salary
Karen	17	32,500
Renee	25	37,500
John	8	85,000
Carl	13	24,000
Denise	32	125,000

Department Table:

Department Number	Department Name
8	Executive
13	Mail Room
17	Human Resources
4	Finance
25	Information Technology

A quick glance at these two tables reveals two inconsistencies: Denise has no matching record in the Department table, and the Finance department has no employees in the Employee table. These two tables are said to lack *referential integrity*—a fancy computer term that simply means the two tables don't completely match up. Fancy term or not, this will be *very* important to you as a report designer. You have to decide how you want to deal with a lack of referential integrity.

NOTE *Many databases can enforce referential integrity, so the situation described previously will never happen. If the database designer chooses to enforce referential integrity between these two tables, an employee cannot be given a department number that doesn't exist in the Department table, and a department record can't be deleted from the Department table if any Employee table records still contain that department. However, enforcing referential integrity often introduces other complexities in the database, and there are many times when the basic function of the database will not allow referential integrity to be enforced. The database designer or administrator should be consulted if you have questions about the way your database is designed.*

A situation in which you would be very concerned about referential integrity is if you were designing a report to print paychecks for employees. Consider the tables previously shown as the basis for your paychecks. If you wish to have the employee's department printed on the check stub to help in check distribution, you would need to link the Employee and Department tables together on the Department Number field. It's a fair assumption that your paycheck run would get at least this far:

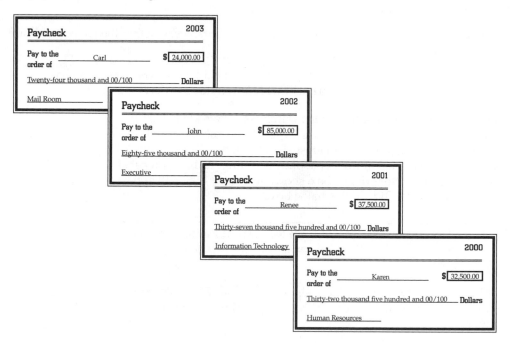

The big question for you, the report designer, is "What happens to Denise?" (the last employee in the Employee table). Considering that she's a highly paid employee, at least from most viewpoints, she will probably be very interested in being paid, regardless of referential integrity. Another interesting question is "Will any checks print for the Finance department?" The answers to your questions are dependent upon which *join type* you use when linking these two tables together.

The following are the two join types that you will be concerned with most of the time:

- **Inner join (sometimes referred to as an** *equal join***)**   Includes records from both tables *only when the joining fields are equal.*
- **Left outer join (sometimes simply referred to as** *outer join***)**   Includes *all* records from the left table, and records from the right table only when the joining fields are equal.

Even though Denise probably doesn't know what a left outer join is, she probably will be much happier if you choose it. This will result in her receiving a paycheck that doesn't have just a department name printed on it. This is particularly important in Crystal Reports, because the default join type for SQL databases is an inner join.

Two other types of joins that you may use less frequently are the following:

- **Right outer join**   Includes *all* records from the right table, and records from the left table only when the joining fields are equal.

Denise would be as displeased with this choice as she would with an equal join. You would also get a wasted paycheck with the Finance department on the pay stub, but no employee or salary printed on it.

- **Full outer join**   Includes all records from *both* tables, whether the joined fields are equal or not.

Denise wouldn't mind this joint type—she'd get paid. However, you'd also have a wasted check for the Finance department with no employee information on it.

Choosing the Join and Link Type in the Database Expert Links Tab

Choose the join type in the Database Expert Links tab by double-clicking the link line between the two tables you are interested in, by right-clicking the link line and choosing Link Options from the pop-up menu, or by selecting the link and clicking the Link Options button. The Link Options dialog box, shown in Figure 15-6, will appear. Select the desired join type from the left side of the dialog box.

NOTE   *If tables are linked by more than one field, choosing a join type for any of the links will set the same join type for all the links. You cannot have different join types for multiple links between the same tables.*

Although most typical business reporting can be accomplished with inner joins and left outer joins, you may have occasion in specialized reporting situations to use these other join types.

Crystal Reports Link Types   In addition to a join type, Crystal Reports provides the additional choice of a *link type* that can be chosen along with a join type.

- **Equal (=)**   Returns records from the tables, matching records from the right table every time the joining field in the left table *is equal to* the joining field in the right table.

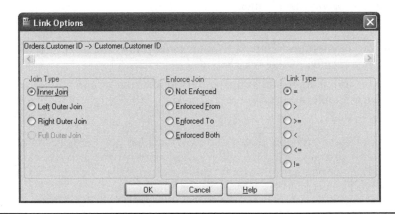

FIGURE 15-6   Link Options dialog box

- **Greater than (>)**   Returns records from the left table, matching records from the right table every time the joining field in the left table *is greater than* the joining field in the right table.

- **Greater than or equal (>=)**   Returns records from the left table, matching records from the right table every time the joining field in the left table *is greater than or equal to* the joining field in the right table.

- **Less than (<)**   Returns records from the left table, matching records from the right table every time the joining field in the left table *is less than* the joining field in the right table.

- **Less than or equal (<=)**   Returns records from the left table, matching records from the right table every time the joining field in the left table *is less than or equal to* the joining field in the right table.

- **Not equal (!=)**   Returns all combinations of records from the two tables where the joining fields *are not equal.*

Various combinations of join and link types can return very interesting combinations of data. For example, choosing an Inner Join but a Less Than link type will return a much larger set of records than an Inner Join with an Equal link type. However, it still won't return records where there is no match at all between link fields. But if you choose a Left Outer Join and a Less Than link type, you'll receive a larger number of matching records, as well as records from the left table that have no match in the right table.

You can choose Database | Show SQL Query from the pull-down menus to see how the combination of join and link types will affect the SQL Query. If you are familiar with the structure of the SQL query, you'll notice that the combination of join and link types will change different portions of the query. For example, an Inner Join with an Equal link type will create this type of query:

```
FROM    "xtreme"."dbo"."Employee" "Employee" INNER JOIN
"xtreme"."dbo"."Orders" "Orders" ON
"Employee"."Employee ID"="Orders"."Employee ID"
```

And, a Left Outer Join using a Less Than link type will return this type of query:

```
FROM    {oj "xtreme"."dbo"."Employee" "Employee" LEFT OUTER JOIN
"xtreme"."dbo"."Orders" "Orders" ON
"Employee"."Employee ID"<"Orders"."Employee ID"}
```

Of course, the exact format of the SQL query and where the joins are performed (the FROM clause in some cases, the WHERE clause in others) is dependent upon the database type and driver being used. Also, you'll see *very* different sets of returned data for the different join and link types you choose. If you aren't extensively familiar with join and link types, you'd be best advised to stick with tried and true Inner or Left Outer join types and Equal link types. In any event, you are well advised to validate the results of your report against your original data source to ensure that all the proper data is being returned by the report once you make join and link choices.

NOTE *Some join and link types won't be available, depending on the types of databases you have chosen for your report. In those cases, the unavailable join and link types will be dimmed in the Link Options dialog box.*

Crystal Reports Join Enforcement

The Link Options dialog box (shown previously in Figure 15-6) includes the Enforce Join category. The four radio buttons in this category allow you to choose whether to include tables you've added to the Database Expert in the eventual SQL query sent to the database, even if you *haven't used any fields from the table* on the report.

By default, joins are not enforced. In this scenario, if you add several tables to the Database Expert but only include fields from one table on the report, the other tables aren't even referenced in the SQL query and any joins and links you choose in the Links tab won't take effect. The Enforce Join options give you the choice of whether to enforce the joins and links, even if fields from all tables aren't included on the report.

Consider an example of two Oracle tables—Orders and Customer—that are being used on a report (Orders is the *from* table and Customer is the *to* table). The tables are linked together on one common field (Customer_ID) using an Inner join and an Equal link. By default, the join is not enforced. The final important piece of this example is what fields are placed on the report, used in a formula or record selection, or otherwise added to the report.

Depending on the choice you make by clicking one of the Enforce Join radio buttons, you'll potentially see different database records on the report, as well as a different SQL query being sent to the Oracle server:

- **Not Enforced**   This choice does not add any extra tables to the SQL query that are not used elsewhere on the report. For example, if only the Order_ID field from the Orders table is added to the report, but no fields from the Customer table are used, the following SQL query will result:

```
SELECT  "Orders"."ORDER_ID"
FROM    "XTREME"."ORDERS" "Orders"
```

  Notice that the Customer table is not included in the query and the join and link types chosen *will not* affect the set of data returned from the database.

- **Enforced From**   This choice will include the FROM table in the query, enforcing its joins and links, even if no fields in the FROM table are used on the report. For example, if only the Customer_Name field from the Customer table is added to the report, and no fields from the Orders table are added, the following SQL query will result:

```
SELECT  "CUSTOMER"."CUSTOMER_NAME"
FROM    "XTREME"."ORDERS" "ORDERS",  "XTREME"."CUSTOMER" "CUSTOMER"
WHERE   ("ORDERS"."CUSTOMER_ID"="CUSTOMER"."CUSTOMER_ID")
```

  Notice that the Orders table is still included in the query and the join and link types chosen *will* affect the set of data returned from the database, even though no Orders table field is used on the report. The result is the inclusion of duplicate Customer Names in order to match each order record.

- **Enforced To**   This choice will include the TO table in the query, enforcing its joins and links, even if no fields in the TO table are used on the report. For example, if only the Order_ID field from the Orders table is added to the report, and no fields from the Customer table are added, the following SQL query will result:

```
SELECT  "ORDERS"."ORDER_ID"
FROM    "XTREME"."ORDERS" "ORDERS", "XTREME"."CUSTOMER" "CUSTOMER"
WHERE   ("ORDERS"."CUSTOMER_ID"="CUSTOMER"."CUSTOMER_ID")
```

Notice that the Customer table is still included in the query and the join and link types chosen *will* affect the set of data returned from the database, even though no Customer table field is used on the report. The result is the inclusion of only order IDs that have a matching Customer table entry (because of the Inner Join), even though no Customer information is included on the report.

- **Enforced Both**   This choice will include the FROM table and TO table in the query, enforcing their joins and links, regardless of which tables are included on the report. So, while the SELECT clause will be affected by whether you include fields from the Orders table, the Customer table, or both, the FROM and WHERE clauses will always refer to both tables:

```
FROM    "XTREME"."ORDERS" "ORDERS", "XTREME"."CUSTOMER" "CUSTOMER"
WHERE   ("ORDERS"."CUSTOMER_ID"="CUSTOMER"."CUSTOMER_ID")
```

The results will be a combination of only orders that have a matching customer record and repetition of customer fields for each matching order.

Which Should Be the Left "From" Table, and Which Should Be the Right "To" Table?

When you use the Links tab, you begin to draw a link by clicking a "from" table. You then drop the link onto the desired field in the "to" table. Initially, you may not be able to tell which table was dragged from and which table was dropped onto. In many cases, Crystal Reports won't indicate this if you are using the default Inner Join and Equal link types.

However, if you change to alternate join or link types, or you use certain databases or database drivers, you'll be able to see which table is the "from" and which is the "to" by looking carefully at the link line—the "from" side of the line will display a small block, while the "to" side will display an arrow.

This begs the question, "Does it make any difference which is the 'from' and which is the 'to' table?" The answer, again, relates to the join and link types you choose, and whether you choose to enforce joins. Generally speaking, if you select an Inner Join and an Equal link and don't enforce them, it doesn't make a great deal of difference. However, if you use any other join or link types, or enforce the joins, it makes a great deal of difference, because the "from" or left table and the "to" or right table determine how the SQL query is formed and what records are returned.

Because left-outer joins return records based on which table is the "left" table and which table is the "right" table, the order in which you join tables together becomes particularly crucial when using this join type. If you use a left-outer join but have the join logically reversed, you'll not receive the proper set of records on the report.

If you're concerned that the link may be in "reverse" order, and you'd like to switch the "from" and "to" tables, you can simply delete and redraw the link, or right-click the link and choose Reverse Link from the pop-up menu.

Viewing the SQL Query

Because Crystal Reports works with SQL databases, it must eventually translate the tables, fields, links, sorting, and grouping that you've used to design your report into SQL. You can view the SQL statements Crystal Reports creates by choosing Database | Show SQL Query from the pull-down menus.

Consider the following report Design tab that uses data from the XTREME sample database, converted from Microsoft Access to Microsoft SQL Server, accessed via ODBC. This report uses the Orders and Customer tables, linked with a left outer join and equal link on Customer ID. The join isn't enforced, but fields from both tables are included on the report. The Select Expert is limiting the report to U.S.A. customers only. Notice the fields that have been placed in the details section. Also, notice that a group based on Customer. Region has been created.

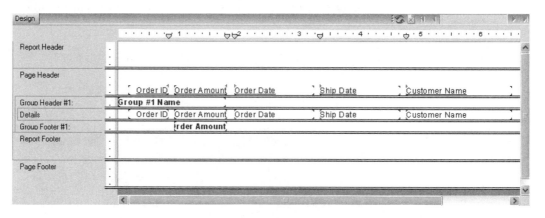

To view the SQL statement that Crystal Reports creates to query the database, select Database | Show SQL Query. You will see the dialog box illustrated here.

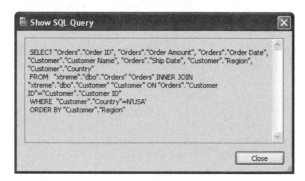

Notice the different parts, or *clauses*, of the SQL statement:

- **SELECT**   Matches the database fields that your report needs (for the details section, formulas, grouping, record selection, and so on).

- **FROM**   Chooses the tables to use and specifies the join type for table linking.
- **WHERE**   Supplies record selection to the server.
- **ORDER BY**   Requests that the SQL server sort records in Customer.Region order (for the Region group) before sending them back to the client.

The SQL syntax may change, depending on the type of database you are reporting against and whether you're using ODBC or direct database drivers to communicate with it. You'll also see different syntax for joining tables. And, you may see the actual table join appear in either the FROM or WHERE clause.

Here is the exact same Show SQL Query dialog box based on a database connection to Oracle using a native driver (notice, among other things, that the join and link is done in the WHERE clause and not the FROM clause):

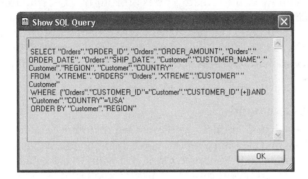

and based on the XTREME.MDB Microsoft Access database via ODBC (this is similar to the SQL Server query, with the exception of different punctuation around field names and the missing "N" character in the WHERE clause):

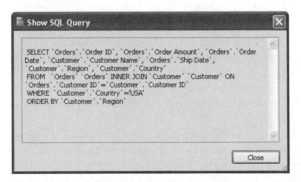

Although you may not consider yourself a database expert and might not make a habit of writing huge SQL statements off the top of your head, there is one advantage to being able to see the SQL query that Crystal Reports is sending to the server: this is useful if you are experiencing performance problems or other peculiarities when running the report. In particular, you want to ensure that as much as possible, if not all, of the report's record selection is translated into a WHERE clause in the SQL query. This will maximize the work performed by the database server and minimize the amount of data and amount of processing left for Crystal Reports to deal with once data is returned from the server. More details on performance considerations can be found later in the chapter.

Crystal Reports SQL Commands

As shown previously, you may see the SQL query created by Crystal Reports in the Show SQL Query dialog box. This query is designed internally by Crystal Reports according to choices you make in the Database Expert, the Select Expert, the report Design tab, and so forth. However, if you are versant in your particular database's version of the structured query language, you may find a need to create your own SQL query and base a report on it. This can be accomplished with the *SQL Command.*

SQL Commands allow you to create a "pass-through" SQL statement that performs more database-specific query processes on the database server, such as aggregate functions, UNION queries, or sub-SELECT queries. Once you've created a SQL Command, you can base a report on it (it looks like a table) or add it to the Crystal Reports Server/BusinessObjects Enterprise repository so that other report designers sharing the same repository can base their reports on it.

Creating the SQL Command

Before you can create a SQL Command, you must log on to the database that the Command will be based on. When first creating a report, you can log on to a database from the Database Expert as described earlier in the chapter. Or, if you want to create a SQL Command after you've already commenced report design, redisplay the Database Expert with the toolbar button or Database | Database Expert menu option.

Once you've logged on to a database, notice the "Add Command" option that appears above the tables, views, and stored procedure categories of the Database Expert Available Data Sources list. Double-click the Add Command option to display the Add Command To Report dialog box, shown in Figure 15-7.

Begin by typing the SQL statement you wish to use for the command in the appropriate box. Note that there is no "Expert" or "Build" functionality in this dialog box—you're on your own for typing correctly formatted SQL particular to the driver or database connection you're using. If you are unsure of proper SQL syntax, you may wish to develop the SQL in another tool provided by your database vendor. Once you've debugged the SQL query in that tool, copy the SQL code to the Windows clipboard and paste the statement into this dialog box.

When you click OK on the Add Command To Report dialog box, Crystal Reports will submit the command to the database to be checked for proper syntax. If you have made an error, the database driver will return a message indicating the particular problem with the SQL statement submitted. The Add Command To Report dialog box will then return, where you may correct the SQL statement and click OK again. Once you've submitted a correct SQL statement, the dialog box will close and "Command" will appear as a table name on the Selected Tables side of the Database Expert. If you wish to give your SQL Command a more descriptive name, select it in the Selected Tables list and then hold your mouse button down for a few seconds. This will place the command name into edit mode, where you may

Type SQL statement here

Remove run-time parameter

Modify run-time parameter

Add run-time parameter

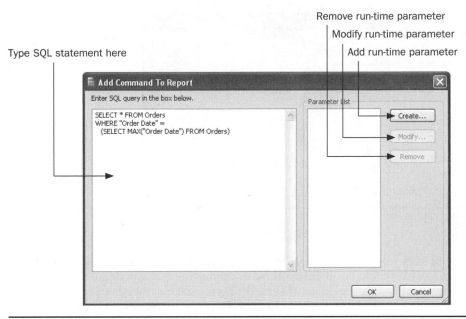

FIGURE 15-7   Add Command To Report dialog box

replace the word "Command" with a new name (note that you cannot include spaces in the new name).

If you wish to view or edit the contents of a command you've created previously, select the command in the Selected Tables list and then right-click. Choose Edit Command or View Command from the pop-up menu. Both options will display the SQL Command in the same dialog box it was created with. If you choose View Command, the command will not be editable—Edit Command will allow the command to be changed; parameters to be added, changed, or deleted; and the command to be added to the Crystal Reports Server/ BusinessObjects Enterprise repository.

CAUTION   To delete a command that you no longer wish to use, select the command in the Selected Tables list and click the left arrow. Be aware; this is a permanent deletion. The command won't move to the left side of the Database Expert where you can add it back to the report. It will be permanently deleted.

Adding a Parameter to the Command

As with reports, you may wish to have the SQL Command prompt a viewer for one or more variable pieces of information when it's submitted to the database. This will allow, for example, the SQL Command to run for a specified department, date range, or sales level threshold. You may accomplish this by creating a parameter in the Command dialog box, and then placing that parameter within the SQL statement.

To add a new parameter, click the Create button next to the parameter list. The Command Parameter dialog box will appear, as shown in Figure 15-8.

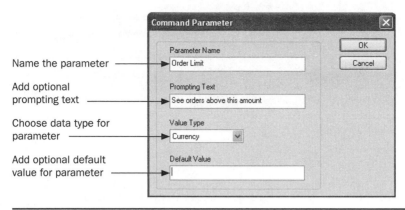

Name the parameter

Add optional prompting text

Choose data type for parameter

Add optional default value for parameter

Figure 15-8   Command Parameter dialog box

Supply desired options in this dialog box. You must, at least, choose a name for the parameter and a value type. The other two choices, prompting text and default value, are optional. Type a name for the parameter that hasn't been used by any other parameters in the SQL Command. And, ensure you choose a data type that matches the use you have in mind for the parameter—if you are going to use it to compare to a numeric database field, choose Number as the value type for the parameter. Once you've made these choices, click OK. The parameter will be added to the Parameter List.

If you later wish to modify or delete a parameter, select the parameter in the Parameter List that you wish to work with. Then, click the Modify or Delete button. Delete will simply remove the parameter from the list (make sure you also remove any references to the parameter from the SQL statement). Modify will redisplay the Command Parameter dialog box, where you may change any of the parameter elements.

Once you've created the parameter, you must now reference it somewhere in the SQL statement for it to have any effect. For example, if you wish to replace a hard-coded number in the WHERE clause with the parameter, edit the SQL statement and replace the hard-coded number with the name of the parameter. You can either type the parameter name in directly (including curly braces around the parameter name and a question mark preceding the name) or simply place the cursor where you want the parameter name to be placed and then double-click on the parameter in the Parameter List.

Thus, a previous WHERE clause with a hard-coded number:

```
WHERE "Order Amount" > 1000
```

can be replaced with a parameter-driven version:

```
WHERE "Order Amount" > {?Order Limit}
```

Once you've added one or more parameters to the SQL Command, click OK. You will then be prompted to supply values for any parameters, and again, the command will be submitted to the database to check for proper SQL syntax. Any errors generated by adding the parameter will appear in an error message, and you'll be returned to the Add Command

To Report dialog box, where you may fix the problem. If the command is syntactically correct, the Database Expert will reappear.

TIP *If you'd like to share the SQL Command with others in your organization, you may copy and paste the SQL text to a shared text or word processing file on your network. Or, if you have Crystal Reports Server/BusinessObjects Enterprise installed, you can store the SQL Command in the repository. Using SQL Commands with the repository is covered in Chapter 17.*

Using a SQL Command in a Report

Once you've created a SQL Command, it will appear in the Selected Tables list of the Database Expert just like a "native" table from a database. Once you close the Database Expert, any fields that the SQL Command returns will appear in the Field Explorer—just drag and drop them onto the report as you would any other database field.

You can even link a SQL Command to another database table in the Database Expert before you proceed to report design. And, you can add an additional table to the report later, linking it to the existing SQL Command on one or more common fields. If you link additional tables to the SQL Command, be aware that you'll be limited in your join and link type choices, as described earlier in the chapter, under "Using Multiple Database Types in the Same Report."

Using a Parameter-Based SQL Command   If you added one or more parameters to your SQL Command, you'll find that the command will prompt you for parameter values as you create the command, and later when you refresh a report based on the command. Notice, also, that the parameter will appear in the Field Explorer as though you added it to the report (Chapter 13 discusses report-based parameter fields).

When you refresh the report, you'll be prompted to choose whether to rerun the report with existing parameter values or to specify new parameter values. If you choose to specify new, the familiar parameter prompt will appear asking for values for the SQL Command parameters. You can even place the parameters you added to the command right on the report, or use the command parameters in report formulas.

CAUTION *When you create a SQL Command–based parameter, you don't have the choice of advanced parameter types, such as multivalue or range. Even if you edit the resulting parameter from within the Field Explorer, you probably won't be able to make such choices. You can, however, create static and dynamic pick lists for SQL Command parameters, as well as use the resulting data from a SQL Command as a data source for dynamic/cascading pick lists. See Chapter 13 for more information on these options. You can even rename a command-based parameter in the Field Explorer the same way you would rename a regular parameter field (although this won't change the name of the parameter in the SQL Command).*

Using SQL Stored Procedures

Most SQL database systems include the capability to use stored procedures. A *stored procedure* is a SQL query that has been evaluated, or "compiled," by the database server in advance and is stored on the server along with regular database tables. Because the stored procedure is compiled in advance, it often performs faster than a SQL query submitted on the fly. Stored procedures can be created by the database designer or administrator for specific queries that will be run on a frequent basis.

To enhance flexibility, stored procedures can contain one or more stored procedure *parameters* that prompt the user to enter a value. The stored procedure then uses the value to run the query. For example, if you have a stored procedure that returns several fields from linked tables, based on Country and Order Date parameters, you'll be prompted to enter a particular country and order date when the stored procedure runs. The procedure will then return a result set containing only records matching the two-parameter values you supplied.

Choosing Stored Procedures

Crystal Reports treats stored procedures almost identically to regular database tables. Stored procedures appear in the Database Expert and are used in a report just like regular database tables. The only difference is that a stored procedure may have parameters associated with it. However, you do have a choice of whether or not stored procedures will appear in the Database Expert in the first place. The quickest way to ensure that they show up is to right-click in the Available Data Sources portion of the Database Expert and choose Options from the pop-up menu. Then, ensure that the Stored Procedure check box in the Database Options dialog box is checked (shown earlier in Figure 15-3). You may also make the change permanent for all new reports in the future by checking the same option on the Database tab after choosing File | Options from the pull-down menus.

Now, when you open a SQL database, you'll see stored procedures appear along with regular database tables.

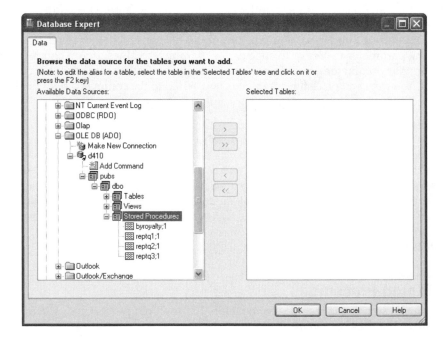

TIP *Crystal Reports allows you to link other database tables to Stored Procedures. Just be aware of limited join and link types, as discussed earlier in the chapter, under "Using Multiple Database Types in the Same Report."*

Working with Stored Procedure Parameters

After you choose a stored procedure to report on, you are prompted to supply any values for any stored procedure parameters in the Enter Parameter Values dialog box. This dialog box is largely identical to the one that prompts for report parameter fields, discussed in Chapter 13.

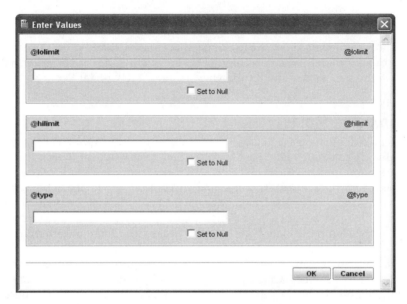

Type your desired parameter values and click OK. You can then simply continue your report design process normally. The stored procedure will supply a list of fields you can use in your report, just like a normal database table.

Stored procedure parameters behave almost identically to Crystal Reports parameter fields. The stored procedure parameters will appear in the Parameter Fields category of the Field Explorer. You can edit a stored procedure parameter like a regular report parameter (except you cannot delete it from the Field Explorer). As with SQL Command–based parameters (discussed earlier in the chapter), you don't have the choice of advanced parameter types, such as multivalue or range.

You can, however, create static or dynamic/cascading pick lists, set length limits or an edit mask for string parameters, or set range limits for number or date parameters. See Chapter 13 for more information on these options. You can even rename a stored procedure–based parameter in the Field Explorer the same way you would rename a regular parameter field (although this won't change the name of the parameter in the stored procedure).

When you refresh the report, you receive the same prompt as when using parameter fields.

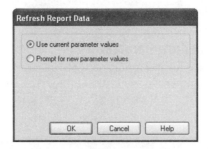

You can choose whether to use the existing values for the stored procedure parameters or to prompt for new values. When you prompt for new values, the server will run the stored procedure with the new values and return a new result set to Crystal Reports.

Using SQL Expression Fields

Sometimes you'll want to have the database server actually perform some calculations for you, sending the already calculated field back with the database result set. This is accomplished with SQL expression fields, which can be created right from the Field Explorer. A *SQL expression* is like a formula, except that it's made up entirely of database fields and SQL functions that are supported by the language of the particular SQL server that you're working with. Sometimes there are advantages to using a SQL expression instead of a Crystal Reports formula. The expression is evaluated on the server, not by the client, which may improve performance.

A particular advantage involves calculations or other specialized functions that are used in record selection. If you use a Crystal Reports formula in record selection, the database server typically won't be able to perform the selection, because it doesn't understand the Crystal Reports formula language. However, when you create a SQL expression and use that in record selection, the SQL server will fully understand the expression, and the record selection will be performed by the database server.

Creating SQL Expressions

The first prerequisite for using SQL expressions is that you must be using a SQL or ODBC database. If you're using a PC-style database that doesn't utilize a SQL-based interface, SQL expressions don't apply and you won't even see the SQL Expression category in the Field Explorer. You also won't be able to use SQL Expressions if your report is based on one or more SQL Commands, stored procedures, or Business Views.

However, when you are using a single SQL database connection, the Field Explorer includes an additional category, labeled SQL Expression Fields. Click the Field Explorer button in the Standard toolbar, or use View | Field Explorer from the pull-down menus to display the Field Explorer (or, if you've shrunk the Field Explorer using the push pin, point to it to expand it). Then, click the SQL Expression Fields category and click the New button in the Field Explorer toolbar or right-click the SQL Expression Fields category and choose New from the pop-up menu.

Creating a SQL expression is very similar to creating a Crystal Reports formula (discussed in detail in Chapter 5). You first are asked to give the SQL expression a name. As with formula names, you should make the SQL expression name reasonably short and easy to understand. You may include spaces as well as upper- and lowercase letters in the name. The name you give the SQL expression will also be the column heading if you place the SQL expression in the report's details section.

After you give the SQL expression a name and click OK, the SQL Expression Editor appears, as shown in Figure 15-9.

Note the similarities between the SQL Expression Editor and the other Crystal Reports formula editors. Creating SQL expressions is essentially the same as creating other formulas: you can type the expression directly into the Formula text box or double-click in the top three boxes to help build the expression. Notice that, as when dealing with formulas, parameter fields, and running total fields, Crystal Reports appends a special character to the beginning of the SQL expression's name. The percent symbol (%) is used to denote SQL expression fields.

The functions and operators available in the SQL Expression Editor change, depending on the database and database driver in use. If you look at the Function Tree box in Figure 15-9, you'll notice a certain set of available SQL functions. This example is for a report using

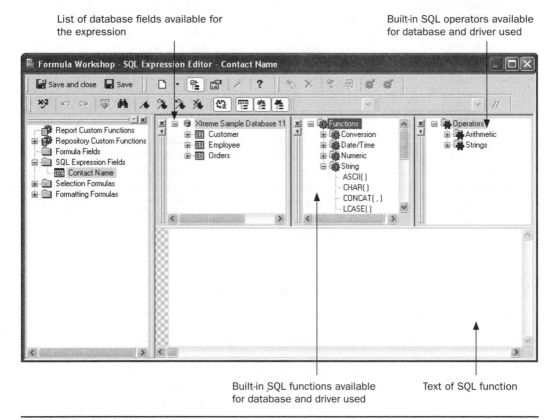

FIGURE 15-9   SQL Expression Editor

Microsoft Access via ODBC. If you use another method to connect to the same database, or another type of database, the SQL Expression Editor will show a completely different set of SQL functions. For this reason, you will probably have to edit or modify some SQL expressions if you change your report from one database to another using Set Location from the Database pull-down menu. To get detailed descriptions of the different built-in SQL functions for your particular database or driver, consult documentation for that database or driver.

For example, you may want a report viewer to be able to specify with just one parameter field a full or partial contact name to search for. If a customer exists whose contact matches what's entered, the customer will be included on the report. In the Customer table of the XTREME sample database that's included with Crystal Reports, the contact information is actually split into separate first and last name database fields. Without using a SQL expression, you have two choices for setting up this search:

- Create two parameter fields—one for first name and one for last name—and try to compare those to database fields.

- Create a Crystal Reports formula that combines the contact's first and last names, and compare the formula to the parameter field.

There are problems with both approaches, however. If you choose the first option, it's much harder for the viewer to simply type a full or partial contact name, such as "Chris" (to find both Christopher and Christine, for example), because some additional logic will be necessary to ignore the last name parameter field if the viewer just wants to search for full or partial first names. Or, if the viewer wants to see everyone whose last name is "Jones," regardless of first name, then similar logic will have to apply for the first name parameter field. It would be much simpler for the viewer to be able to type **Chris*** or ***Jones** to search for their desired customers.

If you choose the second option, the full or partial searches mentioned in the previous paragraph will work; but because the first and last names are combined in a formula, the record selection will not take place on the database server (remember that most Crystal formulas can't be converted to SQL, so the client will perform record selection).

By using a SQL expression, you can have the best of both worlds. The first and last names can be concatenated into one object and compared to the parameter field. But because the concatenation takes place on the database server, it will still perform the record selection, sending only the resulting customers back to the client, not all customers.

The SQL expression to accomplish this is surprisingly similar to a Crystal Reports formula:

```
`Customer`.`Contact First Name` + ' ' +
`Customer`.`Contact Last Name`
```

Notice that a couple of differences exist, however:

- There are no French or "curly" braces around the field names.

- The literal string that separates the first and last name fields must use apostrophes— quotation marks won't work.

Once this SQL expression has been created, it can be dropped onto the report just like a database field, formula field, or other object. It can also be used inside regular report formulas or in conditional formatting formulas. Notice the change to the SQL query (viewed with Database | Show SQL Query) after placing this SQL expression in the details section:

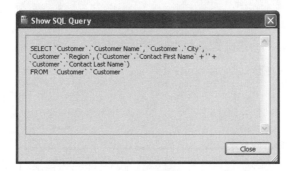

Even though the SQL expression field was given a name in the report, Crystal Reports just adds the SQL expression formula itself right into the SQL statement. The name is simply used by Crystal Reports in the Select Expert or elsewhere on the report.

To now use this SQL expression in record selection, you use the Select Expert's Like operator to allow a wildcard search on the combined first and last names of the contact. If you have already created a string parameter field called {?Contact Prompt}, the Select Expert will look like this:

When you refresh the report and are prompted for the Contact Prompt parameter field, entering the Chris* wildcard will return the following records:

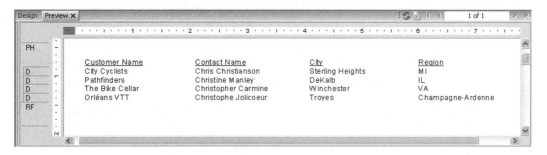

Now, look at the SQL query being sent to the database server:

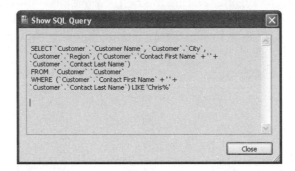

Notice that the WHERE clause includes the SQL expression formula text and a SQL comparison operator that allows wildcard searches. The end result: the flexibility of Crystal Reports formulas with the speed of server-based record selection.

Grouping on the Database Server

Another powerful feature of SQL database servers is server-side processing, or server-based grouping. *Server-based grouping* refers to the ability of the SQL server to perform aggregate calculations on groups of records, returning only subtotals, summaries, and other aggregates to the client. If you are creating a summary report (very often the case), this server capability can significantly decrease the amount of data being passed over the network. Also, the summary calculations can be performed on the server rather than on the client.

Consider the following simple Sales by Region report:

Customer Name		Last Year's Sales	City
AL			
The Great Bike Shop		$15,218.09	Huntsville
Benny - The Spokes Person		$6,091.96	Huntsville
Psycho-Cycle		$52,809.11	Huntsville
3 customers	**Subtotal**	**$74,119.16**	
AR			
Bikefest		$5,879.70	Little Rock
1 customers	**Subtotal**	**$5,879.70**	
AZ			
Bicycle Races		$659.70	Tempe
Biking and Hiking		$65.70	Phoenix
2 customers	**Subtotal**	**$725.40**	

This is the beginning of a report that simply shows all U.S.A. customers, grouped by region, with a customer count and sales subtotal for each group. Because the details section is shown, the database server will need to send all customers in the U.S.A. to Crystal Reports. Crystal Reports is actually calculating the subtotal and count for each group on the client machine as the report processes. This is confirmed by looking at the SQL query for this report:

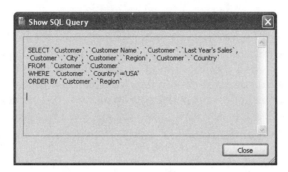

Notice that this fairly simple SQL statement just selects database fields and limits records to the U.S.A. The only server feature used here that helps with grouping is the ORDER BY clause, which presorts the result set into Region order before sending it to the client.

To create a summary report, simply hide the details section by right-clicking in the gray details area in the left of the Design tab and choose Hide (Drill-Down OK) from the pop-up menu. The report will now show just the summary data, with no individual customers appearing on the report.

Customer Name		Last Year's Sales	City
AL			
	3 customers	Subtotal	$74,119.16
AR			
	1 customers	Subtotal	$5,879.70
AZ			
	2 customers	Subtotal	$725.40
CA			
	6 customers	Subtotal	$211,479.24
CO			
	1 customers	Subtotal	$7,874.25

However, if you look at the SQL query, even after refreshing the report, you'll notice that it hasn't changed, because server-based grouping is turned off by default. The server is still sending all customers in the U.S.A. to Crystal Reports, and Crystal Reports still has to cycle through the individual customer records to calculate the customer count and sales subtotals. Database fields in the details section are hidden, but the database returns them anyway.

Enabling Server-Based Grouping

There are several ways to turn on server-based grouping:

- To turn it on for the current report only, choose Database | Perform Grouping On Server from the pull-down menus. You can also choose File | Report Options from the pull-down menus and check Perform Grouping On Server. And, you can choose the same option when you right-click in the Available Data Sources area of the Database Expert and choose Options from the pop-up menu.

- To turn it on for all new reports you create from this point forward, choose File | Options from the pull-down menus and check Perform Grouping On Server on the Database tab.

Once this option is enabled, the report should look the same. There will be some significant changes to the SQL query, however.

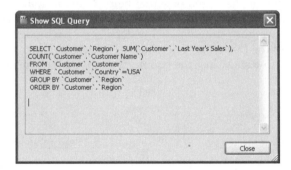

You will see that the SELECT clause now includes only the group field (in this case, Region) and two *aggregate functions* that perform the sum and count functions right on the database server before data is sent to the client. You will also see a new GROUP BY clause that you have not seen before. This new SQL function tells the server to group database records and perform the summary calculations all on the server. Only the summary totals will be sent to the client.

What's Required to Use Server-Based Grouping

Your report must meet certain criteria and be designed in a certain way to use server-based grouping. When you think about the way the server groups and summarizes records, you'll begin to realize why your report must meet these requirements, as shown in Table 15-1.

Requirement	Reasoning
There must be at least one group on the report.	For the GROUP BY clause to be added to the SQL query, there needs to be at least one group defined on the report.
The details section must be hidden or suppressed.	If the details section is visible, no grouping will occur on the server, because the server must send down individual database records to show in the details section.
Include only the group fields or summary fields in group headers and footers.	If you include any other database fields (or formula fields that contain anything other than group fields or summary fields), the server will have to send detail data to the client to properly display the report.
Don't group or base record selection on Crystal Reports formulas.	Because most Crystal Reports formulas can't be converted to SQL, they must be calculated on the client before the report can select or group on them. Because of this requirement, the server has to send detail records to the client. This is another reason you may want to use SQL expressions as an alternative to formulas, as SQL expressions can still be used for server-based grouping.
Running totals must be based on summary fields.	If running totals (described in Chapter 5) are based on detail fields, Crystal Reports needs the detail data to calculate them as the report processes. This prevents grouping from being done on the server.
The report can only contain Sum, Maximum, Minimum, and Count summaries.	Crystal Reports can't convert other summary types to SQL. Therefore, the grouping will be performed by the client if other functions are used.
Report groups can be sorted only in ascending or descending order. Specified-order grouping won't work.	Since Crystal Reports bases specified-order grouping on its own internal logic, it needs detail records to properly evaluate what specified groups to place them in. This requires detail records to be sent by the server.

TABLE 15-1   Server-Based Grouping Requirements

Effects of Drill-Down

When Crystal Reports is performing its own grouping, the concept of report drill-down is fairly straightforward. Even though the details section or lower-level group headers and footers aren't being shown, Crystal Reports is still processing them and storing the data they create. When a viewer double-clicks to drill down on a group, Crystal Reports simply opens a new drill-down tab and displays the data it had previously not displayed.

However, when you enable server-side grouping, there is no detail data to display when a viewer drills down—only the summary data has been sent to the client! Crystal Reports still enables drill-down, however; it just sends another query to the SQL server whenever a viewer drills down. This second query requests just the detail data for the group that was drilled into by adding additional criteria to the WHERE clause. This method provides the benefits of server-based grouping, while still allowing the powerful interactivity of drill-down. The price a viewer pays is the additional time the SQL server may take to process the drill-down query.

Look at the following example. Notice that a viewer has drilled down on a particular region. A new drill-down tab appears, showing detail data for that region. Notice the new SQL query that was created on the fly.

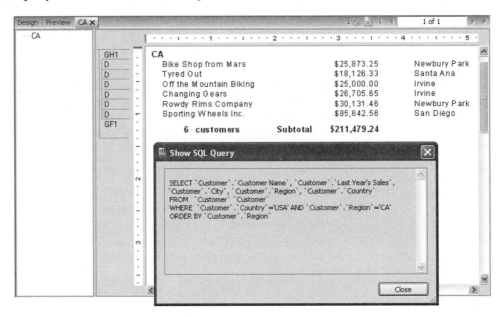

You can view drill-down SQL queries by choosing Database | Show SQL Query when viewing the drill-down tab. If you return to the main Preview tab and show the query, you'll once again notice the GROUP BY clause.

Performance Considerations

SQL databases (or PC-style databases accessed via ODBC) present a very different set of performance considerations than do PC-style databases. As has been discussed throughout the chapter, one of the main benefits of SQL databases over PC databases is the ability of the database server to perform record selection and grouping locally as soon as a SQL query is received from Crystal Reports. Only when the database server has performed record selection or grouping itself will it return the result set back to Crystal Reports.

Let the Server Do the Work

As a general reporting rule, you want to always have the database server perform as much of the processing as possible. Database server software is designed and tuned to perform just such operations, and server software is often placed on very high-end hardware platforms to enhance this performance even further. Any glitch that might cause the database server to send back every record in its database (million-plus-record SQL databases are not at all uncommon) to be selected or summarized locally by Crystal Reports will often result in unsatisfactory performance.

To see how much (or if any) of the query is being evaluated on the database server, view the query by choosing Database | Show SQL Query from the pull-down menus. Look at the SQL statement for the WHERE clause. If you don't see one, no selection at all will be done on the server—every record in the database will come down to the PC, to be left to Crystal Reports to sort through. This can be *very* time-consuming!

Look for an ORDER BY clause if you are sorting or grouping your report. If you see this clause, the database server will presort your data before sending it to Crystal Reports. This can speed the formatting of your report. If you don't see an ORDER BY clause but you specified grouping or sorting in your report, the server will send records to Crystal Reports unsorted, and the client will have to sort the records.

If you wish to use server-based grouping, make sure you see a GROUP BY clause in the query. This ensures that the server is grouping and aggregating data before sending it to Crystal Reports. If you don't see this clause, check back to the server-based grouping requirements in Table 15-1 earlier in this chapter.

To ensure record selection occurs on the server, Crystal Reports must convert your record-selection formula to a SQL WHERE clause. Several rules of thumb help to ensure that as much record selection as possible is converted to SQL and that it is done on the server:

- Don't base record selection on formula fields. Crystal Reports usually can't convert formulas to SQL, so most record selection based on formula fields will be passed on to Crystal Reports. Most *first-pass* formulas can be converted to SQL, while the remainder cannot. Look at the SQL query to ensure that any formulas you use in record selection are converted into WHERE clause SQL.

NOTE *See Chapter 5 for more information on what constitutes first-pass formulas.*

- Don't use the Crystal Reports formula language's built-in functions, such as ToText, in your selection criteria. Again, Crystal Reports usually can't convert these to SQL, so these parts of record selection won't be carried out on the server. You may be able to find a similar function in a SQL Expression field and use the expression in record selection.

Use Indexed Fields

In Crystal Reports, you'll typically see colored arrows in the Links tab of the Database Expert indicating fields that have been indexed by the database designer. Although you aren't typically required to link only on indexed fields, you may want to attempt links on indexed fields if possible anyway (provided the core design of the database will properly link tables if you do). Depending on the database system that you're using, linking to non-indexed fields or performing record selection on non-indexed fields can prove detrimental to the performance of your report. Most SQL database systems have indexing capabilities that the database designer probably considers when designing the database.

If at all possible, work with the database designer to ensure that indexes are created to solve not only your database application needs, but your reporting needs as well. Try to use indexed fields as much as possible as "to" fields in linking, and for record selection.

Also, it may improve performance to select records using as many fields as possible from the main or driving table. For example, you may have a main transaction table that is linked to five lookup tables, and you may want to use the descriptions from the lookup tables in record selection. Instead, consider using the fields in the *main* table for record selection (even if you have to use the codes in the main table, and not the descriptions from the lookup table). Again, if these fields in the main table are indexed, you'll probably see a performance improvement.

Creating and Using Business Views

As you work with a database reporting or querying tool, such as Crystal Reports, you often find yourself facing two tasks: learning the ins and outs of the reporting or query tool itself and learning the underlying database that you need to report or query against. While there are usually resources (such as this book) available to help you learn the reporting or querying tool, there are probably not nearly as many comprehensive sources for information on your particular database.

Complex database designs are not unusual. It's not uncommon to encounter databases that consist of hundreds of different tables, or tables that contain 100 or more fields. Adding to this difficulty are database designers who may attempt to ensure job security by creating table and field names that are far from intuitive. In these situations, you are either forced to look for comprehensive database documentation (which may or may not exist), or to just experiment in a haphazard manner, eventually discovering proper database table and field requirements by hook or crook.

One tool that can greatly reduce the complexity of direct database access is a dictionary or *metadata* tool that organizes the core database table and field structure into a much simpler and easy-to-understand organization. This middle layer can be set up to include only relevant tables, pre-join tables on their proper fields, expose only desired fields from the database, store commonly used formulas, and apply database row and column security to individual report designers and viewers to provide access to only data fields and records that they are permitted to see.

The *Business Views* product is the Business Objects answer to this middle-layer requirement for a Crystal Reports environment. This approach, introduced in Crystal Reports 10, replaced earlier Crystal Dictionary and Seagate Info View tools for reporting against simplified views of the database. And, Crystal Reports XI's new dynamic and cascading pick list capability is also enhanced within Business Views. By adding a shared pick list to a Business View, you obtain centralized control and sharing of pick lists available to reports in your entire organization.

NOTE *Crystal Reports XI can also work with traditional Business Objects universes, the metadata tool from the original Business Objects product set. Using Crystal Reports with universes is discussed in Chapter 20.*

Business Views Overview

You'll want to consider a Business Views implementation if you have any combination of complex databases and report designers who don't want to learn all the intricacies of these databases. This combination probably describes the environment at a fairly large number of organizations, yours very possibly included. Creative use of Business Views will allow Crystal Reports designers to get access to organizational data with minimal difficulty, allowing data fields to be presented in a simple, intuitive fashion. And, Business Views also allows Crystal Reports Server/BusinessObjects Enterprise reports to implement *row security* (tailoring the set of data viewed online to just that allowed for a particular viewer), and *column security* (lack of access to certain fields for a particular viewer). For example, you can design a single company-wide Crystal Report using a Business View and have individual departments see only their data when they view the report. And, only the Human Resources and Payroll departments will be able to see salary fields.

The first concept that will impact many potential Business Views users is where it's based. While the older Crystal Dictionaries tool could be used by itself with stand-alone copies of Crystal Reports, Business Views *requires* installation of Crystal Reports Server/BusinessObjects Enterprise (CRS/BOE)—in fact, it's integral to these tools and cannot be used without them. Each report designer who wishes to use Business Views must first log on to Crystal Reports Server/BusinessObjects Enterprise with a valid user ID and password. This requires your organization to consider CRS/BOE licensing and cost issues when considering whether, and how much, to rely on Business Views. And, unlike the older Crystal Dictionaries tool, Business Views and Crystal Reports Server/BusinessObjects Enterprise require knowledge and infrastructure within your organization to support the more complex Crystal Reports Server/BusinessObjects Enterprise environment (more general Crystal Reports Server topics can be found in Part II of this book).

Once you've properly installed Crystal Reports Server/BusinessObjects Enterprise (or, as part of the CRS/BOE planning process), you'll want to think about where Business Views capabilities will be important for you. In some cases, more experienced report designers may prefer to bypass Business Views and report directly against the production database. In others, you may wish to provide Business Views access to simplify report design for introductory report designers. And, there may be other situations that call for Business Views use with all users to take advantage of row and column security features limiting data to that required for individual department or job functions. As with a report design project, Business Views implementation requires some forethought and planning.

And, Crystal Reports XI dynamic and cascading parameter pick lists also must be considered when looking at a Business Views implementation. While reports that are stored outside of CRS/BOE can maintain their own dynamic and cascading pick lists, any report that you publish to CRS/BOE that makes use of this new type of pick list *must* use pick lists stored in a Business View.

Business Views Objects

Business Views are more complex and flexible than similar tools, including older Crystal Dictionaries or Info Views. While familiarity with these older products, or metadata tools in general, will be helpful in designing Business Views, the steps involved to use the tool vary widely from other products and will take some time to become familiar with.

When you first create a Crystal Report and look for data in the repository (where Business Views are stored), you'll find only one type of Business View object: the Business View itself. When you connect your report to the Business View, the set of fields that the Business View exposes will appear in the Field Explorer. If the Business View includes row or column security, you'll see a limited set of field and record data when you run the report.

However, there are many additional objects that actually go into creating the Business View:

- **Data Connection**   This is a core connection to the actual production database. Like Crystal Reports, Business View Data Connections can be made via native database drivers, ODBC, OLE DB, and other standard Crystal connection methods.

- **Dynamic Data Connection**   This is similar to a Data Connection but can actually encompass *two or more* connections to like database structures. A Dynamic Data Connection allows you to connect to multiple databases, allowing the report designer or report viewer to choose which connection to use when running the report. This is helpful for "test database/production database" environments where a report viewer may want to choose an alternate database to report against on the fly.

- **Data Foundation**   This portion of Business Views is where much of the capability of the tool comes to light. Here, you connect one or more Data Connections or Dynamic Data Connections together to provide a combined set of database fields. You may also create formulas, SQL expressions, filters, and parameter fields to further customize your view. When complete, the Data Foundation contains a combined set of all fields (both database fields and "derived" formulas) that can be used to form your ultimate customized data view.

- **Business Element**   This portion of Business Views equates to a "virtual" table that is ultimately exposed to the report designer. Here, you choose only those fields that you actually wish a report designer to see. You may also rename fields here to be more meaningful.

- **Business View**   This portion, which is ultimately available to a Crystal Report designer, combines one or more Business Elements together to form the ultimate "table and field" structure available to the report designer.

- **List of Values**   This portion, new to Crystal Reports XI, contains a shared dynamic or cascading pick list that can be used among multiple parameter fields in reports stored in CRS/BOE. This pick list can be updated from the source database in real time, or it can be completely or partially scheduled for update within the CRS/BOE scheduling environment. A List of Values depends on an existing Business View.

- **Prompt Group**   This portion, new to Crystal Reports XI, consists of a series of one or more dynamic or cascading pick lists from within the Business View treated as a single "prompt" unit. This can be shared among one or more reports contained within CRS/BOE. A Prompt Group depends on one or more existing Lists of Values.

Each object in Business Views is dependent upon another, and at least one of each object (except a Dynamic Data Connection) must exist before a report designer can make use of a Business View. A Business View (the object that a report designer actually uses, and the portion that List of Values and Prompt Group objects use) requires one or more Business Elements. Business Elements are based on Data Foundations. Data Foundations are made up of one or more Data Connections or Dynamic Data Connections. And, Dynamic Data Connections are based on Data Connections.

Creating Business Views

The process of creating a Business View that can be accessed by a Crystal Reports designer or used to create a pick list, involves creating many of the objects mentioned previously in a logical order. You must, for example, create at least one Data Connection before you can create a Dynamic Data Connection or a Data Foundation. You must use existing Data Connections to make up a Dynamic Data Connection. You must have at least one Data Foundation before you can create a Business Element. And, you must have one or more Business Elements to make up the final Business View. If you are creating a dynamic pick list, you must create a Business View before you can create a List of Values. And, you must have at least one List of Values before you can create a Prompt Group.

Because of this required hierarchy, you must create these individual Business View objects in the proper order. Once you've created them (and added them to the repository), you may then base the higher-level Business View objects on them. And, after you've created a variety of different Business View objects, you are free to create as many dependent objects as you need later on. For example, you may initially create four or five Data Connections to your organization's core data sources and then use them in any variety of Data Foundations now, or in the future.

The Business View Manager

Despite the web-based nature of CRS/BOE, a Windows "thick client" application, called the *Business View Manager,* is used to create and maintain Business Views. The Business View Manager is installed by default when you perform a complete Crystal Reports Server/ BusinessObjects Enterprise installation. If you need to install the Business View Manager on additional computers outside the Crystal Reports Server/BusinessObjects Enterprise server environment for additional Business View designers, you'll need to perform a custom installation from the CRS/BOE program CD and choose the Business View Manager from the list of available client options.

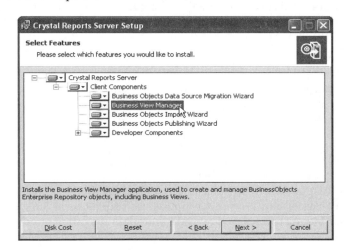

Once you've installed the Business View Manager (if necessary), start it by choosing the appropriate choice from the BusinessObjects 11 program group after clicking the Start button. The Business View Manager will appear, with an initial dialog box requesting you to log on to Crystal Reports Server/BusinessObjects Enterprise. As Business Views are an integral part of the Crystal Reports Server/BusinessObjects Enterprise repository, you must supply a valid CRS/BOE Central Management Server name, user ID, password, and authentication type in order to create or modify Business Views.

Once you've logged in to CRS/BOE, the Welcome to Business Views dialog box will appear inside the Business View Manager. This dialog box allows you to create new Business View Objects, open existing objects, and work with recently used objects (tabs in the Welcome dialog box allow you the choice). Since all Business View objects are stored in the repository, it may be helpful to display the Repository Explorer (when you initially start the Business View Manager, it is not displayed).

You may display the Repository Explorer by closing the Welcome dialog box and then choosing View | Repository Explorer from the pull-down menus. The Repository Explorer will appear, and will continue to appear when you start the Business View Manager from this point forward. You may now either close and restart the Business View Manager to redisplay the Welcome dialog box, or just display it immediately by choosing Help | Welcome Dialog from the pull-down menus. This is illustrated in Figure 16-1.

NOTE *Sample repository objects, including a sample Business View, can be installed by using the Tools | Install Repository Samples option from the Business View Manager pull-down menus.*

If you wish to work with the Business Views Manager toolbars and pull-down menus, you may simply cancel the welcome screen (you can display it later by choosing Help | Welcome Dialog from the pull-down menus). Or, you may click one of the three tabs to create a new Business View object, open an existing object from within the repository, or choose from a list of recently used objects.

If you wish to modify or examine any existing Business View objects, you may either choose the Open or Recent tab in the initial dialog or close the dialog and use the Business View Manager's pull-down menus or the Repository Explorer. For example, to use the Repository Explorer to open an existing Data Connection, simply navigate the folders of the Repository Explorer until you find the Data Connection you wish to open. Double-click the Data Connection to open it inside the Business View Manager.

NOTE *More detailed information on the Repository Explorer can be found later in the chapter, under "Using the Repository Explorer."*

You may have any number of different Business View objects open inside the Business View Manager at a time. Each object will display a tab with the corresponding object type icon and object name across the middle portion of the Business View Manager. Simply click the desired tab to display that particular object. If there isn't sufficient room to display all the object tabs, left- and right-arrow icons will be enabled to the right of the tabs. Use these to display tabs that may have scrolled away. When you're finished working with a particular object, you may click the small X to the right of the tabs and arrows to close the currently displayed object. Choices available in the Business View Manager pull-down menus and toolbar will vary, depending on the type of Business View object currently displayed.

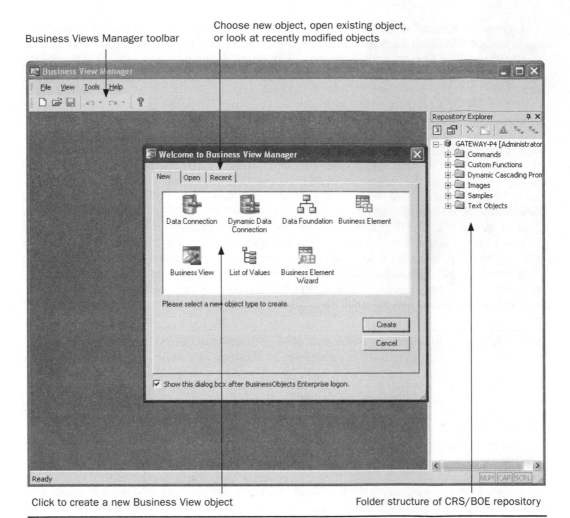

Business Views Manager toolbar

Choose new object, open existing object,
or look at recently modified objects

Click to create a new Business View object

Folder structure of CRS/BOE repository

Figure 16-1   Business View Manager welcome screen

You'll also notice several Business View Manager windows that typically appear, no matter what type of Business View object you are working on. The Object Explorer, Property Browser, and Repository Explorer windows appear within the Business View Manager. If you don't want to see any of these windows, simply click the *X* in the upper right-hand corner of the desired window. You can also uncheck the window name from the View menu. If you wish to redisplay the window, simply recheck the window name in the View menu.

While these windows are initially "docked" to one side or the other of the Business View Manager, you may undock them by clicking in their title bar and dragging. The chosen window will become free-floating, whereby it can be freely moved around your screen, even outside of the Business View Manager. To redock the window, drag it back into the Business View Manager until it snaps to a border of the main window—you may need to try several times to snap the window back where you want it.

If you click the push-pin icon next to the X in the upper right-hand corner of a window, you will shrink the window. If you move your mouse pointer away from the window, it will eventually shrink to the side of the Business View manager, only appearing as a tab. Shrinking windows allows more room for the core design portion of the Business View manager to appear. Pointing to a hidden window tab will expand the window for a few seconds, whereby you can manipulate any items within the window. When you wish the window to shrink again, simply click outside the window with your mouse and wait a few seconds. If you wish a window to reappear permanently, show the window again by pointing to its tab. Then, click the push-pin icon to show the window.

Click pushpin to shrink various
Business View Manager windows

Move between tabs

Click tab to display object

Close current object

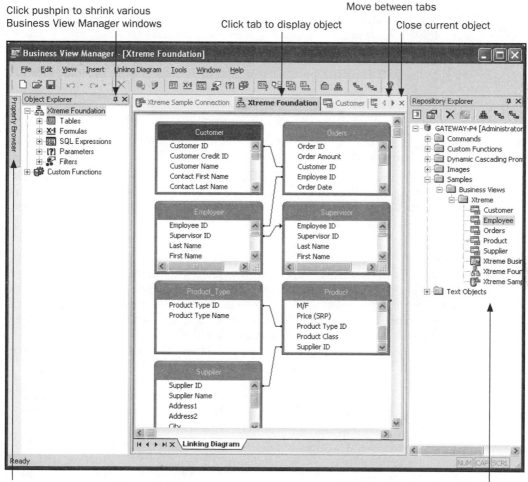

Point to tab to display shrunk window

Open Business View object by double-clicking in Repository Explorer

You may create a new Business View object by clicking the desired object type in the welcome screen. If you've closed the welcome screen, click the New button in the Business View Manager toolbar to redisplay it. You may also choose File | New from the pull-down menus, choosing the desired type of Business View object from the submenu.

Each type of Business View object is described in the following sections of this chapter. These sections illustrate a sample Business View that combines various data elements from the sample XTREME Mountain Bike database included with Crystal Reports, along with other related data sources. The sample Business View illustrated in the rest of this chapter includes the following characteristics:

- Database connections to a "test" XTREME database stored on a local hard disk and to a "production" XTREME database stored on Microsoft SQL Server. When a report is created or run, the designer or viewer is given the choice of using test or production data.

- A database connection to a Microsoft Excel spreadsheet that contains sales quotas for XTREME sales staff (the standard XTREME database doesn't contain any quota information).

- A database connection to a comma-delimited text file dividing XTREME customer states into geographic regions, such as Northwest, Southwest, and so forth. The XTREME database doesn't include any geographic area designations.

- A filter that limits the Business View to returning USA data only.

- Column-level security that limits an employee annual salary field and employee monthly salary formula to members of the Human Resources department.

- Row-level security that limits order display to a regional sales manager's geographic area. For example, a Western Regional Sales Manager will only be able to see orders placed by customers in the Northwest and Southwest. The National Sales Manager, however, will see orders in all regions when viewing the same report.

Data Connection

The first type of Business View object that you must create when starting a new Business View from scratch is a Data Connection. A *Data Connection* is simply a connection to a single database or data source that you can use to build on later in the Business View design process. The Data Connection will consist of a single connection to a single data source. If your entire organization's database can be accessed via a single database connection, then you may need to create only one Data Connection for all your Business Views. However, if you want your Business View to tie together several different databases, you'll need to create a new Data Connection for each database.

To create a new Data Connection, choose the Data Connection icon from the welcome screen when starting the Business View Manager or clicking the New toolbar button, or choose File | New from the pull-down menus, choosing the Data Connection submenu item. The Choose A Data Source dialog will appear after a new Data Connection is displayed in the Business View Manager, as illustrated in Figure 16-2.

Navigate through the folder structure of this dialog box to find your desired data source (navigating this dialog box is similar to using the Crystal Reports Database Expert). Once you've chosen the necessary data source, you may be prompted to log on to a secure database server. Provide proper logon credentials to do so.

If you don't find the particular data source connection you're looking for, you may need to run a separate database utility (such as the ODBC Administrator from the Windows Control Panel) to create the correct data source. Once you've done this, you may refresh the contents of the Choose A Data Source dialog box by clicking the lightning bolt refresh

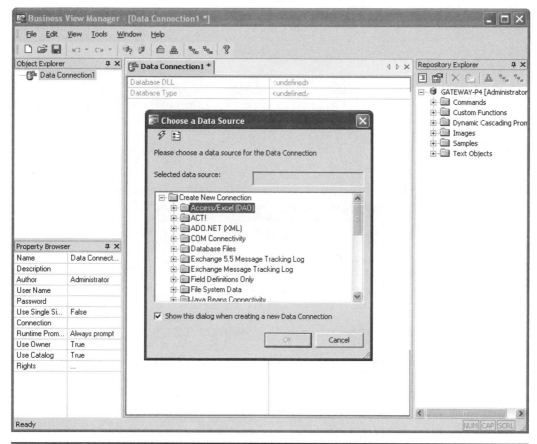

Figure 16-2   Creating a new Data Connection

button at the upper left-hand corner of the dialog. (The F5 key will also refresh this dialog box.) Also, the available data source categories that appear in the Choose A Data Source dialog box depend on what data connection choices you made when installing Crystal Reports Server/BusinessObjects Enterprise components on your PC. If you don't see a desired database type, rerun Crystal Reports Server/BusinessObjects Enterprise installation from the Control Panel or CRS/BOE program CD and choose additional data sources.

NOTE   *The Edit Options button to the right of the Refresh button will display a dialog box allowing you to limit the types of and names of tables you see in the Choose A Data Source dialog box. Since choosing tables is generally irrelevant when creating a Data Connection, you'll probably have little use for this option here.*

Once you've logged on to the data source, you will be able to expand the data source you just connected to in order to see any tables, views, or stored procedures that are contained in that data source. Don't let this ability confuse you—even though you may be able to click one of these items within the data source, you *are not* able to choose any individual tables, stored procedures, or views here. The Data Connection object is merely a connection to the database and individual database elements, such as tables and views, are chosen and linked when you later include the Data Connection in a Data Foundation.

Once you've chosen a data source (and you can only choose one per Data Connection object), you'll be presented with the Set Data Connection Password dialog box. Use this dialog box to confirm the user ID and password you want the Business View to use when connecting to this data source in the future. If the database you chose is not secure (perhaps an Excel spreadsheet or unsecured Microsoft Access database), you may just cancel this dialog box. Or, if you always want the report designer or viewer to be required to specify a user ID or password whenever they use this Data Connection in a Business View, you may also cancel the dialog box.

Once you've specified the user ID and password, and confirmed the password, you may choose whether to prompt the report designer or viewer for the ID and password to this data source whenever the Business View is used. Note that if you choose to Never Prompt, the ID and password you specify here will be stored in the Crystal Reports Server/BusinessObjects Enterprise repository and the Business View user won't have to specify the ID and password when they use the Business View.

New XI Single Sign-On Capability

CRS/BOE XI adds single sign-on capability to Business View Data Connections. If you check Use Single Sign On When Viewing (or set the Use Single Sign On When Viewing property to True), reports based on this data connection will not prompt a viewer for database connection information when the report is viewed in CRS/BOE. Instead, the user ID/password combination the viewer used to connect to CRS/BOE will be passed directly to the database connection. This reduces the number and frequency of ID/password requests report viewers will encounter.

Note that this single sign-on capability only applies to reports viewed within the CRS/BOE InfoView web interface. Reports using associated Business Views in Crystal Reports itself will not recognize the single sign-on property and will still prompt for a user ID and password, even if the ID/password combination used to connect to Business View is the same as that required by the data source.

CAUTION *If you plan on using this Data Connection as part of a Dynamic Data Connection (described later in this chapter), you should make sure to choose the Never Prompt option. Otherwise, you'll be unable to use this Data Connection object as part of a Dynamic Data Connection. Data Connections that are specified to Never Prompt for an ID and password can be further secured by setting Crystal Reports Server/BusinessObjects Enterprise rights. This is discussed later in the chapter, under "Setting Rights for Business View Objects."*

Once you've specified the data source and user ID/password settings, the Data Connection will appear inside the Business View Manager. You'll see information pertaining to the particular data source you chose (such as the database DLL used, time-out properties, and so forth) in the center portion of the Business View Manager. An automatically generated name for the Data Connection will appear in the tab above these properties, displayed with an asterisk (the asterisk indicates that this object has not been saved to the CRS/BOE repository since being created or modified). Two boxes will appear on the left: the Object Explorer and the Property Browser.

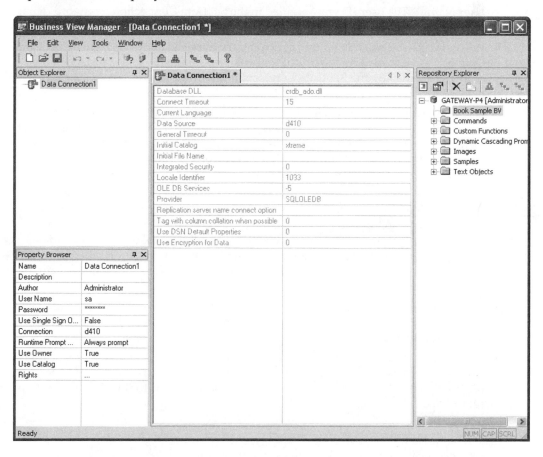

While the Object Explorer is of limited usefulness in a Data Connection (since the Data Connection doesn't contain any "child" objects, such as tables or fields), the Property Browser plays an important role when working with a Data Connection. Here, you may specify various properties for the Data Connection that determine its appearance within the CRS/BOE repository and its behavior. Click in the text area to the right of the property and type your desired value, click the drop-down list to choose from various options, or click the ellipses button to be prompted for additional values.

- **Name**   Type the descriptive name you wish this Data Connection to have when you save it to the repository.

- **Description**   Type an optional description to more fully explain the usage of this Data Connection.

- **Author**   Your CRS/BOE user ID is specified here by default. You may change this text to something else, if you choose.

- **Parent Folder**   This read-only item will appear if you've already saved the Data Connection, or you're modifying an existing Data Connection. It simply shows the location in the repository where the object is located.

- **User Name**   The user ID you specified in the Set Data Connection Password dialog box will appear. You may change the user ID in this box if you choose.

- **Password**   Asterisks will appear indicating the password you chose in the Set Data Connection Password dialog box. If you wish to change the password, click the ellipses to redisplay the Set Data Connection Password dialog box to set a new password.

- **Use Single Sign On When Viewing**   Allows you to choose whether to use single sign-on when a report viewer views a report in the CRS/BOE InfoView. If this is set to True, the viewer will not be prompted for a data source user ID/password when they view the report. Instead, the ID/password combination the viewer used when initially connecting to CRS/BOE will be passed to the data source.

- **Connection**   The data source name you initially chose from the Choose Data Source dialog box will appear here. Click the ellipses to redisplay the Choose Data Source dialog box to change the data source for the Data Connection to a different data source. Alternatively, you may click the Edit Connection toolbar button or choose Edit | Edit Connection from the pull-down menus. You may also right-click the Data Connection name in the Object Explorer and choose Edit Connection from the pop-up menu.

- **Run-time Prompt Mode**   Allows you to choose whether to prompt for a user ID/ password combination whenever a report designer or viewer uses this Data Connection in a Business view.

- **Use Owner**   Determines whether the database owner is included in any SQL query generated by this data source. For example, if the database is owned by "dbo" (database owner), the resulting SQL query may look similar to this if Use Owner is set to True:

```
SELECT  "Customer"."Customer Name"
FROM    "xtreme"."dbo"."Customer"
```

whereas a False setting for Use Owner would result in:

```
SELECT  "Customer"."Customer Name"
FROM    "xtreme"."Customer"
```

- **Use Catalog**   Determines whether the database name is included in any SQL query generated by this data source. For example, if the database name is "xtreme," the resulting SQL query may look similar to this if Use Catalog is set to True:

```
SELECT  "Customer"."Customer Name"
FROM    "xtreme"."dbo"."Customer"
```

whereas a False setting for Use Catalog would result in:

```
SELECT  "Customer"."Customer Name"
FROM    "dbo"."Customer"
```

If both Use Owner and Use Catalog are set to False, the result would be:

```
SELECT  "Customer"."Customer Name"
FROM    "Customer"
```

NOTE *The Use Owner and Use Catalog options should typically be set to True. However, when using Data Connections within a Dynamic Data Connection, these settings may need to be set to False to ensure that data sources that expose supposedly identical organizations will return identical SQL queries even if owner and database names are different.*

- **Rights**   Click the ellipses to set rights for this Data Connection. Setting Business View rights is discussed in detail later in the chapter, under "Setting Rights for Business View Objects."

Saving the Data Connection to the Repository

Once you've set any desired properties, you should save the object to the repository. In fact, you must save new objects to the repository before you set certain properties, such as rights, or perform additional functions, such as checking dependent integrity. To save the Data Connection, click the Save button in the toolbar, press CTRL-S, or choose File | Save from the pull-down menus.

The Save As dialog box will appear, which consists of an object name text box and an embedded copy of the Repository Explorer (discussed in more detail later in the chapter, under "Using the Repository Explorer"). Choose the desired location for your Data connection by navigating to the desired folder, creating an additional folder, or selecting the root-level Central Management Server. If the name of the Data Connection isn't appropriate, change it in the object name text box. Then, click Save to save the Data Connection to the repository.

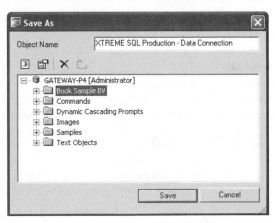

Testing Data Source Connectivity

At any time, either before or after you've saved your Data Connection, you may want to double-check that the data source can be connected to successfully. By clicking the Test Connectivity button in the toolbar or choosing Tools | Test Connectivity from the pull-down menus, you can ensure that the data source name, user ID, and password you've supplied will connect to the data source properly. A message will appear indicating a successful connection or a descriptive error message.

You may also want to ensure that any changes you've made to existing Data Connections don't adversely affect dependent objects. For example, if you created a Data Foundation or Business Element that depends on certain tables and fields in a Data Connection, that Data Foundation and Business Element will fail if you remove the original tables from the database the Data Connection references. More information on checking dependency can be found later in the chapter, under "Object Integrity and References."

CAUTION *Ensure that any data sources you choose when building your Data Connections are also installed on the Crystal Reports Server/BusinessObjects Enterprise servers (Report Job Server, Page Server, Report Application Server, List of Values Server) that will be running the target reports or scheduling dynamic pick lists. If you use a data source when building the Business View that isn't available on these servers, reports will fail when the Crystal Reports Server/ BusinessObjects Enterprise viewer attempts to run them.*

Recall that the sample Business View discussed earlier in the chapter will require connections to a production XTREME database on SQL Server, a test XTREME database from a local Microsoft Access database, an Excel spreadsheet containing sales quotas, and a comma-delimited text file defining geographic regions. Thus, a total of four Data Connections will need to be created to accomplish the ultimate Business View requirements:

- **XTREME Server – Production**   A connection, via OLE DB, to a Microsoft SQL Server.

- **XTREME Local – Test**   A connection, via ODBC, to the XTREME Sample Database 11 Access database.

- **Quotas – Excel**   A connection, via the Access/Excel (DAO) driver, to the Excel spreadsheet containing quotas for each salesperson.

- **Regions – Text File**   A connection, via ODBC, to a comma-delimited text file assigning a region of the country to each state.

Dynamic Data Connection

A useful feature of Business Views is the Dynamic Data Connection. A *Dynamic Data Connection* allows the report designer or viewer to choose from two or more Data Connections to use whenever designing or running a report. This capability often satisfies the "test vs. production" requirement that organizations often have when running reports against multiple databases.

A Dynamic Data Connection is optional within a Business View. While you can create a Dynamic Data Connection if you want to, you don't have to. However, because Dynamic Data Connections are based on existing Data Connections, you must create at least two or more Data Connection objects to make any use of Dynamic Data Connections.

To create a new Dynamic Data Connection, choose the Dynamic Data Connection icon from the welcome screen when starting the Business View Manager or clicking the New toolbar button, or choose File | New from the pull-down menus, choosing the Dynamic Data Connection submenu item. The Choose A Data Connection dialog box will appear after a new Dynamic Data Connection is displayed in the Business View Manager, as illustrated in Figure 16-3.

The Choose A Data Connection dialog box will simply show the folder structure of the repository. Navigate through the folder structure of this dialog box to find your desired Data Connection object (only Data Connections will appear when you open repository folders). If your repository contains a large number of Data Connections, you may use dialog box filters to narrow down the list of displayed Data Connections. Right-click anywhere within the repository folder or object list and choose Advanced Filtering from the pop-up menu. The dialog box will display text boxes where you may specify a combination of object name text or author. When you click the Apply button, only Data Connections that include the supplied text or author names will appear. If you wish to turn off any existing filters, simply right-click and click the Advanced Filtering option again. The complete list of Data Connections will reappear.

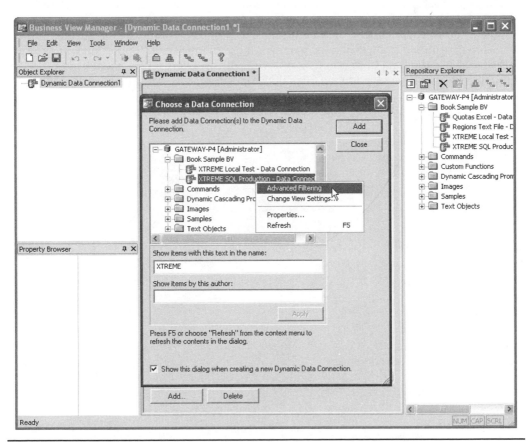

FIGURE 16-3   Creating a new Dynamic Data Connection

Once you've selected your first desired Data Connection, click the Add button. You can also just double-click a desired Data Connection. As you add Data Connection objects, you'll see them appear in the middle of the Business View Manager under the Dynamic Data Connection tab (you may need to move the Choose A Data Connection dialog box out of the way to see this). Once you've chosen desired Data Connections, close the Choose A Data Connection dialog box.

CAUTION *Only Data Connection objects that don't prompt for database logon credentials can be used within a Dynamic Data Connection. If you attempt to add a connection that does prompt, you'll receive an error message. If you encounter such a connection, you'll need to edit it within the Business View Manager and set the Runtime Prompt Mode property to Never Prompt. Then, you may add it to the Dynamic Data Connection.*

Make sure that the Data Connections you are adding to your Dynamic Data Connection expose applicable database objects that are identical to the other Data Connections you add. For example, if you are planning on using the Orders, Customer, and Products tables from one Data Connection, ensure that other Data Connections also expose the same table names with the same set of relevant fields. The entire concept of a Dynamic Data Connection is to provide the exact same database organization, or "schema," from multiple data sources.

Once you've chosen your Data Connections, they will appear inside the Business View Manager. An automatically generated name for the Dynamic Data Connection will appear in the tab above the Data Connections, displayed with an asterisk (the asterisk indicates that this object has not been saved to the CRS/BOE repository since being created or modified).

You may discover that you either have added a Data Connection that you don't want or need to add additional Data Connections. To delete an existing connection, select it in the list (you may select more than one connection with CTRL-click or SHIFT-click) and press the DEL key. You may also click the Delete button at the bottom of the connections list, click the Delete toolbar button, or choose Edit | Delete Data Connection from the pull-down menus.

If you need to add an additional Data Connection, click the Add button at the bottom of the connections list, click the Add toolbar button, or choose Edit | Add Data Connection from the pull-down menus. The Choose A Data Connection dialog box will reappear. Navigate through the repository folders to find the desired Data Connection or Connections to add. Or, if you already see the Repository Explorer elsewhere within the Business View Manager, you can simply drag a Data Connection object from it directly to the list of connection objects.

When the report designer or viewer uses a Business View based on a Dynamic Data Connection, they will be given the choice of Data Connections from within the Dynamic Data Connection in a pick list, similar to that of a standard Crystal Reports parameter field. Data Connections will appear in the pick list in the same order as they appear here. If you wish to change the order that connections will appear in the pick list, click the desired connection and use the up or down arrows at the top of the window to move the connection up or down in the list. You can also sort the entire list in ascending or descending order by choosing an option for the Sort drop-down list to the right of the up and down arrows.

When dealing with Dynamic Data Connections, the Object Explorer is of limited usefulness (since the Dynamic Data Connection doesn't contain any "child" objects, such as tables or fields). However, the Property Browser plays a more important role. Here, you may specify various properties for the Dynamic Data Connection that determine its appearance within the CRS/BOE repository and its behavior. Click in the text area to the right of the property and type your desired value, click the drop-down list to choose from various options, or click the ellipses button to be prompted for additional values.

- **Name**   Type the descriptive name you wish this Dynamic Data Connection to have when you save it to the repository.

- **Description**   Type an optional description to more fully explain the usage of this Dynamic Data Connection.

- **Author**   Your CRS/BOE user ID is specified here by default. You may change this text to something else, if you choose.

- **Parent Folder**   This read-only item will appear if you've already saved the Dynamic Data Connection, or you're modifying an existing Dynamic Data Connection. It simply shows the location in the repository where the object is located.

- **Prompt Text**   Much like a Crystal Reports parameter field, a Dynamic Data Connection will prompt the report designer or viewer for their choice of Data Connection. Any text you type here will appear as prompting text to help the report viewer make the proper connection choice.

- **Rights**   Click the ellipses to set rights for this Dynamic Data Connection. Setting Business View rights is discussed in detail later in the chapter, under "Setting Rights for Business View Objects."

TIP *Even if the Data Connections you add to a Dynamic Data Connection expose supposedly identical data schemas, you may encounter problems later in the Business View design process when browsing sample data or using the finished Business View in a report. This may be due to the data sources within the Dynamic Data Connection adding extra items, such as database catalog name, or database owner, to various portions of the resulting SQL statement. If you suspect this problem, edit the source Data Connections that are referenced by the Dynamic Data Connection and set the Use Catalog or User Owner property to False.*

Saving the Dynamic Data Connection to the Repository

Once you've set any desired properties, you should save the object to the repository. In fact, you must save the object to the repository before you set certain properties, such as rights, or perform additional functions, such as checking dependent integrity. To save the Dynamic Data Connection, click the Save button in the toolbar, press CTRL-S, or choose File | Save from the pull-down menus. As with other Business View objects, you may use various features of the Repository Explorer within the Save As dialog box to save the Dynamic Data Connection to the repository.

You may also want to ensure that any changes you've made to existing Dynamic Data Connections don't adversely affect dependent objects, such as existing Data Foundations or Business Elements. More information on checking dependency can be found later in the chapter, under "Object Integrity and References."

Consider that one of the requirements of the sample Business View discussed earlier in the chapter is the ability to choose between a test database and a production one when designing or viewing reports. Thus, a Dynamic Data Connection containing the XTREME production connection via SQL Server and the XTREME test connection via ODBC will provide this capability.

Data Foundation

Once database connectivity has been organized with either Data Connections or Dynamic Data Connections, you'll need to begin the process of tying the data together and determining what data elements you ultimately want report designers and viewers to be able to see. This portion of Business View design is largely carried out within a Data Foundation.

A *Data Foundation* is a collection of one or more tables, stored procedures, views, SQL Commands, and so forth, which make up a single set of available data. Furthermore, additional data in the form of formulas and SQL Expressions can be added to a Data Foundation. And, parameter fields can be added to prompt the report designer or viewer for variable information. These parameters can be used within Data Foundation filters and formulas to customize Data Foundation behavior. Also, the Data Foundation is where row and column security can be specified to limit the set of fields or records that a report designer or viewer sees.

As you may gather from the large number of features that are controlled by a Data Foundation, creating it can often be the most complex portion of overall Business View design. You'll want to think carefully about what your ultimate goals for Business View design are before getting too deep into Data Foundation development. While you can always come back and edit a Data Foundation later, you'll save time and aggravation by planning ahead before initial design.

There are some fundamental Data Foundation rules you should keep in mind when planning Business View design:

- **Every table or data element must be "linkable"**   Even though you can add more than one Data Connection or Dynamic Data Connection to a Data Foundation, all tables you add to a single Data Foundation from any of these connections must be able to be linked to another table. Just as when designing a Crystal Report directly against multiple data sources, any mismatched data types or nonmatching field contents will render tables unlinkable. The Data Foundation must ultimately be able to return a single record consisting of fields from all tables added to it. Therefore, all tables must be able to be properly linked.

- **Your ultimate Business View must be based on a single Data Foundation**   The "all tables must be linked" caveat at the Data Foundation level may cause you to attempt to link unlinkable data higher up in the Business View hierarchy. For example, maybe you have one Data Foundation that includes a base table with separate first and last name fields. You may create a formula within the Data Foundation to concatenate them into a single combined field, expecting to be able to link the formula to a combined first/last name field in another Data Foundation when you eventually create the top-level Business View object. However, when you attempt to create the Business View, you'll receive an error message if you attempt to add data from multiple Data Foundations. This is a core limitation of the Business View product. So, while you can create multiple Data Foundations in the repository for various Business View requirements, you may only include data from a single Data Foundation when you create a top-level Business View object.

To create a new Data Foundation, choose the Data Foundation icon from the welcome screen when starting the Business View Manager or clicking the New toolbar button, or choose File | New from the pull-down menus, choosing the Data Foundation submenu item. The Choose A Data Connection dialog box will appear after a new Data Foundation is displayed in the Business View Manager, as illustrated in Figure 16-4.

The Choose A Data Connection dialog box will simply show the folder structure of the repository. Navigate through the folder structure of this dialog box to find your desired Data Connection or Dynamic Data Connection object (only Data Connections or Dynamic Data Connections will appear when you open repository folders). If your repository contains a large number of connections, you may use dialog box filters to narrow down the list of displayed connections. Right-click anywhere within the repository folder or object list and choose Advanced Filtering from the pop-up menu. The dialog box will display text boxes where you may specify a combination of object name text or author. When you click the Apply button, only connections that include the supplied text or author names will appear. If you wish to turn off any existing filters, simply right-click and click the Advanced Filtering option again. The complete list of connections will reappear.

Once you've selected your desired Data Connection or Dynamic Data Connection, click OK. You can also just double-click a desired Connection. If you choose a Dynamic Data Connection, you'll be prompted to pick which Data Connection from within it to use for the Data Foundation design process. The Insert Data Tables dialog box will now appear, as shown in Figure 16-5.

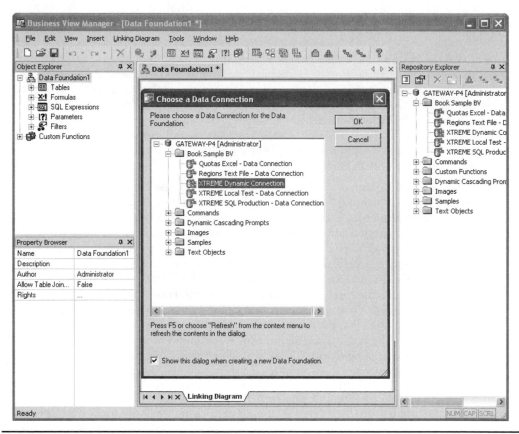

FIGURE 16-4 Creating a new Data Foundation

FIGURE 16-5
The Insert Data
Tables dialog box

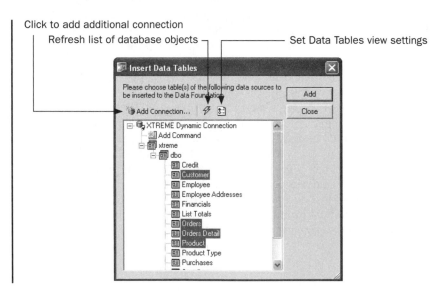

Click plus signs, as necessary, to expand the database connection to see available tables, views, and stored procedures. Choose one or more database items (you may CTRL-click or SHIFT-click to choose more than one item) and click the Add button to add them to the Data Foundation. You may also just double-click a desired item. As you add them, you'll see the items appear inside the Business View Manager (you may need to move the Insert Data Tables dialog box out of the way to see them).

If you wish to add an additional Data Connection or Dynamic Data Connection, click the Add Connection button. This will display the Choose A Data Connection dialog box, where you may navigate through the repository folder structure to look for additional connections. If you choose an additional Dynamic Data Connection, you'll be prompted to pick which connection to use. Once you choose the additional connection, the Insert Data Tables dialog box will appear with the new connection appearing as another category with a plus sign. Click the plus sign to choose database items from the new connection.

If, for some reason, the database connection you are using may change while the Insert Data Tables dialog box is being displayed, you may refresh the list of database items by pressing the F5 key, clicking the Refresh button above the list of tables, or right-clicking in the dialog box and choosing Refresh from the pop-up menu. Any changes to the database will be reflected in the dialog box.

You may also wish to customize display of the Insert Data Tables dialog box. By using options in the Database Explorer Options dialog box, you can choose to limit display to certain types of database items (just tables and views, for example, or all types of database items); only include tables that match a table name or owner character pattern; choose whether to list tables by name, description, or both; and sort table names alphabetically. Display this dialog box by clicking the Edit Options button above the list of tables, or right-clicking in the dialog box and choosing Options from the pop-up menu. After making choices in this dialog box, you'll need to click the Refresh button to redisplay the Insert Data Tables dialog box with the changes.

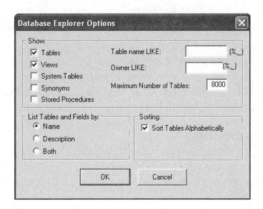

Once you've chosen your tables and closed the Insert Data Tables dialog box, you'll see all chosen database items inside the Business View Manager. An automatically generated name for the Data Foundation will appear in the tab above the Data Connections, displayed with an asterisk (the asterisk indicates that this object has not been saved to the repository since being created or modified).

Saving the Data Foundation to the Repository

While you may still have many options to choose within the Data Foundation, you may want to save it to the repository fairly quickly after choosing the first set of tables. To save the Data Foundation, click the Save button in the toolbar, press CTRL-S, or choose File | Save from the pull-down menus. The Save As dialog box will appear, where you may use options similar to those for other Business View objects to save the Data Foundation.

You may also want to ensure that any changes you've made to the Data Foundation don't adversely affect dependent objects, such as existing Business Elements or Business Views. More information on checking dependency can be found later in the chapter, under "Object Integrity and References."

While other Business View objects may be relatively simple to manipulate or modify, there is a lot more to the Data Foundation portion of Business Views than may initially meet the eye. Once you've chosen an initial set of tables, there is still much to be done:

1. Additional tables may be required, or existing tables may need to be removed. You may also want to change the initial data source that a table is based on, if you have multiple data sources with the same table. You may also need to set the alias name for a table, particularly if you have added two tables with the same name from different connections.

2. You'll need to link all your tables on one or more common fields. You may also need to change link and join types for various table links.

3. You may want to add customized data to your Data Foundation by way of formulas, custom functions, or SQL Expressions.

4. If you want to prompt report designers or viewers for variable information that can affect filters or formulas, you can create parameter fields. You may then use the parameter fields in other portions of the Data Foundation.

5. You can create filters that limit the Data Foundation to a certain set of records. Filters can either be "hard-coded" (such as setting the Country equal to USA) or based on parameters.

6. Row and column security can be set within a Data Foundation, limiting the set of fields or records that are available when reports are designed or run. This row and column security is based on filters and field rights, both being controlled via Crystal Reports Server/BusinessObjects Enterprise user and group security.

Working with Connections and Tables

While earlier discussions in this section revolved around choosing a single Data Connection or Dynamic Data Connection and picking tables, you may often need to add more tables from the first, or additional, connections. You may also need to remove tables that you added by mistake or no longer need.

Adding Additional Tables and Connections   If you need to add additional tables from an already-existing connection, or add more connections and add tables from them, redisplay the Insert Data Tables dialog box that appeared when you first created the Data Foundation. You may do this by clicking the Insert Data Tables toolbar button, by choosing Insert | Insert Data Tables from the pull-down menus or by right-clicking the Tables category of the Object

Explorer window and choosing Insert Data Tables from the pop-up menu. The Insert Data Tables dialog box (shown previously in Figure 16-5) will appear.

For example, the sample Business View described throughout the chapter requires data from two XTREME sample databases (provided by a Dynamic Data Connection), and an Excel spreadsheet and comma-delimited text file (each provided by its own Data Connection). So, the Data Foundation used in this sample Business View will require a Dynamic Data Connection and two Data Connections to all be added to the Data Foundation. Various tables from the XTREME Dynamic Data Connection, as well as a single table each from the Excel and text file connection, will be added to the Data Foundation.

TIP *The Referenced Data Connections window provides the same capabilities as the Insert Data Tables dialog box, but it appears inside the Business View Manager alongside other windows. If you prefer to use this option, choose View | Referenced Data Connections from the pull-down menus.*

Removing Tables   If you inadvertently add tables in the Insert Data Tables dialog box that you don't want, you may remove them from the main Business View Manager window. There are, as you might expect, several ways to do this. You may simply click the table window title bar in the main Data Foundation window, right-click, and choose Remove Table from the pop-up menu.

 You may also click a table name from within the Object Explorer window. Then, simply press the DEL key, choose Edit | Delete from the pull-down menus, or click the Delete toolbar button.

TIP *You won't be able to remove a table if it is linked to any other tables. Delete any table links to or from the desired table before you attempt to remove it.*

Setting Table Locations   If you initially add a table from a particular Data Connection or Dynamic Data Connection and then wish to replace it with an alternate table (most probably, with an identical structure to the first table), you can set the table's location to a different connection. To do this, select either an individual table within the Tables category of the Object Explorer, CTRL-click or SHIFT-click to select multiple tables, or click the word Tables above the entire set of tables that you wish to change (clicking the word Tables is, in essence, the same as SHIFT-clicking all tables within the Tables category). Then, right-click and choose Set Table Location from the pop-up menu, choose Edit | Set Table Location from the pull-down menus, or click the Set Table Location toolbar button. You may also click the ellipses button next to the Data Connection property in the Property Browser (provided you have selected at least one individual table within the Tables category). The Set Table Location dialog box will appear.

This dialog box is identical to the Insert Data Tables dialog box (shown earlier in Figure 16-5), with the exception of having a different name in the title bar and displaying a Set button in place of the Add button. Click either an individual database item (such as a table or stored procedure) or click the connection name—clicking anything else will dim the Set button. If you want to add a new connection to look for a database item, click the Add Connection button.

Choose the new table or connection you want to use and click Set (you can also just double-click the new table or connection). If you selected multiple tables in the Object Explorer before setting location, or chose a single table and then clicked a connection name, only the source connection will change for all the tables—the Business View Manager will look for tables with identical names in the new connection. An error message will appear if matching tables aren't found. If you selected a single table before setting location, and then choose a different single table, Set Table Location will replace the first table with the one just chosen.

Once you set new table locations, you'll be asked if you wish to verify the database. If you reply Yes, the core database will be read in order to display any field name or data type changes in the Business View Manager. You may also wish to do this without changing a table location if the core database schema changes through normal maintenance. Do this by choosing Tools | Verify Database from the pull-down menus or clicking the Verify Database toolbar button. Any changes to the underlying data tables will be reflected in the Object Explorer and the Data Foundation linking diagram window.

If you verify the database and discover that even moderate changes have been made to the underlying data structure of the database, you should probably check the integrity of any dependent objects within the Business View. For example, if Business Element and Business View objects are dependent upon the field names and data types that have now changed, you may need to modify them to accommodate the core database changes. See "Object Integrity and References" later in the chapter for details.

NOTE *If field names have changed between the two tables, you'll be prompted to map new field names to existing fields. This is necessary to ensure that any field names that have changed can be "connected" to existing fields that may already be used in the Data Foundation. The Map Database Fields dialog box displayed in the Business View Manager is identical in appearance and behavior to that displayed in Crystal Reports. Look in Chapter 18 for more information.*

Setting Table Aliases   As a general rule, when you add a database item (table, stored procedure, view) to a Data Foundation, it is stored and displayed with the name it was given when the database was designed. There are two potential issues with using this predefined item name: (1) The name may not be intuitive or easy to understand, and (2) another table with the same name may be added from a different connection. The solution to either of these problems is to use an alias for the table.

An *alias* is simply a different name that refers to the original table in the connection. By assigning an alias, table names may be easier to understand or may differentiate multiple tables with the same core database name (such as a lookup table that needs to be added to the Data Foundation multiple times). The first opportunity to change a table's alias will be presented to you when you attempt to add a table to the Data Foundation with the same name as an existing table. A message box will indicate the duplicate table name, giving you the option to rename the incoming table or cancel the table addition. If you choose to rename the table, the Rename Table dialog box will ask you to specify a new table name.

You may set the alias for an existing table (if the name is confusing, for example) by selecting it in the Object Explorer. Then, select the Table Alias property in the Property Browser and type in a new table name.

TIP *Setting table aliases in the Data Foundation is largely beneficial only to the Business View designer. The actual "table" names that the report designer will see are determined when you create Business Elements (covered later in the chapter).*

Linking Tables   Once you've added tables from the various Data Connections to the Data Foundation, you must link all the tables together. As discussed at the beginning of the Data Foundations section, a core requirement of a Data Foundation is that all tables must be linked on at least one common field. By linking tables together, each table will "follow" another as records are read, returning combined records with matching fields from all linked tables to the report designer or viewer.

Linking tasks are accomplished when viewing the Linking Diagram screen in the Business View Manager. If you don't see the Linking Diagram screen, click the Linking Diagram tab at the bottom of the center Business View Manager window (other tabs may appear for formulas, parameter fields, and so forth). Once the Linking Diagram screen is displayed, you may choose linking options either from the Linking Diagram pull-down menu, from various toolbar buttons, or by right-clicking in the Linking Diagram window and choosing options from the pop-up menus.

NOTE *Table linking concepts in Business Views are almost identical to linking concepts in Crystal Reports. Look in Chapter 15 for table linking concepts, steps, and fine points. Only linking features not common to Crystal Reports will be covered in detail in this chapter.*

Use steps similar to those discussed in Chapter 15 to link tables. For example, you can simply drag and drop from the desired field in one table to the desired field in another to draw a link line. If your database design lends itself to automatic linking (either by field name or by key), you may choose the Smart Linking By Name or Smart Linking By Key choices to link automatically. To change options for an individual link, click the link line, right-click, and choose link-related options from the pop-up menu.

While most linking features are similar or identical to those in Crystal Reports, a few differences exist in Business Views:

- **Locate Table**   If you have added a moderate to large number of tables to your Data Foundation, it may be difficult to locate the table in the Linking Diagram window. The Locate Table option displays a dialog box listing all tables that you've added. Choose this option by choosing Linking Diagram | Locate Table in the pull-down menus, with the Locate Tables toolbar button, or by right-clicking in the Linking Diagram window and choosing Locate Table from the pop-up menu. Click a table name in the dialog box to highlight the table in the Linking Diagram window. Once you've finished, click Done to close the Locate Table dialog box.

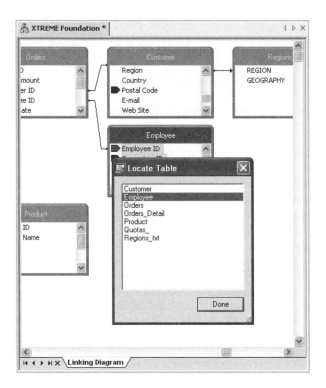

- **Fetch Table Indexes** In Crystal Reports, tables in the Database Expert Links tab show colored arrows next to indexed fields. In Business Views, however, you must specifically request that indexes be read before index arrows appear in the Linking Diagram window. Choose Linking Diagram | Fetch Table Indexes to perform this step. If the database driver you used to create the Data Connections supports exposed indexes, and your database has been indexed on several fields, you'll see colored arrows appearing next to indexed fields in the Linking Diagram window. If you'd like to see a legend that indicates the significance of the colors of the arrows, choose Index Legend from the Linking Diagram pull-down menu or from the pop-up menu you'll see after right-clicking in the Linking Diagram window.

- **Select Visible Tables** If you added many tables to your Data Foundation, it may be difficult for you to navigate all of them in the Linking Diagram window. If you would prefer that a limited set of tables be visible for certain linking choices, you can choose which tables appear or don't appear in the Business View Manager. Do this by choosing Linking Diagram | Select Visible Tables from the pull-down menus or by clicking the Select Visible Tables toolbar button. The Choose Visible Tables for Linking Diagram dialog box will appear. Either select individual tables, click the Select All button to select all tables, or click the Clear button to deselect all tables. When you click OK, those tables that were selected will appear in the Linking Diagram window while those that weren't selected won't appear.

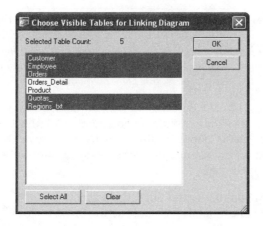

- **Change Linking View**   By default, the Business View Manager shows an individual window consisting of both the table name and all fields in the table, for each table within the Linking Diagram window. This is typically appropriate when you are initially linking tables, as you can see individual table fields for dragging and dropping links. However, you may prefer a more compact view that shows only table names without all fields. Display this alternate view by choosing Linking Diagram | Change Linking View from the pull-down menus, by clicking the Change Linking View toolbar button, or by right-clicking in the Linking Diagram window and choosing Change Linking View from the pop-up menu. A more concise view showing just table names without fields and associated link lines will appear. To return to the original tables-with-fields view, simply choose the Change Linking View option again.

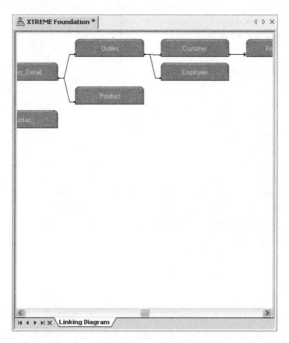

PART I

TIP The Allow Table Joins Override property will appear in the Property Browser when you select the Data Foundation name in the Object Explorer. If you set this property to True, you will be able to modify table linking already set in the Data Foundation when you create a Business View. If you leave this option set to False, the linking you choose in the Data Foundation will always be enforced in any Business Views based on this Data Foundation.

Continuing with the XTREME Business View example discussed earlier in the chapter, the XTREME Dynamic Data Connection (based on the two XTREME Mountain Bike Data Connections), the Quotas Data Connection (based on the Excel spreadsheet), and the Regions Data Connection (based on the comma-delimited text file) should be added to the Data Foundation. Tables will be linked on common fields.

Using Formulas, Custom Functions, and SQL Expressions

One of the main benefits of a "metalayer" tool such as Business Views is the ability to pre-create custom calculations and logic to provide to report designers. This ability allows you to create organization-specific calculations, custom fields, and other special data elements specific to your reporting requirements. These custom fields can be added to the Business View to appear alongside regular database fields. As far as the report designer is concerned, these custom fields are just another available field to drag and drop onto the report.

Two different types of custom fields can be created and placed in your Data Foundation: *Formulas* and *SQL Expressions*. Both can be used to create custom calculations, specially formatted fields, and complex logical expressions. The main difference is that formulas are ultimately evaluated and calculated by the report they're placed in, whereas SQL expressions make use of Structured Query Language functions from your database server and are processed and calculated by the server before being sent back to the report. Typically, there are many more available functions and operators you can use with formulas. However, because SQL expressions are evaluated on the database server, you'll often find improved database query performance when using SQL expressions in filters and other record selection situations. Also, because SQL Expressions are server-based, you can use them to link to other tables in the Business Views Manager.

NOTE Creating formulas and SQL expressions in Business Views is almost identical to creating them in Crystal Reports. Detailed information on formula creation can be found in Chapter 5. Detailed information on SQL expressions can be found in Chapter 15. Because of these similarities, only differences in formulas and SQL expressions between Crystal Reports and Business Views will be highlighted in this chapter.

Creating Formulas   To create a new formula in your Data Foundation, right-click the Formulas category of the Object Explorer and choose Insert Formula from the pop-up menu. You can also choose Insert | Insert Formula from the pull-down menus, or click the Insert Formula toolbar button. The Formula Editor will appear in the middle portion of the Business View Manager. Use the Formula Editor field, function, and operator boxes, as well as the formula text box, to create your formula.

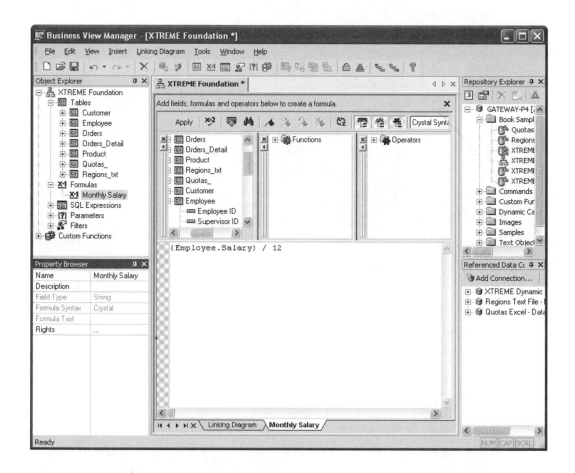

Creating SQL Expressions   To create a new SQL expression in your Data Foundation, right-click the SQL Expressions category of the Object Explorer and choose Insert SQL Expression from the pop-up menu. You can also choose Insert | Insert SQL Expression from the pull-down menus, or click the Insert SQL Expression toolbar button. Because a SQL expression is processed by the database server, it is limited to including fields from a single database connection (unlike a formula, which can include fields that cross database boundaries). Accordingly, you'll be prompted to choose which Data Foundation connection to use for the SQL Expression. Once you make that choice, the SQL Expression Editor will appear in the middle portion of the Business View Manager. Use the SQL Expression Editor field, function, and operator boxes, as well as the formula text box, to create your SQL expression.

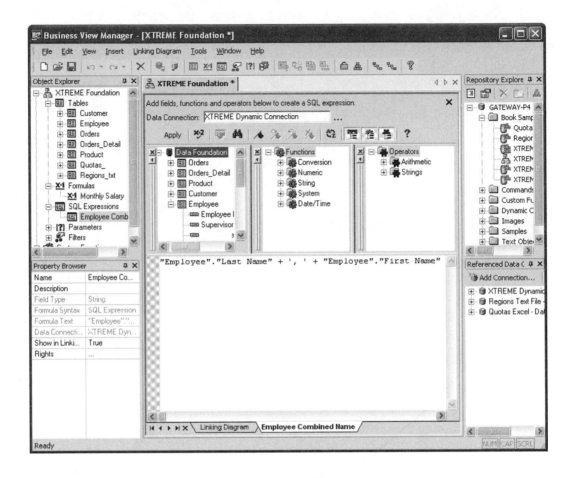

CAUTION *In order to create a SQL Expression, the Data Connection you choose must be based on a SQL Database or a connection via ODBC, as these connections make use of Structured Query Language. Other types of connections, such as "native" PC-style databases or proprietary data connections that don't use SQL, won't be available for use with a SQL Expression.*

With either a formula or a SQL expression, you can check for proper syntax by clicking the Check button in the Editor toolbar. You may click the Apply button to save the contents of the formula or SQL expression to the Data Foundation. To give the formula or SQL expression a meaningful name in the Data Foundation, select the Name text box in the Property Browser when the formula or SQL expression is selected in the Object Explorer. Then, type in an appropriate name and click outside the Name property to save the change. Make sure you save the Data Foundation itself with the Save toolbar button or File | Save menu option to ensure that your new formula or SQL expression is actually saved to the repository with the remainder of the Data Foundation.

One exciting feature of the Business View Manager is the ability to link to other tables on a SQL expression. This improves the ability to link to other data sources that may not contain exactly the same type of data. For example, if one table contains separate first and last name fields, while the other contains a combined first/last field, you can create a SQL expression in the first table that concatenates the first and last name fields together. Then, by selecting True for the Show in Linking Diagram property that appears for the SQL Expression in the Property Browser, you can return to the Linking Diagram and link the SQL expression to another table. SQL expressions will appear with a small icon next to them inside the source table.

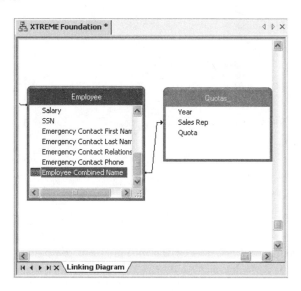

CAUTION *Creating SQL expressions when using Dynamic Data Connections may be problematic, as SQL expression syntax changes depending on the database and database driver used. For example, if you include a database from Microsoft Access via ODBC and one from SQL Server via OLE DB in a Dynamic Data Connection, the data source you choose when first editing the Data Foundation will determine the syntax for SQL expressions. If you then attempt to use the SQL expression after choosing a different data source, the expression may fail because of the different SQL syntax used by the alternate database.*

Importing and Using Custom Functions   Custom functions are reusable pieces of formula language code that are available to every formula in your Data Foundation (they cannot be used in a SQL expression). Because they are stored in the Crystal Reports Server/BusinessObjects Enterprise repository, they can also be centrally maintained. If a particular piece of business logic that a custom function exposes needs to be changed, a single change in the repository will propagate the change through all formulas created using the custom function.

Before you can use a custom function in a Data Foundation formula, you must first import the custom function into the Business View Manager from the repository. Do this by choosing Insert | Import Custom Function from the pull-down menus, right-click the Custom Function category of the Object Explorer and choose Import Custom function from the pop-up menu, or click the Import Custom Function toolbar button. The Choose Custom Functions dialog box will appear.

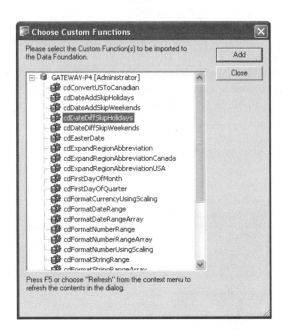

Select the custom function you want to add and click the Add button. You may select as many custom functions as you'd like and click Add (although, you can only click one at a time). When finished, close the Choose Custom Functions dialog box. You'll now notice that the custom functions you chose appear in the Custom Functions category of the Object Browser, as well as the Custom Functions category of the Function tree in the Formula Editor (you'll see the Formula Editor when creating or editing a formula). If any of the custom functions you import refer to additional custom functions, they'll be imported automatically and you'll also see them appear in custom function lists. To use a custom function in a formula, simply double-click the custom function name in the Formula Editor function tree to add the function to your formula. Then, supply any necessary arguments.

NOTE *Complete information on creating custom functions in Crystal Reports and adding them to repository can be found in Chapter 6. Also, if you would like to use sample custom functions that are included with Crystal Reports Server/BusinessObjects Enterprise, choose Tools | Install Repository Samples from the Business View Manager pull-down menus to install sample custom functions to the repository.*

Editing and Deleting Formulas, Custom Functions, and SQL Expressions   Once you've added a formula or SQL expression to the Data Foundation, you may later decide to edit it or delete it. To edit an existing formula or SQL expression, simply double-click it from within the appropriate category of the Object Explorer. You can also single-click the desired formula or SQL expression and choose Edit | Edit Formula or Edit | Edit SQL Expression from the pull-down menus. You can also right-click in the Object Browser and choose Edit from the pop-up menu. To rename a formula or SQL expression, select it in the Object Explorer and change the Name property in the Property Browser. You may also add a description for the object in the Property Browser, if you so desire.

To delete a formula, SQL expression, or custom function, select it in the Object Browser and press the DEL key. You may also right-click the desired object and choose Delete from the pop-up menu. Or, simply select the object and click the Delete toolbar button. If you attempt to delete a formula or SQL expression that is used in other formulas or SQL expressions, or if you attempt to delete a custom function that is used in a formula, you'll receive an error message. Remove the reference to the object from any other object before attempting to delete it. Also, if you attempt to delete a custom function that is being referenced by another custom function, you'll encounter an error message.

As you add formulas and SQL Expressions to your Data Foundation, you'll notice that the Linking Diagram and editors used for each formula and SQL expression all take up the same window in the middle of the Business View Manager. Notice, also, that a tab appears at the bottom of this center window for each formula and SQL expression, as well as for the Linking Diagram. You may click a tab to display that particular object in the Business View Manager. If more tabs appear than can be shown at one time, click the arrow buttons to the left of the tabs. To remove a tab for a formula or SQL expression, click the small X to the left of the first tab or in the upper right-hand corner of the window—double-clicking the formula or SQL expression from the Object Explorer will redisplay it. You cannot close the Linking Diagram window with the X button.

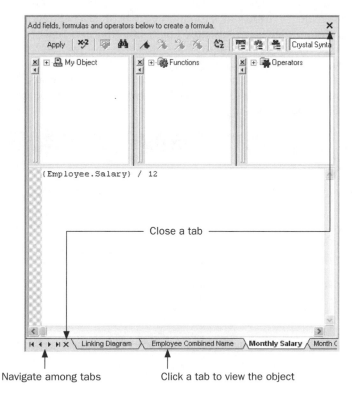

NOTE *You may notice the Rights property for individual formulas and SQL expressions in the Object Browser. Setting rights limits formula and SQL expression availability to certain report designers. More information on this capability is available later in the chapter, under "Row and Column Security." However, you may notice that no Rights property is available for custom functions in the Property Browser. Rights for custom functions are set in the Repository Explorer instead. See "Using the Repository Explorer" later in the chapter.*

Creating Parameters

While Business Views allows a fair amount of flexibility in creating various Data Foundations that return different sets of data, you may want to provide the report designer and viewer various options that tailor Data Foundation behavior at run time. For example, you may wish to prompt for a date range to limit records or prompt for a country to limit data returned by the Data Foundation. As with Crystal Reports, this variable behavior can be accomplished with parameters.

CAUTION *Business Views only allow parameter field use with Data Foundation filters (discussed later in the chapter). Parameters cannot be used inside a formula or SQL expression created within the Data Foundation.*

A *parameter* is a prompt that appears every time a Business View based on the Data Foundation is used as a source for report data. The report designer or viewer provides a response to each parameter prompt, which modifies the way the Data Foundation returns data. When Crystal Reports are viewed or scheduled in Crystal Reports Server/BusinessObjects Enterprise, parameter values can be supplied to customize the way the report runs.

To create a parameter, click the Parameters category of the Object Explorer, right-click, and choose Insert Parameter from the pop-up menu. You can also choose Insert | Insert Parameter from the pull-down menus, or click the Insert Parameter toolbar button. The Create Parameter Field dialog box appears.

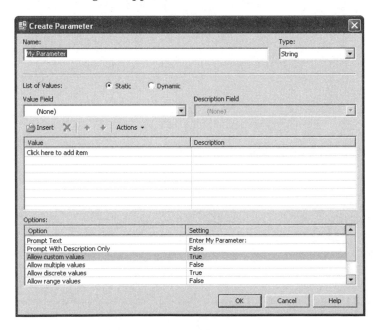

Give the parameter a name (the default "My Parameter" name probably isn't appropriate) and choose a type. Optionally, create a static or dynamic/cascading pick list in the List of Values section. You may also make choices in the Options section, where you can set length limits for string parameters, set range limits for numeric parameters, and so forth. When you are finished creating the parameter, click OK on the Create Parameter Field dialog box. The parameter will now appear within the Parameters category of the Object Explorer. You are now able to use the parameter in a Data Foundation filter (discussed later in the chapter).

NOTE *Creating parameters in Business Views is almost identical to creating them in Crystal Reports. Detailed information on parameter creation can be found in Chapter 13. Because of these similarities, only parameter differences between Crystal Reports and Business Views will be highlighted in this chapter.*

Using Dynamic and Cascading Pick Lists with Data Foundation Parameters   New version XI dynamic and cascading pick lists can be used with Data Foundation parameter fields, the same as they can with Crystal Reports parameter fields. To do this, begin by selecting the Dynamic radio button in the List of Values section. However, unlike Crystal Reports parameter fields, Data Foundation dynamic/cascading pick lists *must be* based on another Business View in the repository (they cannot be based on fields within the Data Foundation they're contained in). You may either create new List of Values and Prompt Group objects for a dynamic pick list or choose existing objects already in the repository (steps for creating these objects are discussed later in this chapter).

To base a dynamic or cascading pick list on existing objects in the repository, click the Existing radio button in the Choose A Data Source section. Then, choose the desired choice for your pick list from the adjacent drop-down list. Choose either an existing List of Values entry or a Prompt Group underneath an existing List of Values entry.

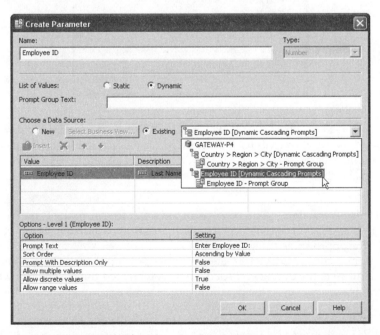

If no appropriate List of Values or Prompt Group exists in the repository, you may create new objects to populate the dynamic/cascading pick list you wish to associate with your Data Foundation parameter field. To do this, click the New radio button in the Choose A Data Source section. Then, click the Select Business View button to display the Select Business View dialog box (in essence, a folder view of the repository). Navigate through repository folders until you find the Business View you wish to use as the data source for your pick list (note that you *cannot* use any Business Views based on the Data Foundation that contains the parameter field you are currently working with—you must choose a separate Business View).

Once you've chosen a Business View that contains desired fields to populate your pick list, choose the desired field for the pick list in the Value column in the middle of the dialog box. If you wish to choose a matching description field, make that choice in the Description column. Then, click the Parameters column to attach the parameter field you are working on to the pick list fields you've just chosen. When you are finished defining your new dynamic pick list, click OK to save the new parameter field in the Data Foundation. The Business View Manager will prompt you for a repository location to store the List of Values and Prompt Group objects that will be created. Either choose the Central Management Server itself (to store the objects in the "top level"), choose an existing folder, or create and choose a new folder. The List of Values object that contains the pick list, and the Prompt Group object that contains the prompting text and associated properties, will be saved to that location.

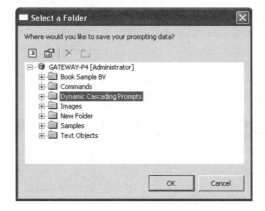

CAUTION *If you later delete the List of Values or Prompt Group objects used in a dynamic pick list, or any dependent objects (such as the Business View the pick list objects are based on), you'll receive a cryptic error message when you attempt to edit the parameter field. Once you clear the error, the dynamic pick list will no longer appear in the Edit Parameter dialog box.*

Editing and Deleting Parameters Once you've added a parameter to the Data Foundation, you may later decide to edit or delete it. To edit an existing parameter, simply double-click it from within the appropriate category of the Object Explorer. You can also right-click in the Object Browser and choose Edit Parameter from the pop-up menu. The Edit Parameter dialog box (identical to the dialog you used when you created the parameter) will appear, where you may make changes to the parameter. To rename a parameter, select the parameter in the Object Explorer and change the Name property in the Property Browser.

To delete a parameter, select it in the Object Browser and press the DEL key. You may also right-click the parameter name and choose Delete from the pop-up menu. Or, simply select the object and click the Delete toolbar button. If you attempt to delete a parameter that is used in a filter, you'll receive an error message. Remove the parameter from all filters before attempting to delete it.

TIP You can create parameters either when creating a Data Foundation, or when creating a Business Element (covered later in the chapter). The difference is that parameters you create in a Data Foundation will appear in all Business Elements that use the Data Foundation, whereas parameters created at the Business Element level will only appear in that one Business Element.

Creating Filters

It is a rare report that benefits from including every record in an entire database. In fact, inadvertently including every database record may result in excessive network traffic, shortage of temporary disk space on your computer, and, at the very least, a useless report of gigantic proportions. While Crystal Reports that are based on Business Views can make use of the Select Expert and the Crystal Reports record selection formula, limiting records to a meaningful set at the Business View level not only avoids "runaway" reports but allows only a limited set of data that's pertinent to the Business View to be returned to the report. In addition, the creation of Data Foundation filters is the cornerstone of Business Views row-level security that limits report data based on Crystal Reports Server/BusinessObjects Enterprise user and group settings.

A *filter* (sometimes referred to as a "Business Filter" in Business Views documentation) is a limit placed on records that are returned from the database. Filters can take the form of "only customers in the USA," "only orders placed within the {?Order Date Range} parameter," and so forth. Filtering is a basic requirement of virtually all database query and reporting tools. You may create as many filters within a Data Foundation as you'd like, applying one or more of them to individual Crystal Reports Server/BusinessObjects Enterprise users or entire groups of users.

NOTE While the filter process in Business Views is different from the Crystal Reports Select Expert, basic filtering and record selection concepts are the same. Get more detailed information on general record selection concepts by reading Chapter 4.

To create a filter, click the Filters category of the Object Explorer, right-click, and choose Insert Filter from the pop-up menu. You can also choose Insert | Insert Filter from the pull-down menus, or click the Insert Filter toolbar button. The filter window fills the middle of the Business View Manager, as shown in Figure 16-6.

Begin by choosing the field you want to use for the first (or only) part of your filter from the top portion of the filter window. Add it to the filter text box by either double-clicking it, dragging and dropping it to the filter text box, or selecting it and clicking the Add Selected Tree Item to Filter button from the filter toolbar (located in the middle of the filter window). The field will be added to the filter text box with an "is any value" criteria chosen by default.

Select the field in the filter text box. A drop-down list of available comparisons will appear below the filter text box. Click it to choose from the available comparison operators,

Pick field to filter on ———
Delete selected portion of filter
Check for proper filter syntax

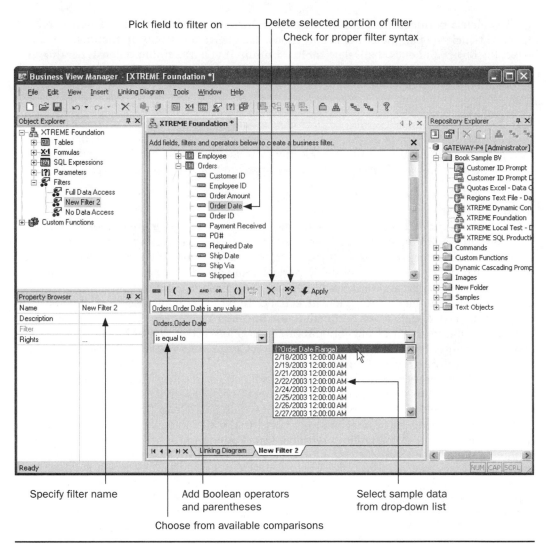

Specify filter name

Add Boolean operators
and parentheses

Select sample data
from drop-down list

Choose from available comparisons

Figure 16-6 Creating a Business View filter

such as equal to, less than, and so forth. Based on the comparison choice you make, additional drop-down/text box combinations will appear to the right of the comparison drop-down. Click the drop-down arrow to browse sample data for the field. If you wish to base this filter on a parameter, choose it from the drop-down list (only parameters that match the data type of the filter field will appear in the list). Or, you may just type in your desired comparison value (such as USA) in the list. Once you've completed this first filter "expression," you may either click the Check Filter Validity button to ensure that the filter meets proper syntax requirements, or click the Apply button to finalize choices you made for this expression.

If you only require a single filter expression, you are now finished creating the filter. Give your filter an appropriate name by typing it in the Name property text box in the Property Browser. However, if you need to create a *compound filter* that contains more than one expression connected with an AND or OR Boolean operator, click the desired AND or OR Boolean operator from the filter toolbar. The word AND or OR will appear after your first filter expression in the filter text box.

Then, repeat the steps described previously to add an additional field to the filter text box and choose a comparison choice and value for it. You may add additional AND or OR Boolean operators and additional field criteria as many times as necessary to create your desired compound filter. You may even reference another filter within this filter. As an existing filter ultimately results in a True or False value, you will simply add the existing filter to this filter connected with a Boolean AND or OR—no comparison operation will be available for the existing filter. If you initially add an AND operator and wish it to, instead, be an OR (or vice versa), simply click the desired operator and click the Toggle And/Or Operator toolbar button.

If you wish to remove any portions of the filter in the text box (such as a particular field/comparison expression or Boolean operator), simply select it in the filter text box. Then, press the DEL key or click the Delete toolbar button from the filter toolbar.

As the default "order of operations" for Boolean operators is from left to right as they're encountered in the filter text box, you may wish to force the evaluation of one or more expressions before the rest of the filter by surrounding the expression or expressions with parentheses. As you cannot type any text directly into the filter text box, you must place the cursor in the text box where you wish to place a single left or right parenthesis, and then click the left or right parenthesis button in the filter toolbar. If you wish to place a left-right parentheses combination around multiple expressions, you may select the expressions, including the Boolean operators, by SHIFT-clicking each expression and Boolean operator that you wish to surround with parentheses. When all the desired expressions are highlighted, click the double-parentheses toolbar button.

Once you've finalized your filter, click the Check Filter Validity button to ensure that it is syntactically correct—any errors will be noted in a message. Click the Apply button to finalize the filter. Then, give the filter a meaningful name by typing it in the Name property in the Property Browser. If you wish to create additional filters within the Data Foundation, simply create a new filter using steps discussed previously. You may add as many different filters to the Data Foundation as you desire, assigning each to a Crystal Reports Server/ BusinessObjects Enterprise user or group of users via rights assignment (discussed later in the chapter, under "Row and Column Security").

CAUTION *You may be confused when you create a filter but find that it doesn't affect any data that ultimately comes from the Business View. This, very probably, is because the filter has not been applied by setting rights for the filter. Steps to apply the filter by setting rights are discussed later in this chapter.*

If you create multiple filters and apply them all to a Data Foundation, Business Views applies a logical OR among the filters. While this is an understandable requirement to properly allow row security within a Business View, it will often give you results that are far different from multiple selection criteria added to the Crystal Reports Select Expert, which uses a logical AND between criteria. If you wish to apply a logical AND to multiple criteria, add multiple expressions to *one* filter and apply an AND operator between the expressions *within* the one filter.

As with any other Business View object, you'll most probably want to save the entire Data Foundation after you create filters. Click the Save toolbar button, or choose File | Save from the pull-down menus to save the updated Data Foundation.

TIP   You can create filters either when creating a Data Foundation, or when creating a Business Element (covered later in the chapter). The difference is that filters you create in a Data Foundation will appear in all Business Elements that use the Data Foundation, whereas filters created at the Business Element level will only appear in that one Business Element. Also, in some cases, you may need to create filters at the different levels to achieve proper combinations of filters for correct row security.

Row and Column Security

One of the most exciting features of Business Views is row and column security. *Row security* allows filtering to be applied to database records "on the fly" to specific Crystal Reports Server/BusinessObjects Enterprise users or groups. For example, when viewing a sales report, the Western Region Sales Manager can be limited to seeing only orders in the Northwest and Southwest. When viewing the same sales report, the National Sales Manager can view orders in all regions. The beauty of row security is that two different reports with two different sets of record selection aren't required to accomplish this. Row security applies the extra filters at run time to all reports based on the Business View supplying the row security. Row security is provided in Business Views by creating filters (described earlier in the chapter) and applying those filters selectively to certain Crystal Reports Server/BusinessObjects Enterprise users and groups.

Column security allows data from certain fields within a data source to be available only to specific Crystal Reports Server/BusinessObjects Enterprise users or groups. For example, when viewing an employee roster report, the HR Manager will be able to see data in the Annual Salary and Monthly Salary fields, along with other employee fields. When any other user views the same employee roster report, the Annual Salary and Monthly Salary fields will display null values, while other employee fields will still display the proper contents. While column security doesn't prohibit a user from adding fields to reports at design time, no data will ever appear in those fields if the user isn't granted the field's right via column security. Column security is provided in Business Views by selecting individual fields in the Object Browser and limiting their rights.

NOTE   You can set row and column security with field limits and filters either when creating a Data Foundation, or when creating a Business Element (covered later in the chapter). The difference is that security you specify in a Data Foundation will apply to all Business Elements that use the Data Foundation, whereas security settings at the Business Element level will only appear in that one Business Element.

Setting Row Security   Business Views row security is accomplished by defining Data Foundation filters, and then applying those filters to the desired Crystal Reports Server/BusinessObjects Enterprise users or groups. First, define an appropriate filter to limit records as desired (as discussed earlier in the chapter, under "Creating Filters"). For example, if you wish to limit records for the Western Regional Sales Manager to only orders placed by Northwest and Southwest customers, create a filter that limits records where "Region = 'Northwest' OR Region = 'Southwest'" (you may create a filter where Region "is one of" Northwest and Southwest).

Once the filter has been defined, it must be applied to one or more Crystal Reports Server/ BusinessObjects Enterprise users or user groups. Otherwise, the filter will never have any effect on a Business View. To apply a filter to a CRS/BOE user or group, you must first save the filter and save the Data Foundation. Then, set rights for the filter from within the Business View Manager. Begin by expanding the Filters category of the Object Browser. Notice that Full Data Access and No Data Access filters appear, even though you didn't create them. These filters, as their names imply, provide full access and no access to records from the Data Foundation. You may apply these built-in filters to users and groups to allow or deny broad access to Data Foundation records.

NOTE *Defining actual Crystal Reports Server/BusinessObjects Enterprise user and user groups is accomplished in the Crystal Reports Server/BusinessObjects Enterprise Central Management Console. More information on general Crystal Reports Server/BusinessObjects Enterprise administration can be found in Part II of this book.*

To apply filters (either your own or Full Data Access/No Access) to CRS/BOE users or groups, begin by selecting the filter that you wish to apply. Then, click the Edit Rights toolbar button, choose Edit | Edit Rights from the pull-down menus, or right-click the selected filter and choose Edit Rights from the pop-up menu. You can also select the Rights property in the Property Browser and click the ellipses button. The Edit Rights dialog box will appear, as shown in Figure 16-7.

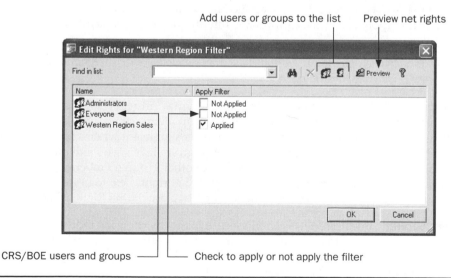

FIGURE 16-7   Edit Rights dialog box

This dialog box will initially show two Crystal Reports Server/BusinessObjects Enterprise groups added by default: the Everyone group and the Administrators group. Each group will be followed by a single check box indicating whether or not the filter is applied to that group (the filter won't be applied to Administrators or Everyone initially). If you want the filter applied to every Crystal Reports Server/BusinessObjects Enterprise user, simply check the box next to Everyone to apply the filter to that group. If, however, you want the filter applied to a smaller set of Crystal Reports Server/BusinessObjects Enterprise users, you must add additional groups or users to the list to apply the filter to. Do this by clicking the Add Groups or Add Users toolbar button. The Add Groups or Add User dialog box will appear.

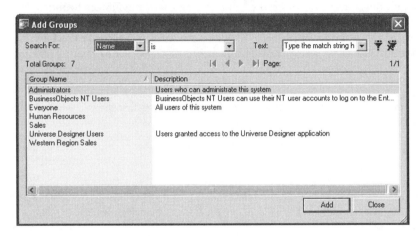

Choose the user or group from the list that you wish to add to the Edit Rights dialog box. You may either double-click the user or group name, or choose the name and click the Add button. Add as many users or groups as you wish to apply the filter to. When you're finished, close the Add Groups or Add User dialog box to return to the Set Rights dialog box. Then, click the Apply check box to apply the filter to the new groups or users.

NOTE *More information on the Add Users and Add Groups dialog boxes can be found later in the chapter, under "Using the Repository Explorer."*

Once you've applied the filter to various groups, you may find it beneficial to preview the "net" rights (that is, rights that take into account group membership, higher-level CRS/BOE folder rights, and so forth). While net rights aren't as significant when applying filters, as filters are simply applied or not at individual user or group levels, you still may find a filter being applied when you don't intend it because of other group membership. Click the Preview button in the Set Rights dialog box to display the net rights next to users and groups. Once you're satisfied that you've applied the filter properly, close the Set Rights dialog box.

Setting Column Security   Business Views column security is set by choosing individual fields, formulas, or SQL expressions in the Object Browser and then setting rights for them. Rights can be set for individual Crystal Reports Server/BusinessObjects Enterprise users or Crystal Reports Server/BusinessObjects Enterprise user groups.

To apply column security to a desired field, formula, or SQL expression, expand the desired field category in the Object Browser and select the desired field within the category. Then, click the Edit Rights toolbar button, choose Edit | Edit Rights from the pull-down menus, or right-click the selected field and choose Edit Rights from the pop-up menu. You can also select the Rights property in the Property Browser and click the ellipses button. The Edit Rights dialog box will appear, as shown in Figure 16-8.

As with the Set Rights dialog box used for applying filters, this dialog box will initially show two Crystal Reports Server/BusinessObjects Enterprise groups added by default: the Everyone group and the Administrators group. Each group will be followed by a View Field Data check box indicating whether or not the field's data is available to that group (the right will indicate "Inherited" initially). Clicking the check box will cycle through three possible choices: Inherited, Granted, or Denied. If you specifically want to deny the field to everyone, click the check box next to Everyone until it indicates Denied (this is of limited usefulness, as this will automatically prevent everyone in CRS/BOE from viewing field contents).

More likely, you'll want the field to be available to a certain set of CRS/BOE users or groups and not available to everyone else. Therefore, you must add additional groups or users to the list to set rights for. Do this by clicking the Add Groups or Add Users toolbar button. The Add Groups or Add User dialog box will appear.

Choose the user or group from the list that you wish to add to the Edit Rights dialog box. You may either double-click the user or group name, or choose the name and click the Add button. Add as many users or groups as you wish to set rights for. When you're finished, close the Add Groups or Add User dialog box to return to the Edit Rights dialog box. Then, click the View Field Data check box to cycle through the three choices for each new group or user.

While setting row security is a simple matter of applying or not applying a filter, setting column security is complicated by the concept of inheritance. *Inheritance* regards the ability of CRS/BOE users and groups to "inherit" rights from higher-level groups, or settings made at the Central Management Server "top folder" level. For example, the rules of inheritance might cause a problem when applying column security to the HR Manager user.

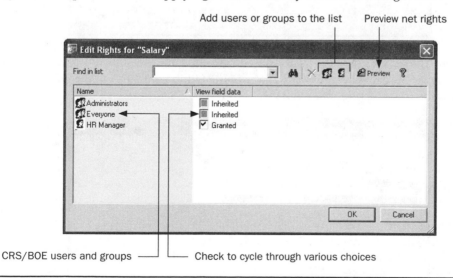

FIGURE 16-8   The Edit Rights dialog box

If you have previously *explicitly denied* rights to the field for the Everyone group, you would be unable to grant rights to the field for the HR Manager even if you *explicitly granted* the right for the HR Manager user. This is because the HR Manager is automatically a member of the Everyone group and explicit denial takes precedence, via inheritance, over explicit granting. The solution is to not explicitly grant or deny the right to the Everyone group, but to explicitly grant it to the HR Manager user. By not explicitly granting the right to the Everyone group, everyone still won't be able to see the field's contents, as not explicitly granting a right automatically denies it. However, because the Everyone group is not explicitly denied the right, the HR Manager will be able to see the field's contents if explicitly granted it, as the rules of inheritance don't consider an unspecified right at a higher group level to be explicitly denied.

The Preview button, which shows net rights for a user or group, is more helpful when setting column security than when setting row security. By clicking this button, you'll see the net rights assigned to users or groups after taking inheritance into account. Take the previous example of explicitly denying a field's right to the Everyone group, but then explicitly granting it to the HR Manager. Notice that the Preview button shows that the HR Manager still won't have rights to the field because of inheritance.

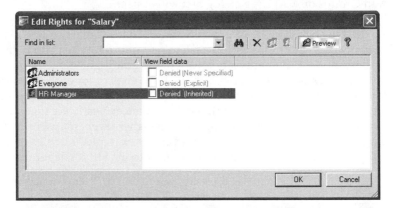

However, if you leave the Everyone group unspecified and grant the right to the HR Manager, you'll notice that everyone *still* can't see the field's contents, but the HR Manager can. This results from the rules of inheritance.

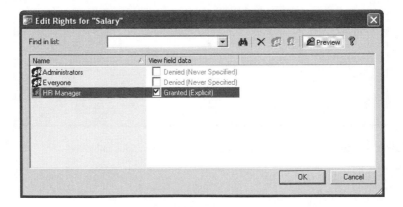

If you think the concepts of inheritance can be a bit confusing, you may be right. While inheritance is designed to make administration of user and group rights simpler, it can also cause confusion. Get more information on the rules of inheritance later in the chapter, under "Using the Repository Explorer."

Once you're satisfied that you've applied proper rights to the field, close the Set Rights dialog box. You may receive a warning indicating that you should check other fields that may be related to the field you just set rights for. For example, even if you limit the Salary database field to the HR Manager, sensitive information still may be available to other report viewers if you have used the Salary field elsewhere in a formula or SQL expression. Ensure that all fields, formulas, and SQL expressions that require column security are specifically addressed using the Edit Rights dialog box.

TIP *It goes without saying that testing your row and column security model is of utmost importance. Often, because of the idiosyncrasies of the Business View Manager (the OR logical connection between multiple Data Foundation filters and rules of inheritance are examples), you may not initially achieve the row or column security you anticipate after your first attempt. For example, you may need to create different filters at both the Data Foundation and Business Element levels to achieve proper combinations for correct row security. You should use Crystal Reports or Crystal Reports Server/BusinessObjects Enterprise to test your row and column security model to ensure that data limits do apply to users that should have limits, and that users who shouldn't be limited, in fact, are not.*

Continuing toward the sample XTREME Business View discussed earlier in the chapter, two filters will need to be created. The first will limit order dates to a value supplied by a date range parameter field and will be applied to all users. While the second filter to limit customer regions to the Northwest or the Southwest used to apply row security to the Western Region Sales Manager may be done here, it will probably need to be done at the Business Element level, due to the Boolean OR value applied between multiple Data Foundation filters. Furthermore, column security will be set so that only the HR Manager has rights to the Salary field from the Employee table, as well as the Monthly Salary formula (which divides the Salary field by 12).

Business Element

As you discovered if you read through much of the previous section on creating Data Foundations, a great deal of the data "abstraction," calculation, and security application is done at the Data Foundation level. However, you may have noticed that unwieldy field names couldn't be changed. You may also have noticed that you had no way of limiting the Data Foundation's set of exposed fields—if you added a table, all fields were available in the Data Foundation (even if you apply column security, a field will still appear inside Crystal Reports even if no data will appear for the field). And, you probably noticed that fields were still organized within their core database tables—you couldn't group fields from different tables together in a more logical fashion.

The Business Element object within your overall Business View allows you to organize your data to your liking. A *Business Element* is simply a smaller set of fields from an underlying Data Foundation. Business Elements determine what set of "virtual tables" ultimately appear in Crystal Reports when a report designer makes use of your Business View. So, even if your underlying Data Foundation consists of 15 different physical database tables that expose 150 fields, you can set up three Business Elements to show 35 significant fields from the Data Foundation in three more logical organizations. Business Elements provide the ability to include any field in any Business Element regardless of what original table it came from, as well as giving the field a more appealing name. When you have created your various Business Elements, you simply add one or more of them to Business View objects (discussed later in the chapter) to determine which set of tables will appear in Crystal Reports.

There are several core concepts to keep in mind when creating Business Elements:

- A Business Element must be based on a Data Foundation. If you have yet to create any Data Foundations in the CRS/BOE repository, you will be unable to create any Business Elements.

- A Business Element can only be based on a single Data Foundation. If you wish to include fields from more than one Data Foundation in a single Business Element, you will find that you are unable to do so. You will need to modify one of the Data Foundations to add additional fields that you wish to use in the Business Element.

There are two different ways of creating Business Elements: by creating them manually within the Business View Manager's typical user interface, or by using the Business Element Wizard to create them via a step-by-step process. As is often the case, you gain more control over individual portions of the Business Element by using the Business View Manager manual method, but you can create multiple Business Elements more quickly using the wizard. You may want to try a combination of methods, perhaps creating a core set of Business Elements quickly with the wizard, and then making any granular modifications to them manually with the Business View Manager itself.

Creating a Business Element Manually

To create a new Business Element, choose the Business Element icon from the welcome screen when starting the Business View Manager or clicking the New toolbar button, or choose File | New from the pull-down menus, choosing the Business Element submenu item. The Choose A Data Foundation dialog box will appear after a new Business Element is displayed in the Business View Manager, as illustrated in Figure 16-9.

The Choose A Data Foundation dialog box will simply show the folder structure of the repository. Navigate through the folder structure of this dialog box to find your desired Data Foundation object (only Data Foundations will appear when you open repository folders). If your repository contains a large number of foundations, you may use dialog box filters to narrow down the list of displayed connections. Right-click anywhere within the repository folder or object list and choose Advanced Filtering from the pop-up menu. The dialog box will display text boxes where you may specify a combination of object name text or author. When you click the Apply button, only foundations that include the supplied text or author names will appear. If you wish to turn off any existing filters, simply right-click and click the Advanced Filtering option again. The complete list of foundations will reappear.

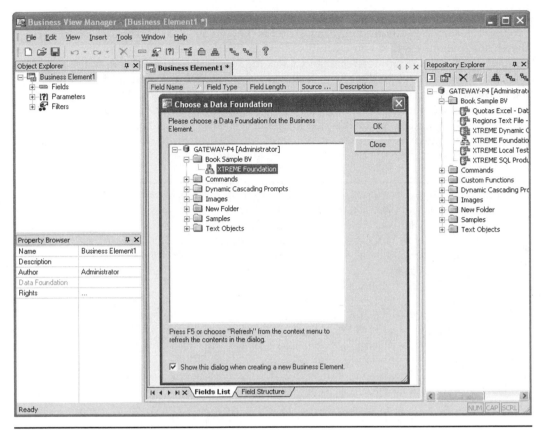

FIGURE 16-9   Creating a new Business Element

Once you've selected your desired Data Foundation, click OK. You can also just double-click a desired foundation. The Insert Business Fields dialog box will now appear.

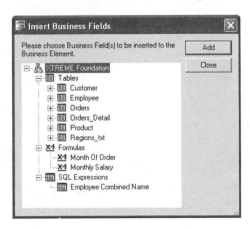

Click plus signs, as necessary, to expand the available tables, formulas, and SQL expression categories. Choose one or more fields (known as "Business Fields" in Business Views documentation) that you wish to add to this Business Element. You may CTRL-click or SHIFT-click to choose more than one field. Click the Add button to add them to the Business Element. You may also just double-click a desired field to add it. As you add them, you'll see the items appear inside the Business View Manager (you may need to move the Insert Business Fields dialog box out of the way to see them). If you add a field that duplicates a field name already added to the Business Element, you'll be given the opportunity to change its name (also known as an alias) as to not conflict with another field. Once you've added all your desired fields, close the Insert Business Fields dialog box.

TIP *The order in which you insert fields from the Insert Business Fields dialog box will be the same order fields appear in when you use the Business Element in a Business View, and eventually in Crystal Reports. This may be deceptive, as fields in the Business View Manager appear in sorted order regardless of the order you inserted them. As you can't reposition fields in a different order, ensure you place them into the Business Element in the correct order if you have a preference. In Crystal Reports, you have the choice of viewing Field Explorer fields in the order they appear in the Business View, or in alphabetical order.*

Once you've added fields, the middle of the Business View Manager will show the Fields List. This simply shows a list of fields you've added to your Business Element, including the field name, data type, field length, source field from the Data Foundation, and any description provided by the Data Foundation or underlying database. You may change the sort order of the Fields List by clicking a column heading. Both ascending and descending sort orders are available for the columns.

Arrow indicates ascending or descending sort   Click column heading to sort fields

Field Name	Field Type	Field Length	Source Data Field	Description
Address1	String	122	Customer.Address1	
Address2	String	42	Customer.Address2	
City	String	42	Customer.City	
Country	String	62	Customer.Country	
Customer N...	String	82	Customer.Custome...	
Postal Code	String	22	Customer.Postal C...	
Region	String	62	Customer.Region	

⟨ **Fields List** ⟩ ⟨ Field Structure ⟩

Notice that an additional Field Structure tab appears next to the Fields List tab at the bottom of the window. Clicking this will display a different view of Business Element fields known as the Field Structure. Initially, this is simply the same set of fields as seen in the Fields List view. However, if you drag one field and drop it onto another, the field you dragged will be placed below the field you dropped onto and indented to create a hierarchy.

Hierarchy created by dragging and dropping fields

This capability is of little use when creating Business Elements for use with Crystal Reports, but it may be useful when creating Business Elements for multidimensional or OLAP types of data cubes (Business Views does not currently create these types of data structures). To reset the field structure so that no field hierarchies exist, choose Edit | Reset Field Structure from the pull-down menus, right-click the Business Element name in the Object Browser and choose Reset Field Structure from the pop-up menu, or click the Reset Field Structure toolbar button. Fields will reappear in the original order of the Business Element with no hierarchy shown.

One of the first Business Element capabilities you'll probably want to take advantage of is the ability to rename fields, or set a field's *alias*. By renaming a field, you can make the ultimate Business View more meaningful and intuitive by eliminating confusing field names from the original data source. Expand the Object Explorer's Fields category and select the field you want to rename. Then, simply click the Name property in the Property Browser and type in a new field name. When you click outside of the Name property, the new name you typed will appear throughout the Business View Manager. If you are curious what the original source field name is for the newly aliased field, view the Fields List in the middle of the Business View Manager. The Source Data Field column will indicate the original field name for the aliased field. You will also notice the original field name in the Source Data Field property in the Property Browser.

As with any other Business View object, you'll most probably want to save the entire Business Element as you progress. Click the Save toolbar button, or choose File | Save from the pull-down menus to save the updated Data Foundation. If you have not saved the Business Element previously, you'll be asked to confirm a name and folder location in the repository.

Adding and Deleting Fields

Once an initial set of fields has been added to your Business Element, it's a foregone conclusion that you'll want to delete some existing fields or add new fields from the Data Foundation. To delete a field, just select it in the Object Browser (you can't delete fields from the Fields List or Fields Structure windows). Then, press the DEL key, right-click the field and choose Delete from the pop-up menu, or click the Delete toolbar button.

Inserting a new field from the Data Foundation is equally simple. Choose Insert | Insert Business Fields from the pull-down menus, right-click the Fields category of the Object Browser and choose Insert Business Fields from the pop-up menu, or click the Insert Business Fields toolbar button. The Insert Business Fields dialog box will reappear. Choose additional fields to add to your Business Element.

Using the Referenced Data Foundation Window   Another way of adding fields, as well as filters, from the underlying Data Foundation is by displaying the Referenced Data Foundation window. Choose View | Referenced Data Foundation from the pull-down menus. The window will appear as another explorer-like window attached to the right side of the Business View Manager. Expand the various categories of the Data Foundation to see available fields. Add a field to the Business Element by dragging and dropping it from the Referenced Data Foundation window to the Object Explorer, the Fields List, or the Fields Structure (you can drop filters only onto the Filters category of the Object Explorer, and parameters cannot be dropped at all). When you're finished, you may close the Referenced Data Foundation window by clicking the small X in the upper right-hand corner.

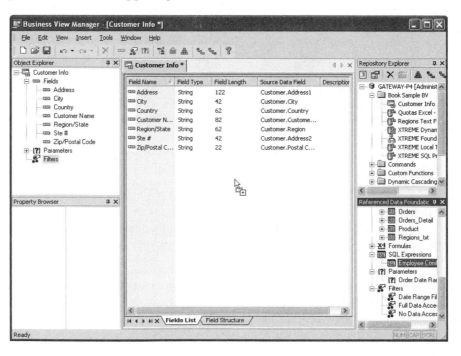

Creating Parameters and Filters

As with an underlying Data Foundation, you can create Parameters and Filters in the Business Element. Steps to create these items are identical to steps for creating them in Data Foundations. Look earlier in the chapter in the Data Foundations section for exact steps.

The difference between creating parameters and filters at the Business Element level and the Data Foundation level is that these items will apply to all Business Elements based on a Data Foundation if they're created at the Data Foundation level. However, if they're created at the Business Element level, they will only apply to this one Business Element.

Using the Business Element Wizard

As mentioned at the beginning of this section, there are actually two ways of creating a Business Element. The second way is the *Business Element Wizard,* which provides a step-by-step approach to creating one or more Business Elements.

To create one or more new Business Elements with the Business Element Wizard, choose the Business Element Wizard icon from the welcome screen when starting the Business View Manager or clicking the New toolbar button, or choose File | New from the pull-down menus, choosing the Business Element Wizard submenu item. The Business Element Wizard will appear, with the Choose Data Foundation screen appearing first.

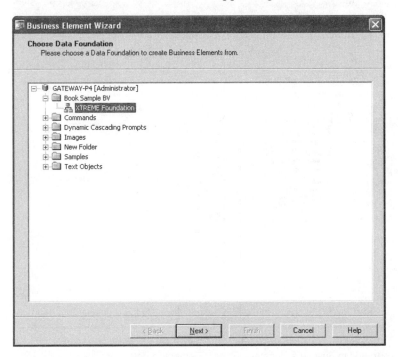

The Choose Data Foundation screen will simply show the folder structure of the repository. Navigate through the folder structure of this dialog box to find your desired Data Foundation object (only Data Foundations will appear when you open repository folders). If your repository contains a large number of foundations, you may use dialog box filters to narrow down the list of displayed connections. Right-click anywhere within the repository folder or object list and choose Advanced Filtering from the pop-up menu. The wizard will display text boxes where you may specify a combination of object name text or author. When you click the Apply button, only foundations that include the supplied text or author names will appear. If you wish to turn off any existing filters, simply right-click and click the Advanced Filtering option again. The complete list of foundations will reappear.

Once you've selected your desired Data Foundation, click Next. The Create Business Elements screen will appear within the wizard, as shown in Figure 16-10.

Click plus signs, as necessary, to expand the available tables, formulas, and SQL expression categories in the left From Data Foundation list. Select the items you'd like to add to the right Business Elements list. You can choose an individual field, formula, or SQL expression. You can also choose entire tables. You can even choose all tables by just clicking the Tables

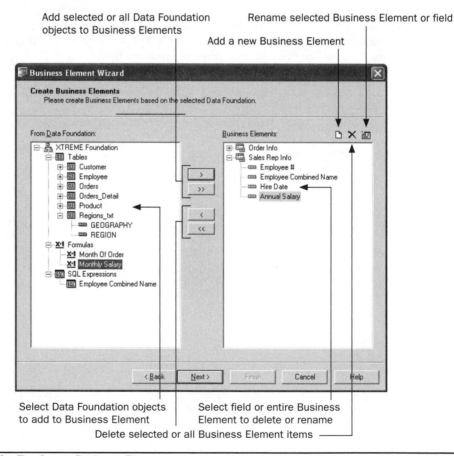

FIGURE 16-10   The Create Business Elements screen

category before you click the right arrow. You may CTRL-click or SHIFT-click to choose more than one object.

Click the right arrow to add the selected objects to the Business Elements list. You may also just double-click a desired field to add it (only fields can be double-clicked; tables cannot). The type of object you selected in the From Data Foundation list determines the type of object that appears in the Business Elements list. If you choose an entire table, the table will become a separate Business Element in the Business Elements list, with all its fields appearing underneath. If you choose one or more fields, they will simply be copied to the Business Elements list within the currently selected Business Element. If you click the Tables category and click the right arrow, or click the double-right arrow, all tables will be copied as individual Business Elements with their fields appearing underneath.

TIP *The order in which you see fields in the Business Elements list will be the same order fields appear in when you use the Business Element in a Business View, and eventually in Crystal Reports. As you can't reposition fields in a different order in the Business Elements list, ensure you place them into this list in the correct order if you have a preference. In Crystal Reports, you have the choice of viewing Field Explorer fields in the order they appear in the Business View, or in alphabetical order.*

Once you've created Business Elements and fields in the Business Elements list, you may use the left arrows or the Delete button above the Business Elements list to remove either entire Business Elements or individual fields. Just select the Business Elements or fields (you can SHIFT-click and CTRL-click in this list, too) that you wish to delete and click the left arrow or Delete button to remove them.

If you prefer to manually create an entire Business Element, just click the New Business Element toolbar above the Business Elements list. A new Business Element with an automatically generated name will be added to the Business Elements list. Select it and then add individual fields from the From Data Foundation list.

To rename either entire Business Elements or individual fields, select the desired Business Element or field in the Business Elements list. Then, click the Rename button. The Business Element or field name will be placed into edit mode. Simply type in a new name and click outside the object. The selected object will take on the new name (you'll be given an error if you attempt to assign a name that already exists).

Once you've designed your Business Elements and added and renamed all pertinent fields, click Next. The wizard will display the Save To Repository screen, showing the folder structure of the repository (this screen is similar to the Repository Explorer, discussed later in the chapter). Navigate through the folder structure to see any existing Business Elements already in the repository (only Business Elements will appear when you open repository folders). If your repository contains a large number of elements, you may use dialog box filters to narrow down the list of displayed elements. Right-click anywhere within the repository folder or object list and choose Advanced Filtering from the pop-up menu. The wizard will display text boxes where you may specify a combination of object name text or author. When you click the Apply button, only elements that include the supplied text or author names will appear. If you wish to turn off any existing filters, simply right-click and click the Advanced Filtering option again. The complete list of elements will reappear.

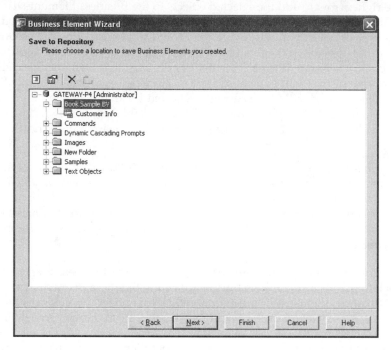

If you want to create a new repository folder to place the Business Elements in, click the New Folder button above the repository list. Or, select an existing folder to place all your new Business Elements in (you cannot save multiple Business Elements in different folders here). Click Finish to save the Business Elements, or Next to be given a choice of options after the elements have been saved.

If you click Next, the wizard will display the What To Do Next screen, giving you four choices. Select the desired choice and click Finish.

- **Create a Business View**   Saves the Business Elements and immediately creates a new Business View containing the newly created Business Elements.

- **Create More Business Elements**   Saves the Business Elements and returns to the Choose Data Foundation screen at the start of the wizard to repeat the Business Element creation process.

- **Edit the Created Business Elements**   Saves the Business Elements and returns you to the Business View Manager where all the just-created Business Elements will be open for manual editing.

- **Exit**   Saves the Business Elements and returns you to the Business View Manager in the same state it was when you initially started the wizard.

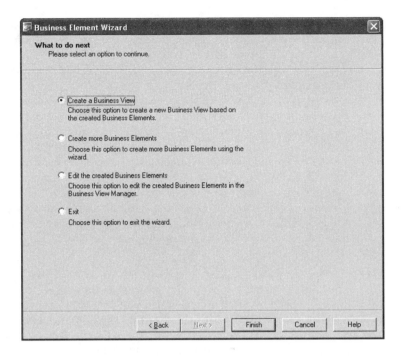

CAUTION *It's advisable to examine existing Business Elements in the repository before you save a large number of Business Elements from the wizard, in case any existing elements have the same name as elements the wizard will try to save. The wizard will save elements until it encounters a duplicate name. It will then present an error message. However, if you click the Back button and delete or rename the offending element, you may receive additional errors if you try to save again. This is because the first set of elements that didn't have duplicate names may have been saved the first time.*

Row and Column Security

As with Data Foundations, you can set row and column security settings at the Business Element level. Steps are the same as they are for Data Foundations: creating filters and applying them to Crystal Reports Server/BusinessObjects Enterprise users or user groups, and selecting individual fields and setting rights for them by user or group.

The difference between setting row and column security at the Business Element level and the Data Foundation level is that Data Foundation row and column security affects all Business Elements based on the foundation, whereas security set at the Business Element level affects only that particular Business Element. One important issue to remember is that you can't turn off existing row and column security supplied by the Data Foundation in the Business Element. For example, even if you apply a "Full Data Access" filter to the Everyone group within the Business Element (you'll need to copy the Full Data Access filter to the Business Element from the Referenced Data Foundation window), any more restrictive filters applied at the Data Foundation level will still apply to the Business Element. Also, setting a View right for a field in a Business Element will not give access to that field if it has been restricted at the Data Foundation level. However, you can create *additional* row and column security at the Business Element level that is not provided at the Data Foundation level.

Steps to creating row and column security by way of filters and field rights is the same with Business Elements as it is with Data Foundations. Look in the Data Foundations section under "Row and Column Security" for information on the process.

Continuing the discussion of the XTREME sample Business View discussed throughout the chapter, several Business Elements are created containing a limited set of relevant data from the XTREME Data Foundation. In particular, XTREME Customer Info, XTREME Order Info, and XTREME Sales Rep Info Business Elements are created. Relevant fields and formulas are added to these Business Elements, being renamed as appropriate. Existing row and column security from the Data Foundation will be used, propagating the order date range filter and salary column security to the Business Element. However, because of the way Business Views applies multiple filters at the Data Foundation level, the row security setting limiting the Western Region Sales manager to the Northwest and Southwest may need to be moved from the Data Foundation to this Business Element.

Business View

The ultimate goal of the entire Business View design process is the actual Business View object itself. This is the only object that will appear when you connect to the repository with Crystal Reports. This object is what exposes the set of virtual tables to the report designer, including all row and column security, renamed fields, and so forth. Because you add existing Business Elements to a Business View, you'll need to make sure you've created one or more Business Elements before attempting to create the Business View.

To create a new Business View, choose the Business View icon from the welcome screen when starting the Business View Manager or clicking the New toolbar button, or choose File | New from the pull-down menus, choosing the Business View submenu item. The Insert Business Elements dialog box will appear after a new Business View is displayed in the Business View Manager, as illustrated in Figure 16-11.

The Insert Business Elements dialog box will simply show the folder structure of the repository. Navigate through the folder structure of this dialog box to find your desired Business Element objects (only Business Elements will appear when you open repository folders). If your repository contains a large number of elements, you may use dialog box filters to narrow down the list of displayed connections. Right-click anywhere within the repository folder or object list and choose Advanced Filtering from the pop-up menu. The dialog box will display text boxes where you may specify a combination of object name text or author. When you click the Apply button, only elements that include the supplied text or author names will appear. If you wish to turn off any existing filters, simply right-click and click the Advanced Filtering option again. The complete list of elements will reappear.

Select Business Elements that you want to appear as tables within your Business View. You may just double-click a Business Element to add it to the Business View, or select the element and click the Add button. Business Elements will be added to the Business View window in the Business View Manager (you may need to move the Insert Business Elements dialog box to see them). Once you've finished adding desired Business Elements, close the Insert Business Elements dialog box.

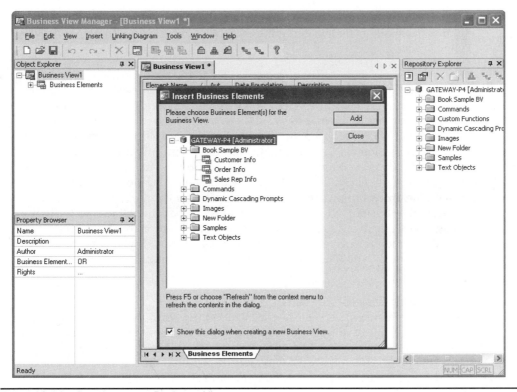

FIGURE 16-11   Creating a new Business View

There are very few properties in the Property Browser that you can change when editing a Business View. If you click the Business View name at the top of the Object Explorer, the following properties will appear in the Property Browser:

- **Name**   Type the descriptive name you wish this Business View to have when you save it to the repository.

- **Description**   Type an optional description to more fully explain the usage of this Business View.

- **Author**   Your CRS/BOE user ID is specified here by default. You may change this text to something else, if you choose.

- **Business Element Filter Combination**   This property allows two choices: AND and OR. Since individual Business Elements that make up the Business View can have their own filters, you may choose how to apply the filters together to get a final set of returned records. If you choose AND, a Boolean AND operator will be used when applying all the filters in the included Business Elements—a record will have to meet all the filter requirements to be returned. If you choose OR, a Boolean OR operator will be used and a record will only have to meet any one of the filter requirements to be returned.

- **Rights**   Click the ellipses to set rights for this Business View. Setting Business View rights is discussed in detail later in the chapter, under "Setting Rights for Business View Objects."

By default, the list of Business Elements you added to the Business View appears in the middle window of the Business View Manager. If you find that more detail on certain Business Elements might be handy to view, you may view individual field detail for a selected Business Element in the middle window as well. Just double-click the desired Business Element in the Object Explorer, or right-click the desired Business Element and choose Show Business Element Detail from the pop-up menu. An additional tab will be added to the middle Business View Manager window showing fields within the chosen Business Element. You can navigate among multiple tabs, including closing Business Element detail tabs, with the arrow buttons and X button at the bottom of the middle window.

As with any other Business View object, you'll most probably want to save the entire Business View object as you progress. Click the Save toolbar button, or choose File | Save from the pull-down menus to save the updated Data Foundation. If you have not saved the Business View previously, you'll be asked to confirm a name and folder location in the repository.

Inserting and Deleting Business Elements

Once an initial set of Business Elements has been added to your Business View, you may later decide to delete some existing Business Elements, or add new Business Elements from the repository. To delete an element, just select it in the Object Browser (you can't delete elements from the middle Business View window). Then, press the DEL key, right-click the element and choose Delete from the pop-up menu, or click the Delete toolbar button.

Inserting a new Business Element from the repository is equally simple. Choose Insert | Insert Business Elements from the pull-down menus, right-click the Business Elements category of the Object Browser and choose Insert Business Elements from the pop-up menu, or click the Insert Business Elements toolbar button. The Insert Business Elements dialog box will reappear. Choose additional elements to add to your Business View. You may also expand folders in the Repository Explorer and simply drag a Business Element from the repository to the middle Business Elements list. The element will be added to the Business View.

CAUTION   *A core requirement of Business Views is that all Business Elements added to a single Business View must be based on the same Data Foundation. If you attempt to add elements from different foundations, an error message will result. If you find that you need to add Business Elements to a single Business View that aren't based on the same Data Foundation, you'll need to edit the Data Foundation and Business Elements to add the additional data items. If this is not possible (due to "unlinkable" data, for example), you may want to consider creating Crystal Reports subreports based on the different Business Views.*

Overriding Data Foundation Linking

If you look closely at the Business View Manager menus while editing a Business View object, you may notice the Linking Diagram pull-down menu, as well as a few toolbar buttons that relate to table linking. However, you may also notice that the toolbar button and all options on the pull-down menu are dimmed.

If the Business View designer so desires, a Business View object can be set to override any table linking that is set in the underlying Data Foundation. This may be handy, for example, if you wish to create two separate Business Views based on the same Business Elements but change table linking within each Business View to return a different set of records.

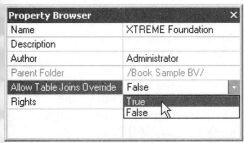

The first requirement to override Data Foundation Linking is to set the Allow Table Joins Override property to True in the Data Foundation itself. If necessary, edit the Data Foundation that the Business Elements are based on and change this property in the Property Browser. Then, save the updated Data Foundation to the repository.

When you reedit the Business View, you'll now notice that the Linking Diagram | Override Linking pull-down menu option is enabled. If you choose it, a Link Override window and tab will appear in the middle of the Business View Manager. When you display the Link Override window, you'll see the underlying tables that make up the Data Foundation the Business View is based on. All the remaining options on the Linking Diagram pull-down menu, as well as link-related toolbar button, will now be enabled.

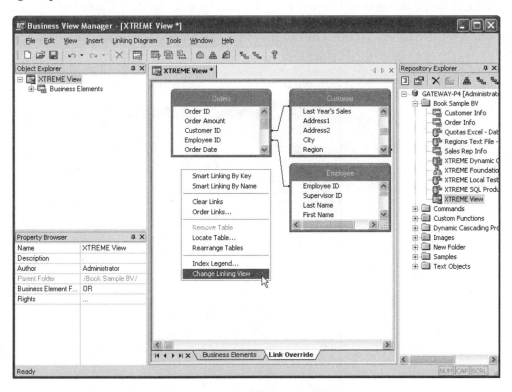

Use techniques described in the section "Data Foundation" of this chapter, as well as in Chapter 15 of this book, to change table linking for this Business View object. If you later decide you wish to return to table linking stored in the Data Foundation, simply choose Linking Diagram | Revert Linking from the pull-down menus. After a confirmation message, linking will revert to that stored in the underlying Data Foundation.

Using the Rights Test View

Since so many different forms of security (including row and column security) can apply to the Business View object, the Rights Test View dialog box can be used to check a variety of rights for chosen Crystal Reports Server/BusinessObjects Enterprise user IDs. The Rights Test View can show if the current Business View object is even able to be used by the user, and if so, what row and column security will be applied.

Display the Rights Test View dialog box by choosing Tools | Rights Test View from the pull-down menus, by right-clicking the Business View name in the Object Explorer and choosing Rights Test View from the pop-up menu, or by clicking the Rights Test View toolbar button. The Rights Test View dialog box will appear, as shown in Figure 16-12.

Select a Crystal Reports Server/BusinessObjects Enterprise User ID to test for rights. You may click the User Name drop-down list at the top of the dialog box and choose any user ID that has been used recently for a rights test. If the desired ID isn't in the list, click the Select User button. The Add User dialog box will appear showing all user IDs in Crystal Reports Server/BusinessObjects Enterprise. Use the dialog box to choose the desired user and then close the dialog box. The user ID will then appear in the User Name list.

The first indication will be whether or not the chosen user can even use the Business View. If not, the Business View Visible text will indicate False and nothing else will appear

FIGURE 16-12
Rights Test View dialog box

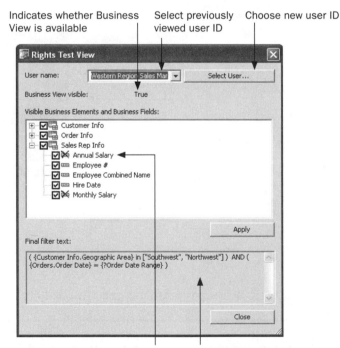

Indicates whether Business View is available

Select previously viewed user ID

Choose new user ID

"X" over field name indicates column security applied

Filter indicates row security applied

in the dialog box. If the Business View is visible for the user, a list of Business Elements will appear in the box, each displaying a plus sign. Click the plus sign to see individual fields within the Business Element.

If any column security is applied for this chosen user, you'll see red *X* indicators displayed next to field names that are unavailable to this user ID. Furthermore, row security will be indicated by the Final Filter Text displayed at the bottom of the dialog box. Because row security can be affected by different Business Elements and fields, you may redisplay any row security filters for a limited set of fields or Business Elements by unchecking the check boxes next to certain fields or Business Elements and clicking the Apply button. The updated row security filter (if any) based on just the checked fields and elements will appear in the Final Filter Text area.

When finished, simply close the Rights Test View dialog box. Wrapping up the XTREME sample Business View, then, simply consists of adding the three previously created XTREME Business Elements into the single Business View object and saving it to the repository. The XTREME Business View is now ready to be used with Crystal Reports.

Creating Business View-Based Pick Lists

One of the exciting new features of Crystal Reports XI and Crystal Reports Server/ BusinessObjects Enterprise XI is dynamic and cascading pick lists. A *dynamic pick list,* when used in conjunction with report-based and Business View–based parameter fields, allows a drop-down list of available parameter field values to be populated from the database in real time. An extension of a dynamic pick list is a *cascading pick list,* which allows a relationship to be set up among multiple pick lists where one pick list restricts the next. For example, a Sales Rep pick list may query the database in real time to gather the current set of employed sales reps. When a specific sales rep is chosen in the first pick list, the second Order Number pick list will query the database in real time for current order numbers but will only show order numbers that belong to the sales rep chosen in the first pick list.

In previous Crystal versions, only *static pick lists* were available (pick lists that contained a fixed set of sample values that were not derived from the database in real time). While static pick lists remain as an option in version XI, dynamic and cascading pick lists are a long sought-after feature that greatly increases flexibility of Crystal Reports and its associated enterprise products.

While Crystal Reports XI can create reports that contain individual dynamic and cascading pick lists and use those reports outside of Crystal Reports Server/BusinessObjects Enterprise, reports published to CRS/BOE *must* make use of pick lists contained in the CRS/BOE repository. This is an important concept to keep in mind when planning a CRS/BOE implementation, as you'll want to coordinate pick list creation to avoid duplicate efforts and uncoordinated creation of excessive pick lists in the repository.

NOTE *Business Objects documentation refers to various portions of dynamic and cascading pick lists as "Lists of Values" (the actual values retrieved from the database that appear in the drop-down list) and "Prompt Groups" (the series of one or more drop-down boxes that make up a dynamic or cascading pick list). However, this book refers to these items more generically as pick lists, an industry-standard term for drop-down lists that a report viewer can choose from.*

There are two general ways of creating dynamic/cascading pick lists in CRS/BOE. First, if you publish a report to CRS/BOE that contains dynamic or cascading pick lists that were created in the report before it was published, the pick lists will automatically be converted to Business View–based pick lists. Or, you may create dynamic or cascading pick lists directly in the Business View Manager and then use them in existing or new reports (you may even use Business View–based pick lists in reports that will not be published to CRS/BOE).

Publishing Crystal Reports with Pick Lists

The first way of creating dynamic/cascading pick lists in CRS/BOE is to publish an existing pick list–based Crystal Reports XI report not currently contained in CRS/BOE (referred to in Crystal documentation as an "unmanaged" report) to the Central Management Server. Because of the requirement for any report stored in CRS/BOE (referred to in Crystal documentation as a "managed" report) to use dynamic/cascading pick lists based on Business Views, publishing a report will automatically create necessary pick list objects in the repository when the report is created.

Consider a report that contains a cascading pick list consisting of a sales rep/order number combination described earlier in this book section. In this particular scenario, the cascading pick list consists of two different drop-down lists (what Business Objects refers to as a "List of Values"), combined together to populate one parameter field (the two related drop-down lists are combined in what Business Objects refers to as a "Prompt Group"). The sales rep pick list consists of the Employee ID field as the actual value, with the Employee Last Name selected as the description. The order number pick list is based on the Order ID field and accepts multiple values. The cascading pick list's data is provided by a SQL Command that returns sales rep/order number combinations only for orders placed in 2004.

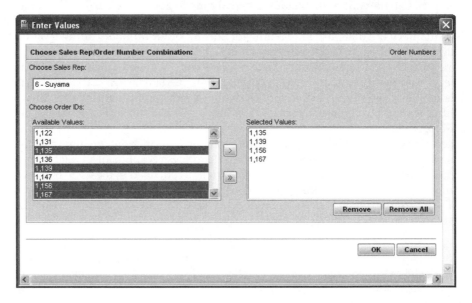

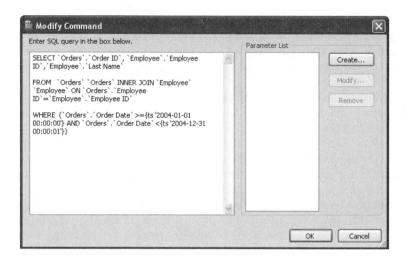

NOTE *Complete details on creating dynamic/cascading pick lists with Crystal Reports parameter fields are discussed in Chapter 13.*

When this report is published to Crystal Reports Server/BusinessObjects Enterprise (various methods of publishing reports are discussed in Part II of this book), several new Business View objects appear in the Dynamic Cascading Prompts folder in the repository. Icons next to the items are indicative of the type of object represented. Also, Crystal Reports will use short abbreviations to indicate what types of objects are created (DF for Data Foundation, BE for Business Element, and so forth). You may explore them in the Business View Manager.

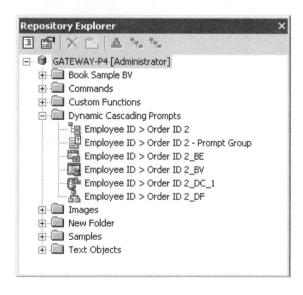

You'll notice components that are discussed earlier in this chapter: a Data Connection, a Data Foundation, a Business Element, and a Business View. These items are all required to supply a data source for the pick lists. You'll also notice two additional components not yet discussed: a List of Values and a Prompt Group (definitions for these types of objects are discussed earlier in this section).

The Data Connection consists of the same data source as the report that was published (ODBC connection, OLE DB connection, and so forth). The Data Foundation mirrors the tables and joins that exist in the report. The Business Element includes fields that were used in the original SQL Command that populated the pick list in the original report. And, the Business View simply contains the Business Element that populates the pick list.

The two additional components determine the actual data that appears in the drop-down lists (the List of Values component) and the way the drop-down lists appear (the Prompt Group component). You may view or edit the objects the same way you do any other Business View items from the repository (double-clicking them in the Repository Explorer is one way). The List of Values exhibits the "cascading" nature of the pick list, exposing the Employee ID field first, followed by the Order ID field. And, the Prompt Group specifies the prompting text, adds the Last Name description to the Employee ID, and designates the Order ID as accepting multiple values.

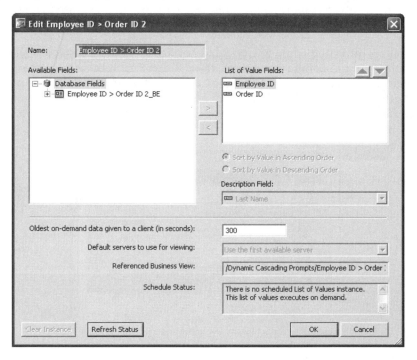

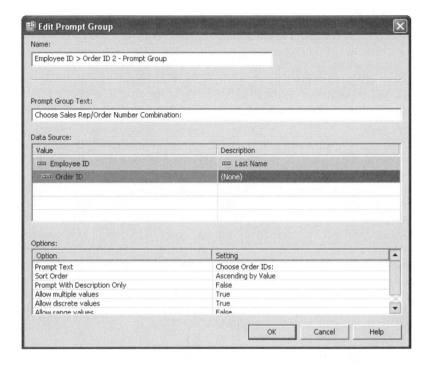

If you later edit the report from within CRS/BOE, you'll notice that parameter fields that make use of dynamic/cascading pick lists have been slightly modified to make use of the repository, rather than database tables/SQL commands that the report is based on.

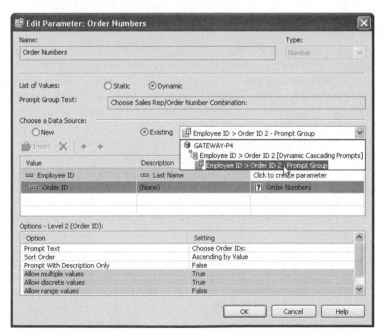

While this method of creating Business View–based pick lists may be preferable (you may be more familiar with Crystal Reports than with the Business View manager, for example), there are several issues to be familiar with:

- You may not have proper rights in the CRS/BOE system to create the various components that make up the pick list. In this case, you'll receive errors when you attempt to publish the report to CRS/BOE and the pick lists won't be created.

- An unchecked number of report designers publishing myriad reports to CRS/BOE may result in a large number of pick list objects in the Dynamic Cascading Prompts folder of the repository. While Crystal Reports will look for existing pick lists in the repository that exactly match that of reports being published (and will just connect to the existing lists rather than creating new ones), even a slight difference from an existing list will cause a large number of new Business View objects to be created for the new report.

If you are planning on allowing publication of reports containing dynamic/cascading pick lists, you may wish to carefully coordinate procedures to ensure minimal pick list duplication. You may also want to consider creating pick lists in the Business View Manager and instructing report designers to use existing lists, rather than creating new ones (creating pick lists in the Business View Manager is discussed next and using existing repository pick lists in reports is discussed later in the chapter).

Creating Pick Lists in the Business View Manager

Another way of making Business View–based dynamic/cascading pick lists available to report designers is to create them directly in the repository using the Business View Manager (dynamic/cascading pick lists in the repository can be used by reports not published to CRS/BOE, and *must* be used by reports published to CRS/BOE). Once these have been created in the Business View Manager, they are available to everyone who can connect to the CRS/BOE system.

Because CRS/BOE-based pick lists use Business Views as their source of data, you must first have available a completed Business View component before you create the pick list. If you don't have a suitable Business View available, perform steps described earlier in the chapter to create all necessary Business View pieces. The Business View object itself is what's used to populate a pick list, so you must create all necessary Business View elements, including the Business View object itself.

While there are two components in the repository that make up a dynamic/cascading pick list (the List of Values and the Prompt Group), only the List of Values can be created directly in the Business View Manager. Prompt Groups are created when you make use of a dynamic/cascading pick list when creating a parameter field in a Data Foundation or Business Element, or in Crystal Reports.

To create a new List of Values, choose the List Of Values icon from the welcome screen when starting the Business View Manager or clicking the New toolbar button, or choose File | New from the pull-down menus, choosing the List Of Values submenu item. The Select Business View dialog box will appear. Navigate through various repository folders until you find the desired Business View (only Business View objects will appear in the dialog box). Once you've made the choice, the Create List Of Values dialog box will appear, as illustrated in Figure 16-13.

Choose from Business View fields   Supply List of Values name

Multiple fields will create cascading hierarchy

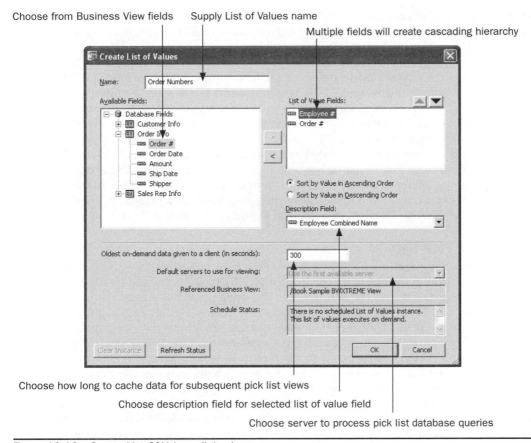

Choose how long to cache data for subsequent pick list views

Choose description field for selected list of value field

Choose server to process pick list database queries

FIGURE 16-13   Create List Of Values dialog box

Begin by navigating through the available Business Elements in the Available Fields list. Select the desired field in the list and click the right arrow to add the field to the List of Values fields list on the right of the dialog box. You may add more than one field if you would like multiple fields to act as pick list data sources (when you create a parameter field, you may choose just one field to act as the pick list—you needn't use all fields). However, if you want to use the fields for a cascading pick list, you must add fields in the order of the "cascade" (for example, you'll add the Employee # field first, followed by the Order # field if you want to display a cascading pick list that limits order numbers to those taken by the chosen employee).

If you want to add a description field (perhaps a text field that matches a numeric field that you added to the List of Value Fields list), select the field to match the description within the List of Value Fields list. Then, choose the matching description field from the Description Field drop-down list. You may also choose to sort the pick list in ascending or descending order by making the appropriate radio button choice.

You may also make one or two choices toward the bottom of the dialog box. While the 300-second setting for Oldest On-Demand Data is typically adequate, you may want to change it to a higher or lower number, depending on how "fluid" the database is that the pick list is based on and on how long a database query to fill the pick list may run. The first time this pick list is used, the database will be queried and the values from the database will be stored in memory on the CRS/BOE system. Any subsequent requests for the same pick list within the time period specified here will be supplied from memory, rather than being re-queried from the database. If your system administrator has configured more than one server system to process pick list queries, you will be able to choose from various servers in the Default Servers drop-down list (although most often you'll probably want to just leave the First Server option chosen).

When you've completed the Create List Of Values dialog box, click OK to save the list of values. The Select A Folder dialog box will appear. Select an existing folder or create and then select a new folder to store the List of Values in. The pick list will be stored in the repository. You may now use the pick list with a parameter field created in another Data Foundation or Business Element, or in Crystal Reports (described later in the chapter).

Scheduling Pick Lists

Another advantage of using CRS/BOE-based pick lists, instead of those based solely on report data sources, is the ability to schedule the pick lists to be populated by a batch process at regular intervals. This may be handy when you design pick lists against large database tables. These pick lists may return large numbers of values, or they may require a large, slow query to run on the database server every time a pick list needs to be populated in real time. This can increase the workload on the database server, as well as slowing pick list generation for report viewers when they run reports based on dynamic/cascading pick lists.

By scheduling a pick list to be populated during a batch process, the slow query can run, perhaps, during off-hours when the database will not be as heavily impacted. The values in the pick list are stored in the CRS/BOE system and displayed in the pick lists much faster than if the underlying query is run every time a pick list is displayed. This both reduces database load and increases response time for report viewers. Furthermore, the Business View Manager allows pick lists to be *partially scheduled*. For example, if you wish the Sales Rep portion of a cascading pick list to be refreshed with a nightly database query, with the Order Number portion of the cascade always running in real time, you may make this choice when you schedule.

TIP *Scheduling of pick lists obviously reduces the real-time availability of pick list values. When scheduling pick lists, choose a schedule interval that will not unduly burden the database but will still provide a reasonably "fresh" set of values from the database.*

To schedule a pick list, select it in the Repository Explorer within the Business View Manager. Choose Schedule List Of Values from the pop-up menu. If the pick list contains multiple fields (perhaps it has been designed to support a cascading pick list), you may specify how many levels in the pick list to schedule. For example, in the previously described scenario, you can choose to schedule only the Sales Rep portion of the pick list, or both the Sales Rep and Order Number portions. Once you've made this choice (and you won't be presented it if the pick list consists of a single field), the Schedule dialog box will appear.

PART I

Use this dialog box to choose how often to refresh (or schedule) the values for the pick list. Various scheduling intervals will appear in the Run Report drop-down list. Based on the selection you make in this drop-down, the rest of the dialog box will change, allowing you to specify, for example, the number of days to separate schedules, and the time to run the refresh. If this pick list is based on a Business View that requires database logon credentials to be supplied (the Always Prompt property is set to True in the pick list Business View's underlying Data Connection), then click the Database Logon button and supply valid database credentials to use when refreshing the pick list. And, if the pick list's Business View is based on a parameterized Data Foundation or Business Element, click the Parameter Values button to supply desired parameter values. Once you've made desired choices, click OK to schedule the pick list refresh process.

NOTE *Unlike other scheduling options discussed in Part II of this book, pick lists will only retain a single "instance" from the last schedule. Any time a new pick list refresh runs, the previous pick list is discarded.*

The pick list will be added to the Central Management Server's schedule to be run at the desired interval. When the pick list is used in a parameter field, values from the last scheduled refresh will appear in the drop-down list, rather than values queried from the database in real time. To check the status of the scheduled pick list (or, to stop the schedule and return to a real-time pick list), edit the List of Values object in the Business View Manager. The status of the latest schedule (success or failure) will appear in the Schedule Status box. Clicking the

Refresh Status button will update this box. To clear the schedule and return the pick list to run in real time, click the Clear Instance button.

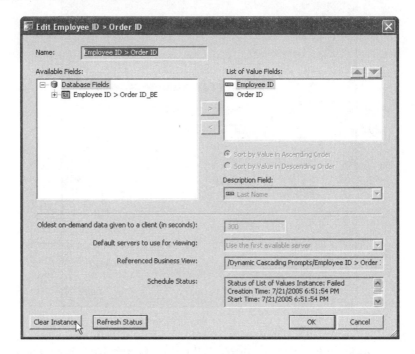

Navigating and Maintaining Business Views

As you can probably deduce from reading previous sections of this chapter, there are many different components that go into making use of CRS/BOE Business Views. Several tools exist in the Business View Manager to help you navigate through, and ensure the integrity of, all these components. Once you've created various Business View components, such as various pieces of the Business View process, List of Values objects, and so forth, you'll probably find the need to ensure that deleting one object won't affect other objects that you wish to retain. And, you may want to copy some or all of your Business View components to an external file (for backup purposes, or to transfer to another CRS/BOE system). Various other objects besides Business Views (such as text objects, bitmap images, custom functions, and SQL Commands) are also contained in the Crystal Reports Server/BusinessObjects Enterprise repository. You may encounter a need to manage them with the Business View Manager as well.

Object Integrity and References

Because of the hierarchical nature of Business Views (as discussed elsewhere in the chapter, Business View objects are dependent on Business Elements, Business Elements are based on Data Foundations, and so forth), there is a very real possibility that changes you make to one object will affect another object (perhaps catastrophically). For example, if you base a series of Business Elements and Business Views on a certain set of tables and fields in a Data Foundation, and then remove them from the Data Foundation, the dependent Business Elements and Business Views will cease to work properly.

There are three different options available throughout the Business View Manager to check for these possibilities: Show Dependent Objects, Show Referenced Objects, and Check Dependent Integrity. Show Dependent Objects and Show Referenced Objects are always available, while Check Dependent Integrity is available for every object type except a Business View, List of Values, and Prompt Group. The choices are available from the Tools pull down menu, as well as via toolbar buttons.

TIP *You can also make use of these options from within the Repository Explorer. Select the desired object within the repository and click the appropriate toolbar button. More information on the Repository Explorer appears later in this chapter.*

Showing Dependent and Referenced Objects

Dependent objects are those that depend on the current object you have selected or are editing. For example, if you are editing a Data Connection, virtually every object "above" the connection in the Business View hierarchy (Dynamic Data Connections, Data Foundations, Business Elements, and Business Views) relies on it. Conversely, referenced objects are objects that the object you have selected or are editing references in one form or another. For example, if you have selected a Business View in the Repository Explorer, at least one Business Element, Data Foundation, and Data Connection (perhaps more) will be referenced by it.

 To show dependent objects for a selected object, choose the Show Dependent Objects menu option or toolbar button. The Dependent Objects dialog box will appear, showing the hierarchy of dependent objects. Click plus signs to see the different objects within the repository that depend on the object you originally selected.

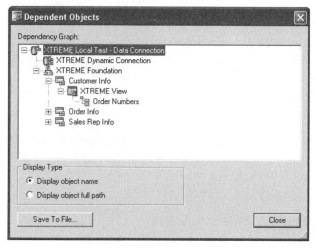

 To show referenced objects for a selected object, choose the Show Referenced Objects menu option under the Tools menu or toolbar button. The Referenced Objects dialog box will appear, showing the hierarchy of referenced objects. Click plus signs to see the different objects within the repository that are referenced by the object you originally selected.

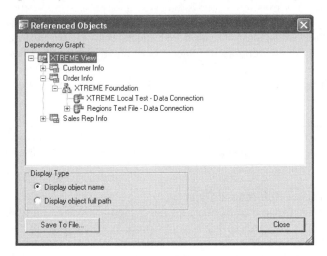

Checking Dependent Integrity

While the steps just described will show you a list of dependent or referenced objects, they don't necessarily indicate that all objects that depend on, or are referenced by, each other are actually "whole." The situation described previously where Business Elements and Business Views may reference fields or tables that have been removed from an underlying Data Foundation is an example that won't be exposed by just showing references or dependencies. To avoid this situation, you need to check to see that all the tables, fields, and other internal elements that are passed back and forth among different Business Views objects are contained in all objects.

To check dependent integrity for a selected object, choose the Check Dependent Integrity menu option or toolbar button. The various dependent objects will be checked to ensure that all referenced fields and tables are accounted for. If no problems are found, a message will so indicate. If, however, tables or fields are missing that are expected in other objects, a dialog box indicating the problem will appear.

CAUTION   *The Check Dependent Integrity feature will not detect a mismatch between a Data Connection and other objects further up the Business View hierarchy. If you encounter data errors in other Business View objects, ensure that the Data Connection that the objects are based on is properly returning the required tables and fields.*

Exporting and Importing Business Views

Once you have gone about the steps of creating the individual objects that make up your Business Views, you may wish to export them for use in another CRS/BOE system (perhaps you have test and production systems), or export them to keep as an extra backup. The Business View Manager allows entire Business View object hierarchies to be exported to XML format and re-imported later.

To export an existing Business View, choose Tools | Export from the pull-down menus. The Export dialog box will appear. The Select Business Views To Export box on the left side of the dialog shows the repository folder structure. Navigate through the folder structure of this dialog box to find your desired Business View objects (Business Views, Lists of Values, Prompt Groups, and Crystal Reports repository objects will appear when you open repository folders). If your repository contains a large number of Business Views, you may use dialog box filters to narrow down the list of displayed Business Views. Right-click anywhere within the repository folder or object list and choose Advanced Filtering from the pop-up menu. The dialog box will display text boxes where you may specify a combination of object name text or author. When you click the Apply button, only Business Views that include the supplied text or author names will appear. If you wish to turn off any existing filters, simply right-click and click the Advanced Filtering option again. The complete list of Business Views will reappear.

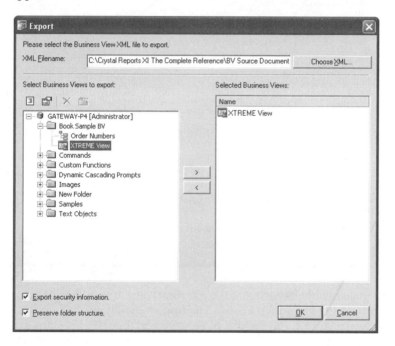

As you can export more than one Business View, select as many as you wish to export, clicking the right arrow after each. If you determine that you've added Business Views that you don't want to export, select the desired Business View in the Selected Business View list and click the left arrow.

Type an XML path and filename to store the exported Business Views in the XML Filename box at the top of the dialog. If you prefer to navigate to a particular folder, click the Choose XML button. Check the Export Security Information check box at the lower left of the dialog to export any row and column security settings and object rights along with the Business View objects (for safety, any embedded Data Connection passwords are not exported). And, checking the Preserve Folder Structure check box will export folder information from the repository along with Business View Objects.

Click OK when you are ready to export the selected Business Views. A message will appear once the export is complete. Examining the exported XML file illustrates the way Business View objects are stored in the repository.

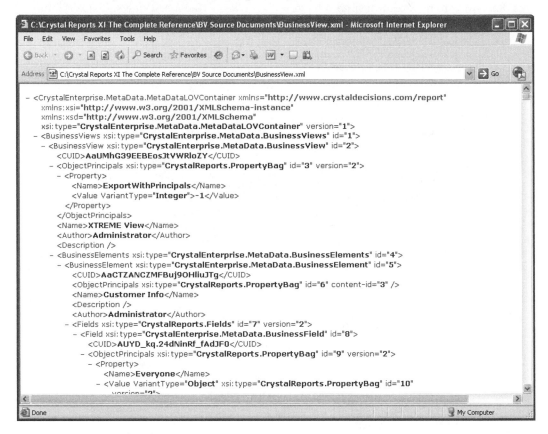

Importing Business Views back into the repository is similarly straightforward. Choose Tools | Import from the pull-down menus. The Import dialog box will appear, showing the repository folder structure in the middle. Note that even though plus signs exist, you will only see subfolders if you click them—no actual existing Business View objects will appear. Click the folder you want to import the Business Views into, or click the New Folder button to create a new folder.

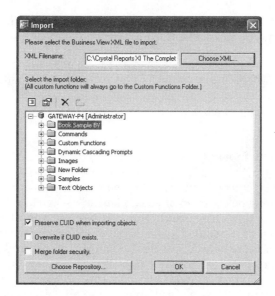

Type the source XML path and filename containing the Business Views you want to import in the XML Filename text box. If you'd prefer to navigate to the file, click the Choose XML button. Check the Preserve CUID When Importing Objects check box at the bottom of the dialog to use the same Crystal Reports Server/BusinessObjects Enterprise unique identifier numbers used when the Business Views were exported. This is important if you are planning on using existing Crystal Reports with the imported Business Views, as the Business View unique identifiers are stored with the reports. The Overwrite If CUID Exists option will overwrite any existing Business View objects with the same unique ID. And, checking the Merge Folder Security option will combine folder security settings between the folders that the original Business Views were in and the destination folder you choose to import the objects (if there is a conflict between settings, the settings already existing in the destination folder in the repository will take precedence).

Finally, if you need to import the Business Views into a different Crystal Reports Server/BusinessObjects Enterprise system than you logged on to when you first started the Business View Manager, click the Choose Repository button. A new Crystal Reports Server/BusinessObjects Enterprise logon dialog will appear, where you can choose a different Central Management Server, user ID, password, and authentication type. Once you've specified all necessary information, click OK.

TIP *Exporting is not limited to Business Views objects. Other Crystal Reports objects stored in the repository (such as bitmaps, text objects, and so forth) can be exported and imported using these steps.*

Using the Repository Explorer

When you first start the Business View Manager, you'll initially see the Repository Explorer window appear on the right. As you continue to edit Business View objects with the Business View Manager, the Repository Explorer always appears (unless you shrink it with the push-pin button, or turn it off from the View menu). Also, when you are prompted to save an object to the repository, you'll see an embedded version of the Repository Explorer in the Save dialog box.

Because Business Views is such an integral part of Crystal Reports Server/BusinessObjects Enterprise and the repository, you'll find it helpful to understand how to make best use of the Repository Explorer. Also, because you can specify Business View object rights from the Repository Explorer, as well as when editing the object, it's helpful to know how to make these settings.

Navigating the Repository Explorer

Notice that the folder structure of the repository is exposed in the Repository Explorer: your CRS/BOE Central Management Server name appears at the top of the folder hierarchy, with top-level folders appearing below them. If you click the plus-sign next to a folder, it expands to show any subfolder or repository objects within it. Notice an additional folder labeled Custom Functions. This is the dedicated folder within the repository where all custom functions created in Crystal Reports are held. You'll also find a Dynamic Cascading Prompts folder dedicated to storing pick lists created when publishing Crystal Reports with dynamic/ cascading pick lists based on report fields.

Notice that, at least initially, you see all folders and all object types (even though not applicable to Business Views) in the repository. You may choose to apply a filter to limit objects shown, or choose options to limit the Repository Explorer to certain types of objects. To apply filters to limit the objects displayed in the explorer, click the Advanced Filtering toolbar button. You can also right-click anywhere within the repository folder or object list and choose Advanced Filtering from the pop-up menu. The Repository Explorer will display text boxes where you may specify a combination of object name text or author. When you click the Apply button, only repository objects that include the supplied text or author names will appear. If you wish to turn off any existing filters, simply click the Advanced Filtering toolbar button again, or right-click and click the Advanced Filtering option again. The complete list of objects will reappear.

You may also limit the types of repository objects that appear. For example, if you are working exclusively with Business Views for the time being, you may not wish to see text objects, bitmaps, or other Crystal Report–related objects in the Repository Explorer. To change view settings, click the Change View Settings toolbar button. You can also right-click anywhere within the repository folder or object list and choose Change View Settings from the pop-up menu. The View Settings dialog box will appear.

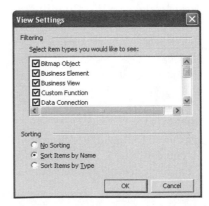

Uncheck repository object types that you prefer not to see. You may also choose how to sort objects in the Repository Explorer. Once you've made your choices, click OK. The Repository Explorer will reappear with your new settings taking effect.

There are additional options for working with the Repository Explorer. The first option you have is to delete objects or folders from the repository. Simply choose the desired object or folder and press DEL. Or, right-click the object or folder and choose Delete from the pop-up menu. You can also click the Delete toolbar button. If the object you attempt to delete is not referenced by any other objects, you'll see a simple confirmation request. However, if you attempt to delete a folder or a Business View object that is referenced elsewhere, you'll see a more elaborate dialog box indicating what else will be deleted if you proceed. Click Yes if you're sure you want to delete the objects.

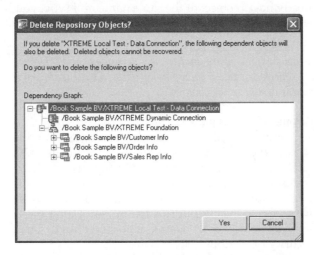

You may also desire to create a new folder within the repository to store Business View objects, or objects added from within Crystal Reports. You may either create a folder directly below the Central Management Server (known as a *top-level folder*), or a subfolder within a top-level folder. In fact, you can create subfolders in subfolders. The key is what you have selected in the Repository Explorer before you click the New Folder button. If you select the Central Management Server, you will create a top-level folder. If you select an existing top-level folder or a subfolder, you will create a subfolder within the selected folder.

Once you've selected the desired location for your new folder, right-click and choose New Folder from the pop-up menu. Or, click the New Folder toolbar button. A new folder will be created with the name "New Folder." You'll be placed into edit mode on the New Folder name—type the desired name for the new folder and click outside it to save the new name.

To rename an existing folder or object, select it. Then, simply hold your mouse button down for a few seconds until the object enters edit mode. You can also right-click an object and choose Rename from the pop-up menu. Or, select an object and press F2. The object will be placed into edit mode. Type a new name for the object (remembering that you can't use the same name as another object of the same type in the same folder) and click outside the object to save the new name.

And finally, you may choose to move or copy either individual repository objects, or entire repository folders, from one place to another in the Repository Explorer. Simply select the object or folder you want to move, hold your mouse button down, and drag it on top of another folder (or the Central Management Server itself to make it a "top-level" folder or object). If you wish to copy an object rather than move it, hold the CTRL key down when you drag. Once you drop the object in its new location, the Repository Explorer will show the new organization immediately. Note that if you attempt to move or copy a folder or object to a location that already has an object of the same name and type, you'll either receive an error message, or be warned that the move or copy will overwrite the existing object.

NOTE *The last three toolbar buttons are used to view dependent and referenced Business View objects, as well as to check dependent integrity for the selected Business View object. Discussions of these options appear earlier in the chapter.*

Setting Rights for Business View Objects

Although this chapter has already discussed applying row and column security via field and filter rights, you also have the ability to specify rights at the Business View object level. For example, you may prefer that only a limited set of Crystal Reports Server/BusinessObjects Enterprise users or groups see a Business View when opening Crystal Reports. Or, perhaps you want to allow several members of your organization to design Business Views, but only the HR group to have access to the HR Information System Data Connections. By setting rights for the Business View object or the Data Connection object, you can control who can see, modify, or set security for various objects.

Not only can you set rights at the object level, but also at the folder and Central Management Server levels. When you set rights at a higher level, they are automatically inherited at lower levels. For example, you may set a certain set of rights at a Business Views folder level to have them "trickle down" to any Business View objects within the folder. This inheritance model (at least in theory) can simplify your administrative tasks by reducing the amount of rights setting that you have to accomplish throughout the repository.

You can set rights on Business View objects in two places within the Business View Manager:

1. When editing a Business View object, by selecting the object name in the Object Explorer and clicking the ellipses button next to the Rights property in the Property Browser.

2. By clicking the object in the Repository Explorer, right-clicking, and choosing Edit Rights from the pop-up menu.

Once you've made this choice, the Edit Rights dialog box will appear, as illustrated in Figure 16-14.

Type in group or user name and
click button to find group or user

Displays list of CRS/BOE groups
or users to add to rights list

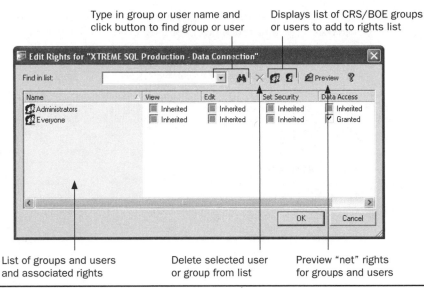

List of groups and users
and associated rights

Delete selected user
or group from list

Preview "net" rights
for groups and users

FIGURE 16-14   The Edit Rights dialog box

You'll see a list of Crystal Reports Server/BusinessObjects Enterprise groups and users and their existing set of rights (initially, you'll see just the Administrators and Everyone group here). Note that, depending on the type of object, three or four different rights can be set for each user or group:

- **View**   The ability to use the object within a Business View
- **Edit**   The ability to modify and delete the object
- **Set Security**   The ability to change repository security settings for the object using this dialog box
- **Data Access**   The ability to view the set of data coming from this data source

Further, if you cycle through the available options for each right by clicking the check box, you'll notice that a right can be granted, denied, or inherited. *Granting* the right explicitly gives that right to the chosen group or user. *Denying* the right explicitly takes the right away from the chosen group or user. And, allowing the right to be *inherited* will grant or deny the right based on higher-level security settings.

If you wish to specifically grant or deny rights to additional groups or users, you'll need to add the group or user to the list by clicking the Add Groups or Add Users button in the Edit Rights dialog box toolbar. These buttons will display an additional Add Groups or Add User dialog box showing all Crystal Reports Server/BusinessObjects Enterprise groups or users (to actually create additional CRS/BOE groups or users, you must use other CRS/BOE

administrative tools, such as the Central Management Console—you can't add these here).
Use this dialog box to choose an additional group or user to add to the Edit Rights dialog box.

Filter the list of groups or
users based on criteria

Clear any filter to show
all users or groups

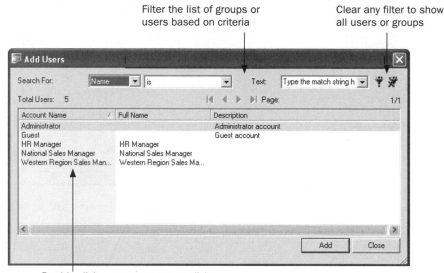

Double-click a group or user or click
Add to add it to the Edit Rights dialog

Once the additional groups or users you've added appear in the Edit Rights dialog box,
you can grant or deny rights to that group or user by clicking the appropriate check boxes.
If you wish to remove a group or user that you previously set rights for, simply select the
user or group and click the Delete button in the toolbar.

Because of inheritance from upper-level folders, you may ultimately not assign the set
of rights you expect. To understand what rights are ultimately given, you may want to see
the set of "net" rights, which take inheritance into account. Do this by clicking the Preview
button in the toolbar. The list of users and groups will change, showing the actual combination
of rights that result from explicit settings and inheritance. If you need to change any rights,
click the Preview button again to return the list to its "editable" state.

Once you've set rights for all necessary groups and users, just click OK to close the Edit
Rights dialog box. If you are editing a Business View object, you should save the object to
ensure that the new rights settings are saved to the repository. Click the Save toolbar button
or choose File | Save from the Business View Manager pull-down menus.

NOTE *A more thorough discussion of repository rights, including the rules of inheritance, can be
found in Chapter 17.*

Using Business Views with Crystal Reports

Once you've created your Business Views, you will probably want to test them in Crystal Reports itself (or, perhaps you are not charged with actually creating Business Views, but just need to use them in report design). Basing a report on a Business View is essentially the same as basing it on a regular database or SQL Command.

When you initially create a new report, you'll find Business Views in the Repository category of the Database Expert. When you click the plus sign next to the category, you'll be prompted to log on to Crystal Reports Server/BusinessObjects Enterprise. Provide valid logon credentials to connect to the repository. The BusinessObjects Enterprise Explorer dialog will appear showing the repository folder structure. Click plus signs next to folders to look for any Business Views (you'll also see SQL Commands inside folders). Once you've found the desired Business View, double-click it or select it and click Open.

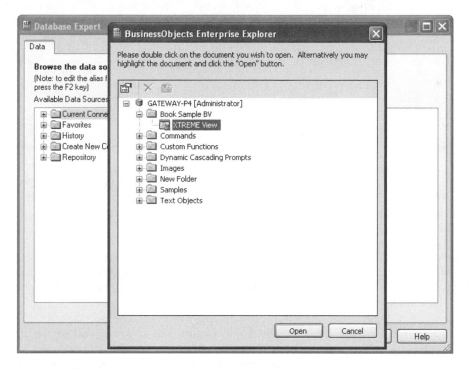

The Database Expert will show the Business View in the Available Data Source box on the left side. Clicking the plus sign next to it will reveal the Business Elements or "tables" included in the Business View. As with other database choices, select one or more of the Business Elements and add them to the Selected Tables list on the right. When finished adding Business View tables, click OK to close the Database Expert.

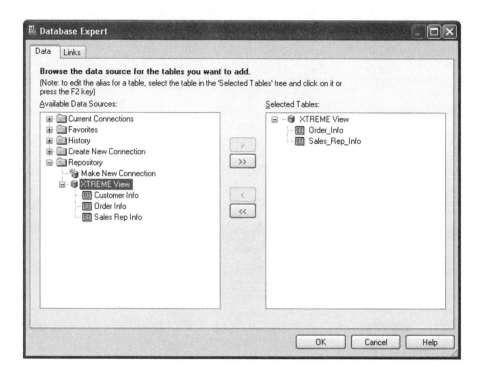

NOTE *Even though you will see the individual tables in the Links tab in the Database Expert after adding multiple Business View tables, you won't be able to actually link the tables together. You'll see link lines drawn between the table names, not particular field names. Linking is handled automatically within the Business View.*

When the Field Explorer is displayed, you'll notice that the Business View tables you chose will appear just like a regular database table. Clicking plus signs next to the tables will reveal the fields from within the Business View. Drag and drop them to the report just like regular database fields.

Even though the Business View may already apply filters or row security, you may still create your own record selection using the Select Expert, just as you would with a regular database connection. Most other report design capabilities also exist with Business Views, such as formatting and formula creation (you may not be able to create SQL Expressions, however).

CAUTION Crystal Reports presents two important Business View limitations that you should be aware of. First, you cannot mix any other data sources in a report that's based on a Business View. Attempting to add any additional data sources to a Business View–based report will result in an error message. Second, once you base a report on a Business View, you can't change the report to be based on a non–Business View data source with the Set Datasource Location option. You'll only be able to change the report to work with a different Business View.

Row and Column Security

One of the benefits of using Business Views with Crystal Reports is row and column security. *Row security* will limit your reports to only the database records applicable to you. For example, when viewing a sales report, the Western Region Sales Manager is limited to only seeing orders in the Northwest and Southwest. When viewing the same sales report, the National Sales Manager can view orders in all regions. The beauty of row security is that two different reports with two different sets of record selection aren't required to accomplish this. Row security applies the extra filters at run time to all reports based on the Business View supplying the row security. So, you can design a single report that will return different sets of records automatically based on the Crystal Reports Server/BusinessObjects Enterprise user ID.

If row security is assigned to the Business View you've based your report on, you may see different records than another user. For example, the exact same report based on the sample XTREME Business View discussed earlier in the chapter will return a complete set of regional customers to the National Sales Manager:

while returning only Northwest and Southwest customers to the Western Region Sales Manager.

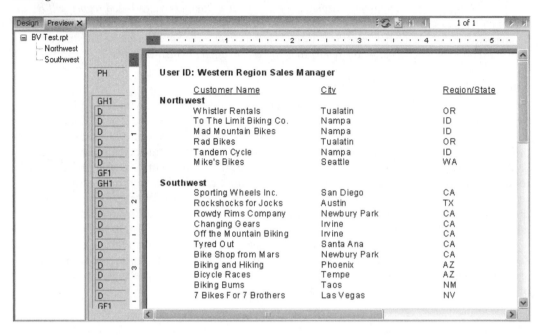

Column security allows data from certain fields within a Business View to be hidden to certain Crystal Reports Server/BusinessObjects Enterprise users. For example, when viewing an employee roster report, the HR Manager will be able to see data in the Annual Salary and Monthly Salary fields, along with other employee fields. When any other user views the same employee roster report, the Annual Salary and Monthly Salary fields will display null values, while other employee fields will still display the proper contents. The one issue with column security to be aware of is that, even if you aren't granted the rights to see fields, you'll still be able to drag them onto your report. When you preview the reports, however, you'll see nothing in them.

For example, the exact same report based on the sample XTREME Business View discussed earlier in the chapter will display salary data for employees when viewed by the HR Manager:

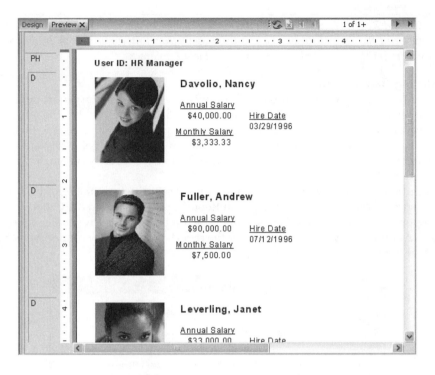

while showing null values for the fields when viewed by any other user.

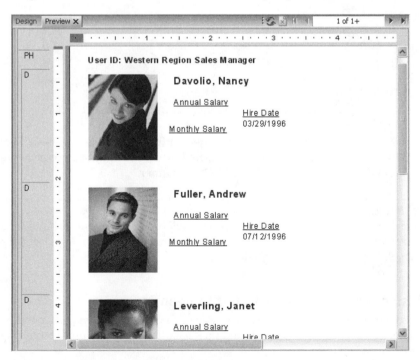

> **TIP** *One Crystal Reports feature you may find handy is the Current CE User Name special field. This will print the Crystal Reports Server/BusinessObjects Enterprise user name on the report. Choose it from the Special Fields category of the Field Explorer.*

Disconnecting View Security

You may encounter a potential problem if you wish to send a Crystal report developed against a Business View to a Crystal Reports user who is not connected to the same Crystal Reports Server/BusinessObjects Enterprise system, or who doesn't have CRS/BOE in their organization at all. This issue is compounded when row and column security are involved with the report, as there will be no CRS/BOE user ID to base security on when the report is opened by the other user.

The solution to this problem is to disconnect view security from the report when saving it. First, ensure that the File | Save Data With Report option is turned on. Otherwise, the non-CE report viewer won't be able to see anything but the report's Design tab. Then, choose File | Save As and specify a new filename for the report. Notice the Disconnect View Security check box at the bottom of the dialog box.

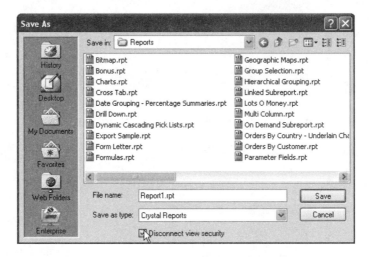

When the report is saved, it will be disconnected from the Business View. The report can be opened and viewed, but no longer refreshed. Also, you cannot reconnect a report to a Business View that has been disconnected in this manner.

> **CAUTION** *Be aware that if you have row and column security settings that permit you to see sensitive data, such as salaries, the sensitive data will be saved with the report when you disconnect view security. Other report viewers will see this data when they open the report, even though they won't be able to refresh the report.*

Using Business View–Based Pick Lists in Reports

As discussed earlier in the chapter, an advantage of a centralized Crystal Reports Server/ BusinessObjects Enterprise system is shared pick lists. The new dynamic/cascading pick list capability of Crystal Reports XI is further enhanced by the ability to share these pick lists in the repository. Once you create a shared pick list (either by publishing a Crystal Report to CRS/BOE or by creating a List of Values object based on a Business View—both discussed earlier in this chapter), you may then make use of it with Crystal Reports parameter fields. Even if you are not planning on publishing your report to CRS/BOE, you may still prefer to use a shared pick list. And, if you are planning on publishing your report, you *must* use a shared pick list (even if you create a report-based dynamic/cascading pick list, it will be converted to a Business View–based pick list when you publish the report, as discussed earlier).

Once one or more shared pick lists are available in the repository, it's a fairly simple process to make use of them in a Crystal Report. First, ensure you are logged on to the desired CRS/ BOE system by displaying the Crystal Reports Repository Explorer. The Repository Explorer can be displayed by clicking the Repository Explorer button in the standard toolbar, or by choosing View | Repository Explorer in the pull-down menus. Click the Logon button in the explorer to log on to CRS/BOE. Once you have logged on, you may close the Repository Explorer to regain screen space, if you'd like. Or, if you've already logged on to CRS/BOE to use a Business View as a report data source, you won't need to use the Repository Explorer.

Begin by creating a parameter field as you normally would (complete discussion of creating Crystal Reports parameter fields is contained in Chapter 13). Give the parameter field a name. While you may wish to choose a data type, you don't have to—the dynamic pick list you use in CRS/BOE will determine the data type automatically. Choose to create a dynamic pick list by clicking the Dynamic radio button in the List of Values section. To use a Business View–based pick list, click the Existing radio button in the Choose A Data Source section. The drop-down list next to the Existing radio button will then expand. The name of the CRS/BOE Central Management Server you logged into earlier will appear, with a list of all shared pick lists appearing underneath it.

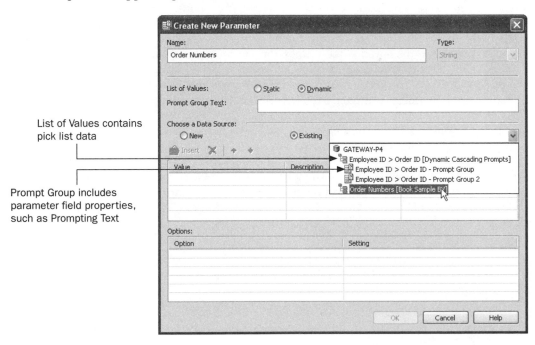

List of Values contains pick list data

Prompt Group includes parameter field properties, such as Prompting Text

You'll notice two different types of entries in the drop-down list: List of Values and Prompt Groups (both defined earlier under "Creating Business View–Based Pick Lists"). The List of Values entry (which you may have created earlier in the Business View Manager) contains the values that will appear in the drop-down pick list. Any Prompt Group entries below the List of Values (there can be one or more Prompt Groups, or none, depending on parameter fields that have been created against the List of Values so far) will include existing parameter field options, such as Prompting Text and settings for Allow Multiple Values and Allow Range Values.

If you wish to use an existing Prompt Group for your parameter field (perhaps you created other parameter fields against this pick list earlier and wish to reuse the settings you made for the earlier parameter field), choose the desired prompt group from the Existing drop-down list. If you wish to define your own options for the parameter field, just choose the List of Values object from the Existing drop-down list. If the List of Values contains more than one data field, you'll see multiple rows in the Value/Description/Parameters table (perhaps the List of Values was designed to accommodate a cascading pick list). Determine which of these rows you wish to attach to your parameter field by clicking the Parameters column in the desired row. Crystal Reports will add a parameter field name that consists of the name you initially gave your parameter field, followed by the name of the pick list field you chose (you may rename your parameter field back to its original name after you save it). If multiple parameter fields happen to be defined because you click the Parameters entry for multiple rows, you may click the entry again until the "Click to create parameter" message returns—no additional unwanted parameter fields will be created.

If you wish to customize any additional parameter field behavior, such as Allow Multiple Values or Prompting Text, make desired choices in the Options section of the Create New Parameter dialog box. Note that if you make any changes to these entries (or, if this is the first time you've created a parameter field with the List of Values entry), an additional Prompt Group containing the options you've chosen will be created in the CRS/BOE repository underneath the original List of Values—the next time you create a parameter using the same pick list, you'll find the additional Prompt Group in the drop-down list.

Click OK to create the parameter field with the pick list from the repository. If Crystal Reports renamed the parameter field inappropriately, you may rename it in the Field Explorer using the rename toolbar button, right-click options, or by holding the mouse button down for a second or two while selecting the parameter field name. When you refresh the report, you'll be prompted for the parameter field and the dynamic/cascading pick list will show you appropriate values in the drop-down list.

If you wish to publish the report to Crystal Reports Server/BusinessObjects Enterprise, you may do so (techniques for publishing are covered in Part II of this book). However, if you choose not to publish the report but just save it on your hard disk or a network drive, the pick list will still be connected to CRS/BOE. The next time you open the report, you will be prompted to log on to CRS/BOE before the report appears.

Tip *In the initial Crystal Reports XI release, you cannot delete a parameter field from the report if it is based on a CRS/BOE pick list, even if the parameter field is not used on the report. To delete the parameter field, edit it and click the Static radio button in the List of Values Section. Then click OK. Now you can delete the parameter field from the report.*

Sharing Report Items with the Repository

O ne of the most often-heard questions asked by users of Crystal Reports prior to version 9 (especially users in larger organizations) was "Can I share parts of this report with other users or other reports?" While some use of creative copying and pasting to shared word processor or text files might have provided a piecemeal answer to this question, the general response was usually "No."

Users of later Crystal Reports versions have enjoyed much broader flexibility to share report items with the repository. The repository allows several types of report objects to be stored in a central database for sharing among other reports and other users. Not only does this greatly reduce the need for repetitive report design steps, it also affords a simple, centralized way of automatically updating common portions of shared reports.

The repository in Crystal Reports XI is only available if you are using Crystal Reports Server/BusinessObjects Enterprise (abbreviated in this book as *CRS/BOE*). While Crystal Reports 9 supported a stand-alone repository database, later versions require the companion Crystal enterprise reporting product to be installed (the repository is stored in the CRS/BOE Central Management Server database). This arrangement provides for tight integration with the enterprise reporting environment, including full support for the integrated CRS/BOE security model.

TIP *More detailed coverage on Crystal Reports Server, its various capabilities, and implementation scenarios, can be found in Part II of this book.*

The Repository Defined

Simply put, the Crystal Reports *repository* is a common place where report objects can be stored. Once you store a report object in the repository, it's available to be added to other reports you create. If you connect to your CRS/BOE-shared repository that other users in your organization also share, objects you add to the repository are available to other Crystal Reports users, and objects they add are available to you.

The repository stores all of its items in the CRS/BOE Central Management Server database. Any Crystal Reports user who has a valid user ID and connectivity to your CRS/BOE system will be able to connect to the repository. Even if you have just a few report designers who share a common repository, the benefits of shared report design and automatically updated report objects will soon become evident.

You make use of the repository in Crystal Reports with the *Repository Explorer,* a separate "un-dockable" dialog box inside the report designer, similar to the Field Explorer. To display the Repository Explorer, choose View | Repository Explorer from the pull-down menus, or click the Repository Explorer toolbar button in the Standard toolbar.

The Repository Explorer window will appear. If this is the first time you've displayed the Repository Explorer since you started Crystal Reports (and you haven't already logged into Crystal Reports Server/BusinessObjects Enterprise), the Repository Explorer won't display any contents. Click the Logon button in the Repository Explorer toolbar to log on to CRS/BOE. You may also right-click the No Server Connection entry and choose Logon Server from the pop-up menu. Once you've supplied proper logon credentials, the Repository Explorer will display the repository contents in a folder structure.

If you initially log on to CRS/BOE with the wrong user ID or password, or you wish to later log off CRS/BOE and log on again with a different ID, Crystal Reports XI now provides this capability without requiring you to close and reopen Crystal Reports. Simply click the Logoff Server toolbar button in the Repository Explorer toolbar, or right-click the CRS/BOE server name at the top of the Repository Explorer and choose Logoff Server from the pop-up menu. You'll be logged off CRS/BOE, and the repository folder structure will disappear.

Click the Logon button again to redisplay the logon dialog box. Enter desired credentials to again log on to CRS/BOE.

As with other "explorer" windows in Crystal Reports XI, you may dock the Repository Explorer to the side of the Crystal Reports designer, may undock the window so that it floats free, or may dock the window, but shrink it, by clicking the push-pin icon in the upper right-hand corner. You may also close the Repository Explorer completely by clicking the small *x* in the upper right-hand corner. If you close the Repository Explorer, simply use the toolbar button or View | Repository Explorer menu option to redisplay it.

The New Repository Explorer Enterprise Items Category

Crystal Reports XI now includes the Enterprise Items category in the Repository Explorer. This folder contains a list of CRS/BOE report folders and subfolders, as well as objects within the folders and subfolders (the folders cannot be created, renamed, or deleted in the Repository Explorer—these types of functions must be performed using other CRS/BOE techniques described in Part II of this book). Click the plus sign next to a folder to open it and see its subfolders and objects. You may also right-click a folder within the Enterprise Items folder and choose Expand All from the pop-up menu. This will expand all subfolders within the selected folder, showing all available objects in them.

NOTE *Although all objects stored in the Enterprise Folders category (such as PDF files, hyperlinks, and so forth) will appear in the Repository Explorer, only Crystal Report objects are usable from within Crystal Reports XI. You'll note the "piece of paper" icon that denotes such an object. You'll also notice report "instances" that were previously scheduled underneath the associated report object.*

There are two general actions you can perform on a report in the Repository Explorer: open it in Crystal Reports, or "manage" it (schedule it, view its scheduling history, and so forth). To open the report you select in the Repository Explorer, just double-click it. You may also right-click the desired report and choose Open Report from the pop-up menu. The report will appear inside the Crystal Report designer, where you may refresh it, modify it, and use the Save toolbar button or File menu option to update the CRS/BOE version (provided your CRS/BOE user ID has sufficient rights). You may also use the File | Save As option to save the report you opened to your local hard drive or a network drive.

To manage a report in the Repository Explorer Enterprise Items category (report instances underneath a report can't be managed), right-click the desired report and choose Manage Object from the pop-up menu. Provided the user ID you logged on to CRS/BOE with has sufficient rights, a dialog box will appear with several tabs, allowing viewing and control of the CRS/BOE report from within Crystal Reports. Among other things, you may view report properties, set scheduling options, and schedule the report to run on a recurring basis. Make choices in the manage dialog box, depending on the actions you want to perform. You must close the dialog box to make any additional use of Crystal Reports.

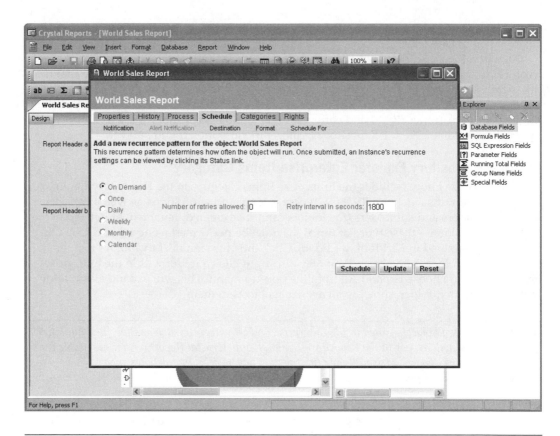

NOTE *More information on available choices in the Manage dialog box can be found in Part II of this book.*

The Repository Explorer Repository Items Category

The portion of the repository that contains "sharable" objects is displayed as the Repository Items category. The Repository Explorer shows this section categorized into folders. Although the sample repository that ships with Crystal Reports Server/BusinessObjects Enterprise shows folders for specific types of objects (text objects, bitmaps, SQL commands), you don't have to organize folders this way—you may put any type of object that the repository supports into any folder. You may add any of the objects in the repository to appropriate areas of your report.

The repository supports several types of Crystal Reports objects:

- **Text objects**   Standard text objects containing static text (no embedded fields)
- **Bitmaps (pictures)**   Bitmap pictures, such as logos, photos, and signatures
- **Custom functions**   Functions or "subroutines" that can be used inside report formulas. Note that repository custom functions appear only in the Formula Workshop, not in the Repository Explorer.
- **SQL commands/queries**   Server-based SQL commands that reports can be based upon

- **Business Views**   Crystal Reports Server/BusinessObjects Enterprise–based metalayer "views" of database connectivity that reports can be based upon (Business Views are covered in more detail in Chapter 16.)
- **Lists of Values**   Portions of new Crystal Reports XI dynamic/cascading parameters that display real-time values in a pick list
- **Prompt Groups**   Portions of new Crystal Reports XI dynamic/cascading parameters that organize one or more Lists of Values in a group

Text objects and bitmaps can simply be dragged from the Repository Explorer onto the report, just as you would drag and drop fields from the Field Explorer. Repository custom functions must be added to report formulas from within the Formula Workshop (covered in Chapter 5). Repository SQL commands and Business Views must be added to the report from within the Database Expert (SQL commands are covered in more detail in Chapter 15, and Business Views are covered in Chapter 16). And, Lists of Values and Prompt Groups are used when creating parameter fields (see Chapters 13 and 16 for more information).

TIP *You can install sample objects into your Crystal Reports Server/BusinessObjects Enterprise repository by using the Business View Manager's Tools | Install Repository Samples menu option. More information on using the Business View Manager is discussed later in this chapter, as well as in Chapter 16.*

The Repository Explorer toolbar contains four buttons, besides the Logoff Server button: Change View Settings, Advanced Filtering, Delete, and Add Folder. The Delete and Add Folder buttons, described later in the chapter, perform fairly self-explanatory functions. The Change View Settings and Advanced Filtering buttons allow you to customize what appears in the Repository Explorer.

Clicking the Change View Settings button, or right-clicking anywhere inside the Repository Explorer and choosing Change View Settings from the pop-up menu, will display the View Settings dialog box. By un-checking any of the repository object types, you can eliminate them from appearing in the Repository Explorer. For example, you may prefer not to see SQL commands (since you can't add them to the report from the Repository Explorer anyway). Just un-check Report Command to eliminate them from the Repository Explorer. You can also sort repository objects by name or type by clicking the desired radio button.

If you click the Advanced Filter button, or right-click anywhere inside the Repository Explorer and choose Advanced Filtering from the pop-up menu, the Repository Explorer will expand to show two filter text boxes and an Apply button. Type in a combination of full or partial object name in the "Show items with this text in the name" box and full author name in the "Show items by this author" box. Then, just click the Apply button or just press ENTER. The Repository Explorer will redisplay showing just repository objects matching the criteria you typed. To remove the criteria, just delete the text on the filter boxes and click Apply or press ENTER. If you no longer wish to see the filter text boxes, just click the Advanced Filtering toolbar button again, or right-click and choose the Advanced Filtering pop-up menu option.

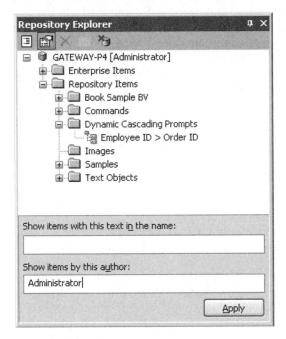

NOTE *Even though folders may show plus signs next to them after setting filters, nothing will appear inside the folder if it doesn't meet the filter requirements.*

Adding To/Updating the Repository

Once you've installed your initial Crystal Reports Server/BusinessObjects Enterprise system with its default database, you'll need to begin to populate it with your shared objects. And while it's not required, you'll probably gain more usability with the repository if you organize the repository into folders.

NOTE *The ability to add, change, and delete repository objects and folders is based on Crystal Reports Server/BusinessObjects Enterprise security. If your CRS/BOE user ID hasn't been granted these rights, you'll receive errors when you attempt these operations. Steps to control these rights are discussed later in this chapter, under "Controlling Repository Rights."*

Creating Folders

You may create as many folders in the repository as you like. And you're not limited to creating a single level of folders—you may create subfolders within other folders to build a hierarchy for repository objects. Once you've created your folder structure, you can place text objects, bitmap graphics, or SQL commands in the folders (custom functions are placed in a separate part of the repository reserved just for themselves—they won't appear in the Repository Explorer).

From within Crystal Reports, you can create, delete, or modify folders from the Repository Explorer. You may create a top-level folder that appears directly underneath the Repository Items category, or a subfolder that exists within another folder. If you wish to create a top-level folder, ensure that you've selected the Repository Items category first. Click the folder button in the Repository Explorer toolbar, or right-click the CRS/BOE server and choose New Folder from the pop-up menu. A folder will be added to the repository with the default name of "New Folder," and you'll be placed immediately into edit mode, where you can type your own name for the folder. Type the new folder name and press ENTER or click elsewhere with your mouse.

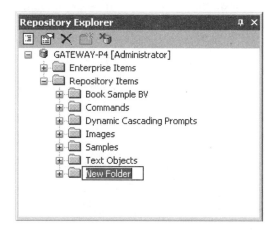

If you wish to create additional folders, you may create top-level folders by repeating the previous steps (just make sure you've selected the Repository Items category prior to clicking the folder toolbar button). If you wish to create a subfolder below an existing folder, select the higher-level folder first. Then, click the folder button in the Repository Explorer toolbar or right-click and choose New Folder from the pop-up menu. You'll see a lower-level folder within the higher-level folder you right-clicked, again with the default name of New Folder, which you can rename immediately.

If you wish to rename a folder you've already added, select the folder you wish to rename and then hold the mouse button down on the folder for a few seconds. You may also select the folder and press F2, or right-click the desired folder and choose Rename from the pop-up menu. In all cases, the folder name will go into edit mode and you can type a new name for the folder.

Deleting folders is similarly straightforward. First, ensure that all subfolders and objects within the folder have been deleted, as you cannot delete a folder that contains any subfolders of objects. Select the folder you wish to delete and simply press the DEL key. Or, you may click the X button in the Repository Explorer toolbar or right-click the desired folder and choose Delete from the pop-up menu. You'll be prompted to confirm the deletion.

CAUTION *Deleting folders, like deleting individual objects in the repository, cannot be undone. Make sure the object or folder you want to delete is no longer needed before you delete it.*

Adding and Deleting Objects

You may add report objects to the repository at any time, even if you haven't yet created any folder structure (moving objects into or among folders will be discussed later in the chapter). The method for adding an object to the repository is dependent on the type of object you wish to add.

Text Objects or Bitmap Graphics

A text object or bitmap graphic can be added to the repository by simply dragging and dropping it from the Design or Preview tab of the report into the Repository Explorer. You may add the object at the very top level by dropping it on the Repository Items category. If you wish to place the object into a particular folder, drag and drop the text object or bitmap on top of the folder you wish to add it to. You may also add a text object or bitmap by right-clicking the desired object and choosing Add To Repository from the pop-up menu.

Specify a name for the object to appear in the repository. Make sure you don't use a name already used for another repository object of the same type in the same folder (you'll be warned if you do this and will overwrite the repository object with the same name if you proceed). You can, however, add a repository object with the same name into a different folder, or an object with the same name, but of a different type, in the same folder.

Although they are not required, you can also add an author name and description for your entry. If you choose the pop-up menu method to add the object, the Repository Explorer will appear within the Add Item dialog box. If you wish to place the object in a folder, choose the folder where you want to place the new object. If you select the name of CRS/BOE server instead of a folder, the object will be placed directly in the top level (the Repository Items category) in the Repository Explorer. Click OK when you've specified all information to add the object to the repository.

If you wish to rename an object you added to the repository previously, you may simply select the object inside the Repository Explorer and then hold the mouse button down for a few seconds. The object will go into edit mode, where you can type in a new name (you'll receive an error if you try to use a name of another object of the same type and name in the same folder) and press ENTER or click away from the object name. The object will be renamed.

If you initially place an object in a particular folder (or in no folder, but right below the Repository Items category itself), you may move or copy it to another location with a simple drag-and-drop operation. Select the object you wish to move and hold your mouse button down. Then, drag the object on top of its new preferred location (a folder if you wish to move the object to that folder, or the Repository Items category if you wish to move the object out of a folder and place it in the repository top level). When you drop the object in its new location, it will then appear where you dropped it. Holding the CTRL key down while dragging will copy the object to its new location, also leaving the object in its original location. If there is already an object with the same name in the destination folder, you will be warned that it will be overwritten.

NOTE *You cannot drag and drop any repository items to the Enterprise Items category, or any folder in this category, from within the Repository Explorer. You'll receive a "no-drop cursor" (a circle with a line through it) if you attempt to drop into this portion of the Repository Explorer.*

Deleting a text object or bitmap from the repository is similar to deleting folders. Just select the object you want to delete and press the DEL key. You may alternatively click the X button in the Repository Explorer toolbar or right-click the object and choose Delete from the pop-up menu. And as with folders, deleting text objects or bitmaps can't be undone. Make sure you really want to delete the object from the repository before proceeding. Note that deleting an object from the repository won't delete it from reports that had originally made use of it. It will still remain in those reports, but it won't be available to add to any new reports.

While you can't add a SQL command to the report from the Repository Explorer (you must do this in the Database Expert), you can rename or delete it from there. And, although you must add Lists of Values or Prompt Groups to the repository from the Business View Manager, you may rename them from the Repository Explorer. Use the same steps mentioned previously for deleting or renaming text objects and bitmaps to delete or rename SQL commands, or to rename Lists of Values or Prompt Groups.

NOTE *If you delete an object from the repository that may be part of existing reports, users will receive an error message when they open the report and attempt to "Update Repository Objects." The object on the report will then appear as it did when the report was last saved.*

Custom Functions

 Add custom functions to the repository from the Formula Workshop. With the Formula Workshop displayed, select the report custom function you wish to add to the repository and click the Add To Repository button. You may also right-click the custom function name and choose Add To Repository from the pop-up menu. And you may also simply drag the custom function name from the Report Custom Functions category of the Formula Workshop to the Repository Custom Functions category (drop on top of any item in the category).

NOTE *You won't be prompted for a folder to place the custom function in. The folder structure discussed earlier doesn't apply to custom functions, which are placed in a separate area of the repository just for them. If you assigned categories to your custom functions when you created them, the categories will be retained when you place the custom function in the repository.*

Deleting a custom function from the repository is quite straightforward. Simply expand the Repository Custom Functions category of the Formula Workshop, select the custom function that you wish to delete, and press the DEL key. You may alternatively right-click the custom function name and choose Delete from the pop-up menu. In either case, you'll be warned that deleting a custom function from the repository can't be undone. Confirm that you want to delete the function and it will be permanently removed from the repository. Note that deleting an object from the repository won't delete it from reports that had originally made use of it. It will still remain in those reports, but it won't be available to add to any new reports.

TIP *The sample repository shipped with Crystal Reports Server/BusinessObjects Enterprise contains a few sample text objects, SQL commands, and bitmaps. These are for demonstration only and will be of little or no use to you when designing your own reports. There are, however, some useful custom functions supplied with the CRS/BOE repository that you may find of use in your own reporting tasks.*

SQL Commands

Add SQL commands to the repository in the Database Expert (creating SQL commands is discussed in more detail in Chapter 15). First, create the SQL command so that it appears in the Selected Tables list of the Database Expert. Then, right-click and choose Add To Repository from the pop-up menu.

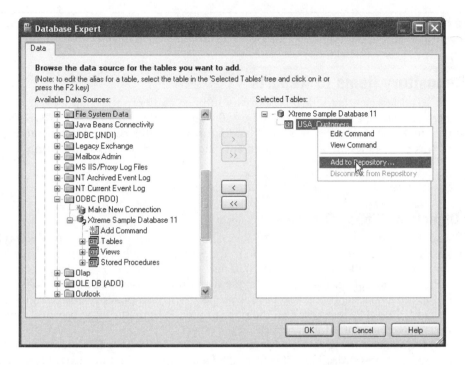

If you haven't previously logged on to CRS/BOE, you'll be prompted to do so. You'll be presented with a dialog box similar to previously described dialogs prompting you to name the object and choose a location in the repository for the object (SQL commands can be stored in the same folder structure you set up in the Repository Explorer). You may optionally specify the author, as well as changing the description for the SQL command to something other than the SQL statement that makes up the command (which is placed in the description text box by default). When you click OK, the SQL command will be added to the repository. It will then appear in the Repository section of the Database Expert.

NOTE *You'll also be able to see SQL commands in the Repository Explorer alongside text objects and bitmaps—they'll just be displayed with a different icon. However, you won't be able to just drag and drop them to the report as you can text objects or bitmaps. You can, however, rename and delete SQL commands from the Repository Explorer using the same techniques described for other objects.*

Renaming or deleting a SQL command from the repository must be done in the Repository Explorer—you cannot rename or delete a SQL command from the repository in the Database Expert. Once you've closed the Database Expert and have arrived at the report Design tab, display the Repository Explorer. Navigate the folder structure to find the desired SQL command. Use techniques described earlier in the chapter to rename or delete the SQL command. Note that deleting an object from the repository won't delete it from reports that had originally made use of it. It will still remain in those reports, but it won't be available to add to any new reports.

NOTE *CRS/BOE Business Views are also stored and managed in the repository. Complete details on how to maintain repository-based Business Views are available in Chapter 16.*

Adding Repository Items to Reports

Once you've added objects to the repository as outlined earlier in the chapter, you, along with other users sharing the same repository, will want to add the items to reports. Repository versions of text objects, bitmap graphics, custom functions, SQL commands, dynamic pick lists, and Business Views are added in different places throughout Crystal Reports.

TIP *Repository-based dynamic pick lists are discussed in more detail in Chapter 16.*

Text Objects or Bitmap Graphics

Add these items to your report from the Repository Explorer (which can be displayed by clicking the Repository Explorer button in the Standard toolbar or with the View | Repository Explorer pull-down menu item). If necessary, log on to Crystal Reports Server/ BusinessObjects Enterprise. Then, simply expand any folders to reveal the text objects and bitmaps that are available. If you want to see properties for a repository object, right-click the object and choose Properties from the pop-up menu. A small dialog box will appear showing various pieces of information about the object.

To add the object to the report, simply drag it from the Repository Explorer to the report. As when dragging and dropping fields from the Field Explorer, an outline will appear as you drag. When you've reached the desired position for the object, release your mouse button. The text object or bitmap graphic will be placed on the report.

TIP *Don't be alarmed when you are unable to format or resize objects you add to the report from the repository. These objects are "connected" to the repository and can't be edited, resized, or formatted until they have been "disconnected." This is discussed later in the chapter.*

Custom Functions

Make use of repository custom functions in the Formula Workshop. You may add a custom function to the report from the repository directly, which will place it in the Formula Editor's function tree for use like built-in Crystal Reports functions. Alternatively, you can use the Formula Expert to create a formula based on a custom function from the repository.

To add a custom function to the report directly, so that it appears in the Formula Editor's function tree, begin by displaying the Formula Workshop. You may do this by clicking the Formula Workshop button in the Expert Tools toolbar, or by choosing Report | Formula Workshop from the pull-down menus.

Expand the Repository Custom Functions category of the Formula Workshop until you find the custom function that you wish to use (you may need to log on to Crystal Reports Server/BusinessObjects Enterprise if you haven't previously). Select the function you wish to add and click the Add To Report toolbar button in the Formula Workshop toolbar. You can also right-click the function name in the Formula Workshop tree and choose Add To Report from the pop-up menu. And finally, you may simply drag the custom function you wish to add to the report from the Repository Custom Functions category to the Report Custom Functions category of the Formula Workshop tree.

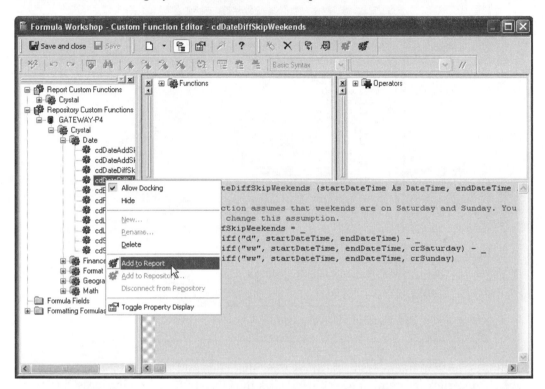

Since a repository custom function can potentially call other custom functions within the repository, you may be asked to confirm the addition to the report of other custom functions. Once you do this, all custom functions you've added from the repository will now appear in the Custom Functions category of the function tree for you to add to formulas.

TIP   *More details on creating formulas with the Formula Expert and using custom functions in formulas can be found in Chapters 5 and 6.*

SQL Commands and Business Views

Add repository-based SQL commands and Business Views to your report from the Database Expert, the Set Location dialog box, or another data-related dialog box that you typically use to add database tables to the report. In these dialog boxes, you'll see a Repository folder. When you click it, you may be prompted to log on to CRS/BOE. Then, the BusinessObjects Enterprise Explorer dialog box will appear, showing the repository folder structure. Expand the folders to reveal SQL commands or Business Views that are located in the repository. An example of the BusinessObjects Enterprise Explorer from the Database Expert is shown next.

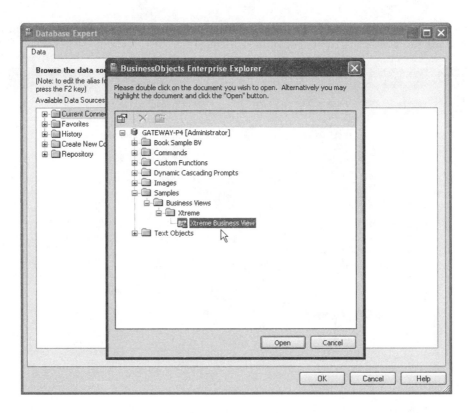

Choose the SQL command or Business View that you want to add to the repository. Then, double-click the item, or select it and click the Open button. The BusinessObjects Enterprise Explorer will close, and the original dialog box will reappear with the item you chose added to the Repository folder. Select the desired item and click the right arrow to add it to the report, right-click the item and choose Add To Report from the pop-up menu, or just drag it from the left side of the Database Expert to the right side. Similar procedures will add SQL commands and Business View "tables" to the report from the repository in other data-related dialog boxes.

Changing Repository Items on Your Report

As indicated earlier in the chapter, you may become confused once you add an object from the repository to your report. This might occur if you attempt to change the format of a text object you added from the repository, resize a bitmap graphic you added from the repository, or change the text of a SQL command or custom function that's been added to the repository. In all these cases, you'll discover that the objects are "locked" or set to a read-only status—you won't be able to make these kinds of changes.

This behavior is by design. In order to ensure that the repository controls the appearance and behavior of these objects, they remain *connected* to the repository once you've added them to the report. As long as they're connected, the repository will control their appearance and size (in the case of text objects and bitmap graphics), or their text (in the case of SQL commands and custom functions). Probably the most obvious clue that an object is connected is the inability to change it. However, in some dialog boxes, you'll also notice a small vertical-bar-with-link icon next to the object's name, which indicates that the object is connected to the repository.

The main benefit of leaving objects connected to the repository is to allow them to be updated automatically if anybody else makes changes to the repository. For example, if you have added a common company logo and slogan to your report using a repository-connected bitmap graphic and text object, you'll probably want all reports using those objects to automatically reflect changes to the repository should your logo or slogan change. In order to ensure consistency with this behavior, individual changes to the objects once they've been added to reports shouldn't be allowed.

TIP *To ensure connected objects will be updated when you initially open your reports, you must make one of two choices. By choosing File | Options from the pull-down menus and checking the Update Connected Repository Objects on Open option on the Reporting tab, you ensure all reports automatically update connected objects when opened. If you only want to update connected objects on a report-by-report basis, leave this global option off and instead check the Update Repository Objects check box on the Open File dialog box when opening a Crystal Report.*

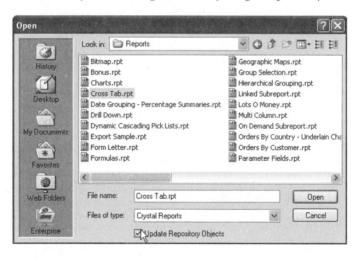

To change this behavior and manually make changes to objects you've added from the repository, you must *disconnect* them from the repository. Begin by right-clicking the object. In the case of text objects or bitmap graphics, right-click directly on the object in the Design or Preview tabs. For SQL commands or custom functions, right-click the command or function name in their respective dialog boxes. From the pop-up menu, choose Disconnect From Repository. Notice that you may now resize or reformat text objects or bitmap graphics, as well as changing the contents of SQL commands or custom functions. Also, you'll notice the previously mentioned vertical bar "connected" icon is no longer visible.

Be aware, though, that these objects will now behave as though you just added them to the report—they won't be automatically updated by the repository any more. Using the company logo and slogan example mentioned previously, if you disconnect the objects from the repository and save the report, they won't reflect any repository changes the next time you open the report.

Updating Repository Versions of Objects

Continuing with the company logo and slogan examples referred to previously in this chapter, what if you are in charge of updating the repository copies of the company logo and slogan? Or, you may have a company-wide custom function that requires changing for a new fiscal year or a new bonus program. In these situations, you must add the object from the repository to your report, make changes, and update the repository with the changed object.

As mentioned previously, you can't edit or modify an object that's connected to the repository. This may cause confusion if you are required to update the repository copy of an object. To get around this confusion, consider the steps required to update the repository copy of an object:

1. Add the object to a report from the repository.
2. Disconnect the object from the repository.
3. Make necessary changes to the object.
4. Save the object back to the repository in the same folder and with the same name as the original object.

Step 4 will exhibit behavior that is slightly different than the first time you added the object to the repository. When you attempt to add an object to the repository in the same folder with the same name, you will be warned that an object already exists and given the opportunity to update the version in the repository with the version that you're saving. If you choose to do this, the old repository object will be replaced with the updated version.

Once you've performed these steps, note that the updated object you just added back to the repository will once again be connected—you won't be able to change formatting or contents. To make future changes to the object, you must once again disconnect it from the repository.

NOTE   *Business Views, including new XI dynamic pick list objects, are modified using the Crystal Reports Server/BusinessObjects Enterprise Business View Manager—you cannot update Business Views from inside Crystal Reports. The Business View Manager is discussed in detail in Chapter 16.*

Controlling Repository Rights

With a shared repository, as with company database connections and network resources, you may wish to limit the ability to update or delete repository objects to a certain set of key users, while permitting the rest of those sharing the repository to just add existing repository items to their reports. As the Crystal Reports repository is managed by Crystal Reports Server/BusinessObjects Enterprise, you make use of CRS/BOE user and group permissions to accomplish this.

While typical Crystal Reports Server/BusinessObjects Enterprise user and group right assignment is accomplished in the Central Management Console (more detail on Crystal Reports Server/BusinessObjects Enterprise architecture and management is discussed in Part II of the book), repository rights are maintained in the CRS/BOE Business View Manager. If you don't already have access to the Business View Manager in an existing Crystal Reports Server/BusinessObjects Enterprise installation, you must specifically install the Business

View Manager on a Windows computer from the CRS/BOE product CD. And, needless to say, since the repository is part of Crystal Reports Server/BusinessObjects Enterprise, you must have a functional Crystal Reports Server/BusinessObjects Enterprise system in place to make use of the Business View Manager.

NOTE *Other Business View capabilities of the Business View Manager not relating to repository rights are covered in Chapter 16.*

Start the Business View Manager from your Windows start menu. You will be prompted to log on to Crystal Reports Server/BusinessObjects Enterprise. Ensure that you use a CRS/BOE user ID (initially, the Administrator ID or a member of the Administrators group will be required) that provides sufficient rights to change repository security. The Business View Manager will appear. If necessary, display the Repository Explorer within the Business View Manager by choosing View | Repository Explorer from the pull-down menus. This window, similar in appearance to the Repository Explorer in Crystal Reports, may be "undocked" and moved around as a free-floating window.

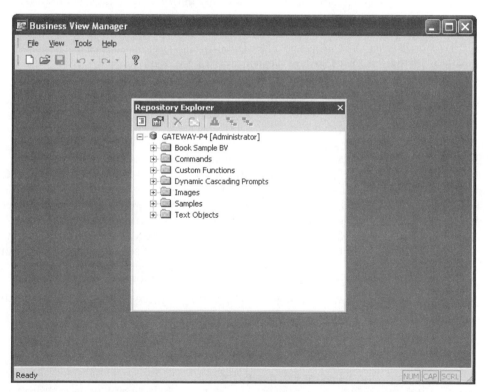

Notice that the folder structure of the repository is exposed in the Repository Explorer: your CRS/BOE Central Management Server name appears at the top of the folder hierarchy, with top-level folders appearing below them. If you click the plus sign next to a folder, it expands to show any subfolder or repository objects within it. The initial difference between the Repository Explorer contained in the Business View Manager and that contained within

Crystal Reports is lack of the Enterprise Items and Repository Items categories in the Business View Manager version. Here, only repository items are shown—no report objects are visible.

Notice an additional folder labeled Custom Functions that you may not have seen before in other versions of the Repository Explorer or Formula Workshop. This is the dedicated folder within the repository where all custom functions are contained. As you can't specify a folder name in the Formula Workshop when adding a custom function, they will all be placed in this single repository folder.

Consider this repository folder and object hierarchy carefully when planning your repository security plan. If you simply want to supply a single set of repository rights for the entire repository (perhaps you want Administrators to have full repository rights, but everyone else to have only read rights), you may set repository rights at the *Central Management Server level*. However, if you want to provide more granular rights (perhaps you want a Sales group to have full rights to the entire Sales repository folder or just certain objects or subfolders within the Sales folder), then you may set rights at the *folder and object level*.

Furthermore, you will want to consider the concept of *rights inheritance,* the capability to set rights at a higher level in the repository (perhaps on the Central Management Server or a top-level folder) and have the rights automatically *inherited* by folders, subfolders, and objects at lower levels. By creative use of different levels of rights and inheritance, you have very tight control (perhaps more than you'll need) over repository rights.

Controlling Rights at the Central Management Server Level

Begin by considering the overall set of rights you want to give to repository as a whole; these will be the rights you set at the Central Management Server level. All folders, subfolders, and objects in the repository will inherit the rights you set here. If, as discussed previously, you only wish to have a single set of rights apply to the entire repository, you need only set rights at this level.

Begin by selecting the top-level Central Management Server name in the Repository Explorer. Then, right-click and choose Edit Rights from the pop-up menu. The Edit Rights dialog box will appear, as illustrated in Figure 17-1.

You'll see a list of Crystal Reports Server/BusinessObjects Enterprise groups and users that have already been granted or denied rights at the Central Management Server level (a freshly installed Central Management Server will initially show the Administrators and Everyone group here). Note the three different rights that can be set for each user or group:

- **View**   The ability to add objects in the repository to reports
- **Edit**   The ability to add new objects to the repository, or update and delete existing objects in the repository
- **Set Security**   The ability to change repository security settings for others

Further, if you cycle through the available options for each right by clicking the check box, you'll notice that a right can be granted, denied, or inherited. *Granting* the right explicitly gives that right to the chosen group or user. *Denying* the right explicitly takes the right away from the chosen group or user. And, allowing the right to be *inherited* will grant or deny the right on the basis of higher-level security settings (at the Central Management Server level, inherited rights apply only to the Administrators group, which is automatically granted all rights to the repository).

List of groups and users
and associated rights

Type in group or user name and
click button to find group or user

Delete selected user
or group from list

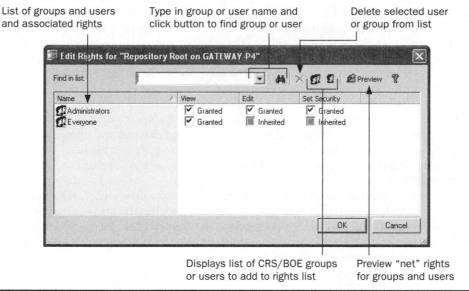

Displays list of CRS/BOE groups
or users to add to rights list

Preview "net" rights
for groups and users

FIGURE 17-1   The Edit Rights dialog box

If you wish to specifically grant or deny rights to additional groups or users, you'll need
to add the group or user to the list by clicking the Add Groups or Add Users button in the
Edit Rights dialog box toolbar. These buttons will display an additional Add Groups or Add
User dialog box showing all Crystal Reports Server/BusinessObjects Enterprise groups or
users (to actually create additional CRS/BOE groups or users, you must use other CRS/BOE
administrative tools, such as the Central Management Console—you can't add these here).
Use this dialog box to choose additional groups or users to add to the Edit Rights dialog box.

Filter the list of groups or users by criteria

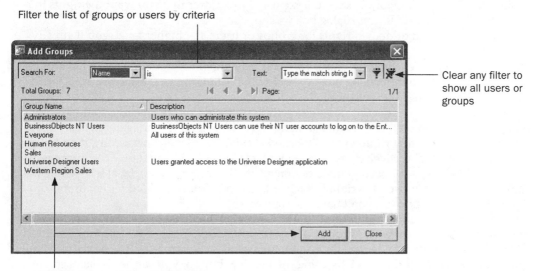

Clear any filter to
show all users or
groups

Double-click a group or user or click
Add to add it to the Edit Rights dialog

Once the additional groups or users you've added appear in the Edit Rights dialog box, you can grant or deny rights to that group or user by clicking the appropriate check boxes. The next time you set rights for the Central Management Server, the new groups and users you added will reappear with the specific rights you granted or denied appearing next to them. If you wish to remove a group or user that you previously set rights for, select the user or group and click the Delete toolbar button (the X).

Although it's not as relevant at the Central Management Server level, you may still want to see what the ultimate or *net* set of rights is for each group or user. Do this by clicking the Preview button in the Edit Rights dialog box toolbar. The list of users and groups will change, showing the actual combination of rights that result from explicit settings and inheritance. If you need to change any rights, click the Preview button again to return the list to its "editable" state.

Once you've set rights for all necessary groups and users, just click OK to close the Edit Rights dialog box. The rights you set will be saved on the Crystal Reports Server/ BusinessObjects Enterprise system and will take effect immediately for all repository users. The rights you set at the Central Management Server level will automatically be inherited by all folders and objects in the repository.

CAUTION *Be careful when denying rights at the Central Management Server level. If you deny a right to a group or user at this level, that user or group won't have the right anywhere in the repository, even if you explicitly grant it at a lower level. Because of the repository's inheritance rules, denial of rights takes precedence over granting of rights when rights are inherited.*

Controlling Rights at the Folder and Object Level

If you wish to take advantage of Crystal Reports Server/BusinessObjects Enterprise's folder- and object-level repository security, perform similar steps to those discussed previously for setting repository security at the Central Management Server level. However, prior to choosing the Edit Rights option from the pop-up menu, ensure that you've selected the desired folder, subfolder, or object in the Repository Explorer that you want the rights to apply to. The same Edit Rights dialog box will appear.

If you've granted or denied rights for groups or users at a higher level, you'll already see the group or user listed in the Edit Rights dialog box. You may either change rights that may be inherited by clicking the check boxes for existing groups or add additional groups or users to the Edit Rights dialog box by clicking the Add Groups or Add Users button in the Edit Rights dialog box toolbar.

The important thing to consider when setting rights at this level is inheritance. If a right has already been granted or denied at a higher level (the Central Management Server or a higher-level folder), that right will be inherited at this lower level. Specifically, if a right has been denied at a higher level, even granting it at this lower level won't give the group or user the right. If a right hasn't been granted or denied at all, granting at this level will enable the right for the group or user. If a right has never been specifically granted (either at this or a higher level), then the user won't have the right.

Once you've specified rights at the lower level, click the Preview button to see the set of net rights granted to users and groups. This net rights display takes into account inherited rights from higher-level folder and the Central Management Server, as well as rights specifically granted and denied at this level. By using the Preview button, you can see what each group and user will ultimately be able to do within this folder or to this object. If you need to modify rights after viewing net rights, click the Preview button again to return the list of groups and users to an "editable" state.

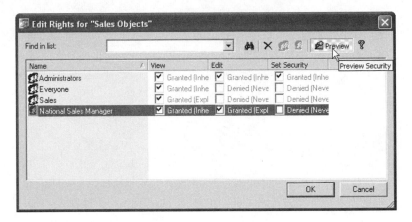

NOTE *Preventing users from updating or deleting repository objects will still allow them to "detach" objects from the repository and change them once they've been placed on the report. However, if they make any changes to such objects, they still won't be able to update the repository with their updated versions.*

Accommodating Database Changes and Field Mapping

There are many situations in which the database you initially developed a report against will change. Perhaps the database is in a state of flux and will be changing dynamically as your report design proceeds. Or, you may develop a report against a test database and then change the report to point to a production database later. Possibly the database has been moved to a different server for network efficiency. Or, you may determine that a different database driver should be used to connect to the database. For true flexibility, you need to be able to accommodate these changes easily so that you don't have to re-create any features or functions of your report just because the database has changed.

With some of these database changes, the database designer or administrator may rename fields. When Crystal Reports detects these changes, it gives you the opportunity to change the field references inside your report, so the new field names can be automatically associated with the previous field names. This field mapping prevents you from having to add fields to the report again or modify formulas that refer to changed fields.

In addition to the Database Expert, which is discussed in Chapter 15, Crystal Reports provides three functions for efficient management of database changes:

- Verifying the database
- Setting the data source location
- Mapping fields

When you use either of the first two functions, and Crystal Reports detects changes that it is unable to resolve, such as field name changes or deletions, the field mapping function is automatically displayed.

Recognizing Database Changes

If the database layout changes (field names change, data types are altered, and so forth), if the database is moved to a new location, or if you want to point your report to a different database than it was originally designed with, you need to use Crystal Reports' functions to recognize these changes.

Verify Database

If the database your report is based on changes (perhaps the database designer adds new fields, deletes old fields, or gives existing fields new names or data types), your report won't automatically recognize these changes when the report is opened. Even if you refresh the report, Crystal Reports won't detect the changes, unless a specific field used in the report no longer exists in the database (it has been removed or renamed). To detect changes to the database the report is based on, you must verify the database.

Choose Database | Verify Database from the pull-down menus. If the database has not changed, you'll see a dialog box indicating so:

However, if the database has changed, you'll receive a message like this:

When you click OK at this prompt, Crystal Reports will read the database structure and make any changes to field names and data types. When you display the Field Explorer, you'll notice the changes. And if you have previously linked tables together and table structures have changed significantly, you may need to relink tables in the Database Expert, as discussed in Chapter 15. If field names have changed, you will see the Map Fields dialog box (discussed later in the chapter).

Verify on First Refresh

If the database changes and you don't verify the database thereafter, your report may show incorrect data if fields have been moved or renamed, or it may display an error message if tables have been removed or renamed. Be very careful when working with a database that may be changing. You'll want to verify the database often to catch any changes.

One way to accomplish this is to check the Verify On First Refresh check box after selecting File | Report Options from the pull-down menus. When you check this option, Crystal Reports will verify the database the first time the report is refreshed in any given report session. The on/off state of Verify On First Refresh will be saved with the report—if it was turned on when a particular report was saved, it will be turned on when that report is opened. If you wish to change this choice for all new reports you create in the future, you may modify the same check box on the Database tab after choosing File | Options.

Using Set Datasource Location

Crystal Reports provides a single menu function for changing the connection to the database (database driver), recognizing a change to the physical location of a database or table, or changing the actual database to be used. All of these types of changes are accomplished via the Set Datasource Location function.

Choose Database | Set Datasource Location from the pull-down menus. The Set Datasource Location dialog box will appear. This dialog box contains two main sections: the Current Data Source box and the Replace With box. Begin by choosing the existing database or table that you wish to alter—you may choose either the entire database name by choosing an entry to the right of the database barrel icon, or an individual table within the database by choosing the table name to the right of the table icon.

Then, expand the appropriate category in the Replace With box to find the new data source you wish to use in place of the selected data source in the Current Data Source box. If necessary, you'll need to provide log on credentials to the new server. Choose a replacement object similar to that selected in the Current Data Source box; if you selected an entire database in the top box, select an entire database in the bottom box. If you selected an individual table above, choose a single table below. Only if you select like object types, will the Update button be enabled.

Select the table or database
the report will be pointed to

If necessary, update
subreports

Select current table or database that needs to change

When you click Update, Crystal Reports will log on to the identified replacement data source. If the database name is different on the replacement, the database will be verified (as discussed previously in this chapter), and you may see the Map Fields dialog box (discussed in the section "Mapping Old Fields to New Names" later in this chapter). But as long as the database names match, Crystal Reports assumes that the databases are the same and does not prompt for further input; it simply makes the change. The new data source is now displayed in the Current Data Source list, and you can click Close on the Set Datasource Location dialog box or make other data source location changes.

If your report contains one or more subreports, a separate category below the main report data source will appear in the Current Data Source box. Simply select the subreport data source as you did the main report data source and choose an alternate data source from the bottom list. All subreports that share the original data source will be directed to the new data source.

NOTE *If database structures have changed significantly, you may need to relink tables in the Database Expert for either the main report or affected subreports. Double-check links by displaying the Database Expert and clicking the Links tab.*

Not only can you use these steps to point your report from one database of a particular type (SQL Server, Informix, etc.) to another of the same type, but you may also change database types in the process. For example, if you've built a report based on a test Microsoft Access database, you can use Set Datasource Location to point the report to a production database hosted on Microsoft SQL Server.

Three special features in Set Datasource Location apply only to reports based on PC-style data source connections (such as the Access/Excel DAO connection type). They provide quick ways to identify and modify the name, local directory, or network path for a database. If necessary, click the plus sign to the left of the PC database name in the Current Data Source box. Then, expand the Properties category by clicking the plus sign next to it. You'll notice several properties for the chosen database, including the database type, physical file location, user ID, and so forth. While some of these properties are display-only, many of them can be changed. In particular, the Database Name property has several options you can choose from a pop-up menu. Right-click the Database Name property to see the three options:

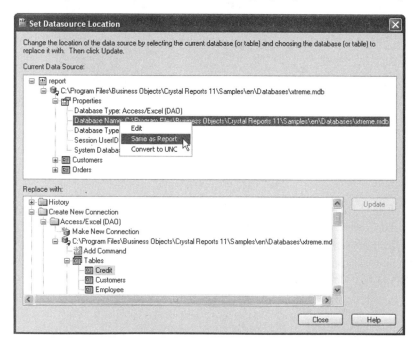

Editing Database Name

The Edit option allows you to change the path to the PC-style database used in the report. If the location or name of the database has changed, or will be different for the person to whom you are sending the report, you can change the path here. Changing the database filename in this path tells Crystal Reports to point to a database with the new name.

Same As Report Option

The Same As Report function will remove any drive letter and path name from the PC-style database location. From that point forward, Crystal Reports will look for the database on the same disk drive and in the same folder as the report.

This allows you to create and save a report for distribution to other report viewers. The other viewers can place the report on any drive and in any folder that they choose. As long as the database the report is based on is in the same folder as the report, the report will be able to find it.

Converting to a UNC Name

The Convert To UNC function will change the hard-coded drive letter and path name for the PC-style database to a Uniform Naming Convention (UNC) name that can easily be found by any computer on the network, regardless of its drive mapping. UNC is a way of pointing to a file on a network disk drive without using a drive letter. Consider the following scenario:

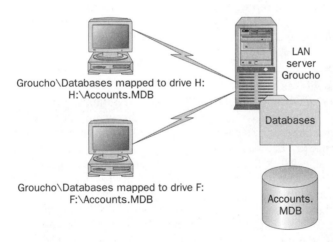

The two PCs are connected to the same LAN server, but are using different drive letters to reach the server. If the first PC creates a report based on Accounts.MDB, the report will have the drive letter and filename H:\Accounts.MDB hard-coded into it. When the second PC opens the report, the report will fail—the database won't be found on drive H.

To avoid this kind of problem, you can use a UNC name to replace the drive letter. A UNC name appears in the following format:

\\<Server Name>\<Share Name<ISA>>\<Path and Filename>

- *Server Name* is the actual name of the computer or server where the file is located (in this case, Groucho). Two backslash characters precede the server name.

- *Share Name* is a name that the LAN administrator has given to a particular group of shared files and folders on the server. When a PC maps a drive letter to a LAN server, the drive letter is mapped to a particular share name (in this case, Databases). A single backslash character separates the *Server Name* from the *Share Name*.

- *Path and Filename* are similar to path names and filenames used on a local PC hard drive, except they are located on the LAN server. In this case, the Accounts.MDB file is in the root of the Databases share name. A single backslash character separates the *Share Name* from the *Path and Filename* (and this path may contain additional backslash characters).

Based on these rules, the corresponding UNC name for the Accounts.MDB file will be as follows:

```
\\Groucho\Databases\Accounts.MDB
```

Notice that the drive letter has been removed. Now, any PC on the network can find the file based on the UNC name—the PC doesn't have to have a drive letter mapped to the LAN server.

Dealing with Table Name Changes

If a database designer or administrator changes the name of a table in the database, the next time you try to refresh your report, you will receive an error indicating that the table can't be found. Unfortunately, refreshing the report or verifying the database will not solve this problem—the message will persist and the report will not print properly.

Table Names vs. Aliases

When you first create a new report based on certain database tables, you'll notice that the actual name of the table you originally chose shows up in the Field Explorer, the Database Expert, and other places in the report. Although it may appear that Crystal Reports must refer to a database table by its physical name, this name is actually an *alias* assigned to the table. While the alias takes on the physical table name by default, it doesn't have to always keep that name. You have the flexibility to change the alias Crystal Reports uses to refer to this table.

To change the alias, display the Database Expert with the appropriate toolbar button or Database | Database Expert menu option. Choose the table you wish to assign a new alias by clicking it in the Selected Tables box on the right side of the Database Expert. Then, press the F2 key, right-click, and choose Rename from the pop-up menu, or simply hold your mouse button down on the table name for a few seconds. The table name will be placed in edit mode. Simply type a new alias name in for the table.

In some cases, Crystal Reports will require you to choose an alias for a table. In particular, if you try to add the same table to a report more than once (perhaps your database contains a shared lookup table that must be added to a report multiple times), Crystal Reports will display a message indicating that duplicate table names aren't allowed. You'll then be required to choose an alias for the table.

To solve this problem, perform the following simple steps:

1. Use the Set Datasource Location function as described in this chapter to connect to the new data source (this may be as simple as contracting and re-expanding the category of the Database Expert where the original database was). Select the old table name in the Current Data Source list and the new table name in the Replace With list. Click Update. This will correctly point the report to the new table name. However, the table will still be referred to by the old name in the report.

2. If you want the new name to appear throughout the report, use the Database Expert to change the alias of the old table to the new table name, as described earlier in the chapter. This will change the name of the table as well, avoiding confusion as to which physical table is actually being used.

Mapping Old Fields to New Names

Database changes can cause a mismatch of field names in your report. For example, your original report may be developed against a Microsoft Access database that includes a field named "Account Number" (note that the space between the words is significant to Crystal Reports). You may need to eventually have the same report work with a SQL Server database where the field is known as "Account_Number" (notice that the space has been replaced with an underscore).

Whenever Crystal Reports detects these kinds of database changes, it can't be sure which new database field the old report object should be associated with. By using Field Mapping, you can point the old object to the new database field. Field mapping simply allows you to change the field name that a report refers to so that, for example, all objects that used to be associated with "Account Number" will now be associated with "Account_ Number." No formulas have to be changed, no old objects have to be removed, and no new objects need to be added.

The Field Mapping function cannot be chosen from a menu. It is triggered when Crystal Reports detects any field name changes in the source database. Crystal Reports will check for these changes whenever you verify the database or use the Set Datasource Location function to change the database or data source connection. When Crystal Reports detects that fields in the report are no longer in the database, it displays the Map Fields dialog box, as shown in Figure 18-1.

The Map Fields dialog box is divided into four boxes or lists. The upper-left Unmapped Fields list shows report fields that don't match up to any field names in the new database. The upper-right list shows a choice of fields in the new database that you can map the report fields to. To map the report field to the new database field, select the report field you want to map in the upper-left box, select a matching database field in the upper-right box, and then click the Map button. The fields will be moved from the upper boxes to the lower boxes.

The list of database fields will change according to whether or not you click the Match Type check box on the right side of the dialog box. If the box is checked, only fields of the same data type (string, number, date, and so forth) as that of the selected report field will show up. This helps to ensure that you're making the correct match of fields, by not inadvertently mapping a string field on the report to a number or date field in the new database (although you may want to do this sometimes). There may be times that you won't

List of fields in the new database
that can be mapped to

Map the field selected in the upper-left list
to the field selected in the upper-right

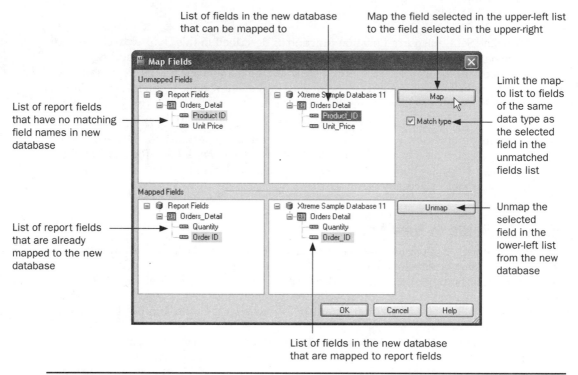

List of report fields
that have no matching
field names in new
database

List of report fields
that are already
mapped to the new
database

Limit the map-
to list to fields
of the same
data type as
the selected
field in the
unmatched
fields list

Unmap the
selected
field in the
lower-left list
from the new
database

List of fields in the new database
that are mapped to report fields

FIGURE 18-1   Map Fields dialog box

see the field you want to map to in the right list, however, because of data type mismatches. For example, if you're remapping fields originally from a Microsoft Access database to a SQL Server database, you may not find any SQL Server field that matches a currency field in the Access database. In this situation, uncheck Match Type and look for the field to map to.

When the Map Fields dialog box first appears, some fields probably will already be present in the lower two Mapped Fields boxes. The lower-left list shows report fields that already have a matching field in the new database. And once you've mapped fields from the upper lists, they will be moved to the lower lists as well. If existing mapping was assumed by Crystal Reports (because of identical field names), or you mistakenly mapped fields that don't belong together, you can select a field in the lower-left or lower-right list. The mapped field will appear highlighted in the other box. You can then click the Unmap button to unmap the fields and move them back to the top lists.

Once you have finished mapping fields, click the OK button to close the Map Fields dialog box. Crystal Reports will now associate the mapped fields with the new database. The Design tab, as well as any formulas, will reflect the new field names. If additional tables have mismatched fields, you'll be presented with the Map Fields dialog box for each subsequent table.

CAUTION *Any fields that no longer exist in the source database must be remapped to new fields. If you don't map old field names to new fields, the old fields and objects they're based on will be deleted from your report.*

Reporting from OLAP Cubes

Relational database systems provide the vast majority of the data analysis and reporting capabilities that most organizations need. However, a smaller segment of many organizations can benefit from more flexible and sophisticated analysis tools. In many cases, an organization's higher-level analysts are still using spreadsheet tools in combination with relational databases to make strategic company decisions.

Online analytical processing (OLAP) is a newer analysis technique that provides much more flexibility in analyzing company data. Crystal Reports supports most standard OLAP tools and enables you to create reports based on these database systems.

What Is OLAP?

Most typical company data is viewed in two dimensions, whether it is viewed by a reporting tool such as Crystal Reports or a spreadsheet program such as Microsoft Excel. In the case of a spreadsheet, the rows and columns constitute the two-dimensional analysis. You may be viewing product sales by state, salesperson volume by product category, or customer totals by demographics. In each of these cases, you typically can see only two dimensions at any one time, even though you actually may prefer to analyze a combination of three or more of these factors.

Region			
Product	USA	CAN	UK
PROD 1	534	212	231
PROD 2	45	21	12
PROD 3	321	324	112
PROD 4	204	120	40
PROD 5	78	43	31
PROD 6	32	12	2
PROD 7	786	512	49
PROD 8	123	23	17

Online analytical processing is a leading-edge analysis approach that allows data to be analyzed and viewed in multiple dimensions in real time. With a typical OLAP tool, you may initially be presented with a spreadsheet-like view that shows information using two dimensions, such as product sales dollars by state (or perhaps by country or region, allowing drill-down to the state level). This initial two-dimensional view is natural despite the ability of OLAP tools to analyze multiple dimensions, most human beings still readily conceive data only in two dimensions.

Even though only two dimensions are visible, additional dimensions are available "behind the scenes" to control the two dimensions you are viewing; you can limit dollars by state by using other dimensions. Perhaps you want to see dollars by state limited to just certain sales reps, certain customer demographics, or certain product categories—you still see the original Dollars and State dimensions, but the numbers are filtered by the other dimensions. You may also want to quickly see sales by product category, demographics by state, or some other combinations of dimensions. Using an OLAP analysis tool, "slicing and dicing" through the different dimensions is typically as easy as dragging and dropping one dimension on top of another. Figure 19-1 shows the multidimensional "FoodMart" database included with Microsoft SQL Server 7.0 OLAP Services or Microsoft SQL Server 2000 Analysis Services.

Whereas relational databases represent data in a two-dimensional, row-and-column (or field-and-record) structure, OLAP databases utilize a multidimensional structure known as a cube (which, despite its name, is capable of storing more than three dimensions of data).

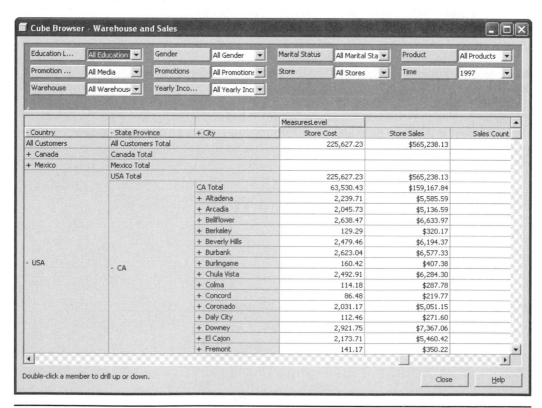

FIGURE 19-1   SQL Server Analysis tool viewing OLAP cube

Often, cubes are built on the basis of regular relational database systems—the relational database is populated using typical data-entry or data-import techniques, and a cube is built that is based on the relational database. Cubes can be refreshed or repopulated on a regular basis to allow multidimensional, real-time analysis of the data in the relational database.

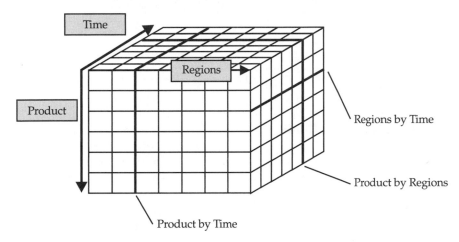

Crystal Reports OLAP Capabilities

You might ask, "Where does Crystal Reports fit into all of this?" Crystal Reports, obviously, can report on the data stored in the two-dimensional relational database. However, Crystal Reports also allows reporting against many industry-leading OLAP cubes. In fact, Crystal Reports can combine reports that are based on both relational databases and OLAP cubes, all in the same report. You have several choices:

- Create a standard report against the relational database the cube is based on.

- Create an OLAP-only report based solely on the cube.

- Create a standard report against a relational database (either the same database the cube is based on or an entirely different database) and include an OLAP report based on a cube inside the standard report.

- Create several different OLAP reports based on the same, or different, cubes. These OLAP-based reports can exist individually, or be included together inside a standard report based on a relational database.

Supported OLAP Systems

While OLAP technology has been somewhat fragmented and proprietary until recently, industry standards are starting to emerge. Crystal Reports will work with leading proprietary OLAP databases, as well as with the emerging Open OLAP standard. Thus, Crystal Reports can create OLAP reports based on the following tools:

- Hyperion Essbase
- Crystal Holos

- IBM DB2 OLAP Server
- Microsoft SQL Server 7.0 OLAP Services or SQL Server 2000 Analysis Services via OLE DB
- OLE DB for OLAP sources (or other "Open OLAP" sources)
- SAP BW
- Crystal Analysis Professional or BusinessObjects OLAP Intelligence (.CAR file)

TIP   The Standard Edition of Crystal Reports XI does not support OLAP. The OLAP-related functions will be inactive on all screens.

OLAP Report Creation Methods

There are several ways Crystal Reports can be used to report on your OLAP data. While all OLAP reporting in Crystal Reports will be based on the same type of object (the OLAP grid), there are several ways to create it. An OLAP grid is very similar in appearance and functionality to a cross-tab object (discussed in detail in Chapter 9). An OLAP grid displays one or more cube dimensions in rows and columns on the report. As with a cross-tab, you may format individual rows and columns to appear as you wish. You may also easily swap, or pivot, the rows and columns to change the appearance of the OLAP grid. And, you can launch the OLAP Analyzer, an interactive viewer similar to the Crystal Analysis and OLAP Intelligence products, to conduct real-time "slice and dice" analysis of your OLAP data right from within Crystal Reports.

Creating reports with OLAP cubes is straightforward and very similar to creating reports with regular relational databases. You may either use the OLAP Report Creation Wizard right from the Start Page or File | New menu option, or add an OLAP grid object to a report you've already created using a standard relational database. The OLAP Report Creation Wizard leads you step-by-step through choosing the cube and dimensions you want to use in the row and column of your report. It will then create a report containing an OLAP grid. If you add an OLAP grid object to your report manually, you can make similar choices to that of the OLAP Report Creation Wizard to construct the OLAP grid (this is similar to creating a cross-tab object).

Using the OLAP Report Creation Wizard

The OLAP Report Creation Wizard is available from the Start Page that appears when you start Crystal Reports. Just click the OLAP Cube Report Wizard link under the New Reports category. You may also choose File | New | OLAP Cube Report from the pull-down menus.

The OLAP Data dialog displays first in the Report Creation Wizard, to allow you to identify the OLAP cube you wish to base your OLAP report on.

OLAP Report Creation Wizard

OLAP Data

Choose the data to be your On Line Analytical Processing (OLAP) source

Choose an OLAP Server type then select the Cube that contains the data.

| Select Cube... | Select CAR File... |

Cube:

Type:

Server:

< Back   Next >   Finish   Cancel   Help

Click the Select Cube button to display the Crystal OLAP Connection Browser, where you can choose from the OLAP cube connections available. If you wish to report on a Crystal Analysis Professional/BusinessObjects OLAP Intelligence .CAR file, you can click the CAR button; CAR files are found through the standard Open dialog, rather than the OLAP Connection Browser used for most OLAP connections.

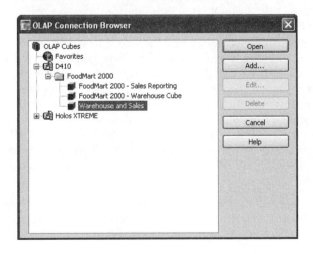

OLAP Connection Browser

- OLAP Cubes
  - Favorites
  - D410
    - FoodMart 2000
      - FoodMart 2000 - Sales Reporting
      - FoodMart 2000 - Warehouse Cube
      - Warehouse and Sales
  - Holos XTREME

Open
Add...
Edit...
Delete
Cancel
Help

Use the OLAP Connection Browser tree to navigate to the OLAP cube you want to report on, then select it and click the Open button, or simply double-click the OLAP cube. If you don't see the desired OLAP cube, you may need to click the Add Server button to browse, log on to, and add a new OLAP server in the New Server dialog.

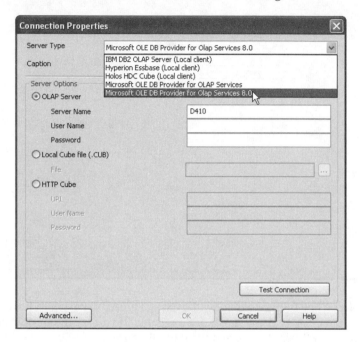

Depending on the type of cube and location of the OLAP database, complete the fields in the Add Server dialog box. If you are using a Microsoft Analysis Services cube with SQL Server 2000, choose the Microsoft OLE DB Provider for Olap Services 8.0 server type. If you are using Microsoft OLAP Services with SQL Server 7, choose the Microsoft OLE DB Provider for OLAP Services item. In either case, you'll then need to specify the server name, user ID, and password in the following three fields. If you have been provided with an Analysis Services local cube (.CUB) file, select the Local Cube file radio button and type in or navigate to the .CUB file. Or, if you've been instructed to connect to the Analysis Services server via HTTP (the standard Internet protocol), select the HTTP Cube radio button and type in the URL to the server, along with your user name and password.

If you choose other OLAP Server Types, appropriate options will appear in the New Server dialog box for connecting to the associated cube. If you are unsure of how to connect to your particular cube type, consult with the administrator of your OLAP database.

TIP   *If your OLAP server doesn't appear in the Server Type drop-down list, you may need to install client software specific to your particular OLAP system, such as a cube-viewing application, on your PC. After you install this software, restart Crystal Reports and try creating the report again.*

Once you've successfully logged onto and connected to the proper cube, you'll be returned to the OLAP Connection Browser and the cube will appear in the OLAP Cubes list—you won't have to go through the Add Server process again, as the cube will remain in the list from this point on. If you made errors in the connection process in the New Server dialog box and the cube can't be connected to, right-click the cube definition in the list and choose Remove Server from the list. The server will be removed, and you can click the Add Server button to add the server again (you can also rename the server from this pop-up menu, as well as adding individual cubes within the server to the Favorites entry in the browser).

Once you've selected the desired cube in the OLAP Connection Browser, the Data dialog of the Report Creation Wizard redisplays, and the Cube, Type, and Server fields on the Data tab of the Expert will be filled in.

After you make these choices, click the Next button to show the Rows/Columns section, shown in Figure 19-2, to choose the dimension or dimensions you want to include in the rows and columns of your report.

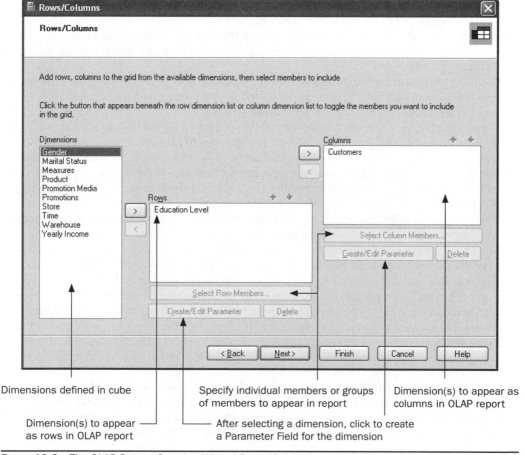

FIGURE 19-2 The OLAP Report Creation Wizard Rows/Columns section

NOTE *Crystal Reports XI includes a sample Holos OLAP cube for the Xtreme Mountain Bike company that you can use to experiment with OLAP reporting. XTREME.HDC can be found below the Crystal Reports program directory in \Samples\en\Databases\Olap Data. However, the examples in this chapter are based on the sample Foodmart OLAP cube provided with Microsoft SQL Server Analysis Services.*

If the default dimensions already in the Rows and Columns list aren't correct, choose from the Dimensions list the dimension that you want to appear as the row in your OLAP report. Then, simply drag and drop it into the Rows box or click the right arrow next to the Rows box.

Use the same drag-and-drop method to add to the Columns box the dimension you want to appear as the column in your OLAP report. Or, select a dimension and click the right arrow next to the Rows or Columns list.

You aren't limited to placing just one dimension in the Rows and Columns boxes. If you add multiple dimensions, Crystal Reports will "group" the dimensions in the OLAP report. For example, if you add a State dimension, followed by a Customer dimension, Crystal Reports will print states and show customers broken down within each state. If you place the dimensions in the Rows or Columns box in the wrong order, you can simply drag and drop the dimensions into the correct order within the Rows or Columns box. Alternatively, you can select the dimension you want to move, and use the up and down arrows above the Rows and Columns boxes.

If you wish to remove a dimension from the Rows or Columns box, drag the dimension back to the Dimensions list. Or, you can select the desired dimension and click the left arrow (you won't be allowed to leave a row or column empty).

Depending on the cube you choose for your report, you may find dimensions that contain many levels or members. A member (sometimes referred to as a generation) is a lower level of information that breaks down the higher level above it. For example, a Products dimension could contain several members: product type, product name within product type, and size within product name. Each member further breaks down the information shown by the member above it, creating a hierarchy for data in the dimension.

By default, if the dimension you choose for your OLAP report contains multiple members, Crystal Reports will show only the highest member in a group hierarchy when it displays the dimension. While this may be the way you want the report to appear, it may actually display a data level that is too high. Often, you'll add dimensions to a report's Rows and Columns boxes, only to have the OLAP report show just one number at the intersection of one row and column. If you need to increase the number of members shown inside a dimension that appears on the report, you can use the Select Members buttons to select the additional members that you want to see. First, select the dimension in the Rows or Columns list that you wish to work with, and then click the Select Row Members or Select Column Members button. You may also just double-click a dimension in the list. When you do either, the Member Selector will appear, as shown in Figure 19-3.

The Member Selector dialog box shows the dimension members in a hierarchy, with pluses and minuses to the left, much like the display of folders and files in Windows Explorer. You can expand the hierarchy to see lower members by clicking the plus signs next to the members. If you want to see just the higher-level members, click the minus sign to collapse them.

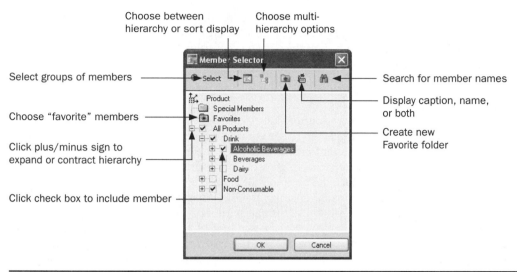

FIGURE 19-3   The Member Selector

Once you've expanded the dimension's members sufficiently, you can simply click the check box next to individual members to select or deselect them. Those that are checked will be included in the report—those that aren't won't. If you want to select multiple members at the same time, you may CTRL-click or SHIFT-click on multiple member names to highlight them (multiselect or range-select, respectively), and then click one check box. All the members that are highlighted will be selected.

If you want to be more systematic in member selection, particularly for very large hierarchies, click the down arrow attached to the Select button in the Member Selector's toolbar to display a pull-down menu (you can also right-click a member name to get a similar set of choices). You'll see various options for selecting groups of members (such as all, none, all members at a certain level, and so forth). Notice that once you choose one of the options in the select menu, the Select button will display an icon similar to the choice you made from the menu. By just clicking the Select button, you can repeat that selection without displaying the drop-down menu again.

You can also control other aspects of the Member Selector by choosing other toolbar buttons:

- Select Display Mode will change from viewing members in a hierarchy to sorting them in ascending or descending order.

- Select Hierarchy will provide additional options if the particular dimension you've chosen encompasses more than one hierarchy.

- New Favorite Group will add an additional category underneath the Favorites folder where you may drag "favorite" members.

- Display Members Using chooses between displaying dimension captions, names, or both (if your cube makes a distinction).

- Search displays a dialog box to allow you to search for members using text searches. You can either use a simple search or click the Advanced tab to create a more complex Boolean search. When the search is complete, you can search again from the resulting list of members, add the selected members to those already selected, or replace selected members with this list.

After you choose the members you want included in the report, click OK. You won't notice any difference in the Rows/Columns tab—you'll need to double-click the dimension or click the Select Member button again to see what members you've chosen.

You may also create a parameter field to allow the viewer to choose members to include in the OLAP grid whenever the report is refreshed. Click either the row or column dimension you wish to parameterize and click the Create/Edit Parameter button. The Create Parameter Field dialog box will appear. Steps for creating an OLAP parameter are similar to those for a regular report parameter, except that you must set default values before you save the parameter field (and, there are no dynamic or cascading pick lists available when you create an OLAP parameter). When you click the Default Values button, the Set Default Values dialog box will appear. Within this dialog box, clicking Select Default Values will again display the Member Selector, where you can choose members to add to the parameter's pick list.

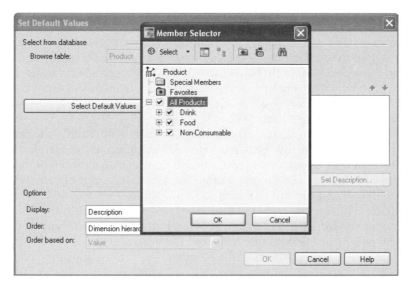

NOTE *More information on parameter field creation is available in Chapter 13.*

Once you've chosen dimensions and members, click the Next button to advance to the Slice/Page section, shown in Figure 19-4, to determine how the remaining dimensions included in the cube will affect your OLAP report.

In the Slice/Page section, you'll see all the other dimensions in the cube that you didn't include in the Rows or Columns boxes. You can use these dimensions to either slice or page your OLAP report. Slicing (similar to filtering) the OLAP report limits the report to certain occurrences of data in these dimensions. Paging the OLAP report is very similar to setting

Limit view to particular member of dimension   Dimensions not included in row or column

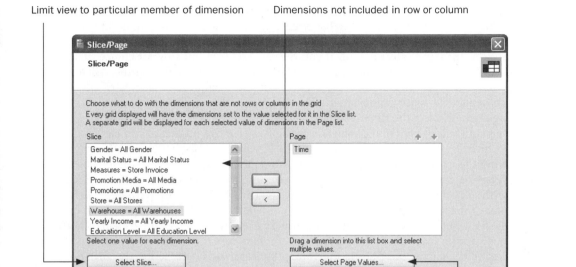

FIGURE 19-4   The Slice/Page section

up report grouping. Like the grouping of other reports, discussed in Chapter 3, this creates a new section of the OLAP report showing a different OLAP grid every time the value of the chosen dimension changes. Each resulting OLAP report section will contain data just for that one member.

To slice the report according to a dimension, look at the Slice part of the dialog box. You'll notice that each dimension displays a filter criterion, such as Store = All Stores. Typically, this default value will be either All or a particular general value that was set as the default when the OLAP cube was defined. Either double-click the dimension you want to slice, or select the dimension and click the Select Slice button. The Member Selector dialog box, described earlier, will appear, in which you can choose a particular value to limit the OLAP report. After you make your choice and click OK, the criterion in the Filter list will change to indicate the value you picked. The OLAP report will now be limited to only values that are included in the dimension you chose.

TIP *Unlike in the previous example with the Member Selector dialog box, you can choose only one value in the box here. Selecting a new value deselects the preceding value.*

To page the OLAP report according to a dimension, select the desired dimension in the Slice list and either drag it to the Page list or click the right arrow. Once again, the Member Selector dialog box appears, in which you can again select any combination of members (using options from the Select menus, if you'd like). After you make your choices, click OK to close the Member Selector dialog box. The dimension you chose for paging will appear in the Page list at the right of the Slice/Page section. If you wish to later change the members you chose to page the report, return to the Slice/Page section and double-click the dimension in the Page list, or select the dimension and click the Select Page Values button.

You can add more than one dimension to the Page list. If you do so, you can change the order in which Crystal Reports will group the OLAP report, by selecting one of the dimensions and clicking the up or down arrow. If you want to remove one of the Page dimensions, select it in the Page list and click the left arrow button or drag the dimension back to the Slice list.

As with the previous section of the wizard, you can base pages on parameter fields. To do this, select the slice or page dimension that you want to create a parameter field for and click the Create/Edit button. The Create Parameter Field dialog box will appear, where you may choose options to prompt the report viewer when the OLAP report is refreshed. Then, the value that the viewer supplies to the parameter field will be passed to the slice or page dimension to control how the OLAP report appears. Once you've added a parameter to a dimension, you'll notice the parameter field to the right of the equal sign in the Slice or Page list. If you later want to edit the parameter field, click the desired dimension and then the Create/Edit button. To delete the parameter and return to a fixed value or values chosen in the Member Selector, choose the desired dimension and click the Delete button.

Once you've made any slicing and paging choices, you're ready to display the OLAP report if you're satisfied with the default formatting Crystal Reports will apply. Click the Finish button if you're ready to view the report. However, you have additional choices in the OLAP Report Creation Wizard if you wish to choose them. You may choose from a set of preformatted styles for the OLAP report, as well as adding charts to show data plotted in your OLAP report.

To customize the formatting of the OLAP grid objects the wizard will create (very similar to the cross-tab object discussed in Chapter 9), click Next to display the Style section of the wizard. Choose from one of the predefined grid styles to apply to the OLAP report.

You may then click the Finish button to display the report, or click Next to create a chart based on your OLAP data. There is a minimal set of charting choices on this section (more detail on charting on OLAP grids is discussed in Chapter 10).

Click the Finish button in the OLAP Report Creation Wizard to run the report and show it in the Preview tab. Depending on any page dimensions you chose, you'll see a few simple objects on the report, such as the print date and page number. You'll also see one or more OLAP grid objects, plus any report sections and groups that were created to accommodate the page dimensions.

If you need to make changes to the Rows/Columns or Slice/Page values in the OLAP cube, you can rerun the Report Creation Wizard by clicking the OLAP Design Wizard button in the Expert toolbar or by choosing Report | OLAP Design Wizard from the pull-down menus.

Alternatively, to display the full OLAP Expert with all possible options (discussed in the next section, "Adding an OLAP Grid to an Existing Report"), you can select the OLAP grid object by clicking in the blank area of the object's upper-left corner (if there is more than one, select the particular one you want to change). Then, right-click and select OLAP Grid Expert from the pop-up menu.

Adding an OLAP Grid to an Existing Report

You probably will encounter situations in which you want to create a standard database report that includes one or more OLAP grids. By choosing the Blank Report option or other wizards from the Start Page or File | New menu, you have more flexibility in creating this type of report. Simply create the base report using the techniques discussed elsewhere in the book.

You may even find it useful to base the main report on some fields from your OLAP database. To use the OLAP database for the main report, choose the OLAP entry under the Create New Connection category of the Database Expert. The OLAP Connection Browser (shown earlier in the chapter) will appear, where you can choose an OLAP cube. You can add as many of these cubes or tables as necessary for the report. Depending on the type of OLAP database you've chosen, the Field Explorer will show the dimensions and members for your chosen cubes, or the fields in the chosen tables. You can add these fields to your main report as you would a regular database field. You may need to try some experimentation to determine which dimensions or fields can be used—OLAP data often doesn't behave the same as relational database data. Once the main part of your report is finished, you can add the necessary OLAP grid objects.

CAUTION   *Even though you can access the OLAP cube by using the Blank Report option, you won't be able to actually include any cube values in any report sections. You'll only be able to include and manipulate dimension names. The only way to actually include the numeric values from the cube is to create an OLAP grid object.*

Adding an OLAP Grid Object

To create an OLAP grid on an existing report, click the OLAP grid toolbar button in the Insert Tools toolbar or choose Insert | OLAP Grid from the pull-down menus. The OLAP Expert appears.

The tabs in the OLAP Expert behave almost identically to the same sections in the OLAP Report Creation Wizard, described earlier in the chapter. Follow the same steps for the Data and Rows/Columns tabs to choose the cube and dimensions for your OLAP grid. You may also use the Style and Customize Style tabs to format the OLAP grid, similar to formatting a cross-tab object (covered in detail in Chapter 9). Three of the tabs deserve more discussion, however: the Slice/Page tab, the Customize Style tab, and the Labels tab.

Slice/Page Tab

Notice that the Page dimension list and the Parameter field buttons that appear with the OLAP Report Creation Wizard are unavailable here, and a note suggests that you use the Wizard if you want to use these features. If you want to have several cubes work as pages, you can either re-create the report using the Wizard or add multiple OLAP grids to your report, specifying a different slice for each grid to mimic the Paged dimension process discussed in the Wizard portion of this chapter.

Customize Style Tab

This tab is identical to the same tab used to format Cross-Tab objects (see more information on this tab in Chapter 9). Options you choose on this tab change formatting options, such as background color, grid line formatting, and "Alias for Formulas," which lets you give a shorter, more meaningful name to a column or row for use in conditional formatting.

OLAP Labels

Many OLAP cubes of even moderate complexity often contain many dimensions. However, unlike a "slice and dice" OLAP analysis tool, the OLAP grid object that initially appears in the Preview tab or appears when you print or export the report doesn't offer a high level of interactivity (although the OLAP Analyzer, discussed later in the chapter, under "The OLAP Worksheet," does provide high interactivity). Accordingly, you'll probably use only a few (if not just one) dimensions for a row and column. The remainder of the dimensions not actually appearing as a row or column (often called qualified dimensions) can simply be ignored, used as Slice dimensions, or used as Page dimensions. Of particular interest is how the report viewer will know what settings have been made for Slice dimensions: if the OLAP grid is limited to just one product, one gender, and one store, how will this be known? The answer is OLAP labels.

When you create an OLAP grid object either with the OLAP Wizard or by inserting an OLAP grid manually, OLAP labels are added to the OLAP grid by default, as shown here:

All Customers	All Education Lev	All Marital Status	Profit		All Media
All Promotions	All Stores	All	All		1997
All Yearly Income					

		All Gender		
		F	M	
All Products	Drink	14,706.27	14,652.70	29,358.98
	Food	122,100.72	123,664.15	245,764.87
	Non-Consuma	31,641.74	32,845.31	64,487.05
		168,448.73	171,162.17	339,610.90

Notice that any Filter dimensions, such as 1997, are listed. Otherwise, the All designations appear. This indicates to the report viewer what limits have been placed on the OLAP grid. You may choose to limit the set of OLAP labels that appear—perhaps to just the ones that are used as a Filter dimension. Or, you may want to otherwise customize the way the OLAP labels appear. To do this, click the Labels tab, shown in Figure 19-5.

By default, all qualified dimensions (those that are in the cube, but not included as a row or column on the grid) are placed in the right Labeled Dimensions box. You can change the order in which they will appear next to the OLAP grid by selecting a label and using the small arrows above the box to move it up or down in the list. If you don't want a particular label to appear with the grid, select it and click the left arrow to move it to the Unlabeled Dimensions box.

You can also customize the amount of white space Crystal Reports will place between the labels by specifying a new value in the Vertical Gap and Horizontal Gap text boxes. You can choose to place the entire set of labels on the top or left side of the OLAP grid (or not have the labels show up at all). And finally, you can check the Display Dimension Name check box to replace the "All <value>" label with "<Dimension> = <value>" for labels.

After you make your desired choices in the OLAP Expert, click OK. An outline of the OLAP grid object will be attached to the mouse cursor. Drop the object in the desired section of the report.

You may make changes or additions to the OLAP grid object by selecting it and then formatting the OLAP grid by using pull-down menu options, the Format button in the Expert Tools toolbar, or format options from the right-click pop-up menu. You can also format individual parts of the OLAP grid, as discussed later in the chapter, under "Controlling OLAP Grid Appearance."

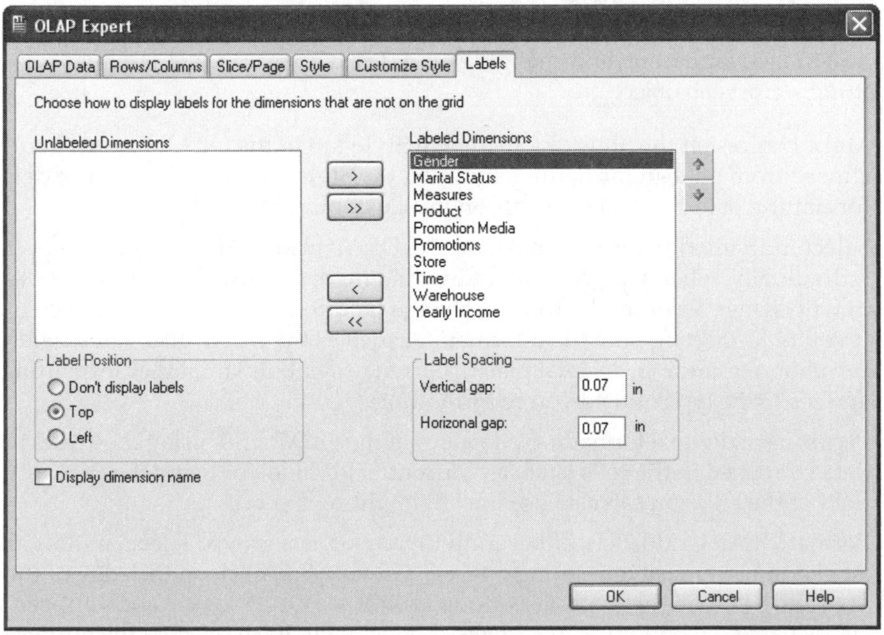

FIGURE 19-5   The Labels tab

Changing the OLAP Database Location

An OLAP grid "points" to a specific OLAP cube location on a server. If that location changes, or if you want to report on a different cube without redesigning the entire OLAP grid, you need to change the location of the OLAP database that the grid refers to.

Select the OLAP grid you want to change by clicking its upper-left corner. Right-click and choose Set OLAP Cube Location from the pop-up menu, or choose Database | Set OLAP Cube Location from the pull-down menus. The Set OLAP Cube Location dialog box appears.

Click the Select button to choose the new OLAP cube or new server location for the associated OLAP database. Then click OK.

Controlling OLAP Grid Appearance

An OLAP grid organizes cube information in a row-and-column format, much as a cross-tab object does. In fact, formatting and changing OLAP grid appearance is essentially identical to formatting a cross-tab object:

- Make choices on the Style or Customize Style tab in the OLAP Expert. You can choose from built-in formatting styles on the Style tab or perform more detailed formatting of individual elements on the Customize Style tab.

- Select individual fields that make up the OLAP grid, and resize or format them individually. When you resize an individual field, the row or column that the field is in will change accordingly. You can change field font face, font size, and color. And if you're formatting numeric information, such as the OLAP grid value fields, you can choose rounding, decimal places, currency symbols, and other formatting that applies to the type of field you're formatting.

- Perform conditional formatting on values in the OLAP grid, using the actual numeric data contained in the cells (such as CurrentFieldValue), or using the Row or Column field of the cell. You can also use the Highlighting Expert.

- Format OLAP Grid labels, either individually or as a group. Select an individual label and use typical formatting options. Or, you may click on the edge of the label area and select all the labels as a group (you'll see OLAP Grid Labels appear in the status bar at the bottom of the screen). You actually have selected the border around all the labels, and you can add a border, drop shadow, or other "border-oriented" formatting options. You can also suppress the labels on the Format Editor common tab if you don't want to see them (this can be done conditionally, as opposed to making a similar choice in the OLAP Labels tab of the OLAP Expert).

Tip *Formatting OLAP grids is virtually identical to formatting cross-tab objects. Refer to Chapter 9 for a thorough discussion.*

Virtual Page Formatting Options

Crystal Reports deals with OLAP grids that span multiple pages in an inconsistent manner between the Preview tab and what actually is printed or exported from the finished report. If an OLAP grid contains a sufficient number of columns that it exceeds the chosen Crystal Reports page width, it simply expands the Preview tab horizontally and shows the OLAP grid across a single page. However, when you print or export the report, the OLAP grid will actually be broken into multiple pages that print one after the other.

Crystal Reports provides specialized formatting options that make OLAP grids that span pages easier to view. A formatting option in the Format Editor, as well as a page number special field, are designed to enhance OLAP grid appearance.

The Repeat on Horizontal Pages formatting option appears on the Format Editor Common tab. You may select this formatting property for virtually all Crystal Reports object types, such as database fields, bitmap graphics, text objects, and so forth. Any object that you apply this formatting option to will repeat on each subsequent page that a OLAP grid object appears on, whether in the Preview tab or on a printed or exported report.

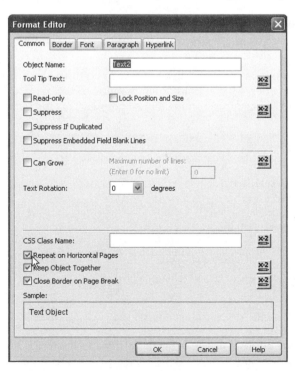

The other feature that's helpful with multi-page OLAP grids is the Horizontal Page Number special field. Available along with other special fields in the Field Explorer, Horizontal Page Number will increment as OLAP grids span multiple pages, whereas the standard Page Number special field won't. Simply drag and drop the Horizontal Page Number special field onto the report as you would any other field. The page numbers will increment as OLAP grids span pages.

Figure 19-6 illustrates these features. Notice that the text object title appears on multiple horizontal pages displayed in the Preview tab. Also, notice that the Horizontal Page Number special field automatically increments when the OLAP grid spans multiple pages.

Interacting with the OLAP Grid

Although you don't have quite the "slice and dice" flexibility with Crystal Reports that you may have with your particular OLAP analysis tool, you might be surprised by how easy it is to rearrange the appearance of an OLAP grid object. When you first create the OLAP grid, you choose which dimensions you want to use as rows and which you want to use as columns. If you choose multiple row or column dimensions, the order in which you add them determines the grouping order for the rows or columns.

You may want to change the order of the OLAP grid's row or column grouping, or you may want to swap or pivot the rows and columns, drill down on higher-level dimensions, and so forth. There are a large number of manipulation choices in Crystal Reports (many of these options are only available when viewing the OLAP grid in the Preview tab—limited options exist in the Design tab):

- **Pivot the rows and columns**   Select the OLAP grid. Then, right-click and choose Pivot OLAP Grid from the pop-up menu. You can also choose Format | Pivot OLAP Grid from the pull-down menus.

- **Reorder dimensions**   Simply click the row or column heading of the dimension you want to reorder. As you hold down the mouse button, you will notice a little "piece of paper" icon appear on the mouse pointer. This indicates that the dimension

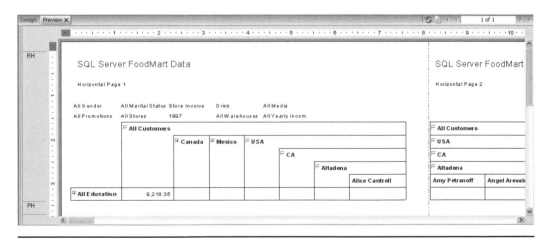

Figure 19-6   Multi-page OLAP grid

can be dragged and dropped below or above another dimension to reorder the dimensions. You can even drag and drop a dimension from a row to a column, or vice versa, provided that at least one dimension will be left in the row or column of the OLAP grid.

Drill down and drill up   Double-click a higher-level member, or click the plus sign next to the member (the plus sign will not appear if you've suppressed drill-down indicators from the Grid Options pop-up menu). This, in essence, is the same as rerunning the OLAP Expert and using the Select Row Members option to show the next level of the hierarchy. You can then drill down on the lower levels that you just exposed, until there are no more lower levels to show. To drill up (hide the lower levels you already showed), just double-click the higher-level member again or click the minus sign next to the member (the plus sign will not appear if you've suppressed drill-down indicators from the Grid Options pop-up menu)—the lower-level members will disappear. You can also select the member name, right-click, and choose Expand Member or Collapse Member from the pop-up menu.

- **Total columns or rows**   Select any row or column member (you can't total when you've selected an individual number "cell") and right-click. Choose Automatic Totals from the pop-up menu. A submenu will appear giving you totaling choices.

- **Add custom calculations**   You may add one or more additional rows or columns (members) based on a calculation. These additional calculated members can consist of such calculations as contribution, growth, ranking, variance, or other statistical calculations that you can create using the MDX query language derived from Microsoft Analysis Services.

To create the calculated member, select the member row or column heading that you want to use as the basis for your calculation. Right-click and choose Add Calculated Member from the pop-up menu. The Calculated Members dialog box will appear.

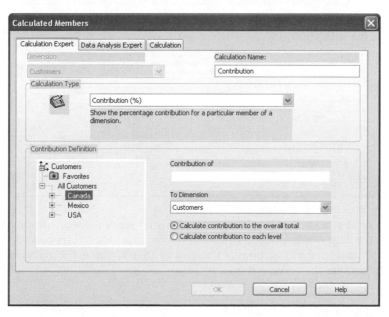

There are three choices: the Calculation Expert tab, the Data Analysis Expert tab, and the Calculation tab. You can create a calculation using one of the three tabs, depending on the type of calculation you want to create.

The Calculation Expert tab allows calculations using contribution, growth, ranking, and variance. The Data Analysis tab allows calculations using trend line, moving average, and linear regression. And, the Calculation tab allows you to create a more complex calculation from scratch using the MDX calculation language.

Once you've finished your calculation, an additional member will appear in the grid showing your calculation. To edit or delete the calculated member, select the member name at the left or top of the grid, right-click, and choose Edit or Delete options from the pop-up menu.

NOTE   *For more in-depth coverage of OLAP calculations and MDX calculations, consult Crystal Reports online help or documentation with your online OLAP analysis tool, such as Microsoft Analysis Services books online.*

- **To create "on-the-fly" filters**   Even though you may have limited your OLAP grid by using a Slice, you can further filter the OLAP grid interactively while you're viewing it. Your filter, based on the "numbers" rather than on the member hierarchy, can consist of a comparison to the numbers, or a top or bottom "N" or percentage.

To add a filter, select the member name column or row that you want to use as a filter (you can't click a number in a cell—it has to be at the edge of a column or row, and only a member name that shows some "filter-able" numbers—not all rows or columns—can be filtered) and right-click. Choose Add Filter from the pop-up menu. The Define Filter dialog box will appear.

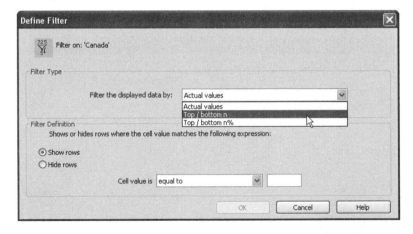

Once you've applied your filter, you'll see a reduced set of rows or columns in the grid, with the filter limiting what appears. You'll know you've added a filter to a row or column if you point to it and your mouse pointer changes to an X. If you want to modify or remove the filter, right-click on the column or row again and choose Edit Filter or Remove Filter from the pop-up menu.

- **Sort the rows or columns by numeric values**   Normally, rows and columns are ordered according to the member name at the top of the column or the left of the row. However, you can sort the rows or columns by "the numbers" if you choose. To do this, select the row or column member name you want to sort (you can't click a number, and the row or column you choose must be "sort-able"—not all columns or rows will offer the option), right-click, and choose Add First Sort from the pop-up menu. A submenu will appear with sorting options. Choose your desired sort option. Notice that the selected row or column is now sorted by the numbers. Also notice that you'll see a double-arrow cursor appear when you point to the row or column member name, indicating that a sort exists.

If you have duplicate values in a row or column and you wish to add a second level of sorting, click the next column or row member name that you want to sort, right-click, and choose Add Next Sort. Choose similar options.

To change or remove an existing sort, select a row or column member name (one with the double-arrow cursor, indicating an existing sort), right-click, and choose Change Direction of Sort or Remove Sort.

The OLAP Worksheet

If the interactivity options discussed previously in the chapter aren't enough, Crystal Reports includes even more OLAP interactivity with the OLAP Worksheet. The OLAP Worksheet is actually largely based on the Crystal Analysis Pro and BusinessObjects OLAP Intelligence OLAP Analysis tools, providing a great deal of "slice, dice, swap, and analyze" interactivity right in Crystal Reports.

To display the OLAP Worksheet, select the desired OLAP grid object in the Preview tab (you can't launch the OLAP Worksheet in the Design tab). Then, right-click and choose View Cube from the pop-up menu. The OLAP grid will be displayed in an additional tab in Crystal Reports labeled Cube View, as shown in Figure 19-7.

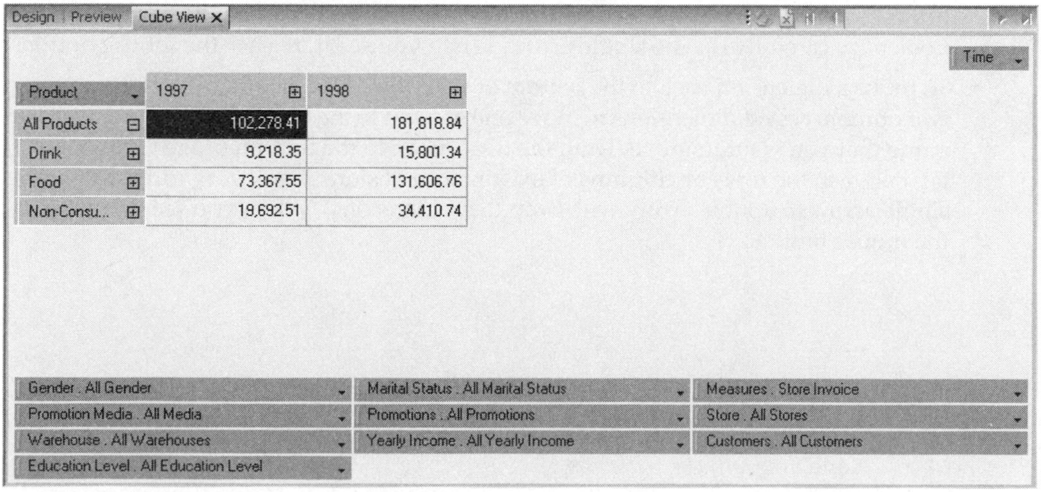

Figure 19-7   OLAP Worksheet Cube View tab

Once you've launched the OLAP Worksheet, you may return to the report's regular Design or Preview tabs by just clicking them, and then return to the Cube View tab by clicking it. To close the Cube View tab and return to a regular report view, click the x on the Cube View tab.

Interactivity in the OLAP Worksheet is somewhat similar to that of the OLAP grid in the preview tab discussed earlier in the report. There is also additional functionality to swap and nest dimensions.

These are among the highlights of OLAP Worksheet interactivity:

- Click plus or minus signs to drill down or drill up (expand or compact members).

- To "drill through" to base relational database data that makes up an individual cell number, right-click on the cell and choose Drill Through from the pop-up menu (only limited OLAP cube servers provide this functionality, so this option may not be available).

- Right-click a member name (row or column name) to choose options from the pop-up menu. Many of these options are similar to those discussed earlier in the chapter relating to the OLAP grid. Some notable additions to the pop-up menu include formatting options, including the Highlighting Exception option, which will color cells that fall within selected numeric ranges.

- Click down arrows next to a dimension to launch the Member Selector (Figure 19-3 earlier in the chapter) where you can choose to display individual members of the hierarchy in the grid, or slice the grid (if you choose a dimension at the bottom of the grid).

- To swap a row or column dimension with another row or column dimension, or a filter dimension (at the bottom of the Cube View tab), click the dimension name that you wish to swap. Then, drag the dimension to the other dimension that you wish to swap with. When you see the double-arrow, release the mouse button.

- To nest or "stack" dimensions (add an additional row or column dimension within another dimension), click the dimension name that you wish to nest. Then, drag the dimension to the existing row or column dimension that you wish to nest it under. Look very carefully for the single arrow. When you see it, release the mouse button.

- To move a dimension back to the bottom of the Cube View tab (there must be at least two or more nested dimensions to move one of them to the bottom), click the dimension name that you want to move. Drag the dimension to the bottom of the Cube View tab between the rows or columns of existing dimensions. Look very carefully for the single arrow (a double arrow will swap the dimensions). When you see it, release the mouse button.

Reporting from Proprietary Data Types

C rystal Reports is best known as the "reporting tool of choice" for use with any standard corporate database. "Standard" databases might generally be thought to include Microsoft Access or SQL Server, Sybase, Oracle, Informix, IBM DB2, and others that are well known in the mainstream of corporate database technology.

But, what do you do if your data is contained in some other form of database or data file? Well, if the database or data file system is very proprietary and out of the mainstream, and the vendor doesn't provide an ODBC (open database connectivity) or OLE DB driver for the database, then you may be, quite simply, out of luck. However, many proprietary databases can be accessed via ODBC or OLE DB, which Crystal Reports will work with. You can also create reports against regular ASCII-delimited text files and against XML files that conform to certain standards. And, Crystal Reports supports other data types directly, without even requiring an ODBC driver. You can create reports based on Microsoft Exchange Server and Systems Management Server databases, the ubiquitous ACT! contact manager, Microsoft Outlook, Windows Server and XP event logs, Microsoft Customer Relationship Management data, and web server activity logs.

The general approach for creating reports against these proprietary types of data sources is similar, regardless of the data source:

1. Ensure that the Crystal Reports Data Access driver you wish to report from is installed. If you're unsure, rerun Crystal Reports setup and expand the Data Access area to ensure that proper drivers have been installed. If you haven't done this in advance, you may be prompted to insert the Crystal Reports XI CD when you initially try to create a report based on a certain type of data.

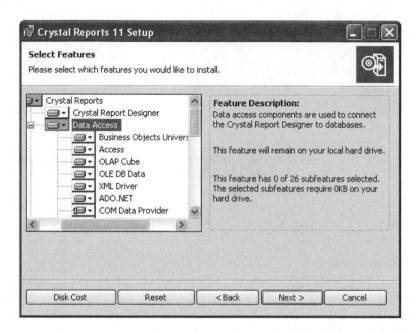

2. Ensure that the software you want to report from (such as Microsoft Outlook), or the vendor's "client" application to access data (such as an Oracle database client), is installed on the same PC as Crystal Reports. Crystal Reports automatically detects these software packages and will list them when you choose a data source.

3. Create a new report using either the report wizards or the Blank Report option. Using either a wizard or the Blank Report option, expand the Create New Connection category of the Database Expert. Then, look for the type of data you want to report against. So, if you want to write reports against a Microsoft Exchange server, choose one of the Exchange data types in from the Create New Connection category, such as Exchange Message Tracking Log. To report against Lotus Domino, expand the More Data Sources folder from within the Create New Connection category and choose the Lotus Domino entry.

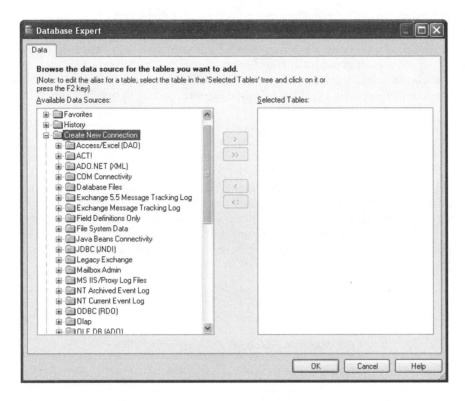

4. Follow any prompts specific to the data source, such as choosing an Exchange server and profile. You'll then see a list of tables and/or fields that are specific to that data type. Use them in your report just as you would use other database tables and fields.

Although Crystal Reports supports many popular data types, most of this chapter will focus on four of the most often used: Microsoft Outlook, the file system data (basically, the disk directory on a PC or network disk drive), the Windows NT/2000/XP event log, and standard web server activity logs.

In addition, the chapter also focuses on reporting from an XML data source, handled through an ODBC driver provided with Crystal Reports, or through a new "native" XML driver added to Crystal Reports XI. And, you'll also find an example of connecting to a BusinessObjects Enterprise Universe, another new capability provided by version XI.

Reporting from Microsoft Outlook

Microsoft Outlook has become a popular standard on office desktops, because it smoothly integrates e-mail, contact management, and calendar maintenance in one package. Outlook's folder metaphor is handy for organizing your office affairs, and it's also handy for reporting.

The first requirement for creating a Crystal Report based on your Outlook folders is rather obvious—you must have Outlook installed on your PC. More specifically, you must have Outlook installed on the same computer on which you will be running Crystal Reports. Crystal Reports won't report on any other Outlook systems on the network—just your own.

To report on your Outlook data, start a new report just as you would for a standard database. You can use the report wizards or the Blank Report option. In either case, expand the Create New Connection category and then expand the Outlook folder. If you have not reported from Outlook before, or there is more than one Outlook Profile on your system, you'll be presented with the Choose Profile dialog box and will need to select your profile (or the default Microsoft Outlook profile) from the drop-down list and click OK. Then you'll be presented with the Choose Folder dialog box, showing the folder hierarchy of your Outlook data. Choose the folder that you want to report on and click OK.

NOTE   *In order to use Outlook as a data source with Crystal Reports, you need to use the full version of Microsoft Outlook. Outlook Express is not available for use in Crystal Reports.*

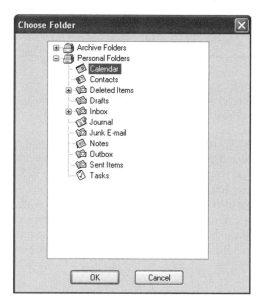

CAUTION   *You cannot report on the Notes folder. You'll receive an error message if you try to select it.*

After you choose the folder and click OK, a "table" will appear in the Available Data Sources list. Select and add the folder just as you would any database table. When you close the Database Expert or advance to the next wizard area, the list of Outlook fields you can report from will appear in the expert or in the Field Explorer.

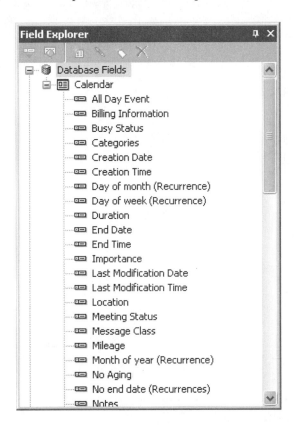

Use the Outlook fields just like other database fields to create your report. You can sort, group, and format the report as you normally would. You can also create formulas, if necessary, to calculate or modify the way Outlook material appears in the report. Figure 20-1 shows a sample report based on the Calendar folder from Outlook.

NOTE *The field names you see in the Crystal Reports Field Explorer may not always match the field names you see in Outlook. If you don't see the field you expect, look for a reasonable alternative field name. Also, you may need to add other Outlook folders (such as the Contact folder and the Inbox folder) and link the two together to get all the data you expect. Make sure you link on correct fields—Auto Linking typically won't pick the correct fields to perform an Outlook link.*

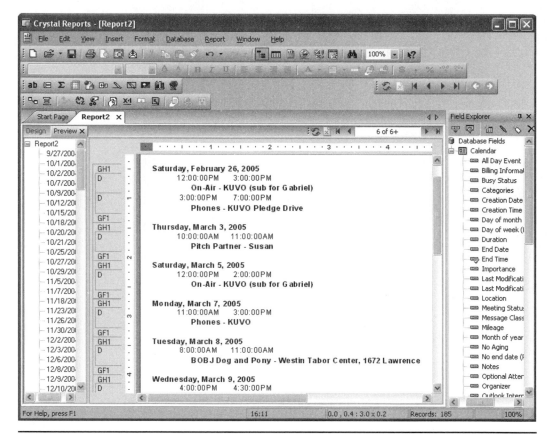

FIGURE 20-1   Crystal Report based on the Outlook Calendar folder

Reporting from the File System Data

You are probably familiar with Explorer, the Windows application that helps you view the hierarchy and layout of your local and network drives, as well as locate one or more particular files you may be looking for. However, if you want a more powerful reporting-type tool to search or report on drive contents, you need another software solution.

Crystal Reports provides the file system data option, allowing you to write powerful reports against any local or network drive on your PC. By choosing a drive and folder or directory, as well as specifying some detailed criteria (if you choose), you can create reports that select and sort files and folders with the complete power and flexibility of Crystal Reports.

To report on your file system data, start a new report just as you would for a standard database. You can use the report wizards or the Blank Report option. When choosing a database, expand the File System Data folder in the Create New Connection category.

You'll be presented with the File System Data dialog box, shown in Figure 20-2. If you simply want to supply a drive or path name, you can either type it or click the ellipses button to navigate to the desired drive and directory. You may also add some additional criteria to narrow down the files and directories you want to see.

Choose whether to include all files or
only those that match wildcard pattern

Type or choose a
directory to report on

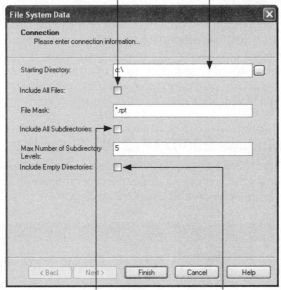

Choose whether to include all subdirectories, or only *N* levels
deep (you must uncheck Include All Subdirectories to see this)

Include directory names
even if they contain no files

FIGURE 20-2   The File System Data dialog box

Make your choices and click Finish. A table entry in the Database Expert Available Data
Sources list will appear, showing the directory you chose. Add it to the Selected tables list to
proceed.

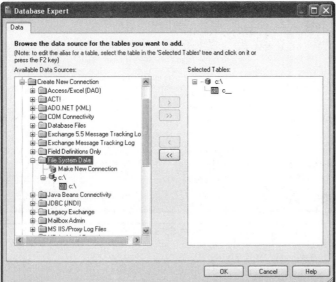

The Field Explorer will expose many different fields containing information you might not have previously been familiar with. Some fields apply only to certain types of files, such as .EXE or .DLL files. Others apply only to files that belong to certain applications (for example, Number of Words generally applies only to Word or other word processing documents). Use these file system fields just like other database fields to create your report. You can sort, group, and format the report as you normally would. You can use the fields to create flexible selection criteria to narrow down your report. You can also create formulas, if necessary, to calculate or modify the way file system material appears in the report. Figure 20-3 shows a sample report based on a local C disk drive.

Reporting from the Windows 2000/XP/2003 Event Log

As Windows 2000, XP, and 2003 Server replace former desktop leaders Windows 95 and Windows 98 and Windows NT server systems, reporting off these operating system logs becomes an even more important capability of Crystal Reports.

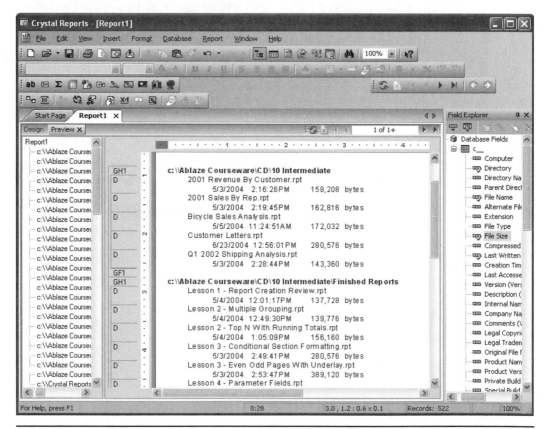

Figure 20-3   Crystal Report based on file system data

An integrated part of the original Windows NT, and its successors Windows 2000, XP, and Windows Server 2003, is the event log. The event logs are files that document events that occur during the general operation of Windows. Several different types of event logs are available, and different types of entries are placed in the event logs as users log on and off, and programs start, stop, and operate. Crystal Reports includes the capability to create flexible reports on these event logs.

NOTE *Although designing reports against the event logs won't harm the computer containing the log, you probably won't find the information returned to be of much use if you're not generally familiar with Windows 2000/XP/2003 and its components. This Crystal Reports capability will probably be most useful to system administrators and other technical personnel.*

To report on event logs, start a new report just as you would for a standard database. You can use the report wizards or the Blank Report option. In either case, expand the NT Current Event Log folder in the Create New Connection category to report on current active event logs on Windows computers. Or, you can click the NT Archived Event Log folder to display an Open File dialog box in which to search for archived (.EVT) event log files. If you use this option, upon selecting an event log you will be presented with the Select Archived Event Log dialog box, and you must identify the type of event log you selected (System, Security, or Application).

If you choose the NT Current Event Log folder, you'll see the Select Current Event Log dialog box, shown in Figure 20-4. This allows you to select an event log on a remote computer—it doesn't have to reside on the computer that you are running Crystal Reports on. You can even include event logs from more than one computer at a time in your report, if you choose.

If you know the domain and computer name, you can simply type it in the Computer(s) text box at the top of the dialog box. If you include more than one computer name, separate the names with commas. If you're not sure which computers to include, you can use the Explorer-like hierarchy to select the computers you wish to use. When you see the computer list, you can select one or more computers.

FIGURE 20-4
The Select
Current Event Log
dialog box

Type in one or more
computer names,
separated by commas

Use the plus and minus
signs or double-click to
navigate through your
network hierarchy

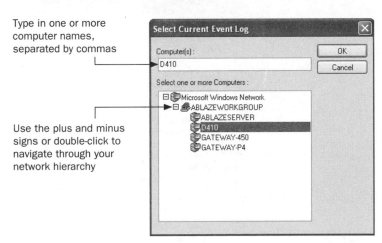

Make your choices and click OK. A new level in the Database Expert will appear for the computer you've chosen, showing the three event logs that are available as tables: Application, Security, and System.

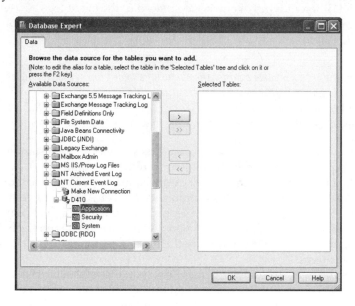

Depending on the types of events you want your report to be based on, choose the appropriate log. If you'd like a better idea of what types of events are contained in each log, use the Event Viewer application from the Windows Control Panel to view the different event log entries. Once you've made your log choice, the list of event log fields you can report on will appear in the expert or in the Field Explorer.

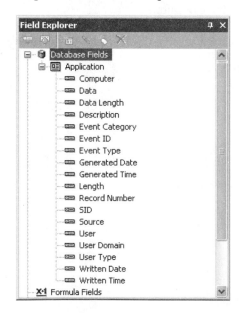

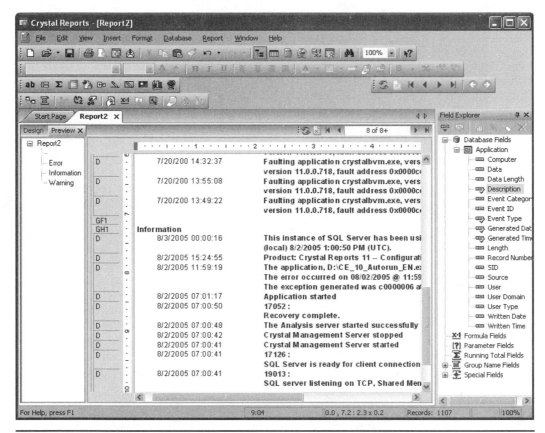

Figure 20-5   Crystal Report based on event log

Use these event log fields just like other database fields to create your report. You can sort, group, and format the report as you normally would. The Event Viewer application can help you identify what some of the available fields contain. You can use the fields to create flexible selection criteria to narrow down your report, and you can also create formulas, if necessary, to calculate or modify the way event-log material appears in the report. Figure 20-5 shows a sample report based on a Windows NT application event log.

Reporting from Web Server Logs

It's now a given that most organizations need to document what pages web users are pointing their browsers to, as well as when and from where. Most web servers, such as those from Microsoft, Netscape, and others, keep various amounts and levels of data about web site visits. What better tool to create web activity reports than Crystal Reports?

There are several types of web server logs that you may encounter, depending mostly on the web server that you are using. Most web server logs are standard delimited ASCII files (a term you don't necessarily need to be familiar with, but it is a common denominator for data-file formats). However, the layout of fields in the files and the information they contain can vary from server to server. There are several "standard" types of log files, including a file type simply known as Standard, and another known as the NCSA Standard, defined by the National Center for Supercomputing Applications for its original web server. Other web server developers have adopted both standards. In addition, if you are using Microsoft Internet Information Server (IIS), you'll find additional types of log files available, such as Microsoft's extended log format. When you configure IIS, you can choose the type of log file that is generated, as well as the fields that are kept in the log file.

As a general rule, web servers will create a new log file every day, adding statistics to the daily log file as they occur. The filenames consist of variations of the date on which they were created, with a standard file extension. For example, you may see a file named EX050302.LOG, indicating a Microsoft extended-format log for March 2, 2005. These files will be located in a standard directory, such as WINDOWS\system32\LogFiles\W3SVC1 (this is the default location for Microsoft IIS versions running on Windows Server 2003).

To report on web server logs, start a new report just as you would for a standard database. You can use the report wizards or the Blank Report option. In either case, expand the Create New Connection category of the Database Expert to proceed. You'll see two categories that may interest you: MS IIS/Proxy Log Files and Web/IIS Log Files. MS IIS/Proxy Log Files will report on "standard" formats, the various Microsoft IIS formats, and Web proxy and Winsock Proxy formats. The Web/IIS Log Files folder will simply report on "standard" and NCSA formatted logs.

Regardless of whether you're using a wizard or the Blank Report option, the rest of the prompts will be consistent. If you choose the more generic Web Log option, you'll simply be prompted to choose a drive and directory where the standard or NCSA Web logs are located. You can type or browse to select a local or network drive and directory. If you choose the IIS option, you'll see the Select Log Files And Dates dialog box, as illustrated in Figure 20-6.

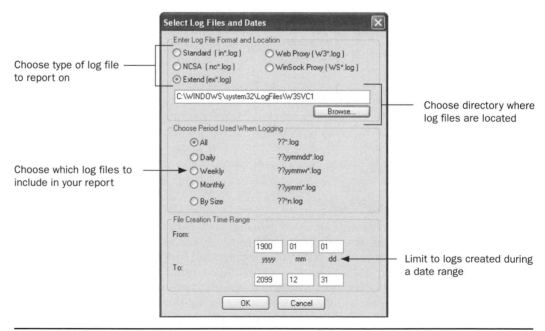

FIGURE 20-6 IIS Select Log Files and Dates dialog box

Choose the type of log file your Web server uses (look for files in a standard location with the .LOG extension to help determine this). You can also choose the format your web server uses when writing log files, based on how often it creates a new log file. And, if you prefer to limit Crystal Reports to using only log files within a certain date range, make that selection as well.

When you're finished with your choices, click OK. A new database entry will appear in the Available Data Sources list of the Database Expert showing the directory name of the log files. Underneath this category, a table-type entry will appear, showing a somewhat cryptic entry for the log files you just chose. Add this table to your report (by double-clicking the table name, dragging it to the Selected Tables list, or selecting the table name and clicking the right arrow) and close the Database Expert. The list of web server log fields you can report from will appear in the wizard or in the Field Explorer.

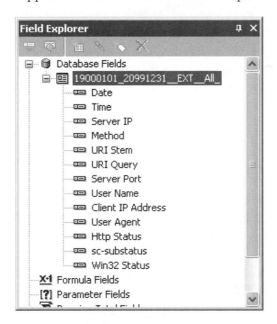

NOTE *The log fields you see here will vary, depending on the web server you are using and the log settings you've chosen for that web server. If you're using Microsoft IIS with Windows 2000, XP, or 2003 Server, you can configure the server to include a variety of helpful statistical fields.*

Use these web server log fields just like other database fields when creating your report. You can sort, group, and format the report as you normally would. You can use the fields to create flexible selection criteria to narrow down your report. You can also create formulas, if necessary, to calculate or modify the way web server log material appears in the report. Figure 20-7 shows a sample report based on a Windows 2003 Server web server log.

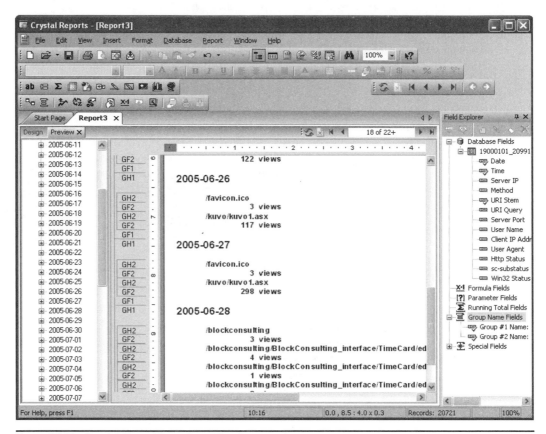

FIGURE 20-7 Crystal Report based on IIS web server log

Crystal Reporting with XML

As Extensible Markup Language, or *XML*, becomes more of a standard data interchange format (both in Windows and Unix/Linux environments), the need for a robust reporting tool increases as well. Crystal Reports includes flexible and comprehensive support for reporting from XML data sources.

Crystal Reports XI adds additional XML support with the inclusion of a new "native" XML driver. This new driver doesn't make use of ODBC for connection to an XML data source. Instead, it reads XML data directly (either from a data file located on a local or network drive, or from a network or Internet "stream") and processes the XML data as though it were a standard database with consistent table and field formats. And, the DataDirect ODBC driver for XML data sources that existed in previous Crystal Reports versions is still available to use with version XI as well.

XML ODBC Driver

The DataDirect ODBC driver is one way to base a Crystal Report on an XML data source. In addition to XML ODBC drivers that may be included with Crystal Reports, other ODBC drivers (including XML drivers) may be downloaded from the Business Objects web site. Once the drivers have been installed on your computer, you may use the ODBC Administrator from the Windows Control Panel to set up an ODBC driver for your specific XML data source. Once you've chosen various options particular to your environment, such as locations for the XML data files and optional schema files they conform to, you can return to Crystal Reports and begin the report design process.

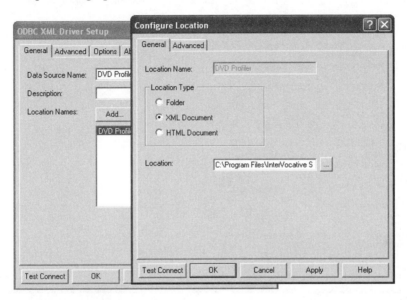

NOTE *The Merant DataDirect ODBC drivers have some limitations that may preclude connecting to your XML file. For more information about these limitations, as well as general information about this ODBC driver, see "DataDirect XML Driver" in Crystal Reports online help.*

Figure 20-8 shows an XML file exported from a personal video library database program, to which the XML ODBC driver can connect. The file consists of a DVD collection data, with tags identifying the different data elements.

To report on a supported XML file, start a new report just as you would for a standard database. You can use the report wizards or the Blank Report option. Expand the Create New Connection section of the Available Data Sources list, and then expand the ODBC (RDO) entry. From the Data Source Selection dialog box, choose the XML data source name that

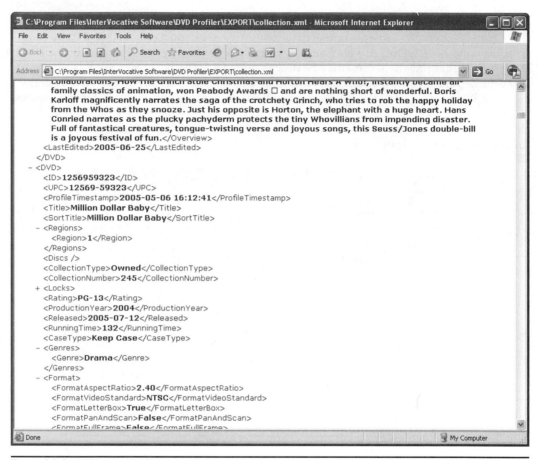

FIGURE 20-8 XML sample file

you defined for XML reporting. The ODBC XML Driver Connection dialog box appears. If you specified a user ID and password requirement when you defined the ODBC data source, specify them on this dialog box.

Once you've completed this dialog box, the Database Expert will return with a new database entry appearing under the ODBC category. If you expand the database and subsequent entries, you'll eventually see a "table name" that corresponds to the XML data that the ODBC data source refers to.

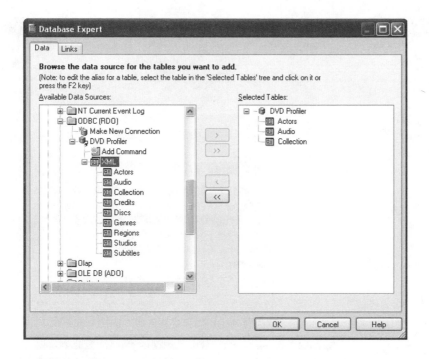

CAUTION *Depending on how you set up the ODBC data source, you may see multiple XML tables listed. However, they will not necessarily return valid data to Crystal Reports if they are not organized in a supported XML format.*

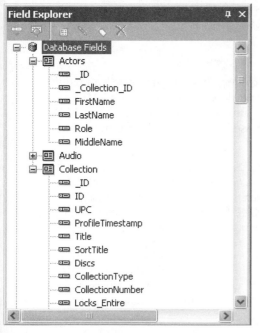

Select the desired XML file from the list and add it to the report (by double-clicking the table name, by dragging the table name to the Selected Tables list, or by selecting the table name and clicking the right arrow). If you add multiple tables, link them on the Links tab. Then, close the Database Expert. The list of fields you can report from will appear in the expert or in the Field Explorer.

From this point forward, designing an XML-based report is virtually the same as designing a report based on another data source. You can sort, group, and format the report as you normally would. You can use the fields to create flexible selection criteria to narrow down your report. You can also create formulas, if necessary, to calculate or modify the way XML data appears in the report. Figure 20-9 shows a sample report based on the XML DVD collection data.

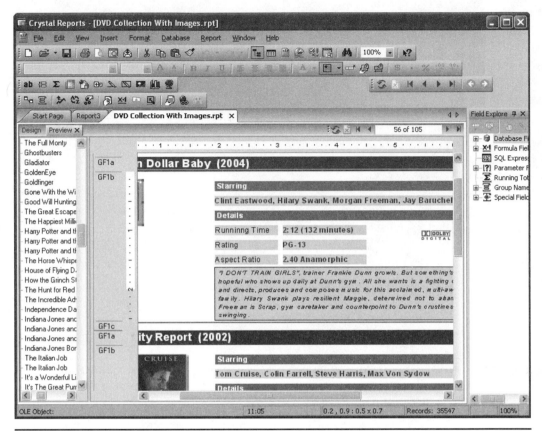

Figure 20-9   Report based on XML data

New XML Native Driver

Crystal Reports XI now includes a "native" XML data driver. This new driver doesn't require any ODBC data source configuration but can directly work with local/network XML data files, as well as network/Internet-based XML data streams from such "providers" as XML web services. These various XML data sources can be used with any of the report wizards of the Blank Report option.

NOTE   *The Crystal native XML driver is Java-based. As such, there are certain prerequisites that must be met for the driver to work properly, such as presence of a necessary Java Software Development Kit and configuration of the CRConfig.XML file. Information on these requirements can be found in online Crystal Reports help. Search for "XML Driver."*

To report on XML data with the native driver, start a new report just as you would for a standard database. Expand the Create New Connection section of the Available Data Sources list, and then select the XML entry. The XML dialog box will appear, where you can make various entries and choices, depending on the source of your XML data.

There are various options to choose on the initial screen, depending on the type of XML data you wish to report on:

- **Use Local Data Source**   Choose this option to base your report on an XML file located on your hard disk or a network drive. You may then type the full path/file name into the box below the radio button, or click the ellipsis button to find the file from a standard Open dialog box.

- **Use HTTP(S) Data Source**   Choose this option to base your report on an XML "stream" from a network data source (such as a data coming from a web page hosted by an outside provider). You may then type in the URL that resolves to the XML data source.

- **Specify Schema File**   If you choose either the Local Data Source or HTTP(S) Data Source option, you may check this box if a separate schema file (a file describing the table/field data layout of the source XML data) is required. You'll specify the actual filename or URL of the schema file in later screens in the XML dialog box.

- **Use Web Service Data Source**   Choose this option to base your report on an XML web service from a local server, or a remote web service provided by an outside provider. Specific connection information for the web service—such as WSDL file, service, and port—is specified in screens later in the XML dialog box.

Depending on which data source you choose on the first screen, additional screens in the XML dialog box will vary when you click the Next button. For example, you may be prompted for a user ID and password for the HTTP(S) data source you chose. Or, you may be prompted to supply a WSDL file location for a web service. You may also be prompted to supply a schema file location (you may choose to supply a local schema file located on your hard drive or a network drive, or a network schema file supplied with a URL). Additional screens will prompt for other required or optional items, such as user ID/password combinations required to access the schema file. And, if you are using an HTTP(S) data source, you'll have the option to supply different values for portions of the URL that Crystal Reports detects (known as *HTTP Parameters*). You may supply fixed values for these, or even supply an @PROMPT formula that will create a report parameter field to prompt for a variable value every time the report is refreshed (exact argument descriptions for the @PROMPT formula can be found in online help).

Once you've completed all XML dialog screens, click Finish. The list of XML "tables" will appear in the Database Expert. Choose desired tables and add them to the report, as you would any other database tables. Then, close the Database Expert. The list of fields you can report from will appear in the expert or in the Field Explorer.

From this point forward, designing an XML-based report is virtually the same as for a report based on another data source. You can sort, group, and format the report as you normally would. You can use the fields to create flexible selection criteria to narrow down your report. You can also create formulas, if necessary, to calculate or modify the way XML data appears in the report.

BusinessObjects Enterprise Universes

As Crystal products are gradually merged with the Business Objects product line following the Business Objects acquisition of the Crystal product suite, more integration options are appearing in the various Crystal products. One example is that the Business Objects *Universe* has been added as an available data source to Crystal Reports XI. By selecting the Universes option in the Database Expert (either in a report wizard or with the Blank Report option), you may base a Crystal Report on a Business Objects universe.

PART I

NOTE *Only universes contained within a BusinessObjects Enterprise (BOE) system may be used as a Crystal Reports data source. Older versions of universes not contained in a BusinessObjects Enterprise system are not available as Crystal Reports data sources.*

To base a report on a universe, start a new report just as you would for a standard database. You can use the report wizards or the Blank Report option. Expand the Create New Connection section of the Available Data Sources list and select the Universes category. If you are not already logged on to a BusinessObjects Enterprise system, you'll be prompted to log on. Supply valid logon credentials to co nnect to the desired BOE system.

The BusinessObjects Enterprise Explorer dialog box will appear, showing only universe objects from the BOE system you've logged on to. Select the desired universe and click Open. The Business Objects Query Panel will appear, as shown in Figure 20-10.

If you've used previous Business Objects products, you may be familiar with the Query Panel. Ultimately, you make choices in this panel to create SQL (Structured Query Language) that will be returned to the Database Expert as a SQL Command (covered in more detail in Chapter 15). Simply drag objects from the left-hand pane to the Result Objects pane (you may also double-click a desired object) to include the object on the report. To add a filter to limit the report to a specific set of database records, drag an object from either the object list or the Result Objects pane to the Query Filters pane. A separate dialog box will appear

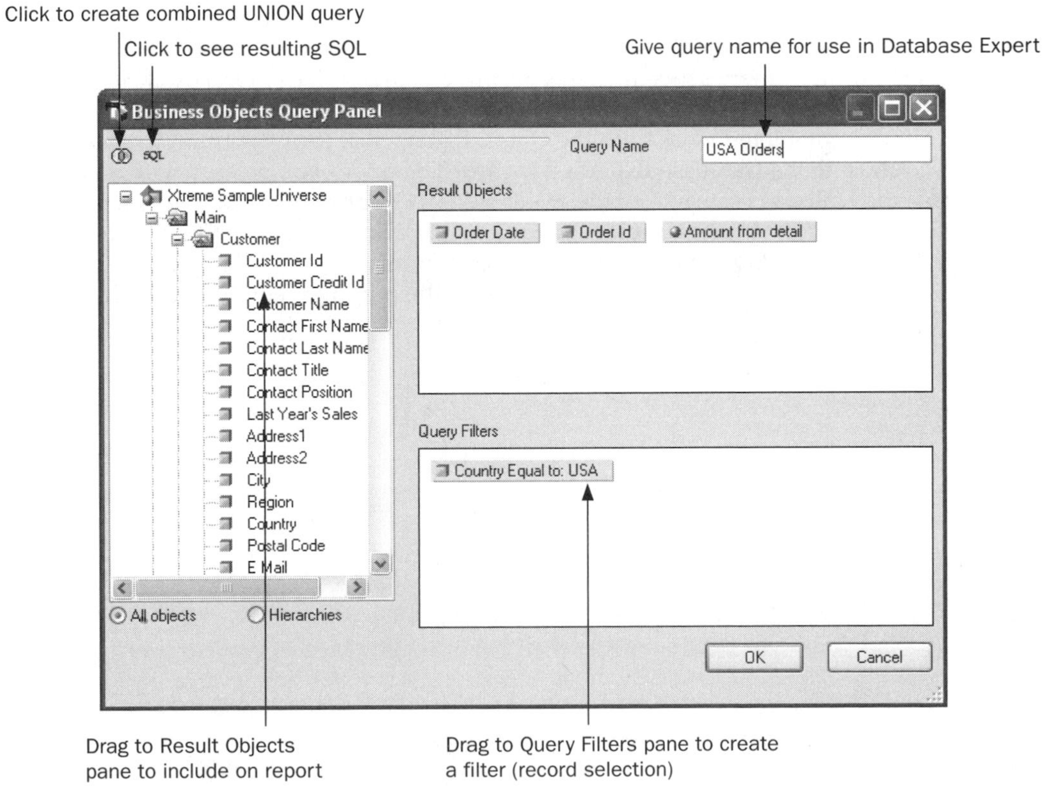

Click to create combined UNION query

Click to see resulting SQL

Give query name for use in Database Expert

Drag to Result Objects pane to include on report

Drag to Query Filters pane to create a filter (record selection)

FIGURE 20-10 Query Panel based on universe

where you may specify filter criteria (including the ability to base the filter on a prompt, as you do when creating a parameter field with a SQL Command or in a report).

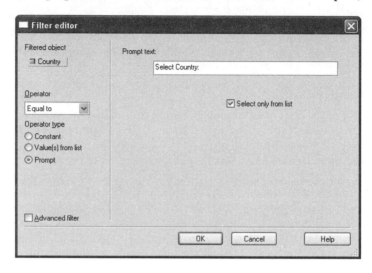

Additional features on the Query Panel include the ability to see the SQL that your query will produce by clicking the small SQL button in the upper left-hand corner. You may also combine multiple queries together (specifically, create a SQL UNION) by clicking the Combine Queries button in the upper left-hand corner of the Query Panel.

Once you've completed work with the Query Panel, click the OK button to save the query and return to the Database Expert or wizard. The query you created will appear underneath the Universes category of the Available Data Sources list. Add it to the report, as you would any other database table (Crystal Reports will treat it as a SQL Command). If you wish to view the SQL that the query creates, you may right-click the query in the Selected Tables list and choose View Command from the pop-up menu. If you wish to edit the query, right-click the query in the Selected Tables list and choose Edit Command from the pop-up menu. The Query Panel will reappear, where you may make changes to the query.

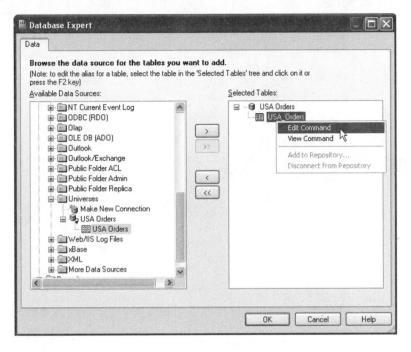

Crystal Reports XI on the Web

Crystal Reports Web Alternatives

S o far, this book has discussed many techniques for creating sophisticated reports with the Crystal Reports XI designer. Part III of the book discusses methods for integrating those reports into your custom web and Windows applications using custom programming tools with Active Server Pages, Visual Basic, and Visual Studio .NET. But, as both large and small business organizations are moving even more to web-based technology for both internal corporate intranets and the Internet, ways to display your Crystal reports in a web browser without custom programming is crucial.

Various alternatives to get your reports on the Web are available, based on Crystal Reports edition, your particular web environment, and your budget (many options require upgrades or additional licenses). From simple HTML exports, to third-party utilities, to a multitier, multiserver enterprise-wide implementation of Crystal Reports Server, you have many choices to consider when looking toward web distribution and customization of Crystal Reports.

These different options give you many ways to place a Crystal Report on the Web—either on your internal corporate intranet or on the entire Internet. Some require custom programming (covered in other chapters), and others are out-of-the-box solutions:

- **Export static reports to HTML format (covered in this chapter)** In this case, you just export your report to one of several different HTML formats, much as you would export a Word or Excel file. Viewers can simply open the HTML file in their browser, or the file can be placed on a web server for viewing.

- **Use the Report Designer Component from Crystal Reports XI Developer Edition with Microsoft Active Server Pages (covered in Chapter 25) or Java Server Pages** This Report Designer Component is the same programming interface used with Visual Basic and provides a high level of web integration for reports. This approach requires ASP or JSP custom programming. The Report Designer Component offers several advantages to web programmers, such as the ability to create or modify reports on the fly in web pages and then save the resulting .RPT files on disk.

TIP   *The Report Application Server (introduced as a stand alone web integration option in Crystal Reports 9 and included with Crystal Reports 10 as Crystal Enterprise Embedded Edition) is still an option for web-based reporting with ASP and JSP. However, it is now only available as part of Crystal Reports Server XI and can no longer be installed as a stand alone product. As such, you have more architectural, licensing, and cost considerations when considering an upgrade of your RAS application to version XI.*

- **Use the Java Reporting Component**   This reporting engine provides some (but not all) of the capabilities of other Microsoft-oriented reporting engines for web customization. Using custom-programmed Java Server Pages, this approach allows connecting to a report directly, or through an existing Crystal Reports Server installation. This SDK, along with its associated documentation, is included with Crystal Reports XI Developer Edition and Crystal Reports Server XI.

- **Use Visual Studio .NET with Web Forms (covered in Chapter 26)**   Visual Studio .NET (VS.NET) incorporates a special version of Crystal Reports as its included reporting tool. The VS.NET object model exposes Crystal Reports functionality, allowing complete control of reports at run time in a web browser. Crystal Reports XI Developer edition expands on VS.NET functionality by adding additional capabilities and features to the base VS.NET Crystal Report functionality.

- **Using Third-Party Tools for Web-based Reporting**   Several third-party software developers have created tools that allow Crystal Reports to be placed in various web-based environments. This book's companion web site (www.CrystalBook.com) includes *Crystal: The Complete Toolset*, a web portal constantly updated with the latest available Crystal Reports utilities.

- **Using Crystal Reports Server (covered in Chapters 22, 23, and 24)**   Crystal Reports Server provides a rich, multitier/multiserver method of hosting real-time and automatically scheduled Crystal Reports on the Web. You can use the standard out-of-the-box user interface provided by Crystal Reports Server, or you may completely customize the user interface using HTML and various development technologies, such as ASP.NET or JSP.

NOTE   *While some discussion of customizing the full Crystal Reports Server/BusinessObjects Enterprise environment is discussed later in Part II of this book, almost all web integration methods discussed in this book pertain to Crystal Reports alternatives that don't require installing or using the full Crystal Reports Server product (with the exception of the Report Application Server using the RAS SDK).*

Exporting to Static HTML

More and more, organizations are looking to distribute Crystal Reports to a large audience in a web format, through a company intranet or the Internet. To provide this capability, you need to convert your report to Hypertext Markup Language (HTML) format—the "markup language" understood by web browsers. If you've decided to provide only static, non-interactive reports in a web browser, you simply need to export the report from Crystal Reports, just as you'd export to a Word document or an Excel spreadsheet.

Simply start Crystal Reports and open or create the report you want to export to HTML. Remember that whatever is visible on your screen is what will be exported to HTML. If you want to export the main report, make sure the Preview tab is clicked. If you want to export just a drill-down tab, select the correct drill-down tab before exporting. Then, choose File | Export from the pull-down menus, or click the Export button in the Standard toolbar. Figure 21-1 shows a sample report, consisting of a report containing a title surrounded by a border on all four sides and a drop shadow, and a chart placed alongside data with the "underlay" section formatting option.

When you choose the Export command, the resulting dialog box allows you to choose the format and destination of your report. You'll be concerned with the two HTML format options available in the Format drop-down list: HTML 3.2 and HTML 4.0. The different versions refer to the different extensions of the HTML language that Crystal Reports can use. To determine which version of HTML you want to use, experiment with your own exports and the browsers that your report viewers will use. Typically, version 4 (dynamic HTML) will better represent the actual formatting of the report in the web browser. However, older versions of a web browser (Internet Explorer or Netscape Navigator/Communicator versions prior to 4) may not be able to properly interpret DHTML. If you're using an older version of these browsers, you may see better results with HTML 3.2.

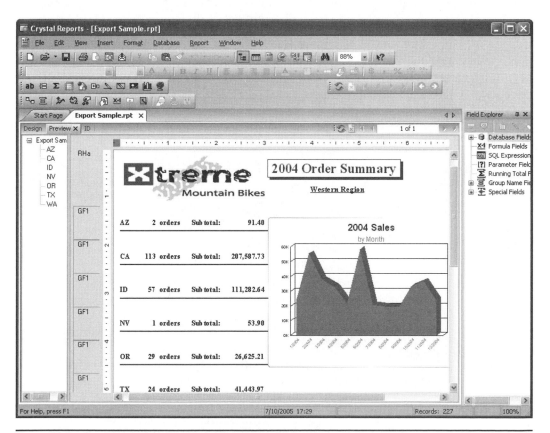

FIGURE 21-1 Sample report with special formatting features

Note   *The HTML export drivers are not installed by default when you install Crystal Reports. If you see a small number 1 beside the export format (indicating "install on first use"), you'll be prompted to insert the Crystal Reports program CD the first time you export to HTML.*

No matter what destination you ultimately choose from the Destination drop-down list, Crystal Reports must write the HTML code and any associated graphics files (for charts, maps, and bitmaps) to a disk folder. You will be asked to make several choices about how and where you want your report exported, as illustrated in Figure 21-2.

Crystal Reports will create a whole new directory to contain the HTML and graphics files that will make up your report. The drive and folder boxes will let you choose an existing directory *under which* a new directory will be created. Type the name of the new directory in the Directory Name box (Crystal Reports will name the new directory HTML by default). If you wish to place the HTML in a specific folder referred to by a web "home" page, make sure you export to the predetermined folder on the web server referred to by the page. Crystal Reports will place the name of the report into the Base File Name box by default. You may want to change this filename to something your web server expects (for example, DEFAULT.HTM), if you are exporting to a web server folder.

You may also use the Page Navigator and Separate HTML Pages check boxes (which typically are helpful only with reports that are more than one page in length). If you check Separate HTML Pages, Crystal Reports will export sequentially numbered HTML pages, one for each page in the report. For example, if you're exporting a drill-down tab that consists of four pages, and you choose DEFAULT.HTM as the base filename, the first page of the report will be exported to DEFAULT1.HTM, the second to DEFAULT2.HTM, the third to DEFAULT3.HTM, and the fourth to DEFAULT4.HTM. If you don't check this box, all three report pages will be combined into one larger DEFAULT.HTM.

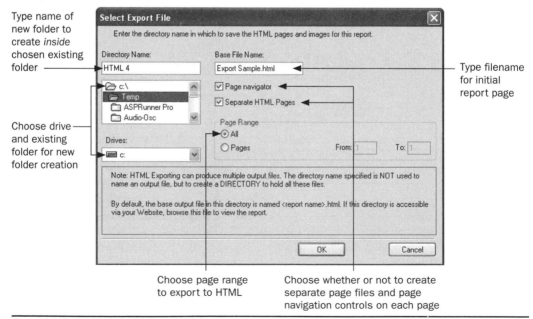

FIGURE 21-2   Export to HTML dialog box

CAUTION *This numbering behavior when using the page navigator may cause unintended results by appending numbers onto each HTML file. Keep this behavior in mind if your web server expects a default filename, such as DEFAULT.HTM. You may wish to actually export your report with a different filename and create a DEFAULT.HTM file that immediately redirects the viewer to the "number 1" exported filename.*

If you check Page Navigator, Crystal Reports will place First, Next, Previous, and Last navigation hyperlinks at the bottom of each page that is exported. If you export to separate HTML pages, these links will navigate to the proper separate HTML page. If you don't export to separate HTML pages, the navigation links will still appear inside the one large HTML page, simply moving the viewer to different locations within the one HTML page.

Once you've specified all export options, click OK. If the folder you specified doesn't exist, Crystal Reports will automatically create it. If the folder already exists and contains an HTML file with the same name as you specified, you'll be prompted to overwrite the existing file. In addition to the HTML report file, Crystal Reports will create uniquely numbered .PNG graphics files—one for each bitmap, chart, or map contained in the report.

When you point your browser to the folder and view the HTML file, you'll see the exported report in the browser window, as shown in Figure 21-3.

Notice the difference between the HTML 3.2 and 4.0 exports. HTML 3.2, for example, didn't display the report title properly and didn't include the horizontal lines between state totals. And, even though the displayed chart appeared beside text, there were significant vertical spacing issues introduced in an HTML 3.2 export. Even HTML 4.0 doesn't always perform perfect exports, but you'll often find a much better rendition of your original report formatting. It's a good idea to try sample exports as you're developing your report, to make sure you don't depend on any features that may not export properly. If your organization has standardized on Adobe Acrobat format files, you can also export to .PDF in the same manner. You'll typically find that Acrobat files exhibit a very accurate representation of your original report formatting.

NOTE *Remember that with HTML, particularly HTML 3.2, some "fancy" report formatting (such as drop shadows or special fonts) may not export to HTML properly. You'll want to try some test exports and view the resulting reports in the web browser that will be used by the majority of your report viewers. That way, you can see what your reports will ultimately look like.*

Don't forget that reports exported to HTML or PDF are static. They will simply show database information as it existed when the report was exported. The only way to update the exported reports is to refresh the report in Crystal Reports and export again. Also, drilling down and using group trees won't work with exported HTML or PDF reports. If you want viewers to be able to refresh reports on their own, as well as interact with the report by drilling down and using the group tree, use other Crystal Reports web options, such as the Report Application Server, Visual Studio .NET, available third-party utilities, or Crystal Reports Server. And, giving web users the ability to print reports on their local printers with accurate pagination also becomes a challenge. The options that best provide this capability are PDF export, the ActiveX or Java report viewers (available with the Report Application Server, some third-party utilities, or Crystal Reports Server), or the ActiveX print control in the Report Application Server or Crystal Reports Server XI.

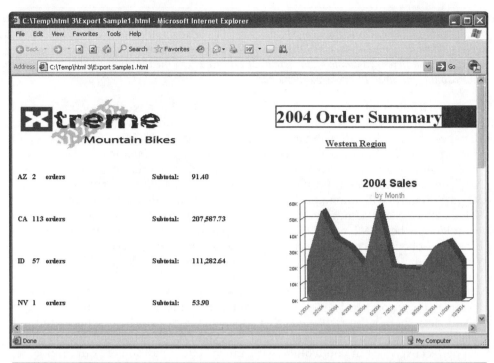

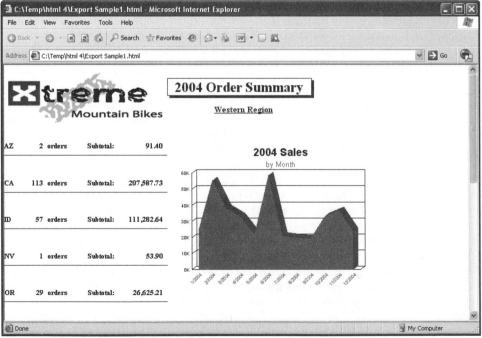

FIGURE 21-3   Export comparison between HTML 3.2 and HTML 4.0

Hyperlink Capabilities

Crystal Reports provides hyperlink capabilities so that you can build hyperlinks into your reports. Virtually any objects on your report, such as text objects, database fields, charts, maps, or bitmap objects, can be linked to web pages, e-mail addresses, other Crystal Reports, or other Windows programs. When you point to an object with an attached hyperlink, your mouse cursor turns into the now-familiar pointing finger. Click, and your web browser will launch the web site, your e-mail program will launch a new message window, or the Windows program or file that is specified will be launched.

Hyperlinks are created right in the Crystal Reports designer. In either the Design or Preview tab, select the object you want to create the hyperlink for. Then, choose Format | Hyperlink from the pull-down menus, right-click, and choose Format Field (or a similar format option) from the pop-up menu, or click the Hyperlink toolbar button from the Expert Tools toolbar. The Format Editor will appear. If it's not already selected, click the Hyperlink tab, shown in Figure 21-4.

Choose the type of hyperlink you'd like to create:

- **No Hyperlink**   If a hyperlink has already been assigned to this object, clicking this radio button will clear the hyperlink.

- **An E-Mail Address**   Click this radio button and add the e-mail address you want the hyperlink to send e-mail to in the Hyperlink Information text box after the mailto: text. If you'd like to create a conditional string formula to customize the hyperlink according to a database field or conditional value, click the conditional formula button next to the text box.

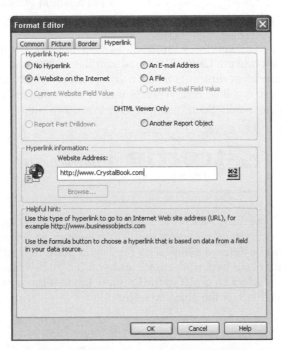

FIGURE 21-4   The Format Editor Hyperlink tab

- **A Web site on the Internet**   Click this radio button and add the web site URL you want the hyperlink to launch in the Hyperlink Information text box after the http:// text. If you'd like to create a conditional string formula to customize the hyperlink according to a database field or conditional value, click the conditional formula button next to the text box.

- **A File**   Click this radio button and add the path and filename of the file you want the hyperlink to launch or the command you want to execute in the Hyperlink Information text box. Type the same command or path/filename you'd type after choosing Start | Run in Windows. If you'd like to create a conditional string formula to customize the hyperlink according to a database field or conditional value, click the conditional formula button next to the text box.

- **Current Web site Field Value/Current E-mail Field Value**   These options are available only if you've chosen a string database or summary field on the report. In this case, the hyperlink will simply be the value of text from the database. To correctly use this option, the database field must return a complete web site URL (including the http:// prefix), or an e-mail address, depending on which option you've chosen.

NOTE *The "DHTML Viewer Only" options in this dialog box are used to control Guided Navigation and Report Part viewing. More details can be found later in this chapter.*

To further benefit the report viewer, you may wish to click the Common tab on the Format Editor and add a tool tip indicating what the hyperlink does. Either type the tool tip into the tool tip text box directly, or click the conditional formula button next to the text box and enter a string formula that will display when the viewer moves his or her mouse over the object.

Once you've specified all necessary information, click OK to close the Format Editor. When you preview the report in Crystal Reports, you'll see the mouse cursor change to a familiar pointing finger hyperlink cursor when you point to the object. If you added a tool tip, it will appear in a small yellow box. When you click your mouse button, the hyperlink will launch the web page, e-mail Send dialog box, or Windows file.

After you create a hyperlink, follow the same steps you used to create it to modify or remove it. If you are modifying your report in the Preview tab, you may find it difficult to select an object that you've defined a hyperlink for. If you point to it with your mouse, your mouse cursor will change to a hyperlink cursor and you'll actually execute the hyperlink if you click. If you need to select an object in the Preview tab that has a hyperlink associated with it, SHIFT-click or right-click the object to select it.

TIP *Hyperlinks aren't applicable only to reports exported or viewed on the Web. When you view reports in the Crystal Reports Preview tab or view a report integrated with a custom program, hyperlinks will work as you expect. Just remember that a viewer who is using Crystal Reports needs a network connection to your corporate intranet or the Internet to successfully use web or e-mail hyperlinks.*

Cascading Style Sheet Support

If you are a web developer, an option on the Format Editor Common tab may catch your eye. The CSS Class Name text box/conditional button allows you to specify a Cascading Style Sheet (CSS) class name for most any object on the report (boxes and lines are notable exceptions). By specifying a CSS class name for the object, you can control formatting "globally" from a style sheet in an HTML document that includes the report.

Either type a CSS class name directly into the text box or click the conditional formula button. A conditional formula editor will appear, where you may type in a string formula that can dynamically set the CSS class name according to database fields, formula functions, and so forth.

NOTE *CSS class names specified in the Format Editor will be exposed in the "native" HTML report viewers used with Crystal Reports integration tools and Crystal Reports Server, but not when reports are simply exported to HTML, as outlined earlier in the chapter.*

Navigating and Viewing Report Parts

Crystal Reports includes features that enhance web-based reporting, particularly when using Crystal Reports Server/BusinessObjects Enterprise. Crystal Reports "online" web viewers used with the Report Application Server, Java Reporting Component, and Crystal Reports Server/BusinessObjects Enterprise support standard Crystal Reports drill-down capabilities (discussed in detail in Chapters 3 and 8). Also, they support hyperlinks to standard "web" items, such as web pages and e-mail addresses. However, these standard drill-down capabilities are limited to drilling down within groups in the same report or using other non–Crystal Report web resources as hyperlink targets. However, there are two additional features that provide more flexibility for drill-down and navigation.

The first feature is known as Guided Navigation (or just *Navigation* for short). Navigation allows you to designate certain objects on your report, such as charts, summary fields, and so forth, to act as hyperlinks to *other* objects on a report—either the same report where the original object resides, or an entirely separate report. The second feature is *Report Parts*, the ability to display just certain portions of a report in a web page, rather than the entire page of a report. Navigation gives you much more flexibility to navigate through reports—you are no longer limited to hyperlinking to web pages or e-mail addresses. And, by using report parts, you can develop web applications that show just specific parts of a report that you may be interested in, such as a single chart or a single grand total in a portal application (report parts can often make web-based Crystal Reports more useful on handheld devices with small screens).

Using Navigation

The first requirement for using Navigation is that your reports must be used in some version of Crystal Reports Server/BusinessObjects Enterprise—either the full version of CRS/BOE, or reports hosted in a custom Report Application Server environment. Navigation can be used in several ways in the DHTML-based report viewers available with these systems (you cannot use the feature in older viewers, such as the ActiveX viewer). By using navigation, you can set up two types of hyperlinks:

- **Report Part Drill-down**   A hyperlink to another part of the same report. Only the object or objects that you choose as the destination of your hyperlink will appear when you drill down—not the entire report. Only available when using the Report Part viewer, this option is discussed later in the chapter, in the section "Displaying Report Parts."

- **Another Report Object**   A hyperlink to another report object, either in the same report as the calling object, or in a completely separate report. If you use this option with the Report Part viewer, only the object or objects you choose as the destination of your hyperlink will appear when you click. If you use one of the page-oriented DHTML viewers, the entire report will appear when you click, but the object you choose as the destination will be navigated to and highlighted.

Tip *Crystal Reports Server/BusinessObjects Enterprise XI includes a report navigation "package" in a sample folder when the product is first installed. You may view the package to see how navigation works, as well as opening the two reports that make up the package in the Crystal Reports designer to see how the navigation has been set up.*

First, if you will be hyperlinking from one report to another, it's helpful to begin the process by opening *both* reports in the Crystal Reports designer. This comes in handy when you need to reference the destination object in the Format Editor Hyperlink tab of the source object. If you are only hyperlinking within the same report, you need only have one report open.

1. Select the object that you wish to be the destination of the hyperlink. For example, if you wish to click a group name field in one report to display related detail data from another report, select the object in the detail report that you wish to navigate to.

2. Right-click the destination object and choose Copy from the pop-up menu. While you will actually be able to paste a copy of the object onto the Design tab if you choose, if you "paste" the object into the Hyperlink tab of the Format Editor, a *reference* to the object will be pasted.

3. If you are working with multiple reports, use the Window menu to choose the report that will contain the original hyperlink. If you are hyperlinking from the same report, you can obviously skip this step.

4. Select the object that you wish to act as the hyperlink. Click the Insert Hyperlink toolbar button in the Expert Tools toolbar, or choose Format | Hyperlink from the pull-down menus.

5. When the Format Editor Hyperlink tab appears, click the Another Report Object radio button in the DHTML Viewer Only section.

6. Click the Paste Link button. You may also click the down arrow next to the Paste Link button to choose from available "contexts" (options in this drop-down list will vary, depending on what type of object you copied in step 2).

Several (if not all) of the text boxes will be populated based on the object you originally copied.

- **Select From** will show the name of the report that the copied object resided in. If you opened the "source" report from within Crystal Reports Server/BusinessObjects Enterprise, an Enterprise "identifier" will appear in this box. While you cannot type over what is placed in this box, you can click the conditional formula button to the right of the box to create a string formula that sets this value.

- **Report Title** will display the value placed in the Report Title field of the Summary Info dialog box (displayed with File | Summary Info) when the source report was created. If this field was not filled, the filename of the report will appear here. You cannot type over what is placed in this box.

- **Object Name** will contain the name of the object that will appear and be highlighted when you click the hyperlink. This object name can be set in the source report by typing a name into the Object Name text box on the Format Editor common tab. You may wish to give relevant objects more logical names (TopProductsChart instead of

Chart1) when preparing them to act as hyperlink targets. You may also find it helpful to use the Report Explorer (discussed in Chapter 1) to determine object names. If you want to navigate to and highlight additional objects beyond what you had originally copied in the source report, type a semicolon after the existing object name and type in additional object names. You will also want to specify multiple object names here if you are only displaying report parts via the Report Part viewer (discussed later in the chapter).

- **Data Context** indicates the location in the destination report that will initially be displayed. For example, if you preview a report and, in the preview tab, click a group name field displaying "1/2004", you'll notice a data context string similar to /Order Date[1/2004] when you paste the object reference into the Hyperlink tab. Data Context strings require some getting used to. The best approach is to experiment with various permutations of "copy and paste" operations to see the resulting Data Context strings. These context strings will vary (or may not even appear), depending on whether you copied the source object when displaying the Design tab or Preview tab, and what choice you make from the Paste Link button drop-down list. You may either type over what has already been placed in this box or click the conditional formula button to the right of the box to create a string formula that sets the context.

Displaying Report Parts

By default, reports are always displayed a full page at a time when viewed in the various Crystal "native" web viewers. While the "page on demand" architecture that's familiar to most Crystal Reports users is very effective at displaying only the currently required page of the report, an entire page is always displayed. However, there is an additional choice available to those who use Crystal Reports Server/BusinessObjects Enterprise as their web reporting method. The *Report Part Viewer* allows individual objects on a particular report page (such as charts, summary fields, cross-tabs, text objects, and so forth) to be specifically chosen as report part targets. When you use the Report Part Viewer, only those objects specifically chosen as Report Part hyperlink targets will be shown in the viewer.

The general idea in using report parts is to show only limited sets of report objects in a web browser (perhaps inside a larger web application, such as a portal or on a mobile device) and allow those limited sets of objects to act as hyperlinks to other limited sets of objects. The stark difference between the Report Part Viewer and the other DHTML viewers is that the other viewers all maintain the "whole report page at a time" approach, whereas the Report Part Viewer can now display just individual objects on a report.

NOTE *In Crystal Reports Server XI, the Report Part Viewer is used with the My InfoView dashboard, or it must be implemented with custom programming web code. More information on using the Report Part Viewer within a My InfoView dashboard can be found in Chapter 23.*

Initial Report Part Setting

The first step in setting up a report to use the Report Part viewer is selecting initial report part settings. These indicate what specific object or objects will initially appear when you view a report in the Report Part viewer. If you don't specify these, the report will appear as an empty web page when you attempt to view it. Initial report part settings are chosen in the Report Options dialog box. Choose File | Report Options from the pull-down menus to display this dialog box.

Complete the Object Name and Data Context fields with appropriate report object names and data context strings (discussed earlier in the chapter). You'll probably want to use the same "copy and paste" approach to place an object reference in these fields. If you wish to initially display more than one object in the Report Part Viewer (perhaps a chart along with a text object describing the chart or multiple summaries and text objects), either CTRL-click the objects before copying or type in each separate object name in the Object Name field, separating them with semicolons. As discussed previously, you may find it helpful to give report objects more meaningful names in the Format Editor before using them, as well as using the Report Explorer to locate specific objects.

NOTE *It's important to remember that you can only display objects in the same report section when working with the Report Part Viewer. For example, if you want to display a chart and a text object side by side in the Report Part Viewer, they must be in the same section of the originating report—the chart can't, for example, be in the report header if the text object is in a group header. This limitation also pertains to Report Part Drill-down, discussed in the following section.*

Report Part Drill-down
While showing an initial limited set of objects in the Report Part Viewer may be sufficient for simple applications, the drill-down capabilities of the Report Part Viewer give you

tremendous flexibility in controlling how end users navigate through your report. While the page-oriented viewers use the grouping hierarchy of your report to determine drill-down logic, you can more closely control individual objects that appear when you drill down with the Report Part viewer.

This is accomplished by setting up a specific drill-down "path" in your report. For example, you may choose to have a group chart contained in the report header be the initial report part object that appears when you first view the report. If a viewer then clicks on a particular pie wedge or bar in that chart, your drill-down path will take them to a lower-level summary field or advanced chart that appears in a lower group level. In this situation, you are mimicking the regular drill-down capabilities of the page viewer, but you are completely controlling the specific objects that appear when the user drills down. You can go a step further and combine report parts and Navigation (discussed earlier in the chapter) to drill down to a predetermined set of objects in *another* report.

Once you've defined your initial report part object or objects, you may then further define your path by creating a Report Part Drilldown hyperlink for these objects. For example, you may want to select a group name field as your initial report part object and then click the Hyperlink toolbar button to set up the report part drilldown. Click the Report Part Drilldown radio button in the DHTML Viewer Only section. The Format Editor will expand, showing available report sections, and fields within it, that can be drilled down on (only sections and objects in a logical report section just below your selected object will appear).

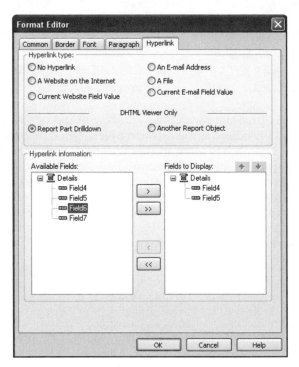

NOTE *Report Part Drilldown is only available if you've chosen a group chart or map or a summary field in a group header or footer. Other objects will not allow a Report Part Drill-down to be chosen.*

Choose the field or fields you'd like to appear when the report viewer drills down. You may click on one field, or CTRL-click to choose multiple fields, clicking the right arrow to add them to the Fields to Display list. Or, click the double-arrow to add all fields. The order the fields are displayed in the Fields to Display list is the order the fields will appear when a viewer drills down. If you need to change the order of the fields, select a desired field and click the up or down arrows above the Fields To Display list to change the order.

When you view the report in a custom application using the Report Part Viewer, you'll see that the initial report view shows only the object or objects that you chose in the initial report part settings. If you then click the initial object (assuming you've defined a Report Part Drill-down for the object), only the resulting objects for that Report Part Drill-down will appear in the browser.

PART II

Introduction to Crystal Reports Server

If you have previous Crystal experience, you may know or remember a product called Crystal Enterprise. That product has been renamed with the XI release and is now known as BusinessObjects Enterprise XI. And, as with previous versions of Crystal Reports, a "lite" version of the BusinessObjects Enterprise product is included with the Professional and Developer editions of Crystal Reports XI. But here's the tricky part: that lite version is now named Crystal Reports Server. Don't be confused—despite the totally different names, they are simply different "editions" of the same product.

NOTE *This chapter refers specifically to Crystal Reports Server. However, all of the concepts also apply to other editions of BusinessObjects Enterprise.*

Crystal Reports Server Defined

As the World Wide Web has become not only a more integral part of consumer computing, but an important consideration for business computing platforms as well, Crystal Reports has continued to offer more and more web-based reporting solutions as each new version is released. Version 7 featured the Web Access Server (WAS) for running reports in web pages. Version 8 introduced a more robust version of the same feature, called the Web Component Server (WCS). And, while Crystal Reports 8.5 eliminated the WCS as a Crystal Reports–only web solution, Active Server Pages and the Report Designer Component), as well as basic HTML exports remained as Crystal Reports–only web options. Crystal Reports 10 included another web-based reporting feature (Crystal Enterprise Embedded Edition) to provide further web-based reporting options. All of these options allow end users who wish to view reports to do so from within their web browsers. A stand-alone copy of Crystal Reports or a custom Windows application integrating Crystal Reports is not required on each of the workstations. And, the workstations don't all have to have connectivity to the corporate database.

However, as these early web reporting options began to unfold, there was an increasing demand for more enterprise-oriented, high-capacity web reporting capabilities. As larger organizations looked more and more toward web-based solutions, solutions needed to be made available that moved beyond the limited-user, web-server-centric tools that were offered in the past for real-time web reporting. Companies needed a reporting solution that would scale to potentially support hundreds, or even thousands, of web-based report viewers.

While the earlier Crystal Info/Seagate Info multitier reporting tool eventually offered a web-based interface that could be used in place of its typical Windows front end, the direction in enterprise solutions was clearly web based. Crystal Enterprise 8, introduced alongside Crystal Reports 8.5, was the first entry in the next generation of unified, enterprise-oriented reporting and analysis tools.

The Two-Tier Web Reporting Method

Crystal Reports 7 and 8 included a limited web server–based reporting system that could be described as *two-tier architecture*. The basic premise of this architecture is to route the report viewing audience through a web browser and a web server, rather than placing an individual copy of Crystal Reports or a Crystal Reports–based custom application on each user PC. Only the web server requires connectivity to the corporate database for ad hoc reporting. This architecture is illustrated in Figure 22-1.

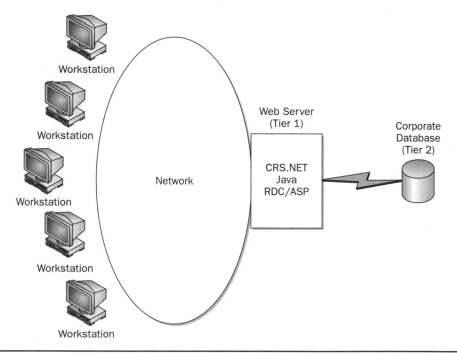

Figure 22-1 The existing two-tier processing architecture

NOTE *Yes, the argument could be made that the architecture being described here is in fact a three-tier architecture—web browser to web server to database. However, by basically moving all of the previous client-based processing to the web server and transforming clients to simple viewer status, the previous two-tier client/server architecture is just being moved around. It can still be argued that in the typical database/query client/server model, the web server has become the client and the database remains the server.*

By centralizing this approach via the Web, much reduced software maintenance on client-side computers is required. New versions of reports or reporting systems do not require any new software to be installed on individual client computers—only the web pages that compose the application need to be updated on the web server. As long as a compatible web browser can be used, Crystal Reports can be viewed on a computer or workstation.

The Multitier Reporting Method

While the existing architecture just described is an overall improvement beyond the classic client/server computing model of an application on a client with a network connection to a server, there are still bottlenecks and disadvantages that limit this architecture's capacity for large reporting environments. In particular,

- The web server suddenly becomes a concentrated reporting and query client instead of the web page distribution server it's designed to be. Every request for an ad hoc report requires the web server to send a query to the database, wait for a result set, and format the result set before sending the report back to a web browser.

- The network connection between the web server and the database can become overloaded, depending on the types of queries and reports that the web server submits to the database and the size of the return result sets.

- There is limited sharing or caching of report requests (particularly for ad hoc real-time reports). If 25 users request the same report (particularly if there are parameter fields or different database user IDs involved), the web server oftentimes will have to submit the report's query to the database 25 times.

- Earlier Crystal Reports web systems do not allow reports to be automatically scheduled to run at regular intervals, such as once per day, once per month, and so on.

The answer to these inherent limitations of existing Crystal web reporting alternatives lies in the Crystal Reports Server multitier report processing architecture, as illustrated in Figure 22-2. Built largely on the existing multitier structure of the Crystal Info/Seagate Info reporting product, this multitier structure allows report distribution scalability far greater than the "classic" two-tier architecture used previously. By creating multiple software functions and creating the ability for them to be rolled out or "scaled" to multiple processors, Crystal Reports Server immediately offers a dramatic improvement in reliability, load capability, and fault tolerance. The web server can return to its core requirement to serve up web pages. Additional components now work together to run ad hoc report and query requests, schedule automatically recurring reports, convert completed reports pages to "page-on-demand" viewing files, handle security, and cache recently reviewed report pages for delivery to the next report viewer. The result is a completely scalable multitier structure that dramatically improves the capabilities and capacity of web-based reporting.

> **NOTE** *Complete discussions of the different server components shown in Figure 22-2 are found in the section "Crystal Reports Server Architecture" later in this chapter.*

Crystal Reports Server Licensing

Crystal Reports Server allows only either named user licenses or concurrent access licenses. A *named user* license allows one specific user to log on, and that license is reserved for that particular user. A *concurrent access* license allows any user to log on using the license, but that license is not reserved for any particular user. Concurrent access licenses allow for an unlimited number of potential users, provided that the total number of users logged on at any one time doesn't exceed the concurrent access license limit.

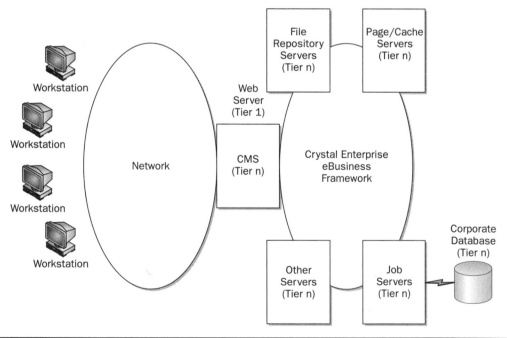

FIGURE 22-2 Crystal Reports Server multitier processing architecture

The license for Crystal Reports Server that is included with the Developer or Professional version of Crystal Reports XI is for five named users. Separately, you can purchase concurrent access licenses for Crystal Reports Server up to a maximum of 20 users. Also, all licenses of Crystal Reports Server are limited to use on a single machine with up to four processors.

The full BusinessObjects Enterprise product features a wider array of licensing options that you may choose from. The full product allows combinations of named user licenses and processor licenses, and it allows for scaling the system through the use of multiple machines.

Study and consider these varying options carefully to have the proper number of licenses for all potential user combinations, without undertaking extra expense that may be incurred for an "overkill" license structure.

CAUTION Not only is evaluating Crystal Reports Server and BusinessObjects Enterprise editions a challenge, but licensing scenarios present their own myriad alternatives. Some features may or may not initially be available in a particular edition. In most cases, you must upgrade to a higher edition to get the feature. Typically, all these features are made available simply by adding additional keycodes to the initial keycode used when installing your system.

Crystal Reports Server New Features

There are several new features of note in Crystal Reports Server, including support for one highly anticipated (and much-requested) feature in Crystal Reports XI.

Dynamic Prompts and Cascading Lists of Values

One of the most important new report design features in Crystal Reports XI is dynamic prompts and cascading lists of values. Support for that feature has also been added to Crystal Reports Server. Now, when a report is run through Crystal Reports Server, the end user can be prompted for parameter values using a dynamic prompt, with default values pulled from a live data source at that time. This is a powerful new feature that will solve many long-standing issues and produce smiles on the faces of many report administrators. Also, several parameters may have default values that "cascade."

For example, a report user can initially be presented with a list of default values for a Country parameter. The user selects USA. The next parameter is Region, and the list of default values is produced using the USA selection—the list contains the states in the USA. The user selects North Carolina. The next parameter is City, and the list of default values is produced using the North Carolina selection—the list contains the cities in North Carolina. The user selects Chapel Hill.

Categories

In the Crystal Reports Server system, reports and other objects are stored in a hierarchical set of folders, much as files are stored in a Windows system. The new Categories feature provides a second, and more flexible, method for organizing objects. Administrators and users both may create an unlimited number of categories and subcategories. Then, shortcuts to objects are placed in the categories, making it possible for a single report to be placed in multiple categories by multiple users without redundancy. Using categories, users may create their own personal and customized organization scheme(s) for the reports and other objects of interest.

Discussions

Discussions are basically mini–message boards that are added to reports, report instances, and other objects. Users can read messages previously posted by other users and can add their own messages to the discussion. The Discussions feature was introduced as an add-on to Crystal Enterprise 10 and was only partially supported. Now, Discussions are part of the Crystal Reports Server standard distribution package and are fully supported.

Traditionally, users that have comments or questions about a report instance will send e-mails to other users. Replies are then created, scattered, and typically deleted and/or lost. Users that subsequently view the report instance may have similar comments or questions but have to begin the entire cycle once again. With Discussions, the original comments and questions, along with all of the replies, are saved alongside the report instance so that future users will be able to review what was written. This can save a lot of time and energy, especially when a group of users is very large and/or geographically dispersed.

InfoView

InfoView is the new web application for Crystal Reports Server users. It replaces the web application previously known as ePortfolio and the Web Desktop. But this is much more than a simple renaming—InfoView is an entirely new application. The user interface was substantially improved, making it much easier for new users to learn and master. And InfoView comes in two versions (.NET and J2EE), giving system architects a choice of application environments.

Universes

Business Objects originally developed Universes as a metadata layer for their report design product, Web Intelligence. As part of the product consolidation plan after the acquisition of Crystal Decisions, Crystal Reports was updated to work with Universes. Now, Universes may be stored in the Crystal Reports Server repository.

Crystal Reports Server Architecture

Crystal Reports Server is a monumental change from the previous single-server approach of the Crystal Reports web component server. As discussed previously in this chapter, one of the huge benefits of Crystal Reports Server over earlier tools is its multitier, multiserver approach to web reporting. By spreading the processing load over multiple software and hardware layers, it enables much higher numbers of users and much better sustained performance.

If you are an end user of Crystal Reports Server, there are several software components that you may encounter as you view reports. Depending on your particular Crystal Reports Server implementation, you may also be required to design, publish, and schedule reports as well. You'll want to be familiar with the different components that are required to use Crystal Reports Server in these various ways. If you are an administrator who is responsible for installing, maintaining, and supporting Crystal Reports Server, you'll want to be familiar with not only the end-user tools available to your user community, but also the particular server components, communications methods, and administrative tools available for your use.

NOTE *More detailed information about end-user components and their usage can be found in Chapter 23. Chapter 24 contains more technical discussions and coverage of administrative tools and processes.*

End-User Components for Reporting

As a web-based reporting tool, Crystal Reports Server provides interaction almost entirely within a web browser. If you are using a Windows PC, an Apple Macintosh, or a Unix/Linux workstation, all you need to work with the majority of Crystal Reports Server features is a standard web browser (a newer browser that supports HTML Version 4 and JavaScript is required). The only exception to the web browser rule is for designing reports in the stand-alone Crystal Reports product—Crystal Reports XI is used to design reports and must run in a Windows environment. And, there are several ways of publishing reports to Crystal Reports Server. One way, the Crystal-supplied Publishing Wizard, is also a Windows-only program.

As an end user, you'll normally start using Crystal Reports Server from InfoView (referred to in previous versions as "ePortfolio" and the "Web Desktop"). InfoView is a web page that can be viewed by pointing your browser to a standard location specified by your Crystal Reports Server administrator. But because Crystal Reports Server is web-based, it's entirely possible to customize the web interface to the Crystal Reports Server system. Your organization may still use the standard locations for Crystal Reports Server pages (but may have customized the pages), or it may have created an entirely customized interface (such as an internal intranet or portal) that interfaces with Crystal Reports Server.

If you wish to add newly designed Crystal reports to InfoView, you can save them directly to Crystal Reports Server folders from Crystal Reports XI, or use either the Central Management Console or the Windows-based Publishing Wizard (both discussed in Chapter 24).

InfoView

InfoView comes in two flavors: .NET and Java. To the end user, these two versions are essentially the same. But the two versions are provided to allow the system administrators the choice of underlying server technologies. While the system administrators may allow both to remain available to end users, they may also decide to disable one version due to security, standardization, and/or maintenance issues.

You may select the appropriate InfoView from the Start menu (located in a default location of BusinessObjects 11/Crystal Reports Server) or type in the location (known in web parlance as a Universal Resource Locator, or URL) of the appropriate InfoView to display the actual starting point for Crystal Reports Server report viewing.

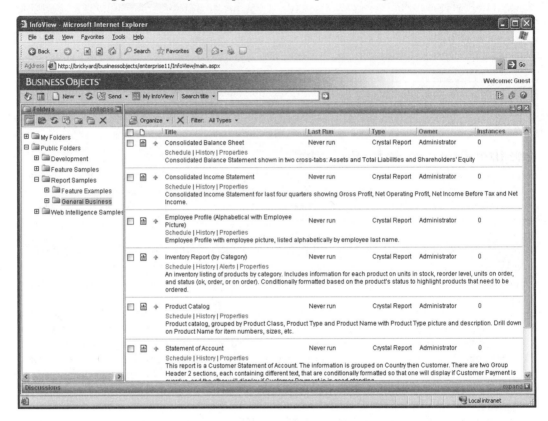

From InfoView, you can create a new user account; log on as a different user; navigate through report folders; view reports, report alerts, PDF documents, Word documents, and so forth; and schedule reports, packages, or programs to run on a recurring basis. (InfoView will most likely appear identical to the preceding illustration, but it may have been modified to more closely align with your organization's standard web look and feel.)

Customized Web Interface

InfoView is a Business Objects–designed interface to Crystal Reports Server. Based on one of two standard programming interfaces (.NET or Java), all InfoView source code is provided for perusal and modification. You may modify the existing InfoView to more closely match your standard web interface, or create a completely new set of web pages to expose Crystal Reports Server features. If a customized intranet page or portal has been created, your administrator may give you a completely different URL to launch your Crystal Reports Server system.

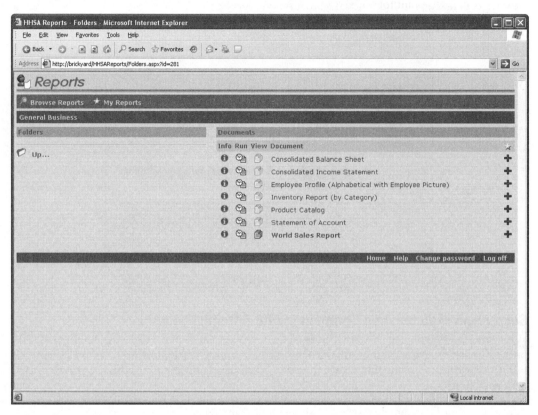

Publishing Wizard

Depending on how responsibilities for maintaining your Crystal Reports Server system are divided within your organization, you may need the ability to post reports you've designed with Crystal Reports XI to your Crystal Reports Server system. There are two ways to accomplish this: using the Central Management Console or the Publishing Wizard (both discussed in Chapter 24).

The Publishing Wizard provides certain advantages over the Central Management Console and is designed to be easier to use overall. This is a Windows program that does require installation on your individual computer from a Windows Setup routine.

You may also edit existing Crystal Reports Server reports or add new reports right from Crystal Reports XI. When you choose File | Open or File | Save As from the Crystal Reports XI pull-down menus, the file dialog box will contain an extra icon labeled Enterprise Folders. Click this icon and log on to the Central Management Server. If your user ID and password allows editing or adding, you'll be able to open existing CRS reports for modification, or add new reports directly to the Central Management Server.

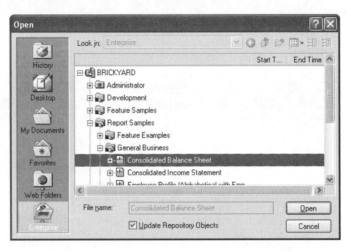

NOTE *More detailed information on connecting to and using InfoView can be found in Chapter 23.*

Server and Maintenance Components for Administrators

While end users will probably stick close to the InfoView (and, perhaps to Crystal Reports XI or the Publishing Wizard if they are in charge of maintaining reports), administrative personnel will find additional items that they can use to administer and maintain the Crystal Reports Server system.

Administration Launchpad/Central Management Console

The Administration Launchpad is the administrator's "portal" into the Crystal Reports Server system. The most commonly used tool from this home page is the Central Management Console, which is used to maintain Crystal Reports Server. There are other administrative tools available from this starting point as well.

Because the Central Management Console is web-based, you can run it on any computer on the network that has a web browser. You don't need to run it on any of the physical components that make up Crystal Reports Server. You can even run it in a remote location from the Internet, provided your internal network security allows an outside browser to navigate to the proper location.

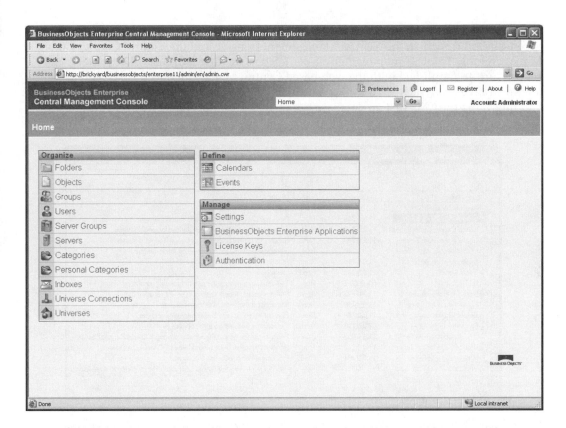

Here, administrative personnel can add and edit user IDs; organize users into user groups; change passwords and grant and deny rights to users; manage back-end servers; add, remove, and modify folders to logically organize reports; and add and remove reports in existing folders.

TIP *More detailed information about Central Management Console functions and capabilities can be found in Chapter 24.*

Central Configuration Manager

Administrative tasks in Crystal Reports Server are split between the web-based Central Management Console (discussed previously) and the Windows-based Central Configuration Manager. When you install a Crystal Reports Server component on a back-end server, the Central Configuration Manager will be installed on that machine as well (although you can connect to another server remotely with the Central Configuration Manager).

While some administrative tasks or viewing of certain server information can be accomplished from both the Central Management Console and the Central Configuration Manager, more "global" management tasks, such as dealing with user IDs, folders, and reports, are accomplished with the web-based Central Management Console. More technical administrative tasks, such as adjusting start-up parameters, changing network port numbers, and migrating the CMS system database to a shared server to enable CMS clustering, are accomplished with the Central Configuration Manager.

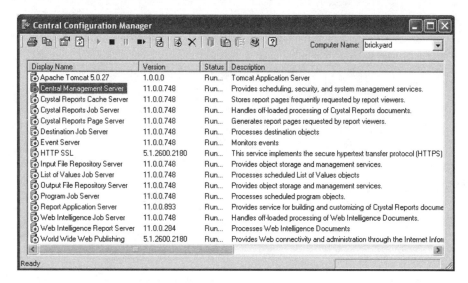

As well as changing server properties, the Central Configuration Manager allows you to add additional servers to the Crystal Reports Server system, stop and start servers, disable particular servers, and configure Web Connectors.

TIP *More detailed information about Central Configuration Manager functions and capabilities can be found in Chapter 24.*

Import Wizard

If you are a user of the original enterprise reporting tool, Crystal/Seagate Info, you may need to migrate this system to Crystal Reports Server. Or, you may have set up an initial test version of Crystal Reports Server but wish to copy the existing set of user IDs, the same report and folder structure, and other characteristics to a newer production Central Management Server.

To prevent an administrator from having to manually reenter all Crystal/Seagate Info or Crystal Enterprise information into a new Crystal Reports Server system, Business Objects supplies the Import Wizard. The Import Wizard reads the contents of an existing Crystal/Seagate Info APS database, an existing Crystal Enterprise APS or CMS database, or an existing Crystal Reports Server CMS database, and copies it into your Crystal Reports Server system.

It will then allow an administrator to choose which users, user groups, folders, and reports to automatically transfer to a new Crystal Reports Server CMS database. When completed, the Import Wizard will have created a new CRS system that closely mirrors that of the previous Seagate Info, Enterprise, or Crystal Reports Server system.

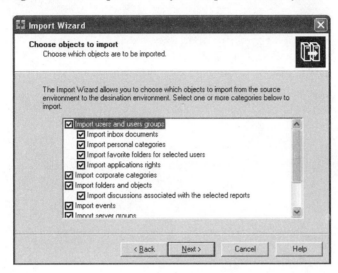

NOTE *For complete information on the Import Wizard, including descriptions of how users and reports may be affected by a migration, consult the online Administrator's Guide. Also, the Import Wizard is discussed in Chapter 24.*

Using InfoView

As a web-based application, Crystal Reports Server can be customized extensively to integrate with your organization's own intranet or Internet look and feel. However, many organizations don't have the resources or can't justify the effort to undertake serious custom Crystal Reports Server integration. For these organizations, Crystal Reports Server XI (CRS) provides out-of-the-box applications that provide full CRS capabilities.

The primary user interface that end users in charge of day-to-day operation of CRS will probably encounter is InfoView. *InfoView* (known variously as ePortfolio and Web Desktop in previous Crystal Enterprise releases) is the actual end-user application that report and document viewers and schedulers use on a day-to-day basis to interact with Crystal Reports Server XI.

NOTE *With version XI, Business Objects introduced two separate enterprise reporting products: BusinessObjects Enterprise XI and Crystal Reports Server XI. The two products are largely the same, with Crystal Reports Server XI being designed exclusively for use with Crystal Report document types. This chapter, while discussing concepts and features that may apply to BusinessObjects Enterprise, concentrates solely on a Crystal Reports Server XI system.*

Connecting to InfoView

Your intranet may already have a link that launches CRS InfoView. If so, merely click the link. However, you may need to navigate directly by typing a specific web address into your browser. In this case, point your browser directly to the URL provided by your administrator. By default, you can navigate directly to InfoView by browsing to

```
http://<web server>/businessobjects/enterprise11
```

where *<web server>* is the name of the web server where CRS is installed.

NOTE *As Crystal Reports Server can be heavily customized, it's possible that your organization has implemented a unique version that will not use the default URL. Check with your Crystal Reports Server Administrator if you are unsure of the proper URL to use.*

If your CRS Administrator has enabled single sign-on, you may be taken directly to the InfoView homepage (the same user ID and password you logged on to your network with will be used to connect you to CRS). If single sign-on isn't enabled, you'll be presented with the Log On To BusinessObjects screen. If you've logged on to CRS previously, a computer name will already appear in the System field. Otherwise, you'll need to type in the correct name of your CRS computer name (in particular, the CRS Central Management Server)—get this from your CRS Administrator. Provided that the administrator hasn't disabled it, you can log on to CRS with the Guest account. Merely leave the user ID and password field blank, leave the Authentication choice set to Enterprise, and click Log On.

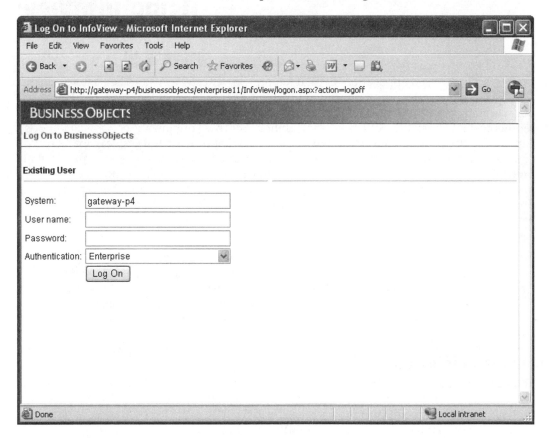

If you know the Guest account is unavailable, or you've been given logon credentials to use, enter them into the logon screen. You may need to choose an authentication type, such as Windows NT, Windows AD, or LDAP, from the drop-down list (again, your administrator will inform you of the proper authentication type). Once you've successfully logged on to CRS, you'll see the initial InfoView screen, as illustrated in Figure 23-1.

If you mistakenly log on with the Guest account, or you need to log off CRS and log on with a different account, click the padlock icon in the upper right-hand corner to log off. This will log you off InfoView and redisplay the logon screen. Enter the new logon information and click the Log On button.

Perform various folder actions   Search for documents within CRS

Perform various CRS actions   Log off InfoView

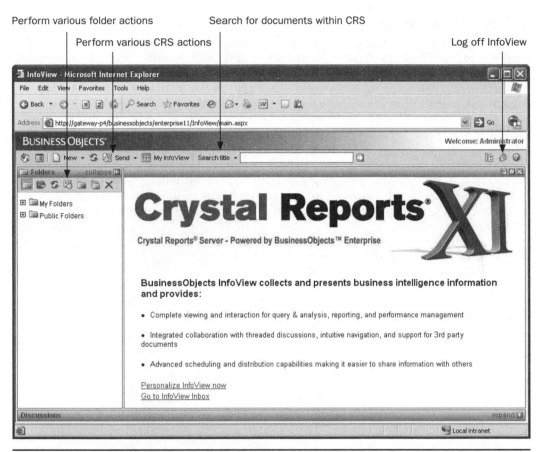

FIGURE 23-1   InfoView home page

The Most Important CRS Component: The CMS

The Central Management Server, or *CMS*, is the heart of Crystal Reports Server. Every other component communicates through the CMS—other servers won't know about each other without the CMS. The CMS also acts as the central security point for Crystal Reports Server logon—all user IDs, passwords, and rights lists are maintained on the CMS. And, the CMS also keeps track of report scheduling. If a report is scheduled to automatically run every day at midnight, the CMS sets the report processing cycle in motion at the prescribed time.

While a substantial number of different software components go into making CRS work, the one you'll be concerned with as a regular report viewer or scheduler is the CMS. You must first log on to the CMS when you start to use CRS. If the CMS isn't working, you won't be able to use Crystal Reports Server (and neither will anybody else, for that matter).

CRS Security Model

Crystal Reports Server includes a robust security model that works behind the scenes in InfoView to control what you can or cannot do. For example, you may find you have the ability to schedule a report and view the resulting "saved instance," but not run the report in real time. Or, you may find the opposite—you may be able to run a report in real time, but not schedule it. Or, you may have the even higher restriction of being allowed to view only a report instance that another user has scheduled—you will not be able to schedule your own reports nor view a report on demand.

This security is quite granular. It can be assigned to an individual user or to a group of users (such as the Accounting group, the Finance group, the Power Users group, or the Administrators group). And, you may have a combination of rights granted or denied you by being a member of more than one group. In addition to this group and user-based security, certain security settings can also be applied to certain folders or individual reports.

Suffice it to say that you may find a variety of capabilities provided to you, depending on various settings and configurations of your particular CRS system. Your CRS Administrator is your source of information on your current security model. Contact him or her if you wish to have additional capabilities provided to you.

Folders, Categories, Inbox, Objects, and Instances

InfoView provides a more robust organization when compared to previous Crystal Enterprise versions. However, it's still quite easy to locate a particular report or document you'd like to view or program object you'd like to schedule. Through a series of folders, subfolders, categories, an inbox, third-party documents, report and program objects, and report and program instances, you can find a particular object, run it on demand for a current view of your data, or view a recent instance of the report or program that resulted from a schedule.

In addition to standard Crystal Reports, Crystal Reports Server XI also allows you to view many "third-party" documents, such as Word documents, .PDF files, and PowerPoint presentations, from within InfoView. And, while you will notice a certain "look and feel" of InfoView when it is first installed, you have the capability of customizing several behavioral characteristics of InfoView to your own liking.

NOTE *As CRS hosts more than just Crystal Reports, the generic term object can apply to a Crystal report, a third-party document (such as a .PDF file, Word document, or Excel spreadsheet), or a program object that performs some sort of logic or script. You'll see the term "object" used generically throughout this chapter to refer to any of these types of documents.*

InfoView Hierarchy

In order to manage organization of InfoView, objects can appear in a variety of organizations. While the folder/subfolder hierarchy familiar to previous Crystal Enterprise users remains, additional ways of organizing Crystal Reports and other objects are now available in Crystal Reports Server. Items can be displayed in categories (both personal categories just for you and "corporate" categories for the entire organization). And, like the e-mail program you may be using, Crystal Reports Server also now includes an Inbox where various consolidations of items can be placed for you to view.

Navigating Folders and Subfolders

Initially, you'll see InfoView organized in a series of folders and subfolders on the left side of InfoView in the *navigation panel*. Top-level folders are the first things you see in the navigation panel when logging on to InfoView (initially, you'll see two top-level folders: My Folders and Public Folders). You can either click a folder name directly to see objects within the folder (if any) or click the plus sign next to a folder to expand the navigation panel to show subfolders. Subfolders can contain other subfolders and objects as well. To see more subfolders within a subfolder, expand the navigation panel again with the plus sign. Or, click a subfolder name directly to see any objects in the subfolder. Once you click a folder or subfolder, a list of objects in that folder will appear to the right of the navigation panel in what's called the *objects area*.

If you expand the My Folders top-level folder, you'll notice a special Favorites folder (it's denoted with an asterisk). This folder is set aside especially for you when your user credentials are initially created on the CMS. Unless the administrator adds objects to your Favorites folder, you'll find nothing in it when you click it. You can, however, copy or move existing objects from other folders to your Favorites folder, as well as creating your own subfolders in your Favorites folder (provided the administrator hasn't restricted this right). You can also add new objects to your favorites folder, as described later in the chapter, under "Adding Objects to InfoView."

Click folder button to show folders in navigation panel

Click to display navigation panel, if it's not visible

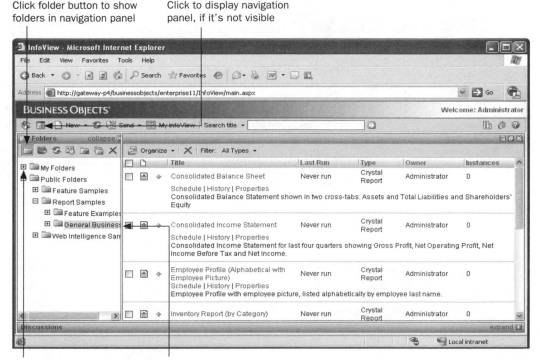

Click plus-sign to expand folder

Click folder to see contents

Categories

Crystal Reports Server XI provides an alternative way of organizing objects: categories. *Categories* can be assigned to an object already contained in CRS—an object can be assigned to one or more categories at the same time. To display categories, switch the navigation panel to category view by clicking the Show Categories toolbar button in the navigation panel toolbar. A category view will appear that behaves similarly to the folder view discussed previously—click the plus sign to expand a category to see subcategories, and click a category itself to fill the objects area with objects assigned to that category.

There are two initial "top-level" categories: *personal categories* and *corporate categories.* Personal categories are those that you create and that only you can see. Corporate categories are created by the CRS Administrator (or other users, provided they have sufficient rights) and are available for all users of CRS.

Click category button to show
categories in navigation panel

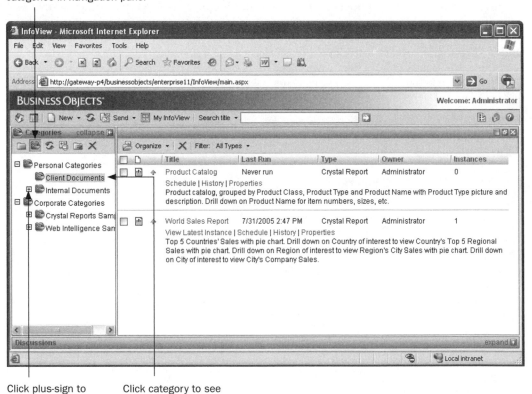

Click plus-sign to   Click category to see
expand category   assigned objects

Your Inbox

Another organizational method new to Crystal Reports Server XI is the inbox. Your *inbox,* as the name might suggest, is similar to the inbox you probably use with an e-mail program. It is designed as a placeholder for new objects or instances that may be placed there by you, by the administrator or another authorized user, or automatically by a report schedule. You'll probably want to designate the inbox as a single place to hold new report instances that you want to see as soon as they have run. If you schedule them to appear in your inbox, all new report instances will be viewable in a single location, regardless of the original location of the report.

You must display the navigation panel in folder view to see the inbox—the inbox won't be available in category view. If necessary, click the folder button in the navigation panel toolbar. Then, expand the My Folders top-level folder and click the Inbox folder. The objects and instances contained in your inbox will appear in the objects area.

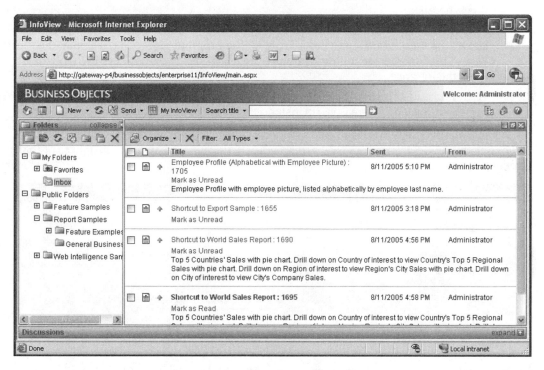

TIP *If the navigation panel displaying folders or categories isn't visible in InfoView, click the Toggle Navigation button in the main toolbar at the top of InfoView. Also, you can resize the navigation panel by pointing to the gray line between the panel and the objects area.*

Objects and Instances

Obviously, just seeing folders and subfolders does you little good if you're trying to make business decisions. Your ultimate goal is to view a report or document within one of the folders. Reports inside InfoView can actually take on two different forms: a report object or a report instance. Likewise, CRS program objects (such as executable programs, Java programs, or scripts) can also appear as objects or instances. And, third-party objects, such as Word documents, PDF files, and Excel spreadsheets, only appear as objects—there will never be a third-party instance.

- A *report object* is a report "template" or design—there's no actual live data contained in the report.

- A *report instance* only appears after a report has been scheduled. An instance is one of the occurrences of a scheduled report.

- A *program object* is a "pointer" to an executable program, Java program, or script file (JScript or VBScript) that can perform some sort of administrative or functional operation, such as updating a data warehouse. The object will perform its task when it is scheduled.

- A *program instance* only appears after a program object has been scheduled. An instance shows the output of the particular "run" of the program object. In particular, the "standard" and "error" output from the program object will be shown when you view the instance.

- A *third-party object* is simply a document that you can view in your web browser. It cannot be scheduled. For this reason, no instances will ever appear for a third-party object.

When a report or program object is first added to InfoView, only an object will be available. Only after the report or program has been scheduled at least once, will any instances of that object be available.

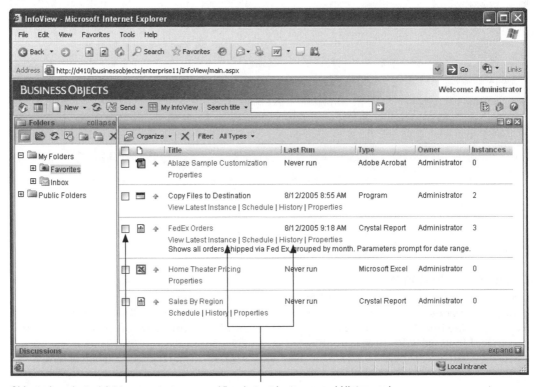

Objects in selected folder or category   View Latest Instance and History only
                                                 appear when object contains instances

NOTE The folders, subfolders, and objects that are available to you will most likely vary according to Crystal Reports Server security. You may, for example, see a completely different set of folders, subfolders, and objects than a coworker sees. Or, you may see some items in common with others in your organization, but everyone may not see the same set of items.

Viewing Reports: On Demand or Instance

Your ultimate goal in using InfoView will no doubt be to view output from various types of objects. In particular, you'll almost certainly want to view reporting results in your web browser. There are two general ways to view reports in InfoView: on demand or as a report instance.

- Viewing a report *on demand* will actually load the report object into one of the CRS servers and run it against the database at the time you request it—you'll see the most current view of the data.

- Viewing a *report instance* requires the corresponding report object to have been previously run at least once via a schedule. One of the occurrences of that scheduled report will be viewed, showing the view of the data as of that point in time.

There are advantages and disadvantages to both methods. For the most current view of the data, you'll probably want to view the report on demand—especially if the database the report is based on is fluid and changes rapidly. However, the load on the database and network can be heavily impacted if a large number of CRS users are viewing reports on demand. And, if the report requires a large database query or lots of report processing, viewing on demand can be slow.

Viewing report instances greatly reduces demand on the database, as viewing an instance shows you a set of "saved data" current as of the time the instance was run. Because the report has already run by the time you view the instance, viewing instances is typically faster than viewing on demand—sometimes by a huge factor. By use of instances, a single database query can populate a report instance that can then be viewed by hundreds or thousands of viewers. Of course, any changes to the underlying database won't be reflected in an instance. However, if the database changes infrequently or up-to-the-minute analysis of the database isn't required, instances can provide accurate data views without impacting the network or database with repetitive queries.

View a report object or instance by performing several simple steps:

1. After logging on to InfoView, choose a folder, a category, or your inbox that contains reports you want to view.

2. If you click the report object name itself, the report will be viewed on demand with current database data, *provided you have the proper rights to view on demand*. If you don't have the proper view-on-demand right, and the report contains instances that you have the right to view, clicking the report name will view the latest instance.

3. If you want to view the latest report instance (the report that ran on a schedule most recently), click the View Latest Instance link below the report name.

4. If you want to examine all report instances that have run, including information on instances that may run in the future, you'll need to view the History List. Click the

History link below the report name. A separate window will appear showing all instances of that report:

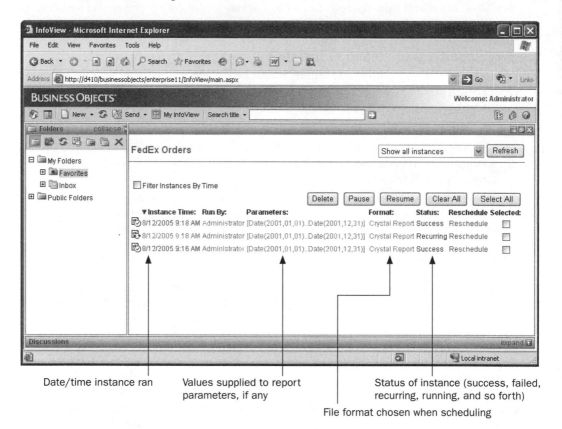

Date/time instance ran   Values supplied to report parameters, if any   Status of instance (success, failed, recurring, running, and so forth)

File format chosen when scheduling

5. To get details on the status of an instance (perhaps you wish to find out more information on a failed instance), click the status value (Success, Failed, and so forth) of the instance you want more information about.

6. To view the instance itself, click the date/time of the desired instance.

NOTE *Your right to view reports on demand or view instances is controlled by CRS security. You may not have the right to view reports on demand—you may only be able to view instances. Or, you may be able to view some reports on demand, but not others. If you have questions about your on-demand versus instance capabilities, check with your CRS Administrator.*

Viewing Third-Party Objects

Crystal Reports Server XI allows additional document types (beyond Crystal Reports documents) to be added to InfoView. These document types, known as *third-party objects*, include standard office documents (such as Word, Excel, and PowerPoint documents), text files, Rich Text Format documents, and Adobe PDF files. You'll notice an appropriate icon appearing next to a third-party object indicating the type of document that the object represents.

Viewing third-party objects is a very straightforward process. Simply click the name of the document that you wish to view, which will download the document to your web browser as though you were downloading it from a regular web site. Depending on what viewers or office software packages are loaded on your computer, the document may immediately be displayed in the right side of InfoView. If not, you may be prompted with several options, such as saving the document to disk.

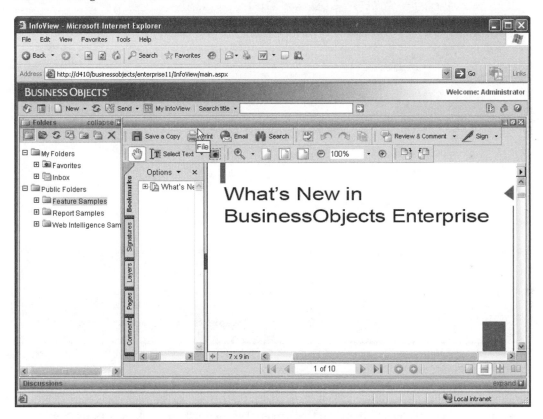

TIP *Viewing program object instances is similar to viewing report instances. However, there is no equivalent to an on-demand program object. As such, program objects must be scheduled before any output can be viewed at all. Scheduling is covered in more detail later in this chapter.*

Setting InfoView Preferences

InfoView is installed with a default look and feel, default color set, and default report viewer. You, however, can change quite a few of these features to match your own particular preferences.

Choose your own InfoView preferences by clicking the Preferences icon in the upper right-hand corner of the InfoView screen. The General Preferences screen will appear.

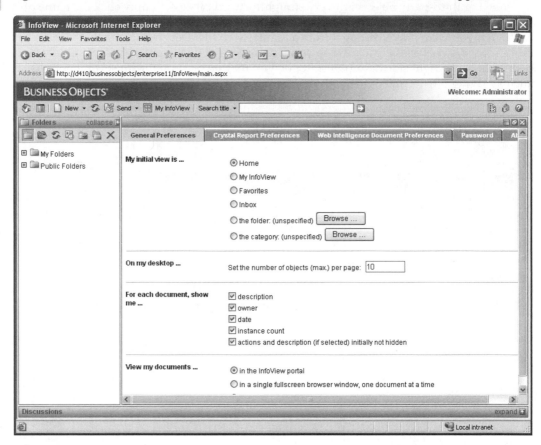

General Preferences

The General Preferences screen is one of two applicable preferences screens (Crystal Reports being the other). Preferences you set here are general in nature, applying to InfoView overall. Make any desired changes to items on this screen. When finished, click the OK or Apply button at the bottom right of the screen (you may need to expand the size of your browser window to see the buttons) to save your changes and return to InfoView.

TIP   *Initially, you may not be able to see all available preference on the screen. If you don't see all available options, either expand the overall width of your browser, hide the navigation panel by clicking the Toggle Navigation button in the top toolbar, or use your mouse to make the navigation panel narrower. You'll then be able to scroll down through all available preferences.*

Available General Preferences options follow.

My Initial View Is   This option determines the first set of folders or categories you see when you log on.

- **Home**   This will show the list of top-level folders defined on the CMS. If CRS security limits your user ID to seeing a certain set of top-level folders, this setting will show them.

- **My InfoView**   This will show the customized "dashboard" view you have set up using the My InfoView option (described later in the chapter).

- **Favorites**   The Favorites view will show you a customized set of folders and objects set up just for you (more information on customizing your Favorites view can be found later in this chapter).

- **Inbox**   This will display the Inbox (discussed earlier in the chapter) where report objects and instances specifically scheduled or copied to your private Inbox will appear.

- **The Folder**   Click the Browse button to choose a specific folder or subfolder to display immediately upon logging on to InfoView.

- **The Category**   Click the Browse button to choose a specific category or subcategory to display immediately upon logging on to InfoView.

On My Desktop   Set a value indicating the number of report or third-party objects to display on a single page when you open a folder, a category, or your inbox. If more objects are available than you specify here, a small set of "navigation numbers" will appear in the bottom right-hand corner of the objects area. For example, if you set this value to 5 and there are 15 objects in a chosen folder, you'll see "1 2 3" navigation numbers appear in the lower right-hand corner. Clicking the number 1 will display objects one through five, clicking the number 2 will display objects six through ten, and so forth.

For Each Document Show Me   Check options in this section to indicate which report properties you wish to see in the InfoView objects area. One option of particular note is the Actions And Descriptions check box. If you leave this option checked, all available actions for an object (such as Schedule, History, or View Latest Instance) will appear for each object on the screen. However, if you uncheck this option, only the object name (and other properties you check in this section) will initially appear, along with a small down-arrow icon. Only if you click the down-arrow icon next to an object will additional action choices appear.

View My Documents   Choose how reports and objects should be displayed. You may display them within the "InfoView Portal" (report or object output will replace the list of objects in the object area), or you may choose to launch a separate browser window to display them. You may choose to launch separate browser windows for each report or object output viewed, or a single separate browser window, where each subsequent report or other object will appear, replacing any that were viewed previously.

My Current Locale Is   Choose available options from the drop-down list indicating the country you are viewing InfoView in. This will affect several behavioral aspects of InfoView, including certain language settings and the way dates and times are formatted.

My Current Time Zone Is This determines the time zone that your current web browser session is operating in. The default, Local to Web Server, assumes that you and the web server are located in the same time zone. If, however, you are in an enterprise environment where the web server is in a different time zone, you'll want to choose your specific time zone from the drop-down list.

This setting ensures that any reports or program objects you schedule will execute at the time you choose. For example, if you are several time zones away from the web server and you don't change the default time zone setting, scheduled jobs will run according to the web server time zone, not your time zone.

Crystal Reports Preferences

The second preferences screen you may choose is the Crystal Reports Preferences screen, which applies only to Crystal Reports views in InfoView. Set these preferences by clicking the Crystal Reports Preference tab to the right of the General Preferences tab. The Crystal Reports Preferences screen will appear.

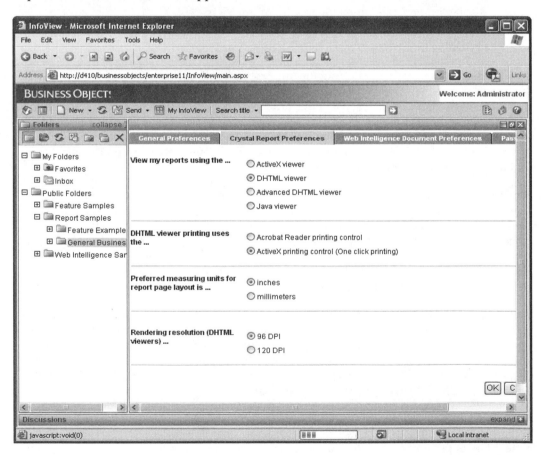

When finished, click the OK or Apply buttons at the bottom right of the screen (you may need to expand the size of your browser window to see the buttons) to save your changes and return to InfoView.

Available Crystal Reports preferences are described next.

View My Reports Using The   Since Crystal Reports can create highly formatted reports (including such features as various fonts, foreground/background color schemes, bitmap graphics, line and box drawing, drop shadows, and so forth), displaying all possible formatting options in a web page is often a challenge. Also, printing reports with their original formatting and pagination intact can also be challenging. As such, several ways of viewing and printing reports are available. This choice determines how reports are viewed within your web browser.

- **ActiveX Viewer**   This choice will download a small ActiveX control to your browser (Internet Explorer is the only browser that supports ActiveX controls). The ActiveX report viewer shows report formatting almost exactly as it was originally created, as well as allowing you to print a perfectly formatted report on your local printer.

- **DHTML Viewer**   This is the default choice when InfoView is initially installed. This choice converts the Crystal Report to Dynamic Hypertext Markup Language (DHTML)—the language used to format web pages. When you use DHTML, no extra controls or objects need to be downloaded to your web browser—the report can be displayed in the browser's native "language." However, some formatting compromises may be made in certain situations. Also, if you click the Print button in your web browser toolbar or choose Print from your web browser menu, only what's currently showing in the browser window will print—not an entire paginated and formatted report (two "native" printing options are discussed later in this section, under "DHTML Viewer Printing Uses The").

- **Advanced DHTML Viewer**   Similar to the DHTML Viewer, this viewer uses "pure" HTML to display reports—no additional controls need to be downloaded to your browser. The Advanced DHTML Viewer provides additional capabilities for report viewers that want to perform additional "subquery" analysis on the report they are currently viewing. These additional capabilities are discussed later in the chapter, under "Navigating the Report Viewers."

- **Java Viewer**   This viewer will use the built-in "Java Virtual Machine" from your web browser (different browsers and operating system installations contain various forms of Java Virtual Machine support). The Java "applet" or control that will appear in your browser shows report formatting almost exactly as it was originally created, as well as allowing you to print a perfectly formatted report on your local printer.

DHTML Viewer Printing Uses The   This setting allows you to choose how to print reports from either the DHTML or Advanced DHTML report viewers. While the ActiveX and Java viewers include their own "native" Print button, pure HTML reports cannot be printed in their native form by using just the Print button from your browser. This choice determines what happens when you click the Print button contained in the DHTML viewers.

- **Acrobat Reader Printer Control**   This choice will cause the report to be downloaded to your browser as an exactly formatted Acrobat .PDF document. Assuming you have a properly configured Acrobat viewer installed on your computer, you'll then be able to print the report using the Acrobat viewer's Print button.

- **ActiveX Printing Control**   This choice will download a small ActiveX control that displays a Print dialog box (the first time you use this, you may be prompted to accept the ActiveX control). Choose desired options for printing, such as a page range or number of copies. The ActiveX print control will then stream the Crystal Report in its native format to the chosen printer.

Preferred Measuring Units For Report Page Layout Is   Choose whether to have CRS display any associated report measurements (if any) in inches or millimeters. You may wish to customize this setting to match the generally-accepted unit of measurement in your locale.

Rendering Resolution (DHTML Viewers)   Choose a resolution (in dots per inch, or DPI) for CRS to use when rendering text and images in your web browser. The optional 120 DPI setting may result in higher-resolution images and text, but it will cause the overall report to appear larger on the screen and may require slightly more time to be downloaded and formatted.

Password and About Screens

Clicking the Password tab will display a change password screen. Type in your CRS user ID and existing password, followed by the new password you wish to assign to your CRS user ID. You will need to type the new password twice. Provided your new password meets any minimum password requirements set by your CRS Administrator (perhaps you need a minimum number of characters, and so forth), your password will be changed.

Clicking the About tab will simply display an informational screen about the current version of CRS, consisting largely of Business Objects patent and copyright notices. There is typically no useful information for using or troubleshooting InfoView on this screen.

NOTE   *The Web Intelligence Document tab only applies to the full version of BusinessObjects Enterprise that supports Business Objects Web Intelligence document types. Its settings are irrelevant in Crystal Reports Server and Crystal Reports document types.*

Controlling, Printing, and Exporting Reports

Often, when you choose to view a report on demand (or schedule a report, for that matter), you need to supply additional information before the report will run properly. In many cases, the report will need to connect to a secure database as its data source—this database will typically require a user ID and password for proper access.

Also, many reports of moderate to high sophistication will be based on Crystal Reports parameters. A parameter will prompt the viewer for customized information each time the report is run on demand. This information, such as one or more departments, a date range, a region, one or more sales people—the list can go on and on—is used to limit or customize the report to the chosen parameter items.

Supplying Database Credentials and Parameters

If a report is based on a secure database, you'll probably need to supply one or more database credentials, such as user ID, password, server name, or database name, when you view the report on demand or schedule the report (scheduling is covered later in this chapter, under "Scheduling Objects"). If you don't supply a proper set of credentials, the report will be unable to connect to the database. The set of database credentials required in your particular organization can vary depending on what database system your reports connect to. If you have a variety of different databases that reports can be based on (for example, some reports are based on Microsoft SQL Server, while others are based on Oracle and yet others are based on Informix), you may find that different sets of credentials are required for different reports.

If any Crystal Reports parameter fields have been added to the report, you will probably be prompted to supply one or more parameter values when you run a report on demand or schedule it. Parameter fields may ask for a variety of values, such as one or more regions, a salesperson number, or a date range.

NOTE *Default values for database credentials and parameter fields can be set in the Central Management Console, negating the need for them to be entered when scheduling or viewing certain reports. Information on this process is covered in Chapter 24.*

Parameter fields can vary widely in data type (text, dates, numbers, and so forth) and parameter type (multiple value, range, and so forth). For example, a single text parameter may be required to specify the country to be used in the report. In this case, you might supply "USA" as the value for the parameter. Another parameter might request one or more salesperson numbers. You, therefore, might supply just salesperson number 5. Or, you might want to see the report for several salespeople—you would then supply salesperson numbers 5, 10, 15, and 17. Or, you might encounter another parameter that needs a date range to be supplied. You would, for example, supply dates between January 1, 2002, and May 31, 2002.

In each case, InfoView will prompt you differently for each parameter. For the most part, experimenting and experience will help you supply parameter values properly.

To respond to InfoView prompts for database credentials or parameter values, when viewing reports on demand, follow some simple steps:

1. Choose a report that requires database credentials or parameter values to be supplied.

2. Click the report name in the objects area.

3. InfoView will prompt for database credentials and/or parameter values (depending on how the report is designed) before showing the report.

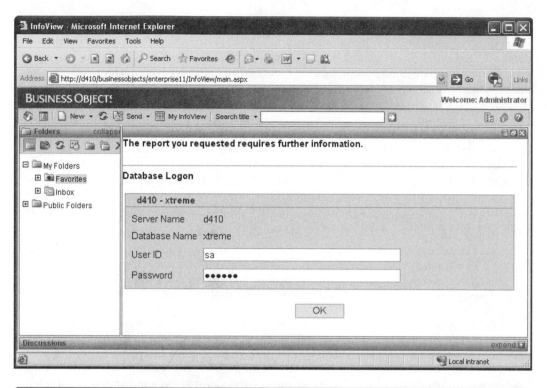

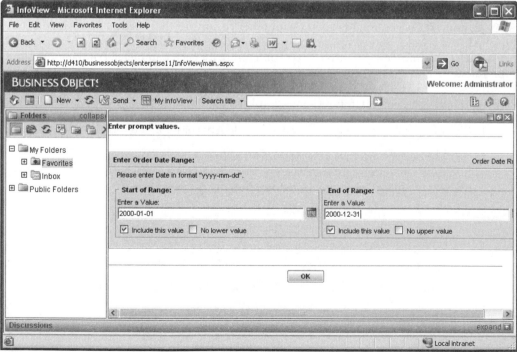

4. Type in any necessary values for database user ID, password, and so forth. If parameter values are requested, add necessary values to customize the report for this particular view, clicking OK after each prompt.

5. The report will be viewed with the supplied values.

NOTE *Date or Time parameter values require adherence to a specific CRS format. For example, if you wish to supply a date of January 1, 2002, you can't simply type "1/1/02" or "1/1/2002"—an error message will appear. You must supply dates in the format yyyy-mm-dd, including the hyphens. So, you would specify a parameter value of January 1, 2002, as 2002-01-01. Note that a small "date picker" icon also appears when prompting for a date parameter. If you click this icon and specify a date in the corresponding calendar box, the properly formatted value will be filled in for you.*

Navigating the Report Viewers

When you view a report, InfoView will display the report in a new browser window using the report viewer specified in Crystal Reports Preferences (discussed earlier in the chapter). The report viewer contains many features that enhance your ability to navigate through the report and perform other useful functions, such as searching the report or exporting the report to another file format. Viewer toolbars and buttons will vary, depending on the report viewer you are using. Here's an example of a report displayed in the default DHTML viewer:

Group tree   Report Viewer toolbar

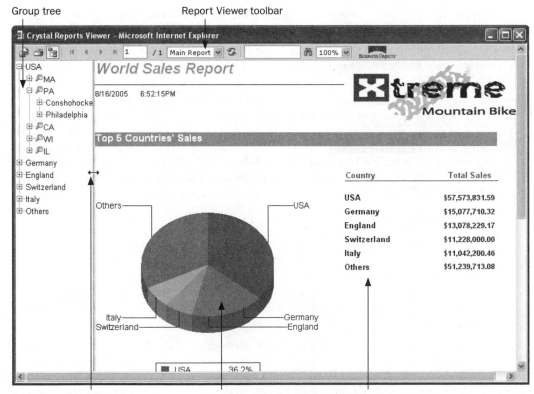

Narrow or widen group tree   Point to chart, summary name, or summary
data to see drill-down "hand" cursor

Toolbar buttons available in various report viewers consist of the following:

- **Export**   You have the option to export a report from the viewer to several different file formats, including Crystal Reports, Microsoft Excel, Microsoft Word, Rich Text Format, and Adobe Acrobat. If you are using the DHTML Viewer, the chosen format will be "downloaded" to your browser, much as you download a file from a web site. If you are using other viewers, a Save As dialog box will appear giving you the opportunity to save the exported file on your hard disk. You will also be able to choose a page range to export.

- **Print**   Print the report currently displayed in the viewer on a printer configured on your computer. If you are using the ActiveX or Java viewers, or the ActiveX print control in one of the DHTML viewers, a print dialog box will appear where you may choose page range, number of copies, and so forth. If you are using the Acrobat PDF print option with one of the DHTML viewers, the report will be downloaded as an Acrobat .PDF file. Use the Acrobat Viewer's Print button to actually print the report.

- **Group Tree**   You can turn the group tree on and off with this button. The group tree, which appears at the left of the report in the viewer, is a powerful navigation tool that shows you an outline of the grouping levels on the report and allows you to click directly to an item and display that page.

- **Page Navigation**   Click the arrow buttons to navigate to the first page, previous page, next page, or last page.

- **Go To Page**   Type in a specific page number and click the Go To Page button to navigate directly to that report page.

- **Drill Down**   If the report has further detail supporting some of the data on the report, you may be able to drill down to the detail by clicking the summary information on the report or on a chart element (such as a pie wedge or bar). The cursor will change when it is rolled over clickable areas, just as it does when rolled over a link on a web page. When you click on a drill-down area, a drill-down page opens in the browser. You can then toggle between the main report page and any open drill-down pages by either selecting them in the current view drop-down box (in the DHTML viewers) or clicking the drill-down tab (ActiveX or viewers). You may also close an open drill-down page in the ActiveX or Java viewers by clicking the red X button when the drill-down page is the current view.

Main Report

- **Refresh**   Refresh an older instance or a recent view to reflect the latest data. Note that your CRS Administrator may deny you the refresh right. If you try to refresh it without this right, you will receive an error message in the browser.

- **Find**   Search the report for certain text or data content. Some viewers have the search text box in the toolbar, and others prompt for the text string after you click the Find button.

- **Zoom**   Choose the zoom level to view the report by choosing various options from the zoom drop-down list. Choices may include percentage numbers, or standard view choices, such as Page Width or Whole Page.

Using Advanced DHTML Viewer Features

Crystal Reports Server XI gives you two DHTML viewer options when choosing a report viewer (discussed earlier in the chapter). The *Advanced DHTML Viewer,* while showing you a report in a pure HTML format like the regular DHTML Viewer, also includes extra subquery features that allow you to further refine and analyze the core underlying data that makes up the report you are viewing. You can choose a subset of fields on the report, choose some additional selection criteria, and display the results in a row-and-column subview (which can also be exported to Word, Excel, or HTML formats).

First, ensure that the Advanced DHTML Viewer is chosen as the desired viewer in Crystal Reports Preferences (this is discussed earlier in the chapter). Then, view the desired report object by clicking the report name, or the desired report instance with the View Latest Instance or History option from InfoView. The report will be displayed inside the Advanced DHTML Viewer.

The Advanced DHTML Viewer looks almost identical to the regular DHTML Viewer with two exceptions: the small header at the top of the viewer that indicates you are using the advanced viewer, and the extra binoculars-with-plus-sign Advanced Search Wizard button in the viewer toolbar. The benefit of the Advanced DHTML Viewer is realized when you use the Advanced Search Wizard. Display it by clicking the Advanced Search Wizard button in the viewer toolbar. The viewer will redisplay the report below the Fields tab of the wizard.

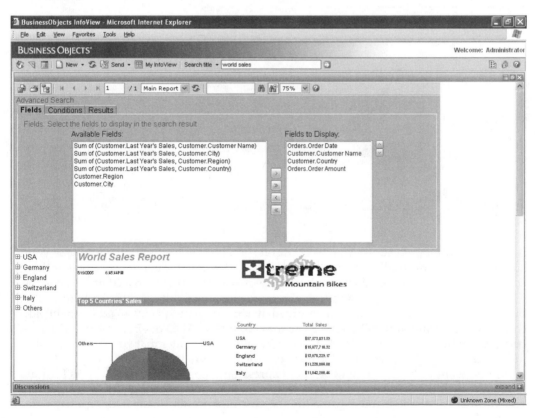

The list of fields that make up the report will appear in the left Available Fields list. Choose one or more fields you want to appear in your subquery (you may CTRL-click or SHIFT-click in the list to select multiple fields). Then, click the right arrow to add the chosen fields to the right Fields To Display list. You may remove any fields you later decide you don't want to include in the subquery by selecting them in the Fields To Display list and clicking the left arrow. To reorder fields in the Fields To Display list, click the desired field and reorder it with the up or down arrows above the list. Once you've chosen the desired set of fields, click the Conditions tab.

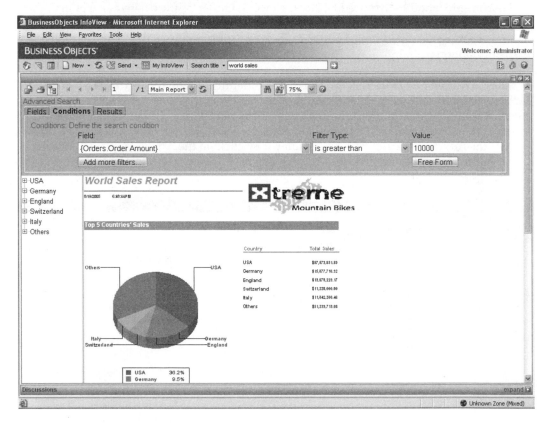

The Conditions tab allows you to choose one or more fields to filter the results of your subquery. Pick a desired field from the Field drop-down list. Then, choose one of the comparison operators from the Filter Type drop-down list and type in a comparison value in the Value text box. If you want to filter on more than one field, click the Add More Filters button. An additional filter line will be added, where you may specify an additional field, condition, and value. You will also be given the choice of an AND or OR Boolean "connector" between the two filters. If you decide you don't want to use a filter that you've already added, just remove any entry from the Value text box. The filter will be ignored.

If you want to type in a manual filter expression using the Crystal Reports formula language, click the Free Form button. A text box will appear showing any existing filters you've already supplied. You may modify the existing formula, delete it, or type in a new formula. Use standard Crystal Reports formula language syntax, as discussed in Chapters 4 and 5. If you want to redisplay the original search "expert," click the Expert button. The filters will be redisplayed in the expert format (providing you haven't specified a free-form formula that is too complex for the wizard to convert to an expert display).

Once you've specified all desired filters, click the Results tab to see the results of your subquery. The Results tab will show the records that compose the result in a row/column format, without formatting.

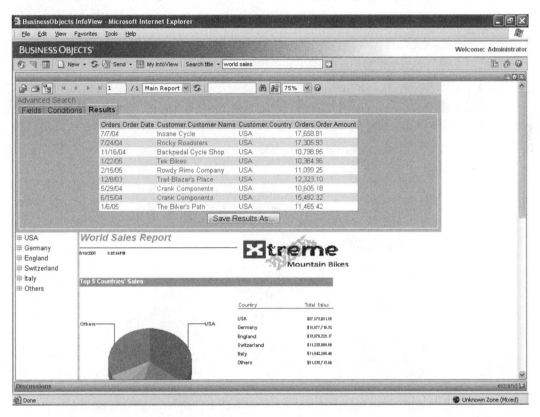

If no results are shown because of invalid filters, or you wish to add or remove fields from the subquery, click the Fields or Conditions tab to make any desired changes. Once the query results are satisfactory, you may export them to Word, Excel, or HTML format. Note the MS Word, MS Excel, and HTML links next to the Export label above the query results. Click the Save Results As button to download the query results.

Even while the Advanced Search Wizard is displayed, you may continue to view and navigate through the original report inside the viewer (this may be helpful when comparing subquery results with the original report data). When you are finished using the wizard, just click the original toolbar button you used to display the wizard in the first place. It will close, and only the report will remain in the viewer window.

NOTE *Remember that the subquery you create with the Advanced DHTML Viewer is only being applied to the records already included in the report you are viewing. The underlying database that the report was originally based on will not be queried again. For example, if the report you are viewing is already limited to USA customers, specifying a filter on the Condition tab that searches for customers in Canada will not return any results.*

Exporting and E-Mailing Reports

You may wish to save a copy of a report from InfoView to your own local computer. Perhaps you wish to include it in a Word document, perform some more unique analysis in Microsoft Excel, or attach an Adobe Acrobat file to an e-mail to send to a colleague who doesn't have access to InfoView. All of this can be accomplished by exporting reports from a report viewer:

1. View the report or instance you wish to export.

2. Click the export button in the viewer toolbar. The Export dialog box will appear (the following example is from the DHTML Viewer).

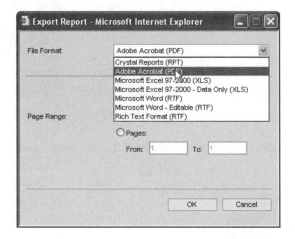

3. If you are using the DHTML or Advanced DHTML Viewer, choose the desired export format from the drop-down list of formats and the page range you wish to export. Then, click OK to start downloading the report to your browser.

4. If you are using the ActiveX or Java viewers, a dialog box will appear where you may choose the location and filename of the exported file, as well as the file format you wish to use and page range you wish to export. Make the desired choices.

5. The file will be saved on your local hard disk.

6. If you wish to e-mail the file to a colleague, attach the file you just downloaded to an e-mail message using typical steps to send e-mail attachments.

Printing Reports on Your Local Printer

Often, you'll want to print a full or partial copy of the report you're viewing on a locally attached printer. And, you'll most probably want it printed with the original formatting and pagination that was used when the report was designed. There are varying ways to accomplish this, depending on the report viewer you've chosen in Crystal Reports Preferences.

If you are using the ActiveX or Java viewers, the viewer will display a Print button right in the toolbar. When you click this button, a typical Print dialog box will appear, allowing you to choose various printing options, such as page range. The report will be printed in "native" format on the chosen printer.

However, if you are using the DHTML or Advanced DHTML Viewer (the DHTML Viewer is the default report viewer used when first installing CRS), you'll find two print buttons: one in the viewer toolbar, as well as the standard browser print button that appears in any web page you view. Ensure that you click the print button in the viewer toolbar, as the browser print button will only print the current browser screen, not the entire report.

In addition, you'll need to make an additional choice about how you want reports printed. As discussed earlier in the chapter, Crystal Reports Preferences gives you two options for printing from the DHTML viewers: Adobe Acrobat format or the ActiveX print control. Adobe Acrobat format will simply download the fully paginated and formatted report in .PDF format to your browser. You may print the report from the Acrobat Reader that displays the report.

NOTE *You must have the Adobe Acrobat Reader installed on your computer for this method of local printing to work. If you don't have the application installed, you will simply be prompted to save the .PDF file on disk, which won't ultimately accomplish your print requirement. Check with your Information Technology department, or visit www.adobe.com to get a copy of the Acrobat Reader for your particular computer and operating system.*

Crystal Reports Server XI also provides the ActiveX print control. If you make this choice in Crystal Reports Preferences, then a small ActiveX control will be downloaded to your browser the first time you print a report from the DHTML Viewer (typically, you can only make use of ActiveX controls if you are using Microsoft Internet Explorer as your browser). You may be prompted to accept this control when it is first downloaded (or, you may be notified that it can't be downloaded if your browser's security settings prohibit ActiveX control download). Once the control is downloaded and registered, it will simply display a standard print dialog where you can specify print settings, such as page range and number of copies. The report will then be streamed to your printer with all original pagination and formatting.

Scheduling Objects

One of the many benefits of using Crystal Reports Server for managing your organization's reporting and analysis infrastructure is its ability to schedule reports. This allows automatic running of reports on a daily, weekly, or monthly basis, or on other regular schedules that suit your particular environment. CRS XI also introduces program objects (executable programs, Java programs, or script) that can also be scheduled on a regular basis. And, CRS XI Object Packages, consisting of groups of related reports or program objects, can be scheduled as well.

NOTE *The majority of scheduling discussions in this section pertain to reports. Program object scheduling options are generally limited to specifying the frequency of the schedule, any command-line arguments supplied when run, and the destination of the program's output text. The remaining scheduling options apply to reports only.*

When you schedule a report or program object, you are setting a time to run it—either once or on a recurring schedule. You can schedule a report to run immediately, if desired; the difference between doing this and viewing on demand is that Crystal Reports Server saves the "instance" of the report when it is run, and makes it available to other users. Unlike the temporary copy that's available only to you for a little while, after you view a report, the Schedule action puts the report instance in history, and these instances are typically available for a much longer time. Scheduling of program objects allows some sort of executable program or script (such as a data warehouse update or CRS administrative task done with JScript or VBScript) to be run on a regular recurring basis. The "instance," in the case of a scheduled program object, is a text view of the standard and error output from the program object when it runs.

Using scheduled reports has several advantages:

- Scheduling instances can optimize database and network performance by avoiding excess network and database requests.

- The scheduling function provides the ability to enter embedded parameter values, database logon, report format, and/or selection criteria, so that viewers aren't prompted for these values.

- Scheduling instances can significantly reduce the time it takes to support a large group of users requesting reports.

So, scheduled instances are flexible and informative while still protecting databases from uncontrolled access, protecting the database servers from unnecessary repetitive queries, and maximizing sharing of common reports.

NOTE *The ability to schedule objects is controlled by CRS security. Your CRS administrator may not have granted you this right for some or all objects. If you don't see the Schedule option in the InfoView pop-up menu, check with your CRS administrator to see if you have this right.*

Scheduling Options

When you schedule an object in InfoView, there are several sets of options you must choose from to customize your schedule. These options may vary depending on whether you're scheduling a report or program object, how the report you're scheduling is designed (reports based on secure databases or with parameter fields must have database credentials or parameter values supplied when scheduling), what output destination you want the object sent to, and so forth. And, you have several other scheduling options, such as how many times and when the report should run.

When you click the Schedule link from the object area, the Schedule dialog box will replace the objects area. Various scheduling options will appear, each preceded with a plus sign. Click the plus sign to expand the desired scheduling option and make your preferred choices.

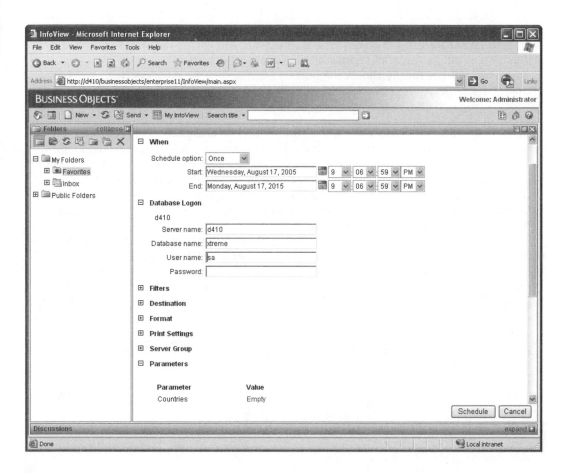

When

The first choice you'll have when scheduling an object is when and how often to run it. These values determine how often and at what time a report instance will be created or a program object will execute. The default option is "Now," meaning the object will run immediately. The second option, "Once," means it will run only once—at the time specified and within 24 hours. It defaults to the current time, so accepting the defaults provides an immediate run. The other options run the object regularly at the time specified or based on a calendar that your administrator has defined (calendar-based scheduling is new in CRS XI).

Other options include Hourly, Daily, Weekly, Monthly, and Calendar. Once you've chosen one of the options from the Run Report drop-down list, the remainder of the schedule dialog box will change, depending on the first choice you made. Depending on the choice you make, you may have additional flexibility in scheduling. For example, if you choose Monthly scheduling, you'll also be able to choose the "Nth day of the month," the last day of the month, the first or second Monday or Tuesday, and so forth.

Fill in necessary items for the chosen scheduling interval. Note that you'll often be prompted to specify both starting and ending dates and times. Even if you schedule an object to run, for example, once a day at the current time, you may still be prompted to specify an end time. This comes into play if an object, for some reason, doesn't run at the exact time you specify (perhaps a CRS component is down at that time, the object initially fails and needs to be retried, and so forth). By specifying an end time, you ensure that any such schedules will not occur after a "point of no return" time during the day.

Also, even if you simply choose a regular schedule, such as "once per day," you may choose to have the object not run past a particular day. While the default end date is far in the future, you may choose to stop the recurring process at an earlier date.

Scheduling Based on a Calendar Crystal Reports Server XI also provides for calendar-based scheduling. With this feature, you may simply choose to run an object on specific days defined in one of any number of calendars defined by your Crystal Reports Server administrator. For example, you may find that your particular organization's payroll processing is on a somewhat irregular schedule that the built-in scheduling periods don't quite fit. In these cases, calendars can be defined that identify specific pay days, regardless of holidays, two- or three-payday months, and so forth.

To schedule according to a calendar, choose Calendar from the When drop-down list. A list of predefined calendars that have been created on the CMS (creating calendars is covered in Chapter 24). Choose the desired calendar. The screen will redraw once again, showing several months in advance with days identified in green acting as days the object will run. Make any desired adjustments to start time, start date, and end date to customize the schedule within the calendar.

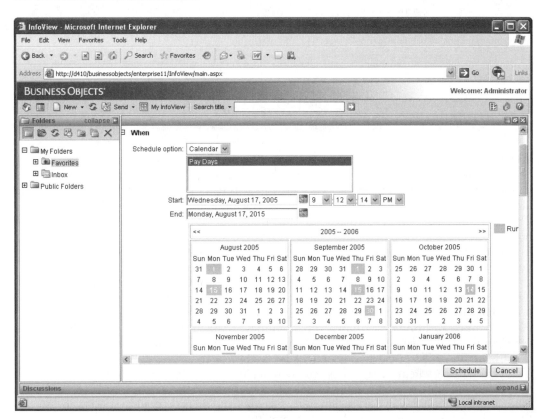

CAUTION Make sure you specify all necessary scheduling options from the various choices in the schedule dialog before you click the Schedule button. If you don't specify all necessary items, the instance will fail or return incorrect results when it is run prematurely.

Logging on to a Database

Depending on the database, or databases, the report you are scheduling is based on, you must specify database credentials as part of the scheduling process (this is not required when scheduling program objects). If proper credentials aren't provided, or a pre-stored set of database credentials haven't been set by the CRS Administrator, the instances will fail when they attempt to connect to the database.

Items you may need to specify include the data source name (an ODBC data source, server name, etc.), the database you wish to connect to, the user ID, and a password. If there is more than one database, you'll be able to make these choices for each database included in the report.

Filters

Most reports contain a record selection formula that you may wish to modify when scheduling (program objects do not make use of a Filters option). A record selection formula is a Crystal Reports–specific statement that filters database records so that a limited set of data will be included on the report.

You can also modify a group selection formula. A group selection formula is similar to a record selection formula, except that it uses subtotal or summary functions at the end of report groups to limit the report to only groups that contain certain values.

You can modify any existing selection formula this instance uses (either record selection or group selection), as well as adding additional criteria to the formulas. Make sure you supply proper Crystal Reports formula syntax in the selection formula (Record and Group Selection formulas are covered in Chapters 4 and 5).

NOTE If the report's existing record or group selection formulas are based on parameter fields, you need not modify the selection formulas themselves—the parameter fields will take care of customizing report filtering for you. However, if you do need to modify the selection formulas manually, be careful. Your formulas must strictly adhere to Crystal Reports formula language syntax or the instances will fail.

Destination

By default, InfoView will run a scheduled report against the database, save the set of data returned from the database with the instance, and allow it to be viewed online in one of the report viewers. And, a scheduled program object's standard and error output is saved as a text file, which can be viewed online after the object has run.

However, in the case of report output, you may prefer to have the instance attached to an e-mail message in a different file format (such as Adobe Acrobat format). Or, you might want to save the instance as an Excel .XLS file to a specific location on a LAN server. Or, you might want to send the instance as a Word document to another site via File Transfer Protocol (FTP). You may prefer to route the report instance to one or more Crystal Reports Server inboxes. Finally, you may simply want the report printed on a printer whenever the instance runs.

If you are in charge of several program objects that, perhaps, perform data warehouse updates or other administrative functions, you may want the standard and error output of the program objects to be e-mailed to you whenever the object runs. Or, you may prefer that the text comprising the object's output be placed in a fixed location on your corporate LAN so that, at any given time, the output from the latest instance of the program object can always be found.

When scheduling, you can specify that Crystal Reports Server send the instance to any number of these destinations. The Destination drop-down allows you to choose various default or specific destinations, including inbox, a file location, FTP server, and e-mail. Of the default choices, Default Enterprise Location indicates that the instance will be automatically saved on a CRS server with a filename managed by CRS. Whenever you view the instance, CRS automatically knows where to find the right files for online viewing. The other default locations are defined in advance by the CRS Administrator. The remaining specific destination choices all produce a set of additional options related to that particular destination, such as inbox choice, e-mail address, or specific file location and filename. Consult your Crystal Reports Server administrator for more specific instructions on which destinations are configured on your CRS system and what choices you may make for them.

Format

You have a choice of file format when scheduling a report (format choices aren't available for program objects). Rather than saving the report in Crystal Reports' proprietary .RPT file format, you have a number of format choices, including two Excel formats, Word, Acrobat, and various text formats.

Depending on your format choice, the dialog box will change with prompts for various format-related options, such as page range or how to convert report formatting to spreadsheet formatting.

TIP *Choosing a format other than "Crystal Report" when using the Default destination will cause different behavior when you attempt to view an instance with a report viewer. Rather than launching the report viewer chosen in Crystal Report Preferences, CRS will download the instance in the file format chosen in the Format drop-down list. If a matching application (such as Excel or the Adobe Acrobat Viewer) is installed on your PC, the application will be launched and the instance displayed in that application. Otherwise, you'll be prompted to save the file to disk.*

Print Settings

If you are scheduling a report, you may desire that the report simply print on a printer configured on the CRS server (for example, you may migrate mainframe-based production reporting to Crystal Reports Server and wish regular printing jobs, such as invoices and accounts payable checks, to be scheduled by CRS).

Regardless of the Destination and Format settings you make, you can choose to print a copy of the report in Crystal Reports format on a printer when the report is run (Print Settings don't apply to program objects). If you choose Crystal Report from the Print drop-down list, the dialog will redraw with additional options, such as a page range and number of copies. You may allow the CRS server to use its default printer, or you may specify a printer name (the name you supply must be properly configured or recognized on the CRS server—check with your CRS administrator if you're unsure of what printer name to use).

Server Group

If the CRS Administrator has defined multiple report job servers (the particular CRS server that processes Crystal Reports), then you may choose which of these servers processes this particular report. Other than the default "Use First Available Server," you may choose to give preference to a specific group of servers, or force only a specific group of servers to be used.

Parameter Values

If the report you are scheduling uses Crystal Reports parameter fields, you'll need to supply parameter values in order for an instance to run successfully, unless default parameter values have been set in the report or set in advance by the CRS Administrator. These defaults may be acceptable to you; if they are, you won't have to change them before scheduling the report. However, if you need different values for this instance, you'll need to supply the new values you wish the instance to use every time it runs.

Click the plus sign next to the Parameters entry to see all parameters included in the report you are scheduling. If default values are already specified, they will appear next to the associated parameter name. If no default is specified, the parameter will indicate Empty. Click the default value or the word Empty to assign a new value. The parameters displayed will vary, depending on what types of parameters exist on the report you're scheduling. Generally, you'll see each parameter listed with its user prompt, and beneath that you'll see an area for adding values for that parameter. You may be able to choose from a set of possible values from a "pick list"—a drop-down list that will show all available values. New Crystal Reports Server XI dynamic and cascading pick lists may appear here, too.

Special types of parameters that you should be on the lookout for are date or date/time parameters. These parameter values require adherence to a specific CRS format. For example, if you wish to supply a date of January 1, 2002, you can't simply type "1/1/02" or "1/1/2002"— an error message will appear. You must supply dates in the format yyyy-mm-dd, including the hyphens. So, you would specify a parameter value of January 1, 2002, as 2002-01-01. Note that a small "date picker" icon also appears when prompting for a date parameter. If you click this icon and specify a date in the corresponding calendar box, the properly formatted value will be filled in for you.

NOTE *If you are scheduling a program object, the Parameters entry will display a single text box where you may specify command-line parameters for the program object.*

Once you're satisfied with all your various scheduling choices, click the Schedule button. The instance will be submitted to the CMS for scheduling.

The History dialog box will appear showing the newly scheduled instance. Click the Refresh button in the History dialog toolbar to update the status of any scheduled or processing instances. The History dialog box initially shows instances sorted by date/time run in descending (newest to oldest) time. You may alternatively sort instances in ascending date/time order, or in ascending or descending order by the user who ran the instance (as noted in the Run By column), or by status (as noted by the Status column). Simply click the column heading of the desired sort item—an "up arrow" or "down arrow" will appear next to the column heading, indicating which column instances are currently sorted by, and in what order.

Check to specify a time range to limit instances

Click status for more information

Sort by Date/Time, Run By, or Status column

Choose between all or only complete instances

Click date/time of successful instance to view

Check desired instances and click option buttons

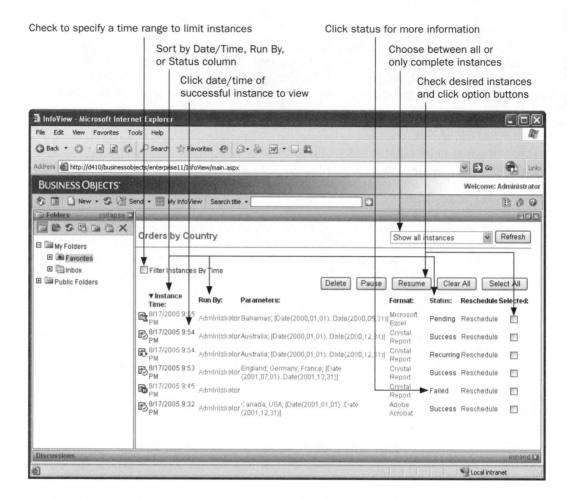

The History dialog will show several different status entries that you may notice:

- **Recurring** The instance is set up to run on a regular basis, such as every day. When the recurring instance's next run time approaches, the CMS will copy the recurring instance to a new Running instance. By clicking the Recurring status, you can see what the instance's recurrence pattern is and when the next instance is scheduled to run.

- **Paused** A recurring or pending instance has been "paused" so that it will not run on its schedule for the time being. These instances can be paused by clicking the check box to the right of a recurring instance and clicking the Pause button. To resume a paused instance, check the paused instance and click the Resume button. The original status will reappear.

- **Pending** The instance is scheduled to run at some point in the future, or is waiting for some sort of "dependency" to be satisfied (dependencies are discussed in more detail in Chapter 24). Clicking the Pending status will show you the time the instance is scheduled to run, as well as any dependencies the instance is waiting for.

- **Running**   The instance is being processed by the CRS server at this time. Clicking the Refresh icon in the History screen toolbar will update the running status as the instance processing progresses.

- **Success**   The instance has completed successfully. By clicking the Success status, you can find out more information about the completed instance.

- **Failed**   The instance failed when it attempted to run. Failed instances can occur for many reasons, such as lack of proper database credentials, failure to supply parameter fields, or incorrect database connectivity on the CRS server. By clicking the Failed status, you'll find out more information on the failed instance, including a description of the reason for the failure (sometimes helpful and descriptive, sometimes not).

To view a successful instance, simply click the date/time entry for the instance. The instance will be displayed in the format chosen when the report was scheduled (to view the latest instance, you can simply choose the View Latest Instance option from the objects area—you needn't even display the History list first). You may also pause, resume, or delete one or more instances by checking the box to the right of the desired instance or instances and clicking various buttons above the instance list. Note that rights to pause, resume, and delete instances may be denied to you by the CRS administrator.

Scheduling Reports Containing Alerts

Crystal Reports can be designed to make use of report alerts. *Report alerts* are settings in a report that trigger a "red flag" when certain conditions are met. Examples would be alerts that would be triggered if sales exceeded a certain goal, customer support calls exceeded a critical level, and so forth (designing Crystal Reports with alerts is discussed in Chapter 7).

When you view a report containing alerts on demand (that is, you simply click the report name in the objects area), the report runs just like any other report and alerts *are not* triggered. However, reports containing alerts behave a little differently when scheduled.

Reports containing alerts will display a special icon in the History list if alerts were triggered when the report ran (you'll notice a small yellow exclamation point added to the report's icon). However, viewing report instances from the History list still will show the entire report, without any indication of what alerts were triggered or what report records triggered them.

However, reports containing alerts will provide an additional Alerts option in the objects area. Click it to see any report instances that have run that contain triggered report alerts. A list of instances that triggered alerts will appear. The original report name, the report's folder or category, the date and time the instance completed, as well as the defined alert or alerts that were triggered will appear. Clicking the report name will simply display the report instance, just as if you would have clicked it in the History list—no alert information will be displayed. However, clicking an alert name will display the report instance showing *only* report records that conform to the alert.

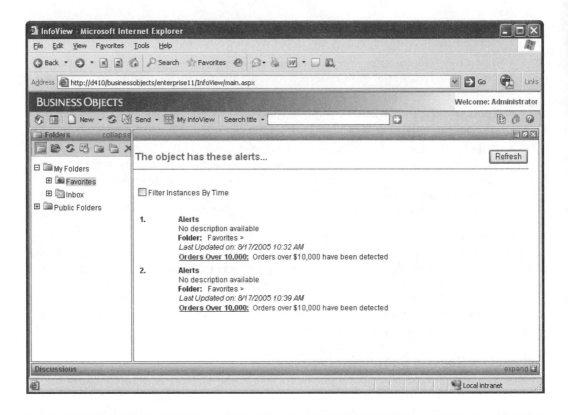

TIP *Crystal Reports Server can also be configured to send an e-mail when a report alert is triggered. This is discussed in Chapter 24.*

Rescheduling Existing Instances

One feature missing from earlier Crystal Enterprise versions has finally arrived in Crystal Reports Server XI. The ability to either change some aspect of an existing scheduled object, or to copy an existing scheduled object to another scheduled instance with changes, is now available in CRS XI. This new feature allows easy changes to be made to existing scheduled items without having to cancel them and completely restart the scheduling process.

First, display the History List by clicking the History link below the desired report in the objects area. Then, find the existing instance that you want to change or copy (this can be any instance that displays a Reschedule link under the Reschedule column). Click the Reschedule link to change or copy the instance. The original schedule dialog box you used when originally scheduling the object will reappear.

If the instance can still run in the future (it's a Pending or Recurring instance, for example), you will be given two choices at the top of the schedule screen: Replace Existing Schedule and Create A New Schedule From Existing Schedule. Choose the Replace Existing Schedule option to change some aspect of the original schedule (such as the end date and time or the destination options) that will affect any future instances that run. Choose the Create A New Schedule option to copy this instance to a new instance with the changes you make elsewhere in the dialog box. The original instance will remain unchanged. If the original instance you choose to reschedule has already completed its scheduling cycle (for example, it has failed or run successfully), the choice to Replace or Copy will be dimmed and you'll only be able to copy the changed instance to a new instance.

Choose whether to modify existing schedule or copy
updated scheduling information to a new instance

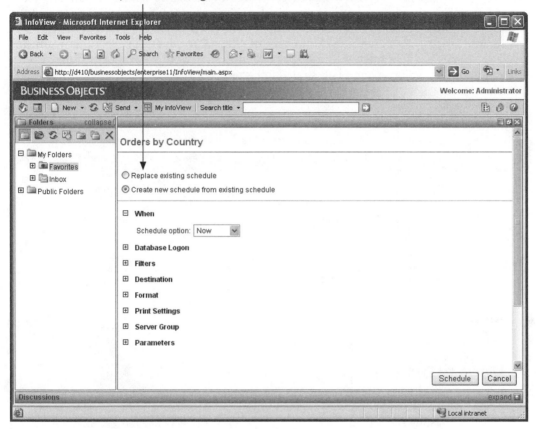

Make any desired changes to scheduling options (such as When, Destination, or Parameters) and click the Schedule button. Either the existing instance will be updated to reflect the new scheduling options, or the copied instance with your new options will appear in the History List.

Using Discussions

Introduced as an add-on for Crystal Enterprise 10, the threaded discussion feature is now an integral part of Crystal Reports Server XI. *Discussions* allow CRS users to enter text comments that are attached to any object within CRS. "Threaded" discussion capabilities indicate the ability to respond to a specific initial comment, with another response to that response, and so forth, creating a *thread* of related messages. This discussion technique is common to many web-based support applications.

NOTE *The ability to add notes to discussion threads can be denied by the CRS Administrator. If you are unable to post messages, check with the administrator to see if you have proper rights.*

Begin by selecting the object you wish to "discuss." This can be any type of CRS object, including a report, program object, or third-party object. You may view either the object itself or any associated instance (remember, however, that a discussion thread will apply to the object and all instances—separate threads can't be created for individual instances of the same object). Once the desired object is selected, click the word Expand or the associated arrow icon on the Discussions panel at the bottom of InfoView. The panel will expand upward. To make the panel larger, point to the line separating the panel from the rest of InfoView and drag up. The Discussions panel is illustrated in Figure 23-2.

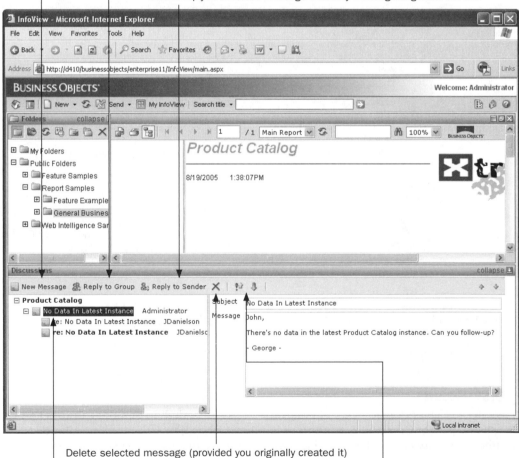

Create new thread for chosen object

Create public reply to selected message

Create reply to selected message that only message originator will see

Delete selected message (provided you originally created it)

Series of messages known as "thread"

Flag message with high or low importance

FIGURE 23-2   Discussions panel

Any existing message threads will appear in the left side of the Discussions panel. You'll notice the hierarchy of messages—initial messages in a thread will appear at the top, replies will appear underneath with plus signs, replies to replies will also appear with plus signs, and so forth. Expand the hierarchy by clicking the plus signs or contract them by clicking minus signs. Any messages you have not yet read will appear in a bold font. Click a message title to display the message in the right side of the Discussions panel.

To create a new thread (this can be done whether any existing threads appear or not), click the New Message button at the top of the Discussions panel. A new top-level thread message will be created on the left side of the panel, with the subject and message fields appearing on the right side of the panel. An automatic subject will be created based on your CRS user ID and the date you create the thread. You may leave the default subject as-is or type a different subject in the field. Then, type the message you wish to add in the message field. If you wish to assign the message a high or low priority, click either the high priority or low priority button at the top of the Discussions panel. A similar high- or low-priority icon will be added to the message you are creating.

Once you are satisfied with the subject and message, click the Post button below the message field on the right side of the panel. The message will be posted to the CRS Central Management Server database. Once the message is posted, other users who view the same object and who also expand the Discussions panel will see the message you created.

CAUTION *It's easy to add a new message and click some other item in InfoView without actually posting the message. If you do this, the message will not be saved. Make sure to click the Post button when you are satisfied with your message to actually save it.*

If you wish to reply to an existing message, select the message that you wish to reply to. Then, click either the Reply To Group or Reply To Sender button at the top of the Discussions panel. Reply To Group will cause your message to be visible to all users who view the thread, while Reply To Sender will cause your message to be visible only to the user who created the original message you are replying to. Once you click either button, a new message will be created indented underneath the message you are replying to. If you are not satisfied with the default subject, you may change it in the subject field. You may also assign the message a high or low priority with the appropriate button at the top of the panel. Then, type your reply in the Message field and click the Post button to add your new message to the thread.

Modifying or Deleting Existing Messages

After you've created a message, you may desire to change the text or subject of the message, or perhaps delete it entirely. Provided that you originally created the message, and provided that it has not been responded to, you may change or delete the message. Merely select the message in the thread hierarchy that you wish to change. The subject and message will appear on the right side of the Discussions panel.

If the message can be edited, you'll be able to change entries in the subject and message fields, you'll be able to assign a high or low priority, and the Post button will appear. Make any changes to the subject or message, assign a priority if you wish, and click the Post button to post the changed message to the Central Management Server database. To delete the message, click the X button at the top of the Discussion panel toolbar. You'll be prompted to confirm the deletion. Once you confirm the deletion, the message will be deleted.

Organizing InfoView

There are many ways to organize and view folders and categories and their associated objects in InfoView. Not only will CRS security determine what folders, categories, and objects you can and cannot see, but there are different ways of displaying those folders and objects that you can see (such as by category, by folder, in the Favorites folder, and your inbox). Crystal Reports Server XI adds additional features over previous Crystal Enterprise versions as well, including the ability to assign categories to objects and to add your own Crystal Reports directly to InfoView without having to use other methods.

You may consider sticking with the folder/category and object/instance organization undertaken by your CRS Administrator (in fact, the administrator may require this, not allowing you much leeway in organizational capabilities by limiting your right to add and move things). However, if you are given the freedom to organize InfoView, you will need to know the various ways of accomplishing this. In any case, you will probably be given free reign to at least your own personal Favorites folder and categories, so you'll still benefit from the ability to create subfolders and categories within it, as well as moving or copying objects and instances to the Favorites folder, creating shortcuts in your Favorites folder, and creating and assigning personal categories.

NOTE *Your CRS administrator may have limited the right to create, modify, or delete folders or objects in Crystal Reports Server. If you are unable to perform actions that you need, contact the administrator for assistance.*

Working with Folders and Categories

 Most organizational tasks revolving around folders and categories are undertaken by clicking toolbar buttons at the top of the navigation panel at the left of the InfoView screen. If the navigation panel is hidden, you must display it before you can move or delete folders or categories. If necessary, click the Toggle Navigation button in the main InfoView toolbar to redisplay the navigation panel. You may also add new folders or categories to InfoView by using the New drop-down button at the top of the InfoView screen (you'll see this toolbar even if the navigation panel is hidden).

Moving, Copying, and Deleting Folders

Before you can move, copy, or delete a folder, you must ensure that the navigation panel is displaying CRS folders (instead of categories). If necessary, click the Show Folders toolbar button in the navigation panel toolbar. This will display the initial My Folders and Public Folders top-level folders. Click plus signs next to these top level folders to view subfolders within them. Once you've found the folder you wish to delete or move, select it. You'll know you've selected the proper folder when it's highlighted with a light shade (and, you'll also notice any objects within the selected folder in the objects area on the right side of the InfoView screen).

 Moving a folder to a new location will move the folder and its contents (objects and instances) to a new location. To move the selected folder, click the Move button in the navigation panel toolbar. This will replace the objects area with the Move screen. Select the desired destination where you want the folder moved. You may select the Favorites folder or any subfolders you may have created in it within the Personal Folders top-level folder, or any folder or subfolder within the Public Folders top-level folder. You'll know which folder you've selected when it appears with a light shade. You may also create a new folder directly in this screen by typing a new name in the New Folder field and clicking Add. You may then select the new folder you just created as the destination.

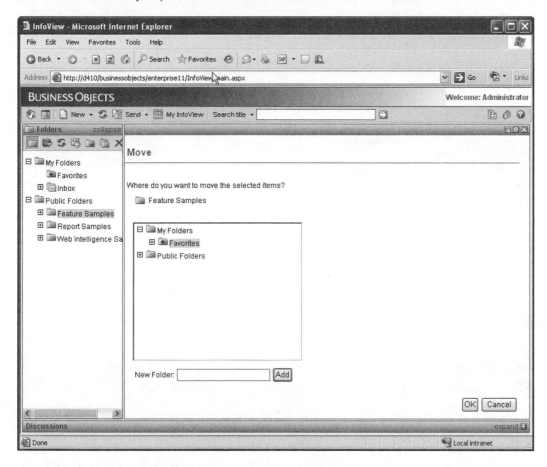

Once you've chosen the desired destination location, click OK. The folder will be moved from its original location to the new location. The objects area will reappear for the folder you just moved.

Copying a folder to a new location will leave the original folder and its contents (objects and instances) unchanged, while making a copy of the folder and its contents in the new location. The initial step is the same: ensure the folder you want to copy is selected within the navigation panel. Then, click the Copy toolbar button in the navigation panel toolbar. This will replace the objects area with the Copy screen. Select the desired destination where you want the folder copied. You may select the Favorites folder or any subfolders you may have created in it within the Personal Folders top-level folder, or any folder or subfolder within the Public Folders top-level folder. You'll know which folder you've selected when it appears with a light shade. You may also create a new folder directly in this screen by typing a new name in the New Folder field and clicking Add. You may then select the new folder you just created as the destination.

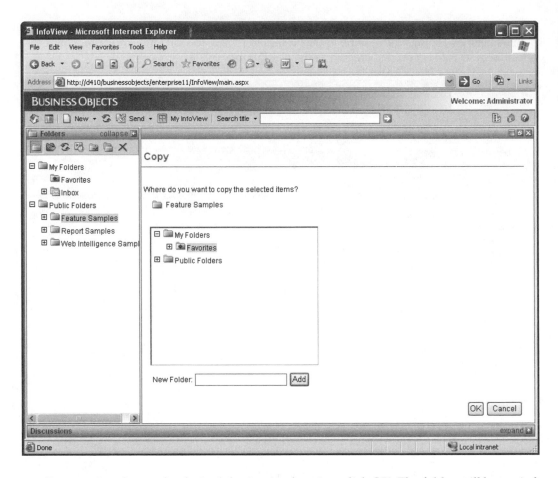

Once you've chosen the desired destination location, click OK. The folder will be copied from its original location to the new location. The objects area will reappear for the folder you just copied.

 Deleting a folder will remove the folder and all its contents (objects and instances) from CRS. The initial step is the same: ensure that the folder you want to delete is selected within the navigation panel. Then, click the Delete toolbar button in the navigation panel toolbar. You'll be prompted to confirm the folder deletion. If you reply Yes, the folder and its contents will be removed.

CAUTION *Deleting folders is a permanent operation—there is no Undo capability. Make sure you really want to delete a folder and its contents before you undertake these steps. You may wish to check with your CRS Administrator to see if he or she has a regular backup procedure in place before you delete valuable folders.*

Moving or Deleting Categories

As discussed elsewhere in the chapter, Crystal Reports Server XI adds the ability to organize objects in categories as well as folders. If you've been granted the right by your CRS Administrator, you can move or delete categories that already exist in CRS. Before you can move or delete a category, you must ensure that the navigation panel is displaying CRS categories (instead of folders). If necessary, click the Show Categories toolbar button in the navigation panel toolbar. This will display the initial Personal Categories and Corporate Categories top-level categories. Click plus signs next to these top-level categories to view subcategories within them. Once you've found the category that you wish to delete or move, select it. You'll know you've selected the proper category when it's highlighted with a light shade (and, you'll also notice any objects within the selected category in the objects area on the right side of the InfoView screen).

Moving a category, in essence, relocates it within another top-level category or subcategory. For example, if you initially have a category defined directly underneath the Corporate Categories high-level category and wish to make it a subcategory of another category directly underneath Corporate Categories, you may move it to the other category. To move the selected category, click the Move button in the navigation panel toolbar. As when moving folders, this will replace the objects area with the Move screen. Select the desired destination where you want the category moved. You'll know which category you've selected when it appears with a light shade. You may also create a new category directly in this screen by typing a new name in the New Category field and clicking Add. You may then select the new category you just created as the destination.

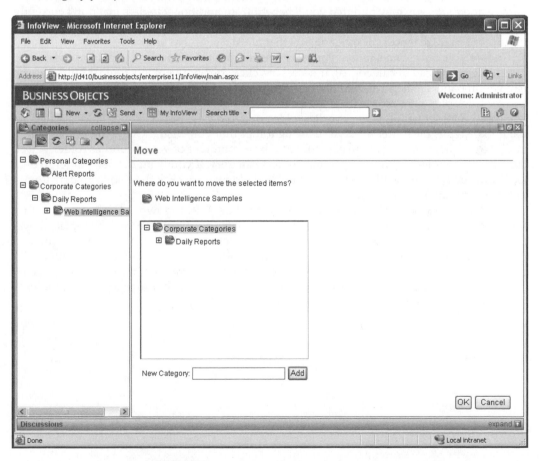

Once you've chosen the desired destination location, click OK. The category will be moved from its original location to the new location. The objects area will reappear for the category you just moved.

NOTE   *There are a few restrictions on moving categories: you may not move your top-level personal category or the top-level corporate category, and you may only move categories to another location within their existing "level" (in other words, you can't move a personal category to a corporate category or vice versa).*

Deleting a category will remove the category from CRS. Unlike removing folders, removing a category will not remove any objects. However, objects that were assigned to the category will obviously no longer be assigned to it once it is deleted. The initial step is the same: ensure that the category you want to delete is selected within the navigation panel. Then, click the Delete toolbar button in the navigation panel toolbar. You'll be prompted to confirm the category deletion. If you reply Yes, the category will be removed.

Creating New Folders

While the existing set of folders you encounter when logging on to Crystal Reports Server may be adequate, you may find that you'll benefit from additional folders that don't currently exist. In particular, you may want to create additional folders within your Favorites folder to further organize reports or other objects that are stored in Favorites.

Before you can create a folder, you must ensure that the navigation panel is displaying CRS folders (instead of categories). If necessary, click the Show Folders toolbar button in the navigation panel toolbar. This will display the initial My Folders and Public Folders top-level folders. Click plus signs next to these top level folders to view subfolders within them. Whether you create a folder within your Favorites folder, or a folder within the Public Folders category, the initial step is the same: select the existing folder that you wish the new folder to reside in. For example, if you want the new folder to be a subfolder of your Favorites folder, select the Favorites folder within the Personal Folders category. If you want the new folder to be located directly underneath the top-level Public Folders area, click the Public Folders item in the navigation panel.

Click the New button in the main InfoView toolbar. A drop-down list will appear with several options for creating new items. Choose Folder. The objects area will be replaced by the New Folder screen. Type the name for your new folder in the Folder Name field (note that you cannot use the same name as an existing folder already in the same location). Optionally, provide a description for the folder in the Description field. And, if you wish to use the Search capability at the top of the InfoView screen to later search for this folder by keyword, type appropriate keywords in the Keywords field.

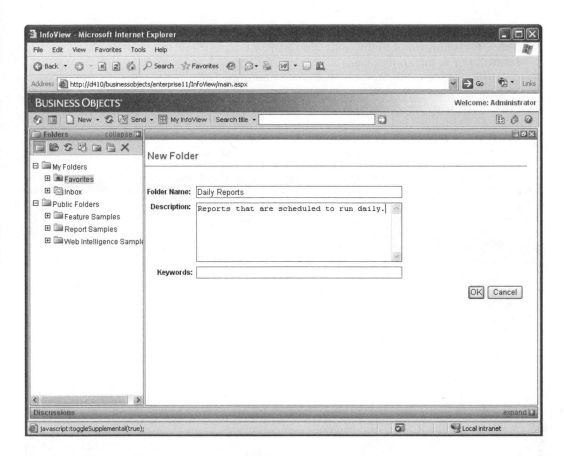

Once you've supplied folder information, click OK. The folder will be created within the desired location. The original location you chose before creating the folder will appear, with the objects area showing the original folder's contents. You'll notice the new folder in the navigation panel within the original location.

Creating New Categories

Before you can create a new category, you must ensure that the navigation panel is displaying CRS categories (instead of folders). If necessary, click the Show Categories toolbar button in the navigation panel toolbar. This will display the initial Personal Categories and Corporate Categories top-level categories. Click plus signs next to these top-level categories to view subcategories within them. Whether you create a category within Personal Categories or within Corporate Categories, the initial step is the same: select the existing category that you wish the new category to reside in. For example, if you want the new category to be a subcategory within Personal Categories, select the Personal Categories entry. If you want the new category to be located directly within the top-level Corporate Categories, click the Corporate Categories item in the navigation panel.

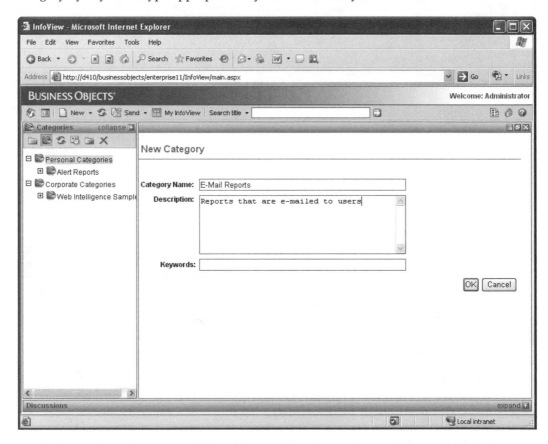

Click the New button in the main InfoView toolbar. A drop-down list will appear with several options for creating new items. Choose Category. The objects area will be replaced by the New Category screen. Type the name for your new category in the Category Name field (note that you cannot use the same name as an existing category already in the same location). Optionally, provide a description for the category in the Description field. And, if you wish to use the Search capability at the top of the InfoView screen to later search for this category by keyword, type appropriate keywords in the Keywords field.

Once you've supplied category information, click OK. The category will be created within the desired location. The original location you chose before creating the category will appear, with the objects area showing the original category's contents. You'll notice the new category in the navigation panel within the original location.

Organizing Objects and Instances

Once you've created folders and categories to your liking, you'll probably want to place desired reports, program objects, and third-party objects in the folders and assign them desired categories. You may wish to delete objects that you no longer need. Or, you may wish to copy or move objects from one folder to another. And, you may find creating Shortcuts to be helpful if a single report needs to be accessed from more than one folder.

Organizational tasks revolving around objects or instances within a folder or category are undertaken with a combination of check boxes next to the desired objects and the Organize or Delete button at the top of the objects area. The first step in organizing objects is to choose the folder or category that the objects you wish to manipulate are contained in. Once you've selected the proper folder or category, objects within it will appear in the objects area. Begin by clicking the check box next to the object or objects that you wish to move, copy, delete, or create a shortcut to. Then, use the Organize or Delete button at the top of the objects area, as illustrated in Figure 23-3.

Deleting Objects

If you determine that you no longer wish to keep a report or other object, you may delete it. If the report or program object contains instances, they will be deleted as well. Once you've selected the desired object or objects that you wish to delete, click the Delete button in the toolbar at the top of the objects area. A dialog box will display asking you to confirm the

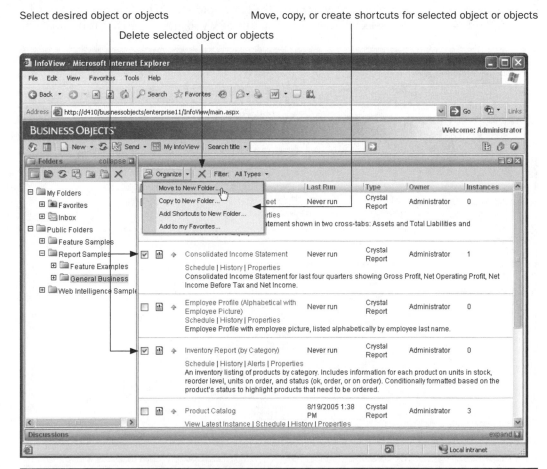

FIGURE 23-3   Organizing objects within a folder or category

deletion. Once you respond Yes, the object (and any associated instances) will be permanently deleted.

CAUTION *Deleting objects is a permanent operation—there is no Undo capability. Make sure you really want to delete an object and its instances before you undertake these steps. You may wish to check with your CRS Administrator to see if he or she has a regular backup procedure in place before you delete valuable objects.*

Copying or Moving Objects

To copy or move one or more objects to another folder, ensure that the desired object or objects have been checked. Then, click the Organize button in the toolbar at the top of the objects area. A drop-down menu of available options will appear. Click either the Move To New Folder or Copy To New Folder choice, depending on what you want to do. The objects area will be replaced with the Copy or Move screen. Select the desired destination folder or category where you want the object moved or copied. You'll know which folder or category you've selected when it appears with a light shade. You may also create a new folder or category directly in this screen by typing a new name in the New Folder or New Category field and clicking Add. You may then select the new folder or category you just created as the destination.

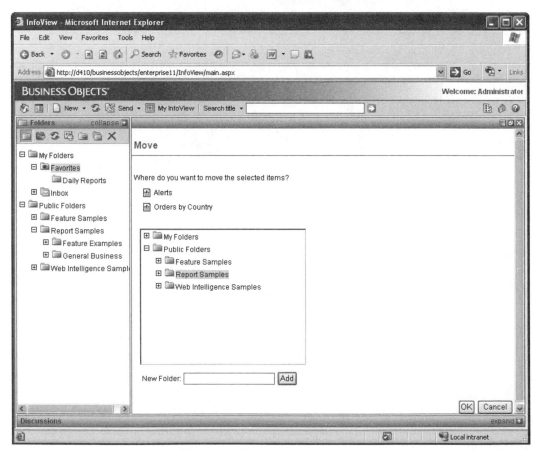

Once you've chosen the destination, click OK. The object or objects will be moved or copied to the desired location. The original folder or category you chose before the copy or move will reappear, showing the results of the move or copy (for example, if you move objects, they will no longer appear in the objects area). To double-check that objects were moved or copied to their new location, select the destination folder or category in the navigation panel.

NOTE *The difference between copying and moving an object is based on whether the object remains in its original location and whether instances are moved to the new location. If you move an object, it will not remain in the original location, and any related instances will be placed in the new location along with the object. Copying an object will leave it intact in its original location with no instances copied to the new location.*

Creating Shortcuts

One issue that may face you is how to deal with a report or other object that you wish to be available in multiple folders. While you could copy the object to multiple folders, as described earlier, CRS makes separate copies of reports or objects in each folder. Thereafter, if you want to modify the original report or object, the modification will only be made to the particular object you select—the others that were copied to other folders will remain unchanged. And, if you schedule one of the copied objects, the instances will only be available within the one folder—other folders won't include the instances.

Crystal Reports Server provides a way to deal with this situation. The Shortcut option creates a shortcut, or link, to the original object. When you schedule the shortcut, the instances you create are accessible in the History lists in the original folder where the object is located. And when other users schedule the object, you will see those instances in the History list within all folders where shortcuts are placed. Much as with Windows itself, an InfoView shortcut is merely a "pointer" to the source object in another location.

To create a shortcut, ensure that the desired object or objects have been checked. Then, click the Organize button in the toolbar at the top of the objects area. A drop-down menu of available options will appear. Click the Add Shortcuts To New Folder choice. The objects area will be replaced with the Shortcut screen. Select the desired destination folder or category where you want the shortcut placed. You'll know which folder or category you've selected when it appears with a light shade. You may also create a new folder or category directly in this screen by typing a new name in the New Folder or New Category field and clicking Add. You may then select the new folder or category you just created as the destination.

PART II

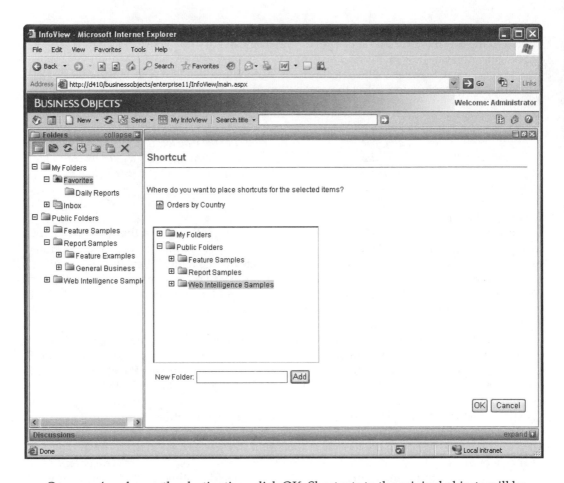

Once you've chosen the destination, click OK. Shortcuts to the original objects will be placed in the desired location. The original folder or category objects area will reappear. To double-check that shortcuts were created in the new location, select the destination folder or category in the navigation panel. You'll notice object names identical to the originals. However, the words "Shortcut To" will appear at the beginning of the object names.

TIP *The Add To My Favorites option in the Organize drop-down menu will actually create a shortcut just as the Add Shortcuts To New Folder option will. However, it will preselect your Favorites folder when the Shortcut screen appears.*

Assigning Categories

A new Crystal Reports Server XI feature is the ability to place an object in one or more categories, regardless of the folder the object is contained in. When you change the navigation panel to Category View, you will see objects organized in their categories completely separate from their folder location. Once you've organized categories as described earlier in the chapter, you'll want to place objects in their desired categories.

Begin by locating the object you want to categorize. This can be done by clicking the folder that contains the object, or the category containing the object (if the navigation panel is already displaying Category View). Locate the object in the objects area and click the Properties link underneath the object name. The Properties screen will appear in the objects area. Categories will appear at the bottom of the properties screen. If necessary, click plus signs to expand available categories to see any subcategories. Once you've displayed all desired categories and subcategories, check the box next to the category or categories that you wish to assign this object to (you may assign an object to as many categories as you'd like).

Check one or more categories to assign object to

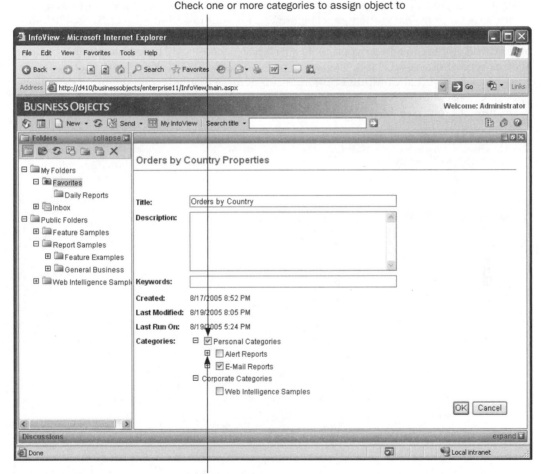

Expand to see subcategories

Click OK to close the properties screen. The objects area will reappear as it was prior to displaying properties. To confirm that the object was assigned to the desired categories, click the Show Categories button in the navigation panel toolbar and navigate to the desired category. You'll see the objects you assigned in the objects area.

Adding Objects to InfoView

In previous versions of Crystal Enterprise, you could move or delete reports and objects from InfoView's predecessor. You could not, however, actually add new reports or objects. This has changed in Crystal Reports Server XI. Provided you have been given the right by the administrator, you can add your own reports, hyperlinks, and third-party objects (such as Word documents, PowerPoint presentations, or Acrobat PDF files) directly to InfoView. The only object that still must be added by other means is a program object (executable program, JavaScript, and so forth).

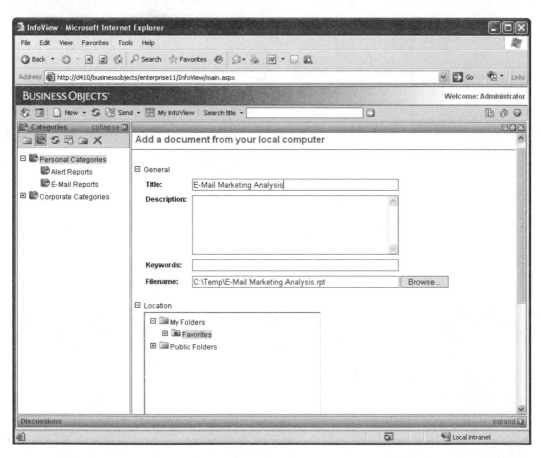

The first step in adding an object is to select the folder or category where you want the object to be copied. For example, if you are only permitted to add objects to your Favorites folder, select it in the navigation panel before you attempt to add the object. Then, click the New button in the very top toolbar of the InfoView screen. A drop-down menu of available options will appear. To add a hyperlink to a web page, choose the Hyperlink option. To add another type of file-based object (such as a Crystal Report or Word document), choose the Document From Local Computer option. A submenu of available document types will appear. Choose the desired document type. The objects area will be replaced with the Add A Document From Your Local Machine screen.

Specify the file path and name of the document you wish to upload to Crystal Reports Server in the Filename field. If you prefer, you may click the Browse button to launch a standard File Open dialog box. Locate the desired file in this dialog box and click Open. The full path and filename will be filled in the Filename field for you. While Crystal Reports text saved in the .RPT file with the File | Summary Info option may appear in the Title and Description fields automatically, you may wish to specify these items for other document types or reports that don't have this information specified. Additional options that must be chosen are Location and Categories (with Categories being optional). Select the desired destination folder from the Location list. Plus signs will allow you to navigate to subfolders. If you wish to assign one or more categories to the object when it's uploaded to CRS, expand the categories list and check any desired categories (you may assign as many categories as you'd like).

Once you've made the desired choices, click OK (you may need to scroll down in your browser to see the OK button). The file will be uploaded to Crystal Reports Server (be patient—this may take some time, depending on the size of the file). The objects area will reappear with your new object now appearing in the object list.

The My InfoView Dashboard

The previous Crystal Decisions product line, while it was quite flexible, didn't include a true "dashboard" product. Business Objects, however, has added functionality from its Dashboard Manager product to Crystal Reports Server XI. Now, it's easier to create a dashboard interface to multiple Crystal Reports and web pages using the new *My InfoView* feature.

A *dashboard* can be loosely described as a series of separate high-level presentations that appear on the same physical screen. Often presented as part of a Key Performance Indicators (KPI) system, dashboards may present several charts, separate sets of high-level totals or metrics, and combinations of current information. Typically, dashboards are highly interactive, allowing drill-down on the higher-level data to expose lower-level data that makes it up. While a Crystal Report consisting of charts, summaries, and subreports has good potential to offer dashboard functionality, the new CRS XI InfoView dashboard capability may provide a better solution.

Crystal Reports Server can maintain a single dashboard in My InfoView. To display My InfoView, click the My InfoView toolbar button in the very top InfoView toolbar. If My InfoView has already been defined, the custom dashboard will appear in place of the objects area. Click on any pane to further interact (a pane can consist of a Crystal report or a web page). If My InfoView has yet to be defined, the Define Content screen will appear, initially showing a single pane available for customization.

Creating the My InfoView Dashboard

My InfoView consists of a series of "panes," or subwindows, which can each contain a full or partial Crystal Report, a third-party document (such as an Excel spreadsheet, a Word document, or an Acrobat PDF file) and a header and footer (consisting of text or a web page link). Initially, a single pane will appear when you first start customizing My InfoView. You may either add panes manually one at a time or choose a predefined pane layout by clicking one of the Choose Template buttons at the top of the My InfoView window. For example, if you click the third Choose Template button (the three-pane vertical layout button), the screen will be divided into three vertically organized panes. This is illustrated in Figure 23-4.

If you wish to manually lay out your set of dashboard panes, you may begin by splitting the single initial pane horizontally or vertically. Click the Split Vertically or Split Horizontally

Click template button to use predefined layout

Delete pane

Display the contents of pane in a separate browser window

Split pane vertically to create another pane

Split pane horizontally to create another pane

Define the content for pane

FIGURE 23-4   My InfoView with three-pane layout

button in the upper right-hand corner of the pane. The pane will be split in half horizontally or vertically with another pane appearing. The new pane will contain the same set of buttons so it, as just discussed, can also be split horizontally or vertically. If you wish to resize a pane, point to the right or bottom border (you can't resize a pane from the top or left). Your mouse cursor will change to a double-arrow cursor—drag to resize the pane, adjusting adjacent panes to fit.

If you wish to delete a pane that you've already created and sized (whether or not you've defined content for it yet), click the small *X* close button at the top of the pane. After a confirmation message, the pane will be deleted, with other panes resizing to fill the space. This process of splitting and resizing existing panes and deleting unwanted panes is how you define the layout of the My InfoView dashboard. You may also use the same techniques to modify the dashboard layout that resulted from clicking one of the predefined template buttons.

To define the content that will appear in each pane, click either the Define Content link or the Properties button at the top of the pane. The Dashboard Properties dialog box will appear, as illustrated in Figure 23-5. Choose either a web address or Crystal Reports Server object to appear in the pane. Click the appropriate radio button and either type the web address in directly or choose the desired object from the CRS folder structure.

In addition to the choice of web address or CRS object, you may specify a header and footer for the pane. Text can be typed that will appear at the top and bottom of the pane. Optionally, if you supply a web address for the header or footer, the text you type will become a hyperlink to the web address you supply.

If you choose a Crystal Report object from the folder list, the Dashboard Properties dialog box will expand to show an additional set of choices to display the Crystal Report.

- **Select a Viewer to use with this Report**   Choose the report viewer to display the report within the pane. The Page Viewer will display the entire report within the pane, while the Parts Viewer will display the initially defined report part in the pane (defining report parts is covered in Chapter 21). In either event, any report part navigation or drill-down defined in the report can be used from within the pane.

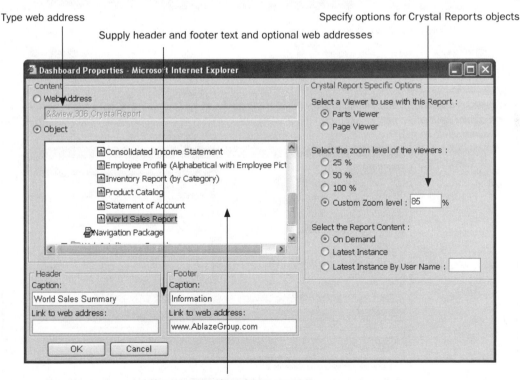

Type web address

Supply header and footer text and optional web addresses

Specify options for Crystal Reports objects

Choose object from folder structure

FIGURE 23-5   The Dashboard Properties dialog box

- **Select the zoom level of the viewers**   Select or specify the initial zoom level when viewing the report. You may need to adjust this choice after initially viewing the report to accommodate the size of the objects on the report.

- **Select the Report Content**   Choose whether to view the report on demand (that is, run it against the database as soon as My InfoView is displayed) or to show the latest instance overall, or else the latest instance run by a specified user. Note that if you specify a latest instance option and the report has not yet been scheduled, an error message will appear within the pane.

Once you've specified all necessary properties, click OK. The Dashboard Properties dialog box will close and the pane will show the contents just specified. Continue to specify contents for remaining panes until all panes have been supplied with content. Click the Save button in the upper right-hand corner to save My InfoView. It will now appear in your Favorites folder—you may view it from there or by clicking the My InfoView button in the main InfoView toolbar. You may also set My InfoView as the initial InfoView display with Preferences (discussed earlier in the chapter). And, if you wish to assign My InfoView to one or more categories, select the Properties link for it within the Favorites folder—you may assign categories just like you can for any other object.

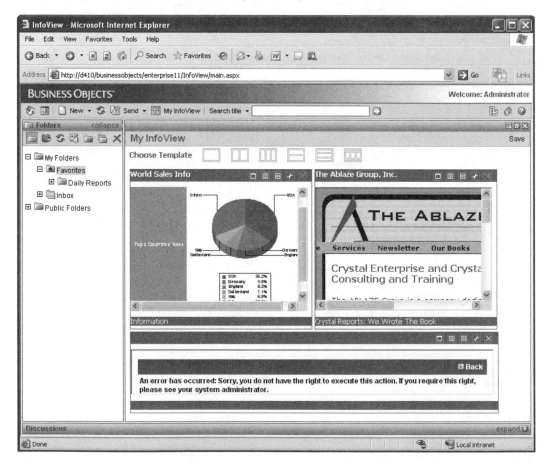

CAUTION *Make sure to click the Save button after you've defined content. If you fail to save the dashboard definition and click an alternative object in the navigation panel, you'll lose your dashboard definition.*

Modifying the Existing My InfoView Dashboard

Once you've defined the initial My InfoView dashboard, you'll no doubt wish to make changes at some point in the near or far future. You may simply want to change the zoom level of a Crystal Report viewer. Or, you may wish to delete the entire My InfoView definition and start over.

To delete the entire My InfoView dashboard, simply click the check box next to it in your Favorites folder and click the Delete button. To change the content of one or more panes, you must first display the My InfoView dashboard (the Modify link in the objects area will just display the screen—it will not begin any modification). Then, just click the Properties button at the top of the pane you wish to modify. The Dashboard Properties dialog box will reappear. Make any desired changes to the pane's contents and click OK to update My InfoView.

ending Objects and Instances to Destinations

While Crystal Reports Server XI retains the previous Crystal Enterprise capability to schedule reports to be sent to a destination outside the system (for example, to an FTP server, specified network file location, or e-mail address), additional capabilities for sending report and third-party objects to external destinations are available in CRS. Notice the Send button in the main InfoView toolbar at the top of the screen. This button, when clicked after selecting objects or instances in the objects area, will send objects to outside destinations or other CRS users' inboxes.

Send ▼   Begin by displaying the folder or category that contains objects you wish to send. If you wish to send the object itself (such as a Crystal Report that won't be run and won't contain saved data, or a third-party object), click the check box next to the object or objects that you wish to send. You can send more than one object at a time. If you wish to send one or more report or program object instances, click the History link next to the object containing the desired instances. Once the History list appears, click the check box next to the instance or instances you wish to send. You can send more than one instance at a time. Then, click the Send button in the main InfoView toolbar. A drop-down list of available destinations will appear. Choose the desired destination.

The objects area will be replaced with a Send dialog box particular to the destination you chose. For example, if you choose to send to an e-mail destination, the Send dialog will include from and to e-mail address fields, subject and message fields, and options for attaching the selected items to the e-mail. If you choose to send to a CRS inbox, a list of CRS users and groups will appear. You may choose one or more user inboxes to send the objects to. And, if you choose an FTP or File location, you'll need to specify FTP server and filename information.

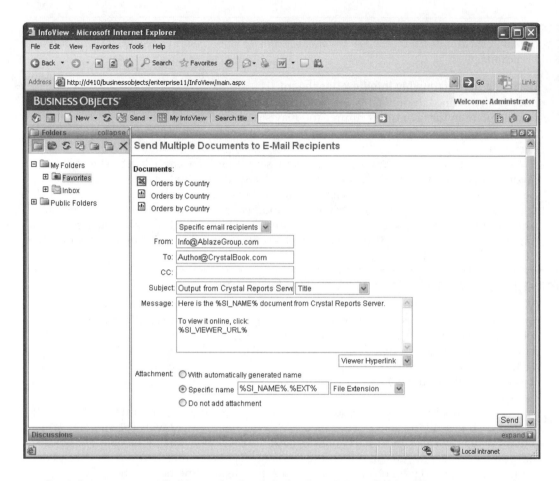

Complete necessary fields on the Send dialog box. Many fields allow you to specify "placeholders" for certain CRS properties specific to the object or instance that you are sending. For example, if you'd like to attach a file to an e-mail message that contains the object name and file extension specific to the file type being attached, you may choose Title and File Extension placeholders to insert into the filename field. CRS will substitute the actual object name and file extension when the e-mail is sent.

When you've completed the Send form, click OK to send the objects. The objects area will return in the same state as it was before you clicked Send. If you chose multiple objects or instances, multiple e-mails will be sent, multiple files will be placed in the specified network file location, or multiple files will be sent to the chosen FTP server. Or, if you chose the inbox destination, multiple items will be placed in the destination inbox or inboxes.

NOTE *The Destination Job Server must be configured for sending objects and instances to work properly. If you discover that the sending process does not work properly, contact your CRS Administrator regarding configuration of the Destination Job Server.*

Administering Crystal Reports Server

C rystal Reports Server (CRS) presents a fairly complex approach to web-based report automation and distribution. Its ability to schedule reports to run on a regular basis, and then make those reports available to viewers in a variety of ways, has made CRS an increasingly popular method for automating corporate reporting. CRS XI has improved upon previous versions by allowing additional document types (such as Adobe PDF files, Microsoft Word and Excel documents, and so forth) to be added to the system, by allowing script and executable programs to be scheduled, and so on. (An overview of new CRS XI features can be found in Chapter 22.)

NOTE *Throughout the Crystal Reports Server system, the product will frequently refer to itself as BusinessObjects Enterprise in dialog boxes, help files, etc.*

As is usually the case, the more flexible and capable a software system is, the more complex its infrastructure becomes. Crystal Reports Server is no exception. Its scalable, flexible, feature-rich foundation for information automation and dissemination results in a more complex and complicated hardware and software combination in the "back end." Part of the initial process of implementing CRS, as well as a continuing requirement of organizations that put it in place, is CRS administration.

This chapter, while not covering every possible combination of CRS implementations and administrative tasks, will give those tasked with implementing, troubleshooting, and maintaining their CRS systems a good background on common administrative tasks. Working with various software components, user management, and server configuration are among the common tasks taken on by CRS administrators.

NOTE *This chapter refers specifically to Crystal Reports Server. However, all of the concepts also apply to other editions of BusinessObjects Enterprise.*

Crystal Reports Server Architecture

Crystal Reports Server's multitier architecture lends itself to a much more flexible, higher-capacity system for web reporting. It also lends itself to more complexity when it comes to initial setup, operation, and administration. This increased complexity comes, in large part, from the increased number of components that make up the server portion (or "back end") of the system. While a CRS end user simply sees web pages that allow scheduling and viewing of reports, there are many separate server components working together to provide this capability to the user. These various server components that make up CRS share its overall processing requirements, passing information among themselves as required.

Administrators of the CRS predecessor, Crystal/Seagate Info, will see many similarities between CRS server architecture and Info server architecture—Crystal Reports Server architecture was borrowed from Info. However, if you are in charge of administering CRS and this is your first experience with a multiserver configuration, there is much to learn about how all these different server components work together and pass information back and forth.

Crystal Reports Server consists of several "back end" servers. Each server acts as an individual Windows NT "service." In the case of Windows NT, 2000, or 2003 Server, you can see each CRS server by displaying the Windows Control Panel Services applet from the Administrative Tools folder. You can also launch CRS's own Central Configuration Manager from the BusinessObjects 11/Crystal Reports Server program group to see only services related to Crystal Reports Server (including the web server).

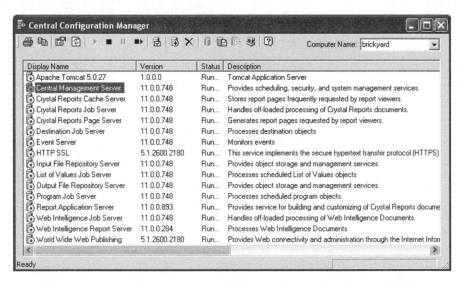

Central Management Server (CMS)

The Central Management Server, or *CMS,* is the heart of Crystal Reports Server. (This component was known as the Automated Process Scheduler [APS] or Crystal Management Server [CMS] in previous versions of Seagate/Crystal Info and Crystal Enterprise.) Every other component communicates through the CMS (the CMS acts as a name server, keeping track of the locations and statuses of the other server components). The CMS also acts as the central security point for Crystal Reports Server logon—all user IDs, passwords, and rights lists are maintained on the CMS. And, the CMS also keeps track of report scheduling. If a report is scheduled to automatically run every day at midnight, the CMS sets the report processing cycle in motion at the prescribed time.

Because the CMS is so critical to the operation of Crystal Reports Server (the entire system is completely "dead in the water" without it), CRS provides for fault tolerance and increased processing capacity with *CMS clustering.* With CMS clustering, multiple physical computers can run as CMS servers. Sharing a common system database hosted on a standard server platform, such as Microsoft SQL Server or Oracle, all CMS machines appear as one *logical* CMS to the entire Crystal Reports Server system. They share processing load, sending processing requests to the least-busy machine in the cluster. If one machine should fail, the remaining CMS machines pick up the load and continue to operate—the end user will not even know that one of the CMS machines has failed.

File Repository Servers

As Crystal Reports Server reporting is based on Crystal Reports, procedures for handling the Crystal .RPT files that are published, scheduled, and viewed must be established. Also, CRS XI program objects and third-party objects (.PDF files, .DOC and .XLS files, executables, Java programs, and script) must be managed for scheduling and viewing. This is where the file repository servers come in. These servers store .RPT files that can be viewed on demand and .RPT files that are to be scheduled on a regular basis (perhaps every night, every week, and so on), as well as the finished copies of scheduled reports—the .RPT files with saved data that can be viewed after they've successfully run. They also manage stored copies of third-party files, such as Word and Excel documents and PDF files, as well as script and program files.

There are actually two different file repository servers. The *Input File Repository Server* (or Input FRS) is where Crystal Report .RPT files, third-party files, and executable/script files are stored after they've been published with Crystal Reports XI, the Publishing Wizard, the Central Management Console, or the Import Wizard. In the case of Crystal Reports, these "not-yet-run" reports are known as Crystal Reports Server report *objects.*

When a request is received to view a published report on demand, or when the CMS runs a scheduled report on a regular basis, the Input FRS is queried for a copy of the .RPT file to run. Also, when a shared third-party object, such as a Word document, Excel spreadsheet, or Adobe PDF file, is requested for viewing, the Input FRS provides access to the file. And, when program objects are scheduled to be executed, the object is supplied by the Input FRS.

The *Output File Repository Server* (or Output FRS) keeps all the finished .RPT files with saved data (known as *report instances*) that result from reports that are scheduled by the CMS on a regular basis. When an end user wishes to view a report instance, the other Crystal Reports Server components query the CMS, which keeps track of report instances in the Output File Repository Server. The .RPT file with saved data is transferred from this server to other components for caching and HTML formatting, eventually appearing in the end user's web browser. The Output FRS also keeps track of the status of scheduled program objects, such as text files containing the output from the executable or script object that was run. These *program instances* can be viewed much the same way as report instances are.

Crystal Reports Page Server

The Crystal Reports Page Server is dedicated to two tasks: creating EPF files and running on-demand .RPT files. This first task comes into play whenever an end user requests to view a completed report. The Page Server communicates with the Crystal Reports Cache Server and may be asked to create individual page image files (known as encapsulated page files, or EPF files) that are stored by the Cache Server and delivered to the end user one page at a time. This "page-on-demand" architecture has been a cornerstone of Crystal Reports performance for several versions. This way, if a report actually encompasses several hundred pages, only the page requested by the viewer will be sent across to the web browser.

The other task given to the Page Server is the processing of *on-demand* reports. On-demand reports differ from reports scheduled by the CMS on a regular basis, which are handled by the Crystal Reports Job Server. While the automatic scheduling of reports is a very powerful feature of Crystal Reports Server, certain reporting environments require near-instantaneous access to a current set of data. In these situations, the Page Server is used to run reports against the database in real time whenever a user requests them. By utilizing both on-demand and scheduled reports (and by dedicating servers to each), Crystal Reports Server can satisfy a broad mix of regular production reporting needs versus on-demand ad hoc reporting needs.

Because the Page Server may need to connect to production databases in real time to run on-demand reports, the Page Server is one of the Crystal Reports Server back-end servers that may require special configuration. For example, you'll need to ensure that all possible ODBC data sources and necessary database client software are installed on the computer running the Page Server software. Also, the Page Server may need to be modified to use something other than the default NT System account in order to provide necessary network security credentials. If, for example, a file-based Microsoft Access database is contained on a network share somewhere in your network, the NT System account probably won't have rights to the shared folder where the Access database is located. You'll need to assign the Page Server NT Service an alternate account that exposes the desired network share.

Crystal Reports Job Server and Report Application Server

While the Page Server can run on-demand reports, another set of servers may also end up running Crystal Reports, depending on how you want the report to run. These two servers, the Crystal Reports Job Server and the Report Application Server, run reports that are scheduled or designed on the fly, respectively. Also, the choice of report viewer that you make in CRS XI InfoView will sometimes determine which server is used.

The Job Server is dedicated to running reports that are scheduled by the CMS. Only reports that run on a regular basis (every day, every week, the first day of the month, and so forth) and create report instances are submitted to the Job Server. When the CMS needs to schedule a report to run, it passes the request on to the Job Server. The Job Server obtains the .RPT file to run from the Input FRS, actually connects to the database to run the report, and sends the completed report instance (an .RPT file with saved data) to the Output FRS.

The Report Application Server, or RAS, processes on-demand reports that are viewed in the Advanced DHTML Viewer. And, the Advanced DHTML viewer's subquery capabilities make use of the RAS's own caching capabilities, which are separate from the Page Server/ Cache Server interaction discussed elsewhere in this chapter.

Because the Job Server and Report Application Server may need to connect to production databases to run reports, they may require special configuration. For example, you'll need to ensure that all possible ODBC data sources and necessary database client software are installed on the computers running the Job Server or Report Application Server. Also, these servers may need to be modified to use something other than the default NT System account in order to provide necessary network security credentials. If, for example, a file-based Microsoft Access database is contained on a network share somewhere in your network, the NT System account probably won't have rights to the shared folder where the Access database is located. You'll need to assign the Job Server or Report Application Server NT Service an alternate account that exposes the desired network share.

Program Job Server

Crystal Reports Server has the ability to schedule program objects, as well as report objects, on a regular basis (every day, the first day of the week, once a month, and so on). Program objects (consisting of executable programs, Java programs, and JScript or VBScript code) allow you to run maintenance tasks, data warehouse imports, or anything else that can be custom-coded, within the Crystal Reports Server environment.

The Program Job Server is responsible for running program objects that are scheduled by the CMS. Much as with the Crystal Reports Job Server, the Program Job Server intercepts requests for program object schedules from the CMS. It then queries the Input FRS for the necessary program object files, runs the program object, and sends the standard and error output from the program object to the Output FRS, where it is stored as a program instance.

Destination Job Server

The Destination Job Server is used when objects are sent to other destinations using the Send feature of Crystal Reports Server. It does not actually run reports but rather simply manages the sending of the report objects. Users may send existing reports and report instances to other users via e-mail, to other users' Inboxes, to an FTP server, or to a file location on an accessible drive.

Crystal Reports Cache Server

As discussed earlier in the chapter, one of the benefits of Crystal Reports Server (and of several versions of Crystal Reports before it) is the page-on-demand architecture. This approach to delivering report pages to the end user's web browser significantly improves performance, especially with larger reports that comprise many pages. The page-on-demand process will deliver only the page of a report that a viewer currently needs to see. When a report is first viewed, only page 1 is delivered to the viewer. If, for example, the viewer then clicks an entry in the group tree that requires page 210 of the report to be delivered, only page 210 is sent to the browser—pages 2 through 209 are ignored.

As discussed previously, part of this page-on-demand process is the creation of EPFs, which is handled by the Crystal Reports Page Server. The other very important part of this process, however, is storing already-viewed EPFs for later reuse (known as "caching"). This process is handled by the Crystal Reports Cache Server. The Cache Server keeps track of pages that may have already been viewed (and that are already cached). When a page is requested from the Cache Server, the Cache Server checks to see if the page already exists in its cache. If the Cache Server can find an already-generated EPF, it simply sends it for viewing. If the Cache Server needs the EPF to be generated (a user, for example, has asked for a report page that hasn't been viewed previously), it asks the Page Server to generate the EPF, which it then caches and sends for viewing.

NOTE *As discussed earlier, if a viewer uses the Interactive DHTML Viewer to view a report, the Cache Server/Page Server interaction discussed here does not apply. Instead, the Report Application Server handles the page-on-demand viewing procedures for the report viewer.*

Event Server

When you schedule a report or program object to run, you may choose to base the schedule on an event. This event might be triggered by the successful completion or failure of another report or program object. Or, the event may by triggered by the creation of a certain file somewhere on your network. While the first type of event is managed entirely by the CMS, a separate server is used to manage file-based events.

The Event Server manages file-based events. When a job is scheduled on the basis of a file event, the Event Server is charged with looking on the network in a specified location for the existence of the file (the contents of the file are irrelevant—the Event Server is only concerned with whether the file exists or not). If the file exists, the Event Server notifies the CMS and the dependent job is processed.

Because of the need to navigate various folders and file structures on your network, the Event Server may be required to use something other than the default NT System account. If, for example, a file that will be used as a trigger for a file event is contained on a network share somewhere in your network, the NT System account probably won't have rights to the shared folder where the file is located. You'll need to assign the Event Server NT Service an alternate account that exposes the desired network share.

List of Values Job Server

One of the important new features of Crystal Reports XI is the ability to create dynamic pick lists for the parameter value entry. Crystal Reports Server also has new features to support and extend this capability. Using the Business View Manager, users can now create dynamic Lists of Values, which are stored in the repository.

When a Crystal Report using a dynamic List of Values from the repository is run, the pick list may be created on the fly. However, depending on the nature of the pick list, this may be a slow process, and it may also be inefficient if many different users are requesting the same pick list. The List of Values Job Server exists to schedule the creation of dynamic pick lists, which in turn eliminates the time lags and inefficiency.

NOTE *The Web Intelligence Job Server and Web Intelligence Report Server are installed with Crystal Reports Server but are not used. In BusinessObjects Enterprise systems, those servers support the classic Business Objects report design program, Web Intelligence (often referred to as Webi).*

Managing Users and Groups

Crystal Reports Server contains its own security system, separate from the operating system underneath. Maintained by the CMS, this allows the CRS administrator to build a unique security model to control access to the reports in the system. Your security model system can be as simple or as complex as needed, providing complete flexibility for the system architect and administrator.

Crystal Reports Server security is designed to closely mimic many security models, with the security model in Windows NT being particularly close. There are individual user accounts that include a user name and password. Those user accounts may be placed into one or more groups that incorporate similar users. For example, all sales users can be placed in a National Sales group. Groups can also be placed within other groups to create a parent/child relationship between groups. For example, all Western Region Sales users can be placed in a Western Region Sales subgroup, contained within the National Sales main group. This allows the administrator to define a hierarchical setup for easier application of security rights across the system.

Users are not limited to being placed in one group. If a user crosses multiple group boundaries, such as being assigned a CRS administrative position, while also being employed in the Sales department, the user can be placed in both the Administrators and National Sales groups.

Introducing the Administration Launchpad and Central Management Console

Most of the administration work in Crystal Reports Server, including adding users and groups or integrating with an existing Windows NT, Active Directory, or LDAP security system (discussed later in the chapter), is performed in the Central Management Console, or *CMC*. This is a web-based application that may be accessed from any computer that has access to the CRS network. One way to access the CMC is through the Administration Launchpad, which is basically a home page for CRS administrators.

NOTE *You'll see that there are two separate Administration Launchpads listed in the BusinessObjects 11/Crystal Reports Server program group: one for .NET and one for Java. These are basically identical pages, but they are based on the two different underlying technologies. For the purposes of this book, we will assume the use of the .NET Administrative Launchpad.*

To display the .NET Administrative Launchpad, choose it from the BusinessObjects 11/Crystal Reports Server program group (if you performed a full stand-alone installation on a single computer). Or, you may navigate directly to

```
http://<web server>/businessobjects/enterprise11/WebTools
```

The Administrative Launchpad will appear.

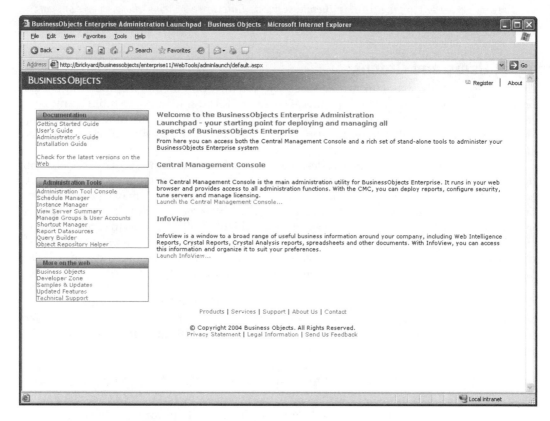

The Administrative Launchpad is a basic home page that doesn't provide any true administrative capabilities directly. However, it does contain links to online CRS documentation and other administrative web pages that perform various subsets of maintenance (and that showcase the Administrative Software Development Kit, which you can also use for your own custom administrative applications). The particular link on the Administrative Launchpad that you'll probably use most often is the Central Management Console.

When you launch the CMC, you'll be prompted to log on to the CMS (which, as discussed earlier, is the heart of Crystal Reports Server). Supply a valid administrative ID and password (when you first install CRS, a default account is created with a user ID of "administrator" and a blank password using Enterprise authentication). Once you log on to the CMS, the Central Management Console main page will appear.

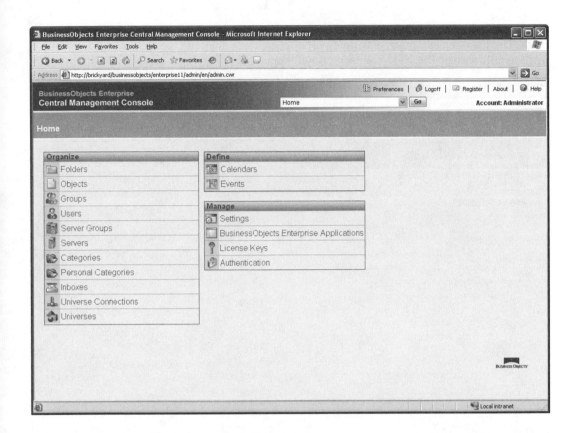

TIP You can click the main links on the CMC page to navigate to various administrative screens. However, you can also navigate directly from any screen to the top of any section by choosing the section from the drop-down list in the upper portion of the CMC. Once you've chosen the desired section, you'll go directly to that section's main page.

Adding, Modifying, and Deleting User Accounts

Two user accounts are created automatically when Crystal Reports Server is installed: Administrator and Guest. The Administrator account is used as the "all access" account for managing your CRS system. The Guest account is set up for general use for users that don't have a specific account, and it may be disabled once security is set up to disallow "anonymous" users. Both of these accounts are set to use Enterprise authentication.

NOTE Various authentication types are covered later in this chapter.

To add a new user account, click Users within the Organize category of the CMC home page. The list of existing user accounts will appear. Then click the New User button in the upper-right corner. The New User screen will appear.

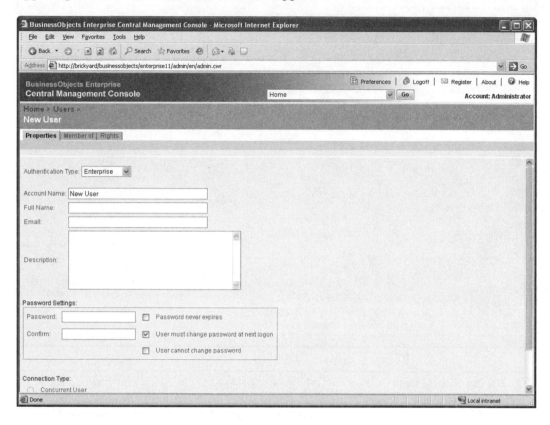

Most fields on the user screen are self-explanatory, and some are optional. Some fields or options may be of particular concern:

- **Password Settings**   While entries you choose here may conflict with overall password requirements set in the Enterprise Authentication screen (viewed by clicking the Authentication link from the Manage area of the main CMC screen), the CMC will generally allow them to be ignored. For example, if you have set requirements for mixed-case passwords, or passwords of a minimum length in the Authentication screen, you'll be able to set initial passwords for users that fall outside of these requirements. The users, however, will need to adhere to the password requirements when they change their own password.

- **Connection Type**   Because Crystal Reports Server only supports concurrent licenses, the connection type will always be concurrent. The named option will be dimmed.

When finished specifying user information, click the OK button. The screen will refresh, showing the new user information you just entered. You'll notice that some new items appear toward the bottom of the page. First, there is now an Account Is Disabled check box that may be used to disable a user account at any time without actually deleting the user account. Also, you'll notice that an alias has been assigned to the account (aliases are used to assign a single user ID to more than one CRS authentication type or other user ID).

If you've made a mistake or would like to make a change to the user account, you may now edit any of the user options. If you do so, make sure you click the Update button to apply the changes. Otherwise, the changes will not be saved. You may do this at any time in the future by simply selecting the user account from the Manage Users page.

To delete a user account, click Users from the Organize category on the main CMC page. In the list of users, select the check box next to the user you wish to delete. Then, click the Delete button in the upper-right corner. You will be prompted to confirm the deletion. Note that some users won't present a Delete check box. The Administrator and Guest accounts can't be deleted. And, any accounts provided by other authentication methods (Windows NT, Active Directory, or LDAP) must be deleted in their original locations—they cannot be deleted here.

NOTE *The preceding steps assume you are using Enterprise authentication and will be adding and maintaining users directly in Crystal Reports Server. If you prefer to use an existing Windows NT, Windows Active Directory, or LDAP system to authenticate users, create users and groups in these systems and use steps described later in the chapter to integrate CRS with your existing security system.*

Adding Groups

Crystal Reports Server groups can be created to organize users together. Users can be placed in one or more groups. Groups can also be made subgroups of other groups. Access rights in CRS can be assigned to groups, in addition to individual users. Users inherit rights from their group membership, which often makes group organization and security key to a good security model with minimal effort. If you use an external authentication method (Windows NT, Active Directory, LDAP), user groups will also be imported into CRS. You may merely accept these existing imported groups, or create additional groups within CRS itself to group all users.

Three groups are created automatically when CRS is installed: Administrators, Everyone, and BusinessObjects NT Users (you'll notice you are unable to delete these default groups). You'll find the Administrator user in the Administrators group, all users in the Everyone group, and no one in the BusinessObjects NT Users group. Place users that will need to perform administrative tasks into the Administrators group—these users will be able to perform most administrative tasks automatically. By default, every user of Crystal Reports Server will be placed in the Everyone group (and, you can't remove this group or take a user out of this group)—you'll set the most basic set of rights for this group. And, the BusinessObjects NT Users group is used in conjunction with Windows NT authentication (which is discussed later in this chapter).

Disabling the Guest Account

By default, when you first install Crystal Reports Server, the Guest account is enabled. This very "open" model allows anyone who has the proper URL or link to connect to CRS using InfoView (discussed in Chapter 23) or a custom web interface that you may have designed. While you may "lock down" the Guest account to, for example, prevent deletion or addition of objects or viewing of certain folders and objects, you still may potentially open up your CRS system to unwanted users by leaving it enabled.

If you want complete control over who uses Crystal Reports Server, you may disable the Guest account, in which case users must specify a specific user ID/password combination to gain access to CRS. To disable the Guest account, click Users from the Organize area of the CMC main screen. You'll be presented with a list of existing users in the system. Click the Guest account. On the user screen, simply click the Account Is Disabled check box. Then, click Update.

You'll be presented with a warning message indicating that any attempts at anonymous access will fail (this may be an issue if you've developed custom CRS applications that don't provide any particular user ID/password combination within the custom code).

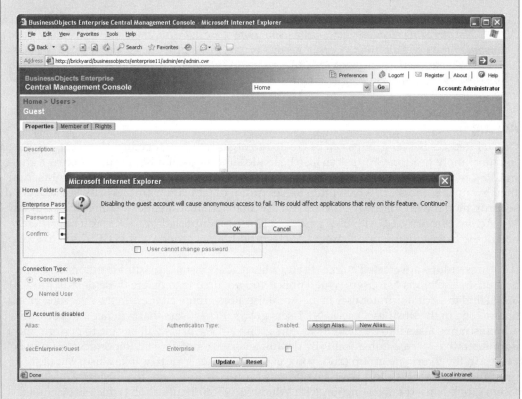

From this point forward, users will immediately be presented a sign-on screen when they get to InfoView, rather then being presented the introductory set of folders and objects provided to the Guest account.

While the three default groups that are created by default when CRS is installed are convenient for certain basic security tasks, they are probably not sufficient for even mildly sophisticated security models. As the administrator, you'll want to think about the best way to group your users for security purposes. For example, some organizations group users by their job functions, with groups such as Sales, Executive, and Human Resources. Other organizations group the users by region, such as East Coast, Midwest, and West Coast. Or, organizations may use a combination of both, or other similar scenarios. There is no right or wrong way to group users, but well-thought-out grouping can make applying access rights much, much easier.

To add a new group, click Groups from the Organize category on CMC home page. A list of existing groups will appear. Click the New Group button in the upper-right corner. Fill in the Group Name and Description. Then, click OK. The group will be added, and the screen will refresh, with the OK button replaced with an Update button.

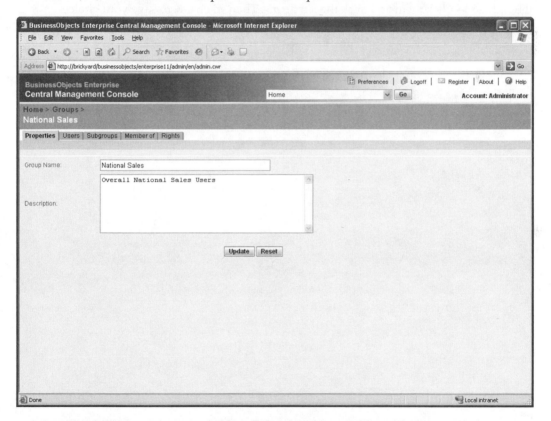

Creating Subgroups

Part of the flexibility of groups is the ability to set up hierarchies, whereby one group can reside inside another group (become a subgroup of the parent group). While there's no practical limit to the numbers and levels of groups to subgroups (a subgroup can be contained within a subgroup or a top-level group, and so forth), nesting groups too deeply may not make for a reasonably simple group structure.

If you plan on nesting groups, you must create all the initial groups (both parent groups and subgroups) using steps mentioned previously in this section. Only after groups have been created can they be nested. Once you've created groups, you may set up a parent/ subgroup relationship by clicking either group name from the main list of groups in the CMC. You'll notice two applicable tabs appearing in the screen for the chosen group: Subgroups and Member Of. If you wish to add a subgroup to the current group, click the Subgroups tab. If you wish to make the current group a subgroup of another group, click the Member Of tab.

Once you've clicked the proper tab, click either the Add/Remove Subgroups button (in the Subgroups tab) or the Member Of button (in the Member Of tab). A new screen will appear showing all other groups in the Available Groups list on the left side of the screen, and any subgroups or parent groups already assigned (if any) on the right side. Click one or more groups (CTRL-click to select multiple groups) from the Available Groups list and click the right arrow button to add them to the right side. If you wish to remove any groups from the right side, click them and click the left arrow. Then, click OK to save your choices.

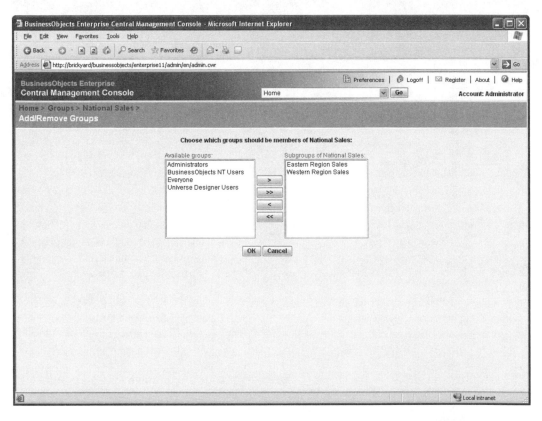

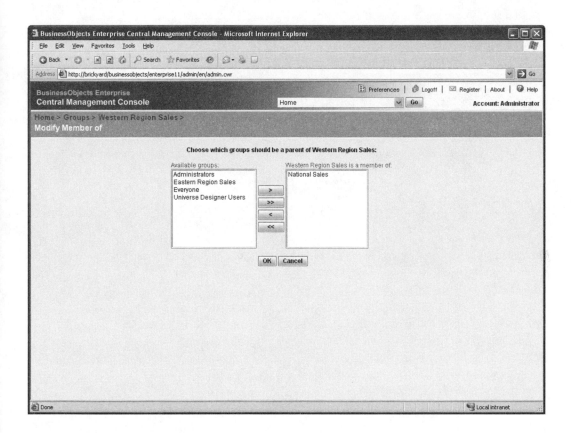

Placing Users in Groups

Once you've created groups and subgroups, you'll want to add users to the groups. There are two general approaches to placing users in one or more groups: either add one or more groups for a user on the CMC Users screen or add one or more users to a group on the CMC Group screen.

To add groups for a user, click Users in the Organize category of the CMC page. Then, choose the user you wish to set group membership for. Click the Member Of tab on the user's screen to see existing group memberships (you'll always see the Everyone group listed here). Click the Member Of button to choose which groups to make the user a member of. A screen will appear showing all groups on the left side and existing group membership on the right side. As discussed earlier in the chapter, select groups to add or remove for the chosen user.

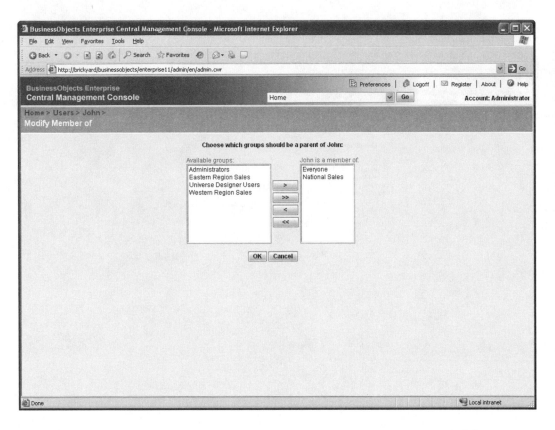

To add users to a particular group, click Groups in the Organize category of the main CMC page. Then, choose the group you wish to add users to. Click the Users tab to see a list of existing users (if any) that already belong to the group. Click the Add Users button to pick from a list of users to add to the group.

Because large numbers of users can appear in the Available Users list, this screen has an additional Look For text box and Find Now button that allow you to enter either a few characters or a full user name to search for. Once you click the Find Now button, only users that contain the characters typed in the Look For list will appear below. As with other, similar, dialog boxes, select users to add to the group in the left list and click the right arrow to add them.

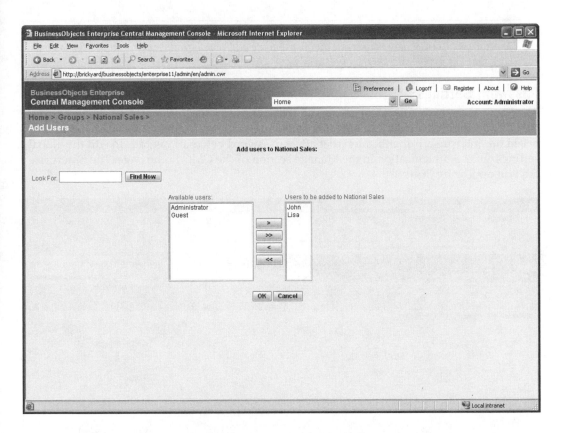

Again, because a large CRS installation can involve large numbers of users, a separate option is used to delete users from a currently selected group. After clicking the Users tab from a group's display, you'll find a separate Remove Users button in the upper right-hand corner. Click this button to display a list of existing users in a group. Choose existing users in the left list and use arrow buttons to add them to the right-hand Users To Be Removed list. If you'd like to find specific users, you can use the Look For text box and Find Now button. Enter either a few characters of a user name or a full user name to search for in the Look For text box. Once you click the Find Now button, only users that contain the characters typed in the Look For list will appear below. Once you've added users to the right list, click OK to remove them from the group.

> **NOTE** *Even if you integrate CRS with an outside authentication method (Windows NT, Active Directory, or LDAP), you may create and manipulate additional groups within the CMC, beyond those that are imported from the outside server.*

Password Settings

As noted earlier, each individual user account has its own password and several check boxes that affect that password. But, there are also global password settings for user accounts based on Enterprise authentication that affect password behavior overall. To edit the global settings, click Authentication in the Manage section of the CMC home page. The Enterprise tab will appear by default.

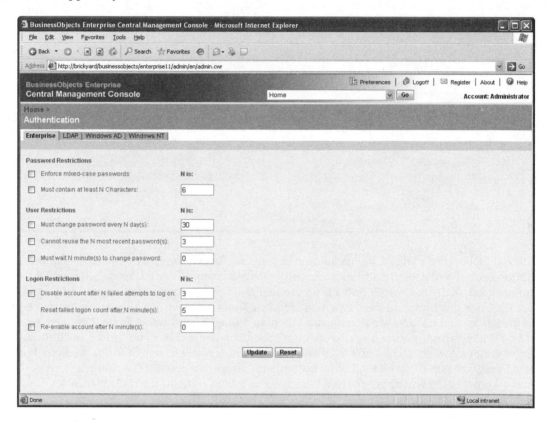

Password Restrictions allow the administrator to force a mixed-case password, as well as a password of a certain character length. User Restrictions allow the administrator to force users to change their passwords every so often, as well as require a series of different passwords. And, Logon Restrictions allow the administrator to shut down the account if a number of unsuccessful logons are attempted. You may use any combination of these choices to enforce password standards and practices for an organization.

Integrating Crystal Reports Server with Existing Security Environments

So far, everything previously discussed is part of Enterprise Authentication, which is Crystal Reports Server's native stand-alone security system. However, if you prefer to integrate CRS security with another authentication system already in place in your organization, you have three additional authentication methods: Windows NT, Windows Active Directory, and LDAP.

You may use the built-in security model that's part of the CMS, and/or if you already have a security system in place within your organization, you may tie CRS to it, provided you are using one of the three standard security models. As such, you have four overall security/authentication choices:

- **Enterprise authentication**   In this scenario, you manage all users and groups entirely within the Crystal Reports Server CMS—no external security system is used. This is separate from any existing network or server security you may already have in place. Enterprise authentication is discussed earlier in this chapter.

- **Windows NT authentication**   Existing Windows NT and 2000 local or domain groups can be used to populate your CRS security model. Members of these groups are automatically granted access to CRS, and users supply their existing network credentials to log on to CRS.

- **Windows Active Directory**   If you've set up Active Directory (AD) security with a Windows 2000 or Windows Server 2003 environment, you can use AD groups and users to authenticate CRS users. AD members are automatically granted access to CRS, and users supply their existing network credentials to log on to CRS.

- **LDAP**   If your organization's security model is based on the open LDAP (Lightweight Directory Access Protocol), you can integrate users maintained by your existing LDAP server into CRS. LDAP members are automatically granted access to CRS, and users supply their existing network credentials to log on to CRS.

NOTE   *You are not limited to choosing just one authentication method. You may use more than one method (or all four methods) to build your total complement of CRS users and groups.*

Windows NT

In some Crystal Reports Server environments, it may be easiest to use the same users and groups that are already defined in your Window NT or Windows 2000 environment. CRS supports this by "mapping" those users and groups into the Enterprise security system. There are two basic methods for this: add the desired NT users or groups into the Crystal NT Users group inside of Windows NT or map the desired NT groups into CRS from within the CMC.

By default, when you install a CRS CMS onto a Windows NT or Windows 2000 computer, a local NT group called BusinessObjects NT Users is created. To map NT users in the BusinessObjects NT Users group, run the Windows NT User Manager (or other similar tool, depending on your operating system). Select the BusinessObjects NT Users group. Click Properties, then Add, and then select the users and/or groups to be added. Click OK to add the selected users and groups, and then click OK to complete the process. Once the new accounts are added, the users can log on with the user name format of *NTDomain**NTUserName* and their standard NT password. They'll need to ensure that they select the Windows NT authentication method when they log on.

To map existing NT groups into the CRS system, click Authentication in the Manage category of the CMC home page. Then, click the Windows NT tab. Confirm that NT Authentication Is Enabled is checked. The default NT Domain shown will allow users to simply supply their user ID and password without full machine name/domain qualification if they're in the default domain. If you need to change the default domain, click it and specify a new default domain when prompted.

Enter the path to the NT group you wish to add in the Add NT Group text box. For global groups, use the format *NTDomain**NTGroup*. For local groups, use the format *Machine*\ *Group*. Click Add to add that group. Enter as many NT groups as desired to the list box in this manner. If you later wish to delete an existing domain, select it in the list of existing domains and click Delete.

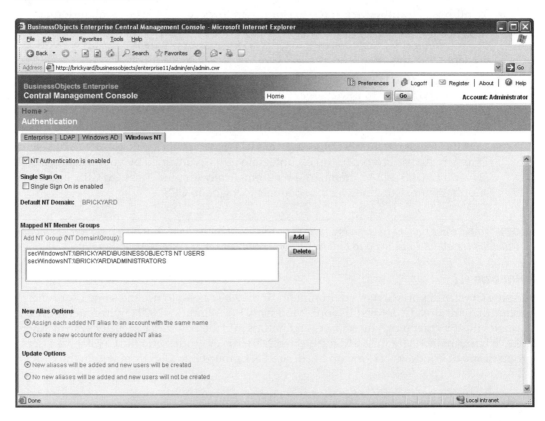

Select various radio button options for dealing with New Alias, Update, and New User options:

- **New Alias Options**   If you choose the first option, CRS will assign an "alias" to any existing CRS accounts that have the same name as an account being imported from the security server. If an imported account does not duplicate an existing account, a new account will be created. If you choose the second option, new accounts will be created even if an existing account with the same name already exists. In the case of duplicate account names, a sequential number will be added to the new account name to distinguish it from the existing account.

- **Update Options**   If you choose the first option, CRS will create a new account (or assign an alias based on your choice in New Alias Options) for every account contained in the groups being imported. This may create a large number of users if the imported groups contain large numbers of users. If you choose the second option, users in the imported groups will be created in CRS once they log on to CRS for the first time. If they never log on, their account will never actually be created in CRS.

- **New User Options**   When new user accounts are created from imported groups, this choice determines which license type they use by default. Note that you must have enough licenses of the chosen type for all users that will be created by the import. If you don't, not all user accounts will be created. If you later decide you want to change the license type for certain imported users, you may select the individual users from the Users link and change their license type.

Once you've made all desired choices, click Update to complete the process. If you chose to immediately create users and groups from the imported groups, you can now navigate to user and group lists to see the newly added users and groups.

Windows Active Directory

Similar to Windows NT authentication is Windows Active Directory (AD) authentication. AD authentication can connect using "native" AD protocols (NT authentication can use AD "mixed mode") to connect to existing Windows 2000 or Windows Server 2003 Active Directory security models.

To map existing AD groups into the CRS system, click Authentication in the Manage category of the CMC home page. Then, click the Windows AD tab. Confirm that Windows Active Directory Authentication Is Enabled is checked. Click the ellipses to specify an AD administrator name and password for CRS to use when authenticating AD users and groups. Also, click the ellipses to specify a default AD domain. You won't have to fully qualify groups in this domain when adding them. And, users in that domain won't have to provide a fully qualified user ID when signing on to CRS.

Enter the path to the AD group you wish to add in the Add AD Group text box. Click Add to add that group. Enter as many AD groups as desired to the list box in this manner. If you later wish to delete an existing group, select it in the list of existing groups and click Delete.

PART II

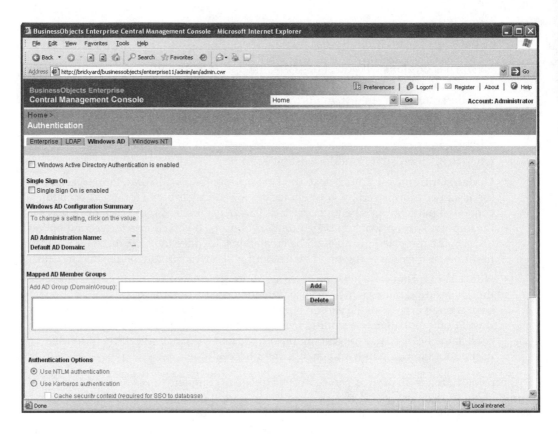

Select various radio button options for dealing with New Alias, Update, and New User options:

- **New Alias Options**   If you choose the first option, CRS will assign an "alias" to any existing CRS accounts that have the same name as an account being imported from the security server. If an imported account does not duplicate an existing account, a new account will be created. If you choose the second option, new accounts will be created even if an existing account with the same name already exists. In the case of duplicate account names, a sequential number will be added to the new account name to distinguish it from the existing account.

- **Update Options**   If you choose the first option, CRS will create a new account (or assign an alias based on your choice in New Alias Options) for every account contained in the groups being imported. This may create a large number of users if the imported groups contain large numbers of users. If you choose the second option, users in the imported groups will be created in CRS once they log on to CRS for the first time. If they never log on, their account will never actually be created in CRS.

- **New User Options**   When new user accounts are created from imported groups, this choice determines which license type they use by default. Note that you must have enough licenses of the chosen type for all users that will be created by the import.

If you don't, not all user accounts will be created. If you later decide you want to change the license type for certain imported users, you may select the individual users from the Users link and change their license type.

Once you've made all desired choices, click Update to complete the process. If you chose to immediately create users and groups from the imported groups, you can now navigate to user and group lists to see the newly added users and groups.

TIP *A potentially useful feature for environments with Microsoft-only servers and browsers is NT Single Sign-On. When properly configured, this allows CRS users to pass their already-supplied Windows user ID and password to the CMS without actually specifying them—the web browser supplies them automatically. This requires, however, that Microsoft IIS be running as the web server and that users use the Internet Explorer browser. This option requires special settings on the IIS web server and changes to various CRS files. Information about enabling NT Single Sign-On is available in the CRS Administrator's Guide.*

LDAP

Another authentication method supported by Crystal Reports Server is via Lightweight Directory Access Protocol, or LDAP. LDAP users and groups maintained in your organization's LDAP server are mapped to CRS, with LDAP user accounts being used either to create a new CRS account or to map to an existing CRS account.

The first step in enabling LDAP authentication is to be sure your LDAP directory is set up and operating properly. Then, click Authorization in the Manage area of the CMC home page. Click the LDAP tab. If you have not previously set up LDAP authentication, a message indicating such will appear with a button to start the LDAP Configuration Wizard. Click the button.

The wizard will proceed through various screens asking for specific information relating to your particular LDAP server. These screens allow you to supply the hostname (or hostnames, if you want to add failover LDAP servers), the server type, the base LDAP distinguished name, the ID and password the CMS should use when querying the server, the type of secure connection to use, and the same CRS account and licensing options specified when using NT or AD authentication. Details on LDAP server settings can be found in the online Administrator's Guide, and details on the CRS account and licensing options are described in the previous NT and AD authentication sections.

Once you've successfully specified all wizard options, click Finished. The wizard will gather necessary information from your LDAP server and display the LDAP summary page in the LDAP tab. Now, you can specify existing LDAP groups to map to CRS. Enter the name of the LDAP group you wish to add in the Add LDAP Group text box. Click Add to add that group. Enter as many groups as desired to the list box in this manner. If you later wish to delete an existing group, select it in the list of existing groups and click Delete.

Once you've made all desired choices, click Update to complete the process. If you chose to immediately create users and groups from the imported groups, you can now navigate to user and group lists to see the newly added users and groups.

Controlling Access Using Rights

The Crystal Reports Server security model includes a series of rights that control a user's access to the various CRS objects such as folders and reports. For example, a user may be able to view a report and schedule it to run at a particular time, but may not be able to refresh the data or delete report instances. As another example, you may imagine a CRS system where company executives have access to all folders, the sales team has access only to the Sales and Inventory folders, and the head of the Human Resources department is the only non-executive with access to the Salary and Compensation Reports folder.

NOTE *This chapter discusses rights from a report and folder perspective. Separate rights exist for objects in the Crystal Reports Server repository, as well as for the CRS Business Views feature. Repository details can be found in Chapter 17. Business Views are covered in detail in Chapter 16.*

There are more than 20 rights that may be individually set, if so desired. However, these individual rights have been conveniently grouped into predefined access levels that can greatly ease the administration of rights. These access levels have been set up to create several commonly used combinations of rights in increasing order of access capabilities:

- No Access
- View
- Schedule
- View On Demand
- Full Control

These rights and access levels may be set for both individual users and groups, as well as for CRS folders, subfolders, and objects within the folders.

One very important concept with CRS security is that of inheritance. Users may inherit their rights from their groups, subgroups may inherit rights from their parent group, and both users and groups may inherit rights from parent folders. Group inheritance is most useful when CRS users are grouped according to their position in the organization, such as in groups called Sales, Marketing, and Human Resources. Parent folder inheritance is most useful when the reports are organized in folders that represent the organization, such as Sales, Inventory, and Vendors. For example, if the right to delete instances is specifically granted to the Sales group, that right would also be inherited by each user member of the Sales group and could also be inherited by a subgroup of Sales called Sales Assistants. If necessary, inheritance from the parent folder may be turned off for a user or group in order to explicitly define rights for that object. As you can probably imagine, inheritance can greatly reduce the number of settings required to control access across the entire CRS system.

Another important concept is the ability to grant or deny rights. Each right may be set as Explicitly Granted, Explicitly Denied, or Not Specified. Using these settings, an administrator can specifically allow one user to print reports, while specifically disallowing another user to refresh reports. If a right is Not Specified, the default is to deny that right unless the right is inherited. And if a right is inherited as granted from one parent group and denied from another parent group, that right is denied. The purpose of denying rights as a default is to be sure that no user is given rights that are not explicitly granted at some level by the administrator.

The combination of user/group, inheritance, and explicitly granted and denied rights produces an extremely flexible (and sometimes confusing) security system. For example, the right to Delete objects may be Explicitly denied for the Everyone group at the group level, so that no user may delete a folder or report anywhere in the system. For most folders and reports, the Delete objects right is Not Specified, and therefore the right is inherited as Denied. However, for the VP of Sales user, the Delete objects right may be Explicitly Granted for the Sales folder so that she may delete older sales reports that are no longer needed. And the Administrators group may have Full Control set at the top user/group level, giving them all rights for all objects, regardless of other rights settings.

NOTE *This chapter covers procedures to set rights for existing folders and reports. Information on how to add new Folders and Reports is covered later in this chapter. Once additional folders and reports are added, use steps discussed here to set their rights.*

Setting Rights

Crystal Reports Server rights can be set at two high levels within CRS: at the overall group or user level (this level is sometimes known as the CRS root folder), and at the folder/subfolder/object level. You don't have to set rights at either level; you may set rights at one level or the other, or at both levels. Just remember the rules of inheritance: top-level folder rights are inherited from group- and user-level rights, subfolder rights are inherited from parent folders, and report object rights are inherited from the folders in which they reside.

Setting Group- and User-Level Rights

When you initially install Crystal Reports Server, a set of group-level rights are already applied for the Everyone and Administrators Groups at the highest (sometimes referred to as "Root Folder") level. These rights can be inherited throughout the rest of the folder and object levels within the CMS. You may merely leave these default rights as-is, change the default rights, or set rights for new users and groups at this same high level.

To display or set Group Level and User Level Rights, click Settings from the Manage category of the CMC home page. Then, click the Rights tab.

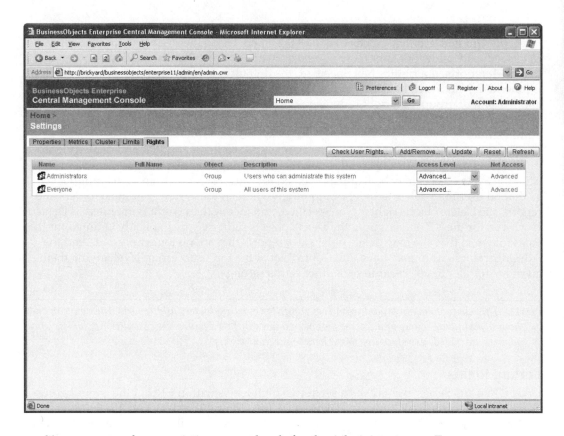

You may now change existing access levels for the Administrators or Everyone groups, or click the Add/Remove button to add or remove groups or users. Once you've added the additional groups or users, you'll be returned to the Rights tab, where you may set rights for the new group or user. Make sure to click Update when you've set new rights to save the changes to the CMS.

Setting Folder- and Object-Level Rights

Once you've set group- and user-level rights (or even if you haven't), you may set rights at the folder and object levels. The process of setting the rights is identical for both folders and report objects.

First, click the desired Folders or Objects links from the Organize category of the CMC home page. Browse to the desired folder or report object you want to change rights for. Then click the Rights tab. You'll immediately see rights inherited from the group and user levels (for example, you'll see the Administrators and Everyone groups listed with their rights set to Inherited Rights). You'll also notice that the display includes a column entitled Net Access. This column displays the final rights setting for that user or group after all inheritance and explicitly set rights have been combined.

Setting rights involves two processes: selecting the users or groups you want to set rights for, and then setting their actual rights. To choose groups or users for the chosen folder or object, click the Add/Remove button in the upper-right corner. If you would like to add a group, select the group from the left-hand list box and click the right arrow button. If you would like to add a user, select Add Users from the Select Operation drop-down. You may then either select a visible user or use the Find option to narrow down the list of users. Select the desired user from the left-hand list box and click the right arrow button. Once you've added your desired users and groups, click OK.

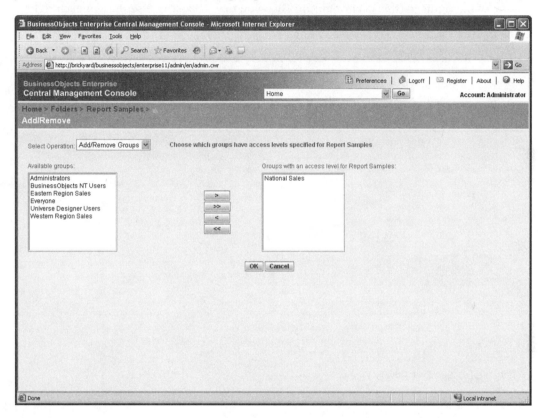

You will be returned to the folder or report Rights tab screen, where you will see that your newly chosen users or groups have been added to the list. You'll note the default access level of Schedule. If this is the desired access level, then click the Update button in the upper-right corner to save the new settings. Or, you may set the rights by choosing a different access level from the drop-down list. If you wish to simply inherit rights from the group and user levels, or from higher-level folders, choose (Inherited Rights). You may also choose one of the predefined access levels. Or, you may set individual rights with the Advanced option.

CAUTION *Don't forget to click the Update button after making any changes. If you don't, your changes won't be saved to the CMS.*

To set individual rights, select Advanced from the Access Level drop-down. You will automatically be taken to the Advanced Rights page. You'll see four columns: Inherited, Explicitly Granted, Explicitly Denied, and Not Specified. The first thing you may want to do is view the inherited rights by checking the boxes at the top of the screen and clicking on the Apply button. This will display the rights as they are inherited so that you see a more complete picture of the rights for this user or group. Then you may choose one setting for each right listed on the right-hand side. Finally, click the OK button to complete the process.

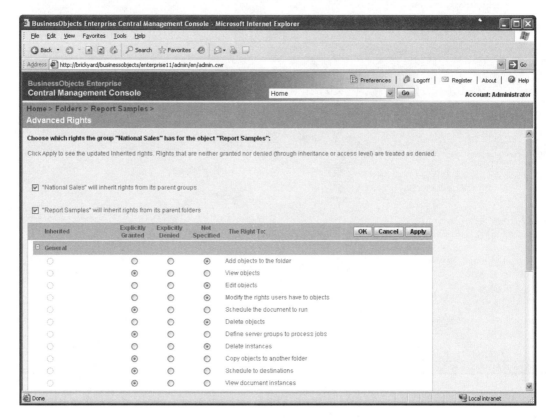

TIP *To get back to the Advanced Rights page for a user or group that you've previously set, you must click the word Advanced in the Net Access column. Because the Advanced option is already selected in the Access Level drop-down, you must click the Advanced hyperlink to go back to the Advanced Rights page.*

One of the most important aspects of setting up your CRS system is assigning rights to various folders and objects. This is the key to displaying only desired folders for certain users and groups; allowing only certain reports to be viewed or scheduled; preventing unauthorized deletion of folders, objects, and instances; and so forth. The CRS security model is very flexible. As is often the case, flexibility can also introduce confusion. More detailed security discussions and scenarios are found in the online CRS Administrator's Guide. Also, you'll want to take the time to test your security model to ensure that users are being granted and denied proper rights at the proper folder and object levels throughout your CRS system. In many cases, you may not be able to determine the exact ramifications of various security and inheritance settings until you actually test behavior by logging into InfoView with various user accounts.

Creating Folders and Adding Objects

The Crystal Reports Server environment uses the tried-and-true hierarchical folder method of organization similar to Windows and other operating systems. Reports and other CRS objects may be placed in these folders to organize the objects into logical groups and simplify navigation for the users. Also, the folder structure can be set up to intelligently apply rights settings using folder inheritance to ease security maintenance.

NOTE *If a user does not have the rights to a particular folder, that folder is not displayed as the user browses the CRS system.*

Upon installation of CRS, there are three folders at the top level: Feature Samples, Report Samples, and User Folders. The Feature Samples folder contains examples of CRS object types, such as executable script, hyperlinks, and third-party file types (in this case, a PDF file). The Report Samples folder contains two subfolders containing several sample reports (of course), while the User Folders folder contains subfolders for each user in the system. The folders under User Folders are special, as they contain the user's InfoView Favorites, and are marked with a blue asterisk. When a new user is added to the system, a new special folder under User Folders is created for that user.

Creating Folders and Subfolders

To create a new folder, click Folders under the Organize area of the CMC. A list of all existing top-level folders will appear. To create a new folder at the top level, select the New Folder button in the upper-right corner. Fill in the new folder name and the description (if so desired) and click OK. After the new folder is created, you will remain on that folder's page with the Properties tab selected. The most common next steps are to add reports to the folder, create subfolders, or set the rights for the folder. These options are all available as tabs across the top of the page.

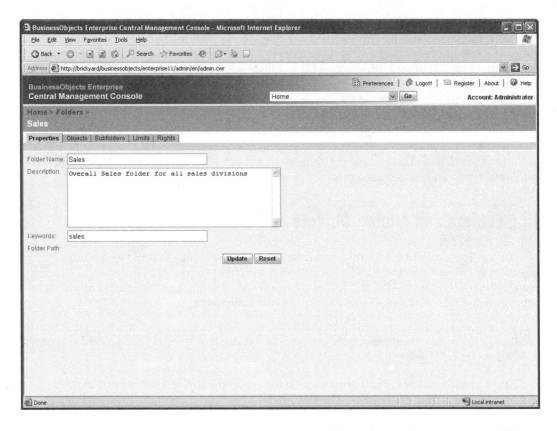

To create a new subfolder, you must first select the folder under which the new subfolder will be created (if you haven't already selected it or just created it). When you initially select the folder, either the Objects or Subfolders tab will be displayed, depending on whether or not there are objects in the folder. If the Objects tab is displayed, click the Subfolders tab.

Any existing subfolders already contained in the folder will be displayed. If there are none, you'll simply see column headings with no subfolders below them. Click the New Folder button in the upper-right corner, which will take you to the now familiar New Folder page. Complete the form and click OK to create the new subfolder.

Adding Reports

One of the main reasons Crystal Reports Server exists, of course, is to manage reports. Therefore, one of the most common and important tasks is to add reports to the system. There are several ways to accomplish this task: with the CMC, directly from Crystal Reports XI, and by using the Publishing Wizard.

Adding Reports with the CMC

You may add new reports to CRS one at a time via the CMC. You may add reports via either the Objects or Folders option from the Organize area of the CMC.

Click Objects to display the list of all existing objects (reports, program objects, third-party objects) already in the CMC, regardless of what folder they are in. To add a new report, click the New Object button in the upper-right corner. The New Object page appears with a list of available object types on the left, and specific details about the selected object type appear on the right. Report is the default object type, so it should already be selected.

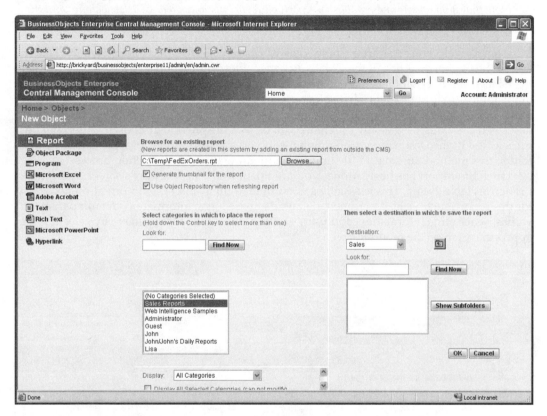

The first step is to specify the location and filename for the .RPT file you wish to add. You may simply type the whole pathname/filename into the text box. However, you may prefer to click the Browse button to display a file dialog (the Browse button also ensures that the correct full pathname and filename are specified). If you chose the Save Preview Picture option in File | Summary Info from within Crystal Reports, you may display the thumbnail in CRS by checking Generate Thumbnail For Report. If the report contains objects connected to the CRS repository, be sure to check Use Object Repository When Refreshing Report. Then, use the lower right section of the form to select the CRS folder or subfolder that you wish to place the report in. You may also use the lower-left section of the form to place a shortcut to the report in a category or categories. (Categories are discussed later in this chapter.) Finally, click OK to finish the process. The file will be copied to the Input FRS from its source location and added to the CMS.

CAUTION *Don't forget that adding a report to CRS copies the .RPT file from the source location to the Input FRS. Any changes you make to the original report in its source location will not be reflected in CRS. If you wish to change an already-published report, you must open the report through the Enterprise Folders option of Crystal Reports XI. Alternatively, you may change the report in its source location, delete the original report from CRS, and publish the updated report. Note that if you delete and republish a report, all report instances will be deleted along with the original report.*

Alternatively, you can start the process by browsing to the desired folder from the Folders link in the Organize section of the CMC. Click the folder you wish to add the report to. Either the Objects tab or Subfolders tab will display, depending on whether or not there are objects in the folder. If the Subfolders tab displays, click the Objects tab. Click the New Object button in the upper-right corner to add a new report. You will see the same New Object page as described previously—the only difference will be that the previously chosen folder will be preselected in the Destination drop-down list. If you are adding several reports to the same folder, this method can save a little time by eliminating the folder selection process.

Once the report has been added, you are taken to the new report's screen with the Properties tab selected. This is usually a good time to fill in any other information necessary for this report, such as the description, default database logon information, default parameter values, scheduling information, and user/group rights. Make these choices by selecting the appropriate tab on the report's screen.

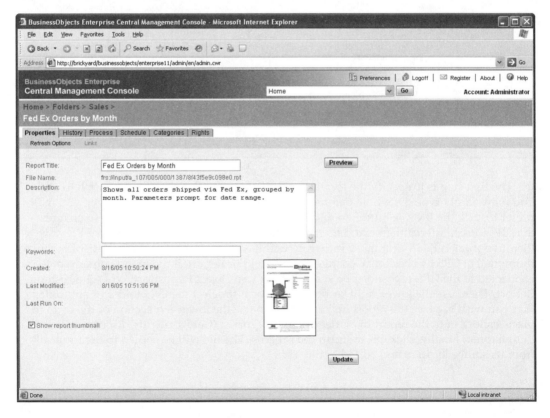

Adding Reports from Crystal Reports XI

One of the simplest methods for adding a report to the system is to save it directly to
Crystal Reports Server from the Crystal Reports XI designer. Once the report you've opened
or designed is ready to publish to CRS, choose File | Save As from the Crystal Reports pull-
down menus. A file dialog will appear. Notice a series of icons along the left side, including
the Enterprise Folders icon. Click this icon to log on to CRS (a CRS logon screen will appear).

Once you've properly logged on, you'll notice the CMS folder structure in the dialog
box. Navigate to the appropriate folder or subfolder where you wish to save the report.
Once you've chosen the desired folder, type in the name for the report in the filename box
(note that no .RPT file extension is required—you are actually specifying a descriptive name
here, and not the actual filename that the Input FRS will use when saving the report). If the
report contains objects from the CRS repository, check Enable Repository Refresh. Click
Save to complete the process. The file will be saved into the Input FRS from Crystal Reports.

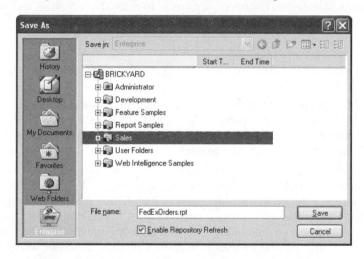

You may also open an existing report on a CRS system by using File | Open from within
Crystal Reports XI. Again, clicking the Enterprise Folders icon will allow you to log on to
CRS and choose existing reports (including instances) from CRS folders. Once you've made
changes, you can update the report on the Input FRS by simply clicking the Save toolbar
button, or using File | Save. This is the only way to modify an existing report object in CRS
without deleting and re-publishing it (and, deleting all report instances in the process).

NOTE *Remember that when you save a report directly to the CRS system from Crystal Reports, you
may have to still use the CMC later to set additional information (default database logon information,
default parameters, rights, and so forth) required for the report.*

Adding Reports with the Publishing Wizard

The Publishing Wizard is a stand-alone Windows application designed with one purpose in
mind: to publish reports and third-party objects (such as Word documents, PDF files, and so

forth) into a Crystal Reports Server system en masse. It works in standard "wizard fashion," taking you from one dialog to the next, showing only those dialogs that are necessary to complete the task at hand. It is most useful when you are adding multiple reports and objects to the system, including objects from multiple folders. In fact, you can even preserve the folder structure from the original source location when you publish objects with the Publishing Wizard. Another benefit of the wizard is that it prompts for much of the "extra" information for a report, such as parameter fields and database logon and scheduling information.

Because the wizard is a stand-alone Windows application, you must specifically install it from the CRS program CD if you want to run it on a computer that doesn't already contain a full CRS installation. You will then launch the wizard directly from the Start menu. If you used the default installation location, you will find it in the BusinessObjects 11/Crystal Reports Server program group. Once you've started the wizard, simply follow the instructions from screen to screen. There are many steps, and some portions and steps are optional.

Here are some of the more common steps used in publishing reports and objects once you've started the Publishing Wizard.

1. Click Next to proceed past the welcome screen.

2. Log on to the CMS with an appropriate account that has publish rights on the CMS. Click Next.

3. Click the appropriate button to add files or a folder. The Add Files button allows you to add one or more individual files (.RPT, .DOC, .PDF, and so forth). The Add Folder button will add all files in a folder on a disk drive (optionally including files in subfolders below the chosen folder).

4. If you click Add Files, a file dialog box will appear. Choose one or more files to add (you may CTRL-click or SHIFT-click to choose multiple files). If you wish to change the type of file shown in the dialog (instead of .RPT, perhaps you would like to choose .PDF), make your choice from the Files Of Type drop-down list. Files you choose will appear in the file list once you close the file dialog. You may click the Add Files button as many times as necessary to add additional sets of files to the list.

5. If you click Add Folder, a folder dialog will appear where you may choose a specific folder. If you would like to publish files in subfolders below the chosen folder, check Include Subfolders. And, you may also choose the type of file you'd like to publish (.RPT, .PDF, .DOC, and so forth) from the drop-down list. You may click the Add Folder button more than once if you wish to add additional folders.

6. Once you've clicked the Add Files and/or Add Folders buttons as necessary, a complete list of files that are ready to be published will appear. Delete excess files you don't want to publish by selecting them individually or CTRL-clicking or SHIFT-clicking to select multiple files. Then, click Remove Files.

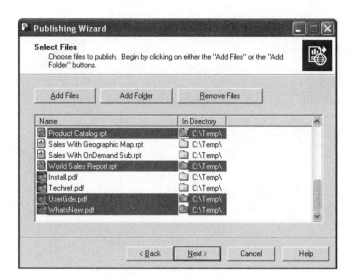

7. Once you've chosen the right set of files you want to publish, click Next. The Publishing Wizard will read the various files to obtain information it needs to continue. It will then present the Folder Hierarchy screen.

8. If you wish to preserve the folder names that the original source files come from, select Yes. The same folder structure will be created on the CMS when files are published. If you select No, all the files chosen in the previous step will be published in the same CMS folder. Click Next.

NOTE *You'll notice an indication that you can't create an object package if you preserve the folder hierarchy. An object package is a series of objects, such as reports, that are published together as a unit. When a report object package is scheduled, all reports within it are processed at the same time.*

9. Select the CRS folder where the objects are to be added (select the CMS name to add the reports to the root folder or to begin your folder creation at the root folder). You may create new folders directly in this dialog box if so desired. You may also create an object package by clicking the appropriate icon. Once you've chosen the desired destination folder, click Next.

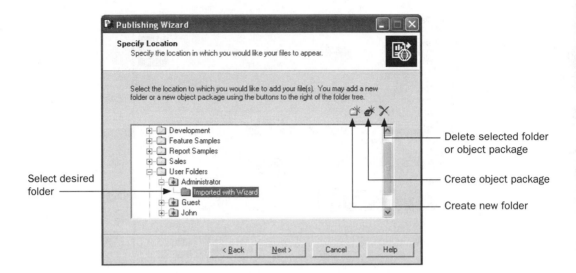

Delete selected folder or object package

Create object package

Select desired folder

Create new folder

10. The Location Preview screen shows you where the objects you are publishing will appear within the CMS. If you chose to preserve the original source folder hierarchy, you'll see the source folder names here, with objects contained in them. You may use this screen to move objects into other folders, create additional folders, and so forth. You may select an object and use the up and down arrows to move it, or you may simply drag the object and drop it "into" the desired folder. The Show File Names/Show Titles button will toggle between displaying source filenames and the title that will appear once the objects are published to the Input FRS. When satisfied with the location of your published files, click Next.

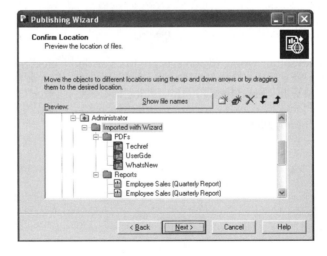

TIP *You will only be able to delete folders and object packages that you have previously added with the wizard (these will be denoted with a green folder icon). You won't be able to delete any folders that existed on the CMS before you started the wizard.*

11. The Schedule Interval screen will now appear, provided you are publishing at least one Crystal Report .RPT file. Select one or more reports that you wish to set scheduling options for. You have the option to specify limited scheduling options for the reports. Let Users Update The Object will simply publish the report object with no scheduling options. Run Once Only will create a single instance of each new report. Run On A Recurring Schedule will allow additional limited scheduling options to be chosen. Make these choices by clicking the Set Recurrence button and choosing options from the resulting dialog. Once you've made desired choices, click Next.

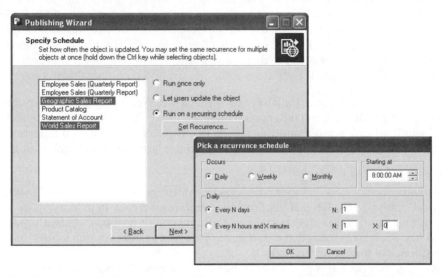

12. The Repository Refresh screen will appear, provided you've published at least one report. Choose reports from the list that contain CRS repository objects that you'd like refreshed. Then, check Enable Repository Refresh. You may also select the option for all or no reports by clicking the Enable All or Disable All button, respectively. Click Next.

13. The Change Default Values screen gives you the choice to modify additional items for any reports that you may be publishing. If you choose to Publish Without Modifying Properties, you won't have the chance to specify the report title, comments, parameter values, database logons, and so forth, for selected reports. You'll proceed immediately to step 18. If you do want to edit these items, choose Review Or Modify Properties. Click Next.

14. The Review Object Properties screen allows you to alter the title and description of each report. To edit the values, select a report from the list box on the left and change the information in the text boxes on the right. Click Next.

15. The Database Logon Information screen allows you to alter the database logon information for each report. To change the information, select a report in the list box, click the plus sign to the left of the report to expose database connections, select a database from that report, and then change the logon information. Continue for each report and database before moving on. Click Next.

16. The Set Report Parameters screen allows you to alter parameter field information for each report that contains at least one parameter field. In this dialog, reports appear in the left list box. When you select a report, the individual report parameters are

listed in the right list box. To edit the parameter information, select a parameter and click the Edit Prompt button. You'll be presented another dialog box, where you may supply a value or values for the chosen parameter field. Once you've specified all parameter field values, click Next.

17. The Schedule Format screen allows you to set the output format for scheduled instances of each report. Again, select a report in the left list box and set that report's format with the drop-down on the right. Click Next.

18. Finally, objects are ready to be published to Crystal Reports Server. You'll see a final list of objects that will be copied to the Input FRS and added to the CMS folder structure. Click Next to begin the publishing process. After the objects are added, the wizard displays a final screen with a summary of add folders and objects. You may click a folder or object to display an indication of whether it was properly published or not. Click Finish to exit the wizard and complete the process.

The Publishing Wizard may initially seem tedious when compared to quick publishing capabilities of the CMC or Crystal Reports. However, using the wizard can be considerably more efficient if you are adding multiple objects to the system, especially if reports share similar characteristics or you wish to maintain the folder structure when publishing.

Reports with Saved Data

An option of particular note to Crystal Reports Server users is Crystal Reports' Save Data With Report option on the Crystal Reports File menu. It is an easy item to overlook when producing a report, but it is an extremely important consideration when that report is published to CRS. It is essential that report developers and system administrators understand the consequence of that little check mark.

When a report is saved with data after being previewed, it saves a snapshot of the underlying data in the Preview tab along with the .RPT file. When you publish the report to CRS via the CMC, the saved data is published along with the report. Whenever that report is run on demand (that is, the user chooses the View option from InfoView instead of the View Latest Instance Or Schedule option), the saved data will be used and the report will *not* connect to the database for new data. This may be desirable in situations where the report is meant to produce a snapshot of data at the time of the report's creation or when you want to limit database queries for a particular report. However, it can very easily lead a report viewer to think they're seeing a current snapshot of database data when they're not. And, if the report includes parameter fields, a viewer running the report on demand will never be prompted to supply them. To confuse things even further, if you add Data Date or Data Time Crystal Reports special fields to the report with saved data, they will be updated as viewers look at the report on demand, even though no new data is coming from the database.

When a report is saved without data, only the definition of the report is maintained, with no additional data saved along with it. Whenever that report is run on demand, the report *must* connect with the database to retrieve data (and, any parameter fields will be prompted for). Most reports should probably be designed this way so that the report produces the most current possible view of the data.

NOTE *When you install Crystal Reports XI, Save Data With Report is turned on by default. This default can be changed using File | Options. Select the Reporting tab on the options dialog and uncheck Save Data With Report.*

Adding Program Objects

A *program object* is an executable program (for example, a program with a .COM, .EXE, .BAT, or similar file extension) that can be run from a command line, a Java program, or a file containing executable script, such as VBScript or JScript. This feature allows you to schedule executable programs and scripts on a regular basis the same way you schedule reports on a regular basis. This new feature greatly improves the flexibility of Crystal Reports Server, allowing you to schedule such tasks as data warehouse updates, server or database maintenance tasks, or other CRS maintenance tasks.

When you schedule a program object to run, the Input FRS transfers the files that make up the program object to the Program Job Server, which actually runs the program object in a shell process. The Program Job Server captures the error and output streams from the process and passes them on to the Output FRS to store as a program instance. Therefore, you can actually view instances for program objects much as you would for a report. However, what will be shown when you view the program instance is the output and error streams from the particular execution of the program object.

The first step in preparing for program object support is determining which types of program objects can be run on a global basis. Click Objects from the Organize area of the CMC main screen. A list of all objects will appear. Click the Object Settings button in the upper right-hand corner of the page. The Object Settings screen will appear. Click the Program Objects tab.

Check appropriate check boxes to run executables (binaries) and scripts, as well as Java programs. These settings apply globally to the entire CMS—no one will be able to run these types of program objects if the corresponding item is unchecked. You may also choose to supply default operating system credentials to run program objects if the user scheduling the object doesn't supply them (this is somewhat of a security compromise, so you should provide default credentials judiciously). Once you ensure proper settings on this page, click Update. You are now ready to add program objects to the desired folder.

Initial steps to add a program object are identical to those used to add reports. Begin by clicking either Folders or Objects from the Organize area of the CMC, depending on whether you want to initially choose the folder to place the object in before adding the object, or after. Once you've displayed the list of existing objects, click the New Object button above the list. The New Object screen will appear, with the list of available object types appearing on the left. Click Program in the list.

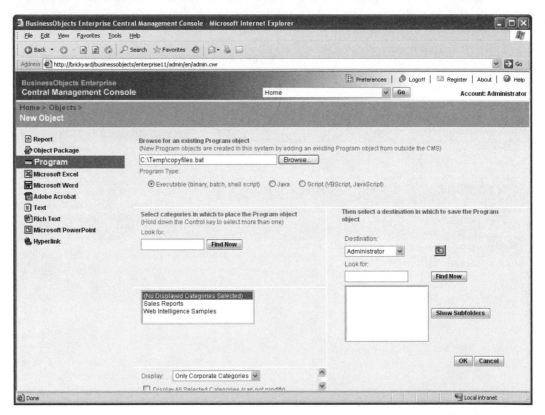

If you know the full pathname/filename of the program object (.BAT file, .EXE file, VBScript, Java program, and so forth) that you want to add, type the full pathname/filename into the text box. You can also click the Browse button to search for the file via a file dialog box. Choose the type of object you are adding by selecting the desired radio button. And, if necessary, choose the folder you wish to publish the object to. Click OK to copy the object to the Input FRS.

The new program object's properties page will appear. Make any desired changes to the object's title and description. If you wish to change access rights to something other than those inherited from the object's parent folder, make your choices on the Rights tab. You may also want to specify additional information specific to the just-added program object on the Process tab. You'll find various options there that can copy additional files required by your program object to the Input FRS (perhaps dynamic link library files, initialization files, and so forth), set the operating system user ID/password that the Program Job Server will use when running the program object, and so forth. Look closely (they're small and hard to see) for Auxiliary Files, Logon, and Parameters links on the Process tab. At the very least, you'll probably want to specify an operating system ID/password combination to use when the Program Job Server runs the program. If you don't (and no default was set when you initially enabled program objects), the program object will fail when scheduled.

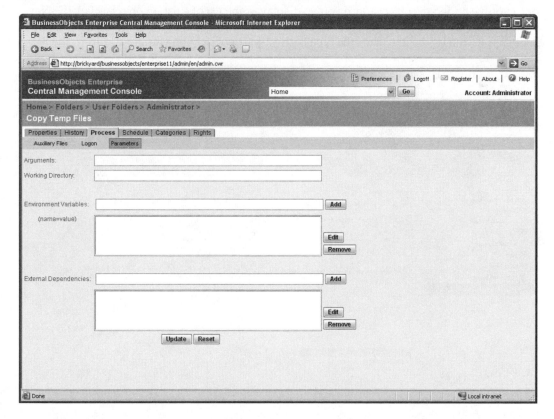

NOTE *There are many fine points to providing specific information to various program objects, such as environment variables, supplementary files, and such. Get complete information on these finer program object points by viewing the online CRS Administrator's Guide from the CRS Admin Launchpad.*

Adding Third-Party Objects

Early versions of Crystal Reports Server only supported adding and viewing Crystal Reports and Crystal Analysis documents. Version 10 expanded this capability significantly with program objects (discussed earlier in the chapter) and common office-type documents, including Acrobat PDF files, Microsoft Word documents, Excel spreadsheet files, Microsoft PowerPoint documents, Rich Text files, standard text files, and web hyperlinks. These additional document types, sometimes referred to as *third-party objects,* can be copied to the Input FRS, where they will be available for viewing by anyone using CRS (provided they have rights to the object).

Initial steps to add a third-party object are identical to those used to add reports. Begin by clicking either Folders or Objects from the Organize area of the CMC, depending on whether you want to initially choose the folder to place the object in or to choose the folder once you've added the object. Once you've displayed the list of existing objects, click the New Object button above the list. The New Object screen will appear, with the list of available object types appearing on the left. Click the type of third-party object you want to add from the list.

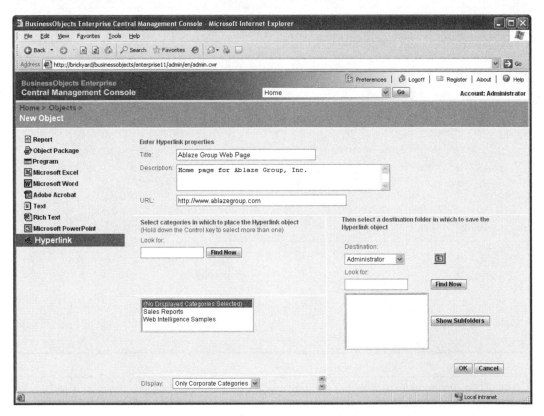

If you chose to add a hyperlink, specify the URL to the web page, and other associated information. File-based third-party objects will require you to specify the filename of the document. If you know the full pathname/filename of the third-party object (.DOC file, .PDF file, and so forth) that you want to add, type the full pathname/filename into the text box. You can also click the Browse button to search for the file via a file dialog box. If necessary, choose the folder you wish to publish the object to. Click OK to copy the object to the Input FRS.

The new third-party object's properties page will appear. Make any desired changes to the object's title and description. If you wish to change access rights to something other than those inherited from the object's parent folder, make your choices on the Rights tab.

NOTE *In essence, viewing a third-party object from CRS is identical to viewing or downloading a similar document from a web page. You should ensure that your user community has appropriate client software (such as Microsoft Office or Adobe Reader) installed on their computers for the types of third-party objects you add to CRS.*

Working with Categories

The Categories feature is one of the new additions to the XI version of Crystal Reports Server. This new feature provides a new method for organizing reports and other objects in a customized ways. In essence, you can use Categories to create an unlimited number of "virtual" folder structures.

There are two types of categories: Corporate Categories and Personal Categories. Corporate Categories are created by system administrators, while Personal Categories (as the name might suggest) are created by individual users. Administrators can use Corporate Categories to provide alternate groupings or create easier browsing for their entire audience of users. And as with folders, administrators can set rights for Corporate Categories to restrict access. Individual users can use Personal Categories to create their own custom organization of reports and other objects, perhaps to assemble and group the set of reports that are specific to their particular job function. Personal Categories can only be accessed by that specific user.

One important note: a category contains only shortcuts to reports and other objects. The reports and objects themselves are stored in the main folder structure. This setup eliminates redundancy, storing each report in a single location. This also allows the same report to be "contained" in an unlimited number of different categories.

Why Categories? An Example...

You may be thinking, "Why would I need to use Categories if I already have Folders?" That's a good question, and sometimes the answer may be, "You don't need to use Categories." However, consider the following example.

A company decided to create their Crystal Reports Server folder structure to mimic their organization. Sales reports went in a Sales folder, HR reports went in an

HR folder, etc. Some of the departments have a few subfolders, while others have an entire hierarchy of subfolders under the main folder. Wisely, this folder structure was created in conjunction with appropriate groups to simplify the application of security rights.

For many users (such as the Director of West Coast Sales), the folder structure works just fine for browsing reports and accessing other documents. The reports that are relevant to their job function are found in the same folder or at least the same section of the hierarchy. However, there are some users (such as the Chief Operating Officer) that need to access reports from many different folders in the hierarchy. Because the reports are so spread out (especially in a system with a large hierarchy and/or a large number of reports), browsing to them is tedious and time-consuming.

To help alleviate this issue (especially for the COO), the CRS administrator created a Corporate Category called "Executive Reports." Shortcuts to reports from various locations in the folder structure were placed in the category. Now, the executive staff can go to a single location and find all of the reports they typically need to view. Those reports are still stored in their original folder locations, and they are still governed by the security rights assigned using those folders, but the executive staff can get to them with a minimum of clicking and in a lot less time.

The Director of Web Coast Sales likes to start each morning by taking stock of a piece of the business, and viewing a series of reports is a great way to do that. Various sales reports are viewed, of course, but the Director also likes to see an inventory status report, a manufacturing status report, and several financial reports. So the Director created a Personal Category called "Daily Morning Reports" and put shortcuts to all of those reports in the category. Now the Director can go to a single place for all the reports, making the morning routine easier and less error-prone.

Creating Categories

As an administrator, you can create both Corporate Categories and Personal Categories, and the process for each is nearly identical. One difference is that you can create new top-level Corporate Categories, but you cannot create new top-level Personal Categories. Top-level Personal Categories are automatically created by the system for each user when that user is created (and all other Personal Categories are created as subcategories of that top-level category). Also, you may assign rights to a Corporate Category, but not to a Personal Category (since only that user may view that category by default).

To create a category, select either Categories or Personal Categories from the Organize section of the CMC. Then click the New Category button in the upper-right corner. Fill in the Category name (and the description and keywords, if so desired) and click OK.

After the new category is created, you will remain on that category's page with the Properties tab selected. The most common next steps are to add objects to the category, create subcategories, or set the rights for the category (if it is a Corporate Category). These options are all available as tabs across the top of the page.

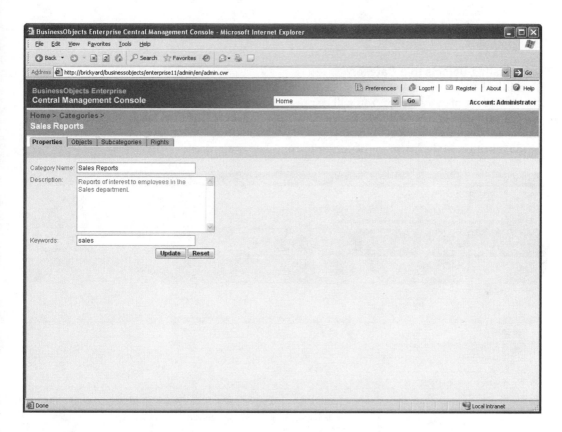

To create a new subcategory, you must first select the category under which the new subcategory will be created (if you haven't already selected it or just created it). When you initially select the category, the Properties tab will be displayed. Click the Subcategories tab.

Any existing subcategories already contained in the category will be displayed. If there are none, you'll simply see column headings with no subcategories below them. Click the New Category button in the upper-right corner, which will take you to the now familiar New Category page. Complete the form and click OK to create the new subcategory.

Adding Reports and Other Objects to Categories

There are two ways to add reports and other objects to categories: 1) add new objects to the system and at the same time add those objects to one or more categories, or 2) select existing objects to place in a category.

Add New Objects to a Category

To add new reports or other objects to a category, click the New Object button in the upper-right corner of the Category screen. You'll see that the process is exactly the same as adding a new object to a folder (since that is actually what is happening). The object itself is added to the folder that you select in the lower-right section of the screen, and a shortcut to the object is added to the category or categories that you select in the lower-left section of the screen. (For more information, see the section "Adding Reports with the CMC" earlier in this chapter.)

Add Existing Objects to a Category

To add existing reports and/or objects to a category, click the Add button in the upper-right corner of the Category screen. You will be presented with a list of all objects in the CRS system. You can use the Look For text box and Find Now button to filter the list for easier selection. Use the check boxes to select the objects you wish to add to the category, and then click the Update button in the lower-right corner to complete the process.

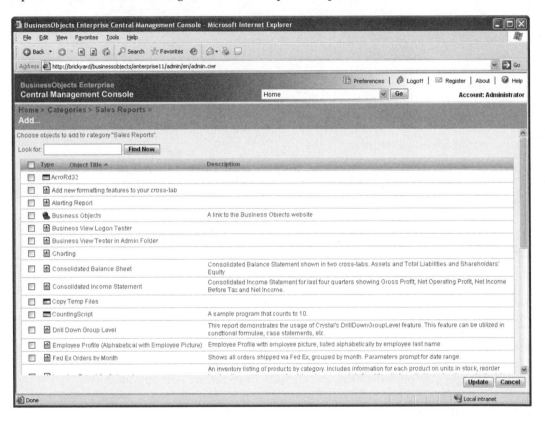

Defining Output Destinations

When you schedule a report or program object to run at a later time or on a recurring basis (third-party objects cannot be scheduled), the report instance or output of the program object is saved to the Output FRS by default. When you then view the instance, the file from the Output FRS is passed on for viewing. However, you may prefer to distribute reports to alternative destinations such as an FTP server, attach them to an e-mail message in an alternate file format, or write them to a specific file location somewhere on your network. You may also prefer to have a program object's output and error streams distributed the same way. This requires you to set destination settings on either the Crystal Reports Job Server (for report instances) and the Program Job Server (for program object instances).

As these destinations are disabled when CRS is first installed, you must both enable the destinations and set specific parameters to configure each output destination. Begin by clicking Servers from the Organize area in the main CMC screen. A list of all CRS servers will appear. Choose either the Program Job Server (to configure destinations for program objects) or the Crystal Reports Job Server (to configure destinations for reports). The properties screen will appear for the chosen server. Click the Destinations tab.

Four destinations will appear: Email (SMTP), FTP, Inbox, and Unmanaged Disk. If a red circle with a minus sign icon appears over the icon next to the destination, that destination is disabled. To enable it, check the check box under the Selected column for all destinations that you want to enable. Then, click the Enable button in the upper right-hand corner.

You must also configure specific settings for each destination type. Do this by clicking the actual destination name to the right of the icon. A specific screen will appear for each destination type.

- **Email (SMTP)**   This destination is for automatically e-mailing instances. Options include the SMTP server information, the default e-mail field values, and file naming conventions for the attached files.

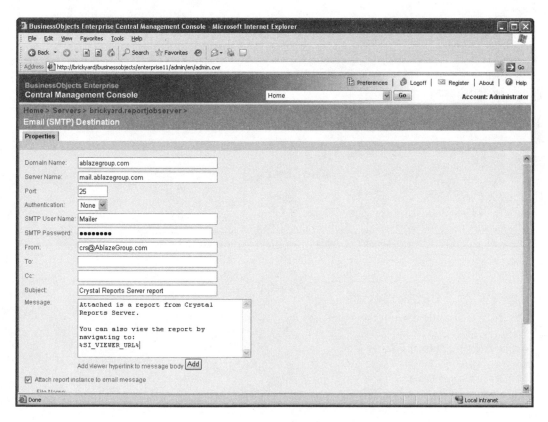

TIP *Crystal Reports Server supports e-mail servers that adhere to the Internet-TCP/IP SMTP standard. If you are using a proprietary e-mail system, such as Microsoft Exchange or Novell GroupWise, you'll need to use SMTP gateway products that allow your e-mail system to send e-mails via the SMTP protocol.*

- **FTP** This destination is for automatically sending instances to an FTP server. Options include the FTP account and logon information, the target directory, and file naming conventions.

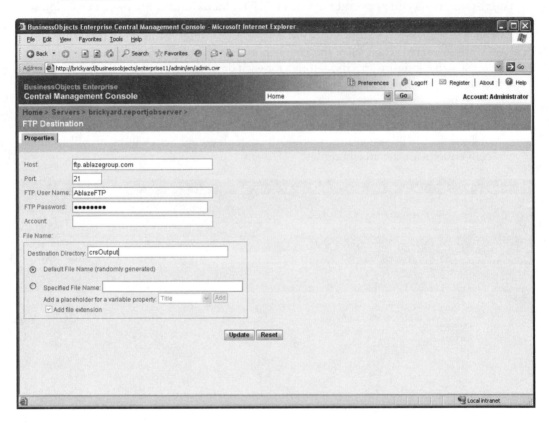

- **Inbox** This destination is for automatically sending instance to a user's Inbox inside of CRS. Options include sending the instance as a shortcut or a copy, and the default list of recipients.

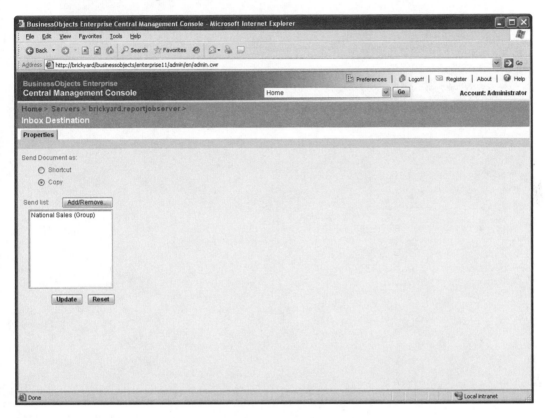

- **DiskUnmanaged** This destination is for saving report or program object output to hard drive files outside of the Output FRS. Options include the target directory, file naming conventions, and logon credentials for the service.

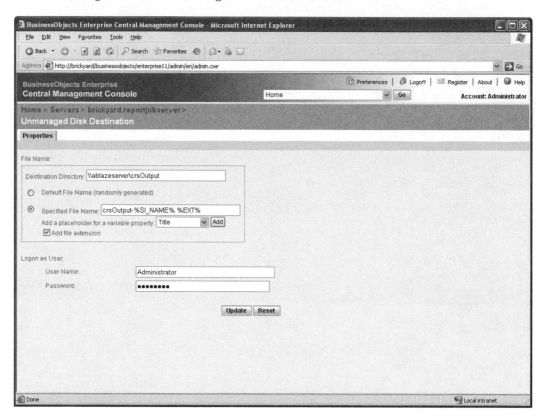

Using Inboxes

The Inbox feature is another new addition to the Crystal Reports Server system with the XI release. It provides an internal mail system for sending reports and other objects directly to particular users. Previously, a report instance intended for a particular user would simply be stored in the CRS system in a specified location, and the user would be notified in one of several ways of its existence. When the user was finished with the instance, it could be deleted, either by the user, the administrator, or automatically by the system when certain limits were reached. Now, that report instance can be sent directly to the user's Inbox, and the instance can be automatically and immediately deleted from its temporary location within the system.

An inbox is automatically created for each user in the CRS system. No other inboxes may be created, and inboxes cannot be manually deleted. A user's inbox is automatically deleted when that user is removed from the system.

Security rights may be set for inbox, similar to the way security rights may be set for a folder or category. By default, the inbox's user has Full Control. Rights for the Everyone group are set at the top-level Inboxes screen; by default, they deny access for that group, allowing only the inbox's user to see their inbox. However, rights could be added to allow additional users into the inbox. For example, a group manager may want everyone in her group to have access to her inbox, which would allow them to view reports and other documents sent to her, an ability that could be especially useful during her vacations or sick days.

Browsing to an inbox in the CMC will open up that inbox's Objects tab, which lists all of the objects in the inbox. This list contains a Read/Unread flag to help the user manage the inbox (the white flag displays when the object is unread and disappears when the object has been read). Objects may be selected from the list, then either marked as Read or Unread, sent to other destinations, copied or moved, or deleted.

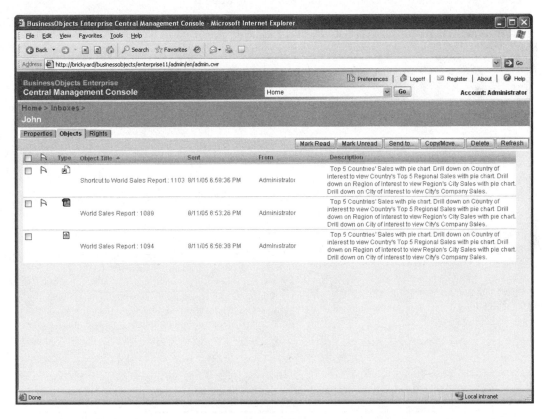

Administrators and users alike will find Inbox as one of the destination options when scheduling an object or when using the Send To button. In both cases, an object may be scheduled to or sent to any number of inboxes, and either a copy of the object or a shortcut to the object may be delivered.

Creating Calendars

One of the features that Crystal/Seagate Info users sorely missed in earlier versions of Crystal Reports Server was calendar-based scheduling. CRS XI includes this capability, allowing reports and program objects to be scheduled according to a particular user-defined calendar. This is handy for scheduling by your own organization's specific processing cycles, such as pay days, accounting periods, and so forth.

The first step in allowing calendar-based scheduling is to define your particular calendars to reflect your individual processing cycles. Begin this process by clicking Calendars from the Define area of the main CMC screen. The Calendars screen will appear, showing any existing calendars you have already created (just column headings will appear if no calendars have yet been created). Click the New Calendar button in the upper right-hand corner to create a new calendar. The New Calendar screen will appear.

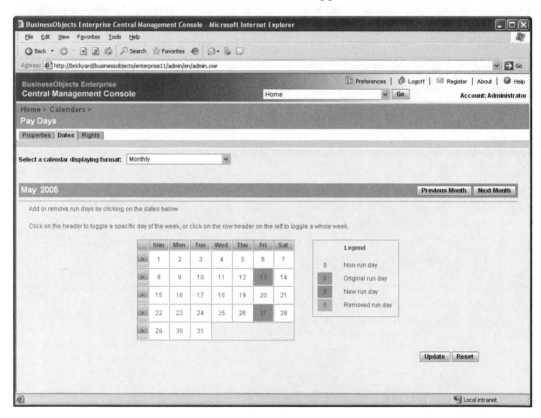

Give the calendar a meaningful name (such as Pay Days), as well as an optional description, on the Properties tab. Then, click OK to actually create the calendar (you cannot select the other tabs until you do so). The Dates tab will then appear automatically. The Dates tab will initially show a yearly view of months, which can be changed by choosing various options from the Select A Calendar Displaying Format drop-down list. Choose the desired display options, or just click one of the displayed months to set run days for that particular month.

Once the desired specific period (or a generic month by day of week or day of month) is displayed, simply click the days you wish objects to run. The day will be shaded in an "Original Run Day" color. If you are modifying an existing calendar, you can click original run days to deselect the day from future schedules (a different color will indicate that the day has been removed). As necessary, click Next Month and Previous Month buttons to display different months to select or deselect additional days. When finished, click the Update button to save the calendar to the CMS.

Once you've created your desired calendar or calendars in the CMC, you may schedule reports and programs based on them. This is carried out in the Organize | Objects area of the CMC, or when scheduling in InfoView (covered in Chapter 23).

TIP   *As with most other features in the CMC, you may also wish to set rights for the calendar by clicking the Rights tab. You may then choose users or groups that you wish to have rights to the calendar and set those specific rights, as described earlier in the chapter, under "Controlling Access Using Rights."*

Using Events

A powerful feature of Crystal Reports Server is the ability to base report and program object scheduling on events. An *event* consists of one of three different general occurrences: the existence of a file somewhere on a drive, the completion of another scheduled job (either just the completion, or specifically the success or failure of the job), or a simple "trigger" that an administrator can initiate from within the CMC. Events allow very powerful control of scheduling from within CRS. For example, you could potentially schedule a program object to execute a custom data warehouse update program, which writes data extracts to a specific file location. Reports based on the new data warehouse files will run after a specific file is detected in that location. And, given the successful completion of the reports, another program object could run a batch file that deletes the data warehouse files.

Before they can be used for scheduling, events must be defined in the Central Management Console. Begin by clicking Events in the Define area of the main CMC screen. The Events screen will appear showing any existing events that have already been defined (just column headings will appear if no events are yet defined). Click the New Event button in the upper right-hand corner. The New Event screen will appear. Select the type of event you wish to create from the drop-down list at the top of the screen.

- **File** Specify a descriptive name and optional description for the file-based event. If your CRS system includes more than one Event Server, choose the server you wish to look for the existence of the file from the Server drop-down list. Then, type the full pathname and filename of the file that the Event Server will look for to trigger the event. Remember that the filename will be used by the Event Server, not necessarily the computer you are accessing the CMC from. So, if you specify a C: drive, the file will need to reside on the chosen Event Server's C drive in order for the event to be triggered. Click OK to save the event when you're finished.

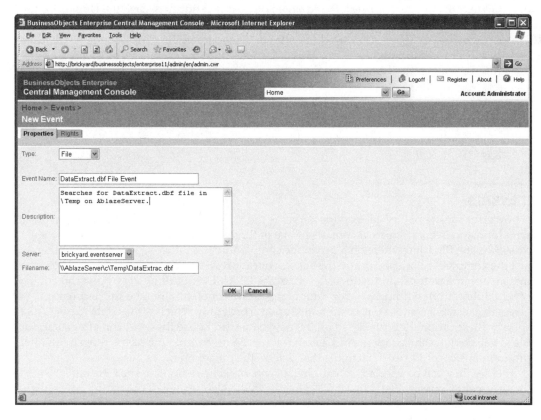

CAUTION *Remember that the Event Server's sole task is to trigger file events. In order for it to do this successfully, the Event Server NT Service must have sufficient rights to read any network file shares that may be specified in a file event. You may need to change the NT account the Event Server uses to something other than the System account for it to properly access network shares. This can be done in the Windows Control Panel's Administrative Tools | Services area, or using the Central Configuration Manager (discussed later in this chapter).*

- **Custom** Specify a descriptive name and optional description for the custom event. No other specifications are necessary. Once you click OK, the event will be saved and the screen will reappear with a Trigger This Event button displayed below the event description. Any time you wish to trigger the custom event, you need merely select the event from the CMC Events link and click the Trigger This Event button.

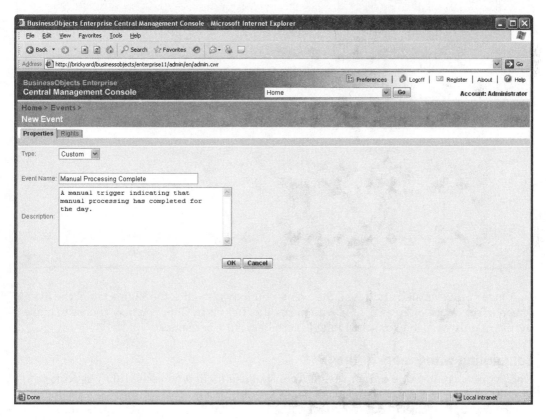

- **Schedule**   Specify a descriptive name and optional description for the schedule event. Then, choose whether the event will be triggered only if the "source" job runs to success, fails, or simply completes in success or failure. Click OK to save the event.

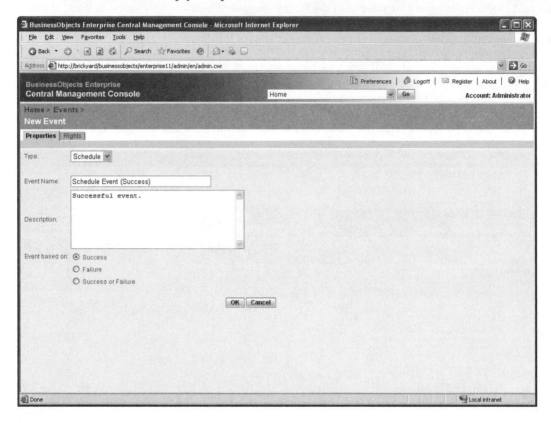

Once you've created and saved the event, you may also click the Rights tab in the Event screen to set rights for the event. As with most other objects in CRS, you may choose to make the event only available for scheduling to certain groups or users.

Scheduling with Events in the CMC

Once you've created one or more events, you can use them when scheduling reports or program objects in the Central Management Console. This is accomplished by selecting the report or program object you wish to schedule with events, and making choices from the Schedule tab after choosing Organize | Objects.

NOTE   *Events can only be used for scheduling from the Central Management Console or a custom web application developed with the development SDK. You cannot schedule with events in InfoView.*

To schedule an object with events, begin by locating the report or program object you wish to schedule according to an event. Click either Folders or Objects from the Organize area of the main CMC screen. If you click Objects, you'll see all objects added to the CMS. If you click Folders, choose the desired folder, which will show only objects contained within that folder. Once you've found the object you wish to schedule, click its name. The object's Properties screen will appear. Click the Schedule tab. The schedule screen will appear, as shown in Figure 24-1.

Begin by choosing some sort of recurring schedule with one of the displayed radio buttons (even choosing Once will suffice—you must choose something other than On Demand). From the Run drop-down list, choose one of the available options that contains the words "With Events" (you won't be able to use any event dependencies without choosing a With Events choice). Once you make this choice, the screen will redraw with Available Events and Available Schedule Events boxes appearing below the Run drop-down list. All defined events that you have rights to will appear in the Available Events list. All schedule events you have rights to will appear in the Available Schedule Events list.

Choose schedule
recurrence

Choose a "with events" option
from drop-down list

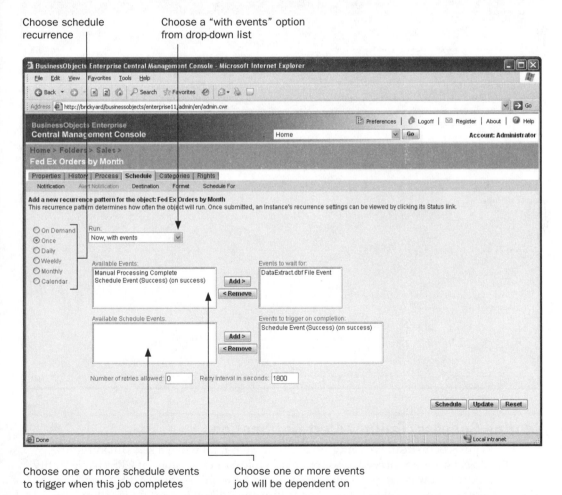

Choose one or more schedule events
to trigger when this job completes

Choose one or more events
job will be dependent on

FIGURE 24-1 Scheduling with events in the CMC

Select one or more events you want this job to be dependent upon in the Available Events list and add them to the Events To Wait For list by clicking the right arrow (*all* events you add to this list must be triggered in order for this job to run). If you want this job to trigger a schedule event (on simple completion, or on specific success or failure, depending on how the schedule event was defined), choose one or more schedule events from the Available Schedule Events list. Then, add them to the Events To Trigger On Completion list by clicking the right arrow.

Once you've made all desired selections, click the Schedule button. The object's History screen will display with the instance you just scheduled appearing at the top (most probably with a Pending or Recurring status). If you want to ensure that the instance is waiting for an event to be triggered, click the status (the words Pending, Recurring, and so forth). The Instance Properties screen will appear, with any pending events noted at the bottom next to the Waiting for Events label.

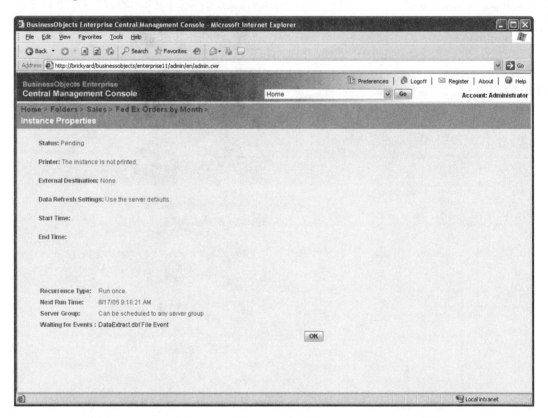

Configuring Success/Failure/Alert Notification

Crystal Reports Server can be configured to send an e-mail when a scheduled report or program object instance succeeds and/or fails. While earlier versions of CRS would notify you if a report alert was triggered (this is covered later in this section), CRS XI will notify of simple report or program object success or failure, in addition to alert notification.

There are one or two prerequisites for notification to work, depending on how you want to be notified of success/failures or report alerts. If you wish to be notified via e-mail, make sure the Crystal Reports Job Server and Program Job Server are properly configured to send e-mail. The Crystal Reports Job Server must have an e-mail server properly configured to send notification of report alert triggers, as well (you can only be notified of report alerts via e-mail—alerts cannot be audited). Information on setting up e-mail procedures can be found earlier in this chapter, under "Defining Output Destinations."

Success/Failure Notification

You may control success/failure notification at the object level from within the Central Management Console. Once you've determined how you want to be notified, any instances for the configured object that succeed or fail may be noted via e-mail.

NOTE *Although Audit Notification is available in an object's Notification tab, auditing is not available with Crystal Reports Server. Auditing is only available with BusinessObjects Enterprise licenses.*

Begin by navigating to the object you want to set notification information for. You may begin by clicking either Objects or Folders in the Organize area of the main CMC screen (depending on whether you want to start from a list of all objects in the system, or just objects in a specific folder). Once you've found the object you wish to set up notification for, click it. The Properties tab will appear. Click the Schedule tab to display scheduling options for the object. Look carefully just below the tabs for the Notification link (it's somewhat hard to see). Click it. The Set Notification screen will appear.

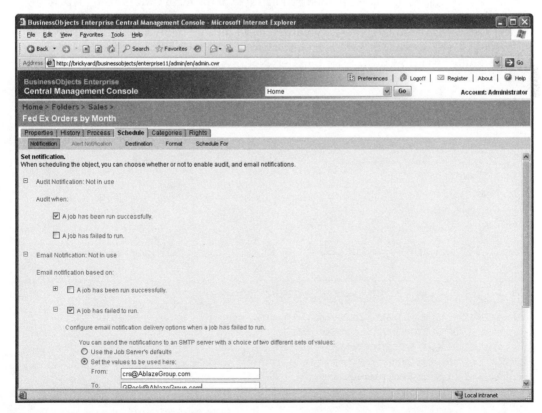

If no previous notification settings have been made for the object, both e-mail and audit notification will indicate "not in use." Click the plus signs next to Email Notification to enable it. You may then select to notify on success and/or failure.

Notifying via e-mail requires specifying more detailed e-mail information, such as from address, to address, e-mail subject, and message body. You may choose to use default settings for these values you set up when configuring the e-mail destination on the server, or specify settings individually here.

Once you've made desired settings, click Update to save the notification information. When you schedule the object in the future (either from the CMC or InfoView), notification will be enabled. For example, a failed job may result in an e-mail being sent.

Alert Notification

If you have designed reports that contain alerts, Crystal Reports Server can send e-mail notification any time a scheduled report triggers the alert (creating reports with alerts is discussed in detail in Chapter 7). For example, if you've built a report that triggers an alert if a customer service representative's open call numbers exceed a predetermined level, you may notify the Customer Service Manager of the alert when the report runs on its regular schedule. Furthermore, you can place a hyperlink in the e-mail that, when clicked, will display the alerting report with just the records that triggered the alert.

Alert notification is set at the object level in the Central Management Console. Begin by navigating to the object you want to set alert notification information for. You may begin by clicking either Objects or Folders in the Organize area of the main CMC screen (depending on whether you want to start from a list of all objects in the system, or just objects in a specific folder). Once you've found the object you wish to set up alert notification for, click it. The Properties tab will appear. Click the Schedule tab to display scheduling options for the object. Look carefully just below the tabs for the Alert Notification link (it's somewhat hard to see). Click it. The Set Alert Notification screen will appear.

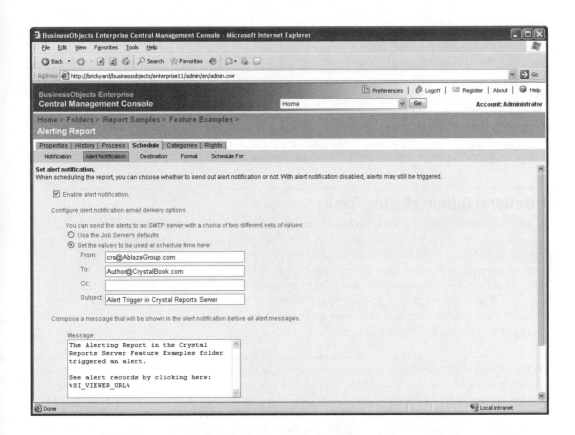

CAUTION *You will only be able to configure alert notification for reports that contain report alerts. If the report does not contain alerts, the Alert Notification link will be disabled. Chapter 7 contains information on how to create alerts when designing a report.*

Check Enable Alert Notification. Then, specify detailed e-mail information, such as from address, to address, e-mail subject, and message body. You may choose to use default settings for these values you set up when configuring the e-mail destination on the server, or specify settings individually here. You may also designate a URL to include in the e-mail that will direct the recipient directly to the report that triggered the alerts, showing only the record in the report that triggered the alert. Typically, you'll want to click the Use Default button to add a mnemonic to the URL that will resolve to the default location from the CMS for the alert report.

Once you've made desired settings, click Update to save the alert notification information. When you schedule the object in the future (either from the CMC or InfoView), an e-mail will be sent if the report triggers alerts.

TIP *You must set up the default viewer URL (typically, you'll at least need to specify your web server name) for the Use Default button to work properly when adding a URL to an alert e-mail. Set the default URL by clicking Objects from the Organize area of the main CMC screen. Then, click the Object Defaults button in the upper right-hand corner.*

Other General Administrative Tasks

In addition to steps discussed previously in this chapter, other administrative tasks of a general nature will probably be required. For example, you may need to add additional license keys to the CMS to allow additional users or features to be enabled. You may choose to view metrics indicating how many users are currently logged on to the CMS. You may need to set limits on the number of report or program object instances that are retained by the CMS. Or, you may desire to change some default behavior of InfoView, which is the primary user interface for non-administrative users who view and schedule reports (InfoView is covered in detail in Chapter 23).

NOTE *As a Crystal Reports Server Administrator, you may also be responsible for maintaining the repository or Business Views. While both of these features are also maintained in the Central Management Server database, they are not administered with the Central Management Console. Instead, you must use the Business View Manager Windows application. Business Views are discussed in detail in Chapter 16. Using the Business View Manager to work with the repository is discussed in detail in Chapter 17.*

Adding Additional Licenses

When you first install Crystal Reports Server, you are prompted to supply a single keycode by the CRS Setup. That keycode will provide the initial set of licensing options available to you. However, should you ever buy additional licenses (to add more concurrent users), you will merely need to supply replacement or additional keycodes—no reinstallation will be required.

You specify additional keycodes in the Central Management Console. Click License Keys from the Manage area of the main CMC screen. The License Keys screen will appear.

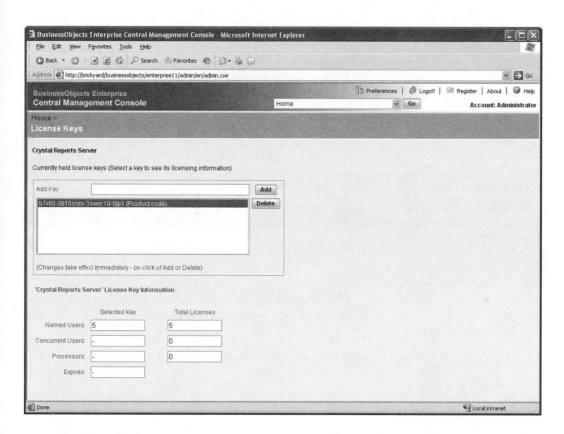

The initial keycode you used when you installed Crystal Reports Server will appear here. You may click the existing keycode in the list to display the type of keycode and number of licenses it provides in the Selected Key column below. To delete a keycode, select the existing keycode and click Delete. To add a replacement or additional keycode, type it in the Add Key box (include the dashes) and click Add.

CAUTION   *In some instances, you may need to replace an initially specified keycode with another keycode (when upgrading from a trial to fully functional version, for example). In this situation, you will need to remove the first keycode before adding the replacement keycode. Otherwise, you may receive an error that you are attempting to add a conflicting keycode.*

Viewing Server Metrics

Various server metrics and settings are available from various screens in the Central Management Console. You may, for example, determine the version of Crystal Reports Server installed, as well as see indications of service packs of version dates. You may also see how many users are currently logged on to the system, what license complements are currently being used, and so forth.

The first set of metrics you may want to view are current license usage and processing job status (successful instance count, failed instance count, and so forth). Click Settings from the Manage area of the main CMC page. The Properties tab will appear, showing version information for the current CMS you are logged on to. Click the Metrics tab to see license usage and processing job information.

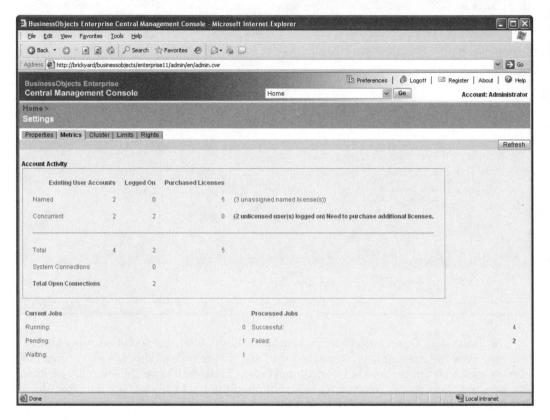

While this screen indicates the number of licenses in use, it doesn't indicate which accounts are using them. This information might be helpful, for example, if you need to track down who is using excessive licenses or you need to request users to log off so that you can perform some system maintenance. Individual user information is available from another screen specific to the CMS.

To see this metric, and similar metrics for other servers, click Servers from the Organize area of the main CMC screen. A list of all configured servers will appear. Click the desired server to further examine details (for example, click the CMS to see current users). The Properties screen for the particular server you chose will appear. Information on the Properties screen will vary with the server you chose (for example, the CMS Properties screen will show currently logged-on users).

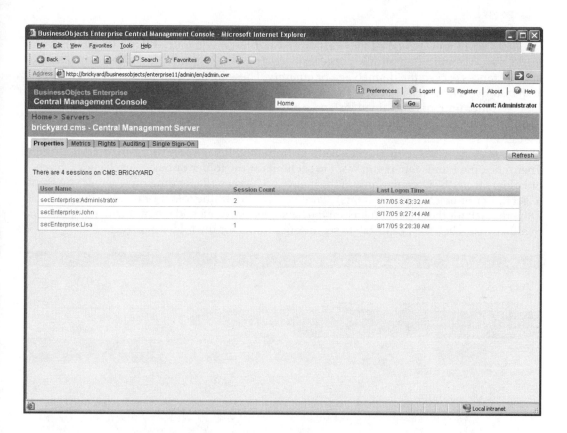

Each server screen also has a Metrics tab. Click it to see various metrics, such as server software version, number of open files, and so forth, particular to that server.

NOTE *Specific information on various options exposed by server Properties tabs can be found in the online Administrator's Guide.*

Setting Instance Limits

As you might imagine, an even moderately "busy" Crystal Reports Server system can use up disk resources rapidly if many reports and program objects are being scheduled on a frequent basis. If you recall architecture discussions earlier in the chapter, you remember that the Output File Repository Server is charged with keeping all report instances that have been scheduled, as well as the text output from all scheduled program object instances. If reports and program objects are scheduled on a frequent basis, the number of instance files can grow rapidly, as can usage of Output FRS disk space. Furthermore, a report object may not be particularly useful if hundreds of saved instances appear in the History list when a user views it.

The CMS includes the capability to automatically purge report and program object instances when they exceed either a certain age or a certain quantity. Once these settings are made, the CMS will automatically purge instances from the Output FRS and its own database once instances exceed the defined age or quantity. These instance limits can be set globally at the CMS level, as well as at both the folder and object levels. For example, you may choose to set a folder limit of 25 retained instances but allow a certain report that runs every hour to retain 50 instances. Furthermore, these settings can be specified for individual users and user groups.

To set global CMS settings, click Settings from the Manage area of the main CMC screen. Then, click the Limits tab. If you want to set limits at the folder or object level, click Objects or Folders from the Organize area of the main CMC screen (depending on whether you want to set folder or object instance limits). Once you've chosen the folder or object, you'll see the Properties tab for the object or folder (or the Subfolders tab for a folder that contains subfolders). In either case, click the Limits tab to set instance limits for the folder or object.

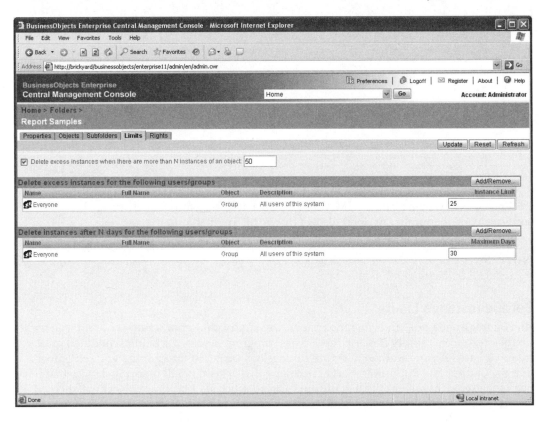

The overall number of instances retained for a folder or object can be set by checking the Delete Excess Instances check box and typing in the number of instances to retain in the text box that follows. If you do nothing else, this will set an instance limit for all objects in the folder. You may either leave this unchecked and specify individual quantity and age limits by user or group, or set a global instance limit and specify more restrictive limits by user and group.

To specify either a quantity or an age limit by user or group, click the Add/Remove button next to the Delete Excess Instances section (to limit by quantity) or the Delete Instances after N Days section (to limit by age). A list of groups will appear. Choose one or more groups that you want to set limits for and click the right-arrow button to add the groups to the chosen list. If you want to set limits for individual users, choose Add Users from the top drop-down list. You can then either pick one or more users directly or use the Find feature to locate a specific user.

Once you've finished choosing users and/or groups, click OK. The Limits tab will reappear with the groups and users you chose now appearing. Set the instance quantity or time limits by typing numbers in the appropriate Instance Limit or Maximum Days text boxes. When finished, click Update in the upper right-hand corner to save your settings.

NOTE *An instance will be deleted if it meets any one of the criteria. So, for example, if you set an overall instance limit of 50, an instance limit for the Administrators group of 25, and a 10-day limit for the Everyone group, any instance over 10 days will be deleted, regardless of who owns it and how many instances there are overall. Administrator-owned instances will be deleted if they exceed a total of 25, and all other users will see their instances deleted if they exceed 50. Also, if you set instance limits at the object level, they will take precedence.*

Specifying Default InfoView Settings

The out-of-the-box user interface for Crystal Reports Server, InfoView, contains a default look and feel when initially installed (InfoView is covered in Chapter 23). While each user can customize their InfoView appearance, you may want to control some more specific InfoView items, such as whether or not to show the Business Objects logo, what custom colors to use for headers, and so forth.

To customize InfoView, click Crystal Applications from the Manage area of the main CMC page. InfoView is among the application options that will appear. Click the InfoView item to customize various options. Choose from the available choices for appearance and behavior. When finished, click Update to save the changes.

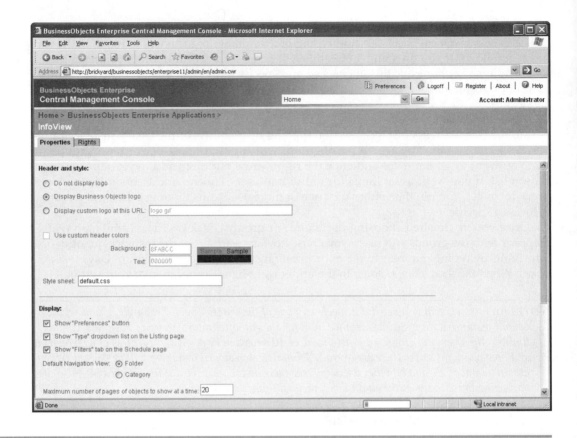

Managing Servers

Part of your administrative duties will include managing the various server components that make up your Crystal Reports Server system (look earlier in the chapter, under "Crystal Reports Server Architecture," for a complete overview of all CRS server components). Management tasks may merely mean making sure all servers are running after you reboot the CRS computer. Or, you may need to migrate the CMS database to a different database server. As your needs grow, you may decide to add multiple CRS servers to improve performance. These all fall under the realm of server management.

While a small amount of attention has been paid to other management tools so far, the majority of CRS administration has been undertaken with the Central Management Console, or CMC. However, another management tool (discussed just briefly so far) is the Central Configuration Manager, or CCM (and, yes, the two acronyms are often confused). Some operations may be performed with either tool, while others require one or the other. In general, the CCM is required to perform configuration that requires the CRS system to be offline, or stopped, while the CMC can be used while the system is up and running. For example, configuring the CMS data source must be done in the CCM with the system offline, while setting the Crystal Reports Page Server processing parameters can be done in the CMC with the system running.

Every server in the CRS system displays management screens in both tools. So, you'll probably find yourself alternatively working with the CMC in some cases, and the CCM in others. Also, while various servers will require various levels of attention as you administer your CRS system, you'll probably find yourself spending more time with the CMS than other servers.

Enabling Servers

There are two parts to making sure a CRS server is fully up and running: 1) make sure the service is running, and 2) make sure the server is enabled. Unfortunately, the CCM "hides" the second part of this equation, so it is easy to forget to make sure that all CRS servers are enabled. This is especially true upon installation, as the CRS servers are *not* enabled by default. The issue is further complicated because the same icon is used in two different places to denote "running" and "enabled."

Make Sure the Service Is Running

The icons in the left-hand column of the CCM show whether the particular server's service is running. A green up arrow means that the service is running; a red down arrow means that it is not running. To start a server, select that server and click the Start button in the toolbar, or right-click and select Start from the context menu. (You may CTRL-click or SHIFT-click to choose multiple servers.)

Make Sure the Server Is Enabled

Click the Enable/Disable Servers button in the toolbar. You will be asked to log on before configuring the servers. Once logged on, you will be presented with a new dialog box listing the CRS servers, each with an icon representing its enabled/disabled status. A green up arrow means the server is enabled; a red circle with a dash means that it is disabled. To enable a server, put a check in that server's check box. To disable a server, clear the check. Or, you may use the Enable All or Disable All buttons at the bottom of the dialog box.

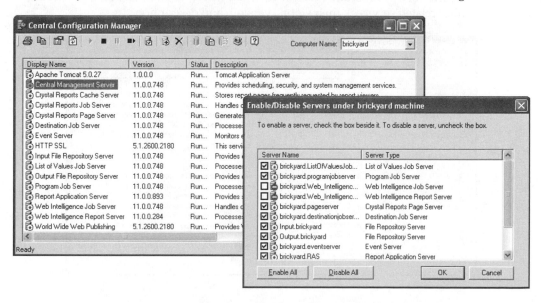

NOTE *You may also enable and disable servers from within the Central Management Console.*

Managing the CMS

The Central Management Server (CMS) is the heart of the Crystal Reports Server system. The CMS authenticates users upon logon, controls security, manages all user requests, handles scheduling, and coordinates the viewing of reports. To do all this, the CMS becomes the center of all communications between the various servers in the CRS system. Each server must register with the CMS so that they can "talk" to perform all of their necessary functions.

To handle all of these tasks, the CMS must keep track of a variety of data, and it does so via a proprietary internal database. The database is stored in Microsoft Data Engine (MSDE) format by default, but it may be stored in SQL Server, Oracle, Sybase, or DB2/UDB. The type of database to use may be chosen at installation, or the database may be migrated to a different platform at a later time (as is discussed later in this section).

Obviously, the configuration of the CMS is of the utmost importance. That configuration is handled by the Central Configuration Manager (CCM) and not the Central Management Console. While other servers may be configured using the CMC from within CRS, the CMS cannot—stopping the CMS to change configuration parameters would stop the CRS system entirely, including the CMC.

CCM Settings for the CMS

The Central Configuration Manager (CCM) is a stand-alone Windows application installed on the physical CMS computer. Most of the CMS configuration is done with this program outside of the CRS environment, since the CMS itself is required to run that environment. The CCM may be used to migrate the CMS database to a new database format or alter several technical configuration parameters such as the port number, SOCKS firewall settings, and account logon information.

The CCM is available from the BusinessObjects 11/Crystal Reports Server program group on the physical CMS computer. When you initially start it, it shows all CRS services (as well as other related services), their status, version, and description.

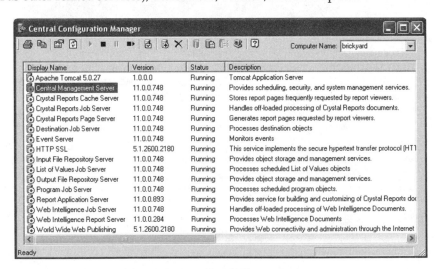

While you may view all CMS settings from the CCM while the CMS is running, you must stop it before changing any settings. Before you do this, ensure that all CRS users are aware that the system will be brought down—you may wish to view CMS properties from the CMC to see which users are still logged on to the CMS. Once you are sure that you may safely stop the CMS, select the Central Management Server in the CCM and click the Stop button in the toolbar.

With the CMS still selected, click the Properties button in the toolbar, or right-click the CMS and select Properties from the context menu. The resulting dialog box exposes five tabs: Properties, Dependency, Connection, Configuration, and Protocol.

The Properties tab contains general information about the CMS, including the server type, display name, server name, command, and startup type. One possibility is to alter command-line parameters at the end of the CMS startup command (details on available command-line parameters are provided in the online Administrator's Guide). By default, the CMS is assigned the NT System account and is set to automatically start when the CMS computer boots.

The Dependency tab contains a list of the services that the CMS is dependent upon. The dependency relationship indicates that the services listed here must be running in order for the CMS to run. These services will vary depending on the type of database system that is used for the CMS database. You may add and/or remove services from the dependency list, but it is highly unlikely that you will ever need to do so.

The Connection tab allows configuration of SOCKS servers. A SOCKS server may be used to allow communication between the web server and the CMS in architectures that involve a firewall. For more information on configuring SOCKS servers, see the Administrator's Guide.

The Configuration tab contains some very important parameters. First, the Port Number may be changed, if necessary, to work with firewalls between the CMS and other CRS servers. Be sure to work closely with the network administrator if you change this number. Second, the CMS Datasource may be changed should you desire to migrate the CMS database to another server, or cluster this CMS with other CMSs (database migration and CMS clustering are discussed later in this chapter).

The Protocol tab allows configuration of the Secure Socket Layer (SSL) for all network communication in the CRS environment. For more information on configuring the SSL, see the Administrator's Guide.

Migrating the System Database to a New Server

When you initially install the Crystal Reports Server CMS, the Microsoft Data Engine (MSDE) is installed to host the CMS database (the exception to this rule is if Microsoft SQL Server is detected in the CMS computer—in that case, SQL Server is used and MSDE is not installed). While MSDE (a "lite" version of SQL Server) is often perfectly acceptable for stand-alone, simple CRS installations, many system architects make the decision to migrate the database to another database system for improved performance, ease of maintenance, backup simplicity, staff knowledge, or other reasons.

NOTE *The following procedure assumes that you are copying an existing CRS XI CMS database to a new, fresh database in another database system. Upgrading from a previous version of CRS involves a different process that is detailed later in this chapter.*

As with most operations of this magnitude, the initial step in the process is to back up the current environment. First, back up the current CMS database just in case you need to restore it later. By default, MSDE installs the CMS database in .MDF and .LDF files in C:\Program Files\Business Objects\BusinessObjects Enterprise 11\ODBCSupt. Then, back up the entire Input and Output File Repository Server directory structures. By default, these are located in C:\Program Files\Business Objects\BusinessObjects Enterprise 11\FileStore.

The next step is to prepare the new destination database. First, define a new database in the destination database system. Do not create any new tables, as this will be done automatically by CRS when the CMS database is migrated. Ensure a database user ID and password combination exists that allows Create, Update, and Delete privileges. Then, create an ODBC data source for the new database on the CMS machine (note that certain databases, such as Oracle and DB/2, can be accessed via native drivers and don't require an ODBC connection). Finally, be sure that you can connect using the appropriate account and data source from the CMS machine.

Then, open the CCM and follow these steps:

1. Select the CMS and stop the CMS server.

2. With the CMS still selected, click the Specify CMS Data Source button in the toolbar. You can also select the Configuration tab in the Central Management Server Properties dialog box and click the Specify button in the CMS Data Source category. The CMS Database Setup dialog box will appear.

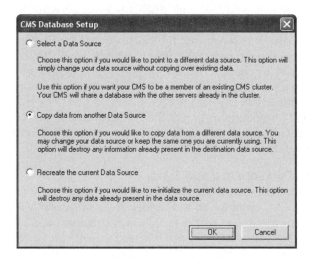

3. Select Copy Data From Another Data Source and click OK. The Specify Data Source dialog box will appear.

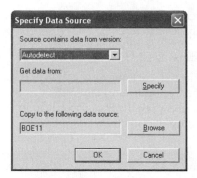

4. Select either Autodetect or BusinessObjects Enterprise XI from the Source Contains Data From Version drop-down list.

5. Click the Specify button next to the Get Data From text box and specify your current data source (you may need to choose the database your current CMS data source uses before you pick the actual data source). You may need to enter logon information to complete this step.

6. Click the Browse button next to Copy To The Following Data Source to specify your new destination data source. You will be given a choice of database connection methods, and then given the choice of a new data source name. Again, you may need to enter logon information to complete this step.

7. Click OK, and then click Yes for the confirmation.

8. When the migration is complete, click OK.

After migration, it is best to check for a migration log file to see if any errors or other messages were written. If you installed CRS to the default directories, you will find the log file in C:\Program Files\Business Objects\BusinessObjects Enterprise 11\Logging.

Next use the CCM to start and enable the CMS server. Log on to the CRS system via the CMC. In the License Keys section, check to make sure all of the CRS license keys were transferred properly. Then, if necessary, return to the CCM to start and enable all of the other CRS servers. Because the CRS file system has not changed locations, all server configurations should remain as they were before migration.

At this point, the CRS system should be fully migrated to the new database system. Test the system in a variety of ways to be sure that everything is functioning properly. For example, view a report, view an instance of a different report, and schedule yet another report to be run in the near future.

Upgrading from an Older Crystal Enterprise System

Often a new Crystal Reports Server installation will be an update to an older version, and therefore the original data needs to be copied to the new database. This process is similar to migrating the database to a new database server, but in this case the desired data is being copied out of an original database and into the current database.

As always, the initial step in the process is to back up the database, which in this case is the original database. Then, back up the entire directory structure, starting with the root directories of the Input and Output File Repositories.

Once you've properly backed up your existing database, perform the following steps to migrate to a newer CRS database structure:

1. Select the CMS and stop the CMS server.

2. With the CMS still selected, click the Specify CMS Data Source button in the toolbar. You can also select the Configuration tab in the Central Management Server Properties dialog box and click the Specify button in the CMS Data Source category. The CMS Database Setup dialog box will appear.

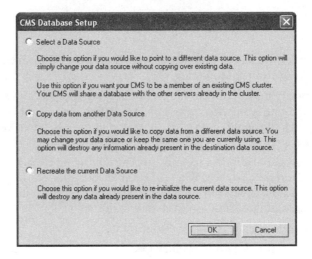

3. Select Copy Data From Another Data Source and click OK. The Specify Data Source dialog box will appear.

4. Select the appropriate version of Crystal Enterprise from the Source Contains Data From Version drop-down list.

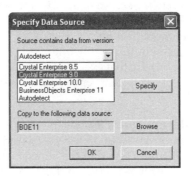

5. Click the Specify button next to Get Data From and specify the original data source (you may need to choose the database your current CMS data source uses before you pick the actual data source). You may need to enter logon information to complete this step.

6. Click the Browse button next to Copy To The Following Data Source to specify the new destination data source. You will be given a choice of database connection methods, and then given the choice of a new dataset name. Again, you may need to enter logon information to complete this step.

7. Click OK, and then click Yes for the confirmation.

8. When the migration is complete, click OK.

After migration, it is best to check for a migration log file to see if any errors or other messages were written. If you installed CRS to the default directories, you will find the log file in C:\Program Files\Business Objects\ BusinessObjects Enterprise 11\Logging.

At this point, there is a new wrinkle: you must make sure the Input and Output File Repository Servers recognize the original file structures. There are two options to accomplish this:

- Copy the complete directory structures from the original file repository locations to the current destination file repository locations.

- Configure the current Input and Output File Repositories so that their root directory locations point to the original root directories. You may do this by making choices in the Central Management Console Servers area for the Input and Output File Repository Servers.

Then, as before, use the CCM to start and enable the CMS server. Log on to the CRS system and open up the CMC. In the License Keys section, check to make sure all of the CRS license keys were transferred properly. If necessary, use the CCM to start and enable the File Repository Servers.

Because the data being imported is from an earlier version of Crystal Enterprise, the Crystal Report Server objects themselves must be updated to conform to the current CRS XI object specifications. Return to the CCM and ensure that the CMS has been restarted. Click the Update Objects button in the toolbar. You will need to log on to the CMS. The CMS will search its database for any objects that require updating. If it finds them, an Update button will be presented to start the process of updating any necessary reports and instances to the CRS XI format. Click the button to perform the update.

If necessary, start any additional services that may not be running. At this point, the original Crystal Enterprise data should be fully migrated to the current database system. Test the system in a variety of ways to be sure that everything is functioning properly. For example, view a report, view an instance of a different report, and schedule yet another report to be run in the near future.

TIP The Import Wizard (discussed in the following section) can also be used to migrate an older Crystal Enterprise database and file structure to a new Crystal Reports Server system.

Upgrading from Crystal/Seagate Info

Crystal/Seagate Info version 7.5 is the precursor to Crystal Enterprise and Crystal Reports Server. While Info had many similar features and functions, the current architecture has changed significantly since its Info-based beginnings. Because of this fact, existing Info databases cannot simply be migrated to the CRS environment as discussed previously. Instead, CRS provides a stand-alone Windows application called the Import Wizard to handle the task.

Because of the fundamental differences between Info and Crystal Reports Server architecture, there are several considerations to keep in mind when running the Import Wizard. For example, while users and groups will typically be imported from Info to CRS, some reports (those based on Info Views, for example) will be handled specially. And, while some instances that are scheduled in Info will be imported into CRS, others based on scheduling concepts not supported by CRS (such as Business Calendars) won't be imported. When the Import Wizard encounters duplicate users, groups, folders, and reports, various things may happen (typically, they're imported with a sequential number added to them).

NOTE *Specific details on how various Info objects are imported with the Import Wizard can be found in the online Administrator's Guide. Look in the index for Importing | From Info.*

The wizard consists of two main processes: specifying the source and target environments, and specifying the objects to be imported. First, make sure you have administrator privileges for both the source and destination environments. Then, as with most wizards, simply proceed through the series of dialogs.

1. Start the Import Wizard from the BusinessObjects 11/Crystal Reports Server program group. Click Next to get through the intro screen.

2. Specify the source environment, including the version, the Info APS name, and the logon credentials.

3. Specify the destination environment, including the CMS name and the logon credentials.

4. Using the check boxes, choose the objects to import. For Info, you'll be given the choices Import Users and Groups; and Import Folders and Objects.

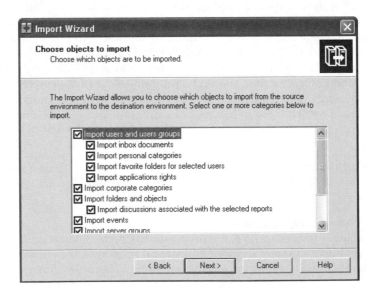

5. You may be given a warning that importing objects with rights requires that users/ groups associated with those also be imported. Click Next.

6. If you chose to import users and groups, choose which users and groups to import with the appropriate check boxes. You may use the Select All and Clear All buttons to select groups and users en masse.

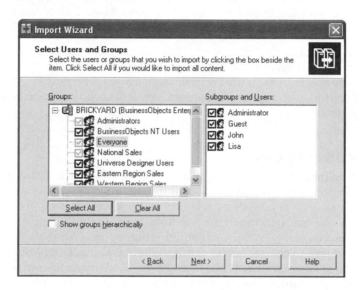

7. If you chose to import folders and objects, choose which folders and objects to import with the appropriate check boxes. You may expand and contract folders with the plus/minus signs. You may also use the Select All and Clear All buttons to select reports and folders en masse. To import existing instances (both complete and recurring), check the Import All Instances check box.

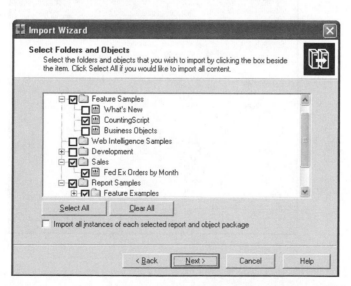

8. When the Information Collection Complete dialog box appears, click Finish to begin the import.

When the import is complete, simply click Done to complete the process. If errors were noted, click View Detail Log to see the log file. The log is also written to the hard drive in a file consisting of "ImportWiz," followed by the date of the import. By default, this file is located in Program Files\Business Objects\BusinessObjects Enterprise 11\Logging.

Check the integrity of your CRS system, comparing to your Crystal/Seagate Info system.

NOTE *If you use the Import Wizard to import into CRS XI something other than an existing Seagate Info system (perhaps you are importing a Crystal Enterprise 9 system or another "test" CRS XI system), you may see additional prompts and slightly different behavior than in the previous example.*

Managing Other Servers

Besides the maintenance and configuration tasks for the CMS that were covered in the preceding section of this chapter, you'll probably find a need at one time or another to perform maintenance or adjustments to other CRS servers as well. As with the CMS, all other CRS servers can be found in the Windows-based Central Configuration Manager. As with the CMS, you can view various configuration options for the servers while they are running. However, to change server configuration, you must stop the server in the CCM and then change its properties. While many of the CMS properties are set in the CCM, most other servers have minimal settings that can be changed in the CCM (the command-line switches used when starting the server being a notable exception).

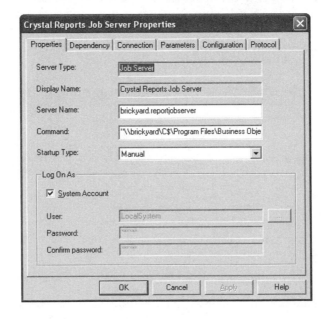

In the CCM, all the servers' Properties dialogs are very similar. For each server, you can set the server name, startup command, and startup type. You can change the NT account that the service uses when the computer boots. You can set dependencies with other NT services, as well as configuring SOCKS server and SSL information when dealing with firewalls and secure network communication. In a few cases, there are additional options relevant to the particular server. In most cases, you will not need to adjust any of these parameters in the CCM.

Another major use of the CCM is adding and deleting additional servers or additional server instances. As a CRS system grows to accommodate more users, more report processing, more viewing, and so forth, the system may be scaled in some ways to adequately handle the load, especially on multiple-processor machines. For example, if there is an increasing need to provide more scheduled report execution, the system may need more Crystal Reports Job Servers to perform the report processing. These new Job Servers may be added, using the CCM, as additional Job Server instances on the same machine.

Unlike the CMS, the other CRS servers also have various properties that appear in the web-based Central Management Console. Begin to work with servers by clicking Servers in the Organize area of the main CMC screen. You may enable or disable one or more servers in the CMC (perhaps you have multiple servers of each type and you wish to limit processing to just one of them for a particular reason). You may also select individual servers and view and change various configuration options on the Properties tab.

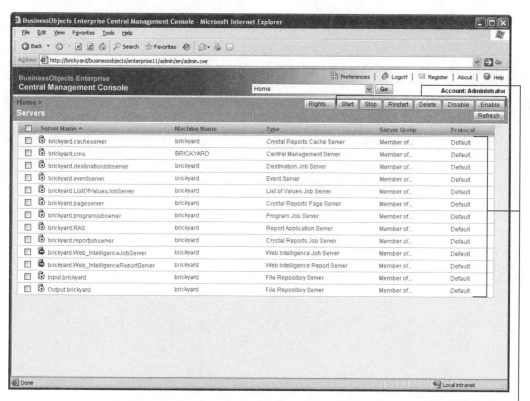

Select servers and use toolbar buttons to start, stop, disable, or enable various servers

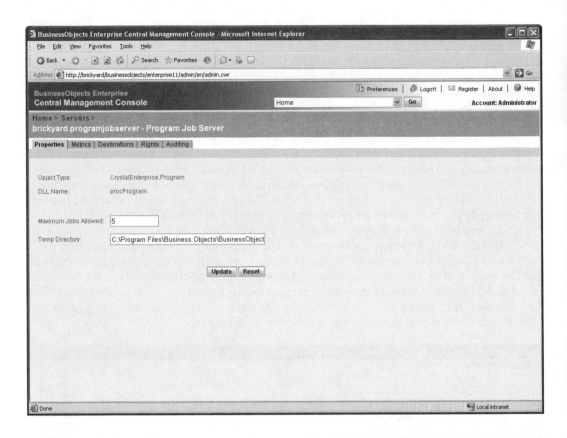

NOTE *Specific details of both CCM and CMC server properties can be found in the online Administrator's Guide. Consult this guide for specific information on the various options available. As the default settings for many of these properties are often adequate, make note of the previous setting before making a significant change. Should your change reduce performance or cause a server to fail, you'll be able to restore the previous setting.*

Server Groups

This feature is available in the Crystal Reports Server system but is really geared for use in full versions of BusinessObjects Enterprise. Server Groups gives administrators a way to group various servers and then use those groups to more efficiently process reports. Due to the single-machine limitation of the CRS license, this is of little use within Crystal Reports Server.

Universes and Universe Connections

Universes (along with Universe Connections) are the metadata layers originally created for use in classic Business Objects products such as Web Intelligence (the report designer). They have been adapted for use with Crystal Reports XI documents as well. Universes are stored in the repository, and are therefore stored in the CRS system database.

Universes may not be added from within the CMC, but administrators can set security rights (similar to other CRS items) and object-level security (particular to Universe development).

PART

Custom Web and Windows Reporting Applications

Integrating Crystal Reports with ASP and Visual Basic

If you've read even a bit of Part I of this book, you've seen some of the power and flexibility of Crystal Reports. By making the vast array of corporate databases accessible with its simple, straightforward user interface, Crystal Reports has established itself as a valuable tool simply by virtue of its reporting and querying capabilities. Part II explored Crystal Reports Server as a method for web-based report scheduling, viewing, and distribution without custom programming requirements. But there's a whole other side of Crystal Reports that has yet to be explored.

Because database reporting and querying is a large part of many standard business applications, you'll often need to include these features in custom applications that you create for your own use. If you develop custom applications for Microsoft Windows in any of the popular Windows development tools, you'll probably soon need some type of database reporting functionality inside the application. And, with the Web becoming an even more popular method for developing custom applications, you may find Crystal Reports capabilities valuable for your web-based business applications as well. While you can develop your own routines to step through the database record by record to generate your own internal reporting mechanism, all the intricacies of formatting, font management, graphics, and other web- and Windows-related printing issues can create a significant, if not impossible, coding challenge.

There are several available options for including Crystal Reports capability in your custom web and Windows applications. Microsoft's Visual Studio .NET editions actually bundle a basic version of Crystal Reports as the reporting tool of choice. By using Crystal Reports XI Developer Edition, you can add to the capabilities provided by the bundled version (developing custom Crystal/Visual Studio .NET applications is covered in Chapter 26). If you are developing Java-based J2EE web applications, Crystal Reports XI includes the Java Reporting Component (not covered in this book). And, if you are using tried and true Component Object Model (COM)–based Active Server Pages (ASP) and Visual Basic development tools, Crystal Reports XI Developer Edition includes an updated version of the Report Designer Component (RDC). This chapter covers using the RDC for your ASP web and Visual Basic Windows custom applications.

Version XI still provides flexibility when it comes to distributing your custom Windows applications as well. While you are not allowed to redistribute the Crystal Reports design components (such as the Crystal Reports design program itself), your custom Windows programs that merely manipulate and customize existing reports can be distributed without charge. You receive a royalty-free license to distribute the Crystal Report Designer Component and associated files, such as associated database and exporting .DLL files. You may purchase a single copy of Crystal Reports XI Developer Edition, develop your custom Windows application, and distribute the run-time files with as many copies of your application as you like, at no additional charge. If you elect to use newer report creation functions or the embedded Report Designer control that is included in version XI Developer Edition, you may redistribute your application as long as each organization you distribute to purchases their own copy of Developer Edition.

RDC-based web applications vary slightly from their Windows counterparts when it comes to distribution requirements. While web applications that you create for use within your own organization have no usage limits or royalty requirements, web-based applications that you distribute outside your organization do require you to purchase a copy of Crystal Reports XI Developer Edition for each additional organization beyond your own that you distribute your application to.

NOTE *Don't forget that Crystal Reports XI is available in three different editions (not including Crystal Reports Server). The Developer Edition will be of interest to you if you plan on using any Windows development features for web or Windows applications. To use any of the developer interfaces discussed in this section of the book, you need to purchase the Developer Edition—the other editions don't provide necessary components for custom Windows integration.*

TIP *Crystal Reports XI's RDC (actually referred to as "Version 11" in object declarations and some documentation) contains a moderate set of upgrades mirroring some new features in the Crystal Reports XI designer and file format. Some new features are of limited benefit. For example, the Table object now exposes an additional Qualifiers collection to retrieve the fully qualified table name. Other new RDC features take advantage of major XI changes. For example, the RDC supports dynamic and cascading prompts that you may have created as part of your new XI reports with the full Crystal Reports XI designer (you cannot create these new prompts in the embedded Visual Basic designer, however). And, XI's new formula-based run-time image locations are exposed in the Visual Basic report designer (but aren't exposed in the object model for run-time modification within code). Look at the section "What's New in the Report Designer Component" of Developer's Help for complete descriptions of version 11 changes.*

Developing ASP Web Applications with the RDC

The "legacy" choice for Active Server Page (ASP) integration of Crystal Reports in a web application is the RDC. The RDC's Component Object Model (COM)–compliant set of objects expose almost every feature of a report to a COM-compliant development environment such as ASP. While Business Objects has relegated this interface to "legacy" status, the RDC is still a very valid development choice for ASP-based applications, and Business Objects has stated they will continue to support the RDC as long as Microsoft supports the COM

What About RAS/Crystal Enterprise Embedded Edition?

The Report Application Server (RAS) as a method of integrating a Crystal report in an Active Server Page web application was introduced in Crystal Reports 9. It continued as an option in Crystal Reports 10 but was known as Crystal Enterprise Embedded Edition. Its usage as a tool for creating a stand-alone web application with Crystal Reports XI is much more questionable.

It is no longer included as a separate CD in Crystal Reports XI Professional or Developer Edition. However, the promotional copy of Crystal Reports Server XI included with the initial release of these editions does include a .PDF document describing how to install a stand-alone copy of the Report Application Server for integrating web-based reports. Unfortunately, this document is in error—the installation program that it refers to does not exist and the Report Application Server cannot be installed without also installing at least the Crystal Reports Server Central Management Server. Furthermore, a descriptive "white paper" outlining the process of upgrading your Crystal Enterprise 10 Embedded Edition applications to Crystal Reports Server XI, available for download from support. BusinessObjects.com (search for crserver_xi_upgrading_from_ce10_embedded.pdf), describes several restrictions (both technical and license-related) that affect your running XI-based RAS applications in a stand-alone environment separate from a Crystal Reports Server installation.

While questions may be raised about "improving capabilities" versus "increasing license revenue" as Business Objects' reasoning for this change in direction with RAS in version XI, it may be a point of concern for those who have relied on the Report Application Server/CE 10 Embedded Edition for stand-alone web applications in the past. If you feel that these applications may benefit from the additional security, organization, and scheduling capabilities of a complete Crystal Reports Server implementation, or you find other XI features a requirement (and, your budget can withstand the expense of the necessary Crystal Reports Server purchase), then your RAS-based application is well positioned to be migrated to Crystal Reports Server XI. However, if your application relies on a stand-alone reporting object model that does not need the greater security and scheduling capabilities of Crystal Reports Server, then you'll probably want to seriously consider leaving the application in its current state and avoiding an upgrade to XI.

Regardless of the direction you may choose to take with your RAS/CE 10 Embedded-based applications, the movement of the XI Report Application Server to a non-stand-alone method of report integration, requiring more Crystal Reports Server components to operate, moves RAS to the realm of a Crystal Reports Server integration method and not a stand-alone Crystal Reports integration method. As such, it moves beyond the scope of this book and is not covered.

PART III

interface (along with several documents that still urge developers to move to .NET or Crystal Reports Server/BusinessObjects Enterprise environments).

As the RDC is a COM-based interface, its primary focus lies with web-based applications utilizing Active Server Pages (ASP) on a Microsoft web server. This technology, which is the predecessor to the current state-of-the-art ASP.NET web environment, can be coded using either VBScript or JavaScript server-side development languages. This chapter concentrates on the Visual Basic, or VBScript, approach.

Active Server Pages and VBScript Overview

The original language of the Web, Hypertext Markup Language (HTML), can be used to create attractive, hyperlinked pages with graphics, various font sizes, and (with the advent of newer HTML extensions, such as dynamic HTML) more interactivity and multimedia features. However, being a "markup language" instead of a true procedural or event-driven development language, HTML falls far short of providing all the flexibility you may need to create full web-based custom applications. To help fill this void, the industry has adopted *scripting* languages that allow browsers to perform much more sophisticated and intricate procedures. Two scripting languages are established: *JavaScript* is a scripting language based on Java, and *VBScript* is a scripting language based on Microsoft's Visual Basic for Applications (VBA). JavaScript is supported by major browser releases, such as Microsoft Internet Explorer (IE), Netscape Navigator, and Firefox. VBScript, generally, is limited to versions of Microsoft IE.

JavaScript and VBScript are *client-side* scripting languages—both being interpreted by the browser after being downloaded in a web page. The scripts are not compiled into machine-executable code and generally cannot make database connections to a corporate database. And because these scripts execute on a browser that can be affected by any number of client-side variables, a developer cannot always expect consistent results.

To provide more flexibility and offer connectivity to corporate databases, Microsoft also implements *server-side* scripting on its Internet Information Server for Windows 2000, Windows XP Professional, and Windows Server 2003. In this instance, the scripting language is interpreted by the web server instead of the web browser client. The results of the server-executed script are then sent to the web browser as HTML. Because the script is executed on the server, you can create much more robust and flexible applications that are browser-independent—all that is sent to the browser is HTML. Microsoft's implementation of server-side scripting is called *Active Server Pages (ASP)*. When a web server has ASP support installed, pages scripted with ASP are given a file extension of .ASP instead of .HTM. The web server will then scan the .ASP file for server-side scripts and execute any it finds, sending the results of the script to the browser.

To enhance ASP even more, Microsoft extends the Component Object Model (COM), which is discussed in more detail in the Visual Basic portion of this chapter, to its web server platform. Because of this, the RDC can be integrated with server-side scripts to create extensive reporting flexibility in web applications. By using the full VBA power of ASP, combined with the ability of the RDC COM object models to control almost every aspect of a report at run time, you can create VB-like applications that integrate reports in a web browser.

NOTE *Both VBScript and JScript (Microsoft's version of JavaScript) can be executed in ASP on a Microsoft web server. However, only VBScript within Microsoft ASP is discussed in this chapter. Information on Java-oriented web development, using either Jscript with ASP or the Java Reporting Component, is available in documentation included with Crystal Reports Server XI Developer Edition.*

Preparing for RDC-Based ASP Applications

When you install Crystal Reports XI Developer Edition, the RDC is installed and registered automatically (the RDC is not included with Standard or Professional Editions). However, sample ASP pages that demonstrate RDC integration with ASP are no longer included with Crystal Reports XI. In fact, some critical support ASPs that handle the various web viewing options and report processing tasks (such as page-on-demand architecture over the Web) are not included with the software.

NOTE *A sample RDC-based ASP application, including several critical support ASPs, can be downloaded from this book's companion web site. Visit www.CrystalBook.com to get these samples. You may also get samples from the Business Objects web site. Browse to support. BusinessObjects.com and search for aspxmps11.exe.*

Once you've created any necessary virtual directories and copied the sample applications, you may use Visual InterDev, Notepad, or another ASP-oriented editor to view the HTML and ASP code in these applications.

What Is RDCrptserver11.ASP?

As you look through the ASP example files downloaded from CrystalBook.com, you'll notice that ASP web reports are displayed in one of several Crystal Report Viewers. Note that the report viewers are always pointed to another file, called RDCrptserver11.ASP. This support ASP is a very important part of Crystal Reports' integration with the RDC.

When you integrate a report with the RDC and Visual Basic (as covered later in this chapter), you use the separate Report Viewer ActiveX control to show the report in a VB window. However, because integrating with the Web means your eventual display target is a web browser, you need to consider some other viewing alternatives when using ASPs. The available web report viewers—ActiveX, Java for Browser JVM, and Java Plug-In—can all be used with ASPs. In fact, the report viewer for ActiveX is the same CRVIEWER.DLL module used to display reports with the RDC in Visual Basic.

Because these viewers use Crystal Reports' page-on-demand architecture, they expect report pages to be fed to them by the RDC's PageEngine object. This rather complicated logic and interaction, including all the necessary post back processing to support page-on-demand, is handled by RDCrptserver11.ASP. Although you might be able to write your own ASP code to replace the function of RDCrptserver11.ASP, one look at the ASP code in this file will probably convince you that it won't be worth the effort.

The RDC Object Model in ASPs

Because Active Server Pages support COM automation servers, you can implement Crystal Reports integration in ASP in much the same way as you do in Visual Basic. The complete RDC object model is available for you to use in your Active Server Pages. You can set properties and execute methods for different objects to customize report behavior. Typically, you'll use controls your user has completed on a form, or perhaps values your ASP is retrieving from a database, to control report appearance at run time.

The Application and Report Objects

As with Visual Basic, two base-level objects must be initially declared in your web project: the Application object and the Report object (the Application object is used in VB only if you are integrating an external .RPT file). The Application object needs to be declared only once, at the beginning of a project. Because Crystal Reports XI continues the recent Crystal Reports tradition of "side-by-side" installations (more than one Crystal Reports version being installed on the same computer), you need to add a version identifier to the ProgID when declaring the Application object.

Once declared, the Application object is then used to open a Report object; it is generally not used again throughout the rest of the project until it is "handed off" to RDCrptserver11. ASP. Because these objects must remain in scope throughout the project and all associated ASP files, they are declared as *session* variables, which retain their values and remain in scope throughout an entire ASP project. Here's sample ASP code to declare them:

```
' CREATE THE APPLICATION OBJECT
If Not IsObject (session("oApp")) Then
   Set session("oApp") = _
      Server.CreateObject("CrystalRuntime.Application.11")
End If

' CREATE THE REPORT OBJECT
reportname = Path & "Xtreme Orders.rpt"
'Path must be physical path, not virtual path
If IsObject(session("oRpt")) then
   Set session("oRpt") = nothing
End If
Set session("oRpt") = session("oApp").OpenReport(reportname, 1)

' Disable error prompts on the Web server
 session("oRpt").EnableParameterPrompting = False
```

A few notes about this sample VBScript code:

- Variables don't need to be identified with DIM or declared before use. In VB terms, no Option Explicit statement has been executed. While this may seem to ease your coding requirements, you need to remember that this means that all variables used in this fashion are variants. Some RDC methods require that variables be passed with a specific data type. In those cases, use VBScript typecasting functions, such as CStr and CInt, to correctly cast variables when passing them.

- The report file has been preceded with a Path variable, which is assigned in previous VBScript not shown here (the Request.ServerVariables("PATH_TRANSLATED") value can be queried for an actual physical pathname to the current ASP). The path must be the physical path to the report file (for example, C:\REPORTS) because the RDC can't resolve web server virtual paths. If you know that the .RPT file will be in a fixed, known location, you can skip this entire section of code and simply supply a physical path and filename to the OpenReport method.

- The Application object is declared only once. To ensure that you use version 11 of the RDC (since more than one version can now reside on a single computer), you should add .11 at the end of the ProgID. If this section of VBScript is executed again, the previous declaration of oApp will remain. However, if there is a previous declaration of the Report object (presumably for a different report that may have been processed in a previous pass through this code), it will be set to Nothing before being set to the new report with the Application object's OpenReport method.

- The EnableParameterPrompting property of the Report object is set to false. This reduces the chances of any prompts appearing on the web server if not supplied by your code. If the RDC displays a prompt on the web server screen while a browser is waiting for a report request, the webmaster likely won't be sitting by, waiting to respond to the web server message. The browser session will hang, or eventually time out, if this happens.

CAUTION *You may see line continuation underlines in the sample code in this book to indicate that a line of code continues from the previous line (this is a Visual Basic standard). However, this is only supported in Visual Basic and is not supported in Active Server Pages. If you type this code in directly, you'll need to keep both lines of code on the same physical line in your ASP.*

Manipulating the Report Object

Once the Report object has been assigned to an .RPT file by setting it to the Application object's OpenReport method, you can use your user interface elements, such as controls on the calling form, to customize the way the report behaves. Use objects, collections, methods, and properties for the Report object to control report behavior. You can also pass logon information for the report (using the RDC connection "property bag" properties) from within your code.

Here are some examples:

```
' Log On to report database connection

Session("oRpt").Database.Tables(1).ConnectionProperties("User ID")_
   = "DBReader"
Session("oRpt").Database.Tables(1).ConnectionProperties("Password")_
   = "DBPassword"
```

This code supplies logon information to the first table of the report (if there is more than one table, you'll need to supply logon information to each table within the tables collection). This makes use of the ConnectionProperties Property Bag collection of the RDC. These various property bags contain variable numbers and types of properties, depending on the particular database connection used for that particular table.

TIP *Specific information on these property bags, as well as the complete RDC object model reference, can be found in Crystal Reports Developer's Help. Navigate to C:\Program Files\Business Objects\Crystal Reports 11\Developer Files\Help\<language> and open DevHelp.CHM.*

```
session("oRpt").DiscardSavedData
session("oRpt").RecordSelectionFormula = "{Customer.Country} = 'USA'"
```

This code first discards any saved data records that may exist within the .RPT file. It then sets the Report object's RecordSelectionFormula property to limit the report to customers in the U.S.A. You could just as easily use some form element or other variable from within your ASP to set the record selection formula.

The following sample code is used to pass a value to a report parameter field:

```
session("oRpt").ParameterFields(1).AddCurrentValue _
CInt(Request.Form("txtTaxRate")))
```

Again, this code is passing the value from the calling form object "txtTaxRate" to the AddCurrentValue method. This method applies to a member of the ParameterFields collection of the Report object. Note that it's a good idea to use a type declaration function (such as CInt) to ensure that the proper data type is being passed to the RDC.

TIP *These are just a few examples of how to manipulate the Report object within your code. For additional RDC object model methods and property examples, refer to the Visual Basic section later in this chapter. Or, look through Crystal Reports Developer's Help.*

After you set all necessary properties for the report object and are ready to process the report, you may need to execute the Report object's ReadRecords method to actually populate the report with data from the database. If the report is based on a PC-style database or an ODBC connection that the web server can reach during the report process, this step may not be necessary. However, if you've used the DataBase object's SetDataSource method to change the data source of the report to an ADO record set or some other data source that's only in scope in the current VBScript procedure, you need to execute ReadRecords so that the report won't fail. If you don't, and the Report object is used in another VBScript procedure (such as RDCrptserver11.ASP) when the record set is no longer in scope, the report won't be able to read records from the record set. Here's sample code to execute ReadRecords:

```
On Error Resume Next
session("oRpt").ReadRecords
If Err.Number <> 0 Then Response.Write _
    "A server error occurred when trying to access the datasource"
```

The PageEngine Object

The RDC exposes a PageEngine object that you normally don't need to worry about in Visual Basic applications because of the report viewer's ViewReport method. However, since you need to pass the Report object to RDCrptserver11.ASP to page out to a Crystal Report Viewer, you need to declare the PageEngine object so that RDCrptserver11.ASP can use it to communicate with the report viewers. If you look at RDCrptserver11.ASP, you'll be able to get an idea (probably after a significant amount of poking around, though) of how the PageEngine works. Declare it with code similar to the following:

```
If IsObject(session("oPageEngine")) Then
    set session("oPageEngine") = Nothing
End If
Set session("oPageEngine") = session("oRpt").PageEngine
```

CAUTION *Because RDCrptserver11.ASP is the ultimate ASP that processes the report, you need to think about it when you declare session variables. It expects three session variables to be declared with specific names: session("oApp"), which is the Application object; session("oRpt"), which is the Report object; and session("oPageEngine"), which is the PageEngine object. Don't use alternative variable names for these session variables, or RDCrptserver11.ASP will fail.*

DC Report Viewers

As discussed in Chapter 21, one of the main benefits of using more robust web reporting methods (such as the RDC and ASP.NET) instead of just exporting reports to HTML from the Crystal Reports designer is that these more robust methods offer full report interaction, such as drill-down and group-tree manipulation. The trick, though, is how to fully implement this interaction in a web browser. One of the continual challenges faced when "web-izing" Crystal Reports is supporting all the formatting and interaction options that Crystal Reports provides.

The options with the most cross-platform support are, as you might expect, HTML-based. While more flexibility and interactivity is added with each new revision of HTML (DHTML 4 has some, but very few, formatting limitations from a Crystal Reports perspective), it still has inherent limitations that make reproducing every element of a Crystal Report difficult. And, dealing with interactive options, such as drill-down and group tree navigation, introduces even more challenges.

While .NET and the full versions of Crystal Reports Server/BusinessObjects Enterprise have largely adopted pure HTML-based solutions, several "thin-client" report viewer applications (as opposed to the "zero-client" HTML viewers) are still used with RDC-based web applications. The *Report Viewer for ActiveX* is a Microsoft-compatible ActiveX control that can be viewed in Internet Explorer 3.02 or greater. The *Report Viewer for Java with Browser JVM* and the *Report Viewer for Java with the Java Plug-In* are Java-based viewers that can be viewed in 32-bit versions of Netscape Navigator 2.0 or greater, Internet Explorer 3.02 or greater, or other Java-compatible browsers such as Firefox and Safari on the Macintosh. The Browser JVM version uses your particular browser's Java Virtual Machine, whereas the Java Plug-In version uses the Sun Java 2 Runtime Environment.

These viewers implement almost all the features and functionality of the regular Crystal Reports Preview tab, although there are some visual differences. All enable you to drill down on group headers and footers, charts, and maps, and both offer full interaction with the group tree. The thin-client viewers maintain most font and object formatting, and they allow you to print reports in their "native" paginated format on an attached printer.

Choosing and Customizing RDC Report Viewers

You'll need to determine which of the report viewers you want to provide to your viewer's web browser. You can include commonly available VBScript code to query the browser for its type. If you encounter Internet Explorer, you can automatically provide the ActiveX viewer. If you encounter Netscape, you can provide the Java viewer. Or, you can create a control on a web page (perhaps a combo box) that allows the viewer to make the choice.

This book's companion web site provides some intermediate ASPs that you may include in your ASP code to choose the desired report viewer. You'll find SmartViewerActiveX.asp, JavaPluginViewer.asp, and SimpleJavaViewerSafari.asp, which instantiate the various viewers. You can just copy and paste the code from one of the ASPs into your own file, or use the HTML *#include file* statement to bring in the proper report viewer code. If you've set up a control on your application form that allows the user to choose a report viewer (similar to the viewer variable in the following example), you might use code similar to this to set the chosen report viewer:

```
viewer = Request.Form("Viewer")
If Request.Form("Viewer") = "ActiveX" then
```

```
%>
<!-- #include file="SmartViewerActiveX.asp" -->
<%
ElseIf Request.Form("Viewer") = "Java using Browser JVM" then
%>
<!-- #include file="SimpleJavaViewerSafari.asp" -->
<%
ElseIf Request.Form("Viewer") = "Java using Java Plug-in" then
%>
<!-- #include file="JavaPluginViewer.asp" -->
<%
End If
%>
```

The sample report viewer ASPs for Java and ActiveX set certain viewer parameters to default settings. When you view the ASP code in these files, you'll notice parameters, such as group-tree display, toolbar button display, enabling of drill-down, and so forth, set with PARAM tags. You may modify this report viewer behavior if you so desire. If you want to make permanent changes to these options, simply change the sample ASP to use your new desired options (perhaps you don't want to offer a Print or Export button to your users at any time). If you want to hard-code a change only for a particular application, while others still use the defaults, you need to copy the code from one of the sample files into your own ASP file and change the parameter in your own file, or set session variables and modify the sample ASPs to look for them.

Look at the following sample code:

```
<%
If session("GroupTree") = "ON" Then
    %>
    <PARAM NAME="DisplayGroupTree" VALUE=1>
    <%
Else
    %>
    <PARAM NAME="DisplayGroupTree" VALUE=0>
    <%
End If
%>
```

The <% and %> characters in the preceding code indicate separation of the server-side ASP script from the actual HTML text to be submitted to the browser. Because the parameters are part of the report viewer Object tag, they need to be returned to the browser, while the If-Then-Else statement will execute on the server. This separation of server-side script from client-side HTML is the basic premise of Active Server Pages.

What Is CleanUp.ASP?

CleanUp.ASP is a sample ASP that "cleans up" the three necessary session variables required by RptServer.ASP. By setting the three session variables to "Nothing," resources on the web server are released. CleanUp.ASP is called by an HTML body tag's onunload event (via a JavaScript function), executing its code when a browser window containing the report viewer closes.

While you may use this sample ASP, you can also code your own procedures to clean up these objects by using alternatives, such as Session.Contents.Remove("*<object name>*"), or Session.Abandon (which will destroy all objects, not just your Crystal Reports objects).

eveloping Visual Basic Windows Applications with the RDC

Crystal Reports developer interfaces have been designed to work with most popular Windows development tools that support Microsoft's standard Component Object Model (or COM). Previous Crystal Reports versions also included "legacy" interfaces that could be used with non-COM environments, such as those that integrated via Windows API calls or Visual Basic ActiveX (.OCX) controls. Most of these older interfaces are no longer supported with Crystal Reports XI, having been given the dubious distinction of "legacy status," indicating that they don't contain newer features that the COM options provide.

The best source of developer-related information from Business Objects is a Windows help file that ships with Crystal Reports. Use Windows Explorer to navigate to the CrystalDevHelp.CHM file in C:\Program Files\Business Objects\Crystal Reports 11\ Developer Files\Help*<language>*. You'll find complete documentation for the Report Designer Component and sample code that you can copy from the Help file.

RDC Object Model Architecture

The RDC conforms to Microsoft's COM. As such, it can be used in any COM-compatible development environment that supports a COM Library (formerly known as an "OLE server"), such as Visual Basic, Visual C++, Delphi, and Microsoft Visual InterDev for web page development (web integration with the RDC is covered earlier in this chapter). While an in-depth discussion of COM is better left to Microsoft documentation, you can consider COM to be a set of standards that allows one software environment to utilize the functions of another software environment by way of objects, properties, methods, and events.

COM development falls under the category of object-oriented programming (OOP). An *object hierarchy* is exposed by the RDC. This hierarchy begins with high-level objects that contain lower levels of objects. These second-level objects can contain lower levels of objects, and so on. If it sounds like the levels of objects can get "deep," they sometimes do. Some objects in the RDC are four or five layers deep in the object hierarchy.

Objects can contain not only additional single objects below them, but also collections of objects. A *collection* is a group of related objects contained inside the parent object. For example, a Report object will contain a collection of Section objects (an object for the report header, page header, and so on). Each of these Section objects itself contains its own collection of Report objects, such as fields, text objects, formulas, lines, boxes, and so on. If the details section of a report has ten database fields, four formulas, and a line drawing, the Details Section object will contain an object collection consisting of 15 *members*—one member for each of the Report objects in the section. And, if a report simply contains the five default sections that are created with a new report, the report's Sections collection will contain five members—one for each section.

If you aren't using the RDC's internal ActiveX report designer but instead are integrating an external .RPT file, the highest level in the object hierarchy is the Application object— everything eventually "trickles down" from it. Although you do need to declare the Application object in your VB code, you will rarely (if ever) refer to it again, or set any properties for it, once it's declared. As a general rule, the highest level of object you'll regularly be concerned with is the *Report* object, created by executing the Application object's OpenReport method (or automatically created if you are using the RDC's internal ActiveX designer). You will then manipulate many of the Report object's properties (such as the RecordSelectionFormula property), as well as work with many objects below the Report object (such as report sections, as just discussed).

Because the RDC is a tightly integrated COM component, you will benefit from Visual Basic's *automatic code completion* when you use it. When you begin to enter code into the VB code window for the Report object, the properties, methods, and built-in constant values become available to you from automatically appearing drop-down lists. If you've used Visual Basic 5 or 6, you're probably already familiar with this feature. You'll enjoy the benefit it provides with the RDC, as well.

Whereas older Crystal Reports integration methods required you to develop the report's .RPT file in the Crystal Reports design tool and *then* integrate it into your VB application, the RDC gives you the choice of actually designing the report right inside VB, as well as integrating existing .RPT files. Not only will you find most of the same design capabilities available from within the RDC that are available in regular Crystal Reports (however, some new XI features, such as dynamic/cascading prompts are supported within the VB designer), but virtually all the fields, formulas, text objects, sections, and other parts of the report will be exposed to VB as objects. Like VB forms and controls, Report objects have properties and methods that can be set at both design time and run time. And, if you still choose to use an external .RPT file, the RDC exposes several COM interfaces, allowing sophisticated object-oriented report integration with both external .RPT files and the RDC's built-in report designer.

NOTE *Even though the RDC adds the ability to create reports completely within the VB IDE, you still may prefer to design reports in the stand-alone copy of Crystal Reports. One of the immediate benefits to this is the Preview tab—you can immediately see how your report will look when making cosmetic changes. If you use the VB ActiveX Report Designer and a report viewer, you'll need to rerun your application every time you want to see how your report design changes will appear.*

TIP *You can find the completed VB application on this book's companion web site. Download the application from www.CrystalBook.com.*

The Xtreme Mountain Bike Sample Reporting Application

The sample application used in this chapter, as well as on the book's companion web site (www.CrystalBook.com), is a sample orders report for Xtreme Mountain Bike, a fictional company used throughout this book. The data for the report comes from the XTREME.MDB Microsoft Access sample database that's included with Crystal Reports XI (connected via ODBC). The application will present a user-friendly, graphical user interface for end users who want to print an Xtreme order report.

This report contains several special features you'll want to enable for your end users in the VB application:

- A user-specified sales-tax rate that is used in the "Order + Tax" formula.
- The ability to group by calendar quarter or customer name, based on user selection.

- A prompt for a highlight value to set orders over a certain amount apart. This value can be either passed to a report parameter field or used in the report details section's Format event.

- An order-date range that will limit the report's record selection.

- A label in the page header of the report indicating the choices the user has made.

- The choice to show detail data, or to just group subtotals and summaries for drill-down. The report contains two different page header sections and two different group header sections, containing column headings that are suppressed and shown according to the summary/detail choice.

- Destination options to preview the report in a window, print the report to a printer, or send the report as a Portable Document Format (.PDF) file, attached to an e-mail message.

If the report is grouped by quarter, given a 5 percent tax rate, and restricted to orders from January 1 through December 31, 2004, and if the value to highlight orders is set to $5,000, the report will appear as illustrated here:

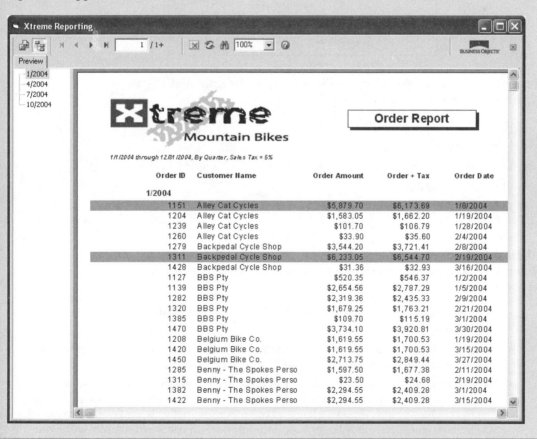

The VB application that will be used to integrate this report is a simple, single-form dialog box that gathers data from the user via text boxes, a combo box, radio buttons, and a check box. When the user clicks OK, the report is previewed, printed, or e-mailed, depending on the selections made. The main form from the application looks like this:

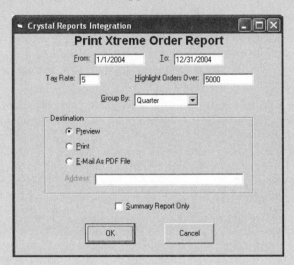

To correctly accomplish the integration, you need to programmatically modify the following report properties from within your VB application:

- Record selection formula
- Report formula
- Parameter field or details section background color in Format event
- Output destination
- Report section formatting (suppress and show)

Different RDC Pieces
The entire RDC actually consists of several parts that work together. In particular, it has four separate pieces:

- **ActiveX designer**   Enables you to actually create and modify reports inside the Visual Basic IDE.

- **Run-Time Library**   After you create the report, the RDC exposes a set of powerful properties, methods, and events via a COM library.

- **Report Viewer**   Because the RDC doesn't include its own built-in preview window, you use another ActiveX component, the Report Viewer, to view reports on the screen. The Report Viewer also exposes a large set of properties, methods, and events, enabling you to have complete control over how your application users can interact with your report in the viewer window.

- **Embeddable Report Designer** This feature allows you to place an ActiveX control on your VB form to allow end users to interactively design reports using features almost identical to the report designer available inside the VB IDE. Once users have finished their report design, the Embeddable Report Designer returns a report object that can be further modified and controlled with the run-time library.

The ActiveX Designer

The first part of the RDC is an *ActiveX designer,* an interface that works with Visual Basic. Whereas other ActiveX controls and libraries generally extend the capabilities of the Visual Basic language, an ActiveX designer actually extends the capabilities of the Visual Basic IDE. Some common examples are the User Connection Designer and the Data Environment Designer, both of which are ActiveX designers for connecting to remote databases that are available with Visual Basic 6.

The designer portion of the RDC allows you to create a complete report right inside Visual Basic. You don't need to use the iterative process of creating or editing a Crystal Reports .RPT file, working with it inside your VB code, going back to Crystal Reports to make changes to the .RPT file, and going back to VB to make changes in the code (although you still may find this process to be preferable—particularly because there's no Preview tab in Visual Basic). The RDC looks similar to the Crystal Reports design screen, with multiple report sections, lists of database fields, formulas, parameter fields, and so on. You interact with the RDC via toolbar buttons and pop-up menus.

What the RDC designer features that Crystal Reports doesn't offer is a complete object model for every report section and every object you place in any report section. Every field, text object, formula, parameter field, or any other type of object has its own set of properties that appears in the property sheet, and many of those properties can be set at run time. With the RDC, you can customize formulas, text objects, section formatting, and most other aspects of report behavior and formatting by using VB coding. By creatively using text objects, you can even create report formulas using the Visual Basic language instead of the Crystal formula language so that the text objects will be under complete VB control at run time. Of course, any Crystal formulas you create will still work, and they can still be modified on the fly from within your application, just as with other integration methods.

The Run-Time Library

The second part of the RDC is the RDC run-time library. This component can accept either a report designed with the RDC ActiveX designer or an external .RPT file created with Crystal Reports XI. The RDC then exposes a large number of properties and methods that can be used to completely customize reporting behavior at run time.

The Report Viewer

The RDC Design Time or Runtime components don't include their own built-in preview window for previewing reports on the screen. Therefore, report previewing is provided by yet another ActiveX component that is available with the RDC, the Report Viewer. This ActiveX control is added to a form, where it exposes a large number of properties in the Properties box displayed in the VB IDE that can be set at design time. When your program is run, the viewer is supplied with a Report object from the RDC Library, which it then displays in its window according to the selections you made at design time.

Not only can many of these properties also be set at run time, but the viewer contains its own COM library, which exposes a large number of other properties, methods, and events that let you completely control report behavior and interaction. You can open drill-down tabs right from within your code, trap a button click in the viewer toolbar, or respond to a drill-down click on a group footer or header. The viewer is versatile enough that conceivably you can design your own container for the Report Viewer window, creating all of your own controls and logic for report interaction.

TIP *The RDC's run-time library and Report Viewer also can be used to develop "thin-client" applications that require only a web browser. Both modules can integrate reports using Microsoft Active Server Pages. This is discussed earlier in this chapter.*

The Embeddable Report Designer

Not only can you modify existing reports at run time from within your code, but Crystal Reports XI offers a fully interactive report design ActiveX control that can be added directly to a VB form. With this control, end users have full interactive capabilities to design new reports or edit existing reports from within your VB application. By providing an already defined Report object to the Embeddable Report Designer, you can allow users to modify an existing report interactively. Or, simply allow an end user to use the Embeddable Designer to create a complete report from scratch, much as you would using the RDC ActiveX designer inside the VB IDE. In either case, when the end user has completed his or her report design process, the Embeddable Report Designer simply returns another Report object that can be further manipulated before being printed, exported, or displayed in the Report Viewer.

Adding the RDC to Your Project

The first step in using the RDC is to add it to your project. After installing Crystal Reports XI Developer Edition, the RDC should be properly registered on your system and ready for use. If you discover that Crystal Reports tools don't appear within the VB IDE, rerun Crystal Reports XI setup from the Windows Control Panel and ensure that the Report Designer Component is selected.

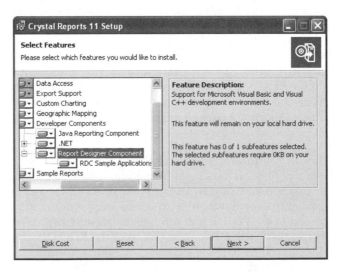

To begin using Crystal Reports with Visual Basic:

1. Start Visual Basic and create a new project, or open the existing project with which you wish to use the RDC.

2. Choose Project | Components from the pull-down menus, or press CTRL-T. The Components dialog box will appear.

3. Click the Designers tab. You'll see a list of ActiveX designers registered on your system. Ensure that the Crystal Reports 11 designer is selected, and then click OK.

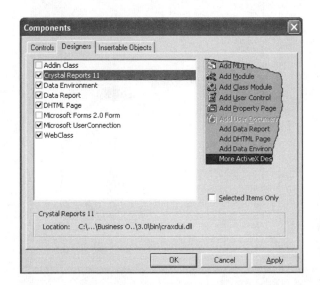

4. Using the Project pull-down menu, choose the Add Crystal Reports 11 option (it may appear on the More ActiveX Designers submenu in VB 5). The RDC will be added to Visual Basic, and the Report Gallery dialog box will appear, as shown in Figure 25-1.

TIP *Crystal Reports XI attempts to add the RDC directly to the Project menu automatically when it's installed. If you need to add it manually with Project | Components, it will "stick" from that point forward. You won't have to add it each time you want to use the RDC with a new VB project.*

The RDC begins by displaying the Report Gallery. The RDC Report Gallery is very similar to the Report Gallery familiar to users of Crystal Reports 10 and earlier with a few changes. For example, there isn't an OLAP report option here, and the From An Existing Report option has been added. Your initial choices in the Report Gallery determine how your main report is designed inside the RDC.

Importing an Existing Report
If you've created an .RPT file in Crystal Reports XI or an earlier version and you want to use that report in the RDC, click the From An Existing Report radio button and click OK. A File

The RDC supplies toolbox icons when
you click the Crystal Reports button

A new Designers folder will contain
ActiveX designers, such as the RDC

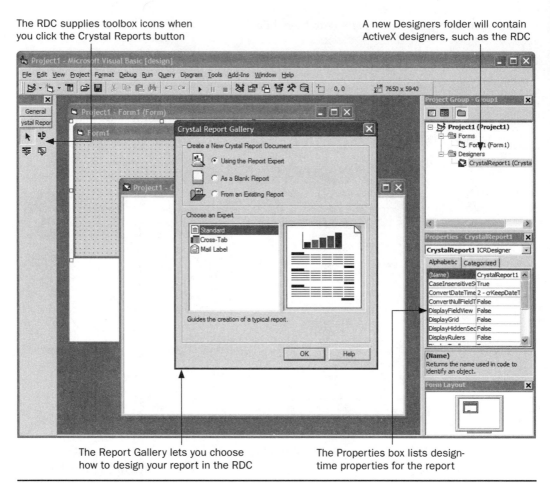

The Report Gallery lets you choose
how to design your report in the RDC

The Properties box lists design-
time properties for the report

FIGURE 25-1 The RDC inside Visual Basic

Open dialog box will appear, in which you can choose the .RPT file that you wish to import.
Once you've chosen the report file, you are prompted to add the Report Viewer to your project.

Here, you can determine whether you want the Report Viewer added to a new form in your project and, if you do, decide whether you want the Report Viewer form to be set as the startup form. If you need to preview the report in a window from within your VB application, you need to add the Report Viewer. Although you can do it later if you need to, the RDC will offer to add it automatically, along with some simple code to tie the report to the viewer. If your report will be used strictly for exporting, e-mailing, or printing to a printer, you don't need to add the Report Viewer control, because it won't be used.

If you import a report and add the Report Viewer to a new form, your screen will look something like the one shown in Figure 25-2.

You'll notice that the RDC design window looks somewhat similar to the regular Crystal Reports design window—many of the features and report design steps apply equally to both environments. There are several ways of carrying out functions in the RDC design window: by using toolbox and toolbar buttons, by choosing items from the Field Explorer at the left of

Field Explorer lets you choose database, formula, parameter, and other fields to add to the report

The RDC design window

Toolbar buttons for common report design functions

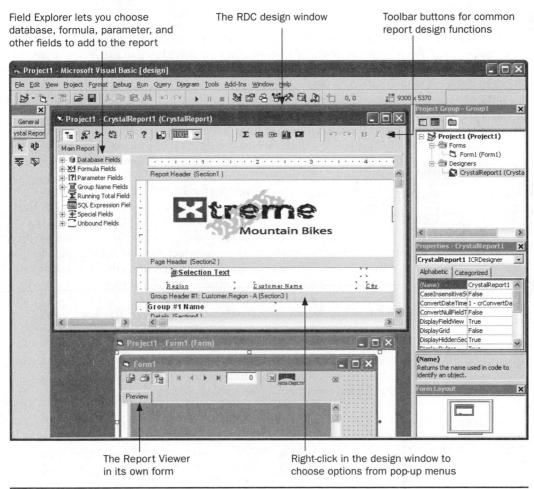

The Report Viewer in its own form

Right-click in the design window to choose options from pop-up menus

FIGURE 25-2   An imported report and the Report Viewer

the report, and by right-clicking in the design window and choosing options from the pop-up menus. As with the regular Crystal Reports designer, you can select objects in the RDC design window and then move, resize, format, or delete them. Steps for these functions are basically the same as they are for regular Crystal Reports (with the exception that all RDC functions must be chosen with toolbar buttons and right-clicks—there are no Crystal-related pull-down menus here, as there are in regular Crystal Reports).

Remember that when you import an .RPT file into the RDC, the RDC simply copies the contents of the .RPT file into the design window and then completely disregards any changes that may later be made to the original .RPT file. Also, if you make any changes to the report inside the RDC, there will be no effect on the original .RPT file. You are not creating a real-time link to the .RPT file.

TIP *If you want to save the contents of the RDC designer to an external .RPT file to use for other purposes, you may do so. Right-click in the design window and choose Report | Save To Crystal Reports File from the pop-up menu.*

While the RDC design window may not provide any particular functional advantage over the regular Crystal Reports designer (except that you don't have to exit VB to use it), the real benefit is the object model that it opens for report contents. When you select an individual Report object, such as a database field or text object, or a report section, such as the report header or details section, you'll see design-time properties in the Properties box. Also, by using the internal report designer, your report design is saved as a .DSR file along with .FRM, .BAS, and other files that make up your VB project. When you compile the project, the report design is embedded in the application's .EXE file—there are no external .RPT files that your end users may inadvertently (or purposely) change.

As you can with properties for a combo box, radio button, form, or other regular VB control, you can set properties at design time for any of these report elements as well. The Properties box and pop-up menu options, such as the Format Editor, interact with each other. For example, you can select a date field, right-click it, and choose Format from the pop-up menu. On the Date tab of the Format Editor, you might choose a spelled-out month and four-digit year, showing no day at all. When you click OK to close the Format Editor and then look in the Properties box, you'll notice that the Day Type property has changed to 2 – crNoDay, the Month Type property has changed to 3 – crLongMonth, and the Year Type property has changed to 1 – crLongYear. The opposite behavior is also true—changes you make in the Properties box will be reflected elsewhere in the RDC dialog boxes.

TIP *Depending on how you plan to integrate your report and how much customization you want to perform at run time, you may want to rename some of the default names given to objects by the RDC. When you begin looking through report objects in your VB code, recognizing what SubHeading represents is easier than recognizing what Text25 represents. If you are using stand-alone Crystal Reports, any name you give an object on the common tab of the Format Editor will remain when the report is imported into the RDC.*

After you modify your report as necessary, save the report design the same way you save changes to a form, module, or project file from within VB. Just click the Save button on the toolbar, right-click the Designer object in the Project Explorer window, and choose Save from the pop-up menu, or just close the project or VB. You'll be prompted to choose a filename for the RDC designer, just as you would for a form or module. Choose a path and filename for the designer file—the default file extension for ActiveX designers is .DSR. When you next open the VB project, the .DSR file will load with the rest of the project files, and all properties and characteristics of the report design window will reappear.

Creating a New Report

Although the ability to import an existing .RPT file into the RDC is an excellent way to integrate an existing .RPT file into a Visual Basic application, you may prefer to maximize the power of the RDC and design the report entirely inside the Visual Basic IDE from scratch. The RDC allows you to do this with one of the Report Gallery choices that appear when you first add the RDC to your project.

If you choose one of the report experts, you'll be led section by section through the expert dialog box, much as you are when you use the report wizards inside regular Crystal Reports (refer to Chapter 1 for more information). If you choose the Blank Report option, you are presented with an empty report design window in which you need to choose database connections, tables, and fields individually to add to the report. Start by right-clicking in the window and choosing Database | Database Expert from the pop-up menu.

Choosing a Report Data Source   When you import an existing .RPT file into the RDC, the report inside your VB application will use the same data source as the imported report did (such as ODBC or a native database driver). These data sources are all provided by Crystal Reports functionality, separate from any database-connectivity features within Visual Basic.

However, when you create a new report from scratch using a report expert in the RDC, you have several choices for how your report will "connect" to a database. Because the RDC is so tightly integrated with Visual Basic, you may want to consider using a database connection that can easily be manipulated from within your VB code. In particular, the RDC can connect to data using various Microsoft data-access methods provided by Visual Basic. These include Data Access Objects (DAO), Remote Data Objects (RDO), and ActiveX Data Objects (ADO). In addition, you'll be able to connect directly to an existing data environment that you may have already defined in your VB application (consult the VB documentation for more information on the Data Environment).

When you're ready to choose a data source, the Database Expert will appear, as shown in Figure 25-3.

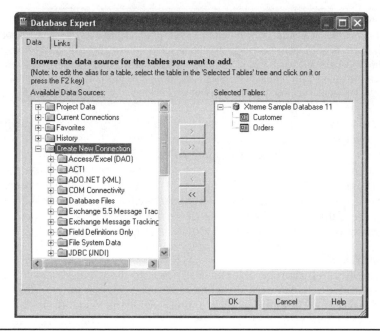

FIGURE 25-3 Database Expert

The Data Environment category, within the Project Data folder, will have entries in it only if you've already added and defined a Visual Basic 6 Data Environment (which is another example of an ActiveX designer) in your project. When you expand this category, the set of connections and commands in the Data Environment will be available to be chosen for your report.

The remaining items in the Database Expert are identical to those displayed in the regular Crystal Reports designer, described in more detail in Chapter 15. Open the desired category, supply logon credentials (if required), and add one or more tables to the Selected Tables list. You can also create SQL Commands in the Database Expert (also discussed in Chapter 15).

If you add more than one table, you must link the tables before proceeding to report design. Click the Links tab of the Database Expert (it will appear only if you add more than one table). Once you've properly linked tables (discussed in detail in Chapter 15), click the Database Expert's OK button to proceed with report design.

Adding Objects   If you are using one of the report experts, you'll design the report by using the simple sectioned dialog box. Since this approach is virtually identical to the technique discussed in Chapter 1, you should refer to that chapter if you're unfamiliar with designing a report with an expert.

If you chose the Blank Report option (or if you've already closed the report expert but want to add additional objects to the report), use the Field Explorer on the left side of the RDC design window to add objects to the report. For example, to add a field from the database, click the plus sign next to the database fields category to display the data source(s) the report is based on. Click the plus sign next to the data source to see the fields contained in it. Then, just drag and drop the fields you want to the desired section of the report design window.

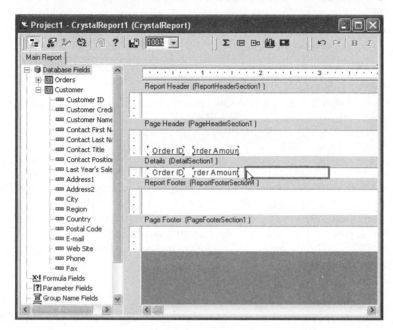

To create new formulas, parameter fields, running totals, or SQL expression fields, right-click their category in the Field Explorer and choose New from the pop-up menu. When the new object has been added, you can drag and drop it on the report. Special fields can also be added to the report by dragging and dropping them from their area of the Field Explorer.

After you add objects, you can select them and move or resize them just as you would in regular Crystal Reports. You can format an object that you've selected by right-clicking and choosing the appropriate choice from the pop-up menu. There are many capabilities and design techniques available that you can apply to the RDC, as you do with regular Crystal Reports. Look at the chapters in Part I of this book for ideas and techniques for designing sophisticated reports. And, don't forget that you also have Visual Basic properties for every object or report section in the report. Select the object or report section and make design-time property choices in the Properties box—that's the power of the VB-integrated RDC.

TIP *The XI version of the VB report designer contains some new XI features, such as the ability to set a graphic file's location with a formula. However, other features won't be available, such as dynamic or cascading parameter pick lists (the dynamic radio button is dimmed in the parameter dialog box).*

The RDC Object Model

As discussed earlier in this section of the chapter, the RDC actually consists of four different main components that may exist in your Visual Basic application: the ActiveX designer, the Run-time Library, the Report Viewer, and the Embeddable Report Designer (not all objects will necessarily exist in every project). When you actually process a report in VB, you design the report within the ActiveX designer window or allow the user to create it with the Embeddable Report Designer and eventually pass a *Report object* to the Report Viewer. The Run-time Library, in essence, appears in the middle to control report customization.

Using the ActiveX Designer Report Object

The first step is to assign the design-window report definition to a Visual Basic object variable, as demonstrated in the following sample code:

```
Public Report As New dsrXtreme
```

In this code, from the modXtreme module in the sample application, *dsrXtreme* is the name given to the ActiveX designer object in the Property Pages dialog box. *Report* is the name of the object that will "point" to the report. Because this object is declared to be Public in a module, it will remain in scope and be accessible throughout the entire application. Then, when the report is going to be viewed in the Report Viewer, the Report object is passed to the Report Viewer's ReportSource property. The following code is from the sample application's frmViewer Form_Load event:

```
CRViewer1.ReportSource = Report
```

In this code, CRViewer1 is the default name of the Report Viewer (and it hasn't been changed to another name). The Report object is given to the ReportSource property so that the Report Viewer knows which report to show.

What the RDC Library does between defining the Report object and assigning it to the Report Viewer is the "meat" of RDC integration programming. After you assign the designer to the Report object variable, an entire object model becomes available to you for modifying and customizing the report. By using the RDC's object model, consisting of objects, collections, properties, methods, and events, you have extensive control over your report behavior at run time.

When you add the RDC to your report, the CRAXDRT (Crystal Reports ActiveX Designer Run-Time) Library is added to your project automatically. This COM interface provides a complete set of properties and methods that you can set at run time. To see the objects, collections, properties, and methods that are exposed by this Library, use Visual Basic's *Object Browser.* The Object Browser can be viewed in Visual Basic any time your program isn't running. Press F2, or choose View | Object Browser from the pull-down menus. Then, choose CRAXDRT in the first drop-down list to see the object library exposed by the RDC.

Although an extensive explanation of COM and its general approach to an object model and object hierarchy is better left to Microsoft documentation, navigating the RDC object model will soon become second nature to you. The highest level in the object hierarchy is the Application object—everything eventually falls below it. In general, throughout the RDC, the Application object is assumed by default, so you don't need to explicitly refer to it (unless you use the RDC without the RDC ActiveX designer report design window). The highest level of object you'll need to be concerned about is the Report object.

TIP *If you are using the Embeddable Report Designer to give your end user interactive report design capability, you'll want to use the combined design-time/run-time library, CRAXDDRT. Look up this library in the Object Browser to explore its objects, collections, properties, and methods. The Embeddable Report Designer is discussed in more detail later in this chapter.*

Using an External .RPT File
One of the main benefits of the RDC is the ability to design a report entirely from within the Visual Basic IDE. When you save this internal report design, the designer specifications are saved in a .DSR file along with the rest of your Visual Basic project. When you compile the project, all of the report design specifications are saved in the compiled modules—there are no external report files to be deleted or modified (either accidentally or otherwise).

However, sometimes you may want to use the flexibility of the RDC and Report Viewer with an external .RPT file, similar to older Crystal Reports integration methods. This is entirely possible, and quite straightforward. Examine the following code module from a VB form.

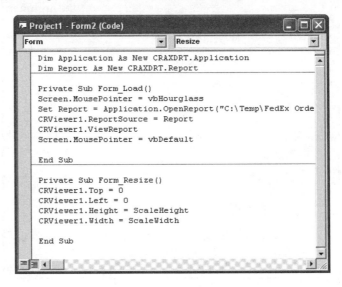

Notice the code that's very similar to the standard code the RDC automatically adds to your project. Notice a couple of differences, however. Rather than declaring and creating one Report object, consisting of an instance of the ActiveX designer, this code declares and assigns two objects: the Application object and the Report object.

The Application Object   When you use the built-in RDC ActiveX designer, you needn't worry about the Application object. However, if you choose to use an external report instead of the built-in designer, you'll need to declare and assign a single "new" instance of the Application object, the highest-level object in the RDC's object hierarchy. Don't forget to fully qualify the Application object by preceding the object type with CRAXDRT (or CRAXDDRT if you're using the combined design-time/run-time library).

The Report Object   The Report object is crucial. You'll use it to perform almost all run-time customization to your reports. You need to declare and assign a Report object for each report you want to have "open" at the same time within your application. For example, if you want to have three separate reports all appearing in their own preview windows simultaneously, you need to declare and assign three different Report object variables. However, if you'll have only one report in use at a time, you can merely declare and assign a single Report object variable, setting it to Nothing and reassigning it as necessary inside your code. Don't forget to fully qualify a "new" instance of the Report object when declaring it with the Dim statement by preceding the object type with CRAXDRT or CRAXDDRT, depending on which library you're using.

Assign the Report object by using the Application object's OpenReport method. Supply the external report's filename, including the full pathname, as the argument.

CAUTION *If you decide to use the RDC with an external .RPT file and don't use the Add Crystal Reports 11 option from the Project menu, you need to ensure that the RDC Run-time Library (or combined Design/Run-time Library) and, optionally, the Report Viewer are added to the project. In order for the proper library to be available, choose Project | References and ensure that the proper library is chosen (either Crystal Reports ActiveX Designer Run-Time Library 11 or Crystal Reports ActiveX Designer Design and Run-Time Library 11). To use the Report Viewer, choose Project | Components and ensure that the Crystal Active X Report Viewer Library 11.0 option is selected (setting this option in Project | References won't be sufficient for the Report Viewer).*

An Introduction to the RDC Object Model

While the Report object has many properties of its own (such as the RecordSelectionFormula property), it contains many objects and collections of objects that fall below it. One available Report object collection is FormulaFields, which contains a set of FormulaFieldDefinition objects, one for each formula defined in the report. Each of these objects contains all the properties for that particular formula, such as the formula name, the text of the formula, the data type that it returns, and other properties.

When you're dealing with a collection of objects, you need to identify which member of the collection you wish to manipulate, by using an index pointer to the appropriate member. In the RDC, indexes are "one-based." That is, the first member is numbered 1, the second is numbered 2, and so on. This is in contrast to the ActiveX control and other VB object models, which often expose "zero-based" indexes. The RDC typically numbers the collection members in the order in which they were added to the report.

For example, to print the formula text from the first formula in the Xtreme Orders sample application, you can type the following code into the Immediate window while the program is in break mode:

```
? Report.FormulaFields(1).Text
```

Here, the object hierarchy is being "navigated" to reveal the Text property of the first member of the FormulaFieldDefinitions collection (referred to simply as FormulaFields) of the Report object. Since the Text property is a read/write property, you not only can retrieve what the formula already contains, but also replace it by setting the Text property to a string value, as in the following:

```
Report.FormulaFields(1).Text = "{Orders.Order Amount} * 1.1"
```

Manipulating Collection Indexes by Name Instead of Number
The RDC will allow you to use string indexes to refer to members of only certain collections, but not all of them. For example, the RDC requires you to set the contents of a formula with

```
Report.FormulaFields(1).Text = "{Orders.Order Amount} * 1.1"
```

while older integration methods, or Visual Studio .NET, might allow

```
Report.Formulas("Order + Tax").Text = "{Orders.Order Amount} * 1.1"
```

You sometimes need to do some experimenting to find the actual member of a collection that you wish to manipulate.

Wouldn't it be nice if, instead of using the numeric index to set the value of a formula, you could use code like this:

```
If SetFormula("Order + Tax","{Orders.Order Amount} * 1.1") Then
   MsgBox "Formula Changed"
Else
   MsgBox "Incorrect Formula Name Supplied"
End If
```

Examine the following function code:

```
Public Function SetFormula(FormulaName As String, _
                           FormulaText As String) As Boolean
Dim intCounter As Integer
For intCounter = 1 To Report.FormulaFields.Count
  If Report.FormulaFields(intCounter).FormulaFieldName = FormulaName
Then
     Report.FormulaFields(intCounter).Text = FormulaText
       SetFormula = True
       Exit Function
   End If  'Report.FormulaFields(intCounter).Name = FormulaName
Next intCounter
SetFormula = False
End Function
```

If you examine this code closely, you'll see that the FormulaFields collection can be cycled through using a For loop, looking for the formula that has the same name as the passed FormulaName argument. Once it's found, the value of the passed FormulaText argument is used to set the value of the formula. If a formula with the same name isn't found, the subroutine returns a false value that can be tested for.

If you have a large number of formulas, parameter fields, SQL expressions, or other objects that may be easier to manipulate by name rather than by index number, use this type of logic to make your coding life easier!

Also, another method exists in various RDC collections (of particular interest are the FormulaFieldDefinitions and ParameterFields collections) that allow you to retrieve an object by name rather than index. Examine the following code for an example of the GetItemByName method:

```
Dim FormulaField As CRAXDRT.FormulaFieldDefinition
Set FormulaField = Report.FormulaFields.GetItemByName("Order + Tax")

FormulaField.Text = "{Orders.Order Amount} * 1.1"
```

In this example, a new object variable is declared to hold a formula. It is then set to an existing formula in the report by calling the FormulaFields collection's GetItemByName method, using the actual name of the formula as an argument. The method returns an actual formula field object, which can then be manipulated by reading or setting properties.

Note that the formula or parameter field name you supply as the GetItemByName argument cannot contain the @ sign, ? sign, or curly braces—just the formula field or parameter field name should be supplied, without any extraneous punctuation. If you supply an invalid name, the RDC will throw a trappable error to VB.

Because the RDC is a tightly integrated COM component, you will benefit from *automatic code completion* (Microsoft refers to it as *IntelliSense*) when you use the RDC with Visual Basic. When you begin to enter code into the VB code window for the Report object, the properties, methods, and built-in constant values will become available to you from automatically appearing drop-down lists. If you've used Visual Basic 5 or 6, you're probably familiar with this feature. You'll enjoy the benefit it provides with the RDC.

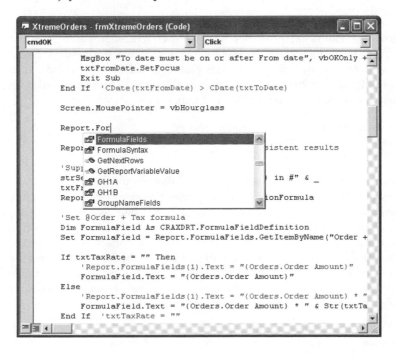

Providing Database Logon Credentials

Many reports you integrate using the RDC will be based on secure databases, requiring a user ID and password to be supplied before the report can retrieve data. In many cases, you will have already established a secure connection with the database through your application before report processing ever begins. In these cases, you'll probably want to pass these credentials directly to the report from within your code. This is particularly important to RDC developers, as the Report Viewer control included with the RDC *will not* prompt the user for logon credentials if they have not been previously provided—the viewer will simply throw an error when attempting to process the report. This is in contrast to other integration methods, such as Visual Studio .NET, which will automatically prompt users for logon credentials if the code doesn't provide them.

Depending on how the report is designed, you may need to approach supplying the user ID and password to the report from several different perspectives. The simplest way to do this is to provide a single user ID and password to the entire report. Even if the report makes use of several database tables, you can supply a single user ID/password combination that will apply to all tables. If, however, you have created a report that mixes tables from separate databases, or you have included subreports in your main report, you may need to perform extra steps to provide logon credentials to individual tables in the main report, or to the subreport.

To supply an all-encompassing user ID/password combination that will apply to all tables originating from the same database, navigate through the RDC object hierarchy to the Database object within the Report object. The LogOnServer method will log on to the database, providing a secure connection to all tables within that database. LogonServer syntax is

```
LogOnServer <databaseDLL>, <Server>, <Database>, <UserID>, <Password>
```

The following code fragment shows how to log on to a Microsoft SQL Server database via ODBC. The ODBC Data Source Name is Xtreme SQL Server, the database name is XTREME, the user ID is DBReader, and the password is DBPassword. No matter how many tables have been added to the report from this database (the main report only—not subreports), this will satisfy logon requirements for all of them.

```
' Login to entire database for main report
Report.Database.LogOnServer "PDSODBC.DLL", _
    "XTREME SQL Server", "XTREME", "DBReader", "DBPassword"
```

If you need to supply different sets of credentials to individual tables (or you just want a more robust way to retrieve and set database properties in general), version XI of the RDC exposes *Connection Information property bags*. A "property bag" is a collection of properties that exist for a certain object. The number of members and names in the collection can change, however, depending on the type of object. In the case of Connection Information property bags, varying sets of properties exist within the DatabaseTable object's ConnectionProperties collection, depending on the particular database DLL being used for a particular table.

An alternative way, then, of supplying logon credentials to an individual report table looks like this:

```
' Login to individual database tables
Report.Database.Tables(1).ConnectionProperties("User ID") = "DBReader"
```

```
Report.Database.Tables(1).ConnectionProperties("Password") = "DBPassword"
```

In this example, two property bag properties from the ConnectionProperties collection (User ID and Password) are set for the first table in the database.

Logging In to Subreports

While the requirement to potentially provide different logon credentials to individual tables in the main report is one consideration, logging in to subreports is another. Because subreports contain unique database connections separate from the main report, you will need to provide logon credentials to each of them separate from the main report. The RDC object model deals with subreports in a fashion that requires a bit of extra coding.

Because a subreport is, in essence, a "report within a report," it possesses its own unique set of properties, methods, and events. Therefore, in order to completely control it, a separate RDC Report object must be declared and assigned to each subreport. Then, that subreport's properties (such as the Database object ConnectionProperties collection) can be manipulated from within their own Report object.

Examine the following sample code:

```
' Login to database for subreport
Dim Top5ProductsSub As CRAXDRT.Report
Set Top5ProductsSub = Report.Subreport1.OpenSubreport
Top5ProductsSub.Database.LogOnServer "PDSODBC.DLL", _
"XTREME SQL Server", "XTREME", "DBReader", "DBPassword"
```

In this example, an additional Report object is declared, using the fully qualified object type of CRAXDRT.Report. It is then "set" to the subreport by navigating to the subreport within the main report object. The subreport object's OpenSubreport method is executed, which creates another RDC Report object (named Top5ProductsSub) just for the subreport. Then, the Database object's LogOnServer method, or ConnectionProperties collection, can be used to supply logon credentials.

TIP *More information on working with subreports can be found later in this chapter, under "RDC Subreports."*

Controlling Record Selection

One of the main benefits of Visual Basic's integration with Crystal Reports is the ability to control report record selection on the fly, based on your user's interactions with the VB application. You can design the exact user interface you need for your application and build the report record selection formula to match how your user interacts with it. Because VB has such powerful user-interface features (such as the VB date picker and other custom controls), you have much more flexibility using VB controls than you do using Crystal Reports parameter fields.

Because the record selection formula you pass to the RDC must still conform to Crystal Reports syntax, you need to be familiar with how to create a Crystal Reports formula. If you are used to using the Crystal Reports Select Expert for record selection, you need to familiarize yourself with the actual Crystal Reports formula that it creates, before you create a selection formula in your VB application. A Crystal Reports record selection formula is a Boolean formula that narrows down the database records that will be included in the report. For example, the following record selection formula will limit a report to orders placed in the first quarter of 2001 from customers in Texas:

```
{Orders.Order Date} In #1/1/2001# To #3/31/2001#
And {Customer.Region} = "TX"
```

TIP *For complete discussions of Crystal Reports record selection and how to create Boolean formulas, consult Chapters 4 and 5.*

Use the RecordSelectionFormula property of the Report object to set the record selection formula for the report. You can set the property to either a string expression or a variable. Here's the code from the sample application to set record selection, based on the contents of the user-supplied From Date and To Date text boxes:

```
'Supply record selection formula based on dates
strSelectionFormula = "{Orders.Order Date} in #" & _
    txtFromDate & "# to #" & txtToDate & "#"
Report.RecordSelectionFormula = strSelectionFormula
```

Record Selection Formula Tips

You need to consider several important points when building a Crystal record selection formula within your application. Specifically, some tricks are available that you can use to make sure that your string values are formatted properly, and that as much of the SQL database query as possible is performed by the database server rather than by the PC.

The string value you pass must adhere *exactly* to the Crystal Reports formula syntax. This includes using correct Crystal reserved words and punctuation. The preceding example shows the necessity of including the pound sign (#) around date values in the selection formula.

Also, it's easy to forget the required quotation marks or apostrophes around literals that are used in comparisons. For example, you may want to pass the following selection formula:

```
{Customer.Region} = 'TX' And {Orders.Ship Via} = 'UPS'
```

If the characters TX and UPS are coming from controls, such as a text box or combo box, you might consider using the following VB code to place the selection formula in a string variable:

```
strSelectionFormula = "{Customer.Region} = " & txtRegion & _
" And {Orders.Ship Via} = " & cboShipper
```

At first glance, this appears to create a correctly formatted Crystal Reports record-selection formula. However, if you supply this string to the RecordSelectionFormula property, the report will fail when it runs. Why? The best way to troubleshoot this issue is to look at the contents of strSelectionFormula in the VB Immediate window, by setting a breakpoint or by using other VB debugging features. This will show that the contents of the string variable after the preceding code executes as follows:

```
{Customer.Region} = TX And {Orders.Ship Via} = UPS
```

Notice that no quotation marks or apostrophes appear around the literals that are being compared in the record selection formula, a basic requirement of the Crystal Reports formula language. The following VB code will create a syntactically correct selection formula:

```
strSelectionFormula = "{Customer.Region} = '" & txtRegion & _
"' And {Orders.Ship Via} = '" & cboShipper & "'"
```

If your report will be using a SQL database, remember also that RDC will attempt to convert as much of your record selection formula as possible to SQL when it runs the report. The same caveats apply to the record selection formula you pass from your VB application as apply to a record selection formula you create directly in Crystal Reports. In particular, using built-in Crystal Reports formula functions, such as UpperCase or ToText, typically causes record selection to be moved to the client (the PC) instead of to the database server. The result can be very slow report performance. To avoid this situation, take the same care in creating record selection formulas that you pass from your application as you would in Crystal Reports. Look for detailed discussions on record selection performance in both Chapters 4 and 15.

TIP *You may also choose to create the SQL statement that the report will use right in your VB application, and then submit it to the report by setting the Report object's SQLQueryString property.*

Setting Formulas

The RDC gives you an extra level of flexibility by allowing you to control the contents of Report objects as each record is processed by the report (see "Changing Text Objects at Run Time" and "Conditional Formatting and Formatting Sections" later in the chapter). Using these techniques, you can actually have objects on your report show the results of Visual Basic calculations and procedures. However, it still may be more straightforward to simply modify the contents of Crystal Reports formulas dynamically at run time. This will be useful for changing formulas related to groups that can also be changed from within your code, for changing a formula that shows text on the report, or for changing a formula that relates to math calculations or conditional formatting on the report.

Setting formulas at run time is similar to setting the record selection formula at run time (described in the preceding section). You need a good understanding of the Crystal Reports formula language to adequately modify formulas inside your VB code. If you need a refresher on Crystal Reports formulas, review Chapter 5.

The RDC provides a FormulaFields collection in the Report object that can be read or written to at run time. This collection returns multiple FormulaFieldDefinition objects, one for each formula defined in the report. Although a great deal of information may be gleaned from the FormulaFieldDefinition object, the simplest way to change the contents of a formula is simply to set the Text property for the particular member of the collection that you want to change. The collection is one based, with each member corresponding to its position in the list of formula fields.

In the Xtreme Orders sample application, the Order + Tax formula is modified according to the user's completion of the Tax Rate text box. The formula is changed using the following code:

```
'Set @Order + Tax formula
If txtTaxRate = "" Then
    Report.FormulaFields(1).Text = "{Orders.Order Amount}"
Else
    Report.FormulaFields(1).Text = "{Orders.Order Amount} * " &_
    Str(txtTaxRate / 100 + 1)
End If  'txtTaxRate = ""
```

You needn't change the property for all formulas in the report—just the ones you want to modify at run time. Remember that you can't specify the formula name directly as the collection index argument—you must use a one-based index number. This is determined by where the formula is in the formula list in the RDC design window—the first formula will have an index of 1, the fifth, 5, and so on. Review the sample code earlier in the chapter if you wish to refer to formulas by name instead of index number.

The Text property requires a string expression or variable, correctly conforming to Crystal Reports formula syntax, which contains the new text you want the formula to contain. Take care when assigning a value to the formula. The Order + Tax formula is defined in Crystal Reports as a numeric formula. Therefore, you should pass it a formula that will evaluate to a number. If the user leaves the text box on the form empty, the VB code assumes no additional sales tax and simply places the Order Amount database field in the formula— the formula will show the same amount as the database field.

If, however, the user has specified a tax rate, the VB code manipulates the value by dividing it by 100 and then adding 1. This creates the proper type of number to multiply against the Order Amount field to correctly calculate tax. For example, if the user specifies a tax rate of 5 (for 5 percent tax), the VB code will change the value to 1.05 before combining it with the multiply operator and the Order Amount field in the formula.

You also may wish to show some form of code-modified text on the report (perhaps the combination of criteria supplied by your application's user interface). Although this can also be accomplished by setting the contents of a string formula, the RDC's capability of manipulating text objects at run time gives you the opportunity to approach this from another angle. Therefore, a formula is not used to accomplish this in the Xtreme Orders sample application with the RDC. The following section explains how this is accomplished by using a text object.

TIP Crystal Reports XI features two formula syntaxes: Crystal syntax, which is compatible with Crystal Reports 7 and earlier, and Basic syntax, which was introduced in Crystal Reports 8. If you need to know which syntax an existing formula is based on, execute some code to access the formula, such as retrieving the Text property. Then, retrieve the Report object's LastGetFormulaSyntax property to determine the syntax of the formula you retrieved before. If you want to assign a specific syntax to a certain formula, set the Report object's FormulaSyntax property first. Then, set the formula's contents by passing formula text in the correct syntax to the Text property.

Changing Text Objects at Run Time

Remember that when you add any object to the report (a field, formula, text object, or other object), the object can be manipulated by VB. It has properties that can be set on the Property Pages dialog box at design time, as well as being modified at run time. If you add a text object to the report, a TextObject object becomes available from within the overall Report object. The TextObject object exposes many properties (you can see most of them in the Properties dialog box) that can be set at run time.

You can access the actual contents of the text object with a property and a method. The Text property can be read during code execution to see what the text object contains. To change the contents of a text object, you need to use the TextObject SetText method at run time.

In the Xtreme Orders sample application, a text object has been placed in the report header and given the name SubHeading. The following code indicates how to set the contents of the text object to indicate what choices the user has made on the Print Xtreme Orders form. This code assumes that the strSubHeading string variable has been declared elsewhere in the application. You'll also notice references to the text object and combo box controls on the form.

```
'Set SubHeading text object
strSubHeading = txtFromDate & " through " & txtToDate
strSubHeading = strSubHeading & ", By " & cboGroupBy
If txtTaxRate = "" Then
    strSubHeading = strSubHeading & ", No Tax"
Else
    strSubHeading = strSubHeading & ", Sales Tax = " & txtTaxRate & "%"
End If   'txtTaxRate = ""
Report.SubHeading.SetText (strSubHeading)
'Note: parentheses around argument to SetText method are optional
```

Because you can change the contents of a text object from your VB code, you can essentially create "VB formulas" in your report by using the RDC. Each section of the report will fire a Format event when it is processed at report run time. You can use the SetText method inside this Format event to change the contents of text objects for each report record (in the details section Format event) or for group or report headers or footers (in their respective Format events). More information on the Format event and conditional section formatting is provided later in this chapter.

The RDC limits some of this ease of individual object control to only reports created with the RDC's internal ActiveX designer. If you use an external .RPT file with the RDC Library, you must sometimes navigate much deeper down the object hierarchy to perform this type of customization. For example, if you have just set up Application and Report objects that point to an external .RPT file (there is no ActiveX designer in your project), and you wish to set the contents of a text object, you'll need to execute code similar to this:

```
Report.Sections("PHb").ReportObjects(1).SetText "Order #"
```

This code will set the contents of the first text object in Report Header b to "Order #". This is accomplished by navigating into the Sections collection (one of the RDC collections that allows string indexes to be used, in addition to numbers). Within the Page Header b section, the first member of the ReportObjects collection (the text object) is being changed by executing the SetText method.

TIP *The RDC also allows you to manipulate embedded fields inside text objects. Using the TextObject object's FieldElements collection, you can add, remove, or query for embedded fields inside text objects.*

Passing Parameter-Field Values

If you are importing an existing .RPT file into the RDC or using an external .RPT file, the report may contain parameter fields that are designed to prompt the user for information whenever the report is refreshed. If you simply leave the parameter fields as they are, the application will automatically prompt the user for them when the report runs. Obviously, one of the main reasons to integrate the report into a VB application is to more closely control the user interface of the report. You'll probably want to alter the mechanism for gathering this data from the user, and then have the application supply the appropriate values to the parameter fields from within the application code.

Because you can control both report record selection and report formulas at run time from within your VB application, there may not be as much necessity to use parameter fields with an integrated report as there might be for a stand-alone report created with regular Crystal Reports. However, if you are using RDC to "share" an external .RPT file with other Crystal Reports users who are not using your custom application, you may need to set the values of parameter fields from within your code.

In this situation, use the Report object's ParameterFieldDefinitions collection to manipulate the parameters. As with formulas, there is one ParameterFieldDefinition object in the collection for each parameter field defined in the report. And as with formulas, the proper member of the collection is retrieved with a one-based index determined by the order in which the parameter fields were added to the report. You can't retrieve a parameter field by using its name as the index (unless you use the looping technique or GetItemByName approaches discussed earlier in the chapter for use with formula fields).

The RDC approach for setting the value of a parameter field being passed to a report is to use the ParameterFieldDefinition object's AddCurrentValue method. This passes a single value to the report parameter field. Because a report can contain multiple-value parameter fields, you can execute the AddCurrentValue method as many times as necessary (for example, in a loop that looks through a list box for selected items) to populate a parameter field with several values.

Although the report included in this sample application (available at www.CrystalBook.com) uses a direct format of the details section during its Format event (discussed later in the chapter) to change section color, this is an example of where a parameter field could be used. If this were the desired approach for conditional formatting, the following code would correctly pass the value to the parameter field:

```
'Set parameter value
'Alternative method is to format Details section within VB
If txtHighlight = "" Then
    Report.ParameterFields(1).AddCurrentValue (0)
Else
    Report.ParameterFields(1).AddCurrentValue (Val(txtHighlight))
End If   'txtHighlight = ""
```

Here, the value is set to 0 if the text box is empty. This is important to note, because the actual parameter field in the report is numeric. Passing it an empty string might cause a run-time error when the report runs. Also, because the AddCurrentValue method is executed at least once, and a value has been passed to the parameter field, the user will no longer be prompted for it when the report is run.

TIP *The RDC object model exposes all the features of Crystal Reports parameter fields, such as range values, multiple values, and edit masks. Look in online developer's help to find the "ParameterFieldDefinition Object" entry. There, you'll find a complete description of the object, as well as all the methods available for manipulating parameter fields.*

Manipulating Report Groups

One of the requirements for the Xtreme Orders report is that the user be able to specify how the report is grouped. A combo box exists on the Print Report form that lets the user choose between Quarter and Customer grouping. In the RDC design window, this is normally accomplished by using the Change Group option from a pop-up menu to change the field a group is based on, as well as the sequence (ascending or descending) that you want the groups to appear in. If the group is based on a date field, such as Order Date, you may also specify the range of dates (week, month, quarter, and so on) that make up the group. To familiarize yourself with various grouping options, refer to Chapter 3.

By being able to change these options from within an application at run time, you can provide great reporting flexibility to your end users. In many cases, you can make it appear that several different reports are available, depending on user input. In fact, the application will be using the same Report object, but grouping will be changed at run time according to user input.

Manipulating groups in the RDC object model requires a bit of navigation "down the object hierarchy." Ultimately, the database or formula field a group is based on is specified by the GroupConditionField property of the Area object. A report contains an Areas collection consisting of an Area object for each area in a report. Consider an "area" of the report to be each individual main section of the report, such as the page header, details section, group footer, and so on. If there are multiple sections on the report, such as Details a and Details b sections, they are still part of the overall details *area*, and there is only one member of the Areas collection for them. The Areas collection has one advantage not shared by most other collections exposed by the RDC—the index used to refer to an individual member of the collection can be a string value or a numeric value. This allows you to specify RH, PH, GHn, D, GFn, PF, or RF as index values, or use the one-based index number. Using the string values makes your code much easier to understand when working with the Areas collection, and you don't have to write extra looping code, like that shown earlier for formula manipulation.

NOTE *The Areas and Sections collections are similar, but not identical. As shown in an example earlier in this chapter, in the section "Changing Text Objects at Run Time," the Sections collection can also accept a string index; but this collection exposes individual sections, with indexes such as PHa for Page Header a and PHb for Page Header b. The Areas collection contains only one member for the Page Header area (referenced with a string index of PH), even if there are multiple page header sections, such as Page Header a and Page Header b.*

However, once you navigate to the specific Area object to specify the GroupConditionField property, you are faced with additional work when approaching the RDC object model. You cannot simply supply a string value containing the actual field name (such as {Orders.Order Date} or {Customer.Customer Name}) to indicate which field you wish to base a group on. Instead, you must specify a DatabaseFieldDefinition object to the GroupConditionField property—you can't just pass a string containing the field name.

The DatabaseFieldDefinition object is found quite "deep" in the object hierarchy—there is one of these objects for each field contained in the DatabaseFieldDefinitions collection in a DatabaseTable object. And, multiple DatabaseTable objects are contained in the DatabaseTables collection of the Database object, contained inside the overall Report object. To make things even more complex, none of the collections just mentioned will accept a string index value—you must specify a one-based index value. You can use the previously mentioned GetItemByName method with the DatabaseFieldDefinitions collection, but not with the DatabaseTables collection.

Although this sounds confusing and hard to navigate, you'll eventually be able to travel through the object hierarchy fairly quickly to find the database table and field you want to provide to the GroupConditionField property. Look at the following code from the Xtreme Orders sample application:

```
'Set grouping
If cboGroupBy = "Quarter" Then
    Report.Areas("GH").GroupConditionField = _
        Report.Database.Tables(1).Fields(5) 'Orders.Order Date
    Report.Areas("GH").GroupCondition = crGCQuarterly
Else
    Report.Areas("GH").GroupConditionField = _
        Report.Database.Tables(2).Fields(3) 'Customer.Customer Name
    Report.Areas("GH").GroupCondition = crGCAnyValue
End If   'cboGroupBy = "Quarter"
```

In this example, notice that the grouping is based on the user choice for the cboGroupBy combo box. In either case, the GroupConditionField property of the GH member of the Areas collection (the group header) is being set. If the user chooses to group by Order Date, the property is set to the fifth member of the Fields collection in the first member of the Tables collection. This indicates that the fifth field (Order Date) in the first table (Orders) will be used for grouping. If the user chooses to group by Customer, the third field (Customer Name) in the second table (Customer) will be used for grouping. As with other collections that don't allow string indexes, you can use quick Print statements in the Immediate window to search through different members of the collection. You can also look at the Database section of the Field Explorer view in the RDC design window to determine which index numbers to use to point to the correct tables and fields. The GetItemByName method can be used. Or, you can write a function that uses looping logic, described earlier, to search through the collections until you find a matching name value.

In addition to choosing the database field you want to use for the group, you may have to choose how the grouping occurs, particularly if you use a date or Boolean field as the group field. This is accomplished by setting the Area object's GroupCondition property, which can be set to an integer value or an RDC-supplied constant (see the explanation for the Area object in the online developer's help for specific constants and integer values). In the sample code shown previously, the group is set to break for every calendar quarter if

Order Date grouping is set (hence, the crGCQuarterly constant that is provided). If Customer Name grouping is chosen, the crGCAnyValue constant is supplied, indicating that a new group will be created whenever the value of the group field changes.

Conditional Formatting and Formatting Sections

You'll often want to present your RDC reports in the Report Viewer to allow report interaction in an online environment, instead of having them printed on paper. The Report Viewer provides complete interactive reporting features, such as drill-down, that are invaluable to the application designer. Having control over these capabilities at run time provides for great flexibility.

The Xtreme Orders sample application gives the user the opportunity to specify whether or not to see the report as a summary report only. When this check box is selected, the VB application needs to hide the report details section so that only group subtotals appear on the report. In addition, you need to control the appearance of the report's two page header sections (Page Header a and Page Header b), as well as the two Group Header #1 sections (Group Header #1a and Group Header #1b). This is done to accommodate two different sections of field titles that you wish to appear differently if the report is presented as a summary report instead of a detail report. If the report is being displayed as a detail report, the field titles should appear at the top of every page of the report, along with the subheading and smaller report title. If the report is displayed as a summary report, you want the field titles to appear in the group header section of a drill-down tab only when the user double-clicks a group. Since no detail information will be visible in the main report window, field titles there won't be meaningful.

And finally, you'll want to show Group Header #1a, which contains the group name field, if the report is showing detail data. This will indicate which group the following set of orders applies to. However, if the report is showing only summary data, showing both the group header and group footer would be repetitive—the group footer already contains the group name, so showing the group header as well will look odd. However, you will want the group header with the group name to appear in a drill-down tab. Therefore, you need to control the appearance of four sections when a user chooses the Summary Report option. Look at Table 25-1 to get a better idea of how you'll want to conditionally set these sections at run time.

You'll notice that, in some cases, sections need to be completely suppressed (so they don't show up, even in a drill-down tab) as opposed to hidden (they show up in a drill-down tab,

Section	Detail Report	Summary Report
Page Header b (field titles)	Shown	Suppressed (no drill-down)
Group Header #1a (group name field)	Shown	Hidden (drill-down okay)
Group Header #1b (field titles)	Suppressed (no drill-down)	Hidden (drill-down okay)
Details (detail order data)	Shown	Hidden (drill-down okay)

TABLE 25-1 Section Formatting for Different Report Types

but not in the main Preview tab). There is a somewhat obscure relationship among areas and sections that make this determination. Specifically, only complete areas (such as the entire Group Header #1) can be hidden, not individual sections (for example, Group Header #1a). However, both areas and sections can be suppressed. To further explain this concept, if you look in the Properties dialog box after you've selected a section in the design window, you'll see a Suppress property but no Hide property.

This presents a bit of a coding challenge for the Xtreme Orders sample application. First, you need to determine the correct combination of area hiding and section suppressing that sets what appears in the Preview window and in a drill-down tab. If an area is set to Hide, none of the sections in it will appear in the main Preview window. And when the user drills down into that section, you will also want to control which sections inside the drilled-down area appear in the drill-down tab. Then, you must find where to set the Hide property for a particular area. You must also find where to set the Suppress property for sections inside the hidden area, or other sections that aren't hidden.

Since the Hide property is available only for an entire area, you need to set the HideForDrillDown property for the appropriate Area object within the Areas collection. Since the Suppress property needs to be set for individual sections, you can just refer to the individual sections in the RDC design window by name, setting the Suppress property for them as needed. Consider that the Page Header b section has been given the name PHb in the Properties dialog box (it was named Section 3 when the report was imported). Other sections have been given more descriptive names in the RDC design window, as well. Group Header #1a is named GH1A, and Group Header #1b is named GH1B.

Keeping in mind the preceding discussion and the hide and suppress requirements outlined in Table 25-1, look at this code from the sample application:

```
'Hide/show sections
With Report
   If chkSummary Then
      .Areas("D").HideForDrillDown = True
      .PHb.Suppress = True
      .Areas("GH1").HideForDrillDown = True
      .GH1A.Suppress = False
      .GH1B.Suppress = False
   Else
      .Areas("D").HideForDrillDown = False
      .PHb.Suppress = False
      .Areas("GH1").HideForDrillDown = False
      .GH1A.Suppress = False
      .GH1B.Suppress = True
   End If   'chkSummary
End With   'Report
```

Notice that both Area objects for the details and Group Header #1 areas are being formatted, as well as individual sections. The areas must be formatted from their collection, whereas sections can be manipulated directly below the Report object by name.

NOTE *You can navigate deeper into the object hierarchy and actually set the Suppress property for members of the Sections collection inside the Area object. Although this is a little more code intensive, it is required if you are using an external .RPT file, which doesn't expose individual section names as does the RDC ActiveX designer.*

The Format Event

Another benefit that only the RDC provides to developers is the Format event. This event is "fired" every time the processing of an individual report section begins. Consider the way the first page of a report might be processed. First, the overall report is "prepared"; then the page header prints, followed, in order, by the report header (since this is the first page of the report), the first group header, all the details sections in that group, the first group footer, and so on. Each time any of these sections begins to print (including when the report is "prepared"), its respective Format event fires.

You can intercept these formatting events and change the behavior of the section, or of objects within the section. This gives you complete Visual Basic functionality when it comes to conditional formatting or section formatting.

TIP *While these format events are automatically exposed when you use the internal RDC ActiveX Designer, you can use them when integrating external .RPT files with the RDC. This can be accomplished by declaring a variable of type Section using the VB keycode WihtEvents. For example, the following code will allow you to use the Format event with an external report:*

```
Dim WithEvents detailSection As CRAXDRT.Section
```

To add code for any Format event, simply double-click a section in the RDC design window. This displays the Format event in the code window for the particular section you double-clicked. You can also right-click the designer in the Visual Basic Project Explorer and choose View Code from the pop-up menu. In either case, each report section appears in the object drop-down list in the upper-left corner of the code window. The only available procedure for each report section is Format, which will appear in the procedure drop-down list in the upper-right corner.

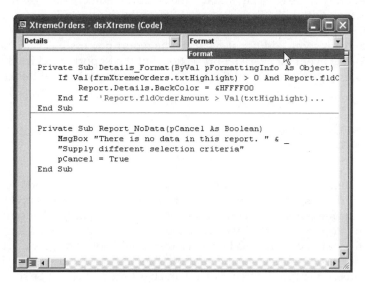

You have all the power of VB at your disposal to control the appearance and formatting of sections and objects, or the content of text objects, while the report is being formatted.

This allows you to write VB code to determine how to format a field in the current section being formatted (perhaps to set the background or font color of an object according to some VB code). You can also change the formatting of the entire section, as demonstrated in the following code from the Xtreme Orders sample application:

```
Private Sub Details_Format (ByVal pFormattingInfo As Object)
    If Val(frmXtremeOrders.txtHighlight) > 0 And _
    Report.fldOrderAmount.Value > Val(frmXtremeOrders.txtHighlight) Then
        Report.Details.BackColor = &HFFFF00
    End If  'Report.fldOrderAmount > Val(txtHighlight)...
End Sub
```

TIP *The pFormattingInfo argument that is passed into the module is an object that exposes three read-only properties that return true or false: IsEndOfGroup, IsStartOfGroup, and IsRepeatedGroupHeader. You can read the contents of these properties to help determine how to handle logic in the Format event.*

This code is contained in the Format event for the details section (notice that the report section has been renamed Details from its default name of Section 6). Every time the details section begins to format, this event fires. At that time, the contents of the Highlight text box on the Print Xtreme Orders form are checked for a value. If the user has supplied a value, and the fldOrderAmount database field from the report is greater than the value the user supplied, the background color of the details section is set. This logic replaces the parameter field and conditional formatting used in many other similar reporting situations.

Obviously, many other flexible and complex types of formatting and manipulation can occur during the Format event. A common use of this manipulation is to replace formula fields on the report with text objects, and use the SetText method to change the contents of the text objects from within the Format event. Essentially, this extends the complete power of the Visual Basic language to objects you place on your report.

The RDC exposes some additional events to the report-processing cycle. Not only can you trap the Format event for every report section, but the Report object itself fires several events as it processes. An event of particular interest is NoData. Look at this code fragment:

```
Private Sub Report_NoData(pCancel As Boolean)
    MsgBox "There is no data in this report. " & _
    "Supply different selection criteria"
    pCancel = True
End Sub
```

If the report contains no data when it processes, the NoData event will fire. You may trap this event and perform special handling. In particular, by setting the pCancel value to true, you can cancel the remainder of report processing. Be aware, though, that canceling report processing won't stop the Report Viewer from appearing—you need to add a global variable or some other flag to indicate that the Report Viewer should not be displayed in this event.

As you search through RDC documentation, you may see references to "Formatting Idle" or other processing time references. Certain object properties can be set only during certain times when the report is processing. This is mostly significant when writing code in the Format event. If you attempt to set a property that can't be set during that particular report-processing time, you'll receive either error messages or unexpected results. Look for a discussion of formatting modes by searching the online Help for "Format event."

CAUTION *Formatting events may fire more often than you might expect because of the multiple passes Crystal Reports must make as it processes the report. This may happen, for example, when the RDC encounters a Keep Together section option at the end of a page. If you place code to accumulate values in the Format event without accounting for these multiple passes, your accumulations will be inaccurate. The RDC includes a feature called Report Variables that can keep track of these reporting passes. If you use Report Variables instead of your own variables, values will accumulate only when an actual "logical" change occurs to a report section. Search the online Help file for "Report Variables" to get complete details.*

Choosing Output Destinations

If your users will have a choice of output destinations (as the user does in the Xtreme Orders sample application), you need to create appropriate code to handle the user's choice. In the Xtreme Orders sample application, radio buttons and a text box allow the user to choose to view the report in the preview window, print the report to a printer, or attach the report as a .PDF file to an e-mail message. If the user chooses e-mail as the output destination, an e-mail address can be entered in a text box. Depending on the user's selection, you need to set the output destination in your VB code.

If the user chooses to view the report on the screen, you need to activate the Report Viewer. In the sample application, this simply entails displaying the form that contains the Report Viewer control, by executing the form's Show method. The Form_Load event of this form will pass the Report object to the Report Viewer and execute the Report Viewer's ViewReport method.

As mentioned earlier, use of the Report Viewer is completely optional—you are free to answer No when you are prompted about whether or not to add it when first adding the RDC to your project. However, if one of the output options will be to the screen (as in the Xtreme Orders sample application), make sure that the Report Viewer is eventually added to your project.

If you respond Yes to the RDC's "Do you want to add the Report Viewer" prompt, the RDC automatically adds the Report Viewer for you. It will create a new form, place the Report Viewer in the form, and automatically add rudimentary code to supply the Report object to the Report Viewer and resize the Report Viewer to be the same size as the form. If the RDC adds the Report Viewer automatically, you can leave this default behavior as is, move the Report Viewer object to another form, or build additional elements into the form that the RDC created automatically. You can also manually add the Report Viewer to your project later and supply code to pass the Report object to the Report Viewer.

If you wish to print the Report object to a printer, execute the Report object's PrintOut method. The syntax is as follows:

```
object.PrintOut Prompt, Copies, Collated, StartPage, StopPage
```

In this statement, *Prompt* is a Boolean value indicating whether or not to prompt the user for printer options, *Copies* is a numeric value indicating how many copies of the report to print, *Collated* is a Boolean value indicating whether or not to collate the pages, and *StartPage* and

StopPage are numeric values indicating which page numbers to start and stop printing on. The parameters are optional—if you want to skip any in the middle, just add commas in the correct positions—but don't include the parameter.

NOTE *The initial Crystal Reports XI release will not prompt for printer options even if the Prompt argument is set to True. You'll need to download a fix or service pack from support.BusinessObjects.com to solve this problem.*

If you wish to export the report to a disk file or attach the report to an e-mail message as a file, use the Report object's Export method. The syntax is as follows:

```
object.Export PromptUser
```

In this statement, *PromptUser* is a Boolean value indicating whether you want to prompt the user for export options. If you choose not to prompt the user for export options, you need to set properties of the report's ExportOptions object. The ExportOptions object contains many properties that determine the output destination (file or e-mail), file format (Word, Excel, PDF, XML, and so on), filename, e-mail address, and more. Many of these properties accept integer values or RDC-supplied descriptive constants. If you choose MAPI as the destination, the user's PC needs to have a MAPI-compliant e-mail client installed, such as Microsoft Outlook or Eudora Pro. Look for all the available ExportOptions properties by searching the online Help for "ExportOptions object."

In the Xtreme Orders sample application, the following code is used to choose an output destination, as well as to specify a file type and e-mail information, based on user selection:

```
'Set output destination
If optPreview Then frmViewer.Show
If OptPrint Then Report.PrintOut (True)
If OptEmail Then
    With Report
        .ExportOptions.DestinationType = crEDTEMailMAPI
        .ExportOptions.MailToList = txtAddress
        .ExportOptions.MailSubject = "Here's the Xtreme Orders Report"
        .ExportOptions.MailMessage = _
"Attached is a PDF file showing the latest Xtreme Orders Report."
        .ExportOptions.FormatType = crEFTPortableDocFormat
        .Export (False)
    End With  'Report
End If  'optEmail
```

CAUTION *If you use the Report object's Export method to export or send the report attached to an e-mail message, make sure you specify all the necessary ExportOptions object properties. If you fail to specify necessary properties or specify them incorrectly, an error may be thrown. Or, the user may be prompted to specify export options, even though you specifically add a false argument to the Export method. If the export takes place at an unattended machine, your application has to wait for a response, even though no user is available to respond.*

Changing the Data Source at Run Time

Obviously, one of the main benefits of integrating a Crystal Report in a Visual Basic program is the ability to tie the report contents to a data set or result set that the program is manipulating. This allows a user to interact with your application and then run a report that contains the same set of data that the user has selected.

One way to accomplish this is to create a Crystal Reports record selection formula or a SQL statement based on your user interface. The formula or SQL statement can then be passed to the report, as discussed elsewhere in this chapter. This allows the user to interact with a data grid, form, or other visual interface in the application and create a report based on its contents.

However, you may encounter situations in which you prefer to have the contents of an actual Visual Basic record set from one of Visual Basic's intrinsic data models act as the data source for a report. The RDC provides for this with the SetDataSource method. Using SetDataSource, you can initially design the report using a particular database or data source, or using a field-definition file (discussed in the online Help). Then, you can pass a Visual Basic DAO, RDO, or ADO record set, snapshot, or result set to the report at run time. The RDC will use the current contents of the VB data set to populate the report.

The syntax for SetDataSource is as follows:

```
[form]Object.SetDataSource data, DataTag, tableIndex
```

In this statement, *Object* is the RDC Database object (residing below the Report object) that you want to supply data to; *data* is the DAO, ADO, or RDO data set that you want to supply data to the report; and *DataTag* and *tableIndex* are parameters indicating, respectively, the type of data and the index of the table that you want to change the data source for. The *DataTag* parameter should always be specified as 3, with *tableIndex* being set according to the table you wish to "point" to the new data source.

Thus, if you have created an RDC report and named the Report object "Report," and you have identified an ADO Recordset object elsewhere in your VB application with the name "ADOrs," the following code will pass the contents of the result set to the report. When the report is printed, exported, or passed to the Report Viewer, the contents of the result set will be used by the report's Database object to populate the report.

```
Report.Database.SetDataSource ADOrs,3,1
```

Notice that the last two parameters to the SetDataSource method are 3 and 1, indicating the only allowable data tag (3), and the first table in the database (1).

There are actually two forms of the SetDataSource method available with the RDC. The method described previously applies to the entire Database object, requiring the third argument indicating a table index. There is also a SetDataSource method available for the DatabaseTable object. The syntax is almost the same—the only difference is that a table-index parameter is not required, because the method applies only to a single Table object.

If you use SetDataSource to change the data source for a database table, make sure the data source you pass to the report remains in scope whenever the report runs. For example, you may define a Report object that's global to your application (by declaring it at the module level). But if you pass it a data source that was declared at the form level, and then try to run the report in another form, the data source will be out of scope and the report will fail. The ReadRecords method is available for reading the contents of the data source into the Report object, if maintaining scope for the data source isn't practical. Search the Developer's Help for information on "ReadRecords."

Tip *The RDC provides two other methods available from the Database object (underneath the Report object) that are similar to SetDataSource. AddOLEDBSource will add an OLE DB table and make its fields available to the report. AddADOCommand will add and pass an ADO record set as a table to the report through an ADO connection and command.*

Unbound Fields

Depending on the reporting application you are designing, you may choose to create a very basic generic report layout that doesn't connect to any particular database at the time you design it. This might be appropriate, for example, for an application that allows a user to choose from a list of database fields and drag and drop them to a pseudoreport outline in your application. When the report is actually printed, your code would need to match the chosen fields to actual field locations on a Crystal Report. Or, you may design one report that a user can choose to connect to either a test database or a production database. Although the SetDataSource method, described previously, may be a good alternative for this example, you may also want to manually assign database values to fields on the report.

The RDC provides capabilities to make this type of customized reporting much easier. *Unbound Fields* can be added to your report in the ActiveX designer just like database fields, formula fields, and so forth. The only difference is that the fields don't actually connect to any particular database table or field. This assignment is made at run time, using automatic or manual binding (discussed later in the chapter).

Adding Unbound Fields to a Report   The first step in using Unbound Fields is to add them to the report in the RDC designer. You'll notice the additional Unbound Fields category in the Field Explorer that you don't see in the regular Crystal Reports designer. When you click the plus sign next to this category, you'll see a list of Unbound Field data types. Drag and drop the desired data types to the report just as you would other Field Explorer objects. Figure 25-4 shows Unbound Fields being placed on a report.

The RDC will apply default object names to the Unbound Fields you drag and drop. Depending on how you're planning ultimately to bind the fields to your data source, you may leave the default names if you so choose. But, it probably makes sense to at least give the Unbound Fields meaningful names, to help you remember what you're binding when you begin to write the binding code. And, if you plan to use the RDC's automatic binding method (discussed in the next section), you need to give them names identical to the field names in the data source that you will be binding to them.

Binding Fields to the Data Source   Once you've created the report with your complement of Unbound Fields, it's time to bind them at run time. First, declare and assign any necessary objects. In the following sample code, a Report object is defined to contain the ActiveX designer report, and an ADO record set is created. Fields from this record set will be bound to the Unbound Fields created in the report.

```
Dim Report As New CrystalReport1
Dim rs As New ADOR.Recordset
rs.Open "select * from orders", "xtreme sample database 11"
Report.Database.AddADOCommand rs.ActiveConnection, rs.ActiveCommand
```

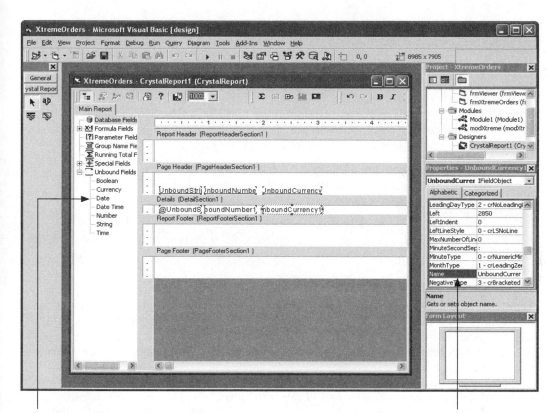

Drag desired data type from Field Explorer   Give the Unbound Field the appropriate object name

FIGURE 25-4   Adding Unbound Fields to a report

Remember that even though the Unbound Fields you added to the report aren't "connected" to any particular database fields, the Report object itself must be connected to your desired data source before you can bind any fields to it. This is accomplished with AddADOCommand, AddOLEDBSource, or some similar method.

After you make the data connection, there are two ways of actually binding the Unbound Fields to a database field: automatic binding and manual binding.

Automatic Binding   *Automatic binding* uses the Unbound Field's data type and, optionally, object name to bind to actual data fields in the data source. To use automatic binding, execute a single line of code similar to this:

```
Report.AutoSetUnboundFieldSource crBMTNameAndValue
```

By supplying the crBMTNameAndValue constant to the AutoSetUnboundFieldSource method, you assure that the RDC will use both the name and the data type of the Unbound Field to try to match to a data source field. If you want to base this object-to-field matching on name only, supply the constant crBMTName. The RDC will then attempt to match Unbound Fields to data source fields solely on the basis of name, regardless of data type.

Manual Binding   If you have disparate data sources that won't always match field names with the names you've given your Unbound Fields, you can assign data source fields to the Unbound Fields one by one. Examine the following code fragment:

```
Report.OrderID.SetUnboundFieldSource "{ado.Order ID}"
Report.OrderDate.SetUnboundFieldSource "{ado.Order Date}"
Report.OrderAmount.SetUnboundFieldSource "{ado.Order Amount}"
Report.ShipVia.SetUnboundFieldSource "{ado.Ship Via}"
```

In this example, individual Unbound Fields are matched to data source fields using the field object's SetUnboundFieldSource method.

Customizing the Report Viewer

If you've added the Report Viewer ActiveX component to your project, you have a great deal of flexibility in customizing the way the Report Viewer appears and behaves. By default, the RDC will add the Report Viewer to its own form and add a small amount of code to supply the Report object to the Report Viewer and resize the Report Viewer whenever the form is resized.

This default behavior uses just a fraction of the Report Viewer's capabilities. The viewer has many options, exposed by its own library, which will meld it more tightly into your application. You can customize how the Report Viewer looks, what controls and toolbar buttons are available, and the Report Viewer's size. You may even perform all the functions from within code that the built-in toolbar buttons would accomplish. This allows you to make the Report Viewer show virtually no controls but the report itself, if you prefer. You can design a completely separate user interface for page control, zoom levels, printing, exporting, and more.

In addition, the Report Viewer contains a flexible event model that will "fire" events as the Report Viewer performs various functions, or as a user interacts with it. You can trap button clicks, drill-down selections, changes in the zoom level, and other events. You can execute extra code when any of these events occur, or intercept the events and cancel them if you wish to not have the Report Viewer complete them.

When you add the Report Viewer to a form (or when it's added automatically by the RDC), you'll see the outline of the Report Viewer appear as an object inside the form. When you select the Report Viewer object, you'll see a large number of design-time properties appear in the Properties box in VB. This is illustrated in Figure 25-5.

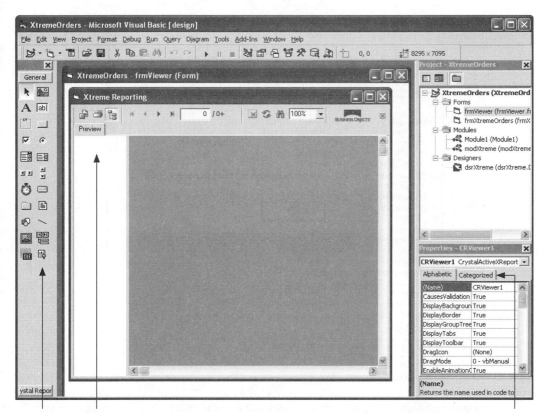

Report Viewer object dragged to form from toolbar   Design-time properties available for the Report Viewer

FIGURE 25-5   The Report Viewer and its design-time properties

If you want the Report Viewer to exhibit consistent behavior during the entire application, you can change properties for the Report Viewer at design time, such as which toolbar buttons are shown, whether a report group tree is displayed, whether a user can drill down, and so on.

Most of these properties can also be set at run time by supplying the appropriate values to the Report Viewer object's properties. Because the Report Viewer object actually adds its own COM library to your project, you can get an idea of the object model, properties, methods, and events that are available by looking at the Object Browser. Press F2, or choose View | Object Browser from the Visual Basic pull-down menus. Then, choose

CrystalActiveXReportViewerLib11Ctl in the library drop-down list to see the object model exposed by the Report Viewer's Library.

Here's some code from the Xtreme Orders sample application that customizes several Report Viewer behaviors. The Print button is turned off on the Report Viewer by setting the EnablePrintButton property to false. The Help button is displayed on the Report Viewer by setting the EnableHelpButton property to true. The Business Objects logo animation control is turned on by setting the EnableAnimationCtrl property to true. And, the EnableDrillDown property determines whether or not a user can double-click a group in the Report Viewer to drill down (if the user chooses to show a detail report, drill-down isn't of benefit).

```
CRViewer1.EnablePrintButton = False
CRViewer1.EnableHelpButton = True
CRViewer1.EnableAnimationCtrl = True

If frmXtremeOrders.chkSummary Then
    CRViewer1.EnableDrillDown = True
Else
    CRViewer1.EnableDrillDown = False
End If   'frmXtremeOrders.chkSummary
```

Trapping Report Viewer Events

The Report Viewer library, in addition to offering a good selection of properties and methods, exposes a large number of events that allow you to trap button clicks, report-processing cycles, and drill-down attempts. These events can be used to modify the behavior of the

Report Viewer, to execute some additional supplementary code when a certain event occurs, or potentially to modify report contents while it is being viewed.

A section of CrystalDevHelp.CHM covers programming the Report Viewers. You'll find complete information about which events are available for custom coding. You may also look at the Object Browser. Or, just open the code window for the Report Viewer object and look at the procedure drop-down list in the upper-right corner of the code window.

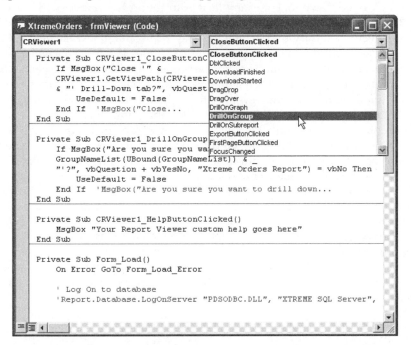

Because you can trap many events that occur during report processing and user interaction with the Report Viewer, you have tremendous power to customize your reporting application. The Xtreme Orders sample application has only three simple examples of these capabilities. If the user clicks the Help button in the Report Viewer, a message box appears indicating "Custom Help Goes Here." When the user drills down on a group, a confirmation message box appears, asking the user to confirm the drill-down. If the answer is Yes, the drill-down will occur. If the answer is No, the drill-down will be canceled. And, after a user drills down and clicks the Close View button (the small X at the very upper right) in the Report Viewer, another confirmation message box appears, asking the user to confirm the closure. As with the original drill-down, the drill-down tab will be closed only if the user answers Yes. Otherwise, the event will be canceled.

One of the more complex parts of these examples is actually determining which group will be affected when the drill-down or drill-down tab closure occurs. Understanding this is crucial for fully exploiting the power of the event model—trapping these events is probably of little use if you can't determine which group is actually being manipulated. The Report Viewer DrillOnGroup event makes this task easier by passing the GroupNameList parameter into the event function. This zero-based array contains an element for each group that has been drilled into previously, with the current group that is now being drilled into being the last element of the array.

If your report contains only one level of grouping (as does the Xtreme Orders sample report), the GroupNameList will always contain just element 0—the group that was drilled down to. However, if your report contains multiple levels of grouping, you'll have the extra benefit of determining how deep and which groups are included in the group that is currently being drilled down to. For example, if your report is grouped on three levels— Country, State, and City—a user may first drill down on Canada. This will fire the DrillOnGroup event, and the GroupNameList array will contain only element 0, Canada. Then, in the Canada drill-down tab, the user might double-click BC. This will again fire the DrillOnGroup event, and the GroupNameList array will now contain two elements, Canada in element 0 and BC in element 1. Then, if the user double-clicks Vancouver in the BC drill-down tab, yet another DrillOnGroup event will fire. Inside this event, the GroupNameList array will contain elements 0, 1, and 2—Canada, BC, and Vancouver.

If you are concerned about only the lowest level of grouping, just query the last element of the GroupNameList array by using the VB UBound function. Even though the Xtreme Orders report contains only one level of grouping (thereby always allowing GroupNameList(0) to be used to determine the group), the UBound function has been used for upward compatibility.

The other argument passed to the DrillOnGroup event is UseDefault. This Boolean value can be set to true or false inside the event to determine whether the drill-down actually occurs. If UseDefault is set to true (or left as is), the drill-down will occur. If it is set to false inside the DrillOnGroup event, the drill-down will be canceled and no drill-down tab will appear for the group in the Report Viewer.

Here's the sample code from the Xtreme Orders application. Note that the actual group being drilled on is included in the message box and that the results of the message box determine whether or not the drill-down occurs.

```
Private Sub CRViewer1_DrillOnGroup(GroupNameList As Variant, _
ByVal DrillType As CrystalActiveXReportViewerLib11Ctl.CRDrillType,_
        UseDefault As Boolean)
    If MsgBox("Are you sure you want to drill down on '" & _
    GroupNameList(UBound(GroupNameList)) & _
    "'?", vbQuestion + vbYesNo, "Xtreme Orders Report") = vbNo Then
        UseDefault = False
    End If   'MsgBox("Are you sure you want to drill down...
End Sub
```

The other Report Viewer event that is used in the Xtreme Orders sample application is CloseButtonClicked. This event fires whenever a user clicks the small X in the upper right-hand corner of the Report Viewer to close the current drill-down tab (known in the Report Viewer object model as the *current view*). Again, the sample application simply displays a confirming message box asking whether or not the user really wants to close the drill-down tab. By setting the UseDefault parameter inside the event code, the drill-down tab is closed or not closed, based on the user's choice.

As when drilling down, the actual drill-down tab that's being closed needs to be known inside the event (it's just being included in the message box in this example). Because the CloseButtonClicked event doesn't pass a GroupNameList or similar parameter into the event, a little more sleuthing has to be done to determine what the current view is. This is where both the Report Viewer's GetViewPath method and its ActiveViewIndex property come into play.

The ActiveViewIndex property simply returns an integer (one based) indicating which drill-down tab is the currently selected tab. While this is helpful, it doesn't return the actual string containing the group name of the tab being viewed. This must be accomplished by using the GetViewPath method of the Report Viewer object. This method accepts one argument, a numeric index indicating the tab in the Report Viewer window for which you want to see the view path. The method returns a one-based string array that includes the actual views (or group names) that are included in the drill-down tab whose index is provided as the argument to GetViewPath. As with GroupNameList, you can then determine the actual name of the current tab being closed by accessing the last element (using the UBound function) of the array.

Examine the following code closely:

```
Private Sub CRViewer1_CloseButtonClicked(UseDefault As Boolean)
    If MsgBox("Close '" & _
CRViewer1.GetViewPath(CRViewer1.ActiveViewIndex)
(UBound(CRViewer1.GetViewPath(CRViewer1.ActiveViewIndex))) _
    & "' Drill-Down tab?", vbQuestion + vbYesNo, _
        "Xtreme Order Report") = vbNo Then
        UseDefault = False
    End If  'MsgBox("Close...
End Sub
```

NOTE *Due to width restrictions in the book, the sample code in the preceding example that demonstrates the CRViewer1.GetViewPath command is broken in various locations. If you look at the sample application from the CrystalBook.com web site, you'll notice that lines are broken in different places, as is required for proper VB interpretation of the code.*

Notice that GetViewPath is supplied with the ActiveViewIndex property. This will return a string array containing all the groups that are included in the current drill-down tab. Even though the Xtreme Orders report contains only one level of grouping, the UBound function is still used to retrieve the last element of the array returned by GetViewPath. This provides upward compatibility if you ever choose to add multiple groups to the report.

The RDC provides additional Report Viewer support for the familiar Crystal Reports Select Expert and Search Expert, as well as a Text Search feature. Buttons for these tools can be enabled or disabled at design time or run time. And, you can programmatically perform both formula-based and text-based searches with the Report Viewer's SearchByFormula and SearchForText methods.

CAUTION *If you are integrating an external .RPT file with the RDC, and you wish to trap drill-down events from within the Report Viewer, ensure that the Create Group Tree option is checked from File | Report Options in Crystal Reports. If you don't specifically set this option, you may get an error when the Report Viewer attempts to trap drill down events.*

Error Handling

You need to set up error-handling code for all aspects of RDC programming. As you manipulate the Report object itself (setting properties and executing methods), you need to plan for the possibility that errors may occur. And if you use the Report Viewer in your application, it can also throw errors for any number of reasons. Add error-handling logic accordingly.

All Report object and Report Viewer errors will appear as regular Visual Basic run-time errors. These need to be trapped with an On Error Goto routine. The hard part is trying to figure out what error codes to trap. Unfortunately, Business Objects has yet to provide comprehensive documentation for the errors that either the Report or Report Viewer objects might throw. In many situations, you'll see typical VB-type error codes for report-related errors. For example, supplying a string index argument to a Report object collection that accepts only integer arguments won't generate an RDC-specific error; instead, Type Mismatch will be returned. However, certain error messages that are Report- or Report Viewer–specific generally throw errors that start with –2147 and are followed by six other numbers.

You'll simply have to test your application thoroughly and create error-handling code appropriately. Try intentionally creating any Report- or Report Viewer–related errors that have even a remote chance of occurring. You can then determine what corresponding error codes the Report or Report Viewer objects throw, and add code to trap those specific errors. Here's sample code from the Xtreme Orders application that traps potential errors when setting Report properties at run time:

```
cmdOK_Click_Error:
Screen.MousePointer = vbDefault
Select Case Err.Number
    Case -2147190889
        MsgBox "Report Cancelled", vbInformation, "Xtreme Order Report"
    Case -2147190908
        MsgBox "Invalid E-Mail address or other e-mail problem", _
                vbCritical, "Xtreme Order Report"
        txtAddress.SetFocus
    Case Else
        MsgBox "Error " & Err.Number & " - " & Err.Description, _
                vbCritical, "Xtreme Order Report"
End Select    'Case Err.Number
```

Other RDC Properties and Methods

This chapter has covered many RDC procedures for handling most common report-customization requirements, but several other areas of RDC functionality deserve some discussion. In particular, RDC functions that pertain to handling SQL database reporting, as well as dealing with subreports, should be addressed. In addition, the RDC DiscardSavedData method for "resetting" or clearing the contents of properties that may have been set in previous VB code should be explored.

The DiscardSavedData Method

If you find yourself displaying a Report object in a viewer, or performing some other output mechanism with the same Report object over and over, you will want to take steps to ensure that any "left over" settings from a previous report process are reset when you run the next report. While you can set the Report object to Nothing and instantiate it again, you may instead want to use the Report object's DiscardSavedData method if you will be running a report multiple times without the Nothing setting.

The Xtreme Orders sample application provides a good example of where this is helpful. The Report object is declared in a global module, and the Print Xtreme Orders form stays loaded during the entire scope of the application. Every time the OK button is clicked, the application sets Report properties based on the controls on the form and then either prints or exports the report, or else displays the form containing the Report Viewer.

The issue of clearing previous settings comes into play when a user runs the report more than once without ending and restarting the application. Because the Report object is never released and reinstantiated, all of its property settings remain intact when the user clicks OK subsequent times. If the Visual Basic code doesn't explicitly set some of these previously set properties, the report may exhibit behavior from the previous time it was run that you don't expect. Executing the Report object's DiscardSavedData method clears many properties of settings from any previous activity, returning them to the state they were in when designed.

Simply execute the DiscardSavedData method for any Report objects that you want to "clean up," as shown in the following sample from the Xtreme Orders sample application:

```
Report.DiscardSavedData 'required for consistent results
```

You may wonder about the significance of DiscardSavedData with the RDC, particularly when you're integrating a report that you designed in the ActiveX designer that does not have a Save Data with Report option. If you are using an external .RPT file that has been saved with File | Save Data With Report turned on, you'll probably want Visual Basic to discard the saved data at run time and refresh the report with new data from the database. Because the RDC is integrating a report that is contained entirely within the VB IDE (even if an .RPT file was imported, its saved data is not imported with it), you may be confused as to how DiscardSavedData applies. The RDC, in essence, "saves" data in the Report object when it is viewed in the Report Viewer, printed, or exported (or when the ReadRecords method is executed). That saved data remains a part of the Report object until it's discarded or the object reference is destroyed.

SQL Database Control

Many corporate databases are kept on client/server SQL database systems, such as Microsoft SQL Server, Oracle, and Informix. Many Visual Basic applications provide front-end interfaces to these database systems and need to handle SQL reporting as well. The RDC contains several properties and methods that help when integrating reports based on SQL databases.

Probably the most common interaction with SQL databases is providing logon credentials. This is discussed elsewhere in this chapter, under "Providing Database Logon Credentials."

Retrieving or Setting the SQL Query   When you submit a record selection formula, as discussed earlier in the chapter, the RDC automatically generates a SQL statement to submit to the database server. However, if the record selection formula contains a Crystal Reports formula or other "complex" characteristics that prevent the RDC from generating a WHERE clause in the SQL statement, report performance can be dramatically and negatively affected. You may, therefore, want to create the SQL statement the report uses directly in your VB application.

As part of this process, you may find it helpful to retrieve the SQL statement that the RDC is generating automatically.

The Report object provides a read/write SQLQueryString property that can be read or written to at run time. By examining the contents of this property, you can see what the SQL query is that the RDC is generating. You can then make necessary modifications to the query, depending on the state of your application and the database on which the report is based. Then, pass the modified query to the SQLQueryString property to be submitted to the server when the report runs.

It's important to note that you can't modify the SELECT clause in the SQL query. Only FROM, WHERE, ORDER BY, and GROUP BY can be modified. However, you must still include the SELECT clause when you return an updated SQL statement to the report, and it must not be changed from the original clause the RDC created. Also, if you create ORDER BY or GROUP BY clauses, you must separate them from the end of the WHERE clause with a carriage return/line feed character sequence. Use the vbCRLF constant to add the CR/LF sequence inside the SQL query.

TIP *Crystal Reports SQL Command capabilities are included in the RDC. One option you have for complete database control is to base your report entirely or partially on SQL commands, rather than manipulating the SQL Query from within your code.*

Reading or Setting Stored Procedure Parameters   If your report is based on a parameterized SQL stored procedure, you will probably want to supply parameter values to the stored procedure from within your code, much as you will want to respond to any RDC parameter fields that may have been created.

With the RDC, SQL stored procedure parameters are treated identically to Report parameter fields. The Report object contains the ParameterFieldDefinitions collection, containing one ParameterFieldDefinition object for each Report parameter field *or* stored procedure parameter contained in the report. The ParameterFieldDefinition object's ParameterType property will indicate whether the parameter is a Report parameter or a stored procedure parameter.

By executing the ParameterFieldDefinition object's AddCurrentValue method, you can pass a value to a stored procedure parameter from within your code. More detailed information on interacting with parameter fields can be found earlier in this chapter.

RDC Subreports

The RDC brings all the flexibility of Crystal Reports subreports to Visual Basic. If you import an .RPT file that contains subreports into the RDC, the subreports will be imported along with the main report. And, you can add your own subreports to the RDC design window at any time by right-clicking a blank area of the report and choosing Insert | Subreport from the pop-up menu (see Chapter 12 for more information on creating subreports).

The unique part of the RDC is the way a subreport fits into the object model. When you are displaying the main report in the RDC design window, a subreport will appear as an object outline, just as it does in regular Crystal Reports. However, if you click the subreport object, it has a set of properties that appears in the Properties box, just like other objects on the report. Figure 25-6 illustrates this.

The subreport design tab   The subreport object "placeholder"   Properties for the subreport object
                                on the main report

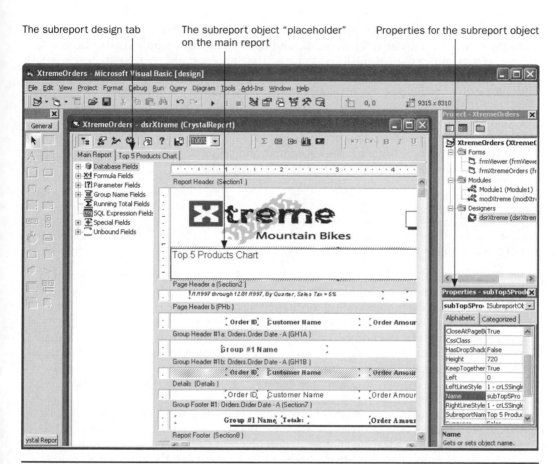

FIGURE 25-6   Subreport in the ActiveX Designer

You can set several design-time properties for the Subreport object, the same way you can for other objects on the report. One of the properties you may want to set as a matter of habit is the subreport name. By giving the subreport a descriptive name, you'll be able to more easily identify and work with it as you write code for your application.

After you add the Subreport object to the main report, it's treated just like a text object, field, line, box, or other object that appears on the main report in the main Report object model. But because the subreport contains its own set of fields and objects that are separate from the main report, the object model can expose them in a number of ways. Subreport objects (fields, formulas, sections, lines, and others) actually appear as part of the main Report object. The RDC precedes the object names with the name of the subreport and an underscore.

Consider a main report that contains several database fields that haven't been renamed since the report was created (Field1, Field2, and so on). The main report also contains a subreport that you've named subTop5Products. The Subreport objects actually become part of the main report. You can now set properties for the Report object named Field1, which will refer to the first field on the main report. If you then set Report properties for an object named subTop5Products_Field1, you are setting properties for the first field on the subreport.

Also, the main report exposes a SubreportObject object for every subreport "placeholder" contained on the main report. This object exposes a variety of properties that can be read and written to at run time to control the appearance and behavior of the placeholder (although not the actual subreport itself). Consider the following code:

```
'Set subreport object borders to blank
Report.subTop5Products.TopLineStyle = 0
Report.subTop5Products.LeftLineStyle = 0
Report.subTop5Products.BottomLineStyle = 0
Report.subTop5Products.RightLineStyle = 0
```

Here, the SubreportObject object is being manipulated from the Report object (referred to with the subreport name subTop5Products). The four line-style properties are all being set to 0, indicating that the border around the Subreport object will be invisible at run time.

Despite this tricky way of sharing objects and setting properties for the subreport placeholder, not all subreport properties, methods, and events are available from the main Report object. And if you're using an external .RPT file, these options won't be available either. Because the subreport is, in essence, an additional report that appears only on the main report, you need a way to control the behavior of the subreport using the same object model as the main report.

To accomplish this, you must declare an object of type Report from the CRAXDRT or CRAXDDRT libraries (the libraries the RDC exposes). You then use the main report's OpenSubreport method to create another Report object variable to contain the subreport. You can then set properties, execute methods, and trap events for the main report using its original object variable, and for the subreport using its own object variable. The following code fragment demonstrates this approach:

```
Dim Subreport as CRAXDRT.Report
...
...
'Put subreport in its own object
Set Subreport = Report.subTop5Products.OpenSubreport

'Set record selection formula for subreport
Subreport.RecordSelectionFormula = "{ado.Unit Price} > 1000"
```

NOTE *You may also have to supply logon credentials for databases in any subreports, separate from databases in the main report. Examples of how to do this appear earlier in the chapter, under "Providing Database Logon Credentials."*

Creating New Reports at Run Time

Not only can the RDC customize existing reports (either those imported from existing .RPT files, or those created directly in the VB designer), but it can also create a new report from scratch in a Windows application. The *Report Creation API*, as Business Objects refers to this feature, allows your VB code to create a new report entirely from scratch, including tables and fields, report sections, and report objects. After you create the base report structure, you can further manipulate report sections or format report objects using code. You can even add the Embeddable Report Designer to your application to allow end users to interactively modify the report, virtually identically to the report design capabilities you have with the RDC's internal ActiveX report designer.

And, once all the code-based design and user manipulation is completed, not only can you view the report in the Report Viewer, or print or export the report, but you can save the completed report as an .RPT file, ready to be opened in Crystal Reports or another custom application. Just be aware that the Crystal Reports license agreement specifically forbids you from using these report design techniques to create "competitive products."

CAUTION *The Report Creation API is only included with Crystal Reports XI Developer Edition. And, if you use these capabilities in your application, the Crystal Reports license agreement states that each organization you distribute the application to must also purchase a copy of Crystal Reports XI Developer Edition.*

There are two general approaches to creating a report at run time:

- Creating all report elements entirely within code
- Using the Embeddable Report Designer ActiveX control within your VB application to allow an end user to create the report interactively

Creating a New Report with Code

Creating a report with code requires the same basic steps that creating a report interactively in the RDC ActiveX designer or in stand-alone Crystal Reports requires:

1. Create a new report.
2. Choose database tables and link them, if necessary.
3. Add fields, text objects, bitmap images, and other objects to various report sections.
4. Add any desired groups.
5. Add subtotals and grand totals.
6. Format objects for desired appearance.
7. View the report in the Report Viewer, print it, or save it as an external .RPT file.

The RDC object model exposes methods and properties to accomplish each of these steps. Initially, you must add the RDC Report Creation library to your application, using Project | References. Check the Crystal Reports ActiveX Designer Design and Run-Time

Library 11.0 (CRAXDDRT.DLL). And, if you will be viewing the completed report in the Report Viewer, add the Crystal ActiveX Report Viewer Library 11.0 with Project | Components.

TIP *You may download a Report Creation API sample application from this book's companion web site, www.CrystalBook.com. The sample code in the remainder of this chapter is taken from this sample application.*

Declare Application and Report objects as you do with applications that use existing external RPT files. Consider this sample code:

```
Public Application As New CRAXDDRT.Application
Public Report As CRAXDDRT.Report
```

Note references to the combined design-time/run-time library (CRAXDDRT). This is in preparation for using the Embeddable Report Designer (described later in the chapter). If you will not be using this designer, but just creating a report entirely within code, you may use the run-time-only library, CRAXDRT.DLL.

The first new step involves assigning an object to the Report object variable. Previously, you've either assigned an existing ActiveX designer object to this variable or used the Application object's OpenReport method to assign an external .RPT file. Now, however, you will be creating a new report from scratch. The Application object exposes the NewReport method to accomplish this:

```
' Create a new empty report
Set Report = Application.NewReport
```

As when creating a new report from scratch in the ActiveX designer or Crystal Reports, you must choose a data connection method and database tables for the report. The Report Creation API requires the same steps. The following sample code illustrates how to assign an ADO connection to the Report object, using the Orders table from the Xtreme Sample Database ODBC data source. The ADO connection string makes this connection (assume that the Microsoft ActiveX Data Objects library has been added to the project, and the ADOConnection and ADOCommand objects have been declared earlier in the Declarations section):

```
' Open the data connection
Set ADOConnection = New ADODB.Connection
ADOConnection.Open "Provider=MSDASQL;Persist Security Info=False;
Data Source=Xtreme Sample Database 11;Mode=Read"

' Create a new instance of an ADO command object
Set ADOCommand = New ADODB.Command
Set ADOCommand.ActiveConnection = ADOConnection
ADOCommand.CommandText = "Orders"
ADOCommand.CommandType = adCmdTable

' Add the data source (the XTREME Orders Table) to the report
Report.Database.AddADOCommand ADOConnection, ADOCommand
```

NOTE *Width limits of this book require that the argument to the ADOConnection.Open method be broken in the middle of the line. Note that the actual sample application maintains the string argument for the Open method all on one line.*

You now have the beginnings of a report, including an assigned Report object with a data connection. Were you to open this report in the Crystal Report designer or supply the Report object to the Embeddable Report Designer at this point, you'd find an empty report, but the Field Explorer would be populated by fields from the Xtreme Sample Database Orders table. You would then drag and drop desired fields into various sections of the report. The next requirement of your Report Creation application is to add objects to different report sections. Examine the following code fragments from the RDC Report Creation sample application:

```
Report.Sections(1).AddTextObject "FedEx Order Detail", 6000, 400
```

This line adds a text object containing the text "FedEx Order Detail" to the report header, at position 6,000/400. This code use methods several levels deep in the RDC object hierarchy. The AddTextObject method is available below an individual Section object within the Sections collection (in this case, the first member in the Sections collection) below the Report object.

Virtually all aspects of report formatting can be undertaken with RCAPI calls. Here's sample code to format the report title object just added:

```
'Format the title
With ReportTitle
    .HorAlignment = crHorCenterAlign
    .LeftLineStyle = crLSSingleLine
    .RightLineStyle = crLSSingleLine
    .TopLineStyle = crLSSingleLine
    .BottomLineStyle = crLSSingleLine
    .HasDropShadow = True
    .Font.Size = 18
    .Font.Bold = True
    .TextColor = &H808000
    .Height = 500
    .Width = 4500
End With
```

The sample application proceeds to add four database fields to the details section of the report:

```
' Add fields to details section
' Note that the Sections collection can be accessed via
' number or string index
Report.Sections("D").AddFieldObject "{ado.Order ID}", 750, 5
Report.Sections("D").AddFieldObject "{ado.Order Date}", 3150, 5
Report.Sections("D").AddFieldObject "{ado.Order Amount}", 5500, 5
Report.Sections("D").AddFieldObject "{ado.Ship Via}", 8850, 5
```

RDC object-hierarchy navigation in the details section is similar to that used to add objects to the report header. The AddFieldObject method used adds a database field, requiring the database field, left position, and top position as arguments. Note that the Sections collection can be accessed via either a numeric or a string index. Should you wish, you could also execute code to format each of these objects.

If you wish to create groups, there are methods exposed in the object hierarchy to allow complete flexibility with group creation. There are also options to create both group summary fields and report grand totals. The RDC Report Creation sample application creates a grand total of Order Amount in the report footer (Section 4) with the following code:

```
' Create and format Order Amount Grand Total in report footer
Dim AmountTotal As CRAXDDRT.FieldObject
' Creating a separate object variable avoids deep navigation
' down the hierarchy when formatting
Set AmountTotal = Report.Sections(4).AddSummaryFieldObject _
Report.Sections(3).ReportObjects(3).Field.Name, crSTSum, 6000, 750)
With AmountTotal
    .Width = 1500
    .Font.Bold = True
End With      'AmountTotal
```

Note several important points about the preceding code fragment:

- A separate object to hold the grand total field was declared and assigned. Note that this wasn't done previously for the text object or field object. While it is possible to create lots of objects, as shown in the preceding example, this requires extra coding and keeping track of all the additional objects. The purpose in this example is to make formatting easier by eliminating navigation into the object hierarchy to set the Width and Font.Bold properties.

- You can apply every conceivable kind of formatting to objects once they have been added to the report. Note that the grand total has been widened from its default size and given a bold formatting attribute. A glance through the sample application reveals the UseOneSymbolPerPage formatting attribute being applied to the Order Amount field, so only one dollar sign will appear at the top of each page:

```
' Format the Order Amount to have one dollar sign per page
Report.Sections(3).ReportObjects(3).UseOneSymbolPerPage = True
```

At this point, a basic report design has been created and is contained in the Report object. Additional RDC methods and properties that you are probably more familiar with can be applied to the Report object as well. For example, the sample application limits the report to orders shipped via FedEx with the following, now-familiar approach:

```
Report.RecordSelectionFormula = "{ado.Ship Via} = 'FedEx'"
```

Now, you're ready to proceed to view, print, export, or perform other familiar functions with the Report object. You can also now supply the partially designed Report object to the Embeddable Report Designer to allow the end user to interactively modify the report you've already started to design in code.

Assuming you've added the Report Viewer to a form, the following code will now display your report in the viewer:

```
CRViewer1.ReportSource = Report
CRViewer1.ViewReport
```

Saving the Report   As discussed earlier in the chapter, the ultimate result of your application can be a saved .RPT file that can be opened in stand-alone Crystal Reports or other applications or custom programs that utilize .RPT files. The RDC exposes a Report object method to accomplish this:

```
Report.SaveAs "Sample.RPT", crDefaultFileFormat
```

Executing the SaveAs method will save the contents of the Report object to the filename supplied as the first argument. The second argument uses an RDC-provided constant to determine what Crystal Reports file format the file is saved in. If the file already exists when SaveAs is executed, it will be overwritten without a warning or any Visual Basic error being thrown. If this is of concern to you, execute additional code prior to SaveAs to check for the existence of the file.

CAUTION   *Online help indicates that the file format argument can be either a Crystal Reports 8 or Crystal Reports 7 format. This is an error in the document. While these arguments will not throw an error (for backward code compatibility), the Version XI RDC will always save a file in a later format (version 10 format, to be exact), unable to be opened by Crystal Reports 8.5 or earlier.*

Using the Embeddable Report Designer

One of the more usable and unique features of the RDC is the *Embeddable Report Designer.* This ActiveX control, when added to a VB form, allows an end user complete interactive report design and modification capabilities, largely identical to the capabilities provided by the ActiveX report designer that appears in the Visual Basic IDE when the RDC is first added to a VB project. The end result from the Embeddable Report Designer is a Report object, identical to the Report object that's been discussed earlier in the chapter. It can be further manipulated from within your VB code, supplied to the Report Viewer, exported with the Export method, printed with the PrintOut method, or saved to an .RPT file with the SaveAs method.

For all the interactive power it gives to your end users, the Embeddable Report Designer is surprisingly simple to implement inside your VB application. To enable the Embeddable Report Designer in your VB application, several general steps are required:

1. Add proper references and components from the Project menu.

2. Add the Embeddable Designer to a form.

3. Supply a Report object to the Embeddable Designer.

4. Do any necessary further manipulation to the Report object, such as printing, exporting, saving, or showing in the Report Viewer.

Begin by choosing Project | Components from the VB pull-down menus. You'll see the list of all registered ActiveX controls on your computer. In particular, you'll want to check the Embeddable Crystal Reports Designer Control Library 11.0. This will place a Crystal Reports icon on the VB toolbar. You may optionally want to choose the Crystal ActiveX Report Viewer Library 11.0 as well, if you will be providing an online viewer for your reports within your application.

You must also add a reference to the Crystal Reports XI combined design-time/run-time library. Choose Project | References from the VB pull-down menus and check the Crystal Reports ActiveX Designer Design and Run-time Library 11.0.

NOTE *This combined design- and run-time library (CRAXDDRT.DLL) is one of two RDC libraries you can use. The run-time-only RDC library (CRAXDRT.DLL) is available as well. When you distribute applications, you'll want to include the combined library if and only if you will be including the Embeddable Report Designer in your application. If you will not require this designer, distribute the run-time-only library (CRAXDRT.DLL).*

Once you've added the proper components and references from the Project menu, you'll notice a new Crystal Reports icon for the Embeddable Report Designer in the VB toolbox. Simply add this control to a form as you would any other VB control. When you do so, you'll see the outline of the designer in your form, along with the designer's design-time properties in the VB Properties box.

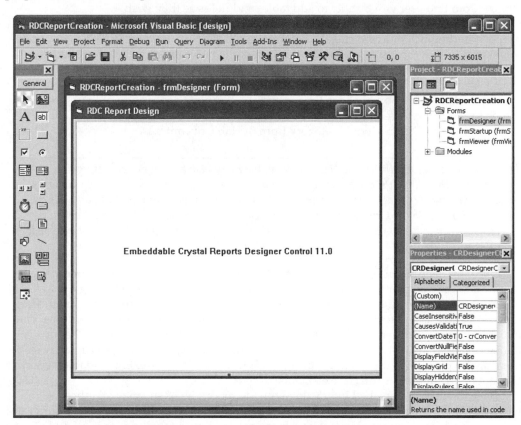

Enabling the designer is as simple as supplying an existing Report object to the designer's ReportObject property, as in the following code:

```
CRDesignerCtrl11.ReportObject = Report
CRDesignerCtrl11.DisplayToolbar = True
CRDesignerCtrl11.EnableHelp = False
```

This code assumes that the Embeddable Designer object has been left with its default name of CRDesignerCtrl11 and that an already declared Report object named Report is in scope within the current procedure. If you wish the end user to modify an existing report, you will have obtained this Report object by using the OpenReport method of an application object, or perhaps used the application object's NewReport method and programmatically added a database connection, fields, text objects, and other items (as in the sample application from this book's accompanying web site, CrystalBook.com). Note, however, that the Embeddable

Report Designer features the capability of displaying the Database Expert with a right-click menu option, so you may provide a completely "empty" report object to the designer if you choose. Your end user will be able to add tables and fields as they wish.

You'll also notice that the designer's EnableHelp property has been set to false. This property setting will hide the Help button from the designer's toolbar, as well as from pop-up menus. In fact, the Embeddable Report Designer exposes an entire set of properties, a single method, and a few Windows-standard events as part of its own library. Most of the report-specific customization of the designer is accomplished by setting properties at design time in the Properties box or at run time in code. A complete description of these properties can be found in the developer's Help file by opening the "Embeddable Crystal Reports Designer Control Object Model" category from the table of contents.

TIP *If you don't disable the online Help button in the Embeddable Designer by setting EnableHelp to false (either in the Properties box or at run time), users will receive a "Help File not found" error message if they attempt to get online help. Information for creating a Windows .HLP file and using it with the Embeddable Designer is available in CrystalDevHelp.chm. Look in the Help file contents and open the "Embeddable Crystal Reports Designer Control Object Model" category. Then, choose "Distributing the Embeddable Designer."*

Once this code has been executed and the form is displayed, you'll note a report designer identical to the designer that appears in the VB IDE when you first begin using the RDC. Users may use the Field Explorer on the left to add fields, create formulas, and so on. They may select objects and format them with right-click pop-up menus or toolbar buttons. The main differences between the Embeddable Report Designer and actual Crystal Reports is that all interaction must be with toolbar buttons, the Field Explorer, and pop-up menus— there are no pull-down menus in the designer. Figure 25-7 shows the Embeddable Report Designer and some of its interface elements.

Once the user has finished interacting with the report, he or she may simply close the window containing the designer, or use some other user interface element you've built into the form, such as a command button or tab control. However, the designer itself *doesn't* contain the Preview tab familiar to Crystal Reports users—you'll have to facilitate viewing of the modified report in your own code.

The designer simply returns the same Report object to your VB code that you initially supplied with any changes the end user made. You may now pass the modified Report object to a Report Viewer control, export it to a file, e-mail it, or execute the Report object's PrintOut method to print it to a printer. These capabilities are discussed earlier in this chapter.

Distributing RDC Windows Applications

After you create an RDC application that integrates Crystal Reports, you'll want to compile and test the application. This process is unchanged with Crystal Reports XI. Unless you're using the application only for yourself, you also need to set up a distribution mechanism to pass your application to your intended audience: the application users.

Because you are distributing Crystal Reports features and components with your VB application, some distribution issues come into play. This section of the chapter discusses both the general points you want to keep in mind when creating your distribution package

Use the Field Explorer to add fields, create formulas, and use other elements of the regular Crystal Reports Field Explorer

Use toolbar buttons to perform commonly required report design functions

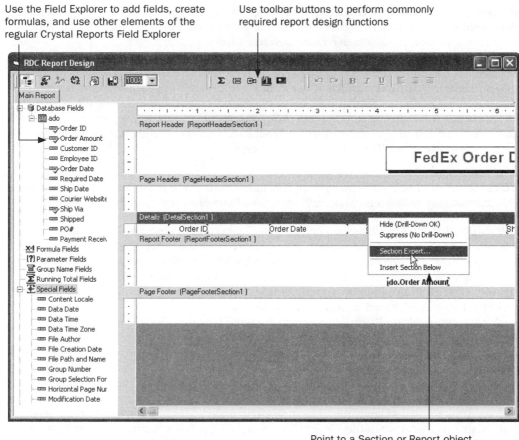

Point to a Section or Report object and right-click to use pop-up menus

FIGURE 25-7   The Embeddable Designer in a VB form

and specific areas that concern certain reporting features you may want to include or exclude from your application.

Distribution Overview

The days of creating a single .EXE executable file that can be easily copied to a single floppy disk are long gone. Standard Visual Basic projects already consist of the main program executable file, run-time files, and a host of support files. Introducing Crystal Reports into the mix adds a fairly large burden to this process. Because Crystal Reports is designed in a very modular fashion, it's easy to add functionality and upgraded features to the tool. However, this modularity also complicates the distribution process because so many different files are involved in the overall Crystal Reports product.

If you prefer to integrate external .RPT files with your RDC application, rather than using the ActiveX designer within the VB IDE, you must include those .RPT files in your distribution package. A variety of support files also are required, depending on several issues such as the database connections the report uses and the export capabilities that the project entails. The best part is that this is all handled pretty much automatically if you use Visual Basic distribution tools to create your distribution package.

In addition to available third-party distribution products, such as InstallShield and Wise, Visual Basic 6 includes the Package and Deployment Wizard, and Visual Basic 5 includes the Application Setup Wizard. All of these tools are designed to gather all the necessary executable and support files required for a project, compress them into a smaller space, and add them to a setup program. When the setup program is run from floppies or a CD-ROM, run from a network share, or downloaded from a web server, all the necessary files are decompressed and installed in the proper locations.

NOTE *Specific instructions for using these distribution tools can be found in the documentation accompanying them—this chapter will not teach you how to distribute VB applications.*

Distribution tools, such as the Package and Deployment Wizard included with VB, look through your VB project file and attempt to determine all the necessary files that must be distributed with the project. Depending on the different RDC libraries and modules you have chosen for your application, a different set of files needs to be included in the distribution process. Having a fundamental understanding of this process will help you tailor your project's distribution, based on its individual needs.

Most tools use *dependency files* to determine what files to include in your distribution package. These files consist of the same base filename as the file used to provide Crystal Reports integration, but contain a .DEP extension. For example, the dependency file for the combined design-time/run-time RDC library (CRAXDDRT.DLL) is CRAXDDRT.DEP. The dependency file is a straight ASCII text file that you can open with Notepad, containing a list of all related DLLs or other files that the "base" file is dependent upon. The distribution package uses the dependency file to include all necessary files (and, in most cases, several that are unnecessary) when the VB application is packaged. If you create VB projects on a regular basis, you may want to customize the appropriate .DEP files to include additional files or exclude files that your applications don't need.

If you let your distribution tool work with default options, you most probably will include necessary files for your application. Simply taking the default options has two potential disadvantages, though:

- More files than you actually need may be included, which likely is a minor inconvenience, eating up a bit more disk space than you really need to use.

- Necessary files may not be automatically detected, which means the application won't work correctly.

By reading on, you'll learn how to selectively remove unnecessary files that are included automatically. However, only by carefully considering your individual application, and the files that it ultimately requires, will you avoid the second problem. In all cases, the rule of thumb is to test and then test again—always try installations on a "clean" machine (similar to what your end users will have in place) to ensure that all files are being installed correctly. Simply installing the package on your development PC (which already has a complete copy of Crystal Reports Developer or Advanced Developer Edition on it) won't be a sufficient test—

you won't detect any missing elements that may be required on a user machine without Crystal Reports already installed.

The RDC is unique among integration methods in that it doesn't use external .RPT files, unless you specifically choose to use them over the internal ActiveX report designer. Report definitions are actually contained in the ActiveX designer (.DSR) files that are added to the project. Because these are an integral part of your application, VB will compile the .DSR files and include them automatically in the project's executable. In addition, the other COM components that make up the RDC will be included in the project.

In particular, the CRAXDRT.DEP or CRAXDDRT.DEP dependency files will include all necessary COM components for the RDC libraries. If you are using the ActiveX Report Viewer to view your reports in a form, CRVIEWER.DEP will be used to include its necessary components. While you probably won't have to worry about including external .RPT files, make sure any required database files are included in your package. You may also want to remove some unnecessary database or export-support files to save disk space.

In some cases, the Package and Deployment Wizard won't be able to find all necessary files. Crystal Reports XI stores many libraries in C:\Program Files\Common Files\Business Objects\3.0\bin. You may need to manually locate files in this folder, or use the Windows Explorer Search function to find them.

TIP *Business Objects now includes newer-standard Microsoft Windows Installer Merge Modules with Crystal Reports XI Developer Edition. These can be found in C:\Program Files\Common Files\Merge Modules. While older-style .DEP files for the Package and Deployment Wizard are still provided, Business Objects will now only support deployments done with newer .MSI technology utilizing these merge modules.*

Database Considerations

The databases that your reports use must be considered when you are deploying your VB application to end users. Obviously, you need to ensure that each end user is able to connect to the database that the reports require. This may be a PC-style database distributed along with the application, a database shared on a common LAN drive, or a client/server database accessed through either a native Crystal Reports database driver or ODBC. You also need to include only the .DLL files specific to the database and access method being used by your reports. Although it won't necessarily hurt to include database driver DLLs for Microsoft Access in your project, even if your reports all connect to an Informix database via ODBC, you can save disk space by eliminating any unnecessary database drivers.

Direct Access Databases If your reports use a PC-style database, such as a Microsoft Access .MDB file or a dBASE for Windows .DBF file, you'll want to make sure that the reports will be able to locate the database when the application is installed. If these files were installed on the C drive when you designed the report, but will reside on a network F drive when the end user runs the application, you need to make sure the reports can still find the file. You can either execute calls inside your VB application to change the data-source location of the reports, or use the Crystal Reports Database | Set Datasource Location command in either Crystal Reports or the RDC ActiveX report designer to point to a different database before distributing the application. You may prefer using the Same As Report option from the Set Datasource Location dialog box to have the report look in the same drive and directory as the report for the database. In this scenario, you need only ensure that the database and reports reside in the same place, regardless of drive or directory, for the reports to be able to locate the database.

You may be able to save disk space by including only the necessary database drivers for your particular Direct Access database. If, for example, you are using only reports that connect directly to a Microsoft Access database, you don't need to include all the other database drivers in your distribution package. If you exclude other database drivers, make sure you test your installation on a machine similar to those found in your end-user environment, to make sure all necessary drivers are being included.

ODBC Data Sources   As a general rule, ODBC is used to connect to centralized client/server databases (although some desktop databases you distribute with your application still may use ODBC as the connection method). Therefore, you probably won't have to worry about distributing the actual database with your application. However, you need to make sure that an ODBC data source is set up so that the report will be able to connect to the database from your end user's machine. Your VB application may take care of this automatically if the application itself will be accessing the same ODBC data source. Also, if your report will be using the Active Data driver to connect to a Data Access Objects (DAO) or ActiveX Data Objects (ADO) record set in the application, special provisions probably won't need to be made.

If your report is the only part of the application that will be using a particular ODBC data source, make sure that the setup application creates the correct ODBC data source. You may even need to install ODBC as part of your setup program, if there's a possibility it won't already be installed on the end user's machine.

You also save disk space if you eliminate other Crystal Reports database drivers that won't be used in your application. Once you exclude other database drivers, make sure you test your installation on a machine similar to those found in your end-user environment, to make sure all necessary drivers are included.

File Export Considerations

The Xtreme Orders sample application that is used in this chapter allows three output destinations to be used: the preview window, the printer, and a .PDF file attached to an e-mail message. Both exporting the report to a .PDF file and selecting e-mail as the output destination create additional file requirements when you distribute the application. Because Crystal Reports is designed with a modular framework, both the file type (PDF, Word, Excel, HTML, and so on) and output destination (disk file, MAPI e-mail, Exchange public folder, and so on) functions are provided in separate .DLL files. If you are using these export formats and methods, make sure the correct files are included in your application.

Conversely, if you are using only a few output types and destinations, or perhaps none at all, you'll save disk space by eliminating these DLLs from your distribution package. Crystal Reports output destinations are provided by U2D*.DLL files. Output formats are provided by CRXF*.DLL and U2F*.DLL files. You need to include only the formats that you specifically call in your application or wish to have available to your end users if they click the Export button in the preview window.

User Function Libraries

If you use formulas in your report that call external User Function Libraries (UFLs), don't forget to include the external UFL .DLL files when you distribute your application. An external

.DLL file is called any time a formula uses any functions in the Additional Functions list in the Formula Editor. If you fail to include the .DLL file with your application, the formula will fail when the report runs on the end user's machine.

By default, Crystal Reports installs several UFLs with the rest of the Crystal Reports package. These are all included in the dependency files that Crystal Reports supplies, so you generally don't have to worry about manually including the UFL files in your distribution package. However, if you've created your own UFLs (a supplementary document appears on www.CrystalBook.com describing how to create your own UFLs with Visual Basic), you'll want to either manually add them to your distribution package or modify the .DEP files to include them in all future distributions. You'll also be able to save disk space by removing UFL files that aren't used in any of your formulas.

UFL files generally adhere to the file format U2*.DLL. If none of the formulas in your report use functions from the Additional Functions list, you can safely remove these UFL files from your distribution package. Again, you should test your installation on a target machine to ensure that your formulas will work properly without the extra UFL files.

PART III

Crystal Reports with Visual Studio .NET

This chapter will discuss using Visual Studio .NET to integrate Crystal Reports into your Windows- and web-based .NET applications. One of the main advantages to the .NET environment in general is the similarity in developing Windows and web apps. That similarity is evident when developing applications involving Crystal Reports.

NOTE *Throughout this chapter, most of the techniques apply equally to Windows and web applications. When there are differences, they will be noted.*

Windows and Web Integration with Visual Studio .NET

Crystal Reports has played a prominent role in Microsoft development environments in the recent past. Crystal Reports has been bundled with previous versions of Microsoft Visual Studio products (perhaps with the sole exception being the concentration on the Microsoft Report Designer included with Visual Studio 6—Crystal Reports was *still* available separately on the program CD). With Visual Studio .NET 2003 (VS.NET), Crystal Reports has once again taken on a prominent role, being an integral part of the VS.NET package right "out of the box."

NOTE *This portion of the book concentrates on the finer points of Crystal Reports integration with Visual Studio .NET using Visual Basic coding techniques. The material assumes you already have a fundamental knowledge of Visual Studio .NET architecture and coding techniques. This portion of the book will not teach you VS.NET fundamentals.*

Crystal/VS.NET Bundle Options

The first distinction to make is between Crystal Reports features bundled with the core Microsoft VS.NET package, and those that are added on by a Crystal Reports XI purchase. If you purchase a copy of Microsoft Visual Studio .NET 2003, Crystal Reports is "bundled" with the VS.NET package. Simply ensure that it is selected when you initially install the VS.NET package to ensure that Crystal Reports features will be available. If you discover that you didn't initially install Crystal Reports, simply rerun VS.NET setup from the Windows Control Panel and select the Crystal Reports option. This will install the core Crystal Reports bundle that provides most all of the Crystal Reports capabilities you'll need from within a .NET application.

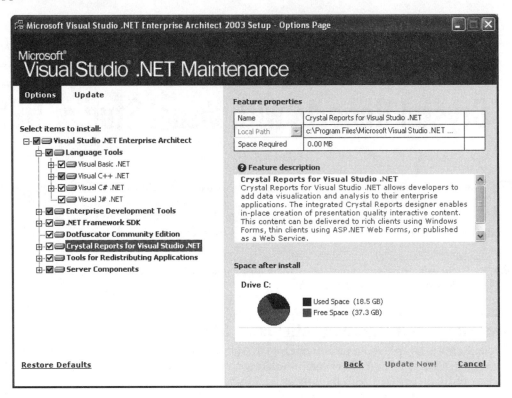

This installs the .NET-bundled version of Crystal Reports, consisting of the Crystal help collection added to the combined VS.NET help collection; and necessary assemblies for designing a report within the VS.NET IDE, integrating the report with a Windows or web application, and creating a Crystal Report web service. This *will not* install a stand-alone copy of Crystal Reports that allows you to design reports outside of the VS.NET IDE.

The version of Crystal Reports installed with VS.NET falls in between Crystal Reports versions 8.5 and 9. While this version will create an .RPT file that can be used outside of VS.NET, it cannot be used with Crystal Reports 8.5 or earlier, as it makes use of the new version 9 .RPT file format that is not backward compatible. However, these .RPT files can be opened and manipulated with stand-alone versions of Crystal Reports 9 or later.

If you install Crystal Reports XI Developer edition, you'll find a .NET option within the Developer Components section of the custom installation option. Ensure that this is chosen when you install Crystal Reports XI. If you don't initially choose this option, rerun Crystal Reports setup from the program CD or the Windows Control Panel and choose the .NET option within the Developer Components category. You'll also need to rerun Setup and choose this option if you install (or reinstall) VS.NET *after* you install Crystal Reports XI. Repairing a Crystal Reports XI installation after reinstalling VS.NET should also work.

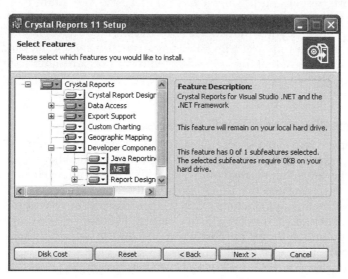

NOTE *You may notice an "Add .NET Components" hyperlink from the initial startup screen that appears when you insert the Crystal Reports XI program CD. Unfortunately, when you click this link, only a message will appear indicating that .NET components are installed from the actual setup program. You'll need to ensure the proper option from the Developer Components section of the setup program is selected to install the extra version XI .NET components.*

Installing Crystal Reports XI Developer Edition will supplement the existing Crystal Reports assemblies installed with VS.NET with newer versions that contain additional capabilities. While not an exhaustive list, these version XI enhancements include some simpler object model calls to perform various report integration functions, an ActiveX printing control for web forms, and additional report data sources. An additional help collection will also be added to the combined VS.NET help collection. You'll notice, in many cases, Crystal-related help options for both "Crystal Reports" and "Crystal Reports 11."

Also, you'll be able to create reports in the stand-alone copy of Crystal Reports XI, including the interactive design/preview process, which will probably be a vast improvement over the VS.NET IDE report designer, which doesn't provide the quick design/preview paradigm that stand-alone Crystal Reports does. You may then merely import your finished .RPT file into VS.NET for integration.

NOTE *Many of the examples in this chapter are taken from a sample VS.NET web application that can be downloaded from CrystalBook.com, this book's companion web site. These examples have been developed with Crystal Reports Developer Edition installed. As such, some object model calls demonstrated require the additional capabilities of Crystal Reports XI. These are noted in the sample code and in the book.*

> **Crystal Reports Server and BusinessObjects Enterprise XI Applications**
> Crystal Reports Server and BusinessObjects Enterprise XI contain their own set of
> object model programming interfaces that also allow you to create Windows and web
> applications. While beyond the scope of this Crystal Reports–oriented book, these
> programming interfaces allow you to completely customize a report viewing, scheduling,
> and distribution system that integrates fully with your organization's portal, intranet,
> or public web site.

Windows Forms Viewer and Web Forms Viewer

The first concept you may need to become familiar with when integrating a Crystal report
into a Windows or web application with VS.NET is the separation between the actual report
itself (the .RPT file you either create within the VS.NET IDE or add to it after creating in the
Crystal Reports designer) and the *viewer* that actually shows the report to the user in the
application. If you are going to include a Crystal report as part of your application, you'll
need to pay close attention to these two distinct objects. If, however, you only wish to include
a report in the application for the purpose of exporting to an external file (perhaps placing
the exported report on the web server for later download or sharing somewhere else within
the web server's network), then you may not even need to add a viewer that presents the
report visually to the user.

However, for most applications you'll need to determine how to present the report to
the user within your Windows or web form. For this, VS.NET includes the *Crystal Windows
Forms Viewer* and *Crystal Web Forms Viewer.* By dropping a Crystal Windows Forms Viewer
onto a Windows form, or a Crystal Web Forms Viewer onto a web form, you can immediately
display a Crystal report, including all embedded formatting. These viewers also support all
typical Crystal Reports interaction, including page-on-demand viewing, group tree navigation,
report group drill-down, on-demand subreport interactivity, and report exporting and printing.

After creating a Windows application or an ASP.NET Web application (the language you
use to create it is irrelevant—Crystal Reports is entirely language independent in VS.NET), add
a viewer to the desired form by dragging it from the Windows Forms or Web Forms section
of the Toolbox. A small outline will initially appear inside the form, and a set of properties
specific to the viewer will appear in the Properties box. This is shown in Figure 26-1.

However, merely adding a viewer to a form won't display anything when the application
is run. This is because you must tie or *bind* an actual Crystal Report object to the viewer so
that there's an actual report to view.

NOTE *Crystal Reports can be integrated in VS.NET applications based on Visual Basic, C#,
Managed C++, or other languages supported in the VS.NET development environment. This
chapter, however, will concentrate on Visual Basic applications and will demonstrate Visual
Basic coding techniques.*

Viewer Binding Options

There are numerous ways to bind reports to the viewer. The option you choose depends
largely on the way your application is designed—whether your reports are "external" to
your application (located at a specific file location or elsewhere on the network connection),

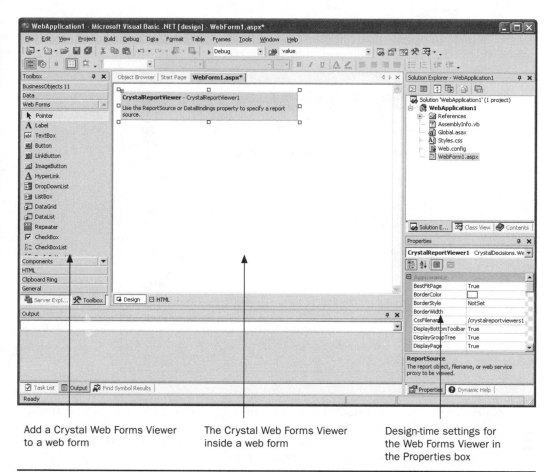

Add a Crystal Web Forms Viewer to a web form

The Crystal Web Forms Viewer inside a web form

Design-time settings for the Web Forms Viewer in the Properties box

FIGURE 26-1   Crystal Web Forms Viewer in a Web Form

designed within the VS.NET IDE, or contained in a Report Component (discussed later); whether you want to use the web-only report caching feature (also discussed later); and so forth.

Probably the simplest way to bind a report to the viewer is to specify the full pathname and filename of an .RPT file located on local or network drive. There are several ways to accomplish this:

- **Specify the Viewer's ReportSource property**   Make sure the viewer is selected in the VS.NET IDE. Navigate to the ReportSource property in the Properties box. Click the down arrow and choose the Browse option. A file open dialog will appear. Navigate through drives and folders until you find the .RPT file you wish to display in the viewer.

- **Specify a filename in the DataBindings dialog box**   Make sure the viewer is selected in the VS.NET IDE. Navigate to the (DataBindings) property. Click the ellipses button to display the DataBindings dialog box. Choose the ReportSource property in the Bindable Properties list. Click the Custom Binding Expression radio button and type the full pathname and filename into the box below the radio button, surrounding the filename with quotation marks.

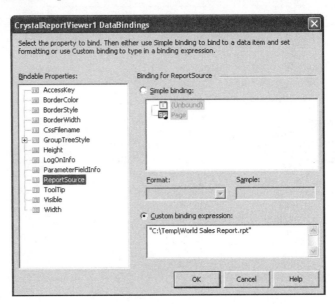

- **Set the Viewer's ReportSource property in code**   The report can be bound at run time by specifying the viewer's ReportSource property. For example, if you display the code window for the form containing the viewer (perhaps the Page_Load event), specify the viewer's ReportSource property as follows:

```
Private Sub Page_Load(ByVal sender As System.Object, _
        ByVal e As System.EventArgs) Handles MyBase.Load
    'Put user code to initialize the page here
    CrystalReportViewer1.ReportSource = "C:\Temp\FedExOrders.rpt"
End Sub
```

In web applications, if you bind the report with either the ReportSource property in the Properties box or the custom binding expression in the DataBind dialog box, the report will actually be displayed in the viewer in the VS.NET IDE. (The report will not display in Windows applications.) If you specify the viewer's ReportSource property in code, the viewer will retain its smaller footprint with no report display inside the form at design time. However, when you run the application, the form will display the report (you may be prompted for database credentials or parameter values first).

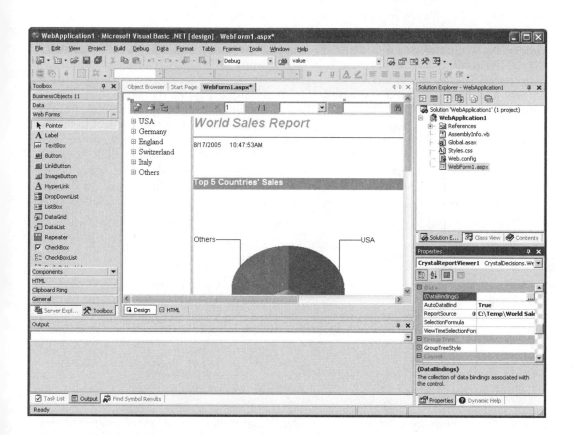

NOTE *The Crystal Web Forms Viewer includes the AutoDataBind property, which is set to True by default. If, for some reason, you choose to set this property to False at design time, or you are using an older Crystal Web Forms Viewer that doesn't include the AutoDataBind property, you must data-bind the viewer at run time by executing the viewer's DataBind method after the InitializeComponent procedure that's executed in the web form's Page_Init event.*

```
Private Sub Page_Init(ByVal sender As System.Object, _
        ByVal e As System.EventArgs) Handles MyBase.Init
    'CODEGEN: This method call is required by the Web Form Designer
    'Do not modify it using the code editor.
    InitializeComponent()
    CrystalReportViewer1.DataBind()
End Sub
```

You may also want to bind a report you've created within the VS.NET IDE to a report viewer (the integrated report designer is discussed later in the chapter, under "Integrated Report Designer"). Or, you may wish to add an existing .RPT file to your project and bind it to a viewer. These types of reports that reside in your project are known as *strongly typed reports*, and a class is added to the project for each strongly typed report. In these cases, you'll eventually see an .RPT filename in the Solution Explorer that represents the strongly typed report you want to bind to the viewer. Surprisingly, though, if you attempt to set the viewer's ReportSource property to the .RPT filename, you won't find the file in the drop-down list of available options—either in the Properties box or in the DataBindings dialog box.

This strongly typed report can be bound using a single line of code in the form's Page_ Load event. By setting the viewer's ReportSource property to a new instance of the desired report class (sans the .RPT extension), you can bind the viewer to the report included in the project.

```
'Binds strongly-typed CrystalReport1.RPT file from Solution Explorer
CrystalReportViewer1.ReportSource = New CrystalReport1
```

In web applications, you can also bind the viewer to a cached version of the strongly typed report. By caching the report, you may improve performance when multiple users access the same web page that contains the report viewer. Whenever you add a strongly typed report to a web project, a cached class of the same report is also created, which can be bound to the Web Forms Viewer.

```
'Binds cached CrystalReport1.RPT file from Solution Explorer
CrystalReportViewer1.ReportSource = New CachedCrystalReport1
```

NOTE *Cached reports are only supported in ASP.NET web applications (not Windows applications). By caching a report, you can potentially improve performance by storing recently viewed report data on the web server for additional users that access the same web form within the prescribed cache time. If, however, you are using a very fluid transactional database that changes frequently, you may choose not to use cached reports to ensure that the user will always see the most current set of data.*

You may also wish to bind a report to the viewer via strongly typed *report component*. In this situation, you add an additional component to the form from the Toolbox and choose an existing strongly typed report in the project for the component to host. Begin by dragging the ReportDocument from the Components area of the Toolbox to the web form. Once you've dropped it on the form, the Choose A ReportDocument dialog box will appear. Click the drop-down list and choose the desired report from the list (you'll see strongly typed reports you've already added to your project). In a web application, if you wish to cache the report, check the appropriate box.

Choose a ReportDocument

Choose a typed ReportDocument class from your project, or the default untyped ReportDocument class.

Name: WebApplication1.CrystalReport1

If no typed ReportDocument exists in your project, you can create one by adding or opening a Crystal Report to your project.

☑ Generate cached strongly-typed report

OK   Cancel

Once you click OK, the report component will appear in a design time–only area of the form (it will not be visible at run time). You may then merely select the viewer in the form and click the drop-down list for the ReportSource property in the Properties box. You'll see all report components you've added to the form in the list. Choose the desired component. Or, you can click the ellipses next to the viewer's (DataBindings) property in the Properties box. Then, select ReportSource in the Bindable Properties list, click the Simple Binding radio button, and expand the Page category. Select the desired report component from the expanded list.

CrystalReportViewer1 DataBindings

Select the property to bind. Then either use Simple binding to bind to a data item and set formatting or use Custom binding to type in a binding expression.

Bindable Properties:

- AccessKey
- BorderColor
- BorderStyle
- BorderWidth
- CssFilename
- GroupTreeStyle
- Height
- LogOnInfo
- ParameterFieldInfo
- ReportSource
- ToolTip
- Visible
- Width

Binding for ReportSource

◉ Simple binding:

- (Unbound)
- Page
  - cachedCrystalReport11

Format: Sample:

○ Custom binding expression:

cachedCrystalReport11

OK   Cancel   Help

TIP *There are yet additional ways of binding reports to viewers. A complete discussion of all viewer binding options, including sample code, can be found in VS.NET help. Search for "Report Binding Options for Windows Forms Viewers" and "Report Binding Options for Web Forms Viewers." There are also additional samples and examples of report binding that can be downloaded from support.BusinessObjects.com or www.BusinessObjects.com/DevZone.*

Integrated Report Designer

One of the more exciting integration benefits of Crystal Reports and Microsoft development environments is the *Integrated Report Designer*. This feature was originally introduced with the Report Designer Component and Visual Basic 6. As Microsoft chose Crystal Reports for its integrated reporting tool in Visual Studio .NET, this capability is brought into the VS.NET environment as well. With this design tool built into the VS.NET IDE, you can perform complex report design tasks, such as adding and joining tables, adding fields, grouping records, and formatting objects, much the same way as you can with the full Crystal Reports designer in an off-the-shelf version of Crystal Reports. When you are finished, the .RPT file you've created or modified will exist within the project as a strongly typed report.

NOTE *One of the initial decisions you'll be making is whether to create reports in the VS.NET IDE or in stand-alone Crystal Reports. While VS.NET allows you to create reports without buying a stand-alone copy of Crystal Reports, your report design choices are more limited in the Integrated Report Designer. For example, you can't simply click a Preview button to see what your finished report looks like—you must place the report in a viewer and run the application every time you want to see any design changes. This, and other differences, may lead you to actually do most of your report design in a stand-alone copy of Crystal Reports and then add the .RPT file to your project with Add | Add Existing Item.*

If you've already worked on another report (perhaps with the full stand-alone copy of Crystal Reports or another VS.NET application), you can add it to your existing project. Simply right-click the project name in the Solution Explorer and choose Add | Add Existing Item from the pop-up menu. An open file dialog box will appear. Change the file type in the drop-down list to Crystal Report—only .RPT files will then appear in the dialog box. Navigate to the location for your desired report and open it. It will be added to the Solution Explorer. To edit the report, simply double-click it in the Solution Explorer window. The report will appear in its own tab in the VS.NET IDE inside the Integrated Report Designer.

NOTE *Adding an existing report to your project will make a copy of the report in your project folder. Any modifications you make to this report in the Integrated Report Designer won't affect the original report you chose when you added the item.*

If you wish to create a new report from scratch for design in the Integrated Report Designer, begin by selecting the project name in the Solution Explorer. Right-click and choose Add | Add New Item from the pop-up menu. The Add New Item dialog box will appear. If necessary, scroll through the available items until you find the Crystal Report icon. Once you select it, a default filename will appear at the bottom of the dialog box. Either accept it or type the desired filename in before clicking Open.

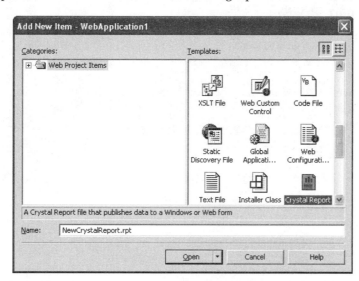

A new tab will appear in the VS.NET IDE for the new Crystal Report, and the Crystal Report Gallery will appear, much as it does when you create a new report in stand-alone Crystal Reports. The Report Wizard and As A Blank Report radio buttons mimic their stand-alone Crystal Reports counterparts. However, the additional From An Existing Report choice appears only in the VS.NET Integrated Report Designer.

Choosing one of the report wizards will display the step-by-step report design dialogs discussed briefly in Chapter 1 of this book. If you choose As A Blank Report, an empty report canvas will appear in VS.NET (the Database Expert won't appear automatically, as it does when using the Blank Report option in stand-alone Crystal Reports). And, if you choose the From An Existing Report choice, an open file dialog will appear where you can navigate to an existing .RPT file to import into the VS.NET Integrated Report Designer.

Once you've made your choices (and, in the case of a report wizard, proceeded through the necessary steps), your report will appear in the Integrated Report Designer inside the VS.NET IDE, as shown in Figure 26-2.

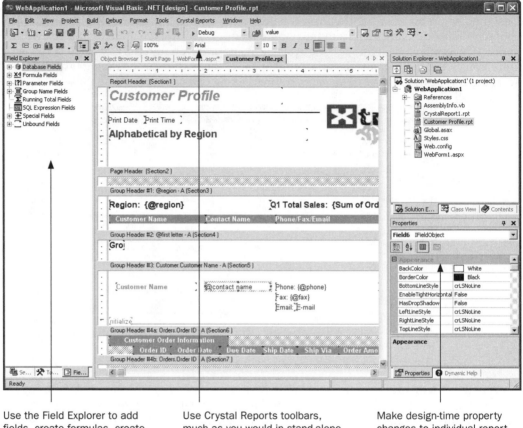

Use the Field Explorer to add
fields, create formulas, create
parameter fields, and so forth

Use Crystal Reports toolbars,
much as you would in stand-alone
Crystal Reports

Make design-time property
changes to individual report
objects in the Properties box

FIGURE 26-2   Integrated Report Designer in VS.NET IDE

Choosing a Data Source

If you are creating a new report from scratch in the Integrated Report Designer, you'll initially
be presented with a blank design screen when you first create the report. As with most report
design scenarios, the first step will be to choose a data source to base your report on.

As with stand-alone Crystal Reports, this is done with the Database Expert. However,
unlike stand-alone Crystal Reports, the Database Expert doesn't automatically appear
when you first create a new report—you need to display it by using a pop-up menu option.
Ensure no existing report objects are selected and right-click in the report design area. Choose
Database | Database Expert from the pop-up menu. The Database Expert will appear.

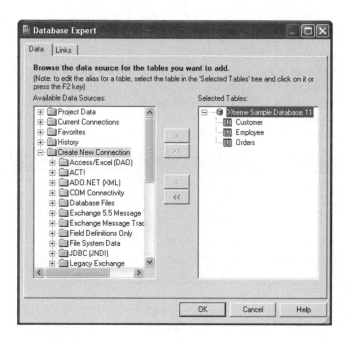

Choose the desired data source category from the list. Note that the choice of categories (and choice of available data source types) may vary, depending on whether you've installed the Crystal Reports 10 Developer or Advanced Developer edition—additional data sources are made available when you do this. Also note that some data sources available in the stand-alone version of Crystal Reports, such as SQL Commands or Business Views stored in the Crystal Enterprise repository, won't be available in VS.NET. You will find a Project Data category, however, that will allow you to connect a report to an existing "project" data source, as an ADO.NET dataset, that has already been defined in your project.

Choose the data source (or data sources) that you wish to use for your report. You may be required to supply logon credentials to a server to make a connection. Expand the various data source categories once you've connected to choose individual tables, views, stored procedures, and so forth that you wish to use in your report. Add each desired table, view, or stored procedure to the Selected Tables list.

If you add more than one item to the Selected Tables list, the Links tab will appear in the Database Expert. Click it and link tables, as described in Chapter 15. Once you've correctly added and linked tables, close the Database Expert by clicking OK.

Selecting Records and Adding Field Objects

Once you've added and linked tables or other data sources, you're ready to add field objects to the actual report canvas. You should also add record selection criteria to ensure that your report will be limited to a meaningful set of data records.

To limit the report to a certain set of records, use the Select Expert or the record selection formula. The Select Expert is displayed by right-clicking on a blank area of the report design canvas and choosing Report | Select Expert from the pop-up menu. You can also click the Select Expert toolbar button in the Crystal Reports toolbar within the VS.NET IDE. If you prefer to edit the record selection formula using the Crystal formula language directly, choose Report | Selection Formulas | Record from the same pop-up menu as the Select Expert. The Formula Editor will appear, where you can create or edit the report's record selection formula. Record Selection is covered in detail in Chapter 4.

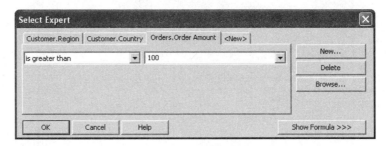

Add field objects to your report from the Field Explorer, which is initially docked at the left side of the report design window. These fields can consist of fields directly from your data source, formulas that you create, parameter fields that prompt the report viewer for a value, and so forth. Expand the desired Field Explorer category and drag the desired field to the appropriate report section. You may also right-click a Field Explorer category, or an individual field, and choose options from the pop-up menu.

You can use the Field Explorer to create report formulas, parameter fields, and SQL Expressions (all are discussed in various chapters in Part I of this book). You can also drag and drop Special Fields, such as page numbers, print date and time, and so forth, to the report from the Special Fields category. The Unbound Fields category is unique to the VS.NET Integrated Report Designer. Opening this category will reveal a field type for each supported Crystal Reports data type (String, Currency, Date, and so forth). By dragging an unbound field to the report, you are merely adding a "placeholder" object that you'll need to fill with data programmatically at run time with a project data source, such as an ADO.NET dataset.

TIP *If you plan to modify your report's behavior at run time (almost a given, since you are most probably integrating a Crystal report with a custom application that will control report behavior from your own UI), you should consider using Parameter Fields to control various aspects of report behavior. By using Parameter Fields when you design your report to control record selection, report formulas, section or object formatting, and so forth, you can control report behavior at run time by passing different values to the parameter fields from within your VS.NET code. These run-time modification techniques are discussed later in this chapter.*

Formatting Objects and Sections

Crystal Reports provides default formatting for individual report objects (fields, formulas, and so forth) and report sections (page header, details, group footer 1, and so forth) when you initially create a report. However, as Crystal Reports is a complete Windows- and web-oriented design tool, you have complete control over a wide variety of properties that affect field and report section appearance.

Format individual report objects by selecting them. Then, make choices from the formatting portion of the Crystal Reports toolbars at the top of the VS.NET IDE. You may also right-click the desired object or objects and choose Format options from the pop-up menu. And, you can also select an object and make choices in the VS.NET Properties box. You'll notice some formatting options change appearance of the report right in the Integrated Report Designer. Other options, however, will only be apparent when you actually run your application and see the report in a report viewer.

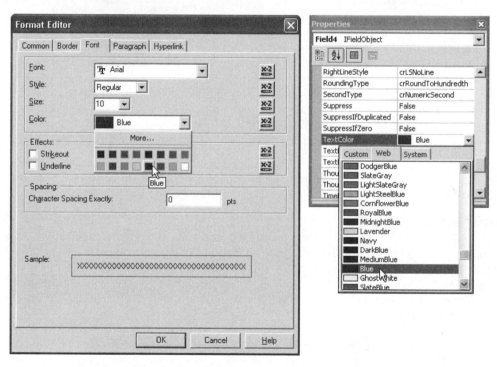

Format entire report sections (such as the Details section, Page Header, and so forth) by clicking the gray section title, right-clicking, and choosing options from the pop-up menu. In particular, you can perform all available section formatting by choosing Section Expert from the pop-up menu. This will display the Section Expert dialog box, which allows control of suppression, page breaks, section background colors, and much more. Make desired choices and click OK. As mentioned previously, some of these changes (especially conditional formatting formulas that you may supply) won't be visible until you run your application and see the report in a viewer.

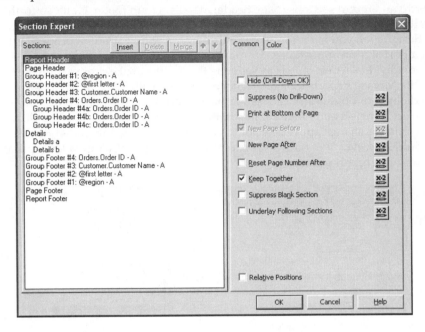

TIP *Formatting report objects is covered in Chapter 7. And, section formatting is covered in Chapters 7 and 8. Refer to these chapters for detailed information on report formatting techniques.*

Sorting and Grouping

While you can just display data records one after the other in the order the database supplies them, your reports become much more powerful if you at least sort the records in a meaningful fashion by one or more relevant fields. Do this by right-clicking on a blank area of the report designer and choosing Report | Record Sort Expert from the pop-up menu. You can also click the Sort Order button in the Crystal Reports toolbar in the VS.NET IDE. The Sort Order dialog box will appear.

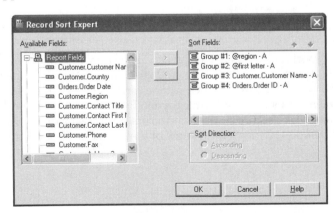

Select a desired sort field from the Available Fields list and click the right arrow to add it to the Sort Fields list. By default, the report will be sorted in ascending (A to Z) order. To change this order, select the desired field in the Sort Fields list and click the Descending radio button at the bottom of the dialog box. The report will be sorted by the chosen field in descending (Z to A) order. You are not limited to sorting the report on a single field—add additional fields in the desired order, choosing ascending or descending sorts for each. If you need to change the priority of fields in the Sort Fields list, simply select the desired field and click the up or down arrow above the Sort Fields list to change the field's priority.

However, you may find that simply sorting the report doesn't provide sufficient flexibility for your needs. In many cases, report grouping is preferable to (or at least helpful in addition to) sorting. By creating report groups, you create "level breaks" that allow placement of summaries and subtotals at the end of each group. Furthermore, these grouping concepts, when used in concert with section formatting (typically, the hiding of report sections), become the basis for sophisticated drill-down reports that maximize the interactive capabilities of Crystal Reports placed in VS.NET applications.

To create a report group, right-click on a blank area of the report designer and choose Insert | Group from the pop-up menu. You can also click the Insert Group toolbar button in the Crystal toolbars in the VS.NET IDE. The Insert Group dialog box will appear.

Choose the desired field on which you wish to group the report from the first drop-down list. Then, choose the order in which you want report groups to appear from the second drop-down list. If you wish to set additional group options, click the Options tab of the Insert Group dialog box and make choices. When you're finished, click OK to close the Insert Group dialog box and add the group to the report. You'll notice that group header and group footer sections appear in the report for your chosen group.

TIP *Complete details on sorting and grouping are provided in Chapter 3.*

Once you've created necessary report groups, you can insert summary and subtotal fields in the group footers for the groups (as well as grand totals in the Report Header or Report Footer). To insert a summary, you may optionally select the field in the Details section you wish to summarize (although you don't have to). Then, right-click the field you've selected and choose Insert | Summary from the pop-up menu. You can also click the Insert Summary toolbar button from the Crystal Reports toolbar in the VS.NET IDE (this button can be used even if you haven't selected a details field first). The Insert Summary dialog box will appear.

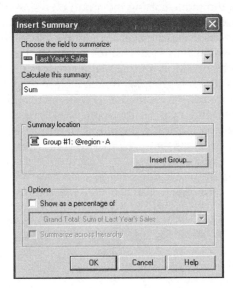

If necessary, choose the field you wish to summarize in the first drop-down list (the proper field should already appear in this list if you selected it first). Then, choose the desired type of summary (sum, average, count, and so forth) from the second drop-down list. In the third drop-down list, choose where you want the summary to be placed. Available options will be a grand total (placed in the report footer), or a subtotal placed in the desired group footer. If you wish to use a Percentage Summary Field or summarize across hierarchical groups (described in Chapter 3), check the appropriate boxes. When you click OK, the summary will be placed in the group footer or report footer.

NOTE *While the user interface in the Integrated Report Designer differs somewhat from that in stand-alone Crystal Reports, the general techniques used to design reports are similar. While this chapter covers very general techniques for report design, Part I of this book covers report design techniques in much greater detail. Refer to chapters in Part I for information on various report design steps that also apply to reports designed with the VS.NET Integrated Report Designer.*

VS.NET Report Customization Object Models

While your application may not require any additional capabilities than are provided by a simple report bound to a viewer, there's a good possibility that you'll need to customize one or more aspects of the report at run time from within your application. These customizations can be as simple as supplying the user ID and password for a report's database connection from within your code (so that the user doesn't have to log on to the report's database again, after they've already logged in to your application). Or, they may require more complex code that changes several report groups, formulas, parameter fields, formatting, or the report's record selection formula all on the fly based on other elements of your application.

Crystal Reports has always been the favorite of developers because of its flexible programming interfaces. And, the versions of Crystal Reports integrated with Visual Studio .NET carry on that tradition by providing rich object models that can control many aspects of report behavior at run time. Installing Crystal Reports XI Developer edition after you've installed VS.NET will improve on this programming flexibility even further.

There are two general ways of customizing your report at run time: using the Crystal Windows or Web Forms Viewer (CrystalReportViewer) object model or using the Crystal Reports Engine (ReportDocument) object model. You should look at both object models, as well as your application requirements, to determine which object model you wish to use for run-time customization. Business Objects documentation discourages mixing object model usage—particularly when changing the same properties in both object models. For example, you will probably encounter confusion (and, possibly application instability) if you change a parameter field using the Crystal Reports Engine object model, and then change the parameter again using the Crystal Web Forms Viewer object model before displaying the report in a viewer.

You'll notice that, in particular, the CrystalReportViewer object model is improved if you install one of the Developer edition of Crystal Reports XI. It's quite possible that the CrystalReportViewer object model will provide all the necessary customization you need. However, certain complex reporting requirements that require more involved section formatting or run-time addition or removal of fields, groups, and so forth will not be satisfied with the CrystalReportViewer object model. These will require use of the ReportDocument object model, which can make significant run-time modifications to a report object *before* it is passed to a report viewer.

Run-Time Customization with the Crystal Windows or Web Forms Viewer

Some of the most obvious run-time customization that you may wish to perform with the viewer is basic viewer appearance. You can, for example, control viewer properties at run time that you see in the Properties box at design time. In addition, commonly used report options, such as the report's record selection formula and parameter field values, can be changed at run time only with calls to the CrystalReportViewer object model.

These CrystalReportViewer object model choices are provided by assemblies installed with VS.NET and Crystal Reports XI. In particular, the *CrystalDecisions.Windows.Forms* or *CrystalDecisions.Web* namespace is added as a reference to your project automatically when you add the respective viewer. This namespace exposes the object model available when using the viewer. When you install Crystal Reports XI Developer edition on an existing computer containing Visual Studio .NET, this namespace is updated with additional version 11 capabilities.

Some initial customization you may wish to perform at run time simply involves viewer behavior, such as visibility of the group tree, appearance of individual toolbar buttons on the viewer toolbar, or complete invisibility of the entire toolbar. VS.NET "intellisense" technology will automatically show you available properties once you type the report viewer class, followed by a period. You can navigate through the various properties and, if necessary, see available arguments for available properties and methods.

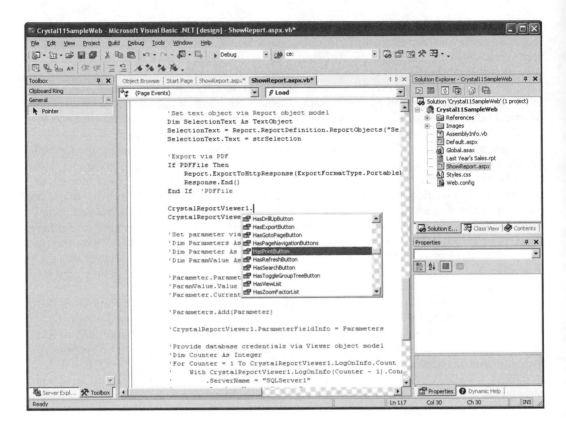

For example, the following code will hide the group tree in the viewer:

```
CrystalReportViewer1.DisplayGroupTree = False
```

And, more involved run-time customization to the viewer can involve instantiating additional objects, setting object properties, and passing the object to a viewer property to change viewer behavior. The following code will result in a group tree displaying an aqua background color and group tree entries in a bold coral color (this is an example of an improvement to the object model provided when you install Crystal Reports XI):

```
Dim GroupTreeStyle As New CrystalDecisions.Shared.GroupTreeStyle
With GroupTreeStyle
  .BackColor = System.Drawing.Color.Aqua
  .ForeColor = System.Drawing.Color.Coral
  .Font.Bold = True
End With
CrystalReportViewer1.GroupTreeStyle = GroupTreeStyle
```

Notice the declaration of the GroupTreeStyle class, taken from the *CrystalDecisions.Shared* namespace. This namespace, also added to your project automatically when you add a viewer, provides an object model that exposes common objects and properties that can be used in both Crystal Windows and web applications.

NOTE *The preceding example shows an object declaration with the fully qualified namespace. If you choose to add an Imports statement to import the namespace, then you would only need to declare the object using its class name without the need to precede it with "CrystalDecisions.Shared."*

Other report properties not related to appearance can also be set with the CrystalReportViewer object model. Some of the most obvious are described in the sections that follow.

Specifying Database Credentials

If the report bound to the viewer is based on a secure database, the viewer will prompt for proper database credentials before displaying the report. If you have already gathered security information elsewhere in your application, you probably won't want your user to be prompted again. You can supply these credentials via the CrystalReportViewer object model as follows:

```
'Provide database credentials via Viewer object model
Dim Counter As Integer
For Counter = 1 To CrystalReportViewer1.LogOnInfo.Count
    With CrystalReportViewer1.LogOnInfo(Counter - 1).ConnectionInfo
        .ServerName = "SQLServer1"
        .DatabaseName = "xtreme"
        .UserID = "sa"
        .Password = "password"
    End With
Next Counter
```

This code loops through the individual ConnectionInfo objects within the report viewer's LogonInfo class, setting credentials for each. All database connections, regardless of original data source, as well as subreport connection objects, will be included in the LogonInfo class. Accordingly, you'll need to take extra steps to properly assign values if the source tables in your main report or subreports come from different databases.

Modifying the Record Selection Formula

This is a very common requirement of report integration applications. You may wish to control report record selection based on some other control on a form or another element of your embedded application logic. This is accomplished by setting the viewer's RecordSelectionFormula property.

```
'Set record selection via Viewer object model
If Countries = "USA Only" Then
    CrystalReportViewer1.SelectionFormula = _
            "{Customer.Country} = 'USA'"
Else
    CrystalReportViewer1.SelectionFormula = ""
End If 'Countries = "USA Only"
```

PART III

Make sure you pass a valid record selection formula, using Crystal Reports Crystal Formula Syntax, to this property. Don't forget to include proper punctuation, such as French braces around field names and apostrophes around string literals. You may find discussions in Chapters 4 and 5 helpful in working with record selection formulas.

Supplying Parameter Field Values

In many cases, you may actually base your report's record selection on a parameter field. Or, perhaps you have created formulas based on parameter fields that change report grouping or formatting. In these cases, the ability to pass values to parameter fields at run time is crucial. Here's an example of passing a value to a single-value (or "discrete") numeric parameter field:

```
'Set parameter via Viewer object model
Dim Parameters As New ParameterFields
Dim Parameter As New ParameterField
Dim ParamValue As New ParameterDiscreteValue

Parameter.ParameterFieldName = "Tax Rate"
ParamValue.Value = CDbl(5.25)
Parameter.CurrentValues.Add(ParamValue)

Parameters.Add(Parameter)

CrystalReportViewer1.ParameterFieldInfo = Parameters
```

Note that additional objects are instantiated to hold a parameters collection, a parameter field, and a parameter field discrete value. The parameter field name is supplied, using the parameter field's name in the underlying report. The actual discrete value for a 5 ¼ percent tax rate is supplied, including a cast to ensure proper data type matching. The discrete value object is added to the parameter's CurrentValues collection. The parameter is added to a parameters collection. And finally, the viewer's ParameterFieldInfo property is set to the parameter's collection.

Report Viewer Events

Not only can you set report viewer properties at run time, but you can also trap report viewer events. As Crystal Reports blends into the entire .NET framework and .NET event processing, you can trap viewer events in the viewer and add code based on them. By selecting the desired viewer in the Class Name list in the code window, you'll then be able to see a list of events that the viewer fires in the Method Name list.

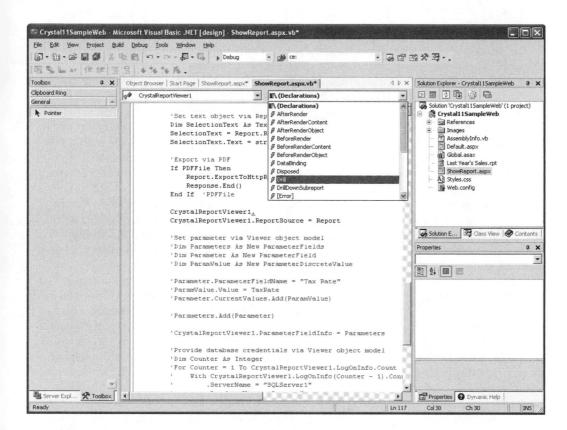

You may, for example, add code that traps a viewer drill-down event and performs some action based on the group that is drilled into.

```
Private Sub CrystalReportViewer1_Drill(ByVal source As Object, _
        ByVal e As CrystalDecisions.Web.DrillEventArgs) _
        Handles CrystalReportViewer1.Drill
    If e.NewGroupName = "USA" Then
        e.Handled = True
    End If
End Sub
```

In this example, the event class exposes DrillEventArgs from the CrystalDecisions.Web namespace, including various properties to indicate what is being drilled into. Here, the code checks to see if the USA group is being drilled into. If so, the drill-down is canceled by setting the class's Handled property to True.

Run-Time Customization with the Crystal Reports Engine (ReportDocument)

So far, this chapter has concentrated entirely on run-time customization with the CrystalReportViewer object model (with classes exposed by the CrystalDecisions.Windows. Forms or CrystalDecisions.Web namespace) and the shared object model (with classes exposed by the CrystalDecisions.Shared namespace). There's still yet another object model/ namespace that exposes classes you can use to customize report behavior at run time.

By using the ReportDocument object model, you can customize report behavior at run time using techniques similar to those discussed previously in the chapter. However, this object model (exposed by the CrystalDecisions.CrystalReports.Engine namespace) offers properties, methods, and events that are strictly limited to the core report object you are integrating in your application, independent of any viewer you may have added to your application. Also, a much larger number of customization options are available with the Report Engine. In addition to setting parameter field values, supplying database credentials, and setting the report's record selection formula, the Report Engine offers the ability to control object formatting, supply new formula contents, export the report to various file formats, and much more.

Any customization you perform here typically takes place *before* you bind a report to a viewer (or, in situations where you don't even add a viewer to your project). Once you've made these customizations to the report object, they will take effect when the report is bound to the viewer (or, in the case of a non-viewing application, whenever you execute a report method to ultimately output the report to a printer, exported file format, and so forth).

As discussed earlier in the chapter, you'll find properties and methods in the Report Engine that duplicate those found in the CrystalReportViewer object model. For example, you can supply database credentials, set the record selection formula, and supply parameter field values via either object model. The decision as to which object model to use is dependent upon your application particulars and how detailed your integration requirements are. Again, Business Objects recommends that you avoid duplicate calls from different object models in the same application. So, as you develop your application, look at which object model provides the best combination of simplicity and functionality depending on your requirements.

To make use of the Report Engine, you must ensure that the CrystalDecisions.CrystalReports. Engine namespace is being referenced in your project. In most cases, you'll also need references to the CrystalDecisions.Shared namespace. Typically, if you add a viewer to the project, these namespaces will automatically be added. If, however, you are designing an application that does not make use of a web viewer, you'll need to use the VS.NET Add Reference option to add these namespaces to your project. Also, you'll need to declare references to several classes from these namespaces in your code and may prefer to use the Imports statement to allow class references without the fully qualified namespace name.

One of the first requirements of using the Report Engine is instantiation of a report object. As discussions earlier in the chapter indicate, there are several ways of adding reports to your project. And, there are several types of reports (untyped, strongly typed, and so forth) that can be added. As an example, you may have added a strongly typed report to your project, either by using Add | Add Existing Item with an existing .RPT file or by using Add | Add New Item and designing a new Crystal report. You then must declare an object to refer to the strongly typed report and expose the Report Engine's object model. Here's an example:

```
Dim Report As New Last_Years_Sales
'refers to strongly-typed Last_Years_Sales.rpt in project
```

Once you've declared this object, you will notice many of the Report Engine properties and methods available via VS.NET's "Intellisense" technology.

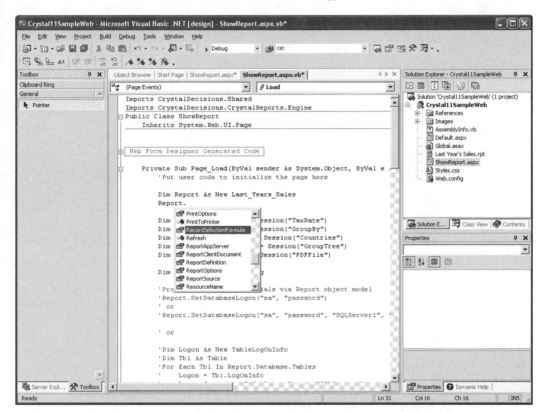

Some of the more common run-time customizations you can make with the Report Engine (but, by no means, an exhaustive list) are described next.

Supplying Database Credentials

If your report is based on a secure database, you will probably prefer that your application code provide database credentials to prevent your report viewer from being prompted, or from your application failing if your report is not bound to a viewer. There are several ways for the Report Engine to supply these credentials. Examine the following:

```
'Provide database credentials via ReportDocument object model
Report.SetDatabaseLogon("sa", "password")
```

This single line of code supplies a user ID and password to every data source in the report, including those contained in subreports. The SetDatabaseLogon method greatly simplifies supplying database credentials if your report is based entirely on a single database connection.

A second permutation of SetDatabaseLogon accept four arguments:

```
'Report.SetDatabaseLogon("sa", "password", "SQLServer1", "xtreme")
```

This allows a database server and database name to also be specified, in case you've made use of several different connections in your report.

If you need a more granular way of supplying database credentials for individual table objects in your main report and subreports, you've got a little more coding ahead of you. Examine the following:

```
Dim Logon As New TableLogOnInfo
Dim Tbl As Table
For Each Tbl In Report.Database.Tables
    Logon = Tbl.LogOnInfo
    Logon.ConnectionInfo.ServerName = "SQLServer1"
    Logon.ConnectionInfo.DatabaseName = "xtreme"
    Logon.ConnectionInfo.UserID = "sa"
    Logon.ConnectionInfo.Password = "password"
    Tbl.ApplyLogOnInfo(Logon)
Next Tbl

'Provide database credentials to subreports
Dim Subreport As ReportDocument
For Each Subreport In Report.Subreports
    For Each Tbl In Subreport.Database.Tables
        Logon = Tbl.LogOnInfo
        Logon.ConnectionInfo.ServerName = "SQLServer1"
        Logon.ConnectionInfo.DatabaseName = "xtreme"
        Logon.ConnectionInfo.UserID = "sa"
        Logon.ConnectionInfo.Password = "password"
        Tbl.ApplyLogOnInfo(Logon)
    Next 'Tbl
Next 'Subreport
```

In the preceding code fragment, a TableLogonInfo class (from the CrystalDecisions.Shared namespace) and Table class (from the CrystalDecisions.CrystalReports.Engine namespace) are instantiated. Then, each table in the main report is cycled through, supplying database credentials via the ConnectionInfo property.

To accommodate subreports, a ReportDocument class is instantiated (this comes from CrystalDecisions.CrystalReports.Engine), which is used to cycle through the main report's Subreports collection. For each subreport, similar loops through the Database.Tables collection are made to supply database credentials.

While the preceding code will work with Crystal Reports 10 and XI, earlier versions (including Crystal Reports included with VS.NET) do not expose a Subreports collection. In this situation, code to deal with subreports must be even more granular, as the following example shows.

```
crSections = Report.ReportDefinition.Sections

For Each crSection In crSections
    crReportObjects = crSection.ReportObjects

    For Each crReportObject In crReportObjects
        If crReportObject.Kind = ReportObjectKind.SubreportObject Then
            crSubreportObject = CType(crReportObject, SubreportObject)
```

```
      subrpt = _
         crSubreportObject.OpenSubreport(crSubreportObject.SubreportName)
      For Each subtbl In subReport.Database.Tables
         str &= subReport.Name & "-" & subtbl.Name & " - "
         objTableLogonInfo = subtbl.LogOnInfo
         objTableLogonInfo.ConnectionInfo = objConnInfo
         subtbl.ApplyLogOnInfo(objTableLogonInfo)
         subtbl.Location = _
          subtbl.Location.Substring(subtbl.Location.LastIndexOf(".") + 1)
         str &= subtbl.TestConnectivity() & vbCrLf
      Next
   End If
Next
Next
```

Setting Record Selection

As with the viewer object model, you can set the report's record selection formula at run time via a simple property setting in the Report Engine. You will probably want to do this in terms of other controls or conditions in your application. For example,

```
Report.RecordSelectionFormula = "{Customer.Country} = 'USA'"
```

will return records where the country is USA. Ensure that you pass a syntactically correct formula using the Crystal Reports Crystal Syntax, including French braces around field names and apostrophes surrounding string literals. Discussions on record selection and formula syntax can be found in Chapters 4 and 5 in this book.

Modifying Existing Formula Contents

One area of report customization that can only be accomplished with the Report Engine is run-time report formula modification. For example, you may wish to change some sort of calculation or string customization contained in a report formula based on a user control or other element of your custom application. By modifying a report formula at run time, you can change report calculations or customized fields based on your application elements. For example,

```
If GroupBy = "Country" Then
   Report.DataDefinition.FormulaFields("Group Field").Text = _
      "{Customer.Country}"
Else
   Report.DataDefinition.FormulaFields("Group Field").Text = _
      "{Customer.Region}"
End If 'GroupBy = "Country"
```

You may navigate directly to the FormulaFields collection of the report's DataDefinition object. Notice that the particular collection member can be retrieved by name, in addition to numeric index (this is a refreshing change from many collections in the older Report Designer Component, which could only be accessed via numeric index). By setting the formula's Text property, you can change the formula contents at run time. In this example, a variable is examined indicating the user's grouping choice. Report grouping is being controlled via a formula that is set to the database field corresponding to the user's choice. Note that you must supply a formula of proper syntax when setting the Text property. Chapter 5 discusses report formulas in greater detail.

Providing Parameter Field Values

A very common requirement of run-time report modification is dealing with parameter fields. As many report customizations can be accomplished by designing reports with parameter fields, you may find this one of the most common run-time modifications you'll be required to perform. While the viewer object model can change parameter field values at run time, you may prefer (or be required) to use the Report Engine to supply parameter values at run time. If you have installed Crystal Reports XI, the report object's SetParameterValue method is a simple way to supply a value to a parameter field:

```
'Set parameter via ReportDocument object model
Report.SetParameterValue("Tax Rate", TaxRate)
```

The SetParameterValue method demonstrated here accepts two arguments: the parameter field to supply a value to (which can be specified either by name or by index), and the value to pass to the parameter field (in this instance, a variable that has been cast elsewhere in the code to match the data type of the parameter field).

The SetParameterValue method is fairly flexible in the data types and parameter field types (such as multivalue parameter fields) that it can accommodate. It can also be used to supply parameter values to subreports. The Crystal Reports XI help collection contains complete details.

If you have more complex parameter requirements that may not be accommodated by the SetParameterValue method, you may modify parameters via an additional object. Here's an example that sets a simple, single-value parameter field:

```
Dim ParamValue As New ParameterDiscreteValue
'CrystalDecisions.Shared.ParameterDiscreteValue if no Imports
ParamValue.Value = TaxRate
Report.ParameterFields("Tax Rate").CurrentValues.Add(ParamValue)
```

A discrete parameter class is instantiated to hold a single-value (discrete) parameter field. The object's Value property is set to a variable (again, properly cast earlier in the code). And, finally, the parameter object is added to the existing parameter field's CurrentValues collection (which, for a single-value parameter field, will contain only one member). The parameter field can be obtained from the report's ParameterFields collection, either by name or by numeric index.

Supplying Text Object Text   While there are several ways to display a custom string or "message" on a report (perhaps you wish to display various run-time options chosen by the report viewer on the report itself), one way is to set the actual text displayed by a text object at run time. This capability is provided by the Report Engine only and cannot be accomplished by using any of the CrystalReportViewer object model calls. Here's an example:

```
'Set text object via ReportDocument object model
Dim SelectionText As TextObject
'CrystalDecisions.CrystalReports.Engine.TextObject if no Imports
```

```
SelectionText = Report.ReportDefinition.ReportObjects("SelectionText")
SelectionText.Text = strSelection
```

Instantiate a TextObject object (supplied by the CrystalDecisions.CrystalReports.Engine namespace). Set it to the proper text object in the report by navigating through the report's ReportObjects collection from the ReportDefinition object. Then, set the text object's Text property to change the actual text contained in the text object on the report.

Exporting Reports in Windows and Web Applications

While the viewer includes an Export toolbar button that allows the user to export the viewed report to various file formats, you may wish to do this programmatically. You may, for example, prefer to limit the formats that the report may be exported to and not allow the user to export with the toolbar button. You might, then, disable the export button in the viewer and export the file to a specified format within code. Examine the following:

```
CrystalReportViewer1.HasExportButton = False
Report.ExportToHttpResponse(ExportFormatType.PortableDocFormat, _
        Response, False, "") 'Crystal Reports XI only
```

Initially, the viewer's export toolbar button is hidden. Then, the report object's ExportToHttpResponse method is used to export the file via the Response object in Acrobat PDF format. There are several versions of this method with arguments documented in the Crystal Reports XI help collection. Note that this particular approach is only supported by the version XI CrystalDecisions.CrystalReports.Engine namespace—if you are using the original out-of-the-box installation of Crystal Reports in VS.NET, you'll need to undertake a more involved export process whereby you export to a file and attach it to an e-mail message (in a Windows application) or export to a local file on the web server and then stream the file to the web browser (in a web application).

Here's an example of the more involved exporting in a Windows application that attaches a file to an e-mail message:

```
Dim ExportOptions As New ExportOptions
Dim EMailOptions As New MicrosoftMailDestinationOptions
ExportOptions.ExportFormatType = ExportFormatType.PortableDocFormat
ExportOptions.ExportDestinationType = ExportDestinationType.MicrosoftMail
EMailOptions.MailToList = strEMailAddress
EMailOptions.MailSubject = "XTEME Orders Report"
EMailOptions.MailMessage = _
   "The XTREME Orders report is attached in PDF format"
ExportOptions.ExportDestinationOptions = EMailOptions
Report.Export(ExportOptions)
```

In this example, both ExportOptions and MicrosoftMailDestinationOptions objects are instantiated (both classes are exposed by the CrystalDecisions.Shared namespace). The ExportOptions export format type is set to Adobe Acrobat Portable Document Format (PDF), and the export destination type is set to Microsoft Mail. Various MicrosortMailDestinationOptions are used to set the e-mail's To address, subject, and message text. The ExportOptions ExportDestinationOptions property is set to the MicrosoftMailDestinationOptions object.

And, finally, the report object's Export method is executed, with the ExportOptions object being supplied as an argument.

Crystal Reports as XML Web Services

One of the new features of Visual Studio .NET is the web service: a web server–based "application" that exposes a set of data based on the Extensible Markup Language, or XML. The web service exposes its actual data, as well as its data layout (or schema), through the Hypertext Transport Protocol, or HTTP. Because the XML data layout is simply an extension of HTML and because HTTP is such a ubiquitous communications protocol, virtually all networks, intranet systems, and Internet connection methods (dial-up, firewalls, and so forth) work with these standards already.

Crystal Reports for Visual Studio .NET fully supports web services—being able to both create and "consume" web services. Creating a web service based on a Crystal report exposes a report via HTTP to anyone who can consume a web service anywhere on an intranet or the Internet. VS.NET also allows you to create projects that use or "consume" published Crystal Report web services. In this scenario, you create a Windows or web application, including a Windows Forms Viewer or Web Forms Viewer, which is then bound to the report exposed by the web service.

Creating a Web Service

Creating a web service based on a Crystal report is a very straightforward process—almost identical to creating a web application using a Crystal report. You must establish a location (by way of a virtual directory) on the web server that you want to use to host the web service. You can do this either by using an existing web application to host the web service or by creating a new ASP.NET Web Service (if all you want to do is host reports in a web service, just create a Web Service, not a Web Application). The web application or web service creation will create the virtual directory with the same name as the service or application.

Once you've opened or created your web service or web application project, add a strongly typed Crystal report the same way you would for another application. Use Add | Add Existing Item and navigate to the desired existing .RPT file, or use Add | New Item and create a new .RPT file from scratch. You may make any design changes and customization to the report in the Integrated Report Designer inside the VS.NET IDE the same as you would for any other report.

CAUTION *Life will be much easier if you add or create a report that doesn't contain any spaces in the filename. If necessary, rename the report in the Solution Explorer, removing or replacing spaces.*

When you're ready to post the report on a web server as a web service, simply right-click the report object in the Solution Explorer that you want to publish. Choose Publish as Web Service from the pop-up menu.

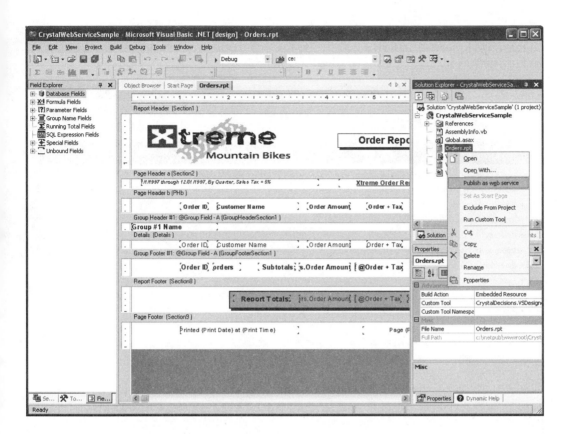

Additional files representing the web service will be created in the Solution Explorer. In particular, an .asmx file (with the word Service appended to the report name) will appear—this is actually the web page that exposes the web service. Also, a language-specific version of the .asmx file (with an appended .vb, for example) will also be created. You'll need to click the Show All Files button in the Solution Explorer to see it. This may be used to add additional custom code to your web service, if you choose.

To actually post the Crystal Report web service on the web server that the web service project was created on, you must compile the application. Choose Build | Build Solution from the VS.NET pull-down menus, or right-click the solution name in the Solution Explorer and choose Build Solution from the pop-up menu.

Consuming Web Service Reports in a Web Application

Once a web service has been created and compiled, you can actually use a web browser to view the properties of the web service. The URL is based on the application or web service you used to publish the report, and the report name. For example, if you created a default web service name of WebService1 and published a report named FedExOrders.rpt, an FedExOrdersService.asmx file will be created in the WebService1 virtual directory. If you type in the following URL in a standard web browser:

```
http://<server name>/WebService1/FedExOrdersService.asmx
```

you'll see the properties exposed by the report web service. You may click various hyperlinks on this page to see the underlying XML that the web report service exposes, but the report will not be viewable in the browser directly using this URL.

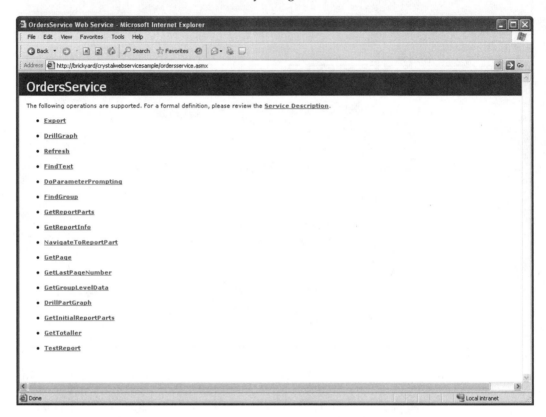

In order to view or "consume" a report web service, you must create *another* web application and add a Crystal Web Forms Viewer to it. You must then bind the Web Forms Viewer to the report exposed by the report web service. As you might expect, there are several ways to reference a report web service in your web application and bind the Web Forms Viewer to it.

Binding by URL as the ReportSource

For Windows applications, binding report web services to the viewer must be done in code. The viewer's Report Source property in the Properties box is unable to accept a URL as a value. For this reason, you'll need to bind the report to the viewer's ReportSource property in the code editor (probably in the parent form's Load event). Here's an example:

```
Private Sub Form1_Load(ByVal sender As System.Object, _
  ByVal e As System.EventArgs) Handles MyBase.Load
    CrystalReportViewer1.ReportSource = _
      "http://localhost/WebService1/FedExOrdersService.asmx"
End Sub
```

This code fragment shows the viewer being bound to a report web service exposed on "localhost" (your own computer's web server). The exposed report is originally entitled FedExOrders.rpt and is published as a web service from a web project named "WebService1."

For web applications, select the viewer you've added to your web form. Then, click the ellipses next to the DataBindings() property in the Properties box. This will display the DataBindings dialog box for the viewer. Click the ReportSource property in the Bindable Properties list and then click the Custom Binding Expression radio button. Type the full URL to the report web service (including the "http://" protocol string), surrounded by quotation marks.

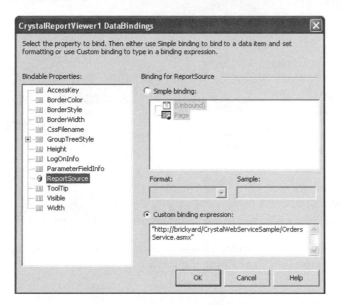

Binding by Adding the Report Web Service as a Reference

You may also add a reference to the web report service to your project and instantiate a copy of any reports exposed by it. To do this, perform the following steps:

1. Add a reference to the web service by clicking the References category of the Solution Explorer. Right-click the References category and choose Add Web Reference from the pop-up menu. The Add Web Reference dialog box will appear.

2. In the Address line of the Add Web Reference dialog box, type the full URL for the web service. For example, to add a reference to the FedExOrders report web service discussed previously, you'd type

```
http://localhost/WebService1/FedExOrdersService.asmx
```

3. You'll see the same web browser display you would see if you navigated to the URL in a standard web browser. Also, a list of all exposed report web services will appear in the box on the right of the dialog box. And, the web server name will appear as the default name for the reference. If you wish to reference the web server by a

different name, type it in the Web Reference Name text box. When you're finished, click OK to add the report web services as references.

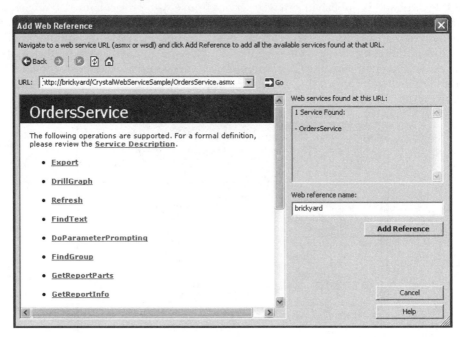

To reference the web service in the viewer, you may execute code similar to the following in the Load event of the form containing the viewer:

```
CrystalReportViewer1.ReportSource = _
New localhost.FedExOrdersService
```

When you run the application, the report exposed by the web service will appear in the form containing the viewer.

Setting Viewer Properties with Consumed Web Services

The actual report exposed by the report web service isn't "strongly typed." For this reason, you don't have the same control you do over a strongly typed report making use of the Report Engine namespace. However, you can still manipulate the report with classes exposed by the viewer (you have a much richer set of choices if you've installed Crystal Reports XI Developer edition).

For example, you can still make use of viewer properties to provide database credentials, set the record selection formula, or supply parameter field values. For example, the following code will supply beginning and ending dates to a date range parameter field included in the report exposed by the report web service:

```
Dim Parameters As New CrystalDecisions.Shared.ParameterFields
Dim Parameter As New CrystalDecisions.Shared.ParameterField
Dim ParamValue As New CrystalDecisions.Shared.ParameterRangeValue
```

```
Parameter.ParameterFieldName = "Date Range"
ParamValue.StartValue = #1/1/2002#
ParamValue.EndValue = #12/31/2002#
Parameter.CurrentValues.Add(ParamValue)

Parameters.Add(Parameter)

CrystalReportViewer1.ParameterFieldInfo = Parameters
```

stributing Crystal Reports .NET and ASP.NET Applications

Custom applications developed in Visual Studio .NET may often need to be prepared for distribution to end users if the application will not be used solely in your organization's environment, or won't be located on the same computer environment it was developed with. Although Visual Studio .NET provides standard features for application distribution, there may be some special considerations you'll still want to make for Crystal Reports-based applications.

Windows Applications

Once you've designed your Crystal Reports Windows application, you'll probably need to package it for deployment to client PCs. Generally speaking, Crystal Reports–based applications are no different than any other application—you can create a typical Setup and Deployment project using standard VS.NET steps to create a Microsoft Installer package to install the Windows application on the target computer.

Web Applications

Once you've designed your Crystal Reports ASP.NET web application, you need to place it on the production web server for use by web viewers. If you happened to install Visual Studio.NET and Crystal Reports XI on the target web server, then you may need to do nothing more than distribute the URL for your application to end users, or place a link containing the URL on another portal or home page.

However, if you need to distribute the ASP.NET web application to a different web server than it was designed on, you have varying amounts of work ahead of you. You could perform a complete install of Visual Studio .NET and Crystal Reports XI Developer on the target server and then simply copy files from the virtual directory. Or, you could create a typical Setup and Deployment project using standard VS.NET steps to create a Microsoft Installer package to install the web application on the target web server.

General Concepts

When deploying .NET or ASP.NET applications that contain Crystal Reports, keep the following general concepts in mind:

- **The target machine must contain the .NET Framework**   Depending on how you create your setup project, you may not include the .NET Framework files in the setup routines. Because Crystal Reports for VS.NET fully integrates with the .NET Framework, you'll need to ensure it is installed on the web server before installing your Crystal web application.

- **You will need Business Objects–supplied merge modules** If you have installed Crystal Reports XI Developer edition on your development machine, you'll need to distribute updated Crystal Reports XI modules with your application. This is accomplished by using one (and, if you are embedding geographic maps in your report, an additional) merge module when you build your setup project. Download the Crystal Reports XI merge modules from http://support.BusinessObjects.com/ MergeModules. You'll find included documentation that specifies what object models, viewers, and features are included with the various merge modules. If you are using the version of Crystal Reports that ships with Visual Studio .NET, merge modules are found in C:\Program Files\Common Files\Merge Modules.

- **Don't forget the keycode** When developing your reporting application, you may have noticed a Crystal screen prompting you to register your copy of Crystal Reports for VS.NET. This appears whether you are using the copy of Crystal Reports included with VS.NET, or if you've installed Crystal Reports XI afterwards (and, sometimes even if you've registered your stand-alone copy of Crystal Reports).

  While you can bypass this screen when developing your application, you won't be so lucky when it comes time to distribute it. If a valid Crystal keycode isn't specified when you build your setup program, your distributed application won't work. You may obtain the necessary keycode by following the steps in the registration prompt (you'll be taken to the Business Objects web site and asked to supply various pieces of personal information).

  Once you're finished with registration, you can display the keycode by choosing Help | About Microsoft Development Environment from the VS.NET menus. Note the three-part keycode that appears next to the Crystal Reports entry in the list. Either write it down or select the Crystal Reports entry and click the Copy Info button to copy the keycode to the Windows clipboard.

  When you build your setup project, you *must* select the primary Crystal Reporting merge module and paste the keycode into the Keycode Properties box.

NOTE *If you installed Crystal Reports XI Developer or Advanced Developer edition, your keycode should be the same keycode on the program CD that you used when you installed stand-alone Crystal Reports XI.*

Formula Language Reference

This appendix provides detailed information for each Crystal Reports formula language function and operator. Functions and operators are categorized by usage (string, numeric, financial, and so forth). The purpose of each function or operator is discussed, along with explanations of various function arguments. An example of each function and operator is provided.

Consider the following points when making use of this reference:

- Crystal Syntax is used in this reference. With very few exceptions, Basic Syntax is not covered, as Visual Basic and Visual Basic for Applications (which Basic Syntax is based on) are commonly documented languages. In many cases, the Basic Syntax version of the function or operator is identical or very similar to the Crystal Syntax version documented here.

- Some more esoteric functions, such as statistical and financial functions, may not be explained in great detail. It is assumed that report designers who need to use these specialized functions will already possess a basic understanding of their usage.

- Although most of the examples in this appendix use "literal" arguments, you may easily substitute database fields, other formulas, and so forth, for function arguments.

- Formatting in examples that follow each function or operator assume standard U.S. settings in the Windows control panel. If you've changed these settings, your default output formatting may be different.

unctions: Additional Functions

This category of the Function tree exposes functions that are provided to Crystal Reports by a set of external dynamic link libraries (DLLs). These DLLs, known as User Function Libraries (UFLs) within Crystal Reports, can be developed in a Windows or Java programming language to provide extensible functions to the Crystal Reports formula language. UFL functions are categorized by their UFL DLL filename.

NOTE *If you have upgraded from previous versions of Crystal Reports, or you have downloaded additional User Function Libraries from Business Objects (or other sources), you'll find additional entries in the Additional Functions category of the Function tree.*

ByteToText

Converts a number to a descriptive string indicating disk or memory storage used.

ByteToText is useful when reporting on the Local File System (or other data source that requires amounts of computer storage to be included on the report). Values less than 1,204 are returned in bytes, values between 1,204 and 1,048,576 are abbreviated to "KB", and values above 1,048,576 are abbreviated to "MB".

ByteToText (n)

n – numeric value.

```
ByteToText(1000)
```

returns "1000 bytes".

```
ByteToText(10000000)
```

returns "9 MB".

DateTimeTo2000

Converts a date-time value that may not be year 2000–compliant to a year 2000–compliant date-time with a four-digit year.

DateTimeTo2000 is "left over" from previous versions of Crystal Reports that may not have dealt with date-time values properly. It is largely not required with current versions, unless you may be dealing with older databases that don't return full four-digit years in date-time fields.

DateTimeTo2000 (dt, n)

dt – date-time value with a two- or four-digit year.
n – numeric value to act as a "sliding scale" year window.

```
DateTimeTo2000(DateTimeValue("1/1/90 1:03 pm"), 95)
```

returns 1/1/2090 1:03:00 PM.

DateTimeToDate

Returns only the date portion of a date-time value.

This function is "left over" from previous versions of Crystal Reports and has been replaced by the CDate and DateValue functions. See **DateValue** for details.

DateTimeToSeconds

Extracts the number of seconds that have passed since midnight.

DateTimeToSeconds evaluates the time portion of the supplied date-time value and returns the number of seconds that have passed since midnight.

DateTimeToSeconds (dt)

dt – date-time value.

```
DateTimeToSeconds(CurrentDateTime)
```

returns 49,980 for a current date-time value that includes the time 1:53:00 P.M.

DateTimeToTime

Returns only the time portion of a date-time value.

This function is "left over" from previous versions of Crystal Reports and has been replaced by the CTime and TimeValue functions. See **TimeValue** for details.

DateTo2000

Converts a date value that may not be year 2000–compliant to a year 2000–compliant date with a four-digit year.

DateTo2000 is "left over" from previous versions of Crystal Reports that may not have dealt with date values properly. It is largely not required with current versions, unless you may be dealing with older databases that don't return full four-digit years in date fields.

DateTo2000 (d, n)

d – date value with a two- or four-digit year.
n – numeric value to act as a "sliding scale" year window.

```
DateTo2000(#1/1/90#, 95)
```

returns 1/1/2090.

DTSTo2000

Returns a string value from a date string or date-time string with a two- or four-digit year.

DTSTo2000 will convert a string formatted in a specific year-month-day-hour-minute-second format to another string with a four-digit year. This function includes a sliding-scale year argument to ready two-digit dates for year-2000 compliance.

DTSTo2000 (s, n)

s – string containing a date in the format "yyyy/mm/dd" or "yy/mm/dd" or date-time in the format "yyyy/mm/dd hh:mm:ss.00" or "yy/mm/dd hh:mm:ss.00".
n – numeric value to act as a "sliding scale" year window.

```
DTSTo2000("90/10/01",95)
```

returns the string "2090/10/01".

DTSToDate

Converts a string formatted in a specific date-time format to a true date value.

DTSToDate is functionally equivalent to CDate and DateValue. See **DateValue** for more information.

DTSToDateTime

Converts a string formatted in a specific date-time format to a true date-time value.

DTSToDateTime is functionally equivalent to CDateTime and DateTimeValue. See **DateTimeValue** for more information.

DTSToSeconds

Extracts the number of seconds that have passed since midnight.

DTSToSeconds evaluates the time portion of the supplied date-time string and returns the number of seconds that have passed since midnight.

DTSToSeconds (s)

s – string containing a date-time in the format "yyyy/mm/dd hh:mm:ss.00" or "yy/mm/dd hh:mm:ss.00".

```
DTSToSeconds("2003/05/28 13:53:00.00")
```

returns 49,980 (the number of seconds between midnight and 1:53 P.M.).

DTSToTimeField

Converts a string formatted in a specific date-time format to a true time value.

DTSToTimeField is functionally equivalent to CTime and TimeValue. See **TimeValue** for more information.

DTSToTimeString

Returns a string containing just the time portion of a date-time string.

DTSToTimeString simply extracts the text after the eleventh character of a string (which does not actually have to be formatted as a date-time string).

DTSToTimeString (s)

s – string containing a date-time in the format "yyyy/mm/dd hh:mm:ss.00".

```
DTSToTimeString("1998/05/28 13:53:00.00")
```

returns the string "13:53:00.00".

NOTE *The preceding series of date-time string (DTS) functions are "left over" from previous versions of Crystal Reports that may not have dealt with date-time values properly. For example, Crystal Reports 6 did not properly recognize a true date or date-time value from a database but returned these values as string fields in a certain format. While you can still make the choice to convert date or date-time values to strings, these DTS functions are generally not required with current Crystal Reports versions.*

EventNumber

Returns a text description of a Microsoft Exchange event number.

EventNumber is helpful when reporting from Microsoft Exchange data sources. Certain supplied event numbers are significant (for example, 1,000 indicates local delivery). Those that aren't recognized will return "unknown event" results.

EventNumber (n)

n – numeric value representing a Microsoft Exchange event number.

```
EventNumber(1000)
```

returns "Local Delivery".

ExchGetId

Extracts the e-mail address from an X400- or X500-formatted string.

ExchGetID is helpful when reporting from Microsoft Exchange data sources. These data sources return certain e-mail address strings that can be passed to ExchGetID to return just the e-mail address.

ExchGetId (s)

s – string containing an X400- or X500-formatted address.

```
ExchGetID("c=US; a= ;p=Ablaze Group;
o=AblazeServer;dda:smtp=Info@AblazeGroup.com")
```

returns "Info@AblazeGroup.com".

ExchGetOrganization

Extracts the organization string from an X400- or X500-formatted string.

ExchGetOrganization is helpful when reporting from Microsoft Exchange data sources. These data sources return certain organization strings that can be passed to ExchGetOrganization to return just the organization.

ExchGetOrganization (s)

s – string containing an X400- or X500-formatted address.

```
ExchGetOrganization("c=US; a= ;p=Ablaze Group;
o=AblazeServer;dda:smtp=Info@AblazeGroup.com")
```

returns "Ablaze Group".

ExchGetPath

Extracts the destination path string from an X400- or X500-formatted string.

ExchGetPath is helpful when reporting from Microsoft Exchange data sources. These data sources return certain destination strings that can be passed to ExchGetPath to return just the destination path.

ExchGetPath (s)

s – string containing an X400- or X500-formatted address.

```
ExchGetPath("c=US;a= ;p=Ablaze Group;ou1=Info;
ou2=Ablaze Group;o=AblazeServer;dda:smtp=Info@AblazeGroup.com")
```

will return "OU1=INFO; OU2=ABLAZE GROUP;".

ExchGetSite

Extracts the site string from an X400- or X500-formatted string.

ExchGetSite is helpful when reporting from Microsoft Exchange data sources. These data sources return certain site strings that can be passed to ExchGetSite to return just the site.

ExchGetSite (s)

s – string containing an X400- or X500-formatted address.

```
ExchGetSite("c=US;a= ;p=Ablaze Group;ou1=Info;ou2=Ablaze Group;
o=AblazeServer;dda:smtp=Info@AblazeGroup.com")
```

will return "AblazeServer".

ExtractString

Extracts the portion of a string that appears between two other strings.

ExtractString will search a string, returning the portion that falls between two other search strings. If the first search string is not found, ExtractString returns an empty string. If the second search string is not found, ExtractString will return the entire portion of the source string after the first search string.

ExtractString (s1, s2, s3)

s1 – source string to be searched.
s2 – first string to search for.
s3 – second string to search for.

```
ExtractString("The rain in Spain falls on the plain",
"rain", "plain")
```

returns "in Spain falls on the".

FRAccRecTurnover

Returns the average turnover of accounts receivable in numeric days.

FRAccRecTurnover calculates the average "turnover" of accounts receivable by dividing accounts receivable by sales, and multiplying the result by the number of days in the year.

FRAccRecTurnover (n1, n2, n3)

n1 – numeric value of total accounts receivable.
n2 – numeric value of total sales.
n3 – numeric value indicating the number of days in a year (default is 360).

```
FRAccRecTurnover(10000,100000,360)
```

returns 36 days.

FRCashFlowVsTotalDebt

Returns the ratio between cash flow and total debt.

FRCashFlowVsTotalDebt determines the ratio of cash flow to debt by dividing cash flow by total debt.

FRCashFlowVsTotalDebt (n1, n2)

n1 – numeric value indicating total cash flow.
n2 – numeric value indicating total debt.

```
FRCashFlowVsTotalDebt(100000,10000)
```

returns a cash flow–to–debt ratio of 10.

FRCurrentRatio

Returns the ratio between current assets and current liabilities.

FRCurrentRatio determines the ratio of current assets to current liabilities by dividing assets by liabilities.

FRCurrentRatio (n1, n2)

n1 – numeric value indicating total current assets.
n2 – numeric value indicating total current liabilities.

```
FRCurrentRatio(100000,10000)
```

returns an asset-to-liability ratio of 10.

FRDebtEquityRatio

Returns the ratio between total liabilities and total equity.

FRDebtEquityRatio determines the ratio of total liabilities to total equity by dividing liabilities by equity.

FRDebtEquityRatio (n1, n2)

n1 – numeric value indicating total liabilities.
n2 – numeric value indicating total equity.

```
FRDebtEquityRatio(10000,100000)
```

returns a liability-to-equity ratio of .1.

FRDividendYield

Returns the ratio between dividend and market price.

FRDividendYield determines the ratio of dividend to market price by dividing dividend by market price.

FRDividendYield (n1, n2)

n1 – numeric value indicating dividend amount.
n2 – numeric value indicating share market price.

```
FRDividendYield(10,50)
```

returns a dividend–to–market price ratio of .2.

APPENDIX

FREarningsPerCommonShare

Returns the ratio of net profit distributable to shareholders to the number of shares.

FREarningsPerCommonShare determines the ratio of net profit to number of shares by subtracting the preferred dividend amount from net profit, and dividing the result by the number of common shares.

FREarningsPerCommonShare (n1, n2, n3)

n1 – numeric value indicating net profit.
n2 – numeric value indicating dividend paid to preferred shareholders.
n3 – numeric value indicating number of issued common shares.

```
FREarningsPerCommonShare (100000, 10, 10000)
```

returns a profit-to-share ratio of 10.

FREquityVsTotalAssets

Returns the ratio between total equity and total assets.

FREquityVsTotalAssets determines the ratio of total equity to total assets by dividing equity by assets.

FREquityVsTotalAssets (n1, n2)

n1 – numeric value indicating total equity.
n2 – numeric value indicating total assets.

```
FREquityVsTotalAssets(100000,500000)
```

returns an equity-to-assets ratio of .2.

FRGrossProfitMargin

Returns the ratio between gross profit and sales.

FRGrossProfitMargin determines the ratio of gross profit to sales by dividing gross profit by sales.

FRGrossProfitMargin (n1, n2)

n1 – numeric value indicating gross profit.
n2 – numeric value indicating sales.

```
FRGrossProfitMargin(10000,100000)
```

returns a profit-to-sales ratio of .1.

FRInterestCoverage

Returns the ratio between cash flow and interest expense.

FRInterestCoverage determines the ratio of cash flow to interest expense by dividing cash flow by interest expense.

FRInterestCoverage (n1, n2)

n1 – numeric value indicating cash flow.
n2 – numeric value indicating interest expense.

```
FRInterestCoverage(100000,2500)
```

returns a cash flow–to–interest expense ratio of 25.

FRInventoryTurnover

Returns the average turnover of inventory in numeric days.

FRInventoryTurnover calculates the average "turnover" of inventory by dividing inventory by sales, and multiplying the result by the number of days in the year.

FRInventoryTurnover (n1, n2, n3)

n1 – numeric value of total inventory.
n2 – numeric value of total sales.
n3 – numeric value indicating the number of days in a year (default is 360).

```
FRInventoryTurnover(10000,100000,360)
```

returns 36 days.

FRNetProfitMargin

Returns the ratio between net profit and sales.

FRNetProfitMargin determines the ratio of net profit to sales by dividing net profit by sales.

FRNetProfitMargin (n1, n2)

n1 – numeric value indicating net profit.
n2 – numeric value indicating sales.

```
FRNetProfitMargin(10000,100000)
```

returns a profit-to-sales ratio of .1.

FROperatingProfitMargin

Returns the ratio between operating profit and sales.

FROperatingProfitMargin determines the ratio of operating profit to sales by dividing operating profit by sales.

FROperatingProfitMargin (n1, n2)

n1 – numeric value indicating operating profit.
n2 – numeric value indicating sales.

```
FROperatingProfitMargin(10000,100000)
```

returns a profit-to-sales ratio of .1.

APPENDIX

FRPriceEarningsRatio
Returns the ratio between share market price and earnings per share.
FRPriceEarningsRatio determines the ratio of share market price to earnings by dividing share market price by earnings per share.

FRPriceEarningsRatio (n1, n2)
n1 – numeric value indicating share market price.
n2 – numeric value indicating earnings per share.

```
FRPriceEarningsRatio (10,100)
```

returns a price-to-earnings ratio of .1.

FRQuickRatio
Returns the ratio between current assets (less inventory) and current liabilities.
FRQuickRatio determines the ratio of current assets (less inventory) to current liabilities by subtracting inventory from assets and dividing the results by liabilities.

FRQuickRatio (n1, n2, n3)
n1 – numeric value indicating current assets.
n2 – numeric value indicating inventory.
n3 – numeric value indicating current liabilities.

```
FRQuickRatio (100000, 10000, 5000)
```

returns a quick ratio of 18.

FRReturnOnCommonEquity
Returns the ratio between net profit and common equity.
FRReturnOnCommonEquity determines the ratio of net profit to common equity by subtracting the dividend amount from net profit, and dividing the result by common equity.

FRReturnOnCommonEquity (n1, n2, n3)
n1 – numeric value indicating net profit.
n2 – numeric value indicating the total preferred dividend amount.
n3 – numeric value indicating common equity.

```
FRReturnOnCommonEquity (10000, 15, 100000)
```

returns a return on common equity ratio of .1.

FRReturnOnEquity
Returns the ratio between net profit and total equity.
FRReturnOnEquity determines the ratio of net profit to total equity by dividing net profit by equity.

FRReturnOnEquity (n1, n2)

n1 – numeric value indicating net profit.
n2 – numeric value indicating total equity.

```
FRReturnOnEquity (10000,100000)
```

returns a profit-to-equity ratio of .1.

FRReturnOnInvestedCapital

Returns the ratio between net profit and invested capital.

FRReturnOnInvestedCapital determines the ratio between net profit and invested capital by dividing net profit by the sum of bank debt and equity.

FRReturnOnInvestedCapital (n1, n2, n3)

n1 – a numeric value indicating net profit.
n2 – a numeric value indicating total bank debt.
n3 – a numeric value indicating total equity.

```
FRReturnOnInvestedCapital (10000,5000,100000)
```

returns a return on invested capital ratio of .1.

FRReturnOnNetFixedAssets

Returns the ratio between net profit and net fixed assets.

FRReturnOnNetFixedAssets determines the ratio of net profit to fixed assets by dividing net profit by fixed assets.

FRReturnOnNetFixedAssets (n1, n2)

n1 – numeric value indicating net profit.
n2 – numeric value indicating net fixed assets.

```
FRReturnOnNetFixedAssets (10000,100000)
```

returns a profit-to-assets ratio of .1.

FRReturnOnTotalAssets

Returns the ratio between net profit and total assets.

FRReturnOnTotalAssets determines the ratio of net profit to total assets by dividing net profit by total assets.

FRReturnOnTotalAssets (n1, n2)

n1 – numeric value indicating net profit.
n2 – numeric value indicating total assets.

```
FRReturnOnTotalAssets (10000,75000)
```

returns a profit-to-assets ratio of .13.

LooksLike

Returns a Boolean (true or false) value based on whether the "mask" is found in the source string.

LooksLike uses DOS-style "wildcards" (the asterisk and question mark) to determine if the source string contains the characters specified in the wildcard-based mask. This is helpful for checking for partial text matches.

LooksLike (s1, s2)

s1 – the source string to be searched.
s2 – the mask string to search against. The mask can include a question-mark wildcard to indicate a single-character substitution and/or an asterisk to indicate a multiple-character substitution.

```
LooksLike("George Peck", "G?orge*")
```

returns True.

Now

Returns the current time from the system clock as a text string.

This function is "left over" from previous versions of Crystal Reports and is similar to the CurrentTime function. The only difference between Now and CurrentTime is the data type returned. CurrentTime returns a time data type, while Now returns a string data type.

Picture

Formats a string based on the supplied formatting "mask" string.

Picture reformats a string value, inserting literal characters supplied within the "mask" formatting string. Picture is helpful for adding characters to an existing string, such as parentheses and hyphens to string database phone numbers without such punctuation.

Picture (s1, s2)

s1 – source string to format.
s2 – string "mask" to base formatting on. Any occurrence of an *x* character in the mask will substitute a single character from the source string. Any character other than *x* will simply be added to the output string.

```
Picture("8007733472", "Phone: (xxx) xxx-xxxx")
```

returns "Phone: (800) 773-3472".

Soundex

Returns a four-character string indicating how the source string "sounds".

Soundex uses a character-based algorithm to assign a "sound" to the source string. Similar-sounding strings, such as "George" and "gorge", will return the same four-character Soundex result. You may use Soundex in If-Then-Else statements, or similar constructs, where you want to compare the sound of two or more strings.

Soundex (s)

s – a string value to perform the Soundex algorithm on.

```
Soundex("George")
```

returns the string "G620".

```
If Soundex("George") = Soundex("gorge") Then
    "Sound the same"
Else
    "Different sound"
```

returns "Sound the same".

NOTE *An involved description of the Soundex algorithm can be found in Crystal Reports online help.*

---

nctions: Alerts

This set of functions exposes Crystal Reports Alerts to formulas.

AlertMessage

Returns a string containing the message portion of an alert.

AlertMessage returns the message portion of an alert when a particular report record has triggered the alert. If the record has not triggered the alert, AlertMessage returns an empty string.

AlertMessage (s)

s – a string value indicating the name of the alert.

```
AlertMessage("Order Over 5K")
```

returns "Orders over $5,000 exist" (the message for the Order Over 5K alert) if the report record has triggered the Order Over 5K alert.

AlertNames

Shows the name of each alert included in the report.

The AlertNames category of the Function tree (within the Alerts category) will show the names of each alert that has been created on the report. These alert names can be supplied as arguments to other Alert functions (described later in this section). If no alerts have been created, this function category won't appear in the Function tree.

IsAlertEnabled

Returns a Boolean (true or false) value indicating whether or not the "Enabled" check box is checked for the specified alert.

IsAlertEnabled tests to see if an alert will "fire" if records meet its criteria. An alert can be enabled or disabled when the alert is edited.

IsAlertEnabled (s)

s – a string value indicating the name of the alert.

```
If IsAlertEnabled("Order Over 5K") Then
    "Over 5K orders will be tested for"
```

returns "Over 5K orders will be tested for" if the enabled check box is checked in the Order Over 5K alert dialog box.

IsAlertTriggered

Returns a Boolean (true or false) value indicating whether or not an alert is triggered.

IsAlertTriggered is used within a formula to see if a particular alert has "fired" for the current record. The formula can base the remainder of its logic on whether or not the record has triggered the alert.

IsAlertTriggered (s)

s – a string value indicating the name of the alert.

```
If IsAlertTriggered ("Order Over 5K") Then
    "Congratulations--Great Order!"
```

returns "Congratulations—Great Order!" if the Order Over 5K alert is triggered when the formula evaluates.

Functions: Arrays

This category of functions applies to arrays. An *array* is a collection of data items stored in a single "bucket," such as a single variable. If an array contains 15 items, it is said to have 15 *elements*. Arrays can contain any supported Crystal Reports data type, such as number, string, date-time, and so forth.

Average

Returns a number containing the average of the numeric elements in the array.

Average (a)

a – an array. The array must be numeric.

```
Average([1,5,10,20,10])
```

returns 9.2.

Count

Returns a number containing the number of elements in the array.

Count is helpful when performing looping logic through an array. By using Count, you can determine how many array elements to loop through.

Count (a)

a – an array. The array can be of any data type.

```
Count([1,5,10,20,10])
```

returns 5.

NOTE *Count is functionally equivalent to UBound when dealing with arrays.*

DistinctCount

Returns a number containing the number of unique entries in the array.

DistinctCount is different from Count in that a duplicated entry in the array (for example, a second occurrence of the same element) will not increment the count when using DistinctCount, whereas it will with Count.

DistinctCount (a)

a – an array. The array can be of any data type.

```
DistinctCount(["George","Paul","George","John","Ringo","John"])
```

returns 4.

MakeArray

Creates an array.

MakeArray will create an array of values. It can be used to assign an array to a variable or pass a "literal" array to another array-based function. Supplying array elements within square brackets is the equivalent of MakeArray.

MakeArray (v1, v2...)

[v1, v2...]

v1 and v2 – literal values, separated by commas, that become array elements. The literal values can be any Crystal Reports data type, as long as they are all of the same data type. An array can contain, at maximum, 1,000 elements.

```
StringVar Array Beatles :=
    MakeArray("George","Paul","John","Ringo");
Beatles[3]
```

returns "John".

```
StringVar Array Beatles :=
    ["George","Paul","John","Ringo"];
Beatles[3]
```

returns "John".

NOTE *Basic syntax contains the Array function in addition to MakeArray. Array and MakeArray are functionally equivalent in Basic syntax.*

Maximum

Returns the last entry in an array.

Maximum will return the "last" entry in an array. What constitutes the "last" entry is based on the type of data in the array. Maximum will return the highest number in a numeric array, the last string value alphabetically in a string array, and so forth.

Maximum (a)

a – an array. The array can be of any data type.

```
Maximum([#1/1/1990#,#12/15/85#,#5/13/03#,#7/4/2000#])
```

will return 5/13/2003 12:00:00 A.M. as a date-time value.

Minimum

Returns the first entry in an array.

Minimum will return the "first" entry in an array. What constitutes the "first" entry is based on the type of data in the array. Minimum will return the lowest number in a numeric array, the first string value alphabetically in a string array, and so forth.

Minimum (a)

a – an array. The array can be of any data type.

```
Minimum(["Paul","George","John","Ringo"])
```

will return "George".

PopulationStdDev

Returns a number containing the population standard deviation of an array.

PopulationStdDev (a)

a – an array. The array must be numeric.

```
PopulationStdDev([1,10,15,20,25])
```

returns 8.28 (rounded to two decimal places).

PopulationVariance

Returns a number containing the population variance of an array.

PopulationVariance (a)

a – an array. The array must be numeric.

```
PopulationVariance([1,10,15,20,25])
```

returns 68.56 (rounded to two decimal places).

StdDev

Returns a number containing the standard deviation of an array.

StdDev (a)

a – an array. The array must be numeric.

```
StdDev([1,10,15,20,25])
```

returns 9.26 (rounded to two decimal places).

Sum

Returns a number containing the sum of array elements.

Sum (a)

a – an array. The array must be numeric.

```
Sum([1,10,15,20,25])
```

returns 71.

UBound

Returns the number of elements in the array.

UBound is helpful when performing looping logic through an array. By using UBound, you can determine how many array elements to loop through.

UBound (a)

a – an array. The array can be of any data type.

```
UBound([1,5,10,20,10])
```

returns 5.

NOTE *UBound is functionally equivalent to Count when dealing with arrays.*

Variance

Returns a number containing the variance of an array.

Variance (a)

a – an array. The array must be numeric.

```
Variance([1,10,15,20,25])
```

returns 85.70 (rounded to two decimal places).

Functions: Conditional Formatting

This category of functions appears in the Function tree only when you display the Format Formula Editor by clicking a Conditional Formatting Formula button from another Crystal Reports dialog box. Some of these functions will appear only in the proper "context"—for example, the Color or RGB functions will be available only when you are setting a color property conditionally.

Color

Returns a specific red-green-blue color combination.

Color allows you to specify intricate color values for font color, background color, and so forth. Rather than choosing from the limited set of default colors (such as crRed, crAqua, and so forth), you may specify any combination of red-green-blue colors with this function.

Color (n1, n2, n3)

n1 – a numeric value specifying the amount of red. The value must be between 0 and 255.
n2 – a numeric value specifying the amount of green. The value must be between 0 and 255.
n3 – a numeric value specifying the amount of blue. The value must be between 0 and 255.

```
If {Orders.Order Amount} > 5000 Then crRed Else Color(10,100,244)
```

will set the font color to a light blue shade (consisting of a red value of 10, green value of 100, and blue value of 244) if the order amount is not over 5,000.

NOTE *The RGB function is functionally equivalent to Color. RGB also accepts three arguments and may be used interchangeably with Color.*

CurrentFieldValue

Returns the contents of the field being formatted.

CurrentFieldValue will return the value contained in the field being formatted. The data type can vary, depending on the field being formatted. CurrentFieldValue is particularly valuable when conditionally formatting Cross-Tab or OLAP grid cells, as the cells themselves cannot be directly referred to in a formatting formula.

CurrentFieldValue

```
If CurrentFieldValue > 5000 Then crRed Else crBlack
```

will set the color property to red if the value of the object being formatted is greater than 5,000.

DefaultAttribute

Returns the setting of the formatting property from the originating dialog box.

DefaultAttribute returns the value set in the calling dialog box. For example, if you set the "absolute" font color to aqua but then click the Conditional Formatting Formula button, you will be able to recall the aqua value in the formatting formula by using DefaultAttribute.

DefaultAttribute

```
If {Orders.Order Amount} > 5000 Then crRed Else DefaultAttribute
```

will set the font color to that selected in the absolute font color property of the Format Editor if the order amount is not greater than 5,000.

GridRowColumnValue

Returns the value of the row or column name in a cross-tab or OLAP grid object.

GridRowColumnValue will return the contents of a "title" cell of a row or column in a cross-tab or OLAP grid object. By using this function, you may determine which row or column is currently formatting and change formatting logic accordingly.

GridRowColumnValue (s)

s – string value indicating row or column name to query.

```
If GridRowColumnValue ("Orders.Employee ID") = 3 Then
    crRed
Else
    crBlack
```

will determine if the Employee ID row in a cross-tab contain employee number 3. If so, the cell will be formatted in a red color.

Row Or Column Names

Names of the rows or columns in a cross-tab or OLAP grid object.

This category of the Function tree will appear only when you are conditionally formatting a cross-tab or OLAP grid object. The category will contain the names given to rows or columns in the cross-tab or OLAP grid. You may use these values with the GridRowColumnValue function to determine which row or column is currently formatting.

nctions: Date and Time

This set of functions deal with date and time manipulation, including extracting the current date and time from your computer's internal clock, performing date-time math, converting date-time functions to other data types, and so forth.

CurrentDate

Returns a date value with the current date from your computer's internal clock.

CurrentDate

```
CurrentDate
```

returns 5/30/2003 if the current date is May 30, 2003.

CurrentDateTime

Returns a date-time value with the current date and time from your computer's internal clock.

CurrentDateTime

```
CurrentDateTime
```

returns 5/30/2003 2:48:32PM if the current date is May 30, 2003 and the current time is 2:48 P.M.

CurrentTime

Returns a time value with the current time from your computer's internal clock.

CurrentTime

```
CurrentTime
```

returns 2:48:32PM if the current time is 2:48 in the afternoon.

Date

Returns a date value when supplied with various other data types.

Date is functionally equivalent to DateValue (with the exception of its availability only in Crystal Syntax). See **DateValue** for details.

DateAdd

Returns a date-time value in the past or future, depending on supplied arguments.

DateAdd is handy for calculating dates in the past or future, based on a certain number of days, weeks, years, and so forth. DateAdd automatically handles leap years, months with less than 31 days, and so forth.

DateAdd (s, n, dt)

s – string value indicating interval type (days, weeks, and so forth). See **Interval Types** later in this section for recognized values.
n – a numeric value indicating number of intervals to add to the source date-time. This can be a negative or positive number.
dt – a date or date-time value indicating the source date-time to add intervals to.

```
DateAdd("d",5,CurrentDate)
```

returns 6/4/2003 12:00:00AM if the current date is May 30, 2003.

```
DateAdd("m",-2,#1/1/2003 10:00AM#)
```

returns 11/1/2002 10:00:00AM.

DateDiff

Returns a number indicating the number of "intervals" between two dates.

DateDiff is helpful in determining a specified amount of time that has elapsed between two date or date-time values. DateDiff can return the number of years, months, days, minutes, and so forth.

DateDiff (s, dt1, dt2)

s – string value indicating interval type (days, weeks, and so forth). See **Interval Types** later in this section for recognized values.
dt1 – a date, date-time, or time value indicating the start date-time to compare.
dt2 – a date, date-time, or time value indicating the end date-time to compare.

```
DateDiff ("h",#5/2/2003 10:00 AM#,#5/3/2003 2:00 PM#)
```

returns 28.

DateDiff (s, dt1, dt2, n)

s – string value indicating interval type (days, weeks, and so forth). See **Interval Types** later in this section for recognized values.
dt1 – a date, date-time, or time value indicating the start date-time to compare.
dt2 – a date, date-time, or time value indicating the end date-time to compare.
n – a numeric value or constant indicating the first day of the week. If not supplied, Sunday is assumed to be the first day of the week. See **First Day of Week Constants** later in this section for recognized constants or numbers for this argument.

```
DateDiff ("ww",#5/1/2003#,#6/1/2003#,crMonday)
```

returns 4.

DatePart

Returns a number indicating the individual "part" (month, hour, year, and so forth) of a date, date-time, or time value.

DatePart will return just the year, month, day, hour, minute, or second of a supplied date-time value. Other functions that work similarly to DatePart are Year, Month, Day, Hour, Minute, and Second.

DatePart (s, dt)

s – string value indicating interval type (day, week, hour, and so forth). See **Interval Types** later in this section for recognized values.
dt – a date, date-time, or time value to extract the interval from.

```
DatePart ("m",CurrentDate)
```

returns 5, if the current date is May 30, 2003.

DatePart (s, dt, n)

s – string value indicating interval type (day, week, hour, and so forth). See **Interval Types** later in this section for recognized values.
dt – a date, date-time, or time value to extract the interval from.
n – a numeric value or constant indicating the first day of the week. If not supplied, Sunday is assumed to be the first day of the week. See **First Day of Week Constants** later in this section for recognized constants or numbers for this argument.

```
DatePart ("w",#May 30, 2003#,crMonday)
```

returns 5, considering that May 30, 2003, is a Friday.

DatePart (s, dt, n1, n2)

s – string value indicating interval type (day, week, hour, and so forth). See **Interval Types** later in this section for recognized values.

dt – a date, date-time, or time value to extract the interval from.

n1 – a numeric value or constant indicating the first day of the week. If not supplied, Sunday is assumed to be the first day of the week. See **First Day of Week Constants** later in this section for recognized constants or numbers for this argument.

n2 – a numeric value or constant indicating the first week of the year. If not supplied, the week containing January 1 is assumed to be the first week of the year. See **First Week of Year Constants** later in this section for recognized constants or numbers for this argument.

```
DatePart ("ww",#6/1/2003#,crSunday,crFirstJan1)
```

returns 23.

DateSerial

Returns a date value based on year, month, and day arguments.

DateSerial provides similar functionality to a specific usage of CDate, Date, and DateValue. DateSerial differs from these other functions in one significant way: the arguments supplied do not have to fall into a strict "month between 1 and 12, day between 1 and 31" requirement. By supplying other values, such as negative numbers, calculations, and so forth, arguments will be evaluated "relatively."

DateSerial (n1, n2, n3)

n1 – a numeric value indicating the year.
n2 – a numeric value indicating the month.
n3 – a numeric value indicating the day.

```
DateSerial(2003, 6, 1)
```

returns 6/1/2003.

```
DateSerial(2003, 6-10, 1-30)
```

returns 7/2/2002 (10 months before June—which equates to August 1, 2002, and 30 days before the first day of the month, which equates to July 2, 2002).

DateTime

Returns a date-time value based on one of several sets and types of arguments.

DateTime is functionally equivalent to CDateTime and DateTimeValue. See **DateTimeValue** for more information.

DateTimeValue

Returns a date-time value based on one of several sets and types of arguments.

DateTimeValue can accept a wide variety of arguments that will be converted to a date-time. DateTimeValue comes in handy when you need to convert other data types to date-time, such as database fields from older systems that stored dates as strings. DateTimeValue is functionally equivalent to DateTime and CDateTime.

DateTimeValue (d)

d – a date value that will be converted to a date-time value with midnight as the time.

```
DateTimeValue(CurrentDate)
```

returns 5/30/2003 12:00:00AM if today's date is May 30, 2003 (in essence, converting the CurrentDate date-only value to a date-time value).

DateTimeValue (d, t)

d – a date value that will become the date portion of the resulting date-time value.
t – a time value that will become the time portion of the resulting date-time value.

```
DateTimeValue(CurrentDate, Time(#10:30 am#))
```

returns 5/30/2003 10:30:00AM if today's date is May 30, 2003.

DateTimeValue (n)

n – a numeric value indicating the number of days since December 30, 1899.

```
DateTimeValue(35000)
```

returns 10/28/1995 12:00:00AM (35,000 days from December 30, 1899).

DateTimeValue (s)

s – a string value that will be evaluated for particular date and time equivalents.

```
DateTimeValue("January 1, 2003 15:50")
```

returns 1/1/2003 3:50:00PM.

DateTimeValue (n1, n2, n3)

n1 – a numeric value indicating the year.
n2 – a numeric value between 1 and 12 indicating the month.
n3 – a numeric value between 1 and 31 indicating the day of month.

```
DateTimeValue(2002,10,15)
```

returns 10/15/2002 12:00:00AM.

DateTimeValue (n1, n2, n3, n4, n5, n6)

n1 – a numeric value indicating the year.
n2 – a numeric value between 1 and 12 indicating the month.
n3 – a numeric value between 1 and 31 indicating the day of month.
n4 – a numeric value between 0 and 23 indicating the hour of day.
n5 – a numeric value between 0 and 59 indicating the minute.
n6 – a numeric value between 0 and 59 indicating the second.

```
DateTimeValue(2002,10,15,14,35,50)
```

returns 10/15/2002 2:35:50PM.

DateValue
Returns a date value based on one of several sets and types of arguments.

DateValue can accept a wide variety of arguments that will be converted to a date. DateValue comes in handy when you need to convert other data types to date, such as database fields from older systems that stored dates as strings. DateValue is functionally equivalent to Date and CDate.

DateValue (dt)
dt – a date-time value that you wish to strip the time portion away from.

```
DateValue(CurrentDateTime)
```

returns 5/30/2002 if the current date is May 30, 2003, regardless of what time of day.

DateValue (n)
n – a numeric value indicating the number of days since December 30, 1899.

```
DateValue(35000)
```

returns 10/28/1995 (35,000 days from December 30, 1899).

DateValue (s)
s – a string value that will be evaluated for particular date equivalents.

```
DateValue("January 1, 2003")
```

returns 1/1/2003.

DateValue (n1, n2, n3)
n1 – a numeric value indicating the year.
n2 – a numeric value between 1 and 12 indicating the month.
n3 – a numeric value between 1 and 31 indicating the day of month.

```
DateValue(2002,10,15)
```

returns 10/15/2002.

Day
Returns a numeric value indicating the day of the month.

Day (dt)
dt – a date or date-time value.

```
Day(CurrentDate)
```

returns 30 if the current date is May 30, 2003.

DayOfWeek
Returns a numeric value indicating the day of the week.

DayOfWeek returns the day of the week. By default, DayOfWeek assumes Sunday is equal to 1. However, you may provide an extra argument to DayOfWeek indicating a different starting day. DayOfWeek is functionally equivalent to WeekDay.

DayOfWeek (dt)
dt – a date or date-time value.

```
DayOfWeek(CurrentDate)
```

returns 6 if the current date falls on a Friday.

DayOfWeek (dt, n)
dt – a date or date-time value.
n – a numeric value or constant indicating the first day of the week. If not supplied, Sunday is assumed to be the first day of the week. See **First Day of Week Constants** later in this section for recognized constants or numbers for this argument.

```
DayOfWeek(CurrentDate, crMonday)
```

returns 5 if the current date falls on a Friday.

Hour
Returns a numeric value indicating the hour of the supplied time or date-time in military time.

Hour (dt)
dt – a date-time or time value.

```
Hour(CurrentTime)
```

returns 17 if the current time is in the 5 P.M. hour.

IsDate
Returns a Boolean (true of false) value indicating whether or not the supplied number or string can be converted to a date value.
IsDate is helpful in determining if a supplied string or numeric value can be converted to a date with the DateValue (or similar) function. Because these other conversion functions will fail with a run-time error if an invalid value is supplied to them, using IsDate with an If-Then-Else statement can prevent run-time errors.

IsDate (s)
s – a string value to be evaluated for conversion to a date.

IsDate (n)
n – a numeric value to be evaluated as the number of days since December 30, 1899.

```
If IsDate({FromMainframe.OrderDateAsString}) Then
    DateValue({FromMainframe.OrderDateAsString})
Else
    DateValue(0,0,0)
```

returns a true order date if it can be converted, or 0/0/0 if it can't.

IsDateTime

Returns a Boolean (true of false) value indicating whether or not the supplied number or string can be converted to a date-time value.

IsDateTime is helpful in determining if a supplied string or numeric value can be converted to a date-time with the DateTimeValue (or similar) function. Because these other conversion functions will fail with a run-time error if an invalid value is supplied to them, using IsDateTime with an If-Then-Else statement can prevent run-time errors.

IsDateTime (s)

s – a string value to be evaluated for conversion to a date-time.

IsDateTime (n)

n – a numeric value to be evaluated as the number of days since December 30, 1899.

```
If IsDateTime({FromMainframe.IncidentDateTimeAsString}) Then
    DateTimeValue({FromMainframe.IncidentDateTimeAsString})
Else
    DateTimeValue(0,0,0,0,0,0)
```

returns a true incident date-time if it can be converted, or 0/0/0 at midnight if it can't.

IsTime

Returns a Boolean (true of false) value indicating whether or not the supplied number or string can be converted to a time value.

IsTime is helpful in determining if a supplied string or numeric value can be converted to a time with the TimeValue (or similar) function. Because these other conversion functions will fail with a run-time error if an invalid value is supplied to them, using IsTime with an If-Then-Else statement can prevent run-time errors.

IsTime (s)

s – a string value to be evaluated for conversion to a time.

IsTime (n)

n – a numeric value to be evaluated as the number of "24-hour units".

```
If IsTime({FromMainframe.IncidentTimeAsString}) Then
    TimeValue({FromMainframe.IncidentTimeAsString})
Else
    TimeValue(0,0,0)
```

returns a true incident time if it can be converted, or midnight if it can't.

Minute

Returns a numeric value indicating the minute of the supplied time or date-time.

Minute (dt)

dt – a date-time or time value.

```
Minute(CurrentTime)
```

returns 43 if the current time is 5:43 P.M.

Month
Returns a numeric value indicating the month.

Month (dt)
dt – a date or date-time value.

```
Month(CurrentDate)
```

returns 5 if the current date is May 30, 2003.

MonthName
Returns a string value indicating the spelled-out month of the supplied numeric argument.

MonthName (n)
n – a numeric value between 1 and 12 indicating the number of the month.

MonthName (n, b)
n – a numeric value between 1 and 12 indicating the number of the month.
b – a Boolean (true or false) value, indicating whether to abbreviate the month.

```
MonthName (3, True)
```

returns "Mar".

Second
Returns a numeric value indicating the second of the supplied time or date-time.

Second (dt)
dt – a date-time or time value.

```
Second(CurrentTime)
```

returns 45 if the current time is 5:43:45 P.M.

ShiftDateTime
Returns a date/time value in a new time zone.

ShiftDateTime (dt, s1, s2)
dt – the date/time value to be converted to a new time zone.
s1 – a string representing the time zone that *dt* is currently in.
s2 – a string representing the new time zone to convert *dt* to.
　　The *s1* and *s2* time zone strings that are supplied to ShiftDateTime can appear to be quite complex. However, the only relevant portion of a time zone string is the *offset* (the number of minutes that the relevant time zone is offset from Greenwich Mean Time/Coordinated Universal Time). While any other portions of the time zone string that you include must appear with proper data types and within appropriate range limits (for example, the month number

portion of the time zone string must be numeric and must be between 1 and 12), these remaining portions of the time zone string are optional and don't affect the actual ShiftDateTime calculation.

To illustrate, compare this usage of ShiftDateTime:

```
ShiftDateTime (CurrentDateTime,
"Mountain Standard Time,420,Mountain Daylight Time,-60;4.1.0/02:00,10.5.0/02:00",
"Pacific Standard Time,480,Pacific Daylight Time,-60;4.1.0/02:00,10.5.0/02:00")
```

with this one:

```
ShiftDateTime (CurrentDateTime, ",420", ",480")
```

Both return "5/14/2005 8:30:00AM" if your current computer date/time is May 14, 2005 at 9:30 A.M. in the Mountain time zone. Note that the only significant portions of the time zone string are the offsets—the remaining portions are ignored when ShiftDateTime calculates the new date and time.

A more typical use of ShiftDateTime might be:

```
ShiftDateTime(CurrentDateTime, PrintTimeZone, CurrentCEUserTimeZone)
```

which displays the current date and time set on your computer adjusted to the time zone of the BusinessObjects Enterprise or Crystal Reports Server system you are currently logged into. For example, if your computer's current date/time is May 14, 2005, at 9:03:10 A.M. in the Pacific time zone and the BusinessObjects Enterprise or Crystal Reports Server system you're logged into is located in the Mountain time zone, this formula will return "5/14/2005 10:03:10AM".

Time Zone Strings

The following table describes the various portions of a time zone string that you can supply to ShiftDateTime, or that is returned by various other functions that return time zone strings (such as CECurrentTimeZone, DataTimeZone, and PrintTimeZone). Each portion is separated from the next by a comma. If you are supplying a time zone string to ShiftDateTime, you may supply an empty string to signify the local time zone to your computer. Or, if you supply a time zone string, the only required portion is the offset preceded by a comma.

Standard Time Zone	A string description of the standard time zone.
Standard Time Offset	A number indicating the number of minutes that this standard time zone is offset from Greenwich Mean Time/Coordinated Universal Time. This number will be positive for time zones west of Greenwich, England, and negative for those east of Greenwich, England.
Daylight Saving Time Zone	A string description of the daylight saving time zone. If the time zone does not utilize daylight saving time, this string won't appear.
Daylight Saving Time Offset	A number indicating the number of minutes that daylight saving time in this time zone is offset from the standard time offset (the second portion of the time zone string). By default, this value is adjusted 60 minutes from the standard time zone offset. If this time zone does not utilize daylight saving time, this number won't appear.

Daylight Saving Start	A string, in the form of m.w.d/hh:mm, indicating the month, week, day, and time that daylight saving time goes into effect for this time zone. The month number, between 1 and 12, indicates the month; the week number, between 1 and 5, indicates the week during the month; and the day number, between 0 and 6, indicates the day of the week (0 being Sunday). Optionally, the month, week, and day will be followed by a slash and a time indicating the hour that daylight saving time starts. The time consists of a two-character hour, a colon, and a two-character minute (in 24-hour time format). The default is 2 a.m. (02:00).
Daylight Saving End	A string, in the form of m.w.d/hh:mm, indicating the month, week, day, and time that daylight saving time ends for this time zone. The month number, between 1 and 12, indicates the month; the week number, between 1 and 5, indicates the week during the month; and the day number, between 0 and 6, indicates the day of the week (0 being Sunday). Optionally, the month, week, and day will be followed by a slash and a time indicating the hour that daylight saving time ends. The time consists of a two-character hour, a colon, and a two-character minute (in 24-hour time format). The default is 2 a.m. (02:00).

Time

Returns a time value when supplied with various other data types.

Time is functionally equivalent to TimeValue. See **TimeValue** for details.

Timer

Returns the number of seconds since midnight.

Timer may be useful as a "seed" for the Rnd (random number) function.

Timer

```
Timer
```

returns 64,917 at 6:01:57 P.M.

TimeSerial

Returns a time value based on hour, minute, and second arguments.

TimeSerial provides similar functionality to a specific usage of CTime, Time, and TimeValue. TimeSerial differs from these other functions in one significant way: the arguments supplied do not have to fall into a strict "hour between 0 and 24, minute between 0 and 59" requirement. By supplying other values, such as negative numbers, calculations, and so forth, arguments will be evaluated "relatively."

TimeSerial (n1, n2, n3)

n1 – a numeric value indicating the hour.
n2 – a numeric value indicating the minute.

APPENDIX

n3 – a numeric value indicating the second.

```
TimeSerial(17,30,15)
```

returns 5:30:15PM.

```
TimeSerial(17,30-40,15+25)
```

returns 4:50:40PM.

TimeValue
Returns a time value based on one of several sets and types of arguments.
TimeValue can accept a wide variety of arguments that will be converted to a time. TimeValue comes in handy when you need to convert other data types to time, such as database fields from older systems that stored times as strings. TimeValue is functionally equivalent to Time and CTime.

TimeValue (dt)
dt – a date-time value that you wish to strip the time portion away from.

```
TimeValue(CurrentDateTime)
```

returns 6:23:19PM if the current time is 6:23 P.M., regardless of what day.

TimeValue (n)
n – a numeric value to be evaluated as the number of "24-hour units."

```
TimeValue(.25)
```

returns 6:00:00AM.

TimeValue (s)
s – a string value that will be evaluated for particular time equivalents.

```
TimeValue("17:15")
```

returns 5:15:00PM.

TimeValue (n1, n2, n3)
n1 – a numeric value between 0 and 23 indicating the hour.
n2 – a numeric value between 0 and 59 indicating the minute.
n3 – a numeric value between 0 and 59 indicating the second.

```
TimeValue(14,12,0)
```

returns 2:12:00PM.

WeekdayName
Returns a string value containing a spelled-out name of the week.
WeekdayName will spell the name of the weekday ("Monday", etc.), based on a supplied numeric value.

WeekdayName (n)

n – numeric value between 1 and 7.

WeekdayName (n, b)

n – numeric value between 1 and 7.
b – a Boolean (true or false) value indicating whether to abbreviate the weekday name.

WeekdayName (n1, b, n2)

n1 – numeric value between 1 and 7.
b – Boolean (true or false) value indicating whether to abbreviate the weekday name.
n – numeric value or constant indicating the first day of the week. If not supplied, Sunday is assumed to be the first day of the week. See **First Day of Week Constants** later in this section for recognized constants or numbers for this argument.

```
WeekdayName (3, True, crMonday)
```

returns "Wed".

Year

Returns a numeric value indicating the year.

Year (dt)

dt – a date or date-time value.

```
Year(CurrentDate)
```

returns 2,003 if the current date is May 30, 2003.

Interval Types

The following interval types can be used with various date functions, such as DateAdd and DateDiff.

m	Month
d	Day (functionally equivalent to y)
yyyy	Year
y	Day of Year (functionally equivalent to d)
w	Weekday or Number of Weeks
ww	Week or Number of FirstDayOfWeeks
q	Quarter
h	Hour
m	Minute
s	Second

First Day of Week Constants

The following first-day-of-week values can be supplied to various functions that change output based on the first day of the week. Either the numeric value or the constant can be supplied.

crUseSystem	0 (default from Windows)
crSunday	1
crMonday	2
crTuesday	3
crWednesday	4
crThursday	5
crFriday	6
crSaturday	7

First Week of Year Constants

The following first-week-of-year values can be supplied to various functions that change output based on the first week of the year. Either the numeric value or the constant can be supplied.

crUseSystem	0 (default from Windows)
crFirstJan1	1
crFirstFourDays	2
crFirstFullWeek	3

Functions: Date Ranges

The following functions return date ranges based on the current date from the computer's clock. For point-in-time reporting purposes, you may change these ranges to be based on something other than the current date by using Report | Set Print Date/Time. All these functions return range values and must be used with a range operator, such as In.

Aged0To30Days

Returns a range in the last 30 days.

Aged0To30Days

```
If {AR.Due Date} In Aged0To30Days Then {AR.Amount Due}
```

returns the AR Amount due if the due date is in the past 30 days. Otherwise, 0 is returned.

Aged31To60Days

Returns a range between 31 and 60 days in the past.

Aged31To60Days

```
If {AR.Due Date} In Aged31To60Days Then {AR.Amount Due}
```

returns the AR Amount due if the due date is within 31 to 60 days past. Otherwise, 0 is returned.

Aged61To90Days

Returns a range between 61 and 90 days in the past.

Aged61To90Days

```
If {AR.Due Date} In Aged61To90Days Then {AR.Amount Due}
```

returns the AR Amount due if the due date is within 61 to 90 days past. Otherwise, 0 is returned.

AllDatesFromToday

Returns a range from today into the future (including today).

AllDatesFromToday

```
If {Shipments.Ship Date} In AllDatesFromToday Then
    "Product still needs to ship"
Else
    "Product has already shipped"
```

returns the appropriate string, depending on whether the ship date is in the future or the past.

AllDatesFromTomorrow

Returns a range from tomorrow into the future (including tomorrow).

AllDatesFromTomorrow

```
If {Shipments.Ship Date} In AllDatesFromTomorrow Then
    "Product ships tomorrow or thereafter"
Else
    "Product has already shipped"
```

returns the appropriate string, depending on whether the ship date is tomorrow or later.

AllDatesToToday

Returns a range up to, and including, today.

AllDatesToToday

```
If {Shipments.Ship Date} In AllDatesToToday Then
    "Product has been shipped"
Else
    "Product ships later"
```

returns the appropriate string, depending on whether the product shipped today or earlier.

APPENDIX

AllDatesToYesterday

Returns a range up to, and including, yesterday.

AllDatesToYesterday

```
If {Shipments.Ship Date} In AllDatesToYesterday Then
    "Product yesterday or before"
Else
    "Product ships today or later"
```

returns the appropriate string, depending on whether the product shipped yesterday or earlier.

Calendar1stHalf

Returns a range including January 1 to June 30 of the current year.

Calendar1stHalf

```
If {Sales.Sale Date} In Calendar1stHalf Then
    "Group 1: Jan 1 - Jun 30"
Else
    "Group 2: Jul 1 - Dec 31"
```

returns one of two appropriate values, depending on whether the sale took place in the first or second half of the year.

Calendar2ndHalf

Returns a range including July 1 to December 31 of the current year.

Calendar2ndHalf

```
If {Sales.Sale Date} In Calendar2ndHalf Then
    "Group 1: Jul 1 - Dec 31"
Else
    "Group 2: Jan 1 - Jun 30"
```

returns one of two appropriate values, depending on whether the sale took place in the first or second half of the year.

Calendar1stQtr

Returns a range including January 1 to March 31 of the current year.

Calendar1stQtr

```
CurrencyVar Q1Total;
If {Sales.Sale Date} In Calendar1stQtr Then
    Q1Total := Q1Total + {Sales.Amount}
```

increments a variable with a sales amount only if the sale took place in the first calendar quarter.

Calendar2ndQtr

Returns a range including April 1 to June 30 of the current year.

Calendar2ndQtr

```
CurrencyVar Q2Total;
If {Sales.Sale Date} In Calendar2ndQtr Then
    Q2Total := Q2Total + {Sales.Amount}
```

increments a variable with a sales amount only if the sale took place in the second calendar quarter.

Calendar3rdQtr

Returns a range including July 1 to September 30 of the current year.

Calendar3rdQtr

```
CurrencyVar Q3Total;
If {Sales.Sale Date} In Calendar3rdQtr Then
    Q3Total := Q3Total + {Sales.Amount}
```

increments a variable with a sales amount only if the sale took place in the third calendar quarter.

Calendar4thQtr

Returns a range including October 1 to December 31 of the current year.

Calendar4thQtr

```
CurrencyVar Q4Total;
If {Sales.Sale Date} In Calendar4thQtr Then
    Q4Total := Q4Total + {Sales.Amount}
```

increments a variable with a sales amount only if the sale took place in the fourth calendar quarter.

Last4WeeksToSun

Returns a range including the four weeks prior to, and including, the most recent Sunday.

Last4WeeksToSun, unlike some other date and date range functions, considers a week to start on Monday and end on Sunday.

Last4WeeksToSun

```
If {AR.Invoice Date} In Last4WeeksToSun Then
    "Current"
Else
    "Past Due"
```

returns a string indicating the status of an account receivable based on the last four weeks.

Last7Days

Returns a range consisting of the last seven days, including today.

Last7Days

```
If {Sales.Sale Date} In Last7Days Then
    "Eligible for Price Protection"
Else
    "Not Eligible for Price Protection"
```

returns a string indicating if a sale is eligible for price protection because it took place within the last seven days.

LastFullMonth

Returns a range including the first day of last month to the last day of last month.

LastFullMonth

```
If {Sales.Sale Date} In LastFullMonth Then
    "Eligible for Price Protection"
Else
    "Not Eligible for Price Protection"
```

returns a string indicating if a sale is eligible for price protection because it took place within the last month.

LastFullWeek

Returns a range including Sunday through Saturday of the previous week.

LastFullWeek

```
If {Sales.Sale Date} In LastFullWeek Then
    "Eligible for Price Protection"
Else
    "Not Eligible for Price Protection"
```

returns a string indicating if a sale is eligible for price protection because it took place within the previous Sunday through Saturday.

LastYearMTD

Returns a range including the first day of this month last year through today's date last year.

LastYearMTD

```
CurrencyVar LastYearMTDSales;
If {Sales.Sale Date}In LastYearMTD Then
    LastYearMTDSales := LastYearMTDSales + {Sales.Amount}
```

accumulates a sales amount in a variable if the sale took place this month-to-date last year.

LastYearYTD

Returns a range including January 1 last year through today's date last year.

LastYearYTD

```
CurrencyVar LastYearYTDSales;
If {Sales.Sale Date}In LastYearYTD Then
    LastYearYTDSales := LastYearYTDSales + {Sales.Amount}
```

accumulates a sales amount in a variable if the sale took place this year-to-date last year.

MonthToDate

Returns a range including the first day of this month through today.

MonthToDate

```
CurrencyVar MTDSales;
If {Sales.Sale Date}In MonthToDate Then
    MTDSales := MTDSales + {Sales.Amount}
```

accumulates a sales amount in a variable if the sale took place from the first of this month through today.

Next30Days

Returns a range in the next 30 days.

Next30Days

```
If {Shipments.Ship Date} In Next30Days Then
"High Priority - shipping within the month"
```

returns the string value if the shipment date is in the next 30 days. Otherwise, an empty string is returned.

Next31To60Days

Returns a range between 31 and 60 days in the future.

Next31To60Days

```
If {Shipments.Ship Date} In Next31To60Days Then
"Medium Priority - shipping 2 months from now"
```

returns the string value if the shipment date is between 31 and 60 days in the future. Otherwise, an empty string is returned.

Next61To90Days

Returns a range between 61 and 90 days in the future.

Next61To90Days

```
If {Shipments.Ship Date} In Next61To90Days Then
"Low Priority - shipping 3 months from now"
```

returns the string value if the shipment date is between 61 and 90 days in the future. Otherwise, an empty string is returned.

Next91To365Days

Returns a range between 91 and 365 days in the future.

Next91To365Days

```
If {Shipments.Ship Date} In Next91To365Days Then
"No Concern - shipping over 3 months from now"
```

returns the string value if the shipment date is between 91 and 365 days in the future. Otherwise, an empty string is returned.

Over90Days

Returns a range from 90 days in the past and beyond.

Over90Days

```
If {AR.Due Date} In Over90Days Then {AR.Amount Due}
```

returns the AR Amount due if the due date is over 90 days past the current date. Otherwise, 0 is returned.

WeekToDateFromSun

Returns a range starting the previous Sunday through today.

WeekToDateFromSun

```
If {Sales.Sale Date} In WeekToDateFromSun Then
   "Eligible for Price Protection"
Else
   "Not Eligible for Price Protection"
```

returns a string indicating if a sale is eligible for price protection because it took place between this past Sunday and today.

YearToDate

Returns a range including January 1 through today's date.

YearToDate

```
CurrencyVar ThisYearYTDSales;
If {Sales.Sale Date}In YearToDate Then
    ThisYearYTDSales := ThisYearYTDSales + {Sales.Amount}
```

accumulates a sales amount in a variable if the sale took place this year-to-date.

ctions: Document Properties

This category of functions duplicates many of the Special Fields available from the Field Explorer. By making these values available to formulas, you may base formulas on various properties of the report, such as the page number that's currently printing, whether a group header is being repeated, and so forth.

ContentLocale

Returns a string indicating the current regional/language setting from the Windows Control Panel.

ContentLocale

```
ContentLocale
```

returns "en_US" if your computer's regional/language option from Windows Control Panel is set to English (United States). The same value will appear on your report if you insert the ContentLocale special field from the Field Explorer.

CurrentCEUserID

Returns a numeric value indicating the internal ID maintained by BusinessObjects Enterprise/Crystal Reports Server for the currently logged-on user.

CECurrentUserID helps identify who is viewing the report after it has been published to BusinessObjects Enterprise/Crystal Reports Server. While you may find some value in the numeric value this function returns, you'll probably find more value in the actual user name returned by the CurrentCEUserName function. This function returns a numeric zero if the report is not being displayed from within BusinessObjects Enterprise/Crystal Reports Server (if used in stand-alone Crystal Reports, for example).

CECurrentUserID

```
CECurrentUserID
```

returns the number 12.00 if the currently logged-on user's internal ID number is 12. The function returns 0.00 if the report is not being displayed in BusinessObjects Enterprise/ Crystal Reports Server.

CurrentCEUserName

Returns a string value indicating the user name for the currently logged-on user.

CECurrentUserName helps identify who is viewing the report after it has been published to BusinessObjects Enterprise/Crystal Reports Server. You may use this function to change report logic according to who is viewing the report in BusinessObjects Enterprise/Crystal Reports Server. This may be helpful for creating certain limitations (similar to row and column security) based on the user. This function returns an empty string if the report is not being displayed from within BusinessObjects Enterprise/Crystal Reports Server (if used in stand-alone Crystal Reports, for example).

APPENDIX

CECurrentUserName

```
If CECurrentUserName = "" Then
    "Not logged in to BusinessObjects Enterprise/Crystal Reports Server"
Else
    CECurrentUserName
```

returns the user name of the current BusinessObjects Enterprise/Crystal Reports Server user. If the report is being viewed outside BusinessObjects Enterprise/Crystal Reports Server (for example, in the stand-alone Crystal Reports designer), the formula returns "Not logged in to BusinessObjects Enterprise/Crystal Reports Server".

CurrentCEUserTimeZone

Returns a time zone string indicating the time zone of the BusinessObjects Enterprise/Crystal Reports Server system you are currently logged in to.

CurrentCEUserTimeZone

```
CurrentCEUserTimeZone
```

returns "Mountain Standard Time,420,Mountain Daylight Time,-60;4.1.0/02:00,10.5.0/02:00" if the BusinessObjects Enterprise/Crystal Reports Server system you are currently logged in to is in the Mountain time zone. Inserting the CurrentCEUserTimeZone special field from the Field Explorer will display the same information (and, the function and the special field both return an empty string if you are not logged in).

NOTE *A detailed description of all the portions of a time zone string can be found in this appendix under ShiftDateTime.*

DataDate

Returns a date value indicating the last date that data on the report was refreshed from the database.

DataDate will be the same date that appears to the left of the page navigation controls in the Preview tab. Click Report | Refresh Report Data (or use the appropriate toolbar button or keyboard shortcut) to refresh the database and update this value to the current date.

DataDate

```
"Data current as of " & ToText(DataDate)
```

returns the string "Data current as of 5/31/2003" if the report was refreshed on May 31, 2003.

DataTime

Returns a time value indicating the last time that data on the report was refreshed from the database.

DataTime will be the same time that appears to the left of the page navigation controls in the Preview tab. Click Report | Refresh Report Data (or use the appropriate toolbar button or keyboard shortcut) to refresh the database and update this value to the current time.

DataTime

```
"Data current as of " & ToText(DataTime)
```

returns the string "Data current as of 6:15:21PM" if the report was refreshed at 6:15 P.M.

DataTimeZone
Returns a time zone string indicating the time zone of the Data Date and Time (typically, the time zone of the computer running the report).

DataTimeZone

```
DataTimeZone
```

returns "Mountain Standard Time,420,Mountain Daylight Time,-60;4.1.0/02:00,10.5.0/02:00" if the computer running the report is in the Mountain time zone. Inserting the DataTimeZone special field from the Field Explorer will display the same information.

NOTE *A detailed description of all the portions of a time zone string can be found in this appendix under ShiftDateTime.*

FileAuthor
Returns a string value from the Author field in the File | Summary Info dialog box.

FileAuthor

```
"Report written by " & FileAuthor
```

returns "Report written by George Peck", if "George Peck" has been placed in the Author field in the Summary Info dialog box.

FileCreationDate
Returns a date value indicating the date that the report file was first created.
This value will not change if the report is later opened, modified, and resaved.

FileCreationDate

```
"Report first created " & ToText(FileCreationDate)
```

will return "Report first created 5/30/2003" if the report was initially created on May 30, 2003.

FileName
Returns a string value containing the file path and filename of the report stored on disk.

FileName

```
"Report location: " & FileName
```

returns "Report location: C:\Reports\Sales Analysis.rpt" if the report is stored as C:\Reports\ Sales Analysis.rpt.

GroupingLevel
Returns a numeric value indicating a group's location in the grouping hierarchy.
  This function is typically used in combination with the HierarchyLevel function to determine where in a hierarchy a particular group resides (see **HierarchyLevel** elsewhere in this appendix). If the field supplied to GroupingLevel is not used in a report group, GroupingLevel will return 0.

GroupingLevel (f)
f – any database field, formula, or SQL Expression.

```
GroupingLevel ({Customer.Country})
```

  returns 1.00 if Country is the first group on the report.

```
GroupingLevel ({@Grouping Field})
```

  returns 3.00 if the third group on the report is based on the Grouping Field formula.

```
GroupingLevel ({Customer.City})
```

  returns 0.00 if there is no City grouping on the report.

ModificationDate
Returns a date value indicating the date that the report file was last modified.
  This value will change any time the report is opened, modified, and resaved.

ModificationDate

```
"Report last modified on " & ToText(ModificationDate)
```

will return "Report last modified on 5/31/2003" if the report was changed on May 31, 2003.

ModificationTime
Returns a time value indicating the time that the report file was last modified.
  This value will change any time the report is opened, modified, and resaved.

ModificationTime

```
"Report last modified at " & ToText(ModificationTime)
```

will return "Report last modified at 6:33:20PM" if the report was saved at 6:33 P.M.

PrintDate
Returns a date value indicating the date that the report is formatted or printed.
  By default, this value is taken from your computer's system clock. You may change it to another value by choosing Report | Set Print Date And Time from the pull-down menus.

PrintDate

```
"Report printed on " & ToText(PrintDate)
```

will return "Report printed on 5/31/2003" if the report is printed or formatted on May 31, 2003.

PrintTime

Returns a time value indicating the time that the report is formatted or printed.

By default, this value is taken from your computer's system clock. You may change it to another value by choosing Report | Set Print Date And Time from the pull-down menus.

PrintTime

```
"Report printed at " & ToText(PrintTime)
```

will return "Report printed at 6:38:33PM" if the report is printed or formatted at 6:38 P.M.

PrintTimeZone

Returns a time zone string indicating the time zone of the Print Date and Time (typically, the time zone of the computer running the report).

PrintTimeZone

```
PrintTimeZone
```

returns "Mountain Standard Time,420,Mountain Daylight Time,-60;4.1.0/02:00,10.5.0/02:00" if the computer running the report is in the Mountain time zone. Inserting the PrintTimeZone special field from the Field Explorer will display the same information.

NOTE *A detailed description of all the portions of a time zone string can be found in this appendix under ShiftDateTime.*

ReportComments

Returns a string value from the Comments field in the File | Summary Info dialog box.

ReportComments

```
"Report Information: " & ReportComments
```

returns "Report Information: Ablaze Group, Version 1, May 2003", taking the text from the Comments field in the Summary Info dialog box.

ReportTitle

Returns a string value from the Title field in the File | Summary Info dialog box.

ReportTitle

```
"Report Title: " & ReportTitle
```

returns "Report Title: Sales Analysis", taking the text from the Title field in the Summary Info dialog box.

Functions: Evaluation Time

This category of functions is used to force a formula to evaluate during one of Crystal Reports' three available report "passes."

By default, formulas evaluate during a certain pass based on their contents. For example, a formula that makes no reference to database fields, such as

```
"Report printed on " & PrintDate
```

prints in the BeforeReadingRecords (or preread) pass by default.

A formula that makes reference to one or more database fields, such as

```
{Orders.Order Amount} * 1.10
```

prints in the WhileReadingRecords (or first) pass by default.

And, any formula that makes reference to summary functions, report alerts, and various other "second-pass" functions, such as

```
{Orders.Order Amount} %
Sum({Orders.Order Amount}, {Employee. Last Name})
```

prints in the WhilePrintingRecords (or second) pass by default.

While you cannot force a formula to an earlier report pass than its default, you can force it to a later pass. In particular, when using variables in formulas, you'll often need to force formulas that use the same variable to the same report pass to ensure consistent results.

BeforeReadingRecords

Forces a formula to evaluate in the "preread," BeforeReadingRecords, report pass.

BeforeReadingRecords

```
BeforeReadingRecords;
NumberVar Array RegionTotals := [0,0,0,0,0,0,0,0,0,0];
0
```

will create an array variable and fill it with zeros before the report reads records from the database.

EvaluateAfter

Forces a formula to evaluate after another formula has been evaluated.

EvaluateAfter is required when you place two formulas in the same report section that evaluate in the same report pass. In this case, it's not predictable which formula will evaluate first. If both formulas, for example, refer to the same variable, you may get unintended results if one formula doesn't evaluate after the other formula.

EvaluateAfter (f)

f – the name of another report formula.

```
EvaluateAfter({@Show Count});
NumberVar BonusCount := 0
```

resets the BonusCount variable to zero after the @Show Count formula has already processed.

WhilePrintingRecords
Forces a formula to evaluate during the second, WhilePrintingRecords, pass.

WhilePrintingRecords

```
WhilePrintingRecords;
NumberVar GroupBonusCount := 0
```

resets the GroupBonusCount variable to zero during the WhilePrintingRecords pass (presumably because other WhilePrintingRecords formulas make use of GroupBonusCount).

WhileReadingRecords
Forces a formula to evaluate during the first, WhileReadingRecords, pass.

WhileReadingRecords

```
WhileReadingRecords;
StringVar GroupField
```

forces the contents of the GroupField variable to be displayed during the WhileReadingRecords pass. This may be helpful if you wish to create report groups based on this formula.

nctions: Financial

This category of functions supplies many standard financial calculations and algorithms. Many of these functions behave similarly to those available in Microsoft Excel.

ACCRINT
Returns a numeric value indicating total accrued interest for a security.

ACCRINT (d1, d2, d3, n1, n2, n3)
d1 – a date or date-time value indicating the issue date.
d2 – a date or date-time value indicating the date of first interest payment.
d3 – a date or date-time value indicating the date the security was purchased.
n1 – a numeric value indicating the annual interest rate.
n2 – a numeric value indicating the par value.
n3 – a numeric value indicating the number of payments per year: 1 = annual, 2 = semiannual, 4 = quarterly.

ACCRINT (d1, d2, d3, n1, n2, n3, n4)
d1 – a date or date-time value indicating the issue date.
d2 – a date or date-time value indicating the date of first interest payment.
d3 – a date or date-time value indicating the date the security was purchased.
n1 – a numeric value indicating the annual interest rate.
n2 – a numeric value indicating the par value.
n3 – a numeric value indicating the number of payments per year: 1 = annual, 2 = semiannual, 4 = quarterly.

APPENDIX

n4 – a numeric value indicating the day basis system: 0 = US (NASD) 30/360, 1 = actual/ actual, 2 = actual/360, 3 = actual/365, 4 = European 30/360.

```
ACCRINT(#1/1/1995#, #1/1/1996#, #6/1/1995#, .065, 100000, 4, 3)
```

returns 2,711.30.

ACCRINTM
Returns a numeric value indicating total accrued interest for a security that pays interest when it matures.

ACCRINTM (d1, d2, n1, n2)
d1 – a date or date-time value indicating the issue date.
d2 – a date or date-time value indicating the maturity date.
n1 – a numeric value indicating the annual interest rate.
n2 – a numeric value indicating the par value.

ACCRINTM (d1, d2, n1, n2, n3)
d1 – a date or date-time value indicating the issue date.
d2 – a date or date-time value indicating the maturity date.
n1 – a numeric value indicating the annual interest rate.
n2 – a numeric value indicating the par value.
n3 – a numeric value indicating the day basis system: 0 = US (NASD) 30/360, 1 = actual/ actual, 2 = actual/360, 3 = actual/365, 4 = European 30/360.

```
ACCRINTM(#1/1/1995#, #1/1/2005#, .065, 100000, 3)
```

returns 65,053.42.

AmorDEGRC
Returns a numeric value indicating depreciation of an asset.

AmorDEGRC (n1, d1, d2, n2, n3, n4)
n1 – a numeric value indicating the asset's initial cost.
d1 – a date or date-time value indicating the asset's purchase date.
d2 – a date or date-time value indicating the end of the first period.
n2 – a numeric value indicating the asset's salvage value.
n3 – a numeric value indicating the period to calculate the depreciation for.
n4 – a numeric value indicating the depreciation rate.

AmorDEGRC (n1, d1, d2, n2, n3, n4, n5)
n1 – a numeric value indicating the asset's initial cost.
d1 – a date or date-time value indicating the asset's purchase date.
d2 – a date or date-time value indicating the end of the first period.
n2 – a numeric value indicating the asset's salvage value.
n3 – a numeric value indicating the period to calculate the depreciation for.
n4 – a numeric value indicating the depreciation rate.

n5 – a numeric value indicating the day basis system: 0 = US (NASD) 30/360, 1 = actual/ actual, 2 = actual/360, 3 = actual/365, 4 = European 30/360.

```
AmorDEGRC (35000,#5/1/2000#,#1/1/2001#,15000,1,.1)
```

returns 7,292.00.

AmorLINC

Returns a numeric value indicating linear depreciation of an asset.

AmorLINC (n1, d1, d2, n2, n3, n4)

n1 – a numeric value indicating the asset's initial cost.
d1 – a date or date-time value indicating the asset's purchase date.
d2 – a date or date-time value indicating the end of the first period.
n2 – a numeric value indicating the asset's salvage value.
n3 – a numeric value indicating the period to calculate the depreciation for.
n4 – a numeric value indicating the depreciation rate.

AmorLINC (n1, d1, d2, n2, n3, n4, n5)

n1 – a numeric value indicating the asset's initial cost.
d1 – a date or date-time value indicating the asset's purchase date.
d2 – a date or date-time value indicating the end of the first period.
n2 – a numeric value indicating the asset's salvage value.
n3 – a numeric value indicating the period to calculate the depreciation for.
n4 – a numeric value indicating the depreciation rate.
n5 – a numeric value indicating the day basis system: 0 = US (NASD) 30/360, 1 = actual/ actual, 2 = actual/360, 3 = actual/365, 4 = European 30/360.

```
AmorLINC (35000,#5/1/2000#,#1/1/2001#,15000,1,.1)
```

returns 3,500.00.

CoupDayBS

Returns a numeric value indicating the days between the last coupon date and the settlement date.

CoupDayBS (d1, d2, n)

d1 – a date or date-time value indicating the purchase date.
d2 – a date or date-time value indicating the maturity date.
n – a numeric value indicating the number of payments (coupons) per year: 1 = annual, 2 = semiannual, 4 = quarterly.

CoupDayBS (d1, d2, n1, n2)

d1 – a date or date-time value indicating the purchase date.
d2 – a date or date-time value indicating the maturity date.
n1 – a numeric value indicating the number of payments (coupons) per year: 1 = annual, 2 = semiannual, 4 = quarterly.

n2 – a numeric value indicating the day basis system: 0 = US (NASD) 30/360, 1 = actual/
actual, 2 = actual/360, 3 = actual/365, 4 = European 30/360.

```
CoupDayBS (#1/1/2000#, #5/31/2004#, 2, 3)
```

returns 32.

CoupDays

Returns a numeric value indicating the number of days in the coupon period that includes settlement.

CoupDays (d1, d2, n)
d1 – a date or date-time value indicating the purchase date.
d2 – a date or date-time value indicating the maturity date.
n – a numeric value indicating the number of payments (coupons) per year: 1 = annual,
2 = semiannual, 4 = quarterly.

CoupDays (d1, d2, n1, n2)
d1 – a date or date-time value indicating the purchase date.
d2 – a date or date-time value indicating the maturity date.
n1 – a numeric value indicating the number of payments (coupons) per year: 1 = annual,
2 = semiannual, 4 = quarterly.
n2 – a numeric value indicating the day basis system: 0 = US (NASD) 30/360, 1 = actual/
actual, 2 = actual/360, 3 = actual/365, 4 = European 30/360.

```
CoupDays (#1/1/2000#, #5/31/2004#, 2, 3)
```

returns 182.5.

CoupDaysNC

Returns a numeric value indicating the number of days between the settlement date and the next coupon date.

CoupDaysNC (d1, d2, n)
d1 – a date or date-time value indicating the purchase date.
d2 – a date or date-time value indicating the maturity date.
n – a numeric value indicating the number of payments (coupons) per year: 1 = annual,
2 = semiannual, 4 = quarterly.

CoupDaysNC (d1, d2, n1, n2)
d1 – a date or date-time value indicating the purchase date.
d2 – a date or date-time value indicating the maturity date.
n1 – a numeric value indicating the number of payments (coupons) per year: 1 = annual,
2 = semiannual, 4 = quarterly.
n2 – a numeric value indicating the day basis system: 0 = US (NASD) 30/360, 1 = actual/
actual, 2 = actual/360, 3 = actual/365, 4 = European 30/360.

```
CoupDaysNC (#1/1/2000#, #5/31/2004#, 2, 3)
```

returns 151.

CoupNCD

Returns a date value indicating the next coupon date after settlement.

CoupNCD (d1, d2, n)

d1 – a date or date-time value indicating the purchase date.
d2 – a date or date-time value indicating the maturity date.
n – a numeric value indicating the number of payments (coupons) per year: 1 = annual,
2 = semiannual, 4 = quarterly.

```
CoupNCD (#1/1/2000#, #5/31/2004#, 2)
```

returns 5/31/2000.

CoupNum

Returns a numeric value indicating the number of coupon periods between settlement
and maturity.

CoupNum (d1, d2, n)

d1 – a date or date-time value indicating the purchase date.
d2 – a date or date-time value indicating the maturity date.
n – a numeric value indicating the number of payments (coupons) per year: 1 = annual,
2 = semiannual, 4 = quarterly.

```
CoupNum (#1/1/2000#, #5/31/2004#, 2)
```

returns 9.

CoupPCD

Returns a date value indicating the last coupon date before settlement.

CoupPCD (d1, d2, n)

d1 – a date or date-time value indicating the purchase date.
d2 – a date or date-time value indicating the maturity date.
n – a numeric value indicating the number of payments (coupons) per year: 1 = annual,
2 = semiannual, 4 = quarterly.

```
CoupPCD (#1/1/2000#, #5/31/2004#, 2)
```

returns 11/30/1999.

CumIPMT

Returns a numeric value indicating cumulative interest paid on a loan.

CumIPMT (n1, n2, n3, n4, n5, n6)

n1 – a numeric value indicating the interest rate, which must be provided on a per-period basis.
n2 – a numeric value indicating the total number of payment periods, which must be provided
on a per-period basis.

n3 – a numeric value indicating the loan's total or "present" value of the loan.
n4 – a numeric value indicating the first period to include in the calculation.
n5 – a numeric value indicating the last period to include in the calculation.
n6 – a numeric value indicating the type of payment: 0 = end of payment period,
1 = beginning of payment period.

```
CumIPMT (.09/12, 60, 45000, 1, 30, 1)
```

returns –7,640.28.

CumPrinc

Returns a numeric value indicating cumulative principal paid on a loan.

CumPrinc (n1, n2, n3, n4, n5, n6)

n1 – a numeric value indicating the interest rate, which must be provided on a per-period basis.
n2 – a numeric value indicating the total number of payment periods, which must be provided on a per-period basis.
n3 – a numeric value indicating the loan's total or "present" value of the loan.
n4 – a numeric value indicating the first period to include in the calculation.
n5 – a numeric value indicating the last period to include in the calculation.
n6 – a numeric value indicating the type of payment: 0 = end of payment period,
1 = beginning of payment period.

```
CumPrinc (.09/12, 60, 45000, 1, 30, 1)
```

returns –20,174.89.

Days360

Returns a numeric value indicating the number of days between two dates using a 30-day-per-month/360-day-per-year financial calendar.

Days360 (d1, d2)

d1 – a date or date-time value indicating start date.
d2 – a date or date-time value indicating end date.

Days360 (d1, d2, b)

d1 – a date or date-time value indicating start date.
d2 – a date or date-time value indicating end date.
b – a Boolean (true or false) value indicating the basis for the calculation: False indicates US (NASD) 30/360; True indicates European 30/360.

```
Days360(#1/1/2003#, #12/31/2003#)
```

returns 360.

DB

Returns a numeric value indicating depreciation of an asset using the declining balance method.

DB (n1, n2, n3, n4)

n1 – a numeric value indicating the asset's initial cost.
n2 – a numeric value indicating the asset's salvage value.
n3 – a numeric value indicating the useful life of the asset.
n4 – a numeric value indicating the period to calculate the depreciation for.

DB (n1, n2, n3, n4, n5)

n1 – a numeric value indicating the asset's initial cost.
n2 – a numeric value indicating the asset's salvage value.
n3 – a numeric value indicating the useful life of the asset.
n4 – a numeric value indicating the period to calculate the depreciation for.
n5 – a numeric value indicating the number of months in the first year.

```
DB(35000,15000,7,5)
```

returns 2,458.71.

DDB

Returns a numeric value indicating depreciation of an asset using the double-declining balance method.

DDB (n1, n2, n3, n4)

n1 – a numeric value indicating the asset's initial cost.
n2 – a numeric value indicating the asset's salvage value.
n3 – a numeric value indicating the useful life of the asset.
n4 – a numeric value indicating the period to calculate the depreciation for.

DDB (n1, n2, n3, n4, n5)

n1 – a numeric value indicating the asset's initial cost.
n2 – a numeric value indicating the asset's salvage value.
n3 – a numeric value indicating the useful life of the asset.
n4 – a numeric value indicating the period to calculate the depreciation for.
n5 – a numeric value indicating the factor at which the rate declines; 2 indicates double-declining.

```
DDB(35000,5000,7,5)
```

returns 2,603.08.

DISC

Returns a numeric value indicating the discount rate for a security.

DISC (d1, d2, n1, n2)

d1 – a date or date-time value indicating the date the security was purchased.
d2 – a date or date-time value indicating the date of maturity.
n1 – a numeric value indicating the security's value when purchased.
n2 – a numeric value indicating the security's value at maturity.

DISC (d1, d2, n1, n2, n3)

d1 – a date or date-time value indicating the date the security was purchased.
d2 – a date or date-time value indicating the date of maturity.
n1 – a numeric value indicating the security's value when purchased.
n2 – a numeric value indicating the security's value at maturity.
n3 – a numeric value indicating the day basis system: 0 = US (NASD) 30/360, 1 = actual/ actual, 2 = actual/360, 3 = actual/365, 4 = European 30/360.

```
DISC(#1/1/2000#,#12/31/2005#,10000,14000)
```

returns .05.

DollarDE

Returns a number indicating the true fractional value of a financial fractional "representation."

This function is helpful for calculating actual decimal values of such terms as "Five and seven eighths."

DollarDE (n1, n2)

n1 – a numeric value representing the number to be converted (such as 5.7 for "five and seven").
n2 – a numeric value representing the base of n1 (such as 8 for "eighths").

```
DollarDE (5.7, 8)
```

returns 5.88 (5.875 rounded to two decimal places).

DollarFR

Returns a number indicating the financial fractional "representation" of a true fractional value.

This function is helpful for converting actual decimal values into such terms as "Five and seven eighths."

DollarFR (n1, n2)

n1 – a numeric value representing the true fractional number to be converted (such as 5.875).
n2 – a numeric value representing the base to convert n1 to (such as 8 for "eighths").

```
DollarFR (5.875, 8)
```

returns 5.70 (indicating "five and seven eighths").

Duration

Returns a number indicating the duration of a bond (sometimes known as the "Macauley duration").

Duration (d1, d2, n1, n2, n3)

d1 – a date or date-time value indicating the bond's purchase date.
d2 – a date or date-time value indicating the bond's maturity date.
n1 – a numeric value indicating the bond's interest rate.
n2 – a numeric value indicating the bond's yield.
n3 – a numeric value indicating the number of payments per year; 1 = annual,
2 = semiannual, 4 = quarterly.

Duration (d1, d2, n1, n2, n3, n4)

d1 – a date or date-time value indicating the bond's purchase date.
d2 – a date or date-time value indicating the bond's maturity date.
n1 – a numeric value indicating the bond's interest rate.
n2 – a numeric value indicating the bond's yield.
n3 – a numeric value indicating the number of payments per year: 1 = annual,
2 = semiannual, 4 = quarterly.
n4 – a numeric value indicating the day basis system: 0 = US (NASD) 30/360, 1 = actual/
actual, 2 = actual/360, 3 = actual/365, 4 = European 30/360.

```
Duration(#1/1/2000#,#1/1/2030#,.08,.09,1)
```

returns 11.37 years.

Effect

Returns a numeric value indicating the effective annual interest rate.

Effect (n1, n2)

n1 – a numeric value indicating the annual interest rate.
n2 – a numeric value indicating the number of compounding periods.

```
Effect(.1,12)
```

returns 0.10471 (when formatted to show five decimal places).

FV

Returns a numeric value indicating the future value of an annuity.

FV (n1, n2, n3)

n1 – a numeric value indicating the interest rate (must be adjusted to a per-period rate).
n2 – a numeric value indicating the number of annuity payments.
n3 – a numeric value indicating the payment amount.

FV (n1, n2, n3, n4)

n1 – a numeric value indicating the interest rate (must be adjusted to a per-period rate).
n2 – a numeric value indicating the number of annuity payments.

n3 – a numeric value indicating the payment amount.

n4 – a numeric value indicating the present value (the total amount that a series of future payments is worth now).

FV (n1, n2, n3, n4, n5)

n1 – a numeric value indicating the interest rate (must be adjusted to a per-period rate).

n2 – a numeric value indicating the number of annuity payments.

n3 – a numeric value indicating the payment amount (a negative amount indicating paying money "out").

n4 – a numeric value indicating the present value (the total amount that a series of future payments is worth now).

n5 – a numeric value indicating the type of payment: 0 = end of payment period, 1 = beginning of payment period.

```
FV (.04/12, 60, -500)
```

returns 33,149.49.

FVSchedule

Returns a number indicating the future value of an annuity with several compounded interest rates.

FVSchedule (n, a)

n – a numeric value indicating the present value of the annuity.

a – a numeric array containing one or more interest rates.

```
FVSchedule (10000,[.04,.0475,.05])
```

returns 11,438.70.

IntRate

Returns a numeric value indicating the interest rate for a security.

IntRate (d1, d2, n1, n2)

d1 – a date or date-time value indicating the security purchase date.

d2 – a date or date-time value indicating the security maturity date.

n1 – a numeric value indicating the original security value.

n2 – a numeric value indicating the value at maturity.

IntRate (d1, d2, n1, n2, n3)

d1 – a date or date-time value indicating the security purchase date.

d2 – a date or date-time value indicating the security maturity date.

n1 – a numeric value indicating the original security value.

n2 – a numeric value indicating the value at maturity.

n3 – a numeric value indicating the day basis system: 0 = US (NASD) 30/360, 1 = actual/actual, 2 = actual/360, 3 = actual/365, 4 = European 30/360.

```
IntRate(#1/1/2000#,#1/1/2005#,10000,13000)
```

returns .06.

IPmt

Returns a numeric value indicating an interest payment based on fixed payments and interest rate.

IPmt (n1, n2, n3, n4)

n1 – a numeric value indicating the interest rate (must be adjusted to a per-period rate).
n2 – a numeric value indicating the payment period.
n3 – a numeric value indicating the total number of payments.
n4 – a numeric value indicating the present value.

IPmt (n1, n2, n3, n4, n5)

n1 – a numeric value indicating the interest rate (must be adjusted to a per-period rate).
n2 – a numeric value indicating the payment period.
n3 – a numeric value indicating the total number of payments.
n4 – a numeric value indicating the present value.
n5 – a numeric value indicating the future value after the last payment.

IPmt (n1, n2, n3, n4, n5, n6)

n1 – a numeric value indicating the interest rate (must be adjusted to a per-period rate).
n2 – a numeric value indicating the payment period.
n3 – a numeric value indicating the total number of payments.
n4 – a numeric value indicating the present value.
n5 – a numeric value indicating the future value after the last payment.
n6 – a numeric value indicating the type of payment: 0 = end of payment period, 1 = beginning of payment period.

```
IPmt(.09/12,30,60,30000)
```

returns –128.76.

IRR

Returns a numeric value indicating the internal rate of return for a series of payments and receipts.

IRR (a)

a – a numeric array indicating the series of payments and receipts (there must be at least one negative and one positive number in the array). An IRR of 10 percent (.1) is assumed.

IRR (a, n)

a – a numeric array indicating the series of payments and receipts (there must be at least one negative and one positive number in the array).
n – a numeric value indicating the "guess" of IRR.

```
IRR([-1000,-500,2000])
```

returns .19.

ISPMT

Returns a numeric value indicating interest paid during a period (assuming equal installments).

ISPMT (n1, n2, n3, n4)

$n1$ – a numeric value indicating the interest rate (must be adjusted to a per-period rate).
$n2$ – a numeric value indicating the period to calculate interest for.
$n3$ – a numeric value indicating the number of payment periods.
$n4$ – a numeric value indicating the present value.

```
ISPMT(.09/12,30,60,30000)
```

returns –112.50.

MDuration

Returns a number indicating the modified duration of a bond (sometimes known as the modified "Macauley duration").

MDuration (d1, d2, n1, n2, n3)

$d1$ – a date or date-time value indicating the bond's purchase date.
$d2$ – a date or date-time value indicating the bond's maturity date.
$n1$ – a numeric value indicating the bond's interest rate.
$n2$ – a numeric value indicating the bond's yield.
$n3$ – a numeric value indicating the number of payments per year; 1 = annual,
2 = semiannual, 4 = quarterly.

MDuration (d1, d2, n1, n2, n3, n4)

$d1$ – a date or date-time value indicating the bond's purchase date.
$d2$ – a date or date-time value indicating the bond's maturity date.
$n1$ – a numeric value indicating the bond's interest rate.
$n2$ – a numeric value indicating the bond's yield.
$n3$ – a numeric value indicating the number of payments per year: 1 = annual,
2 = semiannual, 4 = quarterly.
$n4$ – a numeric value indicating the day basis system: 0 = US (NASD) 30/360, 1 = actual/
actual, 2 = actual/360, 3 = actual/365, 4 = European 30/360.

```
MDuration(#1/1/2000#,#1/1/2030#,.08,.09,1)
```

returns 10.43 years.

MIRR

Returns a numeric value indicating the modified internal rate of return for a series of payments and receipts.

MIRR (a, n1, n2)

a – a numeric array indicating the series of payments and receipts (there must be at least one negative and one positive number in the array).

n1 – a numeric value indicating interest rate cost.
n2 – a numeric value indicating interest rate return.

```
MIRR([-1000,-500,2000], .9, .6)
```

returns .26.

Nominal

Returns a numeric value indicating the nominal annual interest rate.

Nominal (n1, n2)

n1 – a numeric value indicating effective rate.
n2 – a numeric value indicating number of compounding periods.

```
Nominal(.08,12)
```

returns .07721 (when formatted with five decimal places).

NPer

Returns a numeric value indicating the number of payments, based on a fixed number of payments and interest rate.

NPer (n1, n2, n3)

n1 – a numeric value indicating the interest rate (must be adjusted to a per-period value).
n2 – a numeric value indicating the combined principal/interest payment.
n3 – a numeric value indicating the present value of the loan.

NPer (n1, n2, n3, n4)

n1 – a numeric value indicating the interest rate (must be adjusted to a per-period value).
n2 – a numeric value indicating the combined principal/interest payment.
n3 – a numeric value indicating the present value of the loan.
n4 – a numeric value indicating the future value of the loan after final payment.

NPer (n1, n2, n3, n4, n5)

n1 – a numeric value indicating the interest rate (must be adjusted to a per-period value).
n2 – a numeric value indicating the combined principal/interest payment.
n3 – a numeric value indicating the present value of the loan.
n4 – a numeric value indicating the future value of the loan after final payment.
n5 – a numeric value indicating the type of payment: 0 = end of payment period, 1 = beginning of payment period.

```
NPer(.09/12,-750,40000)
```

returns 68.37 (indicating months).

NPV

Returns a numeric value indicating the net present value of an investment.

NPV (n, a)

n – a numeric value indicating the discount rate.
a – a numeric array indicating payments/receipts.

```
NPV(.05,[1000,2000,1500,1750])
```

returns 5,501.93.

OddFPrice

Returns a numeric value indicating the price of a security that pays interest with regularity, with the exception of a short or long (odd) first period.

OddFPrice (d1, d2, d3, d4, n1, n2, n3, n4)

d1 – a date or date-time value indicating the purchase date.
d2 – a date or date-time value indicating the date of maturity.
d3 – a date or date-time value indicating the issue date.
d4 – a date or date-time value indicating the date of first interest payment.
n1 – a numeric value indicating the interest rate.
n2 – a numeric value indicating the annual yield of the security.
n3 – a numeric value indicating the security redemption value (per $100 face value).
n4 – a numeric value indicating the number of payments per year: 1 = annual,
2 = semiannual, 4 = quarterly.

OddFPrice (d1, d2, d3, d4, n1, n2, n3, n4, n5)

d1 – a date or date-time value indicating the purchase date.
d2 – a date or date-time value indicating the date of maturity.
d3 – a date or date-time value indicating the issue date.
d4 – a date or date-time value indicating the date of first interest payment.
n1 – a numeric value indicating the interest rate.
n2 – a numeric value indicating the annual yield of the security.
n3 – a numeric value indicating the security redemption value (per $100 face value).
n4 – a numeric value indicating the number of payments per year: 1 = annual,
2 = semiannual, 4 = quarterly.
n5 – a numeric value indicating the day basis system: 0 = US (NASD) 30/360, 1 = actual/
actual, 2 = actual/360, 3 = actual/365, 4 = European 30/360.

```
OddFPrice (#2/1/2000#,#1/1/2030#,#1/1/2000#,
   #1/1/2001#,.05,.055,75,1)
```

returns 87.69.

OddFYield

Returns a numeric value indicating the yield of a security that pays interest with regularity, with the exception of a short or long (odd) first period.

OddFYield (d1, d2, d3, d4, n1, n2, n3, n4)

d1 – a date or date-time value indicating the purchase date.
d2 – a date or date-time value indicating the date of maturity.
d3 – a date or date-time value indicating the issue date.
d4 – a date or date-time value indicating the date of first interest payment.
n1 – a numeric value indicating the interest rate.
n2 – a numeric value indicating the purchase price (per $100 face value).
n3 – a numeric value indicating the security redemption value (per $100 face value).
n4 – a numeric value indicating the number of payments per year: 1 = annual,
2 = semiannual, 4 = quarterly.

OddFYield (d1, d2, d3, d4, n1, n2, n3, n4, n5)

d1 – a date or date-time value indicating the purchase date.
d2 – a date or date-time value indicating the date of maturity.
d3 – a date or date-time value indicating the issue date.
d4 – a date or date-time value indicating the date of first interest payment.
n1 – a numeric value indicating the interest rate.
n2 – a numeric value indicating the purchase price (per $100 face value).
n3 – a numeric value indicating the security redemption value (per $100 face value).
n4 – a numeric value indicating the number of payments per year: 1 = annual,
2 = semiannual, 4 = quarterly.
n5 – a numeric value indicating the day basis system: 0 = US (NASD) 30/360, 1 = actual/
actual, 2 = actual/360, 3 = actual/365, 4 = European 30/360.

```
OddFPrice (#2/1/2000#,#1/1/2030#,#1/1/2000#,
    #1/1/2001#,.05,13.23,75,1)
```

returns .0549 (formatted with four decimal places).

OddLPrice

Returns a numeric value indicating the price of a security that pays interest with regularity, with the exception of a short or long (odd) last period.

OddLPrice (d1, d2, d3, n1, n2, n3, n4)

d1 – a date or date-time value indicating the purchase date.
d2 – a date or date-time value indicating the date of maturity.
d3 – a date or date-time value indicating the security's last coupon date.
n1 – a numeric value indicating the interest rate.
n2 – a numeric value indicating the annual yield of the security.
n3 – a numeric value indicating the security redemption value (per $100 face value).
n4 – a numeric value indicating the number of payments per year: 1 = annual,
2 = semiannual, 4 = quarterly.

OddLPrice (d1, d2, d3, n1, n2, n3, n4, n5)

d1 – a date or date-time value indicating the purchase date.
d2 – a date or date-time value indicating the date of maturity.
d3 – a date or date-time value indicating the security's last coupon date.

n1 – a numeric value indicating the interest rate.
n2 – a numeric value indicating the annual yield of the security.
n3 – a numeric value indicating the security redemption value (per $100 face value).
n4 – a numeric value indicating the number of payments per year: 1 = annual,
2 = semiannual, 4 = quarterly.
n5 – a numeric value indicating the day basis system: 0 = US (NASD) 30/360, 1 = actual/
actual, 2 = actual/360, 3 = actual/365, 4 = European 30/360.

```
OddLPrice(#2/1/2000#,#1/1/2030#,#1/1/2000#,.05,.055,75,1)
```

returns 84.64.

OddLYield

Returns a numeric value indicating the yield of a security that pays interest with regularity, with the exception of a short or long (odd) last period.

OddLYield (d1, d2, d3, n1, n2, n3, n4)
d1 – a date or date-time value indicating the purchase date.
d2 – a date or date-time value indicating the date of maturity.
d3 – a date or date-time value indicating the security's last coupon date.
n1 – a numeric value indicating the interest rate.
n2 – a numeric value indicating the purchase price (per $100 face value).
n3 – a numeric value indicating the security redemption value (per $100 face value).
n4 – a numeric value indicating the number of payments per year: 1 = annual,
2 = semiannual, 4 = quarterly.

OddLYield (d1, d2, d3, n1, n2, n3, n4, n5)
d1 – a date or date-time value indicating the purchase date.
d2 – a date or date-time value indicating the date of maturity.
d3 – a date or date-time value indicating the security's last coupon date.
n1 – a numeric value indicating the interest rate.
n2 – a numeric value indicating the purchase price (per $100 face value).
n3 – a numeric value indicating the security redemption value (per $100 face value).
n4 – a numeric value indicating the number of payments per year: 1 = annual,
2 = semiannual, 4 = quarterly.
n5 – a numeric value indicating the day basis system: 0 = US (NASD) 30/360, 1 = actual/
actual, 2 = actual/360, 3 = actual/365, 4 = European 30/360.

```
OddLYield (#2/1/2000#,#1/1/2030#,#1/1/2000#,.05,84.64,75,1)
```

returns .055 (formatted with three decimal places).

Pmt

Returns a numeric value indicating the payment for an annuity with fixed payments and interest rate.

Pmt (n1, n2, n3)

n1 – a numeric value indicating the interest rate (must be adjusted to a per-period rate).
n2 – a numeric value indicating the number of payment periods.
n3 – a numeric value indicating the principal/present value of the annuity.

Pmt (n1, n2, n3, n4)

n1 – a numeric value indicating the interest rate (must be adjusted to a per-period rate).
n2 – a numeric value indicating the number of payment periods.
n3 – a numeric value indicating the principal/present value of the annuity.
n4 – a numeric value indicating the desired future value/balance after the final payment.

Pmt (n1, n2, n3, n4, n5)

n1 – a numeric value indicating the interest rate (must be adjusted to a per-period rate).
n2 – a numeric value indicating the number of payment periods.
n3 – a numeric value indicating the principal/present value of the annuity.
n4 – a numeric value indicating the desired future value/balance after the final payment.
n5 – a numeric value indicating the type of payment: 0 = end of payment period,
1 = beginning of payment period.

```
Pmt(.05/12,36,10000)
```

returns –299.71.

PPmt

Returns a numeric value indicating the principal payment for a specific period of an annuity with fixed payments and interest rate.

PPmt (n1, n2, n3, n4)

n1 – a numeric value indicating the interest rate (must be adjusted to a per-period rate).
n2 – a numeric value indicating the specific period to calculate the principal for.
n3 – a numeric value indicating the number of payment periods.
n4 – a numeric value indicating the present value.

PPmt (n1, n2, n3, n4, n5)

n1 – a numeric value indicating the interest rate (must be adjusted to a per-period rate).
n2 – a numeric value indicating the specific period to calculate the principal for.
n3 – a numeric value indicating the number of payment periods.
n4 – a numeric value indicating the present value.
n5 – a numeric value indicating the desired future value/balance after the final payment.

PPmt (n1, n2, n3, n4, n5, n6)

n1 – a numeric value indicating the interest rate (must be adjusted to a per-period rate).
n2 – a numeric value indicating the specific period to calculate the principal for.
n3 – a numeric value indicating the number of payment periods.
n4 – a numeric value indicating the present value.
n5 – a numeric value indicating the desired future value/balance after the final payment.

n6 – a numeric value indicating the type of payment: 0 = end of payment period, 1 = beginning of payment period.

```
PPmt(.09/12,24,60,35000)
```

returns –551.05.

Price

Returns a numeric value indicating the price of a security (per $100 face value) that pays periodic interest.

Price (d1, d2, n1, n2, n3, n4)
d1 – a date or date-time value indicating the purchase date.
d2 – a date or date-time value indicating the date of maturity.
n1 – a numeric value indicating the interest rate.
n2 – a numeric value indicating the annual yield of the security.
n3 – a numeric value indicating the security redemption value (per $100 face value).
n4 – a numeric value indicating the number of payments per year: 1 = annual, 2 = semiannual, 4 = quarterly.

Price (d1, d2, n1, n2, n3, n4, n5)
d1 – a date or date-time value indicating the purchase date.
d2 – a date or date-time value indicating the date of maturity.
n1 – a numeric value indicating the interest rate.
n2 – a numeric value indicating the annual yield of the security.
n3 – a numeric value indicating the security redemption value (per $100 face value).
n4 – a numeric value indicating the number of payments per year: 1 = annual, 2 = semiannual, 4 = quarterly.
n5 – a numeric value indicating the day basis system: 0 = US (NASD) 30/360, 1 = actual/actual, 2 = actual/360, 3 = actual/365, 4 = European 30/360.

```
Price (#1/1/2000#,#1/1/2005#,.055,.05,50,1)
```

returns 62.99.

PriceDisc

Returns a numeric value indicating the discounted price of a security (per $100 face value).

PriceDisc (d1, d2, n1, n2)
d1 – a date or date-time value indicating the purchase date.
d2 – a date or date-time value indicating the date of maturity.
n1 – a numeric value indicating the discount rate.
n2 – a numeric value indicating the security redemption value (per $100 face value).

PriceDisc (d1, d2, n1, n2, n3)
d1 – a date or date-time value indicating the purchase date.
d2 – a date or date-time value indicating the date of maturity.

n1 – a numeric value indicating the discount rate.
n2 – a numeric value indicating the security redemption value (per $100 face value).
n3 – a numeric value indicating the day basis system: 0 = US (NASD) 30/360, 1 = actual/
actual, 2 = actual/360, 3 = actual/365, 4 = European 30/360.

```
PriceDisc (#1/1/2000#,#1/1/2005#,.055,50)
```

returns 36.25.

PriceMat

Returns a numeric value indicating the price of a security (per $100 face value) that pays interest only at maturity.

PriceMat (d1, d2, d3, n1, n2)
d1 – a date or date-time value indicating the purchase date.
d2 – a date or date-time value indicating the date of maturity.
d3 – a date or date-time value indicating the issue date.
n1 – a numeric value indicating the interest rate.
n2 – a numeric value indicating the security's yield.

PriceMat (d1, d2, d3, n1, n2, n3)
d1 – a date or date-time value indicating the purchase date.
d2 – a date or date-time value indicating the date of maturity.
d3 – a date or date-time value indicating the issue date.
n1 – a numeric value indicating the interest rate.
n2 – a numeric value indicating the security's yield.
n3 – a numeric value indicating the day basis system: 0 = US (NASD) 30/360, 1 = actual/
actual, 2 = actual/360, 3 = actual/365, 4 = European 30/360.

```
PriceMat(#3/1/2000#,#3/1/2005#,#1/1/2000#,.055,.05)
```

returns 101.82.

PV

Returns a numeric value indicating the present value of an annuity.

PV (n1, n2, n3)
n1 – a numeric value indicating the interest rate (must be adjusted to a per-period rate).
n2 – a numeric value indicating the number of annuity payments.
n3 – a numeric value indicating the payment amount.

PV (n1, n2, n3, n4)
n1 – a numeric value indicating the interest rate (must be adjusted to a per-period rate).
n2 – a numeric value indicating the number of annuity payments.
n3 – a numeric value indicating the payment amount.
n4 – a numeric value indicating the future value/balance after final payment.

APPENDIX

PV (n1, n2, n3, n4, n5)

n1 – a numeric value indicating the interest rate (must be adjusted to a per-period rate).
n2 – a numeric value indicating the number of annuity payments.
n3 – a numeric value indicating the payment amount.
n4 – a numeric value indicating the future value/balance after final payment.
n5 – a numeric value indicating the type of payment: 0 = end of payment period,
1 = beginning of payment period.

```
PV (.04/12, 60, -500)
```

returns 27,149.53.

Rate

Returns a numeric value indicating per-period interest for an annuity.

Rate (n1, n2, n3)

n1 – a numeric value indicating the number of annuity payments.
n2 – a numeric value indicating the payment amount.
n3 – a numeric value indicating the annuity's present value.

Rate (n1, n2, n3, n4)

n1 – a numeric value indicating the number of annuity payments.
n2 – a numeric value indicating the payment amount.
n3 – a numeric value indicating the annuity's present value.
n4 – a numeric value indicating the future value/balance after final payment.

Rate (n1, n2, n3, n4, n5)

n1 – a numeric value indicating the number of annuity payments.
n2 – a numeric value indicating the payment amount.
n3 – a numeric value indicating the annuity's present value.
n4 – a numeric value indicating the future value/balance after final payment.
n5 – a numeric value indicating the type of payment: 0 = end of payment period,
1 = beginning of payment period.

Rate (n1, n2, n3, n4, n5, n6)

n1 – a numeric value indicating the number of annuity payments.
n2 – a numeric value indicating the payment amount.
n3 – a numeric value indicating the annuity's present value.
n4 – a numeric value indicating the future value/balance after final payment.
n5 – a numeric value indicating the type of payment: 0 = end of payment period,
1 = beginning of payment period.
n6 – a numeric value indicating your "guess" of the return to use as a starting point for the
calculation. If you omit this argument, 10 percent (.1) is assumed.

```
Rate(36, -750, 35000)
```

returns .0134 (when formatted to four decimal places).

Received

Returns a numeric value indicating the amount received at maturity for a fully invested security.

Received (d1, d2, n1, n2)

d1 – a date or date-time value indicating the purchase date.
d2 – a date or date-time value indicating the date of maturity.
n1 – a numeric value indicating the investment amount.
n2 – a numeric value indicating the discount rate.

Received (d1, d2, n1, n2, n3)

d1 – a date or date-time value indicating the purchase date.
d2 – a date or date-time value indicating the date of maturity.
n1 – a numeric value indicating the investment amount.
n2 – a numeric value indicating the discount rate.
n3 – a numeric value indicating the day basis system: 0 = US (NASD) 30/360, 1 = actual/actual, 2 = actual/360, 3 = actual/365, 4 = European 30/360.

```
Received(#1/1/2000#,#1/1/2005#,10000,.075)
```

returns 16,000.00.

SLN

Returns a numeric value indicating straight-line depreciation of an asset.

SLN (n1, n2, n3)

n1 – a numeric value indicating original cost of the asset.
n2 – a numeric value indicating the salvage of the asset at the end of its life.
n3 – a numeric value indicating the life of the asset.

```
SLN(35000,7500,7)
```

returns a per-year depreciation of 3,928.57.

SYD

Returns a numeric value indicating sum-of-years-digits depreciation of an asset.

SYD (n1, n2, n3, n4)

n1 – a numeric value indicating original cost of the asset.
n2 – a numeric value indicating the salvage of the asset at the end of its life.
n3 – a numeric value indicating the life of the asset.
n4 – a numeric value indicating the period to calculate depreciation for.

```
SYD(35000,7500,7,2)
```

returns a second-year depreciation of 5,892.86.

TBillEq

Returns a numeric value indicating the bond-equivalent yield for a Treasury bill.

TBillEq (d1, d2, n)

d1 – a date or date-time value indicating the purchase date.
d2 – a date or date-time value indicating the date of maturity.
n – a numeric value indicating the discount rate.

```
TBillEq(#1/1/2000#,#12/31/2000#,.08)
```

returns .0864 (8.64%) when formatted with four decimal places.

TBillPrice

Returns a numeric value indicating the price for a Treasury bill (per $100 face value).

TBillPrice (d1, d2, n)

d1 – a date or date-time value indicating the purchase date.
d2 – a date or date-time value indicating the date of maturity.
n – a numeric value indicating the discount rate.

```
TBillPrice(#1/1/2000#,#12/31/2000#,.08)
```

returns 91.89.

TBillYield

Returns a numeric value indicating the yield for a Treasury bill.

TBillYield (d1, d2, n)

d1 – a date or date-time value indicating the purchase date.
d2 – a date or date-time value indicating the date of maturity.
n – a numeric value indicating the price per $100 face value.

```
TBillYield(#1/1/2000#,#12/31/2000#,91.89)
```

returns .087 (8.7%) when formatted with three decimal places.

VDB

Returns the variable declining balance for an asset.
    VDB supports various depreciation options, such as double-declining balance or other method and partial depreciation periods.

VDB (n1, n2, n3, n4, n5)

n1 – a numeric value indicating the asset's initial cost.
n2 – a numeric value indicating the asset's salvage value.
n3 – a numeric value indicating the useful life of the asset.
n4 – a numeric value indicating the start period to calculate depreciation for.
n5 – a numeric value indicating the end period to calculate depreciation for.

VDB (n1, n2, n3, n4, n5, n6)

n1 – a numeric value indicating the asset's initial cost.
n2 – a numeric value indicating the asset's salvage value.
n3 – a numeric value indicating the useful life of the asset.
n4 – a numeric value indicating the start period to calculate depreciation for.
n5 – a numeric value indicating the end period to calculate depreciation for.
n6 – a numeric value indicating the factor at which the rate declines – 2 indicates double-declining.

VDB (n1, n2, n3, n4, n5, n6)

n1 – a numeric value indicating the asset's initial cost.
n2 – a numeric value indicating the asset's salvage value.
n3 – a numeric value indicating the useful life of the asset.
n4 – a numeric value indicating the start period to calculate depreciation for.
n5 – a numeric value indicating the end period to calculate depreciation for.
n6 – a Boolean (true/false) value indicating whether to switch from declining-balance to straight-line if declining-balance is less. True will always use declining-balance. False will switch to straight-line if declining-balance is less.

VDB (n1, n2, n3, n4, n5, n6, n7)

n1 – a numeric value indicating the asset's initial cost.
n2 – a numeric value indicating the asset's salvage value.
n3 – a numeric value indicating the useful life of the asset.
n4 – a numeric value indicating the start period to calculate depreciation for.
n5 – a numeric value indicating the end period to calculate depreciation for.
n6 – a numeric value indicating the factor at which the rate declines – 2 indicates double-declining.
n7 – a Boolean (true/false) value indicating whether to switch from declining-balance to straight-line if declining-balance is less. True will always use declining-balance. False will switch to straight-line if declining-balance is less.

```
VDB(50000,15000,7,2,5)
```

returns 10,510.20 depreciation for years two through five.

XIRR

Returns a numeric value indicating the internal rate of return for a series of payments and receipts.

XIRR differs from IRR in that it calculates internal rate of return for payments/receipts that aren't necessarily periodic.

XIRR (na, da)

na – a numeric array indicating the series of payments and receipts (there must be at least one negative and one positive number in the array).
da – an array of date or date-time values indicating the matching dates for the numeric array. There must be one entry in this array for each entry in the numeric array.

XIRR (na, da, n)

na – a numeric array indicating the series of payments and receipts (there must be at least one negative and one positive number in the array).
da – an array of date or date-time values indicating the matching dates for the numeric array. There must be one entry in this array for each entry in the numeric array.
n – a numeric value indicating the "guess" of IRR.

```
XIRR([-1000,-500,2000],[#1/1/2000#,#5/1/2000#,#6/30/2000#])
```

returns 1.08.

XNPV

Returns a numeric value indicating the net present value of an investment.

   XNPV differs from NPV in that it calculates net present value for payments/receipts that aren't necessarily periodic.

XNPV (n, na, da)

n – a numeric value indicating the discount rate.
na – a numeric array indicating payments/receipts.
da – an array of date or date-time values that correspond to the numeric array. There must be one entry in the date array for each entry in the numeric array.

```
XNPV(.05,[1000,2000,1500,1750],
[#1/1/2000#,#5/1/2000#,#6/30/2000#,#12/31/2000#])
```

returns 6,098.72.

YearFrac

Returns a numeric value indicating what fraction of the year is represented by two dates.

YearFrac (d1, d2)

d1 – a date or date-time value indicating the first date in the year.
d2 – a date or date-time value indicating the second date in the year.

YearFrac (d1, d2, n)

d1 – a date or date-time value indicating the first date in the year.
d2 – a date or date-time value indicating the second date in the year.
n – a numeric value indicating the day basis system: 0 = US (NASD) 30/360, 1 = actual/actual, 2 = actual/360, 3 = actual/365, 4 = European 30/360.

```
YearFrac(#1/1/2003#,#3/31/2003#)
```

returns .25.

Yield

Returns a numeric value indicating the yield of a security that pays periodic interest.

Yield (d1, d2, n1, n2, n3, n4)

d1 – a date or date-time value indicating the purchase date.
d2 – a date or date-time value indicating the date of maturity.
n1 – a numeric value indicating the interest rate.
n2 – a numeric value indicating the purchase price of the security (per $100 face value).
n3 – a numeric value indicating the security redemption value (per $100 face value).
n4 – a numeric value indicating the number of payments per year: 1 = annual,
2 = semiannual, 4 = quarterly.

Yield (d1, d2, n1, n2, n3, n4, n5)

d1 – a date or date-time value indicating the purchase date.
d2 – a date or date-time value indicating the date of maturity.
n1 – a numeric value indicating the interest rate.
n2 – a numeric value indicating the purchase price of the security (per $100 face value).
n3 – a numeric value indicating the security redemption value (per $100 face value).
n4 – a numeric value indicating the number of payments per year: 1 = annual,
2 = semiannual, 4 = quarterly.
n5 – a numeric value indicating the day basis system: 0 = US (NASD) 30/360, 1 = actual/
actual, 2 = actual/360, 3 = actual/365, 4 = European 30/360.

```
Yield (#1/1/2000#,#1/1/2005#,.055,62.99,50,1)
```

returns .087 (formatted with three decimal places).

YieldDisc

Returns a numeric value indicating the yield of a discounted security.

YieldDisc (d1, d2, n1, n2)

d1 – a date or date-time value indicating the purchase date.
d2 – a date or date-time value indicating the date of maturity.
n1 – a numeric value indicating purchase price (per $100 face value).
n2 – a numeric value indicating the security redemption value (per $100 face value).

YieldDisc (d1, d2, n1, n2, n3)

d1 – a date or date-time value indicating the purchase date.
d2 – a date or date-time value indicating the date of maturity.
n1 – a numeric value indicating purchase price (per $100 face value).
n2 – a numeric value indicating the security redemption value (per $100 face value).
n3 – a numeric value indicating the day basis system: 0 = US (NASD) 30/360, 1 = actual/
actual, 2 = actual/360, 3 = actual/365, 4 = European 30/360.

```
YieldDisc(#1/1/2000#,#1/1/2005#,36.25,50)
```

returns .0759 (when formatted with four decimal places).

APPENDIX

YieldMat

Returns a numeric value indicating the yield of a security that pays interest only at maturity.

YieldMat (d1, d2, d3, n1, n2)

d1 – a date or date-time value indicating the purchase date.
d2 – a date or date-time value indicating the date of maturity.
d3 – a date or date-time value indicating the issue date.
n1 – a numeric value indicating the interest rate.
n2 – a numeric value indicating purchase price (per $100 face value).

YieldMat (d1, d2, d3, n1, n2, n3)

d1 – a date or date-time value indicating the purchase date.
d2 – a date or date-time value indicating the date of maturity.
d3 – a date or date-time value indicating the issue date.
n1 – a numeric value indicating the interest rate.
n2 – a numeric value indicating purchase price (per $100 face value).
n3 – a numeric value indicating the day basis system: 0 = US (NASD) 30/360, 1 = actual/
actual, 2 = actual/360, 3 = actual/365, 4 = European 30/360.

```
YieldMat(#3/1/2000#,#3/1/2005#,#1/1/2000#,.055,101.82)
```

returns .05.

Functions: Math

This set of functions performs standard math, algebraic, and geometrical calculations.

Abs

Returns a numeric value indicating the absolute value of a number.

Abs (n)

n – a numeric value to return the absolute value for.

```
Abs(-27.3)
```

returns 27.30.

Atn

Returns a numeric value (in radians) indicating the arctangent of the source number.

Atn (n)

n – a numeric value to return the arctangent of.

```
Atn(45)
```

returns 1.55.

Ceiling

Returns a numeric value rounded up to the nearest multiple (for positive numbers) or down to the nearest multiple (for negative numbers).

Ceiling (n)

n – a numeric value to round.

```
Ceiling(2.18)
```

returns 3.00.

```
Ceiling(-214.83481)
```

returns –215.00.

In the preceding examples, Ceiling rounds up (for positive numbers) or down (for negative numbers) to the nearest multiple of 1 (the next whole number up or down).

Ceiling (n1, n2)

n1 – a numeric value to round.
n2 – a whole or fractional value indicating the multiple to round *n1* to.

```
Ceiling (2.18, 2)
```

returns 4.00, as the next multiple of 2 above 2.18 is 4.

```
Ceiling(-214.83481, -.05)
```

returns –214.85, as the nearest multiple of .05 below a negative .83481 is negative .85. Note that a sign on *n2* is ignored, applying the multiple as an unsigned value.

Cos

Returns a numeric value indicating the cosine of the source number.

Cos (n)

n – a numeric value, in radians, to return the cosine of.

```
Cos(45)
```

returns .53.

Exp

Returns a numeric value indicating *e* (the base of the natural logarithm) raised to a power.

Exp (n)

n – a numeric value indicating the power to raise *e* to.

```
Exp(10)
```

returns 22,026.47 (*e* raised to the power of 10).

Floor

Returns a numeric value rounded down to the nearest multiple (for positive numbers) or up to the nearest multiple (for negative numbers).

Floor (n)

n – a numeric value to round.

```
Floor(2.18)
```

returns 2.00.

```
Floor(-214.83481)
```

returns –214.00.

In the preceding examples, Floor rounds down (for positive numbers) or up (for negative numbers) to the nearest multiple of 1 (the next whole number down or up).

Floor (n1, n2)

n1 – a numeric value to round.
n2 – a whole or fractional value indicating the multiple to round *n1* to.

```
Floor (2.18, 2)
```

returns 2.00, as the next multiple of 2 below 2.18 is 2.

```
Floor(-214.83481, -.05)
```

returns –214.80, as the nearest multiple of .05 above a negative .83481 is negative .80. Note that a sign on *n2* is ignored, applying the multiple as an unsigned value.

Int

Returns a numeric value indicating the integer portion of the supplied number.

Int (n)

n – a numeric value that you want to extract the integer portion of.

```
Int(3.574)
```

returns 3.00.

Log

Returns a numeric value indicating the logarithm of the supplied number.

Log (n)

n – a numeric value to return the logarithm of.

```
Log(22026.47)
```

returns 10.

MRound

Returns a numeric value rounded down to the nearest multiple (for positive numbers) or up to the nearest multiple (for negative numbers).

MRound (n)

n – a numeric value to round.

```
MRound (2.18)
```

returns 2.00.

```
MRound (-214.83481)
```

returns –215.00.

In the preceding examples, MRound rounds to the nearest multiple of 1 (the nearest whole number). In this one-argument permutation, MRound is identical to Round.

MRound (n1, n2)

n1 – a numeric value to round.
n2 – a whole or fractional value indicating the multiple to round *n1* to.

```
MRound (1.4, 3)
```

returns 0.00, as the nearest multiple of 3 to 1.4 is 0.

```
MRound (1.6, -3)
```

returns 3, as the nearest multiple of 3 to 1.6 is 3. Note that a sign on *n2* is ignored, applying the multiple as an unsigned value.

Pi

Returns the value of Pi (approximately 3.142).

Although this function appears as "Pi" in the Function tree, "crPi" will appear when you double-click the function name. If you type in the function yourself, type it as "crPi".

crPi

```
crPi
```

returns 3.142 (when formatted to show three decimal places).

Remainder

Returns a numeric value indicating the remainder of a division operation (not the quotient).

The Remainder function operates similar to the Mod arithmetic operator. Among other things, Remainder can be used with the RecordNumber function to shade every other line of a report in alternating colors.

Remainder (n1, n2)

n1 – a numeric value indicating the numerator of the division.
n2 – a numeric value indicating the denominator of the division.

```
Remainder (10,3)
```

returns 1.00 (the remainder of dividing 10 by 3).

```
If Remainder (RecordNumber, 2) = 0 Then
    crSilver
Else
    crNoColor
```

will shade every other details section silver if used as a conditional formatting formula for the details sections background color.

Rnd

Returns a numeric value between 0 and 1 represented as a random number.

Rnd may be helpful in situations where you wish to add a certain "randomness" to portions of your report. By multiplying Rnd by a larger number (10, 100, and so forth), you may get larger numbers that may be appropriate for other uses.

Rnd

Rnd (n)

n – a number to act as a "seed" to generate the random number.

```
Rnd
```

returns a different fractional number within each record and report refresh.

```
Rnd(Timer)
```

uses the Timer function to generate a "seed" number to increase "randomness" of the numbers returned.

Round

Returns a numeric value rounded to a specified number of decimal places.

Round (n)

n – a numeric value to be rounded to the nearest whole number.

Round (n1, n2)

n1 – a numeric value to be rounded.
n2 – a numeric value indicating the number of decimal places to round *n1* to.

```
Round (1.7821, 1)
```

returns 1.80.

RoundUp

Returns a numeric value rounded up to the next highest positive number, or next lowest negative number.

RoundUp is similar to Round, with the exception of always rounding up for positive numbers and down for negative numbers, regardless of how close to a lower number the number to be rounded may be. Also, when supplying a negative value as the second argument to RoundUp, rounding to the left of the decimal occurs.

RoundUp (n)

n – a numeric value to be rounded to the nearest whole number.

```
RoundUp (100.3)
```

returns 101.00.

```
RoundUp (-7.2)
```

returns –8.00.

RoundUp (n1, n2)

n1 – a numeric value to be rounded.
n2 – a numeric value indicating the number of decimal places to round *n1* to.

```
RoundUp (100.2512, 2)
```

returns 100.26.

```
RoundUp (100.2512, -3)
```

returns 1,000.00, as a negative number supplied to *n2* will round to the left of the decimal.

Sgn

Returns a numeric value indicating the sign of the supplied number.

Sgn returns –1 if the source number is negative, 0 if the source number is zero, and 1 if the source number is positive.

Sgn (n)

n – a numeric value to determine the sign of.

```
Sgn (-25)
```

returns –1.00.

Sin

Returns a numeric value indicating the sine of the supplied angle.

Sin (n)

n – a numeric value indicating the angle to calculate the sine of (in radians).

```
Sin(45)
```

returns .85.

Sqr

Returns a numeric value indicating the square root of the source number.

Sqr (n)

n – a numeric value to return the square root of.

```
Sqr (25)
```

returns 5.00.

Tan

Returns a numeric value indicating the tangent of the supplied angle.

Tan (n)

n – a numeric value indicating an angle (in radians).

```
Tan(45)
```

returns 1.62.

Truncate

Returns a numeric value indicating the source number truncated to a specified number of decimal places.

Truncate is similar to Round in that it removes decimal places. However, Truncate doesn't round the source number in the process—it simply removes the decimal places.

Truncate (n)

n – a numeric value to be truncated to zero decimal places.

Truncate (n1, n2)

n1 – a numeric value to be truncated.
n2 – a numeric value indicating the number of decimal places to truncate.

```
Truncate (1.489,1)
```

returns 1.40.

Functions: Print State

This category of functions exposes a variety of functions that generally pertain to the current state of the report when being formatted or printed. Some of these functions duplicate items found in the Special Fields category of the Field Explorer.

DrillDownGroupLevel

Returns a numeric value indicating how many group levels a viewer has drilled down into when viewing the report online (0 is returned if a viewer has not drilled down).

This function is very helpful when you need to determine where a viewer is in a drill-down hierarchy. You may use this function, for example, to suppress a group header if a viewer has drilled down to the group's first level (showing the series of just group headers and footers for the group). You will see a different DrillDownGroupLevel result and be able to show the group header when the viewer drills down to the next level where they're seeing details sections and just a single group header and footer.

DrillDownGroupLevel

```
DrillDownGroupLevel
```

returns 2.00 if the viewer has drilled into the second group.

```
DrillDownGroupLevel = 1
```

will suppress Group Header #1 when a viewer first drills down when placed in a conditional suppression formula for Group Header #1.

GroupNumber

Returns a numeric value indicating the sequential number of the group that is currently being displayed.

GroupNumber is helpful in various conditional formatting situations, such as conditionally setting a New Page Before property, or shading every other group footer. This function returns the same value as the GroupNumber special field.

GroupNumber

```
GroupNumber > 1
```

when used as a conditional New Page Before formula for Group Header #1, will not start a new page before the report's first group.

GroupSelection

Returns a string value indicating the Group Selection Formula.

This function returns the same information as the Group Selection Formula special field.

GroupSelection

```
GroupSelection
```

returns "Sum ({Orders.Order Amount}, {Orders.Customer ID}) > $15000.00" if a group selection formula is limited to groups on the report.

HierarchyLevel

Returns a numeric value indicating the hierarchy or "indentation" level of a hierarchical group.

HierarchyLevel, when used in conjunction with the GroupingLevel function (described elsewhere in this appendix), is helpful when controlling your own indentation with a formula-driven X position in the Object Size and Position dialog box.

APPENDIX

HierarchyLevel (n)

n – a numeric value indicating the number of the group that is organized hierarchically.

```
HierarchyLevel(GroupingLevel({Employee.Employee ID}))
```

returns 1.00 when the highest hierarchical group "indentation" is printing, returns 2.00 when the second hierarchical group "indentation" is printing, and so forth. This assumes that a hierarchical group based on Employee.Employe ID exists on the report.

InRepeatedGroupHeader

Returns a Boolean (true/false) value indicating whether or not the report is currently exposing a repeated group header.

InRepeatedGroupHeader is helpful when you wish to avoid resetting variables in a repeated group header, when you want to add a "continued" message, or similar conditional behavior.

InRepeatedGroupHeader

```
If Not InRepeatedGroupHeader Then
    NumberVar GroupTotal := 0
```

will reset the GroupTotal variable to 0 only if this is the first group header for the group.

IsNull

Returns a Boolean (true/false) value indicating if the supplied field contains a null value.

Null database values may not appear with all databases. Also, the setting of the Convert Null Database Fields To Default option (from File | Report Options or File | Options) affects whether null database values will exist or not.

IsNull (f)

f – any field name from a database table.

```
If IsNull ({Sales.Cust}) Then
    "No customer for this sale"
Else
    {Sales.Cust}
```

returns the string "No customer for this sale" if the field is null. Otherwise, it returns the field's value.

Next (Crystal Syntax only)

Returns the contents of the supplied field for the next database record.

Next (f)

f – any field name from a database table.

```
If {Sales.Cust} = Next({Sales.Cust}) Then
    {Sales.Cust} & " continues on next page"
```

compares the current customer name to the next customer name. If they're the same, the formula returns a "continues on next page" message.

NextIsNull

Returns a Boolean (true/false) value indicating if the supplied field in the next record contains a null value.

Null database values may not appear with all databases. Also, the setting of the Convert Null Database Fields To Default option (from File | Report Options or File | Options) affects whether null database values will exist or not.

NextIsNull (f)

f – any field name from a database table.

```
If NextIsNull ({Sales.Cust}) Then
   "Last order for " & {Sales.Cust}
```

returns a "last order" string if the next record's customer field is null (this assumes that the report is sorted on {Sales.Cust}).

NextValue (Basic Syntax only)

Returns the contents of the supplied field for the next database record.

This function is equivalent to Next. See **Next** for more information.

OnFirstRecord

Returns a Boolean (true/false) value indicating if the current record is the first record on the report.

OnFirstRecord is helpful for some conditional formatting requirements.

OnFirstRecord

```
Not OnFirstRecord
```

when used as a conditional formula for Group Header #1's New Page Before property, avoids a page break before the first group header on the report.

OnLastRecord

Returns a Boolean (true/false) value indicating if the current record is the last record on the report.

OnLastRecord is helpful for some conditional formatting requirements.

OnLastRecord

```
Not OnLastRecord
```

when used as a conditional formula for Group Footer #1's New Page After property, avoids a page break after the last group footer on the report.

PageNofM

Returns a string value indicating the current page number, followed by " of ", followed by the total number of report pages.

PageNofM returns the same string as the Page N of M special field.

PageNofM

```
PageNofM
```

returns "Page 3 of 20" if the current page being formatted is page 3 of a 20-page report.

PageNumber

Returns a numeric value indicating the current page being formatted or printed on the report.

PageNumber returns the same value as the Page Number special field.

PageNumber

```
PageNumber = 1
```

when supplied as a conditional formula for the Page Header Suppress property, will prevent the Page Header from being printed on the first page of the report.

Previous (Crystal Syntax only)

Returns the contents of the supplied field for the previous database record.

Previous (f)

f – any field name from a database table.

```
If {Sales.Cust} = Previous({Sales.Cust}) Then
    {Sales.Cust} & " continued from previous page"
```

compares the current customer name to the previous customer name. If they're the same, the formula returns a "continued from previous page" message.

PreviousIsNull

Returns a Boolean (true/false) value indicating if the supplied field in the previous record contains a null value.

Null database values may not appear with all databases. Also, the setting of the Convert Null Database Fields To Default option (from File | Report Options or File | Options) affects whether null database values will exist or not.

PreviousIsNull (f)

f – any field name from a database table.

```
If PreviousIsNull ({Sales.Cust}) Then
    "First order for " & {Sales.Cust}
```

returns a "first order" string if the previous record's customer field is null (this assumes that the report is sorted on {Sales.Cust}).

PreviousValue (Basic Syntax only)

Returns the contents of the supplied field for the previous database record.

This function is equivalent to Previous. See **Previous** for more information.

RecordNumber
Returns a numeric value indicating the sequential number of the current record.

RecordNumber can be used for certain conditional formatting situations. RecordNumber returns the same value as the Record Number special field.

RecordNumber

```
If RecordNumber Mod 2 = 0 Then
    crSilver
Else
    crNoColor
```

when supplied as a conditional formula to the Details section background color property, shades every other details section silver.

RecordSelection
Returns a string value containing the report's record selection formula.

RecordSelection returns the same value as the Record Selection Formula special field.

RecordSelection

```
RecordSelection
```

returns "{Sales.State} in ["MT", "ID", "WY", "CO"]" if a record selection formula has been created limiting the report to several states.

TotalPageCount
Returns a numeric value indicating the total number of pages on the report.

TotalPageCount returns the same value as the Total Page Count special field.

TotalPageCount

```
If PageNumber < TotalPageCount Then "report continues on next page"
```

prints a "report continues on next page" message if the report is not printing the last page.

nctions: Programming Shortcuts
This category of functions supplies shortcuts for other, more involved programming constructs (such as If-Then-Else or Select-Case).

Choose
Returns a value (the data type depends on function arguments) from the list of "choices."

Choose (n, c1, c2...)
n – a numeric value indicating which entry in the "choice" list to return.

c1 – the first entry in the choice list. *c1* can be any data type or a range value (arrays, however, aren't allowed).

c2 – the next entry in the choice list. It must be the same data type as *c1*. Additional choice entries can follow *c2*, each separated by a comma.

```
Choose(5,"January","February","March","April","May","June")
```

returns "May".

IIF

Returns a value (the data type depends on function arguments) based on the outcome of a conditional test.

IIF (e, v1, v2)

e – a Boolean expression using comparison operators or other Boolean logic. Returns True or False.

v1 – a value of any data type (excluding an array) indicating what the function returns if *e* is true.

v2 – a value of the same data type as *v1* indicating what the function returns if *e* is false.

```
IIF({Sales.Amount} > 5000,"Bonus Sale","Normal Sale")
```

returns the string "Bonus Sale" for sales over $5,000. Otherwise, returns the string "Normal Sale".

Switch

Returns a value (the data type depends on function arguments) based on the outcome of several conditional tests.

Switch (e1, v1, e2..., v2...)

e1 – a Boolean expression using comparison operators or other Boolean logic. Returns True or False.

v1 – a value of any data type (excluding an array) that's returned if *e1* evaluates to True.

e2 – a Boolean expression using comparison operators or other Boolean logic. Returns True or False.

v2 – a value of the same data type as *v1* that's returned if *e2* evaluates to True.

Additional pairs of expressions and values may be supplied. An equal number of expressions and values must be supplied.

```
Switch ({Sales.Amount} < 100, "Needs Improvement",
        {Sales.Amount} < 5000, "OK Sale",
        {Sales.Amount} < 7500, "Bonus Sale",
        True, "Fantastic Sale!")
```

returns a string value relating to the comparisons of the amount field. If the first three tests fail, the formula returns "Fantastic Sale".

nctions: Ranges

This category of functions test range values to determine if they contain a fixed lower or upper bound.

HasLowerBound

Returns a Boolean (true/false) value indicating whether the supplied range has a defined lower bound.

If you supply a range array to HasLowerBound, *every* element of the array must have a lower bound for HasLowerBound to return True.

HasLowerBound (r)

r – a range or range array.

```
If HasLowerBound ({?Order Amounts}) Then
    "Orders start at " & ToText(Minimum({?Order Amounts}))
```

returns "Orders start at 1,000.00" if the Order Amounts parameter field (defined as a range parameter field) has a lower bound of 1,000 specified.

HasUpperBound

Returns a Boolean (true/false) value indicating whether the supplied range has a defined upper bound.

If you supply a range array to HasUpperBound, *every* element of the array must have an upper bound for HasUpperBound to return True.

HasUpperBound (r)

r – a range or range array.

```
If HasUpperBound ({?Order Amounts}) Then
    "Orders end at " & ToText(Maximum({?Order Amounts}))
```

returns "Orders end at 5,000.00" if the Order Amounts parameter field (defined as a range parameter field) has an upper bound of 5,000 specified.

IncludesLowerBound

Returns a Boolean (true/false) value indicating whether the supplied range has a defined lower bound.

If you supply a range array to IncludesLowerBound, *any* element of the array may have a lower bound for IncludesLowerBound to return True.

IncludesLowerBound (r)

r – a range or range array.

```
If IncludesLowerBound ({?Order Amounts}) Then
    "Orders start at " & ToText(Minimum({?Order Amounts}))
```

returns "Orders start at 1,000.00" if the Order Amounts parameter field (defined as a range parameter field) has a lower bound of 1,000 specified.

IncludesUpperBound

Returns a Boolean (true/false) value indicating whether the supplied range has a defined upper bound.

If you supply a range array to IncludesUpperBound, *any* element of the array may have an upper bound for IncludesUpperBound to return True.

IncludesUpperBound (r)

r – a range or range array.

```
If IncludesUpperBound ({?Order Amounts}) Then
    "Orders end at " & ToText(Maximum({?Order Amounts}))
```

returns "Orders end at 5,000.00" if the Order Amounts parameter field (defined as a range parameter field) has an upper bound of 5,000 specified.

Functions: Strings

This category of functions allows manipulation or testing of string values, database fields, and other string formulas.

AscW

Returns a numeric value indicating the Unicode value of the first character of the supplied string.

AscW (s)

s – a string value.

```
AscW ("X")
```

returns 88.00 (the Unicode code for a capital X).

NOTE *AscW replaces Asc, which is still supported for backward compatibility. Asc behaves identically to AscW.*

ChrW

Returns a string value indicating the Unicode representation of the supplied number.

ChrW (n)

n – a whole number.

```
ChrW(88)
```

returns "X".

NOTE *ChrW replaces Chr, which is still supported for backward compatibility. Chr behaves identically to ChrW.*

Filter

Returns a string array containing only strings that match the search string.

Filter (sa, s)

sa – a string array containing one or more individual strings to search.

s – a string value to search *sa* for.

Filter (sa, s, b)

sa – a string array containing one or more individual strings to search.

s – a string value to search *sa* for.

b – a Boolean (true/false) value indicating whether the search should return partial matches. If True, partial string matches will be returned. If False, only complete matches will be returned.

Filter (sa, s, b, n)

sa – a string array containing one or more individual strings to search.

s – a string value to search *sa* for.

b – a Boolean (true/false) value indicating whether the search should return string matches or nonmatches. If True, strings that match *s* will be returned. If False, strings that *do not* match *s* will be returned.

n – a numeric value indicating whether the search is case-sensitive. 0 = case-sensitive search, 1 = not case-sensitive search.

```
StringVar Array Beatles := ["John","Paul","George","Ringo"];
Join (Filter(Beatles,"o"))
```

returns "John George Ringo" (the Join function concatenates the three elements of the Beatles string array that contain the letter *o*).

InStr

Returns a numeric value indicating the first position in the source string where the search string appears.

InStr (s1, s2)

s1 – a string value indicating the source string to search.

s2 – a string value indicating the string to search for in *s1*.

InStr (n, s1, s2)

n – a numeric value indicating the position in *s1* to start searching for *s2*.

s1 – a string value indicating the source string to search.

s2 – a string value indicating the string to search for in *s1*.

InStr (s1, s2, n)

s1 – a string value indicating the source string to search.

s2 – a string value indicating the string to search for in *s1*.

n – a numeric value indicating whether the search is case-sensitive: 0 = case-sensitive, 1 = not case-sensitive.

APPENDIX

InStr (n1, s1, s2, n2)

n1 – a numeric value indicating the position in *s1* to start searching for *s2*.
s1 – a string value indicating the source string to search.
s2 – a string value indicating the string to search for in *s1*.
n2 – a numeric value indicating whether the search is case-sensitive: 0 = case-sensitive,
1 = not case-sensitive.

```
Instr("The rain in Spain falls on the plain","spain")
```

returns 0.00 (the search is case-sensitive).

```
Instr("The rain in Spain falls on the plain","spain",1)
```

returns 13.00 (the search is not case-sensitive).

InStrRev

**Returns a numeric value indicating the last position in the source string where the search
string appears.**

In essence, InStrRev starts searching for the substring from right to left.

InStrRev (s1, s2)

s1 – a string value indicating the source string to search.
s2 – a string value indicating the string to search for in *s1*.

InStrRev (s1, s2, n)

s1 – a string value indicating the source string to search.
s2 – a string value indicating the string to search for in *s1*.
n – a numeric value indicating the position from the right of *s1* to start searching for *s2*.

InStrRev (s1, s2, n1, n2)

s1 – a string value indicating the source string to search.
s2 – a string value indicating the string to search for in *s1*.
n1 – a numeric value indicating the position from the right of *s1* to start searching for *s2*.
n2 – a numeric value indicating whether the search is case-sensitive: 0 = case-sensitive,
1 = not case-sensitive.

```
InstrRev("The rain in Spain falls on the plain","a",25)
```

returns 20.00 (the search starts at position 25 and proceeds left—finding a lowercase *a* at
position 20).

Join

**Returns a string value consisting of all the elements of the source string array concatenated
together.**

Join is helpful for, among other things, displaying all the values entered into a multivalue
string parameter field in a single formula.

Join (a)
a – a string array.

Join (a, s)
a – a string array.
s – a string value to act as a "delimiter"; it will be inserted between each array element in the output string.

```
Join({?States Chosen},", ")
```

returns "CO, WY, MT, UT" if the four states were supplied to the multivalue States Chosen parameter field.

Left
Returns a string value indicating a limited number of characters extracted from the left side of the source string.

Left (s, n)
s – a string value used as the source string.
n – a numeric value indicating how many characters to extract from *s*.

```
Left ("George", 3)
```

returns "Geo".

Length
Returns a numeric value indicating how many characters are contained in the source string.
    Len is functionally equivalent to Length.

Length (s)
s – a string value.

```
Length ("George")
```

returns 6.00.

LowerCase
Returns a string value indicating a lowercase representation of the source string.
    LCase is functionally equivalent to LowerCase.

LowerCase (s)
s – a string value to be converted to lowercase.

```
LowerCase ("George Peck")
```

returns "george peck".

Mid

Returns a string value indicating a substring extracted from the source string.

Mid (s, n)

s – a string value to extract characters from.
n – a numeric value indicating the position to begin the extraction from *s*.

Mid (s, n1, n2)

s – a string value to extract characters from.
n1 – a numeric value indicating the position to begin the extraction from *s*.
n2 – a numeric value indicating how many characters to extract.

```
Mid("George Peck",8,3)
```

returns "Pec".

NumericText

Returns a Boolean (true/false) value indicating whether or not the source string contains only numeric characters.

NumericText is helpful for testing the contents of a string value before converting it with the ToNumber function, as ToNumber will fail if it encounters any nonnumeric characters.

NumericText (s)

s – a string value to test for numeric content.

```
If NumericText ({FromMainframe.SalesAmount}) Then
   ToNumber({FromMainframe.SalesAmount}) * 1.1
Else
   0
```

checks that the SalesAmount string field contains only numeric values before converting it to a number with the ToNumber function.

ProperCase

Returns a string value converted so that the first character, and any character immediately appearing after a space or nonalphanumeric character, will appear in uppercase. The remaining characters will appear in lowercase.

This function is very helpful when encountering proper names, such as first and last names, that are stored in a database in all uppercase characters.

ProperCase (s)

s – a string value.

```
ProperCase("GEORGE PECK,JR.")
```

returns "George Peck,Jr."

Replace

Returns a string value where a certain set of characters have been replaced by another set of characters.

Replace (s1, s2, s3)
s1 – the source string to search.
s2 – the characters to search *s1* for.
s3 – the characters to replace *s2* with in *s1*.

Replace (s1, s2, s3, n)
s1 – the source string to search.
s2 – the characters to search *s1* for.
s3 – the characters to replace *s2* with in *s1*.
n – a numeric value indicating the position in *s1* to start searching for *s2*.

Replace (s1, s2, s3, n1, n2)
s1 – the source string to search.
s2 – the characters to search *s1* for.
s3 – the characters to replace *s2* with in *s1*.
n1 – a numeric value indicating the position in *s1* to start searching for *s2*.
n2 – a numeric value indicating the number of replacements to make.

Replace (s1, s2, s3, n1, n2, n3)
s1 – the source string to search.
s2 – the characters to search *s1* for.
s3 – the characters to replace *s2* with in *s1*.
n1 – a numeric value indicating the position in *s1* to start searching for *s2*.
n2 – a numeric value indicating the number of replacements to make.
n3 – a numeric value indicating whether the search is case-sensitive: 0 = case-sensitive, 1 = not case-sensitive.

```
Replace("George Peck","George","Gregory")
```

returns "Gregory Peck".

ReplicateString

Returns a string value consisting of multiple duplications of a source string.

ReplicateString (s, n)
s – the source string to duplicate.
n – a numeric value indicating how many duplications of *s* to make.

```
ReplicateString ("*", 15)
```

returns "***************".

Right

Returns a string value indicating a limited number of characters extracted from the right side of the source string.

Right (s, n)

s – a string value used as the source string.
n – a numeric value indicating how many characters to extract from *s*.

```
Right ("George", 3)
```

returns "rge".

Roman

Returns a string value expressing the supplied numeric argument as a Roman numeral value.

Roman (n)

n – a numeric value to convert to Roman numerals.

Roman (n1, n2)

n1 – a numeric value to convert to Roman numerals.
n2 – a numeric value indicating the type of Roman numeral to return; 0 = Classic; 1, 2, or 3 = various levels of precision; 4 = simplified.

```
Roman (1998)
```

returns "MCMXCVIII".

```
Roman (1998, 2)
```

returns "MXMVIII".

NOTE *The best way to explore the various precision choices is to simply try them.*

Space

Returns a string value consisting of a specified number of spaces.

Space (n)

n – the number of space characters to duplicate.

```
"George" & Space(10) & "Peck"
```

returns "George   Peck".

Split

Returns a string array consisting of elements built from the supplied individual strings.

Split (s)

s – a string containing one or more individual strings separated by spaces.

Split (s1, s2)

s1 – a string containing one or more individual strings separated by the delimiter specified in *s2*.

s2 – a string value indicating the delimiter that separates individual values in *s1*.

Split (s1, s2, n)

s1 – a string containing one or more individual strings separated by the delimiter specified in *s2*.

s2 – a string value indicating the delimiter that separates individual values in *s1*.

n – a numeric value indicating how many elements should be placed in the array.

Split (s1, s2, n1, n2)

s1 – a string containing one or more individual strings separated by the delimiter specified in *s2*.

s2 – a string value indicating the delimiter that separates individual values in *s1*.

n1 – a numeric value indicating how many elements should be placed in the array (–1 for all).

n2 – a numeric value indicating how to treat the search for the delimiter. 0 = search is case-sensitive, 1 = search is not case-sensitive.

```
Split("John Paul George Ringo")[2]
```

returns "Paul".

```
Split("John And Paul And George And Ringo","and",-1,0)[1]
```

returns "John And Paul And George And Ringo", as only one element was added the array—the delimiter search is case-sensitive and "And" is not found.

```
Split("John And Paul And George And Ringo","and",-1,1)[1]
```

returns "John"—the delimiter search is not case-sensitive.

StrCmp

Returns a numeric value indicating how two strings compare alphabetically.

StrCmp returns –1 if the first string is less than the second string, 0 if the strings are equal, and 1 if the first string is greater than the second string.

StrCmp (s1, s2)

s1 – the first string to compare.
s2 – the string to compare to *s1*.

StrCmp (s1, s2, n)

s1 – the first string to compare.
s2 – the string to compare to *s1*.
n – a numeric value indicating how to treat the search for the delimiter. 0 = search is case-sensitive, 1 = search is not case-sensitive.

```
StrCmp ("abc","xyz")
```

returns –1.00.

StrReverse

Returns a string value consisting of the source string in reverse order.

StrReverse (s)

s – a string value to be reversed.

```
StrReverse ("George Peck")
```

returns "kceP egroeG".

ToNumber

Returns a numeric value indicating a numeric conversion of another nonnumeric value.

ToNumber converts other numeric and Boolean values, as well as string values, to numbers. ToNumber is functionally equivalent to CDbl and Val.

ToNumber (v)

v – a numeric, string, or Boolean value to be converted to a number.

```
ToNumber ("5642.15")
```

returns 5,642.15 as a number.

NOTE *You may wish to test the value to convert with NumericText before you supply it to ToNumber, as ToNumber will fail if a string is supplied that doesn't contain all numeric values. If you wish to avoid the test, you may use Val, which will always return a result (perhaps 0), even if the supplied argument isn't numeric.*

ToText

Converts any nonstring data type to a string value.

ToText is an immensely valuable function used to convert any nonstring data type to a string. You'll often use ToText within a string formula to concatenate various types of data items into a single string result.

ToText (b)

b – a Boolean (true/false) value to be converted to a string.

```
ToText({Orders.Shipped})
```

returns the string "True" if the Boolean Shipped field holds a true value or "False" if the field is false.

ToText (n1, n2, s1, s2)

n1 – a numeric value to be converted to a string.
n2 – a numeric value indicating the number of decimal places to use when converting *n1*. This argument is optional.
s1 – a string value indicating the character or characters to use as a thousands separator when converting *n1*. This argument is optional.

s2 – a string value indicating the character or characters to use as a decimal separator when converting *n1*. This argument is optional.

```
ToText(21256.1255, 2, ",", "-")
```

returns the string "21,256-13" (showing two decimal places, a comma thousands separator, and a dash decimal separator).

ToText (n1, n2, s1, s2, s3)

n1 – a numeric value to be converted to a string.
s1 – a string value used to format the number. This argument is optional.
n2 – a numeric value indicating the number of decimal places to use when converting *n1*. This argument is optional.
s2 – a string value indicating the character or characters to use as a thousands separator when converting *n*. This argument is optional.
s3 – a string value indicating the character or characters to use as a decimal separator when converting *n*. This argument is optional.

```
ToText(21256.1255, "#,###,###.00000",2)
```

returns " 21,256.13000" (with leading spaces for extra # characters).

Numeric Formatting Strings

Character	Usage
#	Numeric placeholder. A single numeric character will be placed in each occurrence of #. If there are more # characters than numeric digits, leading or trailing spaces will be added for extra # characters.
0 (zero)	Numeric placeholder. A single numeric character will be placed in each occurrence of 0. If there are more 0 characters than numeric digits, leading or trailing zeros will be added for extra 0 characters.
, (comma)	Thousands separator. Indicates where the thousands separator should be placed in the resulting string. The thousands separator used is taken from a Windows default or the s2 argument.
. (period)	Decimal separator. Indicates where the decimal separator should be placed in the resulting string. The decimal separator used is taken from a Windows default or the s2 argument.

ToText (d, s1, s2, s3)

d – a date, time, or date/time value.
s1 – a string value used to format the date, time, or date/time value. This argument is optional.
s2 – a string value used as a replacement label for "a.m." for morning hours. This argument is optional.
s3 – a string value used as a replacement label for "p.m." for afternoon/evening hours. This argument is optional.

```
ToText(CurrentDate, "dddd M d, yyyy")
```

returns "Friday May 9, 2003" if CurrentDate contains May 9, 2003.

```
ToText(CurrentTime, "h:mm tt",
"in the morning", "in the afternoon")
```

returns the string " 4:27 in the afternoon" if CurrentTime is 4:27 P.M.

NOTE *Any nonrecognized characters in the format string will be returned as a literal character. For example, a slash (/) or comma (,) in the format string will simply display within the resulting date string.*

Date/Time Formatting Strings

Character	Usage
M	Month number without a leading zero for single-character month
MM	Month number with a leading zero for single-character month
MMM	Month name as a three-letter abbreviation
MMMM	Month name fully spelled
D	Day of month without a leading zero for single-character day
Dd	Day of month with a leading zero for single-character day
Ddd	Day of week name spelled as a three-letter abbreviation
Dddd	Day of week name fully spelled
Yy	Last two characters of year
Yyyy	Full four-character year
H	Hours without a leading zero for a single-character hour (12-hour nonmilitary format)
Hh	Hours with a leading zero for a single-character hour (12-hour nonmilitary format)
H	Hours without a leading zero for a single-character hour (24-hour military format)
HH	Hours with a leading zero for a single-character hour (24-hour military format)
m	Minutes without a leading zero for a single-character minute
Mm	Minutes with a leading zero for a single-character minute
S	Seconds without a leading zero for a single-character second
Ss	Seconds with a leading zero for a single-character second
T	Single-character uppercase A or P (for A.M. or P.M.)
Tt	Multiple-character uppercase AM or PM (for A.M. or P.M.)

NOTE *CStr is functionally equivalent to ToText. It is provided to maintain compatibility with Basic syntax.*

ToWords

Returns a string value indicating the "spelled out" version of the numeric argument.
ToWords is often used to print checks, but can also be used when required to convert numeric values to text for other situations. For example, ToWords will be helpful if you are required to create a formula, based on numeric data, that returns the string "This contract expires in 30 (thirty) days".

ToWords (n)
n – a numeric value to spell as words.

```
ToWords (1145.31)
```

returns the string "one thousand one hundred forty-five and 31 / 100".

ToWords (n1, n2)
n1 – a numeric value to spell as words.
n2 – a numeric value indicating the number of decimal places to use when converting *n1*.

```
ToWords (100, 0)
```

returns the string "one hundred".

NOTE   *An optional third numeric argument specifying the form type can be supplied. Allowable values for the form type argument are numeric and can be 0 (Classic or Check form), 1 (Daily form), or 2 (Casual form). This argument applies only to Asian language versions of Crystal Reports.*

Trim

Returns a string value consisting of the source string with all leading and trailing spaces removed.

Trim (s)
s – a string value.

```
Trim ("    Leading and trailing spaces    ")
```

returns the string "Leading and trailing spaces" with no extra spaces before or after the string.

TrimLeft

Returns a string value consisting of the source string with all leading spaces removed.
LTrim is functionally equivalent to TrimLeft.

TrimLeft (s)
s – a string value.

```
TrimLeft ("    Leading and trailing spaces    ")
```

returns the string "Leading and trailing spaces   " with no extra spaces before the string, but with any trailing spaces remaining.

TrimRight

Returns a string value consisting of the source string with all trailing spaces removed.
    RTrim is functionally equivalent to TrimRight.

TrimRight (s)
s – a string value.

```
TrimRight ("    Leading and trailing spaces    ")
```

returns the string "   Leading and trailing spaces" with no extra spaces after the string, but with any leading spaces remaining.

UpperCase

Returns a string value indicating an uppercase representation of the source string.
    UCase is functionally equivalent to UpperCase.

UpperCase (s)
s – a string value to be converted to uppercase.

```
UpperCase ("George Peck")
```

returns "GEORGE PECK".

URLDecode

Returns a string with specially defined URL characters converted to readable form.

URLDecode (s)
s – a string to apply URL decoding to.

```
URLDecode("http://www.AblazeGroup.%63%6F%6D")
```

returns http://www.AblazeGroup.com, converting the encoded last three characters to text.

URLDecode (s, n)
s – a string to apply URL decoding to.
n – an integer value indicating what encoding scheme is used in *s*. Allowable values are 0 for RFC 1738 standards (the default), 1 for application/x-www-form-urlencoded standards, and 2 for user-defined encoding (alphanumeric characters are returned as supplied, while other characters are interpreted as coded characters).

```
URLDecode("http://www.AblazeGroup.com/Crystal+Reports.htm", 1)
```

returns http://www.AblazeGroup.com/Crystal Reports.htm (converting the encoded plus sign to a space).

URLDecode (s, n1, n2)
s – a string to apply URL decoding to.
n1 – an integer value indicating what encoding scheme is used in *s*. Allowable values are 0 for RFC 1738 standards (the default), 1 for application/x-www-form-urlencoded standards,

and 2 for user-defined encoding (alphanumeric characters are returned as supplied, while other characters are interpreted as coded characters).

n2 – an integer value indicating the character set, or codepage, to use when interpreting *s*. Allowable values are 0 for UTF-8 (the default), 1 for ISO-8859, and 2 for Shift-JIS.

URLEncode

Returns a string value containing coded characters that are required for certain web browser URL encoding.

This function may come in handy when you need to use hyperlinks within your reports. In order to allow web browsers to fully interpret hyperlink URLs with special characters (such as spaces, hyphens, etc.), you may need to encode the initial hyperlink string with URLEncode.

URLEncode (s)

s – a string value to be encoded into a URL-confirming string.

URLEncode (s, n)

s – a string value to be encoded into a URL-confirming string.

n – an integer value indicating what encoding scheme to use when encoding *s*. Allowable values are 0 for RFC 1738 standards (the default), 1 for application/x-www-form-urlencoded standards, and 2 for user-defined encoding (alphanumeric characters are returned as supplied, while other characters are interpreted as coded characters).

URLEncode (s1, n, s2)

s1 – a string value to be encoded into a URL-confirming string.

n – an integer value indicating what encoding scheme to use when encoding *s*. Allowable values are 0 for RFC 1738 standards (the default), 1 for application/x-www-form-urlencoded standards, and 2 for user-defined encoding (alphanumeric characters are returned as supplied, while other characters are interpreted as coded characters).

s2 – a string value indicating characters to never encode when converting *s* (the default is an empty string).

URLEncode (s1, n, s2, s3)

s1 – a string value to be encoded into a URL-confirming string.

n – an integer value indicating what encoding scheme to use when encoding *s*. Allowable values are 0 for RFC 1738 standards (the default), 1 for application/x-www-form-urlencoded standards, and 2 for user-defined encoding (alphanumeric characters are returned as supplied, while other characters are interpreted as coded characters).

s2 – a string value indicating characters to never encode when converting *s* (the default is an empty string).

s3 – a string value indicating characters to always encode when converting *s* (the default is an empty string).

URLEncode (s, n1, n2)

s – a string value to be encoded into a URL-confirming string.

n1 – an integer value indicating what encoding scheme to use when encoding *s*. Allowable values are 0 for RFC 1738 standards (the default), 1 for application/x-www-form-urlencoded standards, and 2 for user-defined encoding (alphanumeric characters are returned as supplied, while other characters are interpreted as coded characters).

n2 – an integer value indicating the character set, or codepage, to use when encoding *s*. Allowable values are 0 for UTF-8 (the default), 1 for ISO-8859, and 2 for Shift-JIS.

URLEncode (s1, n1, n2, s2)

s1 – a string value to be encoded into a URL-confirming string.

n1 – an integer value indicating what encoding scheme to use when encoding *s*. Allowable values are 0 for RFC 1738 standards (the default), 1 for application/x-www-form-urlencoded standards, and 2 for user-defined encoding (alphanumeric characters are returned as supplied, while other characters are interpreted as coded characters).

n2 – an integer value indicating the character set, or codepage, to use when encoding *s*. Allowable values are 0 for UTF-8 (the default), 1 for ISO-8859, and 2 for Shift-JIS.

s2 – a string value indicating characters to never encode when converting *s* (the default is an empty string).

URLEncode (s1, n1, n2, s2, s3)

s1 – a string value to be encoded into a URL-confirming string.

n1 – an integer value indicating what encoding scheme to use when encoding *s*. Allowable values are 0 for RFC 1738 standards (the default), 1 for application/x-www-form-urlencoded standards, and 2 for user-defined encoding (alphanumeric characters are returned as supplied, while other characters are interpreted as coded characters).

n2 – an integer value indicating the character set, or codepage, to use when encoding *s*. Allowable values are 0 for UTF-8 (the default), 1 for ISO-8859, and 2 for Shift-JIS.

s2 – a string value indicating characters to never encode when converting *s* (the default is an empty string).

s3 – a string value indicating characters to always encode when converting *s* (the default is an empty string).

```
URLEncode("http://www.AblazeGroup.com/Crystal Reports.htm")
```

returns http://www.AblazeGroup.com/Crystal%20Reports.htm, converting the space to a 20 encoded string.

```
URLEncode("http://www.AblazeGroup.com",0,"","com")
```

returns http://www.AblazeGr%6Fup.%63%6F%6D, encoding any occurrence of the characters *c*, *o*, or *m*.

Val

Returns a numeric value indicating the numeric portion of the supplied string.

Val is helpful for converting string database fields that contain numeric data to actual numeric values. In particular, Val will not return an error if it encounters a nonnumeric character in the string—it will simply stop the conversion at that point.

Val (s)

s – a string value to be converted to a number.

```
Val ("12500.1a31")
```

returns 12,500.10 as a numeric value.

ctions: Summary

This category of functions largely duplicates summary functions available via the Insert I Summary option from the Crystal Reports pull-down menus. By using these summary functions, you may include the same summary calculations available from the Insert I Summary option in formulas. In fact, if you add a report summary to a report with Insert I Summary and then double-click it in the Fields tree of the Formula Editor, the following summary functions will be inserted in your report automatically.

Average

Returns a numeric value indicating the average of the supplied database field or formula.

Average (f)

f – the database or formula field to summarize for the entire report. This must be a numeric field.

Average (f1, f2)

f1 – the database or formula field to summarize for a report group. This must be a numeric field.
f2 – the database or formula field indicating the group you wish to summarize for. An existing group on the report must be based on this field.

Average (f1, f2, s)

f1 – the database or formula field to summarize for a report group. This must be a numeric field.
f2 – the database or formula field indicating the group you wish to summarize for. An existing group on the report must be based on this field.
s – a string value indicating how often to "change" the summary for Boolean, date, or date-time grouping. See **Boolean Conditions**, **Date Conditions**, and **Time Conditions** later in this appendix for available choices.

```
Average({Sales.Amount})
```

returns the average of sales amounts for the entire report.

```
Average({Sales.Amount}, {Sales.Date}, "monthly")
```

returns the average of sales amounts for the sales date group, summarized for each month.

Correlation

Returns a numeric value indicating the correlation between the supplied database fields or formulas.

Correlation (f1, f2)

f1 – the first database or formula field to summarize for the entire report. This must be a numeric field.
f2 – the second database or formula field to summarize for the entire report. This must be a numeric field.

Correlation (f1, f2, f3)

f1 – the first database or formula field to summarize for the entire report. This must be a numeric field.

f2 – the second database or formula field to summarize for the entire report. This must be a numeric field.

f3 – the database or formula field indicating the group you wish to summarize for. An existing group on the report must be based on this field.

Correlation (f1, f2, f3, s)

f1 – the first database or formula field to summarize for the entire report. This must be a numeric field.

f2 – the second database or formula field to summarize for the entire report. This must be a numeric field.

f3 – the database or formula field indicating the group you wish to summarize for. An existing group on the report must be based on this field.

s – a string value indicating how often to "change" the summary for Boolean, date, or date-time grouping. See **Boolean Conditions**, **Date Conditions**, and **Time Conditions** later in this appendix for available choices.

```
Correlation({Sales.Amount}, {Sales.Goal})
```

returns the correlation between sales amount and sales goal for the entire report.

```
Correlation({Sales.Amount}, {Sales.Goal}, {Sales.Date}, "monthly")
```

returns the correlation between sales amount and sales goal for the sales date group, summarized for each month.

Count

Returns a numeric value indicating the number of occurrences (count) of the supplied database field or formula.

Count (f)

f – the database or formula field to summarize for the entire report.

Count (f1, f2)

f1 – the database or formula field to summarize for a report group.

f2 – the database or formula field indicating the group you wish to summarize for. An existing group on the report must be based on this field.

Count (f1, f2, s)

f1 – the database or formula field to summarize for a report group.

f2 – the database or formula field indicating the group you wish to summarize for. An existing group on the report must be based on this field.

s – a string value indicating how often to "change" the summary for Boolean, date, or date-time grouping. See **Boolean Conditions**, **Date Conditions**, and **Time Conditions** later in this appendix for available choices.

```
Count({Sales.Amount})
```

returns the count of sales amounts for the entire report (in essence, this is the number of records on the report).

```
Count({Sales.Amount}, {Sales.Date}, "monthly")
```

returns the count of sales amounts for the sales date group, summarized for each month (in essence, this is the number of records in the group).

NOTE *The Count function will count every record where the supplied field contains a nonnull value. If any occurrences of the supplied field contain null values, those records won't increment the count.*

Covariance

Returns a numeric value indicating the covariance between the supplied database fields or formulas.

Covariance (f1, f2)

f1 – the first database or formula field to summarize for the entire report. This must be a numeric field.
f2 – the second database or formula field to summarize for the entire report. This must be a numeric field.

Covariance (f1, f2, f3)

f1 – the first database or formula field to summarize for the entire report. This must be a numeric field.
f2 – the second database or formula field to summarize for the entire report. This must be a numeric field.
f3 – the database or formula field indicating the group you wish to summarize for. An existing group on the report must be based on this field.

Covariance (f1, f2, f3, s)

f1 – the first database or formula field to summarize for the entire report. This must be a numeric field.
f2 – the second database or formula field to summarize for the entire report. This must be a numeric field.
f3 – the database or formula field indicating the group you wish to summarize for. An existing group on the report must be based on this field.
s – a string value indicating how often to "change" the summary for Boolean, date, or date-time grouping. See **Boolean Conditions**, **Date Conditions**, and **Time Conditions** later in this appendix for available choices.

```
Covariance({Sales.Amount}, {Sales.Goal})
```

returns the covariance between sales amount and sales goal for the entire report.

```
Covariance({Sales.Amount}, {Sales.Goal}, {Sales.Date}, "monthly")
```

returns the covariance between sales amount and sales goal for the sales date group, summarized for each month.

DistinctCount

Returns a numeric value indicating the unique number of occurrences (distinct count) of the supplied database field or formula.

DistinctCount (f)

f – the database or formula field to summarize for the entire report.

DistinctCount (f1, f2)

f1 – the database or formula field to summarize for a report group.
f2 – the database or formula field indicating the group you wish to summarize for. An existing group on the report must be based on this field.

DistinctCount (f1, f2, s)

f1 – the database or formula field to summarize for a report group.
f2 – the database or formula field indicating the group you wish to summarize for. An existing group on the report must be based on this field.
s – a string value indicating how often to "change" the summary for Boolean, date, or date-time grouping. See **Boolean Conditions**, **Date Conditions**, and **Time Conditions** later in this appendix for available choices.

```
Distinctcount({Sales.Acct#})
```

returns the number of unique accounts for the entire report.

```
Distinctcount({Sales.Acct#}, {Sales.Date}, "monthly")
```

returns the number of unique accounts for the sales date group, summarized for each month.

Maximum

Returns a numeric value indicating the maximum of the supplied database field or formula.

Maximum returns the largest number, the latest date, or the string value last in the alphabet.

Maximum (f)

f – the database or formula field to summarize for the entire report.

Maximum (f1, f2)

f1 – the database or formula field to summarize for a report group.
f2 – the database or formula field indicating the group you wish to summarize for. An existing group on the report must be based on this field.

Maximum (f1, f2, s)

f1 – the database or formula field to summarize for a report group.
f2 – the database or formula field indicating the group you wish to summarize for. An existing group on the report must be based on this field.

s – a string value indicating how often to "change" the summary for Boolean, date, or date-time grouping. See **Boolean Conditions**, **Date Conditions**, and **Time Conditions** later in this appendix for available choices.

```
Maximum({Sales.Amount})
```

returns the highest sales amount for the entire report.

```
Maximum({Sales.Amount}, {Sales.Date}, "monthly")
```

returns the highest sales amount for the sales date group, summarized for each month.

Median

Returns a numeric value indicating the median of the supplied database field or formula.

Median (f)

f – the database or formula field to summarize for the entire report. This must be a numeric field.

Median (f1, f2)

f1 – the database or formula field to summarize for a report group. This must be a numeric field.
f2 – the database or formula field indicating the group you wish to summarize for. An existing group on the report must be based on this field.

Median (f1, f2, s)

f1 – the database or formula field to summarize for a report group. This must be a numeric field.
f2 – the database or formula field indicating the group you wish to summarize for. An existing group on the report must be based on this field.
s – a string value indicating how often to "change" the summary for Boolean, date, or date-time grouping. See **Boolean Conditions**, **Date Conditions**, and **Time Conditions** later in this appendix for available choices.

```
Median({Sales.Amount})
```

returns the median of sales amounts for the entire report.

```
Median({Sales.Amount}, {Sales.Date}, "monthly")
```

returns the median of sales amounts for the sales date group, summarized for each month.

Minimum

Returns a numeric value indicating the minimum of the supplied database field or formula.
Minimum returns the smallest number, the earliest date, or the string value first in the alphabet.

Minimum (f)

f – the database or formula field to summarize for the entire report.

Minimum (f1, f2)

f1 – the database or formula field to summarize for a report group.
f2 – the database or formula field indicating the group you wish to summarize for. An existing group on the report must be based on this field.

Minimum (f1, f2, s)

f1 – the database or formula field to summarize for a report group.
f2 – the database or formula field indicating the group you wish to summarize for. An existing group on the report must be based on this field.
s – a string value indicating how often to "change" the summary for Boolean, date, or date-time grouping. See **Boolean Conditions**, **Date Conditions**, and **Time Conditions** later in this appendix for available choices.

```
Minimum({Sales.Amount})
```

returns the lowest sales amount for the entire report.

```
Minimum({Sales.Amount}, {Sales.Date}, "monthly")
```

returns the lowest sales amount for the sales date group, summarized for each month.

Mode

Returns a numeric value indicating the mode (the most frequently occurring value) of the supplied database field or formula.

Mode (f)

f – the database or formula field to summarize for the entire report.

Mode (f1, f2)

f1 – the database or formula field to summarize for a report group.
f2 – the database or formula field indicating the group you wish to summarize for. An existing group on the report must be based on this field.

Mode (f1, f2, s)

f1 – the database or formula field to summarize for a report group.
f2 – the database or formula field indicating the group you wish to summarize for. An existing group on the report must be based on this field.
s – a string value indicating how often to "change" the summary for Boolean, date, or date-time grouping. See **Boolean Conditions**, **Date Conditions**, and **Time Conditions** later in this appendix for available choices.

```
Mode({Sales.Acct#})
```

returns the most frequently appearing account number for the entire report.

```
Mode({Sales.Acct#}, {Sales.Date}, "monthly")
```

returns the most frequently appearing account number for the sales date group, summarized for each month.

NthLargest

Returns a numeric value indicating the *n*th largest occurrence of the supplied database field or formula.

NthLargest returns the "*nth*" largest number, the "*nth*" latest date, or the "*nth*" string value last in the ASCII sort order.

NthLargest (n, f)

n – a numeric value (between 1 and 100). 5 returns the fifth largest, 2 the second largest, and so forth.

f – the database or formula field to summarize for the entire report.

NthLargest (n, f1, f2)

n – a numeric value (between 1 and 100). 5 returns the fifth largest, 2 the second largest, and so forth.

f1 – the database or formula field to summarize for a report group.

f2 – the database or formula field indicating the group you wish to summarize for. An existing group on the report must be based on this field.

NthLargest (n, f1, f2, s)

n – a numeric value (between 1 and 100). 5 returns the fifth largest, 2 the second largest, and so forth.

f1 – the database or formula field to summarize for a report group.

f2 – the database or formula field indicating the group you wish to summarize for. An existing group on the report must be based on this field.

s – a string value indicating how often to "change" the summary for Boolean, date, or date-time grouping. See **Boolean Conditions**, **Date Conditions**, and **Time Conditions** later in this appendix for available choices.

```
NthLargest(5, {Sales.Amount})
```

returns the fifth largest sales amount for the entire report.

```
NthLargest(5, {Sales.Amount}, {Sales.Date}, "monthly")
```

returns the fifth largest sales amount for the sales date group, summarized for each month.

NthMostFrequent

Returns a numeric value indicating the *n*th most frequent occurrence of the supplied database field or formula.

NthMostFrequent (n, f)

n – a numeric value (between 1 and 100). 5 returns the fifth most frequent, 2 the second most frequent, and so forth.

f – the database or formula field to summarize for the entire report.

NthMostFrequent (n, f1, f2)

n – a numeric value (between 1 and 100). 5 returns the fifth most frequent, 2 the second most frequent, and so forth.

f1 – the database or formula field to summarize for a report group.

APPENDIX

f2 – the database or formula field indicating the group you wish to summarize for. An existing group on the report must be based on this field.

NthMostFrequent (n, f1, f2, s)

n – a numeric value (between 1 and 100). 5 returns the fifth most frequent, 2 the second most frequent, and so forth.

f1 – the database or formula field to summarize for a report group.

f2 – the database or formula field indicating the group you wish to summarize for. An existing group on the report must be based on this field.

s – a string value indicating how often to "change" the summary for Boolean, date, or date-time grouping. See **Boolean Conditions**, **Date Conditions**, and **Time Conditions** later in this appendix for available choices.

```
NthMostFrequent(5, {Sales.Acct#})
```

returns the fifth most frequently occurring account number for the entire report.

```
NthMostFrequent(5, {Sales.Acct#}, {Sales.Date}, "monthly")
```

returns the fifth most frequently occurring account number for the sales date group, summarized for each month.

NthSmallest

Returns a numeric value indicating the *n*th smallest occurrence of the supplied database field or formula.

NthSmallest returns the "nth" smallest number, the "nth" earliest date, or the "nth" string value first in the ASCII sort order.

NthSmallest (n, f)

n – a numeric value (between 1 and 100). 5 returns the fifth smallest, 2 the second smallest, and so forth.

f – the database or formula field to summarize for the entire report.

NthSmallest (n, f1, f2)

n – a numeric value (between 1 and 100). 5 returns the fifth smallest, 2 the second smallest, and so forth.

f1 – the database or formula field to summarize for a report group.

f2 – the database or formula field indicating the group you wish to summarize for. An existing group on the report must be based on this field.

NthSmallest (n, f1, f2, s)

n – a numeric value (between 1 and 100). 5 returns the fifth smallest, 2 the second smallest, and so forth.

f1 – the database or formula field to summarize for a report group.

f2 – the database or formula field indicating the group you wish to summarize for. An existing group on the report must be based on this field.

s – a string value indicating how often to "change" the summary for Boolean, date, or date-time grouping. See **Boolean Conditions**, **Date Conditions**, and **Time Conditions** later in this appendix for available choices.

```
NthSmallest (5, {Sales.Amount})
```

returns the fifth smallest sales amount for the entire report.

```
NthSmallest (5, {Sales.Amount}, {Sales.Date}, "monthly")
```

returns the fifth smallest sales amount for the sales date group, summarized for each month.

PercentOfAverage

Returns a numeric value indicating what percentage an average calculation in one group is of another average calculation in a later group or the entire report.

This function duplicates a Percentage Summary Field created with the Insert | Summary menu option.

PercentOfAverage (f1, f2, s)

This will show the percentage of the group value compared to the value for the entire report.

f1 – the database or formula field to summarize for the entire report. This must be a numeric field.
f2 – the database or formula field indicating the group you wish to summarize for. An existing group on the report must be based on this field.
s – a string value indicating how often to "change" the summary for Boolean, date, or date-time grouping. See **Boolean Conditions, Date Conditions**, and **Time Conditions** later in this appendix for available choices. This argument is required only if *f2* is a date, date-time, time, or Boolean field.

PercentOfAverage (f1, f2, s1, f3, s2)

This will show the percentage of the group value compared to the value for a later group.

f1 – the database or formula field to summarize for the entire report. This must be a numeric field.
f2 – the database or formula field indicating the group you wish to summarize for. An existing group on the report must be based on this field.
s1 – a string value indicating how often to "change" the summary for Boolean, date, or date-time grouping. See **Boolean Conditions, Date Conditions**, and **Time Conditions** later in this appendix for available choices. This argument (and the comma that precedes it) is required only if *f2* is a date, date-time, time, or Boolean field.
f3 – the database or formula field indicating the later group field to use for the summary. An existing group on the report must be based on this field.
s2 – a string value indicating how often to "change" the summary for Boolean, date, or date-time grouping. See **Boolean Conditions, Date Conditions**, and **Time Conditions** later in this appendix for available choices. This argument (and the comma that precedes it) is required only if *f3* is a date, date-time, time, or Boolean field.

```
PercentOfAverage ({Sales.Amount}, {Sales.CustName})
```

returns the percentage that the average sales amount for each customer group makes up of the average sales amount for the entire report.

```
PercentOfAverage ({Sales.Amount}, {Sales.Date},
"monthly", {Sales.CustName})
```

returns the percentage that the average sales amount for each month makes up of the average sales amount for the higher-level customer name group.

PercentOfCount

Returns a numeric value indicating what percentage a count calculation in one group is of another count calculation in a later group or the entire report.

This function duplicates a Percentage Summary Field created with the Insert | Summary menu option.

PercentOfCount (f1, f2, s)

This will show the percentage of the group value compared to the value for the entire report.

f1 – the database or formula field to summarize for the entire report.

f2 – the database or formula field indicating the group you wish to summarize for. An existing group on the report must be based on this field.

s – a string value indicating how often to "change" the summary for Boolean, date, or date-time grouping. See **Boolean Conditions**, **Date Conditions**, and **Time Conditions** later in this appendix for available choices. This argument is required only if *f2* is a date, date-time, time, or Boolean field.

PercentOfCount (f1, f2, s1, f3, s2)

This will show the percentage of the group value compared to the value for a later group.

f1 – the database or formula field to summarize for the entire report.

f2 – the database or formula field indicating the group you wish to summarize for. An existing group on the report must be based on this field.

s1 – a string value indicating how often to "change" the summary for Boolean, date, or date-time grouping. See **Boolean Conditions**, **Date Conditions**, and **Time Conditions** later in this appendix for available choices. This argument (and the comma that precedes it) is required only if *f2* is a date, date-time, time, or Boolean field.

f3 – the database or formula field indicating the later group field to use for the summary. An existing group on the report must be based on this field.

s2 – a string value indicating how often to "change" the summary for Boolean, date, or date-time grouping. See **Boolean Conditions**, **Date Conditions**, and **Time Conditions** later in this appendix for available choices. This argument (and the comma that precedes it) is required only if *f3* is a date, date-time, time, or Boolean field.

```
PercentOfCount ({Sales.Amount}, {Sales.CustName})
```

returns the percentage that the number of records for each customer group makes up of the total number of records for the entire report.

```
PercentOfCount ({Sales.Amount}, {Sales.Date},
"monthly", {Sales.CustName})
```

returns the percentage that the number of records for each month makes up of the number of records for the higher-level customer name group.

NOTE *PercentOfCount calculations will exclude records that contain a null value in the field being counted.*

PercentOfDistinctCount

Returns a numeric value indicating what percentage a distinct count calculation in one group is of another distinct count calculation in a later group or the entire report.

This function duplicates a Percentage Summary Field created with the Insert | Summary menu option.

PercentOfDistinctCount (f1, f2, s)

This will show the percentage of the group value compared to the value for the entire report.

f1 – the database or formula field to summarize for the entire report.

f2 – the database or formula field indicating the group you wish to summarize for. An existing group on the report must be based on this field.

s – a string value indicating how often to "change" the summary for Boolean, date, or date-time grouping. See **Boolean Conditions**, **Date Conditions**, and **Time Conditions** later in this appendix for available choices. This argument is required only if *f2* is a date, date-time, time, or Boolean field.

PercentOfDistinctCount (f1, f2, s1, f3, s2)

This will show the percentage of the group value compared to the value for a later group.

f1 – the database or formula field to summarize for the entire report.

f2 – the database or formula field indicating the group you wish to summarize for. An existing group on the report must be based on this field.

s1 – a string value indicating how often to "change" the summary for Boolean, date, or date-time grouping. See **Boolean Conditions**, **Date Conditions**, and **Time Conditions** later in this appendix for available choices. This argument (and the comma that precedes it) is required only if *f2* is a date, date-time, time, or Boolean field.

f3 – the database or formula field indicating the later group field to use for the summary. An existing group on the report must be based on this field.

s2 – a string value indicating how often to "change" the summary for Boolean, date, or date-time grouping. See **Boolean Conditions**, **Date Conditions**, and **Time Conditions** later in this appendix for available choices. This argument (and the comma that precedes it) is required only if *f3* is a date, date-time, time, or Boolean field.

```
PercentOfDistinctCount ({Sales.Acct#}, {Sales.CustName})
```

returns the percentage that the unique number of account numbers for each customer group makes up of the unique number of account numbers for the entire report.

```
PercentOfDistinctCount ({Sales.Acct#}, {Sales.Date},
"monthly", {Sales.CustName})
```

returns the percentage that the unique number of account numbers for each month makes up of the unique number of account numbers for the higher-level customer name group.

PercentOfMaximum

Returns a numeric value indicating what percentage a maximum calculation in one group is of another maximum calculation in a later group or the entire report.

This function duplicates a Percentage Summary Field created with the Insert | Summary menu option.

PercentOfMaximum (f1, f2, s)

This will show the percentage of the group value compared to the value for the entire report.

f1 – the database or formula field to summarize for the entire report.

f2 – the database or formula field indicating the group you wish to summarize for. An existing group on the report must be based on this field.

s – a string value indicating how often to "change" the summary for Boolean, date, or date-time grouping. See **Boolean Conditions**, **Date Conditions**, and **Time Conditions** later in this appendix for available choices. This argument is required only if *f2* is a date, date-time, time, or Boolean field.

PercentOfMaximum (f1, f2, s1, f3, s2)

This will show the percentage of the group value compared to the value for a later group.

f1 – the database or formula field to summarize for the entire report.

f2 – the database or formula field indicating the group you wish to summarize for. An existing group on the report must be based on this field.

s1 – a string value indicating how often to "change" the summary for Boolean, date, or date-time grouping. See **Boolean Conditions**, **Date Conditions**, and **Time Conditions** later in this appendix for available choices. This argument (and the comma that precedes it) is required only if *f2* is a date, date-time, time, or Boolean field.

f3 – the database or formula field indicating the later group field to use for the summary. An existing group on the report must be based on this field.

s2 – a string value indicating how often to "change" the summary for Boolean, date, or date-time grouping. See **Boolean Conditions**, **Date Conditions**, and **Time Conditions** later in this appendix for available choices. This argument (and the comma that precedes it) is required only if *f3* is a date, date-time, time, or Boolean field.

```
PercentOfMaximum ({Sales.Amount}, {Sales.CustName})
```

returns the percentage that the highest sales amount for each customer group makes up of the highest sales amount for the entire report.

```
PercentOfMaximum ({Sales.Amount}, {Sales.Date},
"monthly", {Sales.CustName})
```

returns the percentage that the highest sales amount for each month makes up of the highest sales amount for the higher-level customer name group.

PercentOfMinimum

Returns a numeric value indicating what percentage a minimum calculation in one group is of another minimum calculation in a later group or the entire report.

   This function duplicates a Percentage Summary Field created with the Insert | Summary menu option.

PercentOfMinimum (f1, f2, s)

This will show the percentage of the group value compared to the value for the entire report.
f1 – the database or formula field to summarize for the entire report.
f2 – the database or formula field indicating the group you wish to summarize for. An existing group on the report must be based on this field.
s – a string value indicating how often to "change" the summary for Boolean, date, or date-time grouping. See **Boolean Conditions**, **Date Conditions**, and **Time Conditions** later in this appendix for available choices. This argument is required only if *f2* is a date, date-time, time, or Boolean field.

PercentOfMinimum (f1, f2, s1, f3, s2)

This will show the percentage of the group value compared to the value for a later group.
f1 – the database or formula field to summarize for the entire report.
f2 – the database or formula field indicating the group you wish to summarize for. An existing group on the report must be based on this field.
s1 – a string value indicating how often to "change" the summary for Boolean, date, or date-time grouping. See **Boolean Conditions**, **Date Conditions**, and **Time Conditions** later in this appendix for available choices. This argument (and the comma that precedes it) is required only if *f2* is a date, date-time, time, or Boolean field.
f3 – the database or formula field indicating the later group field to use for the summary. An existing group on the report must be based on this field.
s2 – a string value indicating how often to "change" the summary for Boolean, date, or date-time grouping. See **Boolean Conditions**, **Date Conditions**, and **Time Conditions** later in this appendix for available choices. This argument (and the comma that precedes it) is required only if *f3* is a date, date-time, time, or Boolean field.

```
PercentOfMinimum ({Sales.Amount}, {Sales.CustName})
```

returns the percentage that the lowest sales amount for each customer group makes up of the lowest sales amount for the entire report.

```
PercentOfMinimum ({Sales.Amount}, {Sales.Date},
"monthly", {Sales.CustName})
```

returns the percentage that the lowest sales amount for each month makes up of the lowest sales amount for the higher-level customer name group.

PercentOfSum

Returns a numeric value indicating what percentage a sum calculation in one group is of another sum calculation in a later group or the entire report.

   This function duplicates a Percentage Summary Field created with the Insert | Summary menu option.

PercentOfSum (f1, f2, s)

This will show the percentage of the group value compared to the value for the entire report.
f1 – the database or formula field to summarize for the entire report. This must be a numeric field.
f2 – the database or formula field indicating the group you wish to summarize for. An existing group on the report must be based on this field.
s – a string value indicating how often to "change" the summary for Boolean, date, or date-time grouping. See **Boolean Conditions**, **Date Conditions**, and **Time Conditions** later in this appendix for available choices. This argument is required only if *f2* is a date, date-time, time, or Boolean field.

PercentOfSum (f1, f2, s1, f3, s2)

This will show the percentage of the group value compared to the value for a later group.
f1 – the database or formula field to summarize for the entire report. This must be a numeric field.
f2 – the database or formula field indicating the group you wish to summarize for. An existing group on the report must be based on this field.
s1 – a string value indicating how often to "change" the summary for Boolean, date, or date-time grouping. See **Boolean Conditions**, **Date Conditions**, and **Time Conditions** later in this appendix for available choices. This argument (and the comma that precedes it) is required only if *f2* is a date, date-time, time, or Boolean field.
f3 – the database or formula field indicating the later group field to use for the summary. An existing group on the report must be based on this field.
s2 – a string value indicating how often to "change" the summary for Boolean, date, or date-time grouping. See **Boolean Conditions**, **Date Conditions**, and **Time Conditions** later in this appendix for available choices. This argument (and the comma that precedes it) is required only if *f3* is a date, date-time, time, or Boolean field.

```
PercentOfSum ({Sales.Amount}, {Sales.CustName})
```

returns the percentage that the total sales amount for each customer group makes up of the total sales amount for the entire report.

```
PercentOfSum ({Sales.Amount}, {Sales.Date},
"monthly", {Sales.CustName})
```

returns the percentage that the total sales amount for each month makes up of the total sales amount for the higher-level customer name group.

PopulationStdDev

Returns a numeric value indicating the population standard deviation of the supplied database field or formula.

PopulationStdDev (f)

f – the database or formula field to summarize for the entire report. This must be a numeric field.

PopulationStdDev (f1, f2)

f1 – the database or formula field to summarize for a report group. This must be a numeric field.

f2 – the database or formula field indicating the group you wish to summarize for. An existing group on the report must be based on this field.

PopulationStdDev (f1, f2, s)

f1 – the database or formula field to summarize for a report group. This must be a numeric field.
f2 – the database or formula field indicating the group you wish to summarize for. An existing group on the report must be based on this field.
s – a string value indicating how often to "change" the summary for Boolean, date, or date-time grouping. See **Boolean Conditions**, **Date Conditions**, and **Time Conditions** later in this appendix for available choices.

```
PopulationStdDev({Sales.Amount})
```

returns the population standard deviation of sales amounts for the entire report.

```
PopulationStdDev({Sales.Amount}, {Sales.Date}, "monthly")
```

returns the population standard deviation of sales amounts for the sales date group, summarized for each month.

PopulationVariance

Returns a numeric value indicating the population variance of the supplied database field or formula.

PopulationVariance (f)

f – the database or formula field to summarize for the entire report. This must be a numeric field.

PopulationVariance (f1, f2)

f1 – the database or formula field to summarize for a report group. This must be a numeric field.
f2 – the database or formula field indicating the group you wish to summarize for. An existing group on the report must be based on this field.

PopulationVariance (f1, f2, s)

f1 – the database or formula field to summarize for a report group. This must be a numeric field.
f2 – the database or formula field indicating the group you wish to summarize for. An existing group on the report must be based on this field.
s – a string value indicating how often to "change" the summary for Boolean, date, or date-time grouping. See **Boolean Conditions**, **Date Conditions**, and **Time Conditions** later in this appendix for available choices.

```
PopulationVariance({Sales.Amount})
```

returns the population variance of sales amounts for the entire report.

```
PopulationVariance({Sales.Amount}, {Sales.Date}, "monthly")
```

returns the population variance of sales amounts for the sales date group, summarized for each month.

PthPercentile

Returns a numeric value indicating the *p*th percentile of the supplied database field or formula.

PthPercentile returns the "*p*th" percentile value, such as the value that equates to the tenth percentile of the report or group.

PthPercentile (n, f)

n – a numeric value (between 0 and 100). 5 returns the fifth percentile, 2 the second percentile, and so forth.

f – the database or formula field to summarize for the entire report. This must be a numeric field.

PthPercentile (n, f1, f2)

n – a numeric value (between 0 and 100). 5 returns the fifth percentile, 2 the second percentile, and so forth.

f1 – the database or formula field to summarize for the entire report. This must be a numeric field.

f2 – the database or formula field indicating the group you wish to summarize for. An existing group on the report must be based on this field.

PthPercentile (n, f1, f2, s)

n – a numeric value (between 0 and 100). 5 returns the fifth percentile, 2 the second percentile, and so forth.

f1 – the database or formula field to summarize for the entire report. This must be a numeric field.

f2 – the database or formula field indicating the group you wish to summarize for. An existing group on the report must be based on this field.

s – a string value indicating how often to "change" the summary for Boolean, date, or date-time grouping. See **Boolean Conditions**, **Date Conditions**, and **Time Conditions** later in this appendix for available choices.

```
PthPercentile (5, {Sales.Amount})
```

returns the sales amount equating to the fifth percentile for the entire report.

```
PthPercentile (5, {Sales.Amount}, {Sales.Date}, "monthly")
```

returns the sales amount equating to the fifth percentile for the sales date group, summarized for each month.

StdDev

Returns a numeric value indicating the standard deviation of the supplied database field or formula.

StdDev (f)

f – the database or formula field to summarize for the entire report. This must be a numeric field.

StdDev (f1, f2)

f1 – the database or formula field to summarize for a report group. This must be a numeric field.

f2 – the database or formula field indicating the group you wish to summarize for. An existing group on the report must be based on this field.

StdDev (f1, f2, s)

f1 – the database or formula field to summarize for a report group. This must be a numeric field.

f2 – the database or formula field indicating the group you wish to summarize for. An existing group on the report must be based on this field.

s – a string value indicating how often to "change" the summary for Boolean, date, or date-time grouping. See **Boolean Conditions**, **Date Conditions**, and **Time Conditions** later in this appendix for available choices.

```
StdDev({Sales.Amount})
```

returns the standard deviation of sales amounts for the entire report.

```
StdDev({Sales.Amount}, {Sales.Date}, "monthly")
```

returns the standard deviation of sales amounts for the sales date group, summarized for each month.

Sum

Returns a numeric value indicating the sum of the supplied database field or formula.

Sum (f)

f – the database or formula field to summarize for the entire report. This must be a numeric field.

Sum (f1, f2)

f1 – the database or formula field to summarize for a report group. This must be a numeric field.

f2 – the database or formula field indicating the group you wish to summarize for. An existing group on the report must be based on this field.

Sum (f1, f2, s)

f1 – the database or formula field to summarize for a report group. This must be a numeric field.

f2 – the database or formula field indicating the group you wish to summarize for. An existing group on the report must be based on this field.

s – a string value indicating how often to "change" the summary for Boolean, date, or date-time grouping. See **Boolean Conditions**, **Date Conditions**, and **Time Conditions** later in this appendix for available choices.

```
Sum({Sales.Amount})
```

returns the sum of sales amounts for the entire report.

```
Sum({Sales.Amount}, {Sales.Date}, "monthly")
```

returns the sum of sales amounts for the sales date group, summarized for each month.

Variance

Returns a numeric value indicating the variance of the supplied database field or formula.

Variance (f)

f – the database or formula field to summarize for the entire report. This must be a numeric field.

Variance (f1, f2)

f1 – the database or formula field to summarize for a report group. This must be a numeric field.
f2 – the database or formula field indicating the group you wish to summarize for. An existing group on the report must be based on this field.

Variance (f1, f2, s)

f1 – the database or formula field to summarize for a report group. This must be a numeric field.
f2 – the database or formula field indicating the group you wish to summarize for. An existing group on the report must be based on this field.
s – a string value indicating how often to "change" the summary for Boolean, date, or date-time grouping. See **Boolean Conditions**, **Date Conditions**, and **Time Conditions** later in this appendix for available choices.

```
Variance({Sales.Amount})
```

returns the variance of sales amounts for the entire report.

```
Variance({Sales.Amount}, {Sales.Date}, "monthly")
```

returns the variance of sales amounts for the sales date group, summarized for each month.

WeightedAverage

Returns a numeric value indicating the average of the supplied database field or formula, given a weight by another field or formula.

WeightedAverage (f1, f2)

f1 – the database or formula field to summarize for the entire report. This must be a numeric field.
f2 – the database or formula field to use as the weight.

WeightedAverage (f1, f2, f3)

f1 – the database or formula field to summarize for a report group. This must be a numeric field.
f2 – the database or formula field to use as the weight.
f3 – the database or formula field indicating the group you wish to summarize for. An existing group on the report must be based on this field.

WeightedAverage (f1, f2, f3, s)

f1 – the database or formula field to summarize for a report group. This must be a numeric field.
f2 – the database or formula field to use as the weight.

f3 – the database or formula field indicating the group you wish to summarize for. An existing group on the report must be based on this field.

s – a string value indicating how often to "change" the summary for Boolean, date, or date-time grouping. See **Boolean Conditions**, **Date Conditions**, and **Time Conditions** later in this appendix for available choices.

```
WeightedAverage({Sales.Amount},{Sales.Goal})
```

returns the average of sales amounts weighted by goal for the entire report.

```
WeightedAverage({Sales.Amount}, {Sales.Date}, "monthly")
```

returns the average of sales amounts weighted by goal for the sales date group, summarized for each month.

Boolean Conditions

The following string values can be used in a summary function when using a Boolean group field:

"any change"
"change to No"
"change to Yes"
"every No"
"every Yes"
"next is No"
"next is Yes"

Date Conditions

The following string values can be used in a summary function when using a date or date-time group field:

"daily"
"semimonthly"
"semiannually"
"monthly"
"quarterly"
"biweekly"
"weekly"
"annually"

APPENDIX

Time Conditions

The following string values can be used in a summary function when using a time or date-time group field:

"by AMPM"
"by hour"
"by minute"
"by second"

Functions: Type Conversion

This category of functions is used to convert from one data type to another. These functions are modeled after functions of the same name found in Visual Basic and Visual Basic for Applications.

CBool

Returns a Boolean (true/false) conversion of the source field.

CBool will return False for a value of 0 (zero). Otherwise, CBool returns True.

CBool (n)

n – a numeric value.

```
CBool(-1)
```

returns True.

CCur

Returns a currency value.

CCur (v)

v – a value of number, currency, or string data type.

```
CCur ("1125.13894")
```

returns $1,125.14 as a currency value.

CDate

Returns a date value.

CDate is functionally equivalent to Date and DateValue. See **DateValue** for details.

CDateTime

Returns a date-time value.

CDateTime is functionally equivalent to DateTime and DateTimeValue. See **DateTimeValue** for details.

CDbl
Returns a numeric value.

CDbl is functionally equivalent to ToNumber. See **ToNumber** for details.

CStr
Converts any nonstring data type to a string value.

CStr is functionally equivalent to ToText, including returning the same result and accepting the same arguments. See **ToText** for complete information.

CTime
Returns a time value.

CTime is functionally equivalent to Time and TimeValue. See **TimeValue** for details.

---

erators: Arithmetic

This category of operators performs standard arithmetic functions, such as addition, subtraction, and so forth.

Add (+)
Adds two numbers.

n1 + n2
n1 – a numeric value.
n2 – a numeric value.

```
2 + 2
```

returns 4.00.

Divide (/)
Divides two numbers.

n1 / n2
n1 – a numeric value.
n2 – a numeric value.

```
10 / 5
```

returns 2.00.

Exponentiate (^)
Raises a number to a power.

n1 ^ n2
n1 – a numeric value.
n2 – a numeric value to raise *n1* to the power of.

```
5 ^ 2
```

returns 25.00.

Integer Divide (\)

Divides two numbers, returning an integer result.

n1 \ n2

n1 – a numeric value.
n2 – a numeric value.

```
10 \ 3
```

returns 3.00, contrasted with

```
10 / 3
```

which returns 3.33.

Modulus

Performs division on two numeric values and returns the remainder of the division rather than the result of the division.

Use the Mod function for particular situations where the remainder of numeric division is required, rather than the actual result. For example, this operator can be used with the RecordNumber function in a conditional formatting formula to shade every other details section.

n1 Mod n2

n1 – a numeric value
n2 – a numeric value

```
If RecordNumber Mod 2 = 0 Then crSilver Else crNoColor
```

when supplied as a conditional formula for the details section background color, shades every other details section silver.

NOTE *Crystal Reports also includes the Remainder function, which performs a similar operation.*

Multiply (*)

Multiplies two numbers.

n1 * n2

n1 – a numeric value.
n2 – a numeric value.

```
5 * 4
```

returns 20.00.

Negate (–)

Returns the negative equivalent of a number.

–n

n – a numeric value.

```
-14
```

returns –14.00.

```
-{GLDetails.DRAmount}
```

returns a positive debit amount if the DRAmount field is coded as a negative number in the database.

Percent (%)

Calculates the percentage one number is of another number.

n1 % n2

n1 – a numeric value.
n2 – a numeric value.

```
5 % 20
```

returns 25.00.

```
{Sales.Amount} % Sum({Sales.Amount},{Sales.Rep})
```

returns the percentage each individual sale is of a sales rep's total sales.

Subtract (–)

Subtracts one number from another.

n1 – n2

n1 – a numeric value.
n2 – a numeric value.

```
25 - 10
```

returns 15.00.

Operators: Array

This set of operators pertain to arrays. An *array* is a collection of data items stored in a single "bucket," such as a single variable. If an array contains 15 items, it is said to have 15 *elements*. Arrays can contain any supported Crystal Reports data type, such as number, string, date-time, and so forth.

In

Returns a Boolean (true/false) value indicating whether a single value is in an array.

v In a

v – a value of the same data type as the *a* array.
a – an array.

```
5 In [1,3,5,7,9]
```

returns True.

```
If {Customer.Region} In ["CO","MT","UT","WY"] Then
    "Rocky Mountain Region"
Else
    "Rest of Country"
```

returns one of two strings based on the existence of a database field in the supplied string literal array.

Make Array

Creates an array of values.

This is functionally equivalent to the MakeArray function. See **MakeArray** in the Functions: Arrays section for details.

Redim

"Resets" an existing array variable to an empty state with a specified number of elements.

Redim a (n)

a – an existing array variable.
n – a positive number.

```
WhilePrintingRecords;
StringVar Array Beatles;
Redim Beatles [4];
Beatles[1]
```

declares an existing string array and resets it to a string array with four elements, each containing an empty string. The formula returns an empty string to the report (the first element of the reset array).

Redim Preserve

"Resizes" an existing array variable with a specified number of elements, retaining existing contents of the array variable.

Redim Preserve a (n)

a – an existing array variable.
n – a positive number.

```
WhilePrintingRecords;
StringVar Array Beatles;
Redim Preserve Beatles [8];
Beatles[1]
```

declares an existing string array and expands it to contain eight elements, retaining any existing data in the array. The formula returns "John" to the report (the existing data in the first element of the array).

Subscript ([])

Extracts an individual element of an array.

a[n]

a – an array value.
n – a numeric value or range indicating the element or elements to extract.

```
WhilePrintingRecords;
StringVar Array Beatles;
Beatles[3]
```

returns "George", the third element of the Beatles array.

erators: Boolean

This set of operators pertain to Boolean (true/false) values, functions, and expressions.

And

Returns true if both associated Boolean values are true.

b1 And b2

b1 – a Boolean value or expression.
b2 – a Boolean value or expression.

```
2 + 2 = 4 And 10 / 2 = 5
```

returns True.

```
If {Customer.Region} = "CA" And
    {Customer.Last Year's Sales} > 50000 Then
      "California Bonus Customer"
Else
      "Other Customer"
```

returns "California Bonus Customer" if both Boolean expressions in the If test are true.

Eqv (Logical equivalence)
Returns true if both associated Boolean values are the same.

b1 Eqv b2
b1 – a Boolean value or expression.
b2 – a Boolean value or expression.

```
2 + 2 = 4 Eqv 10 / 2 = 5
```

returns True.

```
2 + 2 = 8 Eqv 10 / 2 = 5
```

returns False.

```
2 + 2 = 8 Eqv 10 / 2 = 1
```

returns True.

Imp (Logical implication)
Returns true if both associated Boolean values are the same, or if the second value is true while the first value is false.

b1 Imp b2
b1 – a Boolean value or expression.
b2 – a Boolean value or expression.

```
2 + 2 = 4 Imp 10 / 2 = 5
```

returns True.

```
2 + 2 = 8 Imp 10 / 2 = 1
```

returns True.

```
2 + 2 = 4 Imp 10 / 2 = 1
```

returns False.

```
2 + 2 = 8 Imp 10 / 2 = 5
```

returns True.

Not
Reverses the Boolean value (true becomes false and false becomes true).

Not requires a Boolean value or expression to follow it. As such, you may need to enclose a Boolean expression in parentheses for Not to evaluate properly.

Not b

b – a Boolean value or expression.

```
Not (2 + 2 = 4)
```

returns False.

```
Not 2 + 2 = 4
```

results in an error, as Not expects the first occurrence of the number 2 to be Boolean.

```
If Not InRepeatedGroupHeader Then "New Group Starts Here"
```

returns the "new group" string if InRepeatedGroupHeader is false.

Or

Returns true if either or both associated Boolean values are true.

b1 Or b2

b1 – a Boolean value or expression.
b2 – a Boolean value or expression.

```
2 + 2 = 4 Or 10 / 2 = 1
```

returns True.

```
If {Customer.Last Year's Sales} > 50000 Or
    {Customer.Last Year's Sales} < 0 Then
      "Customer needs attention"
Else
      "Normal customer"
```

returns "Customer needs attention" if either Boolean expression in the If test is true.

Xor (Logical exclusion)

Returns true if the associated Boolean values return opposite values (one true, the other false).

b1 Xor b2

b1 – a Boolean value or expression.
b2 – a Boolean value or expression.

```
2 + 2 = 4 Xor 10 / 2 = 6
```

returns True.

```
2 + 2 = 5 Xor 10 / 2 = 5
```

returns True.

```
2 + 2 = 4 Xor 10 / 2 = 5
```

returns False.

APPENDIX

Operators: Comparisons

This category of operators compares values to each other. You may combine comparison operators together with other Boolean operators, such as And, Or, and Not.

Equal (=)

Returns a Boolean (true/false) value indicating whether the two supplied values are equal to each other.

v1 = v2

v1 – a value of any supported data type.
v2 – a value of the same data type as *v1*.

```
10 = 10
```

returns True.

```
If {Sales.State} = "CO" Then "Colorado"
```

returns "Colorado" if the state field is equal to "CO".

Greater or Equal (>=)

Returns a Boolean (true/false) value indicating whether the first supplied value is greater than or equal to the second value.

This operator compares strings from the perspective of sort order.

v1 >= v2

v1 – a value of any supported data type.
v2 – a value of the same data type as *v1*.

```
"abc" >= "wyz"
```

returns False, based on string sort order.

```
If {Sales.Amount} >= 5000 Then "Great Order"
```

returns "Great Order" if the sale amount is exactly $5,000, or anything greater than $5,000.

Greater Than (>)

Returns a Boolean (true/false) value indicating whether the first supplied value is greater than the second value.

This operator compares strings from the perspective of sort order.

v1 > v2

v1 – a value of any supported data type.
v2 – a value of the same data type as *v1*.

```
#1/1/2000# > #1/1/1999#
```

returns True.

```
If {Sales.Amount} > 10000 Then "Eligible for Bonus"
```

returns "Eligible for Bonus" if the sale amount is greater than $10,000. If the amount is exactly $10,000 or less, an empty string is returned.

Less or Equal (<=)

Returns a Boolean (true/false) value indicating whether the first supplied value is less than or equal to the second value.

This operator compares strings from the perspective of sort order.

v1 <= v2

v1 – a value of any supported data type.
v2 – a value of the same data type as *v1*.

```
100 <= 100
```

returns True.

```
If {Sales.Amount} <= 100 Then "Small Order"
```

returns "Small Order" if the sale amount is exactly $100, or anything less than $100.

Less Than (<)

Returns a Boolean (true/false) value indicating whether the first supplied value is less than the second value.

This operator compares strings from the perspective of sort order.

v1 < v2

v1 – a value of any supported data type.
v2 – a value of the same data type as *v1*.

```
#1/1/2000# < #1/1/1999#
```

returns False.

```
If {Sales.Amount} < 100 Then "Improved Performance Required"
```

returns "Improved Performance Required" if the sale amount is less than $100. If the amount is exactly $100 or greater, an empty string is returned.

Not Equal (<>)

Returns a Boolean (true/false) value indicating whether the two supplied values are not equal to each other.

v1 <> v2

v1 – a value of any supported data type.
v2 – a value of the same data type as *v1*.

```
10 <> 15
```

returns True.

```
If {Sales.State} <> "CO" Then "Out-Of-State Sale"
```

returns "Out-Of-State Sale" if the state field is something other than "CO".

> **NOTE** *Case sensitivity of string comparisons is based on the database case sensitivity setting in File | Report Options (applies to the current report only) and File | Options (applies to all new reports in the future).*

Operators: Control Structures

This category of operators might well exist in a separate section of the Formula Editor called "programming constructs." However, as they don't take "arguments" per se, they've been placed in the Operator tree. These operators are most familiar to computer programmers, as they duplicate typical programming logic and flow within a single Crystal Reports formula.

Do While

Loops through formula logic while a condition is true.

Do While differs from While Do in regard to when the loop condition is evaluated. Do While evaluates the loop condition *after* a loop iteration (so that at least one loop will always occur). While Do evaluates the condition *before* a loop iteration (the logic within the loop may not occur at all if the condition is immediately false).

Do <formula logic> While b

b – a Boolean value or expression.

```
NumberVar Counter := 1;
StringVar Accum;
do
(   Accum := Accum + "-";
    Counter := Counter + 1)
while Counter < 100;
Accum
```

returns a string containing 99 dash characters (the loop iterated while the counter was less than 100—once it reached 100, the loop did not repeat).

> **NOTE** *If you wish to include more than one Crystal Reports statement within the loop, separate statements with a semicolon and surround all statements (between the Do and While) with parentheses.*

Exit For

Exits a For loop before its normal conclusion.

Exit For

```
NumberVar Counter;
StringVar Accum;
for Counter := 1 to 1000 step 2 do
(
    Accum := Accum & ToText(Counter);
    If Len(Accum) > 245 Then Exit For;
);
Accum
```

returns the string in the Accum variable consisting of "1.003.005.007.009.00" and so forth. Within the loop, the Accum variable is tested for a length exceeding 245 characters and the loop is exited if this occurs.

Exit While

Exits a Do or While loop before its normal conclusion.

Exit While

```
NumberVar Counter := 1;
StringVar Accum;
do
(   Accum := Accum + "-";
    Counter := Counter + 1;
    If Length(Accum) = 100 Then Exit While)
while True;
Accum
```

returns a string containing 100 dash characters (the loop iterates until the length of the Accum variable reaches 100 characters and the Exit While statement executes).

For

Loops through formula logic a specified number of times.

For v := n1 To n2 Step n3 Do

v – a numeric variable that the loop will increment as it progresses.

$n1$ – a numeric value indicating the beginning value that will be assigned to v when the loop starts.

$n2$ – a numeric value indicating the ending value in v that will stop the loop.

$n3$ – a numeric value indicating the amount to increment v every time the loop iterates. This value, as well as the Step keyword that precedes it, are optional. If omitted, v is incremented by 1 with each loop iteration.

```
NumberVar Counter;
StringVar Accum;
for Counter := 1 to 100 step 2 do
(
    Accum := Accum & ToText(Counter);
);
Accum
```

returns contents of the Accum variable, consisting of the string "13579111315" and so forth, through "99". The Counter variable increments from 1 to 100, incrementing by 2 every time the loop iterates.

NOTE *If you wish to include more than one Crystal Reports statement within the loop, separate statements with a semicolon and surround all statements (after the Do keyword) with parentheses.*

If Then Else

Performs a Boolean test, returning one value if the test is true and an alternate value if the test is false.

If b Then v1 Else v2

b – a Boolean expression (typically using comparison operators discussed earlier in this section).
v1 – a value of any supported data type that is returned if *b* evaluates to True.
v1 – a value of the same data type as *v1* that is returned if *b* evaluates to False. This value, and the Else keyword that precedes it, is optional.

```
If {Sales.State} = "CO" Then
    "Sales Tax Required"
Else
    "No Tax"
```

returns the string "Sales Tax Required" if the Boolean expression after If evaluates to true. Otherwise, the formula returns "No Tax".

```
If {Sales.Amount} > 5000 Then "Bonus Order"
```

returns "Bonus Order" if the sales amount exceeds $5,000. Otherwise, an empty string is returned.

Option Loop

Specifies how many iterations a loop should go through before an error is returned.

By default, Crystal Reports stops loop processing and returns an error if a loop iterates 100,000 times. This behavior prevents infinite loops from occurring. If you wish to lower the maximum number of iterations, use Option Loop.

Option Loop n

n – a numeric value indicating the number of loop iterations that will occur before an error is returned.

Option Loop must be the first statement in the formula.

```
NumberVar Counter;
Do
    Counter := Counter + 1
While True
```

will iterate 100,000 times before returning an error.

```
Option Loop 100;
NumberVar Counter;
Do
    Counter := Counter + 1
While True
```

will iterate 100 times before returning an error.

Select Case

Returns one of several available values based on a series of conditions.

Select Case duplicates the capabilities of sophisticated If-Then-Else logic. However, Select Case is often easier to understand and maintain than complex If-Then-Else formulas.

Select e Case v1: <formula logic> Case v2 <formula logic>...: Default: <formula logic>

e – a value or expression of any data type to test.

v1 – a value or "list" of values (separated by commas) matching in data type to *e* to test against *e*.

v2 – an additional value or "list" of values (separated by commas) matching in data type to *e* to test against *e*.

Additional pairs of Case/<formula logic> combinations may be added. The Default keyword and colon are optional. Formula logic after each Case statement must return the same data type as all other formula logic.

```
Select {Sales.State}
    Case "OR","ID","MT","WA":
        "Northwest"
    Case "CA","AZ","TX","NM":
        "Southwest"
    Case "ME","MA","NH","NY":
        "Northeast"
    Case "FL","NC","GA","SC":
        "Southeast"
    Default:
        "Rest of Country"
```

examines the state field and begins testing it against each Case statement. Once it finds a match, it returns the value following the case statement. If no matches are found, the value following the default statement is returned. Were the Default keyword, colon, and "Rest of Country" string literal to be left out, the formula would return an empty string if no matches were found.

```
Select {Sales.LastYearRevenue}
    Case Is < 100:
        "Improved Performance Needed"
    Case 100 To 1000:
        "Average Year"
    Case Is > 1000:
        "Excellent Year"
```

examines the Last Year Revenue field and begins testing against the ranges specified in each Case statement, returning the appropriate string following the Case statement that matches. No Default keyword is provided, as any number will fall into one of the three Case statements. Were a number to somehow not fall into one of the existing Case statements, a zero would be returned.

While Do

Loops through formula logic while a condition is true.

While Do differs from Do While in regard to when the loop condition is evaluated. Do While evaluates the loop condition *after* a loop iteration (so that at least one loop will always occur). While Do evaluates the condition *before* a loop iteration (the logic within the loop may not occur at all if the condition is immediately false).

While b <formula logic> Do

b – a Boolean value or expression.

```
NumberVar Counter := 1;
StringVar Accum;
While Counter < 100 Do
(    Accum := Accum + "-";
     Counter := Counter + 1
);
Accum
```

returns a string containing 99 dash characters (the loop iterated while the counter was less than 100—once it reached 100, the loop did not repeat).

NOTE *If you wish to include more than one Crystal Reports statement within the loop, separate statements with a semicolon and surround all statements (between the Do and While) with parentheses.*

Operators: Conversion

A single operator exists to convert to one data type from another.

Currency ($)

Converts a numeric value to a currency value.

The CCur function can also be used to convert from another data type to currency.

```
$
```

```
$100
```

returns $100.00.

```
${Sales.Amount} * 1.1
```

returns 10 percent above the sales amount as a currency value.

NOTE *Crystal Reports prohibits both values in a multiplication formula from being currency—one or the other can be, but not both. If necessary, you'll need to convert one currency value to a numeric value with ToNumber or CDbl.*

Operators: Other

This category of operators contains, in essence, operators that don't fit in any other category and perform miscellaneous functions.

Assignment (:=)

Assigns a value to a variable.

In Crystal syntax, don't confuse the assignment operator (:=) with the equals comparison operator (=). In Basic syntax, equals (=) acts as both assignment and equals comparison.

var := v

var – a previously declared variable name.
v – a value or expression of the same data type as *var*.

```
SalesRepBonus := SalesRepBonus + 1
```

adds 1 to the value already in the SalesRepBonus variable and places the result back into the SalesRepBonus variable.

```
NumberVar SalesRepBonus := 0
```

declares a number variable named SalesRepBonus and assigns it a value of zero in a single statement.

Comment (//)

Treats any text following the two slashes as a comment.

Basic Syntax uses the apostrophe (') or the word Rem to indicate a comment. Crystal Reports allows you to add comment slashes or apostrophes to multiple formula lines at once by highlighting them and clicking the Comment/Uncomment button in the Formula Workshop toolbar.

//

```
//The following formula calculates
//commission based on sale amount
Select {Orders.Order Amount}
    Case Is < 100:
        .01
    Case 100 to 1000:
        .05
    Case Is > 1000:
        .1
```

The first two lines of the formula are ignored by the Formula Editor when evaluating the formula logic.

NOTE *If you are troubleshooting a formula, you may prefer to simply "comment out" certain formula lines that you wish to use again later. For example, you may be working on five different methods of calculating a result. By adding or removing two slashes in front of the various formula lines, you may try various methods of calculations without having to delete and retype each line.*

Date-time literal (#)
Returns a date-time value from the supplied string.

#s#

s – a string that can be interpreted as a date, time, or date-time combination.

```
#1/1/2000 10:15 am#
```

returns a date-time value of 1/1/2000 10:15:00AM.

```
#Sep 10, 02#
```

returns a date-time value of 9/10/2002 12:00:00AM.

NOTE *Crystal Reports is fairly creative in what it will interpret as date or time material between the # characters. If the string can't be understood, an error will occur.*

Parentheses
Used to force evaluation of formula expressions in a certain order.

Parentheses allow you to force calculations to occur in other than the default *order of precedence* (exponentiation, then multiplication/division left to right, then addition/subtraction left to right). In Basic syntax, parentheses are also used to delimit array subscripts.

(<expression>)

```
10 + 10 * 2
```

returns 30.00. The order of precedence causes the multiplication to be done first, then the addition.

```
(10 + 10) * 2
```

returns 40.00. The parentheses force the addition to be performed first, then the multiplication.

Operators: Pattern
This set of operators allow partial string matches to be evaluated.

Like
Returns a Boolean (true/false) value based on a partial string match.

Like uses DOS-style "wildcards" (the asterisk and question mark) to determine if the source string contains the characters specified in the wildcard-based mask. This is helpful for checking for partial text matches. This operator is similar to the LooksLike function.

s1 Like s2
s1 – the source string to be searched.

s2 – the mask string to search against. The mask can include a question mark wildcard to indicate a single-character substitution and/or an asterisk to indicate a multiple-character substitution.

```
"George Peck" Like "G?orge*"
```

returns True.

StartsWith

Returns a Boolean (true/false) value if leading characters match the source string.

s1 StartsWith s2

s1 – the source string to be searched.
s2 – the characters to search for as the first characters of *s1*.

```
"George Peck" StartsWith "Ge"
```

returns True.

NOTE *Case sensitivity of string comparisons is based on the database case sensitivity setting in File | Report Options (applies to the current report only) and File | Options (applies to all new reports in the future).*

•erators: Ranges

These operators either create various ranges of values or test existing ranges. A *range* of values consists of beginning and ending values, and every value in between (some ranges can have no beginning and/or ending value—in other words, the range can be "everything above x" or "everything below y").

Both End Points Excluded Range

Creates a range of values between the two endpoints, not including the endpoints.

v1 _To_ v2

v1 – a value of any data type to act as the lower endpoint.
v2 – a value of the same data type as *v1* to act as the upper endpoint.

```
1 In (1 _to_ 100)
```

returns False, as the lower endpoint (1) is not included in the range.

```
99 In (1 _to_ 100)
```

returns True.

In Range

Returns a Boolean (true/false) value indicating whether the single value is in the range.

v In r

v – a single value of any supported data type.
r – a range value or variable of the same data type as *v*.

```
5 In (1 To 100)
```

returns True.

```
If {Parts.PartNo} In (1000 to 5000) Then
    "Taxable"
Else
    "Non-taxable"
```

returns the string "Taxable" if the part number is in the range of 1000 to 5000 inclusive.

Left End Point Excluded Range

Creates a range of values between the two endpoints, not including the first endpoint.

v1 _To v2

v1 – a value of any data type to act as the lower endpoint.
v2 – a value of the same data type as *v1* to act as the upper endpoint.

```
1 In (1 _to 100)
```

returns False, as the lower endpoint (1) is not included in the range.

```
100 In (1 _to 100)
```

returns True, as the upper endpoint (100) is included in the range.

Make Range

Creates a range of values between, and including, the two endpoints.

v1 To v2

v1 – a value of any data type to act as the lower endpoint.
v2 – a value of the same data type as *v1* to act as the upper endpoint.

```
1 In (1 to 100)
```

returns True.

```
100 In (1 to 100)
```

returns True.

Right End Point Excluded Range
Creates a range of values between the two endpoints, not including the second endpoint.

v1 To_ v2
v1 – a value of any data type to act as the lower endpoint.
v2 – a value of the same data type as *v1* to act as the upper endpoint.

```
1 In (1 to_ 100)
```

returns True, as the lower endpoint (1) is included in the range.

```
100 In (1 to_ 100)
```

returns False, as the upper endpoint (100) is not included in the range.

UpFrom
Creates a range of values including a lower endpoint upward, with no upper endpoint.
    Is >= v is functionally equivalent to UpFrom.

upFrom v
v – a value of any data type to act as the lower endpoint.

```
99999999 In UpFrom 100
```

returns True.

```
HasUpperBound (UpFrom 100)
```

returns False (the HasUpperBound function evaluates whether the supplied range has an upper endpoint).

Up From But Not Including
Creates a range of values from a lower endpoint upward (the lower endpoint not being included), with no upper endpoint.
    Is > v is functionally equivalent to UpFrom_.

upFrom_ v
v – a value of any data type to act as the lower endpoint.

```
100 In UpFrom_ 100
```

returns False (the lower endpoint is not included in the range).

```
HasUpperBound (UpFrom_ 100)
```

returns False (the HasUpperBound function evaluates whether the supplied range has an upper endpoint).

UpTo
Creates a range of values from an upper endpoint downward (including the upper endpoint) with no lower endpoint.
    Is <= v is functionally equivalent to UpTo.

upTo v
v – a value of any data type to act as the lower endpoint.

```
-9999999 In UpTo 100
```

returns True.

```
HasLowerBound (UpTo 100)
```

returns False (the HasLowerBound function evaluates whether the supplied range has a lower endpoint).

Up To But Not Including
Creates a range of values from an upper endpoint downward (not including the upper endpoint) with no lower endpoint.
    Is < v is functionally equivalent to UpTo_.

upTo_ v
v – a value of any data type to act as the lower endpoint.

```
100 In UpTo_ 100
```

returns False (the upper endpoint is not included in the range).

```
HasLowerBound (UpTo_ 100)
```

returns False (the HasLowerBound function evaluates whether the supplied range has a lower endpoint).

Operators: Scope
This set of operators is used when declaring variables (see "Operators: Variable Declaration" later in this appendix). These operators determine how long a variable retains its value during report processing.

Global
Forces a variable to retain its value in this formula, and all other formulas in the current report (but not subreports).
    In Crystal Syntax, this is the default scope for variable declarations that do not include a scope keyword.

Global t v
t – a variable declaration statement.

v – a valid variable name.

```
Global NumberVar BonusCount
```

declares a numeric variable called BonusCount that will retain its value throughout the entire report, but not in any subreports.

```
NumberVar BonusCount
```

is functionally equivalent to the previous declaration, as Global is the default variable scope.

Local

Forces a variable to retain its value in this formula only.

In Basic Syntax, this is the default scope for variable declarations that do not include a scope keyword.

Local t v

t – a variable declaration statement.
v – a valid variable name.

```
Local NumberVar BonusCount
```

declares a numeric variable called BonusCount that will retain its value only during the calculation of this formula. If BonusCount is declared in any other formulas, it will contain zero.

Shared

Forces a variable to retain its value in this formula, in all other formulas in the current report, and in all subreports.

Shared t v

t – a variable declaration statement.
v – a valid variable name.

```
Shared NumberVar BonusCount
```

declares a numeric variable called BonusCount that will retain its value throughout the entire report and in all subreports.

erators: Strings

This set of operators applies to string manipulation, such as string "concatenation" (the process of combining two or more strings into a single string).

Concatenate (& or +)

Concatenates (combines) strings into a single string.

The + operator requires that surrounding values be strings, while the & operator performs an implicit conversion to string of all surrounding values.

s1 + s2

s1 – a string value.
s2 – a string value.

```
"Page Number: " + PageNumber
```

returns an error, as the PageNumber function returns a numeric value.

```
"Page Number: " + ToText(PageNumber,0)
```

returns "Page Number: 1" if the first page of the report is printing.

v1 & v2

v1 – a value of any data type.
v2 – a value of any data type.

```
"Page Number: " & PageNumber
```

returns "Page Number: 1.00" if the first page of the report is printing, performing an implicit conversion of PageNumber to a string data type.

```
"Page Number: " & ToText(PageNumber,0)
```

returns "Page Number: 1" if the first page of the report is printing.

NOTE *When using the & operator to concatenate strings, you may still need to use ToText or CStr to control how values are formatted when they are concatenated.*

In String

Returns a Boolean value (true/false) based on if the first string is contained in the second string.

s1 In s2

s1 – a string value to search for in *s2*.
s2 – the source string to search.

```
"eor" in "George"
```

returns True.

```
If "(303)" In {Customer.Phone} Then "Denver Area Code"
```

returns the string "Denver Area Code" if the characters "(303)" are contained anywhere in the customer phone database field. Otherwise, the formula returns an empty string.

Insert Empty String ("")

Inserts a pair of quotation marks in the formula.

You may use this operator from the Operator Tree, or you may simply type quotation mark pairs in directly.

"" ""

```
StringVar BonusCustomer := ""
```

declares a string variable called BonusCustomer and sets it to contain an empty string.

Subscript []

Extracts a substring from a larger string.

s[n]

s – a string value.

n – a numeric value or range indicating the character or characters to extract.

```
"George Peck"[2 to 4]
```

returns "eor".

erators: Variable Declarations

This category of operators is used to declare variables within formulas. Whenever a variable is used in any formula, it must first be declared using one of the following operators.

BooleanVar

Declares a Boolean (true/false) variable to contain an array or single value.

BooleanVar Array varname

BooleanVar varname

varname – a variable name that is not the same as any other Crystal Reports formula keyword, does not contain a space, and does not start with a number or certain special characters.

```
BooleanVar Array Workdays :=
    [False, True, True, True, True, True, False];
Workdays[DayOfWeek(CurrentDate)]
```

returns True if the CurrentDate is Monday through Friday. The formula declares a Boolean array variable containing seven elements and then extracts the element associated with the day of the week.

```
BooleanVar BonusReached;
If {Sales.Amount} > 5000 Then BonusReached := True
```

declares a Boolean variable and assigns it a value of True if a sales amount is exceeded.

CurrencyVar

Declares a currency variable to contain an array, array of ranges, range, or single value.

CurrencyVar Array varname

CurrencyVar Range Array varname

CurrencyVar Range varname

CurrencyVar varname

varname – a variable name that is not the same as any other Crystal Reports formula keyword, does not contain a space, and does not start with a number or certain special characters.

```
CurrencyVar Range GoodSales := upFrom 5000;
If {Sales.Amount} In GoodSales Then "Good Job"
```

declares a currency range variable and assigns it all values including and above $5,000. If a sale amount is included in the variable, "Good Job" is returned by the formula.

```
CurrencyVar HighAmount;
If {Sales.Amount} > HighAmount Then
    HighAmount := {Sales.Amount}
```

declares a currency variable. If the sales amount is higher than what's retained in the variable from previous records, the variable is assigned the value of the higher sales amount.

DateTimeVar

Declares a date-time variable to contain an array, array of ranges, range, or single value.

DateTimeVar Array varname

DateTimeVar Range Array varname

DateTimeVar Range varname

DateTimeVar varname

varname – a variable name that is not the same as any other Crystal Reports formula keyword, does not contain a space, and does not start with a number or certain special characters.

```
DateTimeVar Range WorkDays :=
    #6/2/2003 8:00am# To #6/6/2003 5:00pm#;
If Not ({Salary.WorkDate} In WorkDays) Then
    {Salary.DailyPay} + {Salary.OvertimePay}
Else
    {Salary.DailyPay}
```

declares a date-time range variable and assigns it a value of Monday at 8 A.M. through Friday at 5 P.M. The variable is then checked against a work date to determine if overtime should be added to an employee's pay.

```
DateTimeVar OutOfTolerance;
If {Meas.Sample Value} > {Standards.Sample} Then
    OutOfTolerance := {Meas.Sample Date Time}
```

declares a date-time variable and tests to see if a sample reading was out of tolerance. If so, the date-time that the exception occurred is assigned to the variable.

DateVar

Declares a date variable to contain an array, array of ranges, range, or single value.

DateVar Array varname

DateVar Range Array varname

DateVar Range varname

DateVar varname

varname – a variable name that is not the same as any other Crystal Reports formula keyword, does not contain a space, and does not start with a number or certain special characters.

```
DateVar Range Array CompanyHolidays :=
    [DateValue("1/1/2003") to DateValue("1/2/2003"),
     DateValue("2/17/2003"),DateValue("5/26/2003"),
     DateValue("7/4/2003"),DateValue("9/1/2003"),
     DateValue("11/27/2003") to DateValue("11/28/2003"),
     DateValue("12/25/2003") to DateValue("12/31/2003")];
If {Salary.WorkDate} In CompanyHolidays Then
    "Bonus Pay Required"
```

declares a date range array and sets it to the individual dates and date ranges that make up company holidays. The variable is then checked to see if a work day qualifies for bonus pay.

NumberVar

Declares a number variable to contain an array, array of ranges, range, or single value.

NumberVar Array varname

NumberVar Range Array varname

NumberVar Range varname

NumberVar varname

varname – a variable name that is not the same as any other Crystal Reports formula keyword, does not contain a space, and does not start with a number or certain special characters.

```
NumberVar SalesRepTotal;
If {Sales.Amount} > {SalesRep.BonusLevel} Then
    SalesRepTotal :=
        SalesRepTotal + {Sales.Amount}
```

APPENDIX

declares a number variable and tests to see if a sales amount exceeded a bonus level. If so, the variable is incremented by the amount of the sale.

```
NumberVar SalesRepTotal := 0
```

declares a number variable and resets it to zero in the same formula statement.

StringVar

Declares a string variable to contain an array, array of ranges, range, or single value.

StringVar Array varname

StringVar Range Array varname

StringVar Range varname

StringVar varname

varname – a variable name that is not the same as any other Crystal Reports formula keyword, does not contain a space, and does not start with a number or certain special characters.

```
StringVar ShippersUsed;
If Not ({Orders.Ship Via} In ShippersUsed) Then
    ShippersUsed := ShippersUsed & {Orders.Ship Via} & ", "
```

declares a string variable. A test is performed to see if the shipper database field is already contained in the variable. If not, the shipper database field is added to what's already in the variable, concatenated with a comma and space.

```
StringVar Shippers;
Left(Shippers, Length(Shippers)-2)
```

declares a string variable and returns all but the right two characters of the variable to the report.

TimeVar

Declares a time variable to contain an array, array of ranges, range, or single value.

TimeVar Array varname

TimeVar Range Array varname

TimeVar Range varname

TimeVar varname

varname – a variable name that is not the same as any other Crystal Reports formula keyword, does not contain a space, and does not start with a number or certain special characters.

```
TimeVar Range WorkHours;
If DayOfWeek({Sales.Date}) In 2 to 6 Then
    WorkHours := TimeValue("9:00 am") To TimeValue("7:00 pm")
Else
```

```
    WorkHours := TimeValue("10:00 am") To TimeValue("5:00 pm");
"Store Hours: " & Minimum(WorkHours) &
            " to " & Maximum(WorkHours)
```

declares a time range variable. The day of the week is checked and the variable is given an hour range for weekdays or weekends. The formula returns a string extracting the lower bound and upper bound of the range.

NOTE   *Some of the previous examples illustrate the capability of declaring a variable and assigning it a value in the same formula statement.*

Index

YOU ARE HOLDING THE DEFINITIVE HOW-TO REFERENCE ON CRYSTAL REPORTS.

NOW, WHY NOT GET DEFINITIVE **PROFESSIONAL SERVICES** FOR CRYSTAL REPORTS AND CRYSTAL ENTERPRISE FROM THE COMPANY THAT WROTE THE BOOK?

THE ABLAZE GROUP is an internationally recognized Education and Consultation Provider that can maximize the benefits of Crystal Reports and Crystal Enterprise in your organization. We can help you use these exciting tools to get the information you need to make critical business decisions—decisions that go right to the bottom line.

Whether it's a single tough report with a tough deadline, a multi-site custom Crystal Enterprise implementation, or a team of report designers who need comprehensive training, George Peck and the whole Ablaze Group team stand ready to make it happen. Correctly. The first time.

Now that you have the book, get the company that wrote the book.

- Web-based or In-person Training
- Crystal Enterprise Customization
- Needs and Implementation Analysis
- Report Design
- Custom Web and Windows® Reporting Applications

THE ABLAZE GROUP, INC.
Crystal Reports®... We Wrote The Book

800.773.3472
www.ablazegroup.com